THE OXFORD HANDBOOK OF

THE BIBLE
IN AMERICA

THE OXFORD HANDBOOK OF

THE BIBLE
IN AMERICA

Edited by

PAUL C. GUTJAHR

OXFORD
UNIVERSITY PRESS

Oxford University Press is a department of the University of Oxford.
It furthers the University's objective of excellence in research, scholarship,
and education by publishing worldwide. Oxford is a registered trade mark of
Oxford University Press in the UK and in certain other countries

Published in the United States of America by Oxford University Press
198 Madison Avenue, New York, NY 10016, United States of America

Library of Congress Cataloging-in-Publication Data
Names: Gutjahr, Paul C., editor.
Title: The Oxford Handbook of the Bible in America / edited by Paul C. Gutjahr.
Description: New York : Oxford University Press USA, 2017. | Series: Oxford handbooks
| Includes bibliographical references and index.
Identifiers: LCCN 2016059216 (print) | LCCN 2017039301 (ebook) | ISBN 9780190258856 (updf)
| ISBN 9780190684839 (epub) | ISBN 9780190258849 (hardcover : alk. paper)
Subjects: LCSH: Bible—History. | Bible—Criticism, interpretation, etc.—United States.
| Bible—Influence. | Religion and culture—United States—History.
Classification: LCC BS447.5.U6 (ebook) | LCC BS447.5.U6 O94 2017 (print)
| DDC 220.09—dc23
LC record available at https://lccn.loc.gov/2016059216

FOR MY MENTORS

Jay Fliegelman, *in memoriam*
Giles Florence Jr.
Wayne Franklin
Stephen A. Hayner, *in memoriam*
Walt "Windy" Newcomb
David Nordloh
C. Gregory Read

Non nobis solum nati sumus.
[Not for ourselves alone are we born.]
Cicero

CONTENTS

PART III: THE BIBLE IN AMERICAN HISTORY AND CULTURE

ACKNOWLEDGMENTS

THERE is a pronounced multivocality to a collection of essays such as this one. More than forty scholars have contributed their time and energy to producing this *Handbook*, and the gathering of so many voices creates a far richer volume than any single author could have created. In a similar manner, a great many people helped make this volume a reality.

Much of the hard work of producing this book fell on the shoulders of my two research assistants. Richard Higgins was with me on this project from its inception, and every single page of this collection bears the mark of Richard's wisdom and professionalism. Megan Dyer joined the project in its latter stages as the final editing of the essays reached critical mass. She was immensely helpful in everything from line editing endnotes to gathering permissions for the varied images found in many of these essays. My editor at Oxford, Steve Wiggins, was a model of what an editor should be—professional, prompt, and an absolute pleasure to work with.

Others walked the road alongside me as this volume meandered toward completion. Bob Brown proved a helpful sounding board on everything from the type of essays to solicit to what to do when certain essays failed to appear. Alex Van Riesen was always there with his ability to make me laugh (often at myself). There are countless others who accompanied me as I made this journey, including Nathan Amos, Cary Curry, Nick Williams, Paul and Donna Konstanski, Matt and Kathie Nussbaum, and Bora and Wes Reed. Long projects like this one are made more bearable by the companionship and support of such friends.

Members of my family, as always, were tremendously supportive fellow travelers as well. My parents and sister, Karen, are—and have always been—great examples in my life of love and generosity. My wife, Cathy, continues to be my greatest advocate and my most valuable counselor. My sons, Isaac and Jeremiah, have come to serve as important models for me when it comes to facing the challenges of life with humility, courage, and perseverance. They constantly stir in me the desire to be a better person, not to mention, a better father.

The multivocality contained within this volume echoes the many voices of those who have mentored me over the years. Windy Newcomb took me under his wing when I was a seventh-grader and through long conversations and taking me to countless Shakespeare plays gave me my first glimpses of the magnificence of language and literature. Giles Florence taught me that there is nothing more powerful than someone who is willing to believe in you. He remains the single best teacher I have ever had . . . or ever known. It is because of Jay Fliegelman and his constant encouragement of my undergraduate work with him at Stanford that I ultimately became a university professor and made my specialty early American literature. Wayne Franklin sponsored my admission to the University of Iowa's graduate program in American Studies when eight other programs turned me down. He then went on to direct my PhD dissertation. I will always be humbled by how he gambled on, and then did everything to help me realize, my potential. Greg Read gave me a love for the Bible, and perhaps more importantly, the tools to study it. Steve Hayner tutored me in so many lessons of leadership and life that I still marvel at how often I find myself asking "What would Steve do in this situation?" And finally, David Nordloh guided me with unceasing kindness some twenty years ago when I first arrived at Indiana University and helped me navigate the often treacherous waters of being an assistant professor.

I am grateful for each of these men and for their wisdom, encouragement, and grace. Words fail me now as I try to express my gratitude for the ways in which they have all given of themselves to help me traverse what the Psalmist once called "the path of life."

P.C.G.

LIST OF CONTRIBUTORS

Rebecca Barrett-Fox is Assistant Professor of Sociology at Arkansas State University. She studies conservative and far-right movements and hate groups, religion, sexuality, and women and gender. She is the author of *God Hates: Westboro Baptist Church, the Religious Right, and American Nationalism* (2016).

James S. Bielo is Assistant Professor of Anthropology at Miami University, in Oxford, Ohio. He is the author of *Anthropology of Religion: The Basics* (2015), *Emerging Evangelicals: Faith, Modernity, and the Desire for Authenticity* (2011), and *Words upon the Word: An Ethnography of Evangelical Group Bible Study* (2009), and editor of *The Social Life of Scriptures: Cross-Cultural Perspectives on Biblicism* (2009).

Jason C. Bivins is Professor of Religious Studies at North Carolina State University, and the author of *Spirits Rejoice! Jazz and American Religion* (2015), *Religion of Fear: The Politics of Horror in Conservative Evangelicalism* (2008), and *The Fracture of Good Order: Christian Antiliberalism and the Challenge to American Politics* (2003).

Robert E. Brown is Associate Professor in the Department of Philosophy and Religion at James Madison University, where he teaches courses on American religious history. He is author of *Jonathan Edwards and the Bible* (2002), and editor of the ninth volume of Cotton Mather's *Biblia Americana*.

Andrew T. Coates is a PhD candidate at Duke University. He studies the visual and material cultures of American fundamentalism from the 1880s to 1920s. His dissertation, "Fundamentalist Aesthetics: Sensation and Scripture in Early Twentieth Century American Fundamentalism," received a Mellon fellowship from the American Council of Learned Societies for 2015–2016.

Elesha Coffman is Assistant Professor of history at Baylor University and a resident scholar in the history of Christianity at the Baylor Institute for Studies of Religion. She is the author of *The Christian Century and the Rise of the Protestant Mainline* (2013).

Dawn Coleman is Director of Graduate Studies and Associate Professor of English at the University of Tennessee. She is the author of *Preaching and the Rise of the American Novel* (2013), of numerous essays on American preaching and nineteenth-century literature, and of the critical introduction to Herman and Elizabeth Shaw Melville's copy of William Ellery Channing's six-volume *Works* for *Melville's Marginalia Online*.

Russell W. Dalton is Professor of Religious Education at Brite Divinity School in Fort Worth, Texas. His publications include *Children's Bibles in America: A Reception History of the Story of Noah's Ark in US Children's Bibles* (2015) and *Marvelous Myths: Marvel Superheroes and Everyday Faith* (2011).

Calvin B. DeWitt is Emeritus Professor of Environmental Studies, University of Wisconsin-Madison, with service on the graduate faculties of Land Resources, Water Resources Management, Conservation Biology and Sustainable Development, and Limnology and Marine Science. His books include *Earthwise: A Guide to Hopeful Creation Care* (2011) and *Song of a Scientist: The Harmony of a God-Soaked Creation* (2012).

Daniel L. Dreisbach is a professor at American University in Washington, D.C. He received a Doctor of Philosophy degree from Oxford University and a Juris Doctor degree from the University of Virginia. He has written extensively on the intersection of religion, politics, and law in American public life.

Linford D. Fisher is Associate Professor of History at Brown University. He is the author of *The Indian Great Awakening: Religion and the Shaping of Native Cultures in Early America* (2012) and the co-author of *Decoding Roger Williams: The Lost Essay of Rhode Island's Founding Father* (2014), with J. Stanley Lemons and Lucas Mason-Brown.

Michael J. Gilmour is Associate Professor of New Testament at Providence University College in Manitoba, Canada. His books include *Gods and Guitars: Seeking the Sacred in Post-1960s Popular Music* (2009), *The Gospel According to Bob Dylan: The Old, Old Story for Modern Times* (2011), and *Eden's Other Residents: The Bible and Animals* (2014).

Paul C. Gutjahr is Ruth N. Halls Professor of English at Indiana University. Among his numerous books and articles, he is the author of *An American Bible: The History of the Good Book in the United States, 1777–1881* (1999), *Charles Hodge: Guardian of American Orthodoxy* (2011), and *The Book of Mormon: A Biography* (2012).

Michael W. Hamilton is a former military chaplain and college professor now serving as the Executive Director of The Mary Baker Eddy Library in Boston. He has written on religions in the United States, including "Reader Response to the Yearning for Zion Ranch Raid and Its Aftermath on the Websites of the Salt Lake Tribune and the Deseret News," in the book *Saints under Siege* and "Mary Baker Eddy's Households: Community Experiments in Early Christian Science History," in the journal *Communal Societies*.

Paul Harvey is Professor of History and Presidential Teaching Scholar at the University of Colorado. Among his many books and publications, he is the co-author of *The Color of Christ: The Son of God and the Saga of Race in America* (2014) and author of *Through the Storm, Through the Night: A History of African American Christianity* (2013).

Craig Hefner is a PhD student at Wheaton College Graduate School, studying the theology of Søren Kierkegaard.

Jason A. Hentschel, PhD, is a recent graduate in theology from the University of Dayton. He has authored chapters for *The Bible in American Life* (2017) and *Preaching Conversations with Scholars* (2016), as well as various journal articles.

David Holland is Associate Professor of North American Religious History at Harvard Divinity School. David's work has appeared in *Gender and History*, the *New England Quarterly*, and *Law and History Review*. He is the author of *Sacred Borders: Continuing Revelation and Canonical Restraint in Early America* (2011).

Teresa J. Hornsby is a Professor of Religion at Drury University. She is a co-author of *Transgender, Intersex, and Biblical Interpretation* (2016), a co-editor of *Bible Trouble* (2011), and author of *Sex Texts from the Bible* (2007), as well as numerous essays, chapters, and encyclopedia entries. She lectures internationally on the topic of the Bible, sexuality, and gender.

Michael J. McClymond is Professor of Modern Christianity at Saint Louis University. He was educated at Northwestern University (BA), Yale University (MDiv), and the University of Chicago (MA, PhD), and has held teaching or research appointments at Wheaton College, Illinois, Westmont College, University of California–San Diego, Emory University, Yale University, and University of Birmingham, UK. He has written or edited nine volumes in biblical studies, theology, church history, and World Christianity.

Nicholas Miller (JD, Columbia University; PhD, University of Notre Dame) is Professor of Church History at the Seventh-day Adventist Theological Seminary at Andrews University, in Berrien Springs, Michigan. His publications include *The Religious Roots of the First Amendment* (2012) and *The Reformation and the Remnant* (2016).

Daniel A. Morris is a lecturer in the Religion Department at Augustana College. His work has appeared in *The Journal of Religion, Soundings, Journal of Religious Ethics*, and *Political Theology*. He is the author of *Virtue and Irony in American Democracy: Revisiting Dewey and Niebuhr* (2015).

Mark A. Noll, Francis A. McAnaney Professor of History emeritus at the University of Notre Dame, is the author of *In the Beginning Was the Word: The Bible in American Public Life, 1492–1783* (2016), *The Civil War as a Theological Crisis* (2006), and *America's God: From Jonathan Edwards to Abraham Lincoln* (2002).

Seth Perry is Assistant Professor of Religion in the Americas at Princeton University. His published work includes "'Go Down into Jordan: No, Mississippi': Mormon Nauvoo and the Rhetoric of Landscape," in *Gods of the Mississippi* (2013), "'What the Public Expect': Consumer Authority and the Marketing of Bibles, 1770-1850," *American Periodicals* (Autumn 2014), and "The Many Bibles of Joseph Smith: Textual, Prophetic, and Scholarly Authority in Early-National Bible Culture," *Journal of the American Academy of Religion* (June 2016).

Emerson B. Powery is Professor of Biblical Studies & Coordinator of Ethnic and Area Studies at Messiah College and an Adjunct Instructor in Bible at Lancaster Theological Seminary. His publications include *Jesus Reads Scripture* (2002) and the co-authored volume, *The Genesis of Liberation: Biblical Interpretation in the Antebellum Narratives of the Enslaved* (2016).

A. G. Roeber is Professor Emeritus of Early Modern History and Religious Studies at The Pennsylvania State University. His many publications include: "The Law, Religion, and State Making in the Early Modern World: Protestant Revolutions in the Works of Berman, Gorski, and Witte," *Law and Social Inquiry* (Winter 2006); the co-authored *Changing Churches: An Orthodox, Catholic, and Lutheran Theological Conversation* (2012); and co-editor and contributor to *The Oxford Handbook of Early Modern Theology* (2016).

William D. Romanowski is the Arthur H. DeKruyter Chair in Communication at Calvin College. He is author of *Reforming Hollywood: How American Protestants Fought for Freedom at the Movies* (2012), *Eyes Wide Open: Looking for God in Popular Culture* (2007), and *Pop Culture Wars: Religion and the Role of Entertainment in American Life* (1996).

Suzanne Rosenblith is Professor and Associate Dean of the College of Education at Clemson University. Her research focuses on philosophical perspectives on the relationship between religion and public education in pluralist democracies. She has published widely in *Educational Theory, Educational Studies, Religion and Education, Philosophy of Education, Religious Education,* and *Theory and Research in Education*.

Jonathan D. Sarna is the Joseph H. & Belle R. Braun Professor of American Jewish History at Brandeis University and chairs its Hornstein Jewish Professional Leadership Program. He is also Chief Historian of the National Museum of American Jewish History. Author or editor of more than thirty books on American Jewish history and life, his *American Judaism: A History* (2004) won six awards.

Jeffrey Scholes is Associate Professor of Religious Studies in the Department of Philosophy and the Director of the Center for Religious Diversity and Public Life at the University of Colorado, Colorado Springs. He is the author of *Vocation and the Politics of Work: Popular Theology in a Consumer Culture* (2013) and co-author of *Religion and Sports in American Culture* (2014).

Kristin Schwain is Associate Professor of American Art at the University of Missouri. In addition to her book *Signs of Grace: Religion and American Art in the Gilded Age* (2008), she has published on F. Holland Day, Carl Gutherz, Henry Ossawa Tanner, and Jacob Lawrence.

Rev. Donald Senior, C.P., is President Emeritus and Chancellor of Catholic Theological Union in Chicago, where he is also Professor of New Testament Studies. He is a frequent lecturer, has served on numerous boards and commissions, and is widely published, including a four-volume work on the *Passion of Jesus* (1985-1997), *The Catholic Study Bible* (2016), and *Why the Cross?* (2014). He is past President of the Catholic Biblical Association of America and of the Association of Theological Schools of the United States and Canada. In 2001, Pope John Paul II appointed him as a member of the Pontifical Biblical Commission, and he was reappointed in 2006 by Pope Benedict XVI.

Claudia Setzer is Professor of Religious Studies at Manhattan College in Riverdale, New York. Her books include *The Bible and American Culture* (with David Shefferman, 2011), *Resurrection of the Body in Early Judaism and Christianity* (2004), and *Jewish Responses to Early Christians* (1994). She serves on the board of *The Journal of Biblical Literature*.

Eran Shalev is an Associate Professor in the History Department at Haifa University, Israel. He is the author of *American Zion: The Old Testament as a Political Text from the Revolution to the Civil War* (2013), and *Rome Reborn on Western Shores: Historical Imagination and the Creation of the American Republic* (2009).

Abraham Smith is Professor of New Testament at Southern Methodist University in the Perkins School of Theology. His major publications include: *Mark: Shaping the Life and Legacy of Jesus* (2015); "Paul and African American Biblical Interpretation," in *True to Our Native Land: An African American Commentary on the New Testament* (2007); *The New*

Interpreter's Study Bible (2003), co-edited with Walter Harrelson, Phyliss Trible, James Vanderkam, and Donald Senior; "Commentaries and Reflections on First and Second Thessalonians," in *The New Interpreter's Bible Commentary* (2000); *Slavery, Text and Interpretation* (1998), co-edited with Allen Dwight Callahan and Richard Horsley; and *"Comfort One Another": Reconstructing the Audience of 1 Thessalonians* (1995).

John G. Stackhouse Jr. serves Crandall University as the Samuel J. Mikolaski Professor of Religious Studies and Dean of Faculty Development. The first of his ten books is *Canadian Evangelicalism in the Twentieth Century* (1993) and the most recent is *Why You're Here: Ethics for the Real World* (2017).

Randall J. Stephens is Reader in History and American Studies at Northumbria University. He is the author of *The Fire Spreads: Holiness and Pentecostalism in the American South* (2008) and *The Anointed: Evangelical Truth in a Secular Age* (2011), co-authored with Karl Giberson. His current book project is titled *The Devil's Music: Rock and Christianity since the 1950s* (under contract, Harvard).

Jan Stievermann is Professor of the History of Christianity in the United States at Heidelberg University, Germany. Among his recent publications are the collections *A Peculiar Mixture: German-Language Cultures and Identities in Eighteenth-Century North America* (2013), *Religion and the Marketplace in the United States* (2014), volume 5 in the edition of *Biblia Americana*, and the monograph *Prophecy, Piety, and the Problem of Historicity: Interpreting the Hebrew Scriptures in Cotton Mather's Biblia Americana* (2015).

Daniel J. Treier is Knoedler Professor of Theology at Wheaton College Graduate School. He is the author or co-editor of numerous books, including *Virtue and the Voice of God: Toward Theology as Wisdom* (2006), which addresses theological education.

Susan L. Trollinger is Professor of English at the University of Dayton. She is co-author of *Righting America at the Creation Museum* (2016), and author of *Selling the Amish: The Tourism of Nostalgia* (2012) and "Heritage versus History: Amish Tourism in Two Ohio Towns," in *The Amish and The Media* (2008).

William Vance Trollinger Jr. is Professor of History at the University of Dayton. He is co-author of *Righting America at the Creation Museum* (2016), and author of *God's Empire: William Bell Riley and Midwestern Fundamentalism* (1991) and "Evangelicalism and Religious Pluralism in Contemporary America," in *Gods in America* (2013).

Edward Waggoner is Assistant Professor of Theology and Rt. Rev. Sam B. Hulsey Chair in Episcopal Studies, at Brite Divinity School. He is the author of "Taking Religion Seriously in the U.S. Military," *Journal of the American Academy of Religion* (September 2014), and co-editor of *Religious Experience and New Materialism* (2016).

John B. Weaver is Dean of Library Services and Educational Technology at Abilene Christian University, in Abilene, Texas. A professor of Early Christianity and Church History, he specializes in the relationship between the Bible and culture, especially Christian practices of information and formation through technology.

Shira Wolosky is Professor of American Studies and English Literature at the Hebrew University of Jerusalem. Her books include *Emily Dickinson: A Voice of War* (1984),

Language Mysticism (1995), *The Art of Poetry* (2008), *Poetry and Public Discourse* (2010), and *Feminist Theory across Disciplines in Feminist Community* (2013). Her awards include Guggenheim, ACLS and Fulbright Fellowships, Fellowships at the Institute for Advanced Studies in Princeton and Israel, and Drue Heinz Visiting Professorships at Oxford.

Patrick Womac is Assistant Professor of Curriculum, Assessment, and Instruction at the University of Maine. His areas of specialization include geographic literacy, social studies teacher education, philosophy of education, and the use of cartography to inform policy. His work has been published in *Research in Geographic Education* and *The Journal of Equity in Education.*

INTRODUCTION

PAUL C. GUTJAHR

It is difficult, if not impossible, to dispute the claim that the Bible holds the place as the single most influential book in America's history. From the earliest European settlements in New England, the Bible has exercised a power over community formation and rule that few books have even approached. So influential has been the Bible that early Americans denominated themselves as "People of the Book." They saw themselves as inseparably tied to Bible. Even today, it is estimated that the Bible remains the most owned, if not read, book in the United States. Some 88 percent of American households report owning at least one Bible.[1]

Within the Bible's absolutely pervasive and powerful presence in American society, it has only been relatively recently that scholars have looked at its influence in more systematic, analytical ways. This collection of essays is intended to offer in a single volume a wide-angle view of how Americans have read, understood, and used the Bible since the early seventeenth century. It is also hoped that this volume will serve as a catalyst as well as a jumping off point for future scholarship on how Americans have used, and continue to use, this holy book.

Before reading these essays, however, it may be helpful to understand some of the broader outlines of how a wide range of students of the Bible have analyzed the book's presence in the colonial and national periods. For such an exercise, it might be helpful to employ a metaphor: Imagine these analytical endeavors as a type of centuries-long interpretative rope of biblical examination. Like any rope, this one is made of individual cords that are woven together. Such an image gives one a picture of the historiography of how the Bible's production, usage, and interpretation in the United States have been studied. To understand the history, the scope, and the individual nature of different schools of scholarship on the Bible, one must both be able to first see the rope's different cords and then the rope as an interwoven whole. No single cord stands alone. The six, interwoven cords detailed in this introduction are forever touching and intermingling, and yet they also never cease to retain a certain character of their own.

What follows is a brief overview of the interpretive rope that characterizes the study of the Bible and its role in American society since the first European settlers touched the country's shores. This introduction in particular, and in many respects this volume more generally, makes no pretense at being a comprehensive account of the Bible's role in North America. Instead, it is intended to serve as a larger conceptual template for how the Bible— a book that has formed, framed, and fractured American society over a series of centuries— has been studied by professional and nonprofessional scholars alike.

The First Cord: Textual Interpretation

When European settlers such as the Puritans from England or the Pilgrims from the Netherlands landed on American shores, they came with their Bibles. These early settlers put such a premium on the Bible that the first colonial publishing endeavors centered on publishing sermons, divine poems, theological tracts, and catechisms all centered on enriching one's knowledge of this holy book. Such dedication to explicating the Bible can be seen in how the colonists established the first printing press in Cambridge, Massachusetts, in 1639 largely to print works tied to the biblical text. The Cambridge press published the first book in British North America, a metrical translation of the Book of Psalms in English entitled *The Bay Psalm Book* (1640), as well as the first complete Bible to be published on American shores, the so-called Eliot Indian Bible (1663).

Throughout the seventeenth century, sermons were a mainstay of early American colonial printing. During this century "34 percent of the New England clergy published at least one tract or treatise" and nearly 70 percent of these works were sermons.[2] In New England's nascent publishing industry, sermons were easy to publish because they were short and required relatively little type and paper. They also sold well because ministers had their own congregations, which served as built-in consumers for these publications. By the early eighteenth century, collections of sermons were being bound together into longer works, and the first large folio volume ever produced in New England was a collection of some 250 sermons on the Westminster Catechism by Samuel Willard entitled *A Compleat Body of Divinity* (1736).

The plethora of sermons and sermon collections produced by seventeenth- and eighteenth-century New England presses helped create the first cord in the interpretative rope of biblical examination. Countless early Americans considered the Bible to be a divinely inspired book sent from God to guide both their thinking and their behavior. As such, it was critical that the contents of the book be rightly interpreted and widely taught. For colonial Americans, careful interpretative analysis of the Bible's text took the form of sermons that explicated certain biblical passages, as well as increasingly common theological tracts that used the Bible to address various political and cultural issues of the day.

Such sermons and tracts eventually grew into longer works of textual interpretation commonly known as biblical commentaries. In the seventeenth and eighteenth centuries, what we might identify as extended biblical commentaries were almost exclusively printed in England because of the expense and resources needed to publish longer printed works. When given the opportunity, American clergy read such European-produced biblical commentaries voraciously, but Americans did not begin to publish their own longer exegetical commentaries on the Bible until their print culture reached a certain level of stability and maturity in the early nineteenth century.[3] Particularly noteworthy when examining the rising presence and influence of American nineteenth-century biblical commentaries is the work of the Presbyterian minister and scholar Albert Barnes (1798-1870). His eleven-volume biblical commentary series was remarkable for the way it increased the reach of biblical scholarship beyond strictly educated clerical circles. An immensely popular Philadelphia preacher and pastor, Barnes was both a scholar and a popularizer. His commentaries sold so many copies during his lifetime that he gained a national reputation as a biblical scholar and paved the way for countless others to write biblical commentaries geared more for mass consumption. Although Barnes undertook to write a series of commentaries encompassing the entire Bible, such comprehensive biblical commentary sets would increasingly move from being the work of a single person in the nineteenth century to groups of scholars in the twentieth and twenty-first centuries. Influential later group-written commentary sets include such collections as the New International Commentary, Tyndale, or The Bible Speaks Today commentary series.

A prime example of the long-standing and persistent cord of biblical examination in the form of textual interpretation can perhaps be best exemplified in the first systematic biblical commentary composed in the American colonies, Cotton Mather's *Biblia Americana*. Mather wrote this mammoth six-volume manuscript work comprising some 4,500 folio pages between 1693 and 1728. In these volumes, Mather synthesized vast amounts of contemporary scholarship on the Bible and complimented the analytical work of others with his own interpretations. Although towering English biblical scholars such as Matthew Poole (1624-1679), Samuel Clark (1626-1701), and Matthew Henry (1662-1714) undertook similar extensive commentaries on the Bible and saw them published in England, Mather's *Biblia Americana* was never published on either side of the Atlantic Ocean. It is only now, some three centuries later, that the *Biblia Americana* is being published under the general editorship of Reiner Smolinski for the first time (2010-ongoing).[4] That America's first biblical commentary was originally undertaken near the turn of the eighteenth century and continues to be worked on by a number of twenty-first century scholars in order to bring it finally to press provides a stunning testimony to the longevity, strength, and interest in American textual interpretative work on the Bible.

As time has passed, however, such interpretative work on the Bible has come to include scholars who view the scriptures as a literary text and often interpret it as a more human than divine text. Works representative of this "Bible as Literature" line of analysis date back to the turn of the twentieth century and include such works as J. H. Gardiner's *The Bible as English Literature* (1907), Laura H. Wild's *A Literary Guide to the Bible* (1922), Charles Allen Dinsmore's *The English Bible as Literature* (1931), Frank McConnell's *The Bible and the Narrative Tradition* (1986), Elizabeth A. Castelli et al.'s *The Postmodern Bible* (1995), and Leland Ryken's *The Complete Handbook of Literary Forms in the Bible* (2014).

Whether the ends of such textual study of the Bible are driven by spiritual or more earthly motivations, the fact remains that such textual interpretation remains the oldest and the most common method for how Americans have analyzed the Bible. The various hermeneutic approaches underpinning such textual interpretation center primarily on what the Bible says, not the analysis of the role that the Bible might play in larger cultural formations. Such studies of the Bible's role in American society would be a product of later scholarship.

THE SECOND CORD: WORKS CONCERNING BIBLICAL TRANSLATION

While the cord of textual interpretation stands as the longest and most robust analytic tradition of studying the Bible in the United States, a second interpretative cord closely linked to work in biblical exegesis appeared in the early nineteenth century. This second cord concerned the increasing biblical translation work being undertaken in both America and Europe. These translation efforts were closely tied to the emergence of the German Higher Criticism, a school of criticism which arose in Germany in the late eighteenth century and eventually migrated to the United States in the early nineteenth. Among other things, the Higher Criticism (as it came to be colloquially known) put a great emphasis on determining the reliability of the biblical text, not as a series of divinely recorded words relayed to humanity directly from the mouth of God, but as an artifact that had been recorded, translated, and reproduced by human hands over the centuries.

Early work in Higher Criticism grew out of the textual scholarship of German scholars such as Johann Gottfried Eichhorn (1752-1827) and Johann Jakob Greisbach (1745-1812). It was Eichhorn who was actually responsible for coining the term "Higher Criticism." As opposed to the so-called Lower Critics, who worked on the Bible primarily by looking at its language and grammar, Higher Critics wished to place the biblical text in historical contexts, exploring its authorship, and what its various passages might have meant to those who originally wrote and received them. The Higher Critics saw the Bible as a textual artifact fashioned by the hands of men, and in doing so, de-emphasized the divinely inspired nature of the text.[5]

Eichhorn and Greisbach worked hard to collate the texts found in known biblical manuscripts and painstakingly work backward to recover the oldest, and therefore the purest, text of the Bible. Such rigorous textual scholarship raised doubts about how a number of biblical passages had been translated into English over time, such as the presence of verses in 1 John concerning the Trinity or how the word "baptism" might best be translated.[6] Such textual scholarship raised doubts both about the reliability of certain biblical translation choices and the biblical manuscripts themselves.

Beginning in the early nineteenth century, Americans began to take a serious interest in making their own translations of the Bible for two major reasons. First, some questioned the reliability of the text found in the omnipresent King James Version (KJV) in light of the Higher Criticism's newer work on biblical manuscripts. Second, there were growing concerns that the KJV's language was simply too archaic to be understood by everyday Americans. Before the Civil War, over twenty different translations of the Bible or portions of the Bible were undertaken and published by Americans.[7] This number would only increase in the decades after the War until new translations of the Bible would appear at a rate of roughly one per year by the end of the twentieth century.[8] A glimpse at the range of English Bible translations can profitably begin by looking at William Chamberlin's *Catalogue of English Bible Translations* (1991), a catalogue that lists both entire editions of the Bible and translations of individual books beginning with John Wycliffe's 1388 translation and working up through translations that appear in the early 1990s.

Over time, a large body of work has come into existence on various translation issues concerning the English Bible in America. Nineteenth-century works on such issues are plentiful, but important pieces within this literature include: Oliver Everett's "Novem Testamentum Graece, ex recensione J. Jac. Griesbachii" (1822), *An Argument Sustaining the Common English Version of the Bible* (1850), Cleveland Coxe's *An Apology for the Common English Bible* (1857), and Richard Chenevix Trench's *On the Authorized Version of the New Testament* (1858).

There are more recent works on translation issues as well, and a broad sampling of such works includes: James Duke's *Horace Bushnell: On the Vitality of Biblical Language* (1984), Kenneth L. Barker's *The Making of a Contemporary Translation: New International Version* (1987), Robert Martin's *Accuracy of Translation and the New International Version* (1989), Richard Kevin Barnard's *God's Word in Our Language* (1989), Kenneth Cmiel's *Democratic Eloquence* (1990), Jack Lewis's *The English Bible from KJV to NIV* (1991), Harry Orlinsky and Robert Bratcher's *A History of Bible Translation and the North American Contribution* (1991), Barclay M. Newman's *Creating & Crafting the Contemporary English Version* (1996), D. A. Carson's *The Inclusive Language Debate* (1998), Robert Hodgon and Paul A. Soukup's *Fidelity and Translation* (1999), Bruce M. Metzger's *The Bible in Translation* (2001), and Wayne Grudem et al.'s *Translating the Truth* (2005).

THE THIRD CORD: BIBLIOGRAPHIC AND TEXTUAL WORK ON THE BIBLE

Growing out of the analytic cords of textual interpretation and translation comes the third cord of biblical analysis, work that concentrates on artifact and text-based, bibliographic examinations of the Bible. Here the physical artifact of various published editions of the Bible is the principal object of study, often in conjunction with the Bible's intellectual design. The standard bibliographic treatments of the Bible in the United States remain: Edward O'Callaghan, *A List of Editions of the Holy Scriptures and Parts Thereof* (1861), and Margaret Hills, *The English Bible in America* (1962). Even a casual perusal of these works will quickly disabuse one of the idea that the Bible is some sort of static, monolithic entity. From its first circulation in the country in the sixteenth century, the Bible has taken myriad forms, appearing in thousands of different editions, which were both imported from Europe and produced in North America.[9] While O'Callaghan and Hills painstakingly record the Bible editions printed in the United States, a great many editions of European origin have also circulated in the United States. The standard bibliographic work on these editions is T. H. Darlow and H. F. Moule, *Historical Catalogue of the Printed Editions of Holy Scripture* (1963).

The Hills bibliography is clearly the most useful bibliographic tool for studying the Bible production which took place in the United States, but her study only covers editions published prior to 1958. Since then, American Bible publishers have continued to produce thousands of new editions of the Bible. It is estimated that over seven thousand different Bible editions had been produced in the United States by the early 1990s, of which Hills's bibliography records only some twenty-five hundred.[10] An attempt to add at least a small coda to Hills's study can be found in Paul Gutjahr's "Chronology of English Bible Translations since 1957," a four-page appendix in Hannibal Hamlin and Norman W. Jones's *The King James Bible after 400 Years* (2010). In general, it is safe to say that the exponential growth rate of Bible editions has gone almost completely undocumented bibliographically for the last half century.

There are a number of shorter bibliographic exposés on American Bibles. These more focused treatments tend to concentrate on specific themes or time periods. Jacquelynn Slee offers the only bibliography interested in charting American Bible illustration in her

"A Summary of the English Editions of Illustrated Bibles Published in America between 1790 and 1825" (1973). Bibles distinctive for the cultural importance or their associations with famous Americans are chronicled in *Presidential Inaugural Bibles: Catalogue of an Exhibition* (1969), John Wright's *Historic Bibles in America* (1905), and P. Marion Simms's *The Bible in America: Versions that have Played their Part in the Making of the Republic* (1936). Wilfrid Parsons offers a much needed bibliographic examination of Catholic scriptures in his "First American Editions of Catholic Bibles" (1937) and Wilberforce Eames's *Bibliographic Notes on Eliot's Indian Bible* (1890) offers a more complete picture of one of the most amazing books in American publishing history, John Eliot's seventeenth-century translation of the entire Bible into a Native American language.

The vast majority of bibliographic studies of the American Bible fall under the purview of different major religious traditions. Most important among these have been versions centered on facilitating the Protestant, Catholic, and Judaic faiths. Among these three, Protestant Bibles have attracted the lion's share of scholarly interest over the years. Significantly less time and bibliographic attention have been given to Catholic and Hebrew versions of the scriptures in American culture.

Work on Catholic editions in America is confined almost entirely to article-length treatments that appear by themselves or as chapters in various books. Broad overviews of the American Catholic Bibles include: Hugh Pope's *English Versions of the Bible* (1952), John Shea's "The Bible in American History," R. E. McNally's "The Council of Trent and Vernacular Bibles," and Gerald P. Fogarty's "American Catholic Translations of the Bible" (in Ernest S. Frerichs, *The Bible and Bibles in America*, 1988), and "The Quest for a Catholic Vernacular Bible in America" (in Nathan Hatch and Mark Noll, *The Bible in America*, 1982).

The phrase "Hebrew Bible" not only refers to the language of the editions, but serves to denote what Christians call the Old Testament. The Jewish community in the United States has long been a multilingual community, primarily using English, Hebrew, Yiddish, and German as its most common languages.[11] Yet Jewish scriptures have a long history of being presented in Hebrew in the United States, and although the revered status of Hebrew would remain, eventually the Hebrew Bible would be translated into English to make it more accessible for American Jewish communities. The first such translation appeared in 1845, when the German-born Isaac Leeser produced a version of the Pentateuch. In 1853, Leeser finished translating a version of the entire Hebrew Bible, which would gain great popularity in American Jewish communities by the time of his death in 1868. The story of Leeser's Bible is lucidly told by Lance J. Sussman in his *Isaac Leeser and the Making of American Judaism* (1995). Other helpful bibliographic discussions on American Jewish publishing include selected entries and essays in Joshua Bloch and others' *Hebrew Printing and Bibliography* (1976) and Maxwell Whiteman's "The Introduction and Spread of Hebrew Type in the United States" (1992).

Within the bibliographic cord of examination stand a number of works that recount the production for Protestants of Bibles used in America. Towering still as the most popular Bible translation in the United States is the KJV, a version that has enjoyed a four-century reign as America's most popular Protestant version of the scriptures. Because of the vast and continuing influence of the KJV in American society, it is worth mentioning that a host of books have been published on the creation and influence of this version. Notable among such works on the KJV are: Adam Nicolson's *God's Secretaries: The*

Making of the King James Bible (2003), Gordon Campbell's *Bible* (2010), Alistar McGrath's *In the Beginning* (2001), and Hannibal Hamlin and Norman W. Jones's *The King James Bible after 400 Years* (2010).

Growing out of the bibliographic school of analysis and its careful attention to the material aspects of Bible production and distribution are studies that focus on how the physical character of different editions complement the text they contain. There are times when a Bible's packaging is as important to its cultural use as the words it contains. Often Americans have "read" a Bible before they have even glanced at the text it contains. The material nature of a Bible can send a message by being displayed on a parlor table, resting on a pulpit or being used to swear in an incoming President. Treatments of the Bible's material nature in the United States include: David Cressy's "Books as Totems in Seventeenth-Century England and New England" (1986), portions of David Hall's *Worlds of Wonder, Days of Judgment* (1989), and a chapter in Colleen McDannell's *Material Christianity* (1995).

Topics concerning Bible illustration and typography have been addressed in a wide range of works including Frank Weitenkempf's "American Bible Illustration" (1958), Paul Gutjahr's "American Bible Illustration: From Copper Plates to Computers" in David Morgan and Sally Promey's *The Visual Cultures of American Religion* (2000), and Susan Sink's *The Art of The Saint John's Bible* (2013). The story behind the appearance of the richly illustrated St. John's Bible is told in Christoph Calderhead's *Illuminating the Word* (2015). An excellent chapter-long treatment of how photographs have been placed in American Bibles can be found in Rachel McBride Lindsey's book, *A Communion of Shadows*. Paul Gutjahr looks at the issue and influence of biblical typography in his "The Letter(s) of the Law" in Paul Gutjahr's and Megan Benton's *Illuminating Letters* (2000).

More modern trends in American religious publishing have brought forth new kinds of Bible formatting. One such format in the early 2000s was the emergence of Bible-zines, or Bibles printed to look like magazines. Studies of such Bible-zines include: Paul Gutjahr's "The Bible-zine *Revolve* and the Evolution of the Culturally Relevant Bible in America" (2008), and Susan Harding's "*Revolve*, the Biblezine: A Transevangelical Text" (2009). The issue of the Bible's form and how that form interacts with its content has become of ever greater importance as computer technology and the Internet increasingly play key roles in publishing and distributing the Bible. Studies touching upon the influence of computer technology on the Bible's form and content include Howard Clark Kee's *The Bible in the Twenty-First Century* (1993) and Robert Hodgson and Paul Soukup's *From One Medium to Another* (1997).

THE FOURTH CORD: HISTORICAL WORK ON THE BIBLE

Growing out of the cords of textual interpretation, translation, and bibliographic studies one finds an extensive body of historical work on the Bible and biblical criticism in the United States. Such historical work has most often partaken of the goals and methods of four different schools of historical scholarship: intellectual history, social history, institutional history, and biography. Intellectual history is so named for its concentration on the life of the mind and often takes the form of concentrating on the influence of ideas and the groups and individuals who championed or resisted those ideas. Social history frequently has a more quantitative component, and while intellectual history is often accused of favoring the study of elites, social history has distinguished itself by its interest in the entire demographic range of a given society. Institutional histories, as the name indicates, focus on the rise and fall of institutions, such as the American Bible Society or broader enterprises such as the railroad industry in the United States.

Intellectual histories bearing on the Bible in America have been many and often concentrate on examinations of American biblical interpretation such as Jerry Brown's foundational study of biblical criticism in early America, *The Rise of Biblical Criticism in America, 1800–1870* (1969). Equally important volumes on topics that have close ties to biblical criticism in the colonial and early national period include: E. Brooks Holifield's *The Gentlemen Theologians* (1978) and *Theology in America: Christian Thought from the Age of the Puritans to the Civil War* (2003), and Mark Noll's *America's God: From Jonathan Edwards to Abraham Lincoln* (2002) and *The Civil War as a Theological Crisis* (2006). More focused historical treatments of biblical interpretation include: Robert E. Brown's *Jonathan Edwards and the Bible* (2002) and Philip Gura's *American Transcendentalism: A History* (2007).

For the twentieth century, equally valuable studies of the larger contours of American biblical criticism can be found in Harold R. Willoughby's *The Study of the Bible Today and Tomorrow* (1947), Mark Noll's "Evangelicals and the Study of the Bible" in *Evangelicalism and Modern America* (1984) edited by George Marsden, several essays in Donald McKim's intellectually ambitious *Historical Handbook of Major Biblical Interpreters* (1998), Walter Elwell and J. D. Weaver's edited collection *Bible Interpreters of the Twentieth Century* (1999), and Cullen Murphy's *The Word According to Eve* (1999).

Melding intellectual history with biography, there have also been studies done on specific figures in the history of American biblical interpretation. Such studies include two works by Roy Harrisville, *Benjamin Wisner Bacon: Pioneer in American Biblical Interpretation* (1976) and *Frank Chamberlain Porter: Pioneer in American Biblical Interpretation* (1976), John Crossan's *A Fragile Craft: The Work of Amos Niven Wilder* (1981), Robert Eccles's *Erwin Ramsdell Goodenough: A Personal Pilgrimage* (1985), and John Giltner's *Moses Stuart: The Father of Biblical Science* (1988).

Several histories have been written on the institutions which have stood behind American Bible production. The oldest and most prominent of these institutions has been the American Bible Society, founded in 1816. Since its inception, the American Bible Society has published over four billion copies of the Bible and portions of scripture.[12] Four institutional histories have been written about it: William Strickland's *History of the American Bible Society* (1849), Henry Dwight's *The Centennial History of the American Bible Society* (1916), Peter Wosh's *Spreading the Word: The Bible Business in Nineteenth-Century America* (1994), and the Society's bicentennial history written by John Fea, *The Bible Cause: A History of the American Bible Society* (2016).

There are other important studies which touch upon of the history and influence of the American Bible Society. In the Society's archives in Philadelphia, Pennsylvania, there are over twenty loose-leaf volumes of internal history, charting an amazing array of the Society's activities from book production to the service of women within the organization. The historian David Nord has produced several important studies on early American Bible publishing and distribution that touch closely on the activities of the American Bible Society, including: *Faith in Reading* (2004), "The Evangelical Origins of Mass Media in America, 1815-1835" (1984), and "Free Books, Free Grace, Free Riders" (1996). John W. Quist's "Slaveholding Operatives of the Benevolent Empire" (1996) also tells an important story of American Bible distribution in the South.

Of course, there have been a number of other nonprofit and for-profit societies and businesses that have produced and distributed Bibles in the United States. The American Bible Society spawned rival societies, and the stories of these rivals can be found in William Wyckoff's *Documentary History of the American Bible Union* and *A Sketch of the Origin and Some Particulars of the History of the Most Eminent Bible Societies* (1857-1866). Surprisingly, only one extended history exists of the Gideons International, an organization centered in Nashville, Tennessee, which currently distributes over 45,000,000 portions of the scriptures annually. This treatment, *Sowers of the Word* (1995), is a broad overview of the Gideons International since its founding in 1899, and was written by one of the organization's former presidents, M. A. Henderson. Institutional studies of for-profit Bible publishing include: James Ruark and Ted Engstrom's *The House of Zondervan* (1981) and Judith Duke's *Religious Publishing and Communications* (1984). Aside from treatments of Bible publishing firms, there have been a number of biographical examinations of American Bible producers as well. Studies of two of the earliest, and most important, Bible publishers are: Richard Hixon's *Isaac Collins: A Quaker Printer in the 18th Century* (1968) and James Green's *Mathew Carey: Publisher and Patriot* (1985).

Various Bible editions and Bible versions have garnered their own biographically oriented treatments. The story of the first English-language Bible published in North American is told by Laton Holmgren in his analysis of the printer Robert Aitken entitled "A 'Pious and Laudable Undertaking': The Bible of the Revolution" (1975). An early nineteenth-century attempt at publishing a new Bible edition took the form of Mormonism's founding prophet, Joseph Smith Jr., reworking parts of the scriptures to fit his new American religious tradition. Robert Matthews's *'A Plainer Translation'* (1972) tells the story of Smith's new translation of the Bible. An impressive feat of American religious publishing came in Julia Smith's translation of the Bible, the first American translation of the scriptures completed by a woman. Smith's quest after a new biblical translation can be found in Kathleen L. Housley's *The Letter Kills but the Spirit Gives Life* (1993). An examination of the incredibly popular and influential Scofield Study Bible can be found in Joseph M. Canfield's *The Incredible Scofield and His Book* (1988).

Two autobiographies provide more recent treatments of American publishers: Kenneth Taylor's *My Life: A Guided Tour* (1991) and Sam Moore's *American by Choice* (1998). Taylor founded Tyndale Publishing House after his immense success as translator of The Living Bible paraphrase version of the scriptures, and Moore served as the president of Thomas Nelson Publishers, the nation's largest for-profit Bible publisher.

THE FIFTH CORD: CULTURAL EXAMINATIONS OF THE BIBLE

In 1980 Oxford University Press published *The Bible in America*, a slender volume of essays edited by two historians of American religion, Nathan Hatch and Mark Noll. In the 1970s

and the 1980s, cultural history was a rising school of scholarship that looked at historical phenomena from a variety of angles, stressing the complexity and interrelated nature
of given historical artifacts and the natural and societal contexts that produced and used
those artifacts. It is a type of history that takes into account the popular and the elite, the
ethereal and the material, the geographical and the natural, the rational and the spiritual. It
is marked by its attempts to bring theoretical and rhetorical sophistication to the analysis of
the deep webs of meaning and cultural expression that surround specific artifacts in given
historical moments.

The appearance of *The Bible in America* marked a turning point in terms of the study of
the Bible in America. While scholars had done a great deal of textually interpretative and
bibliographic work on the Bible prior to 1980, the religious historian Mark Noll stressed
how shockingly little scholarly attention had been paid prior to the 1980s to the "Bible as an
industry of print, the Bible as a complex cultural artifact, the Bible as a standard for competing ideological groups, or even the Bible as a source of Jewish and Christian devotion."[13]
Hatch and Noll's volume inaugurated a new era of studying the Bible in American culture.

Following in the wake of *The Bible in America* came the Centennial Publications Series
of the Society of Biblical Literature, which had produced twenty-one volumes by 1988 on
various aspects of the Bible in the United States.[14] Within this series came the Society of
Biblical Literature's "The Bible in American Culture Series," under the general editorship
of Edwin Gaustad and Walter Harrelson. Titles is this six-volume series include: David
L. Barr and Nicholas Piediscalzi's *The Bible in American Education* (1982), Ernest Sandeen's
The Bible and Social Reform (1982), Giles Gunn's *The Bible and American Arts and Letters*
(1983), James Turner Johnson's *The Bible in American Law, Politics, and Political Rhetoric*
(1985), Allene S. Phy's *The Bible and Popular Culture in America* (1985), and Ernest
S. Frerichs's *The Bible and Bibles in America* (1988). The Society of Biblical Literature has
recently published a new volume in this same vein of studying the Bible in American
society: Mark A. Chancey and Carol Meyer's *The Bible in the Public Square: Its Enduring
Influence in American Life* (2014).

A growing number of more synthetic treatments of the Bible in American culture
appeared in the following three decades after "The Bible in American Culture Series." Such
works include studies of the Bible in early American culture, such as Paul C. Gutjahr's *An
American Bible* (1999) and Mark Noll's *In the Beginning was the Word* (2016). Sophisticated
treatments of the Bible in later American culture include: Peter Thuesen's *In Discordance
with the Scriptures: American Protestant Battles over Translating the Bible* (1999), Penny
Schine Gold's *Making the Bible Modern* (2004), Lori Anne Ferrell's *The Bible and the People*
(2008), and Timothy Beal's *The Rise and Fall of the Bible* (2011).

The early twenty-first century also saw a pronounced growth in the scholarly interest
in the Bible in various cultural formations. A great outpouring of scholarship connected
to the Bible in politics in particular has appeared. These works focus on a wide range of
American political concerns and include such works as Steven Green's *The Bible, the School,
and the Constitution* (2012), James P. Byrd's *Sacred Scripture, Sacred War* (2013), Eran
Shalev's *American Zion* (2013), Paul Hanson's *A Political History of the Bible in America*
(2015), and Carl J. Richard's *The Founders and the Bible* (2016). Another area of scholarship to receive a great deal of recent attention near the turn of the twenty-first century
concentrates on African Americans and the Bible. Studies in this vein include: Theophus
H. Smith's, *Conjuring Culture* (1994), Vincent L. Wimbush's *African Americans and the*

Bible: Sacred Texts and Social Textures (2001), Stephen R. Haynes's *Noah's Curse* (2002), and Allen Dwight Callahan's *The Talking Book* (2006).

THE SIXTH CORD: RECEPTION STUDIES OF THE BIBLE

The last cord in the interpretative rope of biblical examination is that of reception studies. Bible reception studies are focused on examining the actual reading practices and preferences of American Bible readers. Such studies most commonly use surveys or close ethnographic studies of defined Bible reading communities to help determine how Americans have read and used their Bibles. Because of their more direct focus on actual reading practices, one might think that reception scholarship would be widely used in the study of the place and influence of the Bible in the United States. Such is not the case for two reasons.

First, survey data is usually not available for determining readership preferences from the past. Prior to the twentieth-century, no organization was surveying American Bible readers in any systematic, broad-based way to determine their preferences when it came to which version of the Bible they used. Scholars and other professionals were also not undertaking any kind of close study of Bible reading and usage practices among Bible owners through a process of interviews or other means of data collection.

Second, when organizations began to use surveys focused on Bible ownership and usage in the twentieth and twenty-first centuries, the data generated from such surveys was usually a closely guarded secret by those (most often publishers) who had paid for the data to be collected. Publishers commissioned such surveys to help them plan their own Bible development and sales strategies. Simply put, Bible publishing is big business, and like any business, there are trade secrets that publishers guard in order to retain their competitive edge. Surveys cost a great deal of money, and when organizations invest their resources, they wish to exercise tight control over the data they have gathered.

There were notable exceptions to the guarded practices most employed when using surveys and other reception studies techniques when looking at the role of the Bible in American culture. In 1990, George Gallup, president of the hugely influential Gallup polling service published a brief study of survey data concerning American usage of the Bible in his *The Role of the Bible in American Society* (1990) and a more broad-ranging exposé on American religious practices and beliefs in his *Surveying the Religious Landscape: Trends in U.S. Beliefs* (1999). The Barna Group has produced a report on extensive polling data it completed at the behest of the American Bible Society in its *American Bible Society's State of the Bible 2015* (2015). Steve Green, the president of the Hobby Lobby chain of retail stores, has also published a book synthesizing many of the polling studies on Bible usage in America completed by various groups in his *The Bible in America* (2013).

More recently, the Center for the Study of Religion and American Culture at Indiana University-Purdue at Indianapolis was awarded a half-million dollar grant by the Lilly foundation to undertake a study named "The Bible in American Life." This study consisted of several elements, but what concerns us here is the approximately $120,000.00 Lilly provided for the execution of two surveys centered on everyday Americans' Bible usage.

To determine actual American Bible usage patterns, the "Bible in American Life" project bought questions on two large surveys focused on the Bible reading preferences and practices of everyday Americans. For roughly $100,000.00, they commissioned questions on the General Social Survey (GSS) that is conducted every other year by the National Opinion Research Center at the University of Chicago, a survey that is largely funded by the National Science Foundation. The GSS has been used since 1972 to track various American demographics, attitudes, and behaviors. Questions were purchased for the 2012 survey and responses were gathered from a sample size comprising 1,551 Americans. An additional $20,000.00 was spent to place questions on the National Congregations Study III (NCS III). The NCS has been used since 1998 to gather information about religious congregational life in America, and "The Bible in American Life" project focused its attention and questions on Christian Church congregations. The Lilly Foundation's grant to the "Bible in American Life" project provided the resources to execute unprecedented research on American Bible usage habits that were not controlled by a single publishing entity. The results of the surveys are striking and add a much needed reception-oriented dimension to the study of the Bible in America. The project report and a series of scholarly essays that it inspired can be found in Philip Goff et al., eds., *The Bible in American Life* (2017).

Finally, there have been ethnographic studies of Bible usage in America. The most focused study in this regard is James S. Bielo's *Words upon the Word* (2009). Bielo examines Evangelical Bible study groups. Such groups are so immensely popular in contemporary Christian culture that over 30 million Protestants gather weekly in such groups to study the Bible. Other more recent ethnographic studies touching upon Bible usage in the United States include Brian Malley's *How the Bible Works* (2004), a collection of essays edited by James Bielo entitled *The Social Life of Scriptures* (2009), T. M. Luhrmann's *When God Talks Back* (2012), and Rebecca Barrett-Fox's *God Hates* (2016).

CONCLUSION

Just as this volume makes no pretense of being a comprehensive study of the Bible in America, neither does this short bibliographic overview of work on the Bible in America claim to be comprehensive. This bibliographic overview of the various cords that compose a larger rope of analytic interpretation focused on the Bible in America has only sought to introduce the major strains of scholarly work done on the Bible in America. In the forty-two essays that follow, one will find one or more of these strains employed to help examine specific aspects of the Bible and how it has been translated, designed, produced, distributed, and used in the United States. The individual bibliographies at the end of each of these essays will only serve to underline how the works cited in this introduction have but scraped the surface of the much larger corpus of scholarship that exists on the American Bible. Although much scholarship does exist on the American Bible and this body of scholarship continues to grow, it is our hope that these essays will serve as a foundation and a catalyst for future scholarship on the importance and influence of the Bible in America. Taking a cue from the final verse in John's Gospel, there is still so much to be studied when it comes to the Bible's place in American history and culture that the world itself could not contain the books that might be written on the topic. Although the sheer complexity of the Bible's role in American society might seem a daunting study, it is also immensely worthwhile. May this volume help lead the way to yet new eras of scholarship on the Bible in America.

NOTES

1. Barna Group, "The State of the Bible Report 2014" (New York: American Bible Society, 2014), 9, http://www.americanbible.org/uploads/content/state-of-the-bible-data-analysis-american-bible-society-2014.pdf.
2. E. Brooks Holifield, *Theology in America: Christian Thought from the Age of the Puritans to the Civil War* (New Haven, Conn.: Yale University Press, 2003), 26.
3. One of the best short treatments of the coming of age of American religious publishing in the nineteenth century is David Nord's "The Evangelical Origins of Mass Media in America, 1815-1835," *Journalism Monographs* 88 (May 1984).
4. Reiner Smolinski is the editor-in-chief of the Mather Project that is bringing the *Biblia Americana* into print for the first time. Smolinski edited the first volume in the series on the book of Genesis, which was published by Baker Academic in conjunction with Mohr Siebeck in Germany in 2010. Other volumes in the series have followed and others are still waiting to be released.
5. Philip F. Gura, *American Transcendentalism: A History* (New York: Hill and Wang, 2007), 25.
6. Paul C. Gutjahr, *An American Bible: A History of the Good Book in the United States, 1777-1880* (Stanford, Calif.: Stanford University Press, 1999), 95–109.
7. Gutjahr, *An American Bible*, 193–94.
8. Paul C. Gutjahr, "From Monarchy to Democracy: The Dethroning of the King James Bible in the United States," in *The King James Bible after 400 Years*, ed. Hannibal Hamlin and Norman W. Jones (New York: Cambridge University Press, 2010), 172.
9. Both the bibliographies of O'Callaghan and Hills concentrate primarily on different Bible editions. These are Bibles which are set in type for one or more printings. Once the type is reset, the Bible is considered a new edition. These bibliographies do not pay as careful attention to the multiple printings of a given edition, although upon occasion different printings of a specific edition are noted. For example, the American Bible Society may have used one set of type to make 140 different printings of an edition, but these bibliographies would usually only take notice of the first printing.
10. Mark A. Noll, *The History of Christianity in the United States and Canada* (Grand Rapids, Mich.: William B. Eerdmans, 1992), 402.
11. Martin Marty et al., eds. *The Religious Press in America* (New York: Holt, Rinehart and Winston, 1963), 125.
12. Noll, *The History of Christianity*, 402.
13. Mark A. Noll, "Review Essay: The Bible in America," *Journal of Biblical Literature* 106, no. 3 (1987): 496.
14. Noll offers a bibliographic review of the majority of this series in his "Review Essay," 493–509.

Bibliography

An Argument Sustaining the Common English Version of the Bible. New York: J. A. Gray, 1850.

Barker, Kenneth L., ed. *The Making of a Contemporary Translation: New International Version.* London: Hodder and Stoughton, 1987.

Barna Group. "State of the Bible 2015." New York: American Bible Society, 2015. http://www.americanbible.org/uploads/content/State_of_the_Bible_2015_report.pdf.

Barnard, Richard Kevin. *God's Word in Our Language: The Story of the New International Version.* Colorado Springs, Colo.: International Bible Society, 1989.

Barr, David L., and Nicholas Piediscalzi. *The Bible in American Education.* Atlanta, Ga.: Scholars Press, 1982.

Barrett-Fox, Rebecca. *God Hates: Westboro Baptist Church, American Nationalism, and the Religious Right.* Lawrence: University of Kansas Press, 2016.

Beal, Timothy. *The Rise and Fall of the Bible: The Unexpected History of an Accidental Book.* New York: Houghton Mifflin Harcourt, 2011.

Bielo, James S., ed. *The Social Life of Scriptures: Cross-Cultural Perspectives on Biblicism.* Rutgers, N.J.: Rutgers University Press, 2009.

———. *Words upon the Word: An Ethnography of Evangelical Group Bible Study.* New York: New York University Press, 2009.

Bloch, Joshua. *Hebrew Printing and Bibliography: Studies by Joshua Block and Others, Reprinted from the Publications of the New York Public Library.* Selected and with a preface by Charles Berlin. New York: New York Public Library, 1976.

Brown, Jerry Wayne. *The Rise of Biblical Criticism in America, 1800–1870.* Middletown, Conn.: Wesleyan University Press, 1969.

Brown, Robert E. *Jonathan Edwards and the Bible.* Bloomington: Indiana University Press, 2002.

Byrd, James P. *Sacred Scripture, Sacred War: The Bible in the American Revolution.* New York: Oxford University Press, 2013.

Calderhead, Christoph. *Illuminating the Word: The Making of The Saint John's Bible.* 2nd ed. New York: St. John's Bible, 2015.

Callahan, Allen Dwight. *The Talking Book: African Americans and the Bible.* New Haven, Conn.: Yale University Press, 2006.

Campbell, Gordon. *Bible: The Story of the King James Version.* New York: Oxford University Press, 2010.

Canfield, Joseph M. *The Incredible Scofield and His Book.* Vallecito, Calif.: Ross House Books, 1988.

Carson, D. A. *The Inclusive Language Debate: A Plea for Realism.* Grand Rapids, Mich.: Baker Book House, 1998.

Castelli, Elizabeth A., et al., eds. *The Postmodern Bible: The Bible and Culture Collective.* New Haven, Conn.: Yale University Press, 1995.

Chamberlain, William J. *Catalogue of English Bible Translations: A Classified Bibliography of Versions and Editions Including Books, Parts, and Old and New Testament Apocrypha and Apocryphal Books.* Westport, Conn.: Greenwood Press, 1991.

Chancey, Mark A., and Carol Meyers. *The Bible in the Public Square: Its Enduring Influence in American Life.* Atlanta, Ga.: SBL Press, 2014.

Cmiel, Kenneth. *Democratic Eloquence: The Fight over Popular Speech in Nineteenth-Century America.* New York: William Morrow, 1990.

Coxe, Arthur Cleveland. *An Apology for the Common English Bible.* Baltimore, Md.: J. Robinson, 1857.

Cressy, David. "Books as Totems in Seventeenth-Century England and New England." *Journal of Library History* 21, no. 1 (Winter 1986): 92–106.

Crossan, John Dominic. *A Fragile Craft: The Work of Amos Niven Wilder.* Atlanta, Ga.: Scholars Press, 1981.

Darlow, T. H., and H. F. Moule. *Historical Catalogue of the Printed Editions of Holy Scripture.* New York: Kraus Reprint, 1963.

Dinsmore, Charles Allen. *The English Bible as Literature.* London: Allen & Unwin, 1931.

Duke, James O. *Horace Bushnell: On the Vitality of Biblical Language.* Atlanta, Ga.: Scholars Press, 1984.

Dwight, Henry Otis. *The Centennial History of the American Bible Society.* New York: Macmillan, 1916.

Eames, Wilberforce. *Bibliographic Notes on Eliot's Indian Bible and on His Other Translations and Works in the Indian Language of Massachusetts.* Washington, D.C.: Government Printing Office, 1890.

Eccles, Robert S. *Erwin Ramsdell Goodenough: A Personal Pilgrimage.* Atlanta, Ga.: Scholars Press, 1985.

Elwell, Walter, and J. D. Weaver, eds. *The Bible Interpreters of the Twentieth Century: A Selection of Evangelical Voices.* Grand Rapids, Mich.: Baker Book House, 1999.

Everett, Oliver. "Novem Testamentum Graece, ex recensione J. Jac. Griesbachii." *North American Review* 15 (1822): 460–86.

Fea, John. *The Bible Cause: A History of the American Bible Society.* New York: Oxford University Press, 2016.

Ferrell, Lori Anne. *The Bible and the People.* New Haven, Conn.: Yale University Press, 2008.

Frerichs, Ernest S., ed. *The Bible and Bibles in America.* Atlanta, Ga.: Scholars Press, 1988.

Gallup, George, Jr. *The Role of the Bible in American Society.* Princeton, N.J.: Princeton Religion Research Center, 1990.

———, and D. Michael Lindsay. *Surveying the Religious Landscape: Trends in U.S. Beliefs.* Harrisonburg, Pa.: Morehouse, 1999.

Gardiner, J. H. *The Bible as English Literature.* London: Forgotten Books, 2015.

Giltner, John H. *Moses Stuart: The Father of Biblical Science in America.* Atlanta, Ga.: Scholars Press, 1988.

Goff, Philip, Arthur E. Fransley II, and Peter J. Thuesen, eds. *The Bible in American Life.* New York: Oxford University Press, 2017.

Gold, Penny Schine. *Making the Bible Modern: Children's Bibles and Jewish Education in Twentieth-Century America.* Ithaca, N.Y.: Cornell University Press, 2004.

Green, James N. *Mathew Carey: Publisher and Patriot.* Philadelphia: Library Company of Philadelphia, 1985.

Green, Steven. *The Bible, the School, and the Constitution: The Clash that Shaped Modern Church-State Doctrine.* New York: Oxford University Press, 2012.

Green, Steve, with Todd Hillard. *The Bible in America: What We Believe about the Most Important Book in Our History.* Oklahoma City, Okla.: Dust Jacket Press, 2013.

Grudem, Wayne, et al. *Translating Truth: The Case for Essentially Literary Bible Translation.* Wheaton, Ill.: Crossway Books, 2005.

Gunn, Giles, ed. *The Bible and American Arts and Letters.* Atlanta, Ga.: Scholars Press, 1983.

Gura, Philip F. *American Transcendentalism: A History.* New York: Hill and Wang, 2007.

Gutjahr, Paul C. *An American Bible: A History of the Good Book in the United States, 1777–1880.* Stanford, Calif.: Stanford University Press, 1999.

———. "The Bible-zine *Revolve* and the Evolution of the Culturally Relevant Bible in America." In *Religion and the Culture of Print in Modern America*, edited by Charles L. Cohen and Paul S. Boyer, 326–48. Madison: University of Wisconsin Press, 2008.

———, and Megan Benton, eds. *Illuminating Letters: Essays on Typography and Literary Interpretation.* Amherst: University of Massachusetts Press, 2000.

Hall, David D. *Worlds of Wonder, Days of Judgment: Popular Religious Beliefs in Early New England.* Cambridge, Mass.: Harvard University Press, 1989.

Hamlin, Hannibal, and Norman W. Jones. *The King James Bible after 400 Years: Literary, Linguistic, and Cultural Influences.* New York: Cambridge University Press, 2010.

Hanson, Paul D. *A Political History of the Bible in America.* Louisville, Ky.: Westminster John Knox Press, 2015.

Harding, Susan. "*Revolve*, the Biblezine: A Transevangelical Text." In *The Social Life of Scriptures: Cross-Cultural Perspectives on Biblicism*, edited by James Bielo, 176–193. Rutgers, N.J.: Rutgers University Press, 2009.

Harrisville, Roy A. *Benjamin Wisner Bacon: Pioneer in American Biblical Interpretation.* Atlanta, Ga.: Scholars Press, 1976.

———. *Frank Chamberlain Porter: Pioneer in American Biblical Interpretation.* Atlanta, Ga.: Scholars Press, 1976.

Hatch, Nathan O., and Mark A. Noll, eds. *The Bible in America: Essays in Cultural History.* New York: Oxford University Press, 1982.

Haynes, Stephen R. *Noah's Curse: The Biblical Justification of American Slavery.* New York: Oxford University Press, 2002.

Henderson, M. A. *Sowers of the Word: A 95-Year History of The Gideons International, 1899–1994.* Nashville, Tenn.: Gideons International, 1995.

Hills, Margaret. *The English Bible in America.* New York: American Bible Society, 1962.

Historical Account of the Work of the American Committee of Revision of the Authorized English Version of the Bible. New York: Charles Scribner's Sons, 1885.

Hixon, Richard F. *Isaac Collins: A Quaker Printer in the 18th Century.* New Brunswick, N.J.: Rutgers University Press, 1968.

Hodgson, Robert, and Paul A. Soukup, eds. *Fidelity and Translation: Communicating the Bible in New Media.* New York: American Bible Society, 1999.

———, and Paul A. Soukup, eds. *From One Medium to Another: Basic Issues for Communicating the Scriptures in New Media.* New York: American Bible Society, 1997.

Holifield, E. Brooks. *The Gentlemen Theologians: American Theology in Southern Culture, 1795–1860.* Durham, N.C.: Duke University Press, 1978.

———. *Theology in America: Christian Thought from the Age of the Puritans to the Civil War.* New Haven, Conn.: Yale University Press, 2003.

Holmgren, Laton E. "A 'Pious and Laudable Undertaking': The Bible of the Revolution." *American History* 10, no. 6 (October 1975): 12–17.

Housley, Kathleen L. *The Letter Kills but the Spirit Gives Life: The Smiths—Abolitionists, Suffragists, Bible Translators.* Glastonbury, Conn.: Historical Society of Glastonbury, 1993.

Johnson, James Turner, ed. *The Bible in American Law, Politics, and Political Rhetoric.* Atlanta, Ga.: Scholars Press, 1985.

Kee, Howard Clark, ed. *The Bible in the Twenty-First Century.* New York: American Bible Society, 1993.

Lewis, Jack P. *The English Bible from KJV to NIV: A History and Evaluation.* 2nd ed. Grand Rapids, Mich.: Baker Book House, 1991.

Lindsey, Rachel McBride. *A Communion of Shadows: Religion and Photography in Nineteenth-Century America*. Chapel Hill: University of North Carolina Press, 2017.

Luhrmann, T. M. *When God Talks Back: Understanding the American Evangelical Relationship with God*. New York: Vintage, 2012.

Malley, Brian. *How the Bible Works: An Anthropological Study of Evangelical Biblicism*. Walnut Creek, Calif.: AltaMira Press, 2004.

Marsden, George, ed. *Evangelicalism and Modern America*. Grand Rapids, Mich.: William B. Eerdmans, 1984.

Martin, Robert. *Accuracy of Translation and the New International Version: The Primary Criterion in Evaluating Bible Versions*. Carlisle, Pa.: Banner of Truth Trust, 1989.

Matthews, Robert. *'A Plainer Translation': Joseph Smith's Translation of the Bible, a History and Commentary*. Provo, Utah. Brigham Young University Press, 1972.

McConnell, Frank. *The Bible and the Narrative Tradition*. New York: Oxford University Press, 1986.

McDannell, Colleen. *Material Christianity: Religion and Popular Culture in America*. New Haven, Conn.: Yale University Press, 1995.

McGrath, Alistar. *In the Beginning: The Story of the King James Bible and How It Changed a Nation, a Language, and a Culture*. New York: Doubleday, 2001.

McKim, Donald. *Historical Handbook of Major Biblical Interpreters*. Downers Grove, Ill.: InterVarsity Press, 1998.

Metzger, Bruce M. *The Bible in Translation: Ancient and English Versions*. Grand Rapids, Mich.: Baker Book House, 2001.

Moore, Sam. *American by Choice: The Remarkable Fulfillment of an Immigrant's Dream*. Nashville, Tenn.: Thomas Nelson, 1998.

Morgan, David, and Sally Promey, eds. *The Visual Cultures of American Religion*. Berkeley: University of California Press, 2000.

Murphy, Cullen. *The Word According to Eve: Women and the Bible in Ancient Times and Our Own*. New York: Houghton Mifflin, 1999.

Newman, Barclay M. *Creating & Crafting the Contemporary English Version: A New Approach to Bible Translation*. New York: American Bible Society, 1996.

Nicolson, Adam. *God's Secretaries: The Making of the King James Bible*. New York: Harper Collins, 2003.

Noll, Mark A. *America's God from Jonathan Edwards to Abraham Lincoln*. New York: Oxford University Press, 2002.

———. *The Civil War as a Theological Crisis*. Chapel Hill: University of North Carolina Press, 2006.

———. *In the Beginning Was the Word: The Bible in American Life, 1492–1783*. New York: Oxford University Press, 2016.

———. "Review Essay: The Bible in America." *Journal of Biblical Literature* 106, no. 3 (September 1987): 493–509.

Nord, David Paul. "The Evangelical Origins of Mass Media in America, 1815–1835." *Journalism Monographs* 88 (May 1984): 1–30.

———. *Faith in Reading: Religious Publishing and the Birth of Mass Media in America*. New York: Oxford University Press, 2004.

———. "Free Books, Free Grace, Free Riders: The Economics of Religious Publishing in Early Nineteenth-Century America." *Proceedings of the American Antiquarian Society* 106, no. 2 (October 1996): 241–72.

O'Callaghan, Edward. *A List of Editions of the Holy Scriptures and Parts Thereof*. Albany, N.Y.: Munsell & Rowland, 1861.

Orlinsky, Harry M., and Robert G. Bratcher. *A History of Bible Translation and the North American Contribution*. Atlanta, Ga.: Scholars Press, 1991.

Parsons, Wilfrid, S.J. "First American Editions of Catholic Bibles." *Historical Records and Studies* 27 (1937): 89–98.

Phy, Allene Stuart, ed. *The Bible and Popular Culture*. Atlanta, Ga.: Scholars Press, 1985.

Pope, Hugh, O.P. *English Versions of the Bible*. St. Louis, Mo.: Herder, 1952.

Presidential Inaugural Bibles: Catalogue of an Exhibition, November 17, 1968 through February 23, 1969, The Rare Book Library, Washington Cathedral.

Price, Rex Thomas, Jr. "The Mormon Missionary of the Nineteenth Century." PhD diss., University of Wisconsin-Madison, 1991.

Quist, John W. "Slaveholding Operatives of the Benevolent Empire: Bible, Tract, and Sunday School Societies in Antebellum Tuscaloosa County, Alabama." *Journal of Southern History* 62, no. 3 (August 1996): 481–526.

Richard, Carl J. *The Founders and the Bible*. Lanham, Md.: Rowman & Littlefield, 2016.

Ruark, James E., and Ted W. Engstrom. *The House of Zondervan*. Grand Rapids, Mich.: Zondervan Publishing House, 1981.

Ryken, Leland. *The Complete Handbook of Literary Forms in the Bible*. Wheaton, Ill.: Crossway, 2014.

Sandeen, Ernest R., ed. *The Bible and Social Reform*. Atlanta, Ga.: Scholars Press, 1982.

Shalev, Eran. *American Zion: The Old Testament as Political Text from the Revolution to the Civil War*. New Haven, Conn.: Yale University Press, 2013.

Simms, Paris Marion. *The Bible in America: Versions That Have Played Their Part in the Making of the Republic*. New York: Wilson-Erickson, 1936.

Sink, Susan. *The Art of The Saint John's Bible: The Complete Reader's Guide*. New York: The Saint John's Bible, 2013.

Slee, Jacquelynn. "A Summary of the English Editions of Illustrated Bibles Published in America between 1790 and 1825, with Indices of Subjects Illustrated and Engravers." Master's thesis, University of Michigan, 1973.

Smith, Theophus H. *Conjuring Culture: Biblical Formations of Black America*. New York: Oxford University Press, 1994.

Soukup, Paul A., and Robert Hodgson, eds. *Fidelity and Translation: Communicating the Bible in New Media*. New York: American Bible Society, 1999.

Strickland, William P. *History of the American Bible Society, from Its Organization to the Present Time*. New York: Harper & Brothers, 1849.

Sussman, Lance J. *Isaac Leeser and the Making of American Judaism*. Detroit, Mich.: Wayne State University Press, 1995.

Taylor, Ken. *My Life: A Guided Tour*. Wheaton, Ill.: Tyndale Publishing House, 1991.

Thuesen, Peter J. *In Discordance with the Scriptures: American Protestant Battles over Translating the Bible*. New York: Oxford University Press, 1999.

Trench, Richard Chenevix. *On the Authorized Version of the New Testament in Connection with Some Recent Proposals for its Revision*. New York: Redfield, 1858.

Weitenkempf, Frank. "American Bible Illustration." *Boston Public Library Quarterly* 3 (July 1958): 154–57.

Whiteman, Maxwell. "The Introduction and Spread of Hebrew Type in the United States." New York: American Printing History Association, 1992. Offprint from *Printing History* 13 and 14 (1991-1992): 41–58.

Wild, Laura H. *A Literary Guide to the Bible: A Study of the Types of Literature Present in the Old and New Testaments*. Norwood, Pa.: Norwood Editions, 1976.

Willoughby, Harold R. *The Study of the Bible Today and Tomorrow.* Chicago: University of Chicago Press, 1947.

Wimbush, Vincent L., ed. *African Americans and the Bible: Sacred Texts and Social Textures.* New York: Continuum, 2001.

Wosh, Peter J. *Spreading the Word: The Bible Business in Nineteenth-Century America.* Ithaca, N.Y.: Cornell University Press, 1994.

Wright, John. *Historic Bibles in America.* New York: Thomas Whittaker, 1905.

Wyckoff, William H., and C. A. Buckbee, eds. *Documentary History of the American Bible Union.* 4 vols. New York: American Bible Union, 1857–1866.

———. *A Sketch of the Origin and Some Particulars of the History of the Most Eminent Bible Societies.* New York: Lewis Colby, 1847.

THE OXFORD HANDBOOK OF

THE BIBLE
IN AMERICA

PART I

BIBLE PRODUCTION

....

CHAPTER 1

PROTESTANT ENGLISH-LANGUAGE BIBLE PUBLISHING AND TRANSLATION

....

PAUL C. GUTJAHR

Introduction

....

In 1663, a Puritan clergyman and missionary by the name of John Eliot produced what is perhaps the most ambitious book ever published in America. Aided by a few dedicated assistants, Eliot produced a complete translation of the Holy Bible in the language of the Massachusetts Algonquin Native Americans entitled *Mamusse Wunneetupanatamwe Up-Biblum God*.[1] What makes Eliot's Bible such an utterly astounding feat is that he both needed to translate the some 700,000 words of the Christian scriptures into Algonquin and then muster the financial capital and printing expertise necessary to produce the mammoth 1,180-page volume. He first published his New Testament in 1661, the entire Bible in 1663, and then a second edition of the Bible in 1685.[2] Once the Bible was completed, then Eliot needed to find ways to distribute it and teach the Native Americans how to read it. In a time when American publishing was in its infancy, and American printers seldom attempted to produce more than broadsheets, sermons, and short pamphlets by toiling through a laborious hand-press printing process, what became known as Eliot's Indian Bible represented nothing short of a publishing miracle. Before his death in 1690, Eliot helped produce almost four million printed pages of biblical text—an undertaking that represented the constant setting and resetting of some 150,000 pieces of individual type impressed upon millions of pages of handmade, linen paper.[3] By almost any publishing standard of the time, producing this Bible was an astonishing accomplishment.

Eliot's Indian Bible highlights two central lines of thought critical to understanding American Bible publishing. First, such Bible production concerns a variety of cultural factors that range from literacy rates to massive shifts in American methods of transportation combined with considerations of changing publishing technologies that include the design of printing presses, the production of paper, the forging of type, the composition of ink, the evolution of bookbinding techniques, and then later the introduction of various means of digital publishing. Second, religious publishing in general, and Bible production and distribution in particular, have long been driven not solely by market considerations but by religiously guided missionary impulses as well.[4] Eliot dedicated much of his life to producing a printed Bible for a tribe that numbered around nine thousand members in the mid-1670s and far fewer by the time he released his Bible's second edition, but numbers of recipients and financial considerations were never uppermost in his thinking.[5] He was convinced that Native Americans who inhabited the region around his village must have access to God's word in order to have access to God Himself. Eliot's Indian Bible forcefully illustrates the importance Bible publishers have long placed on making available copies of God's Word, regardless of cost, so that people's lives might be changed both in this life and the next. To understand Bible publishing, one must appreciate how it is a process borne of a unique blend of the ever-changing nature of American culture, printing technologies, and religious ideologies.

First Wave: American Independence to the 1820s

Added to the mystique of Eliot's accomplishment is the fact that aside from three German-language editions of the Bible produced by the Pennsylvanian printer Christopher Sauer and his son between 1743 and 1776, an English-language New Testament would not be published in the American colonies until 1777. A complete English-language edition of the Bible would not be published until 1782. Nearly a century separates Eliot's Indian Bible from what might be called the First Wave of North American Bible production, a period that began with the advent of the Revolutionary War in 1776 and ended with America's print culture revolution of the 1820s.

The reason behind the slow appearance of American-printed copies of English-language Bibles lies in the fact that colonial printers were subject to British rules of copyright until they broke from England in the Revolutionary War. In England, the Bible could only be published by printers designated by the King or Queen, and no such printers existed on American shores prior to the Revolution. Of the many consequences born of the colonies' Declaration of Independence was the serious disruption of trade between all of Europe and America. Among the countless items lost to the American marketplace were English-language Bibles. American clergymen became ever more concerned over the Bible's scarcity and sought to address the problem by petitioning the Continental Congress in the summer of 1777 to set about procuring or producing more copies of the English Bible.[6] Congress both considered importing Bibles and having local printers produce Bibles. Ultimately, the Philadelphia printer Robert Aitken decided to make the bold move to produce the first American-printed English-language New Testament (1777) and then the entire Bible (1782).[7] With Aitken's efforts, English-language Bible production in America was born.

By any measure, producing a Bible in eighteenth-century America was a daunting undertaking. Printing establishments in this period often included only a single hand-powered printing press, operated by a master with the help of the journeymen or apprentices he employed. These individuals had to set the type in molds for each individual page, then ink the type, and finally impress those molds on sheets of papers. It was arduous, back-breaking work. Each hand press required at least two, commonly, three, workers to facilitate its operation, as one worker operated the press lever (which lowered the type platen onto the paper), while another worker inked the type, and a third worker fed and extracted the paper.

Especially in this early period, it is essential to remember that the Bible is a large and immensely complex book to produce. With its hundreds of densely worded pages, each volume required significant resources to print and bind. Because of its expense, it is not surprising that American printers left its production to larger British and European pub-lishing houses before the Revolutionary War. Aitken's move to print the Bible in America was as tragic as it was bold. His Bible came out in 1782 just as the war was ending. Peace with England once again allowed imported Bibles to flow on American shores. Thus, Aitken's Bible gave him the distinction of both printing the first English-language Bible edition in America and also printing an edition that financially ruined him.[8]

In the half-century following the appearance of Aitken's ill-fated Bible venture, some 150 other American publishers—working mainly in the publishing centers of Boston, Philadelphia, and New York City—embarked on a wide variety of Bible publishing ven-tures. Principal among these Bible publishers was the Philadelphia master printer and entrepreneur, Mathew Carey. Carey was already a seasoned veteran of publishing when he established his printing shop in Philadelphia in 1785. He had apprenticed in Ireland and then had worked for the innovative French printer, Didot, in Paris followed by a period when he assisted Benjamin Franklin in Philadelphia. Carey's first foray into Bible publish-ing came when he decided to publish an American edition of the Catholic Reims-Douay Bible in 1790. In 1801, he produced his first Protestant edition of the Bible, the first of some sixty editions of the King James Bible he would produce between 1801 and 1824.

Carey's work as a Bible publisher is noteworthy for two reasons. First, he was aggres-sive and savvy in his marketing and distribution practices, making his Bibles prior to the 1820s the most common American-produced set of the scriptures available in the United States. Second, he adopted a printing method that involved "standing type," a process that involved him purchasing enough metal type to keep every page of the Bible standing in its own mold between printings.[9] Standing type had two distinct advantages. It could be stored and thus stood ever-ready to print more copies of a Bible edition without the costly and time-consuming process of resetting the type, and it was also freer of the errors caused by having to constantly reset pages of type. With standing type, Carey was able to make textual corrections each time a mistake was discovered. While other printers were forced to reset the moveable type on each page of the Bible before they printed that page, Carey leapfrogged his competitors by dedicating an entire room of his printing house to storing stacks of type-filled molds ready to be employed at any time to produce a new edition of the Bible.

Mathew Carey was perhaps the last great book publisher of America's hand-press era. As he retired from his publishing business in the 1820s after a four-decade career, a new kind of publishing was coming to the fore in the United States. This new publishing moved away from the centuries-old craft and guild structure of printing to be replaced by far more industrialized printing practices.

Second Wave: The 1820s to the 1870s

When American publishing entered the opening decades of the nineteenth century, the basic contours of how machine-printed books were produced had changed little from the time of Gutenberg. Gutenberg's German hand press had printed pages by impressing individual pieces of metal type onto sheets of paper. The basic principles of this impression method of printing would be used with various mechanical deviations up until the end of the twentieth century. A publishing revolution, however, did strike the United States in the 1820s to create a second wave of American Bible publishing as a number of technological changes combined with the country's increasing literacy rates to create unprecedented access to the printed word throughout the United States. These changes involved four of the basic components of book production: type, paper, printing machinery, and bookbinding.

In the opening decades of the nineteenth century, a process called stereotyping revolutionized the way American printers set their type. Stereotype plates represented a natural extension of standing type where a metal stereotype plate was created by means of setting type in a mold and then making a plaster-of-Paris negative of that mold. This negative plate was then used to make a positive plate via liquid metal. Invented in England, David Bruce of New York brought the process to the United States, becoming the country's first successful manufacturer of stereotype plates. In 1814, Bruce sold his first set of stereotype plates for the King James Version of the New Testament to none other than Mathew Carey.[10] Other publishers, most famously, the American Bible Society and Harper and Brothers, would follow Carey in the use of stereotype plates to mass-produce Bibles.

Changes in the papermaking industry joined with the emergence of stereotyping to transform how American printers produced books in the opening decades of the nineteenth century. Two inventions appeared in this period to change papermaking from a task completed by individual workmen straining and flattening cloth pulp in large wooden molds to a product churned out in unprecedented quantities with unprecedented speed through the use of ever more complex machines. In 1804, the English papermakers Henry and Sealy Fourdrinier established a patent on a variation of a French papermaking machine that had been invented in 1799. The Fourdrinier machine forever changed the way paper was produced on both sides of the Atlantic. It enabled papermakers to quadruple both their speed of production and reduce their cost by two-thirds.[11] By the 1820s, several Fourdrinier machines had been imported to the United States, and American machinists immediately began to manufacture their own improved versions of the invention.[12] At roughly the same time, a Pennsylvania farmer and inventor by the name of Thomas Gilpin developed a second, new papermaking machine that used a giant cylinder mechanism to produce long, continuous sheets of paper. By the 1820s the paper mass-produced from Gilpin's machines came to be used by some of the largest religious publishers of the day, including the American Bible Society and the American Tract Society.[13]

Alongside stereotyping and machine-made paper came the rise of the power printing press. In 1821, the printer David Treadwell introduced the first practical power-press to America. While England and other countries had experimented with steam and other kinds of power-presses, Treadwell's design used horse power.[14] His horse-powered press doubled the speed of the printing process. A proficiently run hand press could produce between 200 to 250 pages an hour; Treadwell's horse-powered press could produce over 500 pages in the same amount of time. Treadwell continued to refine his ideas, and by 1823 had created a working steam-powered press. The most successful steam press of the 1820s and 1830s, however, did not come from Treadwell but from a set of Massachusetts publishing brothers by the names of Isaac and Seth Adams. The presses invented by the Adams required fewer workers to operate them and were capable of producing a 1,000 impressions an hour.[15] Various incarnations of the Adams steam press were so nicely designed, did such high-quality work, and required so little maintenance and oversight that they would dominate book publishing for the next fifty years.[16]

Finally, bookbinding was also changing in the 1820s as ever larger print runs came off the presses. As improved mechanization allowed the volume of printed material to grow, similar changes occurred in the process of bookbinding. Prior to the 1820s, printed books most often reached their buyers as sets of loose or loosely stitched pages, which buyers then had a professional bookbinder sew together and cover with leather or cloth-coated boards.[17] By the 1820s, more sophisticated cutting and sewing machinery encouraged ever more publishers to bring the binding process in-house, and by mid-century it was common for large publishers, such as the American Bible Society and Harper and Brothers, to bind every volume they produced.[18] Publishers still bound their books in a range of styles, but without the individual flourishes and nuances common to the more personal binding practices of previous centuries.

It is important to note that while cloth bindings came to replace leather bindings beginning in the 1830s, Bibles resisted this trend.[19] Bibles remained leather-bound long after the majority of new books were being bound in cloth, underlining the worth, durability, and unchanging nature of the biblical text. It is not until the second half of the twentieth century when one finds large numbers of Bibles being bound in ways that do not include leather, and it is still true that Bibles persist as one of the few leather-bound books widely available in today's print marketplace.

All these changes in book publishing helped create an exponential growth of printed material in the United States beginning in the 1820s. Whereas at the turn of the nineteenth century, a large press run for a book hovered around some 2,000 copies, by the 1830s, print runs of 30,000, 50,000, and even 100,000 copies were common.[20] The absolute explosion of printed material in the antebellum period, however, was not simply a matter of technology. Having the ability to produce a product does not guarantee its production. Such production demands a market, and the changing literacy rates, reading habits, and religious beliefs of Americans provided just such a market.

The rising literacy rates across the United States are of central importance to Bible publishing in this period. The literacy rate for white women came to match that of white men in the United States moving from roughly 45 percent in 1790 to grow to around 90 percent by the time of the Civil War.[21] Such phenomenal growth in American female literacy rates is particularly important in light of the fact that females have always outnumbered males when it comes to American church membership and religious involvement.[22] Alongside this high literacy rate for both white men and women in the United States is the fact that American Christians have always put a premium on being able to read the Bible for themselves, a commitment that had deep historical roots. Beginning with the General Court of Massachusetts, which passed legislation in 1647 to support universal schooling in the colony so that all its inhabitants might be able to read the Christian scriptures, the strong emphasis on being able to read the Bible continued to propel literacy education throughout the nineteenth century.[23] Antebellum America's religious print culture grew in tandem with the country's rising literacy rates and the vibrant revivalist, reform, and missionary movements associated with the Second Great Awakening.[24]

Perhaps no single institution better encapsulates this passion for printed material better than the American Bible Society (ABS). Founded in 1816, the ABS had centralized its publishing operations into a single building in New York City by 1830, which came to be commonly called the Great Bible House. The Bible House was a showcase for the most advanced printing techniques of the day, employing machine-made paper, power presses, and stereotyping to print over 300,000 copies of the scriptures a year. By the 1860s, the Bible House had increased its output to one million Bibles a year.[25]

So great was the ABS's faith in the printed word and its ability to print that word, that in 1828 it set about the incredibly audacious plan known as the "First General Supply," a plan to supply every household in the United States with a copy of the scriptures. The Society would undertake three more "General Supplies" during the nineteenth century, the last being an eight-year endeavor known as the "Fourth General Supply" that began in 1882.[26] Each General Supply, however, fell short of achieving the Society's goal of placing a copy of the Bible in every American home. Yet the sheer audacity of these attempts offers insight into just how committed American Protestants were in their commitment to spreading God's word through the power of publishing.

The ABS was so large and so well financed during the opening decades of the nineteenth century that it virtually monopolized the production and distribution of inexpensive Bibles in the United States.[27] In order to reach across denominational and theological differences, the ABS committed itself to publishing the dominant English-language translation of the Bible, the King James Version, "without note or comment."[28] Its goal was simply to get God's word out to all Americans. The Society was not as interested in the theological inflections that might accompany that word.

While the ABS churned out inexpensive Bibles for the masses, numerous other American publishers forged ahead with their own Bible publishing plans. In many cases, these publishers sought to provide the Christian scriptures that did include notes, comments, and illustrations. Emblematic of the more elegant and expensive Bible editions available to nineteenth-century Americans was Harper and Brothers magnificent—and magnificently popular—*Illuminated Bible* (1846). Using a new printing technique known as electrotyping (a refinement on stereotyping that enabled the inclusion of stunning illustrations on the same page as printed text), the *Illuminated Bible* included over 1,600 illustrations. Prior to the ABS's First General Supply, roughly 27 percent of Bible editions produced in America included some form of commentary on the same page as the biblical text. By the time of the Fourth General Supply in the 1880s, the presence of some form of commentary had risen to over 60 percent of all non-ABS Bible editions. At the same time, by the 1880s roughly 60 percent of non-ABS Bible editions included illustrations. By the end of the century, the often austere ABS editions of the scriptures were in a noticeable minority among the editions found in America's Bible marketplace.[29]

THIRD WAVE: THE 1870S TO THE 1980S

By the end of the nineteenth century, producing Bibles in the United States once again underwent significant changes, creating the Third Wave of American Bible publishing. The first significant change concerned geography. Throughout the first three-quarters of the nineteenth century, American Bible publishing had largely been concentrated in the eastern publishing centers of Philadelphia, Boston, and New York. Beginning in the 1870s, much of American Protestant publishing in general, and Bible publishing in particular, moved into the Midwest as conservative elements among Methodist, Presbyterians, Baptists, Congregationalists, and the Plymouth Brethren, created a new kind of interdenominational sympathy centered on the commitment to a more literalist interpretation of the biblical text. Responding to the German Higher Criticism that offered a biblical hermeneutic that took into account the historical moment in which the biblical text had appeared and the possible corruptions the text had undergone since its original composition, more literal-minded interpreters stressed a view that the Bible's words were undefiled by any human error and could be trusted to mean what they said. This literalist, interdenominational body of Protestants grew into what became known as the "Fundamentalist" movement of the early twentieth century.[30]

New interdenominational publishers rose up to service the interdenominational movement that would eventually coalesce into American Protestant Fundamentalism. These publishers worked hard to avoid denominational labels. Instead, they targeted an audience that shared certain core, theological beliefs. This new type of interdenominational publishing first appeared in the Chicago-based publishing firm of Fleming H. Revell in 1870.[31] A number of other Midwestern and southern firms would follow, including: David C. Cook (1875), Broadman (1891), Moody Press (1894), Kregel Books (1909), William B. Eerdmans Publishing (1910), Zondervan Publishing (1931), Baker Book House (1939), Tyndale House (1962), and a reorganized Thomas Nelson Publishers (1969). By the early twentieth century, many of the most important Christian publishing houses were located in or around three hubs: Chicago, Illinois, Grand Rapids, Michigan, and Nashville, Tennessee. The Midwest and the South had replaced the East as the center of American Bible publishing. Several of these publishers, such as Zondervan, Tyndale House, and Thomas Nelson, would rank among the largest American Bible publishers by the end of the twentieth century.[32]

The Third Wave also involved a significant change in the activities of English-language Bible translators. In the later nineteenth century, the King James Version was significantly challenged for the first time for primacy among English Bible translations in America by a new translation of the scriptures produced under the auspices of an international collection of scholars centered in Britain. In 1881, this body of scholars published the Revised Version (RV).[33] The appearance of the RV was heralded as the publishing event of the century. Even before its release, one million orders were placed for the RV. Three million copies were issued within the first twelve months of its appearance, and newspapers such as the *Chicago Times* and the *Chicago Tribune* reprinted the RV's entire New Testament in their Sunday sections over a number of weeks.[34] Such initial interest, however, did not last, and the RV did not claim more than 10 percent of the American Bible market by the turn of the twentieth century.[35]

Still, the importance of the appearance of the RV cannot be overestimated. Once the RV promised a viable, large-scale alternative to the ubiquitous King James Version, the door was opened to an ever-increasing frequency of new English-language translations. While only four new English-language translations of the entire Bible had appeared prior to the Revised Version, by the 1920s, seven new English-language translations were appearing each decade.[36] As the twentieth century came to a close, new English-language translations appeared at a rate of greater than one per year.[37] Although the dominant popularity of the King James Bible has never been eclipsed in the United States, five new English translations during the Third Wave of American Bible publishing were of particular importance.[38] These five pivotal translations include: American Standard Version (ASV, 1901), the Revised Standard Version (RSV, 1952), Today's English Version (TEV, 1966), *The Living Bible* (1967), and the New International Version (1978).

The ASV was an American extension of the RV. After the British translation committee disbanded in 1885 upon the completion and publication of the RV, the American side of the committee decided to continue to meet and out of their work came a version of the RV rendered in a more American idiom, including some six hundred changes in the text that fit more with American English usage.[39] The ASV was more widely adopted than the RV in the United States, and one of its most widely admired characteristics was its firm commitment to a "formal equivalency" or "essentially literal" word-for-word translation strategy. For much of the twentieth century, the ASV—and later the New American Standard Version (1963, 1995)—was considered the gold standard of those who were serious about the original languages of the scriptures and sought out a word-for-word translation for their biblical studies.[40]

The RSV was the product of an interdenominational group of American biblical scholars interested in updating the RV and thereby providing a more contemporary version of the scriptures for those still committed to the KJV or who had adopted the slightly more accessible ASV. The entire RSV of the Bible was released amid great fanfare in 1952. Initially it was welcomed by a wide range of Protestants who considered it the answer to the archaic language of the KJV and the often grammatically awkward ASV. For many American Protestants, the RSV promised to make God's word more accessible to the masses. The RSV, however, soon came under criticism for some of its translation choices, perhaps most famously for its choice to change the wording of Isaiah 7:14. In this verse, the KJV had chosen to use the word "virgin" while the RSV chose "young woman."[41] Mary was a virgin who conceived the Messiah, not just some young woman. Critics decried this choice—and others like it—to be a movement away from the messianic prophecies found throughout the Old Testament pointing to Jesus as the Messiah. Although the RSV would face criticism from more conservative American Protestant elements because of the way it de-emphasized a link between the Messianic prophecies of the Old Testament with the person of Jesus in the New Testament, the RSV gained a substantial foothold among Bible readers in America's mainline denominations.[42]

The ABS published the New Testament portion of the TEV in 1966 under the title *Good News for Modern Man*. The Old Testament was completed in 1976, and then the ABS published the entire Bible as the *Good News Bible: The Bible in Today's English Version*. The TEV offered a far less literal translation of the Bible than the one found in the RSV. The TEV was primarily the work of Dr. Robert G. Bratcher who worked with a larger translation committee appointed by the ABS. Because he was interested in producing a Bible translation that would use language commonly spoken by educated and non-educated Americans alike, Bratcher adopted a translation theory developed by his ABS colleague Eugene Nida known as "dynamic" or "functional equivalence."[43] Prior to *Good News for Modern Man*, the most common Protestant Bible translations found in the United States (the KJV, RV, ASV, and RSV) had approached Bible translation with a formal equivalence approach. Functional equivalence differed from formal equivalence in that it sought to translate passages from the Bible in a thought-for-thought, rather than formal equivalence's emphasis on translating passages in a word-for-word manner. Functional equivalence aimed at capturing the original meaning of the text for the contemporary audience, not necessarily the text's exact wording and syntax.

The goal of the functional equivalence approach in general, and the TEV in particular, was to make the biblical message accessible to modern readers, not to capture every nuance of the Bible's message. The TEV proved to be a stunning success. The ABS's initial print run of 150,000 copies sold out almost immediately. Within one year, 5 million copies were in print, and by the early 1980s more than 75 million copies were in circulation.[44] Inspired by the TEV's massive success, various degrees of the functional equivalence approach to translation would mark many of the Bible translations that appeared after the 1960s such as the New English Bible (1970), the New Jerusalem Bible (1985), and the Contemporary English Version (1995).

One year after the appearance of *Good News for Modern Man*, Kenneth Taylor, a Baptist layman who worked at the Christian publishing house of Moody Press, released a New Testament paraphrase called *The Living Bible*. Taylor had begun the project as a way to communicate the Bible's stories to his children without having to offer extensive commentary on many of the Bible's difficult theological concepts and arcane wording. By the very nature of it being a paraphrase, Taylor's translation was highly interpretative. It was also highly successful. His translation of the epistles of Paul named *Living Letters* (1962), had been adopted and distributed by Billy Graham through his crusades, setting the groundwork for the massive popularity of *The Living Bible's* New Testament (1967) and complete Bible (1971). Taylor's *The Living Bible* became so popular that for three years, 1972-1974, it held the honor of being the fastest selling book in America. By the late 1990s, more than 40 million copies were in circulation, and it had inspired other popular biblical paraphrases such as Eugene Peterson's *The Message* (2002).[45]

In the wake of *The Living Bible's* astounding popularity, Zondervan Publishing House financed a new English-language translation that it promised would be more theologically conservative than the RSV. This new version appeared in 1978 under the title of the New International Version (NIV). It was a version that mixed the translation strategies of formal and functional equivalency. While it followed many of the translational choices of the RSV, the NIV's editors made more conservative choices in highly contested passages such as Isaiah 7:14. In this particular case, the NIV once again restored the word "virgin" to highlight the prophetic linkages between the Old and New Testaments.[46] It was also a version that self-consciously promoted itself as conservative in its approach to translation issues and unequivocally committed to the idea of biblical inerrancy.[47] The NIV proved itself so popular that by the mid-1980s its yearly sales came to rival the perennially popular King James Version of the scriptures.[48]

The NIV's popularity and mixed translation approach would have great influence in the years to come. Perhaps most notably, it helped clear the way for other translation projects to adopt a similar mixed approach to translation, but with less conservative ends in mind. For example, when the RSV was reviewed and became the New Revised Standard Version (NRSV) in 1990, its translators chose to offer the version with gender inclusive language. While the RSV had rendered Matthew 4:4 as "Man shall not live by bread alone," the NRSV translated the same passage as "One does not live by bread alone."[49] Such choices would outrage many, but it was the ability to mix a word-for-word approach with the more inter- pretative stances available through thought-for-thought translation strategies that allowed the NRSV's gender neutrality to emerge.

The Third Wave was also marked by a pronounced rise in the presence of other non- profit Bible publishers that came alongside the ABS to become major forces in Bible pub- lishing and distribution. Perhaps the most important publisher among these nonprofit organizations is Gideons International. Founded in 1899 by a group of traveling salesmen in Janesville, Wisconsin, Gideons International would establish its headquarters and pub- lishing center in Nashville, Tennessee. By 2015, Gideons International had printed and globally distributed a staggering two billion copies of the scriptures in over one hundred languages.[50]

The Third Wave of Bible publishing also saw the appearance of three material changes to the biblical text that would become so common in the twentieth century that Bibles would be synonymous with these material presentations. The first of these was the use of flexible, soft leather bindings. Such "divinity circuit" bindings provided strength in a lighter-weight package, perfect for making a book as large as the Bible easier to use.[51] Second, editions that printed the words of Jesus in red first appeared in 1899, starting a string of typographi- cal innovations intended to help make the text's meaning more accessible for its readers.[52] Finally, in the 1920s Bibles began to be printed on thinner, less costly, more transportable paper, an innovation that gained such popularity among Bible publishers that the paper came to be known as "bible paper." Such paper was actually the invention of the Jehovah Witnesses whose publishing center in Brooklyn, New York, worked with cigarette manufac- turers in the 1920s to create a paper that would be lightweight yet durable enough to hold printer's ink in a clean and legible manner. All three of these innovations would help distin- guish Bibles from the host of other published material to be found throughout twentieth- century American print culture.

FOURTH WAVE: THE 1980S AND BEYOND

A Fourth Wave of American Bible publishing began in the 1980s with the advent of the widespread use of computer technologies in the publishing industry. Rudimentary comput- ers began to be used in American publishing as early as the 1960s to set type and format pages, but it was not until the 1980s that a true revolution in American printing took hold. Up until the 1980s, book production had followed the basic impression method first used by Gutenberg in the 1440s, namely placing ink on a form of type that was then pressed into a sheet of paper. Computer technology changed both how text could be manipulated before the printing process and how inked type was then set on paper. Textual formatting and page presentation became a digital process controlled by manipulating light on screens, and the process of impressing inked metal type on paper came to be refined and in some cases replaced by a variety of printing methods, including some which involved laser technology that adhered graphite dust to heated spaces on paper to create letters and other images.[53]

Computers vastly improved the speed with which an English-language translation could be completed, as well as improving the speed of special formats used to present the Bible's core text. Prior to computers, editors had used graph paper, light tables, scissors, tape, and glue to manipulate text on a page. Computers allowed for digital formatting and the easy collation and manipulation of text. Concordances placed at the end of a Bible edition could be generated in a matter of minutes, a process that took years in previous centuries. Special footnotes, headers, and endnotes could also be inserted and placed on a page in a matter of minutes. Beginning in the 1980s, Bible editors took full advantage of using new computer software to manipulate features such as sidebars, illustrations, color coded fonts, and marginal commentary notes to make new Bible editions.

By the 1980s, computers were helping to create new English-language translations at the rate of more than one a year, and Bible publishers combined the appearance of these new translations with the ease of creating a multitude of specialty Bible editions (with targeted study aids, highlighting, illustrations, notes, and concordances) to meet the needs of specific readerships. Hence, the 1980s began the era of the specialty niche Bible publishing to a degree never before experienced in the United States. While Bibles in different sizes, translations, and bindings can be traced back to the early nineteenth century, the diversity of Bible editions to be found at the end of the twentieth century is nothing short of astounding. Bible publishers targeted a vast array of reading audiences with their new, computer-generated Bible editions. Thus, Bible editions such as *The Couples Bible, Policeman's Bible, The Green Bible, The Coast Guardsman Bible, Celebrate Recovery Bible, American Patriot's Bible, Extreme Teen Study Bible*, and countless other niche Bible editions emerged in the closing decades of the twentieth century.

Eventually the computerization that so defines the Fourth Wave of American Bible publishing entered the electronic book age. As Bible publishing entered the twenty-first century, publishers increasingly sought to make their Bible editions available to the masses through Internet, electronic book, and mobile app formats. A growing segment of the Bible market included dedicated electronic devices that often mimicked the iPad or were constructed to be no larger than a pocket calculator. Such freestanding electronic Bible devices offered a diverse number of features to complement the text, including interpretative aids such as commentaries and dictionaries, large catalogs of Christian music, the ability to be run off solar power, having the capacity for the reader to record personal audio notes on the text, or providing short video clips to help illustrate the text's meaning.

Computerization also continued to have a profound influence on English-language Bible translation work in the twenty-first century. In 2005, the New English Translation or NET Bible appeared, a project that would eventually be closely tied to scholars at Dallas Theological Seminary. The NET Bible began as a project dedicated to creating an entirely new, academically credible English-language version of the Bible that would be globally accessible through the Internet. While the NET Bible can now be obtained in a shorter, printed format as well, its original Internet design allowed it to become a version distinguished by its over 60,000 footnotes, many of them notable for their length and scholarly attention to the original languages and historical nuances of the text.[54] The digital revolution at the heart of the Fourth Wave left no element of Bible production or translation untouched.

CONCLUSION

To study American Bible publishing in particular is to study American publishing in general, for the country's forays into Bible publishing touch every development in American textual production from the hand-press period to the digital age. Since its first printing in 1777, American Bible publishers have made constant use of the newest technologies to ensure that the Bible's content is accessible to as many people as possible. In a very real sense, the history of American book publishing writ large is powerfully illustrated by American Bible publishing. To trace developments in American typesetting, page formatting, paper production, binding practices, and distribution networks for print-based material, one need look no further than the history of American Bible publishing. Any close look at the over two century-long production of the text that gave early Americans the nickname "People of the Book" provides a plethora of insights into the book publishing practices that mark all the other books of that people as well.[55]

NOTES

1. John Eliot to Edward Winslow, July 8, 1649. As quoted in Wilberforce Eames, *Bibliographic Notes on Eliot's Indian Bible: And on His Other Translations and Works in the Indian Language of Massachusetts* (Washington, D.C.: US Government Printing Office, 1890), 1.
2. For a good overview of the Eliot Indian Bible's publishing history, see George Parker Winship, *The Cambridge Press, 1638-1692: A Reexamination of the Evidence Concerning the Bay Psalm Book and the Eliot Indian Bible as well as Other Contemporary Books and People* (Philadelphia: University of Pennsylvania Press, 1945), 208–44. Eliot produced 1,500 copies of his 1661 New Testament, 1,000 copies of his 1663 edition of the entire Bible, and 2,000 copies of the second edition of his Bible in 1685.
3. Winship, *The Cambridge Press*, 210–11.
4. David Paul Nord, *Faith in Reading: Religious Publishing and the Birth of Mass Media in America* (New York: Oxford University Press, 2004), 7.
5. H. A. S. Dearborn, *A Sketch of the Life of the Apostle Eliot: Prefatory to a Subscription for Creating a Monument in his Memory* (Roxbury, Mass.: Norfolk County Journal Press, 1850), 13.
6. William H. Gaines Jr., "The Continental Congress Considers the Publication of a Bible, 1777," *Studies in Bibliography* 3 (1950): 275–76.
7. There is some dispute on whether or not Aitken's New Testament was the first English-language Bible edition printed in America. Some argue that the firm of Kneeland and Green produced the first such Bible edition, but scholarship on this particular edition is vexed, since no copy has ever been located. Harry Miller Lydenberg, "The Problem of the Pre-1776 Bible," *Papers of the Bibliographical Society of America* 48 (1954): 183–94.
8. Laton E. Holmgren, "A 'Pious and Laudable Undertaking': The Bible of the Revolution," *American History* 10, no. 6 (October 1975): 17.
9. For a discussion of standing type, see Rollo G. Silver, *The American Printer: 1787-1825* (Charlottesville: University of Virginia Press, 1967), 90–91.

10. Philip Gaskell, *A New Introduction to Bibliography* (New York: Oxford University Press, 1972), 199–205. George Adolf Kubler, *A New History of Stereotyping* (New York: J. J. Little & Ives, 1941), 147–226. Silver, *American Printer*, 61.

11. *American Dictionary of Printing and Bookmaking* (New York: Howard Lockwood, 1894), 208.

12. David Paul Nord, "The Evangelical Origins of Mass Media in America, 1815–1835," *Journalism Monographs* 88 (May 1984): 11–12.

13. Nord, "Evangelical Origins," 12. Ronald J. Zboray, *A Fictive People: Antebellum Economic Development and the American Reading Public* (New York: Oxford University Press, 1993), 11. See also Judith A. McGaw, *Most Wonderful Machine: Mechanization and Social Change in Berkshire Paper Making, 1801–1885* (Princeton, N.J.: Princeton University Press, 1987).

14. John C. Nerone, *The Culture of the Press in the Early Republic: Cincinnati, 1783–1848* (New York: Garland, 1989), 31.

15. Ralph Green, "Early American Power Printing Presses," *Studies in Bibliography* 4 (1951): 149.

16. Green, "Early American Power Printing Presses," 152.

17. Sigfrid H. Steinberg, *Five Hundred Years of Printing* (London: Faber and Faber, 1959), 201–2.

18. Zboray, *A Fictive People*, 6–9. Peter J. Wosh, *Spreading the Word: The Bible Business in Nineteenth-Century America* (Ithaca, N.Y.: Cornell University Press, 1994), 7–34.

19. Charles Sellers, *The Market Revolution: Jacksonian America, 1815–1846* (New York: Oxford University Press, 1994), 370. Paul C. Gutjahr, *An American Bible: The History of the Good Book in the United States, 1777–1881* (Stanford, Calif.: Stanford University Press, 1999), 191–92.

20. John Tebbel, *A History of Book Publishing in the United States*, vol. 1 (New York: Harper & Row, 1951), 225–27. Sellers, *The Market Revolution*, 371.

21. Kenneth Lockridge, *Literacy in Colonial New England* (New York: W. W. Norton, 1974), 21, 38–43. Maris A. Vinovskis and Richard M. Bernard, "Beyond Catharine Beecher: Female Education in the Antebellum Period," *Signs* 3, no. 4 (Summer 1978): 863.

22. Roger Finke and Rodney Stark, *The Churching of America, 1776–1990* (New Brunswick, N.J.: Rutgers University Press, 1992), 35.

23. Nila Banton Smith, *American Reading Instruction* (Newark, Del.: International Reading Association, 1965), 10–35. Lawrence Cremin, *American Education: The Colonial Experience, 1607–1783* (New York: Harper & Row, 1970), 181.

24. Sydney Ahlstrom, *A Religious History of the American People* (New Haven, Conn.: Yale University Press, 1972), 415–28.

25. Gutjahr, *An American Bible*, 187.

26. Gutjahr, *An American Bible*, 33.

27. Nord, *Faith in Reading*, 67.

28. American Bible Society, *Eleventh Annual Report* (1827), in *Annual Reports of the American Bible Society*, vol. 1 (New York: Daniel Fanshaw, 1838).

29. Gutjahr, *An American Bible*, 37.

30. George M. Marsden, *Fundamentalism and American Culture: The Shaping of Twentieth-Century Evangelicalism, 1870–1925* (New York: Oxford University Press, 1980), 118–23.

31. Allan Fisher, *Fleming H. Revell Company: The First 125 Years, 1870–1995* (Grand Rapids, Mich.: Fleming H. Revell, 1995).

32. Ted W. Engstrom and James E. Ruark, *The House of Zondervan* (Grand Rapids, Mich.: Zondervan Publishing House, 1981). Kenneth Taylor, *My Life: A Guided Tour* (Wheaton, Ill.: Tyndale House Publishers, 1991), 255–65. Sam Moore, *American by Choice: The Remarkable Fulfillment of an Immigrant's Dream* (Nashville, Tenn.: Thomas Nelson, 1998), 95–103, 123–41.

33. Bruce M. Metzger, *The Bible in Translation: Ancient and English Versions* (Grand Rapids, Mich.: Baker Book House, 2001), 99–102.

34. Margaret Hills, *The English Bible in America* (New York: American Bible Society, 1962), 295. Kenneth Cmiel, *Democratic Eloquence: The Fight over Popular Speech in Nineteenth-Century America* (New York: William Morrow, 1990), 216–17.

35. Cmiel, *Democratic Eloquence*, 219.

36. Gutjahr, *An American Bible*, 193–94. Hills, *The English Bible in America*, 360–86.

37. Paul C. Gutjahr, "Chronology of English Bible Translations since 1957," in *The King James Bible after 400 Years: Literary, Linguistic, and Cultural Influences*, ed. Hannibal Hamlin and Norman W. Jones (New York: Cambridge University Press, 2010), 338–41.

38. Philip Goff, Arthur E. Farnsley II, and Peter J. Thuesen, "The Bible in American Life Report," The Center for the Study of Religion and American Culture, Indiana University-Purdue University Indianapolis, March 6, 2014, 12.

39. Bruce M. Metzger, *The Bible in Translation: Ancient and English Versions* (Grand Rapids, Mich.: Baker Academic, 2001), 102–3.

40. Wayne Grudem et al., *Translating Truth: The Case for Essentially Literal Bible Translation* (Wheaton, Ill.: Crossway Books, 2005), 22–23.

41. Peter J. Thuesen, *In Discordance with the Scriptures: American Protestant Battles over Translating the Bible* (New York: Oxford University Press, 1999), 95–96, 124.

42. Thuesen, *In Discordance with the Scriptures*, 67–91, 121–44.

43. Grudem, *Translating Truth*, 50–55.

44. Folder "Historical Essays TEV—Secondary Material," RG 53, Box 2, Historical Essays, Studies Nos. 1–15, American Bible Society Archives, Philadelphia, Pa., pages 2, 12.

45. Taylor, *My Life*, 381.

46. Robert G. Bratcher, "The New International Version: A Review Article," *Duke Divinity School Review* 44 (1979): 164, 177.

47. Thuesen, *In Discordance with the Scriptures*, 134–35.

48. Metzger, *The Bible in Translation*, 139; Daniel Radosh, "The Good Book Business," *The New Yorker*, December 18, 2006, 56.

49. Metzger, *The Bible in Translation*, 160.

50. M. A. Henderson, *Sowers of the Word: A 95-Year History of the Gideons International, 1899-1994* (Nashville, Tenn.: Gideons International, 1995), 3–4. "About Us: Our History," *Gideons International*, http://www.gideons.org/aboutus/ourhistory.aspx.

51. Hills, *The English Bible in America*, xxi.

52. Hills, *The English Bible in America*, 328.

53. For an overview of the technological changes in printing during this period, see Edward Webster, *Print Unchained: Fifty Years of Digital Printing, 1950-2000 and Beyond—A Saga of Invention and Enterprise* (New Castle, Del.: Oak Knoll Press, 2000), 129–81.

54. "The NET Bible," http://netbible.com. The Net Bible can be easily accessed also through https://lumina.bible.org/bible.

55. Theodore Dwight Bozeman, *To Live Ancient Lives: The Primitivist Dimension in Puritanism* (Chapel Hill: University of North Carolina Press, 1988), 13.

BIBLIOGRAPHY

Ahlstrom, Sydney. *A Religious History of the American People.* New Haven, Conn.: Yale University Press, 1972.

American Bible Society. *Eleventh Annual Report* (1827). In *Annual Reports of the American Bible Society.* Vol. 1. New York: Daniel Fanshaw, 1838.

American Dictionary of Printing and Bookmaking. New York: Howard Lockwood, 1894.

Bozeman, Theodore Dwight. *To Live Ancient Lives: The Primitivist Dimension in Puritanism.* Chapel Hill: University of North Carolina Press, 1988.

Cmiel, Kenneth. *Democratic Eloquence: The Fight over Popular Speech in Nineteenth-Century America.* New York: William Morrow, 1990.

Cremin, Lawrence. *American Education: The Colonial Experience, 1607-1783.* New York: Harper & Row, 1970.

Dearborn, H. A. S. *A Sketch of the Life of the Apostle Eliot: Prefatory to a Subscription for Creating a Monument in His Memory.* Roxbury, Mass.: Norfolk County Journal Press, 1850.

Engstrom, Ted W., and James E. Ruark, *The House of Zondervan.* Grand Rapids, Mich.: Zondervan Publishing House, 1981.

Finke, Roger, and Rodney Stark. *The Churching of America, 1776-1990.* New Brunswick, N.J.: Rutgers University Press, 1992.

Fisher, Allan. *Fleming H. Revell Company: The First 125 Years, 1870-1995.* Grand Rapids, Mich.: Fleming H. Revell, 1995.

Gaines, William H., Jr. "The Continental Congress Considers the Publication of a Bible, 1777." *Studies in Bibliography* 3 (1950-51): 274-81.

Gaskell, Philip. *A New Introduction to Bibliography.* New York: Oxford University Press, 1972.

Goff, Philip, Arthur E. Farnsely II, and Peter J. Thuesen. "The Bible in American Life Report." The Center for the Study of Religion and American Culture, Indiana University-Purdue University Indianapolis, March 6, 2014.

Green, Ralph. "Early American Power Printing Presses." *Studies in Bibliography* 4 (1951-52): 143-53.

Grudem, Wayne, et al. *Translating Truth: The Case for Essentially Literal Bible Translation.* Wheaton, Ill.: Crossway Books, 2005.

Gutjahr, Paul C. *An American Bible: The History of the Good Book in the United States, 1777-1881.* Stanford, Calif.: Stanford University Press, 1999.

———. "Chronology of English Bible Translations since 1957." In *The King James Bible after 400 Years: Literary, Linguistic, and Cultural Influences,* edited by Hannibal Hamlin and Norman W. Jones, 338-41. New York: Cambridge University Press, 2010.

Henderson, M. A. *Sowers of the Word: A 95-Year History of the Gideons International, 1899-1994.* Nashville, Tenn.: Gideons International, 1995.

Hills, Margaret. *The English Bible in America.* New York: American Bible Society, 1962.

"Historical Essays TEV—Secondary Material," RG 53, Box 2, Historical Essays, Studies Nos. 10-15, American Bible Society Archives, Philadelphia, Pa.

Holmgren, Laton E. "A 'Pious and Laudable Undertaking': The Bible of the Revolution." *American History* 10, no. 6 (October 1975): 12-17.

Kubler, George Adolf. *A New History of Stereotyping.* New York: J. J. Little & Ives, 1941.

Lockridge, Kenneth. *Literacy in Colonial New England.* New York: W. W. Norton, 1974.

Lydenberg, Harry Miller. "The Problem of the Pre-1776 Bible." *Papers of the Bibliographical Society of America* 48 (1954): 183-94.

Marsden, George M. *Fundamentalism and American Culture: The Shaping of Twentieth-Century Evangelicalism, 1870–1925*. New York: Oxford University Press, 1980.

McGaw, Judith A. *Most Wonderful Machine: Mechanization and Social Change in Berkshire Paper Making, 1801–1885*. Princeton, N.J.: Princeton University Press, 1987.

Metzger, Bruce M. *The Bible in Translation: Ancient and English Versions*. Grand Rapids, Mich.: Baker Book House, 2001.

Moore, Sam. *American by Choice: The Remarkable Fulfillment of an Immigrant's Dream*. Nashville, Tenn.: Thomas Nelson, 1998.

Nerone, John C. *The Culture of the Press in the Early Republic: Cincinnati, 1783–1848*. New York: Garland, 1989.

Nida, Eugene A. *Toward a Science of Translating, with Special Reference to Principles and Procedures Involved in Bible Translating*. Leiden, Netherlands: Brill, 1964.

——, and Charles H. Kraft. *Message and Mission: The Communication of the Christian Faith*. New York: Harper and Brothers, 1960.

Nord, David Paul. "The Evangelical Origins of Mass Media in America, 1815–1835." *Journalism Monographs* 88 (May 1984): 1–30.

——. *Faith in Reading: Religious Publishing and the Birth of Mass Media in America*. New York: Oxford University Press, 2004.

Radosh, Daniel. "The Good Book Business." *The New Yorker*, December 18, 2006.

Sellers, Charles. *The Market Revolution: Jacksonian America, 1815–1846*. New York: Oxford University Press, 1994.

Silver, Rollo G. *The American Printer: 1787–1825*. Charlottesville: University of Virginia Press, 1967.

Smith, Nila Banton. *American Reading Instruction*. Newark, Del.: International Reading Association, 1965.

Steinberg, Sigfrid H. *Five Hundred Years of Printing*. London: Faber and Faber, 1959.

Taylor, Kenneth. *My Life: A Guided Tour*. Wheaton, Ill.: Tyndale House Publishers, 1991.

Tebbel, John. *A History of Book Publishing in the United States*. Vol. 1. New York: Harper & Row, 1951.

Thuesen, Peter J. *In Discordance with the Scriptures: American Protestant Battles over Translating the Bible*. New York: Oxford University Press, 1999.

Vinovskis, Maris A., and Richard M. Bernard. "Beyond Catharine Beecher: Female Education in the Antebellum Period." *Signs* 3, no. 4 (Summer 1978): 856–69.

Webster, Edward. *Print Unchained: Fifty Years of Digital Printing, 1950–2000 and Beyond—A Saga of Invention and Enterprise*. New Castle, Del.: Oak Knoll Press, 2000.

Winship, George Parker. *The Cambridge Press, 1638–1692: A Reexamination of the Evidence Concerning the Bay Psalm Book and the Eliot Indian Bible as well as Other Contemporary Books and People*. Philadelphia: University of Pennsylvania Press, 1945.

Wosh, Peter J. *Spreading the Word: The Bible Business in Nineteenth-Century America*. Ithaca, N.Y.: Cornell University Press, 1994.

Zboray, Ronald J. *A Fictive People: Antebellum Economic Development and the American Reading Public*. New York: Oxford University Press, 1993.

CHAPTER 2

....

THE AMERICAN
CHILDREN'S BIBLE

....

RUSSELL W. DALTON

CHILDREN's Bibles have been among the most popular and influential religious education publications in America. They have provided many Jewish and Christian children with their first impression of what the Bible is and how it should be read. Children's Bibles also lend insight into the minds of the authors, illustrators, and the cultures that created them. The authors and illustrators of children's Bibles often abridge, illustrate, and embellish Bible stories, frequently adding their own commentary and moral conclusions. In the process, these authors and illustrators, consciously or unconsciously, embed a host of religious, ethical, and cultural assumptions and agendas into their retellings of Bible stories.

Children's Bibles have been written by both lay persons and clergy and a roughly equal number of female and male authors. Such writers also come from a wide variety of faith communities. Because of this authorial range, children's Bibles offer a sort of people's history of the reception of the Bible in America, one that is stripped away from the abstract theological or hermeneutical arguments that concern those in academic circles. A survey of the general trends in the ways that children's Bible authors and illustrators have appropriated the Bible's stories, then, can help index America's changing and diverse approaches both to the Bible and to childhood.[1]

Throughout American history, many Christian and Jewish clergy and adults have seen the Bible as the primary curriculum resource for children's religious education. Children's Bibles, in particular, have arguably been the most common type of religious education publication in the United States. Bibles for children have existed since 1170 and have been published in English at least since the seventeenth century.[2] Early American settlers from Europe brought children's Bibles with them, and most of the earliest children's Bibles published in the United States were simply republications of British children's Bibles. The first of these, John Taylor's *Verbum Sempiternum*, was first published in England in 1614 and was being published in Boston as early as 1693.[3] Taylor's book was published in the tiny hardcover format often referred to as a "Thumb Bible" that proved popular for eighteenth- and early nineteenth-century children's Bibles (see figure 2.1).[4] Taylor's *Verbum Sempiternum* and later children's Bibles such as Benjamin Harris's *Holy Bible in Verse* (1717) were widely available in the American colonies.

FIGURE 2.1 "Verbum Sempiternum," Central Libraries Special Collections, Moody Memorial Library, Baylor University, Waco, Tex.

Children's Bibles of various kinds have continued to be one of the most popular types of publications for children in the United States up to the present day. According to *Publisher's Weekly*, in 1990 Americans spent over $40 million on children's Bibles.[5] The demand for children's Bibles only increased throughout the decade, and by the turn of the century *Publisher's Weekly* reported that "many Bible story books are bankrolling their companies."[6]

Along with publishing children's Bibles in sizes that fit children's small hands, another concession that many children's Bibles have made to their young readership has been to include illustrations of Bible characters and events. Even in the eighteenth and early nineteenth centuries, when the printing technology of the time only allowed for very crude woodcut illustrations in cheaper books, many children's Bibles included illustrations on nearly every page.

Not everyone, however, was happy with the trend. *The Children's Bible*, first published in London in 1759 but republished by Andrew Steuart in Philadelphia in 1763, became the first prose children's Bible printed in America. The frontispiece of the book is a rough woodcut illustration depicting a man reading to young children who are drawn in the same style of clothing and same bodily proportions as adults, only smaller in size (see figure 2.2). This image reflects the approach of many writers at the time who viewed children as tiny adults who, though smaller in size and with less knowledge than their elders, were essentially the same as adults.[7] The rest of the Steuart's edition, however, does not include any illustrations of Bible stories. The unnamed author introduces the book by explaining, "I have chosen rather to give it a strong and handsome binding, than to increase the bulk of the volume by crowding it with ill-executed cuts, attended with a large expense and no manner of service;

FIGURE 2.2 Frontispiece of *The Children's Bible* (Philadelphia: Andrew Steuart, 1763).

which may be necessary notwithstanding to promote the sale of nonsense, but the author apprehends that the BIBLE is no fit PLAY-THING FOR CHILDREN."[8]

The creators and publishers of most children's Bibles throughout American history, however, have disagreed with this sentiment, at least when it came to including illustrations. Whether they are the crude woodcuts of the eighteenth and early nineteenth centuries or the colorful cartoon-style pictures of the twenty-first century, illustrations became a mainstay of children's Bibles in America and a primary part of their appeal. These illustrations arguably carry more powerful and more lasting interpretive power than the texts of children's Bibles.[9]

The illustrations that have been included in US children's Bibles also, perhaps unconsciously, help demonstrate the fact that these Bibles do not tell the whole story of American religion or America's use of the Bible with children. Because children's Bibles are commercial products that require money to produce and access to distribution, they primarily represent the history of privileged class thinking in America. African American adults, for example, often told Bible stories to their children in creative ways, but until recently they were less likely than white adults to publish and sell those stories in the form of children's Bibles.[10] One result of this publication history is that the illustrations included in the vast majority of American children's Bibles, past and present, have depicted the ancient Near Eastern people of the Bible as white people of Western European descent.[11] In the twenty-first century, an increasing number of children's Bibles have begun to illustrate Bible characters with a variety of skin tones and facial features, a trend that carries with it significant cultural weight.[12]

The term "children's Bible" has been used as a designation for a variety of publications of different shapes, sizes, formats, and even genres. This essay describes children's Bibles that fit into five general categories: those that appear to be primarily focused on teaching children biblical literacy; those that appropriate Bible stories in ways that instill a fear and respect for God's power and judgment; those that use Bible stories to call children to salvation in Jesus Christ; those that primarily use Bible stories to teach children morals and virtues; and those that reframe Bible stories as fun and engaging stories for young children that teach them that God is a friendly God who cares for them. Not every children's Bible fits neatly into one of these categories or fits into the chronology of the time frame when each trend emerges. Still, these categories can serve as a useful framework for examining the diversity of children's Bibles throughout American history.

Children's Bibles for Biblical Literacy

In their introductions, many children's Bibles from throughout US history have made the case that their books are designed simply to pass on biblical knowledge and stories to children. Many of these same children's Bibles, however, embellish, abridge, and comment upon those stories in ways that convey to their readers a host of embedded theological beliefs and moral values. Still, many Bible resources that can be broadly categorized as "children's Bibles" indeed appear to be designed primarily to increase children's knowledge of the words or events of the Bible. Before examining children's Bibles and their various presentations of biblical material, a survey of such children's Bibles is in order.

One type of children's Bible especially popular in the late eighteenth and early nineteenth centuries in the United States were tiny three- to five-inch-tall thumb Bibles (such as the *Verbum Sempiternum*), and small, thin pamphlet-style books, known as "chapbooks." These tiny books offered short, whirlwind summaries of what their authors deemed to be the key biblical characters and events.

Children's Bible catechisms were also popular in the nineteenth century. Bible catechisms often contained abridged versions of select Bible passages taken directly from a popular translation of the Bible, followed by a series of questions that encouraged a close reading of the text itself. Rabbi Frederick de Sola Mendes's *The Child's First Bible* (1877), for example, offered children an abridged version of the story of Noah and asked them questions such as "1. What kind of man was Noah? 2. What did God tell him to build? 3. Who were to be taken into the ark?"[13]

One of the more creative ways that American adults encouraged children to learn and remember the words of scripture can be found in hieroglyphical Bibles that used a combination of words and pictures on each page to present a Bible verse or two. The preface of *A New Hieroglyphical Bible*, published in Boston in the late eighteenth century, captures the goals of such children's Bibles when its introduction states: "To imprint on the memory of Youth, by lively and sensible images, the sacred and important truths of Holy Writ, is the object of the following work."[14] A later example of this sort of publication, 1899's *Picture Puzzles or How to Read the Bible by Symbols*, depicts the twenty-third Psalm with the word

"The," followed by the Hebrew letters for Yahweh, the words "is my," a picture of a contemporary shepherd, a picture of a human eye, the letter "s" preceding a picture of a hall, a picture of a knot, and finally a picture of a beggar in want (see figure 2.3).[15] One could make the case that the passages and words included in books such as these reveal subtle theological and cultural agendas. When they are compared to children's Bibles that more freely and elaborately retell the stories of the Bible, however, these resources seem to be designed primarily to increase a child's basic biblical literacy.

Naturally, the most common and direct way that parents and educators have sought to increase their children's biblical literacy has been to present them with the text of the entire Bible from a common translation. Children's editions of the Authorized King James Version, the Jewish Publication Society's translation, translations into languages of a group's nation of origin, or other translations of the Bible, often printed in words with larger type in a single column, have been a mainstay of children's Bibles in the United States.[16] Many of these children's editions include illustrations and omit chapter and verse numberings. Many other children's editions of the Bible do not contain the entire text of the Bible, but only select stories that the editors deem especially appropriate for children. In the twentieth century, some writers and scholars provided children with entirely new contemporary translations of the Bible. Offerings such as Henry A. Sherman and Charles Foster Kent's *The*

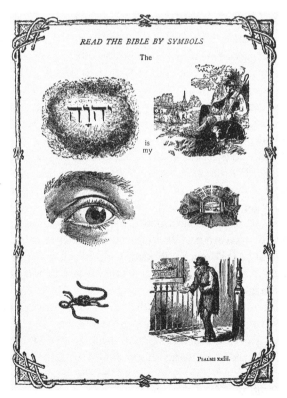

FIGURE 2.3 Psalm 23 from Frank Beard et al., *Picture Puzzles or How to Read the Bible by Symbols (Designed Especially for the Boys and Girls to Stimulate a Greater Interest in the Holy Bible)* (Naperville, Ill.: J. L. Nichols, 1899), 119.

Children's Bible: Selections from the Old and New Testaments (1922) and John Stirling's *The Child's Bible* (1930) provided children with translations that were easier for them to read than the archaic language of the King James Version or Revised Standard Version. [17]

In the second half of the twentieth century, English translations and paraphrases of the Bible such as *Today's English Version, The Living Bible,* and *The New International Version* were created and their contents were accessible to younger readers. In the wake of such biblical translation work, Christian authors and publishers found less need to create entirely new translations for children. Instead, they published a plethora of special children's editions of these translations and paraphrase editions of the Bible. [18]

In the twenty-first century, especially, a growing trend in the United States created separate brightly colored editions of the Bible for children of each gender. Bright pink-covered Bibles marketed to girls include *Shiny Sequin Bible* (2011), *The Precious Princess Bible* (2010), and *The NIV FaiThGirLz! Bible* (2010). [19] Boys, meanwhile, have been presented with titles such as *The NIV Adventure Bible* (2011), *The Super Heroes Bible: The Quest for Good Over Evil* (NIrV) (2002), and the *Compact Kids Bible: Green Camo*, a 2007 international children's Bible with a military-style camouflage cover from Thomas Nelson. [20] The selection of illustrations, packaging, and notes included in these children's Bibles reflect and transmit certain cultural values, norms, and gender roles in particular. They also illustrate the desire of many Christians throughout American history to make the Bible engaging and relevant to their children.

Jewish children's Bibles published in the United States have focused on providing children a readable text that stays close to the words of the Bible itself much more often than their Christian counterparts. To cite one example, Mortimer J. Cohen's *Pathways through the Bible*, published by the Jewish Publication Society of America (JPS) in 1946, uses the Jewish Publication Society Bible translation as its base, but makes it more readable for children "by eliminating difficult words, obscure phrases and archaic expressions, or by substituting modern equivalents for old English words." [21] Similarly, Rabbi Hyman E. Goldin argues for the value of the original wording of the biblical text in his foreword to his *A Treasury of Bible Stories*, also published in 1946. [22] Likewise, Ellen Frankel writes in the introduction to her 2009 *JPS Illustrated Children's Bible* that she sought to anchor her retellings closely to the wording of the New Jewish Publications Society (NJPS) translation. [23] Frankel observes that in Christian children's Bibles, "the biblical stories were expurgated, abridged, rewritten, and more often than not, Christianized. The Bible was thus turned into a morality play for children." Frankel argues, "The Jewish community has also long used the Bible for moral instruction of its children, but it has done so not by rewriting the original text as in Christian children's Bibles." [24] These and many other Jewish children's Bibles have passed on to children knowledge of the words, events, and tone of Bible stories, but do not add morals or explanations to the end of their stories. [25] In doing so, they primarily serve to help children remain aware of their biblical heritage and tradition.

A large number of American children's Bibles, then, have had the primary function of passing on basic knowledge of the words and stories of the Bible. They often execute this knowledge transference by providing children with an engaging and accessible translation of the Bible. Those who produced these books likely had strong opinions on why such knowledge was valuable for children and those assumptions are likely as diverse as the beliefs and values of their creators. In children's Bibles that more freely retell the stories of the Bible, however, those assumptions about what the Bible is and what children should learn from it are more readily apparent.

The Bible as Stories of God's Judgment and Death

In the eighteenth and early nineteenth centuries, the combination of the persistence of Puritan theology's stress on human depravity and the reality of high infant and child mortality rates moved Christian educators to focus on convincing children of their own sinfulness, the righteous judgment of God, and the need to prepare for their own deaths that might come at any time.[26] This practice of teaching children to prepare for death can be seen in the 1777 edition of *The New England Primer*. The popular primer included the well-known prayer:

> Now I lay me down to take my sleep,
> I pray the Lord my soul to keep,
> If I should die before I wake,
> I pray the Lord my soul to take.

Likewise, even while learning the letters of the alphabet in the Primer, children were reminded about death through lessons such as, "T: Time cuts down all, Both great and small," "X: XERXES did die, and so must I," and "Y: While youth do chear, death may be near."[27] This stress on the immanence of death and the theme of God's judgment of sin can be found in many Christian education resources of the time.[28]

These themes can also be found in the ways in which many children's Bibles retell favorite Bible stories. In the early nineteenth century, for example, the story of Noah and the ark was not presented to children as the story of a fun boat ride with animals in which God keeps people safe, but rather as the story of a great deluge in which God punishes the wicked. Many early children's Bible versions of the story include extended descriptions of the plight of the wicked outside of the ark, scrambling to higher ground, screaming to enter the ark, and finally being overcome by the waves. It should be noted that none of these scenes are described in the actual Genesis account of the flood. These descriptions are often accompanied by horrific illustrations of the floodwaters overcoming despairing children and their families. The most common illustration accompanying the story of Noah in late nineteenth-century children's Bibles is not an illustration of fun-loving animals on the ark, as is common in the twenty-first century, but French artist Gustave Dore's "The Deluge," which depicts young children on a mountaintop about to be overcome by the floodwaters (see figure 2.4).[29]

To prevent the possibility that children might miss the message of God's wrathful judgment, authors often made God's wrath quite explicit as can be seen in Lucy Barton's *Bible Letters*, first published in England in 1831 and widely available in America. Barton concludes her story of the flood by warning children, "Oh! how dreadful it is to disobey such a powerful God, who can destroy us in a moment, if he please!"[30] Barton's harsh words seem to

FIGURE 2.4 Gustave Doré's *The Deluge*, ca. 1866, found in many nineteenth-century children's Bibles.

have struck a chord with a number of popular American children's Bible authors who lifted Barton's exact words to conclude their own versions of the story of Noah's ark as well.[31]

Another way that children's Bibles of this era reflected concerns with God's power and judgment was through the stories they chose to include in their children's Bibles. Rather than editing out stories of death and God's wrath, these children's Bibles seemed eager to include them. The story from 2 Kings 2:23–24 of Elisha cursing the children of Bethel and the she-bears killing forty-two of them, for example, is usually only included in the most comprehensive children's Bibles of the twentieth- and twenty-first centuries. In the late eighteenth and early nineteenth centuries, however, if a children's Bible were to include just ten or fifteen stories from the Bible, chances are that this story would be selected and that one of the book's few illustrations would be devoted to a scene of bears eating children (see figure 2.5).[32]

The story is included, for example, in 1763's *The Children's Bible*. The author writes in the book's opening dedication, "For when you hear of GOD's being angry with and punishing people, for their disobedience of his Holy Word, may you not immediately reason with yourself, and think with great justice, that he will punish you likewise, if you disobey him?"[33] The author thus prepares children to read the stories that follow with an eye toward lessons about God's righteous anger and the need to obey God's commandments or suffer the consequences. The book quickly retells the tale of Elisha and the children of Bethel, for example, explaining, "After which, as he was going by Bethel, we are told that some little

BEARS TEARING CHILDREN.

FIGURE 2.5 Woodcut illustration of *Bears Tearing Children* from *Stories from the Bible* (Northampton, Mass.: E. Turner, 1843).

children came out of the city mocking him; the dreadful consequence of which was, that God sent bears to eat them up. And some such curse we may depend upon it, will always attend those who jest at the aged or holy."[34] The author, then, retells the tale in just one sentence, but still takes the time to insert direct commentary to the reader into the text, warning them to be wary of God's judgment even in the present day.

As late as 1877, the children's Bible *Dear Old Stories Told Once More* concluded the story of the children of Bethel by warning, "Oh, how little we think what a dreadful thing it is to disobey and hate the blessed God."[35] Still, for the most part, the harshest stories of God's judgment and the death of sinners began to fade in the late nineteenth century as America's view of childhood had begun to change. For Christian children's Bible authors in particular, the focus shifted from an emphasis on God's judgment to a call for children to accept God's mercy and salvation in Jesus Christ.

THE BIBLE AS THE STORY OF SALVATION IN CHRIST

The Christian revivals that swept through the American colonies during the First Great Awakening beginning in the 1730s and continuing through the so-called Second Great

Awakening of the nineteenth century had a profound and lasting influence on Christianity in the United States. From the 1830s to the end of the nineteenth century, sermons in America focused increasingly on Jesus Christ and his role as the savior to lost sinners.[36] Revival preachers such as Charles Finney, D. L. Moody, and others saw the message of salvation in Jesus Christ in nearly every story of the Bible, including those of the Hebrew Bible. Not surprisingly, those children's Bible authors who grew up hearing the stories of the Bible used in this way retold those stories in a similar manner.

A significant number of Christian children's Bibles published in the United States in the nineteenth century, then, retell Hebrew Bible stories such as those of Adam and Eve, Noah and the Ark, and the binding of Isaac in ways that connect those stories directly to a promise of salvation in Jesus Christ. In the book *Half Hours with the Bible* (1867), for example, an author identified only as "Mrs. Grive" concludes her story of Adam and Eve by explaining that by saying "the seed of the woman shall bruise thy head," God meant "that He would some day send a Savior into the world to cleanse it from sin."[37] She inserts into her story of Noah the comment, "He provided the ark; and the same love provided the Saviour, the ark of our strength—the refuge from the storm of trouble and the flood of sin."[38] Finally, Mrs. Grive concludes her story of Abraham's binding of Isaac by explaining that God's promise to Abraham meant that "the promised Savior should descend from Abraham."[39]

In a similar fashion, Alvan Bond, in his *Young People's Illustrated Bible History* (1878), summarizes his story of Adam and Eve by explaining, "If we, like Adam and Eve, have faith in Jesus, we shall be saved as they were, and made eternally happy when we do."[40] Bond adds to his story of Noah's ark, "And the ark may remind us of the Lord Jesus Christ. If we are in Him, by faith, then we shall be safe for ever from God's anger, as Noah was safe in the ark from the waters of the flood."[41] Bond concludes his story of Abraham's binding of Isaac by explaining, "Abraham gave his son to God, God gave His Son for us."[42] As is often the case in children's Bibles, this commentary is integrated into the flow of the story's narrative so seamlessly that many children would have difficulty distinguishing what aspects of the story appear in the book of Genesis and what are merely the annotations of the children's Bible authors.

These sorts of Christological readings of Hebrew Bible passages seem to have had a resurgence in the twenty-first century as a number of children's Bibles boldly promote the fact that every one of their stories are actually about Jesus. Sally Lloyd-Jones's *The Jesus Storybook Bible: Every Story Whispers His Name* (2007) is a case in point. The book's back cover explains, "From Noah to Moses to the great King David—every story points to him. He is like the missing piece in a puzzle—the piece that makes all the other pieces fit together."[43] In a similar fashion, the publisher's description of Mary Machowski's *The Gospel Story Bible: Discovering Jesus in the Old and New Testaments* (2011) states, "The easy-to-read storybook introduces your family to many captivating people, places, and events from the Bible's Old and New Testaments, showing how each one ultimately points to Jesus."[44] These books, and others like them, follow through on these promises, explicitly reframing each story of the Hebrew Bible and the New Testament as stories that are ultimately about salvation in Jesus Christ.[45]

Concern for children's salvation has been the primary goal of Christian education in the United States. It is not surprising, then, to find many American Christian children's Bible authors using the stories of the Bible to call children to salvation in Jesus Christ. While many children's Bibles in the nineteenth century focused on messages of sin and salvation, by the end of the nineteenth century a growing number of American children's Bibles began instead to focus their retellings on teaching children particular moral virtues.

THE BIBLE AS A BOOK OF VIRTUES

From the late nineteenth century to the twenty-first century, one of the most common ways children's Bibles have appropriated Bible stories has been to teach children personal moral virtues. Up until the late 1800s, religious education materials for Christian children consisted largely of theological catechisms and moralistic short nonfiction stories to impress morals on children.[46] Before the nineteenth century, the Bible was not as commonly used to teach virtues as it would be in later periods. In the late nineteenth century, members of the dominant culture feared that immigrants and freed African Americans would not teach morals to their children, or at least not teach them the type of morals that would make them good factory or farm workers or good citizens who would shore up the status quo. To help teach such morals, Christian adults created children's Bibles—many designed to be used in public schools—that retold Bible stories in ways that taught children obedience and respect for those in authority, contentment with one's station in life, and the value of hard work.

Beginning in the late nineteenth century, children's Bible stories of Noah tended to emphasize not the judgment of God or the salvation of Christ, but the virtue of Noah. Noah is most often lifted up as a role model for either unquestioning obedience or working hard without complaining, but in other children's Bibles he is alternatively used as a role model for gentleness, contentment, kindness, patience, and hopefulness. Various children's Bible authors seem to have their own opinion on which virtue is most important to pass onto children, and they have adapted and embellished the story of Noah accordingly.[47]

In the late nineteenth and early twentieth centuries, children's Bible authors seemed particularly drawn to using the children found in Bible stories as role models for their readers and many collections of the stories of "The Children of the Bible" were produced. In these collections, young Isaac is often presented as a strapping young lad who could easily have escaped being sacrificed by old Abraham, but he knew it was better to submit to his father's will. As the title of one children's book put it, Isaac was *The Boy Who Obeyed*.[48] Likewise, the sacrifice of Jepthah's daughter is frequently presented as regrettable, but she is still lifted up as a wonderful role model of daughterly submission. Young Samuel and "Namaan's Little Maid" had their stories greatly expanded to describe all the chores they had to do and how, though they were servants who were taken from their homes, they happily did their work and loved those whom they served.

The child Jesus was, to many twentieth-century Christian children's Bible authors, the most appealing biblical role model for children. Although the canonical Gospels themselves provide few details of Jesus's childhood, many children's Bibles expand these accounts or invent entirely new stories. Rarely is the young Jesus in children's Bibles presented as the sort of child who would grow up to speak truth to power or resist oppression. Instead, he is presented as a child who joyfully obeyed his parents at all times. This version of a young Jesus worked hard without complaining and was submissive and content with his station in life.[49] In 1785, the Sunday School Society was founded in England with the motto "To prevent vice, to encourage industry, to diffuse the light of knowledge, to bring men cheerfully to submit to their stations."[50] Through the intervening centuries, much religious education in England and the United States continued to be conservative in its nature, encouraging children to submit to authority and be cheerful and content. Even the cultural upheavals of the late 1960s and early 1970s in the United States produced little in the way of children's Bibles that emphasized values such as resisting oppression and working for social justice. Instead, they prompted calls for a return to "family values." Children's Bibles by socially conservative evangelical Christian authors and speakers Dottie and Josh McDowell's *The Right Choices Bible* or the *Focus on the Family Bedtime Bible* have predictably emphasized conservative moral values, but those published by more progressive Christian publishers have as well.[51]

While most Jewish children's Bibles from throughout American history have stayed close to the biblical text itself, with only minimal embellishments, historian Penny Schine Gold notes that several Jewish children's Bibles published from 1915 to 1936, such as Lenore Cohen's *Bible Tales for Very Young Children* and Addie Richman Altman's *The Jewish Child's Bible Stories*, made subtle but significant changes to the biblical text.[52] In her book, *Making the Bible Modern: Children's Bibles and Jewish Education in Twentieth Century America*, Gold argues that some of these changes, such as inserting moral applications to the stories, may have been an attempt by the authors to help Jewish children integrate their faith with the values of American culture.[53] Some examples of twenty-first-century Jewish children's Bibles that teach moral virtues also exist. Ann Eisenberg's *Bible Heroes I Can Be* from 2004, for example, tells young children that they can build things like Noah, welcome guests like Abraham and Sara, and be kind like Rebecca.[54] Still, for the most part, Jewish children's Bibles are much less likely to use the Bible as a book of virtues than their Christian counterparts.

From the late nineteenth century to the present day, then, many Christian children's Bibles and even some Jewish children's Bibles have used the stories of the Bible in a manner similar to Aesop's fables, with each story teaching a particular moral virtue. This same approach to the Bible can be seen as the primary approach to the Bible taken in many Bible studies and religious education curriculum materials for children and adults from throughout American history. Through these children's Bibles and curriculum resources, the Bible has been presented to Americans primarily as a book of virtues.

Fun Stories of a Friendly God of Who Keeps Us Safe

While somber children's Bibles whose stories stay close to the canonical text and contain realistic illustrations certainly do exist in the twenty-first century, a survey of bookstore shelves reveals a growing trend of brightly colored children's Bibles designed for increasingly younger readers that contain cartoonish illustrations of Bible characters and animals. These children's Bibles appear to be designed to be fun and engaging to their young readers and to teach them about a friendly God who keeps them safe.

Throughout the twentieth century, advancements in printing technology made including color illustrations in their books increasingly affordable for publishers.[55] At the same time, publishers of children's books found that they had to make their storybooks entertaining as well as educational in order to compete with the growing variety of visual and electronic media available to children.[56]

America's views of childhood and child-rearing were changing as well. Authors such as Dr. Benjamin Spock told parents that their children were not sinful creatures to be harshly disciplined, but instead kids who should be showered with love and warm affection.[57] Many of these "Baby Boomers," who grew up in the two decades following World War II, recalled their childhoods as a happy time of fun and innocence and sought to assure their own children that they were safe and they were loved.[58] For people of faith, this also meant that rather than teaching their children to fear death and to fear God's judgment upon them—as parents in the eighteenth and nineteenth centuries had done—they sought to teach their children about a God who loved them and would always keep them safe.

As the market for children's literature and picture books for younger children continued to grow in the late twentieth and early twenty-first centuries in America, the number of brightly colored, entertaining Christian children's Bibles were also produced for an increasingly younger readership grew as well. These children's Bibles, with titles such as *The Toddler's Bible* (1992), *The Preschooler's Bible* (1994), *The Beginners Bible for Toddlers* (1995), *Baby's First Bible* (1996), *Baby Blessings Baby's Bible* (2005), and *The Sweetest Story Bible for Toddlers* (2010), tend to present the Bible as something that is fun and God as someone who is friendly, cares for children, and keeps them safe. [59]

Far from being a story of God's harsh judgment upon sinners, the story of Noah in these and many other late twentieth and early twenty-first-century Christian children's Bibles is presented as the story of a fun boat ride with the animals. There is often no mention that God is the cause of the flood or that anyone dies in the flood. Instead, the story of Noah is almost always used to teach children about a God who is their friend and who keeps them safe from dangers such as floods. Instead of illustrations of children and families being drowned amid cataclysmic waves, we find the ubiquitous image of Noah and his animal friends in an overstuffed ark smiling at the reader.

In the same way, stories such as that of David and Goliath, which in past centuries was depicted as a serious and somewhat dangerous and frightening story, more recently have been presented in ways that may be exciting but also put children at ease. David and even Goliath are often depicted as smiling throughout the story (see figure 2.6). As with the story of Noah, the story of David and Goliath is often used to assure children that God is always with them and will always keep them safe.

In the twenty-first century, at least half a dozen Christian children's Bibles have been produced with fuzzy and cuddly false fur and false wool covers. The covers and packaging of these children's Bibles, with titles such as the *Baby Hug a Bible* and *Tiny Bear Story Bible*, instruct parents to have children cuddle and hug their furry Bibles as they think of God.[60] Through such packaging strategies the Bible and God become associated with a literal warm and fuzzy feeling.

One might suspect that the creators of children's Bibles published by more conservative Christian publishers, whose customers tend to have a higher view of the inerrancy and infallibility of the Bible, would be motivated to keep their stories quite close to the canonical texts and their illustrators would be more likely to depict the stories as realistic historical events. A survey of twenty-first-century children's Bibles reveals that this is not the case. Children's Bibles available from evangelical publishers such as Zondervan Publishing

FIGURE 2.6 Artists Peter Grosshauser and Ed Temple's illustration of David and Goliath, from Patti Thisted Arthur et al., *Spark Story Bible* (Minneapolis, Minn.: Augsburg Fortress, 2009), 134–35.

or Baker Books seem more likely to illustrate their books with cartoonish illustrations of anthropomorphic animals and silly characters than their secular or mainline counterparts. Perhaps because the Bible is so central to their faith, and because they hope children will develop a warm connection to their faith at a young age, these children's Bible authors and illustrators appear to be highly motivated to transform the stories of the Bible into fun and engaging children's literature, even if some sense of the stories' historicity may be lost.

Some Jewish children's Bibles in the late twentieth and twenty-first centuries have also told Bible stories in creative and entertaining ways. As I have mentioned, most Jewish children's Bibles stay fairly close to the Bible's text in their retellings and most contain relatively realistic illustrations that avoid the danger of trivializing the stories. When Jewish children's Bible authors do veer from the text, however, they often do so dramatically and explicitly inform their readers that they are drawing on Midrash and other traditions to tell new stories for children. Rabbi Marc Gellman, for example, in the introduction to his 1989 book *Does God Have a Big Toe? Stories about Stories in the Bible*, explains to his young readers, "I am a Jew and I am a rabbi. In my tradition the people who write stories about stories in the Bible are called *darshanim*, and the stories they write about the stories in the Bible are called *midrashim*. A *midrash* is the Jewish name for a story about a story in the Bible."[61] Gellman explains that while he has read the old *midrashim* and learned from them, the stories in his book "are modern *midrashim*."[62] Gellman's retelling of the story of Noah's ark, for example, includes a story about the animals arguing amongst themselves about the nature of God, and two of Noah's friends trying to sneak onto the ark by dressing up in a zebra outfit.[63]

In a similar fashion, Mordecai Gerstein, in the introduction to his 1999 storybook *Noah and the Great Flood*, informs the reader that "in the Jewish tradition, many legends have arisen around the stories of the Bible." He adds, "Here, then, is the story of Noah, enriched by these legends." So, for example, Gerstein's story begins with Noah being born with light of every color streaming from his eyes, which his wise great-grandfather recognizes is a sign "that one day, because of Noah, there will be a bridge of light between heaven and earth, and the world will end and begin again." Gerstein's highly stylized paintings depict

Noah preaching to the cruel giants who roam the land and sneer and jeer at him.[64] Gerstein and Gellman draw upon Jewish legends and other sources to tell children stories that can be seen as more entertaining to children, but their methods differ from their Christian counterparts in that they explicitly tell their readers that they are not simply retelling their stories in ways that remain close to the biblical text. Instead, their goal seems to be to invite children to experience creative, modern-day midrashim.

The late twentieth and early twenty-first-century desire for fun and friendly sacred texts is even reflected in the appearance of a few children's storybooks with stories from the Qur'an in the United States.[65] These children's Qur'ans include colorful illustrations of landscapes and people, but do not show the faces of the prophets. Still, their picture-book format is a concession to the reading habits of American children in the twenty-first century.

As Nikki Bado-Fralick and Rebecca Sachs Norris note in their book, *Toying with God: The World of Religious Games and Dolls*, America is obsessed with having fun, even to the point that they feel compelled to market the practices of their faith as fun and enjoyable activities.[66] The primary goal of many twenty-first-century children's Bibles does not seem to be presenting children with a faithful account of the biblical text or even to pass on particular doctrines or virtues. Instead, the goal seems to be to engage children in a fun and entertaining way that creates warm feelings toward their faith, God, and the Bible itself and that teaches children that God is a friend and helper to them.

CONCLUSIONS

While many children's Bible authors from throughout American history state in their books' introductions that they are merely making the Bible clear and accessible to children, the ways in which many of them adapt and appropriate those stories actually reflect a wide variety of assumptions about what the Bible actually is and what it should mean to children. As has been noted, many children's Bible authors claim to hold to a high view of the authority of the canonical version of biblical texts. The fact that many of them still significantly revise the Bibles' stories speaks to how highly motivated they are to insure that children will draw certain beliefs and values from the Bible. The stakes are high. The first impressions of the nature and purpose of the Bible reflected in children's Bibles often influence a person's view of the Bible well into adulthood.

One significant finding of this study is that, for the most part, the way children's Bible authors have adapted Bible stories appears to have been less affected by the sectarian views of their particular faith communities than by wider American cultural values and sociological trends in general.[67] Changes in childhood mortality rates, advances in child development studies, public schooling, immigration, the industrial revolution, the development of publication technology, and shifts in the children's literature market, in general, seem to explain the types of adaptations and appropriations made in children's Bibles as much or more than scholarly shifts in biblical hermeneutics or their authors' particular denominational affiliations.

For over three hundred years, children's Bibles have been presenting American children with diverse and changing impressions of the Bible and its stories. A survey of children's Bibles in America attests to the remarkable multivalency and malleability of biblical stories.

Furthermore, the study of children's Bibles throughout America's history provides popular cultural snapshots of how Americans have received and appropriated the Bible, and why they have felt that it was important to pass the Bible and its stories on to the next generation.

NOTES

1. This essay is informed by a study of hundreds of children's Bibles published in the United States. My research was partially funded through a Lilly Theological Research Expense Grant distributed by the Association of Theological Schools, which allowed me to travel to the American Antiquarian Society in Worcester, Massachusetts, and the Library of Congress in Washington, D.C., to review many children's Bibles. For a more extensive treatment of many of the trends discussed in this essay, see my book Russell W. Dalton, *Children's Bibles in America: A Reception History of the Story of Noah's Ark in U.S. Children's Bibles* (London: Bloomsbury, 2015).

2. For more on early European children's Bibles, see Ruth B. Bottigheimer, *The Bible for Children: From the Age of Gutenberg to the Present* (New Haven, Conn.: Yale University Press, 1996), 14–52.

3. Bottigheimer, *The Bible for Children*, 45.

4. Ruth Elizabeth Adomeit catalogues over 150 thumb Bibles published from 1750 through the 1800s in the United States, though many of these are second, third, or even twelfth editions of the same texts. See Ruth Elizabeth Adomeit, *Three Centuries of Thumb Bibles: A Checklist* (New York: Garland, 1980).

5. Thomas S. Giles, "Pick a Bible—Any Bible," *Christianity Today*, October 26, 1992, 27.

6. Shannon Maughan, "In the Kids' Corner," *Publishers Weekly* 246, no. 41 (October 11, 1999): 46; LaVonne Neff, "Bible Stories: Facing a Floodtide," *Publishers Weekly* 248, no. 42 (October 15, 2001): 38.

7. Gillian Avery, *Behold the Child: American Children and Their Books 1621–1922* (London: Bodley Head, 1994), 16–21, 65–67.

8. *The Children's Bible* (Philadelphia: Andrew Steuart, 1763), xii. Emphasis in original.

9. See David Gunn, "Cultural Criticism," in *Judges & Method: New Approaches in Biblical Studies*, 2nd ed., ed. Gale A. Yee (Minneapolis, Minn.: Fortress Press, 2007), 205–7.

10. For some recent examples of children's Bibles written and illustrated from an African-American perspective, see *Children of Color Storybook Bible with Stories from the International Children's Bible*, illus. Victor Hogan (Nashville, Tenn.: Thomas Nelson, 2001); *My Holy Bible for African-American Children* (Grand Rapids, Mich.: Zondervan, 2009); and Patricia and Fredrick McKissack, *Let My People Go: Bible Stories Told by a Freeman of Color*, illus. James E. Ransome (New York: Atheneum Books for Young Readers, 1998).

11. See the helpful extended examinations of how children's Bible texts and illustrations treat "otherness" in Bible stories in Caroline Vander Stichle and Hugh S. Pyper, eds., *Text, Image, and Otherness in Children's Bibles: What Is in the Picture?* (Atlanta, Ga.: Society of Biblical Literature, 2012).

12. For examples, see *Children of Color Storybook Bible*, 2001; *My Holy Bible for African-American Children*, 2009; Alice Bach and J. Cheryl Exum, *Moses' Ark*, illus. by Leo and Diane Dillon (New York: Delacorte Press, 1989); *Holy Bible: Children's Illustrated Edition* (New York: American Bible Society, 2000); Desmond Tutu, *Children of God Storybook Bible* (Grand Rapids, Mich.: Zonderkids, 2010).

13. F. De Sola Mendes, *The Child's First Bible: Mainly in Words of One and Two Syllables, for Younger Children with Questions*, 14th ed. (New York: The Author, 1915), 6.

14. *A New Hieroglyphical Bible for the Amusement & Instruction of Children Being a Selection of the Most Useful Lessons; and Most Interesting Narratives (Scripturally Arranged) from Genesis to the Revelations* (Boston: W. Norman, 1794).

15. Frank Beard et al., *Picture Puzzles or How to Read the Bible by Symbols (Designed Especially for the Boys and Girls to Stimulate a Greater Interest in the Holy Bible)* (Naperville, Ill.: J. L. Nichols, 1899), 19.

16. See Bottigheimer, *The Bible for Children*, 46–47.

17. Henry A. Sherman and Charles Foster Kent, *The Children's Bible: Selections from the Old and New Testaments* (1922; repr., New York: Charles Scribner's Sons, 1947); John Stirling, ed., *The Child's Bible* (Indianapolis, Ind.: Bobbs-Merrill, 1930).

18. See, e.g., *The Children's Living Bible* (Wheaton, Ill.: Tyndale House, 1972); *Precious Moments Children's Bible: Easy-to-Read New Life Version* (Grand Rapids, Mich.: Baker, 1999); *NIrV Discover's Bible for Early Readers* (Grand Rapids, Mich.: ZonderKidz, 2002).

19. *Shiny Sequin Bible (ICB)* (New York: Tommy Nelson, 2011); *The Precious Princess Bible (NIrV)* (Grand Rapids, Mich.: ZonderKidz, 2010); *FaiThGirLz! Bible (NIV)* (Grand Rapids, Mich.: Zondervan, 2011).

20. *NIV Adventure Bible* (Grand Rapids, Mich.: Zondervan, 2011); *The Super Heroes Bible: The Quest for Good Over Evil (NIrV)* (Grand Rapids, Mich.: Zondervan, 2002); *Compact Kids Bible: Green Camo* (New York: Thomas Nelson, 2007). See also *NIV Boys Bible* (Grand Rapids, Mich.: Zondervan, 2011).

21. Mortimer J. Cohen, *Pathways through the Bible* (Philadelphia: Jewish Publication Society of America, 1946), x.

22. Hyman E. Goldin, *A Treasury of Bible Stories* (n.p., 1946).

23. Ellen Frankel, *JPS Illustrated Children's Bible* (Philadelphia: Jewish Publication Society, 2009), xii.

24. Frankel, *JPS Illustrated Children's Bible*, xi.

25. For other examples, see Laaren Brown and Lenny Hort, *The Children's Illustrated Jewish Bible* (New York: DK Publishing, 2007); and Alfred J. Kolatch, *Classic Bible Stories for Jewish Children* (Middle Village, N.Y.: Jonathan David, 1994).

26. David E. Stannard, *The Puritan Way of Death* (New York: Oxford University Press, 1977), 171. See also Steven Mintz, *Huck's Raft: A History of American Childhood* (Cambridge, Mass.: Harvard University Press, 2004), 20.

27. *The New England Primer* (Boston: Edward Draper, 1777), n.p.

28. Robert W. Lynn and Elliott Wright, *The Big Little School*, rev. ed. (Birmingham, Ala.: Religious Education Press, 1980), 70–71, 121–22; Anne M. Boylan, *Sunday School: The Formation of an American Institution, 1790–1880* (New Haven, Conn.: Yale University Press, 1988), 147.

29. See, e.g., Charles Foster, *The Story of the Bible from Genesis to Revelation Told in Simple Language* (Philadelphia: Charles Foster, 1873), 19–21; John Howard, *The Illustrated Scripture History for the Young* (New York: Virtue and Yorston, 1876), 11; J. L. Sooy, *Bible Talks with Children: The Scriptures Simplified for the Little Folk* (New York: Union Publishing House, 1889), 16; Carolyn Hadley, *From Eden to Babylon: Stories of the Prophets Priests and Kings of the Old Testament* (New York: McLoughlin Brothers, ca. 1890), 14–15; J. W. Buel and T. DeWitt Talmage, *The New Beautiful Story* (Philadelphia: Historical Publishing Company, 1892), 45; Russell H. Conwell, *Bible Stories for Children* (Philadelphia: W. W. Houston,

1892), 16; Mary A. Lathbury, *Bible Heroes: Stories from the Bible* (Boston: DeWolfe, Fiske, 1898), 5, and many more.

30. Lucy Barton, *Bible Letters* (London: John Souter, London School Library, 1831), 12.

31. Samuel G. Goodrich, *Peter Parley's Book of Bible Stories* (Boston: Lilly, Wait, 1834), 19; *Child's Book of Sunday Reading* (Worcester, Mass.: N. Hervey, 1840), n.p.; and *Bible Stories for the Young with Colored Engravings* (Worcester, Mass.: S. A. Howland, 1842), n.p.

32. See, e.g., *Scripture History* (New York: Wood, 1811), n.p.; *Little Book of Bible Stories for Children: With Numerous Engravings* (Worcester, Mass.: Dorr, Howland & Co. Spooner & Howland, 1839), 19–20; and *Stories from the Bible* (Northampton, Mass.: E. Turner, 1843), n.p.

33. *The Children's Bible*, vi–vii.

34. *The Children's Bible*, 106.

35. Faith Latimer, *Dear Old Stories Told Once More* (New York: American Tract Society, 1877), 100.

36. See Stephen Prothero, *American Jesus: How the Son of God Became a National Icon* (New York: Farrar, Straus and Giroux, 2003), 52–55.

37. Mrs. Grive, *Half Hours with the Bible; or, The Children's Scripture Story-Book* (New York: McLoughlin Brothers, 1867), 8.

38. Grive, *Half Hours*, 21–22.

39. Grive, *Half Hours*, 18.

40. Alvan Bond, *Young People's Illustrated Bible History* (Norwich, Conn.: Henry Bill, 1878), 27.

41. Bond, *Young People's Illustrated*, 28–29.

42. Bond, *Young People's Illustrated*, 37.

43. Sally Lloyd-Jones, *The Jesus Storybook Bible: Every Story Whispers His Name* (Grand Rapids, Mich.: ZonderKids, 2007), back cover.

44. "The Gospel Story Bible," *New Growth Press*, company website, http://gospelstoryforkids. com/portfolio/gospel-story-bible-2/.

45. See, e.g., Sarah Young, *Jesus Calling Bible Storybook*, illus. Carolina Farias (Nashville, Tenn.: Thomas Nelson, 2012); David Helm, *The Big Picture Story Bible*, illus. Gail Schoonmaker (Wheaton, Ill.: Crossway Books, 2004); Rondi DeBoer and Christine Tangvald, *My Favorite Bible* (Grand Rapids, Mich.: Baker, 2011); and *The Big Picture Interactive Bible Storybook* (Nashville, Tenn.: B & H Publishing, 2013).

46. James C. Wilhoit, "The Bible Goes to Sunday School: An Historical Response to Pluralism," *Religious Education* 82 (1987): 395.

47. For a lengthy survey of the diverse virtues of Noah in American children's Bibles, see my chapter in Dalton, *Children's Bibles in America*, 159–236.

48. J. H. Willard, *The Boy Who Obeyed: The Story of Isaac* (Philadelphia: Henry Altemus, 1905).

49. For a longer treatment of the child Jesus in US children's Bibles, see my article Russell W. Dalton, "Meek and Mild: American Children's Bibles' Stories of Jesus as a Boy," *Religious Education* 109, no. 1 (2014): 45–60.

50. Lynn and Wright, *Big Little School*, 26.

51. Dottie and Josh McDowell, *The Right Choices Bible*, illus. by Joe Boddy (Wheaton, Ill.: Tyndale House, 1998); Rick Osborne, Mary Guenther, and K. Christie Bowler, *Focus on the Family Bedtime Bible* (Wheaton, Ill.: Tyndale House, 2002).

52. Lenore Cohen, *Bible Tales for Very Young Children* (Cincinnati, Ohio: Union of American Hebrew Congregations, 1934); Addie Richman Altman, *The Jewish Child's Bible Stories* (New York: Bloch, 1949).

53. Penny Schine Gold, *Making the Bible Modern: Children's Bibles and Jewish Education in Twentieth-Century America* (Ithaca, N.Y.: Cornell University Press, 2004), 117–178).

54. Ann Eisenberg, *Bible Heroes I Can Be* (Minneapolis, Minn.: Kar-Ben, 2004). See also Julie Downing, *A First Book of Jewish Bible Stories* (New York: DLK Children, 2002).

55. John Rowe Townsend, *Written for Children: An Outline of English-Language Children's Literature*, 3rd ed. (New York: J. B. Lippincott, 1987), 304.

56. Leonard S. Marcus, *Minders of Make-Believe* (Boston: Houghton Mifflin, 2008), 136–37.

57. Benjamin Spock, *The Common Sense Book of Baby and Child Care* (New York: Duell, Sloane and Pearce, 1946).

58. Mintz, *Huck's Raft*, 275.

59. See, e.g., V. Gilbert Beers, *The Toddler's Bible*, illus. Carole Boerke (Colorado Springs, Colo.: David C. Cook, 1992); V. Gilbert Beers, *The Preschooler's Bible*, illus. Teresa Walsh (Colorado Springs, Colo.: David C. Cook, 1994); Carolyn Nabors Baker and Cindy Helms, *The Beginners Bible for Toddlers*, illus. Danny Brooks Dalby (Dallas, Tex.: Word, 1995); *Baby's First Bible*, illus. Colin Maclean and Moira Maclean (Pleasantville, N.Y.: Reader's Digest, 1996); *Baby Blessings: Baby's Bible*, illus. Mandy Stanley (Cincinnati, Ohio: Standard, 2005); Diane Stortz, *The Sweetest Story Bible for Toddlers*, illus. Sheila Bailey (Grand Rapids, Mich.: Zondervan, 2010).

60. Sally Lloyd-Jones, *Baby's Hug-a-Bible*, illus. Claudine Gévry (New York: HarperFestival, 2010); Sally Lloyd-Jones, *Tiny Bear's Bible* (Grand Rapids, Mich.: ZonderKids, 2007).

61. Marc Gellman, *Does God Have a Big Toe? Stories about Stories in the Bible* (New York: Harper & Row, 1989), vii.

62. Gellman, *Big Toe*, vii.

63. Gellman, *Big Toe*, 27–29, 32–33.

64. Mordicai Gerstein, *Noah and the Great Flood* (New York: Simon & Schuster Books, 1999), n.p.

65. See Siddiqa Juma, *Stories of the Prophets from the Qur'an* (Elmhurst, N.Y.: Tahrike Tarsile Qur'an, 1998); Saniyasnain Khan, *My First Quran Storybook* (Nizamuddin West, New Delhi: Goodword, 2007); Shahada (Sharelle) Abdul Haqq, *Stories of the Prophets in the Holy Qur'an* (Somerset, N.J.: Tughra Books, 2008).

66. See Nikki Bado-Fralick and Rebecca Sachs Norris, *Toying with God: The World of Religious Games and Dolls* (Waco, Tex.: Baylor University Press, 2010), 107–36.

67. See Bottigheimer, *The Bible for Children*, xii; and Dalton, *Children's Bibles in America*, 260.

BIBLIOGRAPHY

Adomeit, Ruth Elizabeth. *Three Centuries of Thumb Bibles: A Checklist*. New York: Garland, 1980.

Avery, Gillian. *Behold the Child: American Children and Their Books, 1621–1922*. London: Bodley Head, 1994.

Bado-Fralick, Nikki, and Rebecca Sachs Norris. *Toying with God: The World of Religious Games and Dolls*. Waco, Tex.: Baylor University Press, 2010.

Bottigheimer, Ruth B. *The Bible for Children: From the Age of Gutenberg to the Present*. New Haven, Conn.: Yale University Press, 1996.

Boylan, Anne M. *Sunday School: The Formation of an American Institution, 1790–1880*. New Haven, Conn.: Yale University Press, 1988.

Dalton, Russell W. *Children's Bibles in America: A Reception History of the Story of Noah's Ark in U.S. Children's Bibles*. London: Bloomsbury, 2015.

———. "Meek and Mild: American Children's Bibles' Stories of Jesus as a Boy." *Religious Education* 109, no. 1 (2014): 45–60.

Gold, Penny Schine. *Making the Bible Modern: Children's Bibles and Jewish Education in Twentieth-Century America*. Ithaca, N.Y.: Cornell University Press, 2004.

Gunn, David. "Cultural Criticism." In *Judges & Method: New Approaches in Biblical Studies*, 2nd ed., edited by Gale A. Yee, 202–36. Minneapolis, Minn.: Fortress Press, 2007.

Lynn, Robert W., and Elliot Wright, *The Big Little School: 200 Years of the Sunday School*. Nashville, Tenn.: Abingdon, 1971. Reprinted in 1980 by Religious Education Press.

Marcus, Leonard S. *Minders of Make-Believe*. Boston: Houghton Mifflin, 2008.

Mintz, Steven. *Huck's Raft: A History of American Childhood*. Cambridge, Mass.: Harvard University Press, 2004.

Stannard, David E. *The Puritan Way of Death*. New York: Oxford University Press, 1977.

Townsend, John Rowe. *Written for Children: An Outline of English-Language Children's Literature*. 3rd ed. New York: J. B. Lippincott, 1987.

Vander Stichele, Caroline, and Hugh S. Pyper, eds. *Text, Image, and Otherness in Children's Bibles: What Is in the Picture?* Atlanta, Ga.: Society of Biblical Literature, 2012.

Wilhoit, James C. "The Bible Goes to Sunday School: An Historical Response to Pluralism." *Religious Education* 82, no. 3 (1987): 309–404.

CHAPTER 3

....

THE BIBLE AND INDIGENOUS LANGUAGE TRANSLATIONS IN THE AMERICAS

....

LINFORD D. FISHER

THE Abenaki children were taking notes. While listening to Gabriel Druillettes, the young students used bits of charcoal to write characters on thin pieces of white birch bark. Prayers, questions and answers from catechisms, parts of passages from the Christian Bible—all were recorded by these native learners. Notes, yes, but in what language? It was the early 1650s, and Druillettes had only sporadically spent time among the Abenakis at a small French mission town (later Norridgewock) along the Kennebec River in the northern wilderness claimed by Massachusetts and France, but occupied by numerous Abenaki communities and associated native nations. The Jesuit missionary had not taught his catechumens French or Latin, nor did he give them paper, a quill, or ink, nor instruct them to write. Upon inspection, Druillettes realized that his indigenous students were writing in characters that were entirely unfamiliar to him: "Their characters were new, and so peculiar that one could not recognize or understand the writing of another,—that is to say, they used certain signs corresponding to their ideas; as it were, a local reminder, for recalling points and articles and maxims which they had retained."[1]

Druillettes's surprise that the Abenakis had a system of pictographic or hieroglyphic writing—and that they could inventively apply it to new linguistic and religious contexts— is revealing. On the one hand, it illustrates the general bias early modern Europeans had regarding indigenous facility for written communication; namely, they assumed that natives in North America were illiterate and that any kind of writing was foreign to them. Druillettes was surely erroneous in his observation that the characters were entirely new and that the writing could not be comprehended even between native children. On the other hand, and more positively, this example of Abenaki notetaking and writing reminds us that, with regard to the question of the Bible in indigenous languages, the process was not always—or at least not only—one of a Christian missionary translating the Bible into a phonetically rendered version of an indigenous language. In this and many other cases, indigenous people themselves were involved as translators and intermediaries, sometimes even rendering Christian concepts and biblical text into pictographic or other scripts that were initially unintelligible to missionaries.

Scholars have increasingly questioned the sharp line drawn by early modern Europeans between written and oral cultures. In particular, Europeans in the sixteenth and seventeenth centuries (and beyond) elevated alphabetic literacy as the pinnacle of civilized learning—which, unsurprisingly, corresponded with the values, language, and educational models of Europe. Privileging alphabetic literacy blinded them—and us—to other important forms of written communication.[2] Elizabeth Hill Boone and Walter D. Mignolo, in their introduction to *Writing without Words*, argue that we should expand the definition of a written language to include a wider range of intentional and specific communications. Additionally, such writing systems need not be viewed as simply an early phase of a natural progression toward alphabetic literacy. With this expanded definition in mind, then, we can enlarge our understanding of different forms of written communication that were present in a wide variety of pre-contact and immediately post-contact native communities. As Boone and Mignolo note, "pre-Columbian peoples used both glottographic and semasiographic systems. At different times, several cultures in Mesoamerican and Andean South America wrote with hieroglyphics, pictorial images, and abstract signs, combining elements of all three to different degrees."[3] As scholars are realizing, however, this was not just limited to indigenous populations in Central and South America, as is sometimes assumed.

There are several important things to consider when investigating the relationship between natives and the Bible. First, Indian-language translations of the Bible were only one element of a larger program of printing religious materials. This essay takes as a basic starting assumption that most missionary translational efforts contained within them a core of biblical texts and ideas, no matter how fragmentary. This allows us to craft new narratives about Indian Bible translation and helps to decenter what is often seen as the pinnacle of biblical translational history, the Wôpanâak Indian Bible of 1663, often associated with the work of the Roxbury minister and English missionary John Eliot.[4] If one looks strictly at attempts to print the Bible or significant parts of it into native languages, Eliot will continue to stand out, since the 1663 Indian Bible was, in fact, the first complete Bible published in any language anywhere in the New World. But the history of Bible translation and printing in the Americas is larger, more widespread, and more important than just whole printed Bibles. Even Eliot in New England published treatises and catechisms alongside of the biblical text; the entire Bible was just one way of promoting biblical literacy, even for these Bible-centric English Protestants. Taking a wider view of indigenous language translation in the Americas allows for a greater appreciation of the work by Spanish Catholic missionaries and priests in the century prior to English colonization as well as, later, translations undertaken by French missionaries.

Second, any translational efforts in the Americas involved the nearly invisible work of bilingual indigenous linguists. Translating religious texts involved some vocabulary invention, of course, but it also required idiomatic rendering of concepts that would otherwise be impossibly foreign to native cultures. European missionaries and translators did not often highlight or even mention these behind the scenes linguists, but through opaque and a few outright references we are able to more fully understand the culturally hybrid nature of this collaboration.

Third, alphabetic literacy was an idealized goal held by Europeans that was not always shared equally by native communities. Oral knowledge, oral literacy, and—in some communities—pictographic or hieroglyphic literacy had weathered the test of time and were seen as perfectly capable of serving indigenous communities. In many ways, natives only really came to embrace alphabetic literacy for two main reasons: Christianity and the law. Protestants especially placed great value on the printed Bible as the very words of God himself that held great authority. Many Christianized native communities over time embraced this ideal, although not always in alphabetic form (as with the Mi'qmaks). And in the realm of law, natives quickly realized that written documents were required to leverage any power in European contexts (particularly with regard to land deeds). And although the general arc of native history has moved toward increasing written literacy in both European and native languages, some of the written native languages that were developed over time did so explicitly apart from the Latin alphabet. Therefore, the full history of indigenous language Bible translation has to take into account the wider scope of Catholic missionary activity and the involvement of natives in this process, in terms of production as well as reception.

Europeans consistently were amazed at the linguistic diversity they found in the Americas. Europe, too, had a wide variety of languages, but linguistic categories numbered in the dozens at most.[5] Across the Americas as a whole, approximately two thousand languages existed, including hundreds of dialects or branches of each language class or family. In North America alone, there were no fewer than 221 "mutually unintelligible languages, each fractured into myriad dialects that were themselves confounding even to native ears."[6] Early colonists observed that even groups neighboring each other had language dialects that, while perhaps belonging to the same language family, were distinctly different.

As scholars have noted, there were differing levels of effort put forth to understand and reciprocate native and European languages. At almost every sustained point of contact throughout the Americas, Europeans and natives attempted to communicate with each other, whether through hand signs and gestures (as with Columbus in 1492, who fancied himself exceedingly proficient in such communication) or, within a few weeks or months, a sort of rudimentary linguistic pidgin that was formed. Such deliberately limited language devoid of grammatical inflections allowed Europeans and natives to jointly construct a hybrid language for basic communication that drew from both languages.[7] And, in fact, there is linguistic evidence that this hybrid language construction is how some native communities communicated across linguistic lines before European contact as well.[8]

One element (at least) connected all of these various disparate contexts with regard to the experience of colonization: in most locales, missionaries eventually tried to teach basic Christian doctrine to local populations and translate parts of the Bible and catechisms into indigenous languages. This was not the case for every language or every locale, to be sure, but it proved true in dozens of linguistic contexts that affected hundreds of native communities and thousands of indigenous individuals over time. Missionaries—Protestant and Catholic—viewed learning native languages as central to any successful evangelization or conversion program. The Franciscan provincial Jacopo da Testera, writing from Mexico to Emperor Charles V on May 6, 1532, described the linguistic challenges facing missionary efforts as a "wall" that separated the indigenous populations from the newcomers, surmountable only by the difficult and long-term commitment to learning local native languages.[9] The Jesuit linguist Ludovico Bertonio saw it as an ethical imperative to learn native languages in Peru and Bolivia; he once reframed the parable of the Good

Samaritan in linguistic terms, saying that priests who did not learn local indigenous languages were like the priest and Levite who passed by the man who had been mugged.[10] Even in contexts where no official publications emerged, missionaries almost always kept personal, handwritten dictionaries for their own use. Sébastian Rale, the Jesuit missionary in Norridgewock (what is now central Maine), kept a personal dictionary of the Abenaki language, which was only published one hundred and fifty years after his death, and more as an antiquarian specimen than anything else.[11]

European missionaries in the Americas each approached the translation of scripture slightly differently. At times, this was rooted in particular national contexts, since translation of the Bible was prohibited in some European countries and permitted in others. Spanish authorities banned the printing of Bibles in Spanish as early as the mid-sixteenth century, for example. Nonetheless, two early Spanish Bibles were printed outside of Spain, in 1569 (Basel) and 1602 (Amsterdam).[12] Jesuits—who operated transnationally and globally—at times defied imperial mandates, but mostly adhered to this one. At other times, the differences among missionaries were possibly rooted in religious traditions. Recent scholarship has begun to challenge the long-standing caricatures of scripturally ignorant Catholics versus Bible-reading Protestants.[13] Protestants were sometimes more interested in personal interaction with a fuller range of the biblical text, but Catholic missionaries, too, were eager to get catechisms, primers, and portions of the Bible into the hands of their converts. Over time, Catholic missionaries across the Americas were responsible for an enormous indigenous-language literary production that made the Protestant commitment to both the Bible and missionary work look half-hearted and anemic in comparison.

The earliest attempts to render biblical ideas and concepts into forms understandable by natives were neither alphabetic nor printed on a press. From the earliest years of European colonization, early Spanish missionaries in central Mexico built upon pre-contact Mexica pictographic writing to narrate key portions of biblical text.[14] Franciscans would often set up large paintings depicting the Ten Commandments or biblical scenes, such as the creation of the world from Genesis 1–3.[15] Another early attempt to build upon pictographic writing was developed (or at least popularized) by the Franciscan friar Jacobo Testera in the mid- to late-sixteenth century. The *Catechismo Testerinos* (Testerian Catechisms) were an attempt to render the words of the catechism using a rebus system (based on homophony). Each drawn image corresponded with a phonetic component of the desired word, but the individual images and phonetic words did not usually have any correlation with the final word being illustrated. So, for example, a banner (*pantli*) and a nopal fruit (*nochtil*) would be used to suggest *Pater noster* ("Our Father," or the Lord's Prayer).[16] The images used also sometimes utilized Aztec symbols and colors: people pictured in the catechism sometimes wear red robes, the color of Aztec noblemen, and prickly pears (native to Mexico) sometimes appear with the Virgin Mary. Although these *Catechismo Testerinos* were directly based on written, alphabetic catechisms (and therefore possibly meant to supplement them), they were considered to be relatively ineffective—in part because Testera had not learned any indigenous languages—they nonetheless were in circulation into the eighteenth century (figure 3.1).[17]

Over time, however, Franciscans, Jesuits, and other missionaries focused more on alphabetic indigenous and Spanish language catechisms than pictographs. In some cases, these catechisms and educational materials combined phoneticized alphabetic versions of local indigenous languages with older pictographic forms of writing. In 1547, a Tzotzil (Mayan),

FIGURE 3.1 *Catechismo Testerino*, eighteenth century. Courtesy of the John Carter Brown Library at Brown University, Providence, R.I.

Latin, and Spanish book was published that included woodcuts of scenes from the Bible.[18] In this way, missionaries represented pictorially the text of the Bible and the stories it contained even as they encouraged alphabetic literacy. Before printing presses were available, Catholic missionaries translated and circulated manuscript volumes that contained portions of scripture, catechisms, and sermons. One example of this is Maturino Gilberti's "Thema para que se oy galaboz del señor," produced in Mexico in approximately 1559. This 456-page manuscript volume contains scriptural texts and sermons in Latin and Tarasco, or Purépecha, and would likely have been used by natives.[19]

In many other forms, small sections of the Bible were translated and published into a wide variety of languages by Catholic missionaries, including Purépecha, Otomi, Mazahua, Mayan, Zapotec, Huastec, and Nahuatl, among others. This included the numerous *Cartillas* (catechetical booklets), which usually included the Lord's Prayer, the Apostles Creed, the Ten Commandments, and other portions of the catechism. They were often printed in at least two or even three languages, and were used and read widely by native populations in hundreds of mission villages in the Spanish Americas. One example is *Cartilla mayor, en lengua castellana, latina, y mexicana*, a twenty-eight-page booklet in Spanish, Latin, and Nahuatl, published in Mexico City in 1691 (figure 3.2).[20]

In addition to the *Cartillas*, Catholic missionaries and priests in colonial Latin America published hundreds of versions of another catechetical form in the sixteenth and seventeenth

FIGURE 3.2 *Cartilla mayor, en lengua castellana, latina, y mexicana* (En Mexico: en la Imprenta de la Uiuda de Bernardo Calderon en la calle de San Augustin, 1691). Courtesy of the John Carter Brown Library at Brown University, Providence, R.I.

centuries, the *Doctrina Christiana*, sometimes referred to as the "Little Doctrine," usually in local indigenous languages such as Nahuatl, Tzotzil, or Quechua. Both the *Cartillas* and the *Doctrina Christianas* were widely utilized catechistic and doctrinal manuals that were used to communicate basic Christian truths. They also contained within them direct and indirect biblical references and quotations. Even if they were not a straightforward translation of the Bible itself in most cases, they were replete with biblical language, teaching, excerpts, and ideas. As such, they are an important and often overlooked element of translating the Bible and its contents into the indigenous languages of the Americas.

Printing catechisms and portions of scripture unfolded differently in various locations in Spanish territories. In Peru, Jesuits arrived in 1568, largely at the urging of King Phillip II of Spain. From their church and college in Cuzco, the Jesuit fathers undertook to reform Peruvian culture, in part, through linguistic study and teaching centered around Latin and local indigenous languages. By 1576, the Jesuit linguist Alfonso de Barzana had translated into both Quechua and Aymara a vocabulary, grammar, and a long and short catechism.[21] Building on these translations, the Third Council of Lima in 1584 published a text specifically designed to teach Christianity to the Andean natives. Yet another example of the ubiquitous *Doctrina Christiana*, this volume included a "Short Catechism for Uneducated and Busy People" and a "Longer Catechism for Those Who Are More Capable," each in Quechua,

Aymara, and Spanish, both of which likely drew upon Barzana's linguistic work.[22] Perhaps the most widely translated and circulated Catholic Spanish catechism was by Jerónimo de Ripalda: *Catecismo y exposición breve de la doctrina christiana*.[23] First published in Spain in 1591, it was quickly translated into dozens of local indigenous languages in Latin America and reprinted countless times.[24]

Nonetheless, Catholic missionaries and linguists did occasionally publish larger portions of the Bible in native languages. The Franciscan Friar Juan de Zumarraga, given the title of "Protector of the Indians" and who served as the first bishop and archbishop of New Spain, was known for his enthusiasm for translating the Bible into all the languages of the world—so much so that he came under suspicion by the Spanish Inquisition for his translation interests.[25] Another Franciscan, Maturino Gilberti, published *Dialogo de doctrina christiana, enla lengua d[e] Mechuaca* in 1559 (figure 3.3).[26] Published in Mechuaca (Purépecha), this large, 654-page catechism included a version of *Epistolas y Evangelios*, which was essentially readings from the Gospels and various letters of the New Testament for the whole year. The only problem was that *Epistolas y Evangelios*, as compiled by Friar Ambrosio de Montesinos, was banned by Spanish authorities in 1612 and placed on the *Index librorum prohibitorum et expurgatorum*, or the List of Prohibited Books.[27] By the time Gilberti published his *Dialogo* in 1559, he was already coming under the suspicion of the Inquisition for

FIGURE 3.3 Maturino Gilberti, *Dialogo de doctrina christiana, enla lengua d[e] Mechuaca[n]* ([Mexico City]: Fue impresso en casa de Juan Pablos Bressano . . . desta . . . ciudad de Mexico, 1559). Courtesy of the John Carter Brown Library at Brown University, Providence, R.I.

heresy and for having printed books and pamphlets in Purépecha without license. Other missionaries, too, reportedly translated *Epistolas y Evangelios* into other native languages, such as Mixtec, but no copies survived to the present.[28] These restrictions on indigenous language Bible printing reveal the difficulty of printing larger sections of the Bible within Spanish contexts, even in the Americas.

In Paraguay, Jesuits first arrived in 1587 when three missionaries moved to Asunción at the invitation of the Dominican bishop there. A Jesuit mission was established at Loreto in 1610, in the newly created Provincia Gigante de las Indias (1607), part of a larger attempt to protect the Guaraní from the semi-slavery of the *encomienda* system. Nuestra Señora de Loreto, as the mission was called, survived the tumultuous first several decades of tensions between political authorities, slave raiders, and the Jesuits. By 1629, thirteen missions in Guairá included 38,500 natives. After the 1640s, the missions expanded and grew steadily to a peak of 141,182 Indians in thirty mission towns in 1732.[29] In these mission towns, the Jesuits set up fairly autonomous, comprehensive societies that contained elements of socialist utopia and heavy-handed authoritarianism. Land was cultivated to produce surplus crops (some of which were exported), private property was introduced, education was encouraged, and Christianity became a central feature of the mission life.

The first printing press in Paraguay was established in 1700 at Loreto, where Jesuits proceeded to publish a wide variety of religious materials in the Guaraní language, as well as Latin and Spanish. Father Antonio Garriga, a Spanish Jesuit, published *Instruccion practica para ordenar santamente la vidà* in 1713, which was the second book published on the new press.[30] As its title indicated, it contained guidelines for saintly living, although it was entirely in Spanish. A decade later, however, a more fascinating hybrid text emerged from the press. Titled *Explicacion de el catechismo en lengua guarani*, it was a fairly straightforward catechism of the Catholic Church in both Guaraní and Spanish.[31] Like most other Catholic Indian language publications in the early modern era, it also contained snippets of scripture and copious references to biblical texts and ideas. The Lord's Prayer is included, along with catechetical materials relating to Jesus, his death, angels, and living a holy life. What is significant about *Explicacion de el catechismo* is that it was prepared and published by Nicholás Yapuguay, a Guaraní *cacique* (indigenous leader) who seemingly embraced the Jesuits' proffered Catholicism. Yapuguay was born and raised in the Jesuit mission town of Santa María la Mayor, where he grew up speaking Guaraní and eventually became proficient in Latin and Spanish.[32]

In other parts of the Americas, too, missionaries learned local languages and translated catechisms and parts of the Bible. In North America, missionaries and travelers noticed that some native groups had pre-contact forms of written communication. Such native populations included the Abenaki of Maine, the Montagnais of Quebec, and the Hurons of the upper Great Lakes.[33] Perhaps one of the most unique examples of these pre-contact examples of writing comes from the Mi'kmaq, of present-day Nova Scotia and New Brunswick. More pictorial than European in its nature, this hieroglyphic writing, known as *komqwejwi'kasikl*, was clearly rooted in pre-contact native culture.[34] In the summer of 1676, the Recollect missionary Chrestien Le Clercq arrived in Mi'kmaq territory with the goal of converting local native populations to Catholicism. To accomplish this, Le Clercq claimed that he "formed" pictorial writing to communicate the basic truths of Christianity to the Mi'kmaqs. Scholars now largely believe that Le Clercq—much like Gabriel Druillettes among the Abenakis—simply built upon a robust preexisting tradition of hieroglyphic writing among the Mi'kmaqs and adopted characters and concepts for the Christianity he was trying to explain (along with possibly inventing new characters). The Mi'kmaq hieroglyphs that Le Clercq adopted were, he admitted, a bit unsystematic and highly symbolic, "in which each arbitrary letter signifies a particular word and sometimes even two together."[35]

The result was a fascinating and unique set of images and picture words that, with some additional learning by local Mi'kmaqs, communicated basic Christian ideas in written form. These hieroglyphic renditions of basic Christian teaching and bits of scripture were copied and handed down in communities and families from the late seventeenth century through the mid-nineteenth century, when another missionary, Christian Kauder, arranged for the manuscripts to be printed in Vienna using specially made types.[36] A second edition in 1921 is the copy that is most commonly consulted and cited.[37]

Like their South and Central American counterparts, North American missionaries alphabetized and phoneticized local indigenous languages and translated catechisms and primers for local native consumption. In the mid-Atlantic region, Swedish missionary Johannes Campanius translated the 1529 Shorter Catechism by Martin Luther into Pidgin Delaware, which was a hybrid Dutch-Unami language that emerged between the Dutch and the Delaware in the opening years of contact in the 1620s.[38] The catechism contained a range of doctrinally based questions and answers. It also included passages from the Bible, including the Lord's Prayer and the Ten Commandments. In New France, the Jesuit Father Jean de Brebeuf worked on a translation for the Hurons around Montreal, which he published as the *Huron Catechism* in 1630 after his return to Rouen, France.[39] In the early eighteenth century, the Society for the Propagation of the Gospel in Foreign Parts (Anglican) sponsored a collection of Mohawk language publications for missionary use in New York, including specific passages of scripture, catechisms, dictionaries, psalms, prayers, spelling books, and the Book of Common Prayer.[40]

But not all missionary translations in North America made it into publication, largely due to the remoteness of their missionary fields and the lack of access to printing presses. Jesuits, like Father Claude Allouez, working among the Illinois in the Upper Great Lakes region starting in the 1660s translated the Lord's Prayer, the Apostles Creed, and other parts of the catechism into Illinois, but most of these texts were read, recited, and circulated locally, in handwritten form.[41] Similarly, the French Jesuit Father Jean Baptiste Antoine Robert Le Boulanger painstakingly kept a meticulous, handwritten record of the Miami-Illinois language words and their definitions in a large, oversized volume in the eighteenth century. In addition to the approximately 3,000 individual word entries, the manuscript volume also contains prayers, catechisms, the Ten Commandments, translations of readings for the church year in the Gospels, and a translation into Miami-Illinois of the book of Genesis.[42]

In addition to translating catechisms and the Bible (or portions of it, like the Lord's Prayer) into native languages, in some regions missionaries also composed and translated songs into local indigenous languages, many of which were replete with biblical language and imagery. The Moravians (a Protestant Germanic movement with roots in the pre-Reformation era) translated dozens of hymns into the Mahican and Mohawk languages of western Connecticut, western Massachusetts, and eastern New York during the mid-eighteenth century.[43] The Moravians also translated portions of the Gospels into Mahican and Mohawk. In New England, Eliot and his native linguists published the Psalter (intended to be sung) in Wôpanâak as a stand-alone book in 1658, and it was also bound in at the back of the 1663 Indian Bible.[44]

Undoubtedly the most comprehensive effort to provide the entire Bible in a local native language in the colonial period was the Wôpanâak Bible of 1663. Published in Cambridge, Massachusetts, it was the first complete Bible printed anywhere in the Americas. But it is important to stress that Catholic missionaries had been learning, phonetically alphabetizing, and translating parts of the Bible into native languages in Central and South America for almost a century and a half by 1663. It is unclear how aware of these various translation projects Eliot would have been, but it seems impossible that he was entirely ignorant of the fact that Jesuit and Franciscan missionaries already had a well-developed system of phoneticizing and alphabetizing native languages. Therefore, although Eliot was the first to oversee the translation of the entire Bible into an indigenous language, he was a latecomer to indigenous language translation in the Americas more generally.

Eliot began learning the Wôpanâak language in the early 1640s and began preaching to local natives in 1646.[45] Although Eliot's early preaching attempts to local Massachusett natives in 1646 were halting at best, he threw himself into a more full-blown study of the Wôpanâak language, aided by a native servant/slave named Cockenoe, who had been taken as a captive in the Pequot War. Other colonists in New England had learned some of the local languages prior to Eliot, including traders like William Pynchon of Springfield, Massachusetts, and, perhaps more famously, Roger Williams, the religious dissident who founded Providence in 1636 in what later became Rhode Island.[46] Williams's 1643 *A Key into the Language of America* was the first English-indigenous language phrasebook from anywhere in the Americas.[47]

Even as early as the late 1640s, Eliot dreamed of publishing the entire Bible in the Wôpanâak language. Although he started the translation work on the Bible in the early 1650s, the first Indian-language book to emerge from the press in Cambridge was *The Indian Primer*, published in 1654.[48] Eliot sent a few sections of the Bible to press as he worked, including the books of Genesis and Matthew in 1655 and Psalms in 1658, along with printing other primers, catechisms, and other devotional books popular among the English.[49] By December 1658, Eliot reported to the New England Company that the translation of the entire Bible was complete: "the whole book of God is translated into their own language, it wanteth but revising, transcribing, and printing."[50] While Eliot and his native linguists were translating the Bible, Eliot was also slowly building a network of "praying towns," or Christian Indian villages that by 1674 comprised fourteen towns stretching from northeastern Connecticut to northern Massachusetts (this was in addition to the Christian Indian towns on Cape Cod and Martha's Vineyard, under different leadership).[51]

When the entire Bible was finally finished in 1663, it was a serious book, the likes of which the printing presses in North America would not see again for a long time (figure 3.4). The Indian Bible itself is noteworthy for its careful preparation and production. In addition to a painstaking translation by Indian linguists and Eliot, the text of the Bible was lined with marginal cross-references, which were a popular feature of early modern English Bibles, such as the Geneva Bible and the King James Bible. The full text of the Bible—Old and New Testaments—is followed by a version of the metrical psalms, not uncommon for Bibles printed at that time. But included at the back was a short listing of "Rules for Christian Living" designed for natives that included questions like: "How can I walk all the day long with God?" and "What should a Christian do, to keep perfectly holy the Sabbath Day?"[52]

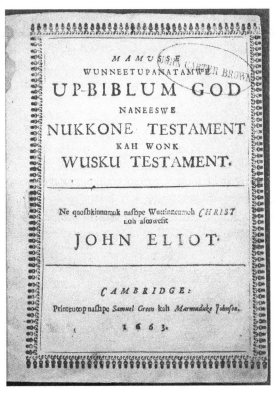

FIGURE 3.4 *Mamusse wunneetupanatamwe Up-Biblium God* title page, 1663 edition. Photograph by Linford D. Fisher. Courtesy of the John Carter Brown Library at Brown University, Providence, R.I.

One of the key considerations is who actually did the translation. As scholars have increasingly realized, native linguists, translators, and cultural mediators were central to any process of alphabetization, phoneticization, or translation.[53] Jesuits in Peru and New France, English ministers in New England, Anglican missionaries in New York, and Recollect fathers in New Brunswick all were able to produce translations and written representations of native languages because of local natives who were able to, first, learn a European language, and second, do the difficult work of idiomatic and literal translation. In Peru, when the Jesuit linguist Ludovico Bertonio worked to refine his understanding of Amyra and translate summaries of scripture and sermons into that language, he relied on literate Andean natives to help with the idiomatic and literal translations of difficult concepts into Amyra.[54] The same appears true of Jesuits in Paraguay, who published Guaraní texts on their printing press in Loreto shortly after 1700. It is likely that bi- and trilingual natives like Nicholás Yapuguay, a local *cacique* and learned individual, helped with most of the translated and published materials in Loreto. Yapuguay published two religious books of his own in Guaraní and additionally helped the Jesuit Father Paolo Restivo with multiple publications, including a 1724 new edition of a 1640 Guaraní grammar by Antonio Ruiz de Montoya.[55]

Native linguists were central to the translation work undertaken by John Eliot as well. Past generations have so venerated Eliot that they have blindly insisted that the work was solely his.[56] But Eliot himself admitted his own linguistic weaknesses from the beginning. In 1649, Eliot wrote a letter to Edward Winslow, in which he noted that, while he desired to translate a primer into the native language, he would need help: "I having yet but little skill in their language . . . I must have some Indians, and it may be other help continually about me to try and examine Translations."[57] Eliot's own vision for this process was a team of native and English linguists, translators, and fact-checkers. Central to this process was, first, Cockenoe, and later, John Sassamon and Job Nesutan. Nesutan was described by Eliot's contemporary, Daniel Gookin, as "a very good linguist in the English tongue, and was Mr. Eliot's assistant and interpreter in his translations of the Bible, and other books of the Indian language."[58]

One of the results of these early attempts to render biblical text and Christian doctrine into native languages was the realization that some things, indeed, might be lost in translation. After one representative of the New England Company (NEC, a London-based missionary society) toured native villages in the early eighteenth century, he reported that "there are many words of Mr. Elliott's forming which they never understood . . . . Such a knowledge in their Bibles, as our English ordinarily have in ours, they seldom any of them have."[59] Such realizations, as Sarah Rivett has argued, led some European philosophers to reconsider their assumptions about the universal ability of language to communicate truth.[60] In New England, this suspicion of the inability of indigenous languages to adequately communicate Christian ideas led the NEC commissioners in Boston to decline Eliot's request to print a third edition of the Indian Bible in the early eighteenth century. As Cotton Mather noted, "the great things of our Holy Religion brought unto them in it, unavoidably arrive in Terms that are scarcely more intelligible to them than if they were entirely in English."[61]

As it turns out, Mather's fears were mostly unfounded in the long term, as native Christian communities seemed to exhibit high levels of theological literacy, even if never completely disconnected from native views of the world. Still, the Indian Bible of 1663 contains mistranslations of varying sorts, some of which evince clear stamps of native translation work. Some seem to be simple mistakes. In 2 Kings 2:23, for example, the young boys who jeer at Elisha for his bald head, in the Indian Bible, say, "Go on up, ball head!" The word that should be "bald" (no hair) is instead rendered as a ball to play with.[62] Others reflect the translation of Christian concepts into native worldviews and language. Native linguists translated "hell" as a long phrase that reflected indigenous epistemologies and theologies, not English ones: *chepiohkomukqut*, which can be translated as "a house of heads without a brain," or "the house of empty skulls."[63] Scholars have noted the presence of "unorthodox" translations in other native contexts as well. The historian Tracy Leavelle, for example, has noted the misrendering of key concepts in the Miami-Illinois language, such as in the Apostles' Creed, where "born of the Virgin Mary" is translated as "the virgin Mary unintentionally gave birth."[64]

It is difficult to know how natives received these primers, prayer books, and even the entire Bible in their languages across the Americas. It is fairly certain that most natives were not instantly awed by alphabetic writing or by published texts. A nineteenth-century native retorted to Moravians who touted written, biblical literacy, "The White people know God from the book . . . we know him from other things."[65] More than the technology of printing, most natives seemed to interact with the content itself. From the surviving evidence, it seems that there was a range of responses to religious publications in Indian language, from apparent acceptance, readership, and use, on the one side, to full out rejection at the other end of the spectrum. In between were a variety of other responses, such as indifference and even unorthodox political uses and appropriations.

Sometimes native linguists took things into their own hands, even apart from the supervision or approval of European missionaries. Hints of this process survive through the centuries. One poignant example of this is the "Nahuatl Bible," produced sometime before 1560 for Aztec communities in Central Mexico.[66] It exists only in manuscript form in the Schøyen Collection, in Oslo, Norway, but presumably represents a larger genre of similar works. Essentially, the Nahuatl Bible is an indigenous-authored, loosely rendered narrative of the conversion of St. Paul from the book of Acts conflated with the ministry of Saint Sebastian (a third-century martyr popular in the medieval period). Although the text is in Spanish, scholarly analysis of the sixteen pages of narrative indicate clear Nahuatl authorship, for reasons both conceptual and textual (like the misspelling of common Spanish words, such as *diaplos* for *diablos*). It is hard to imagine that any Catholic priest would have written or authorized a retelling of the conversion of Paul in the book of Acts that involves a trip to hell during his period of blindness, or a scene in which the Apostle Paul ends up killing Saint Sebastian (not a contemporary of Paul) with a flurry of arrows, followed by a miraculous resurrection. Furthermore, the biblical text contains interjections that reveal deep animosities about Spanish presence: "We [Nahua nobles] no longer believe and still we will love those you [Spaniards] do not yet take to be gods; still before our gods we will kill people; it will again be like it was before you came here."[67]

Another example of such religious literary resistance—although admittedly less unorthodox—took place in the seventeenth and even eighteenth centuries, when religiously trained indigenous linguists revived pictographic literacies to replicate the widely popular *Doctrina Christiana* in pictorial form.[68] Such pictographical renderings of Catholic catechism—presumably unprompted by Spanish missionaries—represented a connection with an earlier era, perhaps an attempt to "archaize" indigenous Christianity by rendering it in pre-contact writing forms. The result was a catechetical form (which, as always, contained portions of biblical text and teachings) that reclaimed non-alphabetic literacy, even as it retained the basic teachings contained in the Catholic catechisms.[69]

One of the most fascinating pieces of evidence we have of native engagement with the Indian Bible are the notes in native languages that are contained in the margins of some extant Indian Bibles. Marginal notations in native languages began early. Although most marginal entries are not dated, the earliest one found so far is from July 17, 1670, only seven years after the publication of the Indian Bible.[70] The marginalia reveal the excitement of owning a book and having open spaces in which to write. For some natives, at least, these Bibles were a big deal. There is clear evidence of tender ownership, of thoughtful engagement with the ideas within it, of honest frustration. The Indian Bibles were loaned out to friends, used to write sermons, written in as journals and for writing practice, and passed down to successive generations. Then again, the majority of New England natives largely ignored the Indian Bible, and nonbelievers even targeted it for destruction during King Philip's War in 1675–1676.[71]

The process of translating the Bible (or parts of it) into indigenous languages picked up considerably in the nineteenth century. In the United States and Europe, this was mostly due to the fact there was a great increase in local, national, and international missionary societies (largely Protestant ones) that carried onto the global mission field a core belief in the importance of having the Bible in local languages. As American and British missionaries translated the scriptures into local languages in India, Burma, the Sandwich Islands, and western Africa, American missionaries renewed their emphasis on indigenous language translation within the boundaries of the United Sates. In particular, the missionaries associated with the American Board of Commissioners for Foreign Missions (ABCFM, founded in 1810) built upon existing linguistic work within the Cherokee Nation of the American Southeast to encourage the translation of the Bible into the Cherokee language.[72]

In the case of the Cherokees, an indigenous silversmith and linguist named Sequoyah devised a non-Latin syllabary for the Cherokee language, starting in 1809.[73] Seemingly apart from any missionary influence, Sequoyah experimented with various kinds of symbols for the written language (including, at first, a symbol for every word). He eventually landed on a system of eighty-six characters that included unique symbols intermixed with Latin, Greek, and Arabic letters. After Sequoyah successfully taught his own daughter to read it, Cherokee leaders became convinced of its utility and adopted it for the whole nation in 1825. With the help of ABCFM missionaries (who were by that time in Georgia among the Cherokees), a Christianized Cherokee named Elias Boudinot had printing type made for the syllabary and in 1828 published the first edition of their own newspaper in both Cherokee and English, the *Cherokee Phoenix*.

Boudinot worked with an ABCFM missionary named Samuel Worcester to begin translating the Bible into Cherokee, and in December 1829, published the first five chapters of Genesis in the ABCFM publication, the *Missionary Herald*. Additional sections of the translated Bible were published over the subsequent thirty years as stand-alone texts and, in some cases, in the *Cherokee Phoenix*.[74] The full Cherokee New Testament was not published until 1860 by the American Bible Society (ABS; founded in 1816, and aided by the Cherokee Bible Society, a local chapter of the national organization).[75] The ABS continued to fund the translation of the Bible—portions of it as well as in its entirety—into North American indigenous languages throughout the nineteenth century and into the twentieth century. This included the Dakota, Seneca, Choctaw, Ho-chunk, and Arapaho languages, among others.

The work of indigenous language translation in the Americas in the twentieth century was intensified by the creation of the Wycliff Bible Translators (1942) and the United Bible Society (1946). Both societies (as well as others) were, in part, dedicated to providing the text of the Bible in indigenous languages globally, including in the Americas. These efforts led to, for the first time, the translation of the full Bible into many indigenous languages in Central and South America. In Peru, where Jesuits had already published catechisms and dictionaries four hundred years prior, United Bible Societies missionaries built upon these earlier efforts to produce translations of the full Bible in Ayacucho Quechua, Cusco Quechua, Huallaga Quechua, and Central Aymara. Additionally, by 2015, the New Testament had been translated into an additional forty-two Peruvian languages.[76]

Although the legacy of such Bible translation projects is contested and ambiguous (in terms of the larger cultural changes that came with Christianization), one of the many ways that these Indian language publications continue to serve native communities in the present is with regard to language revitalization (and, for contemporary translation projects, preservation). From the mid-nineteenth century through the mid-twentieth century, a racially based confluence of regional and national pressures and measures like detribalization, boarding schools, and nullification led to a sharp decline in native languages being spoken, taught, and learned. Perhaps not without irony, the fact that European missionaries all across the Americas alphabetized native languages and printed translations of catechisms, primers, and parts of the Bible into these indigenous languages has meant that, in many cases, these spoken languages never died out or, at the very least, these publications could be leaned upon to recover them in the twentieth century.[77] Although many indigenous languages might have survived without these missionary publications, others were clearly preserved through such translational and publication efforts.

One of the most fascinating examples of language revitalization in New England is among the various communities of Wampanoags on Cape Cod and Martha's Vineyard. Through the work of Mashpee Wampanoag linguist Jessie Little Doe Baird, Wôpanâak is once again being spoken, written, and, for the first time in several generations, being learned as the first language among Wampanoag children. At the center of this language revitalization is the 1663 Indian Bible and the other seventeenth-century Indian language publications. In what can only be described as one of the most supreme ironies of this long history, the very book that was intended to reshape and even eradicate native religion and culture is now being used to rejuvenate it. Although there are other Indian-language publications that Eliot and his native translators and printers produced, according to Baird the sheer length of the Indian Bible makes it indispensable for understanding a wider semantic range of words and their uses in a variety of contexts and different literary genres. In this way, then, Bible-based Indian-language publications from the colonial Americas continue to influence indigenous populations in that hemisphere, although often for cultural revitalization—surely not the intended use by early modern missionaries and translators.

NOTES

This essay was made possible, in part, by the staff at the John Carter Brown Library and the Newberry Library. I am grateful to Jessie Little Doe Baird, Brandon Bayne, Bérénice Gaillemin, Marley-Vincent Lindsey, and Ken Ward for their insights and assistance along the way.

1. Jesuits and Reuben Gold Thwaites, *The Jesuit Relations and Allied Documents: Travels and Explorations of the Jesuit Missionaries in New France, 1610–1791*, vol. 38 (Cleveland, Ohio: Burrows, 1899), 27.

2. Zvetan Todorov has argued that alphabetic literacy gave Europeans an advantage in the conquest in the Americas, although most scholars have rejected that view. For an overview of the debate, see D. W. Soler, "Language and Communication in the Spanish Conquest of America," *History Compass* 8 (2010): 491–502.

3. Elizabeth Hill Boone and Walter D. Mignolo, eds., *Writing without Words: Alternative Literacies in Mesoamerica and the Andes* (Durham, N.C.: Duke University Press, 1994), 11. Regarding the widespread use of pictographs in the Americas, North and South, see Garrick Mallery, *Picture Writing of the American Indians*, 2 vols. (New York: Dover Publications, 2012).

4. John Eliot, *Mamusse Wunneetupanatamwe Up-Biblum God Naneeswe Nukkone Testament Kah Wonk Wusku Testament* (Cambridge, Mass., 1663).

5. Asya Pereltsvaig, *Languages of the World: An Introduction* (New York: Cambridge University Press, 2012), 183.

6. James Axtell, "Babel of Tongues: Communicating with the Indians in Eastern North America," in *The Language Encounter in the Americas, 1492–1800: A Collection of Essays*, ed. Edward G. Gray and Norman Fiering (New York: Berghahn Books, 2000), 16.

7. Sean P. Harvey, *Native Tongues: Colonialism and Race from Encounter to the Reservation* (Cambridge, Mass.: Harvard University Press, 2015), 24. See also Ives Goddard, "The Use of Pidgins and Jargons on the East Coast of North America," in Gray and Fiering, *The Language Encounter*, 64.

8. Harvey, *Native Tongues*, 24.

9. Pauline Moffitt Watts, "Pictures, Gestures, Hieroglyphs: 'Mute Eloquence' in Sixteenth-Century Mexico," in Gray and Fiering, *The Language Encounter*, 83.

10. Sabine MacCormack, "Grammar and Virtue: The Formulations of a Cultural and Missionary Program by the Jesuits in Colonial Peru," in *The Jesuits II: Cultures, Sciences, and the Arts, 1540–1773*, ed. John W. O'Malley (Toronto: University of Toronto Press, 2006), 587.

11. Sébastien Rasles, "Dictionary of the Abenaki Indian Language: Manuscript, 1691–1724," Houghton Library, Harvard University, Cambridge, Mass., http://nrs.harvard.edu/urn-3:FHCL.HOUGH:4630650.

12. Benjamin Wills Newton, *Valera's Spanish Bible of 1602. Appeal to Protestant Christians Respecting the Reprinting of This Version* (London: Houlston and Stoneman, 1856), 3–7.

13. J. H. Elliott, "Religions on the Move," in *Religious Transformations in the Early Modern Americas*, ed. Stephanie Kirk and Sarah Rivett (Philadelphia: University of Pennsylvania Press, 2014), 43.

14. Louise M. Burkhart, "The 'Little Doctrine' and Indigenous Catechesis in New Spain," *Hispanic American Historical Review* 94, no. 2 (May 2014): 186.

15. Elizabeth Hill Boone, "Pictorial Documents and Visual Thinking in Postconquest Mexico," in *Native Traditions in the Postconquest World*, ed. Elizabeth Hill Boone and Tom Cummins (Washington, D.C.: Dumbarton Oaks, 1998), 162, http://www.doaks.org/resources/publications/books-in-print/native-traditions-in-the-postconquest-world.

16. Boone, "Pictorial Documents and Visual Thinking," 161. An example of a *Catechismo Testerinos* can be found at the John Carter Brown Library and online, https://archive.org/details/catecismotesterioocath. Approximately twenty-four such manuscript booklets survive in archives around the world today. Bérénice Gaillemin, "Painting Speech and Speaking to the Eyes: New Insights into Pictorial Catechisms at the JCB Library," talk given at the John Carter Brown Library, March 4, 2015. I am grateful to Bérénice for sharing the manuscript of her talk with me.

17. Gaillemin, "Painting Speech and Speaking to the Eyes," n.p.

18. *[Credo in Deum Patre[m] Omnipotentem Creatorem Celi [et] Terre]*, 1547. Original at the John Carter Brown Library, Brown University, Providence, R.I. Also available from https://archive.org/details/credoindeumpatreoopabl.

19. Maturino Gilberti, "Thema para que se oy galaboz del señor" ([Michoacán de Ocampo, Mexico], 1559), https://archive.org/details/themaparaqueseoyoogilb. Several manuscripts authored by Gilberti also exist, some of which cover some of the same material.

20. *Cartilla mayor, en lengua castellana, latina, y mexicana*, Nuevamente corregida, y enmendada, y reformada en esta vltima impression (En Mexico: en la Imprenta de la Uiuda de Bernardo Calderon en la calle de San Augustin, 1691), https://archive.org/details/cartillamayorenlo1cath.

21. MacCormack, "Grammar and Virtue," 581.

22. *Doctrina Cristiana Y Catecismo Para La Instrucción de Los Indios* (Lima, Peru: Antonio Ricardo, 1584), https://archive.org/details/doctrinachristia00cath. See the discussion in MacCormack, "Grammar and Virtue," 584. For a nice summary of the content of the *Doctrina*, see Nicholas P. Cushner, *Why Have You Come Here? The Jesuits and the First Evangelization of Native America* (New York: Oxford University Press, 2006), 87–93.

23. Jerónimo de Ripalda, *Catecismo Y Exposición Breve de La Doctrine Christiania* (1591; repr. Madrid: Antonio de Sancha, 1783). I am grateful to Ken Ward for this and other helpful references to early catechisms and partial translations of the Bible into indigenous languages in Latin America.

24. Anita De Luna, *Faith Formation and Popular Religion: Lessons from the Tejano Experience* (Lanham, Md.: Rowman & Littlefield, 2002), 34–62.

25. Martin Austin Nesvig, *Ideology and Inquisition: The World of the Censors in Early Mexico* (New Haven, Conn.: Yale University Press, 2009), 121.

26. Maturino Gilberti, *Dialogo de doctrina christiana, enla lengua d[e] Mechuaca[n]* ([Mexico City] : Fue impresso en casa de Juan Pablos Bressano . . . desta . . . ciudad de Mexico, 1559), http://archive.org/details/dialogodedoctrin00gilb.

27. *Index librorum prohibitorum et expurgatorum* (Genevae: sumptibus Iacobi Crispini, 1619). See also Patricia Manning, *Voicing Dissent in Seventeenth-Century Spain: Inquisition, Social Criticism and Theology in the Case of El Criticón* (Boston: Brill, 2009), 97.

28. Personal conversation with Ken Ward, PhD, Maury A. Bromsen Curator of Latin American Books, The John Carter Brown Library, Brown University, Providence, R.I.

29. R. Andrew Nickson, *Historical Dictionary of Paraguay*, 3rd ed. (Lanham, Md.: Rowman & Littlefield, 2015), 327–29.

30. Antonio Garriga, *Practical Instruction to Order One's Life According to Saintly Precepts: Offered by Father Antonio Garriga of the Society of Jesus. As a Brief Memorial and Memento of the Spiritual Exercises of Saint Ignatius Loyola, Founder of the Society* (Loreto, Paraguay: Society of Jesus, 1713), https://www.wdl.org/en/item/2835/.

31. Nicolás Yapuguay et al., *Explicacion de el catechismo en lengua guarani* (En el Pueblo de S. Maria la Mayor : [s.n.], 1724), http://archive.org/details/explicaciondeelcooyapu.

32. Nicholas Ostler, *Passwords to Paradise: How Languages Have Re-Invented World Religions* (New York: Bloomsbury, 2016).

33. Birgit Brander Rasmussen, *Queequeg's Coffin: Indigenous Literacies and Early American Literature* (Durham, N.C.: Duke University Press, 2012), 18–19.

34. David L. Schmidt and Murdena Marshall, eds., *Mi'kmaq Hieroglyphic Prayers: Readings in North America's First Indigenous Script* (Halifax, NS: Nimbus Publishing, 1995), 2.

35. Bruce Greenfield, "The Mi'kmaq Hieroglyphic Prayer Book: Writing and Christianity in Maritime Canada, 1675–1921," in Gray and Fiering, *The Language Encounter*, 195.

36. Bruce Greenfield, "Mi'kmaq Hieroglyphic Prayer Book," 192. See Christian Kauder, *Buch das gut, enthaltend den Katechismus, Betractung, Gesang* [*The Good Book, containing the Catechisms, Meditations, Hymns*] (Vienna: Imperial Printing Office, 1886).

37. Christian Kauder, *Sapeoig Oigatigen tan teli Gômgoetjoigasigel Alasotmaganel, Ginamatineoel ag Getapefiemgeoel; Manuel de Prières, instructions et changs sacrés en Hieroglyphes micmacs; Manual of Prayers, Instructions, Psalms & Hymns in Micmac Ideograms*, new ed. (Ristigouche, Québec: Micmac Messenger, 1921).

38. Martin Luther and Johannes Campanius, *Lutheri Catechismus* (Stockholm: Burchardi tryckeri af J.J. Genath f., 1696). See the discussion in Ives Goddard, "The Use of Pidgins and Jargons on the East Coast of North America," in Gray and Fiering, *The Language Encounter*, 64.

39. Francis P. Dinneen and E. F. K. Koerner, *North American Contributions to the History of Linguistics* (Philadelphia: John Benjamins Publishing, 1990), 68.

40. William B. Hart, "Mohawk Schoolmasters and Catechists in Mid-Eighteenth-Century Iroquoia: An Experiment in Fostering Literacy and Religious Change," in Gray and Fiering, *The Language Encounter*, 233.

41. Tracy Neal Leavelle, *The Catholic Calumet: Colonial Conversions in French and Indian North America* (Philadelphia: University of Pennsylvania Press, 2011), 98ff.

42. Jean Baptiste Le Boulanger, "French and Miami-Illinois Dictionary," n.d., The John Carter Brown Library. For a digital facsimile, see http://www.archive.org/stream/frenchmiamiillinoolebo#page/n7/mode/2up.

43. See, e.g., the collection of hymns in Carl Masthay, *Mahican-Language Hymns, Biblical Prose, and Vocabularies from Moravian Sources, with 11 Mohawk Hymns* (Saint Louis, Mo.: Masthay, 1980). See also Linford D. Fisher, "'I Believe They Are Papists!': Natives, Moravians, and the Politics of Conversion in Eighteenth-Century Connecticut," *New England Quarterly* 81, no. 3 (September 2008): 431–32.

44. Glenda Goodman, "'But They Differ from Us in Sound': Indian Psalmody and the Soundscape of Colonialism, 1651–75," *William and Mary Quarterly* 69, no. 4 (2012): 793–822, doi:10.5309/willmaryquar.69.4.0793; Kathryn N. Gray, *John Eliot and the Praying Indians of Massachusetts Bay: Communities and Connections in Puritan New England* (Lewisburg, Pa.: Bucknell University Press, 2013), 144–66; Eliot, *Mamusse Wunneetupanatamwe Up-Biblum God Naneeswe Nukkone Testament Kah Wonk Wusku Testament.*

45. Although the language of the Indian Bible is often called the "Massachusett" language, it is actually Wôpanâak, according to linguist Jessie Little Doe Baird. Wôpanâak is part of the Eastern Algonquian family of languages indigenous to North America and is spoken by the Wampanoag people of southeastern New England. See also "Wampanoag," Summer Institute of Linguistics' Ethnologue website: https://www.ethnologue.com/country/US/languages.

46. David Powers, *Damnable Heresy: William Pynchon, the Indians, and the First Book Banned (and Burned) in Boston* (Eugene, Ore.: Wipf & Stock, 2015).

47. Roger Williams, *A Key into the Language of America* (London: Gregory Dexter, 1643).

48. As Eliot worked on the Bible, several times the commissioners for the New England Company (a missionary society based in London, often called the NEC) and the United Colonies requested in the 1650s that Eliot's translation of the Bible into the Indian language be done in such a way that it would be understood by as many New England Native nations as possible, which was an unrealistic request. See, e.g., "Commissioners of the United Colonies to John Eliot, August 29, 1655," in *Bibliographic Notes on Eliot's Indian Bible: And on His Other Translations and Works in the Indian Language of Massachusetts*, by Eames Wilberforce (Washington, D.C.: US Government Printing Office, 1890), 5. For more on universal language theories in this time period and how the Indian Bible fit

into them, see Sarah Rivett, *The Science of the Soul in Colonial New England* (Chapel Hill: University of North Carolina Press, 2011), 162–65.

49. For a full listing of the items published in native languages in Massachusetts, see "Books and Tracts in the Indian Language or Designed for the Use of Indians, Printed at Cambridge and Boston, 1653–1721," *Proceedings of the American Antiquarian Society* 61 (October 1873): 45–62.

50. George Parker Winship, *The First American Bible* (Boston: Printed by D. B. Updike at the Merrymount Press for C. E. Goodspeed, 1929), 14.

51. For the Massachusetts and Connecticut missions, see Richard W. Cogley, *John Eliot's Mission to the Indians before King Philip's War* (Cambridge, Mass.: Harvard University Press, 1999). For Martha's Vineyard and the work of the Mayhews, see David J. Silverman, *Faith and Boundaries: Colonists, Christianity, and Community among the Wampanoag Indians of Martha's Vineyard, 1600–1871* (New York: Cambridge University Press, 2005).

52. Justin Winsor and Clarence F. Jewett, *The Memorial History of Boston, including Suffolk County, Massachusetts, 1630–1880*, vol. 1 (Boston: Ticknor, 1880), 470.

53. See, e.g., Harvey, *Native Tongues*, 5.

54. MacCormack, "Grammar and Virtue," 587.

55. Ostler, *Passwords to Paradise*.

56. John Wright, *Early Bibles of America*, 3rd ed. (New York: T. Whittaker, 1894), 1. Even in 1975, one author insisted: "Throughout his work Eliot had no assistance." Edward H. Davidson, "The Eliot Indian Bible," *Non Solus*, no. 2 (1975): 2. See also Hilary E. Wyss, *Writing Indians: Literacy, Christianity, and Native Community in Early America* (Amherst: University of Massachusetts Press, 2000), 42.

57. John Eliot to Edward Winslow, July 8, 1649. As quoted in Wilberforce, *Bibliographic Notes on Eliot's Indian Bible*, 1.

58. Daniel Gookin, "An Historical Account of the Doings and Sufferings of the Christian Indians in New England," in *Archaeologia Americana: Transactions and Collections of the American Antiquarian Society*, vol. 2 (Cambridge, Mass.: Folsom, Wells, and Thurston, 1836), 444. Wilberforce, *Bibliographic Notes on Eliot's Indian Bible*, 1. Increase Mather, Cotton Mather, and Samuel Gardner Drake, *The History of King Philip's War* (Boston: Printed for the editor, 1862), 48–49.

59. As reported by Cotton Mather, in a memorial to the NEC, 1710. Quoted in Wilberforce, *Bibliographic Notes on Eliot's Indian Bible*, 30–31.

60. Sarah Rivett, "Learning to Write Algonquian Letters: The Indigenous Place of Language Philosophy in the Seventeenth-Century Atlantic World," *William and Mary Quarterly* 71, no. 4 (2014): 549–88, doi:10.5309/willmaryquar.71.4.0549.

61. *Collections of the Massachusetts Historical Society* (Boston: The Society, n.d.), ser. 6, 1:8.

62. Winsor and Jewett, *The Memorial History of Boston*, 1:473. There are other supposed mistakes by Eliot and the Indian translators that past generations of historians have noted, particularly with regard to Judges 5:28 ("lattice" translated as "eelpot lattice") and Matthew 25:1–12 (where "virgins" is supposedly rendered in the masculine). Recent linguistic analysis by Jessie Little Doe Baird has revealed these former, older analyses of the translation to be incorrect.

63. I am grateful to Jessie Little Doe Baird for this insight. Taken from personal conversations and a presentation she gave at the Mashantucket Pequot Museum and Research Center, March 1, 2014. See Psalm 9:17, e.g., which reads (in the King James Version) "The wicked

shall be turned into hell, and all the nations that forget God." In the Indian Bible, "hell" in this verse is rendered as *chepiohkomukqut*.

64. Leavelle, *The Catholic Calumet*, 103.

65. Quoted in Phillip H. Round, *Removable Type: Histories of the Book in Indian Country, 1663–1880* (Chapel Hill: University of North Carolina Press, 2010), 126.

66. The following description is drawn from the first chapter of Mark Z. Christensen, *Translated Christianities: Nahuatl and Maya Religious Texts* (University Park, Pa.: Penn State Press, 2014).

67. The Nahuatl Bible, as translated in Christensen, *Translated Christianities*, 23. The brackets are the interpretations of Mark Z. Christensen.

68. Although scholars long thought that these pictographic renderings of Catholic catechetical materials were produced by priests or indigenous converts in the early years of colonization, Louis Burkhart presents convincing evidence of a later authorship. See Burkhart, "The 'Little Doctrine' and Indigenous Catechesis in New Spain," 187–88.

69. Burkhart, "The 'Little Doctrine'," 190–91.

70. The note is in Malachi: "In Boston the 17th of the 5th month (July), 1670." Ives Goddard and Kathleen Joan Bragdon, *Native Writings in Massachusett, Memoirs of the American Philosophical Society*, vol. 185 (Philadelphia: American Philosophical Society, 1988), 383.

71. Wilberforce, *Bibliographic Notes on Eliot's Indian Bible*, 28. During King Philip's War, so many Indian Bibles were destroyed that Eliot confessed to some European travelers seeking a copy that he had none to give them, since most of the Bibles had been burned.

72. For a recent assessment of the ABCFM's global and domestic missionary activities, see Emily Conroy-Krutz, *Christian Imperialism: Converting the World in the Early American Republic* (Ithaca, N.Y.: Cornell University Press, 2015).

73. This summary of the Sequoyah's work is drawn, in part, from April R. Summitt, *Sequoyah and the Invention of the Cherokee Alphabet* (Santa Barbara, CA: Greenwood, 2012); Round, *Removable Type*, chap. 5.

74. James W. Parins, *Literacy and Intellectual Life in the Cherokee Nation, 1820–1906* (Norman: University of Oklahoma Press, 2013), 115.

75. *Cherokee Testament* (New York: American Bible Society, 1860).

76. "Bible Translation Is Key to Peru's Multilingual Society," *United Bible Societies*, September 5, 2014, https://www.unitedbiblesocieties.org/bible-translation-is-key-to-perus-multilingual-society/.

77. Kim Potowski, *Language Diversity in the USA* (New York: Cambridge University Press, 2010), 48.

BIBLIOGRAPHY

Boone, Elizabeth Hill, and Tom Cummins, eds. *Native Traditions in the Postconquest World*. Washington, D.C.: Dumbarton Oaks, 1998.

Boone, Elizabeth Hill, and Walter D. Mignolo, eds. *Writing without Words: Alternative Literacies in Mesoamerica and the Andes*. Durham, N.C.: Duke University Press, 1994.

Burkhart, Louise M. "The 'Little Doctrine' and Indigenous Catechesis in New Spain." *Hispanic American Historical Review* 94, no. 2 (2014): 167–206.

Christensen, Mark Z. *Translated Christianities: Nahuatl and Maya Religious Texts*. University Park, Pa.: Penn State Press, 2014.

Cushner, Nicholas P. *Why Have You Come Here? The Jesuits and the First Evangelization of Native America*. New York: Oxford University Press, 2006.

Fisher, Linford D. "'I Believe They Are Papists!': Natives, Moravians, and the Politics of Conversion in Eighteenth-Century Connecticut." *New England Quarterly* 81, no. 3 (2008): 410–37.

Goodman, Glenda. "'But They Differ from Us in Sound': Indian Psalmody and the Soundscape of Colonialism, 1651–75." *William and Mary Quarterly* 69, no. 4 (2012): 793–822. doi:10.5309/willmaryquar.69.4.0793.

Gray, Edward G., and Norman Fiering, eds. *The Language Encounter in the Americas, 1492–1800: A Collection of Essays*. New York: Berghahn Books, 2000.

Gray, Kathryn N. *John Eliot and the Praying Indians of Massachusetts Bay: Communities and Connections in Puritan New England*. Lewisburg, Pa.: Bucknell University Press, 2013.

Harvey, Sean P. *Native Tongues: Colonialism and Race from Encounter to the Reservation*. Cambridge, Mass.: Harvard University Press, 2015.

Mallery, Garrick. *Picture Writing of the American Indians*. 2 vols. New York: Dover Publications, 2012.

Ostler, Nicholas. *Passwords to Paradise: How Languages Have Re-Invented World Religions*. New York: Bloomsbury, 2016.

Parins, James W. *Literacy and Intellectual Life in the Cherokee Nation, 1820–1906*. Norman: University of Oklahoma Press, 2013.

Pereltsvaig, Asya. *Languages of the World: An Introduction*. New York: Cambridge University Press, 2012.

Potowski, Kim. *Language Diversity in the USA*. New York: Cambridge University Press, 2010.

Powers, David. *Damnable Heresy: William Pynchon, the Indians, and the First Book Banned (and Burned) in Boston*. Eugene, Ore.: Wipf & Stock, 2015.

Rasmussen, Birgit Brander. *Queequeg's Coffin: Indigenous Literacies and Early American Literature*. Durham, N.C.: Duke University Press, 2012.

Rivett, Sarah. "Learning to Write Algonquian Letters: The Indigenous Place of Language Philosophy in the Seventeenth-Century Atlantic World." *William and Mary Quarterly* 71, no. 4 (2014): 549–88. doi:10.5309/willmaryquar.71.4.0549.

———. *The Science of the Soul in Colonial New England*. Chapel Hill: University of North Carolina Press, 2011.

Round, Phillip H. *Removable Type: Histories of the Book in Indian Country, 1663–1880*. Chapel Hill: University of North Carolina Press, 2010.

Soler, D. W. "Language and Communication in the Spanish Conquest of America." *History Compass* 8 (2010): 491–502.

Wyss, Hilary E. *Writing Indians: Literacy, Christianity, and Native Community in Early America*. Amherst: University of Massachusetts Press, 2000, 42.

CHAPTER 4

....

AMERICAN BIBLE BINDINGS
AND FORMATS

....

SETH PERRY

"The Bible"—in America or elsewhere—is an abstraction. It is an imaginary source to which all physical objects called Bibles have an equally imaginary relationship: a timeless, unchanging, and infinitely accessible standard by which those physical objects are made valuable. A variety of theoretical approaches might be marshaled to approach this distinction between the idealized Bible and material Bibles as objects; for the purposes of this essay Roland Barthes's distinction between *text* and *work* will suffice. "The work is a fragment of substance," according to Barthes, "occupying a part of the space of books (in a library for example)." The text, on the other hand, "is a methodological field." Barthes's description of the distinction is characteristically complex, but it can be usefully reduced to material terms: "the one is displayed, the other demonstrated; likewise, the work can be seen (in bookshops, in catalogues, in exam syllabuses), the text is a process of demonstration . . . the work can be held in the hand, the text is held in language."[1] The Bible is the instrumentalized concept of revelation—the practices of identifying, interpreting, and using the word of God. Bibles are books.

With important exceptions, the overwhelming majority of scholarly attention to the Bible in America has been about the idea, not about the books—the text, not the works.[2] Textual practices are not actually separable from the works that facilitate them, though, and looking closely at the changing nonverbal features of American Bibles is crucial. This discussion of Bibles as objects will focus on three changing features: format, binding, and paper. Format is the technical bibliographical term for the size of a book (as distinguished from form, which is my generic term here for talking about overall shape and appearance). Binding will refer to a book's covers and how they are attached to the text pages. Paper will be the stuff that makes up those pages.

These non-linguistic features of printed Bibles have evolved both materially and symbolically since Bibles first came to the Americas with Spanish missionaries, an evolution driven by technological capabilities, economic considerations, aesthetic and practical preferences, and, crucially, a tension between two diametrically opposed but widely shared ideals regarding the Bible's physical presence. Over the course of five centuries, Christians in America with various stakes in Bible production (from church hierarchies to printers to denominational authorities to readers) have had a sense that Bibles should be both materially impressive and widely present. These impulses are at odds. Accessibility demands not just cheapness but the ease of handling and carrying that cheap materials permit. It is this ease that has both allowed Bibles to be present in a variety of scenes of usage and continually conditioned readers to assume that they should be so present—not just in the pulpit and pew, but in the field, on the road, and in the foxhole. The seemingly mundane history of the Bible's format, binding, and paper in America is actually a particularly legible site for thinking about the push and pull between the Bible's transcendence and immanence, a contest very much ongoing in the digital age.

The first printed Bibles were mostly large, imposing volumes. Their sizes are generally referred to as folios and quartos, measuring more than nineteen centimeters (roughly seven and one-half inches), give or take, on the long edge.[3] They were printed on paper made from rags or, less often, vellum (untanned animal skin). They were bound in wooden boards wrapped, generally, in tanned leather. Calf skin, dyed brown, was the most common Bible covering and would be through the nineteenth century. Goat skin (often known as morocco or turkey because of its place of origin) was more expensive and considered fancier because it takes dye better than calf skin and so could be made more dramatically colorful. Design could be added to leather covers using dies and metalwork. What set fine books apart from workmanlike or aesthetically poor ones was the quality of the leather, the way it had been tooled or gilded, the tightness of the binding, and feel of the paper.[4] Throughout the handpress period, moreover, large formats indicated value simply by virtue of marking the consumption of significant resources such as the larger quantity of paper and leather used to make the volumes.[5]

Catholic liturgical practice (not to mention the realities of early-modern literacy) dictated that the scriptures were typically read to the laity rather than read by them, so the visual significance of printed Bibles was important. This would be especially true in the colonial American context. Irving Leonard indexed lists of books ordered by booksellers and sent to New Spain in the sixteenth century and found what he described as a surprising number of Bibles, uniformly requested in large formats (the smallest are octavo) and with bindings "of the best quality."[6] Most of the biblical material brought early to the Americas was in the form of Latin missals in the possession of Spanish Catholic clergy. These books—containing all of the readings necessary for the Mass, including scriptural extracts—were as likely to be in manuscript as print in the early years of contact, and they were often small, portable books.

Such books nevertheless could have visual impact. Jaime Lara draws attention to the affinities of color and style between sixteenth-century missals and pre-Columbian Nahua pictographic codices. Among the Nahua, red and black marked sacred writing to the extent that "Red and Black" was used as a metaphor for knowledge and wisdom generally. Lara suggests that this assisted natives' regard for early-modern Catholic missals, composed of pages replete with black woodcuts and vivid rubrication—red-ink words and numbers that mark points of emphasis and visually organize the text.[7] Where Bibles were present, early Catholic missionaries were conscious of Bibles' possible visual effects when working among native populations that did not possess extensive written culture prior to contact. A French Jesuit among the Iroquois in lower Canada in the 1660s recorded a "formal display" he composed "in order to strike [the natives'] imaginations"—along with a map of the world and a painting of the King of France, he included "the Bible, on a desk covered with a handsome red cloth, below which was to be seen the Image of Our Lord."[8]

Bibles have always been fraught objects for Protestants, obliged to voice both reverence for scripture and disdain for religious things. In *A Briefe and True Report of the New Found Land of Virginia*, Thomas Hariot recounted Powhatan reaction to the Bible he carried there in 1585. "Although I told them the booke materially & of it self was not of anie such vertue, as I thought they did conceiue, but onely the doctrine therein contained; yet would many be glad to touch it, to embrace it, to kisse it, to hold it to their brests and heades, and stroke ouer all their bodie with it."[9]

Hariot's discomfort at inciting reverence for the physical presence of the Bible is, however, a historical outlier among Protestants intent on bringing scripture to subject populations in America.[10] A 1741 list of "books allowed for churches" by the Society for the Propagation of the Gospel in Foreign Parts, the primary Anglican missionary organ to Native Americans and the enslaved in the colonies, called explicitly for an "English Bible in Folio."[11] Even among supposedly austere Puritans, the visual impressiveness of Bibles was of interest where native conversion was concerned. When John Eliot and the native scholars with whom he worked—including Job Nesuton and James Printer—put their Massachusett translation of the Bible to press between 1655 and 1663 it was as a large format volume. The full Bible in Massachusett—the first Bible published in the Americas—appeared in 1663 as a small folio of 1,180 pages. As literary scholar Philip Round notes, the first printing of 1,800 copies was a substantial investment of resources given that paper and type were dear in the colonies.[12] Although many extant copies are roughly bound in plain calf, an embossed presentation copy of the 1680 second edition on fine paper, held by the Lilly Library at Indiana University, underscores the aesthetic aspirations of the book's creators.[13]

The first proposal for an English Bible to be printed in the colonies shared these aspirations—in 1688 Philadelphia printer William Bradford issued "Proposals for the Printing of a large BIBLE," promising a book "in a fair Character, on good Paper, and well bound."[14] That project never came to fruition, probably due to the shortage or expense of resources. In a print environment defined by scarcity, the insistence on such an aggressive outlay of resources for Bible production can at least partially be attributed to shared notions about the Bible's ideal rather than common form. Large formats—quartos and folios—accounted for only about a quarter of all English Bible editions published in the seventeenth century.[15] They were especially rare in the colonies, because until the 1780s all English Bibles were imported and shipping costs were a function of volume. Philadelphia bookseller David Hall imported over 8,000 British Bibles in the 1750s, and fewer than 500 of them were large formats.[16]

The first English Bible printed in the Americas went for presence over grandeur. Philadelphia printer Robert Aitken's 1782 small duodecimo Bible was plain and unimposing; its pages, on poor paper, lacked not just ornament but margins. Aitken's Bible was an outgrowth of an effort to provide Bibles to the colonies during the Revolution and represented a bias toward presence at the expense of visual impact. Tellingly, the market reacted in proportion to the visual quality of Aitken's Bible. As the war ended, it was undercut by cheaper and more appealing imports immediately, and then by a suddenly booming market in domestic Bible printing that highlighted large format, grandly presented Bibles.[17]

After the Revolution, a wide variety of printers turned to Bible production, and quarto "family" Bibles were favorites: after Aitken, eight of the next dozen Bibles printed in

America were quartos or larger, as were nearly one-third of all American editions of Bibles or Testaments through 1840.[18] Printers such as Isaiah Thomas in Worcester, Massachusetts; Isaac Collins in Trenton, New Jersey; and Mathew Carey in Philadelphia became early leaders in domestic Bible printing, primarily through their production and marketing of large Bibles.[19] Beginning with Carey's quarto Douay-Rheims in 1790 and then accelerating with a spate of large Bibles in the 1790s, large family Bibles were everywhere. The suddenly enhanced presence of large-format Bibles reinscribed their iconographic importance: on the title page of a popular Bible reading guide published by the American Sunday School Union in 1827, *Eyes and No Eyes; or, Eyes that See Not: How to Read the Bible Aright*, the paradigmatic Bible appears as a quarto in the clouds, complete with cross-references (figures 4.1 and 4.2).

The preference for large Bibles as authoritative presences could extend even to the subconscious. Late in life, William Miller, who had sifted through his Bible to predict that Christ would return in 1844, recorded a dream in which he was charged with "a curiously wrought casket, about ten inches long by six square." Miller said that in the dream he was given a key to open the box—a dream image of his interpretative methods applied to a Bible—and discovered that it was full of jewels.[20] Miller's own Bible, though, the one from which he preached his apocalyptic message throughout the 1830s and 1840s, is smaller—only seven

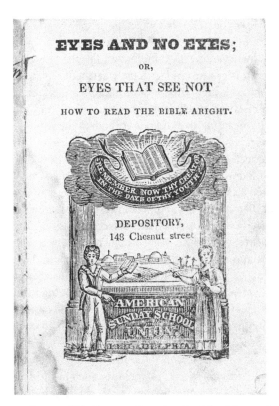

FIGURE 4.1 Title page, *Eyes and No Eyes; or, Eyes that See Not: How to Read the Bible Aright*, American Sunday School Union, 1827. Image courtesy American Antiquarian Society.

FIGURE 4.2 Detail, Title page, *Eyes and No Eyes; or, Eyes that See Not: How to Read the Bible Aright*, American Sunday School Union, 1827. Image courtesy American Antiquarian Society.

by about four and a half inches.[21] The paradigmatic Bible Miller dreamed of explaining was a quarto, much bigger than the Bible with which he actually worked.

Beyond the implications of large formats as such, large Bibles were more likely than smaller ones to be distinguished by fine bindings and paper. Some have suggested that the value of large Bibles in this era was in fact mostly aesthetic. "Standing amid the carefully choreographed furnishing of the parlor, a bible became a piece of furniture, a decorative addition to the room," historian of religious printed material Paul Gutjahr writes, one which "communicated certain meanings that did not depend on the reading or recitation of biblical texts."[22] Gutjahr wonders about the capacity of fine Bibles to distract from reading. In his study of early American reading, William J. Gilmore questioned this sort of worry: "It is ironic that many historians readily assume that hoes and ploughs were used routinely to till fields, that cooking utensils were nearly always used to prepare food, and that clothing was recurrently worn, but then question whether printed texts were habitually read."[23]

Either way, producers' focus on the aesthetics of large Bibles suggests that they, at least, felt that their nonverbal aspects would be "read" as much as the words they contained: advertisements promised accurate texts, informative commentary, and useful illustrations, but they also touted fine paper and, increasingly over the first decades of the nineteenth century, fine bindings.[24] Evidence suggests that customers paid attention. Mason Weems, who peddled Bibles for Carey in the Southeast, was constantly passing on his customers' complaints about flawed bindings and rough cut pages and, with characteristic wit, added his own: "I know 'tis the bread of life but it had no need to be cooked so coarsely."[25] At other times, Weems's customers found Carey's bindings too nice—red morocco Bibles, "some considered & were polite enough to say . . . were too much in the Scarlet whore of babylon colour for a Protestant Bible."[26] Until the nineteenth century, binding was separate from printing—printers like Carey sent their pages out to be bound, and Weems's complaints stemmed from the varying levels of consciousness and skill among binders.

The nineteenth century brought standardization to binding, as the work became mechanized and publishers such as the American Bible Society and Harper Brothers brought it in-house.[27] At the same time, cloth bindings began to replace leather. As Gutjahr has shown, the change to cloth progressed much more slowly for Bibles than for other books, and especially slowly for large formats.[28] The nineteenth-century family Bible reached a nadir in the late nineteenth century with one particular sort of cover. By this time, with the exception of thin scaleboard for small books, actual wooden boards had long since been supplanted by "boards" made out of scrap paper (heavy paperboard could be made out of layered and pressed sheets of scrap, or out of pulped scrap dried into thick sheets).[29]

The later nineteenth century saw a boom in extremely thick pasteboard covers made to look like carved wood. Ostensibly, these were someone's idea of suggesting strength and solidity in a Bible, evoking the kind of imposing Bibles that might have been chained to pulpits in the sixteenth century. If extant copies are any indication, though, these Bibles are anything but solid: the overweight covers of the later nineteenth century made a habit of falling off. An 1874 *Publisher's Weekly* column bemoaned the "imposing exterior and utter uselessness" of these books. "The amount of good morocco spoiled in their bindings is horrible to think of—covers at least an inch thick, beveled, and gilded, and stamped until every natural beauty of the leather is effaced. These solid cubes of ugliness are being sold by the ton."[30]

Bigger and better Bibles answered to one impulse on the part of those invested in Bible production and use. Inevitably, though, idealized attachments to large formats were balanced by practical interests in accessibility and presence. Although stillborn itself, Aitken's plain, small Bible came out of a print-Bible environment in which such Bibles were the most common, if not the most idealized. Duodecimos—about the size of a modern paperback book—were the Bibles of popular preaching, school work, and of much private reading. Aitken's Bible also anticipated the most common Bible forms of the nineteenth century. The first stereotyped Bibles in the 1810s and all of the most massive print-runs produced by the American Bible Society were duodecimos and smaller. While large formats would persist as the ideal in the iconography of American Bibles, duodecimos and the slightly larger octavos were much more common, accounting for more than half of the editions produced by American publishers between 1777 and 1840.

The portability of duodecimos was suited to the itinerant, extemporaneous preaching that defined the Second Great Awakening of the late eighteenth and early nineteenth centuries. Such small Bible editions were easily displayed during those forms of preaching that eschewed pulpits. Lorenzo Dow, the era's best-known itinerant, was converted about 1791 under the preaching of a Bible-wielding Methodist itinerant named Hope Hull, and the presence of Hull's Bible was central to his memory of the occasion: " 'If you don't pray, then you'll be damned,' " Dow records Hull expounding, "and (as he brought out the last expression) he either stamped with his foot on the box on which he stood, or smote with his hand upon the Bible, which both together came home like a dagger to my heart."[31] Dow's account tells us that Hull's Bible was small enough to be held in one flailing hand but stout enough that when it was brought around and punched or slapped for emphasis the impact reverberated (or could at least be confused with stamping on a wooden box). The gesture marks it as a duodecimo: easily gripped in one hand to be pointed like a weapon or waved like a fan at the fires of hell.

Duodecimos are common in salutary depictions of revivalist preaching of the era—note the multiple small books present in J. Maze Burbank's 1839 watercolor "Religious Camp Meeting." Those depictions that framed such preaching in a negative light tended to have no Bibles at all.[32]

In portraiture, Bible size could also have social and class implications. In his youth, Dow was depicted as gaunt man with stringy hair holding a duodecimo New Testament (figure 4.3).

By the time of his death in 1834, however, his image had become that of a hoary-headed prophet standing behind a lectern, resting his arms on a massive pulpit Bible (figure 4.4).

Both illustrations were produced as frontispieces for volumes of Dow's writings, and both may say more about the audience for those writings than about Dow himself. American Methodism (Dow's nominal affiliation) had gentrified considerably over the years between the two publications, and so the itinerant minister and the fleet duodecimo had been replaced by a settled minister with a pulpit on which to rest a symbol of his authority.[33]

The size and relative cheapness of duodecimos answered to the Protestant assumption that the Bible should be present at the expense of making that presence a material answer to the idealization of the Bible's status. While the ABS was unique in making a point of their Bibles' plainness, as noted smaller formats in general were less likely to be differentiated in the market based on features such as paper quality and binding until the later part of

The " *Morning* of LIFE" is passed away, and soon the
" *Evening shades*," will come on apace! I'm travelling
to the " *Land*" whence I shall not return ! !

COSMOPOLITE, Aged 36.

FIGURE 4.3 *Cosmopolite, Aged 36*, unsigned, first published in *Polemical Works of Lorenzo, Complete* . . . (New York: J. C. Totten, 1814). Image courtesy American Antiquarian Society.

LORENZO DOW.

FIGURE 4.4 *Lorenzo Dow*, engraving by A. T. Lee (Philadelphia: Childs and Lehman, 1834). Image courtesy American Antiquarian Society.

the nineteenth century. The smallest Bibles, though, often maintained both. Between 1790 and 1840, American publishers turned out 120 editions of full Bibles and Testaments that could be considered "pockets." These are Bibles small enough to be carried on one's person. Pocket Bibles were ostensibly for ready access and quick reference, but surviving examples (particularly of full Bibles rather than testaments or abridgements) are often printed in such small type that they are difficult to read, even for a scholar in the age of artificial light and widespread corrective eyewear. The extreme compactness suggests that these books were often as much totemic or iconic as functional: often finely bound, they were symbols that invoked reverence and authority by their mere appearance. Because of their relative cheapness and readiness to hand in the early nineteenth century, they were for giving away. At a prayer meeting in central Georgia in February 1802, Dow recorded that he gave his "pocket bible" to a slave woman who had been struck by the Spirit and laid "like a corpse" for an hour and a half under his preaching. When she came to, "I gave her my pocket bible, with orders to carry it home; and if she could not read herself, to get the whites to do it for her."[34] In addition to preachers, Sunday School teachers frequently gave away small Bibles and, more commonly, Bible-abridgements to the students. A popular fictional tract of the early nineteenth century, *Mary the Milk-maid*, depicts a familiar scenario—the pious Mary has received a pocket Bible from her Sunday School teacher and "would not part with it on any account."[35]

The theological underpinnings of the production of duodecimo and pocket Bible editions are driven home by the fact that Catholic Bibles did not often appear in small formats. John Gilmary Shea, author of an 1859 bibliography of Catholic Bibles and Testaments, noted that Catholic Bibles were not "profusely scattered" because Catholics did not treat the Bible as lightly as a school book. "For reverential perusal and devout meditation, a comparatively small number of them suffices."[36] He documented nineteen full Bibles through 1852, some only proposed and not actually printed, none of them smaller than octavo (although he did note that an 1853 pocket Bible published in London sold well in America).[37]

For nineteenth-century Bible users, the intimacy and immediate presence fostered by small formats persisted in tension with the desire to acknowledge the Bible's importance through imposing forms and expensive materials. This tension reached something of a resolution in the last quarter of the nineteenth century through two technological advancements that utterly changed the tactile and visual presence of Bibles of all formats: the development of limp bindings and Oxford India Paper.

Limp bindings are those that lack boards—the book's cover is composed only of heavy cloth, leather, vellum, or paper, making for a floppy, flexible book. Limp bindings of vellum had been common in the sixteenth and seventeenth centuries, and Bible publishers brought back the concept in the late nineteenth century, using treated, untearable papers and other new materials.[38] William Yapp, a London publisher, became known for limp-bound books with covers that extended beyond the pages, with the overlapping bit beveled to protect the paper, and "Yapp binding" became so identified with Bibles and other devotional books that it is also known as "divinity binding."[39]

Oxford India Paper was first marketed on the basis of its durability and practicality and only later became an aesthetic standard for American Bibles. Until the 1840s, paper was primarily made of recycled rags. These seem always to have been in short supply, as desperate printers ran ads constantly offering to buy rags. "*Great* people that are *really great*, save rags" an 1811 ad proclaimed, by way of encouraging contributions, because "even the Bible is made out of rags."[40] Good rags made good paper—white linen the best—but in their absence inferior materials were often substituted. Paper makers used everything from canvas to rope to wool.[41] Paper made from wood pulp dominated by the last decades of the nineteenth century, and Oxford University Press developed the India paper in the 1870s and immediately started using it for Bibles.[42] It promised an intimacy and portability that was the opposite of those "solid cubes of ugliness." "The Oxford University Press has published the smallest Bible ever produced," an 1875 notice proclaimed (probably wrongly). "It is printed on a rough, unbleached India paper, of extreme thinness and opacity; is four and half inches high by two and three-quarters inches high by two and three-quarters inches broad, and half an inch in thickness, and weighs, bound in limp morocco leather, less than three and a half ounces."[43] A decade and a half later Oxford was advertising a full line of "India paper editions" in various formats.[44] Bible paper came into its own, though, with the appearance of the Scofield reference Bible. Cyrus Scofield's extensive notes added considerable bulk to the Bible, but the thinness of India paper allowed the entire apparatus to appear on the pages of the biblical text and, crucially, in a single volume that was only an inch thick.[45] This meant that readers always had the complete text at hand in order to follow Scofield's reasoning as he drew connections among parts of scripture—B. M. Pietsch has argued that India paper was a major factor in the Scofield Bible's success.[46]

Limp-bound, India-paper Bibles transformed the material form of the Bible in America. With the hyper-industrialization of print in the early twentieth century, Bibles reached a new level of diversity. Binding options proliferated (a Bible with a metal cover was produced for soldiers in World War II; one can buy a bullet-proof Bible today), but lightweight materials were favorites of all the major publishers.[47] The combination of light-weight Bible paper and durable limp bindings made for an intimate gestural presence, enabling a rugged, workaday use of the Bible bordering on abuse. Such presence is emblematized by Billy Graham's favored stance at the pulpit—a large-format Bible in one hand, its limp cover curled over on itself (figure 4.5).

In the right hands, this presence has lent grandness to plain Bibles: Martin Luther King Jr.'s battered, Yapp-bound preaching Bible was used for President Obama's Second Inaugural.[48]

It is not just preachers for whom the soft-cover Bible has mattered. The virtual indestructability of twentieth-century binding materials enabled lightweight Bibles to be carried endlessly. Their bindings have bulged with all manner of Sunday bulletins, funeral programs, mementos. The iconic Bible of the twentieth century looks like figure 4.6 used for approximately five decades by one Frances Hutzell of Columbus, Ohio.

Yapp-bound and filled with mementos of life events, marginal notations, and family relics, this one work—one material Bible—is expanded by other works that also participate in

FIGURE 4.5 Billy Graham at the 1970 New York Crusade. ©1970 Billy Graham Evangelistic Association. Used with permission. All rights reserved.

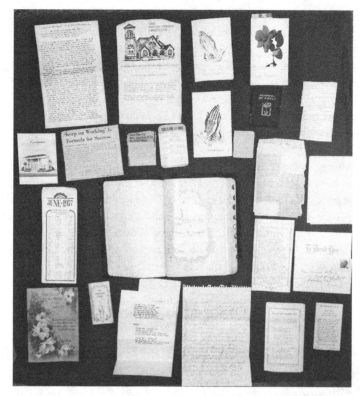

FIGURE 4.6 Twentieth-century Yapp-bound Bible owned by Frances Hutzell and the materials found tucked between its pages (author's collection; image by author).

the textual practice that is the Bible. Many things made that possible; the book's lightness and unbreakable binding are not the least of them.

The cheap but strong materials of its construction made Hutzell's Bible ruggedly present. In recent decades, though, other technologies have made the Bible present "everywhere," as proclaimed by the website of YouVersion, one of the most popular Bible apps.[49] Biola University calls its Bible-search website "The Unbound Bible," emphasizing its potential limitlessness.[50] Electronic Bibles promise a notionally infinite array of translations, text criticism, exegetical commentary, and personalized applications available on one screen, instantly. Like all of those materials tucked into Hutzell's Bible, the expansive content of electronic Bibles is a statement about the importance of the Bible itself.

The material characteristics of Bibles in America are inseparable both from the ways in which Bibles have been used and from arguments about how it should be used. Ultimately, as Barthes realized, texts such as the Bible are not separable from their material iterations: Bibles are both things to be seen and processes of demonstration. Fine paper and heavy covers; light paper and limp bindings; user-friendly apps with exhaustive content— the material features of the Bible's presentation are all rhetorical signifiers of ideological assumptions about the text. They have signaled the Bible's status for countless users as the majestic word of God, a constant companion, and a searchable store of advice.

Notes

1. Roland Barthes, "From Work to Text," in *Image-Music-Text*, trans. Stephen Heath (New York: Hill and Wang, 1977), 155–64. Another useful theoretical approach more closely employing the language of religious studies is laid out by James W. Watts, most importantly in "The Three Dimensions of Scriptures," in his edited volume, *Iconic Books and Texts* (Bristol, Conn.: Equinox, 2013), 9–32. Watts argues for an iconic aspect to scriptural texts created and sustained through ritual. While much of what is important about the material presence of Bibles may be described under this category of the iconic, my own interest is in a broader approach to the importance of the material characteristics of Bibles that does not rely on ritualization per se—both a workaday presence and a figurative usage not necessarily defined by repeatability or the prospect of repeatability.

2. The foremost exception is Paul Gutjahr, *An American Bible: A History of the Good Book in the United States, 1777–1880* (Stanford, Calif.: Stanford University Press, 1999). See also Colleen McDannell, *Material Christianity: Religion and Popular Culture in America* (New Haven, Conn.: Yale University Press, 1995), ch. 3. Historians of the book in America more generally have also paid attention to Bibles as objects—see especially James N. Green, "The Rise of Book Publishing in the United States," in *A History of the Book in America*, vol. 2: *An Extensive Republic: Print, Culture, and Society in the New Nation, 1790–1840*, ed. Robert A. Gross and Mary Kelley (Chapel Hill: University of North Carolina Press, 2010), 1–81. For a descriptive bibliography of American Bibles, see Margaret T. Hills, *The English Bible in America: A Bibliography of the Bible and the New Testament Published in America 1777–1957* (New York: American Bible Society, 1961).

3. Technically, format is a function of the number of times a sheet of paper is folded to make leaves—*quarto*, e.g., means that one sheet of paper was printed such that when it was folded it made four leaves of a book (each side of a leaf is a *page*, then, in bibliographer-speak). Because paper sizes are not exactly standard, exact measurements vary; the point here is that folios (where a sheet makes just one or two leaves) and quartos are the biggest books. For a detailed discussion of all kinds of details like this, see Philip Gaskell, *A New Introduction to Bibliography* (Oxford: Clarendon Press, 1972).

4. The definitive work on historical bookbinding is Julia Miller, *Books Will Speak Plain: A Handbook for Identifying and Describing Historical Bindings* (Ann Arbor, Mich.: Legacy Press, 2010). See also Gaskell, *Introduction to Bibliography*, 149–53.

5. For background on the iconographic status of books in the West, see Michelle P. Brown, "'Images to be Read and Words to be Seen': The Iconic Role of the Early Medieval Book," in Watts, *Iconic Books and Texts*, 93–118. Although he does not talk much about books, on the issues around religious objects as repositories of resources in the early modern period, see Eamon Duffy, *The Stripping of the Altars: Traditional Religion in England, c.1400–c.1580* (New Haven, Conn.: Yale University Press, 2005).

6. See Irving Albert Leonard, *Books of the Brave: Being an Account of Books and of Men in the Spanish Conquest and Settlement of the Sixteenth-Century New World* (1949; repr., Berkeley: University of California Press, 1992), 205–6, 254 (appendix 3). Despite its unfortunate title and disturbing warmth toward Spanish conquest, Leonard's work remains daunting in its breadth, detail, and usefulness. For context, see Rolena Adorno's introduction to the 1992 edition. For a more current study of the history of Latino print culture, see Raúl Coronado, *A World Not to Come: A History of Latino Writing and Print Culture* (Cambridge, Mass.: Harvard University Press, 2013).

7. Jaime Lara, *Christian Texts for Aztecs: Art and Liturgy in Colonial Mexico* (Notre Dame, Ind.: University of Notre Dame Press, 2008), 9. For analysis of pre-Columbian native writing traditions, see Phillip Round, *Removable Type: Histories of the Book in Indian Country, 1663–1880* (Chapel Hill: University of North Carolina Press, 2010).

8. Reuben Gold Thwaites, *The Jesuit Relations and Allied Documents: Travels and Explorations of the Jesuit Missionaries in New France, 1610–1791* (New York: Pageant Book, 1959), 53:214. On the totemic value of scripture books, see Dorina Miller Parmenter, "The Iconic Book: The Image of the Bible in Early Christian Rituals," *Postscripts: The Journal of Sacred Texts and Contemporary Worlds* 2, no. 2–3 (2006): 160–89; Martin Marty, "Scripturality: The Bible as Icon in the Republic," in *Religion and Republic: The American Circumstance* (Boston: Beacon Press, 1987), 140–65; and David Cressy, "Books as Totems in Seventeenth-Century England and New England," *Journal of Library History* 21, no. 1 (Winter 1986): 92–106.

9. Thomas Hariot, *A Briefe and True Report of the New Found Land of Virginia: of the Commodities and of the Nature and Manners of the Naturall Inhabitants* (1590; repr., New York: J. Sabin & Sons, 1871), http://docsouth.unc.edu/nc/hariot/hariot.html. See also Round, *Removable Type*, 11.

10. Whites' encouragement of the "talking book" as a trope among the enslaved suggests as much—see Allen Dwight Callahan, *The Talking Book: African Americans and the Bible* (New Haven, Conn.: Yale University Press, 2006).

11. Society for the Propagation of the Gospel in Foreign Parts, *A Collection of Papers, Printed by Order of the Society for the Propagation of the Gospel in Foreign Parts* (London: Joseph Downing, 1712), 44.

12. Round, *Removable Type*, 26.

13. I am indebted to Rebecca Baumann of The Lilly Library, Indiana University Libraries, for providing research images of this Bible.

14. William Bradford, *Proposals for the Printing of a Large Bible* (Philadelphia: William Bradford, 1688).

15. Calculations for seventeenth-century editions are based on A. S. Herbert, *Historical Catalogue of Printed Editions of the English Bible: 1525–1961*, revised and expanded from the edition of T. H. Darlow and H. F. Moule, 1903 (London: British & Foreign Bible Society, 1968).

16. David Hall Papers, American Philosophical Society Digital Library, Philadelphia, Pa, http://www.amphilsoc.org/collections/view?docId=ead/Mss.B.H142.1-3-ead.xml;query=;brand=default#abstract

17. For details on Aitken's project and the results, see Gutjahr, *American Bible*, 20–23.

18. I have compiled the aggregate data on Bible sizes used throughout this essay from Margaret T. Hills, *The English Bible in America: A Bibliography of the Bible and the New Testament Published in America 1777–1957* (New York: American Bible Society, 1961). Hills recorded dimensions for the Bibles she saw, but did not study the paper in depth to establish technical format. I have used Hills's dimensions to categorize the Bibles she recorded as small, medium, and large. It is not possible to eliminate a subjective element from this appraisal, but I have proceeded by handling selected copies of various sizes and making judgments. I have classed Bibles with a spine height of thirteen centimeters and less as small; between thirteen and twenty-one centimeters as medium; and twenty-two and greater as large. The middle sizes roughly correspond to octavos and duodecimos, with 16mo volumes and smaller classed as small, and quartos and folios identified as

large. Where Hills recorded formats, I have used those. There is an interesting study waiting to be done on the symbolic and practical differences between New Testaments and Bibles in American publishing history. These two are typically lumped together in edition counts—as they mostly are here—but they have very different publishing histories and symbolic resonances. Testaments were much more plentiful and almost always in small, personal, intimate formats. While the Old Testament may have dominated political and theological discourse in early America, there were always more New Testaments than Old in circulation. See Eran Shalev, *American Zion: The Old Testament as a Political Text from the Revolution to the Civil War* (New Haven, Conn.: Yale University Press, 2013).

19. For a thorough examination of this period of American Bible production, see Gutjahr, *American Bible*, especially chs. 1 and 2.

20. William Miller to Joshua Himes, November 1847, in Sylvester Bliss, *Memoirs of William Miller* (Boston: Joshua V. Himes, 1853), 361–63.

21. William Miller's Bible (Oxford: Samuel Collingwood, 1838), Box 2, William Miller Collection (Collection 25), Adventist Heritage Center, James White Library, Andrews University, Berrien Springs, Mich.

22. Gutjahr, *American Bible*, 44.

23. William J. Gilmore, *Reading Becomes a Necessity of Life: Material and Cultural Life in Rural New England, 1780–1835* (Knoxville: University of Tennessee Press, 1989), 269.

24. On early American Bible advertising, see Seth Perry, "'What the Public Expect': Consumer Authority and the Marketing of Bibles, 1770–1850," *American Periodicals: A Journal of History & Criticism* 24, no. 2 (2014): 128–44.

25. Weems to Carey, January 14, 1802, in *Mason Locke Weems: His Works and Ways*, ed. Paul Leicester Ford and Emily Ellsworth Ford Skeel (Norwood, Mass.: Plimpton Press, 1929), 225.

26. Weems to Wayne, August 5, 1906, Ford and Skeel, *Mason Locke Weems*, 340.

27. See Gaskell, *Introduction to Bibliography*, 146–47; Gutjahr, *American Bible*, 42–43.

28. Gutjahr, *American Bible*, 43, 191.

29. Miller, *Books Will Speak Plain*, 107–10.

30. *Publisher's Weekly*, March 21, 1874, 291. See J. W. Tebbel, *A History of Book Publishing in the United States*, vol. 2: *The Expansion of an Industry, 1865–1919* (New York: R. R. Bowker, 1975), 543.

31. Lorenzo Dow, *The Life and Travels of Lorenzo Dow: In Which Are Contained Some Singular Providences of God, Written by Himself* (Hartford, Conn.: Lincoln and Gleason, 1804), 14.

32. See, e.g., John Lewis Krimmel's book-less, grotesquely racialized watercolor, "Negro Methodists Holding a Meeting in a Philadelphia Alley" (ca. 1812). The Metropolitan Museum of Art, Rogers Fund, 1942.

33. See John H. Wigger, *Taking Heaven by Storm: Methodism and the Rise of Popular Christianity in America* (New York: Oxford University Press, 1998).

34. Lorenzo Dow, *The Dealings of God, Man, and the Devil as Exemplified in the Life, Experience, and Travels of Lorenzo Dow* (New York: Nafia & Cornish, 1850), 62.

35. *Mary the Milk-maid* (American Antiquarian Society, n.d.), a slight abridgment of a tract issued by the Philadelphia Female Tract Society in 1817, 8.

36. John Gilmary Shea, *A Bibliographical Account of Catholic Bibles, Testaments, and Other Portions of Scripture Translated from the Latin Vulgate and Printed in the United States* (New York: Cramoisy Press, 1859), 3.

37. Shea, *Catholic Bibles*, 33.

38. Miller, *Books Will Speak Plain*, 162–63.
39. F. J. M. Wijnekus and E. F. P. H. Wijnekus, *Dictionary of the Printing and Allied Industries: In English (with Definitions), French, German, Dutch, Spanish and Italian*, 2nd ed. (Amsterdam: Elsevier Science, 1983), 642.
40. *Reporter* (Lexington, Ky.), August 24, 1811, 2.
41. Gaskell, *Introduction to Bibliography*, 66.
42. P. H. Sutcliffe, *The Oxford University Press: An Informal History* (Oxford: Clarendon Press, 1978), 39–40.
43. *Cincinnati Daily Times*, September 22, 1875, 3.
44. *American Sentinel* (Oakland, Calif.), February 27, 1889, 47.
45. *The Continent*, November 17, 1910, 1627.
46. B. M. Pietsch, *Dispensational Modernism* (New York: Oxford University Press, 2015), 181.
47. On the rapid changes to religious publishing in the early twentieth century, see Matthew S. Hedstrom, *The Rise of Liberal Religion: Book Culture and American Spirituality in the Twentieth Century* (New York: Oxford University Press, 2015); and Daniel Vaca, "Book People: Evangelical Books and the Making of Contemporary Evangelicalism," PhD diss., Columbia University, 2012.
48. Dorina Miller Parmenter has written perceptively about the iconographic significance of battered, obviously well-used Bibles. "Iconic Books from Below: The Christian Bible and the Discourse of Duct Tape," in Watts, *Iconic Books and Texts*, 185–200.
49. "YouVersion," *The Bible App* (Life.Church, n.d.), https://www.youversion.com/. For reflections on the implications of electronic Bibles, see Timothy Beal, "The End of the World as We Know It: The Cultural Iconicity of the Bible in the Twilight of Print Culture," in Watts, *Iconic Books and Texts*, 165–84.
50. *The Unbound Bible* (Biola University, n.d.), https://unbound.biola.edu/.

BIBLIOGRAPHY

Barthes, Roland. "From Work to Text." In *Image-Music-Text*, translated by Stephen Heath, 155–64. New York: Hill and Wang, 1977.
Bradford, William. *Proposals for the Printing of a Large Bible*. Philadelphia: William Bradford, 1688.
Callahan, Allen Dwight. *The Talking Book: African Americans and the Bible*. New Haven, Conn.: Yale University Press, 2006.
Coronado, Raúl. *A World Not to Come: A History of Latino Writing and Print Culture*. Cambridge, Mass.: Harvard University Press, 2013.
Cressy, David. "Books as Totems in Seventeenth-Century England and New England." *Journal of Library History* 21, no. 1 (Winter 1986): 92–106.
Dow, Lorenzo. *The Dealings of God, Man, and the Devil as Exemplified in the Life, Experience, and Travels of Lorenzo Dow*. New York: Nafia & Cornish, 1850.
———. *The Life and Travels of Lorenzo Dow: In Which Are Contained Some Singular Providences of God, Written by Himself*. Hartford, Conn.: Lincoln and Gleason, 1804.
Duffy, Eamon. *The Stripping of the Altars: Traditional Religion in England, c.1400–c.1580*. New Haven, Conn.: Yale University Press, 2005.
Gaskell, Philip. *A New Introduction to Bibliography*. Oxford: Clarendon Press, 1972.
Gilmore, William J. *Reading Becomes a Necessity of Life: Material and Cultural Life in Rural New England, 1780–1835*. Knoxville: University of Tennessee Press, 1989.

Green, James N. "The Rise of Book Publishing in the United States." In *A History of the Book in America*, vol. 2: *An Extensive Republic: Print, Culture, and Society in the New Nation, 1790–1840*, edited by Robert A. Gross and Mary Kelley, 1–81. Chapel Hill: University of North Carolina Press, 2010.

Gutjahr, Paul. *An American Bible: A History of the Good Book in the United States, 1777–1880.* Stanford, Calif.: Stanford University Press, 1999.

Hedstrom, Matthew S. *The Rise of Liberal Religion: Book Culture and American Spirituality in the Twentieth Century.* New York: Oxford University Press, 2015.

Herbert, Arthur Sumner. *Historical Catalogue of Printed Editions of the English Bible: 1525–1961*, revised and expanded from the edition of T. H. Darlow and H. F. Moule, 1903. London: British & Foreign Bible Society, 1968.

Hills, Margaret T. *The English Bible in America: A Bibliography of the Bible and the New Testament Published in America 1777–1957.* New York: American Bible Society, 1961.

Lara, Jaime. *Christian Texts for Aztecs: Art and Liturgy in Colonial Mexico.* Notre Dame, Ind.: University of Notre Dame Press, 2008.

Leonard, Irving Albert. *Books of the Brave: Being an Account of Books and of Men in the Spanish Conquest and Settlement of the Sixteenth-Century New World* (1949). Repr. Berkeley: University of California Press, 1992.

Marty, Martin. "Scripturality: The Bible as Icon in the Republic." In *Religion and Republic: The American Circumstance*, ch. 7. Boston: Beacon Press, 1987.

McDannell, Colleen. *Material Christianity: Religion and Popular Culture in America.* New Haven, Conn.: Yale University Press, 1995.

Miller, Julia. *Books Will Speak Plain: A Handbook for Identifying and Describing Historical Bindings.* Ann Arbor, Mich.: Legacy Press, 2010.

Miller, William. Personal Bible. Box 2, William Miller Collection (Collection 25), Adventist Heritage Center, James White Library, Andrews University, Berrien Springs, Mich.

Parmenter, Dorina Miller. "The Iconic Book: The Image of the Bible in Early Christian Rituals." *Postscripts: The Journal of Sacred Texts and Contemporary Worlds* 2, no. 2–3 (2006): 160–89.

Perry, Seth. "'What the Public Expect': Consumer Authority and the Marketing of Bibles, 1770–1850." *American Periodicals: A Journal of History & Criticism* 24, no. 2 (2014): 128–44.

Pietsch, B. M. *Dispensational Modernism.* New York: Oxford University Press, 2015.

Round, Phillip. *Removable Type: Histories of the Book in Indian Country, 1663–1880.* Chapel Hill: University of North Carolina Press, 2010.

Shalev, Eran. *American Zion: The Old Testament as a Political Text from the Revolution to the Civil War.* New Haven, Conn.: Yale University Press, 2013.

Shea, John Gilmary. *A Bibliographical Account of Catholic Bibles, Testaments, and Other Portions of Scripture Translated from the Latin Vulgate and Printed in the United States.* New York: Cramoisy Press, 1859.

Sutcliffe, P. H. *The Oxford University Press: An Informal History.* Oxford: Clarendon Press, 1978.

Tebbel, J. W. *A History of Book Publishing in the United States*, vol. 2: *The Expansion of an Industry, 1865–1919.* New York: R. R. Bowker, 1975.

Thwaites, Reuben Gold. *The Jesuit Relations and Allied Documents: Travels and Explorations of the Jesuit Missionaries in New France, 1610–1791.* 73 vols. New York: Pageant Book, 1959.

Vaca, Daniel. "Book People: Evangelical Books and the Making of Contemporary Evangelicalism." PhD diss., Columbia University, 2012.

Watts, James W., ed., *Iconic Books and Texts.* Bristol, Conn.: Equinox, 2013.

Wigger, John H. *Taking Heaven by Storm: Methodism and the Rise of Popular Christianity in America*. New York: Oxford University Press, 1998.

Wijnekus, F. J. M., and E. F. P. H. Wijnekus. *Dictionary of the Printing and Allied Industries: In English (with Definitions), French, German, Dutch, Spanish and Italian*. 2nd ed. Amsterdam: Elsevier Science, 1983.

PART II

BIBLICAL INTERPRETATION AND USAGE

CHAPTER 5

··

THE BIBLE IN THE
SEVENTEENTH CENTURY

··

ROBERT E. BROWN

PERHAPS the most notable feature about the Bible in seventeenth-century North America is its ubiquity. From the modeling of large societal institutions to the patterns of everyday speech, the Bible profoundly shaped the ways that European settlers understood and acted in the world around them. While it may be a truism to say that the Bible had a hegemonic authority for nascent colonial societies, truisms exist for a reason. Protestantism was not yet a century old when England began its permanent settlement of the New World. Its establishment in Europe, even among Protestants and the nations they governed, was any-thing but settled. In the wake of this religious and political uncertainty, it was precisely the Protestant doctrine of *sola scriptura* that came to animate so much of the formation of colo-nial life, as settlers sought to work out the societal implications of their biblicist theology.

This was particularly true of the Puritans in New England, whose demographic and set-tlement patterns gave their religious vision an unrivaled ideological heft and an outsized influence on developments in early America. As T. D. Bozeman has characterized it, for Puritans the biblical story was not a mere chronicle of the past but a "living theater" for the present. The Bible served as a lens "projecting an entire realm of experience over against the everyday . . . [exercising] a virtually tyrannical claim upon imagination and belief." Small wonder then that the language of the Bible "became a kind of Puritan dialect" by which their critics distinguished them. Indeed, some have seen the biblicism of the Puritans as their singular contribution to American culture.[1]

It would be a mistake however to see New England as exceptional in this regard.[2] First, settlers with Puritan sympathies if not outright allegiances played formative if often resented roles in the Middle Colonies and the Chesapeake region throughout the seventeenth cen-tury. Furthermore, Puritan attitudes and practices regarding the Bible were widely shared among English Protestants in general, even if less evidently employed. Finally, even in those instances where Puritan biblicism was challenged, it was usually not the authority of the Bible itself that was at issue, but rather the interpretive implications drawn from it by the Puritan establishment. In the end, the primitivism that characterized Puritan ideology and the biblicism that it inspired, while distinctive, were not unique.[3] Quakers, Baptists, Presbyterians, Anglicans, and Catholics—all understood their doctrine, piety, and institutions to hearken back to the teachings of the Apostles, and thus in the deepest sense, as things originating in scripture.[4] The biblicism of the era played a vital and constructive role in the development of characteristically American religious practices and institutions throughout the colonies and across denominational lines.

BIBLICAL LITERACY

Protestants in general, and many colonial Protestants in particular, were keen to advance the ideal of universal literacy, which they saw as fundamental to human salvation and to the advancement of the true church. Illiterate individuals were susceptible to manipulation by false authorities, most notably the papacy. This concern was succinctly stated by the English Puritan Thomas Cartwright: "If all ought to read the scriptures then all ages, all sexes, all degrees and callings, all high and low, rich and poor, wise and foolish have a necessary duty therein." Those seeking a more complete reformation in the English Church believed it would only come by the "propagation of the Word by both private reading and public sermons."[5]

Colonial literacy is typically, if imperfectly, estimated by means of probate documents, with their evidence of writing literacy (signatures). Using these instruments, scholars have generally calculated the writing literacy rates for New England males of sufficient means at about 50 percent in 1650, rising to 70 percent by the end of the century. In the Chesapeake region, male literacy grew from 45 percent to 60 percent in the same period. In New England, the literacy of women rose from 30 percent to 40 percent; in the Chesapeake, perhaps 25 percent to 30 percent. Reading literacy is generally assumed to be higher, though to what degree is difficult if not impossible to measure.[6]

Aware of this state of affairs, the colonies sought to establish communal instruments for universal literacy. In short order nearly all colonies required that children receive instruction in reading and writing. In Virginia this requirement took the form of weekly catechizing of children and servants, mandated from the outset, and periodically renewed in subsequent legislation. In 1642 Massachusetts passed its first of many literacy laws, requiring that selectmen regularly visit homes to enquire about the reading capabilities within households. Connecticut followed in 1650, New York in 1665, and Pennsylvania in 1683.[7] Parents were made chiefly responsible for the basic literacy of their children, but since many were not up to the task, colonial legislation often directed towns of sufficient size to establish petty or grammar schools, the latter often taught by clergy or those with college training. Evidence suggests, however, that most communities were not up to this task either; schools fitfully opened and closed over the century, depending upon the financial resources of towns and parents.

The expressed rationale for literacy was fundamentally religious in nature. As stated in the Massachusetts statute of 1647, literacy was a necessity, it "being one chief project of that old deluder, Satan, to keep men from the knowledge of the Scriptures . . . that so at least the true sense and meaning of the original might be clouded by false glosses of saint-seeming deceivers." So too, the New Haven Code of 1656 required that all children and apprentices should "be able duly to read the Scriptures . . . in some competent measure, to understand the main grounds and principles of Christian Religion necessary to salvation." The

Pennsylvania law (1683) asked that children "be instructed in reading and writing, so that they may be able to read the Scriptures."[8]

Not surprisingly, the curricula employed in both domestic and institutional settings used the Bible as the primary source of instruction. Hornbooks, used to initiate basic literacy, consisted of a single wooden paddle, to which was affixed a sheet containing the alphabet, the syllabary, and, as a practice exercise for both, the Lord's Prayer. Primers advanced the student toward sentence reading, usually by employing biblical or biblically oriented texts such as the Lord's Prayer, the Ave Maria, the Ten Commandments, and the Apostles' Creed, as well as a basic catechism. The variety of primers was abundant if proscribed in seventeenth-century England, and colonials undoubtedly used a number of them, though the more Anglican versions were officially frowned upon in New England.

By the end of the century, the first "American" primer appeared on the scene, the *New-England Primer*, published by Benjamin Harris in Boston no later than 1690. It was an exceedingly simplified adaptation of Harris's *Protestant Tutor* (published in England for a more advanced audience), less anti-Catholic in its rhetoric, and more Calvinist in its theological expression. In addition to the Lord's Prayer, its lessons included the Apostles' Creed, the Ten Commandments, the Westminster Catechism, and a list of the Bible's books. The biblicist ethos of Puritanism is evident throughout, from learning the alphabet ("B: Thy Life to Mend, This Book Attend") to sentence exercises, many of which are biblical citations.[9] Literacy instruction beyond the primer relied on the biblical texts themselves. The first of these was a psalter (the Psalms set to English meter). The first book published in the English colonies was in fact a psalter (the *Bay Psalm Book*), though a common prose psalter, and not this one, was used in educational settings. An American psalter specifically designed for children's education appeared in 1682, as the *New-England Psalter*.[10] After mastering the psalter, students would move on to reading the New Testament, and after that, the Old Testament.

Young men who had sufficiently mastered Latin and Greek in grammar school could matriculate to college; in the seventeenth century this meant Harvard College. While the curriculum was broadly based on the liberal arts, theology and biblical study formed its core. The college by-laws (1642) stated that every student "shall so exercise himself in reading the Scriptures twice a day that they be ready to give an account of their proficiency therein."[11] Significant attention was devoted to the biblical languages. Morning devotions included sight translations of Hebrew and English into Greek (although, as at Yale in the following century, students were known to insert pages of the Septuagint in their Bibles to finesse this task). The two most influential Harvard presidents of the seventeenth century, Henry Dunster and Charles Chauncy (together serving 1640–1672) were able, Cambridge-trained Hebraists; during their presidencies Hebrew, Aramaic, and Syriac, as well as Greek, were core subjects, as was the exposition of the Bible proper.[12] A student was qualified to receive the bachelor's degree only when he was "found to be able to read the originall of the old and New testament into the Latin tongue."[13] No less than eighteen bachelor's and six master's theses were devoted to questions concerning the Hebrew language between 1642 and 1699.[14]

Personal libraries also provide an index of colonial interests and proficiencies in biblical interpretation. Most colonial libraries were relatively small, numbering less than ten books; not surprisingly, the Bible is the most common title found in these in probate documents. The catalogs of some of the more extensive libraries, while atypical in size and scope, more tellingly reveal the depth of interest in matters of interpretation. A number of the founding figures in colonial America had such libraries: William Brewster (d. 1644) and Ralph Partridge of Plymouth (d. 1658), possessed 400 and 420 volumes, respectively—the titles of which were almost entirely religious in nature. Solomon Stoddard's personal library catalog, compiled in 1664 while he was a student, already comprised some eighty volumes. Included in it, among others, are Edward Leigh's *Critica Sacra* (1639/1650), a two-volume commentary on biblical Greek and Hebrew; a translation of Giovanni Diodati's *Pious Annotations upon the Holy Bible* (1643); Henry Ainsworth's *Annotations* on the Psalms (1617); and a "Hebr[ew] bible in 4 parts." The two most prodigious ministerial libraries of the period, those of Increase and Cotton Mather, each numbered upwards of 1,000 by end of the century. Increase's 1664 catalog, already at some 700 titles, included dozens of works on interpretation; Cotton's collection by the end of his life (1728) included hundreds of such titles. This was also true of the libraries of secular and religious figures in the Chesapeake region. Perhaps the best documented of these is that of Anglican minister Thomas Teackle (d. 1695). One-third of his 300-plus volume collection, and the largest single portion of it, was devoted to works of biblical exegesis, including the eight-volume *Critici Sacri* (1660), eight volumes of Joseph Carlyl's commentary on Job (1661), and the Jesuit Joao da Sylveira's four-volume commentary on the Gospels (1672).[15]

LITERATURE AND LITERARY PIETY

Colonial Protestants were not only consumers of religious literature but also important producers, both in print and manuscript form. The Bible figures prominently in that production. This is due in large part to the strong pietism of the era, an interest widely shared in the Protestant world, and indeed, in the Christian world in general. It was perhaps most ardently expressed in the writings of colonial Puritans. For all their notoriety as those obsessed with doctrinal orthodoxy, the theological center of Puritanism was always piety, or godliness. Their preoccupation with orthodoxy was thus driven by their self-understanding as a covenanted people, obligated to a holy and uncompromising God. The purpose of sound doctrine was to create a godly people sufficiently pleasing to the God of the nation.

Sound doctrine came from a right understanding of the Bible: fully two-thirds of the titles published by New England clergy in the seventeenth century were devoted to biblical exposition, in the form of sermons.[16] On occasion, these sermons were collected into distinct (and occasionally posthumous) monographs, as with John Cotton's "Brief Expositions" of Canticles (1642), Ecclesiastes (1654), Revelation (1655), and 1 John (1656), or with Thomas Shepard's *Parable of the Ten Virgins* (1660). The most expansive of these was Samuel Willard's *Compleat Body of Divinity*, 250 sermons structured around the *Westminster Catechism*.[17] By far the most significant work of biblical interpretation originating in the seventeenth century was Cotton Mather's massive 4,500-page commentary, the *Biblia Americana*, a work left unpublished in his lifetime. Begun as a series of notebooks just after the Salem witch trials, the *Biblia* encompasses the breadth and depth of early modern interpretive concerns.

The first book published in America was *The Whole Book of Psalmes Faithfully Translated into English Metre*, the Puritan psalter better known as the *Bay Psalm Book* (1640). Given their precedential status as the only "biblical" songs extant, the psalms became the only songs permissible for Puritan worship. Despite the existence of Puritan psalters, such as Henry Ainsworth's *Book of Psalmes* (1612), the clergy of New England, led by John Cotton, Richard Mather, and John Eliot, desired a song book that was less compromised by paraphrastic concessions to rhyme and meter, paraphrase being, by definition, a departure from the original meaning of the text. They desired a psalter more faithful to the language and meaning of the Hebrew text. The sacrifice of aesthetic sensibilities in the *Bay Psalm Book* was apparently keenly felt, and the third edition, Henry Dunster's *The Psalms, hymns and spiritual songs of the Old and New-Testament* (1651) attempted to restore these features.[18]

Given the scenes of demographic and cultural annihilation that came to characterize European encroachments upon Native American civilization, it is something of a paradox that the first Bible to be published in America was one rendered in the Indian tongue, a work that simultaneously sought to displace native religion while implicitly recognizing the integrity of native culture, by recognizing its language as suitable for religious use.[19] John Eliot (d. 1690) devoted the better part of six decades to missionary work among the Massachusett Indians, by organizing them into Christian communities, the so-called Praying Towns, but more important, by translating Christian works into the native language, above all the Bible.[20] Eliot began his missionary work in 1631, learning Algonquian, establishing the first town of Natick, as well as the first (bilingual) school, in 1651, the latter with the intent "that they may be able to write for themselves such Scriptures as I (may) translate for them."[21] With the help of three native assistants, Job Nesutan, John Sassamon, and James Wowaus, Eliot published a translation of the New Testament in 1661 (1,500 copies), and of the Old Testament in 1663 (1,000 copies). Eliot also published a number of scriptural aids in Algonquian, the so-called Indian Library: a catechism (1653), a psalter (1663), and a primer (1669), as well as two classic devotional works—Richard Baxter's *Call to the Unconverted* (1664) and Lewis Bayly's *Practise of Pietie* (1665). Thus, the corpus of Eliot's translation work sought to aid in the cultural assimilation of Native Americans, by directing them toward a Puritan spirituality, one rooted in religious literacy and the devotional reading of the Bible.[22]

The evangelizing work of Eliot and Thomas Mayhew among New England natives was exceptional in the seventeenth century in the colonies. Still less attention was given by European colonials to the spiritual fortunes of African slaves across British North America. Yet here, too, there is evidence that even from the earliest instances of slavery, Africans were exposed to the Bible, and appropriated its teachings. In New England, where slaves tended to work in domestic settings, they were treated as members of the patriarchal household, and thus included in family devotions, and required to attend church services. In his *Brief Discourse on . . . a Good Servant* (1696), Cotton Mather instructs his readers not to leave slaves "Unacquainted with, and Uncatechised in, the PRINCIPLES OF RELIGION." What such instruction might have looked like is outlined in Mather's *The Negro Christianized* (1706), which included the standard range of biblical catechizing such as the Lord's Prayer and the Ten Commandments. For Mather, this included biblical literacy: "If the Negroes might Learn to Read the Sacred Scriptures . . . Vast would be the Advantage thereof unto them. Until that might be accomplished, would it not be Advantageous to them, to make them Learn by heart, certain Particular Verses of the Scriptures?"[23] Mather occasionally recorded in his diary the spiritual fortunes of his slaves: "This day, my Servant, was offered unto the Communion of my Church . . . Other of my Servants formerly . . . have joined unto my Church." Samuel Willard similarly instructed his flock on the need to teach slaves, since "the Soul of the Slave is, in its nature, of as much worth, as the Soul of the Master."[24] While such relatively enlightened views of the humanity of Africans were probably exceptional in the era, they tended to grow in intensity if not in number as the century progressed. The most trenchant literary example of this is Samuel Sewall's *The Selling of Joseph* (1700), a work dedicated to an abolitionist exposition of the biblical passages relating to slavery.

The Protestant interest in the salvation of individual souls naturally led to the development of a body of literature designed to help the laity assess and improve their spiritual condition: just as there could be no true piety without a knowledge of God, so there could be no true piety without a knowledge of one's self. Protestant devotional works were immensely popular in the colonies. The works most frequently owned included: John Foxe's *Acts and Monuments* (1563), better known as his *Book of Martyrs*; the Royalist cleric Richard Allestree's *Whole Duty of Man* (1658); the dissenter Richard Baxter's *Poor Man's Family Book* (1674); and John Bunyan's *Pilgrim's Progress* (1678). But perhaps the most popular of all titles was Lewis Bayly's *Practise of Pietie* (1612).[25] Bayly (d. 1631) was a Puritan-leaning chaplain to James I, and subsequently bishop of Bangor. His manual is comprised mostly of short theological essays, accompanied by prayers and meditations for daily and special circumstances; in addition, it offers advice on "How to read the Bible with Profit, and Ease," and "Rules to be observ'd in singing of Psalms." All of these are copiously footnoted with scriptural citations; the reader is encouraged to examine these passages to find greater assurance for the practice of piety. The works of Allestree and Baxter are similarly insistent on the priority of scriptural meditation for piety; Bunyan's work was expressly written as a biblical allegory.

Colonial Americans also produced their own oeuvre of devotional literature. Given their pietistic bent, it comes as no surprise that Puritans would turn to self-contemplation, in the form of autobiographical materials, as they wrestled with their concerns about sin and salvation. Many of these were private—diaries, autobiographies, journals—intended only for personal use, or posthumously, for the benefit of families. Thomas Shepard's journal is typical of this literature. In it he records the scripture readings that engaged him, and the reflections on his spiritual journey they provoked.[26] These autobiographical materials, especially diaries, were prevalent in the seventeenth century; they reveal the depth of biblical contemplation in colonial life.[27] Some devotional works, however, often in the form of collected sermons, were intended for public consumption. Thomas Hooker (d. 1647) was a prolific writer of devotional works, including *The Poor Doubting Christian Drawn to Christ* (1629), *The Soul's Exaltation* (1638), and *The Soul's Preparation for Christ* (1632). Hooker's practical theology helped to shape the American Puritan understanding of the morphology of conversion, known as preparationism. Thomas Shepard (d. 1649) also contributed significant works in this vein; among these works is *The Sincere Convert* (1664).

Catechisms were another important source of scriptural contemplation, serving as they did as a template from childhood for rehearsing the great spiritual drama of the biblical narrative. Anglicans, of course, possessed a catechism located in the *Book of Common Prayer*, one that rehearsed the Nicene Creed, the Ten Commandments, the Lord's Prayer, Jesus's Great Command, and the biblical sacraments of the Eucharist and baptism. Puritans naturally felt the need to develop their own catechisms and did so in abundance, although the publication of the *Westminster Shorter Catechism* (1647) served to regularize such instruction to some degree.

In New England ministers tended to write their own catechisms; regarding this proliferation Increase Mather once dismissively acknowledged "no less than five hundred catechisms" circulating in New England in his day.[28] The most popular of these was John Cotton's *Milk for Babes, drawn out of the Breasts of Both Testaments* (1646), republished posthumously as *Spiritual Milk for Boston Babes* (1656). Considered to be the first children's book published in America, it was later appended to the *New England Primer*, where it continued to be printed well into the nineteenth century. It rehearses standard Calvinist themes, with verse citations to buttress their biblical derivation.[29]

Colonial Americans give every evidence of having been inveterate poets, which ought to be of little surprise, given the almost quotidian nature of poetry as a means of expression in the seventeenth century. It appears across the colonies and across a spectrum of publications: in prefaces to monographs, as funeral elegies, and in historical works. It even shows up in unexpected places—much of Roger Williams's *Key into the Language of America* (1643), for example, is rendered in verse. In many instances it also served as an important vehicle for devotional exercise, in the form of meditations on scripture or scriptural themes.

Such can be found in the work of Anne Bradstreet (d. 1672), the first published poet in America. While much of her poetry in *The Tenth Muse* (1650) works within the milieu of Renaissance classicism, it also contains biblical verse, such as "Davids Lamentation for Saul, and Jonathan, 2 Sam. 1.19." Meditations on biblical content became more prominent in the second edition (prepared by her, but appearing posthumously in 1678). Confronted by illness and death in her immediate family, the "Several Poems" section ("Contemplations") finds Bradstreet musing upon the theodicies of human alienation from God.[30]

Others followed Bradstreet in writing spiritual and scriptural poetry in the colonies. Michael Wigglesworth (d. 1705) published perhaps the most elaborate poetic rendition of biblical verse, if not the most terrifying. His *Day of Doom* (1662) became the best-selling work in the colonies, after the Bible and the *Book of Common Prayer*. In it he rehearses with foreboding anticipation the Last Judgement. The most expansive use of the Bible in devotional poetry is that of Edward Taylor (1642-1729). Taylor spent almost sixty years as a minister in Westfield, Massachusetts. During that time, he composed over 200 poems, which he entitled "Preparatory Meditations before my Approach to the Lords Supper." Each centers on the preaching text of the day; the great majority of these are drawn from the Song of Songs (Canticles), which Christians often read as a love song between Jesus and his Church. Explicitly instructing his heirs not to publish them, they remained "lost" until rediscovered and published in the mid-twentieth century.[31]

Another literary genre that can appropriately be thought of as devotional in nature includes captivity narratives, of which four appeared among the English in the seventeenth century. Through this literature, European colonials negotiated their fears of natives and the barbarism that their existence represented to them. A large part of that barbarism was felt religiously. Captives who were absorbed into native society, for however brief a period, faced the potential for spiritual degradation. How could such a shocking instance of captivity and its suffering be comprehended theologically? Did it represent God's judgment? Could God's mercy be seen in the midst of it? Perhaps most important, what sorts of actions could be taken by the prisoner for spiritual sustenance and for the preservation of godliness?

The first of these captivity narratives, and the most iconic of the 300 or so that would follow, was Mary Rowlandson's *The Sovereignty and Goodness of God* (1682), an account of her three-month ordeal during King Philip's War in 1676.[32] In it the Bible figures prominently in her understanding of events and in her preservation through them. The attack and subsequent suffering are described in scriptural metaphor and type. Her captivity becomes the occasion for recognizing her spiritual torpor: "how careless I had been of God's holy time." The Bible serves as the instrument of her restoration. Soon into her ordeal she experienced "the wonderful mercy of God . . . in sending me a Bible" (looted by an Indian in another raid). Over and over again, events bring to mind certain biblical passages, which give her consolation and a settling understanding of their meaning.

Cotton Mather's *Decennium Luctuosum* (1699) recounts the decade-long King William's War (1688–97). Mather includes the narratives of Hannah Swarton and Hannah Duston. They, too, act out what would become scripturally framed spiritual ordeals. Most notorious is the case of Duston, who escaped by bludgeoning her captors in their sleep, in the imitation of "the action of Jael upon Sisera," the Israelite woman who impaled the skull of a sleeping Canaanite warrior (Judg. 4–5).

Finally, Puritans resorted to the Bible to provide the language and interpretive framework for their historical narratives, literary efforts that were also underwritten by a concern for self-scrutiny and for promoting godliness. The Puritans' understanding of themselves as a covenanted people before God, as the new Israel, served to extend their sense of providential history beyond the end of the apostolic age. God continued his covenantal work with his people right up to the present time, giving Puritans a sense that every event was an occasion for deciphering the divine will.

If the early history of New England was an extension of the biblical drama, then it only made sense to record it by means of biblical tropes, most especially in terms of typology. William Bradford's *Of Plymouth Plantation* (the first book of which was published in 1630) and John Winthrop's journal are classic examples of this typological mentality, even though they were not immediately produced for public consumption.[33] The first published historical account of the English colonies, Edward Johnson's *History of New England*, better known by its subtitle, *Wonder-working Providence of Sion's Saviour . . . in New England* (published in London in 1654), fully embraces a typological understanding of the Puritan experience in America. Finally, Cotton Mather's magisterial history, the *Magnalia Christi Americana* (1702), serves, as its title indicates, as a typological rehearsal of God's work among the people of New England, and ultimately, as with all of these historical narratives, as a call to spiritual self-reflection and rehabilitation.

RELIGIOUS DEBATE

For all of the social complexities attending the religious conflicts in the colonies, and they were many, at a fundamental level the participants understood them as conflicts over the proper interpretation of scripture, and in large part conducted their disputes on that rhetorical platform. The first great religious conflict in the colonies, the Antinomian controversy (1636–38), is a classic instance in which we see the nature of Protestant biblicism being negotiated.

The inherent tension in Reformed theology between the prevenient grace of a sovereign God and the instruments of that grace (moral rectitude, scripture, sacraments) meant that Puritans continually struggled to find the right balance between divine and human agency in salvation. Establishment Puritanism insisted that while justification is a wholly divine act, there were certain biblical signs of that act, such as faith and obedience. Scripture, as

God's word, was the chief instrument assuring Puritans of the visible evidence of their faith. Some clergy, particularly John Cotton, wanted to preserve God's sovereignty in justification by limiting assurance to the internal witness of the Holy Spirit, apart from any external (moral) evidence. For his follower Anne Hutchinson and others, the majority of ministers in New England erred on the side of external evidences, or works (and thus not grace), making human actions a sign (and thus a condition) of justification. Such a reading seemed to imply that human actions such as moral behavior and religious piety were superfluous: such an "antinomian" view was perceived as a threat to social order. Moreover, the emphasis of Hutchinson and others on the personal witness of the Spirit seemed to imply that scripture itself was superfluous as a means of structuring the faith of the justified.

The records of the controversy, including the court examinations, demonstrate that at its core, the controversy was couched as a matter of conflicting biblical interpretations. A council of ministers submitted "Sixteene Questions" to Cotton to ascertain his theological position, specifically asking him to ground his answers in scripture. Cotton's initial answers were an effort to finesse the differences of the two sides, subtle enough to agree largely with the clergy, while offering support to the nuances of the antinomian position. Unsatisfied with his response, the "Elders' Reply" to Cotton presents a litany of Bible verses to bolster their critique of his theological positions and asked him again to do the same: dissenters "need bring sound proof from Scripture, or else they tread awry in doing so." Cotton's "Rejoynder" met the challenge to biblical fidelity head on, copiously citing chapter and verse on all the issues at stake.[34]

Finally, the examination of Hutchinson herself shows that biblical interpretation was at the crux of the accusations against her.[35] Winthrop lists a catalog of eighty-two errors marshalled against her, including that she held that "the whole letter of the Scripture is a covenant of works"; that "she wreathed the Scriptures to her owne purpose" in order to mislead others; that she taught men at conventicles in her home, contrary to scripture; that a "knowledge of the holy Scripture, is not a . . . sure way of . . . finding Christ"; that her appeal to the witness of the Spirit was "without any respect unto, or concurrence with the Word"; similarly, that she was advocating that "all doctrines . . . must be tried by Christ the word, rather than by the Word of Christ." Hutchinson's replies to her interrogators reveal her to be equal to the task of biblical reasoning; she is able to cite the Bible in her defense across the line of accusations, in many cases confounding her opponents with her deft handling of scriptural arguments. It was only when she admitted to personal revelations from the Spirit (a claim taken to be prophecy) that the case against her carried the day.

The written records of the Antinomian controversy thus serve as a prototypical example of the way in which colonials sought to resolve their differences. The events of 1636–38 spurred Roger Williams to give full voice to his reservations about the Puritan system, sparking the first substantive debate about the relationship between religion and politics in America. In his *Bloudy Tenent of Persecution* (1644), Williams provided a trenchant critique of the theocracy of Massachusetts and made the argument for the separation of religion and politics. He did so by arguing that the scriptures demanded their separation, since theocracies inevitably lead to the corruption of the church by the state, and thus to the persecution of Christians. Most tellingly, Williams rejected the idea that the "biblical" Israelite theocracy was precedential for Christian "biblical" polities, subverting an idea which sat at the bedrock of Puritan political theory. John Cotton's reply, *The Bloudy Tenent, washed and made white by the Bloud of the Lambe* (1647), and Williams's rejoinder, *The Bloudy Tenent yet more Bloudy* (1652), continue this line of scriptural argumentation.

This mode of argument continued through the century. In the midst of Williams's criticisms as well as those of other dissenters in Massachusetts, authorities produced *A Platform of Church Discipline gathered out of the Word of God* (the so-called *Cambridge Platform*) (1649), in order to decisively state and defend congregational polity and Puritan doctrine; its seventeen chapters contain over 300 scriptural citations. Similarly, the so-called *Half-Way Covenant* (1662) employs a copious scriptural apparatus to justify the changes it introduced into the manner of Puritan church association.[36] Incursions by Quaker and Baptist missionaries into New England show them engaged in public debates with their critics over the scriptural foundations of their dissent. Debates between Quakers and Baptists themselves were similarly conducted.[37]

PUBLIC LIFE

Religious conflicts mattered in the seventeenth century because they held substantive implications for the nature of public life in the colonies: Who was to exercise authority, and how they were to exercise it? In that sense, nearly all religious behavior and belief was public to some degree. English colonial society in the seventeenth century largely assumed a close association of political and ecclesiastical interests, a union of church and state. Even the two colonies that practiced some degree of separation and religious tolerance (Rhode Island and Pennsylvania) did so because their founders were seeking to build an ideal Christian society rooted in scriptural teaching. The Bible was integral to how colonials structured their common life.

Nowhere was this more evident than in New England, where a dissatisfaction with Anglicanism was the highest. Free from political constraint, Puritan clerics rid their church buildings and liturgies of anything not warranted from the Bible. More important, they began to refashion the very foundations of church life according to their biblically drawn convictions. This meant a church polity that recognized the autonomy of local churches (congregationalism), abolished clerical hierarchy (episcopacy), and restrained political interference, all of which had the egalitarian effect of placing final authority with the covenanted laity. The justification for this radical remaking of the church was consistently articulated in biblicist terms: so John Cotton's *True Constitution of a Particular Visible Church* (1642; written in 1635), Richard Mather's *Church-Government and Church-Covenant Discussed* (1643); and Thomas Hooker's *Survey of the Summe of Church Discipline* (1648), as well as others. In the words of Cotton: "God has given us to look for no Laws but his word, and no rules or forms of worship, but such as he hath set down in his word."[38]

Preaching among Puritans had already been refashioned in England prior to emigration to the New World. While colonial clergy did not sense the need to revisit the purpose and structure of the sermon, they did raise its public profile. In addition to Sunday sermons, Puritans held conventicles in private home on Sunday to offer the laity a chance to expound on the Bible. Ministers offered mid-week lectures, which became so popular that the General Court briefly attempted to discourage them as an impediment to the economy. Public events also offered the opportunity for exposition: Puritans employed election sermons, fast-day sermons, and sermons for executions, among others. Virtually any and every public gathering became the pretext for preaching. Some have estimated that a typical colonist in New England might have heard 7,000 sermons during a normal lifetime.[39] As noted earlier, many of these sermons went on to be published, sometimes gathered into treatises. By the end of the century, the sermon became the occasion for communal reflection and repentance in a distinctively American way in the form of the "jeremiad," sermons used to point out communal failings. Thus, sermons became the principal instrument for creating a shared understanding of the meaning of the Bible, and for establishing social mores, shaping public opinion, expressing communal anxiety, and negotiating religious and political disputes.[40]

The conditions that led to the founding of many of the colonies also allowed them to reshape political institutions in increasingly radical directions, and once again, it was a desire to return government to a biblical model that motivated much of this experimentation. This can be seen in the Plymouth Colony's Mayflower Compact (1620), John Winthrop's "Modell of Christian Charity" (1630), the two earliest sketches of a colonial Puritan political theory.[41] Almost immediately, Puritan leaders in Massachusetts set out to articulate a more fulsome political theory. From 1635 to 1636, they produced two manuscripts, the "Modell of Church and Civil Power" and "How Far Moses His Judicials Bind Massachusetts." John Cotton contributed his own work to this end, "Modell of Moses His Judicials," published in 1641 as *An Abstract of the Laws of New England.* These documents decisively shaped the first definitive statement of polity, the *Body of Liberties* (1641). No one would have disagreed with John Eliot, who subsequently published *The Christian Commonwealth; or, The Civil Policy of The Rising Kingdom of Jesus Christ* (1659): Christ will have all people "ruled by the Institutions, Laws, and Directions of the Word of God; not only in Church-Government . . . but also in the Government . . . of all affairs in the Commonwealth."[42] For Puritans, the political precepts of the Bible, and as important, the political actions of Israelites recorded in the Old Testament, held precedential authority, not only for establishing institutions and laws but also to justify day-to-day political actions.[43] Over one-half of the early laws of Massachusetts were premised on the Bible, particularly the Mosaic Law (compared to Virginia, which derived 85 percent of its legal statutes from English law).[44]

Those "Bible commonwealths" that dissented from the Massachusetts way, such as Connecticut and New Haven, did so in order to find an even more perfect expression of biblical politics. They were equally convinced, in the words of John Davenport of New Haven (*Discourse about the Civil Government in a New Plantation Whose Design is Religion* [1638/ 1663]), that the "Scriptures do holde forth a perfect rule for the direction and government of all men in all dueties . . . to God and men [in] commonwealths as in matters of the church."[45]

Even in Rhode Island and Pennsylvania, the move to more radically separate politics and religion was generated by biblicist political theory.[46] Their dissent from the Puritans was not about the importance of the Bible for politics, but rather the misinterpretation of that importance by the founders of the Bay colony. As Roger Williams delineated in *The Bloudy Tenent*, the Bible demanded that politics be kept from religion, in order to preserve the purity of the latter, but this did not mean that religion should not influence public life. While thus rejecting the criminalization of religious acts such as blasphemy, Rhode Island's first Code of Law (1647) was nonetheless premised on a biblical justification (found in 1 Tim. 1:9-10), that the ungodly required legal restraint.[47] Decades later, William Penn structured the governance of his new colony according to his reading of Bible politics, in his *Charter of Liberties* and *Frame of Government* (1682).[48]

NOTES

1. See Theodore Dwight Bozeman, *To Live Ancient Lives: The Primitivist Dimension in Puritanism* (Chapel Hill: University of North Carolina Press, 1988), 16, 34, 38; John Spurr, *English Puritanism, 1603–1689* (New York: Palgrave Macmillan, 1998), 175; Sacvan Bercovitch, "The Biblical Basis of the American Myth," in *The Bible and American Arts and Letters*, ed. Giles Gunn (Philadelphia: Fortress Press, 1983), 219–29.
2. On the widespread biblicism of English colonials, see Mark A. Noll, *In the Beginning Was the Word: The Bible in American Public Life, 1492–1783* (New York: Oxford University Press, 2015), 13.
3. Most of the English sectarian groups in the seventeenth century were primitivist at their core (meaning that they sought to remove embellishments of "original" Christianity that had accrued to the traditions and practices of the church over time) in ways more radical than the Puritans themselves. So William Penn's *Primitive Christianity Revived* (1696). See Christopher Hill, *The World Turned Upside Down: Radical Ideas during the English Revolution* (New York: Viking Press, 1972), 21–30.
4. On early Catholic efforts to promote, translate, and regulate the Bible in the New World, see Noll, *In the Beginning Was the Word*, 22–29.
5. David D. Hall, *World of Wonders, Day of Judgment: Popular Religious Belief in Early New England* (Cambridge, Mass.: Harvard University Press, 1989), 22; see also John Morgan, *Godly Learning: Puritan Attitudes towards Reason, Learning, and Education, 1560–1640* (New York: Cambridge University Press, 1986), 25.
6. These figures compare favorably to the literacy rates in Europe, which ranged between 20 percent (France, Scotland) and 33 percent (England). They reflect the already high literacy of those choosing to emigrate, a result of this theologically motivated interest in Bible literacy among dissenters. Since probate documents only pertained to a relatively small part of the population, however, this data also suggests that the majority of those living in the English colonies were not literate. Thus, most inhabitants would have appropriated the Bible primarily through oral means of communication. See Kenneth A. Lockridge, *Literacy in Colonial New England: An Enquiry into the Social Context of Literacy in the Early Modern West* (New York: W. W. Norton, 1974), 13–15, 77, 97; Hugh Amory and David D. Hall, eds., *A History of the Book in America*, vol. 1: *The Colonial Book in the Atlantic World* (Chapel Hill: University of North Carolina Press, 2007), 69.
7. Lawrence A. Cremin, *American Education: The Colonial Experience, 1607–1783* (New York: Harper & Row, 1970), 125–26.
8. Cremin, *American Education*, 125, 181; E. Jennifer Monaghan, *Learning to Read and Write in Colonial America* (Amherst: University of Massachusetts Press, 2005), 24.
9. Monaghan, *Learning to Read and Write*, 81–85. See also Paul L. Ford, ed., *The New-England Primer: A History of Its Origin and Development* (1897; repr., New York: Teachers College Press, 1962).
10. Monaghan, *Learning to Read and Write*, 85.
11. Samuel Eliot Morison, *The Founding of Harvard College* (Cambridge, Mass.: Harvard University Press, 1935), 333.

12. Samuel Eliot Morison, *Harvard College in the Seventeenth Century* (Cambridge, Mass.: Harvard University Press, 1936), 1:89, 141, 195–206. The textbooks known to have been used by students included a broad range of lexicons and grammars, Christian treatises on rabbinic works, Hebrew and Greek testaments (including in one instance Brian Walton's *Polyglot Bible*), and expositional commentaries; see Arthur O. Norton, "Harvard Text-Books and Reference Books of the Seventeenth Century," *Publications of the Colonial Society of Massachusetts, Transactions 1930–1933*, 28 (1935): 28, 75.

13. Morison, *Founding of Harvard College*, 337.

14. Robert H. Pfeiffer, "The Teaching of Hebrew in Colonial America," *Jewish Quarterly Review* 45, no. 4 (1955): 367–68; Morison, *Harvard College in the Seventeenth Century*, 2:580.

15. Franklin B. Dexter, "Early Private Libraries in New England," *Proceedings of the American Antiquarian Society*, n.s., 18 (1907): 135–47; Norman Fiering, "Solomon Stoddard's Library at Harvard in 1664," *Harvard Library Bulletin* 20, no. 3 (1972): 642–60; Julius H. Tuttle, "The Libraries of the Mathers," *Proceedings of the American Antiquarian Society*, n.s., 20 (1911): 273, 280; Jon Butler, "Thomas Teackle's 333 Books: A Great Library on Virginia's Eastern Shore, 1697," *William and Mary Quarterly* 49, no. 3 (1992): 460.

16. E. Brooks Holifield, *Theology in America: Christian Thought from the Age of the Puritans to the Civil War* (New Haven, Conn.: Yale University Press, 2003), 26.

17. Though not published until 1726, these sermons were delivered at the height of Willard's (1640–1707) ministerial career. One might also consider here Samuel Mather's *Figures or Types of the Old Testament* (1683). Educated at Harvard and a minister in New England until 1650, Mather (d. 1671) spent the last two decades of his life in England and Ireland. As a member of the storied Mather clan, his work enjoyed enormous popularity in New England after its publication.

18. See Bozeman, *To Live Ancient Lives*, 139–50.

19. The reasons for the primacy of an Indian-language Bible are partly accidental, due to the restriction of Bible printing in England by royal fiat, and to the fact that Puritans generally embraced the translations at hand, such as the Geneva Bible and the Authorized Version (KJV).

20. Roger Williams's translation work, *A Key into the Language of America* (1643), while largely secular in its purposes, anticipates Eliot's work in using biblical verses and concepts to render native customs and religious beliefs and practices intelligible.

21. Monaghan, *Learning to Read and Write*, 52.

22. Native Americans early on recognized the assimilative threat of literacy; John Winthrop wrote of an early crisis cult phenomenon in which the native deity Hobbamock gave repeated visionary warnings to natives "to forsake English, and not . . . to learn to read." Monaghan, *Learning to Read and Write*, 47.

23. Cotton Mather, "The Negro Christianized. An Essay to Excite and Assist That Good Work, the Instruction of Negro-Servants in Christianity" (Boston: B. Green, 1706), 29. *Electronic Texts in American Studies*, http://digitalcommons.unl.edu/etas/28.

24. Edmund S. Morgan, *The Puritan Family: Essays on Religion and Domestic Relations in Seventeenth-Century New England* (Boston: Boston Public Library, 1944), 67–70; see also Richard A. Bailey, *Race and Redemption in Puritan New England* (New York: Oxford University Press, 2011), 76–79. Africans in the Chesapeake region were similarly catechized through church attendance, even if less insistently; probate documents attest to some conversions, especially on the part of free blacks. Literacy, especially biblical literacy, came to be much more controversial there and was by the end of the seventeenth

century and early eighteenth century explicitly outlawed. See T. H. Breen and Stephen Innes, *"Myne Owne Ground": Race and Freedom on Virginia's Eastern Shore, 1640–1676* (New York: Oxford University Press, 1980), 87.

25. Cremin, *American Education*, 42. After the Bible, Bayly's work was the most frequently enumerated title in probate documents in Virginia; Amory and Hall, *History of the Book in America*, 1:69.

26. Shepard's journal and autobiography can be found in *God's Plot: The Paradoxes of Puritan Piety*, ed. Michael McGiffert (Amherst: University of Massachusetts Press, 1972).

27. Charles E. Hambrick-Stowe, *The Practice of Piety: Puritan Devotional Disciplines in Seventeenth-Century New England* (Chapel Hill: University of North Carolina Press, 1982), 186; see also David S. Shields, "A History of Personal Diary Writing in New England, 1620–1745" (PhD diss., University of Chicago, 1982).

28. Cremin, *American Education*, 130.

29. For the context of American catechizing, see Ian Green, *The Christian's ABC: Catechisms and Catechizing in England, c. 1530–1740* (Oxford: Clarendon Press, 1996).

30. It also figures prominently in two unpublished manuscripts containing poems and prose; see *The Complete Works of Anne Bradstreet*, ed. Joseph R. McElrath and Allan P. Robb (Boston: Twayne Publishers, 1981), 195–225.

31. See *The Poems of Edward Taylor*, ed. Donald E. Stanford (New Haven, Conn.: Yale University Press, 1960), 5, 83.

32. See *The Oxford Handbook of Early American Literature*, ed. Kevin J. Hayes (New York: Oxford University Press, 2008), 143; *The Norton Anthology of American Literature*, vol. A, ed. Nina Baym (New York: W. W. Norton, 2011), 257; Gary L. Ebersole, *Captured by Texts: Puritan to Postmodern Images of Indian Captivity* (Charlottesville: University of Virginia Press, 1995), 15–60.

33. Bradford's history, covering 1630–51, was used by other historians occasionally (e.g., Thomas Prince's *Chronological History* [1736]), but not "discovered" and published in its own right until 1856. Winthrop's journal did not appear in print until 1825, as *The History of New England, 1630–1640*. See Hayes, *Oxford Handbook of Early American Literature*, 93.

34. David D. Hall, *The Antinomian Controversy, 1636–1638: A Documentary History*, 2nd ed. (Durham, N.C.: Duke University Press, 1990), 43–79. The clergy also turned to public sermons to negotiate this conflict: John Wheelwright using his fast-day sermon to argue the Antinomian cause, Thomas Shepard replying on behalf of the establishment clergy in his sermon before the General Court; see Hall, *The Antinomian Controversy*, 152, 173.

35. The earliest account of this appears in John Winthrop's history of the event, *A Short Story of the Rise . . . of the Antinomians* (1644), and Thomas Hutchinson's *History of Massachusetts* (1767), the latter of which includes a more fulsome edition of the court's transcript of Anne's interrogation.

36. See Robert G. Pope, *The Half-Way Covenant: Church Membership in Puritan New England* (Princeton, N.J.: Princeton University Press, 1969), 14.

37. Hall, *World of Wonders*, 62, 64, 269; Noll, *In the Beginning Was the Word*, 138–39.

38. David D. Hall, *A Reforming People: Puritanism and the Transformation of Public Life in New England* (New York: Knopf Doubleday, 2011), 107–15.

39. Noll, *In the Beginning Was the Word*, 115.

40. On Puritan preaching culture, see Harry S. Stout, *The New England Soul: Preaching and Religious Culture in Colonial New England* (New York: Oxford University Press, 1986);

Lisa Gordis, *Opening Scripture: Bible Reading and Interpretive Authority in Puritan New England* (Chicago: University of Chicago Press, 2002); and Sacvan Bercovitch, *The American Jeremiad* (Madison: University of Wisconsin Press, 1978).

41. See Hayes, *Oxford Handbook of Early American Literature*, 100.
42. Hall, *A Reforming People*, 99.
43. Bozeman, *To Live Ancient Lives*, 153–55.
44. Michael Grossberg, *Cambridge History of Law in America* (New York: Cambridge University Press, 2008), 1:325–26.
45. Hall, *A Reforming People*, 100; Noll, *In the Beginning Was the Word*, 118.
46. Noll, *In the Beginning Was the Word*, 126–48.
47. Grossberg, *Cambridge History of Law in America*, 340.
48. Grossberg, *Cambridge History of Law in America*, 347; Noll, *In the Beginning Was the Word*, 145–48.

BIBLIOGRAPHY

Amory, Hugh, and David D. Hall, eds. *A History of the Book in America*, vol. 1: *The Colonial Book in the Atlantic World*. Chapel Hill: University of North Carolina Press, 2007.

Axtell, James. *The School upon a Hill: Education and Society in Colonial New England*. New Haven, Conn.: Yale University Press, 1974.

Bailey, Richard A. *Race and Redemption in Puritan New England*. New York: Oxford University Press, 2011.

Baym, Nina, ed. *The Norton Anthology of American Literature*. Vol. A. New York: W. W. Norton, 2011.

Bercovitch, Sacvan. *The American Jeremiad*. Madison: University of Wisconsin Press, 1978.

——. "The Biblical Basis of the American Myth." In *The Bible and American Arts and Letters*, edited by Giles Gunn, 219–29. Philadelphia: Fortress Press, 1983.

Bradstreet, Anne. *The Complete Works of Anne Bradstreet*. Edited by Joseph R. McElrath Jr. and Allan P. Robb. Boston: Twayne Publishers, 1981.

Breen, T. H., and Stephen Innes. *"Myne Owne Ground": Race and Freedom on Virginia's Eastern Shore, 1640–1676*. New York: Oxford University Press, 1980.

Brown, Matthew P. *The Pilgrim and the Bee: Reading Rituals and Book Culture in Early New England*. Philadelphia: University of Pennsylvania Press, 2007.

Bozeman, Theodore Dwight. *To Live Ancient Lives: The Primitivist Dimension in Puritanism*. Chapel Hill: University of North Carolina Press, 1988.

——. *The Precisionist Strain: Disciplinary Religion and Antinomian Backlash in Puritanism to 1638*. Chapel Hill: University of North Carolina Press, 2004.

Butler, Jon. "Thomas Teackle's 333 Books: A Great Library on Virginia's Eastern Shore, 1697." *William and Mary Quarterly* 49, no. 3 (1992): 449–91.

Cambers, Andrew. *Godly Reading: Print, Manuscript, and Puritanism in England, 1580–1720*. Cambridge: Cambridge University Press, 2011.

Colacurcio, Michael J. *Godly Letters: The Literature of the American Puritans*. Notre Dame, Ind.: University of Notre Dame Press, 2006.

Coolidge, John S. *The Pauline Renaissance in England: Puritanism and the Bible*. Oxford: Clarendon, 1970.

Cremin, Lawrence A. *American Education: The Colonial Experience, 1607–1783*. New York: Harper & Row, 1970.

Dexter, Franklin B. "Early Private Libraries in New England." *Proceedings of the American Antiquarian Society*, n.s., 18 (1907): 135–47.

Ebersole, Gary L. *Captured by Texts: Puritan to Postmodern Images of Indian Captivity*. Charlottesville: University of Virginia Press, 1995.

Fiering, Norman. "Solomon Stoddard's Library at Harvard in 1664." *Harvard Library Bulletin* 20, no. 3 (1972): 255–69.

Ford, Paul L., ed. *The New-England Primer: A History of Its Origin and Development* (1897). Repr. New York: Teachers College Press, 1962.

Gilpin, W. Clark. "The Creation of a New Order: Colonial Education and the Bible." In *The Bible in American Education*, edited by David L. Barr and Nicholas Piediscalzi, 5–23. Philadelphia: Fortress Press, 1982.

Gordis, Lisa M. *Opening Scripture: Bible Reading and Interpretive Authority in Puritan New England*. Chicago: University of Chicago Press, 2002.

Green, Ian. *The Christian's ABC: Catechisms and Catechizing in England, c. 1530–1740*. Oxford: Clarendon Press, 1996.

Grossberg, Michael, and Christopher Tomlins, eds. *The Cambridge History of Law in America*, vol. 1: *Early America (1580–1815)*. New York: Cambridge University Press, 2008.

Hall, David D., ed. *The Antinomian Controversy, 1636–1638: A Documentary History*. 2nd ed. Durham, N.C.: Duke University Press, 1990.

———. *A Reforming People: Puritanism and the Transformation of Public Life in New England*. New York: Knopf Doubleday, 2011.

———. *Worlds of Wonder, Day of Judgment: Popular Religious Belief in Early New England*. Cambridge, Mass.: Harvard University Press, 1989.

Hambrick-Stowe, Charles E. *The Practice of Piety: Puritan Devotional Disciplines in Seventeenth-Century New England*. Chapel Hill: University of North Carolina Press, 1982.

Hayes, Kevin J., ed. *The Oxford Handbook of Early American Literature*. New York: Oxford University Press, 2008.

Hill, Christopher. *The World Turned Upside Down: Radical Ideas during the English Revolution*. New York: Viking Press, 1972.

Holifield, E. Brooks. *Theology in America: Christian Thought from the Age of the Puritans to the Civil War*. New Haven, Conn.: Yale University Press, 2003.

Lockridge, Kenneth A. *Literacy in Colonial New England: An Enquiry into the Social Context of Literacy in the Early Modern West*. New York: Norton, 1974.

Mather, Cotton. "The Negro Christianized. An Essay to Excite and Assist That Good Work, the Instruction of Negro-Servants in Christianity." Boston: B. Green, 1706. *Electronic Texts in American Studies*. http://digitalcommons.unl.edu/etas/28.

Miller, Perry. *The New England Mind: The Seventeenth Century*. Cambridge, Mass.: Harvard University Press, 1954.

Monaghan, E. Jennifer. *Learning to Read and Write in Colonial America*. Amherst: University of Massachusetts Press, 2005.

Morgan, Edmund S. *The Puritan Family: Essays on Religion and Domestic Relations in Seventeenth-Century New England*. Boston: Boston Public Library, 1944.

Morgan, John. *Godly Learning: Puritan Attitudes towards Reason, Learning, and Education, 1560–1640*. New York: Cambridge University Press, 1986.

Morison, Samuel Eliot. *The Founding of Harvard College*. Cambridge, Mass.: Harvard University Press, 1935.

———. *Harvard College in the Seventeenth Century*. Vols. 1 and 2. Cambridge, Mass.: Harvard University Press, 1936.

Noll, Mark A. *In the Beginning Was the Word: The Bible in American Public Life, 1492–1783*. New York: Oxford University Press, 2015.

Norton, Arthur O. "Harvard Text-Books and Reference Books of the Seventeenth Century." *Publications of the Colonial Society of Massachusetts, Transactions 1930–1933*, 28 (1935): 361–438.

Pfeiffer, Robert H. "The Teaching of Hebrew in Colonial America." *Jewish Quarterly Review* 45, no. 4 (1955): 363–73.

Pope, Robert G. *The Half-Way Covenant: Church Membership in Puritan New England*. Princeton, N.J.: Princeton University Press, 1969.

Shepard, Thomas. *God's Plot: The Paradoxes of Puritan Piety, being the Autobiography and Journal of Thomas Shepard*. Edited and introduction by Michael McGiffert. Amherst: University of Massachusetts Press, 1972.

Spurr, John. *English Puritanism, 1603–1689*. New York: Palgrave Macmillan, 1998.

Stout, Harry S. *The New England Soul: Preaching and Religious Culture in Colonial New England*. New York: Oxford University Press, 1986.

Taylor, Edward. *The Poems of Edward Taylor*. Edited by Donald E. Stanford. New Haven, Conn.: Yale University Press, 1960.

Tuttle, Julius H. "The Libraries of the Mathers." *Proceedings of the American Antiquarian Society*, n.s., 20 (1911): 269–356.

CHAPTER 6

BIBLICAL INTERPRETATION IN EIGHTEENTH-CENTURY AMERICA

JAN STIEVERMANN

THE story of the Bible in eighteenth-century British North America is one of continuity with the earlier period but also one of transformations and complications. Across the colonies Protestant churches dominated and, in theory, agreed on the supremacy of scripture. Underneath its near omnipresence in private and public life, however, there were changes at work that rendered the status and meaning of the Bible much more equivocal by the end of the century. In some regards, the interpretation and use of scripture became fundamentally contested. With the erosion of European-style Christendom, the full dynamic of the two Protestant principles of *sola scriptura* and the priesthood of all believers was unleashed, especially in the middle colonies. New challenges arose to the authority of the Bible and its reach over the increasingly differentiated spheres of society. Who could claim the prerogative to decide what the Bible's revelations meant or demanded by what right or light? These issues were raised with great acuteness and unsettling results as British North America became involved in the two, partly intersecting, partly opposing, movements that reconfigured Protestant Christianity across the Atlantic world: the Enlightenment and the evangelical revivals. Moreover, the entanglement of traditional biblicism with the discourses of British imperialism and later Whig republicanism had ambiguous results, as the sacralization of these essentially secular ideologies at least partly pushed the salvific message of scripture into the background.

COLONIAL LITERARY CULTURE AND THE ESTABLISHMENT BIBLE

By 1800, reading competence had become nearly universal among white males, and white women did not lag far behind. For most colonials, education served religious ends; literacy and biblical literacy went together from the beginning. Primers and simple catechisms remained the chief didactic tools. In the decades prior to the Revolution, however, pedagogy became somewhat more independent and secular, as evinced by the increasing use of less Bible-heavy spelling books, such as *The Child's New Play-Thing* (1750) and Noah Webster's *American Spelling Book* (first published in 1783) eventually displacing the famous *New England Primer*, which had first appeared before 1690.[1] Among certain members of the elite, education metamorphosed into a worldly pursuit, aiming to achieve new ideals of polite culture and civility.

The kind of texts the average colonial most frequently encountered were either religious works based on the Bible or, of course, the Bible itself. "No book was read more often or in so many different ways," as David Hall puts it, "privately in silence, aloud in households . . . and in church services as the text for Sunday sermons."[2] Even though many read the Bible for themselves, their understanding of its contents was mediated through general cultural presuppositions, as well as specific confessional and liturgical traditions inscribed in the catechisms, prayer books, psalters, and hymnals that constituted the very heart of religious life. While Anglicans accessed the Bible chiefly through the *Book of Common Prayer*, Congregationalists, Presbyterians, and Baptists largely anchored their interpretative framework in the *Westminster Shorter Catechism* or simpler catechisms based on it. The biblical psalters formed a key component of worship across the spectrum. Beginning in the 1730s, an emerging innovative biblical hymnody also informed how many colonials, especially those adhering to the Reformed traditions, encountered scripture.

To a large degree, people's understanding of the Bible was still governed by official churches, especially where Anglican or Congregational establishments existed. Diverse ethnic demographics, the Enlightenment, and the Great Awakening did significantly further the tendency of laypeople to challenge prescribed interpretations. But at least in New England and the South, the exegetical authority of ecclesial hierarchies and regular clergy, although diminished, survived. Also, despite the increased circulation of "heterodox" texts, most continued to resort to educational and devotional works that aligned with their denominational traditions' understanding of scripture.

The vast majority of purchased or inherited print items in the American colonies were English Bibles and cheaper religious works in the Anglican or dissenting traditions, with more and more of the latter coming from local production. All the steady sellers of American printers belonged to this category, including various editions of the *New England Psalm Book*, the *Hymns* (first published in 1707), and the biblical *Poems* (first published in 1709) of Isaac Watts, as well as various manuals of piety in the Puritan tradition. The prolific publication of sermons was outranked only by newspapers and items printed for colonial administrations, though almanacs, broadsides, chapbooks, and pamphlets also enjoyed wide dissemination.[3] Since clergymen made up a large portion of the educated elite and colonial colleges were all denominational, those who could afford expensive books typically preferred scripture-related products like commentaries or theological treatises. In contrast, the demand for nonreligious books, such as works by Enlightenment philosophers or English novels, remained modest.

Yet the print record also shows a growing religious diversification that rendered the Word more polyphonous. Overwhelmingly, this diversification was an inner-Protestant affair. The small minority of Catholics that clustered in Maryland and Pennsylvania experienced the scriptures mostly in Latin, within liturgical contexts, and mediated through prayer books and devotional manuals, though some Douai Rheims Bibles in vernacular translations did circulate.[4] Torah scrolls and printed Hebrew Bibles, along with Talmudic and other rabbinic literature, were used among the few colonial Jewish congregations.[5]

Much more sizeable was the number of Dutch and especially German Bibles and biblical literature. The more than 100,000 German-speakers who streamed into the middle colonies created a substantial print market. An essential part of building up Lutheran and Reformed churches in the New World was to provide German translations of the Bible and the main expositional and devotional texts of their respective confessional heritage: the Augsburg Confession, Luther's Small Catechism, the Luther or Lobwasser psalters, the Heidelberg Catechism, and the broadly popular works of biblical theology by Johann Arndt (1555-1621). The pietist center at Halle became a main supplier of imported Bibles in Luther's translation with notes by August Hermann Francke (1663-1727).[6]

A significant minority of German immigrants belonged to "sectarian" groups. Chief among the German printers was the radical pietist Johann Christoph Saur (1695-1758), who in 1743 undertook the first printing of the Bible in a European language on American soil. Based on the revised Halle version of Luther's translation (in the 34th edition), it incorporated materials from the *Berleburger Bibel* (1726-42)—the project of a coterie of scholars with mystical and millennialist beliefs looking for the coming of the Philadelphian age of Christian unity—that was widely suppressed in the Holy Roman Empire.[7]

Across ethnolinguistic and theological divides, colonial Protestants thus shared a bibliocentric culture. Whether in the King James Version (KJV) or the Luther translation, the Bible formed the deep structure of their social formation as individuals and the primary framework for interpreting the world. Scriptural exegesis, formal and popular, was the most important medium of social communication within an evolving public sphere. Although political oratory, poetry, tracts, and newspapers were increasingly influential forms of mass appeal, sermons continued to reign supreme.[8] And even these rivaling genres were often drenched in scriptural language.

IMPERIAL ADJUSTMENTS AND PLURALIZATION

The political, religious, and social adjustments initiated by the Glorious Revolution of 1688-89, which saw King James II lose his English throne to William of Orange, also affected the role of the Bible. As the colonies became more integrated into a restructured empire and were drawn into continuous warfare with France and Spain, a communal British identity was forged. Together with a rampant anti-Catholicism, the sense of a united Protestant interest (based on the Toleration Act of 1689 that allowed freedom of worship to dissenters everywhere in the Empire) was critical to this identity.[9] The Bible served as its touchstone. British colonials were continually reminded that the freedom to read the scriptures constituted the essence of their faith and distinguished them from Catholics. From days of fasting and thanksgiving to the mustering of the militia, public exegesis abounded with invocations of British liberty and the Empire's providential destiny to overturn the tyranny of the popish Antichrist. In some of these discourses the salvific Bible almost entirely recedes behind the imperial Bible.

The growing entanglement of colonial Protestantism with "British imperial Christendom" marks a profound irony.[10] While in some ways it enhanced the stature of the scriptures, it simultaneously signaled the fading of the comprehensive biblicism of seventeenth-century Puritanism. The post-1689 adjustments, together with immigration, the growth of trade and other factors, led to the collapse of New England's "Bible commonwealths," which had aimed at a truly biblical version of Christendom, in which every area of social life was to be ordered according to one official and legally enforced interpretation of God's will. Congregationalism lost its ascendancy. New England societies grew more heterogeneous, and important parts of public life, such as the administration, law, and commerce, developed into more autonomous and secularized spheres. A similar, if less dramatic, transformation occurred in the southern colonies. With the exception of Virginia, the Anglican establishments from Maryland to Georgia left considerable room for Protestant dissent. Although, then, the greatest part of British North America had various established denominational traditions, their hold on society as a whole was weakening in the decades before the Revolution.

Meanwhile the mid-Atlantic colonies followed the Rhode Island model. They created commonwealths without any official church and largely managed to extract themselves from British imperialism until the French and Indian War. Especially in Pennsylvania, an unparalleled degree of religious plurality developed.[11] As with Roger Williams and the seventeenth-century Baptists, the "holy experiment" begun by William Penn's Quakers was animated by a Christian primitivism no less intense than that of the Puritans. Only their version of biblicism opposed the very notion of Christendom. It assumed that coercion in matters of faith was a violation of God's will. Christians ought to gather on a strictly voluntary basis, keep a distance from the evils of "the world," and follow Jesus's ethics of nonresistance. This is what Penn argued in, for instance, *The Great Cause of Liberty of Conscience* (1670) and *Primitive Christianity Revived* (1696).[12]

The German Anabaptist and radical pietist groups shared this alternative form of Christian primitivism and sometimes interpreted it even more strictly. For them, the Constantinian turn toward a state-supported church in the fourth century had been the beginning of the Babylonian captivity. The true heirs of the New Testament church were the suffering witnesses of Christ who for centuries had been persecuted by corrupt state churches, whose dogmatic systems and regimes of creedal coercion were distortions of the Gospel faith. Under the threat of imperial warfare, the Mennonites paid tribute to this scriptural ideal when they commissioned the pietists at Ephrata to produce a High German translation of Thieleman J. van Braght's massive martyrology *Der Blutige Schau-Platz oder Martyrer-Spiegel der Tauffs Gesinnten oder Wehrlosen Christen* (1748).[13]

In other ways, too, the German-speaking "sectarians" greatly diversified the theological spectrum, bringing a plethora of apocalyptic and esoteric readings of the Bible into print. Markedly prolific in this respect was the former baker Johann Conrad Beissel (1691-1768), leader of the quasi-monastic Ephrata community that had separated from the Schwarzenau Brethren (Dunkers)—a transplanted community of German *Neutäufer*—over the question of whether the Bible called for celibacy, poverty, and the celebration of the Sabbath on Saturday. Beissel's interpretative range is on display in his posthumously collected *Deliciae Ephratenses* (1773). Heavily influenced by the radical pietist *Marburger Bibel* (1712) of Heinrich Horch and Ludwig Christoph Schefer, these discourses and letters are bursting with intricate allegorical expositions (especially of the Song of Songs and Revelation) informed by millenarianism, a Philadelphian ecclesiology, spiritual perfectionism and Sophia mysticism in the Boehmian tradition, Paracelsian magic, Hermeticism, Rosicrucianism, astrological and alchemical ideas, as well as the Christian Kabbalah.[14]

The middle colonies thus served as a testing ground for the kind of deregulated exegesis that would subsequently characterize much of American Protestantism. Another crucial force of pluralization in the colonies was the British Enlightenment, which among other things facilitated alternative versions of religiosity and a critical scrutiny of the scriptures.

THE ENLIGHTENMENT BIBLE

In the early decades of the eighteenth century, educated colonials responded to the new empiricism, philosophical rationalism, natural theology, and the emerging historical and textual criticism of the Bible in strikingly different ways.[15] Most embraced a conservative, self-declared Christian Enlightenment stance and interpreted these intellectual trends as largely affirmative of their Protestant orthodoxies. Many readily made use of innovative yet popular biblical commentaries by scholars such as Simon Patrick, Matthew Poole, Matthew Henry, and Philip Doddridge that blended guarded consideration of critical issues with pious exposition and application.

In New England, the most famous early exemplar of this conservative Enlightenment is Cotton Mather (1663-1728). Mather started his career with his notorious defense of the Salem Witch Trials, but he also wrote, among many other things, a treatise on the reasonableness of biblical Christianity (drawing heavily on John Locke), attempts to reduce dogmatics to fundamental Protestant maxims, and the first American compendium of natural philosophy, *The Christian Philosopher* (1721).[16] This work epitomizes a prevalent view among the learned clergy that natural theology supported revealed religion. Moreover, Mather left a massive manuscript entitled "Biblia Americana." When he started the project in 1693, he aspired to synthesize "the Treasures of *Illustrations* for the Bible, dispersed in the Volumes of this Age" so "that all the Learning in the World might bee made gloriously subservient unto the *Illustration* of the *Scripture*."[17] At his death in 1728, he had filled more than 4,500 folio pages with annotations and created America's first comprehensive commentary on the Bible, which is only now being published.[18]

One essential goal of the "Biblia" was to improve the KJV in hundreds of places. To this end, Mather not only compared ancient language versions and modern vernacular translations but also consulted rabbinic glosses and the latest works of academic philology. More important, Mather engaged historical critics and skeptical thinkers who, since the mid-seventeenth century, had challenged the *auctoritas scripturae* and traditional modes of interpreting the Bible in various ways. With considerable intellectual breadth and depth, the "Biblia" discusses contested questions regarding the inspiration, composition, transmission, canonization, and historical realism of the biblical texts, as well as the legitimacy of reading the Hebrew scriptures as prophetically, typologically, and mystically prefiguring Christ. Even though he sometimes modified traditional interpretations, Mather ultimately defended the authority, integrity, and infallible truth of the Bible. Always aiming to help readers grow in piety, he sought to reconcile traditional Protestant biblicism with the scientific advancements of the early Enlightenment.

The "Biblia" thus pioneered a highly learned but apologetically oriented type of biblical criticism invested in a new kind of factualist evidentialism, which would later flower among evangelicals. Other colonial scholars followed the same conciliatory approach. Although less erudite and detailed than the "Biblia," Jonathan Edwards's (1703-1758) extensive corpus of biblical interpretations stands out for its theological originality and philosophical sophistication. He creatively fuses Reformed dogmatics with, among other things, elements of British moral philosophy, idealism, and occasionalism.[19] Also noteworthy is Edwards's extension of traditional Puritan typology to the realm of nature, as well as his innovative postmillennialism that incorporated elements of Enlightenment perfectionism, which would become vitally influential in early America.[20]

Other theologians, however, saw the need to reassess critically received understandings of scripture in the light of reason in order to arrive at a truly "enlightened" Christianity. Latitudinarian Anglicans and even some heirs of Puritanism increasingly felt at odds with Calvinist dogmas and basic Christian teachings. In Boston, renowned educators and clergymen such as Charles Chauncy (1705-1787) and Jonathan Mayhew (1720-1766) rejected Nicean Trinitarianism and argued instead that scripture taught the unity of the Deity and Christ's subordination to God the Father. These proto-liberals also repudiated double predestination, accenting the moral goodness of God and his desire to save all.[21] They branded the imputation of sin and man's total depravity as irrational, immoral, and unbiblical. With these new views of God and human natural ability came a changed understanding of Christ's salvific role as the means for humanity's moral regeneration rather than a substitutional atonement for its sins. Toward the end of his career, Chauncy revived the ancient teaching of *apokatastasis panton* in his work *The Mystery Hid from Ages and Generations* (1784), maintaining that God "will have all men to be saved, and to come unto the knowledge of the truth" (1 Tim. 2:4), either in this life or the next.

Still others found themselves propelled by the dynamics of Enlightenment thought to move beyond the boundary of biblical Christianity altogether. This trajectory was, for the most part, charted by English deism, which supplanted supernatural Christianity with natural religion. Deists posited an impersonal and non-intervening creator, and they were skeptical of prophecy, miracles, bodily resurrection, as well as the incarnation and redemption of Christ. Most deists, however, retained some concept of an afterlife and transcendent justice. The will of the deity was expressed in the universal natural and moral laws that controlled the created order and the course of history, as embodied most purely in the ethics of the historical Jesus. In the deistic view, early followers of Christ and power-hungry priests corrupted these laws and mixed them with superstition and falsehood. Nature was the true Bible, and, illuminated by reason and science, it ought to serve as a corrective to the claims of revealed religion.

One of the first propagators of deist ideas in America was Benjamin Franklin (1706-1790). Franklin might have maintained good relations with most churches, but in his writings he equated the essence of religion with virtue and demonstrated an entirely pragmatic, if not irreverent, approach to the Bible that made reason the ultimate arbiter of its usefulness. Despite its fairly small following and low level of institutionalization (some clubs and Masonic lodges), deism gained a disproportionate influence in the second half of the eighteenth century. It set many of the terms in wider debates about the Bible, Christian teachings, and church-state relations. Crucially, deism informed the outlook and to a certain extent the agenda of many of the political leaders of the American Revolution and architects of the nascent government of the United States.[22]

There was a considerable range of deistic thought. The epitome of the moderate, church-going deist was George Washington. By contrast, Thomas Jefferson (1743-1826) had less patience with traditional Christian religion and was more eager to jettison outdated myths and practices. His skepticism is attested by the famous "Jefferson Bible," an anti-supernaturalist compilation of Christ's life and teachings from the synoptic Gospels that tellingly ends with Matthew 27:60: They "rolled a great stone to the door of the sepulcher, and departed." After the Revolution, Thomas Paine (1737-1809) provoked a storm of rejoinders to his *The Age of Reason* (1794-95), in which he denied "that the Almighty ever did communicate anything to man, by mode of speech, in any kind of language, or by any kind of vision" and decried traditional Christianity as "a fable, which, for absurdity and extravagance is not exceeded by anything that is to be found in the mythology of the ancients."[23] American deists thus mounted a principled contestation of the supernatural authority of the Bible, just as they called into question the exegetical prerogative of clerical elites and the legitimacy of state churches.

THE EVANGELICAL BIBLE

The revivals that swept the colonies during the middle decades of the eighteenth century further contributed to the crumbling of European-style church establishments. This happened, however, under the banner of "the Bible alone." In many ways, the so-called Great Awakening was a revitalization of radical biblicism against the perceived trends of social and intellectual secularization. It was not exactly the biblicism of seventeenth-century Puritanism, though. The experiential hermeneutics propagated and practiced by revivalists caused a momentous individualization as well as democratization of the scriptures. While most early evangelicals were committed to the doctrinal heritage of post-Reformation Protestantism, they stressed an affection-centered conversionist theology (making John 3:3, "Except a man be born again, he cannot see the kingdom of God," their watchword) that hinged on the personal appropriation of the Gospel truths. This prioritization of the personal Bible, however, did not necessarily mean opposition to the imperial Bible. A case in point is Jonathan Edwards, who, especially in his apocalyptical speculations, sounded the trumpet of British exceptionalism.

Along with Puritanism and Continental pietism, Enlightenment thought had a strong influence on evangelical hermeneutics. Its early theological advocates, such as Cotton Mather or Jonathan Edwards, responded to the problems raised by historical-contextual criticism and the distance it put between the scriptural texts and modern exegetes. Eighteenth-century evangelicals, as the biblical scholar Hans Frei has argued, began to create something like an alternative, subjective paradigm of biblical realism that foregrounded the existentially experienced realness of the Word.[24] They thus harnessed empiricism but at the same time circumscribed the boundaries of natural knowledge without God's supernatural revelation and guidance.

A paradigmatic expression of this approach to the Bible can be found in Jonathan Edwards's *A Divine and Supernatural Light* (1734). The sermon distinguishes between normal and spiritual or saving knowledge. While the former is mediated through natural human faculties, the latter is received in confrontation with scriptural revelations. Here God is "not making use of any intermediate natural causes, as he does in obtaining other knowledge." Through illumination by "the gracious distinguishing influence and revelation of the Spirit," God opens up new ways of inwardly understanding and feeling what had been only superficially known before.[25] Having the Word come alive in such a way marked the initiation into a redeeming faith in and intimate relationship with Christ. Albeit to different degrees, revivalists expected the new birth to be a highly emotional event, in which people would live through the whole gamut of Christian experience scripted out in the Bible, ranging from contrition and despair over one's sins to ecstatic delight in God's divine excellency.

At the heart of the Great Awakening and the conflicts surrounding it—was the sharp separation that evangelicals made between their genuine Bible faith and the unbelief or merely nominal Christianity of the larger population. In drawing that line experience and practical piety trumped status and education. As Jonathan Edwards pointed out, Jesus's disciples had been "a company of poor fishermen, illiterate men, and persons of low education." They "attained to the knowledge of the truth; while the Scribes and Pharisees, men of vastly higher advantages, and greater knowledge and sagacity in other matters, remained in ignorance."[26] Although Edwards himself remained committed to learned exposition, there emerged in this period a populist style of revivalist preaching that primarily aimed at a plain but authentic and affective communication of the Gospel message, stressing that all were equally in danger of eternal damnation unless they experienced gracious regeneration in Christ.

Reaching tens of thousands during his whirlwind tours of the colonies (1739–41) that catalyzed the Awakening, George Whitefield (1714–1770) was the master of this affective style. He turned his sermons into dramatic improvisations centered on select scriptural citations, and he performed his sermons in churches and open fields alike. Revivalist preaching also attracted groups hitherto neglected by colonial clergy. Following the lead of such successful preachers as Whitefield, other evangelicals started to spread successfully the Gospel message among African American slaves and revived the flagging Indian missions.[27]

In his spiritual memoir, the black Methodist minister John Marrant (1755–1791) describes his life-changing encounter with Whitefield in Savannah in 1768. He was pushing through the crowd, Marrant writes, "just as Mr. Whitefield was naming his text, and looking round, and, as I thought, directly upon me, and pointing with his finger, he uttered these words, "PREPARE TO MEET THY GOD, O ISRAEL." By the agency of the Spirit, "The Lord accompanied these words with such power, that I was struck to the ground, and lay both speechless and senseless near half an hour." Afterward, the simple quote from Amos 4:12 unlocked to Marrant the whole Gospel truth, and "every word I heard from the minister was like a parcel of swords thrust into me." As Marrant recovers and Whitefield repeatedly prays with him, personal illumination of the Bible leads to joyous conversion, prompting him to devote his life to knowing the Word ("I now read the Scriptures very much") and spreading it first among the Cherokees and then African Americans.[28]

Although his life was exceptional in many ways, Marrant illustrates how the evangelical Bible could empower ordinary and marginalized people by providing not only hope and comfort but also a new sense of self-worth and even spiritual authority. Recent scholarship on the evolution of black Baptists and Methodists and the "Indian Great Awakening" has demonstrated this potential, as well as studies of early evangelical women such as Sarah

Osborn (1714-1796), who by virtue of their piety could rise to positions of informal leadership.[29] Evangelical biblicism also worked to lower denominational bars, diminish the importance of confessional traditions, and undermine support for comprehensive church establishments. As Mark Noll has argued, the "reliance on a personal, existential Bible undercut the patriarchal, ecclesiastical, clerical features of traditional Christendom indirectly and almost inadvertently."[30]

The inadvertent nature of this transformation must be emphasized, for early evangelical leaders were generally focused on deploying scripture to save souls, not reforming the existing order of things. Much more so than with the Puritans, religion was perceived as inward and private. The new emphasis on spiritual equality in Christ usually did not translate into resistance against outward inequality or injustice, even in its most drastic forms. George Whitefield and John Wesley (1703-1791) showed considerable concern for the souls of transplanted Africans and decried their neglect and mistreatment. But they still accepted the institution of slavery and stressed that conversion would make servants more obedient to their masters, if those masters treated them with Christian charity. While some, like Wesley, concluded that "human trafficking" was unscriptural and sought to end the slave trade (following the example of earlier New England theologians like Cotton Mather), an all-out antislavery stance was exceptional among early evangelicals.

Before the Revolution, it was reformist Quakers who led the budding abolitionist cause. In *Some Considerations on the Keeping of Negroes* (1754), the influential itinerant Quaker preacher and writer John Woolman (1720-1772) declared the teachings of Christ to be irreconcilable with slavery, and his friend Anthony Benezet (1713-1784) of Philadelphia formed America's first abolitionist society in 1775.[31] Nevertheless, it was evangelical Protestantism that proved most attractive to blacks. They soon wrested scripture from the hands of their white tutors, directly applying to their lives what would become the biblical leitmotifs of African American theology, such as the exodus from Egypt and the Gospel affirmations that God made all nations "of one blood" (Acts 17:26) and in Christ "there is neither bond nor free" (Gal. 3:28).[32]

Opposition against the revivals in New England and the South had to do with theological differences as much as with fears of ecclesial and social upheaval. In his famous anti-revivalist work *Seasonable Thoughts* (1743), Charles Chauncy chastised the revivalists' arrogance for splitting congregations and whole denominations by discrediting the authority of colleagues who allegedly taught the Bible from mere "head knowledge" and not the internal testimony of the Spirit. Chauncy was thinking here of men like Gilbert Tennent whose *The Danger of an Unconverted Ministry* (1740) stimulated the rift between pro- and anti-revivalist factions within Presbyterianism, or, even worse, itinerant preachers like James Davenport, who seduced congregations from their regular ministers and riled them up against the standing order. The biggest scandal, however, were the self-appointed lay exhorters, who claimed their authority directly from God. Even "*young Persons*," "*Women and Girls*; yea, *Negroes*, have taken upon themselves to do the business of *Preachers*."[33] For Chauncy and the more traditional "Old Light" party in New England Congregationalism, but also for most Anglican ministers in the South, the unbridled emotionalism and enthusiasm of the awakenings disturbed the peace. To claim that the Bible could only really be accessed by fancied supernatural illumination was dangerous. God's will should be explained by educated experts, but everyone could follow it by natural reason.

Recalcitrant lay people and enthusiasm also worried moderate "New Lights" and other generally pro-revivalist ministers. In many a local awakening, attendees would transgress the fine line from experiencing personal illumination to claiming spiritual gifts and revelations. Scholars of the "radical Awakening" have unearthed many reports of phenomena such as hearing divine voices, prophetic foresights, visions of hell, demons, angels, or spiritual journeys to heaven or the New Jerusalem.[34] Some of these revelations exceeded (even if they were rooted in) the canonical texts. In response, champions of orthodoxy like Jonathan Edwards asserted a strictly cessationist position, confining revelation to the closed canon present and available in the Bible. The middle colonies were a particular hot spot for radical groups whose "scripturizing impulse" anticipates subsequent American religious movements like the Shakers or Mormons.[35] Conrad Beissel at Ephrata, for instance, prided himself in having received elaborate visions from God and communicating with spirits and angels.

Significantly, the first rebellion against Congregational establishments in New England was carried forward by evangelical Baptists animated by an intense biblical primitivism. In the 1740s and 1750s, more than a hundred Congregational communities separated from the standing order to create voluntary gatherings of true believers. Testimony of the new birth was made the decisive qualification and lay leaders were often chosen over ordained clergymen. In most cases, these "Separates" came to embrace believer's baptism. A well-known example is Isaac Backus (1724-1806), an untutored farmer from Connecticut who experienced conversion during the height of the Great Awakening in 1741. Backus was called as a preacher to a separatist community in Middleborough, Massachusetts, and in 1751 led part of his congregation to adopt Baptist principles. During the revolutionary period Backus became a champion of the disestablishment movement to separate the church from the state. Backus wrote an elaborate scriptural case supporting his view in his *Government and Liberty Described and Ecclesiastical Tyranny Exposed* (1778). When evangelical Baptists, together with revival-sympathetic Presbyterians, spread to the South, they pushed in the name of the Bible to overthrow the institutionalized Anglican regime there.

THE REVOLUTIONARY BIBLE

Religion undoubtedly played a significant role in the American Revolution. People on both sides and in-between turned to the Bible to define and defend their positions, and to find higher meaning in the turmoil. The flood of sermons and tracts from the period abound with examples of ministers and lay people genuinely searching the Bible for divine guidance. More often, they employed scriptural tropes and narratives to represent their political arguments in a sacred light.[36]

While affiliations cut across denominational lines, members of the dissenting traditions gravitated toward the "Patriots." This is not altogether surprising, given the history of these churches and the Calvinist notion of a divine right of resistance. In the two decades preceding the Revolution, Congregationalist and Presbyterian ministers helped mobilize opposition to the British Crown by justifying resistance to ungodly rulers with scripture. Their sermons increasingly conjoined their theological tradition with the discourse of Whig republicanism, routinely invoking Old Testament examples and parallels such as the

Exodus to highlight themes of liberty and condemn tyranny.[37] Along with the memories of the Puritan Revolution, some also invoked the seventeenth-century tradition of "Hebrew Republicanism" that found especially in Judges and Samuel examples for an original, divinely ordained commonwealth government.[38]

Scholars still debate the specific influence of revivalism on the coming of the Revolution.[39] The intercolonial public sphere with its scriptural framework of reference that the Awakening helped to create was certainly one prerequisite. Also, some of its anti-authoritarian spirit connected with the lay appropriation of the Bible undoubtedly carried over into the political arena. Evangelical ministers, however, were not more involved than their liberal colleagues. And the revolutionary leaders, of course, were mostly deists.

One of the earliest invocations of the duty to resist tyrants came from the Boston minister and political activist Jonathan Mayhew, who delivered his *Discourse Concerning Unlimited Submission* at the one-hundredth anniversary of the beheading of Charles I in 1649. Engaging with those New Testament passages, especially 1 Peter 2:13-14 and Romans 13:1-7, that seemed to demand submission to worldly governments, Mayhew argued that Paul taught obedience only "to such rulers as he himself describes; i.e. such as rule for the good of society." But "Common tyrants, and public oppressors, are not intitled to obedience from their subjects."[40] In the final instance, "We ought to obey God rather than men" (Acts 5:29). Mayhew set an important precedent by finding in the Bible the idea of government by consensus that could and should be revoked if mutual obligations were violated. He also associated the mounting threat of British tyranny with Catholic principles and the forces of the Antichrist himself.

During the pre-revolutionary crisis, anti-Catholic aggression, recently inflamed by the French and Indian War, became redirected at the British Crown. The "Bishop Scare" (the widespread fear that an Anglican bishop for the colonies would be installed) and the 1774 Quebec Act that granted free practice to Catholics in British Canada were taken as evidence that the American colonies could quickly be drowned in a sea of popery.

As protest turned into fighting, sermons and tracts increasingly amalgamated apocalypticism with notions of liberty and progress.[41] The Book of Revelation was taken as a prophetically coded script adumbrating current events. In Samuel Sherwood's (1730-1783) *The Church's Flight into the Wilderness* (1776), King George III characteristically appears as the final manifestation of the Beast, and the "design of the dragon" is "to erect a scheme of absolute despotism . . . and involve all mankind in slavery and bondage." America had become a refuge for the persecuted true church, seeking to realize "that liberty and freedom which the Son of God came from heaven to procure for, and bestow on them." By God's providence, the Patriots would prevail. America was destined to be "a great and flourishing empire," where "unadulterated Christianity, liberty and peace" would thrive together.[42]

In his bestselling pamphlet *Common Sense* (1776), Thomas Paine laced his natural rights arguments with biblical references. From this convergence developed a discourse of Christian republicanism and civic millennialism that would become foundational for America's future civil religion. It transferred the inherited Puritan language of covenantalism first to the revolutionaries and then to the new nation. A prime expression is found in the pioneering biblical poetry of the Connecticut Wits. The festive "rising glory" poems such as David Humphrey's *On the Happiness of America* (1786) propagate an eschatologically inflected proto-nationalism in biblical imagery. And Timothy Dwight's American epic in eleven books of heroic couplets, *The Conquest of Canaan* (1785) is an extended allegory, comparing Joshua's conquest of the promised land with the nation's struggle for independence under Washington.[43]

Loyalists, of course, saw all of this as a willful twisting of scripture and cited chapter and verse for just the opposite stance. One of the most prominent anti-revolutionary ministers was the rector of New York's Anglican Trinity Church, Charles Inglis (1734-1816). In discourses such as *The Duty of Honouring the King* (1780), preached on the day of *"the Anniversary of the Martyrdom of King Charles*,*"* he admonished his audience that Paul's words made it clear that "the powers that be are ordained of God" and "whosoever therefore resisteth the power, resisteth the ordinance of God" (Rom. 13:1-2). Republicanism was an aberration from the divine order, for scripture revealed that God established monarchy as the only proper form of government.

Many in the middle of the country's struggle for independence also voiced concerns with violating God's will for government. Not a few American Lutherans, for instance, were seriously conflicted during the Revolution. While his son Johann Peter Gabriel became a general in the Continental Army, Heinrich Melchior Mühlenberg (1711-1787), the patriarch of American Lutheranism, wrestled with the vexing question of how, during an ongoing power struggle between two regimes, one can know which side was ordained of God. Although Mühlenberg harbored sympathies with the American cause, he could not convince himself that the Bible allowed for pro-active rebellion against a rightful king, and he assumed a public posture of neutrality. In a diary entry from 1777, he arrived at the conclusion that a "Christian People will act most safely in this dangerous crisis if they adhere to God's word and proceed a posteriori according to Romans 13."[44] Many members of the Quakers and German pacifist churches could not follow Mühlenberg's pragmatism when it came to supporting the militia. For them the war became a real test of their faith, as they interpreted Christ's command of nonresistance, as formulated in the Sermon on the Mount (Matt. 5:39-48), to forbid not just direct participation but even commutation fees. Perceiving this as treason, Patriots ostracized and heavily punished Quakers, Mennonites, Dunkers, and Moravians. To the pacifist churches, the patriot Bible was as much a distortion as the imperial Bible.[45]

The Revolution must therefore also be understood as a theological crisis that, like the emerging debate over slavery, demonstrated the pliability of scripture on the most fundamental political and social issues. Moreover, the scripture-saturated rhetoric of American Christian republicanism did not necessarily imply an unequivocal assertion of the Bible's abiding supremacy. One might argue that, as before with British imperialism, the Bible was being pressed into the service of an essentially secular ideology of democratic government, freedom, and pursuit of worldly happiness.

In some ways, the post-revolutionary religious order certainly represents a triumph of the Bible-against Christendom tradition. It must be remembered, however, that disestablishment in the South and on the national level was achieved by the unlikely coalition of revivalist dissenters and deists. The two had quite different visions of the nation's future and the role of Christianity therein. Federalist-leaning evangelicals dreamed of a true Bible civilization based on a voluntary transformation of society by scriptural principles. Jeffersonians and others, however, hoped to build a society based on Enlightenment ideals of tolerance and civic virtue, in which specific beliefs about scripture ought to be a matter of private opinion. People would be protected not only from violations of their religious freedom but also guaranteed a freedom from religion, that is, shielded from any demands that churches might make on them in the name of the Bible. This basic ambiguity in the religious make-up of the United States, together with the proliferation of multiple versions of scripture and the centripetal forces of deregulated, popular exegesis, would profoundly shape the future of the Bible in American culture.[46]

Notes

1. E. Jennifer Monaghan, *Learning to Read and Write in Colonial America* (Amherst: University of Massachusetts Press, 2005).
2. David D. Hall, "Readers and Writers in Early New England," in *A History of the Book in America: The Colonial Book in the Atlantic World*, ed. Hugh Armory and David D. Hall (New York: Cambridge University Press, 2000), 1:117–52, 123.
3. Hugh Armory, "Appendix 1. A Note on Statistics," in *A History of the Book in America*, 1:504–19.
4. In 1790 the Irish Catholic printer Mathew Carey produced a small edition of the Catholic Douai Rheims Bible in English translation. See James Hennesey, *American Catholics: A History of the Roman Catholic Community in the United States* (New York: Oxford University Press, 1981), 83.
5. Jonathan D. Sarna, "Colonial Judaism," in *The Cambridge History of Religions in America*, vol. 1: *Pre-Columbian Times to 1790*, ed. Stephen J. Stein (Cambridge: Cambridge University Press, 2012), 392–409.
6. A. Gregg Roeber, "German and Dutch Books and Printing," in *A History of the Book in America*, 1:298–313.
7. See Douglas H. Shantz, *An Introduction to German Pietism: Protestant Renewal at the Dawn of Modern Europe* (Baltimore, Md.: Johns Hopkins University Press, 2013), 204–36; Stephen L. Longenecker, *The Christoph Sauers: Courageous Printers Who Defended Religious Freedom in Early America* (Elgin, Ill.: Brethren Press, 1981), 52–55.
8. On the growing importance of secular forms of writing, see David. S. Shields, *Civil Tongues and Polite Letters in British America* (Chapel Hill: University of North Carolina Press, 1997); and Michael Warner, *The Letters of the Republic: Publication and the Public Sphere in Eighteenth-Century America* (Cambridge, Mass.: Harvard University Press, 1992). For the abiding centrality of sermonic literature, see Harry S. Stout, *The New England Soul: Preaching and Religious Culture in Colonial New England* (New York: Oxford University Press, 1986).
9. Thomas S. Kidd, *The Protestant Interest: New England after Puritanism* (New Haven, Conn.: Yale University Press, 2004).
10. Mark A. Noll, *In the Beginning Was the Word: The Bible in American Public Life, 1492–1783* (New York: Oxford University Press, 2015), 15.
11. Sally Schwartz, *'A Mixed Multitude': The Struggle for Toleration in Colonial Pennsylvania* (New York: New York University Press, 1988).
12. Melvin Endy, *William Penn and Early Quakerism* (Princeton, N.J.: Princeton University Press, 1973).
13. Richard MacMaster, *Land, Piety, Peoplehood: The Establishment of Mennonite Communities in America, 1683–1790* (Scottdale, Pa.: Herald Press, 1985), esp. 229–48; David L. Weaver-Zercher, *Martyrs Mirror: A Social History* (Baltimore, Md.: Johns Hopkins University Press, 2016), esp. 123–46.

14. See Jeff Bach, *Voices of the Turtledove: The Sacred World of Ephrata* (University Park, Pa.: Penn State University Press, 2003), esp. 25–47.

15. For an excellent survey of the theologies of the American Enlightenment, see E. Brooks Holifield, *Theology in America: Christian Thought from the Age of the Puritans to the Civil War* (New Haven, Conn.: Yale University Press, 2003), 79–255.

16. See Mather's *Reasonable Religion* (Boston, 1700) and *The Stone Cut Out of the Mountain* (Boston, 1716).

17. *The Diary of Cotton Mather*, ed. W. C. Ford, Collections of the Massachusetts Historical Society, 7th series, vols. 7 and 8 (Boston, 1911–1912), 1:169–70.

18. *Biblia Americana: America's First Bible Commentary. A Synoptic Commentary on the Old and New Testaments,* 10 vols., ed. Reiner Smolinski and Jan Stievermann (Tübingen/ Grand Rapids, Mich.: Mohr Siebeck/Baker Academic, 2010–). The *Biblia* is examined from diverse angles in Jan Stievermann, *Prophecy, Piety, and the Problem of Historicity: Interpreting the Hebrew Scriptures in Cotton Mather's Biblia Americana* (Tübingen: Mohr Siebeck, 2016).

19. See Robert E. Brown, *Jonathan Edwards and the Bible* (Bloomington: Indiana University Press, 2002); and Douglas A. Sweeney, *Edwards the Exegete: Biblical Interpretation and Anglo-Protestant Culture on the Edge of the Enlightenment* (New York: Oxford University Press, 2015).

20. Sang Huyn Lee, ed., *The Princeton Companion to Jonathan Edwards* (Princeton, N.J.: Princeton University Press, 2005) and Stephen J. Stein, ed., *The Cambridge Companion to Jonathan Edwards* (New York: Cambridge University Press, 2007) provide helpful access to the vast literature on Edwards. For the development of millennialism in colonial theology, see Reiner Smolinski, "Apocalypticism in Colonial North America," in *Encyclopedia of Apocalypticism*, vol. 3: *Apocalypticism in the Modern Period and the Contemporary Age*, ed. Stephen J. Stein (New York: Continuum, 1998), 36–72.

21. See Charles Chauncy's *The Benevolence of the Deity* (Boston, 1784).

22. David L. Holmes, *The Faiths of the Founding Fathers* (New York: Oxford University Press, 2006), esp. 39–51.

23. Thomas Paine, *The Age of Reason*, ed. Philip S. Foner (Secaucus, N.J.: Citadel Press, 1974), 55.

24. Hans W. Frei, *The Eclipse of Biblical Narrative: A Study in Eighteenth and Nineteenth-Century Hermeneutics* (New Haven, Conn.: Yale University Press, 1974), esp. 152–54.

25. Jonathan Edwards, *Sermons and Discourses, 1730–1733*, in *The Works of Jonathan Edwards*, ed. Mark Valeri (New Haven, Conn.: Yale University Press, 1999), 17:409.

26. Jonathan Edwards, *Sermons and Discourses*, 17:409.

27. A helpful synthesis of the expansive scholarship on the colonial revivals is provided by Thomas S. Kidd, *The Great Awakening: The Roots of Evangelical Christianity in Colonial America* (New Haven, Conn.: Yale University Press, 2007).

28. [W. William Aldridge], *A Narrative of the Lord's Wonderful Dealings with John Marrant, A Black*, 4th ed. (London, 1785), 11–13.

29. See, for instance, Albert J. Raboteau, "The Black Experience in American Evangelicalism," in *African American Religion: Interpretative Essays in History and Culture*, ed. Timothy E. Fulop and Albert J. Raboteau (New York: Routledge, 1997), 89–106; Catherine A. Berkus, *Sarah Osborn's World: The Rise of Evangelical Christianity in Early America* (New Haven, Conn.: Yale University Press, 2013); Linford D. Fisher, *The Indian Great Awakening: Religion and the Shaping of Native Cultures in Early America* (New York: Oxford University Press, 2012).

30. Noll, *In the Beginning*, 195.

31. David Brion Davis, *The Problem of Slavery in the Age of Revolution, 1770–1823*, 2nd ed. (New York: Oxford University Press, 1999).

32. Sylvia R. Frey and Betty Wood, *Come Shouting to Zion: African American Protestantism in the American South and British Caribbean to 1830* (Chapel Hill: University of North Carolina Press, 1998), esp. chaps. 4–5; Albert J. Raboteau, *Canaan Land: A Religious History of African Americans* (New York: Oxford University Press, 1999), esp. chaps. 1–3.

33. Charles Chauncy, *Seasonable Thoughts on the State of Religion in New England* (Boston, 1743), 22.

34. Douglas L. Winiarski, "Souls Filled with Ravishing Transport: Heavenly Visions and the Radical Awakening in New England, 1742," *William and Mary Quarterly* 61 (2004): 3–46.

35. See Stephen J. Stein, "America's Bibles: Canon, Commentary, and Community," *Church History* 64 (1995): 169–84.

36. James P. Byrd, *Sacred Scripture, Sacred War: The Bible and the American Revolution* (New York: Oxford University Press, 2013); James B. Bell, *A War of Religion: Dissenters, Anglicans, and the American Revolution* (New York: Palgrave Macmillan, 2008).

37. See part II of Mark A. Noll, *America's God: From Jonathan Edwards to Abraham Lincoln* (New York: Oxford University Press, 2002); and James H. Hutson, *Religion and the New Republic: Faith in the Founding of America* (Lanham, Md.: Rowman & Littlefield, 2000), esp. 37–48.

38. Eric Nelson, "Hebraism and the Republican Turn of 1776: A Contemporary Account of the Debate over Common Sense," *William and Mary Quarterly* 70 (October 2013): 781–812; Eran Shalev, *American Zion: The Old Testament as a Political Text from the Revolution to the Civil War* (New Haven, Conn.: Yale University Press, 2013).

39. Alan Heimert, *Religion and the American Mind, from the Great Awakening to the Revolution* (Cambridge, Mass.: Harvard University Press, 1966); Jon Butler, "Enthusiasm Described and Decried: The Great Awakening as Interpretative Fiction," *Journal of American History* 69, no. 2 (1982): 305–25; Kidd, *The Great Awakening*, 288–307.

40. Jonathan Mayhew, *Discourse Concerning Unlimited Submission and Non-Resistance to the Higher Powers* (Boston, 1750), 28–29.

41. See Nathan O. Hatch, *The Sacred Cause of Liberty: Republican Thought and the Millennium in Revolutionary New England* (New Haven, Conn.: Yale University Press, 1977); Ruth H. Bloch, *Visionary Republic: Millennial Themes in American Thought, 1756–1800* (Cambridge: Cambridge University Press, 1985).

42. Samuel Sherwood, *The Church's Flight into the Wilderness* (New York, 1776), 17–19.

43. William C. Dowling, *Poetry and Ideology in Revolutionary Connecticut* (Athens: University of Georgia Press, 1990); Michael T. Gilmore, "The Literature of the Revolutionary and Early National Period," in *The Cambridge History of American Literature*, vol. 1: *1590–1820*, ed. Sacvan Bercovitch (Cambridge: Cambridge University Press, 1994).

44. *The Journals of Henry Melchior Mühlenberg*, 3 vols., ed. Theodore G. Tappert and John W. Doberstein (Philadelphia: Evangelical Lutheran Ministerium, 1942–1957), 3:55–56.

45. See Jan Stievermann, "Defining the Limits of American Liberty: Pennsylvania's German Peace Churches during the Revolution," in *A Peculiar Mixture: German-Language Culture and Identities in Eighteenth-Century North America*, ed. Jan Stievermann and Oliver Scheiding (University Park, Pa.: Penn State University Press, 2013), 207–45.

46. See Hutson, *Religion and the New Republic*, 49–114; the essays in Donald L. Dreisbach and Mark David Hall, eds., *Faith and the Founders of the American Republic* (New York: Oxford

University Press, 2014); Jonathan Den Hartog, *Patriotism and Piety: Federalist Politics and Religious Struggle in the New American Nation* (Charlottesville: University of Virginia Press, 2015).

Bibliography

Amory, Hugh, and David D. Hall, eds. *A History of the Book in America*, vol. 1: *The Colonial Book in the Atlantic World*. New York: Cambridge University Press, 2000.

Arndt, Johann, and Johann Christoph Hartwig. *Des hocherleuchteten Theologi, Herrn Johann Arndts*. Philadelphia: Benjamin Fräncklin and Johann Böhm, 1751.

Bach, Jeff. *Voices of the Turtledove: The Sacred World of Ephrata*. University Park, Pa.: Penn State University Press, 2003.

Bell, James B. A. *War of Religion: Dissenters, Anglicans, and the American Revolution*. New York: Palgrave Macmillan, 2008.

Biblia: das ist: Die ganze göttliche Heilige Schrift Alten und Neuen Testaments, nach der deutschen Uebersetzung d. Martin Luthers (1743). Repr. Germantown: Christoph Saur, 1776.

Bloch, Ruth H. *Visionary Republic: Millennial Themes in American Thought, 1756–1800*. Cambridge: Cambridge University Press, 1985.

Brekus, Catherine A. *Sarah Osborn's World: The Rise of Evangelical Christianity in Early America*. New Haven, Conn.: Yale University Press, 2013.

Brown, Robert E. *Jonathan Edwards and the Bible*. Bloomington: Indiana University Press, 2002.

Butler, Jon. "Enthusiasm Described and Decried: The Great Awakening as Interpretative Fiction." *Journal of American History* 69, no. 2 (1982): 305–25.

Byrd, James P. *Sacred Scripture, Sacred War: The Bible and the American Revolution*. New York: Oxford University Press, 2013.

Chauncy, Charles. *Seasonable Thoughts on the State of Religion in New England*. Boston: Rogers and Fowle, 1743.

Cooper, Mary. *The Child's New Play-Thing: Being a Spelling Book Intended to Make the Learning to Read a Diversion instead of a Task* (1743). Repr. Boston: J. Draper, 1750.

Davis, David Brion. *The Problem of Slavery in the Age of Revolution, 1770–1823*. 2nd ed. New York: Oxford University Press, 1999.

Den Hartog, Jonathan. *Patriotism and Piety: Federalist Politics and Religious Struggle in the New American Nation*. Charlottesville: University of Virginia Press, 2015.

Doddridge, Philip. *The Family Expositor; or, A Paraphrase and Version of the New Testament with Critical Notes and a Practical Improvement of Each Section*. 6 vols. London: John Wilson, 1739–1756.

Dowling, William C. *Poetry and Ideology in Revolutionary Connecticut*. Athens: University of Georgia Press, 1990.

Dreisbach, Donald L., and Mark David Hall, eds. *Faith and the Founders of the American Republic*. New York: Oxford University Press, 2014.

Edwards, Jonathan. *The Works of Jonathan Edwards*, vol. 17: *Sermons and Discourses, 1730–1733*. Edited by Mark Valeri. New Haven, Conn.: Yale University Press, 1999.

Endy, Melvin. *William Penn and Early Quakerism*. Princeton, N.J.: Princeton University Press, 1973.

Fisher, Linford D. *The Indian Great Awakening: Religion and the Shaping of Native Cultures in Early America*. New York: Oxford University Press, 2012.

Frei, Hans W. *The Eclipse of Biblical Narrative: A Study in Eighteenth and Nineteenth-Century Hermeneutics*. New Haven, Conn.: Yale University Press, 1974.

Frey, Sylvia R., and Betty Wood. *Come Shouting to Zion: African American Protestantism in the American South and British Caribbean to 1830*. Chapel Hill: University of North Carolina Press, 1998.

Fulop, Timothy E., and Albert J. Raboteau, eds. *African American Religion: Interpretative Essays in History and Culture*. New York: Routledge, 1997.

Gilmore, Michael T. "The Literature of the Revolutionary and Early National Period." In *The Cambridge History of American Literature*, vol. 1: *1590–1820*, edited by Sacvan Bercovitch, 539–693. Cambridge: Cambridge University Press, 1994.

Hatch, Nathan O. *The Sacred Cause of Liberty: Republican Thought and the Millennium in Revolutionary New England*. New Haven, Conn.: Yale University Press, 1977.

Heimert, Alan. *Religion and the American Mind: From the Great Awakening to the Revolution*. Cambridge, Mass.: Harvard University Press, 1966.

Hennesey, James. *American Catholics: A History of the Roman Catholic Community in the United States*. New York: Oxford University Press, 1981.

Henry, Matthew. *An Exposition of all the Books of the Old and New Testaments*. 6 vols. London, 1708–1710.

Holifield, E. Brooks. *Theology in America: Christian Thought from the Age of the Puritans to the Civil War*. New Haven, Conn.: Yale University Press, 2003.

Holmes, David L. *The Faiths of the Founding Fathers*. New York: Oxford University Press, 2006.

Hutson, James H. *Religion and the New Republic: Faith in the Founding of America*. Lanham, Md.: Rowman & Littlefield, 2000.

Jefferson, Thomas. *The Jefferson Bible, or The Life and Morals of Jesus of Nazareth, Extracted Textually from the Gospels in Greek, Latin, French, and English*. Washington, D.C.: Smithsonian Edition, 2011.

Kidd, Thomas S. *The Great Awakening: The Roots of Evangelical Christianity in Colonial America*. New Haven, Conn.: Yale University Press, 2007.

———. *The Protestant Interest: New England after Puritanism*. New Haven, Conn.: Yale University Press, 2004.

Lee, Sang Huyn, ed. *The Princeton Companion to Jonathan Edwards*. Princeton, N.J.: Princeton University Press, 2005.

Longenecker, Stephen L. *The Christoph Sauers: Courageous Printers Who Defended Religious Freedom in Early America*. Elgin, Ill.: Brethren Press, 1981.

MacMaster, Richard. *Land, Piety, Peoplehood: The Establishment of Mennonite Communities in America, 1683–1790*. Scottdale, Pa.: Herald Press, 1985.

Mather, Cotton. *Biblia Americana: America's First Bible Commentary. A Synoptic Commentary on the Old and New Testaments*. 10 vols. General editors Reiner Smolinski and Jan Stievermann. Tübingen/Grand Rapids, Mich.: Mohr Siebeck/Baker Academic, 2010–.

———. *The Christian Philosopher*. Edited by Winton U. Solberg. Urbana: University of Illinois Press, 1994.

———. *The Diary of Cotton Mather*. 2 vols. Edited by W. C. Ford. Collections of the Massachusetts Historical Society, 7th series, vols. 7 and 8. Boston: Massachusetts Historical Society, 1911–1912.

Mayhew, Jonathan. *Discourse Concerning Unlimited Submission and Non-Resistance to the Higher Powers*. Boston, 1750.

Monaghan, E. Jennifer. *Learning to Read and Write in Colonial America*. Amherst: University of Massachusetts Press, 2005.

Mühlenberg, Heinrich Melchior. *The Journals of Henry Melchior Mühlenberg*. 3 vols. Edited by Theodore G. Tappert and John W. Doberstein. Philadelphia: Evangelical Lutheran Ministerium, 1942–1957.

Nelson, Eric. "Hebraism and the Republican Turn of 1776: A Contemporary Account of the Debate over Common Sense." *William and Mary Quarterly* 70 (October 2013): 781–812.

Noll, Mark A. *America's God: From Jonathan Edwards to Abraham Lincoln*. New York: Oxford University Press, 2002.

———. *In the Beginning Was the Word: The Bible in American Public Life, 1492–1783*. New York: Oxford University Press, 2015.

Paine, Thomas. *The Age of Reason*. Edited by Philip S. Foner. Secaucus, N.J.: Citadel Press, 1974.

Patrick, Simon. *A Commentary upon the Historical Books of the Old Testament*. 3rd ed. 2 vols. London, 1727.

Poole, Matthew. *Annotations upon the Holy Bible*. 2 vols. London, 1683–1685.

Raboteau, Albert J. *Canaan Land: A Religious History of African Americans*. New York: Oxford University Press, 1999.

Schwartz, Sally. *'A Mixed Multitude': The Struggle for Toleration in Colonial Pennsylvania*. New York: New York University Press, 1988.

Shalev, Eran. *American Zion: The Old Testament as a Political Text from the Revolution to the Civil War*. New Haven, Conn.: Yale University Press, 2013.

Shantz, Douglas H. *An Introduction to German Pietism: Protestant Renewal at the Dawn of Modern Europe*. Baltimore, Md.: Johns Hopkins University Press, 2013.

Shields, David S. *Civil Tongues and Polite Letters in British America*. Chapel Hill: University of North Carolina Press, 1997.

Smolinski, Reiner. "Apocalypticism in Colonial North America." In *Encyclopedia of Apocalypticism*, vol. 3: *Apocalypticism in the Modern Period and the Contemporary Age*, edited by Stephen J. Stein, 36–72. New York: Continuum, 1998.

Stein, Stephen J. "America's Bibles: Canon, Commentary, and Community." *Church History* 64 (1995): 169–84.

———, ed. *The Cambridge Companion to Jonathan Edwards*. New York: Cambridge University Press, 2007.

———, ed. *The Cambridge History of Religions in America*, vol. 1: *Pre-Columbian Times to 1790*. Cambridge: Cambridge University Press, 2012.

Stievermann, Jan. "Defining the Limits of American Liberty: Pennsylvania's German Peace Churches during the Revolution." In *A Peculiar Mixture: German-Language Culture and Identities in Eighteenth-Century North America*, edited by Jan Stievermann and Oliver Scheiding, 207–45. University Park, Pa.: Penn State University Press, 2013.

———. *Prophecy, Piety, and the Problem of Historicity: Interpreting the Hebrew Scriptures in Cotton Mather's Biblia Americana*. Tübingen: Mohr Siebeck, 2016.

Stout, Harry S. *The New England Soul: Preaching and Religious Culture in Colonial New England*. New York: Oxford University Press, 1986.

Sweeney, Douglas A. *Edwards the Exegete: Biblical Interpretation and Anglo-Protestant Culture on the Edge of the Enlightenment*. New York: Oxford University Press, 2015.

Warner, Michael. *The Letters of the Republic: Publication and the Public Sphere in Eighteenth-Century America*. Cambridge, Mass.: Harvard University Press, 1992.

Watts, Isaac. *Horæ lyricæ. Poems chiefly of the lyric kind*. London, 1706.

———. *Hymns and spiritual Songs. In three Books*. London, 1707.

Weaver-Zercher, David L. *Martyrs Mirror: A Social History.* Baltimore: Johns Hopkins University Press, 2016.

Webster, Noah. [*American Spelling Book*]. *A Grammatical Institute, of the English Language, Part I.* Hartford, Conn.: Hudson & Goodwin, 1783.

Winiarski, Douglas L. "Souls Filled with Ravishing Transport: Heavenly Visions and the Radical Awakening in New England, 1742." *William and Mary Quarterly*, 3rd ser., 61, no. 1 (January 2004): 3–46.

CHAPTER 7

....

NINETEENTH-CENTURY AMERICAN BIBLICAL INTERPRETATION

....

MARK A. NOLL

INTO the middle decades of the nineteenth century, American interpretations of individual biblical passages ranged widely, but the basis for almost all of them remained a traditional Protestant belief in the Bible as divine revelation. Alongside that belief cultural values as shaped by the successful struggle for national independence provided a strikingly important context for interpretation.

FROM THE FOUNDING TO THE CIVIL WAR

....

Thomas Paine's incendiary tract, *The Age of Reason; Being an Investigation of True and Fabulous Theology*, published in 1794, precipitated the first widespread controversy over biblical criticism. As his era's most effective polemicist, Paine less than two decades earlier in his immensely popular *Common Sense* had convinced colonists that monarchy itself meant nothing but tyranny, and by so doing had pushed Americans decisively toward independence. Now in 1794 he took up what he called a logical second step: "Soon after I published the pamphlet, *Common Sense*, in America, I saw the exceeding probability that a Revolution in the System of Government, would be followed by a revolution in the system of religion." Paine attacked deference to scripture with the same passion he had attacked subservience to George III: "Whenever we read the obscene stories, the voluptuous debaucheries, the cruel and tortuous executions, the unrelenting vindictiveness, with which more than half the Bible is filled, it would be more consistent that we called it the word of a demon than the word of God."[1]

If Paine's appeal for independence from traditional views of scripture shared the passion of his proposal for independence from Britain, the American response could not have been more different. Immediately a flood of counterarguments poured from the new country's presses to demonstrate how disastrously Paine's arguments would poison the spiritual and political health of the nation. Even more significantly, in what amounted to an indirect rebuttal, self-sacrificing Methodist itinerants and energetic Baptist lay preachers were putting scripture to use effectively for conversion, church organization, and renovating lives. For every individual won over by Paine, thousands more were reaffirming their confidence in the Bible as truth-telling and life-transforming.

The social situation of the 1790s, when Americans sought moral stability in the face of nearly comprehensive cultural chaos, provided the backdrop for responses to Paine's radicalism. The United States, which had thrown off inherited church establishments, encompassed a huge, lightly civilized geographical domain. The new nation had also embraced a republican vision of political life that identified virtue in the population at large as the sole guarantor of religious and civil liberty. Even as an energetic force of preachers, revivalists, and lay believers found spiritual renewal in scriptural teaching, so too did they look to the Bible for the personal virtue required for a healthy republican society.

As they did so, citizens reflected the nation's deep commitment to liberal values (in the nineteenth-century sense of the term, "liberalism" meant a heightened commitment to notions of freedom, individual rights, and democracy). In practice, the American commitment to liberalism took shape in voluntary associations organized to accomplish educational, religious, social, and political goals. It turned to philanthropy as the prime means for funding voluntary organizations. And it favored middle-class ideals of propriety that grew out of, while also promoting, widespread ideals of respectability. The influence of these values meant that American biblical interpretation would be shaped by popular leaders, institutions that won the trust and captured the wealth of broad constituencies, and influential media, whether elite or popular, that were likewise able to secure the funding and exercise the popular appeal required for broad social acceptance.

To the extent that formal learning influenced biblical interpretation, the dominant intellectual principles came from the Scottish Common Sense philosophy. Early in the eighteenth century, Francis Hutcheson had taught that reliable ethical reasoning could be based on careful introspection of an individual's own innate sense of moral appropriateness. Later in the century, Thomas Reid answered the philosophical skepticism of David Hume by arguing that ordinary experience required humans to take for granted the existence of an external world, as well as real connections between causes and effects. Reasoning from Hutcheson and Reid seemed friendly to theism; it could be used by traditional Christians to support belief in God, but without the need to rely on traditional authorities like established churches or the ancient universities. Leading teachers in the United States rushed to exploit these ideas as the basis for higher learning in the new nation's colleges and theological seminaries. Even more, these common sense principles bolstered the self-confidence of lay exhorters, preachers, and organizers.

A second flurry of agitation over new critical views took place in the 1830s and 1840s. A generation earlier, faculty at the nation's theological seminaries began traveling to the continent for advanced study. They returned with much greater technical competence but also with first-hand knowledge of the advanced European learning that challenged traditional views of the Bible as simply the Word of God.

Yet despite that exposure to advanced European thought, doubts about the divine character of scripture did not gain a substantial American foothold. In 1846 George Noyes, a learned Massachusetts Unitarian, announced that "it is idle to pretend that we have a right to study the Old Testament critically, unless we have a right to judge of its contents according to the laws of critical and historical investigation."[2] Yet Americans barely noticed the critical proposals that Noyes and a few others advanced. As succinctly summarized by historian Jerry Wayne Brown, "The strangest feature of American critical biblical studies in this early period is the fact that they vanished so quickly and made so little impact on the development of American religion."[3]

In a landmark survey of American religion published in 1844, Robert Baird explained why the great majority of what he called the nation's "evangelical" churches could cooperate in so many activities. For Baird it was not only the common trust in scripture inherited from the Protestant Reformation. It was also an approach to the Bible that reflected belief in the intellectual capacity of ordinary readers, fear about relying on external authorities, and trust in the ability of ordinary citizens to interpret scripture for themselves: American Protestants, he wrote, "hold the supremacy of the scriptures as a rule of faith, and that whatever doctrine can be proved from holy scripture without tradition is to be received unhesitatingly, and that nothing that cannot so be proved shall be deemed as an essential point of Christian belief."[4] Baird's generalization explains much about national patterns of biblical interpretation in large part because the churches he regarded as "evangelical" (Methodist, Baptist, Presbyterian, Congregational, Episcopalian, and Restorationist) accounted for more than four-fifths of the country's houses of worship—and because organized religious groups exerted more influence by far on national values than any other center of intellectual influence.

ANTEBELLUM BIBLICAL INTERPRETATIONS

Ongoing near unanimity concerning what the Bible was in itself and could do for society by no means guaranteed unanimity in biblical interpretation. To be sure, patterns of interpretation that had been traditional continued to enjoy a wide influence. Methodists surged during the early history of the United States because of the all-out dedication of the itinerants recruited by Bishop Francis Asbury and because of the message that fueled their surge. It featured biblical interpretations that had become standard in the evangelical revivals of the eighteenth century. Asbury's own preaching reflected this inheritance as it returned relentlessly to passages about personal redemption that he applied with great effect to the existential situations of his hearers—like Luke 19:10 ("For the Son of man is come to seek and to save that which was lost") and 2 Corinthians 6:2 ("For he saith, I have heard thee in a time accepted, and in the day of salvation have I succoured thee: behold now is the accepted time; behold, now is the day of salvation").[5]

Biblical teaching for a wide range of other subjects relied just as much on traditional usage. When in the early 1840s the Presbyterian stalwart J. H. Thornwell polemicized against Catholic treatment of the apocryphal books as scripture, he drew on long-standing Protestant conventions by basing his case on the New Testament record that "Jesus Christ and his Apostles approved of."[6] A different kind of traditional usage also remained important in nineteenth-century America. Passages that had long sustained Bible believers in acute distress continued to provide the same support for the new nation's downtrodden. In an 1817 speech, Jacob Oson, an African-American lay catechist and educator in New Haven, Connecticut, spoke of blacks as "being in a strange land, and in captivity" awaiting

God's deliverance through another Exodus. Oson also attacked the notion seeping in from Europe that Africans constituted a distinctly inferior species by citing the Genesis account of Adam's creation and the Apostle Paul's declaration that God had made "of one blood" all people of the earth (Acts 17:26).[7]

Yet if these historical usages continued to shape interpretation, so also did newer American circumstances. Not surprisingly, connections between biblical interpretations and the new nation's cultural values loomed as most obvious for religious movements that arose in early United States history. Restorationists—groups who were interested in returning the church to its pure New Testament character—were by no means unique, but the boldness of their preaching made cultural-interpretive connections especially prominent. Early leaders of this movement included Thomas Campbell and his son Alexander, who arrived as immigrants from Scotland and Northern Ireland in the first decade of the century. In the Old World, the Campbells had already proclaimed their dedication to scripture, but they had also absorbed the epistemology of John Locke (including a stress on "simple ideas"), the principles of Scottish Common Sense philosophy (including commitment to inductive scientific method), and the anti-tradition stance of Scottish evangelicals James and Robert Haldane (including a profession to live by the Bible as their only guide).

In the New World, the Campbells' devotion to scripture and the elaboration of their interpretive principles proved unusually attractive to Americans moving westward beyond the Appalachian Mountains. For the purpose of restoring the primitive, nonsectarian faith of the Book of Acts, the Campbells deliberately dispensed with the historical Christian creeds, they ridiculed systems of doctrine like Calvinism as mere philosophical speculation, and they denounced traditional rites like infant baptism as simply unbiblical. According to Thomas Campbell's landmark "Declaration and Address" of 1809, authentic Christianity should be characterized by "returning to, and holding fast by, the original standard; taking the divine word alone for our rule; the Holy Spirit for our teacher and guide, to lead us into all truth; and Christ alone, as exhibited in the word, for our salvation."[8] Two decades later, Alexander Campbell expanded upon that foundation by affirming, "I have endeavored to read the Scriptures as though no one had read them before me."[9]

The ways in which distinctly American values informed the Restorationist use of scripture were shared to one degree or another by most of the era's Christian movements. They certainly played a role in the popularity gained by the novel biblical interpretations of William Miller, a Baptist layman from Low Hampton, New York. When Miller's intensive study of apocalyptic passages in the King James translation led him to conclude that Christ would come again in 1843, and when enterprising publicists broadcast these findings in pamphlets and detailed charts, thousands of Americans were convinced. Joseph Smith's 1830 publication of *The Book of Mormon* as a text from God that he was able to translate with divine assistance led to a successful new church instead of the disappointment experienced by Millerites. Yet as with Miller, Smith's credibility was bolstered by cultural values taking for granted the religious capacities of common men, as well as the corruption of religious authority handed down from the past. The important difference was that Smith promoted not a new and definite interpretation of scripture, but a new and definitive scripture.

Similar connections between cultural values and specific interpretations also characterized the work of the era's most highly regarded theologians. In 1819 a landmark sermon by William Ellery Channing spelled out the position of American Unitarians, buttressed by detailed exegesis to support his claim that "the doctrine of the Trinity . . . subverts in effect, the unity of God." In traditional Protestant fashion, Channing based his conclusions on what he called "doctrines . . . clearly taught in the Scriptures [that] we receive without reserve or exception." But as Channing set out what he felt the Bible taught, he did so with conventions indebted to republican political theory and common sense moral philosophy: "We cannot bow before a being, however great and powerful, who governs tyrannically . . . . [Traditional Calvinism shocks] the fundamental principle of morality, and by exhibiting a severe and partial Deity . . . tends strongly to pervert the moral faculty."[10]

A similar combination of implicit trust in both scripture and liberal, common sense conventions tinged the work of Moses Stuart, the nation's antebellum leader in technical biblical scholarship. In 1835 he explained why the Apostle Paul in the Epistle to the Romans did not teach the doctrine of imputation that theologians in his Calvinist tradition had long affirmed (this doctrine saw God as imputing to all subsequent humans the effects of Adam's sin in the Garden of Eden, and likewise imputing to all believers divine grace won through Christ's death and resurrection). According to Stuart, theologians had been misled by their own "philosophizing" and "the speculations of eighteen centuries" that had distorted "the simple facts as stated by the Apostle Paul." Yet as Stuart read those facts, he moved away from Pauline assertions to presuppositions distinctly of his era: "It is in opposition to the immutable principles of our moral nature, to predicate sin in its proper sense of any being that acts without free choice and knowledge of rule."[11]

The era's most respected conservative, Presbyterian Charles Hodge of Princeton Theological Seminary, was quick to critique his peers when he felt that they bent biblical truth to winds of modern thought. Yet Hodge too could rely on common sense intuitions when they suited his purposes. In 1874, after he had published a tract critiquing Darwin for abandoning basic human convictions about purpose in nature, an appreciative Methodist applauded Hodge for appealing repeatedly "to our 'intuitions' as the conclusive stronghold against his materialist opponents." But then the reviewer wanted to know why Hodge in his Calvinism so resolutely resisted "the intuitive pronouncements" that this reviewer saw as so strongly supporting anti-Calvinist Arminianism "against the view presented by [Hodge] of the Divine government."[12]

As central as the Bible remained for theological questions and in the churches, it eventually came to mean almost as much for the nation as a whole. When in the early 1830s slavery emerged as the focus of intense national debate, the question of scriptural interpretation moved front and center. In a national culture where the Word of God enjoyed an exalted place, spokespersons scrambled to enlist scripture as support for their contradictory positions in this hyper-contentious debate.

During the late eighteenth century, the tendency of biblical interpretation had moved steadily against justifications for slavery. In the early nineteenth century, such general biblical arguments received significant reinforcement. Daniel Coker, a colleague of Richard Allen in the early leadership of the African Methodist Episcopal Church, issued one of the most sophisticated renditions of such sentiments in *A Dialogue between a Virginian and an African Minister* (1810). Coker's text was Genesis 17:13 with God's command to Abraham that he circumcise his slaves. To Coker, this command meant that all the blessings of being in covenant with God, symbolized by circumcision, accrued to Abraham's slaves. Therefore, the children of the circumcised had to count simply as Israelites, whom under Mosaic law could not be enslaved. By analogy, when in Christ slaves became adopted children of God, they and their children could never be counted as the "aliens" whom ancient Israel held in bondage.

In 1816, George Bourne's *The Book and Slavery Irreconcilable* offered one of the period's most extensive biblical attacks against the institution. Bourne placed especially heavy emphasis on the biblical prohibition against "man-stealing" (1 Tim. 1:10, along with similar references) as ruling out any exploitation of kidnapped Africans, no matter how many generations removed from the first man-stealing. He also rang the changes on the overarching themes of scripture, including application of the Golden Rule, that in his view made it impossible for Bible believers to hold slaves.

Throughout the rest of the Protestant world at this time—England, Scotland, the Netherlands, British North America, the rest of the continent—very few public voices spoke up to justify slavery. It was different in the United States. From the first widespread contentions over the morality of slavery, its defenders had eagerly turned to the Bible. Already by the 1770s, the main features were fixed in what would become the standard scriptural defense: Leviticus 25 provided for Israel to enslave "the heathen that are round about you" (25:44); Abraham and other Old Testament worthies owned slaves; many other passages in the Pentateuch offered regulations on how to deal with slaves; Jesus revised many teachings from the Old Testament but said not a word against slavery; the Apostle Paul sent a fugitive slave, Onesimus, back to his master Philemon; and the same apostle with several variations told "servants [to] obey in all things your masters according to the flesh; not with eye service, as men pleasers; but in singleness of heart, fearing God" (Col. 3:22).

As soon in the 1830s as agitation over slavery heated up, the biblical defense resurfaced, and with great effect. Some of its effectiveness came from overstatements by abolitionists, like the wildly inaccurate claim that the renowned Henry Ward Beecher of Brooklyn's Plymouth Church made on the eve of the Civil War: "Where the Bible has been in the household, and read without hindrance by parents and children together—there you have had . . . a government that would not have a slave or a serf in the field."[13] More came when those who denounced slavery as incompatible with the general principles of scriptural teachings stumbled in explaining why so many biblical passages took slavery for granted. Most influential was the clarity with which advocates for slavery set forth their case. In 1860, a Virginia Baptist, Thornton Stringfellow, reminded readers "that the subject in dispute is, whether involuntary and hereditary slavery was ever lawful in the sight of God, the Bible being judge." Then followed ten statements beginning "I have shown" that summarized Stringfellow's extensive exegesis of passages from both Testaments that stipulated regulations and duties for slaves or that accepted slavery as a given.[14]

As much as abolitionist overreach and the ability of pro-slavery advocates to quote chapter and verse strengthened the anti-abolitionist cause, hermeneutical conventions that functioned more powerfully in the United States than anywhere else in the world also played their part: democratic empowerment of ordinary people able to read the Bible for themselves, distrust of biblical interpretations from intellectual authorities, and common sense confidence that one's own reading of experience represented universally valid truths.

In debates over slavery, two additional assumptions came into play. First, pervasive white racism made it impossible for most who took part in these disputes to recognize, as one exasperated abolitionist wrote in 1851, that although "the apostles teaching and practice sanctioned slavery, it sanctioned the *slavery of the age* . . . N.B. THIS SLAVERY WAS WHITE SLAVERY . . . the large portion of those enslaved were *as white, and many of them whiter than their masters.*"[15] Identifying the slavery of scripture with race-specific American slavery involved an interpretive leap that all too many made all too easily.

Second was the nation's instinctive liberalism, which foreign observers like Alexis de Tocqueville detailed extensively in his *Democracy in America* (1835, 1840). Although racial prejudice was not a necessary aspect of liberalism, yet liberal values contributed to the fact that the United States was the last major Western nation to permit legalized slavery, and that it practiced systematic forms of racial discrimination longer than most Western countries. Why? Because the racist attitudes that supported first slavery and then segregation rested on popular assumptions about African American inferiority; because voluntary philanthropic forces were not strong enough to overcome broad popular support for slavery and then segregation; and because the nation's free market economy depended on slaves for production of cash crops and on ownership of slaves as the greatest single repository of national wealth. In other words, until the Union armies forced the abolition of slavery, no aristocratic or top-down or anti-democratic forces—no voluntary or philanthropic mobilizations powerful enough—could overcome democratic support for systematic racism and the republican fear of Big Government over-riding local authority.

In the Wake of the Civil War

The third coming of biblical criticism—after Tom Paine and the New England flurry of the 1830s and 1840s—occurred in the 1870s. This one permanently transformed American attitudes toward scripture, which in turn led to significant alterations in biblical interpretation. Assumptions that took for granted the interpretive rights of ordinary readers (democratic empowerment) did not recede, but alongside these assumptions more Americans seemed willing to accept the intellectual authority of scholars credentialed by their university status. Even more important—and with major impact on biblical interpretation—"science" defined as systematic investigation of the natural world increasingly took the place of "science" defined in common sense terms as the systematic observation of one's own intuitions. At the forefront stood the growing acceptance of evolution as a model for all historical development. Along with these tectonic cultural shifts, American biblical interpretation was also being transformed by changes in who counted as "American."

Although Protestant men of British background remained without question the country's dominant religious figures, Catholics led Jews, skeptics, and demographic minorities in asserting their rights as worthy interpreters of scripture. During the Civil War, Catholic newspapers boldly challenged Protestant conventions about the Bible's centrality in American experience. Baltimore's *Catholic Mirror*, for example, called Henry Ward Beecher and Theodore Parker "sensation preachers" who, having "substituted a quasi-Christian code for the immutable laws laid down by the Saviour . . . [,] blasphemously demand an anti-slavery Bible, and an anti-slavery God!" The paper's judgment was harsh: "They are like the plagues of the locusts" responsible for "in great part, the evils that have fallen upon us."[16]

Although Jews were not yet as visible, the fact that Abraham Lincoln enjoyed personal contact and friendship with a large number of Jews spoke of their broadening public presence. In some synagogues the designated Sabbath reading for the day Lincoln died came from Ezekiel's vision of the Valley of the Dry Bones; that vision immediately became a lament for the fallen president. American national purpose phrased in terms of Jewish biblical interpretation continued in heartfelt obsequies for the fallen president, as when a Republican activist Lewis Naphtali Dembitz proclaimed to his Beth Israel Synagogue in Louisville that "of all the Israelites throughout the United States, there was none who more thoroughly filled the ideal of what a true descendant of Abraham ought to be than Abraham Lincoln."[17] Rising recognition for Jewish scholars and increasing protests by Jewish leaders about government support for the King James Bible also increased Jewish visibility on issues concerning scripture.

From another angle, the career of Robert G. Ingersoll also showed how much had changed since Thomas Paine published *The Age of Reason*. In 1879 Ingersoll brought out *Some Mistakes of Moses*, which offered a wider public the gist of speeches he had been delivering as one of the nation's most highly regarded orators. Its advocacy of what Eric Brandt and Timothy Larsen have called "the dethroning of biblical authority" generated considerable opposition, but nothing like the intellectual stone wall and social ostracization that had greeted Paine when he disparaged the Old Testament.[18]

Still more competition came from voices that had long been marginalized in the public use of scripture. In 1876 Julia Smith Parker of Connecticut offered to the public a translation of the Bible that she had accomplished entirely by herself—in large part because she was irritated at how local men had quoted scripture to shut her up. Not long thereafter Elizabeth Cady Stanton and other leading suffragettes published *The Woman's Bible*, a mixed-genre combination of scripture and commentary that advocated the reinterpretation of scriptural texts they believed had worked harm for women. In 1899 Henry McNeal Turner, a bishop of the African Methodist Episcopal Church, appealed for an entire new translation, because, in his view, "the white man" had "colored the Bible in his translation to suit the white man, and made it, in many respects, objectionable to the Negro. And until a company of learned black men shall rise up and retranslate the Bible, it will not be wholly acceptable and in keeping with the higher conceptions of the black man . . . . We need a new translation of the Bible for colored churches."[19]

Among Protestants, biblical criticism steadily gained traction from the mid-1870s, propelled in part by several well-publicized controversies. In 1875 the conservative Free Church of Scotland tied itself in knots when its rising academic star, William Robertson Smith, provided the article on "The Bible" in a new edition of the *Encyclopedia Britannica*. Many Americans noticed that the Scot boldly appropriated German critical theories while trying to hold them together with a still traditional understanding of Christian theology. In 1878 the geologist Alexander Winchell was dismissed from Vanderbilt University for claiming that an intellectually responsible interpretation of the early chapters of Genesis required harmonization with modern theories of evolution. The next year Crawford Toy lost his post as an Old Testament professor at Louisville's Southern Baptist Seminary for promoting a moderate version of German higher criticism.

An address by Charles Briggs at New York's Union Seminary in September 1876 probably signaled the change in critical climate most clearly. The 35-year-old Briggs had enjoyed an excellent education at the University of Virginia, Union Seminary itself, and the University of Berlin before serving briefly as a Presbyterian pastor and then returning to Union as a professor. In Berlin under Isaac August Dorner, Briggs deepened a commitment to disciplined pursuit of Bible-related facts, but he also exchanged the static epistemology of Scottish Common Sense philosophy for an evolutionary conception of ancient history that viewed the Bible as subject to what Dorner described as ordinary historical development. In the years that followed, Briggs remained evangelical, with enduring belief in a God who acted supernaturally to bring about conversion and sustain personal growth in grace. But he had also become a liberal or historicist evangelical who interpreted both God's direction of Israel and his saving work in the present as occurring within evolutionary processes of historical change.

In his 1876 address Briggs contended that Bible believers needed to take up the necessary technical homework required to grasp accurately how the scriptures had been composed. Most important, in carrying out such studies, "we have nothing to do with traditional views or dogmatic opinions." Then Briggs explained exactly what the new scholarship required: "Whatever may have been the prevailing views of the church with reference to the Pentateuch, Psalter, or any other book of Scripture, they will not deter the conscientious exegete an instant from accepting and teaching the results of a historical and critical study of the writings themselves."[20]

After Briggs's address was published in *The Presbyterian Quarterly and Princeton Review* in January 1877, the next issue contained a response by the traditionalist William Henry Green of Princeton Seminary who chastised those who "attacked" the "perpetual authority of the Old Testament" from "within" the Protestant churches, supposedly "in the interests of Christianity itself."[21] Within a half-decade, controversy over biblical criticism engulfed the Presbyterians. Within two decades Briggs had been censured by his denomination for teaching unacceptable views and was forced out of the Presbyterian ministry. By that time Congregationalists, Episcopalians, Methodists, and even some Baptists, who were the least inclined to the innovations of biblical higher criticism, were embroiled in internal debates on the character of scripture, the appropriateness of using modern biblical criticism, and the effects on ordinary Bible readers of the new critical views.

For biblical interpretation, the result was, first, to undermine notions of biblical inerrancy. These critical positions also led some highly visible academics to reinterpret the miracle stories of scripture, to reorient hope for salvation toward immanent processes in history, and to regard the Bible itself as inspiration for ongoing human development rather than a fixed, changeless Word of God for all time.

For American biblical interpretation, however, domestic political, social, economic, and racial developments exerted as much influence as did new scholarship from abroad or high-level debates within theological schools. Among these developments the legacy of antebellum controversy over slavery had the greatest impact.

Hermeneutical assumptions before the Civil War dictated that the Bible be interpreted through common sense popularly understood and that it must stand open to democratic apprehension by all. Yet heated debates over whether scripture permitted slavery had raised fundamental concerns about the overall purposes of scripture and the appropriate ways of guiding Christian life by biblical standards. Antebellum Americans had looked to scripture for a determinative word on slavery, but the strongest defenders of the authority of scripture had delivered cacophony.

In the aftermath of the conflict, many of those who could not accept a biblical sanction for slavery rejected both those hermeneutical notions and the implicit trust in a traditional Protestant scripture. For them, a new approach to the Bible was imperative. Molly Oshatz has well summarized the continuity between the earlier debates and the later turn to a historicist understanding of scripture: "The antebellum world had envisioned a static commensurability between Protestant belief and universal forms of knowledge . . . . The Protestant acceptance of historicism, informed by anti-slavery, evolution, and historical criticism, replaced this relationship with a dynamic, evolving form of commensurability." Earlier arguments against slavery had featured the "spirit" of scripture, an emphasis that after the war became central for liberal Protestants: "scripture could not be taken literally, but had to be interpreted according to the always-developing Christian consciousness." In sum, after the interpretive deadlock of the Civil War, "antislavery, emancipation, Darwinian evolution, and biblical criticism each contributed to the modern conviction that truth and meaning are inseparable from the process of history."[22]

The broader terrain became clearer in other significant developments from 1876, the year of Charles Briggs's initial advocacy for advanced biblical criticism. In the fall of the year, nervous Republicans, desperately trying to hang on to their power in the United States Congress, introduced the blatantly anti-Catholic Blaine Amendment that would have added to the Constitution a provision sponsored by James G. Blaine of Maine. It provided that no public money could be expended on what were called "sectarian [i.e., Roman Catholic] schools," but with a provision added by the Senate that the Amendment would not prohibit the non-sectarian reading of the Bible.

In the debate over this Amendment assumptions once taken for granted wavered. Primary among those assumptions was the conviction that Bible reading in the schools was ideal for strengthening republican government as well as the belief that reading from the King James Version was ideal for promoting republican virtue while preserving the separation of church and state. An even more fundamental assumption held that the United States in a generic Protestant sense was a Christian country where generic Protestant convictions, habits, instincts, and agendas contributed fundamentally to the survival of American liberty. When the United States Congress rejected the Blaine Amendment, many Americans still accepted these assumptions. But no longer did they prevail decisively, universally, or axiomatically.

Where the Bible continued to exert a political presence in 1876, that presence was negative. In the South, spokesmen for what was called the "spirituality of the church" argued that the mandates of scripture pertained exclusively to church bodies and not through the churches to society at large. For church people both South and North, preoccupation with questions of biblical criticism (as in the Briggs controversy) monopolized attention that earlier worked to shape the entire civilization by biblical values.

Three religious initiatives from 1876 also heralded vigorous new competition over individual interpretations as well as general approaches. Early in the year a young minister in Springfield, Massachusetts, put scripture to use in line with those who looked favorably on Charles Briggs's opinions. Washington Gladden, later recognized as a leader of the Social Gospel, appealed in his book, *Working People and Their Employers*, for a broader, not narrower, economic application of the biblical Gospel: "Now that slavery is out of the way," he wrote, "the questions that concern the welfare of our free laborers are coming forward; and no intelligent man needs to be admonished of their urgency."[23] Gladden's desire to find in scripture an antidote to economic distress resonated, however, with only a limited number of his fellow Protestants.

In November, a small group of Presbyterian and Baptist ministers gathered at Swampscott, Massachusetts, with very different purposes. Their convictions stood diametrically opposed to those of Charles Briggs and Washington Gladden. The specific goal of Niagara conveners like James H. Brookes, a prominent Presbyterian minister from St. Louis, was to promote a dispensational and premillennial interpretation of scripture. Because they feared the increasing emphasis in some elite circles on the human character of scripture, these students of biblical prophecy strongly asserted the Bible's supernatural character. They saw these same critics using categories of myth to divide scripture's spiritual message from its literal expression; in opposition, they insisted on reading the Bible literally as a factual historical record.

In earlier decades, advocates of revivalism who appropriated the Bible in mostly literal terms similar to the Niagara organizers had exerted a wide impact on American society. The great antebellum revivalist, Charles G. Finney, was a prime case in point, for Finney had championed social reforms along with revival. By 1876, significant leaders who stood in Finney's revival tradition were using the Bible differently. Their fixation on the supernaturalism of biblical prophecy drove Bible readers away from contemporary social involvement. As had Finney, the Niagara participants treated the Bible as authoritative in all particulars. Unlike the Bible-readers of Finney's generations, those who advanced the Niagara Creed were pushing the Bible out of American history.

Later, just before the turn of the year, the Roman Catholic bishop of Richmond, Virginia, published a book entitled *The Faith of Our Fathers*, but with a subtitle indicating the volume's overarching purpose more clearly: *A Plain Exposition and Vindication of the Church Founded by Our Lord Jesus Christ*. James Gibbons, who in 1870 had been the youngest bishop at the First Vatican Council, would later become the leading figure in the American Catholic Church as the Cardinal Archbishop of Baltimore. His *Faith of Our Fathers* became a multi-million copy bestseller that quoted from the Catholics' Douay-Rheims translation as an essential part of Catholicism, defended the Catholic understanding of scripture with more quotations from the Douay-Rheims, and made sure that readers grasped how well Gibbons felt his Catholic faith accorded with the best American traditions.

The use of a Catholic translation in Gibbons's sensationally popular book was a straw in the wind. Five years later in 1881, the American media, both secular and religious, paid overwhelming attention to the publication of the Revised Version of the New Testament, a well-funded, academically impeccable effort to both modernize KJV usage and base that translation on better ancient manuscripts than had been known in 1611. It and the many later translations that have poured forth in a never-ending stream from American publishers have not by any means done away with the KJV. Yet the unrivaled dominance of this one translation has passed.

That passing is not particularly noteworthy for the Bible considered as a source of spiritual guidance. New translations usually make the Bible clearer than it was in the wording of the KJV. But the passing of the KJV as America's once standard translation destabilized the reliance on scripture that had been so prominent for so long in so much of public life. Where there was for practical purposes only one "*the Bible*," the potential for evocation, allusion, and moral heightening was much greater than in the later situation where there are many "*the Bibles*." The words of the KJV still occupy a surprisingly broad place in American consciousness, but not the unifying place they enjoyed into the 1860s.

From Washington Gladden, the Swampscott dispensationalists, and Bishop Gibbons came forceful proposals for applying scripture to contemporary life. Yet because these proposals operated in such different planes, with almost no shared interpretive conventions, they showed that the once dominant Protestant center of American biblical usage had shattered beyond repair. Instead, fragmentation, novelties, new voices, and reactionary retrievals became the order of the day.

Before about 1876, Americans certainly knew about many of the new ideas that questioned the traditional understanding of scripture as the fully inspired Word of God, but those ideas had been marginalized intellectually and quarantined institutionally. After about 1876, debate over the character of the Bible and over how best to study, understand, and interpret the scriptures moved center stage among all major Christian and Jewish groups. For the broader landscape in which these intra-ecclesiastical debates occurred, there was a more general change. Before the latter decades of the nineteenth century, for most Americans most of the time, the overwhelmingly dominant concern had been how to put the Bible's message to work. Thereafter, among many Americans for much of the time, controversy over what the Bible was and how it should be read absorbed an immense amount of the time and energy that had previously been spent on what the Bible said and how it should be followed.

Notes

1. From *The Age of Reason* in *Selected Writings of Thomas Paine*, ed. Ian Shapiro and Jane E. Calvert (New Haven, Conn.: Yale University Press, 2014), 373, 382.
2. Quoted in Jerry Wayne Brown, *The Rise of Biblical Criticism in America, 1800–1870: The New England Scholars* (Middletown, Conn.: Wesleyan University Press, 1969), 126.
3. Brown, *Biblical Criticism*, 180.
4. Robert Baird, *Religion in the United States of America* (Glasgow: Blackie, 1844), 658.
5. "Index of Sermon Texts," *The Journals and Letters of Francis Asbury*, ed. Elmer T. Clark (Nashville, Tenn.: Abingdon, 1958), 2:818–24.
6. "The Apocryphal Books," in *The Collected Writings of James Henley Thornwell*, ed. John B. Adger (Richmond, Va.: Presbyterian Committee of Publication, 1873), 3:747.
7. Quoted in Laurie Maffly-Kipp, *Setting Down the Sacred Past: African-American Race Histories* (Cambridge, Mass.: Harvard University Press, 2010), 52, 54.
8. Thomas Campbell, *Address of the Christian Association of Washington* (Washington, Pa.: Brown and Sample, 1809), 5.
9. Alexander Campbell, "Reply," *Christian Baptist* 3 (April 3, 1826): 204.
10. William Ellery Channing, *Unitarian Christianity: A Sermon Delivered at the Ordination of Jared Sparks* (Baltimore, Md.: J. Robinson, 1819), 14, 4, 27, 30.
11. Moses Stuart, *A Commentary on the Epistle to the Romans* (Andover, Mass.: Flagg and Gould, 1835), 599, 610, 614.
12. Review of Charles Hodge's *What Is Darwinism*, *Methodist Quarterly Review* 56 (July 1874): 516.
13. Henry Ward Beecher, "Peace Be Still," in *Fast Day Sermons* (New York: Rudd and Carleton, 1861), 289.
14. Thornton Stringfellow, "The Bible Argument; or, Slavery in the Light of Divine Revelation," in *Cotton Is King, and Pro-Slavery Arguments*, ed. E. N. Elliott (Augusta, Ga.: Abbot & Loomis, 1860), 477.
15. John G. Fee, *The Sinfulness of Slaveholding Shown by Appeals to Reason and Scripture* (New York: John A. Gray, 1851), 28.

16. "Sensation Literature Found to be a Nuisance," *Catholic Mirror* (Baltimore), March 9, 1861.

17. Quoted in Gary Phillip Zola, *We Called Him Father Abraham: Lincoln and American Jewry* (Carbondale: Southern Illinois University Press, 2014), 1.

18. Eric T. Brandt and Timothy Larsen, "The Old Atheism Revisited: Robert G. Ingersoll and the Bible," *Journal of the Historical Society* 11 (June 2011): 225.

19. Quoted in Stephen Ward Angell, *Bishop Henry McNeal Turner and African-American Religion in the South* (Knoxville: University of Tennessee Press, 1992), 256.

20. *Address by Rever. Charles A. Briggs* (New York: Rogers and Sherwood, 1876), 14–15.

21. William Henry Green, "The Perpetual Authority of the Old Testament," *Presbyterian Quarterly and Princeton Review*, n.s., 22 (April 1877): 221.

22. Molly Oshatz, *Slavery and Sin. The Fight against Slavery and the Rise of Liberal Protestantism* (New York: Oxford University Press, 2012), 144.

23. Washington Gladden, *Working People and Their Employers* (Boston: Lockwood, Brooks, 1876), 3.

BIBLIOGRAPHY

Barlow, Philip. *Mormons and the Bible.* 2nd ed. New York: Oxford University Press, 2013.

Bassard, Katherine Clay. *Transforming Scriptures: African American Women Writers and the Bible.* Athens: University of Georgia Press, 2010.

Brown, Jerry Wayne. *The Rise of Biblical Criticism in America, 1800–1870: The New England Scholars.* Middletown, Conn.: Wesleyan University Press, 1969.

Callahan, Allen Dwight. *The Talking Book: African Americans and the Bible.* New Haven, Conn.: Yale University Press, 2006.

Fogarty, Gerald P., SJ. *American Catholic Biblical Scholarship.* San Francisco, Calif.: Harper & Row, 1989.

Hatch, Nathan O. *The Democratization of American Christianity.* New Haven, Conn.: Yale University Press, 1989.

Hatch, Nathan O., and Mark A. Noll, eds. *The Bible in America.* New York: Oxford University Press, 1982.

Holifield, E. Brooks. *Theology in America: Christian Thought from the Age of the Puritans to the Civil War.* New Haven, Conn.: Yale University Press, 2003.

Hughes, Richard T. *Reviving the Ancient Faith: The Story of Churches of Christ in America.* Grand Rapids, Mich.: Eerdmans, 1996.

Kern, Kathi. *Mrs. Stanton's Bible.* Ithaca, N.Y.: Cornell University Press, 2001.

Maffly-Kipp, Laurie. *Setting Down the Sacred Past: African-American Race Histories.* Cambridge, Mass.: Harvard University Press, 2010.

Massa, Mark Stephen, SJ. *Charles Augustus Briggs and the Crisis of Historical Criticism.* Minneapolis, Minn.: Fortress, 1990.

Noll, Mark A. *America's God: From Jonathan Edwards to Abraham Lincoln.* New York: Oxford University Press, 2002.

———. *The Civil War as a Theological Crisis.* Chapel Hill, NC: University of North Carolina Press, 2006.

———. *In the Beginning Was the Word: The Bible in American Public Life, 1492–1783.* New York: Oxford University Press, 2015.

Oshatz, Molly. *Slavery and Sin: The Fight against Slavery and the Rise of Liberal Protestantism.* New York: Oxford University Press, 2012.

Taylor, Marion Ann, and Agnes Choi, eds. *Handbook of Women Biblical Interpreters.* Grand Rapids, Mich.: Baker, 2012.

Turner, James. *Philology: The Forgotten Origins of the Modern Humanities.* Princeton, N.J.: Princeton University Press, 2014.

Wacker, Grant. "The Demise of Biblical Civilization." In *The Bible in America*, ed. Nathan O. Hatch and Mark A. Noll, 121–38. New York: Oxford University Press, 1982.

Wimbush, Vincent, ed. *African Americans and the Bible.* New York: Continuum, 2001.

CHAPTER 8

....

TWENTIETH- AND TWENTY-FIRST-CENTURY AMERICAN BIBLICAL INTERPRETATION

....

DANIEL J. TREIER AND CRAIG HEFNER

TWENTIETH- and twenty-first-century American biblical interpretation presents the dual hermeneutical challenge of understanding the present and the recent past. Given the historical detail of many of the other chapters in this volume, we approach the topic of biblical interpretation over roughly the last century as theologians rather than professional historians, and focus our essay on theological hermeneutics: ideas have contexts, but they also have consequences.

Our hermeneutical narrative focuses on theological education.[1] Its formal realm underwent a twentieth-century revolution, with revealing consequences for American biblical interpretation. Beyond its non-formal modes, theological education came to affect all Bible readers through translations, institutional mediation of scholarship, and the ministries of alumni. The moral of the following narrative is that professional theological education has both enriched and fragmented American biblical interpretation.

Theologically speaking, many Americans have misunderstood the traditional Protestant belief in the priesthood of all believers as an absolute right of private judgment. They have neglected the magisterial Protestant reformers' commitment to the leadership of educated clergy and the catechizing of lay biblical interpreters while taking their entrepreneurial history of religious dissent and freedom to individualistic extremes. In return, many scholars have assumed that the American stress on personal biblical interpretation has rendered the traditional Protestant doctrine of all believers' priesthood itself absurd and dangerous—needing replacement by a priesthood of clerics or historical critics. Twentieth-century American theological education is a story of elite efforts not only to inform but often, more boldly, to reform how the populace understands the Bible.

PRECURSORS: THE LONG NINETEENTH CENTURY

Twentieth-century biblical interpretation blazed new trails by spending nineteenth-century cultural capital—accumulated roughly from the American Revolution until World War I in a synthesis of "evangelical Protestant religion, republican political ideology, and common-sense moral reasoning."[2] As American theology became preoccupied with reasonableness and practicality, tension emerged between gradual professionalization and populism, of which Philip Schaff lamented, "Every theological vagabond and peddler may drive here his bungling trade, without passport of license, and sell his false ware at pleasure."[3]

The modern research university emigrated from Berlin in 1810 to Johns Hopkins and Chicago in the later 1800s. A "fourfold pattern" for theological education came in tow: historically oriented exegesis and biblical theology; historical theology; systematic theology; and practical theology. Friedrich Schleiermacher (1768-1834), helping to create the German precursor, recognized that by emerging "critical" standards theology could not qualify as *Wissenschaft*—academically disciplined knowledge. But he sought to maintain theology's university location, positioned as a professional discipline—appropriating historical, philosophical, and "social-scientific" methods to inform clergy training for state churches.

Lacking state churches while being more popularly and professionally oriented, Americans amended this German approach. Nevertheless, many American universities had church-related origins for training clergy. Although research universities eventually replaced theological study with departments of religion, older universities retained divinity schools; both these and freestanding seminaries followed the fourfold pattern. The Bible was distinguished from Christian tradition, but gradually it was recast as a cultural classic rather than inspired scripture, a volume to be studied historically and philologically with religiously neutral discourse having politically irenic goals.[4]

More popularly, Baconian ideals of inductive science shifted the American focus toward proving the integrity of separate biblical books before arranging their various theological facts, while exacerbating appeals for the right of private judgment to restore primitive scriptural religion. Groups like the Mormons took this popular right farther, proclaiming not just individual interpretations but immediate new revelation. Bible conferences spread new emphasis on prophecy.

Nineteenth-century divinity schools evolved into comparatively elite institutions; outside certain denominations many preachers lacked such education. Early on, though, schools still focused on Bible teaching and pastoral training, rather than stressing scholarly production. In the century's latter decades, somewhat controversial work began on a Revised Version of the King James Bible. Further controversy arose as professors adopted "higher criticism" and rejected the "proof texting" theologies frequently associated with biblical inerrancy. Historical scholarship moved beyond establishing original biblical texts and undertaking philological study, challenging traditional ascriptions of authors, settings, and miracles. If the Civil War constituted a crisis of biblical interpretation regarding slavery, then subsequent decades shifted the crisis to the Bible's authority.

Controversy: Modernist Victory and Fundamentalist Retrenchment

Although the fundamentalist-modernist controversy had nineteenth-century precursors, the 1920s and 1930s solidified the decisive shift from broadly evangelical to less traditional engagement with the Bible.[5] The Scopes Trial became emblematic of this shift, alongside differences of social class and formal education.

Earlier "hallmarks of liberalism"—"biblical higher criticism, historical consciousness, and the Social Gospel"—elicited pamphlets defending *The Fundamentals*, supernatural elements of Christianity that secular and religious modernism challenged.[6] The collection's authors included learned clergy and professors alongside popular preachers and a few laymen. Their "fundamentalism" was neither bellicose nor backward. They read biblical critics; they responded primarily with arguments, not *ad hominem* attacks; they advocated not just lower but faith-based higher criticism. Yet they recognized that thoroughgoing historical criticism threatened traditional Christian faith, from Christ's "virgin birth" to his resurrection and miracles in between.

Fundamentalists lost every major denominational battle. "Mainline" Protestant schools produced the constituency of a new journal for progressive Christianity—optimistically named *The Christian Century*—as clergymen longed for ongoing connections with their comfortable educational environs.[7] Leaders of mainline seminaries, though, were not exclusively concerned with clergymen. Yale's Luther Weigle (1880-1976), for example, promoted more professional Sunday Schools—relatively new in their own right—however much laypeople struggled with such initiatives: "Such intimate involvement by a divinity school dean in primary and secondary level religious education would become less common as American universities engaged in ever more specialized, and rarified, research. Yet Weigle lived in an era when the academy optimistically sought to remold the church in its own image . . . . Indeed, the educational agenda of Weigle and others transcended the local congregation and even the denomination to envision a pan-Protestant pedagogical reformation."[8] Early mainline theological education aimed at widely reforming, through clergy trained both classically and practically, how Americans engaged the Bible.

Fundamentalists, exiled from mainline seminaries and alienated from elite culture, retrenched with their own schools; so, for instance, exiles from Princeton Theological Seminary founded Westminster Theological Seminary. Other fundamentalists, associating elite education with liberal reform, supplanted higher education with more populist institutions.[9] So legions of Bible colleges like Moody Bible Institute promoted particular preachers' teaching—with the curricular focus "Bible college" implies. The Scofield Reference Bible and prophecy conferences spread the democratic hermeneutics of dispensationalism, birthing schools like Dallas Theological Seminary to train its pastors. Ironically, dispensationalism popularized inductive Bible study with an intricate system dependent on trusted leaders.[10] Preachers like Billy Graham (b. 1918) filled an apparent vacuum by proclaiming simply, "The Bible says . . . "[11] If modernists aimed to spread historical criticism far and wide, fundamentalists inoculated themselves with systems for unified interpretation of biblical revelation.

Popular contrasts between modernism and fundamentalism concerned "biblical supernaturalism": modernists pursued relevant biblical reinterpretation while fundamentalists embraced modern media to communicate traditional claims about the Bible's teachings. Intellectual contrasts concerned "historical consciousness": conservatives rejected the liberal assumption "that historical process is the bed of human perception, that knowledge is the product of a fluid social process," at least protecting divine revelation from such social fluidity.[12] Despite such contrasts, many claim that fundamentalists and modernists shared commitment to the "objectivity" of the rational individual and, accordingly, apolitical ideals of interpretation.[13] They further shared a tendency toward historical literalism; conservatives tried to answer, while liberals accommodated, the evolutionary and higher critical attacks on the unified truth of biblical narratives.[14] Differing reactions to these attacks nevertheless reflected common assumptions.

MAINLINE: PROFESSIONAL ESTABLISHMENT

As direct controversy ebbed, mainline seminaries focused on developing a professional establishment, albeit still aiming for popular reform. The "Christian realism" of Reinhold Niebuhr (1892-1971) and the pacifism of the *Christian Century* tangled at mid-century, as did so-called neo-orthodoxy and more liberal cultural Protestantism. Karl Barth (1886-1968) eschewed the "neo-orthodox" label, which was hardly enlightening when it also rested on figures like Rudolf Bultmann (1884-1976). Despite Niebuhr's less optimistic anthropology and Barthian overtones, he remained a defining part of the American liberal establishment along with another German émigré, Paul Tillich (1886-1965).

Aided by religion's wartime, bomb-fearing resurgence, theological education surged in a new economy defined by professionalization. Biblical criticism became professional, "far more historical and textually based than the pale denial of Enlightenment scholars."[15] Its achievements were considerable, expanding knowledge of the Bible while enhancing simultaneously the "graduate" and practical character of seminaries.[16] Scholarly societies arose, including the American Academy of Religion (AAR; founded in 1909, renamed 1963) and the Society of Biblical Literature (SBL; founded in 1880), plus an accrediting agency, the Association of Theological Schools (ATS; founded in 1918).

Biblical criticism, however, also generated complications. The mid-century effort to produce an ecumenical Bible translation spawned controversy. Claiming critical neutrality, the Revised Standard Version (1952) changed traditional renderings of key Christological passages—weakening associations of Christ with "God" (e.g., Rom. 9:5), removing proofs for the Trinity (e.g., 1 John 5:8), and threatening verities like the virgin birth (e.g., "young woman" instead of "virgin" in Isa. 7:14, weakening its connection to Matt. 1:23). Popular controversy hindered the RSV's ecumenical aims and elicited numerous alternatives, notably the evangelical New International Version (1978).

Other complications of biblical criticism involved debilitating fractures. Beyond modern fragmentation of theory and practice, scholarly societies shifted biblical study away from church-related schools. Biblical studies no longer served as a feeder discipline for theology, instead constituting a jealously guarded area of professional expertise. Myths of scholarly agreement, spawned by idealized science, left intellectuals reluctant to make

Bible-based claims that would be pluralistically contested. Previously normal disagreement now induced an ever-growing skepticism about the possibility of public, rational discourse concerning important human matters such as religion.[17]

A mid-century study devoted to *The Advancement of Theological Education* already struggled over the Bible's location within tight curricular limits. Even as mainline seminaries professionalized biblical scholarship with more teaching positions, they doubted the necessity of requiring biblical languages. They considered shifting requirements toward enhancing Bible knowledge alongside biblical theology.[18] Although professional theologians, prominently the Niebuhrs, occasionally referred to biblical texts, they did not undertake detailed exegesis as Barth or prior generations did. The "biblical theology movement" quickly faded: scholars recognized the difficulty of appealing to "God's mighty acts in history" with—adopting a "modern" worldview—a drastically different meaning than the Bible's.[19] Such theological change notwithstanding, cultural and institutional realities exerted additional curricular pressure on the quantity of detailed attention to biblical texts.

Thus, amid subsequent discussions of theological education one contributor asserted, however hyperbolically, "It is almost impossible to detect the presence of theological thinking in current biblical scholarship except in its most conservative expressions."[20] The "openly evangelical, even messianic" vision of earlier leaders—"to join the mission of the church with the emerging modern American university"—faced a cloudy future. Despite continuing to pursue popular reform, professionalized biblical criticism and pastoral ministry made theological education increasingly elitist, especially once mainline church attendance and seminary enrollments began declining. Specialization, professionalization, social reform, and pluralism fostered mainline Protestant theological education yet also fractured that American establishment.[21]

OUTSIDERS: CATHOLIC AND JEWISH ASSIMILATION

Immigration brought Judaism and Catholicism into contact with American populism and academic professionalization only after Protestants fostered these new contexts for biblical interpretation. Neither tradition, however, remained a total outsider for long. Both stories, for all their differences, involve some resistance alongside significant assimilation to these American forces.

Shaped by the modernizing movement *Wissenschaft des Judentums*, the first wave of Jewish immigrants assimilated rapidly to the American ideal of individual religious authority.[22] In 1885, a group of rabbis inaugurated the Reform tradition with the Pittsburgh Platform, which denied the traditional confession of the Torah as revelation to Moses on Mount Sinai. In 1937 the Columbus Platform reaffirmed the original Reform position on scripture: "Being products of historical processes, certain of its laws have lost their binding force with the passing of the conditions that called them forth."[23] Openness to popular autonomy arose alongside the professionalization of biblical interpretation.[24] Kaufmann Kohler (1843-1926), second president of Hebrew Union College—America's first successful Jewish seminary—came to the United States because his ideas were too radical for German Jewish communities. Historical criticism entered the curriculum under Kohler's leadership.

He also permitted higher criticism to be applied to the study of the Talmud, forbade head coverings in the chapel, and banned the advocacy of Jewish nationalism.[25]

A symbolic break between the Conservative and Reform traditions arose in 1883, when Hebrew Union College celebrated its first ordination with a banquet serving non-kosher foods. Traditionalist attendees walked out, and soon a Conservative group started New York's Jewish Theological Seminary. Even so, Conservative Judaism continued affirming the Torah's human origins and relating its authority to subsequent historical development. At its establishment in 1902, wealthy sponsors desired that Jewish Theological Seminary be an Americanizing influence.[26]

The largest Jewish exception to American assimilation and professionalization is the Orthodox tradition, which affirms both the Torah's binding nature and its traditional interpretation. In its small immigrant communities, known as *landsmanshaftn*, the traditional chief rabbi oversees a network of synagogues. Wary of both popular and professionalized biblical interpretation, the Union of Orthodox Rabbis refused admittance to those trained in America.[27] Orthodox Judaism comparatively struggles in the United States, the only nation where the Jewish non-Orthodox outnumber the Orthodox.[28]

Early twentieth-century Catholicism similarly resisted the Americanization of biblical interpretation. Yet, as immigration increased, encounters with American Protestants—however awkward—led beyond the entrenchment of the Council of Trent (1545-63) and Vatican I (1869-70), especially once Pope Pius XII's *Divino Afflante Spiritu* (1943) and then Vatican II (1962-65) opened official doors for engaging critical methods and Protestant biblical scholars.[29]

The contrast between the Catholic University of America (CUA) and America's oldest Jesuit seminary Woodstock College is illustrative. In 1883 the Third Plenary Council, meeting to determine a valid English vernacular translation of scripture, decided to establish CUA, which quickly reflected many Catholic scholars' desire to enter mainstream scholarship. As the first trustees discussed the selection of faculty, they specified only one requirement for a professor of scripture: that he be German.[30] CUA hired several progressive biblical scholars, who in dialogue with Europeans developed new theories of scripture's inspiration to accommodate a more critical approach.[31]

Conversely, Woodstock College rejected Americanized biblical criticism. Rector Anthony J. Mass (1859-1927) attacked critical scholars for granting insufficient authority to tradition regarding revealed doctrine. Mass drew especially on Leo XII's rejection of "higher criticism" in *Providentissimus Deus* (1893) and Pius X's condemnation of modernist heresy in *Pascendi Dominici Gregis* (1907). Although Benedict XV declared an end to the aggressive anti-modernist campaign in *Ad beatissimi Apostolorum* (1914), Woodstock College continued promoting conservative biblical scholarship, thwarting widespread acceptance of the critical approach. Hence, Fogarty concludes: "The state of Catholic biblical scholarship in the United States at the end of the 1930s was bleak. Whatever scholarship there had been at the beginning of the century had either been destroyed in the wake of Modernism or had gone underground."[32]

Yet the Catholic Biblical Association began in 1936 to engage mainstream scholarship. World War II made study in Rome difficult, so students began training at secular American schools. *Divino Afflante Spiritu* permitted historical criticism of the Bible and called for translations from scripture's original languages. At Vatican II, *Dei Verbum* clearly approved some use of historical criticism. Catholic biblical scholars in America noticeably became more prominent. In 1967, John L. McKenzie became the first Catholic president of SBL, with others to follow. CUA reinvigorated its engagement with mainstream scholarship, while anti-modernist haven Woodstock College closed its doors in 1974.[33]

Like much of Judaism, mainstream American Catholicism slowly assimilated to the professionalization of biblical scholarship and even aspects of populism. If not futile, resistance was largely unsuccessful. For both traditions, American populism predictably brought fragmentation. In that destabilizing context, professionalization can be seen partly as an attempt to shape (as allowed by traditional clerics), even fundamentally alter (as pursued by critical scholars), newfound popular engagement with the Bible.

RETURN: EVANGELICAL RE-ENGAGEMENT WITH SCHOLARSHIP

Meanwhile Protestant fundamentalists retrenched in sectarian ways, rejecting not just modern culture but eventually each other. Soon some recognized the dangers of isolation and called for re-engagement, reclaiming "evangelical" as their label.[34] Of course, continuities remained with fundamentalists. Dispensationalism remained widespread among evangelicals, despite periodic refinement—first the "revised" version of the system appearing in the study Bible from Charles Ryrie (1925-2016), later the "progressive" form influenced by the "inaugurated eschatology" of George Ladd (1911-1982).[35] "Zionism" garnered particular support from dispensationalist eschatology alongside political support among evangelicals generally.[36] Parachurch ministries such as InterVarsity Christian Fellowship promoted inductive Bible study, with observation-interpretation-application models structuring lay engagement with scripture.

Fundamentalist continuities notwithstanding, the evangelical return to scholarship was genuine. Evangelicals now had to argue for traditional faith against entrenched alternatives, engage new methods, and earn PhD degrees. Crucial to their academic return were British exemplars like F. F. Bruce (1910-1990). These exemplars modeled careful appropriation of historical-critical methods and mentored evangelical students who found the British system more amenable than American universities, where various institutional factors (such as sharper division between divinity and religious studies) apparently made it more difficult for biblically conservative students to complete PhD degrees.[37]

American evangelicals advocated historical-grammatical exegesis pursuing a single meaning determined by authorial intention—appropriating the hermeneutics of secular literary scholar E. D. Hirsch Jr. (b. 1928).[38] This approach authorized the fourfold disciplinary pattern in evangelical colleges and seminaries: exegesis and biblical theology provided the authoritative truth that other disciplines—not just practical but even historical and systematic theology—largely synthesized and contextualized. On the heels of re-engaging biblical scholarship, evangelicals entered other fields. Particularly in the fields of history and philosophy of religion, some evangelical scholars such as Mark Noll (b. 1946) and Alvin Plantinga (b. 1932) became widely influential. Yet these were fields characterized by historical and conceptual analysis assuming author-oriented hermeneutics.

Evangelical scholars faced historical-critical challenges in the context of new institutions and popular controversy. In the 1960s, under Barth's influence, Fuller Theological Seminary (neo-evangelicalism's intellectual alternative to Princeton) removed its commitment to the Bible's inerrancy, restricting biblical "infallibility" to spiritual matters while allowing for historical and scientific error. The backlash, not least from former faculty members leading the new journal *Christianity Today*, was strident. Eventually this "battle for the Bible" resulted in the International Council on Biblical Inerrancy, and Trinity Evangelical Divinity School as an inerrantist alternative to Fuller.[39]

The number, size, and reputations of evangelical colleges and seminaries gradually expanded, while Bible colleges plateaued.[40] As evangelicals entered a wider array of fields, internal debates intensified over biblical boundaries. Overlap ensued between evangelical biblical scholarship and formerly liberal positions. Barth went from virtual anathema in the 1960s to widespread admiration among rising evangelical theologians. Evangelical debates thus expanded from preoccupations with scripture's historical reference to include its theological unity and ethical authority.

Scholarly re-engagement aside, the evangelical populace undergoes continued criticism for biblicist proof-texting. Sociologist Christian Smith (b. 1960), converting from evangelical to Catholic faith, constructed a ten-point construal: evangelical biblicism treats the Bible as (1) "divine writing," offering (2) "total representation" of God's revelation and (3) "complete coverage" of God's relevant will, with (4) "democratic perspicuity" of its plain meaning grasped by (5) "commonsense hermeneutics" rooted in the author's literal sense. Accordingly, (6) "solo scriptura" removes any need for creedal traditions or theological frameworks: the Bible contains (7) "internal harmony" like a puzzle with interlocking pieces, and (8) "universal applicability" apart from internal limitations; thus it can be understood using (9) an "inductive method" and applied according to (10) a "handbook model" of comprehensive guidance for life.[41]

Smith's critique cites progressive evangelical biblical scholars appreciatively. Conservative scholars find such portrayals to be one-sided yet agree about disturbing popular aberrations. Hence, twenty-first century evangelical scholarship is more credible but also more diverse than ever, its audience as divided as ever. Through distance education and social media, the Internet intensifies popular interest and perceived conflict in theological issues, while creating enrollment challenges for theological schools. In a history haunted by the Scopes Trial and a culture rapidly changing its sexual ethics, human origins and homosexuality comprise pressing conflicts. Traditionalist evangelicals—appealing to scripture's historical integrity and theological unity—are accused by progressives of remaining fundamentalist. Progressive evangelicals—limiting biblical inerrancy or otherwise reinterpreting the Bible's historical reference and internal coherence—are accused by traditionalists of revealing themselves to be liberals.

The aims of evangelical theological education are as diverse as its ecclesiologies and entrepreneurs. Yet it successfully imitated mainline professionalization for biblical scholarship and myriad ministries. Looming challenges notwithstanding, evangelical schools maintained greater emphasis on biblical languages and biblical theology, even if some mainline institutions maintained more elite reputations and academic specialization. Professionalized fragmentation affected evangelicals too, but enrollment numbers suggest that—for good and ill—their scholars and students maintained closer connections to America's popular religious marketplace.[42]

Recovery: Mainline Re-engagement
with Tradition

As mainline theological education faced increasing late twentieth-century challenges, discussion arose concerning its "aims and purposes," hoping to heal the aforementioned fractures.[43] That literature partially overlapped with an agenda variously called "narrative theology," the "Yale School," or "postliberalism."

Postliberals hearkened back to Barth's "strange new world of the Bible," wary of Bultmannian "new hermeneutics" and Tillichian "correlation" between Christian tradition and contemporary questions—believing these to focus unduly on human subjectivity and cultural apologetics. Influenced by Hans-Georg Gadamer (1900-2002) and Paul Ricoeur (1913-2005), Catholic priest and University of Chicago professor David Tracy (b. 1939) rearticulated that tradition of "revisionist" liberal hermeneutics, comparing scripture to a "classic text." Readers pass through a threefold arc of initial "understanding"—the text evoking sacred realities and perennial questions in experience—followed by critical, suspicious yet trusting, "explanation" resulting finally in the "second naiveté" of "application." Whether encountering earlier textual audiences or religious others, interpreters exercise an "analogical imagination," negotiating meaningful similarities and differences.[44]

If "Chicago" represented "revisionist" theology following Schleiermacher, then "Yale" represented a more "neo-orthodox" approach. Such categorization is imprecise, not least regarding David Kelsey, whose 1975 analysis of *The Uses of Scripture in Recent Theology* did not toe a Barthian line. Kelsey promoted a "functional" account of scripture's authority, emphasizing its use by the Holy Spirit in shaping Christian identity rather than its traditional revelatory connection to the Logos.[45]

Other Yale figures, though, associated more substantially with Barth. Brevard Childs (1923-2007) pioneered a "canonical" approach, blending historical criticism with attention to the Bible's final form as scripture. Hans Frei (1922-1988) analyzed modern preoccupation with biblical narratives' historical reference to the neglect of their literary world(s). George Lindbeck (b. 1923) popularized the label "postliberal," advocating a "cultural-linguistic" alternative to conservative "cognitive-propositional" and liberal "experiential-expressivist" views of doctrine.[46] On Lindbeck's view, doctrine is the second-order grammar regulating first-order prayer. Since doctrine does not directly make truth claims or express personal experience but instead regulates communal religious language, it is important to move "intratextually" from scripture to theology rather than becoming preoccupied with apologetics. Intratextuality lets biblical categories "absorb the world," not vice versa. Following Frei, the Gospels narrate the divine identity revealed in Jesus, not philosophical themes into which otherwise supernatural elements might be translated.

Debate continues over the category of "postliberalism." Frei and Lindbeck were indebted to the Niebuhrs; hardly anti-liberal, they were reconsidering faithfulness to Christ within modern culture.[47] They recognized that the mainline heritage required meaningful contact with the texts—biblical and theological—of Christian tradition. Beyond "postmodern" emphases on communal language and narrative categories, Yale figures' preoccupations were genuinely theological; yet, Childs aside, they promoted a traditional idiom through formal analyses dominated by historical and philosophical categories. This irony not-withstanding, they created academic space for ecumenical conversation including more distinctive—even evangelical—voices.

Kelsey joined the theological education conversation sparked by Vanderbilt Divinity School's Edward Farley (1929–2014). Farley assumed the collapse of the classic Protestant "house of authority": God as king, speaking to subjects through the Bible, as interpreted through confessional categories. Such an authority structure lacked historical consciousness and critical reflection appropriate to modern inquiry. But newly modern theological edu-cation lacked coherence given its specialized disciplines, fragmentation Farley proposed to address with theology as a *habitus*, the unifying disposition into which students would be edu-cated. While Farley recognized its problems, he only partially resisted the dominant modern paradigm of critical inquiry, continuing to locate theology's *habitus* essentially in the mind, in making judgments. Kelsey demonstrated that the ensuing theme—"wisdom"—masked significant differences among its proponents. Fundamentally different models of education awkwardly intermingled: "Athens," classically pursuing personal formation, and "Berlin," pro-moting critical research.[48]

The narrative theology of Stanley Hauerwas (b. 1940), dominant at Duke Divinity School, reflected his Yale education plus the influence of Mennonite John Howard Yoder (1927–1997) and philosopher Alasdair MacIntyre (b. 1929). Hauerwas championed the nar-rative of Jesus forming virtuous communities through "practices" of Christian nonviolence. Hauerwas insisted that scripture be inseparable from theology rooted in church-centered practice, and vice versa, yet he also appropriated more formal categories. By the late twen-tieth century, historical consciousness and hermeneutical categories were pervasive, even when problematized.[49]

Motivation for recovering a traditional idiom was partly pastoral. Some decried the bibli-cal illiteracy of ministry candidates and seminaries' failure to keep faith with their churches' past.[50] Others highlighted challenges of ministering relevant faith in American culture.[51] Hence, a modest recovery of scriptural and traditional idioms surfaced in some quarters.[52] Yet traditional idioms by no means dominate contemporary mainline theological educa-tion. Calls for their recovery may reflect either increasing attention to, or scholarly alien-ation from, popular faith.

"OTHERS": LIBERALISM AND LIBERATION

Other sectors of the late twentieth-century establishment primarily championed the causes of oppressed persons and groups. Liberationist hermeneutics are more "postmodern," whether appealing to poststructuralism for decentering textual meaning or simply advo-cating "hermeneutics of suspicion" concerning ideological powers. The liberationist focus is not epistemological but ethical—reading for justice for "the other." Such approaches believe mainstream hermeneutics to be too trusting of biblical texts and Christian tradi-tion as well as the people and institutions teaching them. Traditional alternatives are per-ceived as predominantly apologetic, defending culturally privileged positions. Like others, liberationist educators aim to make a popular difference, sometimes adopting different perspectives than those for whom they advocate—often by historically subversive rather than mainstream means.

The sheer plurality of oppressed persons and groups, though, intensifies fragmentation. Appeals for liberation expanded from Latin American Catholics to blacks in South Africa and the United States, suburban and then black womanist and *mujerista* feminists, Native Americans, LGBTQ persons exploring "queer" hermeneutics, and the list goes on. As helpful as deconstructive methods are for challenging oppressors, radical American versions threatened to dissolve public truth claims on behalf of these communities—or so detractors alleged. Moreover, various communities do not always offer complementary readings. For instance, Native Americans highlight the colonizing implications derived from "conquest" narratives following the Exodus—complicating that liberation paradigm.[53] Many "postcolonial" theorists critique liberation theology for not flatly rejecting the Bible's authority, yet the poor themselves frequently choose conservative "Pentecostal" religion.[54]

Liberationist "advocacy" stances create tension with the "diachronic" interpretation that once dominated theological education.[55] Although classical Bible courses have declined in curricular influence and jeremiads decry biblical illiteracy, liberationist emphases are by no means solely responsible. After all, much traditional coursework long ago replaced scripture's theological content with critical study of historical backgrounds.

The African American tradition intersects with liberationist concerns while remaining distinctive. Its oral culture, now celebrated for others to emulate, owes partly to slaves being denied formal education or even literacy. So severe was the long, terrible legacy of this denial that even by the 1990s only about thirty African American biblical scholars had PhD degrees.[56] The African American community developed spiritually creative and ideologically subversive engagement with scripture, not least due to a restricted diet of pro-slavery readings and sermons.

No history of twentieth-century American biblical interpretation would be complete without acknowledging Martin Luther King Jr. and the civil rights movement. King (1929-1968) learned from mainline scholars, while retaining from his church background a stronger sense of human sinfulness and a richer sensibility for appealing to the scriptures—especially prophetic traditions. He powerfully appropriated the sermon form as the broader movement appropriated the scriptures in communal song. Although many mainline Protestants supported the movement, unfortunately others needed confrontation, notably in King's "Letter from Birmingham Jail." Worse still, civil rights were ignored by indifferent evangelicals and opposed by hostile ones.[57]

African American biblical interpretation is uniquely positioned between disparate communities—evangelicals, liberals, and liberationists—given its distinctive blend of scriptural idioms, hermeneutical creativity, and progressive politics. Nevertheless, like others, the black church has fostered increasingly diverse voices. Traditional practice retains a biblical idiom and relatively conservative faith, while many leaders promote liberal, establishment—and riskier, liberationist—verities.[58]

More broadly, twenty-first-century mainline Protestants consume in profitable numbers the claims of the Jesus Seminar and even *The Da Vinci Code*. The Jesus Seminar lent scholarly credibility to a trendy portrait of the "historical Jesus" as a sage of liberated spirituality before Dan Brown's novel lent a popular voice to a pro-heterodox portrait of early Christianity. In both cases, scripture and mainstream tradition gave way to "spirituality without religion." Of course, evangelicals too have favorite decline narratives, blaming "Christendom" rather than its creedal claims. But if evangelical fiction reflects apocalyptic tendencies, mainline spirituality can be more "gnostic"—featuring an American religion of inner spiritual light, tailored for the elite.[59]

A HERMENEUTICAL EDUCATION?

What are the morals of this variegated hermeneutical story? Twentieth-century American theological education blended German university structures and republican religion into a new professional enterprise. This professionalism joined numerous *isms* in American biblical interpretation: Common Sense realism, Baconian inductivism, populism, biblicism, and literalism. What theological education adds to this history are elite efforts not just to enhance, but more fundamentally to alter, how ordinary people understand the Bible. The ensuing question, naturally, is how influential such efforts have been.

The institutional legacy of these educational efforts surely includes deeper understanding of the Bible and its contexts, new professions of teaching and scholarship, more professional clergy, and liberating critiques of oppressive ideas and practices. Yet accompanying this informative legacy are significant fractures: between academy and church, Bible and theology, biblical passages themselves, theological disciplines, and theology's curriculum and other disciplines. Biblical interpretation became marginal to American intellectual life as it became more informed. Many scholars disapproved of much popular interpretation, some with fear or visceral distaste. Scholars frequently bit the religious hands feeding them—with dollars, students, and disciplinary relevance. Still, they nobly filled those hands in return; American biblical scholarship, compared with its German precursor, has remarkably popular aspirations. If there were space here for the subplots of religious publishing and preaching, they could reinforce this informative popular legacy.

When assessing more fundamental reform efforts, we can only gesture at relevant factors to consider. One factor is a distinctive American tendency toward literalism, sometimes explored in parallels between biblical and legal interpretation.[60] Apparently such literalism remains widely resistant to reform, albeit veering inevitably from original meaning into personal and political application. Another factor is the actual quantity of American Bible reading. Periodic surveys claim that legions read the Bible regularly; yet biblical illiteracy may be running ever deeper, with Bible reading generally on the decline.[61] For now such assessments may largely reflect hermeneutical agendas, saying as much about interpretation of the past or ideals for the future as they do about the present.[62]

A third factor to consider is the professional interface of the clergy between scholarly interpretation and popular reading. How substantially have pastoral, priestly, or rabbinic approaches been altered by formal education, and with what trickle-down effects? Catholicism and Judaism retained priestly and rabbinic traditions, but the American context reshaped their training and functions. Among Protestants, both popular appeals to private judgment and professional attempts at reform show striking disregard for the classic "priesthood of all believers."[63] "The priesthood of the believer," its rhetorical substitute pro and con, already manifests America's individualistic turn.

If such morals of this hermeneutical story remain unclear, still an earlier typology underscores the moral agendas at stake: whether "doctrinalist," "pietist," "moralist," or occasionally "culturalist" in focus, most American traditions approach the Bible with distinctively practical-moral aims.[64] Popular literalism, with its embedded distrust of elites, itself reflects distinctive moral commitment.[65] The hermeneutical story embodied in theological education literature is important because it highlights the practical-moral agenda of professionals in return: they nobly seek to inform, frequently even to reform, how Americans approach their Bibles—with historical awareness (however contested its criteria) and theological-political agendas (however various) both ideally displacing literalist private application.

Some mutual popular and professional tensions, then, arise from self-serving private judgments needing reform. Other tensions awkwardly reflect different faith stances concerning biblical supernaturalism, or respective emphases upon historical consciousness versus personal application. Yet still other tension—even resentment—reflects competing ecclesiastical and political agendas. Because these agendas reflect social-class contexts, educational opportunities, and a myriad of other cultural influences, according to elites' own theories those tensions should evoke some scholarly humility.

Such tensions' presence in this history, and impact on its interpretation, cannot be denied.[66] Since twentieth-century histories of American biblical interpretation generally reflect elite sides of the story, the hermeneutical literature on theological education suggests listening more generously to the populace—to what ordinary people hope that they and their pastors, priests, or rabbis might learn of the Bible. For all that professional theological education has informed possibilities for understanding the Bible, how much can or should it actually reform popular habits of mind? That moral of the story remains hard to tell.

Notes

1. Thanks to Linda Cannell, Timothy Larsen, and Mark Noll for commenting on an earlier draft of this chapter. Although none of these three scholars is responsible for any remaining flaws here, Linda has insightfully championed "theological education for the whole people of God" in ways that inspire our theme.
2. Mark A. Noll, *America's God: From Jonathan Edwards to Abraham Lincoln* (New York: Oxford University Press, 2002), 9.
3. Philip Schaff, *The Principle of Protestantism* (Philadelphia: United Church Press, 1964), 150, quoted in E. Brooks Holifield, *Theology in America: Christian Thought from the Age of the Puritans to the Civil War* (New Haven, Conn.: Yale University Press, 2003), 17.
4. Michael C. Legaspi, *The Death of Scripture and the Rise of Biblical Studies*, Oxford Studies in Historical Theology (Oxford: Oxford University Press, 2010); Jonathan Sheehan, *The Enlightenment Bible: Translation, Scholarship, Culture* (Princeton, N.J.: Princeton University Press, 2005).
5. Grant Wacker, "The Demise of Biblical Civilization," in *The Bible in America: Essays in Cultural History*, ed. Nathan O. Hatch and Mark A. Noll (New York: Oxford University Press, 1982), 122.
6. Elesha J. Coffman, *"The Christian Century" and the Rise of the Protestant Mainline* (New York: Oxford University Press, 2013), 35.

7. Coffman, *Christian Century*, 10, 217–18. Glenn T. Miller, *Piety and Profession: American Protestant Theological Education, 1870-1970* (Grand Rapids, Mich.: Eerdmans, 2007), xiv–xv, emphasizes that theological education offered a gateway to the middle class.

8. Peter J. Thuesen, *In Discordance with the Scriptures: American Protestant Battles over Translating the Bible* (New York: Oxford University Press, 1999), 77. Conrad Cherry's title, *Hurrying Toward Zion: Universities, Divinity Schools, and American Protestantism* (Bloomington: Indiana University Press, 1995), illustratively characterizes the grand aims that Chicago's William Rainey Harper (1856-1906) had for popular religious education.

9. Joel A. Carpenter, *Revive Us Again: The Reawakening of American Fundamentalism* (New York: Oxford University Press, 1997).

10. See Timothy P. Weber, "The Two-Edged Sword: The Fundamentalist Use of the Bible," in *Bible in America*, 101–20, 117—despite his overweening claim that fundamentalism produced "so little really independent Bible study."

11. Coffman, *Christian Century*, 202.

12. Wacker, "Demise," 125, 127.

13. Stanley Hauerwas, *Unleashing the Scripture: Freeing the Bible from Captivity to America* (Nashville, Tenn.: Abingdon Press, 1993).

14. Thuesen, *In Discordance*, 10. For his wider frame of reference on these contrasts, see Hans W. Frei, *The Eclipse of Biblical Narrative: A Study in Eighteenth and Nineteenth Century Hermeneutics* (New Haven, Conn.: Yale University Press, 1974).

15. Miller, *Piety and Profession*, xxi.

16. Miller, *Piety and Profession*, 767–68.

17. C. Stephen Evans, "Afterword: The Bible and the Academy: Some Concluding Thoughts and Possible Future Directions," in *The Bible and the University*, Scripture and Hermeneutics 8, ed. David Lyle Jeffrey and C. Stephen Evans (Grand Rapids, Mich.: Zondervan, 2007), 304–10.

18. H. Richard Niebuhr, Daniel Day Williams, and James M. Gustafson, *The Advancement of Theological Education: The Summary Report of a Mid-Century Study* (New York: Harper, 1957), 92–97.

19. Langdon Gilkey, "Cosmology, Ontology, and the Travail of Biblical Language," *Journal of Religion* (1961): 194–205.

20. Thomas J. J. Altizer, "Total Abyss and Theological Rebirth: The Crisis of University Theology," in *Theology and the University: Essays in Honor of John B. Cobb, Jr.*, ed. David Ray Griffin and Joseph C. Hough Jr. (Albany: State University of New York Press, 1991), 171. This book's revealing index exhausts inquiries regarding the Bible with two entries for "God, of Bible," three for "Bible, historical-critical study of," and four for "Bible, inspiration of"—the last containing, "*See also* Authoritarian"!

21. Cherry, *Hurrying Toward Zion*, ix, 2.

22. Michael A. Meyer, *Response to Modernity: A History of the Reform Movement in Judaism* (New York: Oxford University Press, 1988), 75–77, 225–27.

23. Michael A. Meyer and W. Gunther Plaut, eds., *The Reform Judaism Reader: North American Documents* (New York: UAHC Press, 2001), 200.

24. Leon A. Morris, "Beyond Autonomy: The Texts and Our Lives," in *Platforms and Prayer Book: Theological and Liturgical Perspectives on Reform Judaism*, ed. Dana Evan Kaplan (New York: Rowman & Littlefield, 2002), 271–83.

25. Meyer, *Response to Modernity*, 264–95.

THE BIBLE IN TWENTIETH-CENTURY AMERICA   143

26. Lloyd P. Gartner, "American Judaism, 1880-1945," in *The Cambridge Companion to American Judaism*, ed. Dana Evan Kaplan (Cambridge, Mass.: Cambridge University Press, 2005), 51–52.

27. Gartner, "American Judaism," 52.

28. Dana Evan Kaplan, "Introduction," in *Cambridge Companion to American Judaism*, 13.

29. Loyalty to Trent was often (mis)interpreted as an anti-American prohibition of lay Bible reading; Gerald P. Fogarty, "The Quest for a Catholic Vernacular Bible in America," in *Bible in America*, 163–80. Mutual Protestant and Catholic polemics repurposed older attacks in new battles; Thuesen, *In Discordance*, 18–40, 68–69.

30. Gerald P. Fogarty, *American Catholic Biblical Scholarship: A History from the Early Republic to Vatican II* (San Francisco, Calif.: Harper & Row, 1989), 38.

31. Fogarty, *American Catholic*, 47–57.

32. Fogarty, *American Catholic*, 198.

33. Fogarty, *American Catholic*, 233–40, 344–49.

34. The classic sermon "Shall the Fundamentalists Win?" by pastor and Union Theological Seminary professor Harry Emerson Fosdick (1878-1969) illustrates continuing use of "evangelical" (basically denoting Protestant) by twentieth-century liberals.

35. See John A. D'Elia, *A Place at the Table: George Eldon Ladd and the Rehabilitation of Evangelical Scholarship in America* (New York: Oxford University Press, 2008). Inaugurated eschatology has God's kingdom "already" present at Christ's first coming, with some promised aspects "not yet" fulfilled until his second coming. Progressive dispensationalist pioneers include Craig Blaising (b. 1949) and Darrell Bock (b. 1953).

36. See, e.g., Timothy P. Weber, *On the Road to Armageddon: How Evangelicals Became Israel's Best Friend* (Grand Rapids, Mich.: Baker Academic, 2004).

37. Mark A. Noll, *Between Faith and Criticism: Evangelicals, Scholarship, and the Bible in America* (San Francisco, Calif.: Harper & Row, 1986). Carl F. H. Henry (1913-2003) and other early neo-evangelicals gained PhD degrees at Harvard, but most (except Ladd) in history or nonreligious disciplines.

38. E. D. Hirsch Jr., *Validity in Interpretation* (New Haven, Conn.: Yale University Press, 1967) underwrote evangelical rejection of Hans-Georg Gadamer, *Truth and Method*, 2nd ed., trans. Joel Weinsheimer and Donald G. Marshall (New York: Continuum, 1989), for three decades; few read Gadamer himself, while most ignored Hirsch's later nuancing.

39. Definitions of biblical "inerrancy" vary, some generally focusing on the text's trustworthy character as divinely inspired while others pursue specific exegetical or hermeneutical implications. See Daniel J. Treier, "Scripture and Hermeneutics," in *The Cambridge Companion to Evangelical Theology*, ed. Timothy Larsen and Daniel J. Treier (Cambridge: Cambridge University Press, 2007), 35–49.

40. Space prevents defending such claims adequately. Full-time equivalent (FTE) enrollment figures from the American Association of Bible Colleges (AABC) show that the industry leader, Moody Bible Institute, grew between 1991 and 2004, at least through program expansion; other significant schools held steady, declined, changed into universities, or closed. Hence, overall FTE for AABC schools rose modestly, from ~25,000 to ~29,000, while programs departed from narrower Bible-college models. ATS statistics from 1980, 1994, and 2014 for seminaries and divinity schools reflect a blend of tradition- or school-specific factors with generic evangelical fortunes. Such vicissitudes aside, in the broad pattern after 1980 (when fewer than twenty ATS schools would be labeled evangelical) new evangelical schools steadily opened while existing ones pursued and gained full

accreditation. The major evangelical schools of 1980 held fairly steady or sometimes grew in the 1990s; subsequently, enrollments varied according to financial, technological, and regional factors—although generally outpacing mainline strength.

41. Christian Smith, *The Bible Made Impossible: Why Biblicism Is Not a Truly Evangelical Reading of Scripture* (Grand Rapids, Mich.: Brazos, 2011).

42. Mainline schools have seen high-profile mergers or closures as enrollment decline parallels congregational decline. Duke is the only major school with meaningful growth, perhaps due to Stanley Hauerwas's appeal. The ATS includes Orthodox and Catholic schools, whose enrollments testify to the well-known challenges of declining American priestly vocations. The number of ATS schools is growing moderately (from ~190 to 226 to 244, in 1980, 1994, and 2014, respectively), but the core Master of Divinity degree is declining for all traditions, evangelicals included: from 79.5 percent of seminary degrees in 1970 to 58.3 percent in 1980 and under 50 percent by 2014. Traditional biblical and theological study, at least residentially, is giving way to shorter, more thoroughly professional ministry degrees—accordingly more practical, affordable, and achievable than the MDiv, which is increasingly being downsized and refocused. For an illuminating narrative profile of evangelical and mainline schools and students, see Jackson W. Carroll et al., *Being There: Culture and Formation in Two Theological Schools* (New York: Oxford University Press, 1997).

43. Chronicled by David H. Kelsey, *Between Athens and Berlin: The Theological Education Debate* (Grand Rapids, Mich.: Eerdmans, 1993).

44. David Tracy, *The Analogical Imagination: Christian Theology and the Culture of Pluralism* (New York: Crossroad, 1981).

45. Reprinted as David H. Kelsey, *Proving Doctrine* (Harrisburg, Pa.: Trinity Press International, 1999).

46. George A. Lindbeck, *The Nature of Doctrine: Religion and Theology in a Postliberal Age* (Louisville, Ky.: Westminster John Knox, 1984).

47. George Hunsinger, "Postliberal Theology," in *The Cambridge Companion to Postmodern Theology*, ed. Kevin J. Vanhoozer (Cambridge: Cambridge University Press, 2003), 42–57, calls Lindbeck neo-liberal and Frei postliberal. Highlighting Niebuhrian influence while questioning the category "postliberal" is Paul J. DeHart, *The Trial of the Witnesses: The Rise and Decline of Postliberal Theology*, Challenges in Contemporary Theology (Malden, Mass.: Blackwell, 2006).

48. David H. Kelsey's proposal in *To Understand God Truly: What's Theological about a Theological School* (Louisville, Ky.: Westminster John Knox, 1992) remained formal, focusing on study of congregational practices. Highlighting the dearth of engagement with scripture in such literature is Robert Banks, *Reenvisioning Theological Education: Exploring a Missional Alternative to Current Models* (Grand Rapids, Mich.: Eerdmans, 1999), 75–78.

49. Hauerwas frequently asserts hermeneutical assumptions and such categories also appear in other literature appealing to "practices": see Barbara G. Wheeler and Edward Farley, eds., *Shifting Boundaries: Contextual Approaches to the Structure of Theological Education* (Louisville, Ky.: Westminster John Knox, 1991).

50. John H. Leith, *Crisis in the Church: The Plight of Theological Education* (Louisville, Ky.: Westminster John Knox, 1997).

51. Crocker pointedly observes, "A recent study of Genesis and Exodus revealed two things [of his parishioners]: first, their unfamiliarity with the Bible, and second, their

moral distaste for some of the reported actions of God"; Richard R. Crocker, "Why Christian Faith Is Often Impossible, Always Difficult, and Yet Sometimes Happens in Contemporary, Pluralistic, Postmodern American Suburban Life," in *Reading the Bible in Faith: Theological Voices from the Pastorate*, ed. William H. Lazareth (Grand Rapids, Mich.: Eerdmans, 2001), 8.

52. Coffman, *Christian Century*, 219–20, notes a shift in that journal's teaching resources plus the funding of such recovery efforts by the Lilly Endowment.

53. Robert Allen Warrior, "Canaanites, Cowboys, and Indians: Deliverance, Conquest, and Liberation Theology Today," *Christianity and Crisis* 49 (1989-1990): 261–65, reprinted in *Native and Christian: Indigenous Voices on Religious Identity in the United States and Canada*, ed. James Treat (New York: Routledge, 1996).

54. See, e.g., several postcolonial works by R. S. Sugirtharajah, notably *The Bible and the Third World: Precolonial, Colonial and Postcolonial Encounters* (Cambridge: Cambridge University Press, 2001); on global Christianity and biblical interpretation, see the overview in ch. 6 of Daniel J. Treier, *Introducing Theological Interpretation of Scripture: Recovering a Christian Practice* (Grand Rapids, Mich.: Baker Academic, 2008).

55. Mark K. Taylor, "Celebrating Difference, Resisting Domination: The Need for Synchronic Strategies in Theological Education," in *Shifting Boundaries*, 259–93, 266.

56. Cain Hope Felder, ed., *Stony the Road We Trod: African American Biblical Interpretation* (Minneapolis, Minn.: Augsburg Fortress, 1991); the statistics appear in Felder's "Introduction," 1–14. Alongside King's appropriation of mainline education, consider the alienation of James H. Cone, "Martin, Malcolm, and Black Theology," in *The Future of Theology: Essays in Honor of Jürgen Moltmann*, ed. M. Volf, C. Krieg, and T. Kucharz (Grand Rapids, Mich.: Eerdmans, 1996), 185–95.

57. Carl Henry recognized this scandal as early as *The Uneasy Conscience of Modern Fundamentalism* (Grand Rapids, Mich.: Eerdmans, 1947), 16–23, but evangelicals still contribute to racialization decades later through their individualistic "cultural toolkit." See Michael O. Emerson and Christian Smith, *Divided by Faith: Evangelical Religion and the Problem of Race in America* (New York: Oxford University Press, 2000).

58. Peter J. Gomes, *The Good Book: Reading the Bible with Mind and Heart* (New York: Morrow, 1996).

59. See the contrasts between the "Left Behind" novels of Tim LaHaye and those of Dan Brown in light of Philip J. Lee, *Against the Protestant Gnostics* (New York: Oxford University Press, 1987).

60. Explored energetically by Vincent Crapanzano, *Serving the Word: Literalism in America from the Pulpit to the Bench* (New York: New, 2000); and historically by Jaroslav Pelikan, *Interpreting the Bible and the Constitution* (New Haven, Conn.: Yale University Press, 2004).

61. An upbeat tone governs George Gallup Jr. and Robert Bezilla, *The Role of the Bible in American Society: On Occasion of the 50th Anniversary of National Bible Week, November 18-25, 1990* (Princeton, N.J.: Religion Research Center, 1990). John Sullivan, "Reading Habits, Scripture and the University," in *Bible and the University*, 216–39, reflects the anecdotal worries; whereas, Byron R. Johnson, "The Case for Empirical Assessment of Biblical Literacy in America," in *Bible and the University*, 240–52, denies that social-scientific evidence demonstrates deepening biblical illiteracy. See also Philip Goff, Arthur E. Farnsley II, Peter J. Thuesen, *The Bible in American Life: A National Study* (Indianapolis, Ind.: The Center for the Study of Religion and American Culture, Indiana

University-Purdue University, 2014), http://www.raac.iupui.edu/files/2713/9413/8354/Bible_in_American_Life_Report_March_6_2014.pdf.

62. Rodney L. Petersen, "Foreword," in *Theological Literacy in the Twenty-First Century*, ed. Rodney L. Petersen with Nancy M. Rourke (Grand Rapids, Mich.: Eerdmans, 2002), xiii.

63. Until recently the doctrine's only substantial treatment was Cyril Eastwood, *The Priesthood of All Believers: An Examination of the Doctrine from the Reformation to the Present Day* (Minneapolis, Minn.: Augsburg, 1962). Mainline theological education literature assumed the need for an educated clergy, while evangelicals, in particular, oriented pastoral ministry toward cultivating lay initiative. But neither group substantially referenced the initial Protestant claim.

64. Richard J. Mouw, "The Bible in Twentieth-Century Protestantism: A Preliminary Taxonomy," in *Bible in America*, 139–62.

65. Crapanzano, *Serving the Word*, 341.

66. Pietsch offers an important rereading of what we might call early dispensationalism's "popular science," noting that the analytical categories of its historiography have been defined by its theological opponents, with unintentionally distortive consequences; B. M. Pietsch, *Dispensational Modernism* (New York: Oxford University Press, 2015), 6–7. This concern confirms the cautionary moral of our narrative. Such a phenomenon may pertain broadly to popular and professional tensions throughout American theological education.

BIBLIOGRAPHY

Banks, Robert. *Reenvisioning Theological Education: Exploring a Missional Alternative to Current Models*. Grand Rapids, Mich.: Eerdmans, 1999.

Carpenter, Joel A. *Revive Us Again: The Reawakening of American Fundamentalism*. New York: Oxford University Press, 1997.

Carroll, Jackson W., et al. *Being There: Culture and Formation in Two Theological Schools*. New York: Oxford University Press, 1997.

Cherry, Conrad. *Hurrying Toward Zion: Universities, Divinity Schools, and American Protestantism*. Bloomington: Indiana University Press, 1995.

Coffman, Elesha J. *The Christian Century and the Rise of the Protestant Mainline*. New York: Oxford University Press, 2013.

Crapanzano, Vincent. *Serving the Word: Literalism in America from the Pulpit to the Bench*. New York: New Press, 2000.

D'Elia, John A. *A Place at the Table: George Eldon Ladd and the Rehabilitation of Evangelical Scholarship in America*. New York: Oxford University Press, 2008.

DeHart, Paul J. *The Trial of the Witnesses: The Rise and Decline of Postliberal Theology*. Challenges in Contemporary Theology. Malden, Mass.: Blackwell, 2006.

Eastwood, Cyril. *The Priesthood of All Believers: An Examination of the Doctrine from the Reformation to the Present Day*. Minneapolis, Minn.: Augsburg, 1962.

Emerson, Michael O., and Christian Smith. *Divided by Faith: Evangelical Religion and the Problem of Race in America*. New York: Oxford University Press, 2000.

Felder, Cain Hope, ed. *Stony the Road We Trod: African American Biblical Interpretation.* Minneapolis, Minn.: Augsburg Fortress, 1991.

Fogarty, Gerald P. *American Catholic Biblical Scholarship: A History from the Early Republic to Vatican II.* San Francisco, Calif.: Harper & Row, 1989.

Frei, Hans W. *The Eclipse of Biblical Narrative: A Study in Eighteenth and Nineteenth Century Hermeneutics.* New Haven, Conn.: Yale University Press, 1974.

Gallup, George, Jr., and Robert Bezilla. *The Role of the Bible in American Society: On Occasion of the 50th Anniversary of National Bible Week, November 18–25, 1990.* Princeton, N.J.: Religion Research Center, 1990.

Gomes, Peter J. *The Good Book: Reading the Bible with Mind and Heart.* New York: Morrow, 1996.

Griffin, David Ray, and Joseph C. Hough Jr., eds. *Theology and the University: Essays in Honor of John B. Cobb.* Albany, N.Y.: SUNY, 1991.

Hatch, Nathan O., and Mark A. Noll, eds. *The Bible in America: Essays in Cultural History.* New York: Oxford University Press, 1982.

Hauerwas, Stanley. *Unleashing the Scripture: Freeing the Bible from Captivity to America.* Nashville, Tenn.: Abingdon, 1993.

Henry, Carl. *The Uneasy Conscience of Modern Fundamentalism.* Grand Rapids, Mich.: Eerdmans, 1947.

Hirsch, E. D., Jr. *Validity in Interpretation.* New Haven, Conn.: Yale University Press, 1967.

Holifield, E. Brooks. *Theology in America: Christian Thought from the Age of the Puritans to the Civil War.* New Haven, Conn.: Yale University Press, 2003.

Kaplan, Dana Evan, ed. *The Cambridge Companion to American Judaism.* Cambridge, Mass.: Cambridge University Press, 2005.

———, ed. *Platforms and Prayer Book: Theological and Liturgical Perspectives on Reform Judaism.* New York: Rowman & Littlefield, 2002.

Kelsey, David H. *Between Athens and Berlin: The Theological Education Debate.* Grand Rapids, Mich.: Eerdmans, 1993.

———. *Proving Doctrine.* Harrisburg, Pa.: Trinity Press International, 1999.

———. *To Understand God Truly: What's Theological about a Theological School.* Louisville, Ky.: Westminster John Knox, 1992.

Larsen, Timothy, and Daniel J. Treier, eds. *The Cambridge Companion to Evangelical Theology.* Cambridge: Cambridge University Press, 2007.

Lazareth, William H., ed. *Reading the Bible in Faith: Theological Voices from the Pastorate.* Grand Rapids, Mich.: Eerdmans, 2001.

Legaspi, Michael C. *The Death of Scripture and the Rise of Biblical Studies.* Oxford: Oxford University Press, 2010.

Leith, John H. *Crisis in the Church: The Plight of Theological Education.* Louisville, Ky.: Westminster John Knox, 1997.

Lindbeck, George A. *The Nature of Doctrine: Religion and Theology in a Postliberal Age.* Louisville, Ky.: Westminster John Knox, 1984.

Meyer, Michael A. *Response to Modernity: A History of the Reform Movement in Judaism.* New York: Oxford University Press, 1988.

Meyer, Michael A., and W. Gunther Plaut, eds. *The Reform Judaism Reader: North American Documents.* New York: UAHC Press, 2001.

Miller, Glenn T. *Piety and Profession: American Protestant Theological Education, 1870–1970.* Grand Rapids, Mich.: Eerdmans, 2007.

Niebuhr, H. Richard, Daniel Day Williams, and James M. Gustafson. *The Advancement of Theological Education: The Summary Report of a Mid-Century Study.* New York: Harper, 1957.

Noll, Mark A. *America's God: From Jonathan Edwards to Abraham Lincoln.* New York: Oxford University Press, 2002.

———. *Between Faith and Criticism: Evangelicals, Scholarship, and the Bible in America.* New York: Harper & Row, 1986.

Pelikan, Jaroslav. *Interpreting the Bible and the Constitution.* New Haven, Conn.: Yale University Press, 2004.

Peterson, Rodney L., and Nancy M. Rourke, eds. *Theological Literacy in the Twenty-First Century.* Grand Rapids, Mich.: Eerdmans, 2002.

Pietsch, B. M. *Dispensational Modernism.* New York: Oxford University Press, 2015.

Sheehan, Jonathan. *The Enlightenment Bible: Translation, Scholarship, Culture.* Princeton, N.J.: Princeton University Press, 2005.

Smith, Christian. *The Bible Made Impossible: Why Biblicism Is Not a Truly Evangelical Reading of Scripture.* Grand Rapids, Mich.: Brazos, 2011.

Thuesen, Peter J. *In Discordance with the Scriptures: American Protestant Battles over Translating the Bible.* New York: Oxford University Press, 1999.

Treier, Daniel J. *Introducing Theological Interpretation of Scripture: Recovering a Christian Practice.* Grand Rapids, Mich.: Baker-Academic, 2008.

Vanhoozer, Kevin J., ed. *The Cambridge Companion to Postmodern Theology.* Cambridge: Cambridge University Press, 2003.

Volf, M., C. Krieg, and T. Kucharz, eds. *The Future of Theology: Essays in Honor of Jürgen Moltmann.* Grand Rapids, Mich.: Eerdmans, 1996.

Wheeler, Barbara G., and Edward Farley, eds. *Shifting Boundaries: Contextual Approaches to the Structure of Theological Education.* Louisville, Ky.: Westminster John Knox, 1991.

CHAPTER 9

....

THE BIBLE IN DIGITAL
CULTURE

....

JOHN B. WEAVER

THE story of the Bible in electronic society begins in the nineteenth and twentieth centuries with the ability to produce electricity and to take photographs, both of which impacted significantly the media and message of the Bible. These innovations allowed for the capturing and mass reproduction of the senses of sight and sound, so that the Bible was communicated more quickly, more broadly, and increasingly to commercial ends. While mainline Protestantism was more focused on literate-based media, the broad swath of Evangelical churches emphasized the use of electronic media for communication of their faith. Evangelists like Dwight L. Moody, Charles Fuller, Billy Graham, and Oral Roberts became synonymous with electronic means of communicating the Bible. Within the early twenty-first century, and in this present essay, the digital technology of computers and the Web becomes the primary focus of discourse about the Bible and technology. In addition to the use of computers and other electronic production technology in the printing of books, the new media of screen-based communication and Web-based information, enabled primarily by the advance of the microprocessor, are continuing to transform the Bible and related North American (and broader global) culture in epochal ways.

The ongoing shift of the Bible to digital media is the primary story of historical development in the twentieth century. This shift concerns not only the Bible but also a host of other print-based books, from the popular and mass-produced to the specialized and niche-marketed. Previous analyses of electronic books have observed the quantitative and qualitative difference in book production after the advent of digital publishing: "Since the 1980s, when microprocessors moved digital technologies into everyday use, there has been a relentless shift away from writing exclusively in the tangible, intransigent forms of ink and paper and toward the more ephemeral forms of digital text."[1]

In addition to electronic modes of production and distribution of print books, the central trajectory of Bible access in America in recent decades is the expanding accessibility, capabilities, and use of screen-based and Web-based digital media for Bible reading. One indicator of this engagement with digital media is the Barna Group's study "The State of the Bible, 2015," which reveals that the percentage of Bible readers utilizing digital Bibles on the Internet, smartphones, and e-readers has increased annually for at least the past five years, with half of all Bible readers now using the Internet to access the Bible.[2] Similarly, *The Bible in American Life* study reports that among those who have read the Bible in the past year, 31 percent read it on the Internet, while 22 percent employed "e-devices." This study further delineates the identity of these digital readers by age, income, and education, concluding "that younger people, those with higher salaries, and most dramatically, those with more education among the respondents read the Bible on the Internet or an e-device at higher rates."[3] These trends are seen in other, broader surveys of American readers, which indicate increased reading of digital books, but declines in use of "e-readers" to access those digital books and the continued predominance of printed books.[4]

COMPLEXITY AND LOSS IN CONTEMPORARY BIBLE READING

A defining quality of the proliferation of digital Bibles in America is the broader context of hybridity and ambiguity in Bible media. While the use of digital Bibles is rising in a publishing environment that still favors printed Bibles, there is considerable uncertainty about the media trajectory of Bible usage. Despite the growing dominance of digital culture, and relatively high use of screen-based Bibles among Millennials, the practice of reading Bibles in their printed forms in North America remains strong, as does stated preference for printed Bibles over digital Bibles in their various forms. This mixture of reading practices is accompanied, and sometimes occasioned by, the moral ambiguity of digital Bibles, which is the uncertainty of readers toward the ultimate propriety of digital Bibles that both enable good access to scripture and can at times disable good attentiveness to the text by, for example, pushing digital distractions through advertisements and other intrusive notifications. The multimedia environment and the ambiguous value of digital Bibles both contribute, therefore, to an increasingly hybrid reading experience in the early twenty-first century.

In part because of this complex hybridity, the reading of Bibles in our digital culture is subject to the same mournful tendencies that characterize a broader critique of technology within North America literary culture (and beyond). From *Amusing Ourselves to Death* (1985) to *The Gutenberg Elegies* (2006) to *The Late Age of Print* (2011), the moribund state of printed book culture is regularly debated and often lamented. Beyond nostalgia, such discourse accurately names the epochal nature of the current rise of digital books and online reading. The era of printed letters and books might be coming to an end.

Although the Bible existed before the advent of printed texts, the potential loss of the printed Bible is especially acute because of the sacred, even sacramental nature of the Bible in the United States. For many in North America, the Bible is a script for addressing and being addressed by the divine; it is a medium for accessing the power and presence of God. As such, the media of the Bible, whether printed or electronic, serves a sort of sacramental function as an outward and visible sign of inward and spiritual grace. Surveys of Bible readers in North America show that this connection to God is of enduring and central importance. The Bible serves as a critical bridge between the human and the divine. According to a recent survey on the Bible in American life, 72 percent of Bible readers read the Bible "for personal prayer and devotion." The second most common reason for reading the Bible

(62 percent) was "to learn about religion," and the third (44 percent) was "decisions about personal relationships."[5] As these rationale suggest, the reading of the Bible in our digital age remains deeply influenced by a desire to connect with God and with other people.

The digital revolution is new and not new. It is certainly not the first transition in how various forms of media have been used as conduits of divine communication. The conventions of transition, departure, and new arrival that are so often referenced in contemporary discourse around the Bible in digital culture are evidenced in other eras in the histories of Judaism, Christianity, and media.[6]

IDOLATRY IN DIGITAL CULTURE

The modern transition to screen-based Bibles, while lauded for the increased accessibility and searchability of the scriptures, also elicits concern and complaint over the excessive and obsessive attention to the distracting, self-indulgent, and often addictive devices and digital content that accompany and frame many digital Bibles today. A growing commitment and compulsion to the technologies that frame our digital Bible leads to the critique of technology as an idol: "While technology can be an idol in and of itself, far more commonly it serves as an enabler of other idols."[7] The critique of digital Bibles as an enabler of idols results primarily from the location of the electronic Scriptures on multifunctional devices for accessing other information. Although some e-readers like the Kindle allow for dedicated reading of the biblical text, the declining number of such "e-readers" among Americans points to increasingly complex digital environments for Bible reading. This digital technology and content (e.g., banner ads in the Web browser, pop-up notifications on the electronic device, and personalized formatting options in the digital Bible itself) can be thought of as idolatrous because they can easily become more important to readers than God and God's word, absorbing heart and imagination more than does God.

The influence of digital technologies is thought to deceive by overloading and thereby limiting human cognition.[8] The exponentially increasing quantity of information resulting from machine processed data and computer-networked communication has produced what some scholars consider a crisis in literacy and, more specifically, in biblical literacy. The quantity of digital information is indicated by oft-cited and always growing statistics on the number of videos on YouTube, data storage in Facebook, or daily devotion to electronic media by the average American teenager.[9] This information overload is thought to disable human capacity for both deep reading and critical thinking. This is the basic, but often ignored, reality that technology can make some things more difficult.[10]

Two metaphors express the concept of the deceptive and ultimately idolatrous context of digital Bibles: digital overload and digital fog. Images of "information overload" and the "overflowing brain" depict the limits of our cognitive load in digital culture. Like a wire with too much electrical current, our brains short-circuit with too much information. A recent Temple University study showed how information overload shuts off the prefrontal cortex's ability for higher order thinking, concluding: "With too much information . . . people's decisions make less and less sense."[11] Another metaphor, "digital fog," identifies the short-sightedness and disorientation that can result from too much ambient information.[12] Here a too-crowded or overly dense environment of data causes needed information to be unseen and lost. Unfortunately, the prospects for improved capacity are not promising. The rate of our world's datafication is outstripping our innate capacity to adapt to it, and the situation leads contemporary philosophers, such as Byung-Chul Han, to observe how the information society cripples our higher forms of judgment, arguing that "less is better."[13] A pressing question, however, is whether less is possible.

The idolatry of subservience to digital configurations of the Bible is seen in at least three primary contexts: websites and apps, software programs, and social media feeds. Despite the popularity of Bible websites like Bible.com and related mobile apps that seek to simplify and declutter the digital Bible reading experience, smartphones and other Web-enabled devices that mediate these texts are otherwise full of distracting banners and alluring chances to click on various links that lead the reader away from the biblical text. In this digital world, critics warn that readers, in a form of technological idolatry, are subservient to the digital demands of their Bible gadgets.

In addition to the influence of our mobile devices, the fog of digital data displayed by popular Bible software programs can lead users to lose focus on a biblical passage and in losing focus also lose the ability to discover key exegetical insights. In studies of their interactions with Bible study software, which surround and interweave the biblical text with an increasing number of Bible study tools, users of the software report the loss of study focus and the fragmentation of literary context during Bible reading.[14] The simultaneous presentation of (perhaps too many) different study options leads readers away from their ability to do serious study.

Alongside the distractions of multiple study and commentary links within various Bible websites and software packages, the spamming of social media users by automated, computer-generated messages containing Bible verses is generating a digital environment in which verses are falsely represented as "sent" by individuals and also divorced from attention to biblical and social contexts. Twitter bots, for example, are responsible for approximately half of the tens of millions of Bible verses tweeted in a recent year.[15] This growing automation of scripture citations in the social media sphere is a combination of misinformation and information overload, both of which desensitize viewers to the power of scriptures because of their mass quantity and questionable quality.

In addition to overloading the senses, the shift to a digital Bible feeds a social psychology of consumerism that inhibits a productive engagement with the biblical text in service to the church community. The Bible is experienced as a stream of personalized content (as with Facebook posts), which is received in a culture of exhibition and as part of an information economy where negative criticism is limited, optional, and easily terminable without consequence. In a world of device-based Bible apps and online Bible sites, the link to the Bible and its sacred discourse are embedded not in the shared texts of the church or even the observable material world, but in personal preferences and organizations of digital content, with customized selections of configurations of Bible versions, interpretative tools, and sharing applications (such as Facebook).

Disconnection from Authority

Within our digital culture, we are experiencing an epochal transition in the form of the religious text. The shift now is from the printed text to the digital text, with a resulting disembodiment, or excarnation, of the physical, printed Bible as the primary form of Holy Scripture. (There is at the same time a shift from the embodied presence of religious leaders to the ever more distended presence of religious authority through electronic media.) The printed Bible, like any codex, has a body. Its face, back, spine, fore-edges, and leaves are held, turned, and fingered with physical attributes that are essential to its identity and experience. The epochal shift of the Bible from physical "bits" to electronic "bytes" results in a disembodied Bible that has a virtual reality and some material housing in a digital screen and device, but not the same dedicated and tangible tome that was characteristic of the Bible as both an instrument of concrete religious authority and an icon (a material representation of divine presence or power) for both individual and communal devotion.

In addition to the increasing disconnection from the physical presence of the Bible as book, the digital Bible and its online culture has challenged the authority of traditional leaders of religious communities. The challenge comes again from a shifted access to knowledge, namely the ability of viewers to gain uninitiated and unfettered access to (more or less) theological interpretations of the Bible, and also the ability of the technology to have uninvited authority in the lives of religious adherents through advertisement and other pushing of information into otherwise passive and compliant contexts of religious trust and obedience. Commercial promotion through individualized marketing and personal networks or "friend" recommendations are new and central sources of authority for this proactive indoctrination through affinity group—whether the affinity is established through data tracking or online social circle. In both cases, the personalized hold of the digital Bible and related content such as customized reading lists and commentary selections on the attention of readers relocates the source of theological authority and accountability away from the community and community leaders, giving it instead to disembodied voices and individuals. The shift here is of crucial sociological importance as the emphasis of biblical interpretation and guidance moves away from the embodied religious community to the simple consumption of market-driven packages of religious content. Downloading of Bible apps, as well as selection of preacher podcasts and other faith-oriented guides, are individually selected in digital culture so that authority to select, read, and interpret the Bible resides in the digital marketplace and the choice of the individual searcher, with "authenticity" redefined by an app-based culture so that it is a self-expressive application of one's own personal choices regarding scripture, rather than a primary adherence or responsiveness to community-based standards of scriptures that are rooted in traditional notions of canon, tradition, church leadership structures, and especially church leadership figures such as bishops, deacons, and preachers.

The shift in religious authority that parallels the rise of digital Bibles is first and foremost a change in religious practice. Bible readers converse less about the Bible in-person, particularly within religious communities, in large part because the impulse and opportunity for face-to-face Bible conversations are replaced by digital interfaces. Once plugged into their screens, Bible readers spend increasing amounts of time scanning and episodically participating in online Bible sources and chats, which become a primary source of theological information and spiritual formation in their lives. With highlighting of Bibles and theological discussions shifted online and outside the constellations of Christians in churches and other groups, conversation about the Bible becomes a convenience-oriented activity lumped together with secular and mundane consumption of digital information that is valued chiefly due to its accessibility (recommended by the top hit in Web search, ranked highest on the app store, or most promoted on social media) and speed (the page most quickly opened or the app downloaded without expenditure of extra time or money).

This shift in the location of theological authority in reading and interpretation of the digital Bible has a deleterious twofold effect on the importance of the gathered religious community. First, congregational and small-group practices of studying scriptures, reflecting on their meaning, contemplating their significance, and discerning the Holy Spirit's direction for individual and group action—already challenged by limited time and desire—are further challenged by a loss of attention and confidence in the minds and hearts of participants who no longer believe the local community can add anything particularly important to reading, interpretation, and engagement of the digital Bible as presented on the Internet. The wisdom of the local church is thereby subordinated to the broader digital Web of ambient information from and about the Bible.

Second, the particularity of the insight and authority of the local congregation's leadership is, in relationship to digital Bibles, potentially subordinated to the undifferentiated knowledge of the digital network. In a way akin to the ancient heresy of Gnosticism, truth and reality is determined by a disembodied and abstract concept of personal knowledge, without communal authority or accountability. The leader's interpretation and modeling of the Bible is replaced by the wisdom of the crowd, with its crucial disconnection from local discipline and succession, disabling both reliable commitment and continuity in service and leadership.

DEVOTION TO THE WORD: ANCIENT AND MODERN DISCIPLINES OF BIBLE READING

In our contemporary digital world, the move of media from print to electronic has, due to concerns of digital overload and superficiality, lead to an emphasis on the importance of carving out time and attention to reading, especially with recent surveys reporting an ongoing decline in reading rates among youth.[16] Drawing upon traditional spiritual disciplines of Sabbath, *Lectio Divina*, and *Examen*, the reading of the Bible in electronic society is increasingly focused through the use of online sites and mobile apps. I have dubbed these digitally supported religious practices "iDisciplines." These iDisciplines are electronically enhanced habits of religious devotion that seek to maintain a relationship with God by using both old and new media to maintain a focus on God's word as it moves across a cultural transition into a new media. In some cases, these are disciplines of omission that seek to read the Bible more by elimination of digital distractions. For example, such disciplines include the use of Internet blocking software such as https://freedom.to/, which disables access to Web traffic for a specified time. Others are disciplines of commission. Like the Mosaic requirement that God's law be read by the people of Israel every seven years (Deut. 31:9-11), religious authorities today, both in the family and the church, are prescribing digital schedules of Bible reading, often through social media services like Facebook and Twitter.

Screen-based Bibles seem to lead to a division in reading behaviors. A growing body of evidence shows that readers prefer and often use both digital and print Bibles for different purposes. For examples, a recent Barna Group summary of six years of annual "Bible in America" surveys reveals that "reading from a print version on your own" increased at a high rate (89 to 92 percent) from 2011 to 2016, while "searching for Bible verses on a smartphone or cell phone" more than doubled, from 18 to 43 percent during the same time period.[17] As these trends suggest, the scrollable and hyperlinked Bible-in-a-browser is preferred and most often used for rapid searching, scanning, and brief utilization of content—what some have called consumerist reading. Traditional, printed Bibles are most used and preferred for focused discovery and slower consumption of content, actions that Paul Griffiths and others have seen as characteristic of "religious reading" as a behavior that is reverential, ruminative, and reiterative.[18] This differentiation between what is elsewhere distinguished as "extensive" and "intensive" reading is leading to an increasingly hybrid reading experience corresponding to the differences between print and digital. The research of information scientist Ziming Liu, for example, indicates that even as digital reading expands, "readers will continue to use print media for much of their reading activities, especially in-depth reading."[19] This notion of an abiding preference for devotional reading of printed Bibles is supported by national surveys of North American Bible readers and more localized studies of users of Bible-study software. These studies continue to report an enduring use of printed Bibles for intensive reading, even while there is increasing use of Bible software and online apps for browsing, keyword spotting, and other nonlinear reading.[20]

There is increasing recognition of the need to balance deep reading and hyper-reading, the latter of which consumes content as quickly and as little as possible in order to identify needed information.[21] With the rise of digital readers supporting fast reading, and unless digital technology better enables slow reading, we are likely to see the formation of movements advocating for the principled reading of printed Bibles, which, along with other arenas of the contemporary "slow movement," will react intentionally against the product-oriented, speed-obsessed practices of corporatized North American culture and the broader technological drive for greater efficiency, which, as Jacques Ellul famously observed, is the fixed and final purpose of technology.[22]

Bible reading practices are, however, increasingly hybrid and this complexity extends to the relationship between reading of print and digital texts. In contrast to a technological determinism that would see digital technology as necessarily leading to a hyper-efficient or shallower form of knowing the Bible, a preferable methodological approach is to see the digital technology of Bible-making and reading as a social institution that can be shaped and reshaped by religious communities and individuals.[23] The use of digital media for religious reading of printed texts is one example of an iDiscipline, which is a faithful reflection and/or action upon digital technologies for religious information and formation. The importance of such iDisciplines to reading and knowledge of the Bible in our electronic society is seen, for example, in the rise of electronic apps for reading and memorization of scripture. In accord with the injunctions to remember God's words in various religious traditions, contemporary software developers are focusing on the memorization of scripture as spiritual practice. For example, one such development is ScriptureTyper.com. Pictorial and auditory prompts for memorizing either a predefined or personalized selection of scriptures are among the advantages of computer software for memorization of both individual Bible verses and longer passages. Such memorization is an example of what Albert Borgmann has termed a "focal practice," which is a simple, centering, and repeatable action that is an end in itself and guards against technological distraction, using technology only as a means to a more ultimate concern. For Borgmann, both the long distance run, and the common meal at the family table are two examples of such focal practices.[24]

Similarly, remembering and reflecting on scripture (whether in prayer or other practice) is a focal commitment that leads to an intelligent limitation of technology, whether by elimination of distracting media through simplified attention, or diminished need for information technologies to remember biblical passages. In either case, websites and mobile apps can serve as helpful guides to hybrid reading experiences, utilizing the limited strengths of digital tools to engage the strengths of printed media for extensive reading, reflection, and memorization. Stated differently, this synergistic use of digital and printed Bibles and digital Bible-reading apps contributes to our increasingly integrative identity as "social cyborgs," who integrate digital technologies, material technologies, and our human lives to the best and most faithful ends.[25]

DISCONNECTION FROM COMMUNITY

Within our North American culture, digital technology is often associated with increased social isolation and community fragmentation. For example, the reader of a digital Bible on a smartphone in church is separated from other congregants both by attention and by uncertain focus. A phone viewed in worship raises concern: Is the person focused on a Bible or other content that is inappropriate to community and devotion? There are unspoken messages communicated by a wearer of headphones in a public setting ("don't engage me"), or a nearby viewer of a phone screen ("I won't engage you"), or a reader of a tablet screen during a class or other group event ("there is something on my device more engaging than you"). On the one hand, personal technologies are extensions of our bodies, allowing for new connections to other things and people, providing a valuable network of additional ideas and more contacts. (Among the most often cited advantages of digital Bibles are the advantages for searching key words, and for communicating scripture at a distance, especially in foreign languages in overseas contexts.) But the gripping and fixating quality of mobile and Web technologies isolates individuals.

In contrast to the generally approved practice of reading a printed Bible or hymnal during worship, viewing a smartphone during Sunday worship raises questions about our attentiveness and focus, even if it contains our Bible app. Due in part to the taboo of "phubbing"—focusing on a smartphone and snubbing other people—the use of mobile devices in a religious context is viewed with suspicion as a potential phubbing of community and the holy presence of the Divine. The distancing power of digital devices, even when used for reading the Bible, is observed by congregational leaders, especially in economically impoverished areas, who report that when they teach or preach from an electronic tablet there is negative response and separation from other community members due to the leader's perceived technological privilege—a digital divide.

The so-called digital divide that correlates use and non-use of technology to socioeconomic status, age, and other individual and communal characteristics is a central concern in both the creation and communal use of electronic Bibles. Recent studies confirm that, more than any other group, a greater number of wealthy, young, and Caucasian readers utilize the Bible in electronic form.[26] Some recent scholarship suggests gender-based differences in engagement of screen-based books, with men more likely than females to utilize electronic Bibles for prolonged periods.[27]

This distancing of community members due to cultural change and technological shifts is seen in our digital era in the diminishing relationship between the reader and the book's author or donor. This distancing correlates to loss of paratextual and epitextual features that for over five hundred years have mediated printed Bibles to their users, providing both physical and social points of contacts between the book and the broader culture. First, a digital Bible and other electronic books often omit, or allow for easy bypassing of paratextual features such as material found on the flyleaf or in Bible dedications, prefaces, or table of contents. This type of material orients the reader to the book and its author/translator(s) and to its broader creative context. Beyond nostalgia for the printed book, the absence of a textual frame is resulting in ever more fluid encounters with the biblical text. The text is more fluid both in less informed and less purposeful selection of, and adherence to, particular translations and versions of the Bible. A loosening of the boundaries of the biblical canon is also a possible outcome of the loss of foregrounded and tangible controls on the books of the Bible, such as is provided by a bound volume with a table of contents.

The shift in the form of Bibles in our digital culture characterizes and contributes to the increasing decline of one of the distinctive practices of Bible publishing in the modern era: leather (or faux leather) binding. The unique leather binding, gilt page edges, and even the attached bookmark(s) are aspects of the physical book that have marked it out in the modern era as unique and specially authored. In addition to symbolizing the special, sacred status of the Bible in many North American cultures, the leather binding of many American Bibles is a material marker of the social identity of religious communities—a leather book in hand automatically identifies a Bible carrier in North American society. In this way, the digitization of the Bible is disconnecting Bible readers from traditional understandings and symbolizations of Bible culture and commitment. It is unclear and unlikely that digital formats of the Bible in the future will so publicly communicate the identity of Bible ownership.

THE WELCOMING WORD: GATHERING READERS AND WELCOMING STRANGERS

Hospitality, meaningful relationship, and authentic community are central concerns in our digital age. The degree of the adoption of the digital Bible and its corresponding ability to support religious community will depend on its ability to promote or inhibit the hospitable sharing of the scriptures. The value of sharing printed and digital books derives from three ideas and practices: commonality, transferability, and sociability: "We want other people to read the same thing we are reading (commonality); we want to be able to send other people what we are reading (transferability); and we want to be able to talk to other people about what we are reading (sociability)."[28] With extraordinary access to common translations, the greatest concern in digital culture is the ability to give Bibles and converse about them.

The disembodiment of the Bible in digital formats impacts social relationship through its disruption of conventional practices of Bible gifting, namely, personalized purchase, inscription, and presentation. Although the giving of printed Bibles, especially to children, new converts, and potential adherents, is still a widespread practice, the growing preponderance of Bible apps and mobile websites for surveying scripture is causing the reception of a new digital Bible to be more a function of receiving a phone or tablet, rather than an intentional, discrete, and personal gift from one person (often a parent or grandparent) to another. The future of Bible-gifting as a North American cultural practice is in doubt. Will the formal giving of a Bible become as rare as ownership of "family Bibles," which was once a common practice in North American families? At present, most digital Bibles have no convenient options for personalized transmission and dedication of a sacred text that have for generations enabled the symbolic, tangible, and enduring communication, commitments, and concerns of a donor (often a family member or mentor).

Digitization of sacred texts and digital expression of religious community have created a renewed emphasis on the need for intentional hospitality and meaningful dialogue. On the one hand, electronic society has enabled a greater connection to other people, especially through radio, television, and networked computers. On the other hand, this online connection is different than face-to-face conversation, which communicates knowledge and gains insights through relatively uncontrolled and unpredictable exchange of words wrapped in personality and emotional bonds. The importance of this interpersonal dialogue to engagement and application of the Bible is seen throughout history, for example, in the revivalist small group studies of Pietism. These and other face-to-face meetings often emphasized the intimate dialogue and actions of Bible-focused believers as central to Christian revival. As Sherry Turkle observes in her book, *Reclaiming Conversation*, our contemporary digital connections are no replacement for the face-to-face communications that teach the empathy, attentiveness, and civility that studies show to be increasingly rare in supply.[29]

Conclusion

The trans-media environment of our increasingly digital culture is witnessing a complex amalgamation of different technologies and techniques for accessing, interpreting, and applying the Bible. This hybrid environment defies simple answers to the future of Bible production and reading in North America. Within modern digital culture, and especially the Web-based and mobile device environment of North America, the faithful mediation of media difference in sacred text and reading is seen to center on intentional disciplines of reading, reflection (as in memorization), and community hospitality. These spiritual disciplines are not reactionary—not inimical to the inevitable changes in media and its impact on the community—but conserve beliefs and values of religious communities through intentional practices that transform digital Bibles and digital culture.

Notes

1. David Reinking, "Valuing Reading, Writing, and Books in a Post-Typographic World," in *A History of the Book in America*, vol. 5: *The Enduring Book, Print Culture in Postwar America*, ed. David Paul Nord, Joan Shelley Rubin, and Michael Shudson (Chapel Hill: University of North Carolina Press, 2009), 485.

2. Barna Group, "The State of the Bible, 2015," http://www.americanbible.org/uploads/content/State_of_the_Bible_2015_report.pdf.

3. Philip Goff, Arthur E. Farnsley II, and Peter J. Thuesen, *The Bible in American Life* (Indianapolis: Center for the Study of Religion and American Culture, Indiana University-Purdue University Indianapolis, March 6, 2014), 32, http://www.raac.iupui.edu/files/2713/9413/8354/Bible_in_American_Life_Report_March_6_2014.pdf.

4. Pew Research Center, September 2106, "Book Reading 2016," http://www.pewinternet.org/2016/09/01/book-reading-2016/.

5. Goff et al., *The Bible in American Life*, 22.

6. On the concerns expressed "whenever a new medium is brought into religious use," see Peter Horsfield, *From Jesus to the Internet: A History of Christianity and Media* (Malden, Mass.: Wiley Blackwell, 2015), esp. 58–60, 200–207, 222–23. On the epochs of media in human history and human response to these transitions, see Marshall McLuhan, *The Gutenberg Galaxy: The Making of Typographic Man* (Toronto: University of Toronto Press, 1962).

7. Tim Challies, *The Next Story: Life and Faith after the Digital Explosion* (Grand Rapids, Mich.: Zondervan, 2011), 31.

8. Concerns over information overload extend back to Classical Greece and are famously evident after the invention of the printing press in the concerns over the "confusing and harmful abundance of books" as expressed by the Swiss bibliographer Conrad Gesner, *Bibliotheca universalis* (Zurich, 1545). Fear of information overload continues throughout the modern era (especially in relation to newspapers and other periodicals), reaching full contemporary expression in critics of digital culture. In addition to cultural critics, the concept of information overload is applied to interpretation of digital content in the cognitive theory of multimedia learning. See especially Richard E. Mayer, *Multimedia Learning* (Cambridge: Cambridge University Press, 2009).

9. The explosion of Internet users and their online data sources is documented at http://www.internetlivestats.com/. The increasing availability and use of digital media among youth in North America is reported in a variety of multiyear, longitudinal surveys over the past two decades, including (1) The Kaiser Family Foundation's *Generation M²: Media in the Lives of 8- to 18-Year-Olds*, http://kff.org/other/report/generation-m2-media-in-the-lives-of-8-to-18-year-olds/; and (2) Common Sense Media's *Zero to Eight: Children's Media Use in America 2013*, https://www.commonsensemedia.org/research/zero-to-eight-childrens-media-use-in-america-2013.

10. On the negative aspects of technology and what it makes more difficult, see Andy Crouch, *Culture-Making: Recovering Our Creative Calling* (Downers Grover, Ill.: InterVarsity Press, 2008), 29; see also the difficulty of maintaining community with technology as described by Kevin Kelly, "Lessons of Amish Hackers," in *What Technology Wants* (New York: Penguin, 2010), 217–38.

11. Sharon Begley, "The Science of Making Decisions," *Newsweek*, February 27, 2011, http://www.newsweek.com/science-making-decisions-68627.

12. Gary Small and Gigi Vorgan, *iBrain: Surviving the Technological Alteration of the Modern Mind* (New York: Harper Collins, 2008), 19.

13. Byung-Chul Han, *The Transparent Society* (Stanford, Calif.: Stanford University Press, 2015), 4.

14. John B. Weaver, "Accordance Bible Software in Reading and Teaching: The Difference a Digital Text Makes," *Advances in the Study of Information and Religion*, vol. 1, article 12, 230–31, http://digitalcommons.kent.edu/asir/vol1/iss1/12; cf. John B. Weaver, "BibleWorks

Software in Reading and Teaching: The Difference a Digital Text Makes," in "Theological Libraries and the Hermeneutics of Digital Textuality," *American Theological Library Association Summary of Proceedings* (2010), 232–35.

15. Stephen Smith, "The Bible on Twitter in 2015," *Openbible.info* (blog), December 31, 2015, https://www.openbible.info/blog/2015/12/the-bible-on-twitter-in-2015/.

16. A summary of different national research studies of child and young adult reading trends, demonstrating the declining trajectory, has been compiled by Common Sense Media, "Amount and Frequency of Reading," in *Children, Teens, and Reading: A Research Brief*, May 12, 2014, 9–14, https://www.commonsensemedia.org/file/csm-childrenteensandreading-2014pdf/download.

17. Barna Group, *The Bible in America: The Changing Landscape of Bible Perceptions and Engagement* (Ventura, Calif.: Barna Group, 2016), 54.

18. Paul Griffiths, *Religious Reading: The Place of Reading in the Practice of Religion* (New York: Oxford, 1999), 40–45.

19. Ziming Liu, "Reading Behavior in the Digital Environment," in *Paper to Digital: Documents in the Information Age* (Westport, CT: Libraries Unlimited, 2008), 65.

20. Weaver, "Accordance Bible Software in Reading and Teaching"; Weaver, "BibleWorks Software in Reading and Teaching," 232–35.

21. Naomi Baron, *Words Onscreen: The Fate of Reading in a Digital World* (New York: Oxford, 2015), 157–68.

22. Jacques Ellul, *The Technological Society* (New York: Vintage, 1964), 21.

23. Heidi Campbell, "How Religious Communities Negotiate New Media Religiously," in *Digital Religion, Social Media, and Culture: Perspectives, Practices and Futures*, in eds. Pauline Hope Cheong, Peter Fischer-Neilsen, and Stefan Gelfren (New York: Peter Lang, 2012), 82–85.

24. Albert Borgmann, *Technology and the Character of Contemporary Life: A Philosophical Inquiry* (Chicago: University of Chicago, 1984), 196–210, 219–22.

25. On the notion of "social cyborg," see Brad J. Kallenberg, *Gods and Gadgets: Following Jesus in a Technological Age* (Eugene, OR: Cascade, 2011), 115–17.

26. Philip Goff, et. al. *The Bible in American Life*, 31–32, http://www.raac.iupui.edu/files/2713/9413/8354/Bible_in_American_Life_Report_March_6_2014.pdf; cf. Barna Group, *The Bible in America*, 55.

27. Irene Picton, *The Impact of eBooks on the Motivation and Reading Skills of Children and Young People*, September 2014, p.5, http://www.literacytrust.org.uk/assets/0002/3898/Ebooks_lit_review_2014.pdf; cf. John Dyer, *Print Bibles vs. Digital Bibles: Comparing Engagement, Comprehension, and Behavior*, Unpublished Manuscript, (March 2016).

28. Andrew Piper, *The Book Was There: Reading in Electronic Times* (Chicago: University of Chicago, 2012), 84.

29. Sherry Turkle, *Reclaiming Conversation: The Power of Talk in a Digital Age* (New York: Penguin, 2015), 21, 217, 239.

BIBLIOGRAPHY

Barna Group. *The Bible in America: The Changing Landscape of Bible Perceptions and Engagement*. Ventura, Calif.: Barna Group, 2016.

———. "The State of the Bible, 2015." http://www.americanbible.org/uploads/content/State_of_the_Bible_2015_report.pdf.

Baron, Naomi. *Words Onscreen: The Fate of Reading in a Digital World.* New York: Oxford, 2015.

Begley, Sharon. "The Science of Making Decisions." *Newsweek*, February 27, 2011. http://www.newsweek.com/science-making-decisions-68627.

Borgmann, Albert. *Technology and the Character of Contemporary Life: A Philosophical Inquiry.* Chicago: University of Chicago Press, 1984.

Campbell, Heidi. "How Religious Communities Negotiate New Media Religiously." In *Digital Religion, Social Media, and Culture: Perspectives, Practices and Futures*, edited by Pauline Hope Cheong, Peter Fischer-Neilsen, and Stefan Gelfren, 81–96. New York: Peter Lang, 2012.

Challies, Tim. *The Next Story: Life and Faith after the Digital Explosion.* Grand Rapids, Mich.: Zondervan, 2011.

Common Sense Media. *Children, Teens, and Reading: A Research Brief.* May 12, 2014. https://www.commonsensemedia.org/file/csm-childrenteensandreading-2014pdf/download.

———. *Zero to Eight: Children's Media Use in America 2013.* October 28, 2013. https://www.commonsensemedia.org/research/zero-to-eight-childrens-media-use-in-america-2013.

Crouch, Andy. *Culture-Making: Recovering Our Creative Calling.* Downers Grover, Ill.: InterVarsity Press, 2008.

Ellul, Jacques. *The Technological Society.* New York: Vintage, 1964.

Goff, Philip, Arthur E. Farnsley II, and Peter J. Thuesen. *The Bible in American Life.* Indianapolis, Ind.: Center for the Study of Religion and American Culture, Indiana University-Purdue University Indianapolis, March 6, 2014. http://www.raac.iupui.edu/files/2713/9413/8354/Bible_in_American_Life_Report_March_6_2014.pdf.

Griffiths, Paul. *Religious Reading: The Place of Reading in the Practice of Religion.* New York: Oxford, 1999.

Han, Byung-Chul. *The Transparent Society.* Stanford, Calif.: Stanford University Press, 2015.

Horsfield, Peter. *From Jesus to the Internet: A History of Christianity and Media.* Malden, Mass.: Wiley Blackwell, 2015.

Kaiser Family Foundation. *Generation M²: Media in the Lives of 8- to 18-Year-Olds.* http://kff.org/other/report/generation-m2-media-in-the-lives-of-8-to-18-year-olds/.

Kallenberg, Brad J. *Gods and Gadgets: Following Jesus in a Technological Age.* Eugene, Ore.: Cascade, 2011.

Kelly, Kevin. *What Technology Wants.* New York: Penguin, 2010.

Liu, Ziming. "Reading Behavior in the Digital Environment." In *Paper to Digital: Documents in the Information Age.* Westport, Conn.: Libraries Unlimited, 2008.

Mayer, Richard E. *Multimedia Learning.* Cambridge: Cambridge University Press, 2009.

McLuhan, Marshall. *The Gutenberg Galaxy: The Making of Typographic Man.* Toronto: University of Toronto Press, 1962.

Pew Research Center. "Book Reading 2016." http://www.pewinternet.org/2016/09/01/book-reading-2016/.

Piper, Andrew. *The Book Was There: Reading in Electronic Times.* Chicago: University of Chicago Press, 2012.

Reinking, David. "Valuing Reading, Writing, and Books in a Post-Typographic World." In *A History of the Book in America*, vol. 5: *The Enduring Book, Print Culture in Postwar America*, edited by David Paul Nord, Joan Shelley Rubin, and Michael Shudson. Chapel Hill: University of North Carolina Press, 2009.

Small, Gary, and Gigi Voran. *iBrain: Surviving the Technological Alteration of the Modern Mind*. New York: Harper Collins, 2008.

Smith, Stephen. "The Bible on Twitter in 2015." *Openbible.info* (blog). December 31, 2015. https://www.openbible.info/blog/2015/12/the-bible-on-twitter-in-2015/.

Turkle, Sherry. *Reclaiming Conversation: The Power of Talk in a Digital Age*. New York: Penguin, 2015.

Weaver, John B. "Accordance Bible Software in Reading and Teaching: The Difference a Digital Text Makes." *Advances in the Study of Information and Religion*. Vol. 1, article 12. http://digitalcommons.kent.edu/asir/vol1/iss1/12.

——. "BibleWorks Software in Reading and Teaching: The Difference a Digital Text Makes." "Theological Libraries and Hermeneutics of Digital Textuality." *American Theological Library Association Summary of Proceedings*. 2010.

CHAPTER 10

••

FEMINIST INTERPRETATION
OF THE BIBLE

••

CLAUDIA SETZER

WOMEN have always interpreted the biblical text. Within the Bible itself, the prophet Huldah addresses a prophecy in "the book of the law" (probably an early version of Deuteronomy), and Mary of Nazareth is credited with a song of praise that weaves together prophetic and covenantal themes from the Hebrew Bible.[1] Women martyrs and mystics such as Perpetua, Macrina the Younger, Julian of Norwich, Hildegard of Bingen, and Christine de Pizan have visions that appropriate and interpret biblical events. Women expressed themselves not only in exegesis, but in poetry, hymns, painting, and folk art.

A history of feminist interpretation of "the Bible" assumes a canonical text, however, which indicates a period after the first century for the Hebrew Bible and after the fourth century for the New Testament. In the United States, "the Bible" has usually meant the Protestant canon. (Catholics use a Bible with a larger number of books, and Jews do not include the New Testament, ordering the books differently than the Christian Old Testament). Feminist hermeneutics assumes an approach that makes women the subject of analysis and promotes an egalitarian ideal of male–female relations.

The career of the Bible in America had its own peculiar course. From the founding of the Jamestown colony by way of a royal charter in 1606 that included the aim of "propagating of Christian religion" to Native Americans to today's political rhetoric, biblical language and themes have fused with political movements and events. Unsurprisingly, then, the Bible played a larger-than-life role in early movements for women's rights.

Feminism in North America is described retrospectively as three "waves," the result of some feminists of the twentieth century illuminating the legacy of their nineteenth-century pioneers. The first wave is somewhat artificially construed as the period from the Women's Rights convention of 1848 in Seneca Falls to the passing of the Nineteenth Amendment in 1920 granting women the right to vote. In fact, the advocacy for women's rights went back further, involved a set of social and legal issues in addition to the vote, and was an international movement.[2] It was bound up with other transatlantic reform movements including abolitionism and temperance. Second-wave feminism began in the late 1960s and 1970s in the United States, growing up alongside the civil rights and antiwar movements. A third wave includes the present era, but its conscious diversity of expression poses many questions as to whether it should be called a "wave" at all. The word "feminist" is not claimed by all, and its utility as both a term and as an ideology is contested.

Feminists who address biblical issues agree on two fundamentals. First, the Bible in its canonical form is a patriarchal document that promotes and/or has been used to promote a system that subordinates women. Second, it is an androcentric document that puts the male at the center, in particular in its envisioning of a male God as the ultimate authority. Beyond these two fundamentals, feminist biblical hermeneutics contains considerable variety. Its story is one of both fissures and fusions. These differences and alliances have often been generative and honest in their calling the text and its interpreters to account.

CANONS WITHIN AND WITHOUT

First- and second-wave interpreters had their own "canons within a canon," most examining the creation stories in Genesis 1–2, stories of individual women prophets and judges, Paul's conflicting and ambiguous statements about women's comportment versus evidence of fellow preachers, deacons, and apostles in the early churches, and women around Jesus and their status as disciples. Jewish feminist scholars, like Ross Shepard Kraemer, Amy-Jill Levine, Adele Reinhartz, and myself do not regard the New Testament as scripture, but study it for evidence of early Jewish women. We also critique some New Testament scholarship for its misrepresentation of first-century Judaism, especially regarding women. Jesus presents a particular challenge for feminists because he made no statements about women's rights at all and chose twelve men as his inner circle. Yet feminist biblical interpreters almost always endorse him as promoting an egalitarian ideal.

Womanist scholars, who claim the unique experiences of African American women as an interpretive tool, expanded this canon with discussions of Hagar and Gomer, the wife of Hosea, and slavery in the Bible, particularly in the household codes (codes of conduct that mimic Hellenistic conventions of household management).[3] "Texts of terror," as Phyllis Trible has called them, where women are objects of violence, have engendered work by a number of scholars including Trible, J. Cheryl Exum, and Cheryl Anderson.[4] So too, have models of women's friendship and more positive portrayals of women's agency. The prophets offer calls to social justice alongside some of the most misogynist material in the Bible.

Second-wave and third-wave feminists have expanded the canon by promoting awareness of non-canonical texts that offer expansive understandings of gender. *The Gospel of Mary* shows Mary Magdalene as the disciple closest to Jesus, a subject of Peter's envy. The *Acts of Paul and Thecla* lionizes the young woman Thecla for upending gender roles by rejecting marriage, facing martyrdom, and becoming a preacher and healer in Paul's image. The *Passion of Perpetua and Felicity* also disrupts familial loyalties and gender roles, as the young mother has a vision of becoming male and fighting in the arena, as well as leaving her husband and infant in order to embrace martyrdom. Although these texts are later than the canonical New Testament texts, they bring to light a greater diversity of gender roles and relations in early Christian writings. They also force us to recognize that sexism taints not just the content of biblical texts but the process of canonization too.

DEBATES AND DIFFERENCES AMONG
FIRST-WAVE WOMEN ACTIVISTS

The question "Is the Bible useful to women's rights at all?" arose nearly as soon as activists began searching it for liberationist themes. Sarah Grimké, accustomed to speaking publicly against slavery, wrote a series of letters in 1837 to Mary S. Parker, president of the Boston Female Anti-Slavery Society. Published in *The Liberator*, William Lloyd Garrison's abolitionist newspaper, these letters asserted an egalitarian ideal at the heart of the biblical message, particularly in the creation stories. Grimké asserted that inaccurate translation, misunderstanding, and deliberate misuse of the text has rendered it anti-woman. For example, Grimké argues that in the "curse against Eve" in Genesis 3:16, "yet your desire shall be for your husband and he shall rule over you," the word "shall" should be translated as "will" making it a regretful prediction, not a divine command.[5] Frances Willard, the president of the Women's Christian Temperance Union, showed a similar faith in the Bible's liberating message in her *Woman in the Pulpit* (1888), which advocated the ordination of women in the Methodist Church.

At the other end of the spectrum, Matilda Joslyn Gage pronounced the Bible as "evil" and the source of patriarchy.[6] Ernestine Rose, a Polish rabbi's daughter turned atheist, blocked an attempted resolution that declared the Bible's support for women's equality at a women's rights convention in Syracuse in 1852, arguing that women's rights rested on human rights, something more fundamental and earlier than the Bible. Rose illustrated the dilemma of Jewish women, who might support women's equality, but were wary of a strain of Protestant thought that placed the blame for women's subordination on the Jewish origins of Christianity. Saint Paul, for example, is presented as a Christian when he promotes equality in Galatians 3:28 but as an unreconstructed Pharisee when he forbids women to speak in church in 1 Corinthians 14:34-35. Rose rejected religion, but publicly defended Jews and Judaism in a debate with editor Horace Seaver in the *Boston Investigator* in 1863-64.

The most significant treatment of the Bible by women's rights advocates in the Victorian era is *The Woman's Bible*, a commentary edited by Elizabeth Cady Stanton, examining portions of the Bible that deal with women or where women's absence is conspicuous. While the comments vary, from Matilda Gage's condemnation to Stanton's admiring and mawkish statements about Jesus's mother, *The Woman's Bible* commentary is generally negative about the effects of the Bible on women's status in society. The book had an impact and roused passions, but few were ready to engage its remarks seriously. In the political divisions within the suffrage movement, the National American Woman Suffrage Association, a merged group of two suffrage organizations, officially repudiated the work at its convention in January 1896. Consensus on the Bible never was achieved, but as the women's movement in the early twentieth century focused on suffrage alone, it moved away from invoking the Bible or religion. Lucretia Mott, herself an early proponent of biblical equality, later suggested that using the Bible ultimately became a distraction, as it had in the abolitionist cause.[7] Women's rights would not be won or lost on biblical arguments.

AFRICAN AMERICAN WOMEN INTERPRETERS

African American women had their own traditions of biblical study and activism, but racism also helped create one early fissure between African American and other American women. Although black women were part of the different women's suffrage associations, the suffrage movement at times marginalized them, at one point flirting with a "southern strategy" to bring southern states into the movement by suggesting the vote for white women would counter the influence of black voters in the southern states. A linkage between equality of both race and gender in biblical interpretation undergirded the writing and speaking of many African American women, from Sojourner Truth's famous speech for women's rights in Akron, "Ain't I a Woman?" to Anna Julia Cooper's refined *A Voice from the South* (1892). Jarena Lee became a traveling preacher once she was authorized to preach in 1819 by Richard Allen, the founder of the African Methodist Episcopal Church. Virginia Broughton and other African American women traveled through the South creating "Bible bands," groups of women to study the Bible daily. In her reflections, published in 1907, Broughton gathers the biblical texts that authorize women's authority in general and opportunities for African American women in particular.[8]

As biblical scholar Nyasha Junior points out, many relief and organizing efforts were not strictly about suffrage or racial equality, but their effect empowered black women in those directions.[9] She notes that aid societies to improve health, education, and social conditions had been organized since the colonial period according to many affiliations, including racial, ethnic, and religious. The Women's Club movement after the Civil War included black women's clubs like the National Association of Colored Women (NACW) that fought for suffrage and against lynching and Jim Crow laws.

SECOND-WAVE FEMINIST HERMENEUTICS

These early currents are rehearsed, revised, and amplified in the parallel developments of feminist and womanist biblical interpretation in the twentieth century. Second-wave feminists rediscovered and celebrated Cady Stanton's commentary and Anna Julia Cooper's work while recognizing some of their problematic assumptions.[10] Similarly, womanist biblical interpretation saw its own "waves" in the twentieth century, continuing traditions of story-telling that drew from the experiences of African American women in relationship to biblical tropes. Womanist biblical interpretation also drew distinctions between itself and feminist scholarship, seen as dominated by the concerns of white women. Strictly speaking, self-identified womanist biblical scholars are not a large group, if we consider womanist biblical interpretation as a discrete method, and not simply biblical scholarship that is done by African American women.[11] Mitzi J. Smith's recent collection of womanist biblical interpretation is instructive on this score, as it includes twelve interpreters from cognate fields, including theologians and ethicists.[12] Womanist scholarship has always embraced a variety of methods, while white feminist biblical scholars have frequently been more isolated from their feminist peers in other fields.

Although second-wave feminist scholarship emerged in the late 1960s and 1970s, feminist biblical scholarship took time to coalesce. Religious studies professor Judith Plaskow notes the relatively minor and often negative role assigned to biblical studies in the academic and denominational activist conferences and writings of the 1970s.[13] Two early works that brought biblical studies to the table of feminist studies were Leonard Swidler's article, "Jesus Was a Feminist," and Phyllis Trible's, "De-patriarchalizing in Biblical Interpretation." Both attempted to discover within the text itself resources for feminist interpretation.[14] While this struck the radical American feminist philosopher and theologian Mary Daly and others as special pleading, these works provided an impetus for the growth of feminist biblical interpretation in the 1980s. Plaskow's influential 1972 Midrash (creative expansion) on Eve and Lilith, based on the creation narrative and rabbinic tales of Lilith, suggested the Bible and rabbinics might provide resources for feminist theology.[15]

Phyllis Trible is one of the most important of the early feminist biblical interpreters and illustrates the dilemma of many classically trained feminist scholars who enter the field because they love the Bible. While pursuing issues around patriarchy, they are not inclined to dismiss the text or traditional methods *tout court*. Trible's works, *God and the Rhetoric of Sexuality* and *Texts of Terror* interrogate the biblical text, leading her to argue that the text is self-correcting because it offers multiple interpretations and correctives. Song of Songs, for example, is "a midrash on Genesis 2–3." She argues that themes surrounding erotic relationships in the Song of Songs offer an antidote to the brokenness that results from humanity's exile from Eden. She argues for the close relationship between men and women by pointing out that "Adam" is from the same word as earth, "adamah," thus showing it includes males and females in relationship with each other and with the created world.[16]

Tikvah Frymer-Kensky, a professor at the University of Chicago's Divinity School before her death, underlined the possibilities for reading the women of the Bible as widely representative of humanity: some powerful, some subordinate, some victimized. The earlier Ancient Near Eastern setting, with its gods and goddesses, did not present an egalitarian ideal, but relegated women to the domestic sphere. Ironically then, according to Frymer-Kensky, the single male God that emerged in monotheism was a rejection of limiting gender distinctions.[17]

Approaches like Trible's and Frymer-Kensky's were neither naïve nor apologetic in nature, but they did seem to skirt the fundamental suspicion that the Bible had been a supremely negative force for women. Feminist biblical interpretation divided and split into two trends: first, the excavating of women's lives and personhood and, second, the examination of the "ideology of woman" in ancient texts. Those in the first school of "excavators" argue that women's roles and realities show considerable complexity as the search for hidden examples of power and agency renders visible ancient Israelite women as essential to the ancient economy. New Testament feminist scholars reveal women believers as disciples of Jesus as well as deacons, preachers, and patrons of early churches.

The second scholarly approach looks at the assumptions about women that pervade the texts, or how women are constructed. Because this second group is interested in the undergirding values about women as subordinate and marginal in the text, they often reject the results of the first group. Women in the biblical texts, they point out, are not "real" as historical actors, but are ciphers for an idealized version of women in a hoped-for society. Women's subordination then is not a by-product of ancient societies, but a prescription for how the world should operate. Thus, so-called counter-traditions or individual examples of powerful women and prophets do not interrupt the overarching ideology of women. Although these two interpretive trends existed side-by-side in first-wave, and even more clearly in second-wave feminism, the second trend of examination of ideology generally succeeded and undermined the first. The move to consider the ideologies around women was aided by a general turn toward examining the language of the biblical texts.

The Linguistic Turn

As the project of feminist hermeneutics gathered energy, the field took a "linguistic turn" and analysis of women as historical entities gave way to a focus on how gender is constructed in texts. Historian Joan W. Scott's influential article, "Gender: A Useful Category of Historical Analysis," moved historians away from thinking they might reconstruct women's lives from texts to rhetorical considerations such as how women are talked about, placed, depicted, and left out of texts. Influenced by poststructuralism and postmodernism as a whole, gender analysis focused on language and representation, namely what is available at the surface of the text, assuming that any historical reality behind the text cannot be recovered. The category of "gender" meshed with the "linguistic turn" in literary studies and both filtered into biblical studies. Scott has had her critics, but the category of gender was here to stay. Terms like essentialism (that men and women have fixed essences and characteristics throughout time and place) and positivism (that information is accessible and verifiable apart from the orientation of the observer) became terms of critique, if not dismissal.[18]

Yet the linguistic turn has been both good news and bad news for feminist exegetes. Religious studies professors such as Elizabeth Clark and Elisabeth Schüssler Fiorenza worried that an entirely linguistic approach sets aside possible valuable information about earlier women, resulting in what Schüssler Fiorenza calls "a loss of heritage" while continuing to put the male subject at the center of rhetorical analysis.[19] Elizabeth Clark put it succinctly when she states that in such scholarship "the lady vanishes." Schüssler Fiorenza moved the field forward with her "hermeneutics of suspicion," which reads "against the grain," or proposed ideology of the text, maintaining its possibilities for giving up material with liberating tropes. The subtitle of her ground-breaking book, *In Memory of Her*, calls for a "feminist *reconstruction* of Christian origins," implying both a historical project and an interrogation of ideological underpinnings.[20]

Similarly, Elizabeth Clark proposed an integration of gender analysis with historical method, a type of scholarship that many now engage in. Such scholarship proposes that while texts may not tell us directly about "real women," exploring gender construction yields historical information as we "explore the social forces at work in these constructions."[21] Scholarship shifted to examining the underlying ideologies about women and men in texts, recognizing the assumptions and prescriptions about ideal women and men that functioned in the Ancient Near East for the Hebrew Bible and in the Roman Mediterranean world of the New Testament. For example, rather than parsing Paul's worrying and contradictory statements about women's leadership in ancient communities, the emphasis was put on examining the ways in which he used the categories of the female (mother, nurse) and applied them to himself, touting not the masculine ideal of self-control, but taking on categories of weakness and submission. Recent works that exhibit this type of scholarship include Colleen Conway's *Behold the Man* and Stephanie Cobb's *Dying to Be Men*.[22]

A further development in feminist biblical scholarship recognizes that gender did not function in isolation from other factors like race, class, sexual orientation, and able-bodiedness. The term for this turn toward integrative scholarship is "intersectionality," and it comes from legal scholar Kimberlé Crenshaw. Crenshaw considers the multiplying effect of a host of interrelated factors, showing that these different constructions cannot be studied in isolation from one another. *Prejudice and Christian Beginnings*, edited by Schüssler Fiorenza and Laura Nasrallah, brings together essays that explore interlocking natural and societal relationships in early Christian works and in scholarship on early Christianity, arguing that such explorations yield far more complex and nuanced understandings of the biblical text.[23]

THREE FEMINIST INTERPRETERS

Feminist scholarship accelerated in the late 1980s and the 1990s to such a degree that I cannot mention or even list all the women who have participated and continue to participate in such work. Several anthologies gather some of the works of a large cadre of women laboring to bring forth feminist insights from biblical texts, including: Schüssler Fiorenza's 2-volume *Searching the Scriptures; The Torah: A Women's Commentary*, published by the Women of Reform Judaism; The Feminist Companion series to individual books of the Bible, edited by Amy-Jill Levine and others; *Women and Christian Origins*, edited by Ross Kraemer and Mary Rose D'Angelo; and *The Women's Bible Commentary*, edited by Carol Newsom and Sharon Ringe, recently published in its third edition. The Wisdom Commentary series from Liturgical Press, is currently publishing several books per year, with the goal of producing a feminist commentary on every biblical book.

Recognizing that one cannot do justice to all these interpreters, I choose to take a closer look at three North American interpreters who incorporate feminist analysis into their work as examples of the various angles of approach that are being pursued in the field of biblical interpretation. First, the biblical scholar Gail Yee interprets the grisly story of the dismembered concubine in Judges 17-21 from an ideological perspective. The insights of feminist criticism establish the significance of the concubine's actions of leaving her husband and seeking sanctuary, arguing that "stories ostensibly about male-female relations are more often about struggles among men for honor and status."[24] In this particular case, the concubine is judged as a wanton woman, without voice, name, or humanity in the text, whose act of defiance is quashed by the two males in her life. Yee builds on this model by arguing that it is the Deuteronomist's caricature of the Levites and the body of tribes whose cultic acts outside Jerusalem during Josiah's reform defy the monarchy. A fate similar to the concubine's dismembered body awaits the autonomous Jewish tribes' attempt at independence from Jerusalem.

Second, the late religious studies scholar Jane Schaberg was one of the first to argue that Mary Magdalene's legacy was grossly distorted by later Christian tradition. In "How Mary Magdalene Became a Whore" and *The Resurrection of Mary Magdalene*, Schaberg examined the few biblical verses that mention Mary Magdalene and argued that Mary was, in fact, one of the most significant women in Jesus's life and could be fairly called one of his disciples.[25] Schaberg described the extra-canonical traditions that confer on Mary Magdalene an authority in competition with Peter's. Yet, in later Christian tradition, Mary Magdelene is conflated with anonymous women in the New Testament, including adulterous and other penitent women. According to Schaberg, the Mary Magdalene of legend, Church teaching, and Christian art was thus transformed from a follower of Jesus into the penitent whore, a potent symbol of the repression of women's witness and authority.

Finally, the biblical and cultural historian Adele Reinhartz's "Women in the Johannnine Community: An Exercise in Historical Imagination," appears in the Feminist Companion series edited by Amy-Jill Levine.[26] John's Gospel, she observes, is notable for its examples of significant individual women who figure prominently in John's narrative, such as Jesus's mother at Cana, the Samaritan woman, Martha and Mary of Bethany (who engage Jesus at the site of his raising of their brother Lazarus), and Mary Magdalene. Reinhartz suggests that these women may represent "types" who functioned within the Johannine community at the turn of the first century, and by so arguing raises the possibility of women preachers, elders and teachers, healers, and deacons.

Tensions between Biblical Studies and Theology

Feminist biblical scholars and feminist scholars in other branches of the study of religion have not always been in accord. While many interpreters like Schüssler Fiorenza and Elsa Tamez propound a hermeneutics that embraces both biblical scholarship and theology, a certain disconnect exists between feminist biblical scholars and their theologian and ethicist colleagues. Many of the most influential feminist scholars of the 1980s and 1990s were theologians and ethicists who often used biblical material to indict patriarchy, provide alternative readings, or point out "counter-traditions," but their primary interest was not the meaning of the biblical text, its composition, the possible relation of one part to another, or various interpretations suggested by the text. They tended to read biblical texts as unified compositions, finished literary products whose implications were seemingly obvious to any reader. In many ways the general feminist approach was a pre-critical reading, appropriate for discussing the Bible's effect on society. Such societal effects are well within the purview of theologians and ethicists. Moreover, a hallmark of feminist scholarship has been the appeal to experience in responding to cultural and religious institutions and in fashioning authentic responses.

The suspicion directed toward feminist biblical scholars had to do with both the text itself and the methodologies they brought to bear on that text. Susanne Scholz, a professor of Old Testament studies, articulated the suspicions feminist scholars in other fields have directed at feminist biblical scholars.[27] Some, like Mary Daly and Alison Jasper, in echoes of Gage and Stanton, considered the Bible, like other religious institutions, to be irredeemably patriarchal and not salvageable for feminist work. Moreover, the methods of biblical scholarship in which feminist biblical scholars were trained, were suspect. Audre Lorde's famous dictum, "The master's tools will never dismantle the master's house" was directed at traditional historical critical methods of study.[28]

Feminist biblical scholars are suspected of trying to "save" the Bible by exaggerating the number and significance of women and women's history to be gleaned from the text, as well as exhibiting a naïve positivism that takes the appearance of women at face value. This is not really a fair critique. Biblical scholar and archaeologist Carol Meyers, for example, has sought to excavate the daily lives of women in ancient Israel using archaeological and historical data, and argues that women played a more complex and significant role in society than recognized. She agrees that the text should not be the sole source of our picture of ancient Israel and thus identifies herself with those who seek to contextualize biblical material about women.[29] In her presidential address at the Society of Biblical Literature in 2013, Meyers responded to critics from second-wave feminism by invoking third-wave feminist critics who say the term "patriarchy," inherited from nineteenth- and early twentieth-century anthropologists, has outlived its usefulness and is not appropriate for the household-based, agrarian society of most of ancient Israel. She recommends the term "heterarchy," borrowed from the social sciences and used in gender archaeology to designate simultaneous power structures that interact with one another.[30]

Critiques of traditional methods can ignore their uses for feminist work. Christian studies professor Bernadette Brooten gathered inscriptions of women leaders in ancient diaspora synagogues, showing how their meanings were refashioned by translators to deny women's authority.[31] Brooten and New Testament scholar Eldon J. Epp also used text criticism to rediscover the female disciple, Junia, whom Paul calls "prominent among the apostles" (Rom. 16:7). Her name had been corrected in some manuscripts to render it a male name, Junias, and translators followed suit. Without such painstaking work in epigraphy and textual criticism, these ancient women leaders would be unknown. Religious Studies scholar Jennifer Glancy's *Slavery in Early Christianity* combines several forms of analysis to consider the situation of slaves in early Christian circles, subject to the sexual demands of their masters, but schooled in Paul's admonitions against *porneia*.[32] Professor of Philosophy and Religion Clarice Martin explores the translation issues that attend key words like *doulos*, "slave." Its euphemistic translation as "servant" has robbed it of its impact and minimized its cruelty in Paul's time. Like Glancy, Martin insists on speaking to the reality of women's experiences, thus examining the reality of slavery in women's and men's New Testament lives.[33]

Finally, some of the core assertions of feminist scholarship that question the utility of biblical studies include, "the Bible was written by men" or "the texts were written by people in power." Such assertions assume some knowledge of the ancient Near East for the Hebrew Bible and the Mediterranean world for the New Testament. Furthermore, they are buttressed by examinations of the sources, composition, and redaction of the biblical texts.[34]

While most who critiqued feminist scholarship on the Bible came from other fields, Hebrew Bible scholar Esther Fuchs is no less critical than the theologians and ethicists. Her work, *Sexual Politics in the Biblical Narrative* argues that patriarchy cannot be excised from the Hebrew Bible by methods like those of Trible or Meyers. What many feminist biblical interpreters miss, she says, is that patriarchy and androcentrism in the Hebrew Bible are not merely by-products of a certain time and place but are prescriptive of society. In a more recent article, Fuchs argues that the "neo-liberal" brand of interpretation has failed to recognize that the concept of "woman" is a "construct" in the patriarchal project of the Hebrew Bible. Only an entirely new "literary hermeneutics of resistance" will turn the tide. Fuchs's incisive and piquant critique has merit, but her solution is not entirely new in its appeal to experience as arbiter of truth, or in its resistant reading, insisting that "all interpretations be anchored in the reader, not the text."[35]

WITHIN LIBERATIONIST PARADIGMS

With its impetus to recover the voices of women who were not at the center of most texts and its "reading against the grain" of intersecting ideologies, feminist hermeneutics inevitably would not stay confined to one issue or one portion of humanity. Challenges from womanist and Latina (or *mujerista*) interpreters further unsettled taken-for-granted categories. Moreover, scholars in multiple fields have developed questions regarding sexuality, the body, power, and colonizing, which have been incorporated into feminist work. Feminist hermeneutics has come to want to "have it all," to contribute to the liberation of human beings on many fronts and in many parts of the world.

This essay has been discussing biblical interpretation as it has been centered in North America and Europe mostly among academics, therefore elites, but Bible reading flourishes in quite different social climates as well. Increasingly, the Bible is read not by those in established positions of power but by people who find themselves on the margins. The 2014 study on Bible-reading in America done by a team at Indiana University-Purdue University Indianapolis, found that the Bible reader in the United States is most likely to be black, female, older, and low income. Its most striking correlation shows that African Americans read the Bible considerably more than other Americans.[36]

Theologian and seminary professor Kwok Pui-lan notes the dramatic changing global demographics of Christianity in recent years. People who identify as Christian increasingly live in the Global South, while their numbers in Europe and North America shrink. Christianity, at least in terms of population, may become a non-Western religion. As Kwok notes, it is increasingly urgent to bring in other perspectives on the Bible. The New Testament and early Christianity was produced and disseminated throughout the Mediterranean and Asian worlds, often brought to native peoples as a by-product of colonization, so the text is more authentically read "from the underside," its possibilities for liberation enhanced.[37] Musa Dube, a professor of New Testament from Botswana, shows how the image of Jesus as the powerful "man from heaven" in the Gospel of John has helped authorize colonization and subordination of natives in her own country.[38]

Feminist biblical studies developed in Latin America in the shadow of poverty, dictatorships, revolutions, political repression, and imperialism. Elsa Tamez, a Mexican biblical scholar who taught in Costa Rica, describes the feminist scholarly movement as behind the times and is even leery of the term "feminist." Ada Maria Isasi-Diaz's label "mujerista" is not well known. Work on Latina biblical interpretation around women has been centered on the publication *La Rivista de Interpretación Bíblica Latinoamericana* (RIBLA), which began publication in 1988. Like their counterparts in feminist and womanist interpretation, Latin American interpreters put women's experiences at the heart of their work and tend to fuse biblical studies and theology. They use a variety of methods, including traditional historical-critical and literary ones, but with considerable care and from a different perspective.

Distinctive Latin American interpretations include:

(1) The "use of the hermeneutical circle," which begins with experiences in the world, draws in the text and its layers of understanding, and promotes liberating practices in a struggling society. For Latin American women, lived reality includes the experience of poverty and violence on individual bodies, where gender, race, class, and ethnicity collide.

(2) The inclusion of works from African-descendant and indigenous perspectives. Tamez notes the work of several women looking at the African and Asian elements and characters in the Hebrew Bible by scholars such as Maricel Mena and Betty Ruth Lozano and Bibiana Peñaranda. Representations of indigenous cultures in biblical texts are examined by Mercedes López.[39]

(3) They often include a strategy of resistant reading, where nearly automatic readings of the text are read and "de-normalized." Sharing this approach with other feminists, texts are read from perspectives opposed to the authors' intentions. For example, household codes in 1 Timothy, Ephesians, and Colossians that prohibit women's leadership are "de-normalized" to show evidence of women's actual authority. Ivoni Richter Reimer brings to the fore the self-sufficient businesswoman Lydia of Acts 16:14-15, minus the biography attributed to her by male exegetes.[40]

Feminist analysis nearly always has a prescriptive element. It cannot ignore issues of oppression related to categories beyond sex, including nationality, race, sexual orientation, and able-bodiedness. Indeed most feminist scholars include such goals in their work. Ecofeminism, in the words of Brazilian Ivone Gebara "emphasizes the idea that we (all creation) are one sacred Body," and that patriarchy not only promoted injustice in the social sphere but a consumerist approach to nature that led to our current ecological crisis.[41] Tamez uses the book of James and links it to the prophet Amos in light of liberation theology and its "preferential option for the poor." Tamez underscores the idea in James 2:17 "faith without works is dead" as a credo for the work of theology in Latin America.[42]

Hermeneutics, a term with a long and complex pedigree, assumes that interpretation is a process that includes the life-situation and assumptions of the interpreter and is not merely an unlocking of the text. It is not a disinterested search for meaning. Feminist hermeneutics is one of several methods of the twentieth century that demanded recognition of varying meanings and uses of interpretation for different communities, including African Americans, women, and Third World peoples. For these groups, the Bible has been both a source of life and meaning, as well as a tool of their own subordination.

A THIRD WAVE?

The contested term "third-wave feminism" includes at least two rather different brands of feminism. Jennifer Gilley, scholar, librarian, and a self-identified third-wave feminist, describes this flavor of feminism by saying "it celebrates contradiction, complexity, and individual freedom of choice."[43] One brand of third-wave feminism derives its energy from being reactive, rejecting second-wave thinkers as too ideological, and perhaps assuming that many of the gains achieved by twentieth-century feminism meant political struggle was no longer necessary. They may also be endorsing the work of cultural critics like Katie Roiphe and Camille Paglia, who charged earlier feminists with exaggerating images of women as victims. Not surprisingly, women who represent these trends have little interest in religion or the Bible.

The second kind of third-wave feminism continues many of the drives for reforming society and attacking sexism and racism which typified second-wave feminism. Many of its proponents were raised in feminist households and continue to express those values, but in their own style. The term "third-wave" was coined by Rebecca Walker, the daughter of Alice Walker, in an article in *Ms. Magazine* in 1992, called "Becoming the Third Wave." She spoke of her anger at the treatment of Anita Hill during the Clarence Thomas hearings and reminded women of her generation that feminism had not completely remade society, especially vis-à-vis women's rights.[44] Many third-wavers continue the struggle for a just society, but have remade the struggle to reflect their generation. They show a distinct individualism and are more cautious about speaking for all women. They reject strict binaries of male/female in exploring sexuality and difference. These values come across in a third-wave form of biblical hermeneutics, which scholar and preacher Surekha Nelavala calls "an upgraded version of feminism that fits the age and cultures of the postmodern era."[45]

The variety that characterizes third-wave religious feminists is clear in the collection of essays, *Faithfully Feminist*, a book edited by a Jew, a Christian, and a Muslim.[46] These essays are from women in the three traditions who identify as feminists and remain committed to faith communities. Its range is broad and it shows complexity, but the following themes recur:

1. They draw from the teachings and experiences of previous generations. Elise M. Edwards, a professor of Christian Ethics, notes her mother and grandmother who taught her to pray and connect with the divine, and an aunt who encouraged her in the ministry.[47] Many gave thanks for the earlier generation women theologians and scholars who showed them new ways of thinking.

2. These women choose to occupy a liminal, in-between status. One Mormon woman engaged in seeking ordination of women to the priesthood said she was "too feminist for Mormons, and too Mormon for feminists."[48] One spoke of looking for "a sweet spot in the midst of my boundaries as a feminist Orthodox Jewish artist."[49]

3. They see a symbiotic relationship between religion and feminism. Some Christian women draw strength directly from Jesus or identify with him or Mary Magdalene, bypassing patriarchal trappings of the tradition.[50] One woman said, "Feminism birthed the Jew that I am today."[51]

4. They see their religious traditions as both flawed and full of spiritual resources. While several experienced the Bible as a tool that was invoked to argue for women's submission, they found liberating messages elsewhere in the text.[52] Many were attracted by the messages of social justice preached by the prophets, by Jesus's teaching and example, and by the ethics of communal responsibility.[53] Like some nineteenth-century thinkers, some felt a pure divine message could be discerned despite patriarchal settings. "The transcendent Torah," says one, "shines forth from Sinai without ever fully revealing itself."[54]

5. Several note the vitality in struggle. One Orthodox woman suggests it is easier to keep momentum going in non-egalitarian spaces.[55] Miriam Peskowitz remarks that, having come of age in activist Judaism, "when there's no longer as much to argue about, ritual and learning and all the rest feel different; nice, but perhaps a little flat."[56]

Third-wave religious feminists are poised to keep feminism vibrant in the twenty-first century. While some women and men take for granted the gains of the twentieth century in women's rights, religious communities continue to present challenges to equality. Furthermore, the individualism, embrace of diversity, and rejection of rigid gender categories that characterize third-wavers serve them well in creating change in religious communities. Sara Hurwitz has been privately ordained as an Orthodox rabba (a feminization of the title "rabbi"). Kate Kelley is seeking equality within the Mormon Church. Rabbi Danya Ruttenberg writes about parenting as spiritual practice. *Faithfully Feminist* records the experiences of young women in Jewish, Christian, and Muslim communities, who acknowledge their debt to earlier generations of feminist thinkers and continue to remake their religious communities.

At the two recent meetings of the American Academy of Religion, in 2014 and 2015, the "Feminist Theory and Reflection" group presented three and four sections of papers and discussion, respectively, dealing with a book on Foucault, the meaning of work, sexuality, Buddhist Philosophy, and women in indigenous religions. Several were joint sessions with other groups including queer theory, lesbian feminist, and women in Buddhism. In the Society of Biblical Literature for these same years, the Feminist Hermeneutics of the Bible section organized four sessions each year, including responses to Meyers's presidential address, a retrospective on Jacqueline Grant's book *White Women's Christ, Black Women's Jesus*, families in the Bible, and rape culture. Two joint sessions met with African American hermeneutics and with minoritized biblical criticism. Relatively speaking, the word "feminist" does not appear frequently in the paper titles, but the accomplishments of feminist criticism are fundamental to the work of these groups.

There is no specifically American hegemony in feminist biblical hermeneutics. Some of the matriarchs of the field like Elisabeth Schüssler Fiorenza, Athalya Brenner, and Mieke Bal are from Europe and Israel and/or have taught in European institutions. Like most scholarship in the humanities, and especially in religion, feminist hermeneutics includes people from all over the world. The United States, however, disproportionately supports the study of the Bible in its colleges and universities, employs biblical scholars, and witnesses the Bible as part of its public and political rhetoric. This platform allows the field to grow and to continue its global reach.

NOTES

1. 2 Kings 22:14–20; Luke 1:46–55.
2. Margaret McFadden, *Golden Cables of Sympathy: The Transatlantic Sources of Nineteenth-Century Feminism* (Lexington: University Press of Kentucky, 1999).
3. Renita J. Weems, *Just a Sister Away: Understanding the Timeless Connection between Women of Today and Women in the Bible* (Philadelphia: Innisfree Press, 1988); Clarice

J. Martin, "Womanist Interpretations of the New Testament: The Quest for Holistic and Inclusive Translation and Interpretation," *Journal of Feminist Studies in Religion* 6, no. 2 (Fall 1990): 41–61. An example of a household code appears in Colossians 3:18–4:1.

4. Phyllis Trible, *Texts of Terror: Literary-Feminist Readings of Biblical Narratives* (Philadelphia: Fortress, 1984); J. Cheryl Exum, *Plotted, Shot, and Painted: Cultural Representations of Biblical Women* (Sheffield, U.K.: Sheffield Academic Press, 1996); Cheryl B. Anderson, *Women, Ideology, and Violence* (London: Bloomsbury Publishing, 2006).

5. Sarah Grimké, *Letters on the Equality of the Sexes and the Condition of Woman* (Boston: Isaac Knapp, 1838), 7, http://www.archive.org/details/lettersonequalitoogrimrich.

6. Elizabeth Cady Stanton, ed., *The Woman's Bible* (1895-1898; repr., Mineola, N.Y.: Dover Publications, 2002), 209.

7. Elizabeth Cady Stanton, Susan B. Anthony, and Mathilda Joslyn Gage, eds., *History of Woman Suffrage*, vol. 1 (New York: Fowler and Wells, 1881), 540.

8. Virginia W. Broughton, *Twenty Years' Experience of a Missionary* (Chicago: Pony Press, 1907), http://digilib.nypl.org/dynaweb/digs/wwm974.

9. Nyasha Junior, *An Introduction to Womanist Biblical Interpretation* (Louisville, Ky.: Westminster John Knox Press, 2015), 14–15.

10. Elisabeth Schüssler Fiorenza, ed., *Searching the Scriptures*, 2 vols. (New York: Crossroad, 1993), 1–24.

11. Junior, *Womanist Biblical Interpretation*, 122–31.

12. Mitzi J. Smith, *I Found God in Me: A Womanist Biblical Hermeneutics Reader* (Eugene, Ore.: Cascade Books, 2015).

13. Judith Plaskow, "Movement and Emerging Scholarship," in *Feminist Biblical Studies in the Twentieth Century: Scholarship and Movement*, ed. Elisabeth Schüssler Fiorenza (Atlanta, Ga.: Society of Biblical Literature, 2014), 6.

14. Leonard J. Swidler, "Jesus Was a Feminist," *Catholic World* 212 (January 1971): 171–83; Phyllis Trible, "Depatriarchalizing in Biblical Interpretation," *Journal of the American Academy of Religion* 41 (1973): 30–48.

15. Judith Plaskow, *The Coming of Lilith: Essays on Feminism, Judaism, and Sexual Ethics* (Boston: Beacon Press, 2005), 23–32.

16. Phyllis Trible, *God and the Rhetoric of Sexuality* (Philadelphia: Fortress, 1978), 72–143, 144–65. See also *Texts of Terror: Literary-Feminist Readings of Biblical Narratives* (Philadelphia: Fortress, 1984).

17. Tikva Frymer-Kensky, *In the Wake of the Goddesses: Women, Culture, and the Biblical Transformation of Pagan Myth* (New York: Free Press, 1992).

18. Joan W. Scott, "Gender: A Useful Category of Historical Analysis," *American Historical Review* 91, no. 5 (December 1986): 1053–75.

19. Elisabeth Schüssler Fiorenza, *Bread, Not Stone: The Challenge of Feminist Biblical Interpretation* (Boston: Beacon Press, 1984), xii-xiii.

20. Elisabeth Schüssler Fiorenza, *In Memory of Her: A Feminist Reconstruction of Christian Origins* (New York: Crossroad, 1983).

21. Elizabeth A. Clark, "The Lady Vanishes: Dilemmas of a Feminist Historian after the 'Linguistic Turn,'" *Church History* 67, no. 1 (March 1998): 31, doi:10.2307/3170769.

22. Colleen Conway, *Behold the Man: Jesus and Greco-Roman Masculinity* (New York: Oxford University Press, 2008); Stephanie L. Cobb, *Dying to Be Men: Gender and Language in Early Christian Martyr Texts* (New York: Columbia University Press, 2008).

23. Elisabeth Schüssler Fiorenza and Laura Nasrallah, eds., *Prejudice and Christian Beginnings: Investigating Race, Gender, and Ethnicity in Early Christianity* (Minneapolis, Minn.: Fortress Press, 2009).

24. Gale A. Yee, "Judges 17–21 and the Dismembered Body," in *Judges and Method: New Approaches in Biblical Studies*, ed. Gale A. Yee (Minneapolis, Minn.: Fortress Press, 1995), 163.

25. Jane Schaberg, "How Mary Magdalene Became a Whore," *Bible Review* 8, no. 5 (1992): 30–37; and *The Resurrection of Mary Magdalene: Legends, Apocrypha, and the Christian Testament* (New York: Continuum, 2002).

26. Adele Reinhartz, "Women in the Johannine Community: An Exercise in Historical Imagination," in *A Feminist Companion to John*, 2 vols., ed. Amy-Jill Levine and Marianne Blickenstaff (London: Sheffield Academic Press, 2003), 2:14–33.

27. Susanne Scholz, "Second-Wave Feminism," in *The Oxford Encyclopedia of the Bible and Gender Studies*, ed. Julia M. O'Brien (New York: Oxford University Press, 2014), 243–51.

28. Audre Lorde, "The Master's Tools Will Never Dismantle the Master's House," *Sister Outsider: Essays and Speeches* (Berkeley, Calif.: Crossing Press, 1984), 110–14.

29. Carol Meyers, *Rediscovering Eve: Ancient Israelite Women in Context* (New York: Oxford University Press, 2012), 5–16.

30. Carol L. Meyers, "Was Ancient Israel a Patriarchal Society?," *Journal of Biblical Literature* 133 (2014): 8–27.

31. Bernadette J. Brooten, *Women Leaders in the Ancient Synagogue: Inscriptional Evidence and Background Issues* (Chico, Calif.: Scholars Press, 1982).

32. Jennifer Glancy, *Slavery in Early Christianity* (New York: Oxford University Press, 2002).

33. Clarice J. Martin, "Womanist Interpretations of the New Testament: The Quest for Holistic and Inclusive Translation and Interpretation," *Journal of Feminist Studies in Religion* 6, no. 2 (Fall 1990): 41–61.

34. Scholars who recognize the historical bases of such assertions include Schüssler Fiorenza, *In Memory of Her*, xix–xxx; Esther Fuchs, *Sexual Politics in the Biblical Narrative: Reading the Bible as a Woman* (Sheffield: Sheffield Academic Press, 2000), 11–12; and Kwok Pui-lan, "Reading the Christian New Testament in the Contemporary World," in *Fortress Commentary on the Bible: New Testament*, ed. Margaret Aymer, Cynthia Briggs Kittredge, and David A. Sánchez (Minneapolis, Minn.: Fortress Press, 2014), 15.

35. Esther Fuchs, *Sexual Politics in the Biblical Narrative: Reading the Bible as a Woman* (Sheffield: Sheffield Academic Press, 2000), 16.

36. Philip Goff, Arthur E. Farnsley II, and Peter J. Thuesen, "The Bible in American Life Report," The Center for the Study of Religion and American Culture (Indianapolis, Ind.: IUPUI, 2014), http://www.raac.iupui.edu/research-projects/bible-american-life/bible-american-life-report.

37. Pui-lan, "Reading the Christian New Testament in the Contemporary World," 5–30.

38. Musa W. Dube, "Savior of the World but Not of This World: A Postcolonial Reading of Spatial Construction in John," in *Postcolonial Bible*, ed. R. S. Sugirtharajah (Sheffield: Sheffield Academic Press, 1998), 118–35.

39. Maricel Mena, "La herencia de las diosas; Egipto y Sabá en el tiempo e la monarquía salomónica," *La Revista de Interpretación Bíblica Latinoamericana (RIBLA)* 54 (2006): 34–47; Mena, "Hermenéutica negra feminist: De invisible a intérprete y artífice de su propria historia," *RIBLA* 50 (2005): 130–34; Betty Ruth Lozano and Bibiana Peñaranda, "Una relectura de Números 12 desde una perspectiva de mujeres negras," *RIBLA* 50 (2005): 114–16; Mercedes López. "Alianza por la vida: Una lectura de Rut a partir de las culturas," *RIBLA* 26 (1997): 96–101.

40. Ivoni Richter Reimer, "Reconstruir historia de mujeres: Reconsideraciones sobre el trabajo y estatus de Lidia en Hechos 16," *RIBLA* 4 (1989): 47–64.

41. Ivone Gebara, "The Face of Transcendence as a Challenge to the Reading of the Bible in Latin America," in *Searching the Scriptures*, vol. 1: *A Feminist Introduction*, ed. Elisabeth Schüssler Fiorenza (New York: Crossroad Publishing, 1993), 172–86.
42. James 2:17, "So faith by itself, if it has no works, is dead." Elsa Tamez, "Feminist Biblical Studies in Latin America and the Caribbean," in *Feminist Biblical Studies in the Twentieth Century: Scholarship and Movement*, ed. Elisabeth Schüssler Fiorenza (Atlanta, Ga.: Society of Biblical Literature, 2014), 35–52.
43. Jennifer Gilley, "Writings of the Third Wave: Young Feminists in Conversation," *Reference and User Services Quarterly* 44, no. 3 (Spring 2005): 187–98.
44. Rebecca Walker, "Becoming the Third Wave," *Ms. Magazine*, January 1992, 39–41.
45. Surekha Nelavala, "Third-Wave Feminism," in *The Oxford Encyclopedia of the Bible and Gender Studies*, ed. Julia M. O'Brien (New York: Oxford University Press, 2014), 254.
46. Gina Messina-Dysert, Jennifer Zobair, and Amy Levin, eds. *Faithfully Feminist: Jewish, Christian, and Muslim Feminists on Why We Stay* (Ashland, Ore.: White Cloud Press, 2015).
47. Elise M. Edwards, "The Faith of My Mothers and Sisters," in *Faithfully Feminist*, ed. Messina-Dysert, Zobair, and Levin, 20–22.
48. Caroline Kline, "Reflections of a Mormon Feminist," in *Faithfully Feminist*, ed. Messina-Dysert, Zobair, and Levin, 35.
49. Stacy Leeman, "I Still May Push a Little," in *Faithfully Feminist*, ed. Messina-Dysert, Zobair, and Levin, 101.
50. Marcia W. Mount Shoop, "Thy Presence Is My Stay," in *Faithfully Feminist*, ed. Messina-Dysert, Zobair, and Levin, 160–61.
51. Amy Levin, "Beet is the New Orange," in *Faithfully Feminist*, ed. Messina-Dysert, Zobair, and Levin, 64.
52. Emily Maynard, "How Feminism Saved My Faith," 117–19; Amanda Quraishi, "Same Struggle, Different Dogma," 164; Mihee Kim-Kourt, "Tilling the Soil of Faith," 214, in *Faithfully Feminist*, ed. Messina-Dysert, Zobair, and Levin.
53. Jennifer D. Crumpton, "Seeing is Believing," 62; Kathryn House, "Sometimes, the Minister Is a Girl," 190; Christine Stone, "Finding My Faith through Feminist Jewish Values," 201; Kim-Kourt, "Tilling the Soil," 214, in *Faithfully Feminist*, ed. Messina-Dysert, Zobair, and Levin.
54. Leiah Moser, "Speaking Tradition," in *Faithfully Feminist*, ed. Messina-Dysert, Zobair, and Levin, 199.
55. Rachel Lieberman, "Blessed Are You, Who Has Made Me a Woman," in *Faithfully Feminist*, ed. Messina-Dysert, Zobair, and Levin, 43.
56. Miriam Peskowitz, "My Mother's Bat Mitzvah," in *Faithfully Feminist*, ed. Messina-Dysert, Zobair, and Levin, 17.

BIBLIOGRAPHY

Anderson, Cheryl B. *Women, Ideology, and Violence*. London: Bloomsbury, 2006.

Brooten, Bernadette J. "'Junia . . . Outstanding among the Apostles' (Romans 16:7)." In *Women Priests: A Catholic Commentary on the Vatican Declaration*, edited by Leonard Swidler and Arlene Swidler, 141–44. Mahwah, N.J.: Paulist Press, 1977.

Brooten, Bernadette J. *Women Leaders in the Ancient Synagogue: Inscriptional Evidence and Background Issues.* Chico, Calif.: Scholars Press, 1982.

Broughton, Virginia W. *Twenty Years' Experience of a Missionary.* Chicago: Pony Press, 1907. http://digilib.nypl.org/dynaweb/digs/wwm974.

Clark, Elizabeth A. *History, Theory, Text: Historians and the Linguistic Turn.* Cambridge, Mass.: Harvard University Press, 2004.

———. "The Lady Vanishes: Dilemmas of a Feminist Historian after the 'Linguistic Turn.'" *Church History* 67, no. 1 (March 1998): 1–31. doi:10.2307/3170769.

Cobb, L. Stephanie. *Dying to Be Men: Gender and Language in Early Christian Martyr Texts.* New York: Columbia University Press, 2008.

Conway, Colleen. *Behold the Man: Jesus and Greco-Roman Masculinity.* New York: Oxford University Press, 2008.

Crumpton, Jennifer D. "Seeing is Believing." In *Faithfully Feminist: Jewish, Christian, and Muslim Feminists on Why We Stay*, edited by Gina Messina-Dysert, Jennifer Zobair, and Amy Levin, 57–61 Ashland, Ore.: White Cloud Press, 2015.

Dube, Musa W. "Savior of the World but Not of This World: A Postcolonial Reading of Spatial Construction in John." In *Postcolonial Bible*, edited by R. S. Sugirtharajah, 118–35. Sheffield, UK: Sheffield Academic Press, 1998.

Edwards, Elise M. "The Faith of My Mothers and Sisters." In *Faithfully Feminist: Jewish, Christian, and Muslim Feminists on Why We Stay*, edited by Gina Messina-Dysert, Jennifer Zobair, and Amy Levin, 20–26. Ashland, Ore.: White Cloud Press, 2015.

Epp, Eldon Jay. *Junia: The First Woman Apostle.* Minneapolis, Minn.: Fortress Press, 2005.

Exum, J. Cheryl, *Plotted, Shot, and Painted: Cultural Representations of Biblical Women.* Sheffield, UK: Sheffield Academic Press, 1996.

Frymer-Kensky, Tikva. *In the Wake of the Goddesses: Women, Culture, and the Biblical Transformation of Pagan Myth.* New York: Free Press, 1992.

———. *Reading the Women of the Bible: A New Interpretation of their Stories.* New York: Schocken Books, 2002.

Fuchs, Esther. "Reclaiming the Hebrew Bible for Women: The Neoliberal Turn in Contemporary Feminist Scholarship." *Feminist Studies of Religion* 24, no. 2 (2008): 45–65.

———. *Sexual Politics in the Biblical Narrative: Reading the Bible as a Woman.* Sheffield, UK: Sheffield Academic Press, 2000.

Gebara, Ivone. "The Face of Transcendence as a Challenge to the Reading of the Bible in Latin America." In *Searching the Scriptures*, vol. 1: *A Feminist Introduction*, edited by Elisabeth Schüssler Fiorenza, 172–86. New York: Crossroad, 1993.

Gilley, Jennifer. "Writings of the Third Wave: Young Feminists in Conversation." *Reference and User Services Quarterly* 44, no. 3 (Spring 2005): 187–98.

Glancy, Jennifer. *Slavery in Early Christianity.* New York: Oxford University Press, 2002.

Goff, Philip, Arthur E. Farnsley II, and Peter J. Thuesen. "The Bible in American Life Report." The Center for the Study of Religion and American Culture. Indianapolis, Ind.: IUPUI, 2014. http://www.raac.iupui.edu/research-projects/bible-american-life/bible-american-life-report.

Grimké, Sarah. *Letters on the Equality of the Sexes and the Condition of Woman*. Boston: Isaac Knapp, 1838. http://www.archive.org/details/lettersonequalitoogrimrich.

Harper, Ida Husted. *The Life and Work of Susan B. Anthony*. Vol. 1. Indianapolis, Ind.: Bowen-Merrill, 1898. http://archive.org/details/bub_gb_ADgQAQAAMAAJ.

House, Kathryn. "Sometimes, the Minister is a Girl." In *Faithfully Feminist: Jewish, Christian, and Muslim Feminists on Why We Stay*, edited by Gina Messina-Dysert, Jennifer Zobair, and Amy Levin, 188–93. Ashland, Ore.: White Cloud Press, 2015.

Isasi-Díaz, Ada María. *En La Lucha/In the Struggle: A Hispanic Women's Liberation Theology*. Minneapolis, Minn.: Fortress Press, 1993.

Junior, Nyasha. *An Introduction to Womanist Biblical Interpretation*. Louisville, Ky.: Westminster John Knox Press, 2015.

Kim-Kourt, Mihee. "Tilling the Soil of Faith." In *Faithfully Feminist: Jewish, Christian, and Muslim Feminists on Why We Stay*, edited by Gina Messina-Dysert, Jennifer Zobair, and Amy Levin, 212–16. Ashland, Ore.: White Cloud Press, 2015.

Kline, Caroline. "Reflections of a Mormon Feminist." In *Faithfully Feminist: Jewish, Christian, and Muslim Feminists on Why We Stay*, edited by Gina Messina-Dysert, Jennifer Zobair, and Amy Levin, 34–39. Ashland, Ore.: White Cloud Press, 2015.

Kraemer, Ross Shepard. *Her Share of the Blessings*. New York: Oxford University Press, 2002.

Kraemer, Ross Shepard, and Mary Rose D'Angelo. *Women and Christian Origins*. New York: Oxford University Press, 1999.

Kwok, Pui-lan. "Reading the Christian New Testament in the Contemporary World." In *Fortress Commentary on the Bible: New Testament*, edited by Margaret Aymer, Cynthia Briggs Kittredge, and David A. Sánchez, 5–30. Minneapolis, Minn.: Fortress Press, 2014.

Leeman, Stacy. "I Still May Push a Little." In *Faithfully Feminist: Jewish, Christian, and Muslim Feminists on Why We Stay*, edited by Gina Messina-Dysert, Jennifer Zobair, and Amy Levin, 96–101. Ashland, Ore.: White Cloud Press, 2015.

Lerner, Gerda. *The Creation of Feminist Consciousness from the Middle Ages to Eighteen-Seventy*. New York: Oxford University Press, 1993.

Levin, Amy. "Beet is the New Orange." In *Faithfully Feminist: Jewish, Christian, and Muslim Feminists on Why We Stay*, edited by Gina Messina-Dysert, Jennifer Zobair, and Amy Levin, 64–70. Ashland, Ore.: White Cloud Press, 2015.

Levine, Amy-Jill, ed. Various volumes in the Feminist Companion to the New Testament and Early Christian Literature series. Sheffield, U.K.: Sheffield University Press; New York: Continuum; Cleveland, Ohio: Pilgrim Press, 2000–2010.

———, ed. *"Women Like This": New Perspectives on Jewish Women in the Greco-Roman World*. Atlanta, Ga.: Scholars Press/Society of Biblical Literature, 1991. ACLS History E-book Project, 2006.

Levine, Amy-Jill, with Marianne Blickenstaff. *A Feminist Companion to John*. 2 vols. London: Sheffield Academic Press, 2003.

Lieberman, Rachel. "Blessed Are You, Who Has Made Me a Woman." In *Faithfully Feminist: Jewish, Christian, and Muslim Feminists on Why We Stay*, edited by Gina Messina-Dysert, Jennifer Zobair, and Amy Levin, 40–45. Ashland, Ore.: White Cloud Press, 2015.

López, Mercedes. "Alianza por la vida: Una lectura de Rut a partir de las culturas." *RIBLA* 26 (1997): 96–101.

Lozano, Betty Ruth, and Bibliana Peñaranda. "Una relectura de Números 12 desde una per-spectiva de mujeres negras." *La Revista de Interpretación Bíblica Latinoamericana (RIBLA)* 50 (2005): 114–16.

Martin, Clarice J. "Womanist Interpretations of the New Testament: The Quest for Holistic and Inclusive Translation and Interpretation." *Journal of Feminist Studies in Religion* 6, no. 2 (Fall 1990): 41–61.

Maynard, Emily "How Feminism Saved My Faith." In *Faithfully Feminist: Jewish, Christian, and Muslim Feminists on Why We Stay*, edited by Gina Messina-Dysert, Jennifer Zobair, and Amy Levin, 115–20. Ashland, Ore.: White Cloud Press, 2015.

McFadden, Margaret. *Golden Cables of Sympathy: The Transatlantic Sources of Nineteenth-Century Feminism.* Lexington: University Press of Kentucky, 1999.

Mena, Maricel. "La herencia de las diosas; Egipto y Sabá en el tiempo e la monarquía salomónica." *RIBLA* 54 (2006): 34–47.

———. "Hermenéutica negra feminist: De invisible a intérprete y artífice de su propria histo-ria." *RIBLA* 50 (2005): 130–34.

Messina-Dysert, Gina, Jennifer Zobair, and Amy Levin, eds. *Faithfully Feminist: Jewish, Christian, and Muslim Feminists on Why We Stay.* Ashland, Ore.: White Cloud Press, 2015.

Meyers, Carol. *Discovering Eve: Ancient Israelite Women in Context.* New York: Oxford University Press, 1988.

———. *Rediscovering Eve: Ancient Israelite Women in Context.* New York: Oxford University Press, 2012.

Meyers, Carol L. "Was Ancient Israel a Patriarchal Society?." *Journal of Biblical Literature* 133 (2014): 8–27.

Moser, Leiah. "Speaking Tradition." In *Faithfully Feminist: Jewish, Christian, and Muslim Feminists on Why We Stay*, edited by Gina Messina-Dysert, Jennifer Zobair, and Amy Levin, 194–99. Ashland, Ore.: White Cloud Press, 2015.

Nelavala, Surekha. "Third-Wave Feminism." In *The Oxford Encyclopedia of the Bible and Gender Studies*, edited by Julia M. O'Brien, 251–55. New York: Oxford University Press, 2014.

O'Brien, Julia M., ed. *Oxford Encyclopedia of the Bible and Gender Studies.* New York: Oxford University Press, 2014.

Petterson, Christina. "Linguistic Turn Approaches." In *The Oxford Encyclopedia of the Bible and Gender Studies*, edited by Julia M. O'Brien, 436–44. New York: Oxford University Press, 2014.

Peskowitz, Miriam. "My Mother's Bat Mitzvah." In *Faithfully Feminist: Jewish, Christian, and Muslim Feminists on Why We Stay*, edited by Gina Messina-Dysert, Jennifer Zobair, and Amy Levin, 14–19. Ashland, Ore.: White Cloud Press, 2015.

Plaskow, Judith. "Movement and Emerging Scholarship." In *Feminist Biblical Studies in the Twentieth Century: Scholarship and Movement*, edited by Elisabeth Schüssler Fiorenza, 21–34. Atlanta, Ga.: Society of Biblical Literature, 2014.

———. *Standing Again at Sinai: Judaism from a Feminist Perspective.* San Francisco, Calif.: Harper One, 1991.

Plaskow, Judith, and Donna Berman, eds. *The Coming of Lilith: Essays on Feminism, Judaism, and Sexual Ethics.* Boston: Beacon Press, 2005.

Quraishi, Amanda. "Same Struggle, Different Dogma." In *Faithfully Feminist: Jewish, Christian, and Muslim Feminists on Why We Stay*, edited by Gina Messina-Dysert, Jennifer Zobair, and Amy Levin, 164–69. Ashland, Ore.: White Cloud Press, 2015.

Reid, Barbara E., ed. Various volumes in the Wisdom Commentary series. Collegeville, Minn.: Liturgical Press, 2015–2017.

Reimer, Ivoni Richter. "Reconstruir historia de mujeres: Reconsideraciones sobre el trabajo y estatus de Lidia en Hechos 16." *RIBLA* 4 (1989): 47–64.

Reinhartz, Adele. "From Narrative to History: The Resurrection of Mary and Martha." In *A Feminist Companion to the Hebrew Bible in the New Testament*, edited by Athalya Brenner, 197–224. Sheffield, UK: Sheffield Academic Press, 1996.

———. "Jewish Women's Scholarly Writings on the Bible." In *The Jewish Study Bible*, 2nd ed., edited by Adele Berlin and Marc Zvi Brettler, 2086–2091. New York: Oxford, 2014.

———. "Women in the Johannine Community: An Exercise in Historical Imagination." In *A Feminist Companion to John*, edited by Amy-Jill Levine, 2:14–33. London: Sheffield Academic Press, 2003.

Schaberg, Jane. "How Mary Magdalene Became a Whore." *Bible Review* 8, no. 5 (1992): 30–37.

———. *The Resurrection of Mary Magdalene: Legends, Apocrypha, and the Christian Testament.* New York: Continuum, 2002.

Scholz, S. "Second-Wave Feminism." In *The Oxford Encyclopedia of the Bible and Gender Studies*, edited by Julia M. O'Brien, 243–51. New York: Oxford University Press, 2014.

Schüssler Fiorenza, Elisabeth. *Bread, Not Stone. The Challenge of Feminist Biblical Interpretation.* Boston: Beacon Press, 1984.

———, ed. *Feminist Biblical Studies in the Twentieth Century: Scholarship and Movement.* Atlanta, Ga.: Society of Biblical Literature, 2014.

———. *In Memory of Her: A Feminist Reconstruction of Christian Origins.* New York: Crossroad, 1983.

———, ed. *Searching the Scriptures.* 2 vols. New York: Crossroad, 1993.

Schüssler Fiorenza, Elisabeth, and Laura Nasrallah, eds. *Prejudice and Christian Beginnings: Investigating Race, Gender, and Ethnicity in Early Christianity.* Minneapolis, Minn.: Fortress Press, 2009.

Scott, Joan W. "Gender: A Useful Category of Historical Analysis." *American Historical Review* 91, no. 5 (December 1986): 1053–75.

Setzer, Claudia. "First-Wave Feminism." In *The Oxford Encyclopedia of the Bible and Gender Studies*, edited by Julia M. O'Brien, 234–42. New York: Oxford University Press, 2014.

———. "A Jewish Reading of the *Woman's Bible*." *Journal of Feminist Studies in Religion* 27, no. 2 (Fall 2011): 71–84.

Shoop, Marcia W. Mount. "Thy Presence is My Stay." In *Faithfully Feminist: Jewish, Christian, and Muslim Feminists on Why We Stay*, edited by Gina Messina-Dysert, Jennifer Zobair, and Amy Levin, 156–63. Ashland, Ore.: White Cloud Press, 2015.

Smith, Mitzi J. *I Found God in Me: A Womanist Biblical Hermeneutics Reader.* Eugene, Ore.: Cascade Books, 2015.

Stanton, Elizabeth Cady. *The Woman's Bible* (1895–1898). Repr. Mineola, N.Y.: Dover Publications, 2002.

Stone, Christine. "Finding My Faith through Feminist Jewish Values." In *Faithfully Feminist: Jewish, Christian, and Muslim Feminists on Why We Stay*, edited by Gina Messina-Dysert, Jennifer Zobair, and Amy Levin, 200–205. Ashland, Ore.: White Cloud Press, 2015.

Swidler, Leonard J. "Jesus Was a Feminist." *Catholic World* 212 (January 1971): 171–83.

Tamez, Elsa. "Feminist Biblical Studies in Latin America and the Caribbean." In *Feminist Biblical Studies in the Twentieth Century: Scholarship and Movement*, edited by Elisabeth Schüssler Fiorenza, 35–52. Atlanta, Ga.: Society of Biblical Literature, 2014.

————. *The Scandalous Message of James*. New York: Crossroad, 2002.

Taylor, Marion. *Handbook of Women Biblical Interpreters*. Grand Rapids, Mich.: Baker, 2012.

Trible, Phyllis. "Depatriarchalizing in Biblical Interpretation." *Journal of the American Academy of Religion* 41 (1973): 30–48.

————. *God and the Rhetoric of Sexuality*. Philadelphia: Fortress, 1978.

————. *Texts of Terror: Literary-Feminist Readings of Biblical Narratives*. Philadelphia: Fortress, 1984.

Walker, Rebecca. "Becoming the Third Wave." *Ms. Magazine*, January 1992, 39–41.

Weems, Renita J. *Just a Sister Away: Understanding the Timeless Connection between Women of Today and Women in the Bible*. Philadelphia: Innisfree Press, 1988.

Yee, Gale A. "Judges 17-21 and the Dismembered Body." In *Judges and Method: New Approaches in Biblical Studies*, edited by Gale A. Yee, 146–70. Minneapolis, Minn.: Fortress Press, 1995.

CHAPTER 11

....

THE BIBLE AND AMERICAN LGBT INTERPRETATION

....

TERESA J. HORNSBY

INTRODUCTION

....

FOR better and for worse, the Bible has always been central to the persecution and liberation of lesbians, gay men, bisexual persons, transgendered folks, and all who do not seem to "fit" into the sexual categories of what American culture determines to be "normal." These categories, as they intersect with biblical interpretation, take on the status of "natural," and thus are assumed to be divinely ordained. Lesbian, gay, bisexual, and transsexual/transgendered (LGBT) biblical interpretation in the United States tends to focus on: (1) determining the historical contexts of key passages that are usually read to condemn non-heterosexuality; (2) reading the Scriptures with a guiding ideology, such as "love one another" or "do not judge"; and (3) illuminating narratives that feature what may be received as nonconforming genders and sexualities.

HISTORICAL CRITICAL APPROACHES

....

LGBT biblical interpretation is descended from historical critical methods, language studies, feminist hermeneutics, and liberation theology, but has evolved into multilayered, multidisciplinary, and complex approaches to the texts. Once solely within the realm of historical studies, modern LGBT interpretations of the Bible involve literary critical methods (including reader response, critical theory, queer theory, and other postmodernist approaches), the social sciences, semiotics, and ethics. What makes LGBT criticism unique is its subject matter: people whose sexuality and gender expression may differ from what a dominant culture may deem as "normal," which tends overwhelmingly to be a cissexual man and one (cissexual) woman having intercourse within a religiously sanctioned marriage and expressed through a strict gender binary.[1]

Because the Bible is used by many to support a modern model of "normal" sexuality, LGBT biblical criticism employs myriad critical theories to interpret passages such as

Genesis 2-3, Leviticus 18:21, Romans 1:18-36, 1 Corinthians 6:9, and 1 Timothy 1:10, sometimes referred to as the "clobber" passages, to which have been given the vast majority of attention. These passages are typically used to establish heterosexuality as the norm, and to condemn any non-heteronormative sexuality. LGBT interpretations, for the most part, do not argue that the Bible "says" that homosexuality, bisexuality, or another sexuality is acceptable; rather, LGBT criticisms tend to argue that homosexuality (defining a whole person by his or her sexuality) is a modern construction. LGBT Bible scholars tend to assert that a text's "meaning" is located in the intersection of the text itself and the reader. In other words, texts can change meanings depending upon the social, geographical, and/or historical location of the reader. The initial forays in LGBT scholarship relied heavily upon historical critical methods and philology to try to understand what meanings some of the "clobber" texts may have had for their original communities.

Examples of such historical and philological work include the scholarship of Dale Martin. In his exploration of the Greek word *arsenokoites* (1 Cor. 6:9; 1 Tim. 1:10), Martin argues that no one really knows what *arsenokoites* means.[2] When modern translators choose "men who have sex with men" (NIV), "sexual perverts" (RSV), "Sodomites" (NKJV), and "homosexuals" (NASB) as translations of *arsenokoites*, Martin posits a disconnect with how the word was used and understood in other Greco-Roman vice lists similar to the one Paul produces in 1 Corinthians 6:9-10. Similarly, Martin's examination of the word *malakos* (1 Cor. 6:9) reveals that the word was understood to mean "effeminate" in Paul's contemporary literature. Modern interpreters, however, are uncomfortable with this interpretation, because, Martin argues, we tend to realize that expressions of gender change from time to time, and from place to place. In other words, while Paul might consider certain gender transgressions (a woman with short hair, for example) to be "unnatural," thus against God's will, modern readers do not see occasional gender expressions (choices about hair style, clothing, jewelry, or physical mannerisms) as something that would deserve being excluded from the kingdom of God (1 Cor. 6:9). Martin's work shows that in Paul's time as it is today, being "effeminate" had no bearing at all on one's sexuality. A man could be labeled effeminate if he took too much pride in his appearance, even if his goal were to attract women suitors.

Thus, when the 1769 edition of the KJV does indeed use the word "effeminate" for *malakos*, it is closest to Paul's worldview about the word lacking a concerted inflection of one's sexuality. Such a distinction, however, creates a theological dilemma in that to be "effeminate" is equated with being unmanly. What is "unmanly"? What does it mean to be a "real man"? Is it the same everywhere? Always? Who decides? As Martin concludes, most modern Christians would be reluctant to condemn a man to Hell for ambiguous expressions of his masculinity. Translators are more comfortable with a word that renders one's sexuality as sinful (such as "homosexual" or "sodomite"), as opposed to "effeminate," which would be problematic for contemporary readers due to the countless ways in which one expresses masculinity today, but historically and ideologically more appropriate to Paul.[3]

There are two influential, initial historical studies in the area of American LGBT biblical interpretation that were published in the early 1980s: John Boswell's *Christianity, Social Tolerance and Homosexuality* (1980), and Robin Scroggs's *The Bible and Homosexuality* (1983). It would not be a gross overstatement to say that much of the LGBT Bible work after 1983 has been in response to these two seminal works. Although Boswell is more a historian of the Middle Ages than a Bible scholar, the influence of his book on American LGBT Bible scholarship is enormous. Matthew Kuefler published a book of essays in 2006,

The Boswell Thesis, in which scholars from a wide range of disciplines considered the impact that Boswell's book had exercised, concentrating on the fundamental arguments the book engendered. Most notable among Boswell's arguments were his contributions to the "essentialism vs. social constructionist" debate. While Boswell's book became a fountainhead of scholarship on the "essentialism vs. social constructionist" debate, Scroggs's book became equally important for its thesis that Paul's references in 1 Corinthians 6:9 were to the ancient practice of pederasty (an erotic relationship with an adolescent boy who was often a slave) and not homosexuality per se.

Another example of innovative and rigorous historical-critical work in LGBT Bible interpretation is Bernadette Brooten's book, *Love between Women* (1996). Brooten first published a precursor to this book as a 1985 article, "Paul's Views on the Nature of Women and Female Homoeroticism." This work stands as a pivotal landmark for lesbian historical-critical Bible scholarship. Brooten argues that "yes," the apostle Paul does not approve of homoeroticism between women, but that disapproval is based firmly in culture. Paul, like his contemporaries, assumes gender normatives are "natural." If a woman steps outside her so-called God-given passive nature, such as being the sexual actor (a male role), she is being unnatural and against God, regardless of whether her sexual partner is a woman or a man.[4] Paul uses this language in Romans 1:26 (*para phusis*—"against nature").

"POPULAR" LGBT BIBLICAL INTERPRETATION

Another genre of LGBT biblical/historical scholarship emerged in the late 1970s with Letha Scanzoni's and Virginia Ramey Mollenkott's, *Is the Homosexual My Neighbor?*, and continued unto the present with works such as *My Tribe*, by Nancy Wilson (1995) and *Jesus, the Bible, and Homosexuality*, by Jack Rogers (2006). These books are written primarily for non-academic Christians, but are founded on linguistic studies and historical criticism. They tend to move from the study of the usual texts like Romans 1:18-36, or 1 Corinthians 6:9 in order to synthesize a broader theological reading that insists on love and acceptance of all people. One strategy, found most prominently in Wilson's work, is to identify biblical characters who could be read through a homoerotic lens. For example, the narrative of the relationship between David and Saul's son Jonathan (1 Sam. 18) seems wrought with what could be interpreted today as homoeroticism: "When David had finished speaking to Saul, the soul of Jonathan was bound to the soul of David, and Jonathan loved him as his own soul" (v. 1, NRSV). The language continues in verses 3-4:

> Then Jonathan made a covenant with David, because he loved him as his own soul. Jonathan stripped himself of the robe that he was wearing, and gave it to David, and his armor, and even his sword and his bow and his belt. (NRSV)

It is, perhaps, the comparison of Jonathan's love and "the love of women" that has, according to Ken Stone, "stimulated much reflection on the possibility of a homoerotic relationship between David and Jonathan."[5] The comparison to "the love of women" (2 Sam. 1:26) seems to distinguish Jonathan's love for David from what Stone understands to be a more common, ancient Near Eastern "political" love.[6]

Another narrative that bears much fruit for LGBT biblical interpretation is the story of Ruth (David's grandmother) and her mother-in-law Naomi. Indeed, the words spoken at countless (heterosexual) wedding ceremonies are the words spoken by Ruth to Naomi:

> Where you go, I will go;
> Where you lodge, I will lodge; your people shall be my people,
> And your God, my God.
> Where you die, I will die—
> There will I be buried.
> May the Lord do thus and so to me, and more as well,
> If even death parts me from you! (Ruth 1:16–17, NRSV)

Mona West sees this as a "coming out"; it is the moment at which Ruth declares her love and devotion to Naomi.[7] At this point, Ruth becomes a "Queer ancestress" and "provides us with an example of self-determination, refusing to accept a marginalized status based on heterosexist patriarchal definitions of marriage, family and procreation."[8]

In addition to finding possible models of same-sex erotic relationships, LGBT scholars have also identified biblical characters who can be understood as intersex or transgendered individuals. For example, Peterson Toscano, a gay activist who stages and performs his biblical interpretations at universities and churches around the United States, focuses on narratives in which the primary actor could be read as "other gendered." In a performative series that depicts gendered others as the saviors of Israel, he tells the story of Hegai, Queen Esther's chief eunuch and his role in putting Esther in the position to save her people. Toscano also performs the narrative of an Ethiopian eunuch (Ebed Melech) who leads a "black op" unit to rescue the prophet Jeremiah from a cistern (Jer. 38). One of Toscano's longest, and most provocative performance pieces, however, is the story of Joseph, as told by his uncle Esau. Toscano tells the story in such a way that it is easy to imagine Joseph as a gay or possibly trans adolescent. Esau, as narrator, is disgusted by Joseph's effeminate affect; Toscano points out, for example, that the Hebrew phrase used to describe Joseph's well-known "coat of many colors" (Gen. 37:3) is a phrase that is used in only one other place in the Hebrew Bible: it is the garment that the king's virgin daughters would wear (2 Sam. 13:18), and that Joseph "flits about" in it. Toscano encourages the reader to imagine that Joseph is sent to his brothers as they tend the flocks, and that Joseph insists on wearing this "dress." Toscano invites the reader to imagine that it was this act that drove his brothers to beat him, violently rip the garment from him, and throw him into a pit, later to be sold into slavery in Egypt (Gen. 37:23–28). Finally, the family is forced to approach Joseph, who is the overseer of Egypt's food provisions during a time of famine, to beg for food. Esau declares that Joseph, "sissy boy that he is," is the savior of Israel (as was Hegai and Ebed-Melech).[9]

These popular representations of biblical characters are what Dale Martin refers to as "the gay imagination."[10] Martin argues that all one can do, really, is imagine who and what biblical characters were. One can recreate and argue one's point of view based on thorough historical or linguistic analyses, but in the end, even the best-researched ideas cannot be proven or discredited. More, Martin claims that no reconstruction of these historical figures can claim any more validity or legitimacy than another. In other words, there is nothing more or less implausible (or plausible) than Toscano's queer representations of biblical characters; they are based on sound historical, philological, and sociological information.

The popular and the scholarly representations I have mentioned tend to be produced by believers, both clergy (as is the case with Nancy Wilson and Jack Rogers), and lay persons alike. These works are generally produced for use in progressive faith communities, in many instances, to mitigate damage that certain readings of the Bible have done to LGBT Jews and Christians. More progressive interpretations seek to redeem the Bible as good and relevant to LGBT communities and their allies. These progressive interpretations, however, are not without their critics. By far, the most outspoken academic opponent of the LGBT Bible interpretation summarized in this project thus far is Robert Gagnon. Gagnon, an Associate Professor of New Testament at Pittsburgh Theological Seminary, and an ordained elder of the Presbyterian Church (USA), has published extensively on the topic of "Homosexuality and the Bible" since 2000. Although there are countless works that oppose the idea of LGBT acceptance, Gagnon is the most vehement and prolific.

Gagnon's central theses rest upon the conviction that the Bible's prohibitions against homosexuality are moral in nature, not historically contingent, thus timeless and divinely sanctioned. Gagnon, for whom Christian Scripture is inerrant, that is, it contains no mistakes and is completely divinely inspired, posits that the Bible clearly expresses that God's view of any sexuality that is non-heterosexual, and any expression of gender that is apart from a dualist paradigm set up by God in creation, are abhorrent.[11] Gagnon's methodology is anchored in historical-critical method and language studies. Due to these methodological and doctrinal convictions (that biblical texts are timeless, inerrant, and divinely produced) and his ideological stance (truth is singular, objective, and knowable), there is an unresolvable impasse between Gagnon and the progressive Jewish and Christian LGBT scholars, as well as the postmodern biblical interpreters in the following section.

Gagnon makes clear that there is no possible compromise regarding the Bible's (thus God's) condemnation of "homosex" in his response to one of the most theologically conservative (conservative in that it closely reflects Gagnon's own brand of Christianity: non-ecumenical, somewhat exclusivist) defenses of LGBT people of faith—Mark Allan Powell's "The Bible and Homosexuality."[12] In this response, Gagnon is clear: Compromise is not an option when it comes to biblical interpretations of God's view on homosexuality. If good Christians agree to disagree, "Jesus Christ himself would be dethroned from the status of Lord . . . and the Church is left with complete and utter moral chaos."[13] In short, Gagnon's worldview is representative of a cadre of anti-LGBT Christians: Truth is absolute and timeless, and meaning (regardless of your social or temporal location) is clear and knowable. It is a modernist understanding of history based on a belief that one can actually know what words meant in their original context; it is a belief system that is incompatible with the majority of LGBT scholars in the Academy, and in particular with those scholars who are working in postmodernist critical theory.

POSTMODERNISM AND QUEER THEORY

The most recent and dynamic work in the area of LGBT interpretation of the Bible is from literary-critical scholars, particularly those working within postmodern theoretical frameworks. Postmodernism, briefly, posits that meaning lies mostly with the receiver (the listener, the reader, the watcher), and partly in the intersection of text and its reception.

In postmodernism, there is no "natural" or normal way of being; everything (e.g., sexuality, gender) is culturally determined; there are no clear lines of definition, no "binaries." Postmodern biblical scholars read biblical texts (including its cognates—Midrashic and Talmudic studies, intertestamental material, and early Christian documents) through the lenses of influential postmodern/poststructuralist thinkers like Michel Foucault, Judith Butler, Jacques Derrida, Eve Kosofsky Sedgwick, and others. This methodology, for LGBT scholars of the Bible, seeks to expose the artifice of hegemonic ways of defining sexuality. For these scholars, there is no morally superior, or more "natural" sexuality. Heterosexuality is as culturally constructed as any other sexuality and can lay no firm claim to be more divinely sanctioned than any other form of sexuality. It posits that structuralist, historical-critical hermeneutics determined meaning (particularly as it pertains to sexuality) through the biases of the interpreter. In other words, in poststructuralism, meaning itself is not discovered by the scholar, it is created by the scholar. Furthermore, postmodernist interpreters see that the meanings most often created by scholars are imbued with a heteronormative bias.[14]

A postmodern literary critical approach to LGBT Bible texts analyzes the intersections of the production of meaning, institutional and cultural power, and the formations of modern Judaism and Christianity. "Queer" recognizes that there is no stable or natural "normal" and reveals that various power structures determine the temporal normative. Postmodernism suggests that not only is meaning located in the interaction of the reader with the text, the reader (and the reader's sense of "self") is also produced by a dynamic community. In direct conflict with modernist (or structuralist) understandings of history and recovery, postmodernists posit that original authorial intent is forever lost, and following Foucault, meaning, self, and power structures are produced by and through the dissemination of knowledge through social organizations (medical, juridical, psychological, economic, and religious).

Hence, LGBT Bible scholars understand that a wide range of biblical interpretation over the centuries has been central to producing modernist notions of "natural" sexuality. By deconstructing, or exposing, the different ways in which various Bible interpreters have argued the meaning of the Bible, LGBT Bible scholars argue that constructed sexual heteronormative beliefs have produced and maintained a diverse range of powerful societal beliefs and ideologies. By the same token, LGBT scholars also argue that "Queer" sexualities are also cultural constructions that change from time to time and from place to place. Thus, in this type of LGBT postmodern interpretational work, sexuality is stripped of its "essentialness" or "naturalness." These LGBT Bible scholars argue that there is no "normal" human sexuality; the Bible has been used by defined faith communities over long periods of time to produce and preserve a monogamous heterosexuality (as sanctioned in marriage) as something "normal" ordained by God.

The burgeoning field of Queer (or postmodern LGBT) biblical studies has produced compelling scholarship, which seeks to show the heteronormative biases that inflect a wide spectrum of biblical interpretation. For example, as one reads Genesis, apart from the example of Rebecca and Isaac, there is no other example of one man married to one woman, and apart from the purity codes of Leviticus, there is no literal condemnation of homoeroticism in the Christian Old Testament (and those instances are not as "literal" as one might assume). Instead, LGBT scholars bring to light such narratives as Ebed-Melech (Jer. 38:7), an Ethiopian eunuch (intersex, perhaps, meaning he could have been born with ambiguous genitals, or as a hermaphrodite—these terms were often interchangeable) who rescues

Jeremiah and is blessed by God.[15] It reveals that a prominent (and dominant) reading of the relationship of God to Israel (and later, Jesus to the Church) is one of husband and wife, the groom and the bride. Yet, ironically, as queer readers point out, the "people" of Israel, and the "church" are also presented in masculine terms (as are God and Jesus). Thus, if one holds on to that metaphor of marriage, both examples are same-sex marriages. As postmodern LGBT scholars of the Bible suggest, the reader makes meaning. Heteronormativity is not IN the text, waiting to be discovered; the interpreter, or reader, brings the assumption of heteronormativity to the text, and uses the text to justify heteronormativity.

Although LGBT Bible interpretation is as diverse, multidisciplinary, and complex as all of the various biblical methods of interpretation, the postmodernists seek in part, as do other LBGT scholars, to reverse the damage that other Bible interpretations have done to the LGBT community. Here are four of the most notable and recent works in postmodernist/poststructuralist LGBT biblical interpretation:

(1) *The Queer Bible Commentary*, **edited by Deryn Guest et al. (2006).** This is a compilation of the most notable scholars working with postmodern ideologies and queer theory. The book is organized in the same order as the books found in the Christian Bible from Genesis to Revelation. The collection includes many of the principal and original LGBT scholars who worked with poststructuralist ideology, such as Ken Stone, Deryn Guest, Jennifer Koosed, Roland Boer, and Stephen Moore, to name but a few.

(2) *Bible Trouble: Queer Reading at the Boundaries of Biblical Scholarship*, **by** Teresa Hornsby and Ken Stone (2011). This is a recent example of LGBT scholars choosing specific examples of biblical texts and "queering" them. Following the work of Judith Butler (from whose seminal work *Gender Trouble* the text forms its name) and of Teresa de Lauretis, who, in 1991, coined the phrase "queer theory," *Bible Trouble* seeks to trouble not only the boundaries between biblical scholarship and queer theory but also trouble the boundaries between different rubrics used currently in the analysis of biblical literature such as sexuality, gender, class, race, and ethnicity. The queer readings found in these essays do not simply spell "trouble" for gender and sexuality but also trouble (complicate) the norms of biblical scholarship and widespread assumptions about the ways in which biblical scholars ought to turn biblical texts into proper objects to be decoded with proper tools. Queer reading is characterized not simply by attention to diverse genders and sexualities but also by diversities of style, form, and critical approach.[16]

(3) *Intersex, Theology, and the Bible: Troubling Bodies in Church, Text, and Society*, **by Susannah Cornwall (2015).** As LGBT scholarship advances and moves away from the dominant paradigm of a gender binary, Cornwall's book *Intersex, Theology and the Bible* looks specifically at the reality of an intersex body. While gender has long been accepted as culturally constructed (which, as Bernadette Brooten has argued, is contradictory to the apostle Paul's world view), "sex," the physical markers such as genitals, remains anchored in the assumption that there are two, and only two such markers. Again, following Butler's claim that gender produces sex (i.e., we have constructed a two-sex system in order to give a "natural" foundation for a gender binary), Cornwall and the contributors of this volume produce essays that confirm,

affirm, and reconfigure bodies that cannot be confined to a two-sex system. Cornwall writes: "Intersex bodies, not easily classifiable as male or female, challenge the binary sex system operative in Western societies. They have often been pathologized, problematized, or altered via surgical intervention to make them less exceptional."[17] Such bodies have been figured as troubling by doctors, parents, religious institutions, and by society at large. In this volume, scholars engage with intersex ideas from a range of perspectives, including constructive and pastoral theologies, biblical studies, and sociology of religion. This volume suggests that intersex's capacity to "trouble" might also be understood positively, challenging often unquestioned norms and dubious assumptions in religion and beyond. Cornwall's collection reflects postmodernism in that it seeks to deconstruct the sex binary with multidisciplinary and diverse methodologies.

(4) *Transgender, Intersex, and Biblical Interpretation*, by **Teresa J. Hornsby and Deryn Guest (2016).** This book gathers in one place every aspect of gender/sexuality theory and LGBT biblical interpretation discussed previously, and focuses on applying those exegeses to the lives of transgendered individuals. It gives an introduction to terms for the various identities of "trans" people and also offers thoughts on how the Bible can be an affirmation of those deemed sexually other by communities. This book posits readings of well-known passages such as the first chapter of Genesis and John's Revelation, and not so well-known passages such as those found in 2 Samuel 6 and Jeremiah 38 to illustrate that the Bible has been translated and interpreted with a bias that makes heterosexuality and a two-sex, two-gender system appear to be "natural" and divinely ordained. *Transgender, Intersex, and Biblical Interpretation* argues through a range of examples that gender was never a "binary," even at creation, and that gender and sex are always (even in the Bible) dynamic categories that do (and must) transition.

THE ACADEMY AND LGBT INTERPRETATION

The annual meeting of the Society of Biblical Literature (SBL), the principal professional organization for roughly 8,500 international Bible scholars, is by far the largest conference for LGBT scholars in the United States.[18] Founded in 1880, the SBL is devoted to critical investigation of the Bible and is divided into groups by area of scholarship. Although still predominantly a white, male organization, the 1970s saw a great deal of social change for the SBL. There was a concerted effort to be more inclusive of African Americans and of women.[19] As the SBL moved away from a modernist historical critical center to be more inclusive of "new" methods like sociological and literary criticism, these new groups of scholars brought forth considerations on the role of gender in biblical interpretation, not only in reconstructing the historical world of the Bible but also in how that interpretation affects current gender roles.

At its centennial celebration in 1980, Phyllis Trible chaired the first panel specifically investigating gender, titled: "The History and Sociology of Biblical Scholarship: The Effects of Women's Studies on Biblical Studies." These first appearances of a focused examination of gender and the Bible provided the impetus of what would later branch off into LGBT scholarship in the Academy. But first, just as it was with the SBL itself, there was an ideological schism among women scholars: the group "Women in the Biblical World"—the first section devoted to the study of women in the Bible—was situated wholly within historical criticism. Later, under the leadership of Elizabeth Schüssler-Fiorenza, a less historical, more socio-methodology group formed: "Feminist Hermeneutics of the Bible." The first papers to address sexuality specifically occurred in these "Women's Studies" sessions. Although the records are unclear, Bernadette Brooten was presenting papers in these groups on the first chapter of the Book of Romans concerning Paul's attitudes toward female homoeroticism as early as 1983.[20]

Today, there are two groups in the SBL devoted to the study of the Bible and sexuality: LGBTI/Queer Hermeneutics (added in 2006), and Gender, Sexuality and the Bible (added in 2007). The SBL's sister organization, the American Academy of Religion (AAR—founded in 1909), developed two "consultation" groups in the 1980s: "Gay Men's Issues in Religion" and "Lesbian-Feminist Issues in Religion." These consultation groups later became formalized sections within the AAR, and although not solely focused on the Bible per se, these two groups often collaborate with SBL members for joint sessions. The AAR also added a LGBT/Queer Hermeneutics consultation group in 2006. The state of the academic professional organizations (SBL and AAR specifically) is such now that almost any group can have a paper that includes an LGBT hermeneutic for biblical interpretation.

Closely related to the academic institutions, American LGBT biblical scholarship has exploded on the Internet, and specifically, on social media sites. SBL and AAR LGBT scholars have a significant online presence. Many have their own web pages or participate in Facebook, Twitter, and blog sites such as Huffington Post and "Jesus in Love." "Queer Biblical Studies and Theologies," and "Feminist Sexual Ethics," for example, are Facebook groups that feature online discussions of LGBT biblical interpretations.

CONCLUSIONS

As a way to alleviate oppression and to find hope for "queer" Jews and Christians, American LGBT biblical scholarship can indeed be considered a brand of liberation theology. LGBT scholars follow the paths of those who have long searched the Scriptures to show that God is on the side of the oppressed. Such groups have included abolitionists, civil rights workers, suffragists, womanists, and feminists. The strategy is the same: the Bible ought to be studied in such a way to show that it, above all else, illuminates love, respect, and justice. LGBT scholars seek to debunk the claim that the Bible calls for divine punishment against sexual and gendered others. LGBT interpretation seeks to expose the interpretive biases that have produced such conclusions and show that there is a plethora of ways in which the Bible can be read to affirm LGBT Jews and Christians as an equally loved and integrally precious part of God's creation.

NOTES

1. A "cissexual" is someone who lives one's life in the gender that matches (or is assigned by) one's (binary) birth genitals.

2. Dale Martin, "*Arsenokoites* and *Malakos*: Meanings and Consequences," in *Sex and the Single Savior: Gender and Sexuality in Biblical Interpretation*, ed. Dale B. Martin (Louisville, Ky.: Westminster John Knox Press, 2006), 37–50.

3. Martin, "*Arsenokoites* and *Malakos*," 48.

4. Bernadette Brooten, *Love between Women: Early Christian Responses to Female Homoeroticism* (Chicago: University of Chicago Press, 1996), 267–98.

5. Ken Stone, "1 and 2 Samuel," in *The Queer Bible Commentary*, ed. Deryn Guest et al. (London: SCM Press, 2006), 206.

6. Stone, "1 and 2 Samuel," 206.

7. Mona West, "Ruth," in *Queer Bible Commentary*, 191.

8. West, "Ruth," 191.

9. "Peterson Toscano at Open Door Ministries ," YouTube video, 47:19, posted by "Open Door Long Beach," June 12, 2012, https://youtu.be/mAkdmzHqGSs.

10. Dale Martin, *Sex and the Single Savior: Gender and Sexuality in Biblical Interpretation* (Louisville, Ky.: Westminster John Knox Press, 2006), 99.

11. Robert Gagnon, "Does the Bible Regard Same-Sex Intercourse as Intrinsically Sinful?," in *Christian Sexuality: Normative and Pastoral Principles*, ed. Russell E. Saltzman (Minneapolis, Minn.: Kirk House, 2003), 106–55.

12. Mark Allan Powell, "The Bible and Homosexuality," in *Faithful Conversations: Christian Perspectives on Homosexuality*, ed. J. M. Childs (Minneapolis, Minn.: Fortress Press, 2003), 19–40.

13. Gagnon, "Same-Sex Intercourse," 151.

14. For more examples of postmodern biblical interpretation, see Teresa J. Hornsby and Ken Stone, eds., *Bible Trouble: Queer Reading at the Boundaries of Biblical Scholarship* (Atlanta, Ga.: Society of Biblical Literature, 2011); and Deryn Guest, Robert E. Goss, Mona West, and Thomas Bohache, eds., *The Queer Bible Commentary* (London: SCM Press, 2006).

15. Susannah Cornwall, ed., *Intersex, Theology, and the Bible: Troubling Bible in Church, Text and Society* (New York: Palgrave/Macmillan, 2015).

16. Hornsby and Stone, *Bible Trouble*, x.

17. Cornwall, *Intersex, Theology, and the Bible*, 11.

18. These statistics come from the Society of Biblical Literature's web page: https://www.sbl-site.org/. According to SBL's 2014 annual report, women make up 24 percent of the organization. "Society Report, November 2014," http://sbl-site.org/assets/pdfs/SR2014_online.pdf.

19. Earnest W. Saunders, *Searching the Scriptures: A History of the Society of Biblical Literature* (Chico, Calif.: Scholars Press, 1982), http://sbl-site.org/assets/pdfs/SearchingScriptures.pdf.

20. Bernadette J. Brooten, "Curriculum Vitae," http://people.brandeis.edu/~brooten/cv.html.

Bibliography

Boswell, John. *Christianity, Social Tolerance and Homosexuality*. Chicago: University of Chicago Press, 1980.

Brooten, Bernadette. "Paul's Views on the Nature of Women and Female Homoeroticism." In *Immaculate and Powerful*, edited by C. Atkinson, C. Buchanan, and M. Miles, 61–87. Boston: Beacon, 1985.

————. *Love between Woman: Early Christian Responses to Female Homoeroticism.* Chicago: University of Chicago Press, 1996.

Butler, Judith. *Gender Trouble.* New York: Routledge, 1990.

Cornwall, Susannah. *Intersex, Theology and the Bible: Troubling Bodies in Church, Text, and Society.* New York: Palgrave Macmillan, 2015.

Foucault, Michel. *The History of Sexuality.* Vol. 1. New York: Parthenon Press, 1978.

Gagnon, Robert. *The Bible and Homosexual Practice: Texts and Hermeneutics.* Nashville, Tenn.: Abingdon, 2001.

————. "Does the Bible Regard Same-Sex Intercourse as Intrinsically Sinful?." In *Christian Sexuality: Normative and Pastoral Principles*, edited by Russell E. Saltzman, 106–55. Minneapolis, Minn.: Kirk House, 2003.

Gagnon, Robert, and Dan O. Via. *Homosexuality and the Bible: Two Views.* Minneapolis, Minn.: Fortress Press, 2003.

Guest, Deryn, Robert E. Goss, Mona West, and Thomas Bohache, eds. *The Queer Bible Commentary.* London: SCM Press, 2006.

Helminiak, Daniel. *What the Bible Really Says about Homosexuality.* Estancia, N.M.: Alamo Square Press, 2000.

Hornsby, Teresa J., and Deryn Guest. *Transgender, Intersex, and Biblical Interpretation.* Atlanta, Ga.: Society of Biblical Literature, 2016.

Hornsby, Teresa J., and Ken Stone. *Bible Trouble: Queer Reading at the Boundaries of Biblical Scholarship.* Atlanta, Ga.: Society of Biblical Literature, 2011.

Lauretis, Teresa de. "Queer Theory: Lesbian and Gay Sexualities." *Differences* 3 (1991): iii–xviii.

Martin, Dale B. *Sex and the Single Savior: Gender and Sexuality in Biblical Interpretation.* Louisville, Ky.: Westminster John Knox Press, 2006.

Nissinen, Martti. *Homoeroticism in the Biblical World: A Historical Perspective.* Minneapolis, Minn.: Augsburg Fortress, 1998.

Powell, Mark Allan, "The Bible and Homosexuality." In *Faithful Conversations: Christian Perspectives on Homosexuality*, edited by J. M. Childs, 19–40. Minneapolis, Minn.: Fortress Press, 2003.

Rogers, Jack B. *Jesus, the Bible, and Homosexuality.* Louisville, Ky.: Westminster John Knox Press, 2006.

Scanzoni, Letha, and Virginia Ramey Mollenkott. *Is the Homosexual My Neighbor?: Another Christian View.* San Francisco, Calif.: Harper and Row, 1978.

Saunders, Earnest W. *Searching the Scriptures: A History of the Society of Biblical Literature.* Chico, Calif.: Scholars Press, 1982.

Scroggs, Robin. *The New Testament and Homosexuality.* Philadelphia: Fortress Press, 1983.

Stone, Ken. "1 and 2 Samuel." In *The Queer Bible Commentary*, ed. Deryn Guest et al., 195–221. London: SCM Press, 2006.

West, Mona. "Ruth." In *The Queer Bible Commentary*, ed. Deryn Guest et al., 190–94. London: SCM Press, 2006.

Wilson, Nancy. *Our Tribe: Queer Folks, God, Jesus and the Bible.* New York: HarperCollins, 1995.

CHAPTER 12

THE BIBLE IN AFRICAN AMERICAN CULTURE

ABRAHAM SMITH

Out from the gloomy past,
'Til now we stand at last

James Weldon Johnson[1]

INTRODUCTION

WHATEVER the original "ancestral heritage[s], culture[s], language[s], and traditions" of the Africans who were displaced and enslaved in what is now called the United States, the horrors of the transatlantic passage and the harsh physical, legal, and psychological conditions that followed in the colonies deleteriously (though not irretrievably) affected these socio-formative factors, the kinds of factors that otherwise would have fostered traditional patterns of interaction, rituals of solidarity, and communities of belonging.[2] In the passage itself, sable flesh was tightly packed in the hulls of ships and classified as insurable goods on voyages threatened by dangerous winds and epidemic outbreaks. In the colonies, slavers exploited free black labor for the work of capitalist ventures: for clearing land and constructing roads in Massachusetts, pruning or packing tobacco in the Chesapeake, cultivating rice fields all year long in the low country, and planting and picking cotton in the lower South.[3] Then, especially by the second half of the seventeenth century, legal codes brought a fresh torrent of abuses: assigning children born of an enslaved woman to the same status; granting masters the power to maim, sexually abuse, or otherwise torture their "chattel" real estate; and limiting the traveling, educating, and corporate assembling of the African captives.

The full toll of these abuses exacted unspeakable pain and psychological trauma. The result was the beginning of a sojourn in which such Africans were dehumanized, treated as non-subjects, or as soulless victims. They were regarded as if they were fated without the appropriate spiritual or intellectual wherewithal deemed necessary for self-determination.[4] Fated—or better caricatured—thusly, these Africans in the British North American colonies and later in the United States and its territories were brought into the web of a modern "world economy" as the latest victims in a long succession of subjugations that began with, and were justified by, Catholic nations like Spain, Portugal, France, and later Protestant England.[5] In the colonies and later in the United States and its territories, moreover, slavery would be justified—as elsewhere—on "religious, philosophical, and political" foundations, including the Bible.[6]

The casual observer, then, may find it odd that African Americans seem to have internalized many general motifs (such as the Exodus-wilderness-Promised Land trope) and specific texts (such as Ps. 68:31 on Ethiopia) from a book so widely embraced by the same larger cultures that enslaved them and justified such brutalities with that book.[7] How could those who came out from what James Weldon Johnson would later lyricize lamentably as "the gloomy past" internalize the contents of such a book?[8] The products of that internalization, moreover, have not been limited to sermons, songs, or scholarly commentaries. Rather, from colonial to contemporary times, biblical texts have richly saturated the whole of African arts and letters within and beyond ecclesiastical, religious, and educational domains. As the theologian and seminary Professor Stephen Breck Reid has noted: "The Bible has been the source of inspiration for poetry and song, as well as the inspiration for drama and sermon."[9]

Reflecting on such an oddity in the revolutionary era, white abolitionist Samuel Hopkins mused in an antislavery tract (1776) that it was "a very great wonder . . . that any . . . [blacks] . . . should think favorably of Christianity and embrace it," though he himself certainly used the Bible to attack slavery.[10] More striking now, though, is that the affinity continues into the third millennium, when critical study has long noted the Bible's own complicity—let alone its interpreters' complicity—in the violent "construction of the Other."[11] So, why does this book still resonate with so many African Americans as a convenient linguistic shorthand for communicating thoughts, as a call to arms for movement struggles, and as a common register for cultivating piety?

To explain this saturation and answer the aforementioned questions, observers of African American culture must not facilely place African American appropriation(s) of the Bible narrowly in a Procrustean bed of "interpretation" crafts, as if African American engagement with the Bible has been limited to hermeneutics, that is, to what is sometimes known as the "art of interpretation." As the newest wave of African American biblical scholarship has noted for some three decades now, a focus on "interpretation" narrows the scope of uses and often limits observation of biblical appropriation to those instances in which African Americans are seeking to determine "the meaning" or even several "meanings" of these texts supposedly on a pristine laboratory table of objectivity.[12]

What is clear, as captured by Vincent Wimbush, a leading scholar in the study of African Americans and the Bible, is that African American biblical scholars are less concerned with (or ought to be less concerned with) "*what* 'scriptures' mean (in terms of content), but *how* scriptures mean in terms of psycho-social-cultural performances and their politics."[13] I would add that African American biblical scholars should also be concerned with when and why these texts—whether deemed as scripture or not—have preoccupied African Americans. Thus, to explain the everyday, predominantly guilt-free uses of biblical texts by African Americans from the "gloomy past" until now, observers of African American Bible usage must seriously consider three factors that contribute to the saturation of this book in the sojourn of African Americans: the availability of the book, the versatility of the book, and the persuasiveness of the book.[14]

THE AVAILABILITY OF THE BIBLE

Why did some of the colonial, revolutionary era, and antebellum documents written, printed, or published by African Americans allude to the Bible? Why, for example, did the pioneering antislavery activist Caesar Sarter, the poets Phillis Wheatley and Jupiter Hammon, and the political essayists David Walker and Maria Stewart all deploy the jeremiad, a "catalogue of critique" and a call to reform that pronounces the irony between a nation's assumed chosen status as expressed in its foundational creeds or principles and its actual failures to live up to such creeds and principles à la the tradition of Jeremiah the prophet?[15] Why as well did the black spirituals or what W. E. B. Du Bois has called "Negro sorrow songs" (such as "Go Down, Moses" and "Joshua Fit De Battle of Jericho") revel with the imagery of the larger Exodus narrative and why did Presbyterian and activist Henry Highland Garnet take up that imagery when he quipped: "The pharaoh's on both sides of the blood-red waters"?[16] Allen Callahan responds aptly to such questions with a quote from historian of religion Charles Long: "Biblical imagery was used because it was at hand."[17]

Thus, when the earliest enslaved Africans needed idioms, repertoires, and a common fund of language in which to express themselves personally and collectively, they used what was at hand, namely, the King James Bible (KJB). This Bible, of course, had already gained ascendancy over the popular Geneva [English] Bible within fifty years of 1611, when the KJB was first printed, but the KJB was also the first English-language Bible to be printed in the United States.[18] Students in the colonies and later in the United States read from it. School primers quoted from it. Oratorios performed in the states cited it. US presidents were sworn into office on KJBs, and by the nineteenth century, the KJB would be distributed throughout the United States by various Bible societies and other voluntary associations.[19]

Thus, having largely begun to hear about the Bible in the late eighteenth and early nineteenth centuries (as a result of the inclusive evangelicalism of the revivals in the Second Great Awakening), blacks in the eastern seaboard colonies would also have first heard or been taught to read using the KJB (not the Geneva Bible).[20] So, having acquired conversion in the circles of the revivalist movement among the Baptists, Methodists, and Disciples, all of whom stressed a connection between literacy and conversion, blacks would have found in the KJB a site for the construction of black "self-identity and culture," a kind of imaginary framework for interpreting blacks' new, everyday world.[21]

Yet, even in more contemporary times, the language of the KJB has been and continues to be embraced widely in African American arts and letters. At the end of "Sonny's Blues," a 1957 short story about a blues singer, for example, James Baldwin uses the KJB form of Isaiah 51:22 to speak of Sonny's fate or "cup of trembling."[22] In the liner notes to his *A Love Supreme* album (1965), the jazz saxophonist John Coltrane quoted the KJB form of

Luke 11:9 and Matthew 7:7: "seek, and ye shall find."[23] Also, the epigraph of Toni Morrison's 1988 Pulitzer Prize winning novel *Beloved* includes the KJB form of Romans 9:25: "I will call them my people, which were not my people; and her beloved, which was not beloved."[24] In his *Eight Studies for the Book of Genesis* (1989), a series of paintings that illustrate the initial void of Genesis 1 along with the six days of creation and the final day of rest (Gen. 2:2), Jacob Lawrence's captions for each panel mimic the idioms, if not the exact wording of the KJB. In his rap song "Only Begotten Son," the rapper Ja Rule slightly changes the KJB form of John 3:18 to read: "He who believeth in Ja shall not be condemned. But he that believeth not is condemned already. Only because He has not believed in the man and the only begotten son, my Lord."[25] In a sterling and searing critique of the black church's failure to receive and affirm its own black lesbians and gays, though historically it has been an ardent opponent of slavery, segregation, and most other forms of second-class citizenship, moreover, the Episcopal minister Horace L. Griffin slightly modifies the KJB form of John 1:11 ("He came unto his own, and his own received him not") to provide a title for his monograph: *Their Own Receive Them Not: African American Lesbians and Gays in Black Churches.*[26]

Also, notwithstanding the surpassing value of later translations for the accuracy of the manuscript traditions behind them compared to the KJB, even relatively recent niche study Bibles (*The African American Jubilee Edition* [1999], *The African-American Devotional Bible* [2006], *The African American Heritage Bible* [2007], *My Holy Bible for African-American Children* [2010], *The Family Roots Bible* [2013], and *The Children of Color Bible* [2013]) marketed for African Americans have embraced the KJB, though there are African American niche Bibles that also use the Contemporary English Version, the New International Version, and the revised edition of the American Bible.[27] Still, according to religious scholars Emerson Powery and Rodney S. Sadler Jr., "a national study" confirms that African Americans still prefer the KJB compared to "their white counterparts."[28]

Thus, the Bible, specifically the KJB, from colonial times to the present, has been close at hand and therefore immediately accessible. On their sojourn, African descendants have turned to this available book to voice and visualize an order not defined by the "gloomy past" but by a "new day begun."[29]

The Versatility of the Bible

Another contributing factor to African descendants' rich internalization of the Bible has been its versatility or adaptability. That is, the ample mix of narratives and backstories about the struggles and successes of communities—whether about Israel or the early churches and assemblies—was a rich matrix in which African descendants were able to imagine or read themselves. As Allen Callahan has noted, again evoking the renowned religious scholar Charles Long: "[The Bible] was adapted to and invested with the experience of the slave."[30] African descendants were thus able to find in the Bible multiple patterns on which the world of their experiences, anxious fears, and highest aspirations could be mapped time and time again.

This broad figural or typological way of appropriating the Bible, though, did not rise, like a Phoenix, full-blown from a mere pile of ashes. Again, given that many African descendants in the colonies and later United States and territories learned about the Bible in evangelical circles, the ground for the typological or figural approach was prepared first by the Puritans and later by such evangelical communities, both groups of which would give shape to the nascent United States.

Inspired by Calvin and other "magisterial reformers," the sixteenth- and seventeenth-century English Puritans sought to purify the Anglican Church from all vestiges of the Roman Church that could not be warranted by scripture.[31] When their efforts failed in England, and when they repeatedly faced persecution under the rule of James I and his son Charles I, however, the Puritans eventually set their sights on the so-called New World, crossed the Atlantic, and began to realize their religious and political program in New England (first at the Plymouth Colony and later at the Massachusetts Bay Colony).[32]

The Puritans thus saw themselves as the New Canaan or as a chosen people apart from the Old Canaan (England) while the early republic deployed a nationalistic exegesis, claimed the American Revolution as providential, extended the concept of chosenness to the entire republic, and then justified their exploitation of land or bodies on that basis.[33] The evangelicals that followed the Puritans also used a typological approach to the Bible. The evangelicals exercised a Calvinistic outlook, which furnished them with a millennial zeal, an exceptionalist self-understanding, and an "activistic ethos," as Mark A. Noll has indicated.[34]

So, when African descendants were converted in the wake of the evangelical revivals of the eighteenth and nineteenth centuries, they inherited the tenets of post-Revolutionary War evangelical revivalism, including its typological application of biblical images. Equipped with this typological approach, then, African Americans were furnished with a trans-temporal story-world or with what the African American studies scholar Eddie Glaude Jr. has called "vocabularies of agency," which would provide existential imagination, national solidarity, and psychological sustenance for people who continually found themselves trapped in degrading circumstances.[35]

Still, the typological approach provided a broad base, not a narrow one, for African Americans to negotiate meaning and value multiple meanings and values from the Bible in the period that followed the colonial era and Revolutionary War. Notable recent scholarship has analyzed the pliability of the Bible in the African American imagination as various African Americans embraced a well-worn trope of the Bible or turned that well-worn trope on its head. So, on the one hand, in *Martin Luther King, Jr. and the Rhetoric of Freedom*, for example, the communications scholar Gary S. Selby argues that the rhetoric of freedom in the Exodus trope was readily available for King to deploy in his speeches and sermons during the civil rights movement because the repeated deployment of the trope by African Americans had already crystallized into a well-known cultural narrative latent with many rhetorical possibilities and pitfalls for shaping a movement.[36] King could then tap into a narrative already woven into the "collective identity" of African Americans even as King rhetorically steered clear of overidentifying his opponents—whether well-meaning gradualists or ardent segregationists—as "one-dimensional caricatures of evil."[37]

Likewise, in *The African American Jeremiad: Appeals for Justice in America*, the historian David Howard-Pitney has traced a black jeremiad in the writings of several African Americans. These figures include Frederick Douglass (ca. 1818-1895) who used it to critique pro-slavery arguments, Ida B. Wells (1862-1931) who used it to rail against lynching, Malcolm X (1925-1965) who "affirmed Blacks' messianic role and destiny" and near the end of his life dreamt of using his voice to save the entire nation, and Martin Luther King Jr. (1929-1968) who used it (in his famous "I have a Dream" speech) to remind the United

States of its defaulting economic promises and to advance a Second Reconstruction through reformist civil rights legislation.[38] It is also possible to add an earlier gestation period for the development of the black jeremiad, as the historian Christopher Cameron and literary scholar Willie J. Harrell Jr. have argued.[39] Likewise, it is possible to trace the presence of an economic jeremiad in the speeches of then-Senator Barack Obama's first US presidential candidacy, as noted by Harrell.[40]

In her *Transforming Scriptures: African American Women Writers and the Bible*, on the other hand, the literary scholar Katherine Bassard finds two different trajectories for the use and interrogation of the Bible by African American women writers. Some African American women writers (Zora Neale Hurston, Toni Morrison, and Sherley Ann Williams) sharply critiqued the notion of biblical authority. Others (Frances E. W. Harper, Maria Stewart, Hannah Crafts, and Harriet Jacobs) though, merged "cogent social critique with traditional Protestant hermeneutics."[41]

Similarly, in his work *Pillars of Cloud and Fire*, biblical scholar Herbert Marbury has traced two distinctively different approaches to the Exodus trope in the writings of well-known African American thinkers. For Marbury, some of those thinkers (such as Absalom Jones, Frances E. W. Harper, and Martin Luther King Jr.) were advocates of "a pillar of cloud" politics because their readings of Exodus within their specific historical contexts affirmed the larger social norms of the United States. Yet, other thinkers (such as David Walker, John Jasper, Zora Neale Hurston, Adam Clayton Powell Jr., and Albert L. Cleage) were advocates of "a pillar of fire" politics because their readings of Exodus within their own temporal arcs radically challenged the prevailing social norms of the United States.[42]

So, while the black migrants of the decades-long Great Migration period could locate many of their experiences within the Exodus story (and thus view floods or the boll weevil in the South as the plagues sent upon Egypt or the police, sent to arrest "potential migrants as they attempted to board trains," as Pharaoh's army in hot pursuit of a people on its way to freedom), not all African Americans would view the trope in the same manner.[43] Hip-hop era, black youth facing the post–civil rights de-industrialization of urban centers beginning in the 1970s and 1980s and continuing into the new millennium, for example, might look askance at any Exodus promise.[44] Such was the case in the fourth verse of the rap song "The Message," when Melle Mel interrogates the "milk and honey" caricature of the United States as the Promised Land (Exod. 33:3). That is, if one has to "have a con [an underground economy hustle] in the land of milk and honey," as Melle Mel reports, in what sense is the Promised Land a land of promise for the inner cities?[45]

To say that the Christian Bible has been pliable in the hands of African descendants, as the aforementioned studies suggest, moreover, is also to affirm Katherine Bassard's judgment that "African Americans were never a monolithic group of Bible readers but have, from their first encounters with the text, evidenced a range of Bible-reading practices."[46] African Americans historically then have not looked for a singular, sedimented meaning in the Bible. Depending on the need of African Americans in a given temporal arc, for example, African Americans have negotiated texts differently. As historian Albert Raboteau has noted, for example, after the Civil War, blacks interpreted Psalm 68:31 ("Princes shall come out of Egypt and Ethiopia shall soon stretch forth her hands") in three different ways: (1) as a prophecy about the "African race"; (2) as a prophecy about the "redemption of Africa"; and (3) as an indicator of "the mission of the darker races."[47]

Thus, beginning with a wide figural framework, through which many African Americans first read themselves into its pages, African Americans in their arts and letters have negotiated varyingly with the pliable book with the hope that the "gloomy past" would not forever define their existence.[48]

THE PERSUASIVE POWER OF THE BIBLE

Yet another factor contributing to the internalization of the Bible by African Americans throughout the American sojourn was its perceived persuasiveness in the public square. According to Callahan, African descendants found in the Bible: "a penchant for interrogating themselves and others."[49] This stance toward the perceived persuasion of the Bible remains, in Callahan's estimation, moreover, despite the fact that the Bible or the "Talking Book" has also been a "Poison Book," a book with toxicity, as indicated, for example, by those texts that have been used to deny African American survival and flourishing, if not their humanity altogether. Such texts include the so-called curse of Cain, the so-called curse of Canaan, and the passages attributed to Paul that seemingly endorse slavery.[50]

Amazingly, many—though surely not all—African Americans fought against this poison by treating the toxicity with a homeopathic cure: "Their cure for the toxicity of pernicious scripture was more scripture."[51] A few illustrations will show the merit of Callahan's perspective and ultimately the respect that many—though again surely not all—African Americans have for the Bible. Ultimately, behind this respect is a reckoning that in the larger public square this text—despite its toxicity—still sways public discourse and leads many to imbibe its forms, if not also its content.

The Bible and the Case for Black Humanity

Using biblical discourse, some pro-slavers questioned the humanity of African Americans, especially drawing on Genesis 4:11-14 (on the so-called curse of Cain), Genesis 9:25-27 (on the so-called curse of Canaan), or works attributed to Paul—such as Colossians and Ephesians, texts that prescribed the subordination of women and the enslaved to the authority of the free male ascendant in a household. Still, African Americans, viewing the Bible as "the most powerful of the ideological weapons used to legitimate their enslavement and disenfranchisement," countered this discourse of dehumanization both by the act of reading the Bible and by interpreting it differently.[52]

Thus, on the one hand, when blacks first learned to read the Bible, they did more than simply enter, or even enter more deeply, into a new linguistic world (given that literacy must not be defined exclusively in terms of reading and writing).[53] Rather, learning to read and to write was necessary for self-determination and resistance. It was part of a fight for visibility and human dignity. Literacy was an issue of power.[54] To be able to write in an age in which writing was a sign of human reason was to be able to write oneself—as Henry Louis Gates Jr. says—"into being."[55] To be able to read was also testimony to the lie of those who denied black humanity and considered blacks solely as property. Thus, the very acts of reading or writing or speaking (or voicing) in antebellum and postbellum hermeneutics were existential acts of defiance against the structures that denied blacks their existence as human persons.[56] It is with little wonder, then, that the great orator Frederick Douglass used clandestine "Sabbath schools" to teach other blacks to read and write and greatly valued "the written word" as a "pathway from slavery to freedom."[57] In fact, many African Americans began a lifetime of literacy, hearing and then reading the KJB, and thus this initial moment significantly sustained their sense of self-worth, if not also of freedom and human presence. As the historian of literacy Janet Cornelius has noted, "Africans who were enslaved quickly recognized the value of reading and writing—not only for their practical uses (from the beginning of slavery, slaves used reading and writing skills to run away) but because literacy, especially the ability to write, signified an establishment of the African's human identity to the European world."[58]

On the other hand, African Americans also critiqued interpretations of those texts deployed to question their humanity. In his incendiary *Appeal* (1829), for example, David Walker critiqued pro-slavers' declaration that the so-called curse of Cain was blackness, thus claiming that blacks were Cain's progeny:

> Did they [advocates of the claim] receive it from the Bible? I have searched the Bible as well as they, if I am not as well learned as they are, and have never seen a verse which testifies whether we are the seed of Cain or of Abel. Yet those men tell us that we are the seed of Cain, and that God put a dark stain upon us, that we might be known as their slaves!!! Now, I ask those avaricious and ignorant wretches, who act more like the seed of Cain, by murdering the whites or the Blacks? How many vessel loads of human beings, have the Blacks thrown into the seas?[59]

The antebellum African American minister James Pennington likewise questions the logic of an assignment of blackness to Cain's progeny. The attribution, he notes, was "circulated by its framers without once recurring to the textbook fact, that Cain lived before the Deluge, and that all his posterity were swallowed up!"[60]

In a fight against the pseudo-science of polygenesis as proposed by the American School of Ethnology and other supporters of the notion of black inferiority, the minister and journalist George Washington Williams (1883) refuted the so-called curse of Canaan (Gen. 9:20-27) in his two-volume *History of the Negro Race in America (1619-1880)*. Mentioning the so-called curse more than a dozen times, Williams evaluates a drunken post-diluvian Noah's curse as neither a "prophecy" nor something "supernatural."[61] Instead, it was an impulsive, "human" response motivated by Noah's humiliation, and thus not a foundation for condemning a race of people to perpetual degradation even if—for the sake of the argument—Williams had to concede to the false ethnological notion that blacks were descendants of Cush, one of Ham's sons.[62]

Against those who condemned blacks to perpetual slavery or degradation through Paul, moreover, African Americans had several biblical recourses. Many would turn to the "Paul" of Acts 17:26. Thus, before the House of Representatives, educator and minister Henry Highland Garnet evoked the universal parentage of God in Acts 17:26 to denounce slavery as a moral contradiction.[63] M. W. Gilbert, a South Carolina Baptist, wrote: "A true believer in the Scriptures must be equally a believer in the fatherhood of God and the brotherhood of all men. For the divine record declares that God 'hath of one blood created all nations of men for to dwell on the face of the earth.'"[64] Similarly, another Baptist minister, Butler

Harrison Peterson, quipped: "True merit will yet be the worth of the man, under the wise and just government of a beneficent God and Father, who 'of one blood made all nations for to dwell upon the face of all the earth.'"[65] A North Carolina minister, S. G. Atkins, also averred: "There is still a higher authority for a negative answer to the question, 'Should the Negroes be given an education different from that given to the Whites?'" He replied: "God hath made of one blood all nations of men for to dwell on the face of the earth."[66]

In his speeches, Frederick Douglass repeatedly returned to the "Paul" of 1 Timothy to denounce the claim that the Christian Bible supports slavery. [67] Through such allusions, Douglass assayed to illustrate the Christian Bible's pronouncements against "menstealing," which he viewed as tantamount to slavery.[68]

Yet, Douglass also noted the power of the subordinationist codes in the biblical books of Colossians and Ephesians. Thus, in a speech to the British public, Douglass blasts the pro-slavery preacher's "Servants be obedient to your masters" sermon back state-side. As if such a preacher thinks there is nothing else in the Bible to teach, Douglass gibes: "This is the Alpha and Omega, the beginning and ending of the religious teaching received by the slaves of the United States."[69]

William Wells Brown, arguably the first African American novelist, takes a similar tact when he dramatizes a hermeneutics of suspicion through the character Uncle Simon in Brown's novel *Clotel*. That is, Uncle Simon critiqued the limited canon of pro-slavers who seemed to know little beyond Ephesians 6:5: "Servants be obedient to your masters."[70] In Brown's novel, Uncle Simon exposes the preaching of Snyder, a white missionary on a plantation in Mississippi, to be based on repeated citations of a few texts, namely, texts on the submission of slaves. Away from the earshot of his owner, Uncle Simon tells the other African captives: "thars more in de Bible den dat, only Snyder never reads any other part to us. I use to hear it read in Maryland and that was more than what Snyder lets us hear."[71]

The Bible and the Case for Black Women's Rights

In addition to the horrors of slavery, female African descendants faced the triple threat of social oppression based on race, class, and gender. Standing as valiantly against gender oppression as she had against race and class oppression, Maria Stewart read herself into multiple passages about Paul—widely construed—in order ultimately to critique Paul, again widely construed. So, in her "Farewell Address to Her Friends in the City of Boston," she adopts "Paul's" testamentary speech form (Acts 20) and saturates her speech with citations from a broad Paul canon (from the "Paul" of Acts 14:22; an allusion to the "Paul" of Eph. 2:8; the Paul of Rom. 8:38,39; 9:21 15:29; 1 Cor. 3:6; and 1 Thess. 3:1).[72] Yet, she also critiques Paul: "St. Paul declared that it is a shame for a woman to speak in public, yet our great High Priest and Advocate did not condemn the woman for a more notorious offence than this; neither will he condemn this worthless worm . . . . Did St. Paul but know of our wrongs and deprivations, I presume he would make no objections to our pleadings in public for our rights."[73]

A traveling minister of the AME Zion church, Julia Foote faced the same hindrances as other women who desired to preach the Gospel. In her sermon "My Call to Preach" (1886),

Foote uses some parts of Paul's larger oeuvre to correct interpretations of Paul based on another part of Paul, namely, 1 Corinthians 14:34. She notes:

> The Bible puts an end to this strife when it says: 'There is neither male nor female in Christ Jesus' [Gal. 3:28] . . . . Paul called Priscilla, as well as Aquila, his 'helper,' or, as in the Greek, his 'fellow-laborer.' Rom xv.3; 2 Cor viii.23; Phil ii.5; 1 Thess iii.2. The same word, which, in our common translation, is now rendered a 'servant of the church,' in speaking of Phebe (Rom. xix.1 [*sic*]) is rendered 'minister' when applied to Tychicus. Eph. vi.21. When Paul said, 'Help those women who labor with me in the Gospel,' he certainly meant that they did more than to pour tea. In the eleventh chapter of First Corinthians Paul gives directions, to men and women, how they should appear when they prophesy or pray in public assemblies; and he defines prophesying to be speaking to edification, exhortation and comfort.[74]

The Bible and the Case for Black Beauty

In the larger sphere of US culture, "dominant myths" have often decreed "whiteness" as a norm and blackness as deviant.[75] As the work of social critic and philosopher Cornel West and religious studies scholar Kelly Brown Douglas have noted, such myths have also stereotyped blacks as oversexed (as exemplified by Jezebel or the black stud images) or desexed (as seen in the mammy or the Sambo images). The consequence of such stereotypes is psychic scarring on black souls (as typified in *The Bluest Eye* by Toni Morrison's character Pecola who loathes her own sable flesh). Yet another consequence is the rendering of more scaffolding for the construction of the psycho-cultural theater of white supremacy.[76] Yet, all notions of beauty ultimately depend on received traditions. Those traditions may be *visual canons*, that is, the everyday, value-laden representations that are seen day after day in paintings and sculpture such that these visual representations take on the aura of the natural though they are simply representations.

Yet another received tradition, one that has garnered great authority in US culture, though, is the Bible or specific parts of it. Thus, by means of biblical discourse, some cultures have "locate[d] economies of unequal identity *inside* the flesh."[77] For example, although no pictures of the Nazarene Jesus exist, Cornel West notes that the proliferation of images reminiscent of Michelangelo's uncles—even in African American churches—shows the great power of a received tradition and its influence on the formation of black subjectivity.[78] The problem of this received tradition about the value of phenotypes, though, extends wider. As communication and film scholars Catherine Jones and Atsushi Tajima have shown, Hollywood films featuring Jesus perpetuate "the dominant hierarchical racial ideology" without any documentable evidence about Jesus's "phenotype." [79]

Long before Hollywood's popularization of Jesus as Caucasian, however, a translation of a biblical text may have contributed to the projection of a negative aesthetic toward blacks. That text is Song of Solomon 1:5. Jerome translated the text as "I am Black but beautiful," although the Hebrew conjunction between the two expressions "Black" and "beautiful" is a *waw* (meaning "and"). St. Jerome insisted on a translation with a binary, moreover, when he translated the Vulgate Bible even when the Septuagint (the Greek translation of the Hebrew Bible) had rendered the conjunction as *kai* (again meaning "and"). Jerome's translation thus gives the impression that the second clause of the sentence compensates for an acknowledged deformity already expressed in the first clause.[80] This binary then would become the basis for a phenotype prejudice long before the first use of the term "race" in the fifteenth century and certainly long before the rise of the pseudoscience of race in the late nineteenth century.[81] Of critical importance to note, moreover, is that the Geneva Bible, the Bishops Bible, Douai-Rheims Bible, and the KJB all translated the Hebrew conjunction as "but."

Still, several African Americans in the nineteenth and early twentieth centuries appealed to this specific scripture in the vernacular of the KJB to fight against the negative depictions of blacks that they faced elsewhere. From itinerant minister John Jea to itinerant preacher Zilpha Elaw and Baptist minister and historian Rufus Perry, from the abolitionist James McCune Smith to the antislavery lecturer and novelist William Wells Brown, and from the Monrovian pastor Alexander Crummell to the sociologist and philosopher W. E. B. Du Bois and the historian Carter G. Woodson, Song of Songs 1:5 provided a basis for challenging negative depictions of black lives.[82]

Speaking to the British, John Jea (1773-1811) writes, for example, that masters in the United States frequently called blacks "Black devils, not considering what the Scriptures saith in the Song of Solomon, 'I am Black, but comely. Look not upon me, because I am Black, because the sun hath looked upon me; my mother's children were angry with me they made me keeper of the vineyards; but mine own vineyard have I not kept."[83] Also, on the dedication page of her *Memoirs* written to the British, Zilpha Elaw (1790-1846?) wrote: "I feel that I cannot present you with a more appropriate keepsake, or a more lively memento of my Christian esteem, and affectionate desires for your progressive prosperity and perfection in the Christian calling, than the following contour portrait of my regenerated constitution—exhibiting, as did the bride of Solomon, *comeliness* with *Blackness* [Song of Sol. 1:5]."[84]

It is safe to say that not all blacks read Song of Songs 1:5 alike, with some using the "but lovely" translation and yet reading it to insist on black beauty or black desirability while other blacks conceded partially to some of the negative depictions about blacks that were a part of the era. What is more interesting to note, though, is that this text had become authoritative as a resource for persuasion. This text was not simply a text that many felt could be dismissed altogether. Instead, it was viewed as persuasive; it was a text that provided a basis or a framework for reasoning with others (both in Britain and elsewhere) about the beauty of black bodies in the United States.

Thus, the Bible, from colonial times to the present, has also been deemed persuasive. On their sojourn, African descendants have appealed to this book to win arguments in the public square, especially those arguments by which African Americans prepared themselves to move "out from the gloomy past" to a lasting and viable freedom.[85]

CONCLUSION

As noted in the educator and civil rights activist James Weldon Johnson's "Lift Every Voice and Sing," African descendants in the United States have longed for a moment when their "rejoicing could rise high as the listening skies."[86] In search of that moment—a moment when "victory is won," African descendants have frequently and repeatedly appealed to the Christian Bible as a way to voice, imagine, and frame the struggles of their American sojourn. Although many African Americans have also interrogated the Christian Bible and the larger institution of Christianity altogether, the affinity of African Americans with that Bible is unquestionably visible in many parts of African American culture, not exclusively in the traditional religious arenas in which observers of African American culture would be keen to expect to find such appeals. Furthermore, although the casual observer might question why African Americans would continue to appeal to this Bible given the history of its uses against them, from the "gloomy past" until now, a careful study of the nexus between African American culture and the Bible reveals multiple reasons why this book continues to be visible in African American culture.[87] The book has been at hand or available; it has been versatile or adaptable time and time again in the African American imagination; and it has been deemed so persuasive in the larger public square that many African Americans have virtually been compelled to draw on its idioms, even if they do not always—or ever—accept its ideology. To study African American culture carefully, then, is to observe how the Christian Bible has resonated over time with African Americans in a yet unfinished sojourn toward a full and flourishing freedom.

Notes

1. See James Weldon Johnson, *Lift Every Voice and Sing: Selected Poems* (New York: Penguin, 1935), 101. Johnson's song, "Lift Every Voice and Sing," for which his brother Rosamond wrote the music, is also known as the black National Anthem.

2. Forrest G. Wood, *The Arrogance of Faith: Christianity and Race in America from the Colonial Era to the Twentieth Century* (New York: Alfred A. Knopf, 1990), xxi.

3. Christopher Cameron, *To Plead Our Own Cause: African Americans in Massachusetts and the Making of the Antislavery Movement (American Abolitionism and Antislavery)* (Kent, Ohio: Kent State University Press, 2015), 11; Kenneth Chelst, *Exodus and Emancipation: Biblical and African-American Slavery* (Jerusalem: Urim Publications, 2014), 78–80.

4. Wood, *The Arrogance of Faith*, xxi.

5. Howard Winant, *The World is a Ghetto: Race and Democracy since World War II* (New York: Basic Books, 2001), 22; Peter Mancall, *Envisioning America: English Plans for the Colonization of North America, 1580–1640* (Boston, Mass.: St. Martin's, 1995), 4.

6. Winant, *The World is a Ghetto*, 22.

7. See Roy Kay, *The Ethiopian Prophecy in Black American Letters* (Gainesville: University of Florida Press, 2011).

8. Johnson, *Lift Every Voice and Sing*, 101.

9. Stephen Breck Reid, *Experience and Tradition: A Primer in Black Biblical Hermeneutics* (Nashville, Tenn.: Abingdon, 1990), 11, quoted in Emerson B. Powery and Rodney S. Sadler Jr., *The Genesis of Liberation: Biblical Interpretation in the Antebellum Narratives of the Enslaved* (Louisville, Ky.: Westminster John Knox Press, 2016), 10.

10. The 1776 Hopkins tract is quoted in Cameron, *To Plead Our Own Cause*, 39; Eran Shalev, *American Zion: The Old Testament as a Political Text from the Revolution to the Civil War* (New Haven, Conn.: Yale University Press, 2013), 153.

11. Regina Schwartz, *The Curse of Cain: The Violent Legacy of Monotheism* (Chicago: University of Chicago Press, 1997), 5.

12. Thomas Hoyt Jr., "Interpreting Biblical Scholarship for the Black Church Tradition," in *Stony the Road We Trod: African American Biblical Interpretation*, ed. Cain Hope Felder (Minneapolis, Minn.: Fortress Press, 1991), 17–39; Randall C. Bailey, "The Danger of Ignoring One's Own Cultural Bias in Interpreting the Text," in *The Postcolonial Bible*, ed. R. S. Sugirtharajah (Sheffield, UK: Sheffield Academic, 1998), 66–90; Joseph Scrivner, "African American Interpretation," in *The Oxford Encyclopedia of Biblical Interpretation*, ed. Steven L. McKenzie, Oxford Biblical Studies Online, 2013, 7, http://www.oxfordbiblicalstudies.com.proxy.libraries.smu.edu/article/opr/t373/e90; Margaret Aymer, *First Pure, Then Peaceable: Frederick Douglass Reads James* (New York: T. & T. Clark, 2007), 2–13; Vincent L. Wimbush, *White Men's Magic: Scripturalization as Slavery* (New York: Oxford University Press, 2012), 4–12; Valerie Cooper, *Maria Stewart and the Rights of African Americans* (Charlottesville: University of Virginia Press, 2011), 28–38; Herbert Robinson Marbury, *Pillars of Cloud and Fire: The Politics of Exodus* (New York: New York University Press, 2015), xi.

13. Vincent L. Wimbush, "Introduction: Textures, Gestures, Power: Orientation to Radical Excavation," in *Theorizing Scriptures: New Critical Orientation to a Cultural Phenomenon*, ed. Vincent Wimbush (Piscataway, N.J.: Rutgers University Press, 2008), 5 (emphasis in original); quoted in Marbury, *Pillars of Cloud and Fire*, xiii.

14. Johnson, *Lift Every Voice and Sing*, 101. All three of these factors have been addressed in Allen Callahan's *Talking Book: African Americans and the Bible*, arguably a great starting place for any study of the Bible and African Americans as it stands as the most digestible and illustrative exploration of the Christian Bible in African American arts and letters. See Allen D. Callahan, *The Talking Book: African Americans and the Bible* (New Haven, Conn.: Yale University Press, 2006).

15. Sacvan Bercovitch, *The American Jeremiad* (Madison: University of Wisconsin Press, 1978), 5–7.

16. Jon Michael Spencer, *Protest and Praise: Sacred Music of Black Religion* (Minneapolis, Minn.: Fortress Press, 1990), 3–34; Henry Highland Garnet, "An Address to the Slaves of the United States of America of 1843," in *Black Nationalism in America*, ed. John H. Bracey Jr., August Meier, and Elliott Rudwick (Indianapolis, Ind.: Bobbs-Merrill, 1970), 73.

17. Callahan, *The Talking Book*, xx; Charles H. Long, *Significations: Signs, Symbols and Images in the Interpretation of Religion* (Aurora, Colo.: Fortress Press, 1986), 193.

18. Leland Ryken, *The Legacy of the King James Bible: Celebrating 400 Years of the Most Influential English Translation* (Wheaton, Ill.: Crossway, 2011), 52, 54; Alister McGrath, *In the Beginning: The Story of the King James Bible and How It Changed a Nation, a Language, and a Culture* (New York: Double Day, 2001), 297–98; David Daniell, *The Bible in English: Its History and Influence* (New Haven, Conn.: Yale University Press, 2003), 600; Hannibal Hamlin and Norman W. Jones, "Introduction: The King James Bible and Its Reception History," in *The King James Bible after 400 Years: Literary, Linguistic, and Cultural Influence*, ed. Hannibal Hamlin and Norman W. Jones (Cambridge: Cambridge University Press, 2010), 5.

19. Daniell, *The Bible in English*, 635; Gordon Campbell, *Bible: The Story of the King James Version, 1611-2011* (Oxford: Oxford University Press, 2010), 204–5;

20. Albert J. Raboteau, *A Fire in the Bones: Reflections on African-American Religious History* (Boston: Beacon, 1995), 22; Mark A. Noll, "The Bible in Revolutionary America," in

The Bible in American Law, Politics, and Political Rhetoric, ed. James Turner Johnson (Chico, Calif.: Scholars Press, 1985), 49; Albert J. Raboteau, *Canaan Land: A Religious History of African Americans* (New York: Oxford University Press, 2001), 8; Wilson Moses, *Black Messiahs and Uncle Toms: Social and Literary Manipulations of a Religious Myth* (University Park, Pa.: Penn State University Press, 1982), 30; Glenn Miller, *Piety and Profession: American Protestant Theological Education, 1870–1970* (Grand Rapids, Mich.: Eerdmans, 2007), 345–46. The American slaveholders did not initially seek the conversion of African captives, arguing that such evangelization was an economic waste, a precipitant for insurrections, or a tacit assignment of freedom to those slaves who became Christians. See Raboteau, *A Fire in the Bones*, 18. As noted by Raboteau (*A Fire in the Bones*, 19), some slavers eventually consented, however, when the Church of England (1701), through tracts distributed by its Society for the Propagation of the Gospel, argued that conversion would render the captives servile and supported their contention with Ephesians 6:5: "Slaves be obedient to your masters."

21. Daniell, *The Bible in English*, 642; Janet Duitsman Cornelius, *When I Can Read My Title Clear: Literacy, Slavery, and Religion in the Antebellum South* (Columbia: University of South Carolina Press, 1991), 11, 19; Katherine Clay Bassard, "The King James Bible and African American Literature," in *The King James Bible after 400 Years: Literary, Linguistic, and Cultural Influence*, ed. Hannibal Hamlin and Norman W. Jones (Cambridge: Cambridge University, 2010), 297; Jon Sweeney, *Verily, Verily: The KJV: 400 Years of Influence and Beauty* (Nashville, Tenn.: Zondervan, 2011), 36; Campbell, *Bible*, 205.

22. See "Sonny's Blues" in James Baldwin, *Going to Meet the Man* (New York: Vintage Books, 1995), 141.

23. John Coltrane, *A Love Supreme*, Impulse! Label, ABC-Paramount Records, Inc., 1965, 4.

24. Toni Morrison, *Beloved* (New York: Penguin, 1988).

25. Ja Rule, "Only Begotten Son." In *Venni, Vetti, Vecci*. Def Jam Recordings, 1999.

26. Horace L. Griffin, *Their Own Receive Them Not: African American Lesbians and Gays in Black Churches* (Eugene, Ore.: Pilgrim Press, 2010).

27. Mark Fackler, "The Second Coming of Holy Writ: Niche Bibles and the Manufacture of Market Segments," in *New Paradigms for Bible Study: The Bible in the Third Millennium*, ed. Robert M. Fowler, Edith Blumhofer, and Fernando F. Segovia (New York: T&T Clark International, 2004), 70: "niche bible refers to the phenomenon begun in the late 1980s, and still underway, in which a Bible translation is packaged with notes, study aids, and graphics designed to appeal to a fraction of the Bible-buying public."

28. Powery and Sadler, *The Genesis of Liberation*, 9.

29. Johnson, *Lift Every Voice and Sing*, 101.

30. Callahan, *The Talking Book*, xii; Long, *Significations*, 193.

31. Mark Valeri and John F. Wilson, "Scripture and Society: From Reform in the Old World to Revival in the New," in *The Bible in American Law, Politics, and Political Rhetoric*, ed. James Turner Johnson (Chico, Calif.: Scholars Press, 1985), 13.

32. Valeri and Wilson, "Scripture and Society," 21. Robert Warrior, without dismissing the inspirational value of the Exodus story for various liberation theologies—from enslaved African Americans to Latin American base communities—that seek to bring hope to certain communities, avers that the Exodus story must also be read from the perspective of the Canaanites. In so doing, one discovers first that the god of the story is not only "God the Liberator" but "God the Conqueror," that is someone who deploys "the same power used against the enslaving Egyptians to defeat the indigenous inhabitants of Canaan."

One also discovers that in US history, the Exodus narrative (read in conjunction with the Conquest story) supported "American's self-image as a 'chosen people'" even as it justified the genocide of indigenous people, as if the Native Americans were the Canaanites of old. Robert Warrior, "Canaanites, Cowboys, and Indians," *Union Seminary Quarterly Review* 59 (2005): 2–3, 7.

33. Peter J. Gomes, *The Good Book: Reading the Bible with the Mind and Heart* (San Francisco, Calif.: HarperSanFrancisco, 1996), 52; Noll, "The Bible in Revolutionary America," 41.

34. Mark A. Noll, *God and Race in American Politics: A Short History* (Princeton, N.J.: Princeton University Press, 2008), 25; Jackson Lears, *Rebirth of a Nation: The Making of Modern America, 1877–1920* (New York: HarperCollins, 2009), 5–6.

35. Eddie S. Glaude Jr., *Exodus!: Religion, Race, and Nation in Early Nineteenth-Century Black America* (Chicago: University of Chicago Press, 2000), 20.

36. Gary S. Selby, *Martin Luther King, Jr. and the Rhetoric of Freedom: The Exodus Narrative in America's Struggle for Civil Rights* (Waco, Tex.: Baylor University Press, 2008), 34–49.

37. Selby, *Rhetoric of Freedom*, 46.

38. David Howard-Pitney, *The African American Jeremiad: Appeals for Justice in America* (Philadelphia: Temple University Press, 2005), 215–216, 163, 183.

39. Cameron, *To Plead Our Own Cause*, 1–135; Willie J. Harrell Jr., *Origins of the African American Jeremiad* (Jefferson, N.C.: McFarland, 2011), 36–114.

40. Willie J. Harrell Jr., "'A 'Twenty-First Century Economic Agenda for America': Barack Obama's Pre-Presidential Economic Jeremiads," *Canadian Review of American Studies* 41 (2011): 299–324.

41. Katherine Clay Bassard, *Transforming the Scriptures: African American Women Writers and the Bible* (Athens: University of Georgia Press, 2010), 2.

42. Marbury, *Pillars of Cloud and Fire*, 1–200.

43. Milton Sernett, *Bound for the Promised Land: African American Religion and the Great Migration* (Durham, N.C.: Duke University Press, 1997), 67, 63.

44. Hip-hop began in the 1970s as a post-soul cultural aesthetic flowering in the most depressed boroughs of New York City. See Nelson George, *Hip Hop in America* (New York: Penguin, 1998), viii, xl. Thus, the pioneers of this renaissance, arguably young blacks and Latinos, produced hip-hop in the crossfires of the urban underworld— in what S. Craig Watkins describes as "the historic aftershocks of urban renewal, re-segregation, and capital flight." S. Craig Watkins, *Hip Hop Matters: Politics, Pop Culture, and the Struggle for the Soul of a Movement* (Boston, Mass.: Beacon, 2006), 9. The pioneers, though, did not allow the government's disinvestment of their communities to stifle their creativity. Instead, they crafted their own measures of validation and determination by introducing distinctive innovations in multiple artistic venues: in dee-jaying (such as playing turntables with extended rhythmic breaks, producing percussive sounds by scratching or moving a vinyl record back-and-forth, and playing the same section of a piece of music through spinning or the repetition of the segment through the use of two turntables), in poetry (as in MCing, aka rapping), in rhythmic body movements (as in break-dancing), and in graphic art (as in aerosol graffiti [aka tagging]).

45. Grandmaster Flash and the Furious Five's "The Message" (1982) was the first conscious rap song about inner city miseries. Grandmaster Flash and the Furious Five, "The Message," Sugar Hill Records, 1982.

46. Bassard, *Transforming Scriptures*, 2.

47. Raboteau, *A Fire in the Bones*, 42, 45, 51, 51–56.

48. Johnson, *Lift Every Voice and Sing*, 101.

49. Callahan, *The Talking Book*, 242.

50. Callahan, *The Talking Book*, 21–40.

51. Callahan, *The Talking Book*, 40.

52. Vincent L. Wimbush, *African Americans and the Bible: An Interdisciplinary Project* (New York: Continuum, 2000), 17.

53. DoVeanna S. Fulton Minor and Reginald H. Pitts Jr., *Speaking Lives, Authoring Texts: Three African American Women's Oral Slave Narratives* (Albany: State University of New York Press, 2010), 11.

54. Heather Andrea Williams, *Self-Taught: African American Education in Slavery and Freedom* (Chapel Hill: University of North Carolina Press, 2005), 5.

55. Henry Louis Gates Jr., "Writing, 'Race,' and the Difference It Makes," in *The Critical Tradition: Classic Texts and Contemporary Trends*, ed. David H. Richter (Boston: Bedford/St. Martin's, 1989), 1897.

56. Jennifer Fleischner, *Mastering Slavery: Memory, Family, and Identity in Women's Slave Narratives* (New York: New York University Press, 1996), 33.

57. Frederick Douglass, *Narrative of the Life of Frederick Douglass, An American Slave, Written by Himself* (1845; repr., New York: Library of America, 1984), 38.

58. Cornelius, *When I Can Read My Title Clear*, 16.

59. Quoted in Peter P. Hinks, *"To Awaken My Afflicted Brethren": David Walker and the Problem of Antebellum Slave Resistance* (University Park, Pa.: Penn State University Press, 1997), 63.

60. Quoted in Callahan, *The Talking Book*, 27.

61. See George Washington Williams, *History of the Negro Race in America, 1619–1880*, (1883; repr., New York: Arno, 1968), i, vi, xi, 1, 7, 8, 11, 12, 19, 108, 212, 216, 444, 445.

62. Williams, *History of the Negro Race*, i, 1–11; Abraham Smith, "More than a 'Mighty Hunter': George Washington Williams, Nineteenth-Century Racialized Discourse and the Reclamation of Nimrod," in *African American Religious Life and the Story of Nimrod*, ed. Anthony B. Pinn and Allen Dwight Callahan (New York: Palgrave Press, 2008), 74–76.

63. Garnet, "An Address to the Slaves," 189.

64. Quoted in Edward L. Wheeler, *Uplifting the Race: The Black Minister in the New South, 1865–1902* (Lanham, Md.: University Press of America, 1986), 47.

65. Wheeler, *Uplifting the Race*, 51.

66. Wheeler, *Uplifting the Race*, 51.

67. Twentieth-century and twenty-first-century scholars often make a heuristic distinction between an undisputed Paul (one about whom there is not any doubt regarding his authorship of works attributed to his name, for example, 1 Thess., Gal., Phil., Philem., 1 and 2 Cor., and Rom.) and disputed "Paul" (one about whom there is doubt regarding Pauline authorship of yet others works such as 2 Thess., Col., Eph., and the collective group known as the Pastorals: 1 and 2 Tim., and Titus). Such a distinction, though, rarely—if at all—prevailed for African Americans who appropriated Paul in their arguments.

68. See Douglass, *Narrative of the Life*, 49–50, 109, 115, 155, 230, 235, 247, 256, 286, 297–98, 315, 363, 427, 448, 451, 459.

69. Douglass, *Narrative of the Life*, 404–5.

70. William Wells Brown, *Clotel* (New York: Arno, 1969), 82.

71. Brown, *Clotel*, 82.

72. Marilyn Richardson, ed., *Maria W. Stewart, America's First Black Woman Political Writer: Essays and Speeches* (Bloomington: Indiana University Press, 1987), 66–67, 73.

73. Richardson, *Maria W. Stewart*, 68.

74. Quoted in William L. Andrews, *Sisters of the Spirit: Three Black Women's Autobiographies in the Nineteenth Century* (Bloomington: Indiana University Press, 1989), 209.

75. Cornel West, *Race Matters* (Boston: Beacon, 1993), 83; Kelly Brown Douglas, *Sexuality and the Black Church* (Maryknoll, N.Y.: Orbis Books, 1999), 7.

76. West, *Race Matters*, 83–87; Douglas, *Sexuality and the Black Church*, 33–58.

77. Marlon B. Ross, *Manning the Race: Reforming Black Men in the Jim Crow Era* (New York: New York University Press, 2004), 4 (emphasis in original).

78. Anders Stephanson, "Interview with Cornel West," *Social Text* 21 (1989): 284.

79. Catherine Jones and Atsushi Tajima, "The Caucasianization of Jesus: Hollywood Transforming Christianity into a Racially Hierarchical Discourse," *Journal of Religion and Popular Culture* 27 (2015): 202.

80. Rufus L. Perry, *The Cushite or the Descendants of Ham as Found in the Sacred Scriptures and in the Writings of Ancient Historians and Poets from Noah to the Christian Era* (Springfield, Mass.: Willey, 1893), 54.

81. David Theo Goldberg, *Racist Culture: Philosophy and the Politics of Meaning* (Malden, Mass.: Blackwell, 1993), 21.

82. John Jea and George White, *Black Itinerants of the Gospel: The Narratives of John Jea and George White*, ed. Graham Russell Hodges (New York: Palgrave, 2002), 94; Williams, *Self-Taught*, 51; Perry, *The Cushite*, 54; John Stauffer, ed., *The Works of James McCune Smith* (New York: Oxford University Press, 2006), 274; Brown, *Clotel*, 357; J. R. Oldfield, ed., *Civilization and Black Progress: Selected Writings of Alexander Crummell on the South* (Charlottesville: University of Virginia Press, 1995), 38; W. E. B. Du Bois, *The Souls of Black Folk* (1903; repr., New Haven, Conn.: Yale University Press, 2015), 109; Carter G. Woodson, *The Mis-Education of the Negro* (New York: Tribeca Books, 2010), 106.

83. Jea and White, *Black Itinerants*, 94.

84. Williams, *Self-Taught*, 51.

85. Johnson, *Lift Every Voice and Sing*, 101.

86. Johnson, *Lift Every Voice and Sing*, 101.

87. Johnson, *Lift Every Voice and Sing*, 101.

BIBLIOGRAPHY

Andrews, William L., ed. *Sisters of the Spirit: Three Black Women's Autobiographies in the Nineteenth Century*. Bloomington: Indiana University Press, 1989.

Aymer, Margaret. *First Pure, Then Peaceable: Frederick Douglass Reads James*. New York: T&T Clark, 2007.

Bailey, Randall C. "The Danger of Ignoring One's Own Cultural Bias in Interpreting the Text." In *The Postcolonial Bible*, edited by R. S. Sugirtharajah, 66–90. Sheffield, UK: Sheffield Academic, 1998.

Baldwin, James. "Sonny's Blues." In *Going to Meet the Man*, 103–41. New York: Vintage Books, 1995.

Bassard, Katherine Clay. "The King James Bible and African American Literature." In *The King James Bible after 400 Years: Literary, Linguistic, and Cultural Influence*, edited by Hannibal Hamlin and Norman W. Jones, 294–317. Cambridge: Cambridge University, 2010.

———. *Transforming the Scriptures: African American Women Writers and the Bible*. Athens: University of Georgia Press, 2010.

Bercovitch, Sacvan. *The American Jeremiad*. Madison: University of Wisconsin Press, 1978.

Blassingame, James, ed. *The Frederick Douglass Papers, Series One: Speeches, Debates, and Interviews*, vol. 1: *1841-46*. New Haven, Conn.: Yale University Press, 1979.

Brown, William Wells. *Clotel*. New York: Arno, 1969.

Callahan, Allen D. *The Talking Book: African Americans and the Bible*. New Haven, Conn.: Yale University Press, 2006.

Cameron, Christopher. *To Plead Our Own Cause: African Americans in Massachusetts and the Making of the Antislavery Movement (American Abolitionism and Antislavery)*. Kent, Ohio: Kent State University Press, 2015.

Campbell, Gordon. *Bible: The Story of the King James Version, 1611-2011*. Oxford: Oxford University Press, 2010.

Chelst, Kenneth. *Exodus and Emancipation: Biblical and African-American Slavery*. Jerusalem: Urim Publications, 2014.

Cooper, Valerie. *Maria Stewart and the Rights of African Americans*. Charlottesville: University of Virginia Press, 2011.

Cornelius, Janet Duitsman. *When I Can Read My Title Clear: Literacy, Slavery, and Religion in the Antebellum South*. Columbia: University of South Carolina Press, 1991.

Daniell, David. *The Bible in English: Its History and Influence*. New Haven, Conn.: Yale University Press, 2003.

Douglas, Kelly Brown. *Sexuality and the Black Church: A Womanist Perspective*. Maryknoll, N.Y.: Orbis Books, 1999.

Douglass, Frederick. *Narrative of the Life of Frederick Douglass, An American Slave, Written by Himself* (1845). Repr. New York: Library of America, 1984.

Du Bois, W. E. B. *The Souls of Black Folk* (1903). Repr. New Haven, Conn.: Yale University Press, 2015.

Fackler, Mark. "The Second Coming of Holy Writ: Niche Bibles and the Manufacture of Market Segments." In *New Paradigms for Bible Study: The Bible in the Third Millennium*, edited by Robert M. Fowler, Edith Blumhofer, and Fernando F. Segovia, 71–88. New York: T&T Clark International, 2004.

Fleischner, Jennifer. *Mastering Slavery: Memory, Family, and Identity in Women's Slave Narratives*. New York: New York University Press, 1996.

Fulton Minor, DoVeanna S., and Reginald H. Pitts Jr. "Introduction." In *Speaking Lives, Authoring Texts: Three African American Women's Oral Slave Narratives*, 1–38. Albany: State University of New York Press, 2010.

Garnet, Henry Highland. "An Address to the Slaves of the United States of America of 1843." In *Black Nationalism in America*, edited by John H. Bracey Jr., August Meier, and Elliott Rudwick, 67–76. Indianapolis, Ind.: Bobbs-Merrill, 1970.

Gates, Henry Louis, Jr. "Writing, 'Race,' and the Difference It Makes." In *The Critical Tradition: Classic Texts and Contemporary Trends*, edited by David H. Richter, 1891-902. Boston, Mass.: Bedford/St. Martin's, 1989.

George, Nelson. *Hip Hop in America*. New York: Penguin, 1998.

Glaude, Eddie S., Jr. *Exodus!: Religion, Race, and Nation in Early Nineteenth-Century Black America*. Chicago: University of Chicago Press, 2000.

Goldberg, David Theo. *Racist Culture: Philosophy and the Politics of Meaning*. Malden, Mass.: Blackwell, 1993.

Gomes, Peter J. *The Good Book: Reading the Bible with Mind and Heart*. San Francisco, Calif.: HarperSanFrancisco, 1996.

Griffin, Horace L. *Their Own Receive Them Not: African American Lesbians and Gays in Black Churches*. Eugene, Ore.: Pilgrim Press, 2010.

Hamlin, Hannibal, and Norman W. Jones. "Introduction: The King James Bible and Its Reception History." In *The King James Bible after 400 Years: Literary, Linguistic, and Cultural Influences*, edited by Hannibal Hamlin and Norman W. Jones, 1–26. Cambridge: Cambridge University Press, 2010.

Harrell, Willie J., Jr. *Origins of the African American Jeremiad*. Jefferson, N.C.: McFarland, 2011.

———. "A 'Twenty-First Century Economic Agenda for America': Barack Obama's Pre-Presidential Economic Jeremiads." *Canadian Review of American Studies* 41 (2011): 299–324.

Hinks, Peter P. *"To Awaken My Afflicted Brethren": David Walker and the Problem of Antebellum Slave Resistance*. University Park, Pa.: Penn State University Press, 1997.

Howard-Pitney, David. *The African American Jeremiad: Appeals for Justice in America*. Rev. and expanded ed. Philadelphia: Temple University Press, 2005.

Hoyt, Thomas, Jr. "Interpreting Biblical Scholarship for the Black Church Tradition." In *Stony the Road We Trod: African American Biblical Interpretation*, edited by Cain Hope Felder, 7–39. Minneapolis, Minn.: Fortress Press, 1991.

Jea, John, and George White. *Black Itinerants of the Gospel: The Narratives of John Jea and George White*. Edited by Graham Russell Hodges. New York: Palgrave, 2002.

Johnson, James Weldon. *Lift Every Voice and Sing: Selected Poems*. New York: Penguin, 1935.

Jones, Catherine, and Atsushi Tajima. "The Caucasianization of Jesus: Hollywood Transforming Christianity into a Racially Hierarchical Discourse." *Journal of Religion and Popular Culture* 27 (2015): 202–19.

Katz, William Loren, ed. *Five Slave Narratives*. New York: Oxford University Press, 2006.

Kay, Roy. *The Ethiopian Prophecy in Black American Letters*. Gainesville: University of Florida Press, 2011.

Lears, Jackson. *Rebirth of a Nation: The Making of Modern America, 1877–1920*. New York: HarperCollins, 2009.

Long, Charles H. *Significations: Signs, Symbols and Images in the Interpretation of Religion*. Aurora, Colo.: Fortress Press, 1986.

Mancall, Peter. *Envisioning America: English Plans for the Colonization of North America, 1580–1640*. Boston, Mass.: St. Martin's, 1995.

Marbury, Herbert Robinson. *Pillars of Cloud and Fire: The Politics of Exodus*. New York: New York University Press, 2015.

McGrath, Alister. *In the Beginning: The Story of the King James Bible and How It Changed a Nation, a Language, and a Culture*. New York: Double Day, 2001.

Miller, Glenn T. *Piety and Profession: American Protestant Theological Education, 1870–1970*. Grand Rapids, Mich.: William B. Eerdmans, 2007.

Morrison, Toni. *Beloved*. New York: Penguin, 1988.

———. *The Bluest Eye*. New York: Holt, Rinehart and Winston, 1970.

Moses, Wilson. *Black Messiahs and Uncle Toms: Social and Literary Manipulations of a Religious Myth*. University Park, Pa.: Penn State University Press, 1982.

Noll, Mark A. "The Bible in Revolutionary America." In *The Bible in American Law, Politics, and Political Rhetoric*, edited by James Turner Johnson, 39–60. Chico, Calif.: Scholars Press, 1985.

———. *God and Race in American Politics: A Short History*. Princeton, N.J.: Princeton University Press, 2008.

Oldfield, J. R., ed. *Civilization and Black Progress: Selected Writings of Alexander Crummell on the South*. Charlottesville: University of Virginia Press, 1995.

Perry, Rufus L. *The Cushite or the Descendants of Ham as found in the Sacred Scriptures and in the Writings of Ancient Historians and Poets from Noah to the Christian Era*. Springfield, Mass.: Willey, 1893.

Powery, Emerson B., and Rodney S. Sadler Jr. *The Genesis of Liberation: Biblical Interpretation in the Antebellum Narratives of the Enslaved*. Louisville, Ky.: Westminster John Knox Press, 2016.

Raboteau, Albert J. *Canaan Land: A Religious History of African Americans*. New York: Oxford University Press, 2001.

———. *A Fire in the Bones: Reflections on African-American Religious History*. Boston, Mass.: Beacon, 1995.

Reid, Stephen Breck. *Experience and Tradition: A Primer in Black Biblical Hermeneutics*. Nashville, Tenn.: Abingdon, 1990.

Richardson, Marilyn, ed. *Maria W. Stewart, America's First Black Woman Political Writer: Essays and Speeches*. Bloomington: Indiana University Press, 1987.

Ross, Marlon B. *Manning the Race: Reforming Black Men in the Jim Crow Era*. New York: New York University Press, 2004.

Ryken, Leland. *The Legacy of the King James Bible: Celebrating 400 Years of the Most Influential English Translation*. Wheaton, Ill.: Crossway, 2011.

Schwartz, Regina M. *The Curse of Cain: The Violent Legacy of Monotheism*. Chicago: University of Chicago Press, 1997.

Scrivner, Joseph. "African American Interpretation." In *The Oxford Encyclopedia of Biblical Interpretation*, edited by Steven L. McKenzie. 2013. Oxford Biblical Studies Online. http://www.oxfordbiblicalstudies.com.proxy.libraries.smu.edu/article/opr/t373/e90.

Selby, Gary S. *Martin Luther King and the Rhetoric of Freedom: The Exodus Narrative in America's Struggle for Civil Rights*. Waco, Tex.: Baylor University Press, 2008.

Sernett, Milton. *Bound for the Promised Land: African American Religion and the Great Migration*. Durham, N.C.: Duke University Press, 1997.

Shalev, Eran. *American Zion: The Old Testament as a Political Text from the Revolution to the Civil War*. New Haven, Conn.: Yale University Press, 2013.

Smith, Abraham. "More than a 'Mighty Hunter': George Washington Williams, Nineteenth-Century Racialized Discourse and the Reclamation of Nimrod." In *African American Religious Life and the Story of Nimrod*, edited by Anthony B. Pinn and Allen Dwight Callahan, 69–84. New York: Palgrave Press, 2008.

Spencer, Jon Michael. *Protest and Praise: Sacred Music of Black Religion*. Minneapolis, Minn.: Fortress Press, 1990.

Stauffer, John, ed. *The Works of James McCune Smith*. New York: Oxford University Press, 2006.

Stephanson, Anders. "Interview with Cornel West." *Social Text* 21 (1989): 269–86.

Sweeney, Jon. *Verily, Verily: The KJV: 400 Years of Influence and Beauty*. Nashville, Tenn.: Zondervan, 2011.

Valeri, Mark, and John F. Wilson. "Scripture and Society: From Reform in the Old World to Revival in the New." In *The Bible in American Law, Politics, and Political Rhetoric*, edited by James Turner Johnson, 13–38. Chico, Calif.: Scholars Press, 1985.

Warrior, Robert. "Canaanites, Cowboys, and Indians." *Union Seminary Quarterly Review* 59 (2005): 1–8.

Watkins, S. Craig. *Hip Hop Matters: Politics, Pop Culture, and the Struggle for the Soul of a Movement*. Boston, Mass.: Beacon, 2006.

West, Cornel. *Race Matters*. Boston, Mass.: Beacon, 1993.

Wheeler, Edward L. *Uplifting the Race: The Black Minister in the New South, 1865–1902*. Lanham, Md.: University Press of America, 1986.

Williams, George Washington. *History of the Negro Race in America, 1619–1880* (1883). Repr. New York: Arno, 1968.

Williams, Heather Andrea. *Self-Taught: African American Education in Slavery and Freedom*. Chapel Hill: University of North Carolina Press, 2005.

Wimbush, Vincent L. *African Americans and the Bible: An Interdisciplinary Project*. New York: Continuum, 2000.

——. "Introduction: Textures, Gestures, Power: Orientation to Radical Excavation." In *Theorizing Scriptures: New Critical Orientation to a Cultural Phenomenon*, edited by Vincent L. Wimbush, 1–22. Piscataway, N.J.: Rutgers University Press, 2008.

——. *White Men's Magic: Scripturalization as Slavery*. New York: Oxford University Press, 2012.

Winant, Howard. *The World is a Ghetto: Race and Democracy since World War II*. New York: Basic Books, 2001.

Woodson, Carter G. *The Mis-Education of the Negro*. New York: Tribeca Books, 2010.

CHAPTER 13

....

THE BIBLE
AND CREATIONISM

....

SUSAN L. TROLLINGER
AND WILLIAM VANCE TROLLINGER JR.

To understate the case, Charles Darwin's *Origin of Species* (1859) marked a significant challenge to traditional understandings of the Bible and Christian theology. Darwin's theory of organic evolution stood in sharp contrast with the Genesis account of creation, with its six days, separate creations of life forms, and special creation of human beings. More than these particular issues, Darwin's ideas raised enormous theological questions about God's role in creation such as is there a role for God in organic evolution, as well as questions about the nature of human beings such as what does it mean to talk about original sin without a historic Adam and Eve.

Of course, what really made Darwin so challenging to many strains of Christian thought was that by the late nineteenth century his theory of organic evolution was the scientific consensus. That is to say, American Protestants had no choice but to reckon with Darwinism. For many Protestant intellectuals, clergy, and laypersons, this was not an enormous obstacle. That is, and in keeping with previous Christian responses to scientific developments, many Protestants adjusted their understanding of the Bible and their theology to accommodate Darwin's ideas.

But a significant minority of late nineteenth-century American Protestants responded quite negatively to Darwin and would not, or could not, adjust their understanding of the Bible and its authority to fit the theory of organic evolution.[1] They were bolstered in their resistance by the doctrine of inerrancy. Inerrancy was developed in the late nineteenth century by more conservative American Protestant theologians such as those found at Princeton Theological Seminary in response to the rising influence of historicism (or, higher criticism), which—in its determination to examine the Bible as any other historical text would be examined—raised questions about the errors and inconsistencies in the text and highlighted the ways in which aspects of the biblical narrative seemed to involve borrowings from other cultures. In contrast, inerrancy emphasized that the original biblical "autographs" are the errorless product of the Holy Spirit's guidance. While the texts and translations that we have may have a few errors, they are, so it is claimed, so few and so minor that we can trust the Bible that we have as the Word of God. As such, the Bible is factually accurate in all that it has to say, including when it speaks on history and science.[2]

Of course, inerrancy would not mean much if we the readers could not understand what the inerrant text is saying. That is to say, central to inerrancy is the notion that we are to read the Bible plainly, commonsensically, "literally." It bears noting here that—despite all the rhetoric to the contrary—there is no such thing as one and only one literal reading of the Bible. Despite persistent and even frantic efforts by various biblical inerrantists to freeze the interpretation of the biblical text and claim that they have come up with the one true reading of the text, they have not been able to change the fact that there is and will always be a plethora of plain, commonsensical, literal readings of the Bible.[3]

While it is thus certainly possible to imagine an inerrant Bible that is amenable to Darwinism, most late nineteenth-century Protestants who held to inerrancy could see no way to square the theory of organic evolution with the first few chapters of Genesis. Interestingly, however, the idea of an Earth older than the some 4,000 years traditionally attributed to the Old Testament period recorded in the Bible did not pose a problem for these conservative Protestants. This was in good part because the work of squaring a literal reading of Genesis 1 with the notion of a significantly more ancient Earth than pointed to in the Old Testament had already been done for them. In the centuries prior to Charles Darwin there was overwhelming confidence that the findings of modern science did and would square with the biblical text. As Jon Roberts has observed, "Protestant intellectuals . . . conceded that the conclusions of science sometimes seemed to clash with the Scriptures, but they managed to devise a number of formulas that accommodated the meaning and truth of the Bible to the results of scientific investigation."[4] So when it became clear—in the latter half of the eighteenth century and the first half of the nineteenth century—that the Earth was millions of years old, Protestant thinkers instinctively developed ways of reading Genesis 1 to fit this scientific consensus. Two approaches proved to be the most popular: Thomas Chalmers's "gap theory" and Hugh Miller's "day-age theory."

Thomas Chalmers (1780-1847) was an evangelical Scottish minister, a significant figure in the Church of Scotland and leader of the Free Church of Scotland movement, and a professor of moral philosophy at St. Andrews University (1823-28) and then professor of theology at the University of Edinburgh (1828-43). While a minister in his twenties and thirties, Chalmers delivered various lectures in mathematics and the sciences at St. Andrews and the communities where he was pastoring. It was in those years that he advanced his gap theory, which reconciled Genesis 1 with the antiquity of the Earth. As Michael Roberts has ably argued in "Genesis and Geological Time," Chalmers's gap theory is best understood not as a radical departure from established biblical interpretation, but instead as a modification of the chaos-restitution approach to Genesis 1 first articulated by Hugo Grotius and Marin Mersenne in the seventeenth century. In the traditional chaos-restitution exegesis, Genesis 1:1-2 describes an initial creation of chaos or a creation that became chaos—"the earth was a formless void and darkness covered the face of the deep"—that lasted an indeterminate period of time, after which God used six days to order his creation. Specifically citing Grotius, Chalmers took the chaos-restitution interpretation and tweaked it to take into account the recently established antiquity of the Earth. That is to say, Chalmers inserted into the time of chaos, that is, into the gap provided by Genesis 1:1-2, the entirety of geological time and events. This geologically momentous era was then followed by God's six, twenty-four-hour day ordering or restitution of the Earth.[5]

The appeal of Chalmers's gap theory is obvious: one could have an ancient Earth and a literal six-day creation all in one nice-and-neat exegetical package. For the first few decades of the nineteenth century, this was the dominant form of Genesis-geology reconciliation. But after mid-century, it was superseded in popularity by what came to be known as the day-age theory, which, most simply stated, held that the "days" in Genesis 1 are not twenty-four-hour days, but instead periods of time of undefined length. While not the first to make this argument, it was the Scottish geologist, writer, and churchman Hugh Miller (1802-1856) who, particularly in his *The Testimony of the Rocks* (a book he completed on the last day of his life), did the most to advance this argument. While Miller had been an adherent of Chalmers's gap theory, his Scottish compatriot's emphasis on a time of chaos eventually proved unacceptable because, as Davis A. Young has noted, "all the geological evidence indicated to Miller a continuity between the past and the time of the appearance of man." More than this, it seemed to Miller that each of the Genesis days lined up well with (to quote John Hedley Brooke) "sharply differentiated [geological] epochs," at the beginning of each "there had been creative acts of God." As was the case with Chalmers and his gap theory, Miller and others making the case for a day-age approach to Genesis 1 received support from a range of biblical exegetes, who pointed out that in the Bible the Hebrew word for "day" often means a long period of time, that it was very difficult to imagine that the actions described for each of the days could have been completed in discrete twenty-four-hour periods, and that the "seventh day" has not actually ended (and thus is obviously not a twenty-four-hour day).[6]

In the century after Charles Darwin's *Origin of Species*, virtually all Protestants who opposed the theory of organic evolution "readily conceded," as Ronald L. Numbers has observed, "that the Bible allowed for an ancient earth and pre-Edenic life." And virtually all of these "old Earth creationists" utilized either the gap theory or the day-age theory to reconcile Genesis 1 and geology. The most influential representative of the former camp was C. I. Scofield (1843-1921). Scofield was a Congregationalist (and then Presbyterian) minister as well as a prominent figure in the late nineteenth-century Bible and Prophecy movement, which aimed to inculcate American Protestants in biblical inerrancy and dispensational premillennialism. By the turn of the century, Scofield had committed himself to creating an edition of the King James Version Bible that included notes designed to ensure that readers rightly interpreted the scripture.[7]

The first edition of *The Scofield Reference Bible* was published in 1909, with a second edition appearing in 1917. Becoming the unofficial Bible of the fundamentalist movement (which began in 1919), Scofield's Bible was an incredible publishing success story, with two million volumes sold prior to 1945. For our purposes, what is most noteworthy are Scofield's comments on Genesis 1. As regards God's creation of the heaven and the Earth (Gen. 1:1), Scofield noted that this occurred "in the dateless past, and gives scope for all the geologic ages." Then the Earth became "without form, and void" (Gen. 1:2), which according to Scofield "clearly indicate[s] that the earth had undergone a cataclysmic change as the result of a divine judgment," a "catastrophe" which was perhaps due to a "previous testing and fall of angels." But after this time of chaos came the reordering of creation, which on day five included the creation of animal life and on day six the creation of human beings. Regarding the latter, Scofield notes expressly that "man was *created*, not *evolved*," made "in the 'image and likeness' of God," evinced by his "tri-unity" (spirit, soul, and body) and by "his moral nature."[8]

When it came to the gap theory, Scofield's most important disciple was Harry Rimmer (1890-1952), who was the most prominent anti-evolutionist of the 1920s and 1930s. Rimmer tirelessly lectured and wrote against Darwinism, and he was particularly well-known for his fiery debates with proponents of evolution. Rimmer even debated day-age adherent William Bell Riley (1861-1947), the Baptist preacher who founded the World's Christian Fundamentals Association (WCFA) in 1919, and who led the 1920s crusade against modernist theology in the churches and evolutionary teaching in the public schools. But the most famous advocate of the day-age theory was three-time presidential candidate William Jennings Bryan (1860-1925). Interestingly, while Riley held firmly to the special creation of the species—and before his death in 1947 may have been moving toward young Earth creationism (the Genesis days are twenty-four-hour days, and the Earth is approximately 6,000 years old)—Bryan (at least privately) did not have trouble squaring evolution with Genesis as long as the special creation of human beings was maintained.[9]

Bryan's commitment to the day-age theory came into full view at the 1925 Scopes Trial. Bryan had been recruited by Riley to assist in the prosecution of science teacher John T. Scopes for violating Tennessee's law prohibiting the teaching of evolution in the public schools (a law passed in part because of WCFA pressure). Near the end of the trial, defense attorney Clarence Darrow convinced Bryan to get on the witness stand. Darrow was not only determined to make Bryan's biblical literalism look ridiculous—for example, asking where Adam and Eve's son Cain got his wife, or how Joshua survived three days inside a whale—but also inconsistent, pressing Bryan on his day-age theory:

Q—Do you think the earth was made in six days?
A—Not six days of twenty-four hours.
. . .
Q—You do not think that?
A—No. But I think that it would be just as easy for the kind of God we believe in to make the earth in six days as in six years or in 6,000,000 years or in 600,000,000 years . . .
Q—Do you think those were literal days?
A—My impression is that they were periods.[10]

While the gap and day-age theories held sway until the middle of the twentieth century, after the 1950s many or most old Earth creationists have held to some version of "progressive creationism," a term popularized by Bernard Ramm in his 1954 book, *The Christian View of Science and Scripture*. As articulated by Ramm, the six days of creation are not twenty-four-hour days (as in the gap theory), nor are they tied to six particular geological epochs (as in the day-age theory). Instead, "creation was *revealed* in six days, not *performed* in six days. [That is], the six days are *pictorial-revelatory* days, not literal days nor age-days." While this approach allows for much time, God still intervenes in creating "root-species," or "kinds," which then evolve into other species; however, this is only "horizontal" evolution (or, "radiation"), as "vertical progress takes place only by [God's] creation." And, of course, this includes the special creation of a historical Adam and Eve, which for progressive creationists remains "an extraordinary act of God that is not explainable by known natural causes."[11]

In the twenty-first century, perhaps the most well-known advocates of progressive creationism have been astronomer Hugh Ross and his Reasons to Believe ministry. While

Reasons to Believe accepts the Big Bang theory and an ancient universe and Earth, it rejects "macro-evolution"—seeing instead "a single Creator [Who] has generated life throughout Earth's history"—and accepts "the Christian idea that all humanity descended from two historical persons, Adam and Eve." In short, while progressive creationism—in its effort to reconcile a plain, commonsensical, literal reading of Genesis with the findings of science—may have jettisoned virtually all of the gap theory and some of the day-age theory, it remains very much within the tradition of old Earth creationism in its embrace of mainstream geology (and now astronomy) and its rejection of significant components of mainstream biology.[12]

In his preface to *The Christian View of Science and Scripture*, Ramm seeks to take on the "ignoble tradition" within Christianity that "has taken a most unwholesome attitude toward science, and [that] has used arguments and procedures not in the better traditions of established scholarship."[13] As Ramm's chapter on "Geology" makes clear, one of the exemplars of this ignoble tradition was Harry Rimmer and his gap theory. But even more a target of Ramm's academic ire was George McCready Price (1870-1963), who, over the course of six decades, published many articles and numerous books that argued for a six twenty-four-hour-day creation and a young Earth, all supported by "flood geology" (Noah's flood explains the geological strata). Ramm was scathing in his attacks on Price, even using a footnote to mention a "geology professor [who] would not let anybody pass sophomore geology till he had refuted Price." But, as Ronald L. Numbers has wryly noted, "if Ramm thought he was officiating at the funeral of flood geology, he was badly mistaken." In fact, by the latter decades of the twentieth century what goes under the sign of a literal reading of Genesis 1 is the notion of young Earth creationism. As we shall see, Price did much to popularize these claims—but he did not come up with them.[14]

That honor goes to Ellen G. White (1827-1915). In her Methodist adolescence, White became convicted by the arguments of William Miller (1782-1849, of the Millerites) that Jesus would return to Earth in 1843. During the early 1840s, when enthusiasm for the return of Christ and intense religious experience was at a high point, especially among Methodists, White began having powerful dreams and visions. In her second dream, she encountered Jesus who looked piercingly into her eyes and spoke to her directly.[15] To the disappointment of many, including White, Jesus did not return in 1843, or on the later, revised date of October 22, 1844. But White's dreams and visions continued, and many of them were recorded and published. Over time, White attracted a significant following as a prophet in Advent circles and, in 1863, founded with her husband, James White (1821-1881), a new church—the Seventh-day Adventist Church.[16]

To her followers, White's dreams and visions did not merely offer wise commentary on the Bible; they were "on par with the Bible." They spoke God's truth. And one of the truths they spoke was that we live on a very young Earth. White claimed that in her vision, God transported her back to the Creation where she watched as its processes unfolded over the course of a week that was "'just like every other week.'" That is, it consisted of seven twenty-four-hour days. In light of that vision and others, White argued that the Earth was about 6,000 years old (a claim that had by that time been rejected by most evangelicals) and that all signs indicating that the Earth was much older than that could be attributed to catastrophic processes associated with Noah's global flood, which buried the debris from the flood and rearranged the surface of the Earth.[17] For White and her followers, God's revelation to her of a six twenty-four-hour-day creation was important as it grounded the

Seventh-day Adventists' Saturday Sabbath in the Creation—that God created for six days and rested on the seventh.

Price, along with his widowed mother and younger brother, joined the Seventh-day Adventists at about the age of fourteen. Just three years later, he married an Adventist woman and began selling White's books across eastern Canada. Although Price was utterly convinced of White's claims and enjoyed some success at selling her books, he felt called by God to use his own gifts for writing in the cause of White's literal reading of the Genesis account of creation. Unlike White who was deeply interested in many topics important to a good Christian life including diet, hygiene, and overall health, Price was singularly focused on refuting once and for all geologists' claims that the Earth was millions of years old.[18]

Price focused on geology because he was convinced that the whole argument against a special creation rested upon geology's claim for an old Earth. Although his efforts benefited from little formal training in the natural sciences, Price nevertheless set out to undermine geology's dating of the Earth by constructing an alternate science that assumed a six twenty-four-hour-day creation and a young Earth and that explained all evidence that appeared to the contrary by way of Noah's global flood.[19]

On behalf of a young Earth, Price attacked the method he said geologists used to date the Earth. According to Price, geologists dated the Earth by dating rocks according to the content of the fossils contained within them. And they dated fossils by reference to their location in the geological column. Price argued that this reasoning was circular. In addition, he challenged the notion that rocks and fossils had been deposited in a sequential manner over millions of years to form the geological column. Instead, he argued that the processes of Noah's global and catastrophic flood sorted the debris it produced. Since smaller creatures surely died first in the flood, their remains were deposited most deeply. By contrast, larger creatures, including man, headed for the hills to avoid the floodwaters and, thusly, left their skeletons and fossils on higher ground. In addition to forming the fossil record, he argued, the flood also carved out the Grand Canyon, "piled up" the mountains of the Alps and the Himalayas, and transformed great forests into expansive coal deposits.[20]

Later, Price attacked the notion that the location of a fossil amidst a certain layer of rock could indicate the age of the fossil. He did this by pointing to layers of strata that appeared identical yet were identified by geologists through the fossil record as being of vastly different ages. By Price's reasoning, since fossils in and of themselves offer no guarantee of the age of the matter they appear within and since the strata appeared to be identical, one must reject geology's claim that their formation was separated by millions of years. Instead, one must conclude, as one's direct observation would indicate, that the apparently identical strata were created at the same time.[21]

In short, Price argued that the geological column provided no concrete evidence of an old Earth and, further, that there was no evidence to establish the millions of years required for the processes of evolution. Thus, Price concluded, his arguments undermined not only the possibility of evolution but also Darwin's entire argument regarding the origin of species. In so doing, he believed he had restored the Bible to its proper status—as the one literally true account of the Creation, which justified the Saturday Sabbath as a living memorial of a historical event.[22]

Although Price was a Seventh-day Adventist, his new geology, what he called "flood geology," exerted significant influence on fundamentalists in the 1920s and 1930s who were busy crusading against Darwinism. William Bell Riley, the great day-age advocate, proclaimed to his followers that Price was "'one of the real scientists of the day [whose] writings are destined to profoundly influence the thinking of the future.'" At the Scopes Trial, Riley's fellow day-age advocate William Jennings Bryan praised Price as one of but two Earth scientists whose views he respected. And Harry Rimmer, the gap theory firebrand, praised Price's *The New Geology* as "'the most remarkable and up-to-date book of Geology extant today . . . a masterpiece of REAL Science."[23]

What is truly remarkable is that, for all the fulsome praise from fundamentalist leaders, none of them seemed to appreciate fully that Price's literal reading of Genesis undermined their own literal readings of Genesis. While the day-age and gap theories served to reconcile Genesis with an old Earth, Price's flood geology washed away an old Earth altogether. But at the Scopes Trial, Bryan somehow both praised Price's geology and made an extended argument on behalf of the day-age theory. And Bernard Ramm could scarcely contain himself in pointing out that Harry Rimmer completely missed the contradiction between his own approach to reading Genesis and Price's interpretation:

> In regard to geology Rimmer pays due tribute to Price. But this cannot be done with any consistency. First, the gap theory is invoked to account for geologic ages. Price invokes a universal flood to account for geologic ages. Rimmer *appeals to both*![24]

Thus, while Price's notions of flood geology spread through American Protestant fundamentalism in the middle decades of the twentieth century, the logical consequences of his ideas—the rejection of mainstream geology and the acceptance of a young Earth—were in good part ignored until 1961, when Price's arguments were essentially reiterated in the wildly popular book, *The Genesis Flood: The Biblical Record and Its Scientific Implications*.[25] Authors John C. Whitcomb Jr. (a theologian and Old Testament professor at Grace Seminary in Indiana, b. 1924) and Henry M. Morris (a PhD in hydraulic engineering and chair of the civil engineering department at Virginia Tech, 1918–2006) borrowed liberally from Price's work as they mined Genesis to ascertain the facts of the Creation, critiqued modern geological methods, and mobilized Noah's flood to explain how a yearlong global event produced the geological strata that appeared to provide the appearances of an old Earth. Moreover, their aims were, like Price's, to undermine the arguments of mainstream science on behalf of an old Earth and to offer an alternative science—flood geology—that supported their literal reading of the Creation in Genesis. Unfortunately for Price, few reading *The Genesis Flood* appreciated Morris and Whitcomb's indebtedness to his work. Anticipating that evangelicals would likely dismiss out-of-hand arguments borrowed from a Seventh-day Adventist, Morris and Whitcomb kept the origins of their arguments well under the radar. That said, Whitcomb and Morris did take Price's argument on behalf of a literal reading of the Genesis creation account (along, of course, with White's) one step further by claiming that not just the Earth but also the entire universe was created in six twenty-four-hour days less than 10,000 years ago.[26]

The timing of Morris and Whitcomb's volume could not have been better. By the 1960s, evangelicals were ready for a creationist argument that sounded as though it were steeped in the discourse of science. With its footnotes, photographs, and even the occasional mathematical equation, *The Genesis Flood* offered evangelicals what appeared to be a serious scientific alternative to the rhetorical hegemony of mainstream science. Providing an alternative science for the special creation was crucial since by the 1960s science, with its great success in launching rockets and landing manned space ships on the moon, seemed the incontrovertible discourse of Truth. *The Genesis Flood* mobilized its own, albeit curious, science that, at least for many evangelicals, showed that they (and their literal reading of the Bible) were back in the Truth game.

In this regard, Morris and Whitcomb's book was arguably one of the most important American Protestant books of the twentieth century. Not only did it transform the way that evangelicals thought about the Creation, it also transformed their understanding of what it means to hold to the inerrant Word of God. Most of those who held to gap theory or the day-age theory understood themselves to hold to an inerrant Bible. But *The Genesis Flood* persuaded a great many evangelicals that to read the Bible plainly, commonsensically, literally was to believe in a young Earth and universe and a six twenty-four-hour-day creation. Put differently, after *The Genesis Flood* many evangelicals could conclude that those who held to mainstream geology and astronomy—not to mention mainstream biology—did not hold to the inerrant Word of God, and perhaps were not really Christians.

Given the widespread enthusiasm for *The Genesis Flood* and its apparent success in grounding a certain literal reading of Genesis within the discourse of science, it is not surprising that a number of organizations soon appeared after its publication to advance the science of flood geology. Two of the most important were the Creation Research Society (CRS), which was established in 1963, and the Institute for Creation Research (ICR), which emerged in 1972. Notably, both had direct ties to Morris. Although the founders of CRS expressed significant differences about flood geology and its ability to account for the signs of an old Earth, they nevertheless dedicated the CRS to the twin projects of producing real scientific research and science textbooks on behalf of a literal reading of the Creation story.[27] Likewise, the founders of ICR dedicated itself to scientific research and education on behalf of the biblical creation story. Despite their earnest intentions for real scientific research that would prove a literal reading of the creation story found in the Bible, neither organization managed to produce it. On the whole, mainstream science journals found the research that these organizations produced substantively lacking. Thus, the work of the CRS and ICR, limited as it was, largely went unrecognized and unnoticed.[28]

More important than any contribution CRS or ICR made to the research base for the creationist cause was, arguably, their provision of an entrée into the US context for Ken Ham (b. 1951). Born in Cairns, Australia, Ham came to the United States and joined the ICR in 1987 with a bachelor's degree in applied science from the Queensland Institute of Technology, a diploma in education from the University of Queensland, and some experience as a science educator. Ham had also enjoyed significant success as a speaker on young Earth creationism first on his own and then through the Creation Science Foundation (CSF), an organization similar to the ICR. Importantly, Ham never shared the goal of the CRS or the ICR of developing a science of young Earth creationism. Instead, his focus was always on spreading a simple three-pronged message that the teaching of evolution was evil and that it produced terrific cultural decay, that the first eleven chapters of Genesis spoke directly and literally about the origins of the universe as well as about the proper way to organize society, and that true Christians should join earnestly in an all-out culture war for the soul of America against atheistic humanism.[29]

With Henry Morris's blessing and a lot of experience on the young Earth creationist speaking circuit in the United States, Ham and a few of his colleagues from ICR formed Answers in Genesis (AiG) in 1994. In the years since then and with the benefit of Ham's leadership, AiG has become the leading young Earth creationist apologetics ministry in the United States with its extensive online presence (http://www.answersingenesis.org) that includes online magazines, blogs, radio shows, a calendar of speaking events and conferences, and an online store where visitors can find an extensive warehouse of creationist apparel, homeschooling curricula, DVDs, and more.

On May 28, 2007, AiG opened its first bricks-and-mortar presence in the form of the 75,000-square-foot Creation Museum located just south of Cincinnati, Ohio, in Petersburg, Kentucky. By the summer of 2015, the Creation Museum had welcomed 2.4 million people to its many displays, life-size dioramas, and multi-media experiences designed to "point today's culture back to the authority of Scripture and proclaim the gospel message." A second, arguably even more ambitious project, which opened in 2016, features a life-size re-creation of Noah's ark. According to AiG, this ark was constructed as closely as possible to the specifications detailed in Genesis 6–8. Located near Williamstown, Kentucky, the massive wood-framed ark of Ark Encounter (510 feet long and 85 feet tall) has grown to become one of Kentucky's premier visitor sites.[30]

While the Creation Museum clearly reiterates the central arguments of *The Genesis Flood* regarding a six twenty-four-hour-day creation, a young Earth, and a global flood that explains all signs of an old Earth, its real focus is on the question of who or what serves as the ultimate authority for Truth in twenty-first-century US culture. As the museum points out early in its "Bible Walkthrough Experience" (that takes visitors on a visual tour of the first eleven chapters of Genesis), there are only two possible sources for authority: God's Word or human reason. Those who rightly choose the authority of a literal reading of God's Word and are obedient to that Word (by, for example, accepting the claim that marriage can only properly occur between a man and a woman), can in all likelihood look forward to an eternity in heaven. Those who reject that Word and its authority can look forward to being like those who perished in Noah's flood.[31]

As noted earlier, there is not one and only one "literal" reading of the Bible. That said, and as Susan Harding insightfully points out in *The Book of Jerry Falwell: Fundamentalist Language and Politics*, when it comes to fundamentalist discourse, it is a great rhetorical advantage to present one's "biblical interpretation as 'more literal' than another's."[32] This type of argumentation has certainly been used by young Earth creationists when it comes to discounting old Earth creationism. Such an argument has proven to be incredibly persuasive. But it must also be pointed out that—given that there is not one and only one "literal" reading of the Bible—the young Earth creationism of advocates like Morris, Whitcomb, and Ham is not likely to be the final word when it comes to reconciling a plain, commonsensical, and literal reading of Genesis with the findings of science. Given the rules of fundamentalist discourse, it makes sense that what will come next will be an even "more literal" creationism.

Such a creationism is already here, in the form of a geocentric creationism that fully accepts the notion that the universe was created in six, twenty-four-hour days around 6,000 years ago, but also insists that the sun revolves around a stationary Earth. At the heart of this argument is that it is not enough for creationists to take Genesis literally. They must also take literally Ecclesiastes 1:5—"The sun rises and the sun goes down, and hurries to the place where it rises"—as well as Joshua 10:12–13:

> On the day when the LORD gave the Amorites over to the Israelites, Joshua spoke to the
> LORD; and he said in the sight of Israel, "Sun, stand still at Gibeon, and Moon, in the valley

of Aijalon." And the sun stood still, and the moon stopped, until the nation took vengeance on their enemies. Is this not written in the Book of Jashar? The sun stopped in mid-heaven, and did not hurry to set for about a whole day.

Making the case for a biblical "geocentricity" are books with titles such as *He Maketh His Sun to Rise: A Look at Biblical Geocentricity* as well as a host of websites, including the wonderfully titled galileowaswrong.blogspot.com.[33]

Perhaps the most prominent twenty-first-century advocate for an Earth-centered universe is Gerardus Bouw, director of the Association for Biblical Astronomy and author of a number of books on the topic, including *Geocentricity: Christianity in the Woodshed*. While old Earth creationists decry the corruption wrought by the acceptance of the theory of organic evolution, and young Earth creationists decry the decadence wrought by the acceptance of evolution and an ancient Earth, Bouw decries the destructive effects wrought by the acceptance of evolution, an ancient Earth, and a heliocentric universe. More than this, he scores "non-geocentric creationists" for their failure to truly take the Bible literally:

> Is the Scripture to be the final authority on all matters on which it touches, or are scholars, to be the ultimate authority? The central issue is not the motion of the earth, nor is it the creation of the earth. The issue is final authority, is it to be the words of God, or the words of men?[34]

Bouw may be on the creationist fringe at the moment, but he summarizes nicely the issue at hand. In the end, all forms of creationism—old Earth, young Earth, geocentric—hinge on this point of biblical authority. All creationists affirm that they stand on the authority of the Word, but that still leaves open the questions as to what that Word—read plainly, commonsensically, literally—actually means, and to what degree can that plain, commonsensical, literal Word be reconciled with mainstream science. The historical trajectory of creationism suggests that we will see less, not more, reconciliation in the future. Put differently, in fifty years Gerardus Bouw, like George McCready Price before him, may have moved from the fringe to the center of the creationist mainstream.

NOTES

1. Jon H. Roberts, *Darwinism and the Divine in America: Protestant Intellectuals and Organic Evolution, 1859-1900* (Madison: University of Wisconsin Press, 1988), xiii–xx. See the entirety of Roberts' book.
2. Susan L. Trollinger and William Vance Trollinger Jr., *Righting America at the Creation Museum* (Baltimore, Md.: Johns Hopkins University Press, 2016), 2–3.
3. Christian Smith, *The Bible Made Impossible: Why Biblicism Is Not a Truly Evangelical Reading of Scripture* (Grand Rapids, Mich.: Brazos Press, 2011), 3–54; Kathleen C. Boone, *The Bible Tells Them So: The Discourse of Protestant Fundamentalism* (Albany: State University of New York Press, 1989), 71–75; Trollinger and Trollinger, *Righting America*, 109–11, 134–47.
4. Roberts, *Darwinism*, xiii.
5. William Hanna and Dugald Macfadyen, "Thomas Chalmers," in *The Encyclopaedia Britannica*, 11th ed. (New York: Encyclopaedia Britannica, 1910), 5:809–11; Michael B. Roberts, "Genesis Chapter 1 and Geological Time from Hugo Grotius and Marin

Mersenne to William Conybeare and Thomas Chalmers (1620–1825)," in *Myth and Geology*, ed. Luigi Piccardi and W. Bruce Masse (London: Geological Society of London, 2007), 41–42, 46; Michael B. Roberts, "The Genesis of John Ray and his Successors," *Evangelical Quarterly* 74 (2002): 155–57.

6. Roberts, "Genesis of John Ray," 159; Davis A. Young, *Christianity and the Age of the Earth* (Grand Rapids, Mich.: Zondervan, 1982), 58–59; David R. Oldroyd, "The Geologist from Cromarty," in *Hugh Miller and the Controversies of Victorian Science*, ed. Michael Shortland (Oxford: Clarendon Press, 1996), 103–6; John Hedley Brooke, "Like Minds: The God of Hugh Miller," in *Hugh Miller*, ed. Michael Shortland, 172.

7. Ronald L. Numbers, *The Creationists: From Scientific Creationism to Intelligent Design*, expanded ed. (Cambridge, Mass.: Harvard University Press, 2006), 7, 10–11; Trollinger and Trollinger, *Righting America*, 137–38.

8. C. I. Scofield, ed., *The Scofield Reference Bible* (King James Version) (New York: Oxford University Press, 1917), 3, 5, emphasis in original.

9. Edward B. Davis, "Introduction," in *The Antievolution Pamphlets of Harry Rimmer*, ed. Edward B. Davis, vol. 6 of *Creationism in Twentieth-Century America*, ed. Ronald L. Numbers (New York: Garland, 1995), ix–xxviii; Numbers, *Creationists*, 55–58, 81–83; William Vance Trollinger Jr., "Introduction" in *The Antievolution Pamphlets of William Bell Riley*, ed. William Vance Trollinger Jr., vol. 4 of *Creationism in Twentieth-Century America*, ed. Ronald L. Numbers (New York: Garland, 1995), ix–xx.

10. *The World's Most Famous Court Trial: Tennessee Evolution Case*, 2nd rpt. ed. (Dayton, Tenn.: Bryan College, 1990), 298–302.

11. Bernard Ramm, *The Christian View of Science and Scripture* (Grand Rapids, Mich.: Eerdmans, 1954), 195–222, 271–72 (emphasis in the original); Numbers, *Creationists*, 208–11; Pattle P. T. Pun, "A Theology of Progressive Creationism," *Perspectives on Science and Christian Faith* 39 (1987): 9–19.

12. Fazale Rana, "Repeatable Evolution or Repeated Creation?," Reasons to Believe, October 1, 2000, http://www.reasons.org/articles/repeatable-evolution-or-repeated-creation; "Historical Adam," Reasons to Believe, http://www.reasons.org/rtb-101/historicaladam; Eugenie C. Scott, "Antievolution and Creationism in the United States," *Annual Review of Anthropology* 26 (1997): 270–71.

13. Ramm, *Science and Scripture*, 9.

14. Ramm, *Science and Scripture*, 179–88, 195–210 (quote: 181n12); Numbers, *Creationists*, 211.

15. Ann Taves, "Visions," in *Ellen Harmon White: American Prophet*, ed. Terrie Dopp Aamodt, Gary Land, and Ronald L. Numbers (New York: Oxford University Press, 2014), 32–36. To clarify, Ellen Harmon White and Ellen G. White are the same person, as her full name was Ellen Gould Harmon White.

16. Jonathan M. Butler, "A Portrait," in *Ellen Harmon White*, 9–14.

17. Numbers, *Creationists*, 90; Ronald L. Numbers and Rennie B. Schoepflin, "Science and Medicine," in *Ellen Harmon White*, 214–15. Importantly, while White argued for a young Earth, she did not argue for a young universe. In fact, she wrote "of inhabited worlds that antedated the Edenic creation." Numbers, *Creationists*, 228.

18. Numbers, *Creationists*, 92.

19. According to Numbers, Price chose not to take any natural science courses during his two years at Battle Creek College (an Adventist school in Michigan) and took only a few introductory natural science classes in the course of a one-year teacher training course that he took in 1896 at the Provincial Normal School of New Brunswick. Numbers, *Creationists*, 91.

20. Numbers, *Creationists*, 93–94.
21. Numbers, *Creationists*, 95–96.
22. Numbers, *Creationists*, 104–5.
23. Quotes from Numbers, *Creationists*, 115–17. Also Trollinger and Trollinger, *Righting America*, 7.
24. Ramm, *Science and Scripture*, 208, emphasis in original.
25. Numbers, *Creationists*, 114–19.
26. Numbers, *Creationists*, 225–34. Trollinger and Trollinger, *Righting America*, 8.
27. Numbers, *Creationists*, 250–64.
28. Numbers, *Creationists*, 301, 315–19.
29. Trollinger and Trollinger, *Righting America*, 8–10.
30. For further discussion on Ark Encounter, see Bielo's chapter in this volume.
31. Trollinger and Trollinger, *Righting America*, 42–58.
32. Susan Friend Harding, *The Book of Jerry Falwell: Fundamentalist Language and Politics* (Princeton, N.J.: Princeton University Press, 2000), 70–73.
33. Thomas M. Strouse, *He Maketh His Sun to Rise: A Look at Biblical Geocentricity* (Newington, Conn.: Emmanuel Baptist Publications, 2007).
34. Gerardus D. Bouw, *Geocentricity: Christianity in the Woodshed* (Harrison, Ohio: DayStar Publishing, 2013); Gerardus D. Bouw, "Geocentricity: A Fable for Educated Man?," http://www.reformation.edu/scripture-science-stott/geo/pages/12-fable-for-educated%20man.htm.

BIBLIOGRAPHY

Boone, Kathleen C. *The Bible Tells Them So: The Discourse of Protestant Fundamentalism*. Albany: State University of New York Press, 1989.
Bouw, Gerardus D. *Geocentricity: Christianity in the Woodshed*. Harrison, Ohio: DayStar Publishing, 2013.
———. "Geocentricity: A Fable for Educated Man?." http://www.reformation.edu/scripture-science-stott/geo/pages/12-fable-for-educated%20man.htm.
Brooke, John Hedley. "Like Minds: The God of Hugh Miller." In *Hugh Miller and the Controversies of Victorian Science*, edited by Michael Shortland, 171–86. Oxford: Clarendon Press, 1996.
Butler, Jonathan M. "A Portrait." In *Ellen Harmon White: American Prophet*, edited by Terrie Dopp Aamodt, Gary Land, and Ronald L. Numbers, 1–29. New York: Oxford University Press, 2014.
Davis, Edward B. "Introduction." In *The Antievolution Pamphlets of Harry Rimmer*, edited by Edward B. Davis, ix–xxviii. Vol. 6 of *Creationism in Twentieth-Century America*, edited by Ronald L. Numbers. New York: Garland, 1995.
Hanna, William, and Dugald Macfadyen. "Thomas Chalmers." In *The Encyclopaedia Britannica*, 11th ed., 5:809–11. New York: Encyclopaedia Britannica, 1910.
Harding, Susan Friend. *The Book of Jerry Falwell: Fundamentalist Language and Politics*. Princeton, N.J.: Princeton University Press, 2000.
"Historical Adam." Reasons to Believe. http://www.reasons.org/rtb-101/historicaladam.
Numbers, Ronald L. *The Creationists: From Scientific Creationism to Intelligent Design*. Expanded ed. Cambridge, Mass.: Harvard University Press, 2006.

Numbers, Ronald L., and Rennie B. Schoepflin, "Science and Medicine." In *Ellen Harmon White: American Prophet*, edited by Terrie Dopp Aamodt, Gary Land, and Ronald L. Numbers, 196–223. New York: Oxford University Press, 2014.

Oldroyd, David R. "The Geologist from Cromarty." In *Hugh Miller and the Controversies of Victorian Science*, edited by Michael Shortland, 76–121. Oxford: Clarendon Press, 1996.

Pun, Pattle P. T. "A Theology of Progressive Creationism." *Perspectives on Science and Christian Faith* 39 (March 1987): 9–19.

Ramm, Bernard. *The Christian View of Science and Scripture*. Grand Rapids, Mich.: Eerdmans, 1954.

Rana, Fazale. "Repeatable Evolution or Repeated Creation?" Reasons to Believe, October 1, 2000. http://www.reasons.org/articles/repeatable-evolution-or-repeated-creation.

Roberts, Jon H. *Darwinism and the Divine in America: Protestant Intellectuals and Organic Evolution, 1859-1900*. Madison: University of Wisconsin Press, 1988.

Roberts, Michael B. "Genesis Chapter 1 and Geological Time from Hugo Grotius and Marin Mersenne to William Conybeare and Thomas Chalmers (1620-1825)." In *Myth and Geology*, edited by Luigi Piccardi and W. Bruce Masse, 39–50. London: Geological Society of London, 2007.

———. "The Genesis of John Ray and His Successors." *Evangelical Quarterly* 74 (2002): 143–63.

Scofield, C. I., ed. *The Scofield Reference Bible* (King James Version). New York: Oxford University Press, 1917.

Scott, Eugenie C. "Antievolution and Creationism in the United States." *Annual Review of Anthropology* 26 (1997): 263–89.

Smith, Christian. *The Bible Made Impossible: Why Biblicism Is Not a Truly Evangelical Reading of Scripture*. Grand Rapids, Mich.: Brazos Press, 2011.

Strouse, Thomas M. *He Maketh His Sun to Rise: A Look at Biblical Geocentricity*. Newington, Conn.: Emmanuel Baptist Publications, 2007.

Taves, Ann. "Visions." In *Ellen Harmon White: American Prophet*, edited by Terrie Dopp Aamodt, Gary Land, and Ronald L. Numbers, 30–51. New York: Oxford University Press, 2014.

Trollinger, Susan L., and William Vance Trollinger Jr. *Righting America at the Creation Museum*. Baltimore, Md.: Johns Hopkins University Press, 2016.

Trollinger, William Vance, Jr. "Introduction." In *The Antievolution Pamphlets of William Bell Riley*, edited by William Vance Trollinger Jr., ix–xxii. Vol. 4 of *Creationism in Twentieth-Century America*, edited by Ronald L. Numbers. New York: Garland, 1995.

The World's Most Famous Court Trial: Tennessee Evolution Case. 2nd rpt. ed. Dayton, Tenn.: Bryan College, 1990.

Young, Davis A. *Christianity and the Age of the Earth*. Grand Rapids, Mich.: Zondervan, 1982.

CHAPTER 14

....

THE KING JAMES
ONLY MOVEMENT

....

JASON A. HENTSCHEL

I would feel remiss if, in an essay on Americans and their Bibles, I neglected to mention how fashionable it was to burn them. And so, one November evening in 1952, the Reverend Martin Luther Hux, in an odd twist on the fiery passion of his namesake, raised himself up onto the bed of a truck outside his rural North Carolinian church and lit a Bible on fire. The crowd that braved the chilly air to watch the spectacle was a motley blend of both the curious and the sympathetic, not a few of whom carried kitschy American flags, whose slow, pendular waving cast a haze of patriotism over the event. As Hux held aloft that smoldering, recently minted Revised Standard Version of the Bible (RSV), he hissed that it was a fraud, a weapon of the Devil dedicated to the destruction of orthodox Christianity. To condemn it to the ash heap was simply to return it to its hell-bound master.

Such Bible-burnings were and still are relatively rare among King James Only folk, though modern translations like the RSV continue to receive scant quarter today. Even evangelicalism's flagship translation, the New International Version (NIV), fares little better. Only a few years ago I found myself in a small, suburban Ohio church watching a traveling evangelist casually take the pulpit. With a heavy King James Version (KJV) of the Bible in hand, he shocked us all by admitting that, counter to common perception, the NIV, too, was quite useful—so useful, in fact, that he always made sure to keep an emergency copy in his glove box. Sometimes, one simply needed good toilet paper.

Such expressions of scriptural bibliocide, though admittedly extreme, stem from the same ardent biblicism that gives a much more expansive American evangelicalism its shape. We should not be surprised, in other words, to find King James Only Protestant Fundamentalists sharing largely the same story as their evangelical siblings. As historical criticism, which takes the Bible to be as much a product of human ingenuity as of divine inspiration, began to question the historicity of its stories and as a post-World War II influx of new translations fed fears that past certainties were slowly but surely being eroded and undone, a small contingent of America's evangelicals broke free from their brethren to champion the superiority of their old King James.[1] Here, they claimed, was God's true standard, his chosen bulwark against debilitating doubt and inevitable infidelity. Even today, the old Authorized Version (another, more rhetorically meaningful, name for the KJV) continues to be raised up as the one, solid rock of certainty upon which all Christians can rest assured that what they know to be true is really true.

PERCEPTIONS AND REALITIES

As an identifiable entity, the King James Only movement is rather young, overwhelmingly Baptist, and thoroughly American. While its ideological roots stretch back to nineteenth-century Britain and the first calls to revise the KJV, the movement is properly a product of the second half of the twentieth century with its deepening concern to move on from a then 350-year-old translation. Spurred on by significant advancements in textual criticism, institutions and individuals on both sides of the Atlantic, including broad denominational conglomerations such as the mainline National Council of Churches responsible for the RSV, jumped at the opportunity to put forth increasingly up-to-date translations with their promise of heightened biblical understanding, revived religious piety, and, it could be hoped, ever more crowded pews.

This surge of interest in newer biblical translations flooded bookstores with a rising tide of new Bible editions. Americans gobbled up millions of these cutting-edge Bibles, displaying an unprecedented hunger for their clarity and simplicity, as well as their gender, age, or other niche-market commentary apparatuses. While some have come to mourn how this "democratization" of the English Bible, as the religious historian Paul Gutjahr puts it, flattens and narrows biblical meaning, King James Only evangelicals have another complaint. They criticize the vast multiplication of Bible editions for undermining the surety of the King James's time-tested presentation of the truth.[2] One early proponent of the King James Only movement described the dethroning of the KJV as an act of trading in a centuries-old confidence in the content of the Christian faith for a hopeless state of "bewildered confusion."[3] For those who favored the KJV alone, the existence of so many divergent translations undermined the certainty of the faith once delivered by the King James Bible when it alone rang from the pulpit, its accuracy and authority unquestioned.

Although but a tiny percentage of today's evangelicals, the concerns that King James Only folk raise against the Bible enterprise are materially identical to those that have traditionally defined American evangelicalism as a whole. That is, what they fear in this proliferation of Bibles is the widespread collapse of scriptural authority. Such ardent biblicism has long defined American evangelicalism, giving both weight and meaning to its other distinguishing marks of evangelistic outreach, holy living, and an emphasis on Christ's atoning sacrifice on the cross. For those evangelicals in the King James Only camp, the KJV provides a critical commonly accessible material referent.[4] That is to say, they want in their hands—and in the hands of everyone around them—a version of the Word of God they can trust without question. There is little to suggest, of course, that evangelicals as a whole behave any differently toward their own Bibles, whatever the translation, but King James Only adherents unequivocally raise normal evangelical practice to the level of theory, where it faces the challenges of historical criticism especially acutely.

Advocates for the sole authority and sufficiency of the KJV thus place an incomparable amount of stress upon its materiality. A King James Bible is a sacred volume that all can see and touch and, in that seeing and touching, trust. Such scriptural tangibleness proves more than a crutch for faith; indeed, it has become a fundamental doctrine in its own right. If we cannot be certain that every phrase, every word of our Bibles—those we read from, preach from, place on the table in front of us—is wholly true and accurate, then we cannot be certain that our Christian faith is wholly true and accurate. And, if we cannot be certain that our faith is true and accurate, then why should we believe at all?

Across the spectrum of American evangelicalism, biblical authority is put forward as a challenge to any hint of subjectivism. Writing around the same time Hux set fire to his RSV, the British theologian and New Testament scholar J. I. Packer set the stage for conservative Christianity's postwar confrontation with modernity.

> The fact is that here we are faced in principle with a choice between two versions of Christianity. It is a choice between historic Evangelicalism and modern Subjectivism; between a Christianity that is consistent with itself and one that is not; in effect, between one that is wholly God-given and one that is partly man-made . . . . Evangelicals, indeed, are bound to oppose Subjectivism as vigorously as they can. They must do so, in the first place, because subjectivist principles, if consistently worked out, would totally destroy supernatural Christianity.[5]

A flourishing higher criticism, with its litany of historical, scientific, and moral challenges to traditional interpretations of the biblical text, loomed front-and-center in Packer's mind. Indeed, it would continue to do so throughout the battles over biblical meaning and interpretation that did so much to shape and then reshape evangelicalism during the last quarter of the twentieth century and in which Packer would play a central role. But, while evangelicals in general warred against the incursion of higher criticism within their own ranks, believers in the King James Only point-of-view cautioned against an even more fundamental and widespread intrusion into conservative Christianity, insisting that a subtler subjectivism was unwittingly allowed to sneak in through the back door.

As supporters of the movement tell it, no sooner had traditional interpretations of scripture come under attack from higher criticism than did critics begin to challenge the accuracy of the biblical text itself and, in doing so, fuel a similarly burgeoning—and equally, if not more, destructive—textual criticism. The relatively recent discovery of various long-lost biblical manuscripts questioned the authenticity of the foundational texts—together called the *Textus Receptus*, or "Received Text"—underlying the translation work that led to the KJV and fed a professional skepticism intent on determining which textual reading, including substantial additions and omissions, could best lay claim to being original. Disguised as faithful and authentic revision, subjectivism seeped into even the most traditionally conservative sectors of Christian belief, encouraging them to trade God's Word for the efforts of human scholarship. Through such attention to newer biblical manuscripts, American evangelicalism, the last bastion of orthodoxy, had been compromised.

Hence, textual critical issues outwardly dominate the King James Only debate. For today's "liberal" critics, discussions concerning the accuracy and reliability of specific manuscripts involve both external and internal considerations, including the provenance of a particular reading based on its age and location or the status and number of corroborating manuscripts or even the reasons behind the inclusion of various passages when they are considered in light of broader historical and literary contexts. Defenders of the KJV criticize these considerations for being grounded on nothing more than subjective human fancy. They are "excursions into cloud-land," as the nineteenth-century ecclesiastic John William

Burgon, whom those in the King James Only movement have lionized as Britain's arch-critic of textual revision, so colorfully described it.[6] In a word, modern textual criticism commandeered the ancient practice of protecting the biblical text from corruption, only to transform it into a vehicle for naturalistic and humanistic belief.

Due to its much higher volume of textual variants, the New Testament has experienced the lion's share of critical attention. This, coupled with its privileged role in the construction of Christian doctrine, has caused today's critical New Testament texts to come under especially strong fire from the King James Only camp. When these modern texts and the translations based upon them inevitably move away from the KJV and the *Textus Receptus*, those in the King James Only movement cry foul, often charging such alterations of being doctrinally significant corruptions, despite their opponents' assurances to the contrary.[7]

Representative here are complaints raised against the revision of 1 Timothy 3:16. The King James's translators, following the *Textus Receptus*, rendered this passage with the now familiar "God was manifest in the flesh." Most modern texts, however, replace the Greek *theos* of the *Textus Receptus* with *hos*, or who, ostensibly weakening the connection Paul draws between God and the incarnate Christ. Although many today continue to view 1 Timothy 3:16 as advancing a high view of Christology, associating the modern "who" with the "God" of verse fifteen, King James Only evangelicals persist in attacking the revision as an egregious denial of Christ's divinity.

For the Reverend Terence Brown, one-time secretary of Britain's Trinitarian Bible Society, the formative principle underlying the newer critical texts and the translations they spawn can be likened to that of fourth-century Arianism, early modern Socinianism, and today's Unitarianism. "The denial of the eternal Godhead of the Lord Jesus Christ has troubled the Church in every period of its history," a visibly frustrated Brown complained in 1973 when the evangelical establishment suggested that their newly minted NIV be used as the conservative alternative to the mainline RSV. (The New International Version rather innocuously translates 1 Timothy 3:16 as "He appeared in the flesh.") In Brown's eyes, today's translators, even those boasting an otherwise orthodox pedigree, are engaged in the same infernal denial, their translations hardly concealing their willful and malicious intent to deceive. These "opponents of the truth," Brown explains, "have had many things in common, including an intense hostility to the doctrine set forth in this text of Holy Scripture."[8] As with the Reverend Martin Luther Hux, those in the King James Only movement have shown a particularly keen ear for the sinister, accusing modern textual critics of not simply malpractice, but deliberate maliciousness.

Across the movement, though especially on its radical fringes, such accusations quickly took on apocalyptic, even conspiratorial, forms. From sermons and pamphlets to exhaustive book-length treatments, American Christianity—like American democracy and capitalism, to be sure—was engaged in a war of ideologies. Early 1950s McCarthyism, coupled with a more general and persistent Cold War hysteria, virtually guaranteed that King James Only advocates would find evidence of communist propaganda in these new Bible translations, so pervasive and far-reaching was American concern with the Red Menace.[9] But any alternative to the reigning socio-political or religious status quo appeared susceptible to charges that it intentionally sought to defraud Christians of the truth by wrecking their Bibles. In his letter to supporters on the 400th anniversary of the King James, Jack Chick, famous for his polemical tracts, explicitly accused the Vatican—Revelation's "great whore"—of flooding bookstores with "dozens of translations based on the flawed Catholic manuscripts, to destroy our trust in God's Holy Bible."[10]

The imaginative leap for Chick was understandably short. One of the most significant manuscripts fueling modern textual criticism had, in fact, been discovered hidden in the Vatican's archives and, on that account, had come to bear the all too incriminating name "Vaticanus." That said, the height of King James Only conspiratorial rhetoric came in 1993, when Gail Riplinger—now a household name in King James Only circles—unmasked the real culprit behind today's counterfeit Bible translations: the New Age Movement with its blasphemous "Lucifer worship."[11] Riplinger sounded the alarm that Satan once again is pulling the strings in this cosmic battle for souls, thus carrying on today what he had been doing so effectively for ages.

In the end, however, what lies behind all these conspiratorial exposés, tying them together and structuring their most eccentric claims, is a common hostility toward a particular brand of modernism. So central is the denunciation of modernism to the King James Only apologetic that the Presbyterian scholar and great *Textus Receptus* defender Edward Hills, in what quickly became something of an academic manifesto for the movement, identifies modernity with the rise of deism, universalism, and that naturalism said to be at the heart of twentieth-century textual criticism.[12] As an ideology, modernism boils down to one fundamentally anti-biblical claim, that the ultimate authority in our lives is not God's Holy Word but our very own selves. In politics, ethics, and ultimately doctrine, unchecked human reason is the quintessence of modernity's apostasy and the source of today's relativistic uncertainty.

Terry Watkins, the president of "Dial-the-Truth Ministries," a group dedicated to defending the KJV as the best English version of the scriptures, provides one of the more graphic expressions of King James Onlyism's anti-modernism. Watkins attacks the "*per*version" that is the evangelical New International Version of the Bible (NIV), describing the KJV's enemies as those who make light of the biblical text in general, choosing whichever passages they want to believe while changing or even deleting others. Watkins provides his arguments in the form of a little pamphlet, which displays on its cover a shadowy, nearly faceless man literally cutting out objectionable verses of his Bible, thereby evoking popular portrayals of Thomas Jefferson, the great Enlightenment arch-deist himself, who notoriously sliced up the Gospels in an attempt to jettison everything supernatural.[13] Jefferson's Bible and these newfangled translations, Watkins leads readers to believe, are but two heretical peas in the same modernist pod.

For those in the King James Only movement, today's Bible translators and textual critics err when they treat the biblical manuscripts and their development as any other historical text—that is, without recourse to divine providence. For the majority of evangelical scholars today, the authority of the Bible finds its logical ground in the inerrancy of its autographs, or the original writings of the biblical authors themselves. The task of modern textual criticism is to approximate these original autographs by comparing extant manuscripts according to supposedly neutral—and, therefore, universally applicable—philological and linguistic principles.

Here King James Only adherents cry foul and do so on at least three interrelated accounts: First, they take the conventional appeal to a set of long-lost manuscripts to be an epistemological and spiritual dead end. Edward Hills explains this point of view:

> It must be that down through the centuries God has exercised a special, providential control over the copying of the Scriptures and the preservation and use of the copies, so that trustworthy representatives of the original text have been available to God's people in every age.[14]

If we cannot be certain that the words we are reading are the genuine words of God, then we cannot be certain that the truths upon which our salvation is built are even truths at all. If we are then to have any certainty of faith, God must have both inspired the original autographs and preserved them up to today by faithfully overseeing their copying throughout the ages. King James Only followers charge those beholden to modern textual criticism with, in effect, a misplaced faith. Instead of trusting God to preserve his word, those not relying on the KJV pin their hopes on the rationalizations of a small group of scholars who blindly follow a method of interpreting ancient manuscripts according to deceptively neutral and objective principles.

Second, those in the King James Only movement simply reject these claims to neutrality and objectivity. As one of the movement's fellow travelers put it, "when the whole problem of textual criticism is reduced to a series of arguments about the relative merits of this reading over against that reading, we have reached an area where personal opinion—and even personal bias—can easily determine one's decision."[15] Once again, the issue of subjectivism rears its head. In the eyes of those holding a King James Only point of view, decisions regarding which textual variant is authentic always include a significant measure of educated guesswork, more often than not determined by one's professional training or theological upbringing. The King James Only complaint is not that objectivity is an unobtainable fiction, but that textual critics and those who follow their lead are mistaken regarding the location of true objectivity, which lies not in humanly derived principles for textual reconstruction but in the promises of God given in the Word of God.

And so third, and most important, the turn to modern textual criticism reflects ignorance, if not willful negligence, of the Bible's teaching on its own preservation. Here, King James Only believers typically point to Psalm 12, the movement's banner text:

> The words of the Lord are pure words:
> As silver tried in a furnace of earth, purified seven times.
> Thou shalt keep them, O Lord,
> Thou shalt preserve them from this generation forever.

Because they ignore the clear teaching of scripture concerning its providential preservation, most Christians have ironically abandoned the authority of the Bible in their very attempt to uphold it. Hence, the abandonment of the KJV is not simply a product of a subjective method, something that can be chalked up to carelessness or ignorance. God's promise to preserve his word is right there in the Bible, clear as day. To reject the KJV is tantamount to opting for subjective human reason over the promises of God. Modern textual criticism is predicated, then, upon the collapse of biblical authority, the essence of human sinfulness.[16]

Ostensibly, then, the King James Only debate is framed as a discussion of textual critical issues pitting the *Textus Receptus* against constantly evolving newer critical texts.[17] This battle of primary texts gives the King James Only movement an air of genuine truth seeking, if not quite skepticism.[18] It also, rather regrettably, sets King James Onlyism off as simply another arcane debate, the concern of only a few eccentric academics.

Hux's act of fiery bibliocide that November evening is for this reason especially significant, for it sticks out as a prime example of one of those moments of dissonance in the coherency of a position—or, in this case, in the particular way a movement expresses and understands itself. Simply put, Hux's story tells us more about what drives the King James Only movement than any casual glance at the literature ever could. A lay movement as much as an academic one, King James Onlyism is fundamentally concerned with protecting specific doctrines considered central to popular orthodoxy. Its engagement with modern textual criticism is but a means to this orthodox end.

This commitment to certain doctrines of orthodoxy can be seen in the special attention Hux paid to the RSV's translation of Isaiah 7:14, a verse that had long been considered a proof text for Christ's divinity. Needless to say, when the RSV replaced the traditional "virgin" with "young woman," it set off a firestorm of complaints. The new translation made Christ out to be the merely human child of a common whore. No matter that this "new" rendering had precedence stretching back to Martin Luther or that the RSV retained the word "virgin" in Matthew 1:23, which quotes Isaiah 7:14. For conservatives like Hux, there could hardly be more glaring proof that America's liberals were trying to do away with the most cherished doctrines of the faith.

Similar to Hux, those in the King James Only movement consistently find today's new translations to be unorthodox precisely in those places where they suggest interpretations deemed inconsistent with the KJV. Such is the case even when text critical issues do arise, as in 1 Timothy 3:16, which we have discussed as representative of the movement's critical rebuttals (and which, despite King James Only fears, continues to be interpreted in a traditionally orthodox way). A common tactic, powered by its accessibility, is to offer lengthy lists of revisions—often single words ripped out of their contexts—said to represent doctrinal divergence, and then to explain them as the result of either misguided scholarship or liberal treachery.[19]

This particular approach toward defending against doctrinal divergence is well exemplified in Edward Hill's standard argument for providential preservation. Take his defense of the King James's inclusion of 1 John 5:7, the so-called Johannine Comma passage, widely agreed to be a late addition intended to provide explicit and unparalleled biblical support for post-Nicene Trinitarianism:

> [It] was not trickery which was responsible for the inclusion of the *Johannine comma* in the Textus Receptus but the usage of the Latin-speaking Church. It was this usage which made men feel that this reading ought to be included in the Greek text and eager to keep it there after its inclusion had been accomplished. Back of this usage, we may well believe, was the guiding providence of God.[20]

Here providential preservation, if it is to protect the text and authority of the KJV, must baptize the contingencies of history—including, incredibly, those of sinister Rome.

In the end, King James Onlyism, presupposing the King James's orthodoxy, must reverse-engineer its history if there is to be any certainty that what is considered to be the truth is really true. When the influx of new translations shattered this certainty, it cast Christian belief into irredeemable confusion. For those in the King James Only movement, to chase after ancient texts or to pretend that scholars can piece together lost autographs with any measure of certainty is a fool's errand, the unmistakable mark of an unbeliever. As Edward

Hills contends, if God had left his word so vulnerable, then the Christian faith and Christian orthodoxy "would be always wavering."[21] Or, as another follower put it, there would be nothing left but "despair and doubt."[22]

CONSEQUENCES AND IMPLICATIONS

J. I. Packer once defended evangelicalism's quest for certainty, coincidentally during the throes of the RSV controversy, simply by noting its indispensability for Christian belief and practice. "Preaching is hazy; heads are muddled; hearts fret; doubts drain our strength; uncertainty paralyses our action . . . . We know in our bones," he felt certain, "that we were made for certainty, and we cannot be happy without it."[23] The assumption of this need would do much to fuel evangelicals' now distinctive defense of biblical inerrancy, which took shape as their desire for psychological certainty matured into a comprehensive demand for a more fundamental certainty of knowledge, or what I have called a certainty that what we know to be true is really true. That said, the story of King James Onlyism suggests that some unforeseen consequences come attached to this quest for certainty, a number of which question certainty's appeal altogether.

The Quest for Certainty Divorces the Bible from History

In its attempt to lock down its beliefs in the face of rising interpretive uncertainty, King James Onlyism believed that God's providential preservation could successfully deliver the Bible from the contingencies of history—that is, from whatever interpretive subjectivities are the necessary consequence of ordinary attempts at translation. To divorce the Bible from history in this way marks King James Onlyism as a species of biblical originalism that, in the words of Jack Rakove regarding interpretations of the American Constitution, could be described more accurately as "fidelity *through* history" rather than "fidelity *to* history."[24] As an expression of uncertain development and change, King James Only evangelicals imagine history to be something they need to escape. History becomes here the source of that subjectivity from which the Bible itself must be saved if Christians want to see it as God's chosen depository of objective truth. In this view, God and his word stand outside and above history.

Recent developments in the study of the KJV cast this desire to escape history into stark relief. When Jeffrey Alan Miller, professor of early modern literature at New Jersey's Montclair State University, stumbled a few years ago upon a dusty draft of the Apocrypha that had been hidden away for centuries in an old Cambridge archive, he commented that the find offered a rare glimpse into the process by which the King James came to be. Miller's draft is by far the earliest we have of any part of the KJV. In various ways, the find should be inexplicable to adherents of King James Onlyism, for it strongly suggests that different translators used different Greek texts to translate the same biblical book. But even more significantly, it records the evolution of one particular translator's thinking more so than it does any formal recommendation for the committee's review. Simply put, the KJV's translators engaged in a lot of sweaty, albeit informed, guesswork. They made mistakes, changed their minds, and in the end merely offered suggestions.[25] Their translation process was, in reality, strikingly similar to the translation process of newer Bible versions.

To interpret such translational activity along providential preservationist lines would require that one explain away the very contingency of history. Every translational mistake, every change of opinion, must be written off as an inspired blunder, with the result that the God of the Bible begins to look awfully like the king of subterfuge, a divine con artist cleverly marking the Bible as a historical book while actually delivering it from the contingencies of space and time—in other words, from everything human.

The Quest for Certainty Substitutes Epistemic Certainty for Faith

Princeton theologian Ellen Charry once remarked that theology today has found itself increasingly reduced to apologetics. Instead of informing and giving shape to the practice of Christian faith, we offer little more than its justification.[26] The same can be said for King James Only adherents. Especially in their rhetoric, these Protestants redefine faith not as trust in the power and promises of God but as rational assent to a set of objectively certain propositions singularly available in the KJV—including, ironically, the promise of God to preserve his word. What the Protestant Church has traditionally described in terms of faith seeking understanding is here distorted and reversed.

Of course, we might ask at this point why it is assumed that we must have certainty of faith, why we must be certain that what we know to be true is really true. This is simply to ask about the source of that gut feeling J. I. Packer finds so presumably natural. The fact of the matter is that the desire for certainty, especially epistemic certainty, appears more specifically characteristic of Western modernity than it does of our (supposedly) timeless human nature. Packer's deep longing here, which he shares with those in the King James Only movement and with American evangelicalism more generally, is not "in his bones" but simply in his head, a product of a particular time and place. The pragmatist philosopher John Dewey noted as much early in the twentieth century when he observed that the desire for certainty stems from the misguided belief that by attaining it we can escape the risk inherent in all practical and historical action.[27]

That said, we could just as easily have returned to Augustine, whose *Confessions* narrate the reconceptualization of faith as reliance or dependence—a "falling back" upon the person of God rather than strictly knowledge about him—and away from the excessive intellectualism he had previously shown as both a Manichean and a Platonist. Of course, we might have simply reflected a little longer on our Sunday creeds, where we profess to believe in God the Father, not that he is. But, when theological understanding finds itself reduced to the attainment and defense of true propositions, these propositions in turn become a prerequisite to faith, not its object and certainly not in any personal, Augustinian sense.

The Quest for Certainty Disenchants the World

It has become something of a fad to remark on the disenchantment or desacralization of the West. Even a sympathetic Christian theologian such as Alister McGrath worries that the Reformed tradition so dominant in evangelicalism today has had the unintended effect of virtually banishing God from human experience by restricting his voice to that of a dead letter.[28] The past century's Bible battles provide much of the grist for this critique, even if indirectly, and the particular controversies over textual criticism and biblical translation which originally gave rise to the King James Only movement are but a species of these battles. Indeed, what makes such an admittedly small movement especially relevant with regard to the nature and function of the Bible in America is the fundamental struggle against hermeneutical subjectivism and interpretive pluralism it shares with evangelicalism at large. That is to say, King James Onlyism offers a fascinating case study of how evangelicals in their desperate quest for certainty have subtly, if unwittingly, relegated the person of God to a status secondary to scripture and, in doing so, cast him out of their world.

By divorcing the Bible from history while also viewing it as the source—rather than the medium—of divine truth, evangelicalism effectively deified a book. It is ironic, of course, that a people whose piety presupposes a dynamically active God can also boast a theology that paints him as one whose last two acts in the world were to inspire an ancient book only then to pick up and leave. King James Onlyism, thanks to its insistence upon God's continual preservation of the Bible (at least until 1611), escapes some of this critique, but quickly falls back into it when providential preservation is revealed to be an ad hoc measure employed to protect certain favored interpretations. Then, too, the active presence of God in history as the one who will "guide us into all truth" is replaced by a static set of propositions, the meaning of which is said to be universally, eternally, and thus ahistorically clear.

CONCLUSION

In the end, the KJV has become something of a new totem in American religion. As I traveled around to various churches, I was struck that, despite their explicit preference for the KJV, only twice did I hear the translation issue raised apart from my own prompting. That such a defining issue could be so fundamentally significant while at the same time so practically inconsequential seemed odd. I was told the fight had gone cold and had done so without a winner. Indeed, a couple pastors asked that I not speak to the laity at all. They allegedly knew little about the debate and would provide no help to me.

This was not exactly true. On those rare occasions the issue did arise, it appeared as a badge identifying the bearer as safe, even authoritative. When that traveling evangelist, to rounds of laughter and applause, lampooned the NIV as superior toilet paper, he knew what he was doing. When churches today advertise themselves as "KJV-1611" on their signs and in their bulletins, they too are using labels to convey an ideological conformity capable of masking otherwise noteworthy differences. This marker of a commitment to the 1611 KJV, in turn, fosters a sense of socially sustained certainty, but it is nonetheless a certainty built upon a house of cards, one without the widespread, substantial agreement needed to keep it standing. King James Only churches are usually fiercely independent, and they suffer, as sociologist Christian Smith has noted about evangelicalism in general, from an interpretive pluralism that undermines the very claims of certainty so fundamental to the movement's reason for being.[29] The rhetoric of King James Onlyism, however, has proven remarkably resilient, even while the battle that first energized it has largely died out. The question is just how long such an illusion of certainty can possibly last. Of course, if the doctrine of biblical inerrancy is any indicator, the answer is quite a while.

NOTES

1. The story of King James Onlyism's peculiar response to today's translation enterprise, including that of Reverend Hux's Bible-burning, is well told in Peter Thuesen, *In Discordance with the Scriptures: American Protestant Battles over Translating the Bible* (New York: Oxford University Press, 1999).

2. Paul Gutjahr, "From Monarchy to Democracy: The Dethroning of the King James Bible in the United States," in *The King James Bible after 400 Years: Literary, Linguistic, and Cultural Influences*, ed. Hannibal Hamlin and Norman W. Jones (New York: Cambridge University Press, 2010).

3. Jasper James Ray, *God Wrote Only One Bible* (Eugene, Ore.: Eye Opener Publishers, 1983), 1.

4. For one popular catalog of these remarks, which includes the expected emphasis on individual conversion and evangelism, see David W. Bebbington, *Evangelicalism in Modern Britain: A History from the 1730s to the 1980s* (New York: Routledge, 1989, 2005), 2–17.

5. J. I. Packer, *"Fundamentalism" and the Word of God* (Grand Rapids, Mich.: Eerdmans, 1958), 170–71.

6. John William Burgon, *The Revision Revised: Three Articles Reprinted from the "Quarterly Review"* (London: John Murray, 1883), 397.

7. To the chagrin of many of his King James Only opponents, Bruce Metzger, one of the twentieth-century's foremost textual critics, has repeatedly argued that no traditional biblical doctrines are overturned by any of the textual variants discovered by modern textual criticism. Although some doctrines might lose the support of certain individual texts, they receive adequate scriptural support elsewhere. Metzger's emphasis on the canonical character of Christian doctrine—that the truths of the faith draw their support from a range of texts—has proven remarkably difficult for King James Onlyism to accept, a testament to the group's extreme brand of propositionalism. See Metzger's classic text on the subject, originally published in 1964 as King James Onlyism was gaining steam, *The Text of the New Testament: Its Transmission, Corruption, and Restoration*, 3rd ed. (Oxford: Oxford University Press, 1992).

8. Terence H. Brown, "God—Was Manifest in the Flesh . . . I Timothy 3:16," in *True or False: The Westcott-Hort Textual Theory Examined*, ed. David Otis Fuller (Grand Rapids, Mich.: Grand Rapids International Publications, 1973), 25–26.

9. See, for example, the early postwar work of Edward Hills in *The King James Version Defended*, 4th ed. (Des Moines, Iowa: Christian Research Press, 1984), esp. chs. 2–3; Thuesen, *In Discordance with the Scriptures*, 99–106.

10. Jack Chick, customer appreciation letter to Charity Baptist Church, January 1, 2011.

11. Gail Riplinger, *New Age Bible Versions* (Ararat, Va.: A. V. Publications, 1993), 1.

12. Hills, *King James Version Defended*, 68. Hills, a Harvard graduate, first published his defense in 1956 at the beginning of the movement, offering it significant scholarly clout.

13. Terry Watkins, *New International PerVersion* (Pinson, Ala.: Dial-the-Truth, n.d.).

14. Hills, *King James Version Defended*, 2.

15. Zane Hodges, "The Greek Text of the King James Version," in *Which Bible?*, 5th ed., ed. David Otis Fuller (Grand Rapids, Mich.: Grand Rapids International Publications, 1975), 35.

16. One of the movement's early popularizers stated the conflict in expressly patriotic terms, calling the faithful to join ranks against this new tyranny of critical scholars: "Other ages have witnessed vicious and malicious attacks upon the inspired Word of God, but never has *any* other age seen the attacks multiply with such rapidity . . . 'THE BATTLE IS ON!' And Christian, the foundations of your faith and mine are now, *this very moment*, under bitter and vitriolic attack by the enemy of your souls. This is no day for retreat or taking of our time . . . . The men who fled the tyrant's heel in Europe and made America great, suffered for the faith of *their* fathers. Can we do less than the same?" David Otis Fuller, "Introduction," in *True or False? The Westcott-Hort Textual Theory Examined*, ed. D. O. Fuller (Grand Rapids, Mich.: Grand Rapids International Publications, 1973), 19–20, emphasis in original.

17. For a conventional title holding to this line of argumentation, see: Wilbur N. Pickering, *The Identity of the New Testament Text*, rev. ed. (Nashville, Tenn.: Thomas Nelson, 1980).

18. See, for instance, Wilbur N. Pickering, "John William Burgon and the New Testament," in *True or False? The Westcott-Hort Textual Theory Examined*, ed. D. O. Fuller (Grand Rapids, Mich.: Grand Rapids International Publications, 1973), 248–49. To my knowledge, such admissions are rarely, if ever, followed up, thus raising the question if the movement is seeking, as it claims to be, the best text and translation or is simply protecting the text and translation it already believes to be true.

19. See, for instance, Riplinger, *New Age Bible Versions*, vi, 303; Watkins, *New International PerVersion*.

20. Hills, *King James Version Defended*, 209–10.

21. Hills, *King James Version Defended*, 130.

22. Kent Brandenburg, "First Century Textual Attack," in *Thou Shalt Keep Them: A Biblical Theology of the Perfect Preservation of Scripture*, ed. Kent Brandenburg (El Sobrante, Calif.: Pillar & Ground, 2003), 150.

23. J. I. Packer, *God Has Spoken: Revelation and the Bible*, 3rd ed. (Grand Rapids, Mich.: Baker, 1965, 1994), 24.

24. Jack Rakove, "Fidelity through History (Or to It)," *Fordham Law Review* 65, no. 4 (1997): 1591, emphasis in original.

25. Jeffrey Miller, "Fruit of Good Labours: Discovering the Earliest Known Draft of the King James Bible," *Times Literary Supplement* 5872 (October 14, 2015): 14–15.

26. Ellen Charry, *By the Renewal of Your Minds: The Pastoral Function of Christian Doctrine* (New York: Oxford, 1997), 4–5. What Charry has noted about modern theology is especially characteristic of postwar evangelicalism, as evident in the immense popularity of apologetic works like Josh McDowell's *Evidence that Demands a Verdict*, Lee Strobel's *Case* series, and—most explicitly—John Montgomery's *Faith Founded on Fact*.

27. John Dewey, *The Quest for Certainty: A Study of the Relation of Knowledge and Action* (New York: Minton & Balch, 1929), 6.

28. Alister McGrath, *Christianity's Dangerous Idea: The Protestant Revolution—A History from the Sixteenth Century to the Twenty-First* (New York: HarperOne, 2007). Although his thesis has been heavily contested of late, see also Brad Gregory's *The Unintended Reformation: How a Religious Revolution Secularized Society* (Cambridge, Mass.: Harvard University Press, 2012).

29. See Christian Smith, *The Bible Made Impossible: Why Biblicism Is Not a Truly Evangelical Reading of Scripture* (Grand Rapids, Mich.: Brazos, 2011).

BIBLIOGRAPHY

Bebbington, David W. *Evangelicalism in Modern Britain: A History from the 1730s to the 1980s.* New York: Routledge, 1989, 2005.

Brandenburg, Kent, ed. *Thou Shalt Keep Them: A Biblical Theology of the Perfect Preservation of Scripture.* El Sobrante, Calif.: Pillar & Ground, 2003.

Burgon, John William. *The Revision Revised: Three Articles Reprinted from the "Quarterly Review."* London: John Murray, 1883.

Charry, Ellen. *By the Renewal of Your Minds: The Pastoral Function of Christian Doctrine.* New York: Oxford, 1997.

Dewey, John. *The Quest for Certainty: A Study of the Relation of Knowledge and Action.* New York: Minton & Balch, 1929.

Fuller, David Otis, ed. *True or False: The Westcott-Hort Textual Theory Examined.* Grand Rapids, Mich.: Grand Rapids International Publications, 1973.

———. *Which Bible?* 5th ed. Grand Rapids, Mich.: Grand Rapids International Publications, 1975.

Gregory, Brad. *The Unintended Reformation: How a Religious Revolution Secularized Society.* Cambridge, Mass.: Harvard University Press, 2012.

Gutjahr, Paul. "From Monarchy to Democracy: The Dethroning of the King James Bible in the United States," in *The King James Bible after 400 Years: Literary, Linguistic, and Cultural Influences,* ed. Hannibal Hamlin and Norman W. Jones. New York: Cambridge University Press, 2010.

Hills, Edward. *The King James Version Defended,* 4th ed. Des Moines, Iowa: Christian Research Press, 1984.

McGrath, Alister. *Christianity's Dangerous Idea: The Protestant Revolution—A History from the Sixteenth Century to the Twenty-First.* New York: HarperOne, 2007.

Metzger, Bruce. *The Text of the New Testament: Its Transmission, Corruption, and Restoration.* 3rd ed. Oxford: Oxford University Press, 1992.

Miller, Jeffrey. "Fruit of Good Labours: Discovering the Earliest Known Draft of the King James Bible." *Times Literary Supplement* 5872 (October 14, 2015): 14–15.

Packer, J. I. *"Fundamentalism" and the Word of God.* Grand Rapids, Mich.: Eerdmans, 1958.

———. *God Has Spoken: Revelation and the Bible.* 3rd ed. Grand Rapids, Mich.: Baker, 1994.

Pickering, Wilbur N. *The Identity of the New Testament Text.* Rev. ed. Nashville, Tenn.: Thomas Nelson, 1980.

Rakove, Jack. "Fidelity through History (Or to It)." *Fordham Law Review* 65, no. 4 (1997): 1587–609.

Ray, Jasper James. *God Wrote Only One Bible.* Eugene, Ore.: Eye Opener Publishers, 1983.

Riplinger, Gail. *New Age Bible Versions.* Ararat, Va.: A. V. Publications, 1993.

Smith, Christian. *The Bible Made Impossible: Why Biblicism Is Not a Truly Evangelical Reading of Scripture.* Grand Rapids, Mich.: Brazos, 2011.

Thuesen, Peter. *In Discordance with the Scriptures: American Protestant Battles over Translating the Bible.* New York: Oxford, 1999.

CHAPTER 15

....

THE BIBLE AND
THE SERMONIC TRADITION

....

DAWN COLEMAN

So then faith cometh by hearing, and hearing by the word of God.

—Romans 10:17

ALTHOUGH Americans have a long tradition of contemplative Bible-reading, it is in the sacred space of preaching that the Bible has functioned most clearly as a living book with personal and communal significance. The seventeenth-century Puritans set an inimitable standard for the appreciation of preaching—mandatory church attendance, ministerial oratory on all major public occasions, and a meetinghouse on the town square—and, despite innumerable changes over the past 400 years, the practice of preaching and the production of sermons continue to thrive in the United States. As many believers' primary guide to biblical interpretation and practical theology, sermons have been a shaping force in national culture. From Massachusetts Bay Colony Governor John Winthrop's "A Modell of Christian Charity," an origin point for both American preaching and national identity, to Chicago United Church of Christ minister Jeremiah Wright's famous "God damn America!," which brought questions of race to the forefront during Barack Obama's 2008 presidential campaign, sermons have been prime mediators of the Bible in America.

Given the sermon's centrality to American culture, one might expect a rich scholarly literature on the country's preaching. Yet aside from colonial preaching and the sermons of a few titans such as Henry Ward Beecher and Martin Luther King Jr., the sermonic tradition is curiously under-documented and under-analyzed. The problem is partly disciplinary. Historians and religious studies scholars examine denominations, movements, and individuals, but seldom specific genres such as the sermon. Literary and communications scholars, who scrutinize genre, dissect novels, poems, plays, newspapers, and other media, but seldom sermons, which, as discourses delivered to specific faith communities, can seem tangential to theorizations of the public sphere. Above and beyond disciplinary contingencies, the sermonic archive is daunting. Millions of sermons survive as printed books and pamphlets, newspaper reports, longhand manuscripts, television and radio programs, and podcasts and videos. They represent legions of faith traditions: scores of Protestant denominations as well as Roman Catholicism, Judaism, the Church of Jesus Christ of Latter-day Saints, and more, not to mention the ethnic, racial, and regional variants thereof, dozens with worship services in languages other than English.[1] Further, sermons have sacralized an astounding diversity of occasions: weekly services, of course, but also feast days, fast days, baptisms, confirmations, weddings, funerals, militia musterings, election days, and memorial ceremonies. The rhetorical exigencies have been manifold—the communities, multitudinous. Small wonder that Swedish historian of preaching Yngve Brilioth describes the history of American preaching as "an impenetrable forest to the outsider."[2]

Paradoxically, the vast, dense archive of sermons can feel strangely empty. Only a tiny fraction of the sermons delivered in America are extant. Those that survive are not necessarily representative, especially for the seventeenth and eighteenth centuries, when publication strongly favored occasional sermons over the bread-and-butter preaching of weekly worship services. No matter how representative, print sermons are no more than desiccated remnants, the whispering ghosts of long-dead events. A sermon, when preached, is a dynamic rhetorical performance built on the emotion roused by the opening music and hymns, the preacher's voice and bodily movement, and the shared experience of listeners. Sermons extant only on the page are especially inadequate for understanding those traditions that place a high value on extemporaneity, such as Quakers, Methodists, Baptists, and many African American denominations. For listeners, the sermon's full meaning arises in the ritual context and through active participation.[3] Any historical investigation of preaching must thus proceed with humility, recognizing that the archive is immense, fragmentary, and in many respects elusive.

Difficulties notwithstanding, the sermonic tradition is central to understanding how Americans have interpreted the Bible as relevant to their lives. Since the early days of Christianity, and continuous with Jewish tradition, Christian sermons have typically begun with a short biblical text that serves as the basis for the preacher's discourse. But it was Martin Luther's heraldic *sola scriptura* that inaugurated the Reformation and moved the explication of the Bible to the center of Christian worship. In North America, seventeenth-century Puritans advanced Reformation principles through a rigid sermon format derived from William Perkins's *The Arte of Prophesying*. After reading the biblical text and briefly explicating it, the preacher would lay out the doctrine, subdivided into proofs or reasons, then pivot to the application, subdivided as uses, to explain the significance of the doctrine for belief and behavior. Supporting biblical texts were cited liberally throughout.

In the eighteenth century, sermon style relaxed, as ministers cited fewer biblical proof texts and began to blur the line between doctrine and application, with emphasis on the latter. In the next century, sermons became more essayistic still. For most nineteenth-century Protestants, the opening text and a commitment to biblical authority endured, but fewer ministers engaged in sustained exegesis and doctrinal analysis. In the post-Revolutionary environment of religious voluntarism, when ministers had to fill their pockets with tithes and offerings rather than taxes, more and more clergymen made sure that biblical instruction was a pleasure. They told folksy, sometimes sensational, stories drawn from everyday life or illustrated their precepts with memorable metaphors.[4] Yet even as sermon styles evolved and proliferated in the twentieth century, biblical interpretation remained a cornerstone of Protestant preaching.[5]

In this essay, I sketch a road map for navigating American sermons, with a focus on Protestantism due to this tradition's privileging of the preached Word and its persistent hegemony in national life. Working heuristically and historically, I trace the Bible's role in two distinct forms of American preaching. The first is the cultic, which is addressed primarily to believers or potential converts. The mainstay of the American sermonic tradition, these sermons tend to focus on either the salvation of the soul or on spiritual improvement, a difference in emphasis analogous to that in the New Testament between proclamation (*kerygma*) and exhortation (*paraenesis*). Evangelicals have tended to favor the former, and theological liberals, the latter, though this dichotomy is far from absolute. The second form of American preaching discussed here is the civic, which sets forth religious answers to secular national problems. The best-known type of civic sermon is the jeremiad, which calls the nation to righteousness before God, but this form does not exhaust the genre. My closing section directs attention to two less-celebrated strands of civic preaching, namely, those centered on freedom and on love.

SALVATION OF THE SOUL

In a magisterial study of colonial New England preaching, Harry Stout stresses that the dominant theme of Sunday preaching among the Puritans was "the salvation of the soul," in which the individual traveled "from death in sin, to new life in Christ, to the hope of eternal life." This pilgrimage was made possible through the "covenant of grace" (distinct from God's "federal covenant" with nations), in which God in his sovereignty elected, or predestined, whom to save and whom to damn.[6] Even as weekday, or occasional, preaching evolved in response to political events, Sunday preaching remained pietistic, emphasizing how listeners could prepare their hearts for the Holy Spirit through prayer, fasting, sermon-listening, and other means of grace. Into the eighteenth century, sermons were structured according to "sin-salvation-service," supported with a scaffolding of diverse biblical passages drawn from throughout the Bible.[7] Puritan preachers also wove copious proof texts into their arguments. For example, Thomas Shepard in his *Of Ineffectual Hearing the Word* pummeled listeners with more than three dozen discrete texts, often nailing several together in the course of his sermon to support a single point.[8] Truly a people of the Book, the Puritans have few rivals for amplitude of biblical citation.

During the religious revivals of the mid-eighteenth century, the New Testament grew in importance as ministers urged the "new birth" experience as vital to personal and corporate spiritual renewal. The mainspring text was John 3:3, in which Jesus admonishes the Pharisee Nicodemus, "Verily, verily, I say unto thee, Except a man be born again, he cannot see the kingdom of God." Although seemingly at odds with the Calvinistic schema of predestination, the new birth flourished among the Puritan-descended eighteenth-century Congregationalists. Those who wished to be saved submitted to the preached Word and humbled themselves before God, hoping for an experience of divine grace that would reassure them of their salvation.

A path-breaking revivalist and avid, erudite biblical exegete, the fourth-generation Puritan and Northampton, Massachusetts, minister Jonathan Edwards left an impressive record of sermons that drew on every corner of scripture. One of the most rhetorically effective—and notorious—of Edwards's sermons, *Sinners in the Hands of an Angry God*, takes its cue from Deuteronomy 32:35, "Their foot shall slide in due time," and invokes the terrors of Isaiah: "For behold, the Lord will come with fire, and with chariots like a whirlwind, to render his anger with fury, and his rebukes with flames of fire" (Isa. 59:18).[9] Edwards drew the sermon's plentiful metaphors directly from the Bible: "the archer with the drawn bow, the loathsome spider, pent-up waters, unleashed lions."[10] But this sermon represents Edwards imperfectly. Some of his best sermons expound on God's grace, including *A Divine and Supernatural Light*, on Matthew 16:17, and *He That Believeth Shall Be Saved*, on Mark 16:15-16.[11] Edwards would also preach long sermon series that walked listeners through a biblical passage—or a single verse—in painstaking detail. One series on 1 Corinthians 13:1-10 ran to seventeen sermons, and another, on Isaiah 51:8, ran to thirty.[12] After the eighteenth century, such meticulous biblical explication would not come back into fashion in America until the twentieth-century neo-orthodoxy of Karl Barth and Reinhold Niebuhr and the ministers they inspired.

Edwards was the leading theologian of what historians have come to call the "First Great Awakening" (1739-1745). If Edwards was the Awakening's mind, then George Whitefield, its blockbuster preacher, was its voice. Similarly proclaiming the new birth within the context of Calvinism, Whitefield, an Anglican itinerant preacher, led tremendously popular Eastern seaboard revivals during the Awakening, becoming, in the process, "the world's first international celebrity."[13] He preached with theatrical expressiveness in outdoor venues that showcased his charismatic authority. His sermons were calibrated to inspire an immediate conviction of sin and experience of grace, followed by a heaven-sent power to obey the will of God. It was sin-salvation-service with an emotional punch, savvily publicized and promoted via a rapidly expanding network of colonial newspapers.

In the pulpit or in an open field, Whitefield strove to prepare his listeners to recognize and accept God's grace. He drew upon the Bible accordingly. The much-reprinted sermon *The Marks of the New Birth*, for example, begins with the provocation of Acts 19:5, "Have you received the Holy Ghost since ye believed?" Dispatching theological disputes, he focuses on the task at hand: teaching the doctrine of human sin, inspiring listeners to searching self-examination and submission to God, and presenting the signs of piety by which listeners would know whether they had received the Holy Spirit. [14] Again: sin-salvation-service, with an outsize emphasis on salvation. Although Whitefield's sermons drew on the Old Testament, mainly as a repository of stories of heroic, if flawed, individuals, such as Moses, Joseph, David, and Daniel, they seem to have relied more consistently on the New Testament than those of the Puritans. He thus fused Calvinist deferral to God's sovereignty with a strong sense of biblically grounded redemptive hope. His phenomenal success helped establish evangelicalism as a major force in American Protestantism, one that, to this day, privileges the salvific efficacy of Christ's death, the necessity of conversion, and biblical authority.

In the late eighteenth century, after Whitefield's death, conversion sermons waned overall while remaining a keynote among New Light (or evangelical) Congregationalists, some Baptists, and the newly arrived Methodists. But with a new efflorescence of revivals in the early nineteenth century, evangelical preaching again became a driving force in American religion. The so-called Second Great Awakening, which lasted from roughly 1800 up to the beginning of the Civil War, reflected a new democratic ethos in American religion, in which a burgeoning population sought spiritual renewal at extra-ecclesiastical revivals and lent their ears to lay and itinerant ministers.[15] An attenuated, revamped Calvinism held its own on the revival circuit, most notably with the Presbyterians Charles Finney and Lyman Beecher. The most famous preacher of the 1830s and 1840s, Finney relied on "new measures" such as the "anxious bench" and an altar call to encourage on-the-spot conversions. Like Whitefield, Finney tended to preach from short texts that drew sharp contrasts between human depravity and God's grace. Examples include: Ezekiel 18:31, "Make you a new heart, and a new spirit, for why will you die?," Romans 6:11, "Likewise reckon ye also yourselves to be dead indeed unto sin, but alive unto God through Jesus Christ our Lord," and Ecclesiastes 9:3, "The heart of the sons of men is full of evil, and madness is in their heart while they live."[16] Once underway, Finney's sermons were far less likely than those of the Puritans to cite the Bible. They were instead conversational, anecdotal, purposefully repetitive, and, true to his early legal training, relentlessly intent on persuasion.

The Presbyterians boasted Finney, but Methodists led the charge in organizing revivals and preaching conversion, especially in the West and South. Between 1800 and 1850, American Methodism skyrocketed, from 2.5 percent of all religious adherents, to 34.2 percent.[17] The Methodists' success can be attributed to their knack for running camp meetings, organizational infrastructure, circuit-riding ministers, and a dramatic preaching style, which painted the terrors of hell and hallelujahs of heaven in graphic detail.[18] They also offered a winningly democratic message. Unlike Congregationalists and most Baptists, who shared a theological lineage of Calvinism, they held that Christ had died for all, not only the elect. Decried by Calvinists as the heresy of "Arminianism" (after the sixteenth-century Dutch theologian Jacob Arminius), this doctrine put the burden of salvation squarely on sinners: believe in the vicarious atonement of Christ for one's sins, repent of those sins now, and experience God's saving grace. The new birth experience could unfold over weeks or transpire in the space of a sermon; Saul's conversion on the road to Damascus was one prototype of an instantaneous conversion. The urgency and simplicity of this message spilled over to other denominations and energized a generation of believers-turned-preachers. Among Methodists, Baptists, and other denominations that did not insist upon—or scorned—a learned clergy, preachers often felt authorized only by their own conversion experience and a call from God, though, like many a Hebrew prophet, they sometimes hesitated to step forth with their word of truth. In this context, unlettered white men took to the pulpit, along with women and African Americans.[19]

This first wave of evangelical women preachers—white and black, and belonging largely to such upstart sects as the Freewill Baptists, Christian Connection, Northern Methodists, and African Methodists—did not limit themselves to witnessing or exhorting but preached "as teachers who had been divinely inspired to interpret the Bible."[20] Besides using scripture to drive home the familiar Gospel message, they appealed to numerous biblical precedents to defend their right to preach, above all the two "Mothers in Israel": Deborah, the warrior judge who had led Israel to victory, and the "wise woman" who saved her city with a timely word and a diplomatic decapitation (2 Sam. 20:16), and Phebe, commended by Paul and considered by some the first female evangelist (Rom. 16:1-2). Women preachers also stared down Paul's troublesome pronouncement, "Let your women keep silence in the churches: for it is not permitted them to speak; but they are commanded to be under obedience, as also saith the law" (1 Cor. 14:34), countering that this command was specific to the church in Corinth, where women interrupted the preacher. They also perennially defended their calling with Joel 2:28, "And it shall come to pass afterward, that I will pour out my spirit upon all flesh; and your sons and your daughters shall prophesy," and Peter's proclamation of this prophecy at Pentecost (Acts 2:17).[21] Notwithstanding these female pioneers, most denominations did not allow women to preach until the latter half of the twentieth century, and some theologically conservative religious organizations, including Southern Baptists, Roman Catholics, and Latter-day Saints still deny women the pulpit. As the Southern Baptists' most recent statement of faith asserts, "the office of pastor is limited to men as qualified by Scripture."[22]

Despite some eighteenth-century Christians' reservations about preaching to slaves and free blacks—affirming spiritual equality threatened to lead to demands for freedom and other tangible forms of equality—African Americans played a major role in preaching salvation during the Second Great Awakening. Drawing on the energy of evangelicalism, as well as on African traditions that had survived the Atlantic crossing, they constructed vibrant, enduring Afro-Protestant sermon traditions. As W. E. B. Du Bois memorably described the Preacher, one of the three characteristic elements of slave religion (along with the Music and the Frenzy): "The Preacher is the most unique personality developed by the Negro on American soil. A leader, a politician, an orator, a 'boss,' an intriguer, an idealist,—all these he is, and ever, too, the centre of a group of men, now twenty, now a thousand in number."[23] In the antebellum South, laws prohibiting slave literacy did not prevent blacks from acquiring the biblical knowledge regarded as essential to preaching. Many slave preachers learned to read one way or another, others memorized white instruction, and some expounded and riffed on the Bible stories circulating in oral tradition.[24] From slavery to the present day, African American Christians have preached by drawing vividly and dynamically on biblical tropes and stories and by engaging in what has been called "existential exegesis," in which the preacher works with personal and communal experiences to interpret the Bible's meaning.[25]

Preaching "the cross of Christ," or personal salvation through belief in the atoning death of Christ, remains a cornerstone of American Protestantism. Legendary preachers Dwight L. Moody, Billy Sunday, and Billy Graham carried the revival tradition forward, and twentieth-century revivalists ambitious to "win souls for Christ" opted for radio, then television, to broadcast the call to conversion to millions. Salvation remains a perennial theme in the Sunday morning preaching of evangelicals, who, according to a recent survey, constitute about a quarter of the US population and the country's single largest religious group.[26] Even as such preaching has become increasingly sophisticated in its use of music, storytelling, and multimedia, it continues to ground itself in the belief that those who wish to see the kingdom of heaven must, like Nicodemus, be born again.

Spiritual Improvement

As important as salvation has been to the American pulpit, preachers across religious traditions have dwelled even more reliably on personal spiritual improvement. "The end of all preaching is to persuade men to become good," wrote the Scottish rhetorician Hugh Blair, whose influential *Lectures on Rhetoric and Belles Lettres* (1783) went through thirty-seven US editions.[27] Sermons from the Puritans forward have directed listeners to pious behaviors such as prayer, Bible reading, church attendance, and confession, as well as Christian virtues such as perseverance, character, and hope (Rom. 5:2) and the "fruit of the spirit": "love, joy, peace, longsuffering, gentleness, goodness, faith, meekness, [and] temperance" (Gal. 5.22-23). If sermons focused on individual spirituality and virtue risk tedium through over-familiarity, they can also strike listeners as deeply significant for their personal identities and relationships.

Preaching on spiritual development flourished in the eighteenth century, both as a reaction to evangelical preaching and as an extension of it. "Old Light" Congregationalists, who balked at revivalists' insistence on a conversion experience, stressed the faithful development of character. Charles Chauncy, the intellectual leader of this wing, castigated the itinerant revivalists who sprang up in Whitefield's wake and their supposedly born-again followers: "instead of being more kind and gentle, more full of Mercy and good Fruits, they are more bitter, fierce, and implacable."[28] Rebutting the new emotionalism, he preached on 2 Corinthians 5:17, "Therefore, if any man be in Christ, he is a new creature: old things are passed away; behold all things are become new." The marks of being a new creature were a new "inward Frame of Mind" and a new "outward Course and Manner of Life." People could be assured that they were saved, and that their neighbors were, if they lived "soberly, righteously, and godly in the world . . . in the Practice of the whole of their Duty; all that duty they owe, either to God, their Neighbour, or themselves."[29] No agonizing contrition, self-abasement, or flood of grace necessary.

Many evangelical preachers, of course, stressed that the fruits of the Spirit mentioned in the New Testament book of Galatians were inevitable for those who had undergone an authentic experience of grace. Methodists, in particular, taught that "justification," or the sinner's acceptance of the salvific import of Christ's death on the cross, must be followed by "sanctification," in which the Holy Spirit imbued the believer with a sanctifying grace that transformed character and behavior. Like their founder John Wesley, Methodists held that a Christian should strive for—and might actually attain—spiritual perfection, the touchstone verse being, "Be ye therefore perfect, even as your Father in heaven is perfect" (Matt. 5:48). Finney and many other non-Methodist evangelicals would rally to the perfectionist flag as well.

Apart from certain strains of Quakerism such as the Hicksites, who relied on the inward teaching of the Holy Spirit, nineteenth-century Protestants of all stripes claimed to draw their moral and spiritual precepts from scripture. Even the Unitarians, the most liberal of the mainstream denominations, rejecting not only the new birth but also Trinitarianism, original sin, hell, and the idea of a punitive God, turned to the Bible as their primary resource for spiritual and ethical preaching. Although they avoided the Old Testament, with its arcane prescriptions and vindictive deity, they prized the New Testament all the more, especially the Sermon on the Mount and the exemplary life of Christ. For instance, in preaching on the text "Christ also suffered for us, leaving us an example, that ye should follow his steps" (1 Pet. 2:21), father of American Unitarianism William Ellery Channing stressed not Christ's suffering, as the evangelicals might, but his egalitarian spirit and moral grandeur: Jesus "felt that all had a spark of that same intellectual and immortal flame which dwelt in himself." As in his famous sermon *Likeness to God*, Channing called listeners to recognize and share Jesus's belief in humanity's divinity, to feel their own connection with God and one another, and to allow Christ to draw them toward "spotless purity and unconquerable rectitude."[30]

Henry Ward Beecher played a similar tune on a larger stage. An unrivalled pulpit celebrity in the latter half of the nineteenth-century, Beecher used his pulpit at Plymouth Church in Brooklyn, where he served from 1847 until his death in 1887, to address numerous new topics of public concern, including slavery, evolution, consumerism, economic inequality, and historical criticism of the Bible. But much of his conversational, anecdotal, sometimes humorous preaching simply reassured listeners of God's love and sought to rouse their own benevolence and piety. His sermons had a looser, more practical relationship to the Bible than those of his forebears. When a young man on a train once asked Henry Ward whether he had to believe every word in the Bible to be a Christian, the preacher answered with a hearty "No!" and set him straight: "You must believe the *truth* that is in the Bible."[31] Allergic to creeds, especially his father Lyman Beecher's Calvinism, he promoted instead a religion of the heart. In *The Value of Deep Feelings* (1868), for instance, he took the text, "Wherefore I say unto thee, Her sins, which are many, are forgiven; for she loved much: but to whom little is forgiven, the same loveth little" (Luke 7:47).[32] Retelling the story of the prostitute who washed Jesus's feet at dinner, Beecher praised the natural feeling of both Jesus and the woman and critiqued the condemning Pharisee. For Beecher, true emotion should always triumph over religious forms and prejudices.

Nearly as prominent as Henry Ward Beecher in postbellum America was Episcopalian Phillips Brooks, minister of Trinity Church in Boston from 1869 to 1891. Brooks famously called preaching the "bringing of truth through personality," a formulation that cuts out the Bible altogether. His sermon style was inspirational and metaphorical, with scant textual exposition or doctrinal analysis.[33] His much-reprinted sermon "The Candle of the Lord," on the text "The spirit of man is the candle of the Lord" (Prov. 20:27), can be taken as representative. It teaches that everyone can illuminate his or her surroundings through righteous character and behavior, that God is the flame kindling all, and that Jesus is the supreme candle, lit perfectly by God. Here as elsewhere, Brooks extolled Jesus as an incomparable exemplar rather than as an atoning sacrifice.[34] If his theology lacked originality, his relentless use of figurative language and fondness for straightforward biblical texts kept his sermons feeling fresh to his thousands of admirers in Boston and across the country. The mature preacher, he declared, "loves the simplest texts, and the great truths which run like rivers through all life."[35]

Preaching centered on individual morality and spiritual growth has endured across denominations, a counterpoint to the call to repentance. Among liberal Protestants, the most renowned preacher of spiritual improvement in the twentieth century was Harry Emerson Fosdick, pastor of Manhattan's ecumenical Riverside Church and, through the National Vespers Radio Hour, a moral guide to thousands more. A Baptist-turned-Presbyterian who left the Presbyterians before they censured him for his heterodoxy, Fosdick led the early twentieth-century clash between the fundamentalists, who were biblical literalists, and the modernists, who looked to scripture for spiritual direction while developing a faith that kept pace with science and biblical scholarship—a conflict that echoed, in a world buzzing with new knowledge, centuries-old disagreements between liberals and evangelicals.

Although *Shall the Fundamentalists Win?* is his best-known sermon, Fosdick's weekly preaching was seldom polemical. It sought rather to make his listeners feel personally invested in biblical teachings; he famously said that preaching "should be personal counseling on a group scale."[36] In *Handling Life's Second-Bests*, for instance, a sermon he gave six times over thirteen years, then anthologized in two different volumes, he took as his text Acts 16, in which the spirit of Jesus interrupts Paul on his way to Bithynia and sends him instead to Troas. Fosdick used this pericope to springboard into an example-filled sermon about making the best of disappointment: "Well, wanting Bithynia and getting Troas is a familiar experience. But to take Troas, the second best, the broken plan, the remnant of a disappointed expectation, and make of it our greatest opportunity—how much less familiar that is!"[37] Despite his liberal method of interpreting the Bible so as to arrive at a psychological lesson, the short peroration strikes a disarmingly evangelical note. It directs listeners to the cross and tells them to take inspiration from Jesus, who found in Calvary his own "Troas." And what was the soteriological significance of that cross? The final two lines deflect to a nineteenth-century hymn: "All the light of sacred story / Gathers round his head sublime."[38] By alluding to, rather than spelling out, the "sacred story," Fosdick framed traditional biblical belief as so much cherished lore. At the same time, this final gesture affirmed his and his listeners' Christian identity and set the halo of Jesus's venerable example over his listeners' personal disappointments and struggles.

Sermons that draw on the Bible to foster personal development are by no means the exclusive province of liberal Protestantism. Amid the ever-expanding complexities of modernity, ministers across denominations have turned to scripture as a trove of teachings on personal development. If "positive thinking" preachers Norman Vincent Peale and Robert H. Schuller are Fosdick's obvious spiritual heirs, many of the most successful evangelical preachers of the past century can also claim a slice of the bequest. Billy Graham published his sermons on Matthew 5:3–11 as *The Secret of Happiness: Jesus' Teaching on Happiness as Expressed in the Beatitudes* (1955). He exclaims in the introduction that while studying this text he realized that "Christ was giving a formula for personal happiness that applied to anyone, no matter what his race, geography, age, or circumstance!"[39] Southern California megachurch pastor and church growth guru Rick Warren may be most famous for his bestselling *The Purpose Driven Life*, in which evangelical theology is intimately linked to psychological wholeness; it is "a self-help book pitched as an antidote to that very genre."[40] And the African American neo-Pentecostal preacher T. D. Jakes leads a Dallas church called "The Potter's House" (a nod to Jeremiah 18) where he proclaims the therapeutic message of "God's ability to put hurting souls back together again."[41] The most successful of these preachers have exploited new technologies—whether radio, television, the Internet, or social media—while proclaiming a message that is, at its core, a recognizable, often biblically supported call to spiritual growth and well-being.

CIVIC PREACHING

After the passage of the Bill of Rights in 1791 set in motion the disestablishment of religion, erecting what Thomas Jefferson would call a "wall of separation between church and state," preaching became more consistently apolitical.[42] Yet American preachers continued to articulate, especially at moments of national crisis, the moral principles to which the country should aspire. In the most influential theory of the American sermon to date, Sacvan Bercovitch in *The American Jeremiad* argues that Puritan ministers used a type of political sermon known as the jeremiad to advance a coherent myth of self-justification centered on a typological reading of the Hebrew Bible and that this myth endured well after Puritanism itself had withered, into the nineteenth century and beyond.[43] Identifying with the ancient Hebrews, the Puritans held that God had established a covenantal relationship with them and that their "errand into the wilderness" was a divinely sanctioned enterprise, one sacred and secular, religious and civic. Exemplified by such landmark sermons as Increase Mather's *The Day of Trouble Is Near* (1674), the jeremiad called the New Israel back to righteousness by demanding that the people repent of their sins and vices, often catalogued in detail, and warning of incipient divine wrath. In so doing, they would avoid destruction and secure divine approbation.

As Bercovitch's work indicates, this narrative of national identity relied heavily on select biblical passages, above all, Jeremiah 31:31 and 33, in which the Lord establishes a covenant with Israel. Other linchpin passages included Genesis 17:7, God's covenantal promise to bless Abraham and offspring, Deuteronomy 32, or the Song of Moses, celebrating God's faithfulness despite his people's disobedience; Isaiah 44, reiterating the chosenness of Israel and God's saving grace; and, when Indian wars loomed, Psalms 2:8, "Ask of me, and I shall give thee the heathen for thine inheritance, and the ends of the earth for thy possession" (Geneva Bible Translation). Jeremiads also favored eschatological pericopes from Revelation and the Hebrew prophets, which were used to connect the sacred history of New England with the approaching end times.

As a rhetorical pattern that affirms America as a chosen nation and entreats citizens to repent of their sins in order to ensure God's favor, the American jeremiad has outlived the Puritans and overflowed the banks of the sermon's confines. Bercovitch points to its persistence in Revolutionary rhetoric, Fourth of July discourses, and such mid-nineteenth-century writers as Nathaniel Hawthorne, Henry David Thoreau, and Walt Whitman. Extending Bercovitch's analysis into the present, political theorist Andrew Murphy has outlined two types of post-Puritan jeremiad, discernible across sermons, speeches, essays, interview remarks, and so forth: the traditionalist, bound to an often nostalgic vision of an earlier era and intent on returning the nation to an approximation thereof, and the progressive, aimed at purifying the nation through a return not to specific behaviors, beliefs, or lifestyles, but to defining values.[44]

The traditionalist pattern marks, for instance, nineteenth-century sermons and other discourses that opposed slavery by appealing to the Declaration of Independence or arguing that the nation's founders never intended it to persist, the argumentative strategy of such figures as Henry Ward Beecher, Frederick Douglass, and Abraham Lincoln. In the twentieth century, the traditionalist pattern is visible in, for instance, the rhetoric of Christian Right figures such as Pat Buchanan and Jerry Falwell, who exhort Americans to honor the country's putative status as a Christian nation by restoring prayer in schools, ending abortion, and banning gay marriage.[45] In contrast, the progressive pattern defines the rhetoric of antislavery activists who maintained that ending slavery was part of God's unfolding providential plan for the country; of the Civil Rights rhetoric of Martin Luther King Jr., who championed principles of freedom and equality as core to national identity; and of late-twentieth-century communitarian appeals for social commitment and responsibility, like those of Robert Putnam. Regardless of speaker, genre, or mode, the American jeremiad is fundamentally sermonic in that it seeks to inspire people to righteousness by first pulling them into despair over the nation's fallenness, then pointing toward a vision of hope for its redemption. It offers salvation on grand scale.

Fortunately, American preachers have more than one arrow in their quiver, and not every civic sermon is a jeremiad. Freedom, too, has a robust history in American civic preaching, not always with reference to America's status as a chosen nation. Liberty first became a dominant theme of American preaching in the 1770s. As the historian of early American politics and religion James Byrd has detailed, the clergy were essential to galvanizing colonists' support for the American Revolution, with sermons that invoked biblical precedents for divinely sanctioned warfare and republican virtues, especially freedom. Revolutionary sermons on liberty most often took their text from the story of Exodus, as the colonists wove a political narrative in which they were Israelites enslaved by Egyptians (that some colonists were themselves slaveholders was an irony not lost on all).[46] If the Exodus theme dovetailed neatly with the rhetoric of America as the New Israel, other patriotic sermons looked instead to the concept of Christian freedom, especially Paul's counsel to the Galatians, "Stand fast therefore in the liberty wherewith Christ hath made us free, and be not entangled again with the yoke of bondage" (Gal. 5:1). Byrd notes that in the 1770s, "Paul's command to 'stand fast' for liberty was above all a martial command"; the call to courage in the name of freedom was a call to war.[47]

After the Revolution, the preachers who most fervently championed freedom in their civic sermons were, unsurprisingly, African American. To call these sermons "civic" is to acknowledge their importance in creating a black public that transcended particular faith identities.[48] Literally under "the yoke of bondage," African American preachers found their most politically powerful text in Exodus. This motif infuses the spirituals—"Let My People Go," "Go Down, Moses," and many more—with which slave sermons were intertwined, offering a vision of freedom to a nation within a nation. Liberty was not a birthright to safeguard but a vision glimmering on the horizon.

Even after the passage of the Thirteenth Amendment, and in the more than 150 years since, the Exodus story has continued to be a centerpiece of African American preaching: sermons have "identified Pharaoh and Egypt with white slaveholders, racists, and general oppression."[49] The trope reached its apex in the preaching of Martin Luther King Jr., whose driving narrative was "the saga of the enslavement of black people in Africa, their exodus-in-reverse to an alien land, the continued humiliation they endure at the hands of American pharoahs [sic], and now the stirrings of freedom at work among them." King assured his people that God oversaw this process and willed black deliverance.[50] Exodus imagery pervades King's preaching, most memorably in *I See the Promised Land*, a sermon given in a Pentecostal church in Memphis on April 3, 1968, the day before his assassination. He noted previous attacks on his life and the difficulties that lay ahead, then, identifying with Moses gazing at Canaan from Mount Pisgah (Deut. 34:1-4), proclaimed: "But it doesn't matter with me now. Because I've been to the mountaintop . . . . And I've seen the promised land. I may not get there with you. But I want you to know tonight, that we, as a people, will get to the promised land."[51] With this promised land of racial harmony ever on the horizon, African American preachers of the last forty years have regularly turned to the Exodus story and its spirit of liberation.

Another major type of civic sermon that eludes the jeremiad's grasp is that which calls for love and corporate unity. The jeremiad is first and foremost a call to right relationship with God, a renewal of the covenant; civic preaching about love focuses on citizens' relationship to one another. A return to the beginning: *A Modell of Christian Charity*, Winthrop's "city on a hill" sermon, places far greater emphasis on the new community's need for love and mutual care than on the arc of sacred history, notwithstanding Bercovitch's tagging of this sermon, along with John Cotton's *Gods Promise to His Plantation* (1630), as an origin point for the American jeremiad. In his iconic address, Winthrop urged his fellow colonists to look past class differences and to love one another generously, heeding the special demands incumbent on those living in a "Community of perill."[52] Showering them with proof texts, he beseeched them to practice sacrificial love toward one another: to show compassion to the brother in need as evidence that they loved God (1 John), to honor the Lord with their riches (Prov. 3:9), to remember that they were the body of Christ (1 Cor. 12) and that love was the bond of perfection (Col. 3:14).[53] Listeners were to create a holy community by loving one another in word and deed and purse. Assurances of providential care in this sermon are a whisper compared to the sense of impending danger and the admonitions to solidarity.

Notwithstanding sporadic clarion calls, civic sermons pleading for citizens to love one another were sparse until at least the late nineteenth century. Antislavery sermons, for instance, scarcely mentioned love. As historian Molly Oshatz notes, the Bible does not say that loving one's neighbor is incompatible with keeping that neighbor as a slave.[54] Even after the scandalous passage of the Fugitive Slave Law (1850), which required northern- ers to return slaves to their southern owners, most northern ministers counseled obedi- ence to civil authorities; those who took as their text "love thy neighbor as thyself" (Mark 12:31, Matt. 19:19; see also Lev. 19:18, Rom. 13:8, Gal. 5:14) typically interpreted the south- ern slaveholder as the true neighbor.[55] Not until the late nineteenth-century Social Gospel movement, which sought to redress social problems such as urban poverty and worker subjugation, did love for neighbor become a major chord in civic preaching. Social Gospel leader and popular Columbus, Ohio, Congregationalist minister Washington Gladden helped change the tide: few Christians, he wrote, realized that "the law of love governs the whole of life; that it defines our relations to men not only in the home and in the church, but in industry and commerce and politics." He reinforced his point with 1 John 4:20: "He that loveth not his brother whom he hath seen, cannot love God whom he hath not seen."[56]

In the twentieth century, Martin Luther King Jr. was the most powerful minister to enter the public sphere and preach that love could bring about social change. Using rhetoric that drew on both the Black Baptist preaching of his upbringing and on the white liberal preach- ers whose sermons he encountered in his graduate training, especially those of Fosdick and Brooks, King crafted a powerful sermonic voice that rallied both blacks and whites to the Civil Rights movement.[57] "King's code contains a narrative and a precept," Duke Divinity School Professor and systematic theologian Richard Lischer writes. "The narra- tive is the story of liberation, the precept is the command to love."[58] Many of the sermons collected in *Strength to Love* center on self-denying love. In *Love in Action*, on "Father, forgive them; for they know not what they do" (Luke 23:34), he declared that forgiveness like Jesus's on the cross was "love at its best" and that Jesus taught his followers "creative love for their enemies."[59] In *On Being a Good Neighbor*, he took up the perennial ques- tion for civic relations—"And who is my neighbor?" (Luke 10:29)—and directed listeners to Jesus's response, the parable of the Good Samaritan. From this story he derived the spiritual imperative to engage in a risk-taking, integrity-filled altruism that did not limit itself "to tribe, race, class, or nation."[60] In King's social thought and preaching, only such sacrificial love would bring about the "Beloved Community," or an economically just, racially uni- fied society.[61] King famously enacted his philosophy of radical love through the practice of nonviolence; he credited Jesus with supplying the spirit of the Civil Rights movement, and Gandhi, its method.[62] The passage of the Civil Rights Act (1964) and the Voting Rights Act (1965) are testaments to the socially transformative power of King's sermonic rhetoric.

In the generation or so since King's death, no single American minister has played such a colossal role in the national arena or preached civic sermons that so effectively united citizens in a common political cause. One reason may be the reluctance of contemporary ministers to address explicitly political issues from the pulpit, following Lyndon Johnson's 1954 change to the tax code, which prohibits all tax-exempt organizations from openly favoring or endorsing candidates for public office. Nonetheless, religious leaders have continued to rally and fortify the likeminded, generally without naming names or parties. African American ministers such as Jeremiah Wright and the Baptists Jesse Jackson and Al Sharpton have kept alive King's calls for racial justice and liberation but without the overriding emphasis on love or racial unity. White ministers addressing the public have been split along liberal and conservative lines, with conservatives inveighing against America's changing sexual mores and gender norms, and liberals divided across competing priorities, including racial justice, environmental protection, and marriage equality. Further, the proliferation of cable and satellite television and radio channels and the rise of the Web and social media have fragmented the public, making shared, civic space hard to find.

The preeminent civic preachers of the last few decades have arguably not been clergy at all, but politicians: for instance, Bill Clinton in his 1993 Inaugural Address celebrating renewal and calling for sacrifice, closing with the pearl, "And let us not be weary in well-doing: for in due season we shall reap, if we faint not" (Gal. 6:9); George W. Bush consoling the nation and quoting from Psalm 23 in his address to the nation on September 11, 2001; or Barack Obama beginning his remarks at the memorial for the five Dallas police officers slain during a Black Lives Matter protest in 2016 with "Scripture tells us that in our sufferings there is glory, because we know that suffering produces perseverance; perseverance, character; and character, hope" (Gal. 5:3-5).[63] Adorned with biblical citations, the civic sermon lives on most visibly, for the moment, in the uplifting speeches of political ceremony.

Whether focused on national destiny or the new birth, addressed to faith communities or to a pluralistic public, American sermons have served as the country's most widespread and enduring means of biblical interpretation. Taking the Bible as an authority to be understood in light of religious commitment, preachers have offered their hearers the promise of individual and collective salvation, inspired them to live more meaningful, virtuous lives, and catalyzed positive social and political changes. Yet it is surely worth remembering that the power of the Protestant pulpit cuts both ways, that the story of American preaching also includes darker, more troubling subplots, in which preachers traumatize those who diverge from correct belief or practice, support economic and political injustice, and otherwise exert a destructive influence on individuals and the commonweal. Anti-Catholicism, anti-Semitism, racism, imperialism, sexism, xenophobia, and many other noxious prejudices have had their pulpit advocates. These, too, have constituted American preaching, but given the early stage of scholarship in this area, I have sought to highlight instead the narratives of redemption and renewal arguably more central to the sermonic tradition and more vital to listeners and readers across the centuries. One can only hope that future preachers will strive to claim the worthiest, most humane elements of the tradition: that, one might say, a light will shine in the darkness, and that the darkness will not overcome it.

NOTES

1. For example, in 1916, the US census listed nearly thirty languages used for religious services in Catholic parishes. While the Mass was in Latin, the sermon, or homily, was in the listeners' native tongue—or tongues; one parish reported running services in six languages. See Roger Finke and Rodney Stark, *The Churching of America, 1776-2005* (New Brunswick, N.J.: Rutgers University Press, 2005), 134, 137.

2. Yngve Brilioth, *A Brief History of Preaching*, trans. Karl E. Mattson (Philadelphia: Fortress Press, 1965), 171.

3. On listener response to sermons, see, for instance, Meredith Marie Neuman, *Jeremiah's Scribes: Creating Sermon Literature in Puritan New England* (Philadelphia: University of Pennsylvania Press, 2013) and Dawn Coleman, "The Antebellum Sermon as Lived Religion," in *A New History of the Sermon: The Nineteenth Century*, ed. Robert Ellison (Leiden, Netherlands: Brill, 2010), 521–54.

4. The late nineteenth-century increase in sermon illustrations had its roots in Second Great Awakening preaching, especially that of African Americans, and was exemplified in figures such as Dwight Moody and T. DeWitt Talmage; see David Reynolds, "From Doctrine to Narrative: The Rise in Pulpit Storytelling in America," *American Quarterly* 32, no. 5 (1980): 479–98.

5. For an overview of the differences between contemporary sermon structures and the traditional deductive approach, see Thomas G. Long, "Form," in *Concise Encyclopedia of Preaching*, ed. William H. Willimon and Richard Lischer (Louisville, Ky.: Westminster John Knox Press, 1995), 141–51, as well as O. C. Edwards Jr., *A History of Preaching* (Nashville, Tenn.: Abingdon Press, 2004), 798–827. While many denominations leave the selection of biblical texts up to the minister, others use a lectionary, or book of readings, to ensure that the congregation covers a wide range of lections, or biblical passages, over the course of one or more years. One such guide is the Revised Common Lectionary, a three-year cycle of lections for Sundays and holidays, on which more than twenty different denominations consult.

6. Harry S. Stout, *The New England Soul: Preaching and Religious Culture in Colonial New England* (New York: Oxford University Press, 1986), 6, 33.

7. Stout, *The New England Soul*, 41, 148.

8. Thomas Shepard, "Of Ineffectual Hearing the Word," in *American Sermons: The Pilgrims to Martin Luther King Jr.*, ed. Michael Warner (New York: Library of America, 1999), 97.

9. Jonathan Edwards, *The Sermons of Jonathan Edwards: A Reader*, eds. Wilson H. Kimnach, et al (New Haven: Yale University Press, 1999), 49, 59.

10. Michael J. McClymond and Gerald R. McDermott, *The Theology of Jonathan Edwards* (New York: Oxford University Press, 2012), 508.

11. Stephen J. Stein provides a useful précis of Edwards's philosophy of biblical interpretation in "Edwards as Biblical Exegete," in *The Cambridge Companion to Jonathan Edwards*, ed. Stephen J. Stein (New York: Cambridge University Press, 2007), 181–95. On Edwards's preaching, see also McClymond and McDermott's chapter, *The Theology of Jonathan Edwards*, "The Voice of the Great God: A Theology of Preaching," 494–512.

12. Wilson Kimnach, "Edwards as Preacher," in *The Cambridge Companion to Jonathan Edwards*, ed. Stephen J. Stein (New York: Cambridge University Press, 2007), 103–24.

13. Jerome Dean Mahaffey, *Preaching Politics: The Religious Rhetoric of George Whitefield and the Founding of a New Nation* (Waco, Tex.: Baylor University Press, 2007), 213.

14. George Whitefield, *The Marks of the New Birth: A Sermon Preached at the Parish Church of St. Mary, White-Chapel, London* (London, 1739), 13, 15.

15. Classic treatments of this development are Nathan O. Hatch, *The Democratization of Christianity* (New Haven, Conn.: Yale University Press, 1989) and Jon Butler, *Awash in a Sea of Faith: Christianizing the American People* (Cambridge, Mass.: Harvard University Press, 1990).

16. See Charles G. Finney, *Sermons on Important Subjects* (New York: John S. Taylor, 1836) and *Sermons on Gospel Themes* (New York: Revell, 1876).

17. Finke and Stark, *Churching of America*, 56.

18. On Methodist preaching, see Michael K. Turner, "Revivalism and Preaching," *The Cambridge Companion to American Methodism*, ed. Jason E. Vickers (New York: Cambridge University Press, 2013), 119–37, and Coleman, "The Antebellum Sermon as Lived Religion," especially 536–38.

19. The only churches that sanctioned women preachers were in the North. In *Strangers and Pilgrims: Female Preaching in America, 1740-1845* (Chapel Hill: University of North Carolina Press, 1998), Catherine Brekus details women's preaching in early America and explains the resistance in antebellum southern churches to allowing women to preach (130–31). Because her study does not cover the Quakers, it includes only a handful of eighteenth-century preachers. On Quaker women's preaching, see Rebecca Larson, *Daughters of Light: Quaker Women Preaching and Prophesying in the Colonies and Abroad, 1700-1775* (New York: Alfred A. Knopf, 1999).

20. Brekus, *Strangers and Pilgrims*, 132, 208.

21. Brekus, *Strangers and Pilgrims*, 152–53, 217–20, 198, and Chanta M. Haywood, *Prophesying Daughters: Black Women Preachers and the Word, 1823-1913* (Columbia: University of Missouri Press, 2003), 14, 82.

22. Southern Baptist Convention, Article VI, "The Church," The 2000 Baptist Faith and Message, http://www.sbc.net/bfm2000/bfm2000.asp.

23. W. E. Burghardt Du Bois, *The Souls of Black Folk* (Chicago: A. C. McClurg, 1903), 190.

24. On slaves' knowledge of the Bible, see Albert J. Raboteau, *Slave Religion: The 'Invisible Institution' in the Antebellum South*, updated ed. (New York: Oxford University Press, 2004), 231–43.

25. Martha Simmons and Frank A. Thomas, *Preaching with Sacred Fire: An Anthology of African American Sermons, 1750 to the Present* (New York: Norton, 2010), 8.

26. Pew Research Center, "America's Changing Religious Landscape," May 12, 2015, 4.

27. Hugh Blair, *Lectures on Rhetoric and Belles Lettres* (Philadelphia, 1784), 263; James L. Golden and Edward P. J. Corbett, *The Rhetoric of Blair, Campbell, and Whately, with Updated Bibliographies* (Carbondale: Southern Illinois University Press, 1990), 25.

28. Charles Chauncy, "A Letter . . . to Mr. George Wishart, 1742," *The Great Awakening; Documents on the Revival of Religion, 1740-1745*, ed. Richard L. Bushman (Chapel Hill: University of North Carolina Press, for the Institute of Early American History and Culture, 1969), 120.

29. Charles Chauncy, *The New Creature Described and Considered, as the Sure Characteristick of a Man's Being in Christ* (Boston: Edinburgh, 1742), 9.

30. William Ellery Channing, *The Works of William E. Channing, D.D.*, 8th ed. (Boston: James Munroe; New York: C. S. Francis, 1848), 4:147–48.

31. Qtd. in Debby Applegate, *The Most Famous Man in America: The Biography of Henry Ward Beecher* (New York: Doubleday, 2006), 355.

32. Henry Ward Beecher, "The Value of Deep Feelings," in *Plymouth Pulpit: The Sermons of Henry Ward Beecher* (New York: J. B. Ford, 1869), 211–28.

33. Phillips Brooks, *Lectures on Preaching: Delivered before the Divinity School of Yale College* (1877; New York: Dutton, 1907), 5.

34. Gillis J. Harp, *Brahmin Prophet: Phillips Brooks and the Path of Liberal Protestantism* (Lanham, Md.: Rowman and Littlefield, 2003), 123–25.

35. Phillips Brooks, *Lectures on Preaching Delivered before the Divinity School of Yale College* (New York: E. P. Dutton, 1877), 18.

36. Harry Emerson Fosdick, *The Living of These Days: An Autobiography* (New York: Harper & Row, 1956), 94.

37. Harry Emerson Fosdick, "Handling Life's Second-Bests," in Halford R. Ryan, *Harry Emerson Fosdick: Persuasive Preacher* (New York: Greenwood Press, 1989), 118.

38. Fosdick, "Handling Life's Second-Bests," 123.

39. Billy Graham, *The Secret to Happiness: Jesus' Teaching on Happiness as Expressed in the Beatitudes* (Garden City, N.Y.: Doubleday, 1955), v.

40. Steven P. Miller, *The Age of Evangelicalism: America's Born-Again Years* (New York: Oxford University Press), 131.

41. Jonathan L. Walton, *Watch This! The Ethics and Aesthetics of Black Televangelism* (New York: New York University Press, 2009), 104.

42. Thomas Jefferson to the Danbury Baptists, January 1, 1802, *Library of Congress Information Bulletin* 57, no. 6 (1998), https://www.loc.gov/loc/lcib/9806/danpre.html.

43. Bercovitch builds on Perry Miller's pioneering work on the jeremiad in *Errand into the Wilderness* (Cambridge, Mass.: Belknap-Harvard University Press, 1956), while offering a less gloom-and-doom view of the genre and an articulation of its legacy beyond the Puritans.

44. Andrew Murphy, *Prodigal Nation: Moral Decline and Divine Punishment from New England to 9/11* (New York: Oxford University Press), 109–10.

45. On the jeremiads of Southern Baptist minister and Moral Majority founder Jerry Falwell, see Susan Harding, *The Book of Jerry Falwell: Fundamentalist Language and Politics* (Princeton, N.J.: Princeton University Press, 2000), 153–81.

46. James Byrd, *Sacred Scripture, Sacred War: The Bible and the American Revolution* (New York: Oxford University Press, 2013), 47–56.

47. Byrd, *Sacred Scripture*, 116, 129–36, 133.

48. On the function of the black church in creating a public and the key role of the Exodus story, see Eddie S. Glaude Jr., *Exodus!: Religion, Race, and Nation in Early Nineteenth-Century Black America* (Chicago: University of Chicago Press, 2000).

49. David W. Kling, *The Bible in History: How the Texts Have Shaped the Times* (New York: Oxford University Press), 196. Kling details the use of the Exodus motif in the spirituals (209–14). White abolitionist preachers also invoked the motif of freedom, if not always the Exodus story. See, for instance, Quaker Lucretia Mott's *Sermon to the Medical Students* (1849), which cited the Lord's command "to bind up the broken hearted, to proclaim freedom to the captive" (Isa. 61:1) and "Proclaim ye liberty throughout all the land" (Lev. 25:10); *Lucretia Mott: Her Complete Speeches and Sermons*, ed. Dana Greene (New York: Edwin Mellen Press, 1980), 88–89.

50. Richard Lischer, *The Preacher King: Martin Luther King, Jr. and the Word That Moved America* (New York: Oxford University Press, 1995), 212–13.

51. Martin Luther King Jr., *A Testament of Hope: The Essential Writings of Martin Luther King, Jr.*, ed. James Melvin Washington (San Francisco, Calif.: Harper and Row, 1986), 286.
52. John Winthrop, "A Modell of Christian Charity," in *American Sermons: From the Pilgrims to Martin Luther King Jr.*, ed. Michael Warner (New York: Library of America), 33.
53. Winthrop, "A Modell of Christian Charity," 32, 29, 35.
54. Molly Oshatz, *Slavery and Sin: The Fight against Slavery and the Rise of Liberal Protestantism* (New York: Oxford University Press, 2012), 7.
55. Laura Mitchell, "'Matters of Justice between Man and Man': Northern Divines, the Bible, and the Fugitive Slave Act of 1850," in *Religion and the Antebellum Debate over Slavery*, ed. John R. McKivigan and Mitchell Snay (Athens: University of Georgia Press, 1998), 134–65.
56. Washington Gladden, *Social Salvation* (Boston, Mass.: Houghton, Mifflin, and Company, 1902), 10, 12.
57. On King's borrowings, see Keith D. Miller, *Voice of Deliverance: The Language of Martin Luther King, Jr. and Its Sources* (Athens: University of Georgia Press, 1998).
58. Lischer, *The Preacher King*, 210.
59. Martin Luther King Jr., *Strength to Love* (Philadelphia: Fortress Press, 1963), 39, 41.
60. King, *Strength to Love*, 31.
61. Over time, King shifted away from the humanistic "Beloved Community" concept to the theocentric "Kingdom of God"; see Lischer, *The Preacher King*, 234.
62. King, *A Testament of Hope*, 8 and 19, 38.
63. William J. Clinton: "Inaugural Address," January 20, 1993, The American Presidency Project, ed. Gerhard Peters and John T. Woolley, http://www.presidency.ucsb.edu/ws/?pid=46366; George W. Bush, "Statement by the President in His Address to the Nation," September 11, 2011, The White House: President George W. Bush, https://georgewbush-whitehouse.archives.gov/news/releases/2001/09/20010911-16.html; Barack Obama, "Remarks by the President at Memorial Service for Fallen Dallas Police Officers," July 12, 2016, The White House: President Barack Obama, https://www.whitehouse.gov/the-press-office/2016/07/12/remarks-president-memorial-service-fallen-dallas-police-officers.

BIBLIOGRAPHY

Bercovitch, Sacvan. *The American Jeremiad*. Madison: University of Wisconsin Press, 1978.
Bruce, Steve. *Pray TV: Televangelism in America*. New York: Routledge, 1990.
Calloway-Thomas, Carolyn, and John Louis Lucaites, eds. *Martin Luther King, Jr., and the Sermonic Power of Public Discourse*. Tuscaloosa: University of Alabama Press, 1993.
Coleman, Dawn. *Preaching and the Rise of the American Novel*. Columbus: Ohio State University Press, 2013.
Davis, Gerald L. *I Got the Word in Me and I Can Sing It, You Know*. Philadelphia: University of Pennsylvania Press, 1985.
Edwards, O. C., Jr. *A History of Preaching*. Nashville, Tenn.: Abingdon Press, 2004.
LaRue, Cleophus J. *The Heart of Black Preaching*. Louisville, Ky.: Westminster John Knox Press, 2000.
Simmons, Martha, and Frank A. Thomas. *Preaching with Sacred Fire: An Anthology of African American Sermons, 1750 to the Present*. New York: Norton, 2010.

Stout, Harry S. *The Divine Dramatist: George Whitefield and the Rise of Modern Evangelicalism.* Grand Rapids, Mich.: Eerdmans, 1991.

———. *The New England Soul: Preaching and Religious Culture in Colonial New England.* New York: Oxford University Press, 1986.

Walton, Jonathan L. *Watch This! The Ethics and Aesthetics of Black Televangelism.* New York: New York University Press, 2009.

Warner, Michael. *American Sermons: The Pilgrims to Martin Luther King* New York: Library of America, 1999.

William, William H., and Richard Lischer, eds. *Concise Encyclopedia of Preaching.* Louisville, Ky.: Westminster John Knox Press, 1995.

Witten, Marsha G. *All Is Forgiven: The Secular Message in American Protestantism.* Princeton, N.J.: Princeton University Press, 1993.

PART III

THE BIBLE IN AMERICAN HISTORY AND CULTURE

CHAPTER 16

....

THE BIBLE IN AMERICAN PUBLIC SCHOOLS

....

SUZANNE ROSENBLITH AND PATRICK WOMAC

INTRODUCTION

....

PUBLIC schools do not exist in isolation from other institutions and structures in American public life. Even a cursory review of the history of American public schooling beginning in the colonial period, reveals that public schools, and their precursor, the Common School, were constructed as microcosms of society.[1] The earliest conversations about a more organized, state-sponsored public school reveal the symbiotic relationship between American education and American society at large.[2] Public Schools in America have always functioned to reflect the moral, social, and political values of society, to address issues of public concern and to teach the nation's young.[3] As the great American philosopher John Dewey famously asserted, "public schools are laboratories of and for democracy."[4] Public schools, for Dewey, and for so many others, have been spaces in which young citizens hone the skills required to be active participants in the democratic life of the nation. This requires not only discipline-based knowledge but also refining the skills of critical analysis, and it places a premium on the fair and robust interchange of ideas.[5] For these framers of American public schooling, the success or failure of the democratic project rested on the success of the American public school and its ability to cultivate the essential skills necessary for an informed and virtuous citizenry.[6]

Understanding the Bible's role—its varying centrality, irrelevance, and contentiousness—in public schools requires us to place it within the context of American public life. If schools are supposed to reflect and respond to societal norms, beliefs, and trends, as well as solve the problems of society, then the Bible either figures in centrally to these goals or is hostile to achieving these goals. In fact, the history of the Bible in American public schools reveals just this contradiction—the Bible has enjoyed revered status in public schools at times, and at other times has been held as the major obstacle to progress, modernity, and even postmodernity.[7]

In this chapter, we trace the Bible's path through the history of American public education, framing the narrative in the following manner: to understand the role of the Bible in

American public schooling requires understanding the function of public schooling in the context of a republic committed to the principles of democracy and pluralism. That is, an understanding of this educational institution that is at once charged with perpetuating the values of the republic while at the same time addressing societal ills.[8] We trace this arc beginning with some of the earliest Western settlers to America, the Puritans, who saw the Bible as central not only to education, but more important, to their salvation.[9] Complete with laws like the Old Deluder Satan Act, the Bible's central place in Puritan conceptions of life and education (there was not yet an organized or institutionalized schooling) was absolute at this time. For most early white Americans, the only book in the home was a Bible; thereby, the reasons behind the book's centrality were not just spiritual but practical as well.[10]

By the mid-nineteenth century, the advances of society, typically categorized as those of industrialization, immigration, and urbanization required more education for the country's youth. Here we see the first instances of an organized school system (the Common School movement led by Horace Mann), as well as discussions about the function of schools as a direct response to the realities of society.[11] One of the realities of society was the effect of European Enlightenment on American thinking, a type of thinking that caused the Bible to become less relevant.[12] American Enlightenment thinking had a profound impact on the biggest champions of the nation's ever more organized school system, figures including Horace Mann, Benjamin Rush, and Thomas Jefferson. These men, along with others, applied rigorous systems of inquiry and reasoning to everything from politics to scientific thinking. As Enlightenment thinking began to take hold, a new type of non-denominational Enlightenment-inflected Protestantism also rose to prominence.[13] As the nineteenth century wore on, public school curricula shifted away from the Bible as a centerpiece, but it was still a book that was an important institutionalized component for daily reading and prayer, practices that were even mandated in many states.

By the mid-twentieth century and continuing to the present, the Bible's stronghold on schooling has been significantly weakened. What began as an educational and ideological shift in the late nineteenth century was cemented into the foundation of public school practice (mainly through a string of court cases) in the early twentieth century. These court cases helped to divorce irrevocably the Bible from the curricular and policy realms of public education.

COLONIAL AMERICA

Early American education varied significantly in structure depending on the colony concerned. There was no system or uniformity. Schooling in the colonies was typically a local effort guided or administered by the local church. Early colonists' rationale for educating the youth was geared primarily toward instilling religious practices and beliefs.[14] The curriculum was based primarily on the Bible or other lessons guided by denominational doctrine such as the longer and shorter Westminster Catechisms. This type of religious instruction was intended as a safeguard to ensure social stability—inculcating values and therefore forming good citizens who obeyed the laws of the community and "rescue[ing] the children from an incipient savagery."[15]

The first colonies to require some education were Massachusetts and Virginia in the 1640s. The earliest known educationally related law, the Massachusetts Law of 1642, appointed individuals to determine the extent to which children were taught "to read and understand the principles of religion and the capital laws of this country."[16] The "Old Deluder Satan Act" five years later required Massachusetts communities of 100 or more households to provide a grammar school to promote "knowledge of the Scriptures" so that citizens could distinguish true from false religion. The primary mission of schooling (in contrast to Britain) was no longer to transmit intellectual heritage; rather, it was to promote Protestant Christianity.

The Virginia, Maryland, Georgia, and Carolina colonies had church, and thus educational structures that favored the Church of England because in these colonies the British Crown helped fund Church of England activities. In Massachusetts, Connecticut, and New Hampshire, there was a pronounced emphasis on Christian practice marked by Puritan Congregationalism. These allegiances influenced how the Bible was used in various colonies and their classrooms. There were also notable differences between northern and southern colonies. Whether the instruction, however, took place in a church grammar school, a dame school kitchen, or with a private tutor, instruction was primarily religious and authoritarian, typically using the King James Bible.

Through the use of primers, students learned to read scripture and matters of doctrine. Many Puritan beliefs were at odds with the early English primers, hence the eventual development of the *New England Primer* (first edition, 1687), the most widely used textbook throughout the colonies. It was laden with passages of scripture, as well as Protestant catechism and doctrine. An illustrative example from the textbook is presented in its first pages which include "An Alphabet of Lessons for Youth," listing religious adages associated with each letter:

A wise son makes a glad Father, but a foolish son is the heaviness of his Mother.
B etter is little with the fear of the Lord, than great treasure and trouble therewith.
C ome unto CHRIST all ye that labour and are heavy laden, and He will give you rest.[17]

The content of the *New England Primer* is largely representative of the lessons taught in colonial America. Typically, schoolchildren read only from the primer and the Bible. The heavy use of this combination of texts for school instruction is understandable because the overriding reason to teach reading at this time was so that students could read the Bible for themselves.

By the mid-eighteenth century, the increasingly diverse colonial educational landscape mirrored the increasingly diverse religious landscape. There were Lutheran, Quaker, Presbyterian, and Reformed schools, academies, dame schools, and town schools—with no clear distinction between public and private. Public funds often supported religious schools, like the Protestant voluntary association Free School Society.[18] In Delaware, Virginia, and Maryland, these funds were used to build many schools and eventually established a monopoly on funds dedicated toward education. The Bible played a large role in the curricula of these schools.

By the late eighteenth century, the "profound democratic currents that fed the American Revolution greatly increased the concern with popular enlightenment."[19] As cities grew, general education was seen as a means of preventing disorder while fostering civic virtue.[20] Polemics centered on the importance of funding schools and that schools should be full of prayer and ethical instruction would be pervasive for the first 150 years of nationhood.

Madison, Jefferson, and others' adherence to the notion that separation of religion and government was necessary to preserve democracy and liberty would eventually have a more substantial and enduring effect on American education than any other policy in early American history. Jefferson suggested that "instead of putting the Bible and Testament in the hands of children at an age when their judgments are not sufficiently matured for religious inquiries, their minds may here be stored with the most useful facts from Grecian, Roman, European and American History."[21] Politician, teacher, and dictionary composer Noah Webster (1758-1843) was among those who agreed that didactic religious instruction would impede students' critical thinking capacity. In the years following the adoption of the First Amendment, many cities established free public schools, drawing together students from multiple religious backgrounds. As a nonreligious education was unimaginable at this time, religious schools were often subsidized well into the mid-1800s. As public education began to take hold and diversify, so too did a significant opposition to the use of the Bible in the classroom.

By the mid-nineteenth century, industrialization, an influx in immigration, and urbanization all helped change what American society saw as important in educating its youth. Support for public education continued to grow concomitantly with the growth of industry, as greater income provided the means to support the interests and welfare of the general population. It is in the opening decades of the nineteenth century that we see the first instances of an organized school system. In 1827, Massachusetts passed laws to become the first state to establish legislation intended to standardize education in its schools.

When Horace Mann (1796-1859) was appointed the first secretary of Massachusetts's State Board of Education in 1836, he strictly enforced the law, including the stipulation prohibiting the use of sectarian books and proselytization. He "became the nation's most visible and forceful advocate for nonsectarian education." Mann's efforts to remove doctrinal books (such as Calvinist catechisms and various biblical primers) from the classroom were often controversial, but he was eventually successful in his school reform endeavors. While Mann and others still saw the Bible as an important curricular component, teaching specific biblical interpretations and sectarian doctrines eventually fell out of favor "out of respect for freedom of conscience."[22] Eighteenth-century Enlightenment paradigms moved many to believe that increased education would cause religion to "gradually wither away or be confined to the private sphere of life."[23]

By the 1840s, devotional curricula had been significantly reduced due to the efforts of Mann and others leading the Common School movement. While school curricula still integrated a somewhat watered-down, non-sectarian Protestantism, the Bible became less relevant in the classroom—with the exception of the growing number of Catholic schools near the end of the century. The use of the Bible in the classroom changed from an earlier emphasis on conversion and assimilation to a tool to build moral character. For Mann, any doctrinal instruction would foster conflict, while everyone agreed that moral rectitude could only help the nation's democracy thrive. That is not to say there was not Protestant opposition throughout this curricular evolution, but the opposition had increasingly become the minority voice. By the 1840s, the practice of publicly funding private religious schools was no longer common. For many Americans, it was seen as inconsistent with the First Amendment's right to freedom of religious practice to place public monies in the hands of only a select number of ministers and clergyman.

Mann and other Common School leaders succeeded in moving schools away from didactic Bible curriculum without being anti-Bible. In the spirit of Madison and Jefferson, Mann argued that established religion has always led to persecution and tyranny. When considering what he saw in the Massachusetts schools of the 1830s, he noted, "I found books in the schools as strictly and exclusively *doctrinal* as any on the shelves of a theological library. I hear teachers giving oral instructions as strictly and purely *doctrinal* as any ever heard from the pulpit."[24] Mann had a nuanced approach to the use of the Bible in public schools. He did not want to see it gone completely, but he pushed for Bible reading in schools only as long as it was allowed to speak for itself with no doctrinal gloss or denominational interpretation.[25]

Largely on account of the fact that the King James Bible was still read in the classroom (although less frequently), the growing Irish Catholic community established their own parochial school movement in which teachers could help students interpret the Bible—a Catholic approved translation of the Bible, which the King James Bible was not—through a Catholic lens. America's Jewish population joined the Catholics in their disapproval of the lingering Protestant character of the public schools. Meanwhile, many Protestants argued that schools were becoming secularized and "godless."[26] Local disputes of religion's place in the public school continued throughout the nineteenth century, peaking just after the Civil War. The debate "engaged Protestants and Catholics, skeptics and theocrats, nativists and immigrants, educators and politicians," and it reflected larger conflicts regarding the nation's cultural and religious identity.[27] These disputes would only persist throughout the next century.

By the turn of the twentieth century, the Bible had lost its stronghold on school curriculum—with residual usage in parts of the South. Most states forbade using taxes for sectarian purposes. Straightforward Bible reading without direct religious instruction continued to be viewed as non-sectarian in early twentieth-century America, but less so over time. With such religious diversity across the country's entire population, many believed the avoidance of divisiveness would best be brought about by eliminating Bible reading from public institutions. Schools stood at the center of these culture wars, and as the century progressed textbooks included fewer and fewer scripture passages.

The progressive movement in education led by John Dewey (1859-1952) concluded an era of the Bible's use in the classroom. His student Sidney Hook (1902-1989) described a new type of religious ethos in American education. He saw a national shift away from traditional Protestant-tethered notions of education to a society not divided by churches and sects, but a place where "schools can unite becoming the temples and laboratories of a common democratic faith."[28] In Hook's view, the religion of public schools had shifted from Protestantism to the "religion of democracy."

By the early to middle of the twentieth century, public schools in the United States were in a state of transformation. Societal forces once again pressured by growing urbanization, industrialization, and immigration compelled public school officials to consider the degree to which public schools were meeting the needs of the young and of society more generally.[29] In large measure, the consensus was that for varying reasons, public schools needed to do a better job responding to the growing social and economic needs.[30] With respect to the Bible, this meant its use as a curricular resource was less compelling. Learning scripture was viewed by many as a disruption from instruction designed to prepare students for the workforce.

While the non-denominational Protestant ethos of the public schools was still largely present, the utility of the Bible as a curricular resource had waned. Recognizing the need to help students develop the sorts of knowledge, skills, and tools that would prepare them for an ever-changing, increasingly technologically sophisticated world, required a shift in thinking away from absolutist thinking (as embodied in the Bible) and toward a more flexible and innovative thinking (as embodied in technology and science). A move away from the fixity of religion toward the tentativeness of science became the rule of the day.[31] Although the Bible began to lose its stronghold in a curricular sense by the mid-twentieth century, it was still very much a presence in the public school in a symbolic manner.

It was, in fact, still common practice up through the 1950s in many parts of the country for public schools to begin the school day with a prayer or Bible reading. Two significant legal cases decided at the Supreme Court level, however, shifted this practice. In 1962, Steven Engel, a Jewish man, objected to his son bowing his head and clasping his hands while reciting the "Regents Prayer" in a New York State Public School. The Board of Regents created what they believed to be a non-denominational prayer, "Almighty God, we acknowledge our dependence upon thee, and beg Thy blessings upon us, our teachers, our parents, and our country." In a 6–1 decision (two justices did not take part in the case), the Court determined that it was in fact a violation of the Establishment Clause found in the First Amendment (forbidding the establishment of a national church) to require students to take part in this prayer.[32]

One year later, the landmark case, *Abington School District v. Schempp*, determined that a Commonwealth of Pennsylvania statute which read, "Ten verses from the Holy Bible shall be read without comment at the start of each school day," was also a violation of the Establishment Clause.[33] The courts in both cases affirmed the importance of official state neutrality when it comes to matters of religion and public schools. This position holds that the state must maintain neutrality between religion and non-religion. These two lopsided decisions, although unpopular with many citizens, nevertheless firmly divorced religion and the Bible in important ways from public schools. Since these legal barriers were built, those favoring the reintroduction of religion and the Bible into public schools have attempted to do so in several ways: religious advocacy, intellectual advocacy, and alternative policies.

Religious Advocacy

As already mentioned, the Establishment Clause cases of the 1960s severed the hold that Christianity, and the Bible, had long exercised in the nation's public school systems. While the Court's decision set a precedent of state neutrality between religion and non-religion, nevertheless popular opinion departed from this legal opinion and those identifying themselves as the Religious Right made it their mission to reintroduce the Bible into public schools.[34] These efforts can be seen through religious curricular advocacy. Two efforts will be highlighted here. First, there were efforts to introduce biblical creationism into biology classes, and second, there were efforts to create elective classes in which the Bible was to be studied.

Throughout the latter part of the twentieth century until the present day, states like Kansas, Texas, and Tennessee have made several attempts to introduce biblical creationism into biology classes through so-called balanced treatment acts.[35] These efforts argue that limiting lessons on the earth's origins to discussions of Darwinian evolution is tantamount to violating the neutrality principle.[36] Instead these groups argue that schools should teach both "theories" thereby leaving the choice of what to believe up to students.[37] These efforts have institutional support mainly from local and state school boards. Nevertheless, these efforts have not gained widespread support, in part because of the increased emphasis on standards-based instruction. The movement of testing and accountability leaves little room for schools to address anything outside of the material that students are required to know for standardized assessments. Finally, legal scholarship has affirmed that the "neutrality principle" has more to do with the reasons and grounds for introducing a specific academic proposal than it does in what ends up in the curriculum.[38] Such reasoning suggests that the only reason to introduce biblical creationism into a science class is religious and therefore unconstitutional.

A more interesting attempt to reintroduce the Bible into public schools comes through state legislation that allowed for a course entitled, "The Bible and Its Influence on Western Culture." The first of the so-called Bible bills was introduced in Georgia in 2006. Although introduced through Georgia's legislature, the legislation had the backing and widespread endorsement of the National Council on Bible Curriculum in Public Schools (NCBCPS).[39] In just a decade, this organization has worked closely with state legislatures and school districts to insinuate itself into school curricula. While NCBCPS-endorsed legislation takes a decidedly Christian fundamentalist approach to reintroducing the Bible, other curricula take a more intellectual approach like the *The Bible and Its Influence*, by the Bible Literacy project, which has been widely endorsed in many of the nation's local school systems. This curriculum takes a more scholarly approach to biblical literacy, as its goal is to help students become more biblically literate.[40]

NCBCPS-endorsed curricula appear to call for a particular, Protestant interpretation of the Bible. These curricula reject the idea that a textbook would be the most appropriate sourcebook for student learning. Instead the NCBCPS efforts advocate that the Bible be used as the sole curricular resource. Moreover, it proudly endorses the use of one specific bible translation for use in public school courses—the King James Version.[41] In a return to pre-twentieth-century conventions on truth and knowledge, the NCBCPS advocates that its religion curricula will be a return to teaching about the truth. To date there have been two lawsuits challenging the constitutionality of Bible curricula sponsored by the NCBCPS.[42]

INTELLECTUAL ADVOCACY

In contrast to the NCBCPS-supported biblical curricula is a Bible curriculum that is anchored by the Schippe and Stetston textbook—*The Bible and Its Influence* (2005). This text has earned the support of the nonprofit Bible Literacy Project and has been vetted and field tested by over forty-one scholars. The book also has the support of First Amendment advocate Charles Haynes and his well-funded First Amendment Center. The focus of the Schippe and Stetston textbook is on helping students develop a degree of religious literacy that will enable them to navigate a pluralist, democratic state. Those behind this textbook argue that a critical need of twenty-first-century citizens is the ability to understand the religious other.[43] Knowledge becomes a foundational requirement, then, in fostering tolerance, respect, and understanding. In contrast to the NCBCPS-backed curriculum, which has as its goal a "literal" reading of the King James Bible in order to promote a singular, particular right way of believing and behaving, those behind the dissemination of *The Bible and Its Influence* have as their goal the nurturing of religious knowledge and understanding.

Religious studies scholars like Stephen Prothero and Warren Nord have also argued from an intellectual standpoint for consideration of religion in public schools. [44] In much the same way as the Bible Literacy Project argues, they suggest that the Bible, and religion more generally, is a fundamental component of many people's individual and collective identities and that it is difficult not only to understand "the other" without also understanding this consequential part of their identity, but in terms of disciplinary knowledge, religious perspectives and experiences can enrich our disciplinary understandings. As an example, Nord discusses the discipline of economics and how its study benefits from considerations of religion. Since most current discussions of economics use a neoclassical economic framework, economic theory is often thought to be "value-free." Understanding religious points of view and how these impinge upon certain neo-classical assumptions can move economic discussions beyond considerations of "cost-benefit" analysis by looking at the role of conscience, tradition, and the effect economic activity has on the planet.[45]

ALTERNATIVE POLICIES

Recognizing the need to accommodate religious believers—particularly given the "neutrality principle" public schools have invoked—two policies to better meet the needs of religiously identified students have been pursued. The first is the widespread policy of parental "opt outs," though there is no constitutional right to these policies. The first record example of this practice was in 1843 in Philadelphia. Parents could "opt-out" of religious education for their children. The policies of these opt-outs still vary by district and state.[46] Opt-outs allow parents to exempt their children, without penalty, from a particular class or unit they find religiously objectionable.

For some, however, opt-outs are a mere stop gap to prevent their children from being exposed to curricular materials they find personally or religiously objectionable. For parents not satisfied with opt-outs, a more substantive option is Released Time. Many Evangelicals have embraced this policy. It is an arrangement through which students are excused from public schools, during regular hours, to participate in devotional lessons typically conducted by local religious organizations.

Originally conceived as part of an effort to bolster the teaching of morality in public schools without inflaming sectarian passions, the first released time program in the United States was established in Gary, Indiana, in 1914. The Gary Plan, through which pupils were "released" from public school supervision to the care of local religious leaders for instruction in their parents' religion, became a model for released time programs across the country. Interestingly, many Evangelical Protestant organizations originally opposed released time because they thought it encroached upon the parents' right to sole dominion over their children's religious education, that it undermined national unity by highlighting student differences, and that it impeded the assimilation of religious minorities into mainstream American society.[47] Since the Court's 1952 decision in *Zorach v. Clauson* when this practice of Released Time was upheld, religious classes held off public school premises, with parental permission, and without government aid have gained considerable popularity.[48]

Beginning in the 1980s, homeschooling became a more viable option for those parents who objected to any given tenet of the public schools. One of the largest groups to adopt an un-schooling option included those who did so for religious reasons.[49] Arguing that the public schools had grown untenably hostile to Christianity, the Bible, and religion generally, many Christians opted to exit the public school system and educate their children at home in a manner that was more consistent with their personal biblical principles.[50] This movement has enjoyed great popularity. Although today homeschooling is driven by a number of different motivations, many of which have nothing to do with religion, Evangelical Christians are still the largest group to exercise this form of school choice.[51]

CONCLUSION

The Bible's influence on American Education has shifted significantly since the nation's colonial period. Once seen as central to the democratic project, the Bible is now seen as one of the chief obstacles to realizing a version of American Democracy that values diversity, equality, tolerance, and respect. Not only are religion and the Bible too often viewed as inimical to realizing true democratic equality and tolerance, but an increasingly technologically advanced and globalized world seems also to rule out the explanatory power of the Bible as a relevant curricular tool. Yet one thing remains evident: as instability in the name of religion continues to persist across the globe, American students continue to demonstrate a high degree of religious illiteracy, leading to concerns of their inability to understand current geopolitical situations which often have religious inflections. While we are less sanguine that the Bible would be particularly beneficial in helping bridge this illiteracy gap, we suggest that a less hostile, more inviting, consideration of the role of religion in public life more generally could lead to more tolerance, understanding, and respect.

NOTES

1. Carl F. Kaestle, *Pillars of the Republic: Common Schools and American Society, 1780–1860* (New York: Hill and Wang, 1983).
2. Horace Mann, *Horace Mann on the Crisis in Education* (Yellow Springs, Ohio: Antioch Press, 1965); Joel H. Spring, *The Politics of American Education* (New York: Routledge, 2011); Benjamin Rush cited by Frederick Rudolph, *Essays on Education in the Early Republic* (Cambridge, Mass.: Harvard University Press, 1965).
3. Tracy L. Steffes, *School, Society, and State: A New Education to Govern Modern America, 1890–1940* (Chicago: University of Chicago Press, 2012).
4. John Dewey, *Democracy and Education: An Introduction to the Philosophy of Education* (New York: Free Press, 1966).

5. Richard A. Brosio, *Philosophical Scaffolding for the Construction of Critical Democratic Education* (New York: P. Lang, 2000).

6. John Dewey, *Experience and Education* (New York: Macmillan, 1938).

7. Kevin J. Burke and Avner Segall, "Christianity and Its Legacy in Education," *Journal of Curriculum Studies* 43, no. 5 (2011): 631–58; Steven Greene, *The Bible, the School, and the Constitution: The Clash that Shaped Modern Church-State Doctrine* (New York: Oxford University Press, 2012).

8. William Ayers et al., *Teaching Toward Democracy* (Boulder, Colo.: Paradigm Publishers, 2010).

9. Francis J. Bremer, *First Founders: American Puritans and Puritanism in an Atlantic World* (Durham, N.H.: University of New Hampshire Press, 2012).

10. [The Old Deluder Act] The Massachusetts Law of 1647, *Records of the Governor and Company of the Massachusetts Bay in New England* (Boston, 1853), 2:203, https://archive.org/stream/cu31924091024582#page/n221/mode/2up; Mark Noll, *In the Beginning Was the Word: The Bible in American Public Life, 1492–1783* (New York: Oxford University Press, 2015).

11. Burke Aaron Hinsdale, ed., *Horace Mann and the Common School Revival in the United States* (New York: Scribner's, 1898), https://archive.org/details/horacemanncommon00hins.

12. Paul Merrill Spurlin, *The French Enlightenment in America: Essays on the Times of the Founding Fathers* (Athens: University of Georgia Press, 1984).

13. Henry Farnham May, *The Enlightenment in America* (New York: Oxford University Press, 1976).

14. B. Edward McClellan, *Moral Education in America: Schools and the Shaping of Character from Colonial Times to the Present* (New York: Teachers College Press, 1999), 13.

15. Bernard Bailyn, *Education in the Forming of American Society: Needs and Opportunities for Study* (New York: Norton, 1972), 28.

16. Joel H. Spring, *The American School, 1642–1985: Varieties of Historical Interpretation of the Foundations and Development of American Education* (New York: Longman, 1986), 2.

17. Paul Leicester Ford, ed., *The New England Primer: A Reprint of the Earliest Known Edition, with Many Facsimiles and Reproductions, and an Historical Introduction* (New York: Dodd, Mead, 1899), 1, https://archive.org/details/newenglandprimer00fordiala.

18. Leonard Bleecker, "Twentieth Annual Report of the Trustees of the Free-School Society of New York," *American Journal of Education* 1, no. 8 (August 1826): 459–62.

19. Stephen Macedo, *Diversity and Distrust: Civic Education in a Multicultural Democracy* (Cambridge, Mass.: Harvard University Press, 2000), 47.

20. Macedo, *Diversity and Distrust*, 48.

21. Thomas Jefferson and William Harwood Peden, *Notes on the State of Virginia* (Chapel Hill: University of North Carolina Press, 1955).

22. Greene, *The Bible, the School*, 19.

23. James T. Sears and James C. Carper, *Curriculum, Religion, and Public Education: Conversations for an Enlarging Public Square* (New York: Teachers College Press, 1998), 25.

24. Horace Mann, *The Republic and the School: The Education of Free Men*, ed. Lawrence A. Cremin (New York: Teachers College, Columbia University, 1957), 124–25 (emphasis in original).

25. Warren A. Nord, *Religion & American Education: Rethinking a National Dilemma* (Chapel Hill: University of North Carolina Press, 1995).

26. Greene, *The Bible, the School*, 5.

27. Greene, *The Bible, the School*, 6.

28. Sidney Hook, *Education for Modern Man: A New Perspective*, new ed. (New York: Alfred A. Knopf, 1963), 115–16, https://archive.org/details/educationformode011641mbp.

29. James W. Fraser, *The School in the United States: A Documentary History* (Boston, Mass.: McGraw-Hill, 2001), 366; Herbert M. Kliebard, *Changing Course: American Curriculum Reform in the 20th Century* (New York: Teachers College Press, 2002).

30. R. Laurence Moore, "Bible Reading and Nonsectarian Schooling: The Failure of Religious Instruction in Nineteenth-Century Public Education," *Journal of American History* 86, no. 4 (2000): 1581–99.

31. Edward J. Larson, *Summer for the Gods: The Scopes Trial and America's Continuing Debate over Science and Religion* (New York: BasicBooks, 1997).

32. *Engel v. Vitale*, 370 U.S. 421 (1962).

33. *Abington School District v. Schempp*, 374 U.S. 203 (1963).

34. Melissa M. Deckman, *School Board Battles: The Christian Right in Local Politics* (Washington, D.C.: Georgetown University Press, 2004).

35. Deborah Zaberenko, "Tennessee Teacher Law Could Boost Creationism, Climate Denial," Reuters, April 13, 2012, http://reut.rs/HO91UL; Anthony Kirwin, "Toto, I've a Feeling We're Still in Kansas? The Constitutionality of Intelligent Design and the 2005 Kansas Science Education Standards," *Minnesota Journal of Law, Science & Technology* 7, no. 2 (2006): 657–712, http://scholarship.law.umn.edu/mjlst/vol7/iss2/10.

36. Larson, *Summer for the Gods*.

37. Michael B. Berkman and Eric Plutzer, *Evolution, Creationism, and the Battle to Control America's Classrooms* (New York: Cambridge University Press, 2010).

38. Kent Greenawalt, "The Enduring Significance of Neutral Principles," *Columbia Law Review* 78, no. 5 (1978): 982–1021.

39. Brenda Goodman, "Teaching the Bible in Georgia's Public Schools," *New York Times*, March 29, 2006.

40. Cullen Schippe and Chuck Stetson, *The Bible and Its Influence* (New York: BLP Publishing, 2006).

41. Mark A. Chancey, "A Textbook Example of the Christian Right: The National Council on Bible Curriculum in Public Schools," *Journal of the American Academy of Religion* 75, no. 3 (2007): 554–81.

42. American Civil Liberties Union, "Texas School Board Agrees to Stop Teaching Unconstitutional Bible Class in Public Schools," ACLU online. March 5, 2008, https://www.aclu.org/news/texas-school-board-agrees-stop-teaching-unconstitutional-bible-class-public-schools.

43. Bible Literacy Project, "About the Bible Literacy Project," http://www.bibleliteracy.org/Site/Case/.

44. Stephen R. Prothero, *Religious Literacy: What Every American Needs to Know—and Doesn't* (San Francisco, Calif.: HarperSanFrancisco, 2007); Warren A. Nord, *Does God Make a Difference? Taking Religion Seriously in our Schools and Universities* (New York: Oxford University Press, 2010).

45. Warren A. Nord and Charles C. Haynes, *Taking Religion Seriously across the Curriculum* (Nashville, Tenn.: ASCD, 1998), 106–9. Following 9/11, instances of Islamophobia prompted the widely vaunted Banks and Banks handbook of *Multicultural Education* (2006) to include religion (and Islam) for the first time. This was its 6th edition. James A.

Banks and Cherry A. McGee Banks, *Multicultural Education: Issues and Perspectives*, 6th ed. (Hoboken, N.J.: Wiley, 2006).

46. Tommy Kevin Rogers, "Parental Rights: Curriculum Opt-Outs in Public Schools" (PhD diss., University of North Texas, 2010), http://digital.library.unt.edu/ark:/67531/metadc30507.

47. Kenneth S. Volk, "The Gary Plan and Technology Education: What Might Have Been?," *Journal of Technology Studies* 31, no. 1-2 (2005): 43–46.

48. *Zorach v. Clauson*, 343 U.S. 306 (1952); Remalian M. Cocar, "Between a Righteous Citizenship and the Unfaith of the Family: The History of Released Time Religious Education in the United States" (PhD diss., Emory, 2011), http://pid.emory.edu/ark:/25593/bm61b.

49. Milton Gaither, *Homeschool: An American History* (New York: Palgrave Macmillan, 2008).

50. Lee Garth Vigilant, Lauren Wold Trefethren, and Tyler C. Anderson, "'You Can't Rely on Somebody Else to Teach Them Something They Don't Believe': Impressions of Legitimation Crisis and Socialization Control in the Narratives of Christian Homeschooling Fathers," *Humanity & Society* 37, no. 3 (2013): 201–24.

51. Dan Gilgoff, "As Homeschooling Surges, the Evangelical Share Drops," *US News and World Report*, January 9, 2009.

BIBLIOGRAPHY

Bailyn, Bernard. *Education in the Forming of American Society: Needs and Opportunities for Study*. New York: Norton, 1972.

Banks, James A., and Cherry A. McGee Banks. *Multicultural Education: Issues and Perspectives*. 6th ed. Hoboken, N.J.: Wiley, 2006.

Berkman, Michael B., and Eric Plutzer. *Evolution, Creationism, and the Battle to Control America's Classrooms*. New York: Cambridge University Press, 2010.

Brosio, Richard A. *Philosophical Scaffolding for the Construction of Critical Democratic Education*. New York: P. Lang, 2000.

Burke, Kevin J., and Avner Segall. "Christianity and Its Legacy in Education." *Journal of Curriculum Studies* 43, no. 5 (2011): 631–58.

Dewey, John. *Democracy and Education: An Introduction to the Philosophy of Education*. New York: Free Press, 1966.

———. *Experience and Education*. New York: Macmillan, 1938.

Ford, Paul Leicester, ed. *The New England Primer: A Reprint of the Earliest Known Edition, with Many Facsimiles and Reproductions, and an Historical Introduction*. New York: Dodd, Mead, 1899. https://archive.org/details/newenglandprimeroofordiala.

Fraser, James W. *The School in the United States: A Documentary History*. Boston, Mass.: McGraw-Hill, 2001.

Gaither, Milton. *Homeschool: An American History*. New York: Palgrave Macmillan, 2008.

Greene, Steven. *The Bible, the School, and the Constitution: The Clash that Shaped Modern Church-State Doctrine*. New York: Oxford University Press, 2012.

Hook, Sidney. *Education for Modern Man: A New Perspective*. New ed. New York: Alfred A. Knopf, 1963. https://archive.org/details/educationformodeo11641mbp.

Kaestle, Carl F. *Pillars of the Republic: Common Schools and American Society, 1780-1860*. New York: Hill and Wang, 1983.

Kliebard, Herbert M. *Changing Course: American Curriculum Reform in the 20th Century.* New York: Teachers College Press, 2002.

Larson, Edward J. *Summer for the Gods: The Scopes Trial and America's Continuing Debate over Science and Religion.* New York: BasicBooks, 1997.

Macedo, Stephen. *Diversity and Distrust: Civic Education in a Multicultural Democracy.* Cambridge, Mass.: Harvard University Press, 2000.

Mann, Horace. *Horace Mann on the Crisis in Education.* Yellow Springs, Ohio: Antioch Press, 1965.

———. *The Republic and the School: The Education of Free Men.* Edited by Lawrence A. Cremin. New York: Teachers College, Columbia University, 1957.

McClellan, B. Edward. *Moral Education in America: Schools and the Shaping of Character from Colonial Times to the Present.* New York: Teachers College Press, 1999.

Noll, Mark. *In the Beginning Was the Word: The Bible in American Public Life, 1492–1783.* New York: Oxford University Press, 2015.

Nord, Warren A. *Does God Make a Difference? Taking Religion Seriously in Our Schools and Universities.* New York: Oxford University Press, 2010.

Schippe, Cullen, and Chuck Stetson. *The Bible and Its Influence.* New York: BLP Publishing, 2006.

Sears, James T., and James C. Carper. *Curriculum, Religion, and Public Education: Conversations for an Enlarging Public Square.* New York: Teachers College Press, 1998.

Spring Joel H. *The American School, 1642–1985: Varieties of Historical Interpretation of the Foundations and Development of American Education.* New York: Longman, 1986.

———. *The Politics of American Education.* New York: Routledge, 2011.

Steffes, Tracy L. *School, Society, and State: A New Education to Govern Modern America, 1890–1940.* Chicago: University of Chicago Press, 2012.

CHAPTER 17

....

THE BIBLE
IN AMERICAN LAW

....

DANIEL L. DREISBACH

SINCE the first permanent settlements in British North America, Christianity and its sacred text, the Bible, have had a significant impact on American law. The first English colonists in both Virginia and New England brought with them the common law, a system of jurisprudence they had known in England. According to the most influential common law jurists, including William Blackstone and Lord Mansfield, Christianity is and always has been the foundation of the common law, and nothing in the common law is valid that is not consistent with divine revelation. Furthermore, Christianity and the Bible were often the explicit sources of early colonial charters and codes. When free to construct their own legal and political institutions, the New England colonists sought to establish Bible commonwealths and remake political society in conformity with God's laws as they understood them. They borrowed explicitly and extensively from biblical law, especially the laws of Moses. And lest there be any doubt, these codes often included references to specific biblical authority for legal provisions contained in them. The law that emerged in the colonies was a blend of common law, biblical law, and developing local customs.

What does it mean that the Bible influenced American law? It could mean a variety of things, including that the legal system was intentionally founded, in some sense, on the Bible (as is often said of common law), or that biblical values and principles informed the design and content of laws. Such a claim could mean that specific provisions in constitutions, legislation, judicial rulings, regulations, or public policies were influenced by biblical principles or practices, including provisions pertaining to Sunday or Sabbath observance, oaths, marriage and domestic relations, public prayer and Bible reading, religious proclamations, blasphemy, usury, and various sexual practices (e.g., adultery, fornication, incest, sodomy, and bestiality).

The Bible is implicated in American law in other ways. In the body of American case law, for example, there are numerous legal cases involving practices and beliefs that religious adherents contend are prescribed or proscribed by their biblical faith, including conscientious objection to military service, medical treatment (such as blood transfusions), saluting the flag, public displays of religious symbols and sacred texts, religiously mandated garb and grooming, interracial dating and marriage, proselytizing activities, abortion and contraception, polygamous and same-sexed marriage, and handling serpents and drinking poison. Furthermore, advocates have appealed explicitly to the Bible to support or oppose a variety of laws and public policies. On some topics, such as resistance to civil authority, slavery, and immigration, opponents have appealed to the same Bible in support of their respective positions.

The architects of the American legal tradition that emerged in the colonial era and was refined in the founding era looked to the Bible and Christian tradition for general political and legal concepts that they sought to incorporate into their constitutional regimes. They saw in Mosaic law, for example, affirmation of the rule of law and republican government (see Exod. 18:13-27; Deut. 1:9-18). The principles of due process of law (procedural fairness and equality of all persons before the law), explicitly guaranteed in the Fifth and Fourteenth Amendments to the United States Constitution, are sprinkled throughout the laws of Moses, most especially in Exodus 23:1-3, 6-9, which has been called the Decalogue of Due Process (see also Lev. 19:15; Deut. 1:16-17, 16:19-20). Some saw in the form of government described in Deuteronomy 16:18 to 18:22 a separation of powers among the offices of judge, king, priest, and prophet. These brief examples illustrate a few of the many interactions between Christianity and law in American legal culture.

A number of intellectual, legal, and political traditions and perspectives have informed American law and politics. Among the influences scholars have identified and studied are Hebraic, republican (classical and civic), Enlightenment, and the English constitutional tradition. Often overlooked in the scholarship is the role of religion—specifically Christianity—in shaping the American legal system and jurisprudential thought. The Bible had a profound impact on colonial and early national laws and traditions. It is clear, however, that even before the adoption of the US Constitution, influential jurists and jurisprudential perspectives of a significantly secular and at times antagonistic stance toward Christianity began to emerge. These jurists and jurisprudential schools of thought were increasingly in tension with legal perspectives in harmony with traditional Christian thought. By the early nineteenth century and continuing into the present day, increasingly secular and separationist perspectives have challenged the propriety, legitimacy, and constitutionality of lingering biblical influences on law and politics. Thomas Jefferson, for example, disputed the ancient maxim that Christianity was the basis of common law. Also, biblically informed laws regarding Sabbath observance, blasphemy, and, in the twentieth century, the teaching of creation in public schools, were challenged through legislation and litigation. The Bible's influence on law was strongest in the colonial era, but it continued to exert influence in the founding era and the centuries that followed, albeit to a diminishing extent as other, secular jurisprudential perspectives emerged and exerted influence on the legal culture.

This chapter considers the Bible's place in American law, starting with an examination of the Bible's influence on colonial laws crafted in the New World. This is followed by a brief reflection on ways in which the Bible may have informed an emerging constitutional tradition, culminating in the framing of the nation's Constitution of 1787. Attention is then turned to nineteenth- and twentieth-century challenges to vestiges of the Bible's influence on American law as notions of church-state separation and secular perspectives gained ascendancy in public culture. Among the specific controversies briefly mentioned are Thomas Jefferson's rejection of the claim that Christianity was the basis of common law, challenges to Sunday laws designed to preserve the sanctity of the Christian Sabbath, prosecutions for blasphemy, and disputes over teaching creation and evolution in public schools. The chapter's focus on the Bible's influence is not intended to discount, much less dismiss, other sources of influence or schools of thought that shaped American jurisprudence. Rather, casting a light on the Bible's often neglected, yet important, place in legal culture provides a more complete picture of the ideas that informed American law.

THE BIBLE IN THE LAWS OF THE COLONIAL
AND FOUNDING PERIODS

The Bible, especially the laws of Moses, exerted much influence on early colonial law. "Our ancestors" revered the Bible "and endeavored to enact their laws in accordance with it," said Jeremiah Atwater, the president of Middlebury College, in an early nineteenth-century Vermont election sermon.[1] In an 1802 charge to a Massachusetts grand jury, Judge Nathaniel Freeman expressed the deference many in the new nation continued to accord biblical law: "The laws of that system . . . must be respected as of high authority in all our courts. And it cannot be thought improper for the officers of [our] government to acknowledge their obligation to be governed by its rules."[2] The New England Puritans, especially, looked to biblical sources for their laws because they feared that reliance on the mind of man to craft laws—given man's fallen nature—would unavoidably produce corrupted legal codes. The Puritan divine John Cotton wrote in a precursor document to the Massachusetts "Body of Liberties" that "the more any Law smells of man the more unprofitable."[3] Therefore, the only source of proper law, free from the taint of fallen man, was "divine ordinances, revealed in the pages of Holy Writ and administered according to deductions and rules gathered from the Word of God."[4] Moreover, the Bible was a "unifying force" in the law insofar as it "commanded ultimate loyalty and juridical respect" from a Bible-loving people.[5]

The first English settlers in New England were engaged in building Bible commonwealths; accordingly, they looked to the Bible in establishing political and legal institutions. The Bible was often the explicit source of early colonial laws, and colonial judges frequently cited scripture as legal authority. To be sure, the colonists did not enact all aspects of biblical law, and the Bible was not the sole source of their laws, but it was a vital, authoritative source of law in their new political communities. The biblical laws adopted in New England, it should be further noted, "were often enforced after filtration through colonial legislation, common law, or colonial judicial interpretations."[6]

The first charters and constitutions written in New England were explicitly founded on the Word of God. When colonists convened in 1639 to frame the "Fundamental Articles for the Colony of New Haven," the first question they posed was "Whether the Scriptur[e]s doe holde forth a perfect rule for the direction and government of all men in all duet[ies] which they are to performe to God and men as well in the government of famyles and commonwealths as in matters of the chur[ch]." "This was assented unto by all, no man dissenting as was expressed by holding up of hands," according to the report in the Articles.[7] The New Haven colonists agreed "thatt the worde of God shall be the onely rule to be attended unto in ordering the affayres of gouernment in this plantatio[n]."[8] The "Fundamental Orders of Connecticut" (1639), arguably the first written constitution in North America, declared that a governor and his council "shall haue power to administer iustice according to the Lawes here established, and for want thereof according to the rule of the word of God."[9] The

"Massachusetts Body of Liberties" of 1641, sometimes described as the first bill of rights in North America, sets forth "the word of god" as a standard of law.¹⁰ The document further stated that "no custome or prescription shall ever prevaile amongst us in any morall cause, our meaneing is maintaine anythinge that can be proved to bee morallie sinfull by the word of god."¹¹

These early colonists, the late Librarian of Congress Daniel J. Boorstin wrote, looked to the Bible as their guide because through it, they explained, "every man could find the design of life and the shape of the Truth."¹² Historians have long debated the relationship between the colonial codes deliberately based on "the Lawes of God" and the common law the colonists brought with them from the Old World.¹³ As Boorstin observed, "scholarly dispute as to whether early New England law was primarily scriptural or primarily English is beside the point. For early New Englanders these two turned out to be pretty much the same." These pious settlers believed biblical law and English law were in substantial harmony.¹⁴ "They were trying, for the most part, to demonstrate the coincidence between what the scriptures required and what English law had already provided."¹⁵

The scriptures contain legal codes. The Ten Commandments, or Decalogue, is the best known of these codes (Exod. 20:3-17; Deut. 5:7-21), and early colonists apparently framed their codes with a copy of the Ten Commandments before them. The Puritans, however, were not alone among early colonists in their attraction to these biblical passages. Even before the Pilgrims and Puritans set foot on New England's rocky coasts, the Virginians wove the laws of Moses into their "Articles, Lawes, and Orders, Divine, Politique, and Martiall for the Colony in Virginea" (1610-11). Like the legal codes subsequently framed in Puritan commonwealths to the north, it bore the unmistakable influence of the Ten Commandments. It prohibited speaking "impiously or maliciously" against God or the faith, blaspheming God's "holy name," deriding or defying God's "holy word," Sabbath breaking, murdering, bearing false witness, and committing adultery and other sexual sins.¹⁶ The Bible similarly informed early codes in New England. The "Massachusetts Body of Liberties" (1641) borrowed from Mosaic law even more explicitly than Virginia's law, mandating the death penalty for "worship[ping] any other god, but the lord god"; "Blasphem[ing] the name of God, the father, Sonne, or Holie ghost"; witchcraft; murder; rape; adultery; and other sexual sins forbidden in Mosaic law.¹⁷ In short, every commandment in the Decalogue can be found in one of the colonial legal codes. To confirm the source of the law, legal draftsmen often included references to specific biblical authority for provisions in the codes.

Notwithstanding the emergence of Enlightenment influences in the eighteenth century, many important figures in the founding era retained a profound respect for biblical law and its relevance to their legal culture. Significantly, the United States Constitution of 1787 included provisions that were familiar to a Bible-reading people. The Judeo-Christian concept of covenant arguably informed ideas of compact, contract, and constitutionalism. A governmental structure defined by the separation of powers and checks and balances has struck many commentators as an acknowledgment of original sin and the necessity to check the powers exercised by fallen humans.¹⁸ Many in the founding generation, like the New England Puritans, believed that the Hebrew commonwealth described in the Old Testament provided a divinely inspired model for republican government (see Article IV, § 4, cl. 1: "guarantee to every State . . . a Republican Form of Government"). They saw in passages chronicling the experiences of the Hebrew polity support for the notions of consent of the governed and representative government (see Judg. 11:8-11; 1 Chron. 28:1-8).

The Constitution included specific provisions that were almost certainly derived from the Bible and Christian doctrine. The Constitution's oath requirements found in Article 1, § 3, cl. 6; Article II, § 1, cl. 8; Article VI, cl. 3; and Amendment IV entailed a profoundly religious act. Moral philosophers and constitutional architects in the founding era—and well into the nineteenth century—typically defined an oath as a solemn appeal to the Supreme Being for the truth of what is said, by a person who believes in the existence of a Supreme Being, and in a future state of rewards and punishments, according to that form which will bind his conscience most.[19] The Article I, § 7, cl. 2 provision excepting Sundays from the ten days within which a president must veto a bill is an implicit recognition of the Christian Sabbath, commemorating the Creator's sanctification of the seventh day for rest (Gen. 2:1-3), the fourth commandment that the Sabbath be kept free from secular defilement (Exod. 20:8-11, 31:12-17), and, in the Christian dispensation, the resurrection of Jesus Christ from the dead (Matt. 28:1-8; Mark 16:1-8; Luke 24:1-10; see also John 20:1-8). The Article III, § 3, cl. 1 requirement that convictions for treason be supported by "the testimony of two witnesses" conforms to a familiar biblical mandate for conviction and punishment (see Deut. 17:6).[20] For one final example, a maxim of canon law that no man ought to be punished twice for the same offence has been attributed to a fourth-century commentary by Saint Jerome on Nahum 1:9 ("affliction shall not rise up the second time"). From these origins, the principle forbidding a defendant from being tried twice for the same offence entered into canon law and English customary law and was transferred to American colonial law and early state declarations of rights before it was ultimately enshrined in the Fifth Amendment to the US Constitution.[21]

These examples illustrate ways in which biblical law was consistent with and likely influenced the content of the American Constitution. Additional examples could be provided. There is no doubt that Christianity and the Bible informed canon law, civil law, English common law, and the legal traditions crafted by the early colonists. It would be surprising, indeed, if the framers of the Constitution of 1787 were ignorant of this influence or adopted some of these constitutional concepts but wholly disavowed their religious origins. One might argue, of course, that America's founders embraced these legal and political ideas but concluded that their source was neither the Bible nor Christianity. Many of these constitutional concepts found similar expression outside of and apart from the biblical tradition, and, as previously noted, the founders were influenced by a variety of traditions. Tracing the sources of influence can be complicated, but a cursory review of the American constitutional tradition suggests that, at a minimum, Christianity and the Bible had a discernible influence on it.

CHALLENGING BIBLICAL INFLUENCES ON AMERICAN LEGAL CULTURE

Notwithstanding Christianity's expansive influence on the culture and the Bible's lingering influence on municipal law and constitutional tradition, a variety of church-state separationist, rationalist, and secularist individuals and groups in the nineteenth century began to challenge biblical influences on the legal culture. Laws lacking a legitimate secular purpose, critics contended, cannot pass constitutional muster. These challenges, with vary-ing degrees of success, have continued to the present, greatly diminishing the Bible's influ-ence on American law.

A fundamental and enduring question pertaining to the Bible's influence on Anglo-American jurisprudence is whether Christianity is the basis of the common law. As distin-guished from statutory or civil law, the common law comprises the body of laws derived from principles, rules of action, customs, and prior decisions of judicial tribunals. The prin-cipal rule of common law is adherence to legal precedent or *stare decisis* (Latin for "to stand by the decision"), which requires judges to adhere to legal principles set forth in prior cases (precedents). With its profound implications for the relationship between Christianity and law, this question engaged leading intellectuals of the late eighteenth and early nineteenth centuries. A popular, but not unchallenged, notion was that, insofar as the US Constitution accredited the common law, the American people incorporated Christianity into their organic law upon ratification of the Constitution. Throughout his life, but most famously in a posthumously published essay, Jefferson disputed Christianity's seminal contributions to common law, boldly asserting "that Christianity neither is, nor ever was, a part of the com-mon law."[22] In his inaugural lecture as Harvard's Dane Professor of Law, Associate Justice of the US Supreme Court Joseph Story countered that "there never has been a period in which the common law did not recognize Christianity as lying at its foundations."[23] Both sides understood that this debate was fundamentally about whether the laws of civil society are strictly positivistic or whether they are derived from transcendent sources.[24]

Religious traditionalists complained bitterly that Jefferson gave legitimacy to a dis-credited legal theory and, thereby, accelerated the secularization of law and policy by giv-ing plausible grounds to eschew public prayers, fast-day proclamations, religious oaths, Sabbath day observances, and other manifestations of a Christian nation. Jefferson's crit-ics scrutinized constitutional, statutory, and case law, as well as learned treatises on the subject, affirming that in adopting the common law of England, the American people had made Christianity part of their fundamental law. They cited with approval New York Judge James Kent's precedent-setting opinion in the blasphemy case of *People v. Ruggles* (1811) and the influential opinion of the Pennsylvania Supreme Court in *Updegraph v. Commonwealth* (1824). These and many other cases affirmed the proposition that general Christianity is and always has been a part of the common law.[25]

Another controversy in the early republic that raised questions about the relationship between the Bible and law concerned the transportation and delivery of mail on Sundays. Ancient legal restraints on Sunday commerce, which featured prominently in American law, were rooted in the notion that God rested following creation and the commandment to keep the Lord's Day holy. On April 30, 1810, the US Congress adopted a statute requir-ing postmasters "at all reasonable hours, on every day of the week, to deliver, on demand, any letter, paper or packet, to the person entitled to or authorized to receive the same."[26] Before passage of this legislation, no uniform policy or practice governed Sunday business in the nation's post offices. The statute set off an avalanche of protests and petitions from a multitude of religious leaders, denominations, and citizens' committees demanding legisla-tion discontinuing Sunday postal operations. Critics viewed this legislation as the first con-gressional enactment requiring a violation of a biblical command and Christian custom.[27] Petitions were generally referred to the postmaster general. Congress, however, was eventu-ally moved to report on the issue. In 1815, both the Senate and the House of Representatives resolved that it would be "inexpedient" to grant the prayer of the petitioners to prohibit postal services on Sunday.[28]

The controversy subsided for a decade and then exploded in the late 1820s. In March 1825, Congress enacted legislation reaffirming postal obligations spelled out in the 1810 law.[29] Once again, Congress was inundated with petitions and counter-petitions revealing strong sentiment on all sides of the issue.[30] On June 19, 1829, Senator Richard M. Johnson of Kentucky, chairman of the Senate Committee on Post Offices and Post Roads, released a report setting forth fundamental reasons why it would be inappropriate for the US government to yield to demands of religious traditionalists to disallow Sunday mail. Senator Johnson, who later served as vice president of the United States (1837-41), argued that proposed legislation to stop the mail on Sunday "was improper, and that nine hundred and ninety-nine in a thousand were opposed to any legislative interference, inasmuch as it would have a tendency to unite religious institutions with the Government." He further opined "that these petitions and memorials in relation to Sunday mails, were but the entering wedge of a scheme to make this Government a religious instead of a social and political institution."[31] The report provoked lively debate in congressional chambers. To supporters, it affirmed the principle of church-state separation. To detractors, it confirmed the triumph of political atheism and secularism. Representative William McCreery of Pennsylvania drafted a House minority report, released on March 5, 1830: "All Christian nations acknowledge the first day of the week, to be the Sabbath," he wrote. "Almost every State in this Union has, by positive legislation, not only recognized this day as sacred, but has forbidden its profanation under penalties imposed by law."[32] Senator Johnson's view ultimately prevailed, and the campaign to prevent the Sunday mail failed.[33]

The Sunday mail controversy was only one skirmish in a larger conflict over the propriety and constitutionality of Sunday laws. Although religious traditionalists failed to end Sunday mail service, Sunday laws, also known as blue laws, prohibiting or restricting a variety of activities on Sunday, such as commercial transactions, secular employment, and recreational pursuits, remained a feature on the legal landscape.[34] Since the first half of the nineteenth century, these laws have been challenged by, among others, workingmen, free-thinkers, Jews, and Christian Seventh-day Sabbatarians. In 1833, for example, a South Carolina judge upheld an ordinance requiring shops to close on Sundays when two merchants, an avowed infidel and a Jew, contended that the law violated both federal and state constitutional protections for religious liberty.[35] While acknowledging the Christian origins of blue laws, in 1961 the US Supreme Court upheld a state Sunday closing law, arguing that the "present purpose and effect" of the law served the legitimate secular interest of providing "a uniform day of rest for all citizens."[36]

In the first half of the nineteenth century, there were several widely publicized prosecutions for blasphemy. In the Western legal tradition, blasphemy laws, which typically proscribed exposing God, the Christian religion, or the Bible to calumny, contempt, ridicule, or vilification, are rooted in part in biblical injunctions against defiling God's name. A blasphemy conviction for a defendant who said "*Jesus Christ* was a bastard, and his mother must be a whore," was upheld by New York's highest court in 1811. Writing for the Court in *People v. Ruggles*, Chief Justice James Kent, implicitly affirming Christianity's favored position in the law, wrote that such words are "punishable because they strike at the root of moral obligation, and weaken the security of the social ties."[37] This was followed by similar cases in Pennsylvania, Delaware, and Massachusetts.[38] Although blasphemy laws survived well into the twentieth century, these cases served notice that laws widely viewed as rooted in biblical precepts would be challenged in an increasingly secular polity committed to church-state separation. By the mid-twentieth century, a growing number of state and federal courts were declaring traditional state blasphemy laws to be unconstitutional.

Another controversy with implications for the Bible in American law is the teaching of divine creation in public schools. In the 1925 case popularly known as the "Scopes Monkey Trial," a Tennessee high school teacher, John T. Scopes, was convicted of violating a state law that forbade teaching "any theory that denies the story of the Divine Creation of man as taught in the Bible, and to teach instead that man has descended from a lower order of animals."[39] This case was followed by a wave of litigation in state and federal courts raising diverse issues related to the teaching of origins. In 1968, the US Supreme Court weighed in, holding that a state law that forbade teaching evolution, while allowing teaching creation, violated the Constitution's prohibition on the establishment of religion.[40] In 1987, the Court struck down a state law requiring public schools to give "equal time" to "alternative theories" of origins as a violation of the First Amendment because its purpose was "*either* to promote the theory of creation science which embodies a particular religious tenet . . . *or* to prohibit the teaching of a scientific theory disfavored by certain religious sects."[41]

A variety of other controversies involving the Bible in American law have emerged in the twentieth and twenty-first centuries. Although judges since colonial times have cited the Bible in their opinions,[42] in recent decades objections have been raised when judges, prosecutors, and deliberating jurors have invoked the Bible as authority. In a growing number of reported criminal cases, appellate courts have ruled that appeals to the Bible are inadmissible and have even set aside convictions where such invocations may have impacted the outcome of a case.[43] The concern is that references to the sacred text will have a prejudicial impact on those in the judicial system who regard the Bible as divine authority, and such appeals to the Bible constitute an "establishment of religion" in violation of the First Amendment.

CONCLUSION

The Bible has long featured prominently in American law. This is of little surprise given that the common law, which the colonists brought with them from England, bore evidence of Christian influences and that several colonies were established as Bible commonwealths and their laws drew extensively on biblical law as the colonists understood it and adapted it to their time and place. Christianity's influence on the culture and law, however, has waned over time. Biblical laws that were uncontested in the seventeenth century began to be questioned by some rationalists in the eighteenth century and legally and politically challenged in the nineteenth and twentieth centuries as secular and separationist perspectives in law and policy gained ascendancy. That said, vestiges of biblical influence on the law remain a part of the legal culture in the twenty-first century. Many explicitly biblical influences on the law, however, have been stripped from legal codes as unconstitutional establishments of religion, and only those laws that can be justified in secular terms have survived into the twenty-first century.

NOTES

1. Jeremiah Atwater, *A Sermon, Preached before His Excellency Isaac Tichenor, Esq. Governour, the Honorable the Council and House of Representatives of the State of Vermont, at Burlington, on the Day of the Anniversary Election, October 14, 1802* (Middlebury, Vt.: Huntington & Fitch, for Anthony Haswell, 1802), 16.

2. Nathaniel Freeman, *A Charge to the Grand Jury, at the Court of General Sessions of the Peace, holden at Barnstable, within and for the county of Barnstable, March term, A.D. 1802* (Boston, Mass.: Manning & Loring, 1802), 7.

3. John Cotton, "How Far Moses Judicialls Bind Mass[achusetts]," in Worthington Chauncey Ford, *John Cotton's Moses His Judicialls and Abstract of the Laws of New England* (Cambridge, Mass.: John Wilson and Son, 1902), 15.

4. John D. Cushing, introduction to *The Laws and Liberties of Massachusetts, 1641-1691: A Facsimile Edition, Containing also Council Orders and Executive Proclamations*, vol. 1 (Wilmington, Del.: Scholarly Resources, 1976), xvi.

5. John W. Welch, "Biblical Law in America: Historical Perspectives and Potentials for Reform," *Brigham Young University Law Review* 2002, no. 3 (2002): 635, http://digitalcommons.law.byu.edu/lawreview/vol2002/iss3/1.

6. Patrick M. O'Neil, "Bible in American Law," in *Religion and American Law: An Encyclopedia*, ed. Paul Finkelman (New York: Garland Publishing, 2000), 30.

7. "Fundamental Articles of New Haven" (1639), in *Colonial Origins of the American Constitution: A Documentary History*, ed. Donald S. Lutz (Indianapolis, Ind.: Liberty Fund, 1998), 222.

8. Charles J. Hoadly, ed., *Records of the Colony and Plantation of New Haven, from 1638 to 1649* (Hartford, Conn.: Case, Tiffany, 1857), 21.

9. "Fundamental Orders of Connecticut" (1639), in Lutz, *Colonial Origins*, 211.

10. "Massachusetts Body of Liberties" (1641), in Lutz, *Colonial Origins*, 71; see the same language in "Connecticut Code of Laws" (1650), in Lutz, *Colonial Origins*, 242.

11. "Massachusetts Body of Liberties" (1641), in Lutz, *Colonial Origins*, 79.

12. Daniel J. Boorstin, *The Americans: The Colonial Experience* (New York: Random House, 1958), 18.

13. "The Laws and Liberties of Massachusetts" (1647), in Lutz, *Colonial Origins*, 99.

14. Boorstin noted that the New England Puritans made some revisions to English law that aligned colonial laws more closely with Mosaic law. "The most dramatic and most obvious [changes the Puritans made to English law] were in the list of capital crimes. To those crimes punishable by death under the laws of England, the colonists by 1648 had added a number of others, including idolatry (violations of the First Commandment), blasphemy, man-stealing (from Exod. 21.16), adultery with a married woman, perjury with intent to secure the death of another, the cursing of a parent by a child over 16 years of age (Exod. 21.17), the offense of being a 'rebellious son' (Deut. 21.20.21), and the third offense of burglary or highway robbery. These were clear cases where the laws of scripture were allowed to override the laws of England." Boorstin, *The Americans*, 28.

15. Boorstin, *The Americans*, 24. See also William Blackstone, *Commentaries on the Laws of England*, vol. 1 (Oxford: Clarendon Press, 1765), 42 ("no human laws should be suffered to contradict" the "revealed or divine law" found in the "holy scriptures.").

16. "Articles, Lawes, and Orders, Divine, Politique, and Martiall for the Colony in Virginea" (1610, 1611), in Lutz, *Colonial Origins*, 315–18.

17. "Massachusetts Body of Liberties" (1641), in Lutz, *Colonial Origins*, 83–84.

18. Because men are not angels, James Madison famously counseled in *The Federalist No. 51*, "ambition must be made to counteract ambition," in *The Federalist* (Gideon Ed.), ed. George W. Carey and James McClellan (Indianapolis, Ind.: Liberty Fund, 2001), 268, http://oll.libertyfund.org/titles/788. Although this is the most famous passage, it is certainly not the only passage in *The Federalist Papers* that addresses humankind's fallen nature. See the warning in Number 6: do not forget "that men are ambitio[u]s, vindictive, and rapacious." *The Federalist No. 6*, 21. See also *The Federalist No. 15*, 73, 74; *The Federalist No. 24*, 119; *The Federalist No. 37*, 185. It should be acknowledged that various political traditions recognize the fallibility of human actors, but the tradition that most influenced Americans of the founding era on this point was Reformed Protestantism.

19. This standard definition of an oath was repeated in the debates on Article VI of the US Constitution in the state ratifying conventions. See, for example, the July 30, 1788, speech of Judge James Iredell (N.C.), in Jonathan Elliot, ed., *The Debates in the Several State Conventions on the Adoption of the Federal Constitution*, 2nd ed. (Washington, D.C.: Printed for the editor, 1836), 4:196. See also "Kentucky Constitution of 1792," art. VIII, § 5; and "Kentucky Constitution of 1799," art. VI, § 7, *Text of Kentucky Constitutions of 1792, 1799 and 1850* (Frankfort, Ky.: Legislative Research Commission, 1965). Virtually every late eighteenth-century moral philosopher defined oaths in similar terms. See, for example, John Witherspoon, "Of Oaths and Vows," in *Lectures on Moral Philosophy*, ed. Varnum Lansing Collins (Princeton, N.J.: Princeton University Press, 1912), 130.

20. Cf. Deuteronomy 19:15; Numbers 35:30; see also Matthew 18:16; John 8:17; 2 Corinthians 13:1; 1 Timothy 5:19; Hebrew 10:28.

21. See Jay A. Sigler, "A History of Double Jeopardy," *American Journal of Legal History* 7, no. 4 (1963): 284; *Bartkus v. Illinois*, 359 U.S. 121, 152 n. 4 (1959) (Black, J., dissenting).

22. Thomas Jefferson, "Whether Christianity Is a Part of the Common Law?," in *Reports of Cases Determined in the General Court of Virginia. From 1730, to 1740; and From 1768, to 1772* (Charlottesville, Va.: F. Carr, 1829), 140.

23. Joseph Story, "The Value and Importance of Legal Studies: A Discourse Pronounced at the Inauguration of the Author as Dane Professor of Law in Harvard University, August 25, 1829," in *The Miscellaneous Writings of Joseph Story*, ed. William W. Story (Boston, Mass.: Charles C. Little and James Brown, 1851), 517.

24. See generally Stuart Banner, "When Christianity Was Part of the Common Law," *Law and History Review* 16 (1998): 27–62; Bradley S. Chilton, "Cliobernetics, Christianity, and the Common Law," *Law Library Journal* 83 (1991): 355–62; Courtney Kenny, "The Evolution of the Law of Blasphemy," *Cambridge Law Journal* 1, no. 2 (1922): 127–42; and James R. Stoner Jr., "Christianity, the Common Law, and the Constitution," in *Vital Remnants: America's Founding and the Western Tradition*, ed. Gary L. Gregg II (Wilmington, Del.: ISI Books, 1999), 175–209.

25. See *People v. Ruggles*, 8 Johnson 290, 294–97 (N.Y. 1811); *Updegraph v. Commonwealth*, 11 Sergeant & Rawle 394, 399–400 (Pa. 1824).

26. "An Act Regulating the Post-Office Establishment," *Statutes at Large*, vol. 2, sec. 9, 592, at 595 (April 30, 1810).

27. See Jasper Adams, *The Relation of Christianity to Civil Government in the United States*, 2nd ed. (Charleston, S.C.: A. E. Miller, 1833), 33–34, note D.

28. William Addison Blakely, ed., *American State Papers Bearing on Sunday Legislation*, rev. ed. (Washington, D.C.: Religious Liberty Association, 1911), 182–86.

29. "An Act to reduce into one the several acts establishing and regulating the Post-office Department," *Statutes at Large*, vol. 4, sec. 11, 102, at 105 (March 3, 1825).

30. A House committee report on the issue commented: "It is believed that the history of legislation in this country affords no instance in which a stronger expression has been made, if regard be had to the numbers, the wealth or the intelligence of the petitioners." US Congress, House, *Report from the Committee on the Post Office and Post Roads*, 20th Cong., 2nd sess., House Rep. no. 65 (February 3, 1829); reprinted in *American State Papers. Documents, Legislative and Executive, of the Congress of the United States*, Class VII, *Post Office Department* (Washington, D.C.: Gales and Seaton, 1834), 212.

31. US Congress, Senate, 20th Cong., 2nd sess., *Register of Debates in Congress* (January 19, 1829), vol. 5, 42. See also US Congress, Senate, *Report on Stopping the United States Mail, and closing the Post-offices on Sunday, January 19, 1829*, 20th Cong., 2nd sess., Senate Doc. No. 46 (January 19, 1829); reprinted in *American State Papers*, Class VII, 211–12.

32. US Congress, House, *Report of the Minority of the Committee on Post Offices and Post Roads, to whom the memorials were referred for prohibiting the transportation of the Mails, and the opening of Post Offices, on Sundays*, 21st Cong., 1st sess., House Rept. no. 271 (March 5, 1830); reprinted in *American State Papers*, Class VII, 231.

33. It was not until 1912 that Congress enacted legislation closing post offices for most services on Sundays. "An Act Making Appropriations for the Service of the Post Office Department," *Statutes at Large*, vol. 37, 539 at 543 (August 24, 1912). For further discussion on the Sunday mail controversy, see Wayne E. Fuller, *Morality and the Mail in Nineteenth-Century America* (Urbana and Chicago: University of Illinois Press, 2003); Harmon Kingsbury, *The Sabbath: A Brief History of Laws, Petitions, Remonstrances and Reports, with Facts and Arguments, Relating to the Christian Sabbath* (New York, 1840); Richard R. John, "Taking Sabbatarianism Seriously: The Postal System, the Sabbath, and the Transformation of American Political Culture," *Journal of the Early Republic* 10, no. 4 (1990): 517–67; and James R. Rohrer, "Sunday Mails and the Church-State Theme in Jacksonian America," *Journal of the Early Republic* 7, no. 1 (1987): 53–74.

34. See David N. Laband and Deborah Hendry Heinbuch, *Blue Laws: The History, Economics, and Politics of Sunday-Closing Laws* (Lexington, Mass.: Lexington Books, 1987).

35. *Town Council of Columbia v. C.O. Duke and Alexander Marks*, 2 Strobhart 530 (S.C. 1833).

36. *McGowan v. Maryland*, 366 U.S. 420, 445 (1961).

37. *Ruggles*, 8 Johnson at 292, 296.

38. See *Updegraph*, 11 Sergeant & Rawle 394; *State v. Chandler*, 2 Del. (2 Harrington) 553 (1837); *Commonwealth v. Kneeland*, 37 Mass. (20 Pickering) 206 (1838).

39. Tenn. Pub. Acts 1925, ch. 27, § 1.

40. *Epperson v. Arkansas*, 393 U.S. 97 (1968).

41. *Edwards v. Aguillard*, 482 U.S. 578, 593 (1987) (Emphasis in original).

42. See Daniel G. Ashburn, "Appealing to a Higher Authority?: Jewish Law in American Judicial Opinions," *University of Detroit Mercy Law Review* 71 (1994): 295–352; J. Michael Medina, "The Bible Annotated: Use of the Bible in Reported American Decisions," *Northern Illinois University Law Review* 12 (1991): 187–254; Bernard J. Meislin, "The Role of the Ten Commandments in American Judicial Decisions," in *Jewish Law and Current Legal Problems*, ed. Nahum Rakover (Jerusalem: Library of Jewish Law, 1984), 109–20; Sanja Zgonjanin, "Quoting the Bible: The Use of Religious References in Judicial Decision-Making," *New York City Law Review* 9 (2005): 31–91.

43. A growing number of state and federal courts have considered the propriety of prosecutors referencing the Bible in arguments before juries, especially in closing arguments and in capital sentencing proceedings, and juries consulting the Bible in their deliberations. Although these cases often turn on facts specific to the case, the trend would seem to disallow prosecutorial references to biblical authority and the use of the Bible in jury deliberations. See, for example, *Roybal v. Davis*, 148 F. Supp. 3d 958, 1043–52 (S.D. Cal. 2015) ("It is well settled that biblical law has no proper role in the sentencing process" and the "prosecutor's reference to biblical authority was clear misconduct"). For legal analyses of these practices, see Courtney Rachel Baron, "An Eye for an Eye Leaves Everyone Blind: *Fields v. Brown* and the Case for Keeping the Bible Out of Capital Sentencing Deliberations," *Northwestern University Law Review* 103 (2009): 369–99, John H. Blume and Sheri Lynn Johnson, "Don't Take His Eye, Don't Take His Tooth, and Don't Cast the First Stone: Limiting Religious Arguments in Capital Cases," *William & Mary Bill of Rights Journal* 9 (2000): 61–104; "Capital Sentencing—Juror Prejudice—Colorado Supreme Court Holds Presence of Bible in Jury Room Prejudicial. — *People v. Harlan*, 109 P.3d 616 (Colo.), *cert. denied*, 126 S. Ct. 399 (2005)," *Harvard Law Review* 119 (2005): 646–53; Terrence T. Egland, "Prejudiced by the Presence of God: Keeping Religious Material Out of Death Penalty Deliberations," *Capital Defense Journal* 16 (2004): 337–66; Marcus S. Henson, "*Carruthers v. State*: Thou Shalt Not Make Direct Religious References in Closing Argument," *Mercer Law Review* 52 (2001): 731–44; Monica K. Miller, Joseph Dimitrov, Brian H. Bornstein, and Ashley Zarker-Sorensen, "Bibles in the Jury Room: Psychological Theories Question Judicial Assumptions," *Ohio Northern University Law Review* 39 (2013): 579–625; Gary J. Simson and Stephen P. Garvey, "Knockin' on Heaven's Door: Rethinking the Role of Religion in Death Penalty Cases," *Cornell Law Review* 86 (2001): 1090–130; and Cory Spiller, "*People v. Harlan*: The Colorado Supreme Court Takes a Step Toward Eliminating Religious Influence on Juries," *Denver University Law Review* 83 (2005): 613–38.

BIBLIOGRAPHY

Billias, George Athan, ed. *Law and Authority in Colonial America: Selected Essays*. Barre, Mass.: Barre Publishers, 1965.

Clark, H. B. *Biblical Law, Being a Text of the Statutes, Ordinances, and Judgments Established in the Holy Bible—with Many Allusions to Secular Laws: Ancient, Medieval and Modern—Documented to the Scriptures, Judicial Decisions and Legal Literature*. 2nd ed. Portland, Ore.: Binfords & Mort, 1944.

Dreisbach, Daniel L., and Mark David Hall, eds. *The Sacred Rights of Conscience: Selected Readings on Religious Liberty and Church-State Relations in the American Founding*. Indianapolis, Ind.: Liberty Fund, 2009.

Lutz, Donald S., ed. *Colonial Origins of the American Constitution: A Documentary History*. Indianapolis, Ind.: Liberty Fund, 1998.

Meislin, Bernard J. *Jewish Law in American Tribunals*. New York: KTAV Publishing House, 1976.

O'Neil, Patrick M. "Bible in American Law." In *Religion and American Law: An Encyclopedia*, edited by Paul Finkelman, 30–35. New York: Garland Publishing, 2000.

Welch, John W. "Biblical Law in America: Historical Perspectives and Potentials for Reform." *Brigham Young University Law Review* 2002, no. 3 (2002): 611–642. Available at http://digitalcommons.law.byu.edu/lawreview/vol2002/iss3/1.

CHAPTER 18

....

THE BIBLE IN AMERICAN POLITICS

....

DANIEL A. MORRIS

INTRODUCTION

....

THE Bible has had tremendous influence on American politics since before the United States was officially its own country. Perhaps the Bible's earliest influence on politics in the country we now (misleadingly) refer to as "America" were Spanish readings of the *requerimiento* to native people in lands that later became New Mexico and Florida. Written in 1513, the *requerimiento* was designed to inform natives of the provenance and authority of their Spanish-speaking visitors. It also functioned as a legal document to justify warfare in cases of natives' recalcitrance. The *requerimiento* alluded to Genesis, explaining that the Spanish came in service of the God who created all people as descendants of Adam and Eve. It also invoked Matthew 16, claiming that papal authority stretches backward in time all the way to Jesus's conferral of power upon Peter. In 1514 Juan Ponce de León received a contract from King Ferdinand that obligated him to read the *requerimiento* to native populations in *La Florida* such as the Calusa.[1] In 1540 Francisco Vázquez de Coronado read it to the Zuni people in what is now New Mexico.[2] These early examples foreshadowed the ways in which Christians would make political use of the Bible in later American history.

Throughout American history, Christians have turned to the Bible for guidance on political questions. On the one hand, Christian uses of the Bible in politics are typically embedded in more general theological frameworks, which I will call "metanarratives" in this essay. In other words, Christians use the Bible to develop a theological account of what political life is, and relate to the political sphere in light of that account. On the other hand, Christians use the Bible to develop positions on the specific political issues that demand their attention in an ostensibly democratic nation that allows and encourages Christian political participation. In light of these two modes of use, this essay will first explore American Christians' use of the Bible to develop political metanarratives. Next, I will examine American Christians' use of the Bible to inform their positions on specific political issues. Lastly, I will survey the work of three contemporary scholars to show that our understandings of the Bible's place in American politics are contestable, changing, and moving toward greater inclusivity.

THE BIBLE AND POLITICAL METANARRATIVES

Although there have been myriad ways in which American Christians have used the Bible to construct political metanarratives, I will limit my discussion to three types of political theory. These are distinguishable by the central text or theological category around which they are organized. I will survey political stories shaped by Exodus, still other stories that are driven by attentiveness to sin, and a third category of stories informed primarily by eschatology.

Puritan thinkers drew on Exodus to develop one of the earliest and most influential political metanarratives in American history. Exodus seemed to foreshadow several particular features of the Puritans' political circumstances and helped them think about the nature and function of political life. These features include: the political persecution of God's chosen people (the Israelites) under Egyptian rule, God's dramatic liberation of the oppressed over a vast body of water, the Israelites' movement toward the promised land of Canaan, and the frustration of suffering in the wilderness. Many Puritan writers and preachers highlighted specific components of their political situation that seemed to echo, and thus imbue with theological meaning, these facets of Exodus. The hostility of James I and Charles I to dissenting religious views, for example, struck Puritans as a form of political persecution comparable to the Israelites' enslavement in Exodus.³ Increase Mather likened the Puritans' journey over the Atlantic Ocean to God's miraculous deliverance of the Israelites through the parted waters of the Red Sea. In 1674, with King Philip's War looming in the near future, Mather reminded New England Puritans that "God hath culled out a people . . . which he hath also had a great favour towards, and hath brought them by a mighty hand, and an out-stretched arm, over a greater then the Red Sea, and here hath he planted them, and hath caused them to grow up as it were into a little Nation." After linking the parting of the Red Sea to the Atlantic crossing and Canaan to New England, Mather invoked the Exodus theme of trials in the wilderness as his audience considered the coming war.⁴ For Mather, the Puritans reenacted the Israelites' miraculous deliverance, quest for promised land, and suffering in the wilderness. Mather's reading of the Exodus narrative participated in typological hermeneutics common among Puritan preachers. According to such readings, stories narrated in the Hebrew Bible foreshadowed and were fulfilled in New Testament texts and modern events.

Although the Puritans' political theory was shaped most decisively by Exodus, other biblical texts contributed to their vision of politics as well. One of these was Matthew 5. Their readings of Matthew 5 amplified the theme of divine chosenness that they took from Exodus. The NRSV version of this text reads, in part: "You are the light of the world. A city built on a hill cannot be hid. No one after lighting a lamp puts it under the bushel basket, but on the lampstand, and it gives light to all in the house. In the same way, let your light shine before others, so that they may see your good works and give glory to your Father in heaven."⁵ The phrase "city on a hill" became a central motif of American political rhetoric when John Winthrop, the Puritan lawyer and early governor of the Massachusetts Bay Colony, used it in a sermon aboard the *Arbella* in 1630. Entitled "A Model of Christian Charity," Winthrop's sermon articulated the belief that England—and indeed, the entire world—would be watching the Puritans' theological and political experiment at Massachusetts Bay. Like the city on a hill from Jesus's Sermon on the Mount, the Massachusetts Bay Colony would be a model for the world to emulate. Winthrop's invocation of the city on a hill articulated a strong belief that New England's theological and political community was unique among human social arrangements and that God had selected it as a special place with a central role in divine providence. As other societies around the world began to emulate the Puritans' successful community, God's plan of salvation would quicken, making the political society of Massachusetts Bay truly exceptional.

If Exodus and Matthew 5 supplied much of the content of Puritans' political metanarrative, Jeremiah supplied the rhetorical style. The prophet Jeremiah never tires of telling God's people that they are failing to keep their end of the covenant, that their moral fiber is weak, and that God will punish them accordingly. In a memorable exhortation, Jeremiah claims that, given the people's decline into idolatry, God will discipline them through military defeat: if the Israelites do not return to proper, covenantal behavior, God will allow the Babylonian armies to destroy Israel.[6] Puritan leaders made similar claims. Perry Miller shows that Puritan jeremiads served the political purpose of calling New Englanders back to covenantal ideals, primarily by suggesting that the political fate of the community depended on proper moral comportment.[7] Not only would moral decline cause failure for New England's political experiment in a general sense, it could also bring more immediate hardship as God poured out divine wrath in the form of Indian wars, mass illness, and other catastrophes. In all, Puritans used Exodus and Matthew to fashion a political metanarrative emphasizing theological themes of persecution, liberation, chosenness, moral rectitude, and service to the world as an exemplary society. They affirmed their commitment to these ideas in preaching modeled on the rhetoric of Jeremiah.

These themes were modified and renewed in other eras of American history. The themes of chosenness, moral rectitude, and service to the world as an exemplary society played a major role in the grand political narrative of Manifest Destiny. Like the Puritans' notion of the city on a hill, the theory of Manifest Destiny (a term first used publically in 1845) imagined white, English-speaking Protestants as favored by God and superior to other cultures in terms of virtue and language. These attributes validated (in their own minds, at least) English-speaking Protestant Americans' claims to an obvious, divinely appointed "manifest" destiny of westward expansion that included the seizure of lands belonging to Native Americans and Mexicans. The basic themes in the Puritans' political metanarrative have been rearticulated in evangelicalism later in American history. Evangelicals have reaffirmed political stories that emphasize their persecution (especially in the tumultuous decades of the early twentieth century, during which the Scopes Trial took place), chosenness, superior virtue, and status as a model watched by the entire world.

Puritans and evangelicals are not the only American Christians who use Exodus to develop a political metanarrative. Black Christians have done so throughout American history, as well. Christians who were slaves prior to the Civil War referred to the Exodus narrative with great frequency. As slaves embraced Christianity in the colonial period, they found that the book of Exodus spoke directly to their situation. Like the Israelites, they toiled in bondage in a foreign land. Identifying with the Israelites in the Exodus story meant that white, slave-owning Christians played the role of Pharaoh in the Egypt of America. White, slave-owning Christians were uncomfortable with this role reversal not only because they preferred to think of themselves as God's chosen people rather than the agents of injustice and evil in the story but also because thinking of America as Egypt disrupted cherished political notions of America as a land of freedom with divine importance.

Many slave Christians also pursued liberation over a dramatic crossing of water, just as the Israelites had done in Exodus. Slaves seeking to escape slavery in southern states often did so by crossing the Ohio River, and for many of the Christians who did so, this water crossing reenacted the Israelites' dramatic movement across the Red Sea. In addition, slaves imagined themselves as moving toward a promised land, just as the Israelites had done in their departure from Egypt. Slave references to Canaan imagine it both as a physical location (i.e., the North), and also as a social/political reality (i.e., the abolition of slavery).[8]

Black Christians also drew on Jeremiah in the development of a political metanarrative. Eddie S. Glaude Jr. persuasively shows that David Walker's *Appeal* functions as a black Christian jeremiad by denouncing injustice, predicting catastrophe because of moral decline, and calling American society back to the godly ideals it claims to hold dear.[9] Prior to the Civil War, then, black Christians developed a political metanarrative that emphasized similar themes as those the Puritans stressed: persecution, liberation, hope, divine intervention, and the need for collective moral renewal among Christians in the United States. Unlike the Puritans, however, black Christians in the colonial and antebellum periods actually faced slavery. Black Christians also rarely emphasized Matthew 5. For them, America was not some exemplary city on a hill to which other nations should look for guidance.

Although their focus shifted from slavery to other pressing issues, black Christians continued to draw inspiration from the Exodus narrative after the Civil War. This was especially true during the civil rights era. During this time, segregation, the inability to vote, and racial terrorism in the South were fused with poverty, police brutality, and a variety of other challenges nationwide. This network of unjust policies and practices led black Christians to turn once again to the Israelites' persecution in Egypt as a way to describe, understand, and evaluate the frustration of racial politics in the United States. Martin Luther King Jr. linked the United States to Egypt as early as 1954, in a sermon titled "The Death of Evil upon the Seashore."[10] In this sermon, King described both global colonialism and American segregation as suffering akin to the persecution of the Israelites in Egypt. According to King's reading of Exodus, in every instance of human suffering God works through politics for the victory of good over evil. Referring specifically to American segregation, King saw the dramatic moment of liberation in the Supreme Court's ruling in *Brown v. Board of Education*, which marked the *de jure* (if not *de facto*) end of segregation in public education. He wrote that a "world-shaking decree by the nine justices of the United States Supreme Court opened the Red Sea and the forces of justice are moving to the other side."[11]

Fannie Lou Hamer, who was an influential leader in the Mississippi Freedom Summer, frequently used the Exodus narrative in the service of integration and voting rights. She likened southern segregation to slavery in Egypt and to remind listeners that God demands liberation in such situations: "God made it so plain," Hamer said in 1964, "He sent Moses down in Egypt-land to tell Pharaoh to let my people go."[12] For Hamer, the political suffering of Israelites and African Americans alike prepared God's people for trials that would ultimately result in liberation. Indeed, as Hamer's reading of Exodus underscored the redemptive possibilities of racial oppression, it offered these reflections in a style consistent with the basic form of the jeremiad.

Although political metanarratives shaped by Exodus have dominated American Christians' imaginations, the category of sin has also shaped American political theory.

Reinhold Niebuhr's work is a prime example. Niebuhr was the primary American spokesperson for an Augustinian, sin-centered political theology in the twenty-first century.[13] Niebuhr's work emphasized sin and critiqued "liberal" thinkers of both secular and Christian varieties for overlooking this central fact of human nature. Thus, according to Niebuhr, political theorists as distinct as Walter Rauschenbusch and John Dewey shared a dangerous and naïve optimism about the possibilities of human goodness, especially at the levels of national and international politics. Sin, and not virtuous love of neighbor, directs human emotion, thought, and behavior. Therefore, we must remain suspicious of politics, where power amplifies the dangerous possibilities of sin.

And yet, politics is necessary precisely because its basic function is to identify, judge, and restrain sin. In doing so, politics can approximate social justice in a fallen world. Democracy is the most promising political regime because it flattens power to the greatest possible number of people and institutions. For Niebuhr, democracy is preferable to all other regime types because it is the least dangerous. The quotation that best distills Niebuhr's Christian endorsement of democracy is also, perhaps, his most often-quoted: "Man's capacity for justice makes democracy possible; but man's inclination to injustice makes democracy necessary."[14]

Niebuhr bolstered this Augustinian political theory with frequent references to the Bible. As a Christian ethicist writing after the rise of fundamentalist Christianity, he was careful to explain that he read the Bible as "myth," meaning that he did not take all the stories of the Bible to be literally, historically factual. Rather, Niebuhr believed that biblical stories revealed deep truths about human nature and society that resonate with experience, but that reason cannot render immediately intelligible. He also found in the Gospel of Luke pithy and profound advice for human participation in politics. In the parable of the dishonest manager, Jesus quips that "the children of this world are in their generation wiser than the children of light."[15] Niebuhr interprets this statement as a call for Christians (and other participants in politics) to be virtuous enough to support some higher law than unrestrained self-interest but also to possess enough wisdom to know that evil will always seek to overcome that law and act on self-interest alone.[16] Niebuhr's reading of the Bible served an Augustinian political metanarrative that grew out of and responded to a broader theological framework centered on the concept of sin.

Many of Niebuhr's contemporaries used the Bible in service of a political metanarrative shaped more by eschatology than by sin. As American Christians read the Bible and thought about the end of human history, they often came to believe that key events in twentieth-century global politics played a major role in the end times. These events included the Jewish Holocaust, World War II, the establishment of the state of Israel, and the Cold War. Evangelicals often interpreted these events in light of premillennial eschatology, according to which Jesus's second coming would occur prior to the establishment of God's 1,000-year Kingdom on earth. Their reading of Revelation, particularly the verses in chapter 20 that describe God's cosmic defeat over Satan and establishment of 1,000 years of peace and truth, supplied the foundation for premillennial eschatology in general. Beliefs about the specific events of premillennial eschatology and the order in which they occur vary among evangelical Christians, but in the mid-twentieth century, many Americans believed that the Jews' return to their holy land had important eschatological ramifications. Once gathered there, the Jews would begin converting to Christianity in significant numbers. For many American evangelicals, the settlement and conversion of the Jews would signal that the end of human history was imminent. They derived this belief in the eschatological role of the Jews' conversion from biblical texts such as Romans 11:25-26, in which Paul declares that "a hardening has come upon part of Israel, until the full number of the Gentiles has come in. And so all Israel will be saved."

Another angle of political discourse tied to premillennial eschatology was born of a belief that the end times would also include a climactic battle between the forces of good and the forces of evil. Paul Boyer shows that American evangelicals often interpreted the United States' conflict with the Soviet Union in light of these beliefs.[17] Specifically, they focused on Ezekiel 38 as they tried to make sense of global political conflicts within their eschatological vision. In this text, God instructs Ezekiel to prophesy against an obscure character named "Gog of the land of Magog." Ezekiel's message predicts that Gog and Israel will fight a terrible battle, and that God will help Israel destroy Gog. Premillennialist evangelicals found much fodder in this text to fuel a Cold War political metanarrative. The text notes that Gog resides to the north of Israel, which led some to believe that the text predicted a conflict between the young nation of Israel and the Soviet Union. Several linguistic similarities seemed to confirm this connection. For example, some translators rendered Ezekiel 38:2 as saying "Gog of Magog, Prince of Rosh, Meshech and Tubal." The linguistic similarity between "Rosh" (here dubiously taken to be a proper noun) and "Russia" confirmed for premillennialists in the Cold War that the text predicted divine judgment against Russia and the Soviet Union. With Russia playing the role of Gog, American evangelicals became more certain that a conflict between the Soviet Union and the United States over Israel would fulfill one more important piece of the eschatological puzzle that consumed their imagination. Thus, the Jewish Holocaust, World War II, the establishment of Israel, and the Cold War offered raw material for many American evangelicals to reassess and renew their premillennial political metanarrative.

Other Protestants based their political metanarratives on eschatology, but disagreed with premillennialists about the sequence of end-time events. While premillennialists believed that Jesus's second coming would occur before the 1,000-year reign of God's kingdom, postmillennialists believed the opposite. Based on their reading of biblical texts, Jesus would return after the 1,000-year period of God's heavenly kingdom on earth. Postmillennialists anchored their eschatological beliefs on texts such as Isaiah 2:4 ("they shall beat their swords into plowshares, and their spears into pruning hooks; nation shall not lift up sword against nation, neither shall they learn war anymore"), the Lord's Prayer (in which Jesus instructs listeners to pray to God, "Your kingdom come. Your will be done, on earth as it is in heaven"), and the Great Commission (in which the resurrected Jesus charges his followers to "Go therefore and make disciples of all nations, baptizing them in the name of the Father and of the Son and of the Holy Spirit, and teaching them to obey everything that I have commanded you").[18] For postmillennialists, these and other texts suggest that it is possible for human beings to construct God's holy, eschatological kingdom on earth. They reasoned that politics was one avenue to do so. Social conditions could steadily improve through political reforms until sin had been eradicated and a holy society flourished.

In search of such an eschatological society, postmillennial thinkers in the nineteenth century sought to bring American political society in line with God's will through the endorsement of specific policy positions. Walter Rauschenbusch, a leading postmillennial and Social Gospel writer in the late nineteenth and early twentieth centuries, referred to Mark 1:15 to justify a postmillennial politics: "The time is fulfilled; the kingdom of God is now close at hand; repent and believe in the glad news."[19] From such biblical premises, Rauschenbusch developed a political metanarrative according to which participation in politics served the construction of God's kingdom on earth.

THE BIBLE AND POLITICAL POLICY

In addition to their uses of the Bible to develop political metanarratives, American Christians also use the Bible to support stances on specific policy questions. There are many examples of this happening throughout US history, but here I will focus on Christian discussions of three specific political questions: colonial and antebellum debates about slavery, critiques of capitalism in the late nineteenth and early twentieth centuries, and discussions of sexuality in the late twentieth and early twenty-first centuries. I select these examples for their historical and topical variety, although many other biblical engagements of specific policy questions could be included as well.

Long before the United States was an independent nation, Christians had been discussing the institution of slavery through reference to the Bible. As the Civil War crept closer, that discussion grew more intense. Both slave owners and abolitionists defended their political positions by using the Bible, as they had done earlier, but in the mid-nineteenth century, it became clear that appeals to scripture would not alter those positions. As Abraham Lincoln lamented in his Second Inaugural Address, "Both [North and South] read the same Bible, and pray to the same God; and each invokes His aid against the other."[20]

Slave owners found many biblical texts to justify maintaining the institution of slavery. One of these was the story of Noah's curse of Canaan in Genesis 9. In that text, Noah falls into a deep, wine-induced sleep, and his son Ham, who is Canaan's father, happens to see him lying naked in his tent. When Noah learns that Ham has seen him passed out and naked, Noah curses Canaan by declaring all his progeny to be slaves to his uncles' descendants. Many Christian slave owners claimed that this biblical text destined black people (descendants of Canaan) to be slaves.

Furthermore, slave owners appealed to other passages when it came to the institution of slavery. They pointed to Romans 13 where Paul issues a stern warning pertaining to obedience to make clear that every slave should obey rightful authority. "Let every person be subject to the governing authorities," Paul writes, "for there is no authority except from God, and those authorities that exist have been instituted by God. Therefore whoever resists authority resists what God has appointed, and those who resist will incur judgment." Slave owners also pointed to texts in the Hebrew Bible in which God assumes the moral validity of slavery (Deut. 20:10–11), and to texts in the New Testament such as the Household Codes (Eph. 5:22–6:9; Col. 3:18–4:1), which counsel slaves to obey masters. Slave owners were also quick to argue from a lack of evidence against biblical teachings against slavery, pointing out that Jesus never said anything specific about slavery, and therefore must have condoned it.[21]

But for every text that seemed to permit slavery, abolitionists could find another that seemed to prohibit it. Exodus 21:16, for example, seemed to apply to the Trans-Atlantic Slave Trade: "Whoever steals a man and sells him, and anyone found in possession of him, shall be put to death." Abolitionists strengthened their political case by pointing to the dual love command enjoining all people to love God and neighbor. They argued that when Jesus said "you shall love your neighbor as yourself," he likely did not think of enslavement as a work of love.[22] Opponents of slavery also pointed to Paul's soaring rhetoric of equality in Galatians 3:27–29. In those verses, the apostle declares that "as many of you as were baptized into Christ have clothed yourselves in Christ. There is no longer Jew or Greek, there is no longer slave or free, there is no longer male and female; for all of you are one in Christ Jesus." Of course, neither side could convince the other of switching political positions, and the question of slavery would be settled by Supreme Court decisions, simple brute (often military) force, constitutional amendments, legislation, and a host of other non-biblical measures.

American Christians have frequently used the Bible to develop specific positions on economic issues. Social Gospel thinkers, for example, drew on the Bible to critique capitalism and endorse socialist economic policies. The Social Gospel movement, which spanned the late nineteenth and early twentieth centuries, endeavored to realize Christian moral norms in social and economic life, with special attention to the plight of the urban poor. For Rauschenbusch, the establishment of God's millennial kingdom meant primarily economic reform to alleviate poverty and curb the excesses of industrial capitalism. Rauschenbusch drew on prophetic texts from the Hebrew Bible that denounced economic exploitation, such as Hosea, Amos, and Isaiah to ground his economic argument.[23] He highlighted Hosea's critique of priestly "sacrificial ritual" and preference for moral action. Rauschenbusch emphasized the calls for justice for the poor that he found in Amos and Isaiah alike. From Amos 5 he found a message "against the capitalistic ruthlessness that 'sold the righteous for silver and the needy for a pair of shoes.'" And he invoked the first chapter of Isaiah to set the tone for his Christian discussion of economic injustice: "Your hands are full of blood. Wash you! Make you clean! Put away the evil of your doings from before mine eyes! Cease to do evil! Learn to do right! Seek justice! Relieve the oppressed! Secure justice for the orphaned and plead for the widow." For Rauschenbusch, as for many other Christians, these prophetic calls are directly relevant to the exploitation of poor people inherent in America's industrial capitalist society. Thus, according to this view, the Bible indicated socialist policies, cooperative business models, and strong labor unions as a specific set of political responses to the crisis of American economic exploitation.[24]

In the late twentieth and early twenty-first centuries, issues relating to sexuality and reproduction have gained new urgency for American Christians, who sometimes seek political regulation of sexuality in light of their readings of the Bible. The so-called sexual revolution of the 1960s and 1970s challenged many Christians' cherished moral norms elevating monogamy, marriage, and heterosexuality and led to a conservative Christian response from roughly the 1980s onward. The response included political opposition to abortion and LGBTQ (lesbian, gay, bisexual, transgendered, and queer/questioning sexuality) rights from conservative Christians. This common story about Christianity, sexuality, and politics has certain appeal, but merits closer scrutiny. Randall Balmer offers a critique of this narrative, arguing that American evangelicals were not originally opposed to the Supreme Court abortion ruling in Roe v. Wade, and that opposition to abortion is a way for powerful Christian leaders and politicians to motivate evangelicals in service of a different political and economic agenda. According to Balmer, this alternative agenda focuses mainly on minimizing government regulation of church-related institutions and maintaining these institutions' tax exemptions, even when they endorse racially discriminatory policies.[25]

Whatever the reason, some Christians have invoked the Bible in opposition to the legalization of abortion and the movement for LGBTQ equality from the late twentieth century onward. In the case of abortion, they have justified opposition to the *Roe v. Wade* ruling through appeals to Jeremiah 1:5, which reads, "Before I formed you in the womb I knew you, and before you were born I consecrated you." Pat Robertson uses this passage to support the conclusion that "Abortion is definitely wrong" in an online article for the Christian Broadcasting Network.[26] Passages like this one (and others, including Gal. 1:15 and Isa. 44:2) suggest to some Christians that embryos and fetuses have full rights to life attendant to moral personhood, and therefore that a woman has no right to obtain an abortion (or that such a right must be sharply limited). Politically active Christians who read the Bible in this way seek a variety of different political measures to limit abortion. Some endorse changes to the legal articulation of a fetus's viability, which would prohibit women from aborting pregnancies after, say, 20 weeks rather than 24 weeks of gestation. Others hope for a total overturn of *Roe v. Wade* despite the fact that, as Balmer points out, the politicians most likely to pursue such a goal have not done so even when they have controlled all branches of government.[27]

In terms of the politics of homosexuality, Christians who oppose LGBTQ rights frequently draw on the Bible to make their cases. There are five passages in the Bible that appear to mark homosexuality as sinful (tabling, for the purposes of this essay, a discussion of the anachronistic nature of the word "homosexuality").[28] These passages are Leviticus 18:22, Leviticus 20:13, Romans 1:26–27, 1 Corinthians 6:9–10, and 1 Timothy 1:9–11. For Christian opponents of LGBTQ equality, these passages condemn homosexuality as sinful, and therefore require Christian political activity to curtail movements such as the pursuit of same-sex marriage equality. In an influential set of essays, Dale B. Martin argues that Christian appeals to these passages are problematic on linguistic, historical, and moral grounds. He shows that opposition to LGBTQ equality has shaky support when it rests on these biblical passages.[29] Many Christian opponents of LGBTQ equality (especially Catholics) circumvent this problem by appealing less to the Bible and more to natural law reasoning to defend their political positions. The 2015 Supreme Court ruling in *Obergefell v. Hodges* issued a significant defeat to such Christian politics in declaring states' bans of same-sex marriage unconstitutional. Whether Christians continue to voice "biblical" opposition to LGBTQ equality after *Obergefell v. Hodges* remains to be seen.

CURRENT SCHOLARSHIP

In closing, I would like to note two important trends in current scholarship on the Bible and American politics. In the early twenty-first century, scholars writing at the intersection of biblical studies and politics are both challenging dominant political metanarratives and also indicating new concrete political positions for Christians. These trends are welcome because they signal greater inclusivity by giving space to previously unheard voices and because they reveal significant forms of injustice. They make these contributions both at the relatively abstract level of political metanarratives and also at the more specific level of policy. The work of James H. Cone, David A. Sánchez, and Kelly Brown Douglas provide excellent examples of these two trends in scholarship on the Bible in American politics.

Cone has had a long and distinguished career and is widely regarded as a founding thinker of black theology. Cone's work initiated new trajectories in theology, ethics, and Christian history in 1969 and 1970, with the publications of *Black Theology and Black Power* and *A Black Theology of Liberation*, respectively. These texts (and his later work) highlighted black experiences as neglected but vital sources of Christian theology, especially given the ubiquity and depth of black suffering and white supremacy in the United States. Cone's work reminds Christians that God became incarnate in a marginalized community partly in order to demonstrate solidarity with and a preferential option for all who suffer. These positions make his work consistent with other iterations of liberation theology across the globe.

In the United States, Cone's ideas mean that God is in solidarity with black people. Indeed, Cone argues in light of black experiences (and other theological sources) that God is black and Christian "love is a refusal to accept whiteness."[30] Cone's 2008 book, *The Cross and the Lynching Tree*, shows new directions for scholarship on the Bible in American politics by offering a robust challenge to political metanarratives and suggesting new concrete political positions. A concise summary of Jesus's crucifixion from Acts 10:39 supplies the inspiration for Cone's work: "They put him to death by hanging him from a tree." Cone uses this sentence from Acts to link Jesus's death to the lynching of black men throughout American history.

While this book revisits themes from his earlier scholarship, it also issues a deep challenge to Niebuhr's Augustinian political metanarrative. Cone faults Niebuhr for having neglected the scourge of lynching during a career apparently devoted to studying love, justice, guilt, and the social dynamics of sin. Niebuhr's lack of attention to lynching means that he could not sufficiently empathize with black suffering and therefore was incapable of grasping the full import of Jesus's life, death, and resurrection.[31] Niebuhr "was no prophet on race," Cone writes. "Prophets take risks and speak out in righteous indignation against society's treatment of the poor, even risking their lives, as we see in the martyrdom of Jesus and Martin King. Niebuhr took no risks for blacks."[32] Cone's challenge to Niebuhr's political metanarrative carries implications for concrete policy positions, as well. He extends his reflection on the significance of Acts 10:39 to include critiques of America's mass incarceration of black men animated by the war on drugs, the death penalty in the United States, and the tortures and abuses at Abu Ghraib during the Iraq War.[33]

Like Cone, Sánchez challenges American political metanarratives and highlights alternative political stances on the basis of certain readings of the Bible. Sánchez analyzes the ways that Christians have interpreted the Bible to resist and subvert imperial domination at three key historical moments: in first-century Asia minor, in seventeenth-century Mexico, and in the contested land of what is now the Southwestern United States (but was previously Mexican territory) in the twentieth century. For each of these historical moments, Sánchez persuasively shows that marginalized and oppressed people have read Revelation 12 in ways that subvert sacred stories of imperialist powers.

Revelation 12 tells a story about a heavenly, pregnant woman in the throes of labor. The woman gives birth to a boy, who is "taken to God and to his throne," after which a terrifying dragon pursues and tries to kill the woman and "make war on the rest of her children." Following the Mexican-American War and the disastrous Treaty of Guadalupe of Hidalgo, Mexican readers reinterpreted this passage in ways that subverted the American political metanarrative of Manifest Destiny. While English-speaking Protestants understood themselves as superior, divinely chosen people and their Westward expansion as part of God's plan for a special nation, Mexican Christians resisted this metanarrative by invoking the Virgin of Guadalupe, whose appearance to Juan Diego in 1531 fit the exact description of the woman in Revelation 12. The Virgin of Guadalupe has always empowered people on the margins of colonial society, such as indigenous people and peasants. Sánchez shows, though, that Revelation 12 and the Virgin of Guadalupe allow Mexicans to resist domination driven by the United States' vision of Manifest Destiny. The Virgin empowers poor and indigenous people by revealing herself specifically to them, by taking their form, and by giving them a symbolic claim to land. Thus, ever since the US-Mexican War and the Treaty of Guadalupe of Hidalgo, Mexicans have used the image of the Virgin to resist US domination.

César Chávez, members of the Chicana/o movement of the 1960s and 1970s, and Los Angeles muralists all invoke the Virgin of Guadalupe to resist the United States political metanarrative of Manifest Destiny. Indeed, the "Spiritual Plan of Aztlán," a prominent statement from the Chicana/o movement, specifically calls for Mexican reclamation of land wrongly taken under the nineteenth-century pretense of Manifest Destiny.[34] As Sánchez analyzes this interpretation of Revelation 12, he reveals a profound challenge to a metanarrative at the heart of US political identity. But he also underscores some important political positions that follow from this interpretation of Revelation 12. Examining the Chicana/o movement, for example, Sánchez shows that the Virgin of Guadalupe was used in rural contexts to resist "the substandard wages of the farm workers, the lack of education for children (many of whom, because of low-paying jobs, were forced to work alongside their parents), illiteracy, harsh labor conditions, exposure to poisonous chemicals, and the vicious cycle of abject poverty. Some of the most acute urban issues were police brutality, civil-rights violations, land proprietorship, inadequate housing and social services, and being taught that their cultural heritage and language served as a hindrance to their success (English only!)."[35] These political issues are born of American marginalization of Mexicans, which has been a reality since (at least) the US-Mexican War. For Sánchez, Mexican readings of Revelation 12 empower people to confront such difficult problems and resist American domination.

Lastly, Douglas also uses the Bible to challenge dominant American political metanarratives and suggest alternative political stances. Douglas's work has been influential for several decades in the fields of African American theology, ethics, and Christian history. She emphasizes the way that white supremacy has shaped Christian thought in America and the possibilities of black liberation in the face of this problem. In her 2015 book, *Stand Your Ground: Black Bodies and the Justice of God*, Douglas critiques white Christianity's contribution to a culture of violence against black people. She challenges America's political metanarratives of the City on a Hill and Manifest Destiny by showing that these projects have always contained and perpetuated racist ideas about Anglo-Saxon superiority and black inferiority. From Tacitus to Thomas Jefferson and beyond, American political metanarratives have imagined white people as God's morally and politically superior representatives with a special social vision to share with humanity. On the flip side, these political theories have thought of black people as morally stunted, irrational, and dangerous. For Douglas, such theories exalt whiteness as a kind of property to be extended and protected. Alternatively, blackness coincides with character traits that must be controlled and suppressed. This leads to the moral and political ideas that white people can and should protect themselves using deadly force from perceived threats wherever they arise, and that such threats will inevitably come from black people. Thus, the City on a Hill is one in which "stand your ground" effectively means that white people can often kill black people with impunity.

In addition to the deep challenge she issues to the political metanarratives of City on a Hill and Manifest Destiny, Douglas also suggests some concrete political stances for biblically focused Americans in the twenty-first century. "Like the Black Codes of the postemancipation era, laws such as Stop and Frisk, mandatory drug sentencing, Conceal and Carry, and the Stand Your Ground law itself must be brought to an end."[36] These policies are all direct reflections of political metanarratives that have used the Bible to promote white supremacy. For Douglas, both the metanarratives and the specific policies they produce must be challenged. Douglas's work frequently invokes the Bible to make such arguments. In her critique of the City on a Hill and white violence against black bodies, she connects the parable of the sheep and the goats recorded in Matthew 25 to the 2012 killing of Trayvon Martin in Sanford, Florida. "In the stand-your-ground war today, crucifixion comes in the form of gun violence. The Matthean question today might be, 'But Lord, where did we see you dying and on the cross?' And Jesus would answer, 'On a Florida sidewalk, at a Florida gas station, on a Michigan porch, on a street in North Carolina. As you did it to one of these young black bodies, you did it to me.'"[37]

Insofar as scholarship like that of Cone, Sánchez, and Douglas challenges dominant political metanarratives, suggests new policy stances, and includes previously neglected voices, studies of the Bible and American politics in the early twenty-first century demonstrate a praiseworthy democratic impulse. This is not to say that the democratization of scholarship on the Bible and American politics is inevitable. On the contrary, nurturing this democratic impulse will take effort on the part of college and university students, faculty search committees, and administrators, as well as editors of journals and presses. Each of these groups can be reluctant to question the ways Americans have used the Bible to develop political metanarratives and endorse specific policy. But being open to such questions carries the promise of greater forms of inclusion, closer approximations of social justice, and more honest appraisals of the Bible's place in America's political history.

Notes

1. Robert H. Fuson, *Juan Ponce De León and the Spanish Discovery of Puerto Rico and Florida* (Blacksburg, Va.: McDonald & Woodward, 2000), 127–36.
2. David J. Weber, *The Spanish Frontier in North America* (New Haven, Conn.: Yale University Press, 1992), 14–15.
3. Joseph Gaer and Ben Siegel, *The Puritan Heritage: America's Roots in the Bible* (New York: New American Library, 1964), 13–28.
4. Both quotations are from Increase Mather, *The Day of Trouble Is Near: Two Sermons Wherein Is Shewed, What Are the Signs of a Day of Trouble Being Near* (Cambridge, Mass.: Marmaduke Iohnson, 1674), Evans Early American Imprint Collection—Text Creation Partnership, http://name.umdl.umich.edu/N00137.0001.001.
5. Matthew 5:14–16.
6. Jeremiah 20–21.

7. Perry Miller, *Errand into the Wilderness* (Cambridge, Mass.: Harvard University Press, 1984), 1–15.

8. Albert J. Raboteau, *Canaan Land: A Religious History of African Americans* (New York: Oxford University Press, 2001), 48.

9. Eddie S. Glaude Jr., *Exodus!: Religion, Race, and Nation in Early Nineteenth-Century Black America* (Chicago: University of Chicago Press, 2000), 34–43.

10. Martin Luther King Jr., *Strength to Love* (Philadelphia: Fortress Press, 1981), ch. 8.

11. King, *Strength to Love*, 82.

12. Maegan Parker Brooks and Davis W. Houck, eds., *The Speeches of Fannie Lou Hamer: To Tell It Like It Is* (Jackson: University of Mississippi Press, 2013), 49.

13. Niebuhr offered a concise statement on his debts to Augustine in his essay "Augustine's Political Realism." In that essay he calls Augustine "a more reliable guide than any known thinker." See Reinhold Niebuhr, *The Essential Reinhold Niebuhr: Selected Essays and Addresses*, ed. Robert McAfee Brown (New Haven, Conn.: Yale University Press, 1987), 140–41.

14. Reinhold Niebuhr, *The Children of Light and the Children of Darkness: A Vindication of Democracy and a Critique of Its Traditional Defense* (Chicago: University of Chicago Press, 2011), xxxii.

15. Luke 16:8.

16. Niebuhr, *The Children of Light and the Children of Darkness*, 10–11.

17. Paul Boyer, *When Time Shall Be No More: Prophecy Belief in Modern American Culture* (Cambridge, Mass.: Harvard University Press, 1998), 152–80.

18. Matthew 6:10; 28:19–20.

19. Walter Rauschenbusch, *Christianity and the Social Crisis* (Louisville, Ky.: Westminster John Knox Press, 1991), 54.

20. Quoted in Mark A. Noll, *A History of Christianity in the United States and Canada* (Grand Rapids, Mich.: W. B. Eerdmans, 1992), 322.

21. Mark A. Noll, *The Civil War as a Theological Crisis* (Chapel Hill: University of North Carolina Press, 2006), ch. 3.

22. Matthew 22:34–40.

23. All quotations in this paragraph can be found in Rauschenbusch, *Christianity and the Social Crisis*, 5–12.

24. Rauschenbusch, *Christianity and the Social Crisis*, ch. 7.

25. Randall Balmer, *The Making of Evangelicalism: From Revivalism to Politics, and Beyond* (Waco, Tex.: Baylor University Press, 2010), ch. 4.

26. Pat Robertson, "Saving the Unborn," Christian Broadcasting Network, http://www.cbn.com/spirituallife/biblestudyandtheology/perspectives/pat's_perspective_abortion.aspx.

27. Balmer, *The Making of Evangelicalism*, 70–71.

28. Hanne Blank offers a lucid discussion of the first uses and historical development of the concepts "homosexual" and "heterosexual" in her book *Straight: The Surprisingly Short History of Heterosexuality* (Boston, Mass.: Beacon Press, 2012).

29. Dale B. Martin, *Sex and the Single Savior: Gender and Sexuality in Biblical Interpretation* (Louisville, Ky.: Westminster John Knox Press, 2006).

30. James H. Cone, *A Black Theology of Liberation* (Maryknoll, N.Y.: Orbis Books, 2005), 63–66, 74.

31. James H. Cone, *The Cross and the Lynching Tree* (Maryknoll, N.Y.: Orbis Books, 2011), ch. 2.

32. Cone, *The Cross and the Lynching Tree*, 61.
33. Cone, *The Cross and the Lynching Tree*, 163–64.
34. The text of the Spiritual Plan of Aztlán is available at "LATINOPIA DOCUMENT—1969 EL PLAN DE AZTLÁN," March 27-31, 1969, http://latinopia.com/latino-history/plan-de-aztlan/.
35. David A. Sánchez, *From Patmos to the Barrio: Subverting Imperial Myths* (Minneapolis, Minn.: Fortress Press, 2008), 96.
36. Kelly Brown Douglas, *Stand Your Ground: Black Bodies and the Justice of God* (Maryknoll, N.Y.: Orbis Books, 2015), 166.
37. Douglas, *Stand Your Ground*, 180.

BIBLIOGRAPHY

Balmer, Randall. *The Making of Evangelicalism: From Revivalism to Politics, and Beyond*. Waco, Tex.: Baylor University Press, 2010.

Blank, Hanne. *Straight: The Surprisingly Short History of Heterosexuality*. Boston, Mass.: Beacon Press, 2012.

Boyer, Paul. *When Time Shall Be No More: Prophecy Belief in Modern American Culture*. Cambridge, Mass.: Harvard University Press, 1998.

Brooks, Maegan Parker, and Davis W. Houck, eds. *The Speeches of Fannie Lou Hamer: To Tell It Like It Is*. Jackson: University Press of Mississippi, 2013.

Cone, James H. *A Black Theology of Liberation*. Maryknoll, N.Y.: Orbis Books, 2005.

———. *The Cross and the Lynching Tree*. Maryknoll, N.Y.: Orbis Books, 2011.

Douglas, Kelly Brown. *Stand Your Ground: Black Bodies and the Justice of God*. Maryknoll, N.Y.: Orbis Books, 2015.

Fuson, Robert H. *Juan Ponce De León and the Spanish Discovery of Puerto Rico and Florida*. Blacksburg, Va.: McDonald & Woodward, 2000.

Gaer, Joseph, and Ben Siegel. *The Puritan Heritage: America's Roots in the Bible*. New York: New American Library, 1964.

Glaude, Eddie S., Jr. *Exodus!: Religion, Race, and Nation in Early Nineteenth-Century Black America*. Chicago: University of Chicago Press, 2000.

King, Martin Luther, Jr. *Strength to Love*. Philadelphia: Fortress Press, 1981.

Latinopia. "LATINOPIA DOCUMENT—1969 EL PLAN DE AZTLÁN." March 27-31, 1969. http://latinopia.com/latino-history/plan-de-aztlan/.

Martin, Dale B. *Sex and the Single Savior: Gender and Sexuality in Biblical Interpretation*. Louisville, Ky.: Westminster John Knox Press, 2006.

Mather, Increase. *The Day of Trouble Is Near: Two Sermons Wherein Is Shewed, What Are the Signs of a Day of Trouble Being Near*. Cambridge, Mass.: Marmaduke Iohnson, 1674. Evans Early American Imprint Collection—Text Creation Partnership. http://name.umdl.umich.edu/N00137.0001.001.

Miller, Perry. *Errand into the Wilderness*. Cambridge, Mass.: Harvard University Press, 1984.

Niebuhr, Reinhold. *The Children of Light and the Children of Darkness: A Vindication of Democracy and a Critique of Its Traditional Defense*. Chicago: University of Chicago Press, 2011.

———. *The Essential Reinhold Niebuhr: Selected Essays and Addresses*. Edited by Robert McAfee Brown. New Haven, Conn.: Yale University Press, 1987.

Noll, Mark A. *The Civil War as a Theological Crisis*. Chapel Hill: University of North Carolina Press, 2006.

———. *A History of Christianity in the United States and Canada*. Grand Rapids, Mich.: W. B. Eerdmans, 1992.

Raboteau, Albert J. *Canaan Land: A Religious History of African Americans*. New York: Oxford University Press, 2001.

Rauschenbusch, Walter. *Christianity and the Social Crisis*. Louisville, Ky.: Westminster John Knox Press, 1991.

Sánchez, David A. *From Patmos to the Barrio: Subverting Imperial Myths*. Minneapolis, Minn.: Fortress Press, 2008.

Weber, David J. *The Spanish Frontier in North America*. New Haven, Conn.: Yale University Press, 1992.

CHAPTER 19

··

THE BIBLE AND SLAVERY
IN AMERICAN LIFE

··

EMERSON B. POWERY

INTRODUCTION

THE Bible and slavery shared a reciprocal relationship in American life. The Bible provided a religious license for the practice of slavery. Slavery intensified the experience of interpreting the Bible. In nineteenth-century North American life, it would be difficult to understand one without the other.

Many Christians participated in or defended the US slave institution and many did so with the support of Christianity's sacred text. Christian opponents of the "peculiar institution" of slavery also utilized the same Bible to speak against the evilness of the practice. As President Abraham Lincoln would succinctly put it in his Second Inaugural Address, "Both read the same Bible and pray to the same God."[1] Despite Lincoln's words to reconcile disputing parties and warring factions nearing the end of the Civil War, neither side would readily concede his religious point.

The use of the Bible in the cause of slavery did not begin with the nineteenth century.[2] But the formal use of the Bible both in favor and against the institution of slavery intensified during the decades leading up to the Civil War.

PRO-SLAVERY USE OF THE BIBLE

Advocates of the peculiar institution had no reason to make a biblical case for slavery. For centuries, enslavement was a contemporary, global, historical phenomenon that required little defense biblically. Religion participated in the wider American societal (and uncritical) acceptance of this custom. The rise and influence of antislavery arguments would compel pro-slavery thinkers to develop a justification and the latter group would find support available in the Christian Bible.

Slavery was ubiquitous in the ancient world and evidence for its existence is present throughout the biblical story. The story of Genesis includes many references to slaves and masters (cf. Gen. 9:25-27, 12:16, 16:1, 17:12-13, 20:8, 30:43). The laws of ancient Israel assume the presence of enslaved bodies among the people of Israel. While Israel celebrated its very beginnings in terms of liberation from Egyptian oppression and enslavement, this memory of the Exodus event did not lead Israel's leaders to establish a land free of slaves. This memory exercised a more limited and occasional influence, such as hindering the sale of fellow Hebrew slaves to other groups (Lev. 25:39-43), advocating for "fair" payment when masters released Hebrew slaves (Deut. 15:13-15), or, possibly, in the caring for "fugitive" slaves (Deut. 23:15-16). But Israel did not endorse abolition in light of this collective memory.

Ancient Israelite slavery continued into the Greco-Roman period, engulfing both Judaism and Christianity.[3] Jesus told numerous parables assuming the presence of slaves and masters (e.g., Matt. 13:24-30, 18:22-34; Luke 12:35-40, 14:16-24). Early Christian house churches included "free" and "slave" within the developing Christian communities (e.g., Gal. 3:28; Col. 3:22-4:1; Eph. 6:5-9). Paul sent Onesimus back to Philemon, even while encouraging other enslaved Christians to secure their freedom if the opportunity presented itself (Philem. 12; 1 Cor. 7:21-22). The emphasis of the Corinthian passage, for the slavers, lay in the first part of Paul's words that the enslaved believer should "care not for it [freedom]" (KJV) as if it were of great significance in the scheme of the Gospel. Neither could the enslaved own anything or produce legitimate heirs.[4] Racial identity played no factor in slave status in the Greco-Roman world.

The assumption of the compatibility of slave life to people committed to God in these biblical passages encouraged Christian communities, in the centuries to follow, to continue to participate in and support institutions of human bondage. Few Christians would challenge this tradition of the social order. Eventually, the European world, which had instigated a robust transatlantic slave trade, opposed human bondage. Finally, effective change appeared in the United States only in the decades leading up to the Civil War. There was a growing outcry against the peculiar institution in antebellum America and the political landscape followed suit. Leading spokespersons for the continuance of slavery would be forced to argue for its rightfulness in the public square.

The biblical argument in favor of slavery went as follows. The patriarchs of ancient Israel assumed the practice; God's law required the practice; Jesus chose not to condemn the practice; early Christian churches sustained the practice. Noah's curse on Canaan—that he would become a slave and remain in the service of his brothers—was cited often as supporting evidence in the day (Gen. 9:18-27). God's willingness to send Hagar, an Egyptian slave who bore Abraham's first son, back into an abusive situation in Abraham's house was indicative of God's willingness to promote human bondage. Even the Decalogue included injunctions that assumed the presence of the enslaved among the people of Israel: "But the seventh day is a sabbath to the LORD your God; you shall not do any work—you, your son or your daughter, your male or female slave, your livestock, or the alien resident in your towns" (Exod. 20:10). One of the passages most cited to support the peculiar institution was Leviticus 25:44-46: "As for the male and female slaves whom you may have, it is from the nations around you that you may acquire male and female slaves. You may also acquire them from among the aliens residing with you, and from their families that are with you, who have been born in your land; and they may be your property. You may keep them as a possession for your children after you, for them to inherit as property." Advocates commonly viewed other great slaveholders, like Job and Joseph, as biblical exemplars of the institution. As one widely read spokesperson would put it, God "singled out the greatest slaveholders of that age, as the objects of his special favor."[5]

When supporters of the US bondage system turned their attention to the New Testament, they underlined Jesus's silence on the topic to conclude that the founder of Christianity himself recognized the lawfulness of the institution in its Greco-Roman form. Along with his use of the "slave" as a model of the disciple (Matt. 10:24-25), Jesus's relative silence implied consent, not condemnation, of the participation of slaveholders in the house churches. Many advocates, unsurprisingly, emphasized the Pauline command of "slaves obey your masters" as codes for good conduct in these Christian gatherings and clear evidence for the compatibility of Christianity with slavery. With such explicit provisions in both Testaments, the pro-slavery argument based on the Bible was in good stead. Not only does the Bible not label slavery a sin, scripture sanctions the practice as God-ordained. Many would echo Thorton Stringfellow's (a prominent Baptist minister in Virginia) conclusion that Christianity in biblical times "adds to the obligation of the servant to render service with good will to his master, and that gospel fellowship is not to be entertained with persons who will not consent to it!"[6] The Bible not only authorizes human bondage, but those who question the system undermine the very authority of scripture's God.

Furthermore, the Bible's support of slavery was often discussed in terms of skin color and linked to issues of race. Josiah Priest, a popular historian, antiquarian, and defender of slavery, insisted—against the specific evidence of Genesis 9—that Noah's curse was placed upon Ham (Canaan's father) for Ham's action of seeing his father's nakedness and laughing at Noah's drunken condition.[7] More important, for Priest, Ham's immediate, solitary misdemeanor was not the real cause for Noah's curse.[8] Rather, the anathema signified the prophet's recognition of a long history of Ham's wickedness from his childhood, a character flaw central to Ham's personality and his evil actions, a defect that could only stem from someone whose name meant "black":

> The word not only signified *black* in its literal sense, but points out the very disposition of his mind. The word, doubtless, has more meanings than we are *now* acquainted with—*two* of which, however, beside the first, we find are *heat* or *violence* of temper, exceedingly prone to acts of ferocity and cruelty, involving murder, war, butcheries, and even *cannibalism*, including beastly lusts, and lasciviousness in its *worst* feature, going beyond the force of these passions, as possessed in common by the other races of men. Second, the word signifies deceit, dishonesty, treachery, low-mindedness, and malice. What a group of horrors are here, couches in the word *Ham*, all agreeing, in a most surprising manner, with the color of Ham's skin, as well as with his real character as a *man*, during his own life, as well as with that of his race, even now.[9]

Priest's creative etymological scheme was a common, nineteenth-century investigative strategy into biblical characters, drawing on partial assessments of Hebrew meanings through contemporary racialized discourse. This assessment of lexical terms had more to do with race relations in nineteenth-century America than with ancient Israelite history or the etymology of Hebrew words. To maintain a biblically based, pro-slavery stance, it was necessary to insist on Noah's cursing of his "black" son, Ham, rather than on Canaan. For many pro-slavery advocates, the story of Genesis was not simply a historical account of Ham, his character, and his enslavement, but a story about "the color of Ham's skin" and his posterity that justified Priest's "even now" stance concerning the righteousness of slavery in his day.

While Josiah Priest (a northerner) may have popularized these arguments, James Henley Thornwell, the great southern Presbyterian theologian and (arguably) most formidable theologically conservative thinker in the nation, wisely avoided these etymological games and appealed to the Bible's advocacy of social order and social hierarchy as the most significant premise for maintaining support for the slavocracy.[10] The slave institution was part of a larger, southern social order undergirded for centuries by the biblical record: "Is it to be asked of us to renounce doctrines which we believe have come down to us from the earliest ages, and *have the sanction of the oracles of God*? Must we give up what we conscientiously believe to be the truth? The thing is absurd."[11]

Thornwell would not agree with President Lincoln's generous premise that both read the same Bible. It was not sufficient to promote, as abolitionist exegesis would suggest, the "spirit" of that text over against the text itself. For Thornwell, such an approach was hermeneutically catastrophic and signaled the demise of a proper Christian theology of scripture. A statesman, a college president, and a Presbyterian minister, Thornwell advocated for the merciful nature of the peculiar institution as necessary to society, since the maintenance of "slaves" as "property" was not, according to Thornwell, granted by US law, but "it has always been held to be moral by the vast majority of the (human) race."[12] If biblical slavery was dismissed, then why not biblical marriage and all other relationships forged under the social order of biblical patriarchy? Despite his defense of the peculiar institution, he recognized the need for modest reforms to address some southern expressions of slavery that were harshly mandated and conflicted with the Bible; so, he advocated for "the legal sanction of slave marriages, repeal of the laws against slave literacy, and effective measures to punish cruel masters."[13] On these reforms, he was not far removed from the gradual emancipationists of the North.

The Abolitionist Use of the Bible: Gradual Emancipationists

Gradual emancipationists form one wing of the abolitionist movement, although they are less well known in popular American history than their more aggressive "partners," the immediate emancipationists. The former position had wide and influential support in the first half of the nineteenth century. Perhaps this was due to the success of gradual emancipation legislation in northern states following the Declaration of Independence.[14]

The more gradual strategy toward the emancipation of four million enslaved African Americans formed some of its arguments as a mediating view and strategy through the Bible's role in the nation's impasse. Although there were certainly also political reasons for the gradual approach (such as maintaining the Union), the point here is to underscore the role of the Bible and its interpretation in this intermediate position. Of all three opinions, the gradualist was commonly propagated among biblical scholars who taught in the North. Charles Hodge would state the position of the Presbyterian church—and many Christians—as navigating wisely this middle position: "It is now seen that the principles which our church has always avowed on this subject, are as much opposed to the doctrine that slavery is a good institution, which ought to be perpetuated, as to the opposite dogma, that slaveholding is in itself sinful, and a bar to Christian communion."[15]

In a landmark pamphlet, Moses Stuart—a professor at Andover Theological Seminary and one of the leading biblical scholars of the day—also argued for a middle position when it came to American slavery. His *Conscience and Constitution* (1850) was a political treatise in support of Daniel Webster's *Seventh of March* (1850) speech that supported the "Compromise of 1850." Part of the Compromise was, on the one hand, the Fugitive Slave Act of 1850 and, on the other hand, the inclusion of several states such as California as free states. The government considered this agreement as a political effort to maintain the Union in 1850. Stuart provided detailed exegesis of the Bible in order to support his senator's (Webster) position and promote a gradual and voluntary emancipation of the enslaved. On the one hand, against (immediate) abolitionists, Stuart argued that the Bible voiced a pro-slavery stance. From the patriarch Moses to Jesus, the Bible never prohibited holding humans in bondage. Generally, gradual emancipationists considered ancient Israelite slavery more lenient than its counterparts in the ancient Near East. As Stuart would put it, Moses "outstripped all the legislators and sages of antiquity" in understanding human rights and developed "great advances in the matter of humane treatment."[16]

As a unionist, Stuart claimed that "universal and immediate emancipation would be little short of insanity" and that efforts of radical abolitionists have put the cause "back at least half a century."[17] He asserted that this antislavery (and, anti-Bible) position: (1) violates our "national faith"; (2) dissolves the Union; and, (3) begins a war.[18] Yet, unlike his careful attention to the Bible to reinforce slavery as an institution, none of these assertions were accompanied by a sustained exegetical treatment of biblical passages. For example, Stuart declined to address whether or not the Bible supported the idea of a democratic political Union?

Of particular interest—in light of the 1850 compromise—was Deuteronomy 23:15: "Thou shalt not deliver unto his master the servant which is escaped from his master unto thee" (KJV). The "fugitive" of Deuteronomy 23:15, according to Stuart, was a reference to the non-Israelite slave. All Hebrew slaves who escaped, however, should be returned to their fellow Hebrew masters.[19] In the same way, many would argue that black fugitives should be returned to their "Christian" masters in the South, since "these States are not *heathen*."[20] His support of Webster's (and Henry Clay's) 1850 Compromise provisions influenced directly his exegetical conclusions. The literary and historical context of Deuteronomy is less clear on the ethnic background of the escapee.[21] Stuart moves beyond an exegesis of the biblical passage into his own "compromising" interpretation in order to support the divisive political fugitive slave law of 1850. Furthermore, as Mark Noll recognizes, Stuart awkwardly assumed, as many pro-slavers would, "American states were analogous to the tribes of Israel,"[22] which was an assumption not easily discernible from the commonsense interpretation of the day.

On the other hand, in favor of the cause of emancipation, Stuart asserted that if slavery was still practiced, following the laws of Moses, then citizens should also "insist on the liberty of polygamy and concubinage."[23] Clearly other principles for applying ancient texts in contemporary settings were at stake and emancipation had to be the ultimate, if slowly attained, goal. The ultimate goal of emancipation was most importantly framed by how most abolitionists believed that the spirit of Christ's teachings as found in the Gospels was the new "supreme law" for Christian living.

The appeal to the "spirit" of the Bible's Christ-like direction with respect toward eliminating human bondage was further strengthened through the use of supporting references to biblical texts as well. Stuart employed five of the leading verses among abolitionists of all stripes, as he appealed to southern slaveholders through moral suasion: Matthew 22:39 (love your neighbor); Matthew 7:12 (do to others what you would like done to you); Acts 17:26 (one blood doctrine); Romans 3:29 (Is God not also the God of the Gentiles?); and, Ephesians 2:14 (God has broken down the dividing wall).

Along with other abolitionists, gradual emancipationists found the practices of the peculiar institution in the South to be incompatible with a biblical approach to human bondage. Charles Hodge would put it in this manner, "Slaveholding may be justifiable, and yet the laws made by slaveholders be atrociously unjust."[24] Even wise southern advocates of slavery recognized this dilemma and sought to reform the tradition. To hinder access to education, marriage, and family life was an immoral way to treat one's "neighbor." Abolitionists, of all stripes, would often acknowledge the sexual abuse enslaved, female bodies suffered.[25] The Matthean passages were often summoned to support these charges against such offenses. The dismantling of the "dividing wall" of Ephesians 2 encouraged, according to Stuart, religious and spiritual instruction of the enslaved and, despite the cultural context of Romans 3, this verse implied granting full citizenship to free blacks (in their interpretation).[26]

Passages such as Acts 17 and its views of the equality of all humanity in the eyes of God also provided a vibrant counterargument against views of African American racial inferiority. Stuart labeled the pigmentation of ancient Israelites a "yellow-brown hue" and acknowledged many significant ancient African theologians, including Origen, Clement, and Augustine. As a biblical scholar, Stuart disputed the superiority of the "Caucasian race" as an "anti-biblical theory."[27] He may have been well ahead of his contemporaries in utilizing the Bible to discuss issues of racial equality, but his arguments did not mean that Stuart advocated racial amalgamation following emancipation. Instead, he believed that blacks would need to be colonized "as we have the *Indians.*"[28] Many emancipationists desired a colonization plan far from American shores. Such emancipationists argued that "Expatriation . . . is an essential feature of any wise plan of emancipation."[29] Even President Lincoln's original draft of the Emancipation Proclamation included a clause for the African colonization of former American slaves.[30]

For many gradual emancipationists who appealed to biblical authority, Christians could be slaveholders. Slavery was not a biblical sin! Charles Hodge himself was a northern slaveholder who provided religious instruction for those he enslaved.[31] What no Christian slaveholder could do, however, was "deliberately endeavor to keep his slaves in a state of ignorance and degradation in order to perpetuate their bondage."[32] Perpetual slavery, therefore, is a "sin."

THE ABOLITIONIST USE OF THE BIBLE: IMMEDIATE EMANCIPATIONISTS

The so-called radical approach to abolition—that is, the immediate abolition of the enslaved—shared with the "moderate" position an elevation of those biblical texts that called for a common humanity among all people (since God "hath made of one blood all nations" [KJV]) and a fairer treatment of other human beings ("do unto others"). Furthermore, it was not uncommon for antislavery abolitionists to reject the ideas of gradual emancipationists

along with the views of pro-slavers, believing both groups elevated a belief in the maintenance of the institution (even if only for a time) as the only way to preserve the Union.³³
"No Union with Slaveholders" was a battle cry of many immediate abolitionists and occupied the masthead of William Lloyd Garrison's abolitionist newspaper, *The Liberator*
(1831–65).³⁴ Furthermore, against moderates, radicals argued against any compensation for
slaveholding masters.

Even while both emancipationist parties voiced the importance of the spirit of the Bible,
radical abolitionists called into question the conservative approach to the sacred text of
Christian faith. Frederick Douglass had in mind "divinity masters," like Stuart and Hodge,
when he gave his famous speech "What to the Slave Is the Fourth of July?" (1852). Not only
did he challenge the (northern) ecclesial community's support for the 1850 Fugitive Slave Law,
but he called into question their acknowledgment of the Bible's passages on slavery as indicative of the rightfulness of the institution itself in human history.³⁵ For Douglass, "that which
is inhuman, cannot be divine!!"³⁶ One interpretive difference was Douglass's identification
of enslaved, downtrodden bodies with those of ancient biblical Israel who were taken into
captivity, citing Psalms 137: "How can we sing the Lord's song in a strange land?"³⁷ This typological move confronted the view of many white Americans—whatever their opinion of the
peculiar institution—who would associate the nation's Union as a whole with the people of
Israel. For Douglass, only the disenfranchised could claim this link with downtrodden Israel.
If Douglass's hermeneutical approach to the Bible was correct, then slavery must be unjust.

A number of biblical passages commonly appeared in abolitionist literature. Perhaps the
most dominant biblical phrasing highlighted by abolitionists was the association of slavery
with, as the KJV would translate it, "men-stealing" (see Exod. 21:16; 1 Tim. 1:10).³⁸ The slave
trade and slave auctions treated people as property and, by their very practice, cast doubt on
the humanity of the enslaved and called into question the biblical expectations for human
relationships and the human pursuit of happiness, including marriage, family, and education. The Bible cannot support the idea, according to the abolitionist activist and writer
Theodore Weld, that the enslaved is "property," simply a "thing."³⁹ For Weld, God distinguished human beings from property in the Old Testament: "If God permitted man to hold
man as property, why did he punish for stealing that kind of property infinitely more than
for stealing any other kind of property?"⁴⁰

As for the curse of Ham account, more literal-reading abolitionists would commonly
emphasize Noah's precise bondage curse on *Canaan*; in this way, they would suggest that
"contemporary Canaanites" (if any could be found) could be enslaved according to the biblical indictment. Some interpreters would find in Noah's words, as the escaped slave and
abolitionist writer Samuel Ringgold Ward would put it, "the words of a newly awakened
drunken man" not a divine mandate: "I do deny that God is responsible for the words of
Noah at that time, and I also deny that there is any sort of connection between his prediction and the enslavement of the Negro."⁴¹

One crucial exegetical error some abolitionists made was to conclude that the KJV's use
of "servant" was somehow different from the contemporary understanding of "slave." This
argument was easily dismissed by pro-slavers, some of whom understood correctly that
the Hebrew ('*ebed*) and Greek (*doulos*) indeed usually implied a human held in bondage
as property. In any case, many antislavery proponents highlighted the voluntary nature of
ancient Israelite debt slavery, as a system unlike the compulsory, chattel form of human
bondage in the US system.

Finally, many abolitionists elevated God's liberation of Israel from Egyptian bondage as the decisive sacred attitude toward slavery, a divine viewpoint that would overrule any other biblical evidence on the topic. Furthermore, especially surrounding the 1850 Fugitive Slave Act, many radical abolitionists would break with the "gradual" proponents in their interpretation of Deuteronomy 23:15, understanding this passage, rather, as license to protect any escaped fugitive by any means necessary.

Others, in the abolitionist camp, would continue to foster an investigation of biblical texts that supported their arguments of moral suasion. Passages that could speak to the (im)morality of the particulars of the peculiar institution allowed them to make judgments about the larger institution itself. In this respect Jesus was not silent, as many pro-slavers would argue. His own words—"do unto others as you would have them do unto you," "love one's neighbor as oneself," and "do unto the least of these"—served as general moral guides to the dignity of the human individual. They utilized these key verses as wedges to divide the arguments of the pro-slavery cause and develop cases for the larger principles that the abolitionists desired to defend. The African American abolitionist David Walker wrote in his famous *Appeal* (1830) how Jesus's own words attacked slavery and racism:

> Have not the Americans the Bible in their hands? Do they believe it? Surely they do not. See how they treat us in open violation of the Bible!! . . . Our divine Lord and Master said, "all things whatsoever ye would that men should do unto you, do ye even so unto them." But an American minister, with the Bible in is hand, holds us and our children in the most abject slavery and wretchedness.[42]

On many of these points, the gradual emancipations agreed with their more urgent collaborators. As already mentioned, while the Bible advocated slavery, the US example of human bondage failed to fulfill the essence of "loving one's neighbor" by lacking proper avenues for the moral development of the enslaved. Harriet Beecher Stowe's widely read *Uncle Tom's Cabin* (1852) would liberally appeal to biblical passages to stress themes of loving your neighbor. For Stowe, the Bible clearly stood on the side of the abolitionist cause, despite her concern over William Lloyd Garrison's radical rejection of the Bible.[43]

Other abolitionists interpreted, incorrectly, the relative silence of Jesus, on the topic, as never coming into contact with human bondage in the Roman world. Many abolitionists acknowledged that the early church leaders allowed for the presence of slaveholders, but this allowance extended not (in their minds) to Jesus. Wanting to keep Jesus on their side, they would ignore Jesus's regular usage of slave/master accounts in his parables. With respect to the leadership in the early church, abolitionists also claimed that these early leaders, at least, gave commands to masters to manage their households as Christians responsible to God. If all slaveholders were to heed Paul's advice to treat Onesimus "not now as a servant, but above a servant, a brother beloved" (Philem. 16), this type of treatment (they claimed) would lead to the end of human bondage altogether.

Like Frederick Douglass, there were others who continued to separate the Bible, God, and "the Christianity of Christ" from any association with the so-called "Christianity of this land" which practiced slavery.[44] On this point, the radical abolitionists distinguished themselves from their gradualist counterparts. Reverend James Pennington could exclaim, "There is not a solitary decree of the immaculate God that has been concerned in the ordination of slavery, nor does any possible development of his holy will sanctify it."[45] Nancy Ambrose—Howard Thurman's grandmother—could reject certain Pauline texts as

"Scripture" altogether.[46] Sojourner Truth's claim to "read men and nations" was a herme-neutical approach to scripture that depended less on texts than on human actions and the chief subject of the New Testament, Jesus.[47] William Lloyd Garrison would also distinguish between the "Jesus" of the Gospels from other teachings in scripture, declaring the Bible was no less a pro-slavery document than the nation's Constitution.[48] All four—Douglass, Pennington, Ambrose, Truth—spoke on the matter from the perspective of the formerly enslaved. From first-hand experiences, they all understood the degradations to human life associated with the peculiar institution.

Most of these so-called more extreme claims about the Bible's view of slavery did not generally lead to a rejection of the Bible or the Christian God. Rather, they represented a forthright unwillingness to compromise with those who aligned the Bible with the power-ful, who failed to notice the inhumane treatment of their enslaved fellow human beings, and who declined immediate action.

SLAVERY, BIBLICAL AUTHORITY, AND BIBLE DICTIONARIES

One hermeneutical legacy of the enduring challenges of interpreting the Bible in light of US slavery in the nineteenth century is the concern over the Bible's authority with respect to contemporary moral issues in the country's life. Entries on "slavery" in Bible dictionaries in the twentieth century provide insight into these tensions surrounding the understanding of the Bible and slavery from the previous century. On the one hand, the abolitionist position of the nineteenth century is unanimously viewed as the morally superior position. On the other hand, recognizing the advocacy of enslavement in their ancient biblical settings (that is, the pro-slavery position of the previous generation), many of the dictionaries attempt to distance the people of God—whether Israel or Christians—from passages apparently sup-porting human bondage. The implications of this tension were profound. If the Bible was unable to provide a commonly accepted moral rationale for preventing the Civil War and lead effectively to a common ground on the issue of slavery, then how could it impart reso-lution to a wide array of other moral dilemmas that divide people of good will who turn to the sacred text of Christianity to shape their lives? The few dictionaries that have attempted to propose a way through the dilemma are disconcerting.

Less than one hundred years after the Civil War, some dictionaries attempted to distance even the patriarchs from the institution of slavery: "It cannot be said to be a Mosaic insti-tution at all, but being found by the Jewish lawgiver, it was regulated by statute with the purpose and tendency of mitigating its evils and of restricting its duration."[49] This dilemma about how to understand the relationship and meaning of biblical texts for slavery is most clearly exemplified in dozens of biblical dictionaries that continue to shape the field of bibli-cal studies in the twentieth century. As the quotation indicates, a common recent interpre-tive position is to conclude that, often without sufficient comparative evidence, slavery in the community of ancient Israel and in the house churches of early Christianity was in many respects more lenient than the practice that existed in surrounding communities of the ancient Near East.[50] As one writer put it, there was a "redemptive" quality in the traditions

surrounding slavery among the people of God that was absent from its contemporary counterparts.[51] Rather than acknowledge the similar contexts and position of ancient societies on
slavery, as a regular institution of ancient life, these cumbersome entries on slavery struggle
to find positive elements within the biblical practices of slavery in order to maintain the
authority and moral core of the sacred text.

Along these lines, theologian and Christian educator Merrill Unger asserts apologetically, "In so far as anything like slavery existed, it was a mild and merciful system, as compared to that of other nations."[52] Following this line of argument, it is presumed that even
foreign slaves in Israel worked in a system that was caring and just: "All these non Hebrew
slaves were regarded as members of the Commonwealth of Israel . . . and they were equal
before God, participating in religious festivals and sacrifices . . . and enjoying the rest of the
Sabbath day."[53] More recently a number of dictionary entries highlight Deuteronomy 23:15
as representative of Israel's humanitarian effort toward the enslaved: "in contrast to ANE
[ancient Near East] treaties providing for mutual extradition of fugitive slaves, biblical law
prohibited such extradition and granted them asylum."[54] This particular law may be distinctive among the slave laws of ancient Israel's neighbors, but this "humanitarian" practice did
not extend to other enslaved foreigners who resided in their midst.[55]

Reflecting on the position of slavery within the New Testament, there are efforts to
ensure that one's status—whether slave or free—gave no Christian an advantage in the early
Christian communities. Christ was the great equalizer. In reality, it is difficult to ascertain
the exact experience of slaves in and around early house churches since none of our documents originate from the hand of an enslaved Christian. It would have been very complicated for the enslaved to account for two masters, an earthly and a heavenly one. Perhaps
that was the point of Paul's advice to enslaved believers in Corinth to secure their freedom
if it became readily available (1 Cor. 7:21-22).

Yet, many Bible dictionaries—which are expected to represent the common knowledge
of the field of biblical studies—promote the view that the Christian form of slavery constituted a marked improvement over that in other circles within the Roman Empire. While
the New Testament failed to reject the institution, it also did not justify its presence (as is
frequently acknowledged), a holdover idea from nineteenth-century abolitionists. The New
Testament "recognized the equality of slave and master in God's sight . . . (and) exhorted
the master to treat his slaves considerately, reminding him that they had rights which God
will maintain."[56] Decades later, we find the following observation in a dictionary more representative of the critical side of biblical studies, "Paul encourages slaves to be obedient
(Eph. 6:5; Col. 3:22) and he sends the runaway slave Onesimus back to his master (Philem.).
Nonetheless the NT undermines the institution of slavery inasmuch as it proclaims a radical equality in Christ (1 Cor. 7:21-22; Gal. 3:28; Col. 3:11)."[57] Apparently, this "radical equality" was diluted in the communities represented by the Pastoral Epistles, if not other early
Christian circles as well.

There is minimal discussion, in Bible dictionaries, on the role Jesus may or may not have
played in the maintenance of the slave system. Occasionally, a positive insight is drawn
from Jesus's action or teaching. For example, "Jesus' call for his followers to forgive all debts
(Matthew 6:12) would have undermined the basis for debt slavery,"[58] apparently an observation neither Jesus nor the early church promoted. A much more nuanced view has been
recently offered by J. Albert Harrill in his entry on "Slavery." Harrill suggests that Jesus's parables reveal the enslaved as only "stock" characters and do not provide essential observations

about the real treatment of the enslaved in first-century life, even while attempting "to communicate early Christian ethics through the slavery allegory."[59]

Much of the discussion of slavery found in Bible dictionaries in the twentieth century (and beyond) can be traced back to the earlier tense debates that informed the public discussions on slavery, in light of the Bible, in the decades leading up to the Civil War. Many of the entries found in post–Civil War Bible dictionaries provide evidence of the hermeneutical challenges of coming to terms with how the Bible, which often promotes the immoral institution of slavery, can offer moral guidance in other areas for the contemporary community.

Conclusion

In the history of the debates surrounding slavery, many have seen the Bible as speaking on both sides of the nation's greatest moral sin. When the Bible failed to resolve the controversy over slavery on its own, a war that killed hundreds of thousands of Americans determined the direction forward. One could conclude from the slavery debate that the Bible has no compelling authoritative "voice" of its own accord in the making of moral decisions. That claim overstates the reality of its usage in American life. Mark Noll suggests that interpreters turned to the Bible to understand slavery, but failed to return to the Bible to comprehend issues of race.[60] Another way to view it is that they intentionally read their understanding of human bondage in the United States into the biblical passages on slavery, even as they unintentionally read into the Bible their assumptions about race. Interpreters did not always appreciate the historical distance between the Bible's cultural contexts and US society. Whether deliberate or not, "race" and "identity" were often at the forefront of searching the scripture.[61] The history of US slavery and the role the Bible played in justifying its continuance and in arguing against its perpetuation should serve as a reminder that the justice of the Bible is not self-authenticating.[62] The Bible does not have agency, except through its inheritors and interpreters. Scripture has a complex history as it relates to the institution of human bondage, and, at times, the Bible itself has also had a complicated American life.

Notes

1. "Second Inaugural Address," March 4, 1865.
2. See James P. Byrd, *Sacred Scripture, Sacred War: The Bible and the American Revolution* (New York: Oxford University Press, 2013), 55–62.
3. See Catherine Hezser, *Jewish Slavery in Antiquity* (New York: Oxford University Press, 2006); Jennifer Glancy, *Slavery in Early Christianity* (New York: Oxford University Press, 2002).
4. Keith Bradley, *Slavery and Society at Rome* (Cambridge: Cambridge University Press, 1994), 50.
5. Thornton Stringfellow, *Scriptural and Statistical Views in Favor of Slavery* (Richmond, Va.: J. W. Randolph, 1856), 23, http://docsouth.unc.edu/church/string/string.html.
6. Stringfellow, *Scriptural and Statistical Views*, 54.

7. Josiah Priest, *Bible Defence of Slavery; or, The Origin, History, and Fortunes of the Negro Race* (Glasgow, Ky.: W. S. Brown, 1853), 91–92, http://hdl.handle.net/2027/inu.30000005357862. Priest credits the first-century Jewish historian, Josephus, for the additional information of Ham's "laughter" without questioning its authenticity (95). Genesis 9 offers no observation about Ham's demeanor after seeing his father's nakedness: Ham "saw the nakedness of his father, and told his two brothers outside" (NRSV).

8. Priest, *Bible Defence of Slavery*, 92–93.

9. Priest, *Bible Defence of Slavery*, 40, emphasis in original.

10. Eugene Genovese, "James Henley Thornwell and Southern Religion," *The Abbeville Review* (May 5, 2015), n.p., http://www.abbevilleinstitute.org/review/james-henley-thornwell-and-southern-religion/.

11. James Henley Thornwell, "The State of the Country," in *The Life and Letters of James Henley Thornwell*, ed. Benjamin Morgan Palmer (1875; repr., New York: Arno Press, 1969), 597, emphasis added.

12. Thornwell, "The State of the Country," 597. Furthermore, "it has been grounded by philosophers in moral maxims" (597).

13. Genovese, "James Henley Thornwell," n.p.

14. States passed manumission legislation in the following order: Pennsylvania (1780); Massachusetts (1783); Connecticut and Rhode Island (1784); New York (1785, 1799); New Jersey (1786, 1804). See John Hope Franklin and Alfred A. Moss Jr., *From Slavery to Freedom: A History of African Americans*, 8th ed. (New York: Alfred A. Knopf, 2006), 92–93.

15. Charles Hodge, "Emancipation," in *Essays and Reviews: Selected from the Princeton Review* (New York: Robert Carter & Brothers, 1857), 516.

16. Moses Stuart, *Conscience and Constitution* (Boston, Mass.: Crocker & Brewster, 1850), 37 and 41, respectively.

17. Stuart, *Conscience and Constitution*, 112 and 109, respectively.

18. Stuart, *Conscience and Constitution*, 12–13.

19. Stuart, *Conscience and Constitution*, 31.

20. Stuart, *Conscience and Constitution*, 31–32, emphasis in original.

21. Most biblical scholars agree that the "fugitive" in mind was an enslaved foreigner. See also Jeffrey H. Tigay, *The JPS Torah Commentary: Deuteronomy* (Philadelphia: Jewish Publication Society, 1996), 215.

22. Mark Noll, *The Civil War as a Theological Crisis* (Chapel Hill: University of North Carolina Press, 2006), 61.

23. Stuart, *Conscience and Constitution*, 36–37.

24. Hodge, "Emancipation," 532.

25. Stuart, *Conscience and Constitution*, 104.

26. Stuart, *Conscience and Constitution*, 105–6.

27. Stuart, *Conscience and Constitution*, 103.

28. Stuart, *Conscience and Constitution*, 115, emphasis in original.

29. Hodge, "Emancipation," 526.

30. Whether Lincoln eventually relinquished this idea is debated. See John Hope Franklin, *Reconstruction after the Civil War*, 2nd ed. (Chicago: University of Chicago Press, 1995), 26.

31. Paul C. Gutjahr, *Charles Hodge: Guardian of American Orthodoxy* (New York: Oxford University Press, 2011), 174.

32. Hodge, "Emancipation," 533.

33. The relationship between the two emancipation groups was tense. See James Brewer Stewart, *Holy Warriors: The Abolitionists and American Slavery*, rev. ed. (New York: Hill and Wang, 1997), 46–49.

34. Garrison ended his preface to Frederick Douglass's narrative with these words as well, "No COMPROMISE WITH SLAVERY! No UNION WITH SLAVEHOLDERS!" in "Preface," *Narrative of the Life of Frederick Douglass, an American Slave. Written by Himself* (Boston, Mass.: Anti-slavery Office, 1845), xii, http://hdl.handle.net/2027/uc2. ark:/13960/t9x05zk36.

35. Frederick Douglass, "What to the Slave Is the Fourth of July? Speech at Rochester, New York, July 5, 1852," in *Against Slavery: An Abolitionist Reader*, ed. Mason Lowance (New York: Penguin Books, 2000), 43.

36. Douglass, "What to the Slave Is the Fourth of July?," 41.

37. Douglass, "What to the Slave Is the Fourth of July?," 41.

38. The NRSV translates *andrapodistēs* of 1Timothy as "slave traders."

39. Theodore Dwight Weld, *The Bible against Slavery: An Inquiry into the Patriarchal and Mosaic Systems on the Subject of Human Rights* (New York: American Anti-Slavery Society, 1838), 12–13, http://hdl.handle.net/2027/chi.22440439.

40. Weld, *The Bible against Slavery*, 14. See also Exodus 21:16.

41. Samuel Ringgold Ward, *Autobiography of a Fugitive Negro: His Anti-Slavery Labours in the United States, Canada, & England* (London: John Snow, 1855), 270–71, http://hdl.handle.net/10111/UIUCOCA:autobiographyoffooward.

42. David Walker, *Walker's Appeal: In Four Articles* (Boston, Mass.: D. Walker, 1830), 43, https://archive.org/details/walkersappealinfwalk.

43. Nancy Koester, *Harriet Beecher Stowe: A Spiritual Life* (Grand Rapids, Mich.: William B. Eerdmans, 2014), 185.

44. Douglass, *Narrative of the Life of Frederick Douglass*, 118.

45. James W. C. Pennington, *The Fugitive Blacksmith; or, Events in the History of James W. C. Pennington, Pastor of a Presbyterian Church, New York, Formerly a Slave in the State of Maryland, United States* (London: Charles Gilpin, 1850), 76, http://lincoln.lib.niu.edu/islandora/object/niu-lincoln:37490.

46. Howard Thurman, *Jesus and the Disinherited* (New York: Abingdon Press, 1949; repr., Boston, Mass.: Beacon Press, 1996), 30.

47. Elizabeth Cady Stanton, Susan B. Anthony, and Matilda Joslyn Gage, eds., *History of Woman Suffrage* (New York: Fowler & Wells, 1882; repr., Salem, N.H.: Ayer Company, 1985), 2:926–27.

48. In a series of personal correspondences, Garrison admitted to Harriet Beecher Stowe that he remained a follower of Jesus, despite his radical rejection of many biblical themes. See also Koester, *Harriet Beecher Stowe*, 184–89.

49. "Service," in *Unger's Bible Dictionary*, by Merrill F. Unger (Chicago: Moody Press, 1957), 998.

50. Hector Avalos recently published a major critique of this general conclusion: *Slavery, Abolitionism, and the Ethics of Biblical Scholarship* (Sheffield, UK: Sheffield Phoenix Press, 2011).

51. William J. Webb, "Slavery," in *Dictionary for Theological Interpretation of the Bible*, ed. Kevin J. VanHoozer (Ada, Mich.: Baker Academic Press, 2005), 751–52.

52. "Service," 998.

53. "Slave," in *A Dictionary of the Bible*, by John D. Davis (Grand Rapids, Mich.: Baker Book House, 1954), 770. See also Deuteronomy 29:10–13.
54. Barry L. Eichler, "Slavery in the Ancient Near East," in *The HarperCollins Bible Dictionary*, rev. ed., ed. Paul J. Achtemeier and Roger S. Boraas (San Francisco, Calif.: HarperSanFrancisco, 1996), 1030.
55. J. Albert Harrill, "Slavery," in *The New Interpreter's Dictionary of the Bible*, ed. Katharine Doob Sakenfeld (Nashville, Tenn.: Abingdon Press, 2009), 5:300.
56. "Slave," 770.
57. Frank J. Matera, "Servant," in *The HarperCollins Bible Dictionary*, rev. ed., ed. Paul J. Achtemeier and Roger S. Boraas (San Francisco, Calif.: HarperSanFrancisco, 1996), 1001.
58. S. Scott Bartchy, "Slavery in the New Testament," in *The HarperCollins Bible Dictionary*, rev. ed., ed. Paul J. Achtemeier and Roger S. Boraas (San Francisco, Calif.: HarperSanFrancisco, 1996), 1031. I am grateful to Leslie Giboyeaux, my assistant, who located a number of these dictionary entries.
59. Harrill, "Slavery," 306.
60. "On slavery, exegetes stood for a commonsense reading of the Bible. On race, exegetes forsook the Bible and relied on common sense"; Mark Noll, *America's God: From Jonathan Edwards to Abraham Lincoln* (New York: Oxford University Press, 2002), 418.
61. See also Sylvester Johnson, *The Myth of Ham in Nineteenth-Century American Christianity: Race, Heathens, and the People of God* (New York: Palgrave Macmillan, 2004), xiii, 5.
62. Sylvester Johnson, "The Bible, Slavery, and the Problem of Authority," in *Beyond Slavery: Overcoming Its Religious and Sexual Legacies*, ed. Bernadette Brooten (New York: Palgrave Macmillan, 2010), 231–48.

BIBLIOGRAPHY

Avalos, Hector. *Slavery, Abolitionism, and the Ethics of Biblical Scholarship*. Sheffield, UK: Sheffield Phoenix Press, 2011.

Byrd, James P. *Sacred Scripture, Sacred War: The Bible and the American Revolution*. New York: Oxford University Press, 2013.

Franklin, John Hope. *Reconstruction after the Civil War*. 2nd ed. Chicago: University of Chicago Press, 1995.

Franklin, John Hope, and Alfred A. Moss Jr. *From Slavery to Freedom: A History of African Americans*. 8th ed. New York: Alfred A. Knopf, 2006.

Genovese, Eugene. "James Henley Thornwell and Southern Religion." *The Abbeville Review* (May 5, 2015), n.p. http://www.abbevilleinstitute.org/review/james-henley-thornwell-and-southern-religion/.

Gutjahr, Paul C. *Charles Hodge: Guardian of American Orthodoxy*. New York: Oxford University Press, 2011.

Johnson, Sylvester. "The Bible, Slavery, and the Problem of Authority." In *Beyond Slavery: Overcoming Its Religious and Sexual Legacies*, edited by Bernadette Brooten, 231–48. New York: Palgrave Macmillan, 2010.

———. *The Myth of Ham in Nineteenth-Century American Christianity: Race, Heathens, and the People of God*. New York: Palgrave Macmillan, 2004.

Koester, Nancy. *Harriet Beecher Stowe: A Spiritual Life*. Grand Rapids, Mich.: William B. Eerdmans, 2014.

Noll, Mark. *The Civil War as a Theological Crisis*. Chapel Hill: University of North Carolina Press, 2006.

Priest, Josiah. *Bible Defence of Slavery; or, The Origin, History, and Fortunes of the Negro Race*. Glasgow, Ky.: W. S. Brown, 1853. http://hdl.handle.net/2027/inu.30000005357862.

Stewart, James Brewer. *Holy Warriors: The Abolitionists and American Slavery*. Revised ed. New York: Hill and Wang, 1997.

Thurman, Howard. *Jesus and the Disinherited*. Boston, Mass.: Beacon Press, 1996. First published 1949 by Abingdon Press.

CHAPTER 20

··

THE BIBLE AND SPORTS

··

JEFFREY SCHOLES

INTRODUCTION

··

JOHN 3:16 is one of, if not the most beloved verses in the Bible for Christians. Its message is succinct and at the same time, ostensibly comprehensive. But how many Christians who hold the verse so dear would be able to recite its entire text word for word? Given the overall lack of knowledge about religion held by Americans, it is likely that far more Christians would recognize the words "John 3:16" than its full text.[1] Why, if it is the content of the verse that is truly important, is John 3:16 so popular? Perhaps the fact that "John 3:16" was shown on T-shirts and banners worn and held throughout the 1970s and 1980s in prominent locations at the Olympics, the World Cup, NFL playoff games, and the Masters by a man named Rollen Stewart is partially to blame. Wearing his signature rainbow wig and jockeying into a prime position at these major sporting events, Stewart no doubt succeeded in imprinting the Bible verse into the minds of countless viewers and sending more than a few to their Bibles to investigate.

While his strategy could cynically be reduced down to one more example of shameless-exploitation-of-a-television-camera-meets-Christian-evangelism, it is more suggestive of the relationship between the Bible and sports in America than one might think. The fact that John 3:16 has nothing to do with sports and Stewart's sign was likely meant as an invitation to look up the Bible verse indicates something of a tenuous connection between sports and the Bible. Indeed, the link between the Bible and sports is, in one sense, weak. The Bible rarely refers directly to organized games or sports, though there are a handful of biblical references to the engaging in various forms of competition and physical activity.[2] When sports or physical activity are mentioned, they are often used analogously to say something "more important" about spiritual matters. And even when we find the few examples of sports or sports terminology in the Bible, they bear little resemblance to the sports that we know and play today.[3]

Yet, in another sense, the tie between the Bible and sports has been made strong by Americans who have historically searched for and often created bridges from the one to the other. Given the Bible's relative silence on matters directly pertaining to sports—whose power has steadily increased in strength and scope in American culture—it should not come as a surprise that a robust, albeit indirect, relationship has developed between the two.

In the first of two sections of this essay, entitled "Sports in the Bible," I will examine biblical texts that cite physical activity and sports explicitly. The second section, "The Bible in Sports," will look at the ways that the Bible has been used (primarily by Protestant Christians) throughout US history to clarify what sports is, to lend credence to the moral quality of sports, and to measure its closeness to other activities deemed holy and unholy. In conclusion, I will critically examine the primary way in which the Bible and sports are conjoined in America today—sports as vehicle to carry the Gospel to the masses with a Bible verse as the bumper sticker.

Sports in the Bible

Hebrew Bible

The Hebrew Bible makes several direct references to games or play, but little information is given as to the nature or role of these games. Children are encouraged to play (Isa. 11:8), and a confirmation that Zion has been restored post-exile can be seen in how the streets of Jerusalem are "filled with boys and girls playing" (Zech. 8:5). With regard to adults, the extent of games and competition often comes down to the use of dice ("lots") to decide everything from slave allotments to who would care for the Temple. In addition to games, there are several well-known biblical references to physical activity. Prominent among such activity is Jacob wrestling with God (Gen. 32:24-32), David firing an accurate shot with a slingshot at Goliath (1 Sam. 17:48-49), and Samson killing 1,000 Philistines with the jawbone of a donkey (Judg. 15:14-15).

Whether any portion of the Hebrew Bible is used to inform the playing of games that involve physical activity (what we would call "sports") usually hinges on one's hermeneutics. If a dualism is assumed that separates body/flesh from soul/spirit and places the latter far above the former, then sports are typically seen as inimical to the things of God. In such a reading of the Bible, the pursuit of spiritual goals should make one wary of activities which encourage and even valorize one's body and its accomplishments. Alternatively, if one maintains the unification of body and soul, then the kind of physical activity that participation in sports demands is elevated. If body and soul are thought of as indistinguishable within each human being (a view known as monism), then athleticism has a chance to be biblically sanctioned or at least allowed to coexist peacefully with spiritual pursuits.

By and large, the anthropology of the Hebrew Bible is a monistic one. As Shirl Hoffman states, "The Old Testament made no distinction between body and soul, the human person was not body and soul but an undivided unity. The Ancient Israelite would have pointed out: 'I do not *have* a body, I *am* my body.'"[4] The primary source material for such a view is found in the book of Genesis. As the mechanism by which Adam is created and given life in the creation narrative indicates, he becomes a *nephesh*, or soul, upon the divine breath animating the material dust (Gen. 2:7). The conscious body is the spirit, as the remainder of the Hebrew Bible largely reflects.[5] It must be noted that merely unifying body and soul does not stand as either an endorsement of organized play or even as a valorization of physical activity. Despite this, the integration of body and soul found in the characters that animate the Hebrew Bible has inspired many to appropriate a biblical monistic anthropology to the end of promoting the value of sports.[6]

New Testament

The New Testament, while similarly lacking any systematic treatment of athleticism, play, or participation in what we might call sports, does contain more direct references to sporting activity than does the Hebrew Bible. Though the texts have Jesus saying nothing of the virtues or drawbacks of physical activity or of games. And labeling carpentry work, the hike up a mountain, or the overturning tables in the Temple as signs of Jesus valuing physical fitness is a stretch similar to the misapplication of examples of physicality that we find in the Hebrew Bible to the endorsement of sports. As Hoffman notes, when play is addressed, the New Testament authors express a rather bland neutrality toward athletics. They "considered (informal play) to neither confer special advantage nor pose a substantial threat to the spiritual vitality of early adherents to the faith."[7]

Yet the New Testament does present the reader with the opportunity to yoke some of its verses to sports, however incidental the connection might be. For instance, just as links have been made between the embodied Adam to the importance of physical activity, some have argued that the Incarnation sanctifies Jesus's material body and therefore ours as well along with the physical activity that the body must undertake.[8] In addition, at the risk of confusing sports with war or more correctly spiritual warfare, God's followers can expect to "wrestle against . . . rulers of darkness" (Eph. 6:11-13). Or Jesus has competed, struggled, and eventually defeated sin (Heb. 2:14-15) as recounted in the *Christus Victor* theory of atonement. And Jesus will eventually defeat the Antichrist in in the ultimate "game" of life (Rev. 19:17-21).

Some of the absence of a direct endorsement of sport in the New Testament surely has to do with the nature of the ancient Greek and later Roman games.[9] These games were often performed in the nude, were extremely violent (primarily the Roman gladiatorial events), and honored the gods or the Roman Emperor—all violations of Jewish law. They were a serious problem for some early Gentile Christians too. The second-century Christian apologist and polemicist Tertullian warned that attending the Roman games tempts spectators to all kinds of sin. To drive home his point, he pointed to the Gospel of Matthew, "no one can serve two masters."[10] The Roman Emperor Constantine banned gladiator games in 325 C.E., and the later Theodosius I allegedly terminated the Olympic Games in the fourth century for their deep associations with paganism. The games would not appear again until 1896.

Although we do find references to physical activity and sports in the New Testament primarily from Paul and his mouthpieces. It is uncertain whether Paul himself attended the triennial Isthmian games in Corinth, though he was most certainly aware of their existence.[11] Several Pauline and pastoral epistles use the striving in these games figuratively in order to illuminate the more important activity of the spirit in the lives of the readers. Sports-talk in these letters, then, attempts to bridge the material, accessible world of sports to the spiritual world—a bridge that functions only when physical activity is shown to be inferior to the spirit.

It is Paul's first letter to the Corinthians that has the most prolonged discourse on sports in the Bible:

> Do you not know that in a race the runners all compete, but only one receives the prize? Run in such a way that you may win it. Athletes exercise self-control in all things; they do it to receive a perishable wreath, but we an imperishable one. So I do not run aimlessly, nor do I box as though beating the air; but I punish my body and enslave it, so that after proclaiming to others I myself should not be disqualified. (1 Cor. 9:24-27; all biblical passages are from the New Revised Standard Version [NRSV] translation unless otherwise noted)

Here, Paul is exhorting the Corinthians to apply knowledge of athletic preparation to their spiritual lives. Those pursuing the kingdom of God have need of rigid discipline and abstinence much like successful athletes. Yet at the semicolon is where the athletic metaphor ends—the laurel is an eternal one given at the end of the pursuit for God. Paul then picks up the sports metaphor again with a different sport to make a similar point. By invoking the image of a boxer punching the air, Paul calls to mind wasteful, misplaced, or even foolish-looking athletic activity so that his own efforts to preach the Gospel will be judged as "landing its blow."

In his letter to the Philippians Paul again uses the striving toward a prize as a means to highlight the true goal of life, but the explicit reference to a physical race is absent:

> Beloved, I do not consider that I have made it my own; but this one thing I do: forgetting what lies behind and straining forward to what lies ahead, I press on toward the goal for the prize of the heavenly call of God in Christ Jesus. (Phil. 3:13-14)

Likewise in other Pauline and deutero-Pauline epistles as well as in Acts (2 Tim. 4:7-8; Acts 20:24; Heb. 12:1; Gal. 2:2, 5:7; Phil. 2:16), we find the running of a race as a means of making a point about enduring spiritual trials, but little else about the sport of racing or its merits/demerits. Alternatively, there are passages that specifically address the nuance of a sport and seem to place value on athleticism in and of itself. The verse in 2 Timothy 2:5 warns, "and in the case of an athlete, no one is crowned without competing according to the rules." This verse is located in a longer treatise about soldiers and farmers operating properly within their occupational frameworks. Therefore, for the athlete, abiding by the rules constitutes proper behavior. The clearest statement on the relative value of physical fitness comes from 1 Timothy 4:7b-8: "Train yourself in godliness, for, while physical training is of some value, godliness is valuable in every way, holding promise for both the present life and the life to come." Finally, a Pauline passage that has been used repeatedly to champion the care of the body is 1 Corinthians 6:19:

> Do you not know that your body is a temple of the Holy Spirit within you, which you have from God, and that you are not your own? For you were bought with a price; therefore glorify God in your body.

As we will see later, this verse has been propped up by many in the sports world not only to sanctify the activities needed to keep the body in good shape but also to critique the ingesting of harmful substances, both legal and illegal. An athlete may misuse his or her body by eating unhealthy foods, but the use of this verse to curb the behavior is out of context—Paul is referring to sexual immorality and not matters of diet.

Do these verses add up to evidence that Paul and his representatives approve of or even tolerate competitive sports? Victor Pfitzner answers similarly but for non-theological reasons. In *Paul and the Agon Motif*, he argues: (1) athletic metaphors were so common in Greek literature and parlance that they could function quite well without the user ever having to endorse sports at all and (2) Paul-as-Pharisee is almost guaranteed to have possessed an "abhorrence [of] Greek athletics and gymnastics as typical of heathendom." Hence, "one must question Paul's so-called love for, and familiarity with Greek sports."[12] Perhaps it is because of this abhorrence that sporting terminology rarely shows up in rabbinic literature around this same time, which prompts Robert Ellis to ask, "Would he [Paul] not . . . have exercised more restraint in using this rhetorical device"?[13] Restraint may have been expected if Paul's intended audience were fellow Jews. Yet sports metaphors would resonate with Paul's primary target group, the Gentiles, who likely appreciated (or were forced to "appreciate") the pagan games. While Paul's instrumental usage may not constitute approval of sports, it may not indicate disgust either. What it does demonstrate is that Paul is willing to deploy secular tropes if it furthers his real agenda—a tactic that is the subject of the next section.

THE BIBLE IN SPORTS

Puritan Era

Sports as varied as cockfighting, boxing, dice, and rounders (an antecedent to baseball) were carried on the ships from England to the New World along with Puritanical attitudes toward them. King James's *Book of Sports* (1618), which encourages the playing of sports (even on the Sabbath—after church, of course), particularly riled many of the English Puritans who abandoned their homeland for the new land in the seventeenth-century. Once in the colonies, the pronounced emphasis on the twin Calvinist principles of hard work and delayed gratification made Puritans wary of sports.[14] Idle, and therefore nonproductive, action was disparaged, as was any kind of play. Play was predicated on leisure—a luxury enjoyed and honored by King James and British aristocrats but deemed a waste of time by industrious Puritans. Hoffman suggests that play could be deemed perilous as well: "Complete surrender to the illusionary world of play, allowing oneself to be separated from the life of everyday responsibility, seemed to Puritans a very dangerous thing for the Christian to do."[15]

It was the biblical injunction to refrain from labor on the Sabbath (Gen. 2:2–3) and to keep it holy (Exod. 20:8) that most forcefully legitimized the Puritan stance against play and sports. The clear delineation of work from rest that the Sabbath drew could lead to a quick jump from rest to leisure, from leisure to play, and from play to organized sports, so the Puritan chain of logic went. Contrary to the license to play on the Sabbath given in *Book of Sports*, Puritan hermeneutics cast Sunday as a day of devotion to God, not merely rest. Or as Michael Oriard puts it, "Puritan theology set play not just against work, but against piety."[16]

In truth, the American colonies inherited a "bifurcated leisure heritage" which saw Puritan austerity tempered with their own dreams of a "leisured paradise" in the New World.[17] As biblicists, the Puritans would have banned the playing of all sports if the Bible explicitly forbade it. But absent this proscription, if participating in sports could be seen as contributing to a godly life, it could be tolerated or even recommended—just not on Sundays. Therefore while boxing and cockfighting ("blood sports") were rebuked in the strongest terms, certain forms of physical activity, if they could be pressed into the service of godly work, could be justified under the Puritan regime. No less a Puritan than John Winthrop wrote, "I examined my heart, and finding it needful to recreate my minde [sic] with some outward recreation, I yielded unto it, and by a moderate exercise herein was much refreshed."[18] Increase Mather quipped that play for Christians was "very lawful, and in some cases a great duty."[19] And Richard Baxter required sports to be played for one end: "your service to God," so that financial or personal profit from playing sports was effectively prohibited as this would express vanity and/or pride. It is the ambiguous relationship to sports that the Puritans harbored that, perhaps ironically, helped physical activity and competitive sports avoid the kind of wholesale rejection that drinking and gambling suffered for centuries in the United States.

Muscular Christianity

The mid-nineteenth century saw a shift from a Christianity distrustful of sports to a Victorian era "muscular Christianity" that readily incorporated physical fitness and the sports that expressed it. First coined in England in a review of a sports fiction book for young boys, muscular Christianity or the "Christian commitment to health and manliness" entailed the recovery of a "muscular, 'preindustrial' body" that had purportedly been lost by young men.[20] Conspiring to weaken (read: feminize) these young men were lingering Puritan prohibitions on sports, the absence of holistic agrarian labor in the factory, Victorian wives who "controlled" their husbands, the new-found leisure time afforded by industrial production, and after-work drinking at the tavern. The Christianity in Europe and America, it was held, contributed to the problem by only dealing with the health of the soul.

The burgeoning Social Gospel movement helped effect a reversal of this trend by emphasizing societal sin and the ushering in the kingdom of God in this world through human effort. A humble spirit alone could not accomplish this task—brawn and the willingness to put one's faith into action were needed as well. Thomas W. Higginson, in his influential 1858 *Atlantic Monthly* essay, "Saints, and Their Bodies," lamented that too many for too long have believed that "physical vigor and spiritual sanctity are incompatible." Consequently, religious men (and women) resemble "precocious little sentimentalists" who "wither away like blanched potato-plants in a cellar . . . . We distrust the achievements of every saint without a body."[21] The Young Men's Christian Association or the YMCA was founded as a corrective to this state of affairs in England in 1844 and in the United States in 1851. With the intent of bringing together the "body, mind and spirit" (Deut. 6:5) of men, urban gyms were built in which they could gather, strengthen their bodies, collectively build moral character, and then take the Gospel out to the streets with determination.[22] As an early YMCA leader put it, "The gymnasium belonged to the YMCA as a fundamental and intrinsic part in the salvation of man."[23] Charles Kingsley, famed preacher of muscular Christianity in nineteenth-century Britain, similarly cited the intrinsic religious value of sports: "Games conduce not merely to physical, but to moral health; in the playing field boys acquire virtues which no books can give them . . . self-restraint, fairness, honour, unenvious approbation of another's success."[24] Or as another pastor of the gospel of muscular Christianity quipped, it is "easier for a boy to be a Christian in the gymnasium than when in the back of a hymn book."[25]

These acute phrases may have animated muscular Christianity, but what of the biblical justification for the movement itself? If we can locate muscular Christianity within the engine of the Social Gospel movement, then it likely possessed a postmillennial orientation drawn from a certain interpretation of Revelation 20:1-3. Indeed, Tony Ladd and James A. Mathisen aver that "the perceived goodness of masculine activity and sports was implicitly part of the vision to win the world for Christ and thereby usher in the millennium."[26] Or as other historians of American sports Elliot Gorn and Warren Goldstein put it, muscular Christians tied "the growing concern of American churches with man's life in the world with the alleviation of problems in the here and now, with the 'social gospel.'"[27]

For a more direct linking between the Bible and muscular Christianity, Mark 11:15 (Jesus throwing the money changers out of the Temple) and 1 Corinthians 6:19-20 (body as temple for Holy Spirit) are two verses commonly cited by muscular Christians of old and new, as is 2 Timothy 4:7 that references fighting the good fight and finishing the race of faith.[28] As noted earlier, it is a long road from Jesus merely overturning a table to the biblical sanctioning of physical fitness and sports. But a slew of "body-as-temple theologians" in the late nineteenth and early twentieth centuries trumpeted the "compatibility of health and scripture" by pointing to how Moses had to be strong in order to "march over the desert"; Jesus "radiated good health"; and Paul was "one of the great sport lovers of his day."[29] No less a theologian than Walter Rauschenbusch, leader of the Social Gospel movement, similarly declared, "There was nothing mushy, nothing sweetly effeminate about Jesus . . . . He went into the city and the temple to utter those withering woes against the dominant class."[30] And as mentioned earlier, the incarnation (and crucifixion) gave reason to respect one's body, which could lead to keeping it fit through athletic activity. "To dishonor our body is to dishonor His—to crucify Him afresh and to put Him to an open shame," one muscular Christian wrote.[31] For these evangelists, "the body was more than a container for the soul, it was a means of salvation itself."[32]

So while direct biblical support for muscular Christianity is scant and while the Bible has been enlisted to buttress the ideology *post facto*, the Bible has played an important supportive role for muscular Christians. It is, however, a relationship that must fashion Jesus into a fierce athlete while downplaying or disregarding the statement that "the meek shall inherit the earth" and disobeying his command to "turn the other cheek."

Sports Evangelism

The rise of Protestant fundamentalism in the first decades of the twentieth century paralleled a period of separation between religion and sports in America. Billy Sunday, the former baseball player turned evangelical pastor, exemplified the tenor of the times. Sunday had left the game of baseball because the sport's increasing professionalization meant that playing was more and more about money and fame rather than building moral character and saving society. For Sunday, baseball (and all sports for that matter) no longer possessed the capacity to Christianize the world; therefore, it must immediately stop trying.

Ladd and Mathisen contend that Sunday's departure from baseball and his call for Christians to distance themselves from sports reflects "a premillennial emphasis on 'otherworldly' Christian service at the expense of involvement in 'this present world.'"[33] Sports held little intrinsic value for those who held a deep distrust for the things of this present, earthly world and were awaiting the imminent second coming of Christ—the premillenarian interpretation of Revelation 20:1-3. If sports were thought to be able to "make bad people good" through the dogma of muscular Christianity, for Protestant fundamentalists, this present world was in the process of being permanently corrupted by scientism, capitalism, and liberal theology. No worldly activity, including sports, could offer real redemption in the face of such a secular onslaught. The Puritans rejected sports in favor of concrete actions that accorded with God's will; early twentieth-century Protestant fundamentalists rejected anything concrete.

The increasing power of sports turned the Bible into a refuge where literalist interpretations could provide their own response to the rising tide of "the world." Yet as sports continued to occupy more and more popular cultural terrain during the first half of twentieth century in the United States, and as a new breed of Evangelicals sought to disentangle themselves from Protestant fundamentalism, a reunion between Christianity and sports was in the offing. In fact, it is still widely held that hitching a ride to big-time sports in the United States assures a level of cultural relevance from the mid-twentieth century on, while the insistence on biblical literalism has had the opposite effect.[34] "Sports evangelists" after the mid-twentieth century held—as did Paul to an extent—that sports had extrinsic value in that they corralled and carried lost souls to Christ like no other institution could. Unlike the early church, this "church" made peace with spectator sports as those on the sports stage were seen as an invaluable conduits for spreading the Gospel.

It is the overwhelming infiltration of evangelical Christianity into the hallowed halls of American sports that justifies the attention paid to it in this section. Not only do evangelicals give an incredible amount of authority to the Bible, it is estimated that born-again Christians comprise around 40 percent of the players on the teams making up the major sports leagues in the Unites States with little indication that any substantial change is on the horizon.[35]

Any discussion of American evangelicalism in the twentieth century must focus on Billy Graham. In one of his earliest revivals in 1947, Graham had Gil Dodds, the world indoor record holder in the mile at the time, run around the stadium track and then give his testimony before the crowd. The crowd went wild as the separation between sports performance and the preaching to follow thinned substantially. A sports fan himself, Graham held most of his "Crusades" in famous sports stadiums and referred to his close staff as a "team" who "kept score of every convert and then publicized the numbers 'won to Christ.'"[36] The following statement by Graham offers a glimpse of a pugilistic muscular Christianity worldview that characterized his early crusades: "We used every modern means to catch the attention of the unconverted—and then we punched them right between the eyes with the Gospel."[37]

As spectator sports continued to colonize more and more cultural terrain in the United States, the spectacle of sports that relies on loud personalities, faster and faster action, and winning at all costs slowly put its stamp on the evangelical Christianity that was now in tow. As Hoffman notes, "the image of a champion became more salient in the evangelical cause than either the image of the good sportsman or that of the squeaky clean, upright-living, manly man."[38] The discourse of spiritual warfare in evangelical communities took on a new relevance as Christian fervor was often sublimated on the fields of competition. For instance, one of the key verses used by the Fellowship of Christian Athletes (FCA) is Ephesians 6:11: "Put on the whole armor of God, so that you may be able to stand against the wiles of the devil." Similarly, scholar Annie Blazer recounts her time at a 2007 FCA camp: "The ease with which the speaker moved between the concepts 'battle' and 'game' equalizes these two ideas in importance and urgency."[39]

As difficult as it is to find non-analogous scriptural sanction for physical activity, it may be more of a challenge to find biblical backing for the push to win at-all-costs in athletic competitions. Because evangelicalism grounds its beliefs in the word of God, its relatively newfound reliance on sports, its culture, and norms necessitated a new-found function for the Bible. What has unfolded over the last sixty years is that the Bible has become a cheerleader for big time sports in America. Verses, rarely longer passages, either are utilized to motivate athletes and coaches to play hard and win or are presented on the sports-enshrined platform as a vague but provocative invitation to accept Jesus.[40] In both cases, the Bible stands dutifully in the service of promotion and sustenance of sports by largely staying above the fray of its politics, economics, and ethical quandaries.[41]

For motivation on the field, oft-cited Bible verses abound. One such popular verse is Philippians 4:13: "I can do all things through him who strengthens me." As one of the more prominent examples of its presence, the verse graces the Under Armour brand basketball shoe designed by NBA superstar Steph Curry. Major League baseball player Jeff Francoeur has "Joshua 1:9" ("Be strong and courageous. Do not be afraid; do not be discouraged, for the Lord your God will be with you wherever you go") stitched into his batting gloves. During his improbable 2011 football season with the Denver Broncos, quarterback Tim Tebow, in a pregame speech to the team, cited Proverbs 27:17, which reads in the NIV translation, "Iron sharpens iron, so one man sharpens another." NFL quarterback Colin Kaepernick has the entire verse of Psalm 27:3 tattooed on his left bicep: "Though an army besiege me, my heart will not fear; though war break out against me, even then I will be confident." And Sam Bradford, another quarterback, prepares for games by reading the story of the ultimate underdog, David, beating Goliath in 1 Samuel 17.[42]

When sports operate as a stage for presenting the Gospel message, the Bible verses used by those on the stage may have nothing to do with sports but everything to do simple, pithy lines about the Christian faith. Reminiscent of Rollen Stewart, Tebow has scrawled "Mark 8:36," "John 16:33," "Ephesians 2:8-10," "James 1:2-4," and, of course, "John 3:16" on his eye black for games throughout his college career. Tebow claims to have used this tactic to motivate himself, but he admits that there was also the hope spectators would go to their Bibles out of curiosity. In fact, ninety-two million people Googled "John 3:16" during Tebow's national championship game in 2007. Seattle Seahawks quarterback Russell Wilson tweets a Bible verse almost every day with the expressed purpose of bringing people to Christ. And NBA All-Star Dwight Howard has outright stated that he hopes that one day, "the NBA will be [run] by the standards of God."[43] While these and other brazen displays of biblical passages continue to grace our television screens and sports arenas, it bears mentioning that more and more Christian athletes are rejecting this practice in favor of "witnessing without words." Interestingly, one of its most prominent practitioners, Aaron Rodgers of the Green Bay Packers, quotes not the Bible to support this practice but St. Francis.[44]

CONCLUSION: SPORTIANITY, THE BIBLE, AND BEYOND

American sportswriter and novelist Frank DeFord begins his three-part series for *Sports Illustrated* in 1976 called, "Religion in Sport," with a verse from the Bible as the lone epigraph. DeFord's use of Psalm 104:21, "The young lions roar after their prey, and seek their meat from God," suggests that he does not share the same enthusiasm for sport evangelism that its proponents do. In his piece, DeFord dubs the merger of American sports culture and evangelical Christianity "Sportianity."[45] The term is more than a clever mash-up—it is a new denomination of religion for DeFord in which, unfortunately, sports culture now molds large swaths of American Christianity instead of the other way around.

As Sportianity concerns the Bible, some have accused Sportians of a kind of selective literalism in which "cherry-picked Bible verses pre-screened to ensure that they don't conflict with sport's reigning orthodoxies."[46] The overarching orthodoxy of winning with a show of strength—all for the spectacle of it—can, and does, find its Bible verses for proof-texting. As such, after addressing the use of Philippians 4:13 to endorse sports and masculinity, the sports historian Robert Higgs wonders, "why promoters of muscular Christianity think these verses more relevant for the wisdom of the athlete than, say . . . Philippians 4:5, for example, (which) contains this: 'Let your moderation be known unto all men.'"[47] Higgs raises a valid point but an unrealistic one given the almost wholesale surrender of evangelical Christianity to the dictates of the sports world. Sportianity is alive and well in the United States, and any Bible verse that dares gain purchase with athletes must align with the discourse of sports first.

It is true that handpicking verses that serve ulterior purposes is inimical to good exegesis, but does this practice render the Bible impotent to confront issues that it ideally should? DeFord notes that Sportians will call out the bad individual behavior of athletes at times, especially sexual impropriety and illegal drug use. Yet "no one in the movement—much less any organization—speaks out against the cheating in sport, against dirty play; no one attacks the evils of recruiting, racism or any of the many other well-known excesses and abuses."[48] In similar fashion, Hoffman laments that Sportians have rounded off "the sharp, offending edges of the Christian gospel." In order for the Gospel to be domesticated in the way that Hoffmann describes, scripture has to be kidnapped "making it the handmaiden of hypercompetitiveness" which renders it unable "to acknowledge competition's corrosive effects on human relationships."[49]

No one can argue that the emphasis on winning in modern sports has encouraged bad behavior, and that American society has, for the most part, given high-profile athletes a free pass for a wide range and depth of ethical infractions. But as we have seen, the slender connection that the Bible has to physical activity and sports, both two thousand years ago and today, means that it is hamstrung in its ability to frame modern sports and challenge its power when needed head-on. Is it, then, unfair to enlist the Bible to address moral issues that arise out of sports as DeFord desires? Probably not, as ethical violations are ethical violations in spite of the context. Moreover, singling out athletes and coaches as the sole proof-texters in American society ignores the long history of decontextualizing the Bible by pastors, politicians, and pretty much anyone who only cites one verse. Significant, on the other hand, is the tension between the thin association between the Bible and sports and the perpetual need by some to thicken the relationship. It is precisely this yawning gap between the Bible and modern sports, both chronologically and semantically, that allows for innovative, albeit somewhat revisionist, ways of putting them together. And it is some of these ways that could and should be the object of future scholarship rather than question-able hermeneutics of athletes, coaches, and opportunistic evangelists that have, for better or worse, constructed a bridge between the Bible and sports.

NOTES

1. "U.S. Religious Knowledge Survey," Pew Forum on Religion & Public Life, September 28, 2010, http://www.pewforum.org/2010/09/28/u-s-religious-knowledge-survey/.
2. By "sports," I rely on Allen Guttmann's definition. He differentiates sporting activity from other activities; sport is organized play (games) that are competitive and physical. Allen Guttmann, *From Ritual to Record: The Nature of Modern Sports* (New York: Columbia University Press: 1978), 1–14.
3. According to Allen Guttmann modern sports "appear in sharply delineated contrast against the background of primitive, ancient, and medieval sports." Modern sports are largely secular, are promoting of equal opportunity, are rationalized, bureaucratically organized, and quantified based on the need for record keeping (and breaking). None of these qualities were present in games and contests before the seventeenth century. Therefore, the chances of establishing a clearly defined association between the Bible and the kind of sports that Americans are familiar with are slim. Guttmann, *From Ritual to Record*, 15.
4. Shirl James Hoffman, *Good Game: Christianity and the Culture of Sports* (Waco, Tex.: Baylor University Press, 2010), 169 (emphasis in original).
5. After Babylonian exile and especially during the period of Hellenistic Judaism, Israelites adopted a more dualistic perspective.
6. In an address to athletes, Pope John Paul II, who was an avid skier and soccer player in his youth, applies this insight to sports thusly, "Sport, as you well know, is an activity that involves more than the movement of the body: it demands the use of intelligence and the disciplining of the will. It reveals, in other words, the wonder structure of the human person created by God as a spiritual being, a unity of body and spirit." Here, the biblical iteration of the holistic human being as used both to legitimize the "movement of the body" as well as warn against athletics activity that minimizes the spiritual component of it. John Paul II, "Address to Participants of Athletic World Championships," *L'Osservatore Romano*, English ed., no. 36, September 7, 1987, 5. His successor, Pope Benedict stresses a holistic anthropology when it comes to sports but focuses on the necessity of balance. "Body, spirit and soul form a single unity and each component must be in harmony with the other. You know how necessary this interior harmony is in order to reach sporting

goals at the highest levels. Consequently, even the most demanding sports must be rooted in a holistic view of the human person, recognizing his profound dignity and favouring an overall development and full maturity of the person." Here and as with John Paul II, Benedict reminds athletes that cleaving body and soul is not only in opposition to scripture, but it can also hamper performance. Benedict XVI, "Speech to the Austrian National Ski Team, Oct.6, 2007," in *Insegnamenti di Benedetto XVI*, vol. 3 (Vatican: LEV, 2007/2), 423.

7. Hoffman, *Good Game*, 25.
8. See Gregg Twietmeyer, "Religion, Theology and Sport," in *Routledge Handbook of the Philosophy of Sport*, ed. Mike McNamee and William J. Morgan (New York: Routledge, 2015), 250.
9. As a precursor to Paul's response to sports, there is a comment in the deuterocanonical book 2 Maccabees written in the second century B.C.E. that traces the demise of the Jews under high priest, Jason, back to his building of a gymnasium in the town—a clear sign of his shameful compliance with Greek culture (2 Macc. 4:11–17).
10. Tertullian, "On the Spectacles," ch. 26, The Tertullian Project, http://www.tertullian.org/anf/anf03/anf03-09.htm#P991_405231.
11. Jerome Murphy-O'Connor, *St. Paul's Corinth: Texts and Archaeology* (Collegeville, Minn.: Liturgical Press, 2002), 15.
12. Victor Pfitzner, *Paul and the Agon Motif* (Leiden, Netherlands: Brill, 1967), 188.
13. Robert Ellis, *The Games People Play: Theology, Religion, and Sport* (Eugene, Ore.: Wipf and Stock, 2014), 137.
14. Surprisingly enough, John Calvin was somewhat tolerant of play: he bowled on Sundays. Just so that sports did not result in excess or invite immoral behavior such as cheating or gambling, they were tolerated.
15. Hoffman, *Good Game*, 81.
16. Michael Oriard, *Sporting with the Gods* (New York: Cambridge University Press, 1991), 363.
17. Elliott J. Gorn and Warren Goldstein, *A Brief History of American Sports*, 2nd ed. (Urbana: University of Illinois Press, 1993), 16–17.
18. Robert C. Winthrop, *Life and Letters of John Winthrop: Governor of the Massachusetts-Bay Company at Their Emigration to New England, 1630*, 2nd ed. (Boston, Mass.: Little, Brown, 1869), 104.
19. Quoted in William J. Baker, *Playing with God: Religion and Modern Sport* (Cambridge, Mass.: Harvard University Press, 2007), 19.
20. Putney, *Muscular Christianity*, 6, 11.
21. Thomas W. Higginson, "Saints, and Their Bodies," *Atlantic Monthly* 1, no. 5 (1858): 583–88.
22. John 17:21 is cited as the foundational scripture for the YMCA: "As you, Father, are in me and I am in you, may they also be in us, so that the world may believe that you have sent me"—a gesture toward the proselytizing mission of the YMCA.
23. Hoffman, *Good Game*, 117.
24. Quoted in Allen Guttmann, *A Whole New Ball Game: An Interpretation of American Sports* (Chapel Hill: University of North Carolina Press, 1988), 73.
25. Quoted in Hoffman, *Good Game*, 194.
26. Tony Ladd and James A. Mathisen, *Muscular Christianity: Evangelical Protestants and the Development of American Sport* (Grand Rapids, Mich.: Baker Books, 1999), 29.
27. Gorn and Goldstein, *A Brief History of American Sports*, 103.

28. Putney, *Muscular Christianity*, 11. Nick Watson, Stuart Weir, and Stephen Friend, "The Development of Muscular Christianity in Victorian Britain and Beyond," in *Journal of Religion & Society* 7 (2005): 2.

29. Putney, *Muscular Christianity*, 56.

30. Quoted in Stephen Prothero, *American Jesus: How the Son of God Became a National Icon* (New York: Farrar, Straus and Giroux, 2003), 96.

31. Putney, *Muscular Christianity*, 57.

32. Hoffman, *Good Game*, 116.

33. Ladd and Mathisen, *Muscular Christianity*, 81.

34. The YMCA gradually removed most of its explicit Christian language in official organization statements by the middle of the twentieth century in an effort to maintain its broad appeal.

35. Tom Krattenmaker, *Onward Christian Athletes: Turning Ballparks into Pulpits and Players into Preachers* (Lanham, Md.: Rowman & Littlefield, 2010), 13, 26.

36. Baker, *Playing with God*, 196.

37. Quoted in Annie Blazer, *Playing for God: Evangelical Women and the Unintended Consequences of Sports Ministry* (New York: New York University Press, 2015), 7.

38. Hoffman, *Good Game*, 131–32.

39. Blazer, *Playing for God*, 81.

40. Each approach is loosely reflected in the representative missions of the two primary Christian sports ministries in operation today. The FCA started in 1954 to do exactly what its name suggests. Gatherings, or "huddles" as FCA calls them, of Christian athletes are meant to provide support and motivation, both on the field and in one's spiritual life. Athletes in Action (AIA), which began in 1966, on the other hand, makes saving souls its sole purpose. AIA's athletes (which occupy all major sports) are called to give testimonies that add to the organization's "aggressive evangelism and disciple training." Krattenmaker, *Onward Christian Athletes*, 80.

41. For most evangelical athletes, it is difficult to separate one function from the other. Evangelism is always the goal; therefore, using biblical verses to motivate athletic performance can act as a "witness." Or vice versa passages that proclaim the glory of God can also be used for motivation on the field. An example of this found in the story of Eric Liddell, British Olympic sprinter and basis for the movie, *Chariots of Fire*. He chose not to run 100 meters (his best event) on Sunday for religious reasons in the 1926 Olympics and was handed a piece of paper with 1 Samuel 2:30, "Those who honor me I will honor," written on it that he held as he won the gold medal and set the world indoor record in the 400 meters several days later.

42. Curtis Eichelberger, *Men of Sunday: How Faith Guides the Players, Coaches, and Wives of the NFL* (Nashville, Tenn.: Thomas Nelson, 2012), 4.

43. Krattenmaker, *Onward Christian Athletes*, 29.

44. Eichelberger, *Men of Sunday*, 216.

45. Frank DeFord, "Religion in Sport," *Sports Illustrated*, April 19, 1976, http://www.si.com/vault/1976/04/19/614818/religion-in-sport.

46. Hoffman, *Good Game*, 14.

47. Robert J. Higgs, *God in the Stadium: Sports and Religion in America* (Lexington, Ky.: University Press of Kentucky, 1995), 325.

48. DeFord, "Religion in Sport."

49. Hoffman, *Good Game*, 264.

BIBLIOGRAPHY

Baker, William J. *Playing with God: Religion and Modern Sport*. Cambridge, Mass.: Harvard University Press, 2007.

Blazer, Annie. *Playing for God: Evangelical Women and the Unintended Consequences of Sports Ministry*. New York: New York University Press, 2015.

Ellis, Robert. *The Games People Play: Theology, Religion, and Sport*. Eugene, Ore.: Wipf and Stock, 2014.

Gorn, Elliott J., and Warren Goldstein. *A Brief History of American Sports*. 2nd ed. Urbana: University of Illinois Press, 1993.

Guttmann, Allen. *From Ritual to Record: The Nature of Modern Sports*. New York: Columbia University Press, 1978.

———. *A Whole New Ball Game: An Interpretation of American Sports*. Chapel Hill: University of North Carolina Press, 1988.

Higgs, Robert J. *God in the Stadium: Sports and Religion in America*. Lexington: University of Kentucky Press, 1995.

Hoffman, Shirl James. *Good Game: Christianity and the Culture of Sports*. Waco, Tex.: Baylor University Press, 2010.

Krattenmaker, Tom. *Onward Christian Athletes: Turning Ballparks into Pulpits and Players into Preachers*. Lanham, Md.: Rowman & Littlefield, 2010.

Ladd, Tony, and James A. Mathisen. *Muscular Christianity: Evangelical Protestants and the Development of American Sport*. Grand Rapids, Mich.: Baker Books, 1999.

Oriard, Michael. *Sporting with the Gods*. Cambridge: Cambridge University Press, 1991.

Pfitzner, Victor. *Paul and the Agon Motif*. Leiden, Netherlands: Brill, 1967.

Putney, Clifford. *Muscular Christianity: Manhood and Sports in Protestant America, 1880–1920*. Cambridge, Mass.: Harvard University Press, 2001.

CHAPTER 21

··

THE BIBLE AND
THE MILITARY

··

EDWARD WAGGONER

In America, both the Bible and the military are difficult to miss. The Bible sells reliably and profitably, year after year. It consistently tops polls that ask Americans to name their favorite books. No book has been more influential than the Bible in America's political, cultural, and religious history. The military likewise has an exceptional place in the American mindset. In annual polls since the mid-1970s, Americans express more confidence in their military than in any other institution. The Bible has long been used to help justify military actions, and the experience of war and conflict has often shaped how Americans interpret the Bible. Thus, it is sensible to analyze the interrelation of the Bible and the US military. Such an analysis reveals how the nation, the divine, and the military acquire their meaning in relationship with one another. This essay explores military editions of the Bible as material objects, the Bible as an idea that stands as a symbol for Christianity in an increasingly religiously diverse America, and the link between the Bible and the military in the ways that Americans think about doing good for the rest of the world.

A good way to begin thinking about "the Bible" and "the military" jointly is to identify where and how they seem to overlap. Military-edition Bibles are one such "place." Scholars can analyze these editions as material objects, directing their inquiry by asking questions about the visual and conceptual design of these editions. How do producers of these books make them attractive to their intended readers in the military community? How do the materials that supplement the biblical text encourage specific lines of interpretation and theological claims?

A second "place" where the Bible and the military overlap can be located in public controversies. The delivery or distribution of Bibles, testaments, and portions of the scriptures to military personnel by Bible societies and Christian ministry organizations has become problematic for many people inside and outside the military. Has the military given inappropriate access to these distributors? There are also controversies about the use of biblical text in the military workplace. What are the rights and responsibilities of the military and its members in such cases? Controversies such as these raise fundamental questions about the role of religion in public institutions.

A third "place" where the Bible and the military overlap is in various locations beyond our country's borders. For as long as Americans have sent troops abroad, they have also sent Bibles to the hosts, enemies, and vanquished peoples with whom they engage. Scholars can track the movement of Bibles with or through or from the American military to local populations outside the United States. What narratives about the nation and its purpose do Americans tell themselves, and others, about their military actions? How and when do the ultimate aim of Bible societies and Christian ministry organizations converge with—or diverge from—that of the military?

MILITARY EDITIONS OF THE BIBLE

Like other niche Bibles, military editions are crafted to be attractive to a specific population. These Bibles are targeted to those who have some connection to, or affinity for, the American military. Designers use symbols, images, colors, graphics, fonts, page layouts, commentary, marginalia, and supplemental materials (such as endorsements, verse-finders, creeds, hymns, poems, prayers, devotions, testimonies, and articles) to influence the way that such martial Bibles are "read" by their intended military-connected audience. Military editions differ from their civilian counterparts in several respects:

1. Military editions of the Bible draw from especially powerful symbols, images, concepts, and language.

Military symbols are powerful because the military is a formidable institution. It is the best-funded public institution in America. That fiscal prominence alone is enough to place decisions about the military at the very core of congressional politics. The US Department of Defense is also the world's largest employer, and one of the world's largest property owners. The American armed services have the distinction of being the most lethal, globally active, well-resourced, and dominant force the world has ever seen.

The power of the military is not merely fiscal, economic, and martial. It is also social. For example, Americans have learned to index many of their personal, family, and national memories by referring to the dates of major military conflicts. Military color guards solemnize a wide range of American ceremonies, including: graduations, funerals, legislative openings, speeches, and the opening of a wide array of sporting events. In annual polls since the mid-1970s, Americans express more confidence in their military than in any other institution.[1]

At both conscious and unconscious levels, military and national symbols have a remarkable capacity to "move" Americans. Few citizens can think "military" without also thinking, "nation"—and vice versa. Both terms elicit and organize important national and personal memories, concepts, and affective responses. No designer of a niche edition of the Bible has a more potent pool of symbolic resources from which to draw.

2. Military editions of the Bible show a particularly close fit between symbols, images, concepts, and language "inside" the covers of the text and those "outside" it (i.e., in the objects, spaces, and activities of everyday military contexts).

In principle, any social marker of identity including, but not limited to, such things as age, race, gender, as well as any activity or interest, could anchor a niche Bible. The designer of such a Bible will first select the central marker (e.g., "student") and then ask which symbols, images, concepts, and ways of speaking typically attach to that marker. From that reservoir of associations, the designer will decide how to establish relations between these and the biblical text. The stronger the power of the identity marker, the stronger the symbols, images, and vocabularies; and the stronger the symbols, images, and vocabularies, the stronger the conceptual and affective relation that niche-Bible "packaging" can create between the intended reader and the God of the text.

In a Bible intended for students, for example, the designer might insert a text-box on the page where the *Letter to the Hebrews* declares that Jesus had to learn obedience through his suffering. A student who reaches that page might find a two-paragraph commentary, entitled, "God's Schoolhouse," in which she is exhorted to obey her schoolteachers, parents, and God (the hard-nosed, Divine Teacher). If the symbols, imagery, and concepts used to write the commentary build a strong enough cognitive or affective connection between the reader's everyday experience and the biblical text, that connection could influence the student's social imagination and behavior.

One of the distinguishing marks of military-edition Bibles is that they are "read" in contexts carefully constructed and maintained. For example, a military reader will see camouflage not only on the cover of her Bible but also on the tent in which she sleeps, the rucksack that holds her belongings, the netting draped over the equipment that is stacked outside her living quarters, and the transport plane parked near the runway. The reader of that edition's introductory letter from two major generals and a rear admiral will register those military ranks not only when she lifts the cover to her Bible but also when she crosses paths with other military personnel that day in her world of ubiquitous ranks and hierarchies.

It is not merely the case that the soldier's Bible is "packaged" with camouflage and rank—two symbols/concepts that have in themselves a high capacity to carry aesthetic, cognitive, and affective associations. Rather, the further distinction in this edition's capacity to "speak" to the reader stems from its placement in a "world" of objects and spaces and encounters that speak to her using the same syntax, as it were. The "readable" text of a well-crafted, military-edition Bible is larger than the text between its covers—and is so, by a significantly wider margin than is the "readable" text of most other niche Bibles. This is both because the symbols of the nation and the military transcend the material object and because, for those who are reading it while serving in the military, the everyday persons and things that military personnel encounter tend to match the universe of symbols and discourse built into the packaging and supplementary material of these Bibles in obvious ways. Unlike the student who is not always defined by the physical and symbolic space of the classroom, military personnel are surrounded twenty-four hours a day, seven days a week, with obvious visual reminders of the encompassing nature of their military context.

3. Military editions of the Bible suggest some distinctive views about divine providence, atonement, God's identity, and human transformation.

Frequent family moves, risk of death, separation, not-knowing what policymakers will choose or why—military life poses many challenges that personnel and their families cannot control. Devotional writers for military-edition Bibles address this problem by reminding

the reader that God directs everything. Writers sometimes offer direct advice on such matters as respect for military authority or the need to seek out godly friends. More often,
authors "talk out-loud" about their own military experiences, and model how to interpret,
redirect, or reframe thoughts and emotions in God-respecting ways.[2]

What it means for God to be "in control" here is not clear. When authors of supplemental
materials in military editions tell the story of salvation, they nearly always describe Christ's
act as sacrificial. "Jesus willingly gives up his life as a sacrifice on behalf of the nation, on
behalf of the world."[3] The implication is that God's providence has a similar, sacrificial cast
to it. America is called to sacrifice, US military members and their families are called to
sacrifice, and US civilians are expected to reiterate gratitude and admiration for the sacrifices made by their fellow citizens. Personal and national sacrifice seems endemic to God's
governance of the world.

Writers of prose pieces in military-edition Bibles stress divine identities or roles, as often
as they discuss divine attributes. Jesus is "a loving, merciful Lord."[4] But God's love is a "force."[5]
The writers in these editions invoke martial identities for God. God is addressed as a healer,
a "defender and protector,"[6] "our Ultimate Authority," and our "Heavenly Commander."[7]
Jesus Christ is "the Wounded Warrior-King," "God's greatest warrior," and "the Ultimate
Warrior."[8]

The Protestant pedigree of most military-edition Bibles is evident in their accounts of
human transformation. Devotionals and other biblical extra material may encourage military readers, but only "the Bible text" itself will transform them. The words of scripture,
or the principles of scripture, must be internalized. Military wives, for example, should
post scripture verses all around the house in order to stay focused on God's Word.[9] A pithy
line from *The Warrior's Bible* expresses well a message that recurs in many editions: "Your
strength and power to live a victorious, fulfilled life depends exclusively on how much you
get of the Bible in you."[10]

4. Military editions of the Bible offer narratives in which divine, national, military, and
   individual histories align.

The most distinctive, theological contributions that contemporary military editions of the
Bible make are often found in a letter of introduction, preface, or publisher's introduction
to the biblical text. That is where the producers of these editions explain why "the Bible" is
important and relevant to military readers, and why the military and the nation are important to God. To make that case, a Bible publisher often places divine, national, military, and
individual histories into a single narrative. Each military-edition Bible becomes a potential
site for this constructive work.

Operation Worship, Holy Bible: U.S. Air Force [Edition], for example, opens with a letter of introduction addressed to "our Men and Women in Uniform, and to your families."
The author asserts that the Bible is "the greatest book ever written" because it shows God's
loving heart. God's love compels the author and his reader to military service. The author
explains that his military reader and Jesus have much in common. Both are motivated by
selfless regard for the weak. Each in his time participates in a "rescue mission," to a "hostile,"
"foreign country." Jesus has already been willing to die a "sacrificial death" to complete his
mission—and so, implies the author, is his military reader.[11]

On the dedication page of *The Military Bible*, the publisher commends the Bible to military members as "a source of comfort and strength within the chaos and turbulence of combat." The goal of the publisher—and of God, as well—is to help America's military personnel and their families to withstand the rigors of extended deployment to combat zones.[12] The publisher contributes a forty-four paged, "Spiritual Fitness Manual," inserted after the last bit of biblical text. With God's help, through the Bible, and with the instructions in this manual, the military reader will be able to fulfill his or her "high calling" as "a Warrior for our Nation and a Worshipper of God."[13]

The American Bible Society's *Holy Bible Military Edition: National Guard. New International Version* is introduced by a National Guard chaplain. The chaplain builds a parallel between the reader, whom he commends for being a "loyal servant of God, country, and community," and God, who shows "unfailing love and faithfulness." The Guardsperson "defend[s] the United States around the world" and has a duty to go anytime and anywhere his nation calls. The chaplain reminds the reader that "spiritual preparation" is "critical to the success of the mission." That is the lead-in to the chaplain's description of this gift Bible: it testifies to "God's nature, God's actions within our history, and God's love and faithfulness." The implied message to the Guardsperson is clear: our mission is to protect the nation; do not threaten the success of the mission by failing to read your Bible.[14]

Biblica, one of the nation's largest Bible societies, and producer of many military-edition Bibles, takes a different tack. It has created a boiler-plate synopsis of the Bible, entitled, "The Drama of the Bible in Six Acts." The tagline is: "Take Up Your Role in the Drama of the Bible."[15] Each edition in Biblica's current line of military Bibles has that same synopsis section. Supplementary materials that further distinguish one military edition from another in the Biblica line are inserted before the synopsis, in-between sections of biblical text, or after the biblical text. For *The Greatest Warrior,* Biblica adds testimonials from military personnel who suffer from wartime trauma.[16] *Finding Hope Beyond the Battle: A Bible for Military Families* and *Peace for the Military Family: A New Testament* include testimonials from military wives (and one husband).[17] Biblica's standard-issue combat edition adds selected Psalms, prayers, liturgy, and a combatant-centered meditation, entitled, "Jesus, the Son of David, The Wounded Warrior-King."[18]

Biblica's version of the history of salvation is a quasi-imperial, military, nation-building-or-restoring, justice-bringing story. It relates that human beings were created as "significant, decision-making, world-shaping beings," destined to "share in the task of bringing God's wise and beneficial rule to the rest of the world." After the first parents rebelled, humankind lost its capacity to carry out that "ancient mission." God graciously "promises to send a new king . . . who will lead the nation back to its destiny." In due time, Jesus, the promised king, arrives. He "renews the nation" and rebuilds it—but not in the way people expected. He "willingly gives up his life as a sacrifice on behalf of the nation, on behalf of the world." The payment of Jesus's blood restored humankind to its "mission." God's people now "demonstrate God's love across the usual boundaries of race, class, tribe and nation." Even so, there are still persons who "do not acknowledge the rule of the Messiah." But Jesus, the true ruler, "will return to the earth and the reign of God will become an uncontested reality throughout the world." At their resurrection, "the dynamic force of an indestructible life will course through" the bodies of Jesus's followers. "We will pursue our original vocation as a renewed humanity. We will be culture makers, under God but over the world."[19]

What these narratives seem to effect—to various degrees of success—is a fusion of identities, histories, and purposes. In each of the narratives, God, the military, the nation, and the reader are imagined to work together. The military-edition Bible is offered as an orientation guide, or instruction manual, for working confidently and effectively in this God-led effort.

CONTROVERSIES ABOUT THE USE OF
THE BIBLE IN THE MILITARY

How does the Bible—as both a material object and sacred text and symbol of Christianity—function in public debates about religion in the military? In the military, broad cultural and political disagreements about claims for the "Christian" identity of the United States have coalesced around both the distribution of Bibles to military personnel and the use of biblical texts by military personnel in the course of their professional duties. A number of incidents have raised intense public debate about Christianity and the Bible.

As historians and experts on the military point out, the disaffection of many liberal, mainline Christians with US policy in the Vietnam War left the staffing of the military's chaplaincies—the formal "face" of religion in the military—to more socially, politically, and theologically conservative Christian denominations. The military in general was eager to have the support of evangelical Christians at that time—both in chaplain positions and the officer corps. Drug abuse, dereliction, "fragging," and well-publicized ethics violations during the prosecution of the war demoralized many in the military and left its professional core convinced that they needed to shore up discipline, morality, and *esprit de corps* among their ranks. The Bible-focused Christianity of conservative evangelicals seemed conducive to the reform of the military.[20]

The emergence of the "Religious Right" in the politics and society of the 1980s and subsequent decades with its reactionary agenda against such issues as abortion rights and homosexual marriage provided a foundation for a counterattack against what many deemed the rising moral laxity and permissiveness to be found in American culture. This counterattack contributed to what many people call the "culture wars" in American society, creating deep divisions along political and religious lines. Thus, a significant number of Americans (including those in liberal, mainline Christian denominations, those who identify with other religious traditions, and those who claim no particular tradition) felt alarmed by the role that the largely evangelical "Religious Right" played in the administration of President George W. Bush. As chief executive and commander-in-chief, Bush invoked powerful currents in American Christianity by including direct and indirect biblical language in his public remarks about how America should respond to the terror attacks of September 11, 2001.[21] And in a telephone appeal for France's support to French president Jacques Chirac, Bush allegedly cast the larger turn of events in the Middle East, and America's upcoming invasion of Iraq, in biblical, prophetic, and apocalyptic terms.[22]

Beginning in 2005, in response to a proselytization scandal at the US Air Force Academy, political and legal advocacy groups long dedicated to the separation of church and state, joined newer organizations to raise forceful objections to what they viewed as an increasingly sectarian and coercive, evangelical Christian climate in many parts of the armed forces. The distribution, display, and use of Bibles inside the military became a flashpoint for complex questions about religion in national life.

A series of specific questions emerged. Is it permissible for military leaders to cite the Bible in their public remarks? Is it permissible for Bible societies to place Bibles in military lodgings? Is it permissible or appropriate for the military to include copies of the Bible in various displays of military and government programs? Does the military grant Bible distributors inappropriate access to military personnel, such as the stations where new recruits are initially processed, or in basic training, or at the military's major points of embarkation? Is it permissible for military members to publically display scripture verses in their workplace?

The military's sociological power as an institution, its formidable fiscal and political weight in American society, and its prominent place in narratives that Americans construct about their nation all increase the weight and intensity of the visual and conceptual resources from which designers of military-edition Bibles can draw in order to influence the way that such Bibles are "read" by their intended readers. Likewise, these same notable features of the American military—coupled with the general dominance of Christianity in American culture—make the distribution of Bibles, and the public use of biblical texts in the military workplace, occasions for especially intense disagreements.

The distinctive parameters of military life and the military's status as a publicly funded institution make it all the more important that debates about the Bible in the military also be opportunities to discuss the role of religion in general, and Christianity in particular, in American national life. Political and military decisions about such questions may be important contributions to ongoing changes in what national identity means for Americans, and how religious belief bears on that national identity.

BIBLES WITH THE MILITARY, TO THE WORLD

American Bible societies and ministry organizations seek to disseminate Bibles, testaments, and other portions of scripture all over the world. Military action outside the United States sometimes opens or widens doors to regions otherwise hard for distributors to reach. At times, the American government and military have directly promoted Bible distribution abroad. The heyday of this partnership was from the occupation of Japan in World War II through the Vietnam War, yet every new US military conflict stands as a milestone in America's distribution of Bibles to the world.

During the US War with Mexico (1846-1848), the American Tract Society (ATS) told potential donors that the war was providential, as it gave Americans the chance to "regenerate, disenthrall, [and] bless Mexico" with scriptures. In New Orleans, where US troops boarded ships to Mexico, an ATS agent recruited American soldiers to serve as colporteurs. Army officers, as well as Louisiana's governor and several state legislators, lent their support.[23] The board of the American Bible Society (ABS) "deeply deplored" the outbreak of war but also saw God's hand in the conflict.[24] The adversity of war would render many Mexicans "disposed to receive and peruse" the Bible. After crediting divine providence for sending them a well-qualified missionary to serve as their agent, they dispatched him to Mexico with 3,000–4,000 Bibles and testaments. They were pleased to report that the American government—acknowledging the ABS as a benevolent, rather than commercial venture—had exempted them from duty taxes on that shipment.[25]

When America announced itself as a global military power on May 1, 1898, by obliterating the Spanish Pacific fleet at Manila, in the Philippine Islands, Christian ministry groups and Bible societies saw their opportunity immediately. By June 1, the YMCA had secured the US War Department's permission to send two representatives with the first wave of soldiers to sail for the Philippines. The two men were charged with ministering to the troops and sharing the Gospel with Filipinos in Manila. The War Department paid for the cost of shipping these YMCA workers, with their Bibles and other equipment, and it gave them a large building in the heart of the city.[26]

Eight weeks after the YMCA workers arrived in Manila, the ABS' agent in China arrived "for the sake of preliminary inquiries about the possible openings there for the distribution of the holy Scriptures."[27] On the basis of his report, the ABS appointed a newly graduated seminarian from New Jersey, Jay C. Goodrich, to go to Manila as their first agent in the Philippines. Goodrich and his wife arrived at the end of November, 1899, and went immediately to see Major General Otis, who commanded all US forces in the Philippines, and who was therefore its current governor. The ABS and its young agent were worried that the Major General would not permit them to disseminate the scriptures freely. It had been rumored in stateside newspapers that Otis "had hindered Bible distribution" in the newly declared US possession. Goodrich was relieved to learn that the rumor "was absolutely without foundation." General Otis not only encouraged Goodrich in his plans to begin distributing the Bible to the Filipinos but also "granted [him] on special order a free entry for all Bibles and tracts." The ABS also needed, and received, the military's protection. American and Filipino forces were fighting one another less than ten miles outside Manila.[28]

Goodrich established a depository in the YMCA building and immediately enlisted military help to distribute Bibles to Filipinos. "The Army officers, and especially the chaplains," said Goodrich, seemed "friendly to our cause and willing to aid as far as able and taking the Gospels we have printed to the natives." He relied on "Christian men in the Army" for information as he drew up plans to establish "a depository [of Bibles and tracts] in the principal city of each island."[29] By 1904, Goodrich could report good progress in the work of giving scriptures to the Filipinos. The US military and civil governments in the Philippine Islands had improved public services that were vital for America's success in "the highest type of colonization ever attempted."[30]

At the end of World War II, General Douglas MacArthur firmly believed that Japan's recovery from the war would require it to be Christianized. For that task, MacArthur saw two things necessary: missionaries and Bibles. He made it official, government policy to return Western missionaries to Japan as soon as possible. He invited (and the military transported to Japan) several leaders of American Bible societies, denominations, and missionary organizations to hear his pitch in-person.[31]

General MacArthur asked the ABS and the Pocket Testament League to distribute huge numbers of Bibles to the Japanese.[32] When the visiting ABS senior general secretary told him, in 1950, that the ABS had distributed four million scriptures to the Japanese since the end of the war, and that the ABS planned to send twice that amount in the next two years, MacArthur requested that the ABS reset its goal to 30 million.[33] He asked the Pocket Testament League to distribute ten million portions of the scriptures in Japan, and he requested that US and Japanese officials provide any needed help. (Incredibly, the League distributed eleven million portions of scripture in Japan as they acted on MacArthur's request). Because MacArthur was the Supreme Commander for the Allied Powers in the region—the most powerful man in postwar Japan—many Japanese officials took MacArthur's letter of support for the distribution of the scriptures not as a suggestion, but a direct order.[34]

In the Korean conflict of the early 1950s, the US military hired American missionaries and former military chaplains to distribute Bibles to the Chinese and North Korean prisoners of war in the camps. MacArthur, who had become the commander of US military forces in Korea, had already publicly declared in Japan that Christianity would save and protect Asia from communism. The Gideons and the American Bible Society sent scriptures to US military officials for distribution to Chinese and North Korean detainees.[35] For countless Americans, it was welcome news that the Bible was having such a powerful effect among the communist prisoners of war.[36]

The Vietnam War enabled evangelical outreach to the Vietnamese. The war also allowed for record numbers of Bibles and portions of Scripture to be sent to the members of the American military. Pocket Testament League representatives toured the country in US military vehicles and flew in US military helicopters to visit South Vietnamese soldiers. Upon arrival, the League's representative would deliver a message to the whole group, distribute copies of the Bible to the Vietnamese, and then invite them to talk one-on-one with evangelists.[37] The American Bible Society, Gideons, and the International Bible Society also distributed scriptures to the Vietnamese during the war.

Between Vietnam and the Gulf Wars of the 1990s, several factors began to make the relationship between the military and Bible societies and ministry groups somewhat different than before. First, many in mainline, liberal Christian denominations soured on US military involvement in Vietnam. At the same time, these denominations began to suffer a pronounced decline in their stateside membership. The combination of these two factors allowed more theologically conservative evangelical Christians in America to gain a majority status in the military chaplaincy. Chaplains had always been an important link between Bible societies, ministry groups, and commercial publishers of military-edition Bibles. Now, for the first time, conservative, evangelical chaplains would set the tone, and control the basic narrative, for the distribution of the Bible from, with, or through the military, to the world.

Second, in the 1990s, the focus of the nation's military actions shifted to lands with predominantly Muslim populations. In those theaters of operation, where the opposing forces were terrorist organizations with extremist Muslim ideologies, it became counterproductive for the military to openly participate in the distribution of Christian scriptures. Whereas US commander General Norman Schwarzkopf publicly thanked the American Bible Society in 1991 for donating 300,000 copies of the Bible to US troops in operation Desert Storm, he was incensed by the effort of Samaritan's Purse to distribute Arabic translations of the Bible to US personnel as an evangelistic tool for converting Muslims in Saudi Arabia.[38]

The US Military's Central Command—which presided over recent wars in Iraq and Afghanistan—has issued a directive that expressly forbids US personnel from proselytizing in that theater of operation.[39] This policy was tested in 2009, when news organizations all over the world began to run a story (which had come initially from Al Jazeera) about US military personnel in Afghanistan who had received Bibles from stateside groups to send or give away to Afghans. The Bibles had been printed in local Afghani languages. Eventually, the US military had to burn the Bibles in order to quell the uproar among Muslims around the world.[40] But that act of burning the Bibles in turn offended some Christians inside the United States.[41]

In the latest American interventions in the Middle East, the question about the Bible's connection to the activities of the American military has thus come to prominence. Should the Bible be distributed with, through, or after US military actions? It may be the case that domestic struggles over issues of religious status or prerogatives or responsibility in the public sphere will dampen the military-aided Bible distribution that marked previous eras.

Conclusion

Both as material object, sacred text, and symbol of religion, the Bible acquires distinctive characteristics in its association with the US military. Military editions are important barometers for understanding what members of the military community are experiencing. In the first two decades of the twenty-first century, they express the challenges that America's extended "War on Terror" has presented both to those who serve in the military and those who are in close relationship with them. Military editions of the Bible also provide glimpses into ways that many Christians in the military community are coping with these challenges. These citizens are making many adjustments to their lives because American war-making both requires and depends on their doing so.

By investigating why Americans produce these editions of the Bible, how they send them, and how such Bibles function in controversies in the military, we learn something about the self-understanding of many Christian groups and about ongoing debates about the role of religion in public life. Both the distribution of Bibles to American military personnel and the use of such biblical texts in the military have been common practices for more than two centuries. The Bible's shift from commonplace to controversial artifact owes something to increasing religious pluralism and to wider political and legal struggles to clarify religion's role in public institutions, but it relates also to a shift in the military's own center of activity. The interrelation between the Bible and the American military will continue to be an important window onto the interactive material and discursive spaces in which personal and social identities, God, the military, and the nation, acquire their meanings.

Notes

1. Gallup, "Confidence in Institutions," 2016, http://www.gallup.com/poll/1597/confidence-institutions.aspx.
2. For military editions of the Bible that include vignettes of life in the US military community, see, e.g., *The Greatest Warrior* [Holy Bible, New International Version] (Colorado Springs, Colo.: Biblica, 2011), unnumbered pages immediately following cover, and unnumbered pages between 70 and 71, 166 and 167, 326 and 327, 422 and 423, and

unnumbered pages immediately preceding back cover; *Peace for the Military Family: A New Testament* [The Holy Bible, New International Version] (Colorado Springs, Colo.: Authentic, 2009), A1–A32, A33–A64; and *Military Wives' New Testament with Psalms & Proverbs* (Grand Rapids, Mich.: Zondervan, 2012), 69, 88, 120, 139, 297, 298.

3. "Jesus, the Son of David, The Wounded Warrior-King," in *Holy Bible, New International Version* [Digital Camouflage Edition] (Colorado Springs, Colo.: Biblica, 2011), A15. For other passages where Christ's work is described in sacrificial terms, see, e.g., "The Warrior's Bible Managing Editor's Preface," in *The Warrior's Bible: A Military Community Application Bible* [The Holy Bible, New King James Version] (Springfield, Mo.: Life Publishers, 2014), vi; *Operation Worship, Holy Bible* [U.S. Air Force Edition], [New Living Translation, 2nd ed.] (Carol Stream, Ill.: Tyndale House Publishers, Inc., 2009), A6; and *Operation Worship, Holy Bible: Homefront Edition*, [New Living Translation, 2nd ed.] (Carol Stream, Ill.: Tyndale House Publishers, Inc., 2009), A6.

4. *The Warrior's Bible*, vi.

5. *The Warrior's Bible*, v.

6. *HCSB Military Families Bible* (Nashville, Tenn.: Holman Bible Publishers, 2016).

7. *The Warrior's Bible*, 867, 1863; "Spiritual Fitness Manual," *The Military Bible Bible, with the Spiritual Fitness Manual* [New King James Version] (The Military Bible Publisher / The Chiaroscuro Foundation, 2010), 10.

8. *The Greatest Warrior*, A14; *The Warrior's Bible*, vi.

9. *Military Wives' New Testament, with Psalms & Proverbs*, viii.

10. *The Warrior's Bible*, 1372.

11. *Operation Worship, Holy Bible: U.S. Air Force* [Edition], A5–A6.

12. "Spiritual Fitness Manual," *The Military Bible, with Spiritual Fitness Manual*, iii.

13. "Spiritual Fitness Manual," *The Military Bible, with Spiritual Fitness Manual*, 24.

14. *The Holy Bible, New International Version* [National Guard Edition] (New York: American Bible Society, 2007).

15. "The Drama of the Bible in Six Acts," in, e.g. *Holy Bible, New International Version* [Digital Camouflage Edition], iii, v.

16. *The Greatest Warrior*, unnumbered pages immediately following front cover, unnumbered pages between 70 and 71, 166 and 177, 326 and 327, 422 and 423, unnumbered pages immediately preceding back cover.

17. *Finding Hope beyond The Battle: A Bible for Military Families* [The Holy Bible New International Version] (Colorado Springs, Colo.: Biblica, 2011), A1–A24, B3–B24. Testimony of husband is at B17. *Peace for the Military Family: A New Testament.* [The Holy Bible, New International Version] (Colorado Springs, Colo.: Authentic, 2009), A1–A32, A33–A64.

18. *The Holy Bible, New International Version* [Digital Camouflage Edition] (Colorado Springs, Colo.: Biblica, 2011), A14–A16.

19. *NIV Finding Hope beyond The Battle Bible: A Bible for Military Families*, vi–xi.

20. See, e.g., Anne C. Loveland, *American Evangelicals in the U.S. Military, 1942-1993* (Baton Rouge: Louisiana State University Press, 1997); Andrew J. Bacevich, *The New American Militarism: How Americans Are Seduced by War* (Oxford: Oxford University Press, 2005), esp. ch. 5.

21. U.S. President George W. Bush quotes Psalm 23 in his 9/11 national address, "National Day of Prayer and Remembrance for the Victims of the Terrorist Attacks on September 11, 2001" [A Proclamation].

22. Jean-Claude Maurice, *Si vous le repetez, je dementirai . . . Chirac, Sarkozy, Villepin* (Paris: Plon, 2009), 49.

23. For the ATS quotation and description of ATS work, see: John C. Pinheiro, *Missionaries of Republicanism: A Religious History of the Mexican–American War* (Oxford: Oxford University Press, 2015).

24. *Annual Report of the American Bible Society* (New York: American Bible Society, 1847), 56.

25. *Annual Report of the American Bible Society* (New York: American Bible Society, 1848), 70.

26. Stephen D. Coats, *Gathering at the Golden Gate: Mobilizing for War in the Philippines, 1898* (Fort Leavenworth, Kans.: Combat Studies Institute Press, 2006), 185–87; Annual report of the American Bible Society (New York: American Bible Society, 1900), 148.

27. Annual report of the American Bible Society (1899), 126.

28. *Annual Report of the American Bible Society* (1900), 147–149.

29. *Annual Report of the American Bible Society* (1900), 148–149.

30. *Annual Report of the American Bible Society* (1904), 181.

31. William P. Woodard, *The Allied Occupation of Japan 1945–1952 and Japanese Religions* (Leiden, Netherlands: E. J. Brill, 1972), 218–19.

32. MacArthur also commended the work of the American Bible Society, the Gideons, the national conference of Christians and Jews, and the Roman Catholic Church in Japan. See William P. Woodard. *The Allied Occupation of Japan 1945–1952 and Japanese Religions*, 242–45.

33. *The Record*, American Bible Society, Summer 2003, 18.

34. Woodard, *The Allied Occupation of Japan, 1945–1952*, 245.

35. David Dempsey, "In and Out of Books," *New York Times*, December 23, 1951; "'You Shall Have Them, Chaplain,'" *Bible Society Record*, American Bible Society, December 1951, 150.

36. "Among Prisoners of War in Korea," *Bible Society Record*, American Bible Society, May 1951, 68–69.

37. "Under the Guns: Vietnam" [video], The Pocket Testament League, https://www.ptl.org/videopages/historicvideos.php.

38. "General Offers Letter of Thanks," *The Gainesville Sun*, Saturday, April 30, 1991; Norman Schwarzkopf, *It Doesn't Take a Hero: The Autobiography of Norman Schwarzkopf* (New York: Bantam, 1992), 335.

39. General Order Number 1B (GO-1B): Prohibited Activities for U.S. Department of Defense Personnel Present within the United States Central Command (USCENTCOM) Area of Responsibility (AOR), United States Central Command (2006).

40. "'Witness for Jesus' in Afghanistan: U.S. Troops Urged to Share Faith and Filmed with Local Bibles despite Anti-Proselytizing Rules," Al Jazeera, May 4, 2009, http://www.aljazeera.com/news/asia/2009/05/200953201315854832.html; "Military Burns Unsolicited Bibles Sent to Afghanistan," *CNN*, May 22, 2009, http://edition.cnn.com/2009/WORLD/asiapcf/05/20/us.military.bibles.burned/.

41. Todd Starnes, "The Day the U.S. Military Burned the Bible in Afghanistan," FoxNews.com, March 2, 2012, http://www.foxnews.com/opinion/2012/03/02/day-us-military-burned-bible-in-afghanistan.html.

Bibliography

Coats, Stephen D. *Gathering at the Golden Gate: Mobilizing for War in the Philippines, 1898.* Fort Leavenworth, Kans.: Combat Studies Institute Press, 2006.

Finding Hope Beyond Battle for Military Families [Holy Bible, New International Version]. Grand Rapids, Mich.: Zondervan, 2011.

The Greatest Warrior [Holy Bible, New International Version]. Colorado Springs, Colo.: Biblica, 2011.

HCSB Military Families Bible. Nashville, Tenn.: Holman Bible Publishers, 2016.

Holy Bible, New International Version [Digital Camouflage Edition]. Colorado Springs, Colo.: Biblical, 2011.

Holy Bible, New International Version [National Guard Edition]. New York: American Bible Society, 2007.

Loveland, Anne C. *American Evangelicals in the U.S. Military, 1942–1993.* Baton Rouge, La.: Louisiana State University Press, 1997.

The Military Bible, with the Spiritual Fitness Manual [New King James Version]. The Military Bible Publisher / The Chiaroscuro Foundation, 2010.

Military Wives' Bible New Testament with Psalms & Proverbs. Grand Rapids, Mich.: Zondervan, 2012.

Operation Worship, Holy Bible: Homefront Edition [New Living Translation, 2nd. Ed.]. Carol Stream, Ill.: Tyndale Publishers, Inc., 2009.

Operation Worship, Holy Bible: U.S. Air Force Edition [New Living Translation, 2nd. Ed.]. Carol Stream, Ill.: Tyndale Publishers, Inc., 2008.

Peace for the Military Family: A New Testament [The Holy Bible, New International Version]. Colorado Springs, Colo.: Authentic, 2009.

Pinheiro, John C. *Missionaries of Republicanism: A Religious History of the Mexican–American War.* Oxford: Oxford University Press, 2014.

The Warrior's Bible: A Military Community Application Bible [The Holy Bible, New King James Version]. Springfield, Mo.: Life Publishers, 2014.

CHAPTER 22

....

THE BIBLE AND THE
CREATION OF THE NATION

....

ERAN SHALEV

ON July 2, 1776, the day of the signing of the Declaration of Independence, a special committee to design a great seal for the new United States gathered in Philadelphia. The renowned
Benjamin Franklin proposed the image of Moses and the Israelites watching Pharaoh and
his host drowning in the Red Sea, while the young Thomas Jefferson suggested the image
of the Israelites following the cloud of smoke in the desert. A few months earlier, as the
colonies started gearing toward independence, Thomas Paine dedicated a quarter of his
powerful pamphlet *Common Sense* to biblical themes, much more than to any other subject. If such was the mindset of the most deist minds of their era, it is hardly surprising
that more conventional Reformed Christians (who may have constituted up to 85 percent
of the white American population at the time of the Revolution) mobilized the traditional
Puritan image of the American Israel to a remarkable extent. The Bible, particularly the Old
Testament, would continue to saturate the early US culture (especially the political culture)
to such an extent that Perry Miller concluded that by the conclusion of the founding it was
as "omnipresent . . . as . . . the air that people breathed."[1]

Views of following generations confirm such assessments. Harriet Beecher Stowe, the
author of the incredibly influential antislavery novel *Uncle Tom's Cabin*, averred in the mid-
nineteenth century that early Americans "spoke of Zion and Jerusalem, of the God of Israel,
the God of Jacob, as much as if my grandfather had been a veritable Jew; and except for
the closing phrase, 'for the sake of thy Son, our Saviour,' might all have been uttered in
Palestine by a well-trained Jew in the time of [King] David."[2] Similarly, Henry Adams wrote
in the opening pages of *The Education* that to be born to an elite family in eighteenth-
century Boston was similar to being "born in Jerusalem under the shadow of the Temple
and circumcised in the Synagogue."[3] More recently, political scientists were able to back up
quantitatively these assessments regarding the prevalence of the Bible in the early United
States. The political scientist Donald Lutz, for example, observed that during the founding
era (1760-1805) the source most frequently cited in political expositions was the Book of
Deuteronomy.[4] Perhaps even more surprising and significant is that even after counting
off the 75 percent of biblical references that appeared in reprinted sermons, a huge cottage
industry that accounted for 10 percent of all contemporary pamphlets, the non-sermon

source of biblical references was roughly as important as other leading categories such as common law and classical history. In the following decades, the prominence of the Bible would only increase.

The Bible served revolutionary Americans in several ways. During the years surrounding the War for Independence, it provided a fathomless assemblage of war stories, which helped instill courage and martial virtue during times of crisis. Patriots also turned to the Bible time and again to instill ideals such as the sacrifice for their compatriots, or the idea of pursuing a sacred war for liberty. In offering a gallery of virtuous and warlike characters, the Bible proved crucial for making the patriotic case for war and proved an effective tool in inspiring patriotism in revolutionary America. While the patriotic biblical appeals may have begun in New England—mainly but not exclusively through sermons—they quickly spread throughout the Atlantic seaboard. The Revolution may not have been a religious revolt, but it was to a large extent stimulated through repeated uses of and appeals to the Bible, with scripture functioning as a central channel for arousing political sentiments.

Patriots scoured both the Old and the New Testaments for their wartime needs. In the Old Testament, they found themes such as the obscure curse of Meroz for chastising neutrality as sinful cowardice, or the character of King David, the warrior psalmist, to endure the atrocities of war. In the New Testament, they struggled with loyalist claims that Peter and Paul condemned rebellion against civil authority, and they read the apostles, like the rest of the Holy Book, through a republican prism. Many read the apocalyptic book of Revelation to contemplate a millennial future but also to inject into their revolution a dose of militant chiliastic Christianity.

The patriots' rich biblical theo-political cosmology was dominated however by a specific narrative, namely that of the Exodus. The Exodus detailed how the Israelites, led by a charismatic and divinely inspired Moses, roamed the wilderness for forty years after their escape from Pharaoh, and eventually conquered Canaan and settled in a promised land full of milk and honey. The story of the rise of the Israelites from the house of Egyptian bondage captivated much of the political discussion throughout the Revolution.

By the time of the Revolution, Exodus already had a long history in the British North American colonies, especially in New England, where the Puritan immigrants and succeeding generations interpreted the Great Migration of the 1630s as a crossing of the Red Sea and an escape from the British Egypt. In many accounts, the Exodus functioned as a towering narrative and trope, and was fundamental in shaping the form and content of early American biblicism. The story of the enslaved Israelites who fled Egyptian tyranny also narrated their election by God during their long sojourn in the desert as his chosen people on their way to the Promised Land. This story of divine deliverance exerted tremendous influence over various segments of American society.

The Exodian trope was thus readily reshaped to function as a fundamental source for talking about politics and for exploring the meaning of nationhood in revolutionary America. It also enabled Americans engaged in revolutionary politics to construct links between biblical Israel and what they perceived as the new, American Israel. In such prevalent understandings, God seemed to have selected a new (American) people to lead through the Red Sea of the Revolution against the crushing tyranny of Britain. With the creation of the United States, Americans saw themselves as an emergent New Israel, complete with a new

Federal Constitution that signaled a modern covenant, delivered by the hand of another Moses, George Washington.

The Exodus was certainly a story of an astounding deliverance of the children of Israel from the Egyptian bondage. Nevertheless, Revolutionary preachers also portrayed the Exodus, perhaps more significantly, as a republican tale, "a very signal instance of God's appearing in favour of liberty, and frowning on tyrants." The God of Israel was a republican god, who "shews how much he regards the rights of his people, and in how exemplary a manner, hard hearted tyrants, and merciless oppressors, sometimes feel his vengeance."[5] Some, such as the minister Nicholas Street in his remarkable but characteristic sermon, *The American States Acting Over the Part of the Children of Israel in the Wilderness* (1777), referred to the Exodus to elaborate the precarious American situation. Street's impressive typological reading, coming at a time of dire straits for the young American confederacy, lengthily juxtaposed "the history of the children of Israel in Egypt, their sufferings and oppression under the tyrant Pharaoh, their remarkable deliverance by the hands of Moses out of the state of bondage and oppression, and their trials and murmurings in the wilderness." In Street's wartime jeremiad, Americans "act[ed] over . . . the children of Israel in the wilderness, under the conduct of Moses and Aaron, who was leading them out of a state of bondage into a land of liberty and plenty in Canaan."[6]

As the Revolution advanced, it became clear that the Exodus was not a model that applied merely to New England, and so New Englanders were not the only one to employ the tropes of the story. Indeed, different speakers molded New England onto the sacred history of Israel and then extended that history to the whole of the new American nation. Such molding involved making typological sense of the relevance of the Exodus to the young United States. Americans outside of New England, particularly in the middle colonies-turned-states, were becoming accustomed to think that although they, like the Israelites in Egypt, were enslaved in foreign bondage, with "a wilderness still before us," they should expect soon to cross "the Red Sea of our difficulties."[7]

Interestingly, although "crossing the Rubicon" would arguably better describe the stakes before declaring American Independence than crossing the Red Sea, the biblical metaphor seems to have been the patriots' favorite during the early months of 1776 (as proven by Franklin's and Jefferson's aforementioned proposals for the American Great Seal in 1776). Numerous references to the tyrannical English "Pharaoh" and his Israelite-American subjects-turned-enemies during the Revolution attested to that popularity. After the war concluded, it was manifested in Timothy Dwight's epic metaphoric poem, *The Conquest of Canaan* (1785), which he dedicated to the American Moses (and now victorious Joshua), George Washington. Exodus, in short, provided a key trope in the construction of the United States as a New Israel and would continue to exert its influence across centuries of American history, from the Puritans to enslaved African Americans to the Mormons to the civil rights movement.

Beyond the pervasiveness of the image of the American Israel and its centrality to the self-realization and identification of the young American nation, the Bible became a significant vehicle for political reflection during the turbulent late eighteenth century. As Americans struggled on the battlefield and strove to constitute a union out of the colonies-turned-states, they were also forced to come to terms with republican conceptions of politics, particularly with a demanding virtue-based, civic-humanistic ideology. Consequently, they articulated a rich biblical idiom that extended much wider and deeper than the Exodus.

Such an idiom helped them to define the contents and limits of a revolutionary political discourse. The remainder of this essay explores the broad range of biblical tropes and modes of thought that founding era Americans applied to the most urgent tasks of their political lives and the construction of their nation. Those biblical images and ideas consequently helped shape the distinct contours of the new nation's culture.

It has long been accepted that classical republicanism and religion interacted creatively in late eighteenth-century America. The prevalence of the Bible in the American political world was, of course, no accident. It was the consequence of a Protestant theology that emphasized a direct relationship with God's Word as an essential component to salvation and the ability to live a morally correct life. Religion thus occupied a unique role in the formation of American republicanism: While republican fears of corruption echoed with the traditional rhetoric of the jeremiad, the emerging American republic could be associated with the advent of Christ's millennial reign.

In this context, it is evident how the Bible could be converted into a text that reflected and professed a republican worldview. The Bible may not have provided contemporaries with new ideas about the conduct of modern polities (that is, it did not constitute a new political philosophy), but its narratives and tropes could furnish powerful justifications, ideas, and motivations for modes of action which otherwise may not have been accessible, or may have been unacceptable or even inconceivable.

Revolutionary-era Americans frequently discussed, adapted, and absorbed the fundamentals of the republican doctrine through biblical, often Old Testament narratives and figures. This blending of the Bible and republicanism enabled revolutionaries (and successive generations of Americans) to conciliate the distinct scriptural and classical worlds, and harness them to advance immediate political goals. This biblical republicanism thus expands our understanding of the ways in which early Americans constructed their political worldviews in light of the scriptures. It also sheds light on how the Bible helped the nation's founders create a revolutionary ideology and then a meaningful and functional national governmental construct in the years after the Revolution. One of this emerging discourse's big advantages was that virtually every patriot—not merely the formally educated elites—could potentially come to terms with civic-humanistic republicanism (an obscure and harsh creed, at least for the multitudes that lacked formal education) through the use of well-known biblical structures, narratives, forms, and metaphors. The Bible functioned throughout the era, in short, as the nation's *lingua franca*.

A few examples demonstrate this fruitful and pervasive dynamic. The entrenched republican fear of corruption was often absorbed through the examination of the case of the Persian kingdom ("empire") under its king Ahasuerus (Xerxes), the memorable backdrop for the Old Testament Book of Esther. That eastern kingdom was characteristically seen during the years leading to Independence through a republican prism, as a monarchy much like Britain in which luxury and effeminacy raged, which "became prolific in the production of cockatrices and vipers, that began to prey upon the bowles of the empire."[8] The story told in the Book of Esther of the conspiracy against the Jews and their miraculous salvation functioned however not only to condemn the British Empire in general, but specifically to highlight an alleged ministerial plot against America.

After the repeal of the Stamp Act in 1766, Americans almost universally expressed their dismay that the minister (they had in mind the Earl of Bute) who had been "the instrument of conveying to his Majesty such Sentiments of his faithful [American] and loving Subjects . . . is a vile Slanderer and Accuser of the People, and a Traitor to his Prince." Such a man was, they heard, "as great an Enemy . . . as was wicked Haman to the Jews."[9] The recurring appeals to the Esther story, which commonly targeted its villain counselor Haman, became a popular way of demonstrating a biblical mode of interpretation of imperial politics throughout the rebelling colonies. The South Carolinian clergymen Thomas Reese found it convenient in a sermon titled *The Character of Haman* to denounce the conniving biblical courtier who would sacrifice all to achieve his cruel object, the destruction of his innocent enemies. Haman would "stop at no act of cruelty, however horrid, which he thinks may forward his designs. Treachery, poison, daggers, and all the instruments of death are employed without remorse. He cares not how much blood he spills, nor how much misery he causes, if he can only gain his point."[10]

These few lines, similar to numerous other calls across America, underscore the attraction and benefits that Patriots found in the years and months preceding Independence in using the Bible as a guide and manual for oppositional politics in a still monarchical political culture. They aptly framed biblical characters and narratives in the conceptual world of early modern republicanism and situated them in a familiar imperial setting. By reading classical republicanism into Old Testament narratives and figures, American commentators and politicians helped wide local audiences make sense of, and become conversant with, an ideology that was a significant force in shaping their political lives.

The uses of Gideon, Israel's savior and the fifth Judge of the Israelites, provides another illustrative case. While discussions of corruption facilitated a critical view of British policy mostly before Independence, the creation of a new nation required Americans to articulate positive models for the virtuous conduct of their country's citizenry. Gideon, whom the Bible also identifies as Jerubbaal, was renowned for his military leadership, but especially his refusal to become king over Israel—making him an exemplary republican model. Thomas Paine, the man perhaps most responsible for anti-monarchical sentiment in America, was also the one to inject Gideon's model into the American discourse. Paine imparted a civic-humanist flavor on the biblical story of Gideon's rejection of dynastic monarchy in *Common Sense*, pointing out that the Israelites "proposed making [Gideon] a king, saying, Rule thou over us, thou and thy son and thy son's son." As he confronted the basest and most dangerous of sentiments in the republican lexicon, the corrupting lust for political power, the pious Gideon replied: "I will not rule over you, neither shall my son rule over you, THE LORD SHALL RULE OVER YOU." "Words," Paine concluded, "need not be more explicit."[11]

Others followed Paine's reference to Gideon's republicanism, keeping the virtuous Hebrew judge a mainstay in American political speech. A prolonged revolutionary pamphlet, *Jerubbaal* (1784), closely examined Gideon (the titular Jerubbaal) and his rejection of political power and ambition. The author emphasized Gideon's aversion to power and his negative response regarding "the ambition which would prompt some men to court so high an honor—or to grasp the nomination to office." When first approached by God's angel, "the judge-elect modestly declines the appointment—remonstrates the smallness of his tribe—the obscurity of his family—and his own inferiority in it—represents himself as the last person, of the last family, of the last tribe, from which a commander in Israel should be expected—and persists in his doubts."[12]

To the ears of a republican audience, young Gideon's behavior was no demonstration of timidity (which could, after all, be a plausible interpretation of the biblical text). American revolutionaries argued that a much more likely explanation involved Gideon's choice to act the virtuous role of republican self-effacement, thus avoiding the slightest appearance of a self-seeking pursuit of power, of personal gratification, and ambition. Classical republicans, such as this late eighteenth-century Gideon, would accept political power only for upholding the common good. The similarity between the Israelite Judge's refraining from power and George Washington's statement to the Continental Congress upon his appointment as commander of the Continental Army a few years must have struck contemporaries: "Tho' I am truly sensible of the high Honour done me, in this Appointment, yet I feel great distress, from a consciousness that my abilities and military experience may not be equal to the extensive and important Trust."[13] Good republicans, from Gideon son of Joash to George Washington son of Augustine, were supposed to erase the slightest impression that they were power hungry, to act humbly to the point of self-deprecation. Little wonder that Americans would construct George Washington, the master of classical politics of virtue, as a latter-day Gideon.

A republican truism taught that throughout history at the dangerous moment of victory, military leaders capitalized on their battlefield success to solidify and perpetuate their power. Such a threatening moment arrived when Gideon, who had valiantly won a war and saved his people, was consequently "crowned with the blessings of his rescued country— and loaded with laurels." At that dramatic moment the children of Israel invited Gideon to ascend a throne. Not only were the Israelites ready to receive him as their monarch, they also invited Gideon "to settle the crown upon his issue-male, as their hereditary property in lineal succession." Like the Romans who presented Julius Caesar, their republic's destroyer, a dictatorship for life, the Israelites, so the biblical narrative went, wished to crown their victorious general. The biblical Gideon was, of course, not only a Judge but also a military chieftain, a figure that was traditionally suspected of seeking to usurp the republic for personal gratification. Unlike Caesar, however, who was remembered for dishonestly rejecting—thrice—the diadem offered him by the Roman people only to become a monarch *de facto*, Gideon's "patriotic greatness of soul" obliged him to "positively refuse the unadvised present" of a king's throne. Gideon declined perpetual sovereignty and refused rewards "which none ever did better deserve." Not only did the Israelite Judge "accept no pay for his laborious services," he did not even accept "any pension to himself or family."[14]

Once more Americans were supposed to see their leader's conduct reflected through a republican lens of the Gideon story. George Washington, they remembered, famously set a magnificent republican example upon becoming the Continental Army's commander: "As to pay, Sir, I beg leave to assure the Congress, that, as no pecuniary consideration could have tempted me to have accepted this arduous employment, at the expence of my domestic ease and happiness, I do not wish to make any profit from it."[15] With the example of the Washington on their minds, Americans remembered Gideon's "retirement to his farm ... while he withdraws from the command."[16] Here the juxtaposition was sealed: the biblical tale together with the archetypal model of Roman virtue, represented by a Cincinnatian retreat, was recently fulfilled by Washington's retirement from his military command. The world of the Bible was infused with classical ideological meaning to instruct the American nation on its perilous political march.

The Bible was the most read and revered book in North America, and biblical authority was as important as any other source in endowing the Revolution and the nation it created with meaning. To understand the centrality of the Bible in making sense out of the Revolution and the volatile world that it created, one needs to pay attention not only to biblical narratives and characters but also to the uses of its distinct language in political discourse. The language of the King James Bible was as strange and foreign to late eighteenth-century and nineteenth-century Anglophones as it is to twenty-first-century English speakers. The staccato rhythms confined in short and numbered verses, the repetitive use of phrases such as "and it came to pass," and the use of verbs with suffixes such as "—eth," had been long gone from the spoken language by the second half of the eighteenth century. Nevertheless, revolutionary era Americans reverted to that language and its accompanying structures and forms to discuss their difficulties and represent their achievements, past and present.

This "pseudo-biblicism," the tradition of writing in biblical style, was not a predominantly religious idiom as Providence was notably absent from those texts as an active agent. Rather, American authors and commentators used that language as a means to establish their claims for political truth, as well as their authority and legitimacy in public discourse. The distinct use of biblical language and phrasing for a broad range of topics, notably political issues across the ideological spectrum, coincided with the emergence of the United States and provides an indication of the ways in which Americans attempted to understand their role in history in a quickly changing world. While the language of the Bible reiterated Americans' understanding of their collective mission, it also positioned politics as the new religion of their republic, a medium that sanctified the nation and constructed Americans' perception of being a new, divinely chosen people.

The adoption of biblical language for non-religious purposes had English origins, but by the late eighteenth century became a distinct American political expression. The Revolution brought pseudo-biblicism to the forefront of patriot polemics with elaborate and extensive literary pieces (often consisting of dozens of verses and thousands of words) that were reprinted across the colonies. John Leacock's *The First Book of the American Chronicles of the Times* (1774-75) was a characteristic (if particularly elaborate) example of the pseudo-biblical style during the revolutionary years. *The First Book* was written in numbered verses and laden with identifiable phrases such as "And it came to pass . . ." *The First Book* was published serially and reprinted in newspapers and later in several pamphlet editions, attesting to its immense popularity. It was a full-blown exposition of the events in Boston in 1773-74, filled with dozens of biblically named characters (Jedidiah the prophet, for example) and events such as the attempts to make Bostonites "bow down to the TEA CHEST, the God of the Heathen" or camels—a biblical vehicle—loaded with cargoes of tobacco.[17]

Like scores of similar texts *The First Book* consisted of a patriotic narrative of the contemporary events in biblical style and used thoroughly biblical nomenclature (such as Mordecai the Benjaminite for Benjamin Franklin, or Thomas the Gageite for Thomas Gage, the military commander of Boston). The imagery was also densely biblical and so were its idioms, which constantly merged ancient and modern into the kind of anachronism that characterized the pseudo-biblical genre: repeating 2 Samuel 1:20, Americans were urged in the lamenting words of David the son of Jesse, "Tell it not in Gath, nor publish it in the streets of Askalon."[18]

Numerous later post-revolutionary texts adopted similar measures. *Chapter 37th*, for example, published in 1782, began: "And it came to pass in the reign of George the king, who ruled over Albion, and whose empire extended to the uttermost parts of the earth," and went on to versify the history of the Revolution in a thoroughly biblical fashion. The *Chapter* concluded with an American hero singing biblically, "the song of triumph, saying others have slain their thousands, but I have slain my ten thousands."[19] These and other similar pseudo-biblical texts depicted America, implicitly and explicitly, as a latter-day Israel, a chosen nation in the most earnest terms.

The Bible, through the distinct usage of its language, forms, and style, no longer informed early Americans merely of the ancient history of a bygone Israelite society; nor was it solely a typological text that signified, foresaw, and mapped biblical events to corresponding events in American society. Through the popular medium of pseudo-biblicism, the Bible became in late eighteenth-century America a living text, an ongoing scriptural venture that complemented and fortified notions of national chosenness and mission in the early United States. It fostered the intense employment and further construction of biblical politics, each side depicting the other, to take an example from the 1790s, as wrong-doing "Adamites" and "Jeffersonites."[20] Transcending the partisan nature of an immediate political context, however, it helped in further constructing the United States as a biblical nation. American politics were transformed, in texts largely devoid of references to God, into the new religion of the American Republic while the Bible was woven into American life and sanctified the young nation.

As we have seen, the Bible was an instrument for revolutionary teachings that helped guide the American Bible-reading masses through the intricacies of republican politics. In time it also facilitated contemporaries' coming to terms with the greatest innovation of American political philosophy, namely federalism. The idea that stood at the bottom of American federalism, namely the overlapping of state and federal level authority, went against prevailing belief regarding the indivisibility of sovereignty. Detailed discussions regarding a revered "Mosaic constitution" helped clarify and sway a perplexed American public toward the novel doctrine of federalism.[21]

As national independence became a reality, Americans came to view biblical Israel as a "republic" or "commonwealth." Earlier Europeans, notably English and Dutch commentators, have spent much of the turbulent seventeenth century grappling with their respective country's experimentations in republicanism through the examination of the Mosaic constitution and its relevance to their situation. Moses's "constitution" was usually seen as a biblical constitutional arrangement of a divinely sanctioned political scheme, which created a united Hebraic people ruled by law out of tribal disorder. More than a century after the conclusion of the intense European examination of the biblical constitution, Americans would have their turn in making the Mosaic arrangement relevant to their political venture.

After the 1770s, and particularly at the time of the debate over the Federal Constitution, Moses's constitution of Israel became central to attempts to come to terms with the novelties of the nascent American political system. It was first mentioned during the second half of the 1770s as an archetype for the revolutionary state constitutions with discussions spilling from formal sermons to newspaper articles. Even before Independence, in an attack on the institution of monarchy that was not meant to provide a detailed constitutional program for the colonies, Thomas Paine made clear in a passing remark in *Common Sense* that he believed that the Hebrew polity was a republic: the Israelites had no kings and it was held sinful to acknowledge a monarch; also, their form of government was "a kind of republic administered by a judge and the elders of the tribes."[22] In the years following their independence from Britain, Americans would elaborate on the republican nature of the ancient Hebrew form of government and its correlations to its American counterpart.

With the conclusion of the Revolutionary War, Americans continued to find in the political history of the ancient Israelites a model for developing a federal republicanism that they sought to formalize with the Constitution of 1787. Contemporaries long believed that the Mosaic constitution manifested a civic law and the earliest example of a government by law. Yet the Israelite republic offered America something more than a superb and time-proven legal code; ancient Israel, rendered a model federal constitution, which was especially instructive to Americans who were about to adopt the innovative governing system that was proposed by the delegates to Philadelphia in the summer of 1787. American commentators attempted to make sense of, justify, and reconcile the experimental constitutional arrangements of the young United States with hallowed political models introduced through what they commonly called the "Jewish republic." Hence, when Massachusetts braced itself to vote for the ratification of the Federal Constitution in early 1788, Samuel Langdon provided on the eve of his state's eventual adoption of the Constitution a remarkably elaborate, if not uncharacteristic, analysis of the Hebrew constitution and its relevance to the US system of governance.

As the title of Langdon's sermon indicated ("The Republic of the Israelites: An Example to the American States"), he believed that the political history of the Hebrews provided a striking example regarding issues of state formation at the moment of American political and legal reorganization. While the Israelites who fled into the wilderness were merely an unruly multitude that has just escaped captivity, they were seen as suddenly collected into a body politic under the leadership of Moses. Like the Americans who declared independence from their oppressors, the Israelites were transformed in a short space of time after they had passed the Red Sea into a new civil and military order; that order was further enforced by able men being chosen out of the tribes and made "captains and rulers of thousands, hundreds, fifties and tens: and these commanded them as military officers, and acted as judges in matters of common controversy."[23]

The Israelites' quick progress from slavery to a national polity was impressive, perhaps even miraculous. But that was only half the tale. Langdon pointed out that biblical Israel was not established as a simple republic but as a federacy. In the alleged Israelite federacy, every tribe seemed to have elders and a leader with whom Moses did not interfere. Under this federacy, the tribal leaders acknowledged a right to meet and consult together, and with the consent of their tribe to do whatever was necessary to preserve good order and promote the common good. In short, the tribes were autonomous and semi-sovereign entities and thus foreshadowed the American states under the Constitution. As in the United States, the local governments of the Israelites' tribes were structurally similar to the general government: Each had "a president and senate" at its head, while the whole of the Hebrew people "assembled and gave their voice in all great matters."[24]

The arrangement of the Hebrew courts too appeared to resemble the American federal solution. After their settlement in the land of Canaan, the civil government of the Israelites included courts in which elders served as judge. Those judges, it was concluded, had the power to decide cases within their respective jurisdictions. It was further believed that appeals could be allowed in weighty cases from the provincial Israelite courts to higher courts and finally to the authority of the "general senate and chief magistrate."[25] This Hebraic hierarchy of courts seemed too to have perfectly mirrored the complex and layered judiciary branch of the American Constitution.

The Hebrew republic, in short, provided a blueprint for the US federal governmental structure. On the eve of the adoption of the Constitution, the biblical Hebraic political edifice provided a historical example of checks and balances in the executive, legislative, and judicial spheres between periphery and center that reflected the expectations of many when it came to the proposed Constitution of the United States. Such a depiction of biblical Israel as a "prefect republic," and a federal one as such, became a staple in public discussions in America on the virtues and shortcomings of their national political system for decades to come.

Ezra Stiles's renowned election sermon *The United States Elevated to Honor and Glory* (1783) provides a window into the role of the Bible in endowing the young nation with meaning. Stiles, the president of Yale University, delivered his sermon at the close of the War of Independence, and it expectedly reflected a postwar optimism. Yet it also represents an early and recognizable facet of the identifications of the United States as a reincarnation of biblical Israel. The United States was already seen as "God's American Israel" and thus enjoyed the promise for future prosperity and national splendor.[26] This sanguine outlook was based on a biblical history that demonstrated time and again that the welfare of Israel depended on its own conduct. A paramount example of a correct national choice was seen in placing at the head of the Continental Army a leader such as George Washington, "the only man on whom the eyes of all [America's] Israel were placed . . . this American Joshua."[27] Self-reliance thus promised Americans that as long that they continued to maintain their divine sense of virtue, America's future national prosperity would be secure for their Second Israel.

Studying the rich biblical culture of the late eighteenth century through political pamphlets, histories, public orations, private correspondence, sermons, poetry, newspaper essays, and other polemical and partisan writings is how we latecomers may come to terms with the roles of the Bible in the early United States. It also demonstrates how American authors, public speakers, and commentators developed sophisticated modes of probing the new nation's key problems, dynamics, and relationships through the Old Testament, enabling them and their contemporaries to make better sense out of their nascent national project. The Bible, specifically the history of ancient Israel, provided a productive intersection between politics and religion, a political theology which legitimized political novelties but could also help unite a loose union of political entities—the newly formed American states—around well-known and revered scriptural narratives, structures, and models. Such a broad reading provides a sense of the depth of the American political culture's biblicism, as well as the commitment of early Americans in understanding their new nation as a biblical reincarnation of Israel. It also demonstrates how the various ways in which early Americans merged their nation and the Bible, and thus wrote a meaningful new chapter in the history of the American Bible.

Notes

1. Perry Miller, "The Garden of Eden and the Deacon's Meadow," *American Heritage Magazine* 7, no. 1. (December 1955): 54–61, 102, http://www.americanheritage.com/content/garden-eden-and-deacon's-meadow.

2. Harriet Beecher Stowe, *Oldtown Folks, and Sam Lawson's Oldtown Fireside Stories* (Boston, Mass.: Houghton, Mifflin, 1896), 1:306.

3. Henry Adams, *The Education of Henry Adams* (New York: Barnes & Noble, 2009), 13.

4. Donald Lutz, "The Relative Influence of European Writers on Late Eighteenth-Century Political Thought," *American Political Science Review* 78 (1984): 189–97.

5. Gad Hitchcock, *A Sermon Preached at Plymouth December 22d, 1774. Being the Anniversary Thanksgiving* (Boston, Mass.: Edes and Gill, 1775), 20.

6. Nicholas Street, *The American States Acting Over the Part of the Children of Israel in the Wilderness, and thereby Impeding Their Entrance into Canaan's Rest* (New Haven, Conn.: Thomas & Samuel Green, 1777), 3, 9.

7. "From the Pennsylvania Packet," *Continental Journal*, July 18, 1776.

8. Oliver Noble, *Some Strictures upon the Sacred Story Recorded in the Book of Esther* (Newburyport, Mass.: 1775), 7.

9. *Boston-Gazette*, November 24, 1766.

10. Thomas Reese, "The Character of Haman," in *The American Preacher*, 4 vols., ed. David Austin (Elizabethtown, N.J.: Shepard Kollock, 1791-93), 2:331; James Murray, *Sermons to the Ministers of State* (Newcastle upon Tyne, UK, 1781), 52.

11. Thomas Paine, *Common Sense* (Los Angeles: IndoEuropean Publishing, 2010), 10.

12. John Murray, *Jerubbaal; or, Tyranny's Grove Destroyed, and the Altar of Liberty Finished. A Discourse on America's Duty and Danger* (Newburyport, Mass.: 1783), 13.

13. George Washington, "Acceptance of Appointment as General and Commander in Chief," June 16, 1775, in *The Writings of George Washington from the Original Manuscript Sources*, 39 vols., ed. John Clemens Fitzpatrick (Washington, D.C.: US Government Print Office, 1931-44), 3:292–93.

14. Murray, *Jerubbaal*, 20–21.

15. Washington, "Acceptance of Appointment," 3:292–93.

16. Murray, *Jerubbaal*, 21.

17. John Leacock, *The First Book of the American Chronicles of the Times, 1774-1775*, ed. Carla Mulford (Newark: University of Delaware Press, 1987), 14.

18. Leacock, *The First Book*, 58, 61, 54.

19. "Chapter 37th," *Boston Evening Post*, April 20, 1782.

20. See, for example, "The First Book of the Kings," *Alexandria Expositor*, February 21, 1803.

21. The Mosaic Constitution is an early modern concept, which was adopted by modern scholars of political theology. For a recent addition, see Graham Hamill, *The Mosaic Constitution: Political Theology and Imagination from Machiavelli to Milton* (Chicago: University of Chicago Press, 2012).

22. Paine, *Common Sense*, 9.

23. Samuel Langdon, *The Republic of the Israelites: An Example to the American States* (Exeter, N.H., 1788), 8, 15.

24. Langdon, *The Republic of the Israelites*, 9–10.

25. Langdon, *The Republic of the Israelites*, 11.

26. Ezra Stiles, *The United States Elevated to Glory and Honor* (New Haven, Conn.: Thomas & Samuel Green, 1783), 7, http://digitalcommons.unl.edu/etas/41/.

27. Stiles, *The United States Elevated to Glory and Honor*, 5, 37.

BIBLIOGRAPHY

Adams, Henry. *The Education of Henry Adams.* New York: Barnes & Noble, 2009.

Austin, David. *The American Preacher; or, A Collection of Sermons from Some of the Most Eminent Preachers Now Living in the United States of Different Denominations in the Christian Church.* Elizabethtown, N J · Shepard Kollock, 1791–93.

Byrd, James. *Sacred Scripture, Sacred War: The Bible and the American Revolution.* New York: Oxford University Press, 2013.

Gutjahr, Paul. *An American Bible: A History of the Good Book in the United States, 1770–1880.* Stanford, Calif.: Stanford University Press, 1999.

Hatch, Nathan O., and Mark A. Noll, eds. *The Bible in America: Essays in Cultural History.* New York: Oxford University Press, 1982.

Kidd, Thomas. *God of Liberty: A Religious History of the American Revolution.* New York: Basic Books, 2012.

Lutz, Donald S. "The Relative Influence of European Writers on Late Eighteenth-Century American Political Thought." *American Political Science Review* 78, no. 1 (1984): 189–97.

Miller, Perry. "The Garden of Eden and the Deacon's Meadow." *American Heritage Magazine* 7, no. 1. (December 1955): 54–61. http://www.americanheritage.com/content/garden-eden-and-deacon's-meadow.

Paine, Thomas. *Common Sense.* Los Angeles: IndoEuropean Publishing, 2010.

Perl-Rosenthal, Nathan. "'The Divine Right of Republics': Hebraic Republicanism and the Debate over Kingless Government in Revolutionary America." *William and Mary Quarterly* 66, no. 3 (2009): 535–64.

Richard, Carl J. *The Founders and the Bible.* Lanham, Md.: Rowman and Littlefield, 2016.

Shalev, Eran. *American Zion: The Old Testament as a Political Text from the Revolution to the Civil War.* New Haven, Conn.: Yale University Press, 2013.

Stiles, Ezra. *The United States Elevated to Glory and Honor.* New Haven, Conn.: Thomas & Samuel Green, 1783. http://digitalcommons.unl.edu/etas/41/.

CHAPTER 23

....

THE BIBLE IN
THE CIVIL WAR

....

PAUL HARVEY

THE American Civil War is sometimes considered one of the most religious wars in modern history. The contending sides each drew from evangelical ideas of understanding the world and their cause; each experienced great revivals in their respective armies; and each claimed the Bible for its own side. Abraham Lincoln perfectly captured these ironies in his Second Inaugural Address in March 1865. On that day in early March, just a little over a month before his assassination, he reflected on how each side had "looked for an easier triumph, and a result less fundamental and astounding. Both read the same Bible and pray to the same God, and each invokes His aid against the other." Then he twisted the knife: "It may seem strange that any men should dare to ask a just God's assistance in wringing their bread from the sweat of other men's faces, but let us judge not, that we be not judged." Lincoln concluded with a Calvinist uncertainty uncharacteristic for that age of a triumphalist certainty in biblical interpretation: "The prayers of both could not be answered. That of neither has been answered fully. The Almighty has His own purposes."

Lincoln's perception of the limits of human knowledge of divine purposes was rare. More commonly (though not universally), Americans expressed righteous certainty about how biblical passages applied to contemporary events. These might include the results of the latest battle, the "message" God might be sending in the outcome of this or that event, or the meaning of vast social transformations such as emancipation. Clergy, laypeople, and soldiers on both sides freely divined God's purposes in history and suggested scriptures to back up their prognostications. As with the battle for the Bible in the slavery controversy, however, the standard mode of biblical exegesis for mid-nineteenth-century Protestants, common-sense realism (a method which assumed that the plain words of the text would speak plainly to the reader), provided such a plethora of answers about the meaning of contemporary events that there was no clear answer. The Bible did not speak plainly. More than just about any theologian or minister, Lincoln understood that and articulated it in 1865.

On the controverted issue of slavery and the coming of emancipation, however, African Americans found in the Bible the clearest connection to the apocalyptic events they experienced. Verses about Ethiopia stretching out its arms to God came to have a special meaning in an age when the war produced the one thing that most whites had little intention of fighting over when the war came: the freeing of nearly four million slaves. In the spirituals,

African American slaves had developed a profound theology of how contemporary lives and events fit into biblical passages and stories. Those stories came alive in the present tense in the spirituals, and the rituals of those singing these tunes—the bodily polyrhythmic accompaniment bringing the biblical narratives to life.

The Bible served one other, grimmer function as well—to bolster two armies armed with increasingly lethal weaponry. As men learned to place their own actions within a biblical cosmological framework, they also came to understand how crucial their role was in realizing a narrative foretold or sanctioned in the biblical passages. Chaplains carried a similar message to the men in both armies. Thus, soldiers on both sides imbued themselves with memorized verses, poetry, and stories from scripture. So armed, they slugged it out for four years, at the expense of three-quarters of a million lives. None of their prayers were answered fully, not even the desire for a nineteenth-century Victorian "good death."[1] Ultimately, the battle for the Bible during the slavery controversy and over the course of the Civil War helped to displace a world in which the Bible itself was the primary mode of interpreting contemporary events.

BIBLES IN THE CIVIL WAR ERA

The antebellum era was the great age of the mass production of religious print and imagery. Tracts, pamphlets, literature of religious edification, imagery (including, for the first time in American history, mass-produced imagery depicting Jesus as a white man with long flowing locks and a gently expressive face), and Bibles poured off steam printing presses. They traveled on wagons, steamboats, and railroads, blanketing the nation in a sea of Christian literature and pictures. Growing denominations and societies sent their agents—colporteurs—crisscrossing the country, giving away or selling religious literature of all sorts. The American Bible Society (ABS), founded originally in 1816, took up the task of distributing scripture to soldiers during the war. By the end of 1861, the Society claimed success in printing 7,000 pocket New Testaments per day for soldiers; by the end of the war, the ABS claimed to have distributed well over 3,000,000 Bibles to soldiers (including those who had been captured and imprisoned) and civilians.[2] The Bibles came in many varieties and in languages, including German, French, Italian, Spanish, Dutch, Swedish, and Portuguese. Catholic editions were available for pious Catholic soldiers who avoided King James Bibles.

Southerners interested in distributing Bibles to their Confederate soldiers faced serious obstacles. Few Bibles had been printed in the South before the war; most of the Bibles distributed in the region came from the ABS. In 1862, an interdenominational group of southern religious leaders formed the Bible Society of the Confederate States, and they attempted to provide pocket Testaments, at least, to southern soldiers.[3] Ultimately, perhaps one in five or six Confederate soldiers received a Bible or Testament during the war, and few of those had been printed in the South. Many came from England, on ships that attempted to run blockades to bring in supplies for the Confederacy. Some Bibles made it through that way; many did not. A few hundred thousand Bibles made their way from North to South. One Richmond Bible blockade-runner smuggled tens of thousands of Testaments and portions of the Psalms and the Gospel from England to the Confederacy.[4]

How many soldiers read the Bibles distributed is impossible to determine. Religious agencies, chaplains, and sometimes legendarily pious military leaders such as Thomas J. "Stonewall" Jackson provided plenty of coaxing to get young men to crack open the Good Book rather than the deck of playing cards. Confederate soldiers, who were in need of so many more basic things (food, shoes, and other necessaries), sometimes let Bible distributors know how much they valued their product by using the pages to deposit wads of tobacco, or to line sinks in army camps. The limited place of Bibles for some northern soldiers was evident as well. When one Union soldier lost his Bible at the Battle of Shiloh, he simply hoped that "the man that took it will make better use of it than I did."[5]

On the other hand, many soldiers read their Testaments if only because they craved anything at all to read. Publicists for efforts at Bible distribution warned that soldiers lacking scriptures might pick up trashy reading material—or, even worse, Shakespeare. Moreover, the frequently circulating stories in which the Bible stored in a man's shirt pocket performed miraculous feats—usually involving stopping a bullet that otherwise would have been fatal—encouraged some men to keep and read them. Ultimately, who knew which stories were apocryphal and which ones might be real? In this case, the physical object was a talisman. In other cases, soldiers searched scriptures for comfort and solace in hellish situations. Union soldiers stuck at the prisoner-of-war camp in Andersonville, Georgia, understandably looked to scriptures and providence, as they watched their comrades all around them waste away and die. One June morning in 1864, a Connecticut soldier recently captured and sent to Andersonville sat with two others, looking in the Bible for comfort. They came upon St. Paul's words: "I have learned in whatsoever state I am therewith to be content." He concluded, "We all felt it was for us." Another soldier's final diary entry said simply "My only trust is in Christ." Four days later, weakened from multiple illnesses contracted at Andersonville, he passed. Through the Bible, God spoke to the Union soldiers: he was "bidding us prepare for death, bidding us to purify our hearts & Lives & let the Master find us ready & waiting when he calleth for us."[6]

Regardless of who had, owned, or made use of Bibles, Americans more generally lived in a Bible-saturated culture. Scriptural references and assertions of God's providence filled the writings of soldiers and civilians alike, as did assumptions of what lessons God might be teaching through the great conflict. Thus, more important than tabulating statistics about the actual production and distribution of Bible texts, impressive though those are, is understanding the way that Bible narratives, stories, imagery, metaphors, and theological concepts informed the entire way Americans understood the meaning of the Civil War. God had, as Julia Ward Howe wrote for her adaptation of "John Brown's Body" into "The Battle Hymn of the Republic," "Loosed the lightening of his terrible swift sword," but just what was the meaning of that providence? And as each side assailed the other with their own favored passages and interpretations, how could the American common-sense reading of the Bible survive the increasingly brutal and devastating slaughter of the war?

NORTHERN PROVIDENTIALISM

For northern clergymen, the Bible suggested both apocalyptic themes of remaking the world in the new millennium and a conservative emphasis on obedience to the powers that

be. They frequently invoked Romans 13, which enjoins on Christians obedience to the powers that be. Drawing from this, northern clergymen during the secession crisis and early in
the war primarily condemned rebellion rather than slavery. That grew into such a meme
that a few ministers pointed out that an overly enthusiastic application of that chapter of
Romans would effectively disallow all rebellion against constituted authority, including that
which began in America in 1776.[7] Northern clergymen pronounced a fairly authoritarian
view of the prerogatives of the government of the American Republic. Later, they saw there
also a justification for the elimination of slavery, for its abolition became central to the
repression of the rebellion and restoration of the American Republic.

According to James Moorhead's classic study *American Apocalypse*, supporters of the
Union generally shied from making simplistic eschatological readings of the Civil War
by equating it to the end times or believing that biblical readings could closely predict or
interpret current events. One Presbyterian paper in 1861, for example, dismissed "several
communications whose object it is to trace in the present war the fulfillment of certain
prophecies in the Revelation of John." The paper noted how often in the past Christians
had been "wont to seize upon and apply to their own times the predictions that seem so
applicable to our own."[8] Yet, as Moorhead also notes, the majority of Protestants "accepted
the apocalyptic character of the struggle and described it in language suggestive of the ultimate crisis in world history. Or, as the *Christian Advocate and Journal* expressed it, God was
putting America through a moral renaissance that would create "a mountain of holiness for
the dissemination of light and purity to all nations." God would create in America a "new
Mt. Sinai from the Gulf to the St. Lawrence, thundering from its top right, and truth, and
justice, and liberty through the centuries and the millenniums and the aeons and out into
eternity."[9]

The logic of millennialism suggested that the events of the Civil War could not just be
random, for they involved a cosmic struggle of good and evil, Christ and Antichrist. Thus,
extraordinary actions that would have been shocking in any other time became fully justifiable. One sermon, for example, praised Philip Sheridan's epic campaign of destruction of
Confederate supplies in the Shenandoah Valley in 1864: "We are upon Bible ground, therefore, when we invoke God in doing battle for a just cause, and we are following a biblical
precedent when we ascribe to Him the victory." Southerners were waging "unholy war, a
monstrous conspiracy of crime" on the Union.[10]

The Civil War, then, was, in the words of a northern Presbyterian, "the old conflict reenacted of Despotism against Freedom." The southern cause drew from a direct connection
to "the first two great rebellions—that which assailed the throne of heaven directly, and
that which peopled our world with miserable apostates." Part of the Union struggle, too,
involved tamping down appearances of "the fast maturing germs of the last great antichrist" in the modern world, including "Owenism, the Non-Resistance, the Fourierism,
Transcendentalism, and Come-Outerism of our country," even as the inventions of the
modern age made it possible to spread the Gospel more rapidly than ever before. The purpose of America in this millennial time, many believed, was to "stand up before the nations
of the earth as a model nation, to exhibit to them the beauty and glory of free institutions," and thereby to be God's "modern Israel."[11] Henry Ward Beecher put all these themes
together in 1861. He preached to one admiring audience that "wherever you have had an
untrammeled Bible, you have had an untrammeled people." Where the Bible could be "read
without hindrancy by parents and children together," there you would not see "a slave or

a serf in the field. Wherever the Bible has been allowed to be free; wherever it has been knocked out of the king's hand, and out of the priest's hand, it has carried light like the morning sun, rising over hill and vale, round and round the world."[12]

Biblical prophecies also helped shape white northerners' thinking about why a good God had allowed slavery, and what the age of emancipation now required of Christians. God was also fulfilling prophecy by using the war to prepare the way for colonizing blacks to Africa, and thereby exporting the blessings of Christian civilization. Isaiah's vision of the lion and lamb lying together would be realized, and Africa would realize a "higher order of civilization and a better type of Christianity than has yet been known."[13] Without a commitment to abolition, another northern minister said, then "we shall be plagued as were those oldest of slaveholders the Egyptians, and the war shall rage till there be not a house North or South, where there is not one dead. There will be a passage to the Red sea for us also; a deep red sea of blood." But if the mantle of freedom was taken up, then Americans would move through the seas unscathed, "and the nation, washed of its sin, shall learn war no more, but abide in peace to the latest generation."[14] James Moorhead describes such rhetoric as part of the rise of an "American Culture-Protestantism that viewed the national order as a divinely perfected source of religious fulfillment and authority." In this view, "righteous wars" were "means of grace." Clergymen reflected that the battlefield was an "anvil" to forge a people and melt down ethnic identities into a common American one. God used war to shape men to his own design and open new eras for nations.[15] As Moorhead summarizes, "In baptizing the Civil War with the bloody urgency of the Apocalypse, Protestants were fighting for more than the political integrity of the Union; the issue was no less than the survival of corporate identity and purpose."[16]

In his chapter for this volume, Mark Noll demonstrates how commonsense Christian readings of the Bible in a democratic culture simply could not answer the most pressing moral dilemma of the age. They did not prevent the cataclysm of the Civil War or provide any rich or profound answers to the pressing moral issues of the post-emancipation era. In *The Civil War as a Theological Crisis*, Noll concludes, "The theological crisis of the Civil War was that while voluntary reliance on the Bible had contributed greatly to the creation of American national culture, that same voluntary reliance on Scripture led only to deadlock over what should be done about slavery."[17] Ultimately, military might and industrial mobilization defeated what scriptural reasoning could not.

African Americans, the Bible, and the Civil War

During the Civil War, Frederick Douglass noted that: "Nobody at the North, we think, would defend Slavery, even from the Bible, but for this color distinction. Color makes all the difference in the application of our American Christianity.... The same book which is full of the Gospel of Liberty to one race, is crowded with arguments in justification of the slavery of another. Those who shout and rejoice over the progress of Liberty in Italy, would mob down, pray and preach down Liberty at home as an unholy and hateful thing."[18] Perhaps no group had a greater investment in a providentialist reading of the Bible and its impact

on current events of the Civil War era than African Americans. Certainly it was no accident that, following the Union capture of Wilmington, North Carolina, in February 1865,
black members of the town's Front Street Methodist Church (a congregation affiliated with
the Methodist Episcopal Church South) attended a sunrise service one Sunday morning in
which the black prayer leader chose as his text Psalm 9: "Thou hast rebuked the heathen,
thou has destroyed the wicked, thou hast put out their name for ever and ever." He proceeded to tell the people to "study over this morning lesson on this day of Jubilee." A black
Union Army chaplain told the congregation that "the armies of the Lord and Gideon has
triumphed and the Rebels have been driven back in confusion and scattered like chaff
before the wind."[19] Black members of this church responded to an African American version of biblical millennialism, one focused not on some future course of events, but instead
on those places where human history and the divine plan intersected. Rather than drawing
texts from the Book of Revelation, for example, they took as their models the Day of Jubilee,
Exodus, Gideon, and David in the Psalms.

One slave spiritual asked, "Were you there when they crucified my Lord." In placing the
Crucifixion in the present tense, black believers employed strategies of biblical interpretation that hinged on narrative meanings rather than historical chronology. That carried
over into the immediate postwar period, when organizers of a freedmen's convention in
Wilmington published a call for the election of representatives, using a theme from the
book of Isaiah: "Freedmen of North Carolina, Arouse!! . . . These are the times foretold by
the Prophets, when the Nation shall be born in a day . . . . The time has arrived when we
can strike one blow to secure those rights of Freemen that have been so long withheld from
us."[20] African Americans may have read the scriptures providentially, but they also kept
alive the poetry and magic of the texts. More than any other group of nineteenth-century
Americans, biblical narratives carried present-day meanings, for the way truly appeared
as the realization of scriptural prophecy. Their hermeneutical practice, according to Noll,
"featured the Bible as a source of prophecy, magic, conjuring, and dreams; the Bible as a
dramatic, narrative book; and the Bible as a book of grand, controlling themes."[21]

SOUTHERN PROVIDENTIALISM

White southerners carried over into the Civil War era a well-developed and defended intellectual edifice. The top ranks of southern theologians outlined a powerful pro-slavery argument based not on extrabiblical notions of racism, but instead founded on a theological
defense of European conservative ideas of social order. Good order pleased God; anarchy
and theological infidelity did not. Conservative theologians of both regions developed and
presented a coherent pro-slavery argument that could not be refuted successfully with the
commonsense biblical principles of the day.

A powerful force in antebellum America, the biblical pro-slavery argument spoke to the
commonsense biblical literalism of many evangelicals. The pro-slavery argument relied on
the evangelical synthesis to make its points. As one religious southern pro-slavery writer
put it for *DeBow's Review* in 1850, "What we have written is founded solely upon the Bible,
and can have no force, unless it is taken for truth. If that book is of divine origin, the holding of slaves is right; as that which God permitted, recognized and commanded, cannot be

inconsistent with his will." Answering the argument that slavery in the Bible somehow differed from racial chattel slavery which enriched planters, the author insisted that in fact "the condition of the servant of the Roman empire, was much less free than that of the southern negro." Even as biblical masters had much more control, yet the Apostle Paul still insisted that servants were to submit to their masters—"not only to the good and gentle, but to the forward; and to masters to give to their servants what is just and equal." Biblical passages approved the "legality and propriety of the relation of slave and master. "It can not, then, be wrong," he concluded. [22] Baptist minister Thornton Stringfellow of Virginia furthered this point, insisting that the Bible did "much to secure civil subordination to the State, and hearty and cheerful obedience to the masters, on the part of servants." It would seem from the biblical texts, then, that the true "danger to the cause of Christ" came from the side of "*insubordination among the servants*, and *a want of humility with inferiors*, rather than *haughtiness among superiors* in the church." If the cause of Christ suffered, in other words, it was the slaves' fault. [23]

Sermons in defense of slavery became a religious ritual of self-defense in the antebellum South. This pro-slavery sermonic literature began to appear in the eighteenth century, and over time developed into a formidable intellectual edifice. Richard Furman of the South Carolina Baptist Convention contributed one of the earliest expressions of the genre with his address in 1823, just following the abortive Denmark Vesey rebellion. He sought to allay fears among some masters that acquainting slaves with scriptures would disturb domestic peace, only because opposition to slavery has been attributed by abolitionists to the "genius of Christianity." If holding slaves was a moral evil, he asserted, then it "cannot be supposed, that the inspired Apostles . . . would have tolerated it, for a moment, in the Christian Church." The idea that the Golden Rule condemned slavery was absurd. For example, if a son wished that his father would follow his commands, did that mean that fathers were obligated to obey orders from their sons? Furman acknowledged the evils and cruelties that had been attendant upon slavery. But such abuses also had been true of other primary social institutions, such as marriage, and that hardly proved that "the husband's right to govern, and parental authority, are unlawful and wicked." When tempered with "humanity and justice," slavery might provide a state of "tolerable happiness" for those in the lower orders of society. Furman's views seeded the growth of the religious paternalist pro-slavery theology that spread through the antebellum South. [24]

Through the 1850s and the Civil War, the religious pro-slavery argument appeared in its fullest, most well-developed forms. On November 29, 1860, some 2,000 parishioners gathered at the First Presbyterian Church of New Orleans to hear the leading Southern Presbyterian (and founder of what became Rhodes College) Benjamin Morgan Palmer defend secession, and more generally explain the role of the South in God's plan for the world. Southerners, he said, had a "providential trust to conserve and to perpetuate the institution of slavery as now existing . . . a trust to preserve and transmit our existing system of domestic servitude, with the right, unchallenged by man, to go and root itself wherever Providence and nature may carry it." [25] Through the war, Palmer repeated his theological view that God had assigned special missions to nations. The Confederacy's role was to persevere through trials and conflicts to carry out God's will.

As the Civil War progressed, elite southern divines wove ever-more elaborate theories of the meaning of the great conflict, always connecting it with God's will for slavery. Stephen Elliott, the well-known Episcopalian divine, found the meaning of the war in God's plan for the "poor despised slave as the source of our security." He proclaimed that God had "caused the African Race to be planted here under our political protection and under our Christian nurture, for his own ultimate designs"—that being their preparation to return the Christian word to their home continent of Africa. If God kept his own chosen people in the Old Testament enslaved for four hundred years, as part of their preparation to "go forth as a nation among nations," then surely history would teach American slavery was the yoke Africans would be under until God "saw fit to break it and to carry them, a humbled and prepared people, into the land which had been marked out for them as the scene of their future glory." In this sense, the very presence of slaves in the Confederacy was its greatest security.[26]

White southern Christians praised the religiosity of their new government and its leaders. As the "Apostle to the Slaves," Charles Jones explained to his son in March 1862, the new southern government came into being "with fasting, humiliation, and prayer." The Union suffered under burden of a godless Constitution, while southerners had "acknowledged Almighty God in ours—"the God of the Bible, the only living and true God—as our God; and we take Him as the God of our nation and worship Him, and put our nation under His care as such."[27] In 1864, a southern cleric praised the southern revolution for vindicating the word and providence of God, for "slavery and the system of labor which time has built upon it are in a true sense divine." Moreover, he argued, the "dogma, that all men are entitled to equal rights, is a fatal error." Instead, men were entitled to a government suited to their conditions; for Negroes, then, the "system of Bible, domestic slavery is . . . the sum of the African's rights, and the sole condition of his welfare."[28]

Bible verses provided lessons in their very physical presentation. *The Soldier's Pocket Bible*, carried by Confederate soldiers, contained single sentence morals which then led to a series of verses that explicated the lesson. One lesson was that "for the iniquities of God's People, they are sometimes delivered into the hands of their enemies," and "both Soldiers and all God's people . . . must search out their sins." The southern religious press carried the accompanying verses, and sometimes whole Bible chapters, including Deuteronomy 28, which tells of the blessings to be received by Israel if the nation obeys God, and the punishments to come if it did not.[29] In August 1863, one chaplain for General George Pickett's Division of the Army of Northern Virginia had to preach to southern troops who had recently experienced one of the most devastating defeats in Civil War history, when Union defenders repulsed their famous charge across the open field on the third day of the Battle of Gettysburg. John Cowper Granberry, the chaplain, preached from Hebrews 11:6: "But without faith, it is impossible to please him: for them that diligently seek him," as he paraphrased it for his wife. His lesson was that "the independence of our country may be won by this potent principle," if Confederates would only turn back to God through the Bible.[30]

All the more important, then, that southerners paid careful attention to watch for their own sins. "We lay the corner stone of our social system on this Word," the superintendent of public schools in North Carolina noted. He concluded that "in our controversy with the nations about slavery we summon the Word of God to the witness stand; and thus, like the Jews of old, we have as a nation solemnly bound ourselves to take this as our national chart and covenant." Southerners thus were required to "see the spirit of Divine Truth reflected in the laws of the land."[31] That centrally involved continuing the mission to the slaves who "would be so happy if the wicked had left them to their natural and normal position in this country, but who are made so wretched by the false teachings and allurements and practices of our enemies."[32]

White southerners also further ornamented increasingly baroque exegeses of how slavery arose from God's curse on the Negro as a race. Passages from the Old Testament, especially Genesis 9:18–27 (which outlined the curse on Canaan, son of Ham, who had originally espied Noah's naked drunkenness) provided at least a start at a religio-mythical ground-ing for modern racial meanings. With roots in the medieval era, when the "curse" applied to other groups (including Jews), this passage defeated generations of theologians' efforts to downplay it. The "curse" on Canaan, son of Ham––with Ham as a figure considered to represent black people, Shem standing in variously sometimes for Indians, other times for Jews, and Japheth supposedly being the progenitor of white people––was revived as a mode of biblical interpretation during the modern age of exploration, from the sixteenth century forward. It persisted through centuries in spite of "incessant refutation," and was, according to historian Winthrop Jordan, "probably sustained by a feeling that blackness could scarcely be anything but a curse and by the common need to confirm the facts of nature by specific reference to Scripture."[33]

The curse on Ham ultimately fed into and reinforced southern notions of honor. Southerners read the verses of the ninth chapter of Genesis as a story about a violation of family loyalty that showed the transgressor to be without honor, and therefore a subject that could be enslaved. If slavery was consigned to people without status and therefore without honor, then ancient stories explaining the origins of "primal dishonor" could explain the divine sanction for contemporary enslavement.[34]

CONCLUSION

Lincoln was correct in the Second Inaugural Address when he said, "Both read the same Bible." He might have added that American Protestants read the same Bible in the same way (i.e., through the hermeneutic of common-sense realism). By that reckoning, and assuming that the Bible should speak clearly (at the very least) on the most important and pressing social issues of the day, then American Christians should have developed a common reading of the text that might have mitigated or prevented the bloodletting of 1861–1865. But, of course, they did not, nor could they have done so. Because, as they learned, the Bible did not speak plainly. Its morals, lessons, parables, poetry, imagery, and narratives developed over centuries of time and across vastly different societies, never mind the centuries of interpretations and discussions of the scriptures from ancient times to the nineteenth century. During the war itself, the Bible variously provided inspiration, comfort, solace, and motivation both to soldiers and to civilians at home anxiously await-ing news of their loved homes stationed far from home. They saw in their Bibles justifi-cations for their causes, and plenty of reason to hate their enemies further. The inability of scripture to explain, prevent, or even marginally mitigate the greatest social conflict and upheaval of American history created a cognitive dissonance for many nineteenth-century Americans. Ultimately, a war so suffused with Bible readers and biblical imagery led to a displacement of a trust in the Bible as an ultimate and unquestionable source of moral authority.[35] The major exception was for African Americans, whose Christianization (measured in terms of number of churches and church members) increased dramatically in the years after the Civil War. For them, the "terrible swift sword" of God's justice led them to see that his truth was, indeed, marching on.

NOTES

1. Drew Faust, *This Republic of Suffering: Death and the American Civil War* (New York: Vintage, 2004).
2. John Fea, *The Bible Cause: A History of the American Bible Society* (New York: Oxford University Press, 2016), 72–84.
3. For more on the distribution of Bibles among Confederate soldiers, see George Rable, *God's Almost Chosen Peoples: A Religious History of the American Civil War* (Chapel Hill: University of North Carolina Press, 2011).
4. Rable, *Chosen Peoples*, 130.
5. Rable, *Chosen Peoples*, 131.
6. Lesley Gordon, *A Broken Regiment: The 16th Connecticut's Civil War* (Baton Rouge: Louisiana State University Press, 2014), 151.
7. George Frederickson, "The Coming of the Lord: The Northern Protestant Clergy and the Civil War Crisis," in *Religion and the American Civil War*, ed. Randall M. Miller, Harry S. Stout, and Charles Reagan Wilson (New York: Oxford University Press, 1998), 120.
8. James Moorhead, *American Apocalypse: Yankee Protestants and the Civil War* (New Haven, Conn.: Yale University Press, 1978), 63.
9. Moorhead, *American Apocalypse*, 65.
10. Mark Noll, *God and Race in American Politics: A Short History* (Princeton, N.J.: Princeton University Press, 2008), 43.
11. Moorhead, *American Apocalypse*, 53, 60–61.
12. Mark Noll, "The Bible and Slavery," in *Religion and the American Civil War*, ed. Randall M. Miller, Harry S. Stout, and Charles Reagan Wilson (New York: Oxford University Press, 1998), 50.
13. Moorhead, *American Apocalypse*, 106.
14. Moorhead, *American Apocalypse*, 100.
15. Moorhead, *American Apocalypse*, 147.
16. Moorhead, *American Apocalypse*, 164.
17. Mark Noll, *The Civil War as a Theological Crisis* (Chapel Hill: University of North Carolina Press, 2005), 159.
18. Noll, *God and Race*, 41.
19. Matthew Harper, "Emancipation and African American Millennialism," in *Apocalypse and the Millennium in the American Civil War*, ed. Ben Wright and Zachary W. Dresser (Baton Rouge: Louisiana State University Press, 2013), 155.
20. Harper, "African American Millennialism," 155. For the original source, see https://www.newspapers.com/clip/2658515/freedmen_of_north_carolina_arouse/.
21. Noll, "The Bible and Slavery," 53.
22. "Slavery and the Bible," *DeBow's Review* (September 1850): 281–86, in *Defending Slavery: Proslavery Thought in the Old South: A Brief History with Documents*, ed. Paul Finkelman (Boston, Mass.: Bedford Books, 2003), 113–14.
23. Thornton Stringfellow, "The Bible Argument; or, Slavery in the Light of Divine Revelation," in Finkelman, *Defending Slavery*, 128, emphasis in original.

24. Richard Furman, *Rev. Dr. Richard Furman's Exposition of the Views of the Baptists Relative to the Coloured Population of the United States, in a Communication to the Governor of SC* (Charleston, S.C.: A. P. Miller, 1823), 9, 12, 17, 19.

25. Benjamin Morgan Palmer, "Thanksgiving Sermon," reprinted in Thomas Cary Johnson, *The Life and Letters of Benjamin Morgan Palmer* (Richmond: Presbyterian Committee on Publication, 1906), 207–21, quote on 213. The full sermon is easily available at http://civilwarcauses.org/palmer.htm.

26. Stephen Elliott, *Our Cause in Harmony with the Purposes of God in Christ Jesus. A Sermon Preached in Christ Church, Savannah, Georgia, September 18, 1862* (Savannah, Ga.: Power Press of John M. Cooper & Co., 1862), http://docsouth.unc.edu/imls/elliott5/elliott5.html.

27. Rev. C. C. Jones to Lt. Charles C. Jones Jr., March 3, 1862, in *The Children of Pride*, 207.

28. Rev. William A. Hall, *The Historic Significance of the Southern Revolution: A Lecture Delivered by Invitation in Petersburg, Va., March 14th and April 29th, 1864: in Richmond, Va., April 7th and April 21st, 1864* (Petersburg, Va.: A. F. Cruchfield & Co., 1864), 3, 13, 38.

29. Kurt Berends, "'Whole Reading Purifies and Elevates the Man': The Religious Press in the Confederacy," in *Religion and the American Civil War*, 151.

30. Reid Mitchell, "Christian Soldiers? Perfecting the Confederacy," in *Religion and the Civil War*, 306.

31. Calvin Henderson Wiley, *Scriptural Views of National Trials; or, The True Road to the Independence and Peace of the Confederate States of America* (Greensboro, N.C.: Sterling, Campbell, & Albright, 1863), 159.

32. *Journal of the Sixty-Eighth Annual Council of the Protestant Episcopal Church in Virginia, Held in St. Paul's Church, Richmond, on the 20th, 21st and 22nd May, 1863*, 38, http://docsouth.unc.edu/imls/episc68th/episc68th.html.

33. Winthrop Jordan, *The White Man's Burden: Historical Origins of Racism in the United States* (New York: Oxford University Press, 1974), 10.

34. Stephen Haynes, *Noah's Curse: The Biblical Justification of American Slavery* (New York: Oxford, 2001), 67.

35. For more on this, see Faust, *This Republic of Suffering*, 171–211.

BIBLIOGRAPHY

Elliott, Stephen. *Our Cause in Harmony with the Purposes of God in Christ Jesus. A Sermon Preached in Christ Church, Savannah, Georgia, September 18, 1862.* Savannah, Ga.: Power Press of John M. Cooper & Co., 1862. http://docsouth.unc.edu/imls/elliott5/elliott5.html.

Finkelman, Paul, ed. *Defending Slavery: Proslavery Thought in the Old South: A Brief History with Documents.* Boston, Mass.: Bedford Books, 2003.

Furman, Richard. *Rev. Dr. Richard Furman's Exposition of the Views of the Baptists Relative to the Coloured Population of the United states, in a Communication to the Governor of SC.* Charleston, S.C.: A. E. Miller, 1823. http://cdm16821.contentdm.oclc.org/cdm/ref/collection/p16821coll2/id/5593.

Gordon, Lesley. *A Broken Regiment: The 16th Connecticut's Civil War.* Baton Rouge: Louisiana State University Press, 2014.

Harvey, Paul. *Trouble the Waters: Race and Southern Christianities from Jamestown to Katrina.* Chicago: University of Chicago Press, 2017.

Haynes, Stephen. *Noah's Curse: The Biblical Justification of American Slavery*. New York: Oxford, 2001.

Jordan, Winthrop. *The White Man's Burden: Historical Origins of Racism in the United States*. New York: Oxford University Press, 1974.

Moorhead, James. *American Apocalypse: Yankee Protestants and the Civil War*. New Haven, Conn.: Yale University Press, 1978.

Noll, Mark. *America's God: From Jonathan Edwards to Abraham Lincoln*. New York: Oxford University Press, 2005.

——. *God and Race in American Politics: A Short History*. Princeton, N.J.: Princeton University Press, 2008.

Palmer, Benjamin Morgan. "Thanksgiving Sermon." In *The Life and Letters of Benjamin Morgan Palmer*, edited by Thomas Cary Johnson, 206–19. Richmond, Va.: Presbyterian Committee on Publication, 1906. http://civilwarcauses.org/palmer.htm.

Rable, George. *God's Almost Chosen Peoples: A Religious History of the American Civil War*. Chapel Hill: University of North Carolina Press, 2011.

Wiley, Calvin Henderson. *Scriptural Views of National Trials; or, The True Road to the Independence and Peace of the Confederate States of America*. Greensboro, N.C.: Sterling, Campbell, & Albright, 1863.

Wilson, Charles Reagan, Harry Stout, and Randall Miller, eds. *Religion and the American Civil War*. New York: Oxford University Press, 2008.

Wright, Ben, and Zachary W. Dresser, eds. *Apocalypse and the Millennium in the American Civil War*. Baton Rouge: Louisiana State University Press, 2013.

CHAPTER 24

....

THE BIBLE AND
THE RELIGIOUS RIGHT

....

REBECCA BARRETT-FOX

BACKGROUND

....

AT his second inauguration, amid the strife of the American Civil War, President Abraham Lincoln puzzled at the apparent paradox of religious justification for the bloodshed. Both sides, he noted, "read the same Bible, and pray to the same God; and each invokes His aid against the other."[1] Reviewing the situation more than sixty years later, Christian ethicist H. Richard Niebuhr explained the irreconcilability of Confederate and Union Christianity as rooted in their Bibles:

> It was plain to Southern Methodists, Baptists, Presbyterians, and Episcopalians that many of the Old Testament heroes they had been taught to venerate had been masters of slaves, that Paul had given his sanction to the institution . . . . The incompatibility of chattel slavery with the counsel of love was no less evident to the Northern church-goer.[2]

No less today than in Lincoln's and Niebuhr's times do Christians agree that the Bible is authoritative without being able to agree on how its texts bear on contemporary life. For theologically and politically conservative Christians, their faith does not simply allow for, but insists upon, certain readings of biblical texts. These readings tend to be vague enough to allow people from a variety of denominations to share them, but they are also specific enough to support particular types of political thought and action.

Conservative Christians' claim to being Bible-believers is only as strong as their endorsements of the following tenets:

- inerrancy—"the idea that because the Bible is inspired, it is wholly without error and thus completely accurate in all matters, including history, science, and theology,"[3]
- literalism—the idea that the majority of the text (outside of those verses that are clearly figures of speech) should be read literally,
- divine inspiration—the idea that "the books of the New Testament do not owe their authority to any human agency [because their] authority rises organically out of what

these books *are* in and of themselves," that is, a record of real events recorded by trustworthy witnesses,[4]

- the authority of the Bible—the idea that the Bible "makes sense" and continues to be applicable to the world, which must submit to its authority,[5]
- accessible to anyone who can read, for its contents are clear and can be understood in common-sense fashion,
- internally consistent, with all apparent discrepancies between passages harmonized,[6]
- coherent, with the correct hermeneutic, for "there are consistent rules of interpretation for all of us; that we don't like where they might take us is an indictment of our hearts toward God, not intellectual integrity about the meaning of any given passage."[7]

The end result is that the number of interpretations available to readers is limited—ideally to just one interpretation. This particular interpretation aligns with socially conservative politics and is able to be, and often is, ardently defended from attack. Of course, in an understated fashion, the historian and political scientist Benjamin T. Lynerd notes in *Republican Theology*, "it remains feasible to note some ways in which the Hebrew law, as well as the moral teachings of Jesus and Paul, complicate the idea that life, liberty, and property are universal and unalienable rights, or that limited government represents the ideal Christian framework for human politics."[8] In particular, the doctrine of inerrancy "generates a host of strained interpretations," while biblical literalism produces its own set of difficulties, including inconsistencies between science and religious texts.[9] The sociologist of American religion Christian Smith outlines the most common strategies for handling these difficulties in *The Bible Made Impossible*. Literalists may respond by ignoring the "problematic" texts, "essentially pretending that they do not exist," interpreting such passages "as if they say things that *they do not in fact say*," or developing "elaborate *contortions* of highly unlikely scenarios and explanations . . . which rescue the texts from the problems."[10] With these strategies in hand, it is not surprising that northern and southern soldiers could both go to battle armed with full confidence that they were doing God's will.

The destruction of the Civil War challenges the claims that the Bible, if read correctly, will unite the nation in obedience to God. Rob Schwarzwalder, senior vice-president of Family Research Council (FRC), a Religious Right policy effort, claims that conservative Christians "don't need a pope because, instead, we have the authoritative, enscripturated Word of God, which is sufficiently clear (and has been since the completion of the canon) for all believers to understand it's [*sic*] essential teachings."[11] Supporters of the Religious Right can agree on the social and political implications of scripture even when they do not agree on the biblical validity of various doctrines concerning infant baptism, the afterlife, the mechanism of salvation, or the means or meaning of communion. Such agreement comes not because, as Schwarzwalder suggests, the Bible is "sufficiently clear" on issues of US law, but because the Religious Right attracts conservative Christians who approach the Bible with a set of assumptions that are likely to yield readings of the Bible that support its brand of conservative politics. As the religious studies scholar Kathleen C. Boone notes, "strained exegeses not only arise from interpretive strategies" common among conservative Christians; "they are themselves evidence that these strategies exist logically prior to the text itself."[12]

Similarly, the sociologist Aaron B. Franzen's qualitative research indicates that actual engagement with biblical texts does little to sway the politics of conservative Christians. Instead, he argues that it is "the interpretative community and context of literalism" that influence individuals' views on topics such as expanded government and police authority to fight terrorism and engage such social issues as the nature of criminal penalties, protections for the environment, public health, education, welfare, economic inequality, and improving life for minorities. More explicitly religious topics addressed by such interpretative communities include whether the United States should be officially declared a Christian nation, the place of prayer in public schools, and the display of religious symbols in public places.[13] Such interpretative strategies may thus stand at the root of many conservative values.[14] Years of sociological data linking support for conservative politics to conservative theology, at least among the white Protestants who make up the majority of the Religious Right, suggests that this is the case.[15]

Francis Shaeffer, celebrated theologian of the Religious Right, explained why in *The Great Evangelical Disaster*: "Only a strong view of Scripture is sufficient to withstand the pressure of an all-pervasive culture built upon relativism and relativistic thinking."[16] Devalued scripture—that is, readings that allow for the possibility that not every word is "God-breathed," historically accurate, and culturally relevant to the present moment—leads to liberal and progressive policies that in turn undermine faith, freedom, and family. Christians who support more conservative views of the place of faith and family and the role of freedom in the United States must, consequently, choose reading strategies that promote a "strong view" of the Bible.

The result of such conservative readings of the scriptures is the religionization of politics, a path that is potentially "gory in its consequences," as well as the politicization of religion.[17] Conservative politics, economics, and religion blend into one another. In his endorsement of the Faith and Freedom Coalition (a Religious Right organization founded by political activist Ralph Reed), South Carolina Senator Tim Scott expressed his gratitude for the organization by claiming, "Let me just say thank you, because I'm not just a fiscal conservative, I'm not just a social conservative, I'm a biblical conservative."[18] Indeed, for the "biblical conservatives" who comprise the Religious Right, an accurate reading of the Bible will always lead to social and fiscal conservatism. As FRC's Schwarzwalder notes, this stream of American Christianity does not need a pope to enforce correct Bible reading and interpretation; political and social conservatism instead shapes and reinforces believers' interpretations of scripture.

THE RELIGIOUS RIGHT IN POLITICS AND SOCIETY

This essay focuses on conservative theology and the beliefs and actions of its conservative interpretative communities. The ambitious goals of the Religious Right concerning political and social involvement is captured well in the mission and rhetoric of the anti-feminist group Concerned Women for America (CWA), which makes clear its goal to "bring biblical principles into all levels of public policy" and "protect and promote biblical values among all citizens—first through prayer, then education, and finally by influencing our society—thereby reversing the decline in moral values in our nation."[19] "Religious Right" here describes voters, activists, and movement leaders who root their conservative political and social views in their conservative religious—and generally Protestant—faith.

The Religious Right is one of many global "movements of the orthodox which have pursued public agendas of cultural authoritarianism and economic individualism."[20] It traditionally does not include historically black churches, despite the fact that "fundamentalism actually defines, in the main, the theological disposition of most Black churches today."[21] Participants in these churches, in general, do not tend to support socially conservative politics. It should be noted that the Religious Right has attempted to make inroads into black and Hispanic churches and organizations but has enjoyed limited success.

The Religious Right locates its agenda in "the very bedrock of evangelical theology"—the Bible.[22] For conservative Christians, the Bible is "both an ancient text and a how-to manual (more credible because of its ancient, supernatural origins)," and they believe that it can—and indeed must, if the nation is to survive and prosper—inform public policy and private morality.[23] "Now as in the past," the sociologist and renowned scholar of American evangelicalism James Davison Hunter notes, "there is a direct line of reasoning from biblical mandate to public policy recommendation" for such believers.[24]

The Bible is used in multiple ways by the Religious Right. Biblical figures who also served as political leaders, such as Moses, David, and Nehemiah, are held up as models for contemporary leadership.[25] Organizations connected to the Religious Right draw their mission and bylaws from biblical texts and precepts.[26] In general, the movement advocates for increased public display and use of the Bible.[27] The larger goal, however, is to deploy scripture to support what Lynerd identifies as the elements of republican theology: "private morality as a public matter" (that is, opposition to "the enforced privatization of religion and religiously informed morality") and an affinity for republican liberty and libertarian government.[28] For the faithful of the Religious Right who are already "immersed in daily prayer sessions and study," the world appears "always already biblically written, as the Bible becomes the Book of the World."[29]

The links between conservative religious thinking and conservative politics is explicitly taught in churches through curricula such as Summit Ministries' *Thinking Like a Christian: Understanding and Living a Biblical Worldview* and Focus on the Family's small-group DVD study *The Truth Project*. *The Truth Project* includes lessons on how a judge must "always remember his place under the sovereignty of God."[30] It further teaches that "America is unique in the history of the world," a place where "a people holding to a biblical worldview have had an opportunity to set up a system of government designed to keep the state within its divinely ordained boundaries."[31]

The mutual reinforcement of conservative faith and politics has long allied Christian conservatives with the Republican Party, even as both the party and its conservative Christian members have concerns about that relationship.[32] The historian Steven P. Miller sees the Religious Right leaders as "waning, increasingly insular voices."[33] As legal scholar John Dombrink notes in his examination of social conservatism in the Obama era, leaders of the Religious Right "were never the whole story of religion in America, and they certainly now have a diminished profile."[34] This is in part due to the well-established decline in religious affiliation among Americans, especially younger people, and a decline in the number of people who believe in what the sociologists Paul Froese and Christopher Bader call an authoritarian God—one who is engaged with and judgmental of humanity.[35] The idea that God will intervene to punish or reward individuals and nations for their behavior motivates Religious Right engagement, and those who believe in such a God "are always more likely to be Republican . . . [and their] attitudes about social and economic policy are a perfect fit with a conservative policy agenda."[36]

Indeed, for the Religious Right the link between right living (frequently articulated in a policy agenda that opposes feminism, abortion, gay rights, and other so-called anti-family efforts) and national security is clear: "Righteousness exalteth a nation: but sin is a reproach to any people" (Prov. 13:34). Virtuously correct behavior based on correct religious beliefs will lead to a nation that prospers under God, and "Americans who believe in a more judgmental God are the most likely to think that God favors the United States over all other nations," in part because of Americans' high level of faith.[37] As the number of people who view God this way declines, the number of people motivated to political action out of fear of God's punishment likewise decreases. Even as the Religious Right faces challenges from politics and religion, "the propensity of certain Christian organizations and their leadership to politicize their engagement with the world is not likely to diminish any time soon" for at least three reasons.[38]

First, even as the Religious Right makes claims that conservative Christianity is "under attack" and that Christians are "persecuted," many of the ideas of evangelical, if not always conservative, Christianity freely circulate in—and have been absorbed by—mainstream American culture.[39] Conservative politics remain a fertile ground for conservative religious belief. Among registered voters, approximately 38 percent identify as conservative; this predicts "political party affiliation, voting behavior, and attitudes on a host of moral and policy issues."[40] Pessimism about the moral direction of the country, though, extends beyond self-identified conservative voters. Eight out of ten Americans believe that America is facing a moral decline, and 29 percent of those say that "lack of Bible reading is the primary cause." In its 2015 report on Americans' use of the Bible for the American Bible Society, the Barna Group found that 23 percent of adults say that the Bible is the actual Word of God, to be taken literally, and 30 percent say it is the error-free inspired word of God with some verses that are meant to be symbolic.[41] Forty-one percent of practicing Protestants, however, believe that the Bible is the literal Word of God, a rate much higher than among the population in general. They would likely agree that increased Bible reading would do America good—but that is also the position of half of Americans. According to Barna, half of adults (50 percent) believe the Bible has too little influence in US society today, more than three times the proportion of those who think it has too much influence (16 percent). The value of the Bible is clear to many Americans; 50 percent of Americans "strongly agree that the Bible contains everything a person needs to know to live a meaningful life."[42] If the Bible is this highly valued among the general public—and even more highly valued by those who are active in their Christian faith—then the foundation is there to argue that the Bible should be incorporated into politics.

Second, even if the numbers of Christians who hold an authoritarian view of God and a literal view of the Bible are in decline, those who continue to hold such views are not retreating from the public sphere.[43] There is a rising young core of conservative Christians who remain ready to engage society with biblically based political and social views. Young conservative Christians continue to oppose abortion vocally.[44] These young conservative Christians are also more likely to support Bible reading and prayer in public school compared to other young Christians who do not so readily embrace the conservative label.[45] In other words, the next generation of conservative Christians is committed to traditional views on the Bible's role in private and public life.[46]

The young and old among conservative Christians remain firm in their desire to influence society. In response to the Supreme Court's 2015 decision to recognize the legality of marriage between same-sex couples, Albert Mohler, long-time leader in the Southern Baptist Convention, encouraged both young and old conservative believers not to change their understanding of the Bible.

> We are called to be the people of the truth, even when the truth is not popular and even when the truth is denied by the culture around us. Christians have found themselves in this position before, and we will again. God's truth has not changed. The Holy Scriptures have not changed. The Gospel of Jesus Christ has not changed. The church's mission has not changed. Jesus Christ is the same, yesterday, today, and forever.[47]

Mohler is typical of many conservative Christians when he stresses that the Bible is more authoritative in believers' lives than is the law. The question, though, for the declining but still influential Religious Right, is whether that authority can be applied, through the government, to all people.

Third, many prominent and more contemporary politicians have stressed the importance of the Bible for all Americans. Ronald Reagan shared sentiments of this type in his proclamation declaring 1983 the Year of the Bible: "Of the many influences that have shaped the United States of America into a distinctive Nation and people, none may be said to be more fundamental and enduring than the Bible."[48] Reagan argued that Bible stories and the beliefs that they cultivated "inspired many of the early settlers of our country, providing them with the strength, character, convictions, and faith necessary to withstand great hardship and danger in this new and rugged land." The Bible also had a unifying function, as the settlers' "shared beliefs helped forge a sense of common purpose among the widely dispersed colonies—a sense of community which laid the foundation for the spirit of nationhood that was to develop in later decades."[49] Implicit in Reagan's words—and in the occasion for them—was that the Bible needed to be publicly honored so that its beneficial functions for American society could continue. With these sentiments, Reagan was giving voice to an increasing Religious Right resentment in the 1980s as conservative Christians actively involved in politics believed that there was a concerted effort to attack the Bible's role in public sphere. This attack had a long history, beginning with the prohibition of mandatory Bible reading in public schools in *Abington School District v. Schempp* (1963).[50] If the Bible could be honored for its role in American history, though, conservative Christians believed it could regain its proper place in American culture.

Their concern about the diminishing role of the Bible in schools and other public places is just one part of the "litany of concern and complaint" from religious conservatives. In their mythic view of American history, the United States was founded as a Christian nation but is now in danger because of the country's moral failings, including a legally codified rejection of the Bible. Conservative Christians believe that if political power is given over to Protestant Christians and like-minded allies, the tide can be turned and the United States will once again return to God.[51] This desire is rooted in what Hunter concludes is the Religious Right's "clear desire and ambition for dominance or controlling influence in American politics and culture . . . to ensure that public life is ordered on their terms."[52] Such a dream is dependent on the Religious Right's ability to bring every American under obedience to God and punish or ostracize those who fail to obey.

The American Family Association (AFA) argues that God through the Bible "communicated absolute truth to mankind," and since "all people"—not just Christians—"are subject to the authority of God's words at all times," the AFA works for "a culture based on biblical truth . . . in accordance with our founding documents."[53] This return to a society based on biblical truths is the only way for America's course to be correct and its social problems to cease. The religiously conservative CWA explains that with the rise of secularism Western Civilization forfeited "the faith and logic of a biblical worldview for an irrational secularism based on an unthinking and cruel relativism. This foolish exchange is at the root of the glaring injustices of modern American public policy."[54] In their endeavor to reverse this mistake, organizations such as the AFA and CWA support an industry of Bible promotion so that the United States might become a Bible-based society and attain the "mythic connection between the Christian faith and America."[55] In this view, history, in the words of a Religious Right DVD series on the religious founding of the nation, is "the providence of God" and America has a very special role in how God has interacted with the world.[56]

Reclaiming God's blessing for the country is a lot of work. Books, radio broadcasts, conferences and telecasts, sermon series, and seminars and conferences have all appeared with the goal of correcting the secular historians' version of American history, a version that fails in the eyes of the Religious Right to recognize adequately the faith of the founders or their religious intentions. For example, in his analysis of numerous iterations of the curriculum of the National Council on Bible Curriculum in Public Schools (a Religious Right organization promoting the allegedly non-sectarian and thus legal study of the Bible in public schools), the religious studies scholar Mark A. Chancey concludes that the curriculum's objective seems to be "convincing students that the [Protestant] Bible was *the* formative political influence on the Founding Fathers."[57] Indeed, the 2005 curriculum's cover is not decorated with a Bible but with the Declaration of Independence and a US flag.[58]

Others have argued in a similar manner for the Bible's preeminence in early American political thinking. The Religious Right pseudo-historian David Barton heads WallBuilders, an organization that has produced many texts arguing this line of thinking. Barton has remained a popular speaker, despite criticisms by scholars and the recall of one of his books by publisher Thomas Nelson.[59] Other Religious Right participants have been highly invested in the supernatural retelling of American history that places their political desires within a biblical cosmology. The words of American Family Council's Bryan Fischer exemplify the Religious Right's version of our nation's founding:

> The truth is that the Founders themselves recognized the ultimate authority of Scripture. Every part of the Constitution is infused with biblical principles and precepts. The Declaration of Independence is saturated with biblical themes, including the unambiguous affirmations that there is a Creator, that man is a created, not an evolved, being, and that every single one of our fundamental human and civil rights comes to us as a gift from God.[60]

Bryan Fischer's words also hint at the greater goal of the Religious Right's campaign, namely to link the Bible to the moment of the nation's birth and thus insure that the government is under the authority of God.

The theology of the Religious Right, argues the communication studies scholar Tahlia G. M. B. Fischer, "functions as constitutive rhetoric providing fundamental scaffolding that configures American law as biblically based," with the goal "to subsume American law under the figuration of divine authority."[61] Tahlia G. M. B. Fischer argues that the Religious

Right claim that the United States could not be what it is—a land of freedom—unless it were under the authority of God. She also underlines Bryan Fischer's view among those in the Religious Right that government should have a limited role in the lives of the nation's citizens. Bryan Fischer stresses that "the Founders expressed the biblical view that the role of government (Rom. 13) is not to grant us rights but to guarantee them, to secure them and protect them" and punish those who would infringe upon the God-given rights of those who have God-given rights.[62]

Indeed, the nation's current social problems, argued former GOP House Majority Leader Tom DeLay in an interview with Pastor Matthew Hagee (son of apocalyptic-focused evangelist John Hagee) in 2014, began "when we allowed our government to become a secular government . . . when we stopped realizing that God created this nation." DeLay is literal in his meaning that God created the United States, writing that "He wrote the Constitution, that it is based on biblical principles, and we allowed those that don't believe in those things to keep pushing us, pushing us, and pushing us away from the government."[63] Those laws were based on the biblical Ten Commandments, among other biblical texts. In *The Ten Commandments: Foundation of American Society*, FRC author Kenyon Cureton agrees with DeLay's thinking and goes through the commandments, pairing each one with laws of the founding era to illustrate the early republic's commitment to obeying God.[64]

In claiming that the rights of citizens derive from God, not from the government, and that the Constitution (and other founding documents) are divinely inspired, if not in the same exact way as the Bible then in some similar way, Religious Right leaders argue that the government is a lesser authority than the Bible, just as "the Founders themselves recognized the ultimate authority of Scripture."[65] Not only does this open the door for civil disobedience or even outright civil war if the government attempts to require religion to be subordinate to the law, it also makes the government the servant of God. And not just any God, of course, but the authoritarian Christian God of the Religious Right.

Non-Christians must recognize the Christian God if they want to have religious liberty since that God is the deity who gave American religious freedom, according to Judge Roy Moore, who was removed from his post as Chief Justice of Alabama in 2003 (only to win it back in the 2012 election) for his refusal to remove a Ten Commandments monument from the state Supreme Court building. "Religious liberty," he asserts, "is for everyone. But you've got to recognize a particular God. You can't recognize Mohammed because Mohammed doesn't give you religious liberty."[66] By Moore's logic, only Christians—those who have accepted "the Protestant Bible and fundamentalist Protestant notions about that Bible as standard and normative"—are guaranteed the freedoms articulated in the founding documents.[67] Such is the logic that undergirds conservative efforts to deny Muslims, for example, the freedom to build mosques.

In response to God's granting American Christians liberty, God wants obedience to the values of the Bible, as "our culture flourishes when we uphold them."[68] For those unsure of what kind of Christian America the founders intended, David Barton has provided an edition of the sacred book that outlines God's relationship to America and the demands he makes of its people: *The Founders' Bible: The Origin of the Dream of Freedom*. Just as the Scofield Reference Bible offered extensive commentary on the biblical text that reshaped many Protestants' thinking about biblical history since its release in the early 1900s, *The Founders' Bible* offers numerous in-text resources that encourage the reader to view the biblical text through the prism of Religious Right politics. In addition to a full text of the New American Revised Standard version, *The Founders' Bible* includes over 900 pages of commentary, including biographical sketches of figures from American history and quotations as well as "some of the most inspiring history on the founding of America and the destiny and purpose God intended."[69] The "destiny and purpose" for America is for conservative Christians to lead it to freedom (within the constraints of conservative Christianity), free markets, international dominance, and conservative social policy.

This mission aligns with both "soft" and "hard" versions of dominionism, belief that Christians—and especially Christian men, who are assumed to be heterosexual—are called by God to exercise authority (or "dominion") over the whole world, working through (never really) secular social institutions such as politics and business. Although they do not use the word *dominionism*, which is sometimes used pejoratively by journalists, in their own materials, the Religious Right promotes the idea in organizations' communications with supporters.[70] For example, the Faith and Freedom Coalition uses its Facebook feed to encourage supporters to "keep our prayer going that we retake America and restore conservative leadership in Washington, D.C." The Council for National Policy, a large coalition of Religious Right elites, likewise shares its goal of political control in the name of its summertime conference: "Road to Majority." These groups do not argue explicitly for theocracy or theonomy (government that would incorporate both Religious Right interpretations of Christian Scriptures and Mosaic Law, characteristic of "hard dominionists").[71] Instead, they wish that the diffuse influence that ordained America "as a Christian nation" be reclaimed and that Christians exclusively "rule and reign" in a form of soft dominionism, which promotes Christian nationalism while stopping short of calling for a fully theocratic government. While many in the Religious Right are cautious about calling for a theocracy, "the foundational ideas of Dominionism . . . are important to many evangelicals" and appear throughout *The Founders' Bible*.[72]

CONCLUSION

With an understanding of American history that does not just permit but mandates conservative Christian involvement in politics, Religious Right leaders can press for a conservative social and fiscal agenda justified by their interpretations of scriptural passages about limited government, welfare reform, gender roles, mandatory schooling, warfare, and international relations. What undergirds their authority is the idea that they uniquely belong at the helm. In 2012, pastor Larry Huch at New Beginnings in Irvine, Texas, a charismatic megachurch that incorporates some Messianic Jewish practices, preached a sermon series titled "Getting to the Top and Staying There," a "message for us as individuals, the kingdom of God, but also for America . . . God will begin to rule and reign . . . God's people and His kingdom will begin to rule and reign."[73] He slides easily between a rule by God's kingdom and by God's people: today's Religious Right. During the series, evangelist Rafael Cruz, the father of Senator Ted Cruz, spoke to the congregation, referencing the Parable of the Minas from the Gospel of Luke, chapter nineteen. In that passage, a wealthy landowner must leave his land in an attempt to become king in a nearby land. He leaves different servants in charge of some money, commanding them to "occupy till I come" (verse 13). Some carry on with their master's business, and upon his return are rewarded—but one servant instead hides the money, fearful of losing it, and so has no returns to show and is scolded by his master. Scholarly readings argue that "occupy" here is better translated as "trade" or "go into business," but many in the Religious Right have taken up this phrase "occupy till I come" to mean that they are commanded by God to take control of American culture and government. In his comments on the text, Cruz provides directions on doing so: "The majority of you . . . your anointing . . . is an anointing as king."[74] "God has given you an anointing to go to the battlefield. And what's the battlefield? The marketplace. To go to the market-place and occupy the land. To go to the marketplace and take dominion." Conservative Christians thus have found in their Bibles a mandate to take financial, political, social, and cultural control until Jesus's return.

NOTES

1. Abraham Lincoln, "Second Inaugural Address," March 4, 1865, 3, Abraham Lincoln Papers at the Library of Congress, Manuscript Division, American Memory Project, Washington, D.C., http://memory.loc.gov/cgi-bin/query/r?ammem/mal:@field(DOCID+@lit(d4361300)).

2. H. Richard Niebuhr, *The Social Sources of Denominationalism* (New York: Meridian, 1975), 191.

3. Mark A. Chancey, "A Textbook Example of the Christian Right: The National Council on Bible Curriculum in Public Schools," *Journal of the American Academy of Religion* 75, no. 3 (2007): 565. The 2012 National Congregations Study reports that 83.3 percent of key informants (ministers, pastors, priests, etc.) responded affirmatively to the question, *Does your congregation consider the Bible to be the literal and inerrant word of God?* "National Congregations Study, Cumulative Dataset," Association of Religion Data Archives, Duke University, Durham, N.C., 2012, http://www.thearda.com/ConQS/qs_240.asp.

4. "Why the Bible Is Reliable," Focus on the Family, http://family.custhelp.com/app/answers/detail/a_id/26296.

5. Alex McFarland, "The Bible under Scrutiny," The Stand: Official Blog of the American Family Association, March 23, 2015, http://www.afa.net/the-stand/apologetics/the-bible-under-scrutiny.

6. Chancey, "A Textbook Example," 567.

7. Rob Schwarzwalder, "Don't Try to 'Cherry-Pick' the Bible," FRC Blog, July 16, 2013, http://frcblog.com/2013/07/dont-try-cherry-pick-bible.

8. Benjamin T. Lynerd, *Republican Theology: The Civil Religion of American Evangelicals* (New York: Oxford University Press, 2014), 50.

9. Kathleen C. Boone, *The Bible Tells Them So: The Discourse of Protestant Fundamentalism* (Albany: State University of New York Press, 1989), 46.

10. Christian Smith, *The Bible Made Impossible: Why Biblicism Is Not a Truly Evangelical Reading of Scripture* (Ada, Mich.: Baker Publishing, 2012), xii, emphasis in the original.

11. Rob Schwarzwalder, "The Truth about Human Sexuality: It All Comes Down to the Bible," first published at *The Christian Post*, February 2, 2015, http://www.frc.org/op-eds/the-truth-about-human-sexuality-it-all-comes-down-to-the-bible.

12. Boone, *The Bible Tells Them So*, 65.

13. Aaron B. Franzen, "Reading the Bible in America: The Moral and Political Attitude Effect," *Review of Religious Research* 55, no. 3 (2013): 408.

14. Brian Malley, *How the Bible Works: An Anthropological Study of Evangelical Biblicism* (Walnut Creek, Calif.: AltaMira Press, 2004), 87.

15. More than 70 percent of evangelicals have voted Republican every election since 1980. John C. Green, *The Faith Factor: How Religion Influences American Elections* (Westport, Conn.: Praeger, 2007), 43.

16. Frances A. Schaeffer, *The Evangelical Disaster* (Wheaton, Ill.: Crossway Books, 1984), 48.

17. Zygmunt Bauman, *Living on Borrowed Time: Conversations with Citlali Rovirosa-Madrazo* (Malden, Mass.: Polity Press, 2010), 132.

18. Tim Scott, "Sen. Tim Scott at the 2010 FFC Conference," YouTube video, 11:13, Posted by "bkirkland7," December 18, 2012, https://www.youtube.com/watch?v=V_NvSTaw_20.

19. "Who We Are," Concerned Women for America, http://www.cwfa.org/about/who-we-are; see also "About," Concerned Women for America, http://www.cwfa.org/about/vision-mission.

20. Nancy J. Davis and Robert V. Robinson, *Claiming Society for God: Religious Movements and Social Welfare* (Bloomington: Indiana University Press, 2012), 13.

21. Sylvester Johnson, as quoted in Philip Goff, Arthur E. Farnsley II, Peter J. Thuesen, "The Bible in American Life," Center for the Study of Religion and American Culture/The Trustees of Indiana University, Indianapolis, Ind., 2014, http://www.raac.iupui.edu/research-projects/bible-american-life/bible-american-life-report, 24.

22. Robert D. Putnam and David E. Campbell, *American Grace: How Religion Divides and Unites Us* (New York: Simon and Schuster, 2010), 111.

23. Erin A. Smith, *What Would Jesus Read? Popular Religious Books and Everyday Life in Twentieth-Century America* (Chapel Hill: University of North Carolina Press, 2015), 13.

24. James Davison Hunter, *To Change the World: The Irony, Tragedy, and Possibility of Christianity in the Late Modern World* (New York: Oxford University Press, 2010), 114.

25. See, for example, Mike Hurt, "Leadership: More about Availability than Ability," LifeWay Christian Resources, http://www.lifeway.com/Article/leadership-more-about-availability-than-ability; Josh Patterson, "4 Leadership Lessons from Nehemiah," Verge Network, http://www.vergenetwork.org/2014/07/08/four-leadership-lessons-from-nehemiah.

26. For example, Focus on the Family notes that its statement of faith "does not exhaust the extent of our beliefs. The Bible itself, as the inspired and infallible Word of God that speaks with final authority concerning truth, morality, and the proper conduct of mankind, is the sole and final source of all that we believe. For purposes of Focus' faith, doctrine, practice, policy, and discipline, our Board of Directors is Focus' final interpretive authority on the Bible's meaning and application." "Focus on the Family Statement of Faith," Focus on the Family, http://family.custhelp.com/app/answers/detail/a_id/25114.

27. For example, FRC promotes the inclusion of both prayer and non-sectarian Bible use back in public school. William Jeynes, "Putting the Bible and Prayer Back in the Public Schools," FRC University Library, http://www.frc.org/get.cfm?i=ev14f04. The American Center for Law and Justice (ACLJ), a Christian legal counsel organization, is fighting against the Freedom from Religion Foundation's demand that private hotels remove Bibles from rooms (Benjamin P. Sisney, "ACLJ Takes on Angry Atheists Demands," ACLJ.org, http://aclj.org/free-speech/aclj-takes-on-angry-atheists-absurd-demand-that-private-hotels-remove-bibles) and for the right of military staff to display Bible verses at workstations (Laura Hernandez, "ACLJ & Key Members of Congress Urge Armed Services Appeals Court to Uphold Religious Liberty," ACLJ.org, http://aclj.org/

religious-liberty/aclj-key-members-of-congress-urge-armed-services-appeals-court-to-uphold-religious-liberty). The legal organization associated with Jerry Falwell-founded Liberty University, Liberty Counsel, recently worked on behalf of a Bible study leader living in public housing to secure her right to use the community space for a Bible study ("Apartment Complex Resident Will Host Bible Study after Seven Years of Being Denied," Liberty Counsel, November 29, 2007, https://www.lc.org/newsroom/details/apartment-complex-resident-will-host-bible-study-after-seven-years-of-being-denied); in defense of students' rights to distribute the Bible on public high school property ("Religious Freedom Day Celebrated with Bible Distribution," Liberty Counsel, January 18, 2013, https://www.lc.org/newsroom/details/religious-freedom-day-celebrated-with-bible-distribution); in defense of individuals' rights to distribute Bibles in federal parks ("Park Service Reverses Decision and Allows Bible Distribution," Liberty Counsel, April 2, 2013, https://www.lc.org/newsroom/details/park-service-reverses-decision-and-allows-bible-distribution-1); in defense of the right of a children's Bible study leader to distribute flyers for a Good News Club that included the words "Bible stories" in public school ("School District Reverses Prohibition of the Word 'Bible' on a Christian Program's Flyer," Liberty Counsel, October 19, 2011, https://www.lc.org/newsroom/details/school-district-reverses-prohibition-of-the-word-bible-on-a-christian-program-s-flyer); the right of individuals to distribute Bibles on public busses ("Federal Court of Appeals Hears Arguments of a Woman Who Was Booted from a Bus Because She Handed Out the Bible," Liberty Counsel, January 26, 2007, https://www.lc.org/newsroom/details/federal-court-of-appeals-hears-arguments-of-a-woman-who-was-booted-from-a-bus-because-she-handed-0); and more. Foundation for Moral Law—a group once led by Religious Right darling Judge Roy Moore, the current Supreme Court Justice of Alabama, and now led by his wife Kayla Moore—similarly works on legal issues, such as the ability of jurists to consult a Bible ("Bibles in Juries," Foundation for Moral Law, http://morallaw.org/about/our-legal-cases/#Bibles in Juries). In an effort to forestall legal troubles, the American Family Association (AFA) includes an explanation for school administrators about the legality of Bible distribution on public school property on the back of each Truth for Youth Bible it gives to high schoolers to share with "unsaved friends in school." "National 'Truth for Youth' Week—Get Your Free Bible Now!" AFA, http://www.afa.net/action-alerts/national-truth-for-youth-week-get-your-free-bible-now.

28. Richard John Neuhaus, *American Babylon: Notes of a Christian Exile* (New York: Basic Books, 2009), 39. Lynerd, *Republican Theology*, 3.

29. Linda Kintz, *Between Jesus and the Market: The Emotions that Matter in Right-Wing America* (Durham, N.C.: Duke University Press, 1997), 33.

30. Here "Understanding" involves Bible study, while "Living" is both about personal morality and politics. Topics include "SOCIOLOGY: What about society?," "LAW: Who makes the rules?," "POLITICS: What about government?," and more. David Noebel, *Thinking Like a Christian: Understanding and Living a Biblical Worldview* (Nashville, Tenn.: Broadman & Holman Publishers, 2002), 91, 103, 121.

31. Focus on the Family, "The Truth Project Lessons," The Truth Project, http://www.thetruthproject.org/en/about/truthprojectlessons.aspx#top.

32. For example, Jim Shempert of One Million Dads, a conservative Christian group encouraging Christian men to "Lead Them or Others Will," captures some conservative Christians' disappointment with the Republican Party when he grumps,

"Politically, I am an evangelical conservative. You know, that group that no Republican can win without their support, who then is forgotten when they get into office?" Jim Shempert, "On Government and Faith," The Stand: Official Blog of the American Family Association, December 23, 2015, https://www.afa.net/the-stand/government/2015/12/on-government-and-faith.

33. Steven P. Miller, *The Age of Evangelicalism: America's Born-Again Years* (New York: Oxford University Press, 2014), 4.

34. John Dombrink, *The Twilight of Social Conservatism: American Culture Wars in the Obama Era* (New York: New York University Press, 2015), 113.

35. Claude S. Fischer and Michael Hout, *Century of Difference: How America Changed in the Last One Hundred Years* (New York: Russell Sage, 2006), 186–211; Paul Froese and Christopher Bader, *America's Four Gods: What We Say about God—and What That Says about Us* (New York: Oxford University Press, 2010), 166.

36. Froese and Bader, *America's Four Gods*, 123.

37. Froese and Bader, *America's Four Gods*, 157.

38. Hunter, *To Change the World*, 168.

39. Miller, *The Age of Evangelicalism*, 8.

40. Froese and Bader, *America's Four Gods*, 58.

41. Barna Group, "American Bible Society's State of the Bible 2015," American Bible Society, New York, 2015, http://www.americanbible.org/features/state-of-the-bible-2015, 24, 21.

42. "American Bible Society's State of the Bible," 7.

43. "American Bible Society's State of the Bible," 26.

44. Robert P. Jones and Daniel Cox, "How Race and Religion Shape Millennial Attitudes on Sexuality and Reproductive Health," Public Religion Research Institute, Washington, D.C., 2015, 3–4, http://publicreligion.org/site/wp-content/uploads/2015/03/PRRI-Millennials-Web-FINAL.pdf.

45. Philip Schwadel, "Changes in Americans' Views of Prayer and Reading the Bible in Public Schools: Time Periods, Birth Cohorts, and Religious Traditions," *Sociological Forum* 28, no. 2 (2013): 276.

46. According to the 2012 National Congregations Study, 54.8 percent of church leaders identified their congregations as politically conservative. 33.7 percent as politically "right in the middle," and just 11.5 percent as politically liberal. "National Congregations Study," Association of Religion Data Archives, http://www.thearda.com/ConQS/qs_240.asp.

47. Albert Mohler, "Everything Has Changed and Nothing Has Changed," albertmohler.com, June 27, 2015, http://www.albertmohler.com/2015/06/27/everything-has-changed-and-nothing-has-changed-the-supreme-court-and-same-sex-marriage.

48. Ronald Reagan, "Proclamation 5018—Year of the Bible, 1983," February 3, 1983, The American Presidency Project, http://www.presidency.ucsb.edu/ws/?pid=40728.

49. Reagan, "Proclamation 5018."

50. *Abington School District v. Schempp*, 374 US 203 (1963).

51. Hunter, *To Change the World*, 127.

52. Hunter, *To Change the World*, 124.

53. "Our Mission", AFA, https://www.afa.net/who-is-afa/our-mission.

54. "Our Issues," Concerned Women for America, http://www.cwfa.org/about/issues/#sthash.qyzHfV45.dpuf.

55. Hunter, *To Change the World*, 128.

56. "A Comprehensive Defense of the Providence of God in the Founding of America," directed by Douglas W. Phillips (San Antonio, Tex.: Vision Forum, 2007), DVD.

57. Chancey, "A Textbook Example," 571, brackets and italics in original.

58. Chancey, "A Textbook Example," 570–71.

59. Barton's works, all published through his WallBuilders organization, include *The Second Amendment: Preserving the Inalienable Right of Individual Self-Protection* (2000), *Original Intent: The Courts, the Constitution, and Religion* (2000), *The Bulletproof George Washington* (2000), *A Spiritual Heritage Tour of the United States* (2000), *Setting the Record Straight: American History in Black and White* (2004), and *Separation of Church & State: What the Founders Meant* (2007). Christian publishing house Thomas Nelson recalled Barton's *The Jefferson Lies: Exposing the Myths You Always Believed about Thomas Jefferson* in mid-2012 in response to serious criticism about the factual accuracy of Barton's claims from Christian scholars, such as that put forward in Warren Throckmorton and Mike Coulter's *Getting Jefferson Right: Fact Checking Claims about our Third President* (Grove City, Pa.: Salem Grove Press 2012). Although in an undated open letter titled "Defending *The Jefferson Lies*: David Barton Responds to His Conservative Christian Critics," http://www.WallBuilders.com/downloads/newsletter/DefendingTheJeffersonLiesDavidBartonRespondstohisConservativeCritics.pdf, Barton claimed that Simon & Schuster would be picking up the book and delivering it to an audience much larger than it "would have with the Christian publisher Thomas Nelson," a slightly revised version was instead published by the right-wing World Net Daily. John Fea recapped the controversy for the History News Network in "Still Misleading America about Thomas Jefferson," February 7, 2016, http://historynewsnetwork.org/article/161878.

60. Bryan Fischer, "What Ben Carson Should Have Said . . ." The Stand: Official Blog of the American Family Association, August 4, 2015, http://www.afa.net/the-stand/news/what-ben-carson-should-have-said.

61. Tahlia G. M. B. Fischer, "(Re)membering a Christian Nation: Christian Nationalism, Biblical Literalism, and the Politics of Public Memory" (PhD diss., University of Iowa, 2014), 4.

62. Bryan Fischer, "What Ben Carson Should Have Said . . ."

63. Matthew Hagee, "Tom Delay," The Difference with Matthew Hagee, season 2, part 7, aired February 19, 2014, https://www.getv.org/Videos/Watch/ca8e0cd2-e9f1-4909-adec-4290a46b6b7e#.

64. Kenyn Cureton, "The Ten Commandments: Foundation of American Society," Family Research Council, Washington, D.C., no date, http://downloads.frc.org/EF/EF10I86.pdf.

65. Bryan Fischer, "What Ben Carson Should Have Said . . ."

66. Casey Toner, "Alabama Supreme Court Chief Justice Roy Moore: Same-Sex Marriage Ruling 'Destroyed the Institution of God,'" *The Huntsville Times*, July 12, 2015, http://www.al.com/news/mobile/index.ssf/2015/07/alabama_supreme_court_chief_ju.html.

67. Chancey, "A Textbook Example," 558. Generally speaking, Jews are treated differently than other non-Christians by the Religious Right, though the theological treatment of Jews by conservative Christians varies greatly. Roman Catholics are similarly treated very differently among Protestant groups.

68. "Home: Traditional Values," Council for National Policy, http://www.cfnp.org.

69. "About," The Founders' Bible, http://thefoundersbible.com/about.

70. Michael J. McVicar, "'Let them have Dominion': 'Dominion Theology' and the Construction of Religious Extremism in the US Media," *Journal of Religion and Popular Culture* 25 no. 1 (2013):120–45, http://www.utpjournals.press/doi/full/10.3138/jrpc.25.1.120.

71. Theonomist Greg L. Bahnsen argues for the theonomic position, saying, "The Whole Bible God expects us to submit to His every word, and not pick and choose the ones which are agreeable (that is, to ignore the Old Testament) to our preconceived opinions. The Lord requires that we obey everything He has stipulated in the Old and New

Testaments—that we 'live by every word that proceeds from the mouth of God' (Matt. 4:4)." Greg L. Bahnsen, *By This Standard: The Authority of God's Law Today* (Tyler, Tex.: Institute for Christian Economics, 1985), 25, http://www.garynorth.com/freebooks/docs/pdf/by_this_standard.pdf.

72. Jason R. Hackworth, *Faith Based: Religious Neoliberalism and the Politics of Welfare in the United States* (Athens: University of Georgia Press, 2012), 33.

73. Larry Huch and Rafael Cruz, "Sunday Service August 26, 2012—Pastor Rafael Cruz Preaches," YouTube video, 2:46:25, posted by "LarryHuch," August 26, 2012, https://www.youtube.com/watch?v=Qyo74QLV2D8.

74. Hutch and Cruz, "Sunday Service."

BIBLIOGRAPHY

Bauman, Zygmunt. *Living on Borrowed Time: Conversations with Citlali Rovirosa-Madrazo.* Malden, Mass.: Polity Press, 2010.

Barna Group. "American Bible Society's State of the Bible 2015." American Bible Society, New York, 2015. http://www.americanbible.org/features/state-of-the-bible-2015.

Barton, David. *The Second Amendment: Preserving the Inalienable Right of Individual Self-Protection.* Aleda, Tex.: WallBuilders, 2000.

———. *Original Intent: The Courts, the Constitution, and Religion.* Aleda, Tex.: WallBuilders, 2000.

———. *The Bulletproof George Washington.* Aleda, Tex.: WallBuilders, 2000.

———. *A Spiritual Heritage Tour of the United States.* Aleda, Tex.: WallBuilders, 2000.

———. *Setting the Record Straight: American History in Black and White.* Aleda, Tex.: WallBuilders, 2004.

———. *Separation of Church & State: What the Founders Meant.* Aleda, Tex.: WallBuilders, 2004.

Boone, Kathleen C. *The Bible Tells Them So: The Discourse of Protestant Fundamentalism.* Albany: State University of New York Press, 1989.

Chancey, Mark A. "A Textbook Example of the Christian Right: The National Council on Bible Curriculum in Public Schools." *Journal of the American Academy of Religion* 75, no. 3 (2007): 554–81.

Davis, Nancy J., and Robert V. Robinson. *Claiming Society for God: Religious Movements and Social Welfare.* Bloomington: Indiana University Press, 2012.

Diamond, Sara. *Roads to Dominion: Right-Wing Movements and Political Power in the United States.* New York: Guilford Press, 1995.

Dombrink, John. *The Twilight of Social Conservatism: American Culture Wars in the Obama Era.* New York: New York University Press, 2015.

Fischer, Claude S., and Michael Hout. *Century of Difference: How America Changed in the Last One Hundred Years.* New York: Russell Sage, 2006.

Fischer, Tahlia G. M. B. "(Re)membering a Christian Nation: Christian Nationalism, Biblical Literalism, and the Politics of Public Memory." PhD diss., University of Iowa, 2014.

Franzen, Aaron B. "Reading the Bible in America: The Moral and Political Attitude Effect." *Review of Religious Research* 55, no. 3 (2013): 393–411.

Froese, Paul, and Christopher Bader. *America's Four Gods: What We Say about God—and What That Says about Us.* New York: Oxford University Press, 2010.

Goff, Philip, Arthur E. Farnsley II, and Peter J. Thuesen. "The Bible in American Life." Center for the Study of Religion and American Culture/The Trustees of Indiana University,

Indianapolis, Ind., 2014. http://www.raac.iupui.edu/research-projects/bible-american-life/bible-american-life-report/.

Hackworth, Jason R. *Faith Based: Religious Neoliberalism and the Politics of Welfare in the United States*. Athens: University of Georgia Press, 2012.

Hunter, James Davison. *To Change the World: The Irony, Tragedy, and Possibility of Christianity in the Late Modern World*. New York: Oxford University Press, 2010.

Jones, Robert P., and Daniel Cox. "How Race and Religion Shape Millennial Attitudes on Sexuality and Reproductive Health." Public Religion Research Institute, Washington, D.C., 2015. http://publicreligion.org/site/wp-content/uploads/2015/03/PRRI-Millennials-Web-FINAL.pdf.

Kintz, Linda. *Between Jesus and the Market: The Emotions That Matter in Right-Wing America*. Durham, N.C.: Duke University Press, 1997.

Lynerd, Benjamin T. *Republican Theology: The Civil Religion of American Evangelicals*. New York: Oxford University Press, 2014.

Malley, Brian. *How the Bible Works: An Anthropological Study of Evangelical Biblicism*. Walnut Creek, Calif.: AltaMira Press, 2004.

McVicar, Michael J. "'Let Them Have Dominion': 'Dominion Theology' and the Construction of Religious Extremism in the US Media." *Journal of Religion and Popular Culture* 25 no. 1 (2013):120–45. http://www.utpjournals.press/doi/full/10.3138/jrpc.25.1.120.

Miller, Steven P. *The Age of Evangelicalism: America's Born-Again Years*. New York: Oxford University Press, 2014.

Neuhaus, Richard John. *American Babylon: Notes of a Christian Exile*. New York: Basic Books, 2009.

Niebuhr, H. Richard. *The Social Sources of Denominationalism*. New York: Meridian, 1975.

Putnam, Robert D., and David E. Campbell. *American Grace: How Religion Divides and Unites Us*. New York: Simon and Schuster, 2010.

Schaeffer, Frances A. *The Evangelical Disaster*. Wheaton, Ill.: Crossway Books, 1984.

Schwadel, Philip. "Changes in Americans' Views of Prayer and Reading the Bible in Public Schools: Time Periods, Birth Cohorts, and Religious Traditions." *Sociological Forum* 28, no. 2 (2013): 261–82.

Smith, Christian. *The Bible Made Impossible: Why Biblicism Is Not a Truly Evangelical Reading of Scripture*. Ada, Mich.: Baker Publishing, 2012.

Smith, Erin A. *What Would Jesus Read? Popular Religious Books and Everyday Life in Twentieth-Century America*. Chapel Hill: University of North Carolina Press, 2015.

Throckmorton, Warren, and Mike Coulter. *Getting Jefferson Right: Fact Checking Claims about our Third President*. Grove City, Pa.: Salem Grove Press, 2012.

CHAPTER 25

···

THE BIBLE
AND ENVIRONMENTALISM

···

CALVIN B. DEWITT

APPROPRIATELY enough, the Bible begins with the words "In the beginning . . .", and with these words readers are ushered into what one scholar has described as "the theater of God's glory."[1] The first chapter of the Bible's book of Genesis reveals this glory through a creation of dynamic yet ordered immensity. The narrative tells of a geophysical earth in its spheroidal fullness bringing forth vibrant life within an enveloping biosphere. Myriad creatures, great and small, bright and beautiful, drab and cryptic—sustained within the interacting spheres of air, land, and water—fill the creation. The second chapter of Genesis moves on to describe how human beings—created in the image of their creator, God—are formed and then settled in a garden planted eastward in Eden and given the pleasurable assignment to serve and to protect the garden.[2] This garden is their home; it becomes the initial context of their lives and a site of divine service. But over the course of the third chapter of Genesis, these appointed stewards choose to know evil and, tragically, are banished from this garden. The swiftness of this sequence—from creation to stewardship to banishment—can leave one breathless. It also introduces the idea that God created humans to be stewards of the world he created.

One key biblical book in terms of reinforcing the themes of God's creative power and human stewardship is the Book of Psalms. For early, and then later Americans, the book of Psalms became a grand repository of narratives and descriptions of God's glory set forth in His creation and how he placed the care of that creation into human hands. Early American settlers transposed the Book of Psalms into verse and this verse, in turn, was often turned into song. Put to music and metrical rhymed verse, and sung in Sunday worship and mealtime devotions, various Psalms provided a framework that helped the earliest American settlers interpret their place in the New World, a place that for many of them resembled a new Garden of Eden.[3]

For American Christians, the medium of music and its use in describing God's creation with Edenic overtones reaches from the first book printed in North America, *The Bay Psalm Book* (1640), all the way down to songs popular in the twentieth- and twenty-first centuries. Perhaps most famous of these later musical odes to God's creation in the American context is the song "America the Beautiful," penned by Katharine Lee Bates in 1895. Initially a poem

Bates wrote after beholding the glorious view had from the top of Pike's Peak in Colorado, the poem was eventually set to music.[4] The magnificence of God's creation as seen in spacious skies, purple mountain majesty, and fertile plains has continued to be a popular rendition of the power and beauty of God's creation as displayed in the American landscape. For over four centuries, American Christians have in various ways held to a belief that their country formed a new type of Eden where God had bestowed upon them a special land they were to both enjoy and watch over.

PIVOTAL GARDENERS IN THE NEW EDEN

Beginning largely in the nineteenth century, a number of American figures distinguished themselves as particularly important in terms of thinking about issues of God's creation and humanity's stewardship over that creation. Such stewardship came to be known by various names over the years, such as conservancy or environmental care. What is often overlooked in discussions of the critical figures in various American environmental movements is how a stunning array of important environmental leaders in the United States had deep ties to the Bible.

George Perkins Marsh

George Perkins Marsh (1801–1882) is regarded as the originator of American environmentalism with his book, *Man and Nature* in 1864. He was born and raised in a Congregationalist family in Woodstock, Vermont, spoke twenty languages, was the US Minister to Turkey for five years and appointed Minister (Ambassador) to Italy by President Abraham Lincoln where he served his life's final twenty-one years. He had seen the deforestation of Woodstock's Mount Tom in his youth, and as ambassador, the consequences of human action in the Mediterranean and beyond. This and more were described in 1864 in his *Man and Nature*, revised in 1874 as *The Earth as Modified by Human Action: Man and Nature*. For his entire life, he held the basic biblically based conviction that God had given humans the world to care for, not to exploit.[5] The later American naturalist Aldo Leopold declared this work "one of the first to sense that soil, water, plants, and animals are organized collectively in such a way as to present the possibility of disorganization. His case histories describe many degrees of biotic sickness in many geographic regions. They are probably the ultimate source of the biotic ideas now known as conservation."[6]

John Muir

John Muir (1838–1914) followed Marsh and is widely considered the great Godfather of environmental conservation in the United States. Muir gained early training in mountain-climbing when he and his childhood friends scaled the walls of the old castle at the edge of the North Sea at Dunbar, Scotland. At age eleven he came to America where he coupled exceptional skill in traversing wild landscapes with extensive knowledge of the Bible—already having memorized the New Testament and three-quarters of the Old Testament. Besides internalizing the Bible and musically incorporating its Psalms into his life's soundtrack, he was accompanied on his long treks by John Milton's *Paradise Lost*, and "internalized his words and meaning and incorporated them organically into his books and articles."[7] Writing his daughter Wanda in 1893, from Dunbar, Scotland, after a forty-four-year absence from his place of birth, Muir wrote, "You are now a big girl, almost a woman, and you must mind your lessons and get in a good store of the best words of the best people while your memory is retentive, and then you will go through the world rich. Ask mother to give you lessons to commit to memory every day, mostly the sayings of Christ in the gospels, and selections from the poets. Find the hymn of praise in Paradise Lost, 'These are thy glorious works, Parent of Good, Almighty!' and learn it well."[8]

John Muir was born April 21, 1838, and baptized sixteen days later in Dunbar's Ebenezer Erskine Memorial Church.[9] He soon found he "was fond of everything that was wild," later saying, "I loved to wander in the fields to hear the birds sing, and along the seashore to gaze and wonder at the shells and seaweeds, eels and crabs in the pools among the rocks when the tide was low."[10] The pulse that beat at the heart of his boyhood's Presbyterian community was the Scottish Psalter together with the Bible and the *Westminster Shorter Catechism*, all adding to a rich cultural matrix within which his exploration of God's creation was set. Vital to this exploration was the linkage of God's special revelation and general revelation as described in the catechism—no doubt memorized by Muir as a child and laying the groundwork of faith for a budding scientist: "In what *volumes* has God discovered the knowledge of himself to all mankind?" the *Westminster Shorter Catechism* asked. Its answer: "In the great volumes of *creation* and *providence*; which he opens to all the world."[11] For Muir and his community, the book of God's creation and the book of God's word were to be read as one. The vitality of reading and memorizing both volumes of God's revelation was embedded early, and it persisted throughout Muir's life.

Joining this understanding of the great volumes of creation and providence were the Psalms. Sung over the ages since the time of the ancient Israelites, the Hebrew Psalms fostered awe, wonder, praise, and gratitude in the minds of wanderers, prophets, farmers, homemakers, and common folk. Muir sang the 150 psalms from the Scottish Psalter—*The Psalms of David in Metre with Notes by John Brown of Haddington*—during his boyhood and later as he grew up in Wisconsin. Reverend John Brown (1722–1787), who taught himself Latin, Greek, and Hebrew in his early years, wrote notes to the Psalter that linked every Psalm to its New Testament fulfillment in Christ. Muir's psalmic soundtrack was like a vast biblical sea of knowledge. In his 1893 letter to Wanda he wrote, "The waves made a grand show breaking in sheets and sheaves of foam, and grand songs, the same old songs they sang to me in my childhood, and I seemed a boy again and all the long eventful years in America were forgotten while I was filled with that glorious ocean psalm."[12]

Muir's psalm-inflected writing came to saturate wide swaths of American culture, greatly influencing people in their appreciation of America's spacious skies, mountain grandeur, fruitful plains, and shining seas. Both Muir and Milton brought together scripture and God's creation—the Bible and the environment—in psalmic praise. The legacy of these two writers continues to help Americans hold all truth together in lives embedded in nature. Historian Mark Stoll says,

The legacy of the Reformed Protestant yearning for Eden before the Fall still survives, shaped by Milton's vision and transmitted in his poetry to the founders and builders of National Parks, long outliving the theology and popularity of its greatest expositor. This legacy, the idea of national parks, has constituted a great gift to the world, in which places of rare natural beauty have been reserved for the enjoyment of the people, most of whom have nothing to do with Calvin or Milton. In such ways, and to a surprising degree, Yosemite Valley and the parks are Milton's monuments.[13]

Theodore Roosevelt

Theodore Roosevelt (1858–1919), a robust field biologist and hunter, and president of the United States, is widely regarded as the first environmental president. While in office he protected some 230 million acres of public land, including creating 51 bird reservations, 4 wild game preserves, 150 national forests, 5 national parks, and 18 national monuments, including the Grand Canyon national monument. Well-versed in the Bible, he also remained part of a Reformed congregation throughout life. In Washington, this was Grace Reformed Church to which he normally walked each Sunday from the White House. His favorite hymn "How Firm a Foundation" is a richly biblical hymn with its first stanza from 2 Peter 1:4, the second from Isaiah 41:10, the third from Isaiah 43:2, and the fourth from Isaiah 46:4 together with 2 Corinthians 12:9 and Hebrews 13:5.

Like Muir, Roosevelt's Reformed perspective embraced the two books of revelation as given in the Belgic Confession, which states the means by which God is made known to us: "First, by the creation, preservation, and government of the universe, since that universe is before our eyes like a beautiful book in which all creatures, great and small, are as letters to make us ponder the invisible things of God: God's eternal power and divinity, as the apostle Paul says in Romans 1:20." And, "Second, God makes himself known to us more clearly by his holy and divine Word, as much as we need in this life, for God's glory and for our salvation."[14]

Aldo Leopold

Aldo Leopold (1887–1948), an avid reader of the Bible, published "The Forestry of the Prophets" in 1920 based upon his reading of the Bible as a scientist.[15] In it he declared the prophets Ezekiel "a woodsman and an artist," Isaiah "the Roosevelt of the Holy Land," and Joel "the preacher of conservation of watersheds." From his study of Job he named its writer "the John Muir of Judah." Isaiah, said Leopold, "knew a whole lot about everything, including forests . . . and calls the trees by their first names"; "Joel knew more about forests than even Isaiah—he is the preacher of conservation of water-sheds, and in a sense the real inventor of 'prevent forest fires.'" David "speaks constantly and familiarly about forests and his forest similes are especially accurate and beautiful." Ezekiel is a "woodsman and an artist" who "knew a good deal about the lumber business, domestic and foreign." And "the John Muir of Judah" wrote "one of the most magnificent essays on the wonders of nature so far produced by the human race."[16]

Although he had an extensive knowledge of the Bible and ecology, Leopold would be the first to admit he knew little of theology. Yet his observations are consistent with Job scholar, Rabbi Robert Gordis, who says Job's author was

> Gifted with a strong sense of curiosity, keen powers of observation, and a vivid intelligence, the author reveals a high degree of familiarity with the arts and sciences of his day. His unforgettable pictures of beasts and birds and of the great land and sea monsters in the God speeches are impressive proof of his intellectual gifts as well as of his poetic powers. He is familiar with the sea and clouds, snow and hail, rain and ice. He has observed the refraction of light. The stars in their constellations are known to him, as are the paths of the streams of the desert and the mountain. He is familiar with of the wonders of birth for man and beast, his description of the fashioning of the human embryo being unparalleled in poetry. He knows the art of horticulture, including the transplantation of trees, and is at home with the craft of the hunter, using no less than six terms to describe various kinds of traps.[17]

Leopold had explored the wooded bluffs along the Mississippi at Burlington, Iowa, with his father and siblings in his childhood and youth. His profession of forestry, begun as a student at Yale, metamorphosed at the University of Wisconsin into wildlife management and then wildlife ecology from which he emerged as a land ethicist. His major work, "The Land Ethic," "was written in four phases over a fourteen-year period," an essay that "continues to grow in importance," wrote his biographer, Curt Meine. "Students read it. Journalists quote it. Environmentalists live by it. Supreme Court Justices cite it. Scholars criticize it." Meine goes on to comment that "many readers have gained their first exposure to an ecological world view through it," even as "it has become a standard starting point for scholarly discussions of environmental ethics."[18]

"Individual thinkers since the days of Ezekiel and Isaiah have asserted that the despoliation of land is not only inexpedient but wrong," said Leopold in his widely acclaimed essay, "The Land Ethic."[19] But since this ethic was not given in the Bible's Ten Commandments, Leopold extends the Decalogue on societal and social ethics to an ethic for the land:

> The land ethic simply enlarges the boundaries of the community to include soils, waters, plants, and animals, or collectively: the land.
>
> . . .
>
> In short, a land ethic changes the role of *Homo sapiens* from conqueror of the land-community to plain member and citizen of it. It implies respect for his fellow-members, and also respect for the community as such.
>
> . . .
>
> Conservation is a state of harmony between men and land.
>
> . . .
>
> A thing is right when it tends to preserve the integrity, stability, and beauty of the biotic community. It is wrong when it tends otherwise. [20]

Significantly, Leopold had all of his students at the University of Wisconsin read John Muir's book, *The Story of My Boyhood and Youth*, which provided a fine entrée for people aspiring to pursue vocations in ecology and the environment. And it was a book, followed by many others written by John Muir, that resonated with Leopold's love of the Bible.

Rachel Carson

As Muir and Leopold helped build appreciation for landscapes, Rachel Carson (1907–1964) did similar work in building an appreciation for the sea and its vibrant coastal edge of wondrous ecosystems and their intriguing creatures. Carson wrote, "If a child is to keep alive his inborn sense of wonder . . . he needs the companionship of at least one adult who can share it, rediscovering with him the joy, excitement, and mystery of the world we live in."[21] This certainly was true for Rachel, whose mother Maria "impressed her respect and love for wild creatures on all her children" and "enlivened Rachel's lifetime of literary development and study of nature" as her "close mentor."

Maria had been brought up in a strong Presbyterian family whose father was a pastor and minister. She graduated with honors in Latin from Washington Female Seminary in 1887—a United Presbyterian seminary in Pennsylvania—where her classmates "remembered her for her uncommon musical ability, playing the piano, singing, and composing, and winning distinction in each."[22] Maria's two older children were already in school when Rachel was born, and in their country home she gave her full attention to educating Rachel in nature study, natural history, literature and music, all in the context of the Reformed Presbyterian worldview that was a large part of the culture of western Pennsylvania. Important for Rachel was this tradition's concept of vocation or calling, serving God in the whole of the created world, thereby, "to glorify God and enjoy him forever."[23] This tradition has a naturalist catholicity that is directed toward the salvation and caring for the whole creation, not just people.

As it had for John Muir, the Bible and the *Westminster Shorter Catechism* provided a rich cultural matrix for Carson and was accompanied by Maria's habitual singing as she went about her work at home and outdoors. Carson had her Confirmation service just before her tenth birthday in the Cheswick Presbyterian Church, marking a serious vocational development in her life. There is no doubt, that Maria took seriously the Bible's teaching, "Train up a child in the way he should go: and when he is old, he will not depart from it" (Prov. 22:6, KJV). Rachel was a prime example of this nurture.

Upon entry to Pennsylvania College for Women in 1925, Carson wrote in her first college essay, "I am a girl of eighteen years, a Presbyterian, Scotch-Irish by ancestry, and a graduate of a small, but first class, High School," and love "all the beautiful things of nature." She went on to write that "I have come to P.C.W. because I know it to be a Christian college, founded on ideals of service and honor. I believe I will have time to think and to come to a fuller realization of myself, and that the training I receive here will help me to play my part on the stage of my life."[24] Her books *Under the Sea Wind* (1941), *The Sea around Us* (1952), and *The Edge of the Sea* (1955), conveyed wonder for the sea and its dynamic tidal edge, introduced the new field of ecology to thousands of readers, and established the basis for an *ocean ethic*. Remarkably, *The Sea around Us*, was published in thirty-two languages and made the *New York Times* bestseller list for eighty-one weeks.[25]

In June 1962, she wrote a series entitled *Silent Spring* for *The New Yorker* magazine, published as a book in September.[26] "We still talk in terms of conquest," she said April 3, 1963, in a CBS Reports documentary on "The Silent Spring of Rachel Carson," and concluding, said, "I truly believe that we . . . must come to terms with nature and I think we are challenged as mankind has never been challenged before to prove our maturity, and our mastery, not of nature, but of ourselves."[27] A day later, Senator Abraham Ribicoff announced hearings on pollution and pesticides to which he invited her to join. He greeted her: "Miss Carson, you are the lady who started all this."[28] She died from cancer on April 14, 1964.

TROUBLE IN THE GARDEN AND THE RISE OF NEPA

On May 20, 1966, the *Washington Post* published an article by John Chamberlain entitled, " 'Environmentalist' Ribicoff." This date marked the first time *environmentalist* and *environmentalism* in their modern sense were put into print, according to the *Oxford English Dictionary*.[29] Care for Eden in Genesis and for the new Eden in the New World had been christened. And *environmentalism* and *environmentalist* would be applied, however anachronistically, to John Muir, Aldo Leopold, and Rachel Carson; and also to Minister (Ambassador) George Perkins Marsh and President Theodore Roosevelt. The appearance of the term also coincided with a heightened American awareness concerning how more and more problems were facing the country in terms of how natural resources and nature itself was being stewarded by the country's inhabitants.

By the 1960s, widespread awareness and concern across America had grown to such a pronounced degree that many in government were calling for various forms of definitive environmental action. National leaders identified fragmentation in the government's decision-making processes as a major problem when dealing with environmental problems. Such fragmentation made it impossible to deal holistically with the environmental problems facing the nation. The solution pursued in the second half of the twentieth century was grounded in initiatives that worked against such governmental fragmentation of environmental vision and effort.

In the 1960s, Congress passed a series of legislative acts to address these problems, including the Clean Air of 1963, Wilderness Act of 1964, and Water Quality Act of 1965.[30] Such legislative activity intensified dramatically following the rupture of the steel casing of an offshore oil rig on January 28, 1969, at Santa Barbara that poured more than eighty-thousand barrels of petroleum over eleven days into the ocean, spreading broadly and contaminating coastal tide pools and numerous California beaches.[31] Environmental disasters such as the one in Santa Barbara dealt a serious blow to visions of *America the Beautiful*. Such blows became a catalyst for launching the Environmental Decade of the 1970s—bringing with it the National Environmental Policy Act of 1969 (NEPA)—the decade's flagship legislation signed by President Nixon on January 1, 1970. NEPA's stated goal was:

> To declare a national policy which will encourage productive and enjoyable harmony between man and his environment; to promote efforts which will prevent or eliminate damage to the environment and biosphere and stimulate the health and welfare of man; to enrich the understanding of the ecological systems and natural resources important to the Nation; and to establish a Council on Environmental Quality.[32]

Passed unanimously by the Senate and nearly unanimously by the House of Representatives (372-15), this far-reaching policy initiative broadly reflected Americans' deep-seated concern for their planet, and for the more religious, their gratitude and care for God's Creation.

Lynton Keith Caldwell (1913–2006), who came to be regarded as the principal architect of NEPA, was a professor of Government at Indiana University and a distinguished international scholar. In 1950 he explored the American West, covering 11,000 miles by automobile. During his explorations, Caldwell was dismayed by garbage and litter along roadsides, soil erosion from farmlands, polluted rivers along his route, oppressive smog in cities, unsightly development, aftermaths of mining and logging, and negative consequences of river damming. Deeply troubled by his observations, "Caldwell made the decision in 1962 to abandon his career in government and public administration in order to turn his mind to something then entirely novel: the development of environmental policy and administration to achieve better public planning, regulation and protection of the nation's remaining resources."[33]

In his definitive essay, "Environment: A New Focus for Public Policy?" published in 1963, Caldwell sketched the basic architecture of NEPA—legislation that would in time become a widely implemented model worldwide. "Fragmented action and policies affecting natural resources and human environment have brought waste and confusion in their train" he wrote, and "are a result of the lack of recognition of environment as a general subject for public action"—environment being not only "the complex interrelating reality surrounding us" but that which also "includes us."[34] Early in 1968, he began to work with Congress to develop a national environmental policy act to help guide American policy on environmental matters. Widely acclaimed as the hallmark of Caldwell's contributions was his *action-forcing mechanism*—an innovative tool to require every government agency and government-funded project to conduct an *Environmental Impact Assessment (EIA)*—on proposed projects.[35] The EIAs would cause every government agency to incorporate environmental stewardship and human well-being into their actions.

Caldwell understood that the perception "of an interactive world system is important because it is the context within which rational decisions affecting the environment must be made," but he found this to be "seldom the viewpoint of people preoccupied with their immediate day-to-day concerns," because "the holistic environment seems to exceed human comprehension."[36] For him, this *interactive world system* was no less than the entire biosphere—the living fabric of the whole Earth of which all people are part. The meaning of our reality—our most comprehensive environment—encompasses everything, including the Sun and the Cosmos, without which the Earth cannot exist.

Caldwell also made use of the Bible in his thinking and his writing about the environment. In his thirty-year retrospective book on NEPA, he reflected on the Bible's opening to the book of John, "The ultimate mystery—the origin and meaning of reality—may never have been better expressed than in the opening lines of the New Testament Gospel According to St. John: 'In the beginning was the Logos, and the Logos was with God and the Logos was God.'"[37] He notes that "the biblical scholar, Dr. James Moffatt, identifies the Word (*Logos*) as the 'divine principle of creation apart from which the universe is unintelligible.'"[38] And identifying the environment in its absolutely most comprehensive totality, Caldwell brings the Bible and the environment together to embrace one another in his interactive and interrelated notion of God's creation.

Caldwell's cutting-edge 1963 essay had been influenced by University of Wisconsin ecologist Aldo Leopold. And, through curious coincidence he visited Leopold in 1946, after traveling to Madison for a meeting to which he was denied access because it was only for "registered industry representatives." But he met a professor who said Leopold was teaching that morning. Arriving at class, and telling Leopold of his plight and his interest in ecology, he was invited to sit in, and afterwards Leopold invited him to dinner. "It was late when I finally left," he later told his biographer, Wendy Wertz. "I never again met Leopold again face to face but I think he helped to plant a seed in me that day which continued to grow until it emerged fifteen years later when the right time came."[39]

The Garden in the Twenty-First Century

Perhaps the greatest environmental and theological thinker of the early twenty-first century is Jorge Mario Bergoglio (b. 1936), chemist, Jesuit priest, and archbishop of Buenos Aires. Despite all these accomplishments, Bergoglio is best known by the name of Francis (after Francis of Assisi), a name he adopted upon his election as pope on March 13, 2013. In his book, *The Great Reformer*, his biographer Austen Ivereigh writes a narrative, captured in his book's title, "of a church leader who from an early age felt called to be a reformer, and was given the authority to do so."[40] Many of Pope Francis's concerns center on stewardship issues regarding God's creation.

On December 8, 2015, Pope Francis initiated the Jubilee Year of Mercy at St. Peter's Square by opening the Holy Door of the grand basilica. It was fifteen years early, but moved up to coincide with the fiftieth anniversary of the Second Vatican Council—an anniversary that remembered not only its documents but "a genuine *encounter between the Church and the men and women of our time.* An encounter marked by the power of the Spirit, who impelled the Church to emerge from the shoals which for years had kept her self-enclosed so as to set out once again, with enthusiasm, on her missionary journey."[41] It was "the resumption of a journey of encountering people where they live: in their cities and homes, in their workplaces," said Francis. In Argentina, Jorge Bergoglio "engaged in three reforms: of the Argentine Jesuit province, of the Argentine Church, and now of the universal Church. His lodestars are two French theologians, Yves Congar and Henri de Lubac."[42] These two men had been key advisors to the Second Vatican Council at which Congar advocated "a church that should be more evangelical and open to the Word of God"—more open to the Bible, and a church that would also "engage the modern world."[43]

As part of this third reform, Francis published his encyclical letter *Laudato Si': "Care for Our Common Home"* on June 18, 2015, thoughtfully referencing Genesis 2:15: the biblical appointment given Adam to serve and to keep the garden.[44] Covering climate change, biodiversity loss, ocean degradation, atmospheric pollution, and social degradation, its 246 sections address the "excessive anthropocentrism" handed to us as "a Promethean vision of mastery over the world, which gave the impression that the protection of nature was something that only the faint-hearted cared about," thereby exposing the error of interpreting *dominion* (cf. Gen. 1:28) as domination, when it "should be understood more properly"— "in the sense of responsible stewardship."[45] On climate change, Francis proved to be in full accord with the Oxford Declaration on Climate Change, produced by other religious leaders and climate scientists in 2002.[46]

In America, *Laudato Si'* was embraced and broadly supported by the US Conference of Catholic Bishops, whose president, Archbishop Joseph Kurtz, welcomed with "an open heart and gratitude" and whose Archbishop Thomas Wenski affirmed that "The U.S. bishops stand united with the Holy Father in his call to protect creation." [47] Of leaders of American denominations that stem from the "16th-Century Great Reformer," Steven Timmermans, CEO of the Christian Reformed Church in North America, responded to Francis's encyclical, saying, "We confess that for far too long we have shirked our divinely-ordained vocation of earth care, and we lament the ways in which our abuse and neglect of the created world has led to poverty, hunger, and a dangerously changing climate." And affirming the pope's statement, Timmermans wrote that "the Creator does not abandon us; he never forsakes his loving plan or repents of having created us"—that "the gospel must always be both proclaimed in word and demonstrated in deed, and that a central component of this task includes taking seriously God's command in Genesis 2:15 to serve and to protect the rest of the created order and to exercise responsible stewardship." And "we affirm the integrity of creation as an evangelical witness to the power and glory of God and the cosmic scope of God's redemptive work in Jesus as encompassing all of creation . . . . We add our voice to the gathering cry of the global church out of gratitude for the saving work of God in Christ and out of concern for the integrity of God's good creation."[48] Significantly, Timmermans strongly affirmed Francis's reading of Genesis 2:15 as requiring a culture of care that implies a "relación de reciprocidad" (in his Spanish text)—a relationship of reciprocity that expects human beings to return the services of the garden with services of their own—a relationship of *con-service* and *con-servancy*. [49]

The Ecological Society of America—numbering nearly 10,000 ecological scientists—responded to the pope's interest in the natural world, stating that the Society "commends Pope Francis for his insightful encyclical on the environment."[50] It is "an eloquent plea for responsible Earth stewardship" and the pope "is clearly informed by the science underpinning today's environmental challenges," including "climate change, its potential effects on humanity and disproportionate consequences for the poor, and the need for intergenerational equity." And, commending the encyclical as "remarkable for its breadth," the Society commented that

> Today's environmental dilemmas require bold responses, and the pope suggests actions to sustain ecosystems at local to global scales. He sees the need for comprehensive solutions solidly grounded in understanding of nature and society. Because there is no single path to sustainability, he sees generating viable future scenarios as necessary to stimulate dialogue toward finding solutions. We concur . . . . We hope his leadership will lead to serious dialogue among—and action by—the world's religious, political and scientific leaders on the environmental challenges facing this and future generations of humanity.[51]

APPOINTED TO SERVE AND TO KEEP

Examination of the people widely considered the principal leaders in American environmentalism—George Perkins Marsh, John Muir, Theodore Roosevelt, Aldo Leopold, and Rachel Carson—finds them all to have world-and-life views that are expansively integrative, working organically to hold together reciprocity between gardener and garden, between people and the biosphere. Over the course of a century, from Marsh's *Man and Nature* in 1864 to Rachel Carson's death in 1964, each worked to re-establish the lost reciprocity of con-service between people and the biosphere, and to safeguard both in the interest of biospheric integrity. Curiously, it was only in 1966, after their deaths, that they were first called environmentalists and their work, environmentalism. The Bible and its exposition were important to all of them, as also was the biosphere and all its benevolent services to life on earth. They were *two-book people*—not merely readers and students of the Bible but also readers and students of Creation. And not only Creation beautiful and whole, but abused and neglected. And it was this *two-book knowledge* that fueled their passion for stewardship.

John Calvin, the Great Reformer of the sixteenth century, commenting on the stewardship appointment of Genesis 2:15 knew that "the custody of the garden was given in charge to Adam, to show that we possess the things which God has committed to our hands, on the condition, that being content with a frugal and moderate use of them, we should take care of what shall remain."[52] And Pope Francis, the Great Reformer of the twenty-first century, addressing this same biblical text, wrote that it requires a "culture of care" and implies a "relación de reciprocidad"—a benevolent reciprocity between garden and gardener, between people and the earth.[53] As the earth serves and keeps us, so must we serve and keep the earth.[54] This clearly is a basic truth for all people everywhere in all times.

Pope Francis addressed this now-global stewardship in his encyclical released on July 18, 2015, *Laudato Si': On Care for Our Common Home*.[55] This broadened the scope of Earth stewardship, but most important brought it new life. "Now faced as we are with global environmental deterioration . . . I would like to enter into dialogue with all people about our common home," Pope Francis wrote, and he went on to introduce the world to *Integral Ecology*—an ecology that is integratively responsive both to "the cry the earth" and "the cry of the poor."[56] With this vital refreshment of the stewardship tradition, Pope Francis brought the universal human appointment "to serve and to keep" God's creation to the forefront of the Roman Catholic Church's agenda. His desire was to reach out beyond the Catholic Church as well with his encyclical, which he intended as a clarion call for everyone and every institution to return to their appointments to serve and to keep all of God's creation, to be mindful gardeners in a world handed down to humanity since the time of Eden.

NOTES

1. Genesis 1:1. All scripture citations in this chapter are from the New Revised Standard Version (NRSV), unless otherwise indicated. Belden C. Lane, *Ravished by Beauty: The Surprising Legacy of Reformed Spirituality* (Oxford: Oxford University Press, 2011). See esp. ch. 2, "John Calvin on the World as a Theater of God's Glory." Also see Susan F. Schreiner, *The Theater of His Glory: Nature and the Natural Order in the Thought of John Calvin* (Jamestown, N.Y.: Labyrinth Press, 1991).

2. The words "to serve," "to tend," and "to keep" are translations of the Hebrew words, *avad* and *shamar* in Genesis 2:14 that are central to humankinds' stewardship appointment as explained later in this chapter.

3. Sacvan Bercovitch, "The Typology of America's Mission," *American Quarterly* 30, no. 2 (Summer 1978): 155.

4. The first version, "America," was published in *The Congregationalist* 80 (1895): 27.

5. Wayne G. Boulton, *From Christ to the World: Introductory Readings in Christian Ethics* (Grand Rapids, Mich.: Wm. B. Eerdmans, 1994), 526.

6. Aldo Leopold, "The Land Health Concept and Conservation," in *Aldo Leopold: For the Health of the Land: Previously Unpublished Essays and Other Writings*, ed. J. Baird Callicott and Eric T. Freyfogle (Washington, D.C.: Island Press/Shearwater Books, 1999), 219.

7. Calvin B. DeWitt, "The Psalmic Soundtrack of John Muir: Singing from Two Books," *Plough Quarterly* 4 (2015): 46–53; Mark Stoll, "Milton in Yosemite: *Paradise Lost* and the National Parks Idea," *Environmental History* 13 (2008): 261.

8. William Frederic Badè, *The Life and Letters of John Muir* (Boston: Houghton Mifflin, 1924), 30, 316.

9. From his baptismal record obtained through research with Scotland's People's OPR Births and Baptisms Statutory Register, http://www.scotlandspeople.gov.uk/.

10. John Muir, *The Story of My Boyhood and Youth* (Boston: Houghton Mifflin, 1913), 1.

11. Ebenezer Erskine and James Fisher, *The Westminster Assembly's Shorter Catechism Explained* (Edinburgh: John Gray and Gavin Alston, 1765), 20, emphasis in the original.

12. Badè, *Life and Letters*, 316.

13. Stoll, "Milton in Yosemite," 263.

14. "Belgic Confession," Article II in Philip Schaff, *The Creeds of Christendom* (Grand Rapids, Mich.: Baker, 1931), 384. Philip Schaff writes in his preface to this Confession that this was originally composed in French by Guy de Brès in 1561.

15. Curt Meine, *Aldo Leopold: His Life and His Work* (Madison: University of Wisconsin Press, 1988), 183; also Nina Leopold Bradley, personal communication, ca. 1995.

16. Aldo Leopold, "The Forestry of the Prophets," *Journal of Forestry* 18 (1920): 412–19.

17. Robert Gordis, *The Book of God and Man: A Study of Job* (Chicago: University of Chicago Press, 1965), 212–13.

18. Curt Meine, "Building the Land Ethic," in *A Companion to "A Sand County Almanac": Interpretive and Critical Essays*, ed. J. Baird Callicott (Madison: University of Wisconsin Press, 1987), 172–73.

19. Aldo Leopold, "The Land Ethic," in *A Sand County Almanac and Sketches Here and There*, ed. Luna Leopold (London: Oxford University Press, 1949), 203. Leopold also cites Ezekiel 34:18 that in a more recent version asks, "Is it not enough for you to feed on the good pasture? Must you also trample the rest of your pasture with your feet? Is it not enough for you to drink clear water? Must you also muddy the rest with your feet?" (NIV). Due note should be given here to this verse in regard to stewardship being a relation of reciprocity.

20. Leopold, "The Land Ethic," 201–26.

21. Rachel Carson, *The Sense of Wonder* (New York: Harper & Row, 1965), 55.

22. Linda Lear, *Rachel Carson: Witness for Nature* (Boston: Houghton Mifflin Harcourt, 2009), 14.

23. Erskine and Fisher, *Shorter Catechism*, 9.

24. Rachel Carson, "Who I Am and Why I Came to PCW," Chatham University Archives & Special Collections, Chatham University, Pittsburgh, Pa., 1925.

25. "Rachel Carson: National Wildlife Refuge, Maine," *U.S. Fish & Wildlife Service*, http://www.fws.gov/refuge/Rachel_Carson/about/rachelcarson.html.

26. Rachel Carson, *Silent Spring* (Boston: Houghton Mifflin, 1962).

27. "The Legacy of *Silent Spring*," CBS News, http://www.cbsnews.com/news/the-legacy-of-silent-spring/. Also cf. Calvin B. DeWitt, "Ruling Ourselves in Truth and Grace: Lessons from the Elms," *Christian Century* 112, no. 34 (1995): 1116–19.

28. Arlene R. Quaratiello, *Rachel Carson: A Biography* (Westport, Conn.: Greenwood Press, 2004), 113.

29. *Oxford English Dictionary*, s.v. "environmentalism."

30. Nancy E. Marion, *Making Environmental Law: The Politics of Protecting the Earth* (Santa Barbara, Calif.: Praeger, 2011), 12.

31. Marion, *Making Environmental Law*, 92.

32. *Federal Historic Preservation Laws: The Official Compilation of U.S. Cultural Heritage Statutes*, 6th ed. (Washington, D.C.: US Department of the Interior, 2006), 101.

33. Wendy Wertz, "The Shared Vision of Lynton Keith Caldwell and Earth Day Founder Gaylord Nelson," Indiana University Press, http://iupress.typepad.com/blog/2014/04/guest-post-the-shared-vision-of-lynton-keith-caldwell-and-earth-day-founder-gaylord-nelson.html.

34. Lynton Keith Caldwell, "Environment: A New Focus for Public Policy?," *Public Administration Review* 23 (1963): 132, 133.

35. The IEA incorporated the Environmental Impact Statement (EIS).

36. Lynton Keith Caldwell, *National Environmental Policy Act: An Agenda for the Future* (Bloomington: Indiana University Press, 1988), 9.

37. *Word* in John 1:1 is replaced with *Logos*—the transliteration of the original Greek Λόγος. For a comparison of Greek texts of John 1:1, see the Online Parallel Bible Project, http://biblehub.com/text/john/1-1.htm.

38. Caldwell, *Environmental Policy Act*, 8.

39. Wendy Wertz, *Lynton Keith Caldwell: An Environmental Visionary and the National Environmental Policy Act* (Bloomington: Indiana University Press, 2014), 65.

40. Austen Ivereigh, *The Great Reformer: Francis and the Making of a Radical Pope* (New York: Henry Holt, 2014), xv.

41. Francis, "Extraordinary Jubilee of Mercy: Opening of the 'Holy Door of Charity' and Celebration of Holy Mass," December 18, 2015, italics in the original text, https://w2.vatican.va/content/francesco/en/homilies/2015/documents/papa-francesco_20151218_giubileo-omelia-porta-carita.html.

42. Ivereigh, *Great Reformer*, xv.

43. Robert Barron, "Yves Congar and the Meaning of Vatican II," Eternal Word Television Network, 2012, http://www.ewtn.com/.

44. Francis, *Encyclical Letter Laudato Si' of the Holy Father Francis on Care for Our Common Home* (Vatican: Libreria Editrice Vaticana, 2015), http://w2.vatican.va/content/francesco/en/encyclicals/documents/papa-francesco_20150524_enciclica-laudato-si.html.

45. Francis, *Laudato Si'*, ¶ 116.

46. "Oxford Declaration on Global Warming," Au Sable Institute and the John Ray Initiative 2002 Forum Statement, http://www.jri.org.uk/news/statement.htm.

47. "Archbishop Kurtz Welcomes Pope Francis' Encyclical *LAUDATO SI*'," US Conference of Catholic Bishops, http://www.usccb.org/news/2015/15-094.cfm; "Bishops Welcome Constructive Dialogue to Protect Creation and Address Climate Change," US Conference of Catholic Bishops, http://www.usccb.org/news/2015/15-133.cfm.

48. Steven Timmermans, "CRC Celebrates Pope's Call to Climate Action," Christian Reformed Church in North America, June 18, 2015, http://network.crcna.org/.

49. Francisco, *Laudato Si': Sobre el Cuidado de la Casa Común*, Papal Encyclicals, 2015, ¶ 67, http://www.papalencyclicals.net/. (Note that *Francis* is *Franciscus* in Latin, *Francesco* in Italian, and *Francisco* in Spanish).

50. "ESA Commends Pope Francis for Encyclical on the Environment," Ecological Society of America, June 29, 2015, http://www.esa.org/.

51. "ESA Commends Pope Francis."

52. John Calvin, *Commentaries of The First Book of Moses Called Genesis*, vol. 1, trans. John King (Edinburgh: Calvin Translation Society, 1554; repr., Christian Classics Ethereal Library), http://www.ccel.org/ccel/calvin/calcom01.html.

53. Francis, *Laudato Si'*, ¶ 231

54. Francisco, *Laudato Si'*, ¶ 67. (This is the Spanish edition.)

55. Cf. The home page of Pope Francis, https://w2.vatican.va/content/francesco/en.html.

56. Francis, *Laudato Si'*, ¶ 3, 137, 49.

BIBLIOGRAPHY

Beldon, Lane C. *John Calvin on the World as a Theater of God's Glory*. Oxford: Oxford University Press, 2011.

Bratton, Susan P. "The Spirit of the Edge: Rachel Carson and Numinous Experience between Land and Sea." In *Deep Blue: Critical Reflections on Nature, Religion and Water*, edited by Sylvie Shaw and Andrew Francis, 159–77. London: Equinox, 2008.

Bouwsma, William J. "Explaining John Calvin." *Wilson Quarterly* 13 (Winter 1989): 58–76.

———. *John Calvin: A Sixteenth Century Portrait*. Oxford: Oxford University Press, 1987.

Caldwell, Lynton Keith. *Between Two Worlds: Science, the Environmental Movement, and Policy Choice*. Cambridge: Cambridge University Press, 1990.

———. *The National Environmental Policy Act: An Agenda for the Future*. Bloomington: Indiana University Press, 1998.

Cansdale, George S. *Animals of Bible Lands*. Exeter: Paternoster Press, 1970.

Carson, Rachel. *The Sense of Wonder*. New York: Harper & Row, 1965.

DeVos, Peter A., C. B. DeWitt, Vernon Ehlers, Eugene Dykema, Dirk Perenboom, Aileen VanBeilen, and Loren Wilkinson. *Earthkeeping: Christian Stewardship of Natural Resources*. Grand Rapids, Mich.: Eerdmans, 1980.

DeWitt, Calvin B. "Biogeographic and Trophic Restructuring of the Biosphere: The State of the Earth under Human Domination." *Christian Scholar's Review* 32 (2003): 347–64.

———. "Contemporary Missiology and the Biosphere." In *The Antioch Agenda: Essays on the Restorative Church in Honor of Orlando E. Costas*, edited by D. Jeyaraj, R. Pazmiño, and R. Peterson, 305–28. Delhi: ISPCK, 2007.

———. "III. Earth Stewardship and *Laudato Si'*." *Quarterly Review of Biology* 91, no. 3 (September 2016): 271–84.

———. *Earthwise: A Guide to Hopeful Creation Care*. 3rd ed. Grand Rapids, Mich.: FaithAlive, 2011.

———. "The Psalmic Soundtrack of John Muir: Singing from Two Books." *Plough Quarterly* 4 (2015): 46–53.

———. "The Scientist and the Shepherd: The Emergence of Evangelical Environmentalism." In *The Oxford Handbook of Religion and Ecology*, edited by Robert Gottlieb, 568–87. Oxford: Oxford University Press, 2006.

———. "Stewardship: Responding Dynamically to the Consequences of Human Action in the World." In *Environmental Stewardship: Critical Perspectives Past and Present*, edited by R. J. Berry, 145–58. London: T&T Clark International, 2006.

Eccleston, Charles H. *NEPA and Environmental Planning: Tools, Techniques, and Approaches for Practitioners*. Boca Raton, Fla: CRC Press, 2008.

Elder, John. *Pilgrimage to Vallombrosa: From Vermont to Italy in the Footsteps of George Perkins Marsh*. Charlottesville: University of Virginia Press, 2006.

Francis (Pope). *Encyclical Letter Laudato Si' of the Holy Father Francis on Care for Our Common Home*. Vatican: Libreria Editrice Vaticana, 2015. http://w2.vatican.va/content/francesco/en/encyclicals/documents/papa-francesco_20150524_enciclica-laudato-si.html.

Gerrish, Brian A. "Tradition in the Modern World: The Reformed Habit of Mind." In *Toward the Future of Reformed Theology*, edited by David Willis and Michael Welker, 3–20. Grand Rapids, Mich.: Eerdmans, 1999.

Glacken, Clarence J. *Traces on the Rhodian Shore: Nature and Culture in Western Thought from Ancient Times to the End of the Eighteenth Century*. Berkeley: University of California Press, 1967.

Hall, Douglas John. *Imaging God: Dominion as Stewardship*. Grand Rapids, Mich.: Eerdmans, 1986.

Ivereigh, Austen. *The Great Reformer: Francis and the Making of a Radical Pope*. New York: Henry Holt, 2014.

Keynes, John Maynard. *Essays in Persuasion*. Reprint. New York: W. W. Norton, 1963.

Klein, H. M. J. "Roosevelt as a Man." *Reformed Church Review*, 4th series, 24, no. 1 (1920): 90–106.

Lane, Belden C. *Ravished by Beauty: The Surprising Legacy of Reformed Spirituality*. New York: Oxford University Press, 2011.

Larsen, David K. "God's Gardeners: American Protestant Evangelicals Confront Environmentalism, 1967-2000." PhD diss., University of Chicago, Divinity School, 2001.

Leopold, Aldo. "The Forestry of the Prophets." *Journal of Forestry* 18, no. 4 (1920): 412–19.

———. "The Land Ethic." In *A Sand County Almanac and Sketches Here and There*, 201–26. London: Oxford University Press, 1949.

Lowenthal, David. "Introduction to the 2003 Edition." In *Man and Nature; or, Physical Geography as Modified by Human Action*, by George Perkins Marsh, xv–xxxiv. Reprint. Seattle: University of Washington Press, 2003.

Manahan, Ronald E. "A Re-Examination of the Cultural Mandate: An Analysis and Evaluation of the Dominion Materials." PhD diss., Grace Theological Seminary (Winona Lake, Ind.), 1982.

McKim, Donald K. *John Calvin: A Companion to His Life and Theology*. Eugene, Ore.: Cascade Books, 2015.

Mitchell, Nora J., and Rolf Diamant. "The Necessity of Stewardship: George Perkins Marsh and the Nature of Conservation." *Forest History Today*, Spring/Fall 2005, 4–9.

Meine, Curt. *Aldo Leopold: His Life and His Work*. Madison: University of Wisconsin Press, 1988.

———. "Building the Land Ethic." In *A Companion to "A Sand County Almanac": Interpretive and Critical Essays*, edited by J. Baird Callicott, 172–85. Madison: University of Wisconsin Press, 1987.

Ogden, J. Gordon. "Frank W. Very." *Popular Astronomy* 36, no. 7 (1928): 390–97.

Roberts, Jon H., and James Turner. *The Sacred & the Secular University*. Princeton, N.J.: Princeton University Press, 2000.

Schreiner, Susan F. *The Theater of His Glory: Nature and the Natural Order in the Thought of John Calvin*. Jamestown, N.Y.: Labyrinth Press, 1991.

Sideris, Lisa H., and Kathleen Dean Moore. *Rachel Carson: Legacy and Challenge*. Albany: State University of New York Press, 2008.

Simpson, John W. *Visions of Paradise: Glimpses of Our Landscape's Legacy*. Berkeley: University of California Press, 1999.

Stoll, Mark. *Inherit the Holy Mountain: Religion and the Rise of American Environmentalism*. Oxford: Oxford University Press, 2015.

———. "Milton in Yosemite: *Paradise Lost* and the National Parks Idea." *Environmental History* 13 (April 2008): 237–74.

Tansley, Arthur G. "The Use and Abuse of Vegetational Terms and Concepts." *Ecology* 16, no. 3 (1935): 284–307.

Vanhoozer, Kevin J. "At Play in the Theodrama of the Lord: The Triune God of the Gospel." In *Theatrical Theology: Explorations in Performing the Faith*, edited by Wesley Vander Lugt and Trevor Hart, 1–29. Eugene, Ore.: Wipf and Stock, 2014.

Van Houtan, Kyle S., and Stuart L. Pimm. "The Various Christian Ethics of Species Conservation." In *Religion and the New Ecology: Environmental Responsibility in a World in Flux*, edited by David M. Lodge and Christopher Hamlin, 116–47. Notre Dame, Ind.: Notre Dame University Press, 2006.

Very, Frank W. *Atmospheric Radiation: A Research Conducted at the Allegheny Observatory at Providence, R. I., Bulletin 221*. Washington, D.C.: US Government Printing Office, 1900.

Walls, Andrew, and Cathy Ross, eds. *Mission in the Twenty-First Century: Exploring the Five Marks of Global Mission*. London: Darton, Longman and Todd, 2008.

PART IV

··

THE BIBLE AND THE ARTS

CHAPTER 26

....

THE BIBLE AND ART

....

KRISTIN SCHWAIN

A work of fine art picturing biblical subject matter is never a straightforward depiction of a scriptural text. It is a visual translation of it, shaped by available models of interpretation, the aesthetic styles and visual cultures of the era, and the cultural contexts of its production, display, circulation, and reception. An artist's rendition of the Madonna and Child, for example, encompasses official church doctrine and popular devotional practices; the history of its representation in art, cinema, literature, music, popular culture, and theater; and common perceptions of women's cultural role and the family as a social unit. Its meaning, in other words, is conditioned by the reading habits, viewing practices, and cultural beliefs shared by a particular community at a given historical moment.

In this essay, I examine the intersection of the Bible and American fine art by showcasing how and why artists transformed their interpretations of scripture into visual forms. A comprehensive, chronological survey is a nearly impossible task because of the manifold ways that artworks picture biblical subjects and invite religious interpretation. The role of the Bible in American art is so pervasive that it is overwhelming to consider just how often the Bible and its contents have fashioned American artistic expression.

In considering the subtle and not-so-subtle connections between the Bible and American art, examples abound. For instance, while many images may not appear to have scriptural content, their production and reception is shaped by it nonetheless. Protestant America's self-identification as God's "chosen people" and the United States as the "New Israel" infused nearly every nineteenth-century landscape painting with religious meaning. These artworks relied on a typological relationship between a biblical past and a national present to convey the country's cultivation and settlement as the result of its Manifest Destiny.[1]

In addition, many artists mine the history of art to render their subjects sacred. Returning to the example of Madonna and Child for a moment, virtually all turn-of-the-century images of motherhood touched upon the relationship between Mary and her son, since Mary best incarnated contemporary conceptions of womanhood. Mary epitomized chaste maternity and mediated the earthly and heavenly realms.[2]

Finally, many artists appropriate canonical artworks to engage contemporary concerns regarding gender, colonialism, race, and sexual orientation. By doing so, they emphasize the history of discrimination, as well as its sacralization and systemization in cultural institutions like the church, the museum, and the nation-state. While the biblical subject matter is certainly relevant in these objects, it is often the original work itself—its place in the canon, its physical location, and viewers' familiarity with it—that takes precedence.

In what follows, I pay particular attention to fine art paintings and sculptures that directly reference a biblical story or scriptural passage. I employ these works to exemplify four trends woven through the history of American biblical imagery. First, I examine how artists relied on prevalent models of biblical interpretation to infuse their work with moral instruction. Second, I look at how painters and sculptors turned to scripture to comment on political concerns that engaged the American public. Third, I examine how artists turned to biblical imagery to assert communal identity amid sectarian and cultural conflicts. Finally, I showcase artists who turned to scripture to render cultural criticism and call for social change. While many artworks belong in multiple categories, analyzing the manifold ways artists employ the Bible foregrounds its centrality in the production and interpretation of American art and visual culture.

VISUAL EXEGESIS AND MORAL INSTRUCTION

Thomas Eakins (1844-1916), America's preeminent realist painter in the second half of the nineteenth century, embraced German Higher Criticism (with its pronounced emphasis on the human role in the transmission and interpretation of the Bible) and relied on Roman Catholic ways of seeing in *The Crucifixion* (1880) (figure 26.1).

Stripped of beautifying effects, devotional aids, moral sentiment, and traditional iconography pointing to Christ's resurrection, Eakins's life-sized Christ dramatically confronts the viewer. His head falls forward, darkened by shadows; his hands are clenched in rigor mortis, punctured by nails; and the blood from his body collects in his legs, which have turned purple. Christ is dying, isolated in a forsaken, nondescript landscape, and alienated by friends and followers. Eakins's clinical representation of the human body produced what he termed "an objective study of a human being in his last moments."[3]

Eakins's realist idiom and attention to anatomical detail accented Christ's historical reality. The artist's emphasis on the humanity of Christ, rather than his divinity, situated him within a larger American and international context that sought knowledge of the historical Christ: what he looked like, the places he lived, and the roads he walked. Sponsored by liberal Protestants who sought an alternative to a religion based on creeds and dogma, interpretative stances influenced by German Higher Criticism situated Christ in his temporal and physical environments.[4] Despite the prominence of the historical Christ in American fine art and mass culture, most Protestant viewers were uncomfortable with the stark realism of Eakins's canvas because it did not serve what they deemed to be art's proper functions: to serve a good purpose, to stir noble emotion, and to elevate the mind. For these critics, realism had to be tempered with idealism and reverence in religious representation.

Eakins's rendition of *The Crucifixion* did correspond, however, to the Roman Catholic community's advocacy for the educational and edifying role of aesthetic engagement. In a contemporary apology for the role of art in Catholic life, the author wrote that Crucifixion imagery "brings before our minds the mystery of redemption and enable[s] us the more fully to appreciate it."[5] The author's continual use of active verbs in the present tense—"we look," "we see," "we can," "we hear"— highlighted the beholder's dynamic role in looking at art. Far from simply seeing Christ hanging on the cross, the viewer set the historical scene,

FIGURE 26.1 Thomas Eakins, *The Crucifixion* (1880). Oil on Canvas. Philadelphia Museum of Art, Accession number W1899-1-1. Gift of Mrs. Thomas Eakins and Miss Mary Adeline Williams.

entered it, and connected it to the present. The support Eakins received from Philadelphia's Catholic community underscores that his realist style coincided with the Catholic reliance on visual imagery to acknowledge the power of the phenomenal world. Catholic tradition shied away from reducing knowledge to the word rather than the Word and gave precedent often to the visual rather than the aural in matters of religion. By honoring sensory experience, many Catholics foregrounded the physical and material realities of human life.

An artist who came from a decidedly different background than Eakins—a man who drew on contemporary scholarship regarding Christianity and biblical exegesis while working within the fine art tradition—was the African American artist, Harriet Powers (1837–1911). Powers was born a slave in antebellum Georgia and produced two Bible quilts after the Civil War predicated on African American oratory.[6] Powers's brightly colored 1886 Bible quilt (now in the Smithsonian Institution) includes appliquéd figures and animals that reference conventional religious iconography as well as contemporary life. The biblical story appears in eleven episodes that can be read from left to right: Adam and Eve in the Garden of Eden; Eve bears a son; Satan amid the seven stars; Cain kills Abel; Cain, forced to leave, goes to Nod to find a wife; Jacob and the angel; Christ's baptism; the Crucifixion; Judas Iscariot and thirty pieces of silver; The Last Supper; and the Nativity. By beginning with Adam and Eve and ending with Mary, Joseph, and Christ, Powers presented a typological interpretation of the Bible: Christ's birth redeems the sins of Adam and Eve.

The biblical figures she included—Cain, Jacob, the criminal next to Christ on the Cross, and Judas—reinforced her focus on God's mercy and humanity's redemption through Christ.

In her 1886 Bible quilt, Powers also carefully interspersed objects from contemporary life with Christian iconography and biblical stories. For example, in the first panel, she represented original sin through a dressmaker's form. When asked why she carefully worked the trim around the neck of the form, Powers purportedly responded, "To ketch de eye er moral man."[7] In doing so, Powers referenced traditional interpretations of Eve's vanity and, perhaps, directed a warning to the European American women for whom she worked as a seamstress. She also employed preaching techniques practiced by many Protestant and African American religious leaders. She called attention to the presence of God in the natural world; she clothed the biblical protagonists in familiar garb; and she brought the biblical past into the present.[8] Given that Powers probably considered herself a lay minister and described the quilt as a "sermon in patchwork," her Bible quilt testifies to the power of oral tradition and the role of the visual in its transmission.

Finally, contemporary artist and muralist Archie Rand (b. 1949) employs a style often associated with comic books and graphic novels to produce works centered on Jewish life and religious belief. In *Sixty Paintings from the Bible* (1992), Rand appropriates a series of seventeenth-century engravings by the Christian artist, Matthaeus Meroian, entitled *Icones Biblicae* (1630). Translating the Renaissance drawings into comic form, Rand employs vivid colors, loose brushwork, and speech balloons with emphatic texts to challenge standard interpretations of Old Testament stories. For example, in his representation of King Solomon's adjudication of a case concerning two women claiming to be the mother of the same child, he destabilizes the stock interpretation of it as indicative of the king's wisdom. Instead, Solomon stands before his throne at the center of the composition, crying out: "*CUT THE KID IN HALF*!! AND GIVE ONE TO EACH MOTHER!" Even Rand's cartoony style and garish colors cannot mitigate the horror of the scene, as a soldier holds high a sword, ready to slash the naked child in two.

Rand uses the historical images as a framework to, in his words, "reassess the Tanach, get past the standard English translation and find the 'punch' of the original Hebrew."[9] By selecting single verbal expressions from paradigmatic stories, Rand forces viewers to consider them anew. Art historian Samantha Baskind situates this kind of Jewish art in the traditional practice of Midrash—a constant dialog between and among the text, its myriad interpretations throughout history, and the circumstances of contemporary life—that helps maintain the Hebrew Bible's central place in Jewish life and culture.[10]

AMERICAN POLITICS AND THE PURSUIT OF VIRTUE

Washington Allston (1779-1843) was among the young nation's first professional artists trained in the academic tradition. After graduating from Harvard in 1800, he enrolled at the Royal Academy in London and traveled around Europe studying the Old Masters. In 1817, Allston began work on *Belshazzar's Feast*, an almost fourteen by eighteen foot painting based on a passage from the Old Testament (figure 26.2).

According to the biblical text, Belshazzar hosted a great feast and invited the lords and ladies of his court to drink from gold and silver vessels. While doing so, the fingers of a

FIGURE 26.2 Washington Allston, *Belshazzar's Feast* (1817). Detroit Institute of Arts, USA. Gift of the Allston Trust/Bridgeman Images.

man's hand appeared and wrote an inscription on the chamber wall. Neither the king nor any of his wise men were able to interpret the prophecy, so Belshazzar invited Daniel to do so. Daniel told the king that God was displeased with Belshazzar for worshipping gold and silver instead of glorifying God. Belshazzar was slain that evening.

In *Belshazzar's Feast*, Allston focuses on a specific moment in the story: Daniel's interpretation of the inscription.[11] In doing so, Allston drew on contemporary explanations of the biblical story. He acknowledged free will (Belshazzar made a choice not to humble himself before God) but also stressed that people require divine assistance. Consequently, the painting encouraged moral reform, affirming humankind's ability to bring about a new era. At the same time, it served as a warning that unrestrained materialism and the failure of reason to control the passions could invite divine retribution and social anarchy. Indeed, Allston's understanding of the biblical story worked hand-in-hand with his Christian and elite-minded Federalist values. His typological interpretation avowed that if US citizens lived according to God's law, they would bring about the millennium (the thousand-year reign of Christ after he returns to Earth). Allston's Federalist leanings necessitated an opposition to Jacksonian democracy, a form of government that valorized and sought to empower the common man. Allston saw Andrew Jackson as a Napoleonic figure, an embodiment of materialism, skepticism, empiricism, and, above all, hubris. For Allston, Andrew Jackson's belief that ordinary voters, not overeducated aristocrats, should govern the young United States threatened the nation with disaster. In contrast, the painter sought a leader like

Daniel, an emissary between God and humankind, to stave off godless, plebian, avaricious sentiments. In Allston's mind, only a Federalist virtue driven by Christianity could successfully guide American republicanism.

Eakins's student, Henry Ossawa Tanner (1859-1937), was an internationally renowned painter at the turn-of-the-century who focused specifically on religious subjects.[12] His father, Benjamin Tucker (B. T.) Tanner, was a minister, and later a bishop, in the African Methodist Episcopal (AME) Church. The church, described by W. E. B. DuBois in *The Souls of Black Folk* (1903) as "the greatest Negro organization in the world," focused on religious conversion, evangelism, and African American uplift. Along with their European American counterparts, members of the AME Church deemed Christianity the primary means to individual respectability, a civilized society, and the success of American democracy on an international scale. Tanner's upbringing in the AME Church shaped his visual interpretations of the biblical text and led him to create paintings that engaged the viewer's emotions. At the same time, Tanner's paintings modeled a form of religious experience that was disciplined and restrained.

Tanner's biblical paintings posited a relationship between seeing and believing, a theological formulation consistent with Methodism's emphasis on experience as a means to the Divine. Even a cursory glance through the biblical subjects Tanner chose to represent calls attention to God's presence amid humanity's struggles. Daniel sits unharmed in a den of lions; angels appear before the shepherds; Gabriel approaches Mary (*The Annunciation*); Lazarus rises from the dead; and the disciples and the three Marys stare into an empty tomb (figure 26.3).

More specifically, Tanner's work models a form of disciplined piety and Victorian gentility that he and other African American intellects deemed critical to "civilize" the newly freed slaves and attain equality with whites in the United States. Tanner's conviction that art had the potential to inculcate certain values and behaviors underscores the ways in which African American and European American Protestant intellectuals and church leaders turned to religious imagery to nurture and aid in the development of personality.

In 1978, renowned artist and sculptor George Segal (1924-2000) turned to the Old Testament to encourage personal, political, and philosophical reflection when the Cleveland-based Mildred Andrews Fund commissioned him to memorialize the Kent State shootings of May 4, 1970. On that fateful day, members of the Ohio National Guard fired into a crowd of unarmed students—some protesting the Cambodian Campaign, some watching from a distance, and some walking to class—killing four and wounding nine. Segal found a precedent for the massacre in the Old Testament story of Abraham and Isaac. In it, God tests Abraham's love by commanding him to sacrifice his son, Isaac. Only after Abraham built an altar, collected wood for the fire, and laid his son on this altar did God stay Abraham's hand. In his life-sized bronze sculpture, Segal presents Abraham in contemporary clothing, grasping a knife and looming over his college-age son, Isaac, who kneels before him with his hands bound by rope.

Kent State University officials refused Segal's sculpture, declaring it "inappropriate to commemorate the deaths of four persons and the wounding of nine . . . with a statue which appears to represent an act of violence about to be committed."[13] In contrast, Segal interpreted the sculpture as "the eternal conflict between adherence to an abstract set of principles versus the love of your own child."[14] Indeed, he viewed the Kent State shootings through a generational lens, one in which the older generation equated patriotism with obedience.

FIGURE 26.3 Henry Ossawa Tanner, *The Annunciation* (1898). Oil on Canvas. Philadelphia Museum of Art, Accession number W1899-1-1. Purchased with the W. P. Wilstach Fund, 1899.

For university leaders struggling to control the May 4 narrative, the allegorical sculpture appeared to sanction the National Guard's actions against student protestors. For Segal, who purposefully represented the moment before Abraham sacrificed his son, the memorial testified to generational tensions that could never be solved, but nevertheless, obliged old and young to work together to prevent future violence.

GROUP IDENTITY

Edward Hicks (1780-1849), a Quaker preacher from Bucks County, Pennsylvania, painted over sixty versions of the *Peaceable Kingdom*, predicated on a passage in the prophetic book of Isaiah: "The wolf also shall dwell with the lamb, and the leopard shall lie down with the kid; and the calf and the young lion and the fatling together; and a little child shall lead them" (Isaiah 11:6) (figure 26.4).

Hicks included many of the animals cited in the scriptural passage in the foreground of his paintings. An assortment of wolves, lambs, leopards, cows, lions, bears, infants, and children all sit calmly beside one another in a bountiful landscape. In the middle ground, Hicks often included a scene loosely based on Benjamin's West's *Treaty of William Penn with the Indians* (1771-72). He depicts Penn, who founded colonial Pennsylvania as a "holy experiment" in religious freedom, entering into a peace treaty with Tamanend, a chief of the Lenape Turtle Clan in 1683. The painting presents early Quakerism's emphasis on quietism, the belief that true religious experience occurs when a believer empties him or herself of all worldly concerns and becomes open to a peaceful union with God. It also pictured Quakerism's history in the New World through the vision of William Penn.[15]

Despite the bucolic nature of Hick's Peaceable Kingdom paintings, they were sectarian assertions of a particular version of Quaker theology and social life that split the American Quaker community in 1827.[16] Hicks himself was a leading member of the "Hicksite" faction, named for his second cousin, Elias Hicks, who advocated extreme quietism and its attendant emphases on individual spirituality and democratic access to the Divine. Even the Bible was considered worldly. The Bible might be inspired by God, but it was also a human creation that carried with it the potential to impede communication between the believer and God. "Orthodox" Quakers, in contrast, embraced nineteenth-century American Protestantism's evangelical outlook and the authority of the Bible while downplaying the Inner Light so favored by the Hicksites. In this environment, Hicks's familial and theological associations

FIGURE 26.4 Edward Hicks, *Peaceable Kingdom* (1826), Philadelphia Museum of Art, Accession number 1956-59-1. Bequest of Charles C. Willis, 1956.

with Elias Hicks made his paintings partisan arguments for a particular sect of Quakerism and situated it within the heritage of William Penn and the nation's founding.

Hicks's critique of Orthodox Quakerism and mainstream American Protestantism reappears in a related painting, *Noah's Ark* (1846), predicated on Nathaniel Currier's popular 1844 lithograph of the same scene. According to the Genesis story, God was dismayed to see the wickedness and corruption of humankind and decided to start anew with Noah, a faithful and righteous servant. He instructed Noah to build an ark that would house and protect his family and two of every animal during forty days and nights of torrential rain. In Hicks's visual rendition, animals process as a "peaceable kingdom" across the foreground in a calm, orderly fashion. They veer to the right and enter the ark, and birds fly into a window directly above the door. The painting, however, is far from serene. The lion's anxious look, directed at the viewer, suggests the destruction yet to come, as do the ominous clouds darkening the sky and the waves gathering near the front of the boat. By lining the shore with New England-style homes, Hicks updates the biblical story and sets it in the present, inviting the righteous aboard the ark before God cleanses the world once again.

While Hicks's images of the Peaceable Kingdom and Noah's Ark served as apologies for a particular interpretation of Quaker's founding principles, the photographer Gertrude Käsebier (1852-1934) turned to Mary, the mother of Jesus, to convey her belief in certain principles of motherhood that linked woman across time and space. While accusations of "Mariolotry" permeated nineteenth-century Protestant discourse on Roman Catholicism, the writings of English art critic, Anna Jameson, made the Madonna safe for Protestant consumption in the first extensive study of Marian iconography, *Legends of the Madonna as Represented in the Fine Art* (1852).[17] In it, she contended that the cult of Mary stemmed from two separate but related trends: it was the amalgamation of all "types of a divine maternity," and it developed in tandem with new ideas concerning the "moral and religious responsibility of women" in civilized societies. Jameson's conception of the Madonna as the quintessence of Protestant womanhood created a language and usable past that enabled artists such as Kasebier to divorce Mary from her Roman Catholic doctrinal, liturgical, and ritual contexts.

Kasebier created a Marian trilogy with the production of *Blessed Art Thou among Women* (1899) (figure 26.5), *The Manger* (1899), and *The Heritage of Motherhood* (1904). The photographs interpret scenes from the New Testament that feature three scenes from Mary's life: the Annunciation, Nativity, and Crucifixion. The popularity of Marian imagery at the turn-of-the-century and the works' titles ensured viewers would recognize the women as Mary even without customary identifying markers. In an early print of *The Heritage of Motherhood*, for example, Kasebier drew three crucifixes in the lower left hand corner, literalizing the connection between the grieving woman and Mary's lamentation. She removed the crosses in the final version. By drawing on her own maternal experiences, those of her friends, and those of Mary, Kasebier pictured her belief in the transcendent nature of motherhood. When photographing her daughter with her newborn a few years later, she noted: "While posing my daughter there suddenly seemed to develop between us a greater intimacy than I have ever known before. Every barrier was down. We were not two women, mother and daughter, old and young, but two mothers with one feeling."[18]

Between the two world wars, African American artists turned to biblical subjects to assert their American identity and celebrate their unique contributions to American life.[19] In 1927, the African American author, diplomat, and songwriter James Weldon Johnson

FIGURE 26.5 Gertrude Kasebier, *Blessed Art Thou among Women* (1899). Platinum print. Image © The Metropolitan Museum of Art. Image source: Art Resource, N.Y.

(1871–1938) published a series of poems intended to preserve the sermons of "old-time Negro preacher[s]" before they vanished from the American scene.[20] In a volume entitled *God's Trombones*, Johnson continued his larger project of assembling and conserving African American folk creations of all kinds by offering eight poems inspired by the oratory and theology of antebellum ministers. Although the poems are presented in standard type, their titles feature gothic lettering fashioned by one of the nation's leading illustrators, Charles B. Falls, and they are accompanied with illustrations by one of the foremost visual artists of the Harlem Renaissance, Aaron Douglas (1899–1979).

While Johnson's poems locate African American history in the antebellum South, Douglas's modernist artistic idiom was inspired by African art and life in the urban North. In *The Crucifixion*, for example, Douglas presents a number of scenes from Johnson's sermon and the Passion story, including Christ's betrayal in the Garden of Gethsemane and struggle on the road to Golgotha. A large figure buckling under the weight and pressure of the cross, lunges on the earth's horizon and dominates the image. He represents, simultaneously, three different protagonists: Simon of Cyrene, an African man asked to carry Christ's cross; Jesus, the primary subject of the poem; and contemporary African Americans, who identified themselves with both men because of their persecution and suffering. The multivalency of the figure is intensified by the widespread equation of the crucified Savior with lynching victims in contemporary American visual culture.[21] Johnson's poetic debt to southern folk culture served a similar purpose to Douglas's reliance on African art. Both turned to the "primitive" to create histories particular to African Americans that provided a foundation for race pride and emphasized their modern consciousness and progressive development.

A similar tension appears in works by other black artists, including William Johnson (1901-1970), who looked to Western modernism, as well as to the religious heritage of southern blacks for the style and substance of his work. In *Jesus and the Three Marys* (1939), Johnson depicts the Crucifixion as described in John 19:25 (figure 26.6). Christ, the central figure, hangs serenely from the cross while three women—Mary, the mother of Jesus; Mary, the wife of Cleophas; and Mary Magdalene—occupy the foreground. Outlining the protagonists in black and interlocking them through flat blocks of color, Johnson juxtaposes their moderate expressions with exaggerated hands and feet. While compositionally similar to traditional renditions of the same scene, Johnson makes two fundamental changes. First, he renders the sacred figures black, countering standard representations of them as white and European. Second, he predicates their gestures on the religious practices of southern black evangelicals, as well as followers of new religious movements that flourished in urban storefronts following the Great Migration. Importantly, the physicality of the figures is balanced by their serene countenances, allowing the artist to avoid, as art historian Richard Powell argues, "the intellectual trap of a professed objectivity as well as the methodological pitfall of viewing black religion from an essentially European cultural standard."[22]

FIGURE 26.6   William H. Johnson, *Jesus and the Three Marys* (1939). Smithsonian American Art Museum, Gift of the Harmon Foundation.

CULTURAL CRITIQUE

Following in the legacy of Harriet Powers, "Self-Taught" artist Sister Gertrude Morgan (1900-1980) saw herself as a religious visionary who produced art to accompany her evangelical missions.[23] In 1937, Morgan received her second prophetic revelation from God that instructed her to "Go-o-o-o-o, Preacher, tell it to the World."[24] Eventually, this led her to move away from her Baptist congregation in Georgia to New Orleans, where she adopted a white dress uniform, the title "Sister," and traditions from the heavily Holy Spirit-oriented Holiness and Sanctified Movements. She based her ministry in New Orleans's Lower Ninth Ward in a shotgun house painted completely white—except for the brightly painted images she produced on any available surface (even Styrofoam meat trays) inspired by the books of Revelation and Daniel. She developed an apocalyptic iconography that was always accompanied by the scripture that inspired it, creating a baroque, multilayered visual experience.

In many of her works, Sister Gertrude Morgan represents herself as the Bride of Christ, often standing next to a fair-skinned Jesus as groom. One such image is her crayon rendering entitled "Rev. 19 Chap", where a multi-ethnic host joins the wedding couple before God's throne (figure 26.7).

Some of Sister Gertrude Morgan's most potent images present the New Jerusalem, described in Revelation 21:2: And I "saw the holy city, new Jerusalem, coming down from God out of heaven, prepared as a bride adorned for her husband." Once again in an image based on a passage from the book of Revelation, Morgan represents herself as the Bride of Christ, but here the setting resembles New Orleans, the city she sought to save, with stacked row houses or multi-storied apartment buildings outlined in red. Visionary images from the Book of Revelation appear and reappear in Morgan's work, including the Apocalypse and its four horsemen, the Antichrist, the Whore of Babylon, the Beast, and Armageddon (among others), along with the text itself.

Morgan also integrated contemporary music and Christian visual culture into her biblical art. The gospel song, "Jesus is my Air-o-plane," recorded by Mother McCollum in 1930, "appears" in Morgan's works; she regularly pictures herself in a two-seated airplane alongside Jesus. She also borrows heavily from prophecy charts or charters, schematic and diagrammatic illustrations that logically organize and map scripture through uniform correspondences, historical references, and iconographies of prophetic symbols.[25] Historically, preachers employed these charts to demonstrate the unity of the biblical text and to show the clear timeline it establishes for the second coming of Christ. Within the sacred space of her "Everlasting Gospel Mission House," as well as the secular spaces of the French Quarter and the New Orleans Jazz and Heritage Festival, Morgan's paintings, preaching, and singing worked together to advance her mission to save the city of New Orleans in preparation for the arrival of God's New Jerusalem.

While Morgan turned to art as a didactic tool to prepare for the next world, other artists relied on biblical subject matter to call attention to the horrors of the present. Abraham Rattner (1893-1978), like a number of Jewish artists in the United States and Europe, turned to Christological imagery to visualize Jewish suffering the 1930s and 1940s.[26] After spending twenty years in Paris between the World Wars, Rattner returned to the United States in 1939 and was shocked by Americans' indifference to events in Europe. He began to work

FIGURE 26.7 Sister Gertrude Morgan, *Rev. 19 Chap.* (1960). Crayon on paper. Courtesy of the Louisiana State Museum.

on crucifixion imagery to call attention to the victims of fascism and the Holocaust more specifically.

The title for Rattner's 1942 painting, *There Was Darkness over All of the Land*, is taken from a verse in Mark's gospel framed by Christ's crucifixion and his final exclamation, "My God, my God, why have you forsaken me?" In the upper portion of the painting, Christ's bloody body hangs from the cross. Although his head slumps forward, nails in his hands keep his distorted body tethered to the cross. Below, a procession of mask-like figures dressed in armor carry lit torches. Although cubist forms distinguish the figures from one another, the artist uses color to link them together into a united and skeletal mass. The tension between the upper and lower portions of the canvas, the suffering Christ and inhuman mob, echoes Rattner's verbal commentary: "It is myself that is on the cross, though I am attempting to express a universal theme—man's inhumanity to man." He was even more specific on another occasion: "The Crucifixion is not a single incident: it is symbolic of what is the matter with the world today."[27] Indeed, the same frieze of wide-eyed, skeletal figures composes Rattner's 1944 *Among Those Who Stood There*, begging the viewer to consider his or her place among those who stood by watching the crucifixion and the horrific implications of that decision.

Finally, Pop artist Andy Warhol (1928-1987) called attention to the imbrication of American art, religion, and consumption in his images from the mid-1980s, including *The Last Supper (Dove)* (1986) (figure 26.8).[28] Predicated on outline drawings of the

FIGURE 26.8 Andy Warhol, *The Last Supper (Dove)* (1986). Synthetic polymer paint on canvas. © 2016 The Andy Warhol Foundation for the Visual Arts, Inc. / The Museum of Modern Art. Digital Image © The Museum of Modern Art/Licensed by SCALA I Art / Artists Rights Society (ARS), New York.

da Vinci Renaissance masterpiece in a nineteenth-century encyclopedia of art, Warhol's works became part of the image's endless circulation in fine art and popular culture. He emphasized the commodification of the pictures, as well as the Christian traditions they evoked by including the advertising logos of Wise Potato Chips, Dove soap, and General Electric (among others). Warhol's title, "the Pope of Pop," and his use of "contemporary icons" and "commercial logos" (a word referring to corporate identities, on the one hand, and the Incarnation, on the other), suggest that neither art nor religion can be rescued from the sediment of consumerism because all three are intimately tied. While intended for the secular space of a museum rather than a church, and the individual investor rather than a mass of believers, Warhol's art drew on the tradition of devotional art to question the role of art and commerce in America's spiritual life. At the same time, he questioned the transcendence conferred on high art and the beholder's role in endowing this sanctity. The "community" illustrated by Andy Warhol shared an iconography of corporate logos, a hymnal of commercial jingles, and a financial—rather than a theological or experiential—means to salvation.

CONCLUSION

The Bible's dynamic and persistent role in American art, its ability to speak to the past, present, and future, and its status as a cultural and devotional object is embodied in a late work by the acclaimed American artist, Jacob Lawrence (1917–2000).[29] In 1989, New York City's Limited Editions Club commissioned Lawrence to illustrate the first chapters of Genesis from the King James Version (KJV) of the Bible. Standard representations of the Creation in the Western tradition visualize the biblical narrative itself and most often feature a muscular Caucasian God with long white hair and flowing beard fashioning the world with a dramatic flash of the hand. In stark contrast, Lawrence's *The First Book of Moses, Called Genesis* depicts a black preacher's sermonic evocation of it for his parishioners. By selecting the KJV of the biblical text, the artist reinforces the series' commitment to an expansive concept of the black church's social contract and a commitment to black history because of the version's centrality to African American culture.[30] It serves, simultaneously, as a historical account of life in 1930s Harlem, a celebration of the figures and institutions that have shaped—and continue to shape—black life and culture, and a devotional work that interprets the biblical past for contemporary believers.

By shifting the viewer's attention from the written text to its oral performance, from the story's ancient roots to its contemporary retelling, and from traditional modes of representation to a modernist visual language, Lawrence presents the biblical text as a living document that creates community and shapes the lives of those who read, preach, and hear it. Like all the biblical images and objects discussed in this essay, the meaning of Lawrence's work is not contingent solely on the artist's religious affiliation, the scriptural subject matter, or the context in which it is viewed. Rather, it is determined by their interaction, and in this way, underscores the vitality and continuing significance of American fine artists' engagement with the biblical text.

NOTES

1. While the literature on American landscape painting is vast, a classic source is: Angela Miller, *The Empire of the Eye: Landscape Representation and American Cultural Politics, 1825–1875* (Ithaca, N.Y.: Cornell University Press, 1996). See also Gail E. Husch, *Something Coming: Apocalyptic Expectation and Mid-Nineteenth Century American Painting* (Hanover, N.H.: University Press of New England, 2000).
2. Kristin Schwain, *Signs of Grace: Religion and American Art in the Gilded Age* (Ithaca, N.Y.: Cornell University Press, 2008), ch. 4.
3. Elizabeth Milroy, "*Consummatum est* . . . : A Reassessment of Thomas Eakins' *Crucifixion* of 1880," *Art Bulletin* 71, no. 2 (June 1989): 269. For general overviews of Eakins's body of work, see Elizabeth Johns, *Thomas Eakins: The Heroism of Modern Life* (Princeton, N.J.: Princeton University Press, 1983); and Kathleen A. Foster, ed., *Thomas Eakins Rediscovered: Charles Bregler's Thomas Eakins Collection at the Pennsylvania Academy of the Fine Arts* (New Haven, Conn.: Yale University Press, 1997).
4. John Davis, *The Landscape of Belief: Encountering the Holy Land in Nineteenth-Century American Art and Culture* (Princeton, N.J.: Princeton University Press, 1996). See also Burke O. Long, *Imagining the Holy Land: Maps, Models, and Fantasy Travels* (Bloomington: Indiana University Press, 2003).
5. Very Rev. Daniel. I. McDermott, *The Use of Holy Pictures and Images* (Philadelphia: Catholic Truth Society, n.d.), 2, 11–12. Schwain, *Signs of Grace*, ch. 1.
6. Gladys-Marie Fry, "'A Sermon in Patchwork': New Light on Harriet Powers," in *Singular Women: Writing the Art*, ed. Kristen Frederickson and Sarah E. Webb (Berkeley: University of California Press, 2003), 81–94. See also Marie Jeanne Adams, "The Harriet Powers Pictorial Quilts," in *This Far by Faith: Readings in African-American Women's Religious Biography*, ed. Judith Weisenfeld and Richard Newman (New York: Routledge, 1996), 21–31.

7. Lucine Finch, "A Sermon in Patchwork," *The Outlook*, October 19, 1914, 493–95.

8. Religious Studies scholar Albert J. Raboteau describes the general structure of the sermon in "The Chanted Sermon," *A Fire in the Bones: Reflections on African-American Religious History* (Boston, Mass.: Beacon Press, 1996), 141–51.

9. Qtd. in Richard McBee, "Archie Rand: Three Major Works," TheJewishPress.com, November 24, 2011, http://www.jewishpress.com/sections/arts/archie-rand-three-major-works/2011/11/24/.

10. Samantha Baskind, *Jewish Artists and the Bible in Twentieth-Century America* (University Park, Pa.: Pennsylvania State University Press, 2014), 4–5.

11. My understanding of Allston's work is heavily influenced by David Bjelajac, who has written two books on the artist: *Millennial Desire and the Apocalyptic Vision of Washington Allston* (Washington, D.C.: Smithsonian, 1993); and *Washington Allston, Secret Societies, and the Alchemy of Anglo-American Painting* (New York: Cambridge University Press, 1996).

12. Kristin Schwain, "Consuming Christ: Henry Ossawa Tanner's Biblical Paintings and Nineteenth-Century American Commerce," in *ReVisioning: Critical Methods of Seeing Christianity in the History of Art*, ed. James Romaine and Linda Stratford (Eugene, Ore.: Wipf and Stock, 2013), 277–93. See also Dewey F. Mosby, Darrel Sewell, and Rae Alexander-Minter, *Henry Ossawa Tanner* (Philadelphia: Philadelphia Museum of Art, 1991); and *Henry Ossawa Tanner: Modern Spirit*, ed. Anna O. Marley (Berkeley: University of California Press, 2012).

13. Robert McCoy to George Segal, August 23 and 28, 1978, George Segal Papers, Box 38 and Folder 6, Department of Rare Books and Special Collections, Princeton University Library. Qtd. in John Nelson, "Abraham and Isaac," *Nassau Weekly*, May 26, 2010, http://www.nassauweekly.com/abraham-isaac/.

14. George Segal, *Abraham and Isaac: In Memory of May 4, 1970, Kent State University*, 1978–79, The John B. Putnam Jr. Memorial Collection, Princeton University, http://artmuseum.princeton.edu/campus-art/objects/31772. See also John Fitzgerald O'Hara, "Kent State/May 4 and Postwar Memory," *American Quarterly* 58, no. 2 (June 2006): 301–28; and Eve Streicker, "Rejected Remembrance: Commemorating the Contentious Memory of the Kent State Shootings" (Senior thesis, Department of Art History and Studio Art, Williams College, 2009), http://library.williams.edu/theses/pdf.php?id=364.

15. On Edward Hicks and his Peaceable Kingdom paintings, see (among others) David Tatham, "Edward Hicks, Elias Hicks and John Comly: Perspectives on the Peaceable Kingdom Theme," *American Art Journal* 13, no. 2 (Spring 1981): 36–50; and Eleanore Price Mather, *Edward Hicks, His Peaceable Kingdoms and Other Paintings* (Newark: University of Delaware Press, 1983).

16. For an overview of the theological history of the separation, see Thomas D. Hamm, "Hicksite, Orthodox, and Evangelical Quakerism, 1805-1887" and Carole Dale Spencer, "Quakers in Theological Context," in *The Oxford Handbook of Quaker Studies*, ed. Stephen W. Angell and Pink Dandelion (Oxford: Oxford University Press, 2013), 63–77 and 141–57.

17. Jenny Franchot, *Roads to Rome: The Antebellum Protestant Encounter with Catholicism* (Berkeley: University of California Press, 1994); and John Davis, "Catholic Envy: The Visual Culture of Protestant Desire," in *The Visual Culture of American Religions*, ed. David Morgan and Sally Promey (Berkeley: University of California, 2001), 105–28. Anna Jameson, *Legends of the Madonna, as Represented in the Fine Arts* (London: Longman, Brown, Green, and Longmans, 1852).

18. Barbara L. Michaels, *Gertrude Kasebier: The Photographer and her Photographs* (New York: H. N. Abrams, 1992), 82.

19. On American cultural nationalism, see (among others), Wanda Corn, *The Great American Thing: Modern Art and National Identity, 1915–1935* (Berkeley: University of California Press, 1999). On the ways in which African American leaders participated in this discourse, see Mary Ann Calo, *Distinction and Denial: Race, Nation, and the Critical Construction of the African American Artist, 1920–40* (Ann Arbor: University of Michigan Press, 2007).

20. James Weldon Johnson, *God's Trombones: Seven Negro Sermons in Verse* (New York: Viking Press, 1927), 11. On Douglas, see *Aaron Douglas: African American Modernist*, ed. Susan Earle (New Haven, Conn.: Yale University Press, 2007); and Caroline Goeser, *Picturing the New Negro: Harlem Renaissance Print Culture and Modern Black Identity* (Lawrence: University Press of Kansas, 2007).

21. Caroline Goeser, "'On the Cross of the South': The Scottsboro Boys as Vernacular Christs in Harlem Renaissance Illustration," *International Review of African American Art* 19, no. 1 (2003): 19–27.

22. Richard Powell, "'In My Family of Primitiveness and Tradition': William H. Johnson's *Jesus and the Three Marys*," *American Art* 5, no. 4 (Autumn 1991): 32. For a more extended study of the artist by the same author, see *Homecoming: The Art and Life of William H. Johnson* (New York City: W. W. Norton, 1993).

23. The primary work on Morgan is William Fagaly, *Tools of Her Ministry: The Art of Sister Gertrude Morgan* (New York: Rizzoli, 2004). For an in-depth analysis of the artist and her relationship to New Orleans, see Emily Suzanne Clark, "New World, New Jerusalem, New Orleans: The Apocalyptic Art of Sister Gertrude Morgan," *Louisiana History* 55, no. 4 (Fall 2014): 432–59.

24. Eric Newhouse, "Prayers Painted by Sister Gertrude Morgan," *Daily Advertiser*, November 5, 1972. Qtd. in Clark, "New World, New Jerusalem, New Orleans," 433.

25. For an in-depth discussion of Millerite and Adventist charts in mid-nineteenth-century America, see David Morgan, *Protestants and Pictures: Religion, Visual Culture, and the Age of American Mass Production* (Oxford: Oxford University Press, 1999), 123–98.

26. For a discussion of how and why Jewish artists in Europe and the United States turned to Christian iconography to visualize Jewish suffering in the 1930s and 1940s, see Matthew B. Hoffman, "The Artist Crucified," in *From Rebel to Rabbi: Reclaiming Jesus and the Making of Modern Jewish Culture* (Palo Alto, Calif.: Stanford University Press, 2007), 206–51.

27. Allen Leepa, *Abraham Rattner* (New York: Harry Abrams, 1979), 42; and Allen Leepa, ed., *Abraham Rattner, February 14–March 8, 1970* (New York: Kennedy Galleries, 1970). Qtd. in Matthew Baigell, "Jewish Artists in New York during the Holocaust Years," Monna and Otto Weinmann Annual Lecture, May 16, 2001 (Washington, D.C.: United States Holocaust Memorial Museum, 2001), 8, https://www.ushmm.org/m/pdfs/20040908-baigell.pdf.

28. One of the first studies of Warhol's religious imagery was Jane Dillenberger, *The Religious Art of Andy Warhol* (New York: Continuum, 1998). See also Peter Kattenberg, *Andy Warhol, Priest: "The Last Supper Comes in Small, Medium, and Large"* (Boston, Mass.: Brill, 2001).

29. On the series, see Amy Mooney, "Illustrating the Word: Paintings by Aaron Douglas and Jacob Lawrence," in *The Walter O. Evans Collection of African American Art*, ed. Andrea Barnwell Brownlee and Tritobia H. Benjamin (Seattle: University of Washington Press,

1999), 43–54. For a more general discussion of the artist, see Patricia Hills, *Painting Harlem Modern: The Art of Jacob Lawrence* (Berkeley: University of California Press, 2009).

30. While the literature on the Bible's influence on black life is extensive, attention to the versions used by abolitionists, ministers, scholars, and writers is far less studied. For a broad introduction, see *African Americans and the Bible: Sacred Texts and Social Structures*, ed. Vincent Wimbush (New York: Continuum, 2001). See also Cheryl J. Sanders, "The KJV's Influence on African Americans and Their Churches," in *Translation that Openeth the Window: Reflections on the History and Legacy of the King James Bible*, ed. David G. Burke (Atlanta, Ga.: American Bible Society, 2009), 139–54.

BIBLIOGRAPHY

Apostolos-Cappadona, Diane. *The Spirit and the Vision: The Influence of Christian Romanticism on the Development of 19th Century American Art.* Atlanta, Ga.: Scholars Press, 1995.

Baigell, Matthew. *Jewish-American Artists and the Holocaust.* New Brunswick, N.J.: Rutgers University Press, 2001.

Baigell, Matthew, and Milly Heyd, eds. *Complex Identities: Jewish Consciousness and Modern Art.* New Brunswick, N.J.: Rutgers University Press, 2001.

Baskind, Samantha. *Jewish Artists and the Bible in Twentieth-Century America.* University Park: Pennsylvania State University Press, 2014.

Bjelajac, David. *Millennial Desire and the Apocalyptic Vision of Washington Allston.* Washington, D.C.: Smithsonian Institution Press, 1993.

———. *Washington Allston, Secret Societies, and the Alchemy of Anglo-American Painting.* New York: Cambridge University Press, 1996.

Corn, Wanda. *The Great American Thing: Modern Art and National Identity, 1915–1935.* Berkeley: University of California Press, 1999.

Crown, Carol, ed. *Coming Home! Self-Taught Artists, the Bible, and the American South.* Memphis, Tenn.: Art Museum of the University of Memphis and Jackson: University Press of Mississippi, 2004.

Davis, John. *The Landscape of Belief: Encountering the Holy Land in Nineteenth-Century American Art and Culture.* Princeton, N.J.: Princeton University Press, 1996.

Doss, Erika. "Robert Gober's *Virgin* Installation: Issues of Spirituality in Contemporary American Art." In *Visual Culture of American Religions*, edited by David Morgan and Sally Promey, 129–45. Berkeley: University of California Press, 2001.

Elkins, James, and David Morgan, eds. *Re-Enchantment (The Art Seminar).* New York: Routledge, 2008.

Fagaly, William. *Sister Gertrude Morgan: The Tools of Her Ministry.* New York: Rizzoli, 2004.

Frederickson, Kristen, and Sarah E. Webb, eds. *Singular Women: Writing the Art.* Berkeley: University of California Press, 2003.

Greenhouse, Wendy. "Daniel Huntington and the Ideal of Christian Art." *Winterthur Portfolio* 31 (1996): 104–40.

Gutjahr, Paul. *An American Bible: A History of the Good Book in the United States, 1770–1880.* Stanford, Calif.: Stanford University Press, 1999.

Heartney, Eleanor. *Postmodern Heretics: The Catholic Imagination in Contemporary Art.* New York: Midmarch Arts Press, 2004.

Heller, Ena Giurescu, ed. *Reluctant Partners: Art and Religion in Dialogue*. New York: American Bible Society, 2004.

Husch, Gail E. *Something Coming: Apocalyptic Expectation and Mid-Nineteenth Century American Painting*. Hanover, N.H.: University Press of New England, 2000.

Jameson, Anna. *Legends of the Madonna, as Represented in the Fine Arts*. London: Longman, Brown, Green, and Longmans, 1852.

Morgan, David. *Protestants and Pictures: Religion, Visual Culture, and the Age of American Mass Production*. New York: Oxford University Press, 1999.

Morgan, David, and Sally Promey, eds. *The Visual Culture of American Religions*. Berkeley: University of California Press, 2001.

Plate, S. Brent, ed. *Art, Religion, and Visual Culture: A Cross-Cultural Reader*. New York: Palgrave, 2002.

Promey, Sally. *Painting Religion in Public: John Singer Sargent's* Triumph of Religion *at the Boston Public Library*. Princeton, N.J.: Princeton University Press, 1999.

Pyne, Kathleen. *Art and the Higher Life: Painting and Evolutionary Thought in Late Nineteenth Century America*. Austin: University of Texas Press, 1996.

Romaine, James, and Linda Stratford, eds. *ReVisioning: Critical Methods of Seeing Christianity in the History of Art*. Eugene, Ore.: Wipf and Stock, 2013.

Schwain, Kristin. *Signs of Grace: Religion and American Art in the Gilded Age*. Ithaca, N.Y.: Cornell University Press, 2008.

CHAPTER 27

....

ENGLISH CINEMA AND
THE BIBLE

....

WILLIAM D. ROMANOWSKI

FROM the start, the Bible and cinema have made strange bedfellows. While clergy attacked movies for "offering trips to hell," nickelodeon theaters regularly screened Bible stories; *David and Goliath* (1908), *From the Manger to the Cross* (1912), and *Joseph in the Land of Egypt* (1914) are among a spate of Bible-related movies released prior to World War I.[1] These short silent films and others produced during these years made for lively entertainment— *The Life of Moses* (1910) showed the ten plagues and parting of the Red Sea. Producers also hoped that biblical topics would appease religious reformers and boost the coveted patronage of the middle class.

The fate of *The Life of Our Saviour* (1914) is illustrative. Expecting a box-office windfall from respectable churchgoers, the producers spared no expense. Shooting took place on locations in Bethlehem, Nazareth, Gethsemane, Jerusalem, and Galilee. Audiences however, had a decidedly mixed response to the crucifixion being depicted so graphically that "cold chills go coursing up and down one's spine," according to one reviewer. Some thought the film was "sacrilegious" and "ghastly," while others found it "daring" and "wonderful." An exhaustive marketing campaign initially enticed clergy and church groups. But after the first week of release, viewer turnout (and thus the film's commercial prospects) "fell down with a thud," leading a *Variety* critic to conclude that "the people do not care for the big Biblical pictures."[2]

The trade magazine's judgment, however, proved too hasty. With some ebb and flow, expensive Bible-themed films have been a staple of the American cinema. From *Intolerance* (1916), D. W. Griffith's masterful diatribe against censorship, to Paramount's action-packed blockbuster *Noah* (2014), film producers have mined the Bible's stories to explore the human condition, address contemporary preoccupations, or score a box-office hit. In other words, the production and reception of Bible-related movies have been variously motivated, often resulting in clashes between art, moneymaking, and ministry aspirations that get sensationalized by the media and religious groups alike.

The story of the Bible and American cinema has as much to do with the movies themselves as it does with an ongoing struggle between two dynamic institutions—religion and film—over cultural power and the function of entertainment. Aware that the cinema is a vital source of creativity and cultural vitality, religious leaders have kept vigilant regarding depictions of their traditions and beliefs. They have also paid close attention to Hollywood's effect on the moral and religious character of the nation.

Scholars have written extensively about the Bible and cinema utilizing various disciplinary approaches. Movies are probed for insight into contemporary culture and religion, treated as a source of theological reflection or instrument of biblical interpretation, and to foster a dialogue between the fields of religion and culture. An often overlooked, but crucial, aspect is the dynamic between industry and culture, or more specifically the tension between commercial and religious values. For better or worse, anticipated audience and box-office returns frequently outweigh religious concerns about morality or religious orthodoxy.

As prop, subject, quotation, or theme, the Bible appears both explicitly and implicitly in countless movies. Hollywood's large-scale biblical epics are perhaps the best known, but there are also many worthwhile films that are independently produced, and even some financed by churches, denominations, or faith-based organizations. This chapter is so arranged as to provide some historical context, while considering important themes, trends, and events when it comes to the Bible and American cinema. There is an affinity between film and religion; both propagate values and offer visions of life that can—and often do—rival one another. That central dynamic finds a measure of resolution in movies that fuse biblical motifs with American ideals and assumptions. These films, more than explicitly Bible-related fare, demonstrate the significance of Bible and cinema as an expression of American culture.

SCREENING THE BIBLE: PRODUCTION AND RECEPTION

In market terms, Bible-related movies have a "presold" quality; their familiar source material and presumed built-in audience heightens their commercial prospects—at least in theory. The market for Bible-related movies is quite unpredictable. A *New York Times* critic remarked in 1961 that "spiritual hunger is not what draws people to see 'Ben Hur.' The most exciting thing in the picture is that murderous chariot race!"[3] As it is, most moviegoers, whether avowedly religious or not, go to the movies expecting to be entertained and in some sense affirmed (or at least not offended) in their basic beliefs.

Bible-based movies, like *The Ten Commandments* (1956), *Ben-Hur* (1959), and more recently, *The Passion of the Christ* (2004) have been huge box-office hits. Overall, however, films in the genre have a spotty track record, including a number of dismal failures. Based on a bestselling novel by Lloyd C. Douglas, *The Robe* was the top-grossing movie in 1953, while *Salome* released in the same year, an equally lavish production in Technicolor about Herod and John the Baptist, flopped. *The Big Fisherman* (1959), a screen adaptation of Douglas's follow-up novel on the Apostle Peter, was outpaced that year at the box office by *Solomon and Sheba*, an erotic epic starring Yul Brynner and Gina Lollobrigida. Despite high expectations, *The Prince of Egypt* (1998) and *The Nativity Story* (2006) were commercial disappointments. In between, *The Chronicles of Narnia: The Lion, the Witch and the*

Wardrobe (2005), based on C. S. Lewis's allegorical children's stories, struck box-office gold; the next two installments however—*Prince Caspian* (2008) and *Voyage of the Dawn Treader* (2010)—earned only about half of the original and ended the franchise.

While film producers watch over the bottom line, defenders of the faith have different priorities. In their view, box-office success is more a by-product; the cinema's deeper purpose is to instill right values, piety, and reverence in viewers, and perhaps even move them toward deeper religious commitment. Equally important is safeguarding the integrity of scripture and religious traditions.

The specific moral or theological matters that might preoccupy religious leaders are of little interest to most Hollywood producers—other than to alleviate any objections that might impinge on box-office performance. And for that, they often take precautions by enlisting religious authorities to serve as film consultants. The advice of high-profile Protestant, Catholic, and Jewish advisers during production of *The King of Kings* (1927) was to avoid offending any religious group with the expectation that their imprimatur would also boost the film's commercial fortunes.[4] Likewise, to placate criticism and secure pre-release promotion, the producers of the animated *Prince of Egypt* (1998) arranged screenings, seeking feedback—and endorsements—from around six hundred religious experts.[5]

The difficulty for filmmakers is to appease the religiously devout without losing the patronage of moviegoers more interested in love, thrills, and suspense than theological speculation. On the one hand, producers might try to homogenize or tone down particular expressions of religion. Studio executives had the words "Holy Bible" digitally removed from the book cover in a scene in *Soul Surfer* (2011); though restored, the intent of the deletion was to broaden the inspirational film's appeal among non-Christians.[6] On the other hand, finding movies directly targeting the "Christian" audience tricky to market, producers prefer to make a general release more acceptable, for example, by "sanding the edges off dialogue that might offend churchgoers," according to a *New York Times* report.[7] These are rather minor tactics revealing nonetheless the imperative of box-office performance and potential market for any release.

The essentials of Hollywood filmmaking—mystery, adventure, and romance—of necessity weigh heavily in Bible-related productions. The Bible provides basic story inspiration; scriptwriters fill narrative gaps with implied drama. As Cecil B. DeMille, whose name is synonymous with Bible epics, put it, "It is not possible to produce a great and successful film dealing with historic characters and not have a love-interest."[8] *The Ten Commandments* intertwines the Israelite Exodus from Egypt with a love triangle involving Moses, Pharaoh Ramses II, and his wife, Nefertiti. *King of Kings* (1961) gives a fictitious Roman centurion named Lucius a key role in the narrative; the screenplay draws extensively on the work of first-century historian, Flavius Josephus. *Noah* (2014) features earth encrusted, fallen angels called the Watchers, found in a non-biblical source, the Book of Enoch. The creative inclusion of extra-biblical material may boost entertainment value, but this practice also raises questions—and religious concerns—about how much viewers perceive a Bible-related film as being fiction or nonfiction.

Controversies erupt periodically with filmmakers and critics sparring over aesthetic merits. Religious leaders have also weighed in on such matters as depictions of specific religious groups or a film's fidelity to the Bible. Although *Variety* declared *The King of Kings* "the greatest picture ever produced," Jewish authorities insisted on changes to prevent fostering anti-Semitism.[9] With his auburn hair and blue eyes, actor Jeffrey Hunter looked more like a

1950s teen idol than a first-century Galilean Jew in the role of Jesus in *King of Kings*. A *Time* critic derisively dubbed the film, "I Was a Teenage Jesus."[10] Over four years of research to make *The Greatest Story Ever Told* (1965), the most authentic Jesus film to date, went for naught; critics almost universally panned the effort as boring and theologically vacuous. *The Last Temptation of Christ* (1988) and *The Passion of the Christ* (2004), both films the product of director indulgence, were in their own way enormously controversial, irking different constituencies. As these illustrations suggest, artistic, cultural, religious, and industrial concerns factor in curious combination in the discourse of Bible and cinema.

FILMS FEATURING THE BIBLE

The appearance of the Bible in movies, whether quoted by characters or used as a prop, might simply be a matter of verisimilitude. We expect the Pentecostal preacher in *The Apostle* (1997) to be carrying the Good Book. In *Amazing Grace* (2007), the Bible is a key inspiration for William Wilberforce in his political campaign to abolish the slave trade in Britain. A sincere evangelical college freshman takes on—and bests—a seasoned atheistic professor using the Bible to mount an argument for God's existence in *God's Not Dead* (2014).

Inclusion of the Bible is the essential feature of evangelical productions. World Wide Pictures, a subsidiary of the Billy Graham Evangelistic Association formed in 1951, earned acclaim for *The Hiding Place* (1975), based on the true story of Corrie ten Boom, a Christian who hid Jews in Amsterdam and then survived a Nazi concentration camp. But its routine conversion films, like *The Restless Ones* (1965), effectively established the formula for evangelical movies: a clear presentation of the Christian Gospel in a dramatic context with hardly any artistic pretensions. Despite their evangelistic ambitions, these have been faulted for being contrived; characters exhibit little depth and the sanitized stories lack credibility. *Left Behind* (2000), the first film in a series based on the bestselling novels by Tim LaHaye and Jerry B. Jenkins, uses a contemporary setting to dramatize a premillennial dispensationalist reading of the Book of Revelation. One reviewer began with a caveat. "Immediate disclaimer: This is not to denigrate the religious beliefs that inform *Left Behind* . . . This is simply to address the hilariously bad manner in which those beliefs are expressed."[11] Similarly, the aim of *Son of God* (2014) was to provide a clear and unambiguous cinematic statement so that moviegoers "may believe that Jesus is the Messiah, the Son of God, and that by believing you may have life in his name" (John 20:31).

Despite poor production values and lackluster reviews, many evangelical movies were successfully niche marketed to churchgoers. *Facing the Giants* (2006) was made for a mere $100,000. Funded by the Sherwood Baptist Church in Albany, Georgia, this film about a football coach whose spiritual renewal turns his life around earned $10 million. *Fireproof* (2008) cost just $500,000 to produce and earned $33 million in a theatrical run. In this Christian drama, a fireman commits to "The Love Dare," a forty-day Bible-based program to rescue his marriage. *Jesus* (1979), an independent production financed by Campus Crusade for Christ supporters, deserves mention. Shot on locations in the Middle East, this docudrama adheres closely to the Gospel of Luke. Although panned by critics when it was released by Warner Bros. in the United States, the film has reportedly had several billion viewings worldwide since its initial release resulting in over 200 million conversions.[12]

The Bible is also employed as a visual metaphor in myriad films to enrich character or story with artistic flair. Scripture inspires the gifted runner in *Chariots of Fire* (1984), a story of faith and the human spirit that climaxes at the 1924 Olympics. That prison inmate Andy Dufresne conceals his digging tools in a Bible highlights the disparity between the brutal warden's false piety and hypocrisy and the freedom of salvation alluded to in Andy's escape in *The Shawshank Redemption* (1994). Conversely, Max Cady's perverted use of the Bible in *Cape Fear* (1991) and John Doe's calculated murders linked to the seven deadly sins in *Se7en* (1995), convey a twisted religious fanaticism that makes these psychotic killers appear all the more deranged.

Tender Mercies (1983) is a poignant story about a former country singer whose life is in ruins, but who experiences redemption through a renewed faith and devoted wife. Exploring racism in a small town during the 1930s Depression, *Places in the Heart* (1984) closes with a church service as a metaphor for the Kingdom of Heaven: the pastor reads scripture about the primacy of love, a choir hymn is sung as protagonists and antagonists— living and departed—together receive communion. In *American Sniper* (2014), the Bible metaphorically connects the sharpshooter's identity, values, and sense of purpose with American civil religion and the Iraq War. Drawing on the Book of Job, *The Tree of Life* (2011) situates an intimate story of human desire for meaning amidst suffering. The cosmic scope and experimental large-scale shifts in time that span the universe, if only stylistically, recall somewhat the cinematic effort of early Bible epics to deliver spiritual context for human events.

THE HOLLYWOOD BIBLICAL EPIC

To signify the divine presence in history, the Hollywood biblical epics combine cinematic spectacle and melodrama with the aim of eliciting deep emotions and instilling reverence in viewers. These sweeping, big-budget extravaganzas typically feature a star-studded cast, the latest special effects, and a lush orchestral score. Cecil B. DeMille fashioned the basic cinematic conventions for such epics with his pioneering silent trilogy: the key ingredients being religion, sex, and violence (though not necessarily in that order of priority). In his *The Ten Commandments* (1923), which cautioned against breaking God's law, DeMille has Moses receive the commandments on Mt. Sinai while the Israelites go off in a drunken orgiastic feast around the Golden Calf. DeMille's *The King of Kings* (1927) interlaces the life of Christ with a steamy love affair between Judas and Mary Magdalene. *Variety* warned that scenes of violence and a wild Roman orgy in DeMille's *The Sign of the Cross* (1932) would "make the church element dizzy trying to figure which way to turn."[13]

Biblical epics became a staple of Hollywood production—and some of the top-grossing films—in the period after World War II. The trend coincided with an upsurge in church attendance in the United States that peaked during the 1950s and has been identified with a deepening commitment to an American civil religion. As scholars have shown, the belief that the United States has a special character and purpose links the nation's history and destiny to the biblical narrative. The Puritans saw themselves as

God's elect and took their flight from religious persecution in England to the New World as a reiteration of the Israelites leaving Egypt for the Promised Land. Their mission of demonstrating to the world the blessings of a social order based on biblical precepts morphed into a vision of America as a global beacon of freedom, equality, and opportunity. American exceptionalism assumes that God is "actively interested and involved in history, with a special concern for America," and that the archetypal American is a kind of Adamic figure, innocent now by virtue of having shed the baggage of history and ancestry and "poised at the start of a new history."[14] This vision of human innocence and national virtue harbors a future orientation with the country shedding the ignorance and limitations of its past and advancing toward perfectibility. American exceptionalism tends to project to the world a kind of Manichean divide between good (America) and evil (Others).

This vision is most fully realized in DeMille's 1956 remake of *The Ten Commandments*, a quintessential postwar American film. The United States emerged from World War II as the most powerful nation in the world; the Cold War came into being in the 1950s as a new kind of international tension. DeMille envisioned this remake as a cinematic metaphor with the power to unite Protestants, Catholics, and Jews in the common cause of faith and freedom against tyranny—now in the form of atheistic communism. In an unusual onscreen introduction, the director steps from behind a curtain onto an empty stage to address the audience: "The theme of this picture is whether men ought to be ruled by God's law or whether they are to be ruled by the whims of a dictator like Rameses. Are men the property of the state or are they free souls under God? This same battle continues throughout the world today." With this, DeMille joins the biblical Exodus with Cold War geopolitics.

In delivering the Israelites from bondage in Egypt, DeMille's 1956 Moses prefigures, or serves as a type of the Christ who frees believers from slavery to sin and death. Moses's final line of dialogue is "Go, proclaim liberty throughout all the lands, unto all the inhabitants thereof." It is hard to find even a trace of this implied optimism in Moses's diatribe recorded in Deuteronomy, filled as it is with dire warnings and repeated pleas that the Israelites quit their disobedience and submit to God (e.g., Deut. 28). Nevertheless, DeMille's film takes its cue from Leviticus 25:10, a reference to the Year of Jubilee, the ultimate Sabbath year when all debts are to be forgiven, slaves freed, and property restored. DeMille also uses similar imagery of promise used by Isaiah to describe the coming Messiah (Isa. 61:1-2). As such, DeMille's second *The Ten Commandments* and other Old Testament inspired films of the period employ a subtle Christological framework that points to the coming of Jesus, the start of the Christian religion, and beyond that to America as the contemporary fulfillment of the Great Commission: Jesus's post-resurrection charge to His followers to "make disciple of all nations" (Matt. 28:19).

The Roman conversion films, like *Quo Vadis?* (1951), *The Robe* (1953), and *Ben-Hur* (1959), are set during the time of Christ or thereafter as a newly born Christian community struggles to establish itself amidst Roman persecution. Like the Old Testament dramas, the theme of slavery versus freedom is also at the heart of these films. *Quo Vadis?* (Latin meaning, "where are you going?") starts with a voiceover describing the horror and magnitude of Roman brutality and bondage. The introduction also anticipates the overwhelming power of Christianity to affect change: "That any force on earth can shake this pyramid of power and corruption, of human misery and slavery seems inconceivable." *The Robe* begins the same way; in Rome "we traffic in human souls," the voiceover narration informs viewers. The dramatic conversion of the Roman protagonist, typically a virile warrior, signifies the triumph of the Christian ethic of faith, hope, and love over Roman corruption, militarism, and paganism. It also prefigures the transformation of Christianity from a beleaguered sect into an established religion under the Roman Emperor Constantine. By way of analogy, this "redefinition of empire" represents the power of Christian America to transform the world.[15]

The freedom of an oppressed people—Jews in Judea and Galilee—also figures in the postwar Jesus films, not in the overthrow of Roman rule, but in a spiritual sense represented by Christ's resurrection. As religious scholar Adele Reinhartz, who has written extensively on the Bible and cinema, observes, movies like *King of Kings* and *The Greatest Story Ever Told* mark "the beginning of Christianity, a major new player that, from Hollywood's perspective, led in a straight line to America itself."[16]

The postwar Bible dramas met with a decidedly mixed response. While some religious reviewers swooned over *The Ten Commandments* and *Ben-Hur*, many others faulted these films for caricaturing and distorting the Bible, substituting sex and violence for theological grit or cultural relevance, and even undermining the Christian religion. *The Christian Century* went so far as to urge readers to stop patronizing Hollywood's "vulgar efforts to use the Bible against itself."[17] Reflecting on the genre, a *New York Times* film critic concluded, "Not one of them could be considered a penetrating exploration of the mystery and majesty of life."[18]

Generic Transformation

The postwar Bible epics are best understood as reflections of the era's *zeitgeist*. Epic films tend to prosper during times "when a country's national myths are still believed—or, at best, at a time when a nation feels itself slipping into decline, which produces a spate of nostalgic evocations of those myths," a British film critic explains. "Afterward, a period of cynicism sets in, in which the myths are presented in a revisionist manner."[19] To wit, *The Greatest Story Ever Told* (1965) was supposed to set a new course for the Jesus biopic by focusing on the simple, basic story of the life of Christ without the pagan revelry that was typical of the genre. Instead, it marks the end of the era of biblical epics.

The Vietnam War, the civil rights movement, and a powerful, youthful counterculture unraveled the postwar consensus; American society became fragmented over questions about policies at home and abroad. One effect was to question the alignment of national ideology with God and righteousness. Production of Bible-based films waned, then reemerged in the 1970s exhibiting new stylistic and thematic approaches that were far removed from the splendor and reverence of the postwar epics. In other words, the "genre" was being transformed: conventions were parodied, the narrative reappropriated in new contexts, and the traditional story demythologized. A segment in Mel Brook's *History of the World Part I* (1981) pokes fun at Old Testament films; *Life of Brian* (1979), a British comedy about a young Jewish man who is mistakenly identified as the Messiah, includes a scene spoofing Jewish resistance to Roman occupation.

Depictions of direct divine intervention that typified postwar fare were displaced by que-ries about God's relationship to humanity and role in history. This trend is nowhere more evident than in films focused on the life and mission of Jesus; wrestling with the messianic character—the paradox of Christ being fully human and fully divine—became more central and more contentious.

The ascetic depiction in *The Greatest Story Ever Told* was meant to emphasize Christ's divinity, but ultimately suffered artistically and theologically for lacking a point of view and being "completely oblivious of the problem of the historical Jesus."[20] The youth-oriented rock opera, *Jesus Christ Superstar* (1973), represents a shift in perspective. Making Jesus into a pop idol entwines the Gospel story with the trials and temptations of modern celebrity culture. The depiction of the Messiah as bewildered and preoccupied with his superstar status is offset by the ambiguity and intrigue of other characters. A perplexed and vulner-able Mary Magdalene wants to understand her love for Jesus; the struggle of a confused and skeptical Judas to understand the Messiah's mission becomes the story's center with Judas upstaging Jesus in a post-crucifixion epilogue. Along with charges of anti-Semitism, the casting and costuming of a Caucasian Jesus dressed in white, and an African American Judas in red (a color connected to Satan), elicited allegations of racism.[21]

The Last Temptation of Christ (1988) stresses Jesus's humanity even more as an internal battle between flesh and spirit. Jesus seems ill at ease in human form, grappling fiercely with his own nature and messianic mission. He is tormented by fear and doubt; tempted by Satan, he fantasizes about living as a married man with children. Evangelicals blasted the portrayal as sacrilegious and an assault on Christianity and pressured theater owners not to exhibit it—actions that turned dissent and theological debate into a First Amendment issue.[22]

The evangelical and Catholic groups that protested *The Last Temptation of Christ* became a potent consumer force behind *The Passion of the Christ* (2004)—a film that fittingly serves to illustrate key themes highlighted so far. An ultraviolent movie presented in Aramaic with English subtitles, *The Passion of the Christ* defied industry wisdom and became a stun-ning worldwide hit. From the start, however, this independent production was embroiled in sharp controversy that actually resulted in huge publicity for the film.

Its notable aesthetic merits aside, detractors blasted *The Passion*'s excessive depiction of the torture and crucifixion of Jesus as violent pornography. Reading the film as making the Jews responsible for Christ's death, they accused it of anti-Semitism. In contrast, propo-nents defended the film as historically accurate, with one branding faultfinders as "almost all, on the other side" in the religious and culture war "for the soul of America."[23] Evangelical Christians even launched a nationwide grass-roots campaign hoping to capitalize on the film's release as an extraordinary evangelistic opportunity.

If *The Passion*'s brief flashbacks serve to humanize Jesus, they do little to help viewers lacking a theological framework to contextualize and understand the horrific events that unfold. Bible aficionados might take their cue from an opening graphic of Isaiah 53:5 ("He was wounded for our transgressions, crushed for our iniquities; by His wounds we are healed."). But the film itself communicates little more than that Jesus suffered unbearably. In a postmodern twist, viewers are left to impose their own meaning on the film. As one film critic observes, the film "never gets beyond its raw and prolonged depiction of human and demonic cruelty."[24]

Director Mel Gibson claimed, "We've done the research. I'm telling the story as the Bible tells it." Regardless, *The Passion* relies heavily on implied drama; one line from the Gospels—that Pilate "had Jesus flogged" (Matt. 27:26; Mark 15:15; John 19:1)—is the story's dramatic cornerstone. The screenplay utilizes extraneous material, especially the visions of a nineteenth-century Augustinian nun, Anne Catherine Emmerich. Moreover, in crucial ways the depiction of Christ reflects not just Gibson's traditionalist Catholicism but also his penchant for tortured and anguished characters and violence. As a marketing director made clear, "Our job was to make it more *Braveheart*."[25] After beating Jesus almost to the point of losing consciousness, the sadistic Roman soldiers seem satisfied and finished. But then to the astonishment of all, Jesus gets up and stands tall. This "bring it on" display of toughness would seem contrary to the "sheep to the slaughter" attitude in scripture (Acts 8:32), but nevertheless one displayed by the typical Hollywood action hero played by Gibson in movies like the *Lethal Weapon* (1987–1998) franchise and *The Patriot* (2000).

THE BIBLE AND AMERICAN CULTURE

As the attending media hype often enough demonstrates, the occasional Bible-explicit film is hardly in the mainstream of contemporary American cinema. Of greater importance is the extent to which biblical themes and imagery pervade the cultural landscape of conventional Hollywood movies. Scholars have uncovered themes like redemption and self-sacrifice or spotted Christ-figures in movies ranging from the traditional western *Shane* (1953) and the gangster epic *The Godfather* (1972), to science fiction tales, *Close Encounters of the Third Kind* (1977) and *E.T.: The Extraterrestrial* (1982), and dramas like *Cool Hand Luke* (1967) and *Gran Torino* (2008). No doubt, the blending of biblical and American motifs has animated popular genres and had a lasting impact on the American cinema.

The classical Hollywood film foregrounds American cultural values associated with individualism: self-reliance and brave determination. Typically, these self-sufficient individuals have whatever it takes to accomplish their goal; they need only to believe in themselves. The hero's triumph over adversity is sometimes aided with "some magical outside assistance."[26] The sentiment is expressed plainly by Harry Stamper (Bruce Willis), the main character in *Armageddon* (1998): "Come on, God, just a little help. It's all I'm asking." Hints of otherworldly assistance can be found in typical Hollywood fare, like *Rocky* (1976) and *Forrest Gump* (1994), less subtly perhaps in *Groundhog Day* (1993), and more explicitly in *It's a Wonderful Life* (1946) and *The Legend of Baggar Vance* (2000). The main protagonists in these films are basically good, if temporarily wayward, and ultimately responsible for their own destiny. The human problem is that they "keep looking up," God tells Bruce in *Bruce Almighty* (2003). "People want me to do everything for them. What they don't realize is they have the power."

When this synthesis of the Bible and American individualism is applied to biblical figures, the covenantal relationship between God and his people is recast with "a much more intense focus on the individual, and, by implication, attribute primary and often more redemptive agency to them than do the biblical stories as such," as Reinhartz observes.[27] Although the lyrics of the *Prince of Egypt* (1998) theme song ("When You Believe") were apparently changed, the chorus still implies that believers, and not God, are the source of miracles: "Who knows what miracles you can achieve / When you believe." And in *Noah* (2014), at the decisive moment, the ark builder ultimately trusts not God, but the "love in his heart." There is never any doubt that this tribulation-ridden hero will finally do the right thing; reason and apparent goodness trump faith, that is, what Noah believes God expects of him.

BIBLE SUPERHEROES

Scholars have shown that Westerns, action-adventure, and superhero films all adhere to a distinctively American monomyth, which they describe as an American appropriation (and secularization) of Judeo-Christian redemption dramas: "A community in a harmonious paradise is threatened by evil; normal institutions fail to contend with this threat: a selfless superhero emerges to renounce temptations and carry out the redemptive task: aided by fate, his decisive victory restores the community to its paradisiacal condition: the superhero then recedes into obscurity."[28] This narrative pattern echoes the arc of Bible history: creation, fall, redemption, consummation. And if not exactly Christ types, these selfless and reluctant heroes perform a salvific role by "saving" a community of people from a destructive evil through an act of regenerative violence, which is a key metaphor in American mythology.[29]

Apocalyptic movies are a unique expression of this formula and conventions. Films in this genre envisage present-day anxieties as cataclysmic events threatening to end the world as we know it, whether an asteroid striking the earth (*Armageddon* and *Deep Impact*—1998), a pandemic (*Contagion*—2011), climate change (*The Day After Tomorrow*—2004), or alien invasion (*Independence Day*—1996). In Christian eschatology, which looks beyond time and history, a messianic figure triumphs over evil and suffering and ushers in "a new heaven and new earth" (Rev. 21:1). In apocalyptic movies, the eschaton turns on the hero's actions with the catastrophe averted by human ingenuity and determination. By overcoming the cataclysmic threat, the hero prevents the end of world (perhaps with some otherworldly assistance as noted earlier). The effect is to secularize Jewish and Christian apocalyptic literature by investing humans—not God—with ultimate control over time and history.[30] Instead of a new and perfected world to come, the periodic renewal of this world via human agency suggests an ongoing and optimistic movement toward final human control and perfectibility.

The comic-book superhero films provided a recipe for Bible-based dramas and action films in 2014, which was heralded Hollywood's "Year of the Bible."[31] A marketing executive explained, "If you're doing big, epic effects films, you're going to run out of flying superheroes. These are superheroes of the ancient time." Indeed, as one reviewer notes, Jesus causally performs miracles "in a manner befitting a superhero" in *Son of God* (2014). And only a superhero of sorts could possibly endure the incredible torture that Roman soldiers inflict on Jesus in *The Passion of the Christ*. The director of *Noah* even conceived the main character as an American "superhero, a guy who has this incredibly difficult challenge put in front of him and has to overcome it."[32] Noah is the stoic, determined action hero, adroit and capable of violence; faith serves as his superpower. Environmental destruction gives this big-budget, special-effects film an apocalyptic setting. In hopes of starting a trend, the Bible's action-packed stories were repackaged with Bible figures cast as the Hollywood superhero—a potent mythic representation that has become the dominant expression of American cinema worldwide.

Conclusion

Myths define a nation and invest ordinary life with meaning. Their function "is largely utopian," one scholar explains. "Ritual is generally enough to assure the fulfillment of the promise of the myth."[33] Movie going is one such ritual. Insofar as culture is a conversation, the dialogue between the Bible and American cinema has undoubtedly shaped the popular imagination by dramatizing the nation's core mythology, recasting its central themes, characterizations, and conflicts to address—and narratively resolve—new problems and dilemmas. That the Bible as subject, theme, or metaphor continues to inform the American cinema and surrounding discourse testifies to its enduring significance in the national culture.

Films Cited

American Sniper (2014), *Ben-Hur* (1959), *The Big Fisherman* (1959), *Chariots of Fire* (1984), *The Chronicles of Narnia: The Lion, the Witch and the Wardrobe* (2005), *The Greatest Story Ever Told* (1965), *Jesus Christ Superstar* (1973), *The King of Kings* (1927), *King of Kings* (1961), *The Last Temptation of Christ* (1988), *The Life of Our Saviour* (1914), *Noah* (2014), *The Passion of the Christ* (2004), *Places in the Heart* (1984), *The Prince of Egypt* (1998), *Quo Vadis?* (1951), *The Robe* (1953), *The Shawshank Redemption* (1994), *Solomon and Sheba* (1959), *Son of God* (2014), *The Ten Commandments* (1956), *Tender Mercies* (1983), *The Tree of Life* (2011).

Notes

1. Wilbur F. Crafts, *National Perils and Hopes: A Study Based on Current Statistics and the Observations of a Cheerful Reformer* (Cleveland, Ohio: F. M. Barton, 1910), 39.
2. "Life of Our Saviour," *Variety*, April 10, 1914, in *Variety Film Reviews 1907–1920*, vol. 1 (New York: Garland Publishing, 1983); "'Saviour' Film Falls Down," *Variety*, April 17, 1914, 19.
3. Bosley Crowther, "The Good Book Is a Great Script," *New York Times*, December 31, 1961, SM11.
4. William D. Romanowski, *Reforming Hollywood: How American Protestants Fought for Freedom at the Movies* (New York: Oxford University Press, 2012), 57-60.
5. Jeffrey A. Smith, "Hollywood Theology: The Commodification of Religion in Twentieth-Century Films," *Religion and American Culture* 11, no. 2 (Summer 2001): 221.

6. Paul Bond, "Producer Tried to Edit Bible Out of Sony's 'Soul Surfer,'" *Hollywood Reporter*, online edition, April 8, 2011, http://www.hollywoodreporter.com/news/producer-tried-edit-bible-sony-100356.

7. Sharon Waxman, "The Passion of the Marketers," *New York Times*, July 18, 2005, C3.

8. DeMille quoted in William E. Barton, "Chaplain-in-Ordinary to a Film," *Dearborn Independent*, April 9, 1927, 22.

9. "The King of Kings," *Variety*, April 20, 1927, 15.

10. "Cinema: $ign of the Cross," *Time*, October 27, 1961, 55.

11. Desson Howe, "'Left Behind': Heaven Help Us," *Washington Post*, online edition, February 2, 2001, http://www.washingtonpost.com/wp-srv/entertainment/movies/reviews/leftbehindhowe.htm.

12. The Jesus Film Project, http://www.jesusfilm.org/.

13. Quoted in Gregory D. Black, *Hollywood Censored: Morality Codes, Catholics, and the Movies* (Cambridge: Cambridge University Press, 1994), 68.

14. Robert N. Bellah, "Civil Religion in America," *Daedalus* 134, no. 5 (2005): 45; R. W. B. Lewis, *The American Adam: Innocence, Tragedy, and Tradition in the Nineteenth Century* (Chicago: University of Chicago Press, 1955), 1.

15. Paul V. M. Flesher and Robert Torry, *Film & Religion: An Introduction* (Nashville, Tenn.: Abingdon Press, 2007), 56.

16. Adele Reinhartz, *Bible and Cinema: An Introduction* (New York: Routledge, 2013), 79-80.

17. "The Bible against Itself," *Christian Century*, October 28, 1959, 1235.

18. Crowther, "The Good Book."

19. Paul Coates quoted in Allen Barra, "The Incredible Shrinking Epic," *American Film* 14, no. 5 (1989): 43-44.

20. James M. Robinson, "Neither History Nor Kerygma," *Christian Advocate*, March 25, 1965, 7.

21. Jaime Clark-Soles, "Jesus Christ Superstar," in *The Bible and Cinema: Fifty Key Films*, ed. Adele Reinhartz (New York: Routledge, 2013), 140-45.

22. Romanowski, *Reforming Hollywood*, 195.

23. Patrick J. Buchanan, "The Passion and Its Enemies: The Campaign Against the Movie Bespeaks Deeper Animus," *The American Conservative*, April 26, 2004, http://www.theamericanconservative.com/articles/the-passion-and-its-enemies/.

24. Peter T. Chattaway, "Lethal Suffering: The Passion," *Christianity Today* online, February 25, 2004, http://www.christianitytoday.com/ct/2004/februaryweb-only/passionofthe-christ.html.

25. Gibson quoted in Amy-Jill Levine, "Mel Gibson, the Scribes, and the Pharisees," in *Re-Viewing the Passion: Mel Gibson's Film and Its Critics*, ed. S. Brent Plate (New York: Palgrave, 2004), 138. Bob Berney quoted in Erica Orden, "Hollywood's New Bible Stories," *Wall Street Journal*, September 27, 2012, https://www.wsj.com/articles/SB10000872396390444180004578016711320291332.

26. Alan Trachtenberg, *The Incorporation of America: Culture and Society in the Gilded Age* (New York: Hill and Wang, 1982), 81.

27. Reinhartz, *Bible and Cinema*, 43.

28. John Shelton and Robert Jewett Lawrence, *The Myth of the American Superhero* (Grand Rapids, Mich.: Eerdmans, 2002), 6.

29. See Richard Slotkin, *Regeneration through Violence: The Mythology of the American Frontier, 1600-1860* (Middletown, Conn.: Wesleyan University Press, 1973).

30. See Conrad E. Ostwalt Jr., "Hollywood and Armageddon: Apocalyptic Themes in Recent Cinematic Presentation," in *Screening the Sacred: Religion, Myth, and Ideology in Popular American Film*, ed. Joel W. Martin and Conrad E. Ostwalt (Boulder, Colo.: Westview, 1995), 55–63.

31. Andrew Romano, "Hollywood Declares 2014 the Year of the Bible," *Daily Beast*, January 9, 2014, http://www.thedailybeast.com/articles/2014/01/09/hollywood-declares-2014-the-year- of-the-bible.html.

32. Berney quoted in Orden, "Hollywood's New Bible Stories"; Claudia Puig, "'Son of God' Goes by the Book," *USA Today*, February 27, 2014, https://www.usatoday.com/story/life/movies/2014/02/27/son-of-god-review/4990053/; Darren Aronofsky quoted in Kim Masters, "Rough Seas on 'Noah': Darren Aronofsky Opens up on the Biblical Battle to Woo Christians (and Everyone Else)," *Hollywood Reporter*, February 12, 2014, http://www.hollywoodreporter.com/news/rough-seas-noah-darren-aronofsky-679315.

33. Warren I. Susman, *Culture as History: The Transformation of American Society in the Twentieth Century* (New York: Pantheon Books, 1984), 8.

Bibliography

Anker, Roy. *Catching Light: Looking for God in the Movies*. Grand Rapids, Mich.: Eerdmans, 2004.

Babington, Bruce, and Peter William Evans. *Biblical Epics: Sacred Narrative in the Hollywood Cinema*. New York: St. Martin's Press, 1993.

Bach, Alice. *Biblical Glamour and Hollywood Glitz*. Atlanta, Ga.: Scholars Press, 1996.

Baugh, Lloyd. *Imaging the Divine: Jesus and Christ-Figures in Film*. Kansas City, Mo.: Sheed & Ward, 1997.

Exum, J. Cheryl, ed. *The Bible in Film—The Bible and Film*. Boston, Mass.: Brill, 2006.

Flesher, Paul V., and Robert Torry. *Film & Religion: An Introduction*. Nashville, Tenn.: Abingdon Press, 2007.

Forshey, Gerald E. *American Religious and Biblical Spectaculars*. Westport, Conn.: Praeger, 1992.

Reinhartz, Adele. *Bible and Cinema: An Introduction*. New York: Routledge, 2013.

———, ed. *Bible and Cinema: Fifty Key Films*. New York: Routledge, 2012.

———. *Jesus of Hollywood*. New York: Oxford University Press, 2007.

———. *Scripture on the Silver Screen*. Louisville, Ky.: Westminster John Knox Press, 2003.

Scott, Bernard Brandon. *Hollywood Dreams and Biblical Stories*. Minneapolis, Minn.: Fortress Press, 1994.

Shepherd, David. *Images of the Word: Hollywood's Bible and Beyond*. Atlanta, Ga.: Society of Biblical Literature, 2008.

Tatum, W. Barnes. *Jesus at the Movies: A Guide to the First One Hundred Years*, 3rd ed. Santa Rosa, Calif.: Polebridge Press, 2012.

Walsh, Richard G. *Reading the Gospels in the Dark: Portrayals of Jesus in Film*. Harrisburg, Pa.: Trinity Press International, 2003.

Wright, Melanie Jane. *Moses in America: The Cultural Uses of Biblical Narrative*. New York: Oxford University Press, 2003.

CHAPTER 28

THE BIBLE IN AMERICAN LITERATURE

SHIRA WOLOSKY

THE first English settlers to America arrived in a wilderness without the immemorial institutions of England—no feudal, ecclesiastical, state, class, or economic tiers such as had been in place for centuries in Europe. In this undefined territory, the Bible emerged as the major shared cultural institution. It became a thread, or rather, a woven and braided rope, intertwining American history, politics, religion, and literature, with literature itself never quite shedding its ties to biblical exegesis. Consequently, American culture has a paradigmatic identification with biblical textuality. This identification begins with the Protestant groups who defined their venture to America through a specific biblical hermeneutic, as has been most deeply explicated by Sacvan Bercovitch. This biblical textual identity was disseminated, often with striking and startling shifts in position and interpretation, through subsequent groups, denominations, and parties.[1]

The biblical hermeneutic that informs America has a long history in earlier Christian writings, controversies, and heresies. Jerome, Tertullian, Origen, Augustine, each gave different weights and balances to its component elements. Its canonical form took shape as the Quadriga—a fourfold structure divided, first, into the "literal" historical-grammatical level of Hebrew scripture, but then, in a second level, as a prophecy and prefiguration of the New Testament, thus rebaptized as Old Testament. The New Testament on this second level, is the figural-spiritual-allegorical sense fulfilling the prefigurations of the now Old Testament, specifically in the person of Christ. The New Testament, while also historically literal, makes available the all-important event of Christ's crucifixion, an event that reveals the eternal plan of human suffering, death, and resurrection.

All things that happen in the Old Testament, while indeed occurring historically (a status variously evaluated as to its weight and significance), receive their full meaning only in Christ, who alone reveals their true, eternal significance.[2] Old Testament persons and events thus become "types" foretelling and to be fulfilled in Christ. Type, like allegory, signifies a further, Christian meaning, but also takes place in actual history. Allegories symbolize without having actually happened. Types have concrete historicity. Yet this is not what gives them meaning. Their true significance is only available when seen not as historical event but as prophetic prefiguration, "fulfilled" in the "antitype" of the spiritual truth revealed in Christ.

That there is an instability in this literal/figural structure is eloquently attested in medieval exegetical discussions. On one hand, the "literal" Old Testament type is generally downgraded compared to its New Testament spiritual fulfillment, as at best a secondary meaning and at worst one that misleads and even obstructs. Requiring New Testament transfiguration, Old Testament figures risk entrapment in temporal senses as the "carnal" letter that kills against the "spirit" that gives life (2 Cor. 3:6).[3] On the other hand, "literal" and "figural" emerge as shifting terms whose status and hierarchy can blur. The Old Testament "type" is in fact not "literal," but a figure for the New Testament antitype. And the New Testament, as what the type signifies, is in a sense its literal meaning. Indeed, the whole term "literal" is itself a figure: for the "letter" of the Old Testament which the "spirit" of the New Testament at once requires and yet also effaces.[4] Such ambivalence of the literal is an ambivalence to historicity itself. Both in the early church and subsequently, the status of the Old Testament remained controversial as representing time, materiality, and concrete events, whose meaning resides only in an eternity that subsumes them.

The type's role of revealing the eternal design in Christ, both affirms history and absorbs it. Christ as the axis around which time turns, the center of the circle to which all time points, refers time beyond itself to its eternal and unchanging signified meaning. That "types" are also called "shadows" recalls Platonic hierarchy in which what is true is at once indicated but also obscured by its earthly representation. Types, too, both positively attest to the total light of unchanging truth but also block it, remaining only partial, incomplete, and temporal revelation, seen through a glass but darkly.

The literal historical Old Testament, as prefiguration of New Testament spiritual eternity was extended to two further levels: the "tropological" level where each Christian conforms to the pattern in Christ spiritually and to life in the church, and the "eschatological" level of last things, when all time ends, in a mystical sense as the end of each life and, in a prophetic sense as the end of all earthly time. In such a view, time itself will undergo death and resurrection beyond this world. In one sense, this eschatological level marks a return to historicity, since it will actually occur; but it is also the end of history finally subsumed into the eternal pattern. The course of the earthly world itself follows the trifold pattern of Christ: (1) the creation as birth into time; (2) the crucifixion as time's center, revealing exactly God's eternal design for his creation; (3) the ultimate death and resurrection of time and world itself into eternity. All these levels thus refer to and reflect the Christic center, the eternal design, which governs human experience from the creation until the final Apocalypse.

During the Middle Ages, the emphasis remained on the spiritual life of the Christian in the church, with eschatology discouraged as a revolutionary invitation threatening orthodox institutions (including the church itself). In early modernity, the Reformation initiated renewed interest in historical, individual, and earthly experience. This is visible in, for example, the Protestant rejection of monastic life. In Calvinist early America, what emerged is a marked re-historicizing of biblical hermeneutic. Alongside the traditional Old Testament figures, fulfilled in the New Testament events, colonists considered the Bible to prophesy and foretell America itself. Text becomes history, history becomes text. At the same time, the inner Christian life was subjectivized as conscience and a sense of divine calling, and further intensified by constant self-examination and testimony.

Inwardness remains: but a new sense of historical outwardness opens as well. If medieval Christianity is other-worldly, and pure secularism is this-worldly, then Puritan Americans can be called both-worldly. The inward, individual salvation now also takes shape in outward, public history lived as community. In one sense, a further, fifth level of meaning has been introduced to the classical four: a return to a literal level in the events of American history. In another, the Americans were claiming the traditional, eschatological level as their own. They themselves were the ultimate fulfilment of biblical promises. Eschatology pointed to their Puritan communities as the reborn Kingdom of God in America.[5]

What resulted was a renewed identification with Old Testament historicity: an intense and provocative self-naming as the New Israel, the Chosen People in the Promised Land of the New World. Puritans, like the Israelites of old, left Egypt/England, to cross the Red Sea/Atlantic Ocean, in order to enter the Kingdom of God in New England. But instead of apocalyptic world's end or mystical ascent to heaven, eschatology itself became historicized. Historical ultimacy was no longer a closure of time but incorporated into time itself, in ongoing processes of realization. Such ongoing processes for the Puritans were not yet secular progress, nor were they classical Weberian disenchantment and enterprise. Eternity is not eliminated or displaced by time; it is intensely reflected in it. What is desired is religious life both inward and outward, spiritual and historical, individual and communal, with participation both in this world and the next, both dimensions intersecting in the core notion of calling, as religious awakening and also labor in the world.

And yet, the different levels, in this very effort to be mutually confirming, also become mutually betraying. The hermeneutic that bound together pattern and history, structure and event, also traced a fault line opening division and dissension between them. In rejecting the authority of the Catholic Church, the Reformers had turned to that of the Bible, retranslating its text to guard against Church distortions, and making scripture the central religious reference to be available to every Christian. In this way, the Reformers were confident that every reader would receive the same revelation and the same truth.

Faith in a common revelation and understanding, however, shockingly gave way not to a single truth but competing ones. In an America without a centralized church structure, without a ministry trained in sufficient numbers for the increasingly dispersed American settlements, without a civic power to enforce discipline, and with the Protestant doctrines of inner call and conscience, the outcome was multiple exegetical readings and claims, splinter groups, and rival readings. Such diversity led to questions about biblical authority in the very act of claiming it. Moreover, the tensions between different levels within the biblical hermeneutic under evolving American conditions gave rise to a historicity that challenged religious assumptions.

Instead of a unified revelation, scripture and its hermeneutic practices came to generate multiple interpretations with figural levels playing off against each other. This becomes the very stuff of American literature: patterns and correlations inward and outward along with cracks, suspicions, and breakage in these patterns and claims. Into the twentieth century, the Bible remains a backbone across the spine of America religious, cultural, and literary life, but it does so as a cacophony, which American literature records. Biblical exegesis and representation become a scene of clashing versions. On one level, they are held together by common reference to the Bible; on another they are full of conflict and contestations over how biblical references are to be applied and construed, with the very right to contest a mark of American membership. This contest-as-membership can be charted through a range of literary communities. It commences with early American literary traditions and then continues into the literary traditions of African Americans, women, and more secular biblical engagements, claims, and counterclaims.

Literature of the first American century was on the whole a handmaiden to religious textuality, with the Bible the giant at its center. Edward Taylor's "Meditations," discovered centuries after their writing, were written in tandem with his sermons celebrating the Lord's Supper, each based on a biblical verse and deeply typological in structure and image. In them, biblical pattern is immediate experience. There is a strong emphasis on the Old Testament, typologically as figures of Christ but also as an immediate, almost phenomenological reference for daily events. Old Testament community and covenant also deeply inform the colonists' vision of themselves in the image of the ancient Israelites.

Edward Taylor, as did many Puritan ministers, knew (some) Hebrew, which shaped his poetics materially, while the Bible provided image and overarching pattern. In his Meditation II:7, Taylor asks: "Does Joseph type thee out?" and then proceeds to a detailed typological correspondence between Joseph and Christ. Both were thrown into the pit, both sold, both jailed, both tempted, both bread-givers, although in each correlation Christ is more so. The typology then extends to include Taylor and his own immediate community. Taylor speaks for himself and his fellow saints when he proposes his own poem to answer the call to "Haraulds of Angells sing out, Bow the Knee."[6] Taylor's poems thus present a private face to his public sermons and congregation.

Cotton Mather's histories of the colony are thoroughly public both in audience and in vision, with typological pattern joining these together as the very meaning of colonial history. John Winthrop is "chosen for Moses . . . when the noble design of carrying a colony of chosen people into an American wilderness was undertaken." Mathers writes of his *Biblia Americana*: "I considered that the treasures of illustration for the Bible . . . might be fetched all together . . . to have all the typical men . . . accommodated with their Antitypes . . . [and] the histories of all ages, coming in with punctual and surprising fulfilments of divine Prophecies."[7]

In the early eighteenth century, Jonathan Edwards enthusiastically embraced the immediacy of last things. An activist in the First Great Awakening, he preached it as the beginning of end times. "The holy community," wrote Edwards, "must serve as a type of New Jerusalem" and hence as an earthly "instrument for bringing it into being."[8] In Edwards, eschatological prophecy becomes history. As his "Personal Narrative" records: "My heart has been much on the advancement of Christ's kingdom in the world. . . . And my mind has been much entertained and delighted with the scripture promises and prophecies, which relate to the future glorious advancement of Christ's kingdom upon earth."[9] In a parallel and daring extension, his notes on "Images and Shadows of Divine Things" expands typology to nature, attempting to incorporate into the biblical practices of figuration new science and philosophy, the study and interpretation of the material world.

The effect of both Jonathan Edwards's typologized historicism and his naturalism is to invest spirituality in the immediate world; but in doing so it also shifts greater emphasis and meaning to history and nature. In announcing history to be biblical, Edwards also contributed to displacing the Bible into history. Time, instead of being an image of eternity, begins to overtake it. The duplicity of typology—that time mirrors eternity—reverses, so that eternity mirrors time. Here are the first stirrings of secular progress.

The reversibility of typological conversion—from time to eternity or eternity to time—becomes a wild ambiguity in nineteenth-century literature. The Revolutionary period that followed the First Great Awakening of the early eighteenth century instituted another stage in typological America, making biblical promise into concrete politics, through a complex conjunction between religious and Enlightenment humanisms. It is wrong to read this period and its aftermath as straight secularization. What followed the Revolution was the Second Great Awakening stretching from roughly 1800 to 1860. Here the secular and religious mutually infuse and transform each other. A mixture of religion, republicanism, nationalism, and economic expansion provides the context for nineteenth-century writers, interwoven in ways that show their mutual implication as well as tensions.

Emerson, as both ideologist and critic of emerging American identities, offers just such mixed, contested discourses. "Self Reliance," adopted by Henry Ford as a justification for pure economic individualism, was proposed by Emerson as a far broader vision at once religious, philosophical, aesthetic, and humanist. When he invites his audience to "Speak your latent conviction, and it shall be the universal sense; for always the inmost becomes the outmost—and our first thought is rendered back to us by the trumpets of the Last Judgment," Emerson is not pleading megalomania but a Kantian sense of exemplary ethics, in which what each person undertakes should be universalizable for all.[10] The reference to the "Last Judgment" is here a figure for ultimate accountability. Indeed, Emerson warns at the end of the essay against taking self-reliance to mean only Lockean liberty-as-property in mere self-aggrandizement. This would be a failure of republicanism. "The reliance on Property," he warns, "including the reliance on governments which protect it, is the want of self-reliance." It is a failure of the individual in both civic and spiritual senses, in the liberal theological terms Emerson is inventing. Thus, he concludes with the challenge: "Will the God deign to enter and inhabit you . . . . It is only as a man puts off from himself all external support and stands alone that I see him to be strong and to prevail."[11] Here Emerson is at once deeply Protestant, rejecting all "external support" for inward illumination, but also humanist, if not heretical, in identifying his inner self with God. Emerson resists, not endorses, the growing economic individualism around him, in which the invitation to stand alone is taken to mean self-promotion and self-aggrandizement: the material level of experience ceasing to correspond with the spiritual.

Economic expansion in this period was conjoining with territorial expansion, a further conversion of religious promise into material power. America's idea of Manifest Destiny, the belief that its citizens had the right to expand across all of North America, both incorporates and displaces biblical promise. The mid-century response to such expansion is often a type of reflective misgiving, where skepticism itself becomes a moral stance. Religious terms continue to be invoked but also to be accused. As Herman Melville writes of Nathaniel Hawthorne's "great power of blackness," it is impossible to account for the world without "that Calvinistic sense of Innate Depravity and Original Sin [since] no man can weigh this world, without throwing in something, somehow like Original Sin, to strike the uneven balance."[12] To Melville, the world is indecipherable in ways that continue to refer to a religion that no longer completely explains or justifies.

Melville's *Moby-Dick* (1851) invokes biblical types ("Call me Ishmael") and patterns ("And I only am escaped alone to tell thee") but as a trajectory of misappropriations, chastising, among other things, America's imperial extension.[13] Melville's next novel *Pierre* (1852) traces the inversion of the American Adam in American Eden to suicide and dark self-destruction. Its treatise on "Chronometrical and Horological Time" is a parody of, among other targets, typological efforts to correlate time's events with eternity's designs. After the Civil War, Melville directly exposes, now in the nigh-impenetrable verse of *Battle-Pieces* (1866), the dangers of historicized biblical patterns deployed, as was indeed the case, to justify each side claiming for itself the inheritance of America's biblical destinies. Melville's poem "The Martyr" joins with an outpouring of popular verse making Lincoln into a Christ figure in his Good Friday murder, but Melville warns: "The People in their weeping / Bare the iron hand" of vengeance, not mercy.[14] *Billy Budd*, published posthumously in 1924, probes scenes of fallen nature, the characters offered as types where Claggart as unredeemed Old Adam triumphs over Billy Budd as New Adam in Christ. Melville's *The Confidence Man* (1857), the last novel he published in his lifetime, renders all types, patterns, fulfillments, and identities a hoax or scam of discontinuities that suggest the postmodern.

Concomitantly, Hawthorne, in stories such as "Young Goodman Brown" (1835), "The Maypole" (1837), the *Scarlet Letter* (1850), and *House of Seven Gables* (1851), critiques Puritan paradigms as a source of both civic and religious American life. In the very process of this critique, however, he attests to their continued power for interpreting American culture and history. The sense of America as languishing in sin, even if sin is equated with historical and cultural guilt, confirms the very doctrines that Hawthorne at the same time presents as incriminating hallucination.

It is a peculiar power of biblical paradigms in America that they are claimed not only by mainstream white, male Protestants, but by multiple groups who each then adopts and, in the very act of doing so, contends with and transforms biblical authority. Both African American and women's writing emerge within the frameworks of such pluralized and contentious scriptural claims. The Bible came to the African Americans in travail. Many slave owners opposed the Christianization of slaves, which would have meant admitting they had souls. One of the earliest Black Code laws dictated that conversion did not bring manumission, as neither did white male parentage. Missionaries to the slaves met with obstacles. Assembly of slaves, including for the purposes of worship, was strictly controlled. Teaching slaves to read was punishable. The Bible itself was jealously guarded and, once Christianization had nonetheless penetrated through the revivals of the First Great Awakening, carefully restricted. Attempts were made to block access to the Bible or control its interpretation, especially of liberationist texts, notably the Exodus story.

Nevertheless, biblical lore spread into slave communities, with song being one of its central means of dissemination. The slave spirituals only saw publication during the Civil War, when "Go Down Moses" was printed as a "Song of the Contraband," registering the painful status between property and peoplehood of slaves who escaped to join the North's army ranks. What this song and others show is a quite sophisticated typologizing, one source of which was Isaac Watts's hymns sung at revival camp meetings. [15] The Exodus story becomes an important pattern for countless slave narratives, indeed inspiring slave rebellion as white owners feared.

The correlation between the Exodus story and American slavery goes beyond general identification of the Israelites in Egypt and the promise of liberation. Slave spirituals interweave complex counterpoints between Old Testament slavery, New Testament promise, and the slaves' own historical nightmare in ways that adopt and reenact the typological practices of American culture. What is dramatic is the radical redistribution of roles and positions in how these parallels are assigned. Like the Puritans, African Americans identify themselves with the Chosen People, but doing so displaces white Christians from the place of blessing to one of condemnation. White Americans have become the Egyptians. White America is no longer the Promised Land, but instead the cursed land of Egypt.

This claiming/disclaiming/counter-claiming/reclaiming, and inheriting/dispelling of the Bible as shared but contested in white America is given voice in the writings of African American authoress Frances Harper. An active abolitionist, she worked in the Underground Railroad before the Civil War and the freedmen's education after it. She was also—unusually crossing color lines—active in the women's rights movement. In Harper's writings, radical politics conjoins with Christian commitment, as she claims and contests biblical authority. Her poem "Deliverance" (1871), like many slave spirituals, rewrites the Exodus story from the viewpoint of the African American. "Bible Defense of Slavery" (1854) directly reflects and contests the way the Bible was invoked to defend slavery in the southern churches, a practice she exposes as an inversion and betrayal countered by true faith.

Frederick Douglass in his autobiographical slave narrative gives testimony to a religion where the more devout the slaveholder, the more vicious and self-righteous he became; whereas in the case of slaves, a true Christianity helped strengthen resistance and community. At the end of the nineteenth century, Paul Laurence Dunbar in his "Ante-Bellum Sermon" (1895) stages a double message to two distinct audiences: the slave congregation to whom the Exodus story is one of promise and a source of dignity and deliverance; and the overseers sent to enforce submission and obedience, whom he assures he is only "talking about our freedom / In a Bibleistic way."[16] In such writings, it has been argued that there are two Christianities, the true, African American one and the false, white one. Indeed, the churches themselves broke apart in schism in the years leading up to the Civil War, as northern and southern churches fought within themselves and against each other as to whether to sanction or oppose slavery. As Lincoln said in his Second Inaugural Address (1865), "Both sides read the same Bible and pray to the same God. The prayers of both could not be answered."

This split in American religion revolves around two different fundamental understandings of the Bible that emerge in the antebellum period, enacted in debates over abolition and also women's rights and diffused through American literature. On one side was the subordinationist reading, in which the Bible was invoked as teaching hierarchy, authority, obedience, and submission. Christian liberty was for the next world, not this one. What was required in this present world was submission to one's earthly status as a Christian duty. This reading obviously worked better for those with higher status than those with lower. An opposing, liberationist view of the Bible saw its core teaching to be one that emphasized equality, the dignity of each person in the image of God, and liberation from oppression.

These two interpretive approaches to the Bible's central teachings alter and direct every aspect of biblical interpretation and its norms. Each involves choosing different biblical passages as proof texts, different biblical figures as models, and different authorization for interpretation itself. Hierarchical interpretation authorized hierarchies of interpreters, privileging white male ministers. Liberationist principles endorse every person's equal right to interpret the Bible's teachings.

Many women writers embraced the egalitarian rather than hierarchical hermeneutics. Even when their allegiance was apparently traditional, they often undermined hierarchy in claiming the right of interpretation for themselves. In their work, new attention was paid to female biblical figures, rereading their stories, recovering their viewpoint and voice—as Elizabeth Cady Stanton comments in the *Woman's Bible* (1895) at the end of the century, "we never hear sermons pointing women to the heroic virtues of Deborah."[17] Women poets retell biblical stories and reclaim biblical women where they had languished in silence and invisibility through the centuries. (This revisionist project continued into twentieth-century women's writing, although mainly without knowledge of the prior nineteenth-century work, since most women's writings were buried with their authors, going out of publication and circulation on their death.) Harriet Beecher Stowe's *Uncle Tom's Cabin* (1852) marshals biblical authority against slavery. Abolition itself was largely based in Christian principles for the women who were its backbone, in protest against the immorality of sexual abuse, adultery, and assault on the family in slavery, as well as the corruption of white family integrity and sexual morality.

The two great mid-century poets, Emily Dickinson and Walt Whitman, despite their almost opposite poetics and social situations, can be seen as mirror images of each other when viewed through shared figural traditions of American biblicism. The promise of biblical typology is to align spiritual and mundane worlds, and the extensions of such alignment into self, community, history, and God. This correspondence is a promise each poet both practices and tests. Seeing Whitman's poetry in this typological context makes visible a figural complexity otherwise occluded in the (carefully constructed) apparent spontaneity, casualness, and narrative thrust of his work. This is more than hinted in a notebook entry in which he calls his work "The Great Construction of the New Bible."[18] To take one example only, the marvelous sequence of "I Sing the Body Electric" in Whitman's *Leaves of Grass* (1855) works as a commentary on the core biblical text affirming man and woman's creation in the image of God (Gen 1: 27). Section 5 of the poem makes clear reference to the creation of man from the breath of God, speaks of the "divine nimbus" that "exhales" from the "female form . . . from head to foot."[19] But Whitman, in his own New Bible, rejects any traditional dualist split between spirit and matter, soul and body, which inherited typologies assume as a clear hierarchy subordinating body to soul, history to design, time to eternity. Whitman against any notion of immaterial spirit/material body dualism insists in section 6 (as also in *Song of Myself*, sections 5 and 21), that sacrality includes the body. "The man's body is sacred, and the woman's body is sacred / No matter who it is, it is sacred" ("I Sing the Body Electric," 6). Whitman's text extends the divine image to the whole self of all genders, races, and ethnicities, pursuing an egalitarian and liberationist reading of the Bible, if not a full political abolitionism (putting Union first, as did Lincoln). But Whitman also sees the Bible as betrayed in hierarchies that shape American social and economic inequality. These inequalities he exposes. In section 7 of the poem he proclaims: "A man's body at auction;" but then utterly transforms the auctioneer's words: "Gentlemen look on this wonder: whatever the bids of the bidders they cannot be high enough for it" ("I Sing the Body Electric," 7). "Wonder" here means miracle; and what Whitman exposes is the evil of reduction of the infinite person to economic measure. No bid can reach or encompass the infinite value of every human person.

Whitman is here recreating multiple levels of meaning that recall those of typology: soul and body, history and value, spiritual and material spheres that he sees as betrayed by the

American political economy. In his poetry, Whitman heroically and prophetically seeks to realign, and show the unity of, such seeming oppositions. Yet there are striking departures from tradition. There is no eschatology in Whitman. As he writes in section 6 of the poem,

> Each has his or her place in the procession.
> (All is a procession; The universe is a procession, with measured
> and beautiful motion). ("I Sing the Body Electric," 6)

Experience means multiplicity, reflected and celebrated in multiple figurations. For Whitman there is no end to it, but an ongoing creativity and generativity, to which it is Whitman's courage to pledge himself and America.

Emily Dickinson works in reverse. Her texts repeatedly unravel just the correlations that pointing to biblical figures and patterns promises. She takes apart the traditional strands that earlier American biblical hermeneutics proposed as parallels and confirmations of each other. Self, history, society, and divine pattern are all invoked in her work. But then she refuses to let them match and corroborate each other. A poem written in response to the death of Frazer Stearns of Amherst in the Civil War, whose strife frames and penetrates her verse as it does Whitman's, dislocates the theological and biblical promise of eternal care in earthly events. "Victory comes late" she begins his eulogy: too late even for those who fought on the side of the victors, but who are dead and thus "too rapt with frost / to take it." Here is a "historical" level in all its facticity. She then asks: "Was God so economical?" The divine pattern to which events are supposed to point for their justification and significance is invoked, but as accusation not confirmation. Dickinson tends to use economic imagery when she is being critical, not to say assaultive. God may offer bounty, but it remains out of human reach. His communion "Table's spread too high for Us." Earthly and heavenly spheres miss each other. They do not match. As to the speaker herself, far from testifying to the place of the individual in a redemptive pattern, she declares their exclusion. Identifying with the "Sparrows" promised divine care in the New Testament, she declares of them, and herself to be among those "Who of little Love know how to starve."[20]

Whitman and Dickinson already register in their radical poetics trends that will emerge at the end of the century as modernism. Modernism can be defined as a crisis in tradition, where tradition has not been completely abandoned and yet is no longer fully convincing or authoritative. In this crisis, writers either attempt to return to past traditions, to revise them, or, in a move into postmodernism, to reject and abandon them. T. S. Eliot, after staring into the *Waste Land* (1922), pursues the effort of return. In his *Four Quartets* (1941-42), he reconstructs a full-fledged typology. The first quartet, "Burnt Notion," opens by drawing time into the circle of eternity that typology outlines: "Time present and time past / Are both perhaps present in time future / And time future contained in time past." The final section of "Burnt Notion" reiterates:

> Or say that the end precedes the beginning,
> And the end and the beginning were always there
> Before the beginning and after the end.
> And all is always now.

Here words become the Word, in a figuration of timeless time, an unmoving pattern which subsumes movement, a traditional eternal design recast in modern language and rhythm.

End as beginning, beginning as end emerges as a refrain throughout the *Quartets*. The text thus enacts typological schema, reaffirming the beginning of tradition as its present end in an oddly backward-looking modernism. What the *Waste Land* projected as lack, the *Four Quartets* seeks to have restored.[21]

William Faulkner offers a quite different modernism in his biblical, typological reference. "The past is never dead," Faulkner wrote in *Requiem for a Nun* "it isn't even past."[22] But frozen time is not redemptive. It is stifling, entrapping, betraying. For Faulkner, time has been overtaken by secular progress, and as such has come to justify exploitative consumerism, betraying the land biblical time had promised to redeem. Faulkner's *Go Down, Moses* (1942) announces the Bible in its title (specifically Exodus 8:1), but the message here is not one of biblical hope and redemption but one of decline. When Uncle Ike, one of Faulkner's genealogical figures who ties the present to a withering past, muses on God's original creation, he does so as a topos of doom:

> God created man and He created the world for him to live in . . . and maybe he didn't put the desire to hunt and kill game in man but I reckon He knew it was going to be there . . . foreknowing it . . . . The woods and fields he ravages and the game he devastates will be the consequence and signature of his crime, guilt, and his punishment.[23]

Ike—Isaac, in fact, the intended heir who Abraham tried to sacrifice—bears witness as highways and railroads eat away at the forest land, and men break all restraints to hunt and kill. Man is still marked by "crime, guilt, and punishment," but there is no redemption in sight. Time takes shape as betrayal of humanity in ongoing racial hatred and a progress that has proved to be self-consuming. Promise becomes hard to tell from curse.

It is a surprising and distinguishing feature of American literature that the Bible continues to haunt twentieth-century writing, albeit in increasingly pluralized and fractured forms. Splintered dissemination of biblical types and paradigms lurked within biblical hermeneutics from its very outset. Already, in the first generation of Puritans, Anne Hutchinson and Roger Williams claimed an authority to interpret that conflicted with the Colony's official ministers. In the twentieth century, this impulse toward fragmentation becomes an enactment of plural identities in ways increasingly claimed not only to be legitimate but to define the American character. Yet multiple definitions of selfhood continue to include biblical engagement to a surprising extent. Women's writing, African American writing, as well as other ethnic writing draw on a biblical heritage at once common and full of conflict.

American Jewish writing in many ways inaugurated what was to become hyphenated, ethnic American identities as exemplary and not merely odd, deviant, or excluded from "true" American selfhood. In the work of the late nineteenth-century authoress, Emma Lazarus, this hyphenated character takes shape as a mirroring exercise in which early Puritan identification as Israelites circle back to contemporary Jews as Americans. The Statue of Liberty, first conceived as a tribute to French-American friendship, is recast in Lazarus's "The New Colossus" (the poem inscribed on the Statue's pedestal) to be an icon of American immigration. The poem's "mighty woman with a torch" projects the nineteenth-century women's culture of benevolence as the true America, identified with Christic redemption in the (silent) cry "Send me your poor," while also Judaic culture in the (silent) reference to Deborah the prophetess who, in the biblical Hebrew Lazarus had begun to study, appears as "eshet lapidoth," the woman of the torch. The lifted "lamp beside the golden door" of the poem's conclusion is in Lazarus's writing repeatedly associated with the Hanukah Menorah.[24] The poem, one of the few by a woman to circulate in the public sphere, offers an intensive typology of a Hebrew (vs. Greek), Christic America, gendered identity, and ethnic, immigrant diversity.

Lazarus is followed at the turn of the twentieth century by other Jewish American writers including Israel Zangwill, who invents the term "melting pot," and Horace Kallen, who coins "cultural pluralism." Both of these writers register transformations of the self into plural formations that become dominant in the century to come. Jewish American literature is radically metamorphosed when Hebrew reenters as a modern language, alongside the migration of Yiddish with the influx of immigrants at the twentieth century's turn.[25]

Confronting and negotiating social forces in which the very meaning of identity is pluralized, the Bible is no longer an overriding guide. Yet, in a kind of ironic confirmation of American exceptionalism, the Bible continues to play an intrinsic part, even in marking its own displacements. No longer commanding or central, biblical moments are disseminated in more fragmentary ways, intermixed, often without integration, with other strands of social and political energies. Writers self-consciously explore and assert newly pluralized senses of identity and memberships, be they ethnic, gendered, national, racial, or religious. The presence of the Bible in literature no longer amalgamates or consolidates or hierarchizes, but instead serves to deploy multiple commitments, as much in their conflict and as in their corroboration. The experience of migration, transnationalism, multilingualism along with social, religious, and American ideologies forges a matrix into which biblical references resound, but not as the core organizing structure.

What emerges is the Bible's loss of defining cultural authority (in literature, not in certain forms of politics) which both defines connection and dissolves into American discourses. In women's writing, questions of gender become increasingly self-conscious as topic, as well as shaping voice and creative address. Twentieth-century writing continues the earlier rewriting and reclaiming of women's biblical figures, even without direct knowledge of the earlier literary biblical ventures. But there is less identification and self-definition, more experiment, distance, invention in biblical representation. Marianne Moore marks a transition from nineteenth to twentieth century, in a modernism that is liberal and open where Eliot's was conservative and closed, celebrating time and difference rather than consolidation into eternal design. Hers is a modernism of revision rather than return. Drawing on impulses both Protestant and gendered, Moore authors a remarkable series of poems recasting Hebrew prophets including David, Jonah, Habakkuk, "Isaiah, Jeremiah, Ezekial, Daniel," echoing a women's prophetic tradition in which speaking for some larger mission or purpose authorized women to have voices of their own at all.[26] The recurrent figure of Mary in H.D., Sylvia Plath, and Anne Sexton mark syncretist, irreverent, humanized/mythologized reclamations that scatter rather than restore.

African American writing marks an especially fraught biblical turn. What had been in the nineteenth century a strong twine around which African American self-affirmation could assert itself becomes in the twentieth century a far more suspect and contentious resource. As a structure of white America, its contrast with and historical marginalization of African religious forms gives rise to what might be called a fractured syncretism, suspected and represented as adulteration and suppression. The Bible appears in literature as fragmentary flashpoints. Toni Morrison, for example, seeds her texts with biblical names, titles, allusions, but in ways that interrupt as much as they give entry to biblical heritage. The Bible can be said to reside at the hyphen between African and American, as a point of severe pressure that registers the extremes of participation/exclusion of the African in American culture and history, indelibly part yet also apart in the formation of the American narrative.

The Bible remarkably persists in American literary discourses; even as its power is increasingly centrifugal. Yet in some sense even this dispersion continues the work and place the Bible has held from the American outset, which is to straddle the intensely diverse energies unleashed in the American venture. It marks both a transnationalism and an exceptionalism that, rather than being simply at odds, increasingly impact each other in an identity whose very multiplicity defines it as American.

NOTES

1. See Sacvan Bercovitch, "The Typology of America's Mission," *American Quarterly* 30, no. 2 (Summer 1978): 135–55; *Puritan Origins of the American Self* (New Haven, Conn.: Yale University Press, 1975); *American Jeremiad* (Madison: University of Wisconsin Press, 1978); Werner Sollors, *Beyond Ethnicity* (New York: Oxford University Press, 1986).

2. Erich Auerbach classically discloses this tradition in "Figura," in *Scenes from the Drama of European Literature* (Minneapolis: University of Minnesota Press, 1984).

3. J. S. Preus, *From Shadow to Type* (Cambridge, Mass.: Harvard University Press, 1969), 156–65, summarizes that, despite recurrent "literalism," the Old Testament was seen until the Reformation largely as theologically negative, a "letter" that at worst compromises, at best erases itself before Christian spiritual understanding.

4. Jacques Derrida deconstructs the sense of the "literal," *Of Grammatology* (Baltimore, Md.: Johns Hopkins University Press, 1976), 15. For the ongoing instability in the uses of the term "literal" in Christian exegesis, see Preus, *From Shadow to Type*.

5. Richard Niebuhr, *The Kingdom of God in America* (1938; repr., Middletown, Conn.: Wesleyan University Press, 1988).

6. Edward Taylor, *The Poems of Edward Taylor*, ed. Donald E. Stanford (Chapel Hill: University of North Carolina Press, 1989), 92. For further discussion of biblical structures in Puritan writings, see Shira Wolosky, "Edward Taylor's American Hebraism," in *The Turn around Religion in America*, ed. Michael Kramer and Nan Goodman (Burlington, Vt.: Ashgate, 2011), 287–312; "Biblical Republicanism: John Cotton's 'Moses His Judicials' and American Hebraism," *Hebraic Political Studies* 4, no. 2 (Winter 2009): 104–27.

7. Cotton Mather, *Diary of Cotton Mather*, 1681-1708 (Boston: Massachusetts Historical Society), 23–231.

8. Cited in Bercovitch, *American Jeremiad*, 144.

9. Jonathan Edwards, "Personal Narrative," in *Jonathan Edwards, Selections*, ed. Clarence Faust and Thomas H. Johnson (New York: Hill and Wang, 1962), 57–73, 68.

10. Stanley Cavell, *Conditions Handsome and Unhandsome* (Chicago: University of Chicago Press, 1988), 44.

11. Ralph Waldo Emerson, *Selected Prose and Poetry*, ed. Reginald Cook (New York: Holt, Rinehart, Winston, 1969), 72–94, 92–93.

12. Herman Melville "Hawthorne and His Mosses," http://www.sas.upenn.edu/~cavitch/pdf-library/Melville_Hawthorne.pdf, 1159.

13. Herman Melville, *Moby-Dick* (New York: Bobs-Merrill, 1964), 723, quoting Job 1:14–19.
14. Herman Melville, "The Martyr," *Battle Pieces and Aspects of War*, in *Selected Poems of Herman Melville*, ed. Hennig Cohen (New York: Fordham University Press, 1991), 42.
15. Shira Wolosky, "Slave Spirituals and African American Typology," *Poetry and Public Discourse* (New York: Palgrave Macmillan), 83–96, 87–88.
16. Paul Laurence Dunbar, "An Ante-Bellum Sermon," in *The Collected Poetry of Paul Laurence Dunbar*, ed. Joanne M. Braxton (Charlottesville: University of Virginia Press, 1993), 13.
17. Elizabeth Cady Stanton, *The Woman's Bible*, Part II (Boston: Northeastern University Press, 1993), 19.
18. Walt Whitman, *Notebooks and Unpublished Prose Manuscripts*, ed. Edward Grier (New York: New York University Press, 1984), 1:353. Whitman also calls "*Leaves of Grass*-the Bible of the New Religion," in *Notes and Fragments Left by Walt Whitman*, ed. Richard Maurice Bucke (London and Ontario: A. Talbot, 1899), 55.
19. Walt Whitman, "I Sing the Body Electric," cited by sections in *Poetry and Prose*.
20. I am here following the most recent publication of Dickinson's complete poems by Cristanne Miller, *Emily Dickinson's Poems as She Preserved Them* (Cambridge, Mass.: Harvard University Press, 2016), 357.
21. T. S. Eliot "Four Quartets," in *The Complete Poems and Plays, 1909-1950* (New York: Harcourt, Brace & World, 1971), 117, 121.
22. William Faulkner, *Requiem for a Nun,* http://www.potolkimaker.com/second/William-Faulkner/requiem-for-a-nun.html, 229.
23. William Faulkner, *Go Down Moses* (New York: Modern Library, 1970), 348.
24. Shira Wolosky, "An American-Jewish Typology: Emma Lazarus and the Figure of Christ," *Prooftexts* 16, no. 2 (May 1996): 113–25, 113.
25. For discussion of American Jewish languages, see Hana Wirth-Nesher, *Call It English: The Languages of Jewish American Literature.* (Princeton, N.J.: Princeton University Press, 2009).
26. For discussion of Moore's prophetic poems, see Cristanne Miller, *Cultures of Modernism* (Ann Arbor: University of Michigan Press, 2005), 151–60.

Bibliography

Auerbach, Erich. *Scenes from the Drama of European Literature.* Translated by Ralph Manheim. Minneapolis: University of Minnesota Press, 1984.
Bercovitch, Sacvan. *American Jeremiad.* Madison: University of Wisconsin Press, 1978.
——. *Puritan Origins of the American Self.* New Haven, Conn.: Yale University Press, 1975.
——. "The Typology of America's Mission." *American Quarterly* 30, no. 2 (Summer 1978): 135–55.
Cavell, Stanley. *Conditions Handsome and Unhandsome.* Chicago: University of Chicago Press, 1988.
Derrida, Jacques. *Of Grammatology.* Baltimore, Md.: Johns Hopkins University Press, 1976.
Niebuhr, Richard. *The Kingdom of God in America* (1938). Repr. Middletown, Conn.: Wesleyan University Press, 1988.
Preus, J. S. *From Shadow to Type.* Cambridge, Mass.: Harvard University Press, 1969.
Sollors, Werner. *Beyond Ethnicity.* New York: Oxford University Press, 1986.

Wolosky, Shira. "Biblical Republicanism: John Cotton's 'Moses His Judicials' and American Hebraism." *Hebraic Political Studies* 4, no. 2 (Winter 2009): 104–27.

———. "Edward Taylor's American Hebraism." In *The Turn around Religion in America*, edited by Michael Kramer and Nan Goodman, 287–312. Burlington, Vt.: Ashgate, 2011.

———. *Poetry and Public Discourse in Nineteenth Century America*. New York: Palgrave Macmillan, 2010.

CHAPTER 29

THE BIBLE AND GRAPHIC NOVELS AND COMIC BOOKS

ANDREW T. COATES

TELLING BIBLE STORIES WITH IMAGES

A cloud of dust grows behind Jesus. His powerful arm upraised, he tosses boxes, cages, and tables in the air. Terrified shopkeepers clutch their remaining wares, cowering before the muscular Son of God. To their horror, gold coins whiz through the air alongside their merchandise. Jesus is cleaning house. Shown in a jagged speech balloon, he announces, "The scriptures say, 'my house shall be a house of prayer.' But you have turned it into a den of thieves." A pair of frightened white lambs flees the chaos created by the Lamb of God as he drives the merchants out of the Temple. He looks irate, but a caption explains that Jesus is driving the money changers out of the Temple "in righteous anger." The vividly colored image of an angry Jesus visualizes a scene from the Gospel of Matthew as dramatic action. It is a comic book image of a righteously angry superhero. The scene presents itself as sacred scripture, though little text appears on the page.[1]

This scene comes from *The Action Bible* (2010), a Bible created in the style of comic book art. It depicts the Temple cleansing scene found in the Gospels, and it presents Jesus as a holy action hero. He has the appearance and bearing of a superhero, but his actions and speech come straight from the pages of the New Testament. Published by David C. Cook, this heavily illustrated Bible edition was produced by evangelical Protestants. Evangelicals are Christians who take the Bible as the authoritative Word of God. The book's primary artist possessed a serious pedigree in the comic book world, having worked for Marvel and DC Comics on such well-known superhero serials as *Daredevil*, *The Green Lantern*, and *Batman*. As an evangelical book, *The Action Bible* aimed to induce conversions and get people excited about reading the scriptures. In the book's introduction, its editor proclaimed, "God is the original action hero . . . . Superman may save the day with his strength, but Jesus saved the whole world with His death."[2] The Bible, he elaborated, is full of action heroes, such as King David, Samson, and Esther, who make Superman and Batman look like minced meat. Most important, he explained, any person who reads *The Action Bible* and accepts God's "call to action" would perform even more exciting feats than those its pages portrayed. Thus, each reader's story of salvation was itself an exciting, superhero action story.

The history of American comic book Bibles reveals shifting understandings of images in Protestant communities. *The Action Bible* tells its Bible stories almost exclusively with images. While it is not surprising that early twenty-first-century American Protestants imagined the Bible as an action story, it is somewhat unusual that they condoned a Bible edition in which images performed such important religious work as conveying the message of the Bible. Evangelical theologians have long conceived of the Bible as the "Word of God," an authoritative textual message sent directly from God on high. They are wary of images and less inclined to accord religious authority to images than to the text of the Bible. As if preemptively addressing this concern, the publishers of *The Action Bible* offered a justification for their book's use of images on the back cover. As a "blend of clear writing plus dramatic images," they announced, their graphic Bible "communicate[d] biblical truth clearly and forcefully."[3] Its publishers considered the blend of images and scriptural words the secret of the new Bible edition's power. Properly coupled with scriptural words, its comic book images communicated salvific truth.

The Action Bible did not emerge from a vacuum. By the time of its publication in 2010, American Protestants had been producing comic book Bibles for nearly a century. When Protestants deployed the art of comic books to tell Bible stories, it brought readers into a world where the Bible's narrative unfolded right before their eyes. Comic book Bibles immersed readers in the action of biblical narrative. They made biblical characters into speaking, breathing actors who performed actions in real time. They made it fun and exciting to conduct the pious Protestant practice of reading the Bible on one's own.

Comic book Bibles eschewed the formality of liturgical readings and group Bible study, turning individual, silent Bible reading into an entertaining and immersive experience. This made comic book Bibles particularly appealing for those who wanted to train children to read the Bible regularly. Throughout the twentieth century, Protestants frequently marketed their graphic renditions of the Bible as useful for the evangelization and religious education of children. They reasoned that children might actually sit down and read a comic book as opposed to a catechism or manual. Making the Bible into a comic book would help children become lifelong readers and lovers of the Word of God.

But Protestants put comic book Bibles to other uses as well. The many comic book Bibles they produced in the twentieth and early twenty-first centuries demonstrate Protestants' changing understandings of the religious power of images. The evolving visual styles of twentieth-century comic book Bibles show more than just shifting tastes in art. Changing styles of visual representation in comic book Bibles reveal twentieth-century American Protestants' changing cultural values, changing understandings of their relationship to the nation, and changing practices of using the Bible.

What Makes a Bible a Comic Book?

Theorizing Sequential Art

This essay uses the terms "comic books," "comics," "graphic novels," and "sequential art" almost interchangeably. In recent years, scholars have introduced the term "sequential art" to describe the complex and multifaceted artistic medium that includes comic books and graphic novels.[4] This term emphasizes the medium's use of sequentially juxtaposed static images to create narrative in short strips, book-length works, and cartoon-style, single-panel narrative images. "Comics" or "comic books" often denote the same materials, although technically a comic book is a particular type of publishing format and not a type of art. Historically, people often considered comic books to be children's literature because of their simple themes, low cost, and targeted marketing. The term "graphic novel" emerged to describe the longer, adult-level works that used sequential art to tell more complex tales.

Whatever one chooses to call this medium, neither analysts nor artists can provide an easy theoretical definition of it. Comics present a host of conceptual problems for scholars. Historian Jean-Paul Gabilliet observes that the complex nature of comic books manifests in the many European terms for the medium. In German, the word "*Bildergeschichte*" (literally: "picture stories") highlights the visual storytelling inherent to the form. The French term "*bande dessinée*" (cartoon strip) emphasizes the sequentiality of images in comic book art. Italian's "*fumetti*" (bubbles) points to a common stylistic feature of comic books and graphic novels: the omnipresent speech and thought balloons through which readers hear characters speak and watch them think. Finally, the English term "comics" highlights the medium's origins in satirical cartooning and political satire. In an attempt to capture the breadth of these terms, Gabilliet identifies several necessary features of comics as an artistic medium. First, comics are narratives created through images. Second, in the visual narratives created by comics, images form an essential part of the construction of meaning and are never secondary to words. The creation of meaning must occur through a close relationship between a text's words and images. Finally, the term only applies to visual narratives meeting the above criteria produced in the context of mass publication after the 1830s. The role of imagery, the relation between words and images, and the means of production are all significant elements of sequential art.[5]

One of the most defining features of sequential art is its close relationship between words and images. Sequential art is almost a perfect incarnation of what art historian W. J. T. Mitchell called "image-text," which describes "the heterogeneity of representational structures within the field of the visible and readable."[6] Though imbricated with text, images drive the narratives of sequential art. The best sequential artists use images like an alphabet, a set of culturally shared building blocks that generate meaning. Through subtle visual cues, sequential artists convey specific ideas, moods, and character traits. Successful interpretation of comics relies on shared visual assumptions between writer and reader. By juxtaposing images in a particular sequence, a particular story takes shape. According to graphic novelist and theorist Will Eisner, it is possible to tell a complete narrative in sequential art without using any words at all. The artistic devices of perspective, shading, coloring, lines, figuration, size, and sequentiality contribute to the images' narrative.[7]

Images establish the narrative of sequential art, but words are also critically important to the medium. Words help create a sense of time and timing in the narrative imagery. Whether typed or hand-lettered, the words of sequential art are best understood as parts of the images that surround them. Words help provide sequence to the images and can even give the illusion of temporal duration to the two-dimensional pictures on a page. The words of sequential art create the sense that time is unfolding. For example, when a sequential artist strings a vowel several times at the end of a word, as in the exclamation "noooooo," it gives the illusion that a character has made a long, drawn-out cry. This gives pace to the action of a scene. As this example illustrates, another major characteristic of the words of sequential art is that they conjure speech and sound. This contributes still more to the reader's feeling that the narrative imagery of sequential art unfolds in time. When a character "speaks" with words in a speech balloon, readers accept those words as having come after previous utterances in time and having taken a certain amount of time to say.

Reading the words in a series of images from top to bottom and left to right (in Western countries), readers construct a timeline of events in the narrative. Within that basic timeline, the shape, size, style, and relative position of words convey emotions and moods. Shaky lettering might conjure a voice trembling with fear. Large, bold, capital letters might create the sense that a character is shouting. The words of sequential art are not the same as the words of a novel or poem. They are more like the dialogue and sounds in a film or play, conjuring the auditory dimensions of a story that unfolds in time. By using words and images in dynamic relationship, sequential art can explore the full spectrum of human activity, thought, and emotion as events happening in time.[8]

As a medium in which words and images were inseparable, sequential-art versions of the Bible offered Protestants something unique. For those uneasy about the religious use of images alone, this medium offered the built-in safety net of text. The actual words of familiar Bible translations were always present among the splashy images of sequential-art Bibles. Thus, even the most theologically conservative Protestants turned to the medium to present biblical truth. The close relationship between images and the words of the Bible made sequential art seem less theologically dangerous than other kinds of art. The images of sequential-art Bibles held a clear meaning that sacred text helped create. But sequential art also appealed to Protestants because it allowed them to experiment with the religious possibilities of visual representation. As a medium frequently marketed as children's literature, sequential-art Bibles did not have to obey the same conventions of decorum, theological rigor, and scholarly accuracy as other Bible versions. Sequential-art Bibles were free to perform whatever religious work their creators and audiences needed them to do. As a new medium of the twentieth century, sequential art offered Protestants a chance to push the boundaries of what images could do in their communities.

WORD OF GOD AS WORD AND IMAGE: A VISUAL HISTORY OF SEQUENTIAL-ART BIBLES

Sequential-art Bibles emerged out of a long tradition of Protestant Bible illustration. During the nineteenth century, industrial printing technologies allowed Bible publication to reach an unprecedented pace. Old-fashioned Gutenberg-style presses could, at best, produce around one thousand copies of a single page of the Bible per day. The new steam-driven presses of the 1820s churned out thousands of copies of a page per hour. By mid-century, it was possible to generate millions of copies of a page per day. As a result, printed materials like Bibles became extremely cheap and widely accessible. The American Bible Society adopted the new printing technologies to produce inexpensive and durable little Bibles that could fit into a coat pocket. Their express goal was to place at least one copy of the Bible in every American home. In response to such efforts, other Protestant publishers sought to distinguish their Bible versions with increasingly lavish materials and illustrations. The

American Bible Society cornered the market for cheap, inexpensive Bibles comprised only of text, but other publishers realized Protestants wanted big Bibles, Bibles that could be status symbols, and Bibles that contained beautiful pictures. These Bibles sometimes became gilt-edged leather tomes that weighed a hefty twenty pounds. They commonly incorporated hundreds of lavish woodcuts and lithographs of biblical scenes, sometimes from famous artists like Gustave Doré. The images in Protestant Bibles ran the gamut from bare instructional aids, to fine-art colored lithographs, to titillating nudes. Whatever their particular style, almost all illustrations aimed to increase Bible sales, increase understanding of the Bible, increase the "accuracy" of a Bible version, or some combination of the three.[9]

By the turn of the twentieth century, it was commonplace to find illustrations within the covers of Protestant Bibles. Sequential-art Bibles merely pushed one step further than their nineteenth-century predecessors, making images themselves the primary vehicles for the construction of biblical narratives. Sequential-art Bibles were made mostly of images, with just a sprinkling of text. In each iteration of sequential-art Bibles, images served slightly different purposes for Protestants. Using sequential art, Protestants explored a range of possibilities for what narrative images could do when packaged as scripture.

The Jewish Roots of Protestant Sequential-Art Bibles

While the cooperative relationship between words and images made sequential art appealing to Protestants, many of the earliest and most influential comic books were not Protestant at all. In fact, the earliest examples of comic books were the products of Jewish immigrants' children. *Superman*, widely regarded as the first superhero comic book, was created by Jerry Siegel and Joe Shuster in 1938. Both Siegel and Shuster were children of Eastern European Jewish immigrants. Likewise, Bob Kane and Bill Finger, co-creators of the popular superhero *Batman* (1939), grew up in Jewish immigrant families. Stan Lee, the prolific artist behind well-known superhero comics including *The Amazing Spider-Man* (1962), *The Hulk* (1962), and *The X-Men* (1963), was born Stanley Lieber, the son of Jewish immigrants from Romania.[10]

Although their works usually avoided overt references to Judaism or Jewish religious practice, many scholars have noted that early superhero comics reflected deep truths of American Jewish experience. Like Jewish immigrants' children, superheroes were usually regarded as outsiders by American society. Their "secret identity" was that of a normal person who fit into American life, while the truth was that the hero was a bright green giant or an alien who could leap tall buildings in a single bound. Superheroes possessed special abilities that allowed them to perform heroic feats and gain a measure of acceptance from the dominant culture around them.

Many analysts have suggested that such stories mirror the story of second-generation Jewish Americans' struggles with assimilation from the 1880s to 1930s. Just as Clark Kent (Superman's alter ego) hid his powers from his coworkers, Jewish immigrants' children struggled to balance their unique identities as Jews with the demands of the largely Protestant society around them. Others suggest the idea of a superhuman protector drew heavily on the Jewish legends of the Golem. According to legend, this creature was created by a rabbi to protect his community from Christian persecution, but its superhuman powers led it to run amok.

In any case, comic books, cheaply printed and distributed through nontraditional literary channels, offered a platform for artists with Jewish backgrounds to express themselves without suffering the prejudices and exclusions they faced from the mainstream publishing houses. The fact that American Protestants gradually adopted sequential art and superhero stories in the production of their own Bibles speaks volumes about the changing place of Jewish people in American culture. It also demonstrates the warming relationship between American Protestantism and Judaism in the twentieth century.[11]

Sequential Art and Biblical Inerrancy: The Fundamentalist Cartoons of E. J. Pace

Protestants began using sequential art to tell Bible stories almost as soon as people started publishing it. Single-panel cartoons on Christian themes appeared in newspapers and other periodicals beginning at least in the 1870s and, by the early 1900s, cartoons had become a standard fixture of Protestant publications. As debates about the authority of the Bible raged between Protestant modernists and fundamentalists in the early decades of the new century, sequential art became a key battleground for popular opinion. Fundamentalists championed sequential art as a way of teaching the real truth of the Bible in a fun, entertaining way. Using didactic sequential-art images as "illustrations" of biblical text, fundamentalists made their interpretations of the Bible seem self-evident, authoritative, and objective.

Ernest J. Pace (1880-1946) was a Moody Bible Institute professor, traveling evangelist, and also the head cartoonist for the widely circulated fundamentalist journal the *Sunday School Times*. Publishing about one cartoon per week from 1916 until his death in 1946, Pace's work helped solidify sequential art's place in the visual landscape of Protestant fundamentalism. Often appearing alongside short Bible passages and explanatory "lessons" on the pages of the *Sunday School Times*, Pace's images rendered fundamentalist Bible interpretation visually. At least in theory, the Bible's words reined in the meaning of Pace's sequential-art images. His cartoons were not art for art's sake, but appeared alongside sacred text as teaching tools intended to illustrate the Bible's "plain sense" meaning.

Pace's cartoon images reimagined Bible stories as visual narratives relevant for the age of automobiles, airplanes, phonographs, and American interventionism. Pace once illustrated a Bible lesson on Isaiah 13:11 as a tale of America's providential destiny on the world stage (figure 29.1). He quoted the text of Isaiah as reading, "I will punish the world for their evil, and the wicked for their iniquity; and I will cause the arrogance of the proud to cease, and will lay low the haughtiness of the terrible." While the meaning of the prophecy is opaque in its biblical context, Pace's cartoon left no room for interpretation. In his cartoon illustrating this passage, an angel carrying a sword stands over a slain soldier. The soldier's distinctive *Pikelhaube* identifies him as German officer. On the angel's robe appear the words, "The Justice of God." The fallen soldier himself bears a label that says, "The Nation that Forgot God." Appearing in 1919, the cartoon implied that Germany's defeat in World War I was the result of God's justice. By implication, America's victory meant that it stood on God's side—at least for the time being.[12]

The cartoon used the fall of Germany to urge Americans to adopt right thinking, which in this case meant fundamentalist thinking. In order to avoid Germany's fate, America needed

FIGURE 29.1 *"Let the Nations Take Warning!"* Artist: E. J. Pace. Publication: *The Sunday School Times*, 61.10, March 8, 1919, p. 136.

to "remember" God. Fundamentalists considered modernist American biblical criticism to be a direct product of the influence of German academia. Germany was "the nation that forgot God" because it adopted modernist methods of biblical criticism. In other words, America could only avoid the wrath of God by maintaining fundamentalist positions about the authority of the Bible. By presenting his interpretation as single-panel sequential art accompanied by the text of Isaiah 13:11, Pace's image naturalized a very complex fundamentalist argument as straightforwardly and self-evidently "biblical." Images like this set the standard for later Protestant sequential-art Bibles: images appeared merely to teach the text of the Bible, but actually presented densely coded visual information that supported very particular interpretations. Images practically disappeared in biblical sequential art, seen as nothing more than window dressing to lessons about the Bible's "message."

Educational, Exciting Pictures: Bible Stories in the Early Years of Comic Books

As single-panel cartoons left the confines of newspapers and developed into full-length comic books, Protestants seized on the new format to tell longer biblical narratives. The first modern comic book, *Famous Funnies #1*, was published in 1934. Satirical cartoons and comic strips had long been fixtures of the Protestant press, but the advent of the comic book made sequential art a serious, independent force in American art and literature. M. C. Gaines (1894–1947), the Jewish comic book publisher who released *Famous Funnies*, developed one of the first sequential-art Bibles: a comic book series called *Picture Stories from the Bible* (1942–45). The series took popular biblical tales, such as Moses crossing the Red Sea, David and Goliath, and even the crucifixion of Jesus, and rendered them in the style of the emerging superhero genre of sequential art. Bright colors, clear lines, and emphasis on a single hero's story characterized this style of sequential art, which sold for ten cents per issue. In both style and price, the series sought to appeal directly to middle-class boys and girls who had a few extra dimes to spend.

By 1943, the *Picture Stories* comics were collected into "complete" volumes of Old and New Testaments. A banner across the cover of the Old Testament collection boasted that it included, "The ENTIRE Old Testament told chronologically, for the first time, in full color continuity." The edition sold briskly, with the publisher running two printings of one hundred thousand copies in just two years.[13] Gaines himself was Jewish, but he assembled a mainly Protestant advisory committee to oversee the publication of the *Picture Stories* series. His editorial board included the editor of the *Christian Herald*, a representative from the American Bible Society, a radio minister who also pastored Manhattan's Calvary Baptist Church, and positive-thinking preacher Norman Vincent Peale. The project's ecumenical goals were clear from a disclaimer on its title page, which reassured parents that "in preparing these picture stories from the Old Testament, the official Protestant (King James), Catholic (Douay), and Jewish Publication Society versions were consulted."[14]

Picture Stories from the Bible proclaimed itself to be both engaging, modern entertainment and faithful to the text of the Bible. An editorial description on the collected edition's back cover walked a tightrope between modern innovation and textual fidelity. It claimed to offer "for the first time in one volume, all of the glamorous, romantic stories of the old familiar heroes—told in faithful detail—carefully illustrated in fast-moving action continuity—brought to modern life in glorious full color."[15] Bible stories rendered in comic book style, such advertisements suggested, were "romantic" and "fast-moving," tales that fit well into the full color world of modern American life. Marketed specifically for the religious edification of children, however, the *Picture Stories* series had to be more than merely entertaining. This exciting Bible edition, the editors insisted, was also "faithful" to the textual details of the sacred writ. Its illustrations were "careful" in their presentation of scripture as well as entertaining. This balancing act showed both Protestants' wariness and excitement about the new medium of sequential art. Images that were too entertaining, too lavish, might be considered idolatrous. Worse still, they might stray from the accepted meaning of the Bible, adding or omitting important details Protestants expected in their visual renderings of scripture. But if the images were recognized as fun, they presented the possibility that children would actually sit down and read the Bible.

In its style and content, *Picture Stories from the Bible* sought to teach Protestant children valuable wartime attributes like self-sacrifice, obedience to authority, and respect for tradition. The story of King Josiah aimed particularly at the patriotic education of boys. In 2 Chronicles and 2 Kings, Josiah is portrayed as a religious reformer who removes idol worship from the kingdom of Judah, restores the Temple, rediscovers the Torah, and reinstitutes the celebration of Passover. He dies in a battle against Egyptians.

In the *Picture Stories from the Bible* version of his reign, Josiah receives the epithet "the young king of the Jews." He is blonde and muscular, an all-American kid who has been given a divine commission to rule a kingdom under threat. In the first panel of his story, his mother tells him, "My son, you are called to rule in troublesome times!" Just like kids growing up in wartime America, Josiah and his nation faced serious problems. Clenching his fist with a look of determination, young Josiah decides to seek wisdom just like his ancestor King David did. To the acclaim of his people, Josiah eliminates the "national evil" of idolatry. A few panels later, when presented with the rediscovered Torah, Josiah asserts, "How disgracefully we have neglected this book! I'll do something about it immediately!"

American children were supposed to identify the hero Josiah's struggles with their own struggles to obey the Bible. The story teaches them to follow biblical precepts even in the midst of national troubles. The martial character of Josiah's story became especially clear in the story's final four panels. Outnumbered by a vast army of invading Egyptians, Josiah decides to ride out bravely and attack his enemies instead of retreating. Wearing a golden cape and crown, Josiah rides at the head of his army. His war chariot is pulled by two galloping white stallions. Two panels later, Egyptian arrows pierce Josiah and he dies. But his story does not end there. In the final panel of this visual narrative, Josiah's son Jehoahaz sits smiling on his father's throne. He states, "I shall continue to enforce the laws of God from the sacred book Josiah found. Right shall rule!" In short, Josiah's righteous actions as a boy turned him into the kind of man who was willing to die in battle for his country. In so doing, he left a more righteous nation to his own son. The story served a didactic purpose for wartime American Protestants, teaching children that their own obedience to God served the national interest.[16]

The Graphic Truth of Prophecy: The Apocalyptic Bible Comics of Basil Wolverton

By the 1960s, biblical sequential art took a radical turn. Once a medium primarily for the religious education and edifying entertainment of children, a new generation of Protestant artists began using the medium to convince others of biblical prophecy's terrifying reality. When M. C. Gaines died suddenly in 1947, his son William Gaines (1922–1992) took over the Educational Comics (EC) company, publisher of *Picture Stories from the Bible*. The younger Gaines possessed a bold new vision for sequential art and soon began publishing comics for mature audiences that held explicitly sexual and violent themes. EC changed from the "Educational Comics" company to the "Entertaining Comics" company.[17] Alongside such dark series as *Weird Science* and *Tales from the Crypt*, William Gaines published a new satirical magazine that became one of the nation's leading sources for sarcasm and toilet humor: *MAD* magazine (1952). By calling his publication a magazine, Gaines managed to skirt the new censorship laws of the Comics Code Authority. This comic book publishers' self-governing agency forbade depictions of violence and sexuality in comic books in an effort to protect the minds of children.[18]

Basil Wolverton (1909–1978) was one of the most influential artists employed at *MAD* in its early years. Wolverton's artistic style exaggerated human features beyond anything attempted in earlier sequential art. According to one scholar, "Wolverton's special gift was a unique perspective on the grotesqueries of the human anatomy which produced some of the most outlandish caricatures to appear in any print medium."[19] Under Wolverton's pen, bodies warped, bulged, melted, dripped, and ballooned in humorous and disturbing ways. Wolverton's work as an artist for *MAD* helped cement the magazine's prosperity, but he was also a devout Protestant. He drew Bible comics extensively for the publications of Herbert W. Armstrong's (1892–1986) apocalyptic Worldwide Church of God, particularly *Plain Truth* and *Tomorrow's World*. Wolverton believed the Second Coming of Jesus was imminent. He used his sequential art to explore what it might look like if the End of Days happened in his immediate future. He thought it necessary to render every detail of the Word of God in his images, including the gory truth of violent passages.

Basil Wolverton's apocalyptic sequential art visualized the grotesque and horrifying aspects of biblical prophecy. In the vision of Daniel 7:7, the biblical prophet describes seeing a beast with ten horns trampling and devouring people, "dreadful and terrible, and strong exceedingly; and it had great iron teeth" (KJV). Wolverton took this prophetic passage as a visual description of a horrifying creature, so he drew it as best he could (figure 29.2). Resembling a snub-nosed crocodile, Wolverton's "beast" stood on eight warty legs and had ten sharp horns protruding from the center of its back. A small horn, precisely as the prophet describes, also poked out. Demonstrating his faithful visual literalism, Wolverton's beast squishes human flesh under its claws and chomps on human appendages. Terrified onlookers, dressed like modern middle-class Americans, run from the flesh-eating monster. Wolverton's vision of the beast permits no abstraction, metaphor, or historical criticism

FIGURE 29.2 *Daniel 7: The Beast with Ten Horns.* Artist: Basil Wolverton. Image source: *The Wolverton Bible*, ed. Monte Wolverton (Seattle, Wash.: Fantagraphics Books, 2009), 258. Used with permission. All rights reserved.

in the reading of Daniel. When the prophet writes about a beast with ten horns plaguing humanity, Wolverton understood that he actually saw a horrible, horned creature eating people.[20] By this reasoning, readers of the Bible do best to accept such visions at face value because there are terrible consequences for ignoring them.

Wolverton's art implied that biblical prophecy described events in the present or the near future, not the ancient past. With unwavering depictions of nuclear war and God's punishment for the wicked, his images insisted biblical prophecy was a message for contemporary America. The opaque texts of biblical prophecy were not ancient fantasy or myth, but visual descriptions of things that would probably happen within the next decade. In an image titled "Bomb Crater," Wolverton offered his visual interpretation of death riding a pale horse and destroying a quarter of the world, as described in Revelation 6:8 (figure 29.3). The "pale horse" appears as several white, space-age airplanes. They have dropped so many nuclear bombs that they have created a deep void crater that occupies about a third of the image. In the foreground, a massive steel girder appears melting and burned, drooping like a cooked noodle. Around the girder lie dozens of mangled, twisted bodies in a heap. Faces, melted and full of holes, peek from the pile with expressions of severe pain. Some have no eyes left, their cheeks like rippling water. By grimly rendering Revelation's prophetic visions in his own grotesque style, Wolverton's work warned people that they ignored the Bible's predictions at their own peril. They had to get right with God or face the horrifying consequences.[21]

FIGURE 29.3 *Bomb Crater: Revelation 6:8*. Artist: Basil Wolverton. Image source: *The Wolverton Bible*, ed. Monte Wolverton (Seattle, Wash.: Fantagraphics Books, 2009), 269. Used with permission. All rights reserved.

Jughead Finds Jesus: Al Hartley and the Mainstreaming of Conservative Evangelicalism

Wolverton's biblical sequential art acquired limited viewership, but Protestant sequential art of the "Jesus Freak" generation in the 1970s and 1980s aimed to bring conservative Protestantism to the masses. When the Comics Code Authority began its crusade against sex and violence in sequential art in 1954, many publications fell to the censors. Comics had to be squeaky clean under the new rules, promoting wholesome family values and All-American youth activities.

Under the new rules of censorship, one series shone brightly and became one of the nation's longest-running and best-loved comic book series: *Archie* (1941). *Archie* comics told of the wholesome adventures and innocent romantic entanglements of a group of high school students in the fictional American small town of Riverdale. The series centered on Archie Andrews, a freckled, sixteen-year-old redhead who always tried to do the right thing. Archie made harmless mischief with his clumsy, hamburger-gobbling friend Jughead Jones. He found himself at the center of an innocent love triangle, juggling dates with good-natured Betty Cooper and glamorous Veronica Lodge. In the early 1970s, *Archie* artist Al Hartley (1921–2003) acquired a license to use the Riverdale gang for his own side project. A committed born-again Christian, Hartley created an evangelical version of the *Archie* series for the Spire Christian Comics imprint. In this version of Riverdale, Archie, Jughead, Betty, and Veronica were all born-again Christians. The Spire Christian Comics series cast evangelical attitudes, biblical interpretations, and religious practices into the idiom of mainstream comic books, making them seem completely uncontroversial.

Hartley's art reassured evangelicals, particularly evangelical young people, that their values and actions belonged in the American mainstream. In Hartley's Riverdale, a kid did not have to feel strange for conducting the pious evangelical practice of praying a blessing over a meal in the school cafeteria. In fact, the comics singled out those who were not born again as the strange ones. Kids who got their comic books at Christian bookstores were cool, while those who read the "filthy" comics of other bookstores were ostracized by Archie and the gang.

In the Spire Christian Comics universe, evangelicalism was the standard-bearer of cool. But more than just appealing to young people's cultural tastes, the Spire *Archie* series presented conservative evangelicalism as a panacea to the serious social issues facing 1970s America. If people would just accept Jesus as their personal savior and live their lives according to the plain-sense moral precepts of the Bible, Archie and his friends insisted, there would be no racial injustice, no school violence, no premarital sex, no feminism, no drugs, and no need for the counterculture movement. Before the rest of the country came to its senses, however, Christian Archie encouraged conservative evangelical youngsters to continue their distinctive religious behaviors with pride. Evangelical Christianity was "with it," while everyone else's beliefs and actions were not. Besides Christian Archie, other comics in the Spire Christian Comics catalogue promoted similar ideas. These titles included a comic book version of Charles Colson's bestselling book *Born Again*, a sequential-art retelling of the evangelical conversion of musician Johnny Cash, and a comic book edition of Corrie Ten Boom's memoir, *The Hiding Place*.[22]

Along with the "Christian Archie" series and its sequential-art versions of popular evangelical books, Spire Comics published several comics that told biblical stories. Some titles, like *Jesus* (1979), followed closely in the footsteps of *Picture Stories from the Bible*. These sequential-art Bible stories used oriental garb and traditional visual motifs to provide "faithful" renditions of scripture. In *Jesus*, for example, the character Jesus always appears clad in white and scarlet robes. Square-jawed and light-skinned, he has bright blue eyes and bears a strong resemblance to Warner Sallman's famous painting *Head of Christ* (1940). Avoiding unnecessary controversy, not a drop of blood stains Jesus's muscular body at his crucifixion. Nevertheless, the visual style and textual content of *Jesus* aims to make the stories of the gospel entertaining for young people in the 1970s.

Occasionally, Jesus says things that are not contained in the text of the New Testament. When he does so, his words are almost always rendered in the funky patois of 1970s youth culture. Speaking to Nicodemus in the comic's rendering of John 3, Jesus offers a summary of the New Testament tinged with evangelical interpretation. "I've come to CHANGE the lives of all who need HELP!!!" he says, continuing, "Unless you're BORN AGAIN—you'll NEVER understand the kingdom of God!" Nicodemus replies, "But how can I be born again at MY age???" Jesus responds, "I speak of your SPIRITUAL life, Nicodemus!!! You've already had a PHYSICAL birth—now you need a SPIRITUAL birth! That's why God sent me—I bring his love! And all who BELIEVE in ME shall not perish, but have eternal life!!!"[23] Visually cautious, this section renders Jesus's speech in a language that would be familiar to young people in the 1970s. Like the self-described "Jesus Freaks," this Jesus speaks in contractions and brings a message of love, personal belief, and profound life change.

Spire's comic about Jesus did not stray far from the bounds of Protestant iconographical tradition, but other comics in their Bible series reimagined biblical stories as events happening in the 1970s. *Paul: Close Encounter of a Real Kind* (1978) offered a contemporized retelling of the life of the Apostle Paul as told in Acts 26–28 and New Testament epistolary literature. The title of the comic echoed a popular science-fiction movie, *Close Encounters of the Third Kind* (1977). The alien encounters in the movie might have been entertaining, the title suggested, but Paul's "encounter" was real.

In the comic's opening pages, Paul appears with blonde hair, blue eyes, and a strong chin, wearing a military uniform and red beret reminiscent of communist revolutionary Che Guevara's. He is rounding up and killing Christians. Riding in his Humvee to Damascus to stamp out the Christians there, Paul suddenly gets blinded by light. "It's a laser beam!!! A death ray!" he exclaims, but soon realizing the miraculous truth, he cries, "It's not a thing!!! It's a person!!!"[24] Jesus announces himself and demands that Paul stop persecuting him and his followers. Paul immediately agrees. Soon, he starts wearing a suit and tie. He proclaims that Jesus is the Son of God, and finds himself arrested. He gains supernatural power from his conversion, including the power to heal a man in a wheelchair. He writes letters to other "Jesus Freaks." A text balloon explains that Paul's letter-writing constituted much of the New Testament: "The entire world read Paul's mail!"[25] Paul writes to the Christians in Philippi, "Live clean lives in a dark world. Be enthusiastic about life! Don't worry about anything . . . pray about everything! And don't forget to thank God for answered prayer!"[26] Along with these words appear images of a mother and father hugging their children, a surfer riding a big wave, and smiling people dressed in clothing ranging from overalls to power suits. As in the Christian Archie comics, Hartley uses the story of

Paul to make evangelicals' distinctive beliefs, practices, and biblical interpretations seem appealing to young people of the hippie generation.

CONCLUSION: THE VISIBLE BIBLE
OF AMERICAN PROTESTANTISM

Like its predecessors in sequential art, *The Action Bible* used images in very particular ways. In *Picture Stories from the Bible*, Jesus does not bleed at the crucifixion. On the cross, he looks small and pale. In *The Action Bible*, the crucified Jesus looks very different. His massive pectoral and abdominal muscles give him the appearance of a bodybuilder or professional wrestler. His physique makes him appear superhumanly strong, as if the ropes and nails that hold him to the cross serve no real function. He is on the cross by choice. Although he bleeds from his hands, feet, face, and abdomen, he looks more powerful than defeated. He is hypermasculine, a bruised warrior who will not be defeated by death. He was a fitting hero for America in 2010, an international superpower embroiled in two long-standing foreign wars and still hunting for its enemy Osama bin Laden.[27]

For nearly a century, Protestants have presented scripture through sequential art. They used a variety of visual styles, employing images to conduct religious work. At times, the images served as weapons in internecine Protestant wars over the authority of the Bible. Other Protestant sequential-art Bibles had a didactic purpose, educating children about the Bible and about their community's values. Other Protestant sequential art tried to present the graphic realities of a world in sin, a world about to suffer the wrath of God. Still other Protestant sequential art sought to give cultural cachet to a particular style of biblical interpretation. It used popular characters and idioms to make Bible stories appealing for a generation that elevated youth culture. In these and many other ways, Protestants used the images of sequential art to serve their changing religious needs. Translating the Bible into modern English required years of scholarship and valued fidelity to the original languages above all else. By contrast, presenting the Bible as sequential art freed Protestant imaginations. Sequential-art Bibles enabled Protestant Americans to show the Bible as they wished it to be. The Bible of Protestant visual imagination was edifying, educational, terrifying, exciting, engrossing, militaristic, countercultural, transformative, heroic, cool, and even funny.

NOTES

1. Doug Mauss, ed., *The Action Bible: God's Redemptive Story* (Colorado Springs, Colo.: David C. Cook, 2010), 614.
2. Mauss, *Action Bible*, 7.
3. Mauss, *Action Bible*, back cover.
4. Comic artist Will Eisner understands "sequential art" to be "an art and literary form that deals with the arrangement of pictures or images and words to narrate a story or dramatize an idea." Will Eisner, *Comics and Sequential Art: Principles and Practices from*

the Legendary Cartoonist Will Eisner (New York: W. W. Norton, 2008), xi; artist and theorist of comics Scott McCloud elaborates Eisner's definition of "sequential art" to distinguish it from video animation and other forms of sequenced imagery: sequential art is "juxtaposed pictorial and other imagery in deliberate sequence." McCloud explains that "sequential art" is preferable to the term "comics" because the former is "neutral on matters of style, quality, or subject matter." Calling comics "sequential art" thus emphasizes the way the medium's constituent images are arranged and read, rather than their visual content, style, or genre. Scott McCloud, *Understanding Comics* (New York: HarperCollins, 1994), 9, 5.

5. Jean-Paul Gabilliet, *Of Comics and Men: A Cultural History of American Comic Books*, trans. Bart Beaty and Nick Nguyen (Jackson: University Press of Mississippi, 2009), xi xvi.

6. W. J. T. Mitchell, *Picture Theory* (Chicago: University of Chicago Press, 1994), 88.

7. Eisner, *Comics and Sequential Art*, 10.

8. Eisner, *Comics and Sequential Art*, 24.

9. For a concise history of Bible illustration and its effects on American Bible reading and consumption during the nineteenth century, see Paul Gutjahr, *An American Bible: A History of the Good Book in the United States, 1777-1880* (Stanford, Calif.: Stanford University Press, 1999); see also Paul Gutjahr, "American Protestant Bible Illustration from Copper Plates to Computers," in *The Visual Culture of American Religions* (Berkeley: University of California Press, 2001), 267–85; David Morgan has presented detailed analyses of the nineteenth-century Protestant practices of Bible image production, visual reading practices, and mass publication. David Morgan, *Protestants and Pictures: Religion, Visual Culture, and the Age of American Mass Production* (New York: Oxford University Press, 1999), 13–39.

10. Representative histories of Jewish people's contributions to the development of comic books include: Danny Fingeroth, *Disguised as Clark Kent: Jews, Comics, and the Creation of the Superhero* (New York: Continuum, 2008); Arie Kaplan, *From Krakow to Krypton: Jews and Comic Books* (Philadelphia: Jewish Publication Society, 2008); Paul Buhle, ed., *Jews and American Comics: An Illustrated History of an American Art Form* (New York: New Press, 2008).

11. Kaplan, *From Krakow to Krypton*, 2–44.

12. E. J. Pace, "Let the Nations Take Warning!," *Sunday School Times* 61, no. 10 (March 8, 1919): 136.

13. M. C. Gaines, *Picture Stories from the Bible: The Complete Old Testament Edition* (New York: M. C. Gaines, 1943), back cover.

14. Gaines, *Picture Stories*, title page.

15. Gaines, *Picture Stories*, back cover.

16. M. C. Gaines, ed., "The Story of Josiah: The Young King of the Jews," in *Picture Stories from the Bible: The Old Testament in Full-Color Comic-Strip Form* (New York: Scarf Press, 1979), 174–77.

17. Relevant histories of the Comics Code Authority and E. C. Comics include: David Hajdu, *The Ten Cent Plague* (New York: Farrar, Straus and Giroux, 2008); see also Amy Kiste Nyberg, *Seal of Approval: The History of the Comics Code* (Jackson: University Press of Mississippi, 1998).

18. In response to the pressures of the Comics Code Authority, many of sequential art's most daring artists took their work underground. Many self-published their comics

or published them in countercultural magazines aimed at adults. Ironically, the visual style of these comics, pioneered by the likes of R. Crumb's *Zap Comix*, influenced one of the best-known fundamentalist sequential artists of the twentieth century: Jack Chick. Chick's small, sequential-art tracts sold millions of copies from the 1960s to 2000s. His works tried to "scare the hell out of people," inducing conversion through fear of damnation. Much like Wolverton, he graphically depicted the eternal consequences of sin. See Jason Bivins, *Religion of Fear: The Politics of Horror in Conservative Evangelicalism* (New York: Oxford University Press, 2008), 41–88.

19. Ray Zone, "Boltbeak: The Art of Basil Wolverton," *Journal of Popular Culture* 21, no. 3 (Winter 1987): 145.

20. Monte Wolverton, *The Wolverton Bible: The Old Testament and the Book of Revelation through the Pen of Basil Wolverton* (Seattle, Wash.: Fantagraphics Books, 2009), 258.

21. Wolverton, *Wolverton Bible*, 269.

22. Very few scholars have examined Hartley's Spire Comics series. The series receives a brief mention in Kate Netzler, "A Hesitant Embrace: Comic Books and Evangelicals," in *Graven Images: Religion in Comic Books and Graphic Novels* (New York: Continuum, 2010), 221. Evangelical comics artists have written their own history of Hartley's work at http://www.christiancomicsinternational.org/hartley_pioneer.html.

23. Al Hartley, *Jesus* (Old Tappan, N.J.: Fleming H. Revell, 1979), 10–11.

24. Al Hartley, *Paul: Close Encounters of a Real Kind* (Old Tappan, N.J.: Fleming H. Revell, 1978), 5.

25. Hartley, *Paul*, 28.

26. Hartley, *Paul*, 30.

27. Mauss, *Action Bible*, 636.

Bibliography

Barthes, Roland. *Image-Music-Text*. Translated by Stephen Heath. New York: Hill and Wang, 1978.

Bivins, Jason. *Religion of Fear: The Politics of Horror in Conservative Evangelicalism.* New York: Oxford University Press, 2008.

Blankenship, Anne. "Catholic American Citizenship: Prescriptions for Children from *Treasure Chest of Fun and Fact* (1946–63)." In *Graven Images: Religion in Comic Books and Graphic Novels*, edited by A. David Lewis and Christine Hoff Kraemer, 63–77. New York: Continuum, 2010.

Carmody, Thomas. "Converting Comic Books into Graphic Novels and Digital Cartoons." In *Understanding Evangelical Media: The Changing Face of Christian Communication*, edited by Quentin J. Schultze and Robert Woods, 186–97. Downers Grove, Ill.: InterVarsity Press, 2008.

Eisner, Will. *Comics and Sequential Art: Principles and Practices from the Legendary Cartoonist Will Eisner.* New York: Norton, 2008.

Fingeroth, Danny. *Disguised as Clark Kent: Jews, Comics, and the Creation of the Superhero.* New York: Bloomsbury Academic, 2008.

Freedberg, David. *The Power of Images: Studies in the History and Theory of Response.* Chicago: University of Chicago Press, 1989.

Gabilliet, Jean-Paul. *Of Comics and Men: A Cultural History of American Comic Books.* Translated by Bart Beaty and Nick Nguyen. Jackson: University Press of Mississippi, 2009.

Gaines, M. C., ed. *Picture Stories from the Bible: Complete Old Testament Edition.* New York: M. C. Gaines Press, 1943.

———. *Picture Stories from the Bible: The Old Testament in Full-Color Comic-Strip Form.* New York: Scarf Press, 1979.

Gordon, Ian. *Comic Strips and Consumer Culture: 1890–1945.* Washington, D.C.: Smithsonian Institution Press, 1998.

Gutjahr, Paul. *An American Bible: A History of the Good Book in the United States, 1777–1880.* Palo Alto, Calif.: Stanford University Press, 1999.

Hajdu, David. *The Ten Cent Plague: The Great Comic-Book Scare and How It Changed America.* New York: Farrar, Straus and Giroux, 2008.

Hartley, Al. *Archie's Something Else!* Old Tappan, N.J.: Fleming H. Revell, 1975.

———. *Jesus.* Old Tappan, N.J.: Fleming H. Revell, 1979.

———. *Paul: Close Encounters of a Real Kind.* Old Tappan, N.J.: Fleming H. Revell, 1978.

Kaplan, Arie. *From Krakow to Krypton: Jews and Comic Books.* Philadelphia: Jewish Publication Society, 2008.

Laycock, Emily. "Graphic Apocalypse and the Wizard of Grotesque: Basil Wolverton, The Worldwide Church of God and Prophecy." In *The End Will Be Graphic: Apocalyptic in Comic Books and Graphic Novels,* edited by Dan W. Clanton Jr., 20–34. Sheffield, UK: Sheffield Phoenix Press, 2012.

Mauss, Doug, ed. *The Action Bible: God's Redemptive Story.* Colorado Springs, Colo.: David C. Cook, 2010.

McCloud, Scott. *Understanding Comics: The Invisible Art.* New York: HarperCollins, 1994.

Mitchell, W. J. T. *Iconology: Image, Text, Ideology.* Chicago: University of Chicago Press, 1987.

———. *Picture Theory.* Chicago: University of Chicago Press, 1994.

———. "There Are No Visual Media." *Journal of Visual Culture* 4, no. 2 (2005): 257–66.

Morgan, David. *Protestants and Pictures: Religion, Visual Culture, and the Age of American Mass Production.* New York: Oxford University Press, 1999.

———. *Visual Piety: A History and Theory of Popular Religious Images.* Berkeley: University of California Press, 1998.

Netzler, Kate. "A Hesitant Embrace: Comic Books and Evangelicals." In *Graven Images: Religion in Comic Books and Graphic Novels,* edited by A. David Lewis and Christine Hoff Kraemer, 218–29. New York: Continuum, 2010.

Nyberg, Amy Kiste. *Seal of Approval: The History of the Comics Code.* Jackson: University Press of Mississippi, 1998.

Wolverton, Monte. *The Wolverton Bible: The Old Testament and the Book of Revelation through the Pen of Basil Wolverton.* Seattle, Wash.: Fantagraphics Books, 2009.

Wright, Bradford W. *Comic Book Nation: The Transformation of Youth Culture in America.* Baltimore, Md.: Johns Hopkins University Press, 2001.

Zone, Ray. "Boltbeak: The Art of Basil Wolverton." *Journal of Popular Culture* 21, no. 3 (Winter 1987): 145–63.

CHAPTER 30

....

THE BIBLE AND MUSIC

....

JASON C. BIVINS

INTRODUCTION

....

AGAINST what she calls "reductive textualism," Anne Blackburn notes that texts "also shape the world of material culture" and are deeply woven into "ritual and devotion."[1] Blackburn argues that texts move continually outside their institutional or traditional locations, to be appropriated in the interior spaces of reflective deliberation, in the embodied modes of enactment or veneration, or even, I would add, in artistic creations (here as motivation, framework, or devotional object alike). The Bible is not just a repository of narrative, neatly confined to particular institutional or interpretive lineages, or even to limiting readings of its authority and implications. Yet scholarship on the Bible has too seldom focused on these dimensions. In this essay, I show how American music has been a medium through which religious practitioners encounter the Bible with what Zora Neale Hurston once called the "will to adorn."[2] In this, I hope to locate new interpretive possibilities for thinking about the Bible and American music.

The study of North American religions has recently opened up conversations about the centrality of the senses to religious experience, including their engagement with sacred texts. As part of these investigations, scholars have paid more attention to the role of sound and music in religious worlds, often focusing on either "religious music" (i.e., specific song forms belonging to established traditions) or representations of religion in various musical genres (with a consequent focus on lyrical content).[3] In between these two orientations, however, we see how religions intersect with various musical cultures to produce hybrid forms of religio-musical identity, practice, and experience. How, then, can we locate such complexity in one of the more apparently settled areas of religious identity or experience? Can we find in and around the Bible evidence of how religions are, as Colleen McDannell writes, "multimedia events"?[4]

This piece argues that interpretation of the Bible and American music should focus not only on conventional scholarly questions of theme and representation but also on the senses, power, and intersubjectivity. Although there is ample scholarly investigation of expanded textuality, of music and religion, and of the negotiations of identity, these three foci are often held apart. By paying closer attention to the varieties of American music, though, we can "hear" the Bible differently, unpacking the strategies for self-creation and self-understanding American religious practitioners have enacted. In this, we see how, in Blackburn's formulation, texts "model styles of human action and character that inform the imagination, action, and interpretation of those who read, see, or hear them."[5]

I will explore how musical performance has historically integrated these different dimensions of the Bible: as a locus of themes and preoccupations central to American history and as a medium for embodied musical creativity. Consideration of music and the Bible also provides a window, as discussed in this chapter's conclusion, into the sensorium of American religions (how the imagination works with the senses to create religious meaning). While the importance of creative expressivity and biblical authority in American religion is well known, this history looks and sounds different if we chronicle it with a focus on music beyond the textual. More than simply a sourcebook for exhortation or reflection, the Bible in America possesses a social, textual, and emotional generativity that its musical engagements manifest. This chapter first names several interpretive strategies for thinking about this resonance, and from there proceeds to excavate from conventional scholarly and historical foci the kinds of complexity that might facilitate new lines of scholarly questioning and hearing.

METHODS

There are some obvious interpretive similarities between sacred texts and music: formal properties can be mapped, historical contexts identified, and the interests and aspirations of performers documented. Yet music is often defined by, and experienced through, the absence of conventional references and languages, even if key scholarly foci have generally subsisted in various kinds of textual representation.[6] While music's formal properties are compelling, music also plays key roles in shaping identity and community, and in the enactment of norms and values.

With the Bible and American music, despite how apparent the limits of textual (and scholarly) format might appear, the closer we look at genre, community, tradition, and practice, the more we see that Americans have used the Bible to make musical multitudes. Music is not incidental to religious interpretations and convictions, a sonic gloss on antecedent "meaning"; nor, going somewhat deeper, is it the case that biblical themes are represented in song. Rather, the mutual transformations and performances of music and the Bible open up beyond "reductive textualism" (assumptions that texts are somehow separable from materiality, embodiment, practice, and community) into the mutual imbrication of relation, experience, and social power in American history. The key for scholarship, then, is how to realize fully these social worlds without losing the text; and how to acknowledge textual complexity without losing practice and sound.

These aspirations seem reasonable, given that musicologists describe performance as something that helps us organize our experience of the world, in terms of time, social organization, and aesthetics.[7] As McDannell has shown, the materiality of the Bible is ineluctably a part of its practical history in America. As Laurie Maffly-Kipp, Allen Dwight Callahan, and others show, the Bible's role in African Americans' self-determination and political practice exemplifies its enduring social resonance. And as Stephen Marini and David Stowe note, the multivalence of biblical texts has produced an array of creative American musical expressions. As valuable as these individual foci are, I contend that no understanding of the Bible and music can hold apart ritual, politics, experience, and textual creativity, since all are intertwined in performance: sacred texts are articulated in song, hymns are composed to enshrine religious convictions, and rituals shot through with music that establishes boundaries (between self and other, sacred and profane), facilitates communication, and focuses the senses. In subsequent sections, I show how the conventional areas of scholarly inquiry into the Bible and music—historical traditions and musical genres—actually amplify rather than muffle the questions and concerns that can reorient scholarship, focused newly on intersubjectivity and power, the senses, and cultural blendings.

Histories

Blackburn's "reductive textualism" has loomed large in American religious history, whose key questions about the Bible and music have been shaped by a scholarly focus on biblical themes and their place in denominational life.[8] These emphases have generally been employed in studies of the seventeenth to nineteenth centuries, and so I explore the aforementioned new questions and themes in the same period as a way of unpacking alternate interpretations. Beyond the representational link between the two idioms, there is much in even the earliest phases of colonial history showing how music regularly manifested other dimensions of the Bible in practice, as did the Bible of music. We might look first to the way these generative sources were means by which Americans navigated pluralism, teaching them how to read each other and their new setting. For example, in the earliest examples of contact between European colonists and indigenous populations, the Bible and music were co-present. This is true not only in the establishment of Spanish missions in the Southeast and Southwest but also in more far-flung expeditions. For example, accompanying Drake's voyage one encounters reports of Native Americans sitting attentively (perhaps curiously) as colonists sang Psalms and Bible verses.[9] And at Jamestown and other English settlements, psaltery, popular dance, and military music blended frequently.[10] Biblical sound thus emerges historically as a medium of exchange and negotiation between different populations in their discrepant arrangements of power.

As already noted, much scholarship in this area has focused on the development of American hymnody. As Mark Noll and others show, the Puritans wrote regularly about how one of their most important possessions in the New Israel would be their Books of Psalms, whose settings for joyful noise (inspired by Col. 3:16 and the biblical Psalms themselves) sustained their ocean crossings and their beliefs that they would create in America a new Zion.[11] Across colonial American Christianity, there developed a range of compositional contributions to liturgical song. Formal expressions of this work included not only older European religious music but also Wesleyan hymns and varied musical settings for text. From the network of English-speaking "free churches" of the American colonies, a rich musical tradition arose centered on the popular hymns of the Englishman Isaac Watts or the nascent Protestant "shape note" tradition in North America in the seventeenth and eighteenth centuries.[12] As the American cultural historian David Stowe notes, this family of traditions—reaching from the seventeenth to the nineteenth centuries—maintained the importance of psalmody and hymnody (adaptations of specific biblical texts) to early

American religion, in official liturgy and in other arenas like Revolutionary War songs.[13] Beyond the formal and syntactic, though, lies another, even broader current of social power and intersubjectivity that merits further attention.

In a period of not only rising pluralism but also increased awareness of the "sphere" of religion in relation to the state, the market, civil society, and the private, one fascinating arena in which understandings of identity and morality were taught and took shape was religio-musical education. In both public culture and diverse educational locations, ceremonialism and pedagogy both included the regular singing of biblical hymns and psalms that served as reminders of religious identity and affiliation and crucial sensorial, experiential registers for the inculcation of good morality and citizenship. Examples from singing schools and elsewhere included psalters, instructions for youth, and other collections of musical templates, such as John Anderson's 1791 "discourse on the divine ordinance of singing Psalms," Ann Taylor's 1813 "Hymns for Infant Minds," and the fantastically detailed "Psalm C. To be sung at the tea party given in the town-hall at Natick, October 28, 1846, for the purpose of raising means to purchase a copy of Eliot's Indian Bible, to be preserved in the archives of the town."[14] Texts like these oriented listeners in terms of not only sacred knowledge but also in terms of law and identity.

So these and other historical periods and concerns can be remapped more broadly. Beyond the focus on hymnody and representation in discretely bounded religious communities, music and the Bible themselves were woven into—and thus can tell of—an expanding public sphere, with all its related issues of often fractious pluralism, overlapping identities, and protest and power. Not only was adaptation to, and negotiation of, these new realities musical, as I contend, the new religious identities opening up during this period were characterized by particularly intense forms of religious experience that can be appreciated freshly by attending to biblical music and its social location.

As the historian of American religion Ann Taves notes, the revival circuit of the mid-eighteenth century and early nineteenth century facilitated the increased circulation of official hymnody and psalmody in new territories, at revivals and camp meetings, but it is also critical to keep in mind that the rise of evangelicalism also entailed the emergence of new musical and experiential engagements with the Bible.[15] Primitive Baptists sang regularly in what have been called "miniature sermons."[16] Barton Stone led "singing exercise[s]" at Cane Ridge, in order to inculcate Bible sensibilities more thoroughly.[17] It is here that many interpreters locate the emergence of, broadly speaking, American gospel music, as part of what Nathan Hatch describes as the period's more democratic and egalitarian "reordering of preaching and print communications."[18] But as suggestive as these observations are, the key question seems to be less one of communication as such as of the intermingling of emotionality, discourse, and new communities taking shape. The co-resonance of music and the Bible makes clear that these matters cannot be disentangled.

Biblical sound was also the medium for the adaptation and assimilation sought by new religious communities as well, and not simply a feature of their liturgies. Aside from the enduring vitality of more formally traditional hymnody, this kind of proliferation in American music tracked roughly with that of American religion more broadly, as it grew through often contested interactions, frequently involving immigrant populations as they blended into American cities. The Catholic mass, with its rich musical repertoire as a kind of experiential constant, assisted Irish, German, Italian, and East European communities in navigating the complexities of American public life, schooling, and commerce. Similarly, in the adaptations of synagogue life first in Reform Jewish communities and later elsewhere, the ongoing role of the *shemah* and cantorial leadership oriented practitioners even as Jews adapted the language, the location, and the social implication of their practice.[19]

This combination of discourse, social change, and emotionality is seen perhaps most clearly in the emergence of African American spirituals from slave songs, field hollers, and ring shouts, religious rituals involving coordinated song and circular movement. Across multiple generations, the extraordinary appropriations of, and improvisations on, the Bible in African American cultures made this sacred text central to not only artistic culture but also, in Callahan's estimation, to the realization "of the justice of God."[20] This much is known on a general level, but these linkages must also be understood as exemplifying Phillis Wheatley's conviction that sensation was one powerful register in which the Bible could be felt working on the devout.[21] The words did more than simply justify protests or artworks: "the text 'got all up into' their bodies, animating them to respond with music and movement to the transcendent God implied in the iconic text."[22] As the religious historians Edward Blum and Paul Harvey note, exile and exodus were converted into sacred creativity through the very multitudes of the text, and the quickening pulse of music has brought these properties home with particular experiential resonance.[23] Music and expressive culture formed one of the most powerful settings for and mediums of biblical themes of deliverance, even as biblical critics also argued for limiting these practices.[24]

Such examples show that at every historical stage and among disparate communities, the Bible and music open into and exemplify the broader themes that this chapter follows. While general histories of American religion focus perhaps insufficiently on the importance of music, to deepen the focus on music does more than simply fill a scholarly need. As the historian of American religious print Paul Gutjahr and others show, scholarship sensitive to the multivalent use and interpretation of texts demonstrates how, in the late nineteenth century, the Bible begins to inform American culture (and thus music) far more broadly than in the arena of religious traditions alone.[25] So while the stories of the latter continue to inform scholarship of this and other periods—McDannell's focus on the use of vernacular music in Catholic mass following the Second Vatican Council, or R. G. Robins's work on music in Pentecostal services—the post-Civil War birth of multiple strains of distinctively American music, all indelibly shaped by biblical tropes, marks a point in history when biblical music begins manifestly to flow beyond denominational boundaries.[26]

Institutions still mattered, of course, as exemplified by the growth of African American denominations or the power of the Moody Bible Institute; but perhaps more significant was music's increased circulation more broadly, evidenced by the popularity of an 1875 recording of gospel hymns by the Moody Institute's own Ira Sankey and Philip Bliss.[27] And when, on Christmas Eve 1906, "the first wireless radio broadcast in the United States consisted of a religious program of devotional music and Bible reading," the annunciation of technology as central to the new American century announced further changes still.[28] This new moment of circulation marks not just a historical transition, but an opportunity for scholarship to engage more deeply the Bible's implication in hybrid religious identities and contested social spaces. Important work has investigated traveling gospel troupes, Yiddish Theater Music, Sacred Harp players, and new idioms like rag and blues.[29] But collectively, the significance of these developments can be amplified more suggestively by noting how improvisation, that hallmark of American religiosity, led to new and creative fusions of music and biblical themes, increasingly prevalent in ostensibly secular musical genres.

GENRES

Beyond the limits of tradition and scholarly convention, the historical era of denominational flourishing and expanded hymnody reveals complex engagements with pluralism,
power, and the senses. In the interminglings of genre, we encounter sound as broad and
polyphonic as American life itself. This intermingling is a common subject in religious
studies and elsewhere, though the study of popular music has also focused largely on representation and imagery, as with important essay collections such as *Religion and Popular
Culture in America* and *God in the Details*.[30] The idea of the fluidity and cross-pollination
of genres remains important given that new artists and genres of significance emerge,
and deserve documentation. And in the growing literature on the abundance of musical
genres—Paul Griffiths on new music, Robert Walser on heavy metal, Tricia Rose on rap—
religion emerges as a lyrical theme, with comparably little attention to its implications for
community, reception, practice, or power dynamics.[31] As I will note in specific examples,
scholars of American religions have demonstrated appropriate attention to these factors,
but they also often overlook the key textual components of these genres.

So as a counterpoint to the historical section, I suggest that further themes and questions get to what is salient about the Bible and music, and are best exemplified by a focus
on genre music since 1900: the increased fuzziness of the category "religion," the deepened
intertwining of social power and music, the emergence of new communities of sound, and
religio-musical hybrid identities. Each genre of significance contains abundant tropes and
representations, but we might profit by studying them as they link up to a different analytic
that I signal in each instance.

Perhaps the clearest example of the benefits of discourse orientation is in the musical out-
growths of congregational music. Dating all the way back to the eighteenth century, the distinctive African American Baptist and Methodist performance style fused emotionality and
prophetic thematics. In the twentieth century, practitioners like Thomas A. Dorsey, Mahalia
Jackson, Sister Rosetta Tharpe, and the Fisk Jubilee Singers widely popularized these musical forms, whose expressivity amplified the intensity of religious language that spoke to
religio-political oppression (e.g., "Go Down, Moses" or "Joshua Fit' the Battle of Jericho").[32]
As the music business scholar Don Cusic shows, it was largely out of the same milieu that
produced gospel that country and blues emerged.[33] Older African American religious and
musical traditions fed into the emergence of the blues, even if it was often scorned as irreli-
gious. The music's feeling and themes remain indelibly linked to religion (whether in Sonny
Treadway's use of steel guitars in his Florida ministry or in biblical meditations like Blind
Willie Johnson's "John the Revelator"). Many blues musicians strive openly to replicate the
musical feeling of gospel groups like the Golden Gate Quartet without actually performing spirituals; and B. B. King avowed that blues began with slavery and developed through
the sanctified church, its sense of emotional urgency and meaning through suffering both
drawn from the Bible.[34]

Country music's emergence from early twentieth-century "hillbilly music" was associated with troubadours like Hank Williams, June Carter and Johnny Cash, Willie Nelson,
and Loretta Lynn, whose songs often contained religious themes.[35] In certain cases, these
are performances of rearranged traditional music, as with the Carter Family's "Can the

Circle Be Unbroken?" or Jimmie Rodgers' "Just a Closer Walk with Thee." More commonly, country music has narrated the role of the Bible in culture, as with Charles Tillman's "My Mother's Bible" (1893), Don Reno's "I'm Using My Bible for a Roadmap" (1951), Kitty Wells's "Matthew 24," and the influential work of the Louvin Brothers.[36] Other examples abound, and there is complexity in the appropriation of such thematics. But when we turn to other musical forms, fresh interpretive possibilities emerge more clearly.

Most understandings of "classical music" posit its roots in traditional performances of sacred music, whose many developments featured biblical allusions or text settings in both content and inspiration.[37] Early American history substantiates this, with the First and Second New England Schools of composition extending European forms while hewing closely to biblical material. But the history of American classical music shows, despite a persistent engagement with biblical sources, the increased blurring of the boundaries between the religious and the nonreligious, a trend which resonates with scholarly focus on the haziness of the category "religion" itself in contemporary life.[38] We see this blurring in nineteenth-century improvisations on the Bible: William Bradbury scandalized audiences by including biblical characters in an opera; Horatio Parker blended Episcopalian liturgical music with celebrations of place; and James C. Johnson adapted the cantata form for nonreligious usage.[39]

Such boundary-blurrings were facilitated by the emergence of arts organizations in the nineteenth century, many of which, like the Handel & Haydn Society, effectively bridged church communities and the growing, diversifying public spheres alongside them. Perhaps even more exemplary of the changing shape of American culture was the proliferation of composers in the early twentieth century—from Charles Ives to Aaron Copland to Joplin to William Grant Still—who saw the Bible and its musical settings as part of a larger vernacular tapestry of American culture whose breadth and diversity itself would shape their new, cross-genre musical investigations. This absorption of religious song and themes also shaped subsequent compositional developments, like the émigré Kurt Weill's 1946 *Kiddush*. Similar engagements continued throughout the remainder of the twentieth century, with Leonard Bernstein's "Mass," Harry Partch's "Revelation in the Courthouse Park," and Steve Reich's use of Hebrew cantillation, among many examples. Not only were such compositions anything but clear examples of devotional music, the unimpeded, near viral circulation of religious materials for multiple uses parallels the increased regularity with which religious identity and cultural creations develop outside the formal structures of religious traditions and institutions. Further interrogation of these processes, with the Bible both product and facilitator, could help to elucidate the complex relation between genre music and shifting conceptions of what counts as "religion."

Much scholarship has focused on the role the Bible has played in inspiring twentieth-century social movements, especially the civil rights movement.[40] Yet there remain associations and resonances awaiting further excavation, as with the Bible's links to new histories and rituals that facilitate self-determination among African Americans outside of, or alongside, conventional social movement formations. One of the most suggestive of these associations is in jazz music. As I show in my book *Spirits Rejoice!*, one finds in jazz history a reexamination of the intimate links between biblical veneration and expressive music alongside a suspicion that its rhythmic exuberance banished the sacred.[41]

Yet throughout jazz's existence, some of its major composers have turned to the Bible to articulate the liberating dimensions of African American history through sound. Duke

Ellington regularly composed settings for scripture (arrangements for Psalm 23 or God's creation of song).[42] In Ellington's final decades, he composed three Sacred Concerts, extended engagements with biblical materials to be performed in churches. Jazz settings of liturgical materials have since become a semi-regular form of religious expression among musicians including Mary Lou Williams, Louis Bellson, Dave Brubeck, and Deanna Witkowski. Jazz musicians have also regularly narrated the history in which the Bible became central to African American religion. In the works of Charles Mingus, John Carter, and Wynton Marsalis, one hears historical self-consciousness become a part of twentieth-century reinvestigations of the Bible for renewed liberatory potential. And still others, like the bandleader and visionary Sun Ra, fashioned their historical-musical understandings against the Bible, which he described as "a dangerous book" for its doctrine of "salvation through sorrow, suffering and shame."[43]

One finds a related hybridity in rap, which soon after its 1970s inception became known for its incisive social commentary (the rapper and music producer Chuck D called it "black people's CNN") and wide-ranging creative expression.[44] Yet though social and religious panic accrued to the sometimes flamboyant and confrontational sound, often associating it with black criminality and imagined sexual exploits, rappers themselves often embraced religiosity for both social criticism and inspiration. What is more, these religiosities have often been not merely accompaniments to (lyrical pointers) but constitutive of rap's emergence as a kind of alternate public sphere, in Michael Warner's sense that a public is established in part when audiences and interlocutors pay attention.[45]

The ghetto environments that have produced much rap music have been interpreted biblically, with rappers from Kanye West and Coolio, 2pac Shakur, and Nas, likening it to the "valley of death" in Psalm 23:4. West, who infamously calls himself Yeezus and talks to God on his albums, regularly engages biblical texts, as in "Mercy," which refers to Jesus's description of Hell in Matthew 13:42: "It is a weeping and a moaning and a gnashing of teeth." Mos Def and Talib Kweli's Black Star criticizes materialism in rap by alluding to 1 Timothy 6:10: "Money's the root of all evil."[46] KRS-One of Boogie Down Productions nodded to the biblical roots of Afrocentrism, claiming "Genesis chapter eleven, verse ten / Explains the genealogy of Shem."[47] Such analyses are means to establish critical distance, making of the music (despite its varied reception dynamics) a source of identity apart from mainstream conceptions of racial, political, and religious identity.

Rap music has birthed additional explicitly Christian and Jewish idioms, from Stephen Wiley's 1985 "Bible Break" to D.C. Talk, Lecrae, or Matisyahu. These have spawned different kinds of audiences or civic identities, formed largely around questions about the sinfulness of rap as "secular" or "fallen" music as sinful or as enabling positive social change.[48] Thus, questions about the mere presence of biblical referents or the consolidation of religious idioms themselves might illustratively be extended to consider their uses in alternate publics or in negotiations of the distinction between secular and religious.

Similar negotiations are at work in rock music broadly speaking, and some scholarship has reflected suggestively on it.[49] It is not difficult to locate examples of rock music's use of biblical themes, from Bruce Springsteen's ruminations on Genesis in "Adam Raised a Cain" to Bob Dylan's multiple engagements with biblical imagery ("All along the Watchtower" echoes Isaiah 21:5-9 in the line "two riders were approaching"), Leonard Cohen's "Story of Isaac," The Byrds' "Turn! Turn! Turn!," or the Violent Femmes' "It's Gonna Rain." Other musicians have engaged the Bible via criticism, as with punk and metal denunciations of religion (Minor Threat and Slayer), onstage defamations of Bibles (Marilyn Manson), or regular invocations of biblical imagery for nonreligious or anti-religious purposes (such as Metallica's "Creeping Death" or Black Breath's "Black Sin (Spit on the Cross)").[50]

Yet one of the most interesting examples of the Bible's use in religio-musical hybridity comes not just in the deployment of such themes and images but in creative mimesis as an avenue to new collective affective environments. Among the many religio-musical sub-cultures in America, from neo-pagan festivals to performance art collectives or evangeli-cal megachurches, it is in contemporary Christian music's (CCM) often surprising uses of biblical settings that we see evidence of new modes of religious practice that might generate new scholarly interpretations beyond mere examinations of musical text settings. As David Stowe and Eileen Luhr show, when CCM emerged in the 1970s, its emergence could be understood minimally as a "biblical" alternative to popular music.[51] But it also captures the intersubjective and multisensory formation of contemporary religious identities, as is evidenced by the new shapes of community taking shape around "biblical" genre music, from the popular ministry of Rob Driscoll at Seattle's Mars Hill to the emergence of the "alternative" scene surrounding the Cornerstone festival, featuring performers like David Bazan of Pedro the Lion and Rob Lacey, who performs "a three-minute version of the entire Bible" between band sets. Among these performers and audiences, the Bible is understood as protean not just in form but in affect and implication, realized collectively and individu-ally simultaneously.[52]

While contemporary music continues to resound with biblical imagery—in Nickel Creek or Mumford and Sons, U2 or Lady Gaga—the focus on genres in this section shows not only how various historical traditions have developed in conversation with vernacular cultures but also how religious communities themselves are now being reshaped precisely by these idiomatic expressions, with their regular engagements with social issues and intersubjectivity. Against a merely documentarian impulse among scholars, I have sug-gested here that within and alongside the text are multitudes and complexities that can ori-ent future scholarship. These dimensions are sociological and historical as well as textual, and their presence shows how the generativity of religious texts captures something of the larger creativity in American religions. Across genres, the Bible is the impetus for creating music, the background condition for history, or a launchpad into new experiences and social interventions. The shifting uses of the Bible in these genres suggest ways of recon-sidering how sacred texts and music interact, showing that beyond "reductive textualism," these improvisations on form and text reveal the creative possibilities of tradition and interpretation.

CONCLUSIONS

The scholar of comparative religions David Chidester has written that the Bible "marks fundamental oppositions," or meaningful distinctions.[53] Improvising on this notion, there are many implications—both scholarly and otherwise—that emerge from focusing jointly on music and the Bible in American culture. Broadly speaking, this focus ampli-fies several enduring impulses literally and metaphorically. Even when there is minimal lyrical content, the texts are transformed when made musical: they become fluid and interactive, both subjects and objects of musical transformation, and in this interactive fluidity they open up to multisensory engagement. It is precisely to this multivalence and mutual embeddedness that scholarship should attend more regularly, since the textual does more than simply mark an experiential limit; it often is the avenue of a different kind of experience for practitioners. In its incorporation into broader sonic and social environments, whether within formal traditions or not, the Bible not only represents a particular form of religiosity—annunciation, confession, or narration—but also grafts its particular meanings onto other forms such as blessings, praises, purification, or contemplation.[54] Music not only arouses and focuses emotions similar to those denoted in the text; it also situates the text in a more cognitively and experientially immersive milieu.

In American music broadly we see and hear the ongoing potency and resonance of biblical themes and allegories. In the country's songs of longing, in official hymnody, in rap or classical music, we hear reflections on biblical notions of time and history, on sacrifice and redemption, on exaltation and liberation. To a certain extent, the differences in inflection may depend partly on how different modes of reading the Bible figure in music-making, from the allegorical (Dylan) to the literal (the Louvin Brothers) to the prescriptive (often found in CCM). Beyond the enumeration of examples, themes help shape the interaction between text and sound such as the apocalyptic or the providential.

Further still, the Bible and music reveal reflections on and contributions to American assessments of communal and social life. Certainly the historical record in America is, as historians from Sydney Ahlstrom to Perry Miller to James Morone and hundreds more attest, littered with experiments artistic, social, and political reflecting varied understandings of the Bible: messianism, providence, social criticism and the adjustment to norm, liberation and constraint, the peaceable kingdom, and the righteous commonwealth.[55] The Bible is not only a register of social capital, in its capacity to sanctify certain social arrangements, but a vehicle of critique, perhaps most powerful when announced in song.[56] Just as song can become the medium through which text is ritually manifested, so too can it become the embodiment not simply of biblical injunctions about sound, but—in protest music (during the civil rights movement, for example), in debates about commercialization, in reflections on intersubjectivity (as in censorship debates)—about the devout follower's relation to the world and how best to live in it.

The Bible is situated in a confluence of traditions in which Americans have imagined and narrated their complex relation to the past, to civic identity, and to national purpose, among other concerns.[57] To note this is not to suggest that the music discussed here can be reduced to its sociological or historical resonances, in a kind of "reductive sociology." Instead, I have sought in these observations to compel the reader with lines of questioning that begin from the assumption that the sounds themselves simply are the history, the religion, and the society they aim also to evoke, nowhere more vividly than in their improvisations on the Bible.

One finds across a range of American religious creations—visual art and architecture, landscape, and cyberspace—that no area of American life and expression is unmarked by the Bible. But music is perhaps among the most enduring and powerful of these. For in all its varieties, the momentariness of sound and its emotionality provide for a wide range of Americans, across time and place, a means of relating to their sacred texts as revivified, protean, and personal. For these and other reasons, I have striven in this chapter to complicate long-standing scholarly orientations to sacred texts and music. Rather than jettisoning altogether the focus on free-standing genres or historical traditions, I have proposed harvesting from these areas new, cross-cutting inquiries that resonate with current religious studies scholarship while also, more important, getting to the complex textures of the Bible's ever-evolving role in American music.

NOTES

1. Anne M. Blackburn, "The Text and the World," in *The Cambridge Companion to Religious Studies*, ed. Robert A. Orsi (Cambridge: Cambridge University Press, 2012), 151.
2. George Lewis, "Omar's Song: A (Re)construction of Great Black Music," *Lenox Avenue: A Journal of Interarts Inquiry* 4 (1998): 77.
3. See Philip V. Bohlman, Edith L. Blumhofer, and Maria M. Chow, eds., *Music in American Religious Experience* (New York: Oxford University Press, 2006); and Lawrence Sullivan, ed., *Enchanting Powers: Music in the World's Religions* (Cambridge, Mass.: Harvard University Press, 1997).
4. Colleen McDannell, ed., *Religions of the United States in Practice*, vol. 2 (Princeton, N.J.: Princeton University Press, 2001).
5. Blackburn, "The Text and the World," 163, 159.
6. See, for example, J. Cheryl Exum, ed., *Retellings: The Bible in Literature, Music, Art and Film* (Leiden: Brill, 2008); Edwin Good, "The Bible and American Music," in *The Bible and American Arts and Letters*, ed. Giles Gunn (Philadelphia: Fortress Press, 1983), 131–58; and Michael Lieb, Emma Mason, Jonathan Roberts, and Christopher Rowland, eds., *The Oxford Handbook of the Reception History of the Bible* (New York: Oxford University Press, 2013).
7. Robert Walser, ed., *Keeping Time: Readings in Jazz History* (New York: Oxford University Press, 1999).
8. Nathan Hatch and Mark Noll, eds., *The Bible in America: Essays in Cultural History* (New York: Oxford University Press, 1982), while it does not specifically examine music and the Bible, exemplifies a still-predominant scholarly focus on literary themes (rather than experience, materiality, or intersubjectivity) in interpreting the Bible in American religion and culture.
9. See Michael D. McNally, *Ojibwe Singers: Hymns, Grief, and a Native American Culture in Motion* (St. Paul: Minnesota Historical Society Press, 2009).
10. Thomas E. Warner, "European Musical Activities in North American before 1620," *Musical Quarterly* 70, no. 1 (1984): 89–93. See also Nicholas E. Tawa, "Songs of the Early Nineteenth Century, Part 1: Early Song Lyrics and Coping with Life," *American Music* 20, no. 4 (2002): 361–80.
11. See Mark Noll, *In the Beginning Was the Word: The Bible in American Public Life, 1492-1783* (New York: Oxford University Press, 2015), 61–66, 112–14; and David Stowe, *How Sweet the Sound: Music in the Spiritual Lives of Americans* (Cambridge, Mass.: Harvard University Press, 2004), 26–27.
12. See Stephan A. Marini, *Sacred Song in America: Religion, Music, and Public Culture* (Urbana-Champaign: University of Illinois Press, 2003).
13. Stowe, *How Sweet the Sound*, 29, 38.
14. John Eliot, and A.W.T., "Psalm C. To be sung at the tea party given in the town-hall at Natick, October 28, 1846, for the purpose of raising means to purchase a copy of Eliot's

Indian Bible, to be preserved in the archives of the town" (Natick, Mass.: s.n., 1846), https://searchworks.stanford.edu/view/8128423.

15. Ann Taves, *Fits, Trances, and Visions: Experiencing Religion and Explaining Experience from Wesley to James* (Princeton, N.J.: Princeton University Press, 1999).

16. John R. Bowen, *Religions in Practice: An Approach to the Anthropology of Religion*. 6th ed. (New York: Routledge, 2013), 159.

17. Stowe, *How Sweet the Sound*, 255.

18. Nathan O. Hatch, *The Democratization of American Religion* (New Haven, Conn.: Yale University Press, 1989), 146.

19. See Chester Gillis, *Roman Catholicism in America* (New York: Columbia University Press, 2000); and Jonathan D. Sarna, *American Judaism: A History* (New Haven, Conn.: Yale University Press, 2004) for discussions of these and related changes, and of their broader historical contexts.

20. Allen Dwight Callahan, *The Talking Book: African-Americans and the Bible* (New Haven, Conn.: Yale University Press, 2008), 48.

21. See Phillip M. Richards, "Phyllis Wheatley and Literary Americanization," *American Quarterly* 44, no. 2 (1992): 163–91.

22. Richards, "Phyllis Wheatley and Literary Americanization," 82.

23. Edward J. Blum and Paul Harvey, *The Color of Christ: The Son of God and the Saga of Race in America* (Chapel Hill: University of North Carolina Press, 2014), 60–62, 129–30.

24. See Curtis Evans, *The Burden of Black Religion* (New York: Oxford University Press, 2008). See also Samuel Floyd, *The Power of Black Music: Interpreting Its History from Africa to the United States* (New York: Oxford University Press, 1996); and Lawrence Levine, *Black Culture and Black Consciousness: Afro-American Folk Thought from Slavery to Freedom* (New York: Oxford University Press, 1977).

25. Paul Gutjahr, *An American Bible: A History of the Good Book in the United States, 1777-1880* (Stanford, Calif.: Stanford University Press, 1999). For particularly vivid illustrations of this point, see Gutjahr's discussion of the American Bible Society (29–37), illuminated bibles (70–76), and the film *Ben Hur* (166–73).

26. Colleen McDannell, *The Spirit of Vatican II: A History of Catholic Reform in America* (New York: Basic Books, 2011); and R. G. Robins, *Pentecostalism in America* (Westport, Conn.: Praeger, 2010).

27. Candy Gunther Brown, "Practice," in *Religion in American History*, ed. Amanda Porterfield and John Corrigan (London: Wiley-Blackwell, 2010), 308.

28. David Chidester, *Authentic Fakes: Religion and American Popular Culture* (Berkeley: University of California Press, 2005), 30.

29. See Kiri Miller, "'First Sing the Notes': Oral and Written Traditions in Sacred Harp Transmission," *American Music* 11, no. 1 (1993): 90–111.

30. See Bruce David Forbes and Jeffrey H. Mahan, eds., *Religion and Popular Culture*, 2nd ed. (Berkeley: University of California Press, 2005); and Eric Mazur and Kate McCarthy, eds., *God in the Details: American Religion in Popular Culture*, 2nd ed. (New York: Routledge, 2010).

31. See Paul Griffiths, *Modern Music and After*, 3rd ed. (New York: Oxford University Press, 2011); Tricia Rose, *Black Noise: Rap Music and Black Culture in Contemporary America* (Middletown, Conn.: Wesleyan University Press, 1994); and Robert Walser, *Running with the Devil: Power, Gender, and Madness in Heavy Metal Music* (Middletown, Conn.: Wesleyan University Press, 1993).

32. For a useful overview, see LeRoy Moore Jr., "The Spiritual: Soul of Black Religion," *American Quarterly* 23, no. 5 (1971): 658–76. See also Jerma A. Jackson, "Sister Rosetta Tharpe and the Evolution of Gospel Music," in *Religion in the American South: Protestants and Others in History and Culture*, ed. Beth Barton Schweiger and Donald G. Mathews (Chapel Hill: University of North Carolina Press, 2004).

33. Don Cusic, *The Sound of Light: A History of Gospel Music* (Bowling Green, Ohio: Bowling Green State University Popular Press, 1990).

34. William Ferris, *Give My Poor Heart Ease: Voices of the Mississippi Blues* (Chapel Hill: University of North Carolina Press, 2009), 191–92.

35. See Robert M. Shelton, "Doing Theology with Willie Nelson," in *Theomusicology. A Special Issue of Black Sacred Music: A Journal of Theomusicology* 8, no. 1, ed. Jon Michael Spencer (Durham, N.C.: Duke University Press, 1994): 254–64.

36. Charles Reagan Wilson, "A Larger View: Self-Taught Art, the Bible, and Southern Creativity," in *Coming Home! Self-Taught Artists, the Bible, and the American South*, ed. Carol Crown (Jackson: University Press of Mississippi, 2004), 81. See also John Hayes, "Religion and Country Music," in *Religion Compass* 4, no. 4 (2010): 245–52.

37. See Ter Ellingson, "Music and Religion," in *The Encyclopedia of Religion*, vol. 9, ed. Mircea Eliade (New York: MacMillan, 1993), 163–72.

38. See, among many others, Russell McCutcheon, *Manufacturing Religion: The Discourse on Sui Generis Religion and the Politics of Nostalgia* (New York: Oxford University Press, 2003).

39. See Juanita Karpf, "If It's in the Bible, It Can't Be Opera: William Bradbury's Esther, the Beautiful Queen, in Defiance of Genre," *American Music* 29, no. 1 (2011): 1–34; and Jacklin Bolton Stopp, "James C. Johnson and the American Secular Cantata," *American Music* 28, no. 2 (2010): 228–50.

40. See Mark A. Chancey, Carol Meyers, and Eric M. Meyers, eds. *The Bible in the Public Square: Its Enduring Influence in American Life* (Atlanta, Ga.: Society of Biblical Literature, 2014); and Paul D. Hanson, *A Political History of the Bible in America* (Louisville, Ky.: Westminster John Knox Press, 2015).

41. Jason C. Bivins, *Spirits Rejoice! Jazz and American Religion* (New York: Oxford University Press, 2015).

42. John Sanders, liner notes to *Black, Brown & Beige*, Duke Ellington and His Orchestra Featuring Mahalia Jackson, Columbia CK 65566, CD, 1999.

43. Sun Ra, quoted in John Corbett, ed., *The Wisdom of Sun Ra: Sun Ra's Polemical Broadsheets and Streetcorner Leaflets* (Chicago: WhiteWalls, 2006), 115.

44. Jeff Chang, "Rapping the Vote with Chuck D," *Mother Jones*, September 1, 2004, http://www.motherjones.com/media/2004/09/chuck-d.

45. Michael Warner, *Publics and Counterpublics* (New York: Zone Books, 2005).

46. Mac McCann, "The Best Bible Verse-Checks in the History of Rap," *FaithStreet*, July 29, 2014, http://www.faithstreet.com/onfaith/2014/07/29/the-best-bible-verse-checks-in-the-history-of-rap/33362.

47. See Charise Cheney, "Representin' God: Rap, Religion, and the Politics of Culture," *The North Star: A Journal of African American Religious History* 3, no. 1 (1999), https://www.princeton.edu/~jweisenf/northstar/volume3/cheney.html.

48. David L. Moody, *Political Melodies in the Pews? The Voice of the Black Christian Rapper in the Twenty-First Century Church* (Lanham, Md.: Rowman and Littlefield, 2012), 4.

49. See Eileen Luhr, *Witnessing Suburbia: Conservatives and Christian Youth Culture* (Berkeley: University of California Press, 2009); and David W. Stowe, *No Sympathy*

for the Devil: Christian Pop Music and the Transformation of American Evangelicalism (Chapel Hill: University of North Carolina Press, 2011).

50. See Deena Weinstein, *Heavy Metal: The Music and Its Culture*, rev. ed. (Boston, Mass.: DaCapo Press, 2000).

51. See Eileen Luhr, *Witnessing Suburbia: Conservatives and Christian Youth Culture* (Berkeley: University of California Press, 2009); and David W. Stowe, *No Sympathy for the Devil: Christian Pop Music and the Transformation of American Evangelicalism* (Chapel Hill: University of North Carolina Press, 2011).

52. Andrew Beaujon, *Body Piercing Saved My Life: Inside the Phenomenon of Christian Rock* (Boston, Mass.: DaCapo Press, 2007), 15.

53. Chidester, *Authentic Fakes*, 137.

54. See Guy Beck, ed., *Sacred Sound: Experiencing Music in World Religions* (Waterloo, ON: Wilfrid Laurier University Press, 2006).

55. Sydney E. Ahlstrom, *A Religious History of the American People* (New Haven, Conn.: Yale University Press, 1972); Perry Miller, *Errand into the Wilderness* (Cambridge, Mass.: Belknap Press, 1956); and James A. Morone, *Hellfire Nation: The Politics of Sin in American History* (New Haven, Conn.: Yale University Press, 2004).

56. R. Laurence Moore, *Selling God: American Religion in the Marketplace of Culture* (New York: Oxford University Press, 1995), 34–35.

57. Claudia Setzer and David A. Shefferman, eds. *The Bible and American Culture: A Sourcebook* (New York: Routledge, 2011).

BIBLIOGRAPHY

Beaujon, Andrew. *Body Piercing Saved My Life: Inside the Phenomenon of Christian Rock.* Boston, Mass.: DaCapo Press, 2007.

Bivins, Jason C. *Spirits Rejoice! Jazz and American Religion.* New York: Oxford University Press, 2015.

Blum, Edward J., and Paul Harvey. *The Color of Christ: The Son of God and the Saga of Race in America.* Chapel Hill: University of North Carolina Press, 2014.

Bohlman, Philip V., Edith L. Blumhofer, and Maria M. Chow, eds. *Music in American Religious Experience.* New York: Oxford University Press, 2006.

Bowen, John R. *Religions in Practice: An Approach to the Anthropology of Religion.* 6th ed. New York: Routledge, 2013.

Callahan, Allen Dwight. *The Talking Book: African-Americans and the Bible.* New Haven, Conn.: Yale University Press, 2008.

Chancey, Mark A., Carol Meyers, and Eric M. Meyers, eds. *The Bible in the Public Square: Its Enduring Influence in American Life.* Atlanta, Ga.: Society of Biblical Literature, 2014.

Chidester, David. *Authentic Fakes: Religion and American Popular Culture.* Berkeley: University of California Press, 2005.

Clark, Lynn Schofield, ed. *Religion, Media, and the Marketplace.* New Brunswick, N.J.: Rutgers University Press, 2007.

Cusic, Don. *The Sound of Light: A History of Gospel Music.* Bowling Green, Ohio: Bowling Green State University Popular Press, 1990.

Evans, Curtis. *The Burden of Black Religion.* New York: Oxford University Press, 2008.

Exum, J. Cheryl, ed. *Retellings: The Bible in Literature, Music, Art and Film.* Leiden: Brill, 2008.

Ferris, William. *Give My Poor Heart Ease: Voices of the Mississippi Blues.* Chapel Hill: University of North Carolina Press, 2009.

Floyd, Samuel. *The Power of Black Music: Interpreting Its History from Africa to the United States.* New York: Oxford University Press, 1996.

Forbes, Bruce David, and Jeffrey H. Mahan, eds. *Religion and Popular Culture.* 2nd ed. Berkeley: University of California Press, 2005.

Gillis, Chester. *Roman Catholicism in America.* New York: Columbia University Press, 2000.

Griffiths, Paul. *Modern Music and After.* 3rd ed. New York: Oxford University Press, 2011.

Gutjahr, Paul C. *An American Bible: A History of the Good Book in the United States, 1777–1880.* Stanford, Calif.: Stanford University Press, 1999.

Hanson, Paul D. *A Political History of the Bible in America.* Louisville, Ky.: Westminster John Knox Press, 2015.

Hatch, Nathan O. *The Democratization of American Religion.* New Haven, Conn.: Yale University Press, 1989.

Hatch, Nathan O., and Mark Noll, eds. *The Bible in America: Essays in Cultural History.* New York: Oxford University Press, 1982.

Levine, Lawrence. *Black Culture and Black Consciousness: Afro-American Folk Thought from Slavery to Freedom.* New York: Oxford University Press, 1977.

Lieb, Michael, Emma Mason, Jonathan Roberts, and Christopher Rowland, eds. *The Oxford Handbook of the Reception History of the Bible.* New York: Oxford University Press, 2013.

Luhr, Eileen. *Witnessing Suburbia: Conservatives and Christian Youth Culture.* Berkeley: University of California Press, 2009.

Marini, Stephan A. *Sacred Song in America: Religion, Music, and Public Culture.* Urbana-Champaign: University of Illinois Press, 2003.

Mazur, Eric, and Kate McCarthy, eds. *God in the Details: American Religion in Popular Culture.* 2nd ed. New York: Routledge, 2010.

McCutcheon, Russell. *Manufacturing Religion: The Discourse on Sui Generis Religion and the Politics of Nostalgia.* New York: Oxford University Press, 2003.

McDannell, Colleen, ed. *Religions of the United States in Practice.* Vol. 2. Princeton, N.J.: Princeton University Press, 2001.

———. *The Spirit of Vatican II: A History of Catholic Reform in America.* New York: Basic Books, 2011.

McNally, Michael D. *Ojibwe Singers: Hymns, Grief, and a Native American Culture in Motion.* St. Paul: Minnesota Historical Society Press, 2009.

Moddy, David L. *Political Melodies in the Pews? The Voice of the Black Christian Rapper in the Twenty-First Century Church.* Lanham, Md.: Rowman and Littlefield, 2012.

Moore, R. Laurence. *Selling God: American Religion in the Marketplace of Culture.* New York: Oxford University Press, 1995.

Morone, James A. *Hellfire Nation: The Politics of Sin in American History.* New Haven, Conn.: Yale University Press, 2004.

Noll, Mark. *In the Beginning Was the Word: The Bible in American Public Life, 1492–1783.* New York: Oxford University Press, 2015.

Orsi, Robert A., ed. *The Cambridge Companion to Religious Studies.* Cambridge: Cambridge University Press, 2012.

Robins, R. G. *Pentecostalism in America.* Westport, Conn.: Praeger, 2010.

Rose, Tricia. *Black Noise: Rap Music and Black Culture in Contemporary America.* Middletown, Conn.: Wesleyan University Press, 1994.

Sarna, Jonathan D. *American Judaism: A History*. New Haven, Conn.: Yale University Press, 2004.

Schweiger, Beth Barton, and Donald G. Mathews, eds. *Religion in the American South: Protestants and Others in History and Culture*. Chapel Hill: University of North Carolina Press, 2004.

Smith, Christian. *American Evangelicalism: Embattled and Thriving*. Chicago: University of Chicago Press, 1998.

Stowe, David. *How Sweet the Sound: Music in the Spiritual Lives of Americans*. Cambridge, Mass.: Harvard University Press, 2004.

———. *No Sympathy for the Devil: Christian Pop Music and the Transformation of American Evangelicalism*. Chapel Hill: University of North Carolina Press, 2011.

Sullivan, Lawrence, ed. *Enchanting Powers: Music in the World's Religions*. Cambridge, Mass.: Harvard University Press, 1997.

Taves, Ann. *Fits, Trances, and Visions: Experiencing Religion and Explaining Experience from Wesley to James*. Princeton, N.J.: Princeton University Press, 1999.

Walser, Robert, ed. *Keeping Time: Readings in Jazz History*. New York: Oxford University Press, 1999.

———. *Running with the Devil: Power, Gender, and Madness in Heavy Metal Music*. Middletown, Conn.: Wesleyan University Press, 1993.

Weinstein, Deena. *Heavy Metal: The Music and Its Culture*. Revised ed. Boston, Mass.: DaCapo Press, 2000.

CHAPTER 31

....

PERFORMING THE BIBLE

....

JAMES S. BIELO

CONSIDER two moments in American religious history, separated by nearly 130 years. The first moment is set on the shores of Chautauqua Lake, in New York's far southwestern corner. In 1874 the Chautauqua Institution created a 400-foot landscape model of "biblical Palestine," complete with mountains, rivers, seas, and cities in miniature.[1] The model was part of Chautauqua's broader Methodist project to train Sunday School teachers. In this re-created landscape, Chautauqua Lake was transformed into the Mediterranean Sea. Visitors were transported to the model by boat and encouraged to envision themselves stepping off onto scriptural territory.

The second moment transports us to Orlando, Florida. Eleven miles northeast of Walt Disney World, the Holy Land Experience (HLE) opened in 2001. HLE is "a living, biblical museum"—or "biblical theme park" or "theme park cum pilgrimage center"—founded by a Christian Zionist ministry and purchased in 2007 by Trinity Broadcasting Network, a charismatic televangelism ministry. HLE features live Passion Play re-enactments and re-created scenes from a Protestant themed first-century Jerusalem: Old City entrance gates, Western Wall, Garden Tomb, Second Temple on Mount Moriah, and a large floor model of the city circa 66 A.D. (see figure 31.1). [2]

What unites these two moments, separated as they are by century, location, explicit function, self-understanding, institutional affiliation, and technology? They are both Protestant re-creations of "the Holy Land": modern-day Israel-Palestine and the historical setting for the sacred stories of Christian scripture. In this essay, I explore how sites like biblical Palestine and the HLE are much more than the sum of re-created parts. They index a broader phenomenon among American Christians: an impulse to not just read the Bible but to perform it. By closely analyzing the cultural production of sites that perform the Bible, we gain distinctive insight into key dynamics of religious materiality and American religious culture. Ultimately, I argue that performing the Bible is a strategy for actualizing the problem of authenticity, something that animates any and every lived expression of Christianity. All Christians must reckon with the irreducible fact that while they are embedded in tradition, they are separated from their origins temporally and, for most Christians, geographically, linguistically, and culturally. Performing scripture, akin to pilgrimage, works to collapse the distance between present and past, promising a closer bond with an idealized authenticity.

FIGURE 31.1 Jerusalem floor model at Holy Land Experience. Photo by author.

MATERIAL RELIGION

Studies of material religion reflect what has been called the "media turn" in the study of religion.[3] This turn has recalibrated the center of analytical gravity to the forms and processes of religious mediation. A central question for the media turn is how religious actors use different material channels—from physical objects to technological apparatuses and the human sensorium—to shape religious experience, communication, and learning. The organizing theoretical conceit is that mediation is constitutive of religious worlds, not simply a decorative byproduct or practical necessity. Religious actors use material forms to address the central problems that animate their religious tradition(s), such as authority, belonging, and presence. The media turn has put to rest tired ideologies that doubt or dismiss the fact that religious life is at its core entangled in life's gritty and polished materialities.[4]

Acts of performing the Bible exemplify central themes in material religion, such as the cultivation of physical environments (from modified landscapes to elaborately fashioned experiential worlds). They also illustrate the process of trans-mediality (the mobility of a cultural form across multiple media genres). For example, the communications scholar Mark Wolf analyzes the artistic processes and professional industry of fantasy world-making. He argues that "transmedial growth and adaptation enrich an imaginary world beyond what any single medium could present, and also make the world less tied to its medium of origin."[5] In this way, the Bible is not so different from, say, *Lord of the Rings*. When the Bible is performed, it works in a trans-medial fashion, moving among written text, live theater, museum, garden, theme park, and other genres of place and ritualization.[6]

Understanding the Bible as trans-medial resonates with the argument that "the Bible" cannot be reduced to simply being a book.[7] Rather, "the Bible" is an open category that can be variously expressed. A volume of sixty-six translated texts is one expression, but so are other textual versions (children's Bibles, manga Bibles, illustrated Bibles, braille Bibles for the blind), stained glass art, films, television mini-series, live theater productions, board games, video games, and so on. Materialized attractions like Chautauqua's Palestine Park and Orlando's HLE are further trans-medial expressions of the category "Bible."

As a comparative phenomenon of material religion, performing the Bible raises significant questions. For example, how does existing in a trans-medial state shape interpretive and ideological relations with scripture? How do experiences with the performed Bible interact with the experience of Bible reading? What kinds of ritual action do people construct for biblical performances? How do material channels of body, technology, and object intersect amid biblical performances to shape religious experience? The following section prepares the ground for such questions by providing a descriptive tour of selected American sites. In doing so, I hope to re-create something of the experiential promise these attractions offer to visitors.

How Has the Bible Been Performed?

There are more than 200 sites across the United States that perform the Bible. In this descriptive tour, I highlight a few examples from four reoccurring types and a further example that illustrates something of the idiosyncratic possibilities for performing the Bible across genres.[8]

Holy Lands

Perhaps a good place to begin is where our opening moments left off. Palestine Park and the HLE are not America's only Holy Land re-creations. There have been at least fifteen others.[9] Some are no longer operative. For example, in 1869 a parachurch Holiness Methodist movement started a camp meeting in the sleepy Atlantic town of Ocean Grove, New Jersey. Ocean Grove aimed to meld leisure, urban escape, and spiritual regeneration.[10] In 1879, five years after Chautauqua's debut, Ocean Grove added a scale model of nineteenth-century Jerusalem to its attractions. Visitors were led on virtual tours, mimicking the Palestine tours that became popular after the Civil War.[11] A 1919 description by an Ocean Grove Camp Meeting Association trustee boasted that the model had 1,200 miniature trees, cost $2,500 to create (approximately $57,000 in 2015 dollars), and was "so accurate in the reproduction that scores of travelers who have visited Jerusalem have found keen delight in identifying its different sections and even individual buildings."[12]

Other American Holy Lands are still open for business. For example, there is the Biblical History Center (BHC) in La Grange, Georgia.[13] La Grange is a small city of about 30,000

people, one-hour drive southwest of Atlanta. The BHC was founded in 2006 by a theologically trained archaeologist who began working in Israel-Palestine in 1973. The Center sits
on the city's western edge, nestled amid an industrial corridor, and receives around 12,000
visitors per year. The site's self-described mission is to "help people encounter the ancient
biblical world through its history and culture."[14]

The BHC's main display, "the archaeological garden," emphasizes domestic and agri-
cultural elements of ancient biblical life, including a goat hair tent, grape stomping vat,
sheepfolds tombs, threshing floor, olive crusher, watchtower, underground grain silo, and
vineyard (see figure 31.2).

Each replica is explained on a self-guided map and posted signage, and each is linked
to an Old and/or New Testament biblical text. Other features include an archaeological
showcase of over 200 "ancient artifacts" from biblical lands. These artifacts are on loan from
the Israel Antiquities Authority and are housed behind glass in a separate, tornado-proof
enclosure where photographs are not permitted. In the main building visitors in groups of
ten or more can arrange a ninety-minute "biblical meal" in rooms replicating a first-century
dining experience.[15]

The archaeological garden is a thoroughly sensorial experience. The area is mostly outdoors (with partial covering and a few covered replicas), which means visitors feel the day's
weather conditions. As you progress on the self-guided tour, you walk on loose, sandy
gravel. You are surrounded by Levantine botanical varieties, lending the aroma of scriptural
flora. Roosters crow from an enclosed cage and flying birds chirp. There are numerous

FIGURE 31.2 Inside the goat hair tent at the Biblical History Center. Photo by author.

tactile, interactive elements: ascending a hill to stand in the watchtower, descending down steps to the bottom of the grain silo, pushing the olive crusher, touching the coarse and firm goat hair tent.

The Center's next addition was in progress as of summer 2015. The founder has purchased land adjacent to the current site, where he plans to construct a walking map of the Holy Land—from the Negev desert north to the Galilee. Such a landscape model would reprise the strategy of America's first re-created Holy Land at Chautauqua.

Holy Houses and Stairs

"The Holy Land" offers numerous geographic, architectural, and archaeological forms to re-create. But performing the Bible can also concentrate on a single site. Such is the case with replicas of "the Holy House" and "the Holy Stairs."

The Holy House is a reference to the Basilica della Santa Casa in Loreto, Italy. According to Catholic tradition, the Basilica contains the original house from Nazareth where Mary and Joseph raised Jesus. To avoid destruction, angels transported the house from Judea to the location in Italy. As early as 1631, when a replica was built in Prague, re-creations of the site have proliferated and become pilgrimage destinations. In the United States, there are at least four Holy Houses. For example, in Worcester, Massachusetts, a replica site includes relics from Loreto. There is the Our Lady of Walsingham Church and Shrine in Houston, Texas, which is actually a replica of another replica: a Catholic and Anglican replica of Loreto in Walsingham, England, based on a Marian revelation in 1060.[16] A Holy House replica built in 1973 resides at the National Blue Army Shrine of Our Lady of Fatima in Washington, New Jersey. The Shrine's website states that "stones from the actual Holy House in Italy were pulverized and added to the mortar used to construct the Holy House Chapel. The Chapel is the same size as the original Holy House and is constructed similarly."[17]

The Holy Stairs (Scala Santa) are a reference to a set of twenty-eight steps in Rome near the Vatican. According to Catholic tradition, these are the same steps Jesus walked up to meet Pontius Pilate and were transported to Rome in the fourth century by Helen, the mother of Constantine. Pilgrims to the site traditionally ascend the steps on their knees. Replica sites exist throughout the world, including at least five in the United States. For example, there is the National Shrine of the Cross in the Woods in Indian River, Michigan, located just south of the bridge to the Upper Peninsula. The centerpiece of this site is a twenty-eight-foot tall bronze statue of a crucified Jesus. In 1956, three years before the bronze figure was attached to the wooden cross, twenty-eight steps were built on one side leading up to the foot of the cross.

Creation Museums

Performing the Bible is not restricted to re-creating particular biblical scenes. It can also be about performing a particular biblical hermeneutic and worldview. This is most clearly exemplified by the genre of "creation museums" that exist throughout the world. There are at least forty globally, twenty-eight of which are in the continental United States.

What is a creation museum?[18] As a family resemblance of traits, the following interlaced elements define the genre:

- Promotes a young earth creationist worldview, including: the age of the earth is approximately 6,000 years old, human beings are a special creation of God (not the result of biological evolution), humans and dinosaurs co-existed because God created all living things in successive days as recorded in the Book of Genesis, and the Flood of Noah was a literal historical event killing all but the eight people onboard the ark;[19]
- Supports the textual ideology that the Christian Bible is God's inerrant and authoritative revelation to humanity;[20]
- Rejects the legitimacy of evolutionary science (often performed in a vehemently antagonistic register);
- Argues for the legitimacy of "creation science," which is the use of selected scientific theory and method to support creationist tenets;[21]
- Presents an evangelical Gospel message of born-again salvation.

A few creation museums are mobile (i.e., put-up-take-down-in-a-day), but most are brick and mortar attractions. Ranging widely in size and technological quality, all are affiliated with either a ministry, congregation, or youth camp. Most important, creation museums feature curated exhibits that teach the above five points of creationist content.

What do producers and supporters hope for in a creation museum? The genre of "museum" is revealing in itself because it marks the creationist movement's public ambition to wrest cultural authority away from mainstream science by producing their own version of the natural history museum. A significant aim for creation museums is the edification and training of committed creationists, to better equip adherents as witnesses for creationism. Of course, there are also hopes for the religious transformation of visitors, converting non-creationists to creationism and non-Christians to Christianity. For a closer portrait, consider two museums that teach very similar creationist content, but pursue the task with different resources.

Just west of Akron, Ohio, is the Akron Fossils and Science Center. Family owned, this 4,500-square-foot museum opened in 2005 after two years of construction. The building sits at the intersection of small two-lane roads and affords parking for about twenty cars. Outside on the property, there is a small play area for children and a 200-foot zip line. The museum itself offers only tours guided by a staff member. The roughly one-hour experience moves through four spaces: a welcome room that poses creationist questions; a "geology and archaeology" room that combines evidential appeals from these sciences with negative biographic profiles of famous evolutionary scientists and an argument for why dragon legends explain human–dinosaur coexistence; a "biblical authority" room that argues for a literalist reading of the Book of Genesis; and, a gift shop area with one book shelf and small trinkets (including items such as dinosaur figurines). Fluorescent lighting, low ceilings, and a musty smell pervade the space.

Two hundred and fifty miles to the south is the Creation Museum (CM) in Petersburg, Kentucky, just across the Ohio River from Cincinnati. CM is the product of Answers in Genesis (AiG), an internationally known creationist "apologetics ministry." AiG was founded in 1994 and broke ground on CM in 2001. Six years later, the 75,000-square-foot, $30 million project opened to public controversy and media fanfare.[22] CM is at least an all-day experience, if not more, once you explore the petting zoo, botanical gardens, zip line course (twenty different lines, the longest stretching to 1,800 feet), cafe, planetarium, lectures by AiG researchers, large bookstore/gift shop, lobby with exhibits, and the sixteen-exhibit "Museum Experience Walk" (see figure 31.3).

Creationist supporters, media journalists, and critical and sympathetic scholars all recognize that CM is the most elaborate and technologically sophisticated creation museum to date. Indeed, places like the Akron Fossils and Science Center—deeply sincere as they are—force an appreciation of the scale, creative design, marketing savvy, and professionalism of CM. If I were a creationist, and Akron was the going standard prior to 2007, then CM would be an undeniable source of celebratory pride.

Bible as Wax Museum

Along with creation museums and Holy Lands, Houses, and Stairs, the Bible is performed through other re-creations (Noah's ark, Moses's tabernacle), gardens, Passion Plays, and art and archaeology museums. Other sites are more idiosyncratic. Consider a final example, one that appeals to a genre with roots outside the field of religion.

In Mansfield, Ohio (a one-hour drive southwest of Akron), there is BibleWalk: 300 wax figures organized into four themed tours and seventy glass-enclosed scenes.[23] Founded in 1987, BibleWalk is owned and operated by a nondenominational, conservative evangelical

FIGURE 31.3 Allosaurus fossil display at the Creation Museum. Photo by author.

church residing on the same property. The two main tours, each sixty-minutes long and led by museum staff, respectively depict Old and New Testament stories and characters. Most of the scenes are mid-action: Jonah walking away from a beached whale, Noah and family building the ark, Moses parting the Red Sea, Abraham wielding the knife over his son. Visitors progress in timed intervals from one scene to the next, with orchestral music playing overhead throughout and low-level lighting effects during selected scenes.

WHAT HAPPENS WHEN THE BIBLE IS PERFORMED?

Genres of replica, landscape, live theater, theme park, garden, and museum demonstrate the trans-medial capacity of the category "Bible." The question to consider now is what happens when the Bible is materialized. The primary argument I want to advance is that performing the Bible is a strategy for actualizing a virtual problem that animates any and every lived expression of Christianity.

The terms "virtual," "actualize," and "problem" carry precise theoretical meaning. They derive from anthropologist Jon Bialecki's model to account for the dizzying plurality of global Christianities without conceding a coherent and comparative sense of shared Christianity.[24] Bialecki uses philosopher Gilles Deleuze's concept of "the virtual": a state of potential that is not yet actualized but is ontologically real. As a virtual field, Christianity is not defined by formations like belief, ritual, or social institution. These are already actualizations of the virtual; that is, they are realizations of more open potentiality within a particular sociohistorical context. A virtual approach means conceptualizing Christianity as composed of problems that require realization. Problems are not like jigsaw puzzles that are solvable once and for all. They are more like steady churning engines, keeping the tradition in motion by continually producing new formations. In turn, the dizzying plurality of global Christianities (and their attendant range of beliefs, practices, and institutions) are all attempts to resolve a shared bundle of virtual problems.[25]

What virtual problem does performing the Bible actualize? It is the problem of Christian authenticity. All Christians must reckon with an irreducible fact: they are separated from the original version of their faith—all temporally, many geographically, and most linguistically and culturally. This problem is accentuated with each schism. The historian Paul Conkin captures this when writing about new religious movements in America: "In some sense, almost all new Christian movements have advertised their return to an early or pure New Testament church."[26] Actualizations of the problem of authenticity are about constructing and solidifying historical continuity, bolstering intimate claims of connection to a past long gone yet mediated many times over.

In performing the Bible, material channels promise particularly potent actualizing potential because they construct claims to authenticity through indexicality and iconicity. The terms "index" and "icon" come from American philosopher Charles Sanders Peirce and his semiotic model for how signs work.[27] In contrast to symbolic signs, which function according to a conventional relationship between Object and Sign-vehicle, indexical and iconic signs function via natural and mimetic relations. Smoke, for example, is a Sign-vehicle indexing its Object: fire. Sites that perform scripture must confront the question of what relationship their re-creation (Sign-vehicle) has with the Bible (Object). As strategies for claiming an authentic relationship, certain material channels appeal to ideologies of direct connection (indexicality) and resemblance (iconicity).

The most prevalent indexical strategy is to use natural materials from biblical lands as part of a re-creation. For example, the Loreto replica at Our Lady's Blue Army Shrine includes "stones from the actual Holy House in Italy." Holy Land USA in Bedford, Virginia, which ran from 1972 until 2009, included sand from the Negev Desert. The phenomenon of re-creating biblical meals incorporates foods native to Israel-Palestine, such as "fruits, dates, nuts, [and] pita bread."[28] Scriptural indexicality is elaborated most extensively by biblical gardens, of which there are more than fifty in the continental United States.[29] Visitors to biblical gardens walk pathways surrounded by flora mentioned in the Bible. These sites promise a devotional and pedagogical experience of stepping into the Bible, of engaging scripture through the fragrant smell of botanical varieties, the feel of branches and leaves, and the vibrant colors of fruits. If Holy Land pilgrimages invite travelers to walk where Jesus walked, biblical gardens invite visitors to smell, taste, and feel the botanical world that Jesus did.[30] For example, the Warsaw Biblical Gardens in Warsaw, Indiana, is a three-quarter-acre site featuring 115 different trees, flowers, shrubs, and herbs named in scripture.[31] Biblical meals and gardens operate through embodied indexical registers, offering a naturalized connection through sensory experience (see figure 31.4).

The most prevalent iconic strategy in performing the Bible is to stress aspects of size, dimension, and number. Sites emphasize that their biblical replicas are "life-size" and "exact scale models." For example, the Biblical Tabernacle Reproduction at the Mennonite

FIGURE 31.4 Warsaw Biblical Gardens. Photo by author.

Information Center in Lancaster, Pennsylvania, features "a full-size, wax figure of the high priest" and "made-to-scale" replicas of "The Golden Candlestick and Table of Shew Bread."[32] Iconic strategies, much like their indexical counterparts, work ideologically to construct a more direct connection with the past. Through claims of natural and mimetic relation, they promise an unmediated access to biblical history.

Cultural Production

Of the many thought-provoking questions we might pose about performing the Bible, I focus here on matters of production: How are sites made? This question has at least two, interrelated expressions. The first can be glossed as political economy and includes matters of institutional affiliation, legal status, land acquisition, zoning, fundraising mechanisms, construction labor, building and maintenance costs, and so on. These issues are undoubtedly important for how performances of the Bible become available to the public, but I bracket them to concentrate in another direction: the creative processes involved with making biblical re-creations. This choice emerges ethnographically. For two and a half years I conducted fieldwork with the creative team in charge of conceptualizing and designing a creationist theme park in Kentucky.[33]

On December 1, 2010, the Governor of Kentucky held a public press conference to announce a new addition to the state's tourism industry: Ark Encounter. The park is a joint venture between the for-profit Ark Encounter LLC and Answers in Genesis (the same ministry that opened the Creation Museum in 2007). Set on 800 acres of Kentucky rolling hills—forty miles south of Cincinnati, Ohio—the park's centerpiece will be an all-wooden re-creation of Noah's ark, built to creationist specification from the text of Genesis 6–9.

In a room filled with journalists, the governor was joined on stage by local politicians and Ark Encounter personnel. The press conference intended to clarify why a faith-based project was applying for the Kentucky Tourism Development Act's sales tax reimbursement program. The brief question-answer session was dominated by a legal frame, namely inquiries about Ark Encounter's constitutional legitimacy. Is it a violation of the prohibition against state establishment of religion for a faith-based project to receive a taxpayer-based economic incentive? Although, some journalists took a different approach. Given the creationist argument that humans and dinosaurs coexisted and that Noah's ark included pairs of selected dinosaur species ("kinds," in creationist theo-zoology), one journalist sardonically asked if the re-created ark would feature live dinosaurs.

Ark Encounter is a $172 million project that opened in July 2016, not quite six years after it was first publicly announced (see figure 31.5).

The completed ark required nearly four million board feet of timber, stands 85 feet wide, 51 feet tall, 510 feet long, and contains more than 100,000 square feet of themed exhibit space. From October 2011 through June 2014, I conducted fieldwork with Ark Encounter's creative team.[34]

I approach this project as an ethnography of cultural production. By following a process of production, "the making of," distinctive insight is gained about cultural content, aspiration, and identity compared to analyses that are limited to completed products or acts of consumption.[35] Studies in cultural production afford unique access to crucial acts of decision-making, logics for actualizing deeply held commitments, and, for the creative

FIGURE 31.5 Ark Encounter. Photo by author.

team, capturing creative difference and documenting what separates discarded drafts from finalized creations.

The team's daily creative labor was the ethnographic backbone of the project: spending mornings and afternoons at the design studio while they drew freehand, illustrated concept art, worked with raw materials, sketched exhibit schematics, and edited and critiqued each other's work-in-progress. I talked with the artists at their cubicles, took notes during planned and impromptu team meetings, listened to lunchtime work talk, and photographed the ubiquitous art sitting on tables, hanging on walls, and torn up in trash cans. The majority of audio recordings and field notes addressed the work of a small team working from small desks: usually tedious, frequently under deadline, ever-conscious of budgetary constraints, and constantly seeking the next imaginative breakthrough.

Visitors to the park progress through three decks onboard the ark filled with a mix of live animals, animatronic figures, interactive displays, multimedia exhibits, food vendors, and children's play areas. Each deck is designed to produce a particular affective experience. Deck One centers on the emotional drama of Noah and his family following the closing of the ark door. They are relieved to have escaped a terrifying storm, they have just witnessed mass death, and they are anxious about the weeks ahead. The creative team always talked about Deck One as the "darkest" of the decks, sensorially represented by low levels of lighting. The storm is audible; sounds of wind, rain, thunder, and debris bang against the ark's sides via surround sound speakers. Noah and his family comfort the animals and each other amid the difficult conditions.

Deck Two focuses on the tasks and challenges of living on the ark. Noah and his family are settled, going about their liminal living: the daily grind of tending the onboard garden, caring for the animals, and managing daily routines. The creative team envisioned Deck Two as the primary "how-to" deck, addressing numerous "practical" issues about the Noah story. How did they feed all the animals? What did they do with all the animal waste? How were air, water, and sunlight distributed? What did Noah's workshop and library look like? By addressing these questions, Deck Two emphasizes the creationist claim that "ancient" people were capable of incredibly sophisticated technology because of their long lifespans (Noah living to the ripe old age of 950).

Deck Three continues themes from the first two decks and introduces several new experiences. More exhibits teach about many different types of animals. More exhibits address how-to matters, such as what the passengers' living quarters were like and what technology Noah used to build the ark. Deck Three also captures the salvific realization that God's wrath has been expended, the storm is over, the waters receded, the eight passengers spared, and the whole world is now theirs. This affect transitions into further creationist teaching points about post-Flood life, such as the Tower of Babel dispersal of languages and people groups. Deck Three is the place that most explicitly teaches Protestant fundamentalist typological hermeneutics—for example, linking the story of Noah to the story of Jesus.[36]

As visitors move through the decks, 132 exhibit bays (44 per deck) combine to present a creationist narrative about the steadfast faithfulness of Noah and his family, their salvation, and, ultimately, the evangelical Gospel of salvation. The team consciously designed this iconicity of moving from darkness to light, from judgment to salvation, wanting visitors to physically experience this symbolic progression. Through the story of Noah and his family, Ark Encounter teaches creationist history, theology, and the creationist critique of evolutionary science.

Ark Encounter is, among other things, a $172 million testimony. It is missionization, massively materialized, performed in the key of biblical literalism. But the creative team's labor was far more complicated than merely a presentation of the creationist message. First, they were tasked with demonstrating the historical plausibility of reading Genesis as literal history.

They begin with the premise that it was physically and technologically possible for Noah to have built the ark described in Genesis 6. The project claims to use the exact dimensions detailed in scripture and only building materials that would have been available to Noah (namely, timber and iron). Through different exhibits the team portrays tools and techniques Noah might have used, though the project's publicity materials repeatedly explain that modern construction technology (e.g., cranes) is pragmatically necessary (e.g., to complete construction within the timeframe required by building permits).

Plausibility alone, however, is not enough. Noah's story cannot merely be told; it must be felt. What was it like to see the door close? To hear the fierce storm outside? The cacophony of animals? To live on the ark day after day? And what was it like when the dove did not return? To see the rainbow and be the center of God's saving grace? An immersive experience promises to bridge the gap between plausibility and believability, and the logic of immersive entertainment is the engine that propelled the team's creative labor. This conversion model of plausibility-immersion exemplifies how Ark Encounter, like so many attractions that perform the Bible, emerges from the tight entanglement of religion and entertainment.

To be immersed is a primary goal in our modern culture of entertainment. The anthropologist Peter Stromberg defines entertainment as any activity that allows consumers to become physically, emotionally, and/or cognitively "caught up" in a frame of role-play that transports them away from the frame of everyday reality.[37] Echoing scholars and pundits who have asserted that a demand for fun pervades modern life, Stromberg argues that our shared culture of entertainment has become "the most influential ideological system on the planet."[38] As modern consumers, we prioritize and gravitate toward leisure that is interactive, participatory, engaging, experiential—not merely consumptive.

Stromberg argues that entertainment is not just dominant vis-à-vis other cultural forms, but that the logic and values of entertainment have actually infused other cultural forms. "As Darwin argued for the survival of the fittest, we now have survival of the most entertaining . . . . The entertaining politician gets elected, the entertaining class gets the enrollment, the entertaining car is the one that sells, and over time a competition emerges to enhance entertainment value wherever possible."[39] This echoes the "Disneyization of society," in which Disney-style entertainment and leisure imperatives colonize other forms of consumer experience.[40] For example, religious studies scholar David Chidester observes how Disney's influence has created a widespread imperative to "create imaginary worlds that evoke a thematic coherence through architecture, landscaping, costuming, and other theatrical effects to establish a focused, integrated experience."[41] Ark Encounter exemplifies how religious actors are not exempt from this new Darwinian contest. Indeed, they have embraced it as enthusiastically as any other cultural producer if not more so.

Immersion was certainly an organizing imperative for the Ark Encounter creative team. For them, the project's success or failure hangs in the balance of how well they execute this strategy of creating an immersive experiential environment for visitors. Other sites that perform the Bible also demonstrate a commitment to immersion, even if they lack Ark Encounter's $172 million budget and professional talent. For example, the BHC includes a range of immersive strategies, some notably more partial than others. Like biblical gardens, the BHC includes flora indigenous to "the Holy Land," such as olive trees, inviting visitors to smell the Bible's natural aromas. Indexical features like this exist alongside plastic grapes collected in a non-operable replica of a first-century grape crusher. Then, there are more ambiguous mimetic features. As you walk through the outdoor "archaeological garden," you notice white stone scattered throughout the space, conjuring the optical experience of viewing biblical landscapes. This is an indexical illusion. All of the site's white stone is Alabama limestone, which closely approximates the color of Israel-Palestine's geologic material.

Our modern culture of entertainment is clearly at work in the cultural production of performing the Bible. However, we should not be too quick to explain immersive strategies as solely a late modern phenomenon. The goal of creating experiential conditions that transports visitors away from the world of the here-and-now to a biblical time-place has deeper historical roots. Consider again Palestine Park. Along with bringing visitors to the site by boat across the lake-cum-sea and encouraging them to envision stepping onto scriptural territory, Chautauqua capitalized on the effect of role-playing in a themed setting in other ways. Participants would attend onsite lectures dressed in Middle Eastern cloaks and robes. As the religion scholar Burke Long describes it: "Realism was the driving aim, fantasy the enabling impulse."[42]

CONCLUSION

This chapter has explored the phenomenon of performing the Bible in America. Sites that materialize the Bible invite visitors to experience scriptural stories, scenes, and characters. Whatever else their desires might be—conversion or education, devotion or inspiration—they reproduce the ideology that the Bible is a living text and the promise that scripture can always be made real in new ways.

Sites like Holy Land replicas, Creation Museums, biblical gardens, and Ark Encounter exemplify the material character of religious practice and demonstrate the trans-medial capacity of the category "Bible." In exploring these sites, I have presented two inter-related arguments. First, performing the Bible is a strategy for actualizing the virtual problem of authenticity in Christianity. Second, analyzing the cultural production of biblical re-creations reveals the centrality of entertainment imperatives for crafting these attractions.

I close by highlighting another significant question raised by acts of performing the Bible. How does materializing scripture interact with practices of reading? Performing the Bible is obviously not meant to replace the written text, so how do these two kinds of consumption (experiential and literary) interact with one another. Do adherents make them work in concert? Do they pose tensions or confusions? Does one renew energy and excitement for the other, or detract from it? These are open questions deserving ethnographic answers, but perhaps there are some historical clues with which we might begin.

Consider religious historian David Morgan's account of biblical panoramas that were toured through urban and rural churches in the late nineteenth century. He describes the example of a twenty-two-scene panorama of the Book of Revelation created by a Pennsylvania art student that toured the American South in 1880. "Visual spectacle in the form of the panorama's popular version of the sublime rivaled, even surpassed, words, making access to the events portrayed in biblical text immediate and riveting. As one fan put it after seeing the panorama . . . 'a person can learn more of the Book of Revelation in one evening than he would from reading it in a life-time.'"[43] Might contemporary Bible performances exercise this same power, activating visual piety, and elevating the role of embodied experience in internalizing the commitments of faith?

NOTES

1. Burke O. Long, *Imagining the Holy Land: Maps, Models, and Fantasy Travels* (Bloomington: Indiana University Press, 2003).
2. "About the Experience," *The Holy Land Experience*, http://www.holylandexperience. com/about/about.html. Joan Branham, "The Temple That Won't Quit: Constructing Sacred Space in Orlando's Holy Land Theme Park," *Harvard Divinity Bulletin* 36 (2008): 18–31. Ronald Lukens-Bull and Mark Fafard, "Next Year in Orlando: (Re) Creating Israel in Christian Zionism," *Journal of Religion and Society* 9 (2007): 1–20. Yorke Rowan, "Repacking the Pilgrimage: Visiting the Holy Land in Orlando," *Marketing Heritage: Archaeology and the Consumption of the Past*, ed. Yorke Rowan and Uzi Baram (Walnut Creek, Calif.: Alta Mira Press, 2004), 249–66.

3. Matthew Engelke, "Religion and the Media Turn: A Review Essay," *American Ethnologist* 37 (2010): 371–77.

4. Anderson Blanton, *Hittin' the Prayer Bones: Materiality of Spirit in the Pentecostal South* (Chapel Hill: University of North Carolina Press, 2015).

5. Mark J. P. Wolf, *Building Imaginary Worlds: The Theory and History of Subcreation* (London: Routledge, 2012), 267.

6. My thinking on the Bible as trans-medial has been greatly enriched by the work of Timothy K. Beal. For example: *Roadside Religion* (Boston: Beacon, 2005); and *The Rise and Fall of the Bible* (New York: Mariner, 2012).

7. Brian Malley, "Understanding the Bible's Influence," in *The Social Life of Scriptures: Cross-Cultural Perspectives on Biblicism*, ed. James S. Bielo (New Brunswick, N.J.: Rutgers University Press, 2009).

8. For a curated catalogue of sites throughout the world, see the digital scholarship project *Materializing the Bible*, http://www.materializingthebible.com.

9. Long, *Imagining the Holy Land*.

10. Troy Messenger, *Holy Leisure: Recreation and Religion in God's Square Mile* (Philadelphia: Temple University Press, 1999).

11. Stephanie Stidham Rogers, *Inventing the Holy Land: American Protestant Pilgrimage to Palestine, 1865–1941* (Lanham, Md.: Lexington Books, 2011); cf. Hillary Kaell, *Walking Where Jesus Walked: American Christians and Holy Land Pilgrimage* (New York: New York University Press, 2014).

12. Quoted in Messenger, *Holy Leisure*, 106.

13. This description is based on the author's visit to the site in May 2015. The Biblical History Center, formerly the Explorations in Antiquities Center, was relocated to the United States after several attempts to establish it as the Biblical Resources Museum in Jerusalem. See Amos S. Ron and Jackie Feldman, "From Spots to Themed Sites: The Evolution of the Protestant Holy Land," *Journal of Heritage Tourism* 4 (2009): 201–16.

14. Biblical History Center, http://www.biblicalhistorycenter.com/.

15. Amos S. Ron and Dallen J. Timothy, "The Land of Milk and Honey: Biblical Foods, Heritage, and Holy Land Tourism," *Journal of Heritage Tourism* 8 (2013): 234–47.

16. Simon Coleman and John Elsner, "Performing Pilgrimage: Walsingham and the Ritual Construction of Irony," in *Ritual, Performance, Media*, ed. F. Hughes-Freeland (London: Routledge, 1998).

17. "About the Blue Army Shrine," The National Blue Army Shrine of Our Lady of Fatima, http://wafusa.org/the-shrine/about/.

18. The following analysis is based on repeated visits to The Creation Museum in Petersburg, Kentucky. I have also conducted single visits to creation museums in Ohio (September 2014), Tennessee (March 2015), California (April 2015), and Georgia (May 2015).

19. See Ronald L. Numbers, *The Creationists: From Scientific Creationism to Intelligent Design* (Cambridge, Mass.: Harvard University Press, 1992).

20. For a discussion of textual ideology, see James S. Bielo, *Words upon the Word: An Ethnography of Evangelical Group Bible Study* (New York: New York University Press, 2009).

21. Christopher P. Toumey, *God's Scientists: Creationists in a Secular World* (New Brunswick, N.J.: Rutgers University Press, 1994).

22. Ella Butler, "God is in the Data: Epistemologies of Knowledge at the Creation Museum," *Ethnos* 75 (2010): 229–51.

23. This description is based on the author's visit to the site in April 2014.

24. Jon Bialecki, "Virtual Christianity in an Age of Nominalist Anthropology," *Anthropological Theory* 12 (2012): 295–319.

25. This section is revised from James S. Bielo, "Replication as Religious Practice, Temporality as Religious Problem," *History and Anthropology* (2016), doi: 10.1080/02757206.2016.1182522.

26. Paul K. Conkin, *American Originals: Homemade Varieties of Christianity* (Chapel Hill, N.C.: University of North Carolina Press, 1997).

27. Daniel Chandler, *Semiotics: The Basics* (London: Routledge, 2007).

28. Ron and Timothy, "Land of Milk and Honey," 9.

29. Between May 2015 and July 2016, I visited nine biblical gardens in the United States (Arizona, Ohio, Indiana, Michigan), Israel, and Croatia.

30. Kaell, *Walking Where Jesus Walked*.

31. Warsaw Biblical Gardens, http://www.warsawbiblicalgardens.org.

32. "Biblical Tabernacle Reproduction," Mennonite Information Center, http://www.mennoniteinfoctr.org/tabernacle.

33. Portions of this section were previously published in Bielo, "Replication as Religious Practice" and James S. Bielo, "Literally Creative: Intertextual Gaps and Artistic Agency," *Scripturalizing the Human: The Written as the Political*, ed. Vincent L. Wimbush (New York: Routledge, 2015), 20–34.

34. The methodological details of this fieldwork were unconventional in several ways. I was not granted complete access to the team's creative labor. I had to arrange each visit weeks in advance with the team. Throughout the forty-three months of fieldwork, planned visits were canceled or rescheduled on numerous occasions, often with little notice. Ultimately, I logged nearly 130 hours at the design studio. The Ark Encounter website has been an additional data source, in particular, the blog provided publicity-oriented updates on the team's productions and arguments in support of creationist claims. I supplemented this fieldwork with observations at the Creation Museum on numerous visits and observations at other Answers in Genesis events (e.g., the much publicized Ken Ham–Bill Nye debate in February 2014).

35. Matthew Engelke, *God's Agents: Biblical Publicity in Contemporary England* (Berkeley: University of California Press, 2013).

36. Susan F. Harding, *The Book of Jerry Falwell: Fundamentalist Language and Politics* (Princeton, N.J.: Princeton University Press, 2000).

37. Peter G. Stromberg, *Caught in Play: How Entertainment Works on You* (Stanford, Calif.: Stanford University Press, 2009), 2–3.

38. Stromberg, *Caught in Play*, 3.

39. Stromberg, *Caught in Play*, 8.

40. Alan Bryman, "The Disneyization of Society," *Sociological Review* 47 (1999): 25–47.

41. David Chidester, *Authentic Fakes: Religion and American Popular Culture* (Berkeley: University of California Press, 2005), 146.

42. Long, *Imagining the Holy Land*, 30.

43. David Morgan, *The Lure of Images: A History of Religion and Visual Media in America* (London: Routledge, 2007), 164.

BIBLIOGRAPHY

Beal, Timothy K. *The Rise and Fall of the Bible: The Unexpected History of an Accidental Book.* New York: Mariner, 2012.

———. *Roadside Religion: In Search of the Sacred, the Strange, and the Substance of Faith.* Boston, Mass.: Beacon, 2005.

Bialecki, Jon. "Virtual Christianity in an Age of Nominalist Anthropology." *Anthropological Theory* 12 (2012): 295–319.

Bielo, James S. "Literally Creative: Intertextual Gaps and Artistic Agency." In *Scripturalizing the Human: The Written as the Political*, edited by Vincent L. Wimbush, 20–34. New York: Routledge, 2015.

———. "Replication as Religious Practice, Temporality as Religious Problem." *History and Anthropology*. doi: 10.1080/02757206.2016.1182522, 2016.

———. *Words upon the Word: An Ethnography of Evangelical Group Bible Study*. New York: New York University Press, 2009.

Blanton, Anderson. *Hittin' the Prayer Bones: Materiality of Spirit in the Pentecostal South*. Chapel Hill: University of North Carolina Press, 2015.

Branham, Joan. "The Temple That Won't Quit: Constructing Sacred Space in Orlando's Holy Land Theme Park." *Harvard Divinity Bulletin* 36 (2008): 18–31.

Bryman, Alan. "The Disneyization of Society." *Sociological Review* 47 (1999): 25–47.

Butler, Ella. "God Is in the Data: Epistemologies of Knowledge at the Creation Museum." *Ethnos* 75 (2010): 229–51.

Chandler, Daniel. *Semiotics: The Basics*. London: Routledge, 2007.

Chidester, David. *Authentic Fakes: Religion and American Popular Culture*. Berkeley: University of California Press, 2005.

Coleman, Simon, and John Elsner. "Performing Pilgrimage: Walsingham and the Ritual Construction of Irony." In *Ritual, Performance, Media*, edited by F. Hughes-Freeland, 46–65. London: Routledge, 1998.

Conkin, Paul K. *American Originals: Homemade Varieties of Christianity*. Chapel Hill: University of North Carolina Press, 1997.

Engelke, Matthew. *God's Agents: Biblical Publicity in Contemporary England*. Berkeley: University of California Press, 2013.

———. "Religion and the Media Turn: A Review Essay." *American Ethnologist* 37 (2010): 371–77.

Harding, Susan F. *The Book of Jerry Falwell: Fundamentalist Language and Politics*. Princeton, N.J.: Princeton University Press, 2000.

Kaell, Hillary. *Walking Where Jesus Walked: American Christians and Holy Land Pilgrimage*. New York: NYU Press, 2014.

Long, Burke O. *Imagining the Holy Land: Maps, Models, and Fantasy Travels*. Bloomington: Indiana University Press, 2003.

Lukens-Bull, Ronald, and Mark Fafard. "Next Year in Orlando: (Re)Creating Israel in Christian Zionism." *Journal of Religion and Society* 9 (2007): 1–20.

Malley, Brian. "Understanding the Bible's Influence." In *The Social Life of Scriptures: Cross-Cultural Perspectives on Biblicism*, edited by James S. Bielo, 194–204. New Brunswick, N.J.: Rutgers University Press, 2009.

Messenger, Troy. *Holy Leisure: Recreation and Religion in God's Square Mile*. Philadelphia: Temple University Press, 1999.

Morgan, David. *The Lure of Images: A History of Religion and Visual Media in America*. London: Routledge, 2007.

Numbers, Ronald L. *The Creationists: From Scientific Creationism to Intelligent Design*. Cambridge, Mass.: Harvard University Press, 1992.

Rogers, Stephanie Stidham. *Inventing the Holy Land: American Protestant Pilgrimage to Palestine, 1865–1941*. Lanham, Md.: Lexington Books, 2011.

Ron, Amos S., and Jackie Feldman. "From Spots to Themed Sites: The Evolution of the Protestant Holy Land." *Journal of Heritage Tourism* 4 (2009): 201–16.

Ron, Amos S., and Dallen J. Timothy. "The Land of Milk and Honey: Biblical Foods, Heritage, and Holy Land Tourism." *Journal of Heritage Tourism* 8 (2013): 234–47.

Rowan, Yorke. "Repacking the Pilgrimage: Visiting the Holy Land in Orlando." In *Marketing Heritage: Archaeology and the Consumption of the Past*, edited by Yorke Rowan and Uzi Baram, 249–66. Walnut Creek, Calif.: Alta Mira Press, 2004.

Stromberg, Peter G. *Caught in Play: How Entertainment Works on You*. Stanford, Calif.: Stanford University Press, 2009.

Toumey, Christopher P. *God's Scientists: Creationists in a Secular World*. New Brunswick, N.J.: Rutgers University Press, 1994.

Wolf, Mark J. P. *Building Imaginary Worlds: The Theory and History of Subcreation*. London: Routledge, 2012.

PART V

THE BIBLE
AND RELIGIOUS
TRADITIONS

CHAPTER 32

··

THE BIBLE AND JUDAISM
IN AMERICA

··

JONATHAN D. SARNA

WHEREVER Jews migrate, the Bible follows them, for Jewish communal life is impossible without it. So late in 1655, perhaps a year after the first Jewish communal settlement in New Amsterdam (today New York), a Sephardic merchant named Abraham de Lucena (d. ca. 1670) arrived in town bearing a Torah, a handwritten parchment text of the Pentateuch, rolled up into a scroll, borrowed from the Jewish community of Amsterdam. The presence of this Torah scroll served as a defining symbol of Jewish communal life and culture. It created a sense of sacred space.[1]

Wherever Jews later created communities in North America, they either brought Torah scrolls with them from home, which is what the Jews who emigrated as a group to Savannah did in 1733, or they quickly borrowed Torah scrolls from elsewhere, as the Jews of Newport did in 1760. Some individual Jews are known to have brought privately owned Torah scrolls with them to the New World. Jewish religious life in smaller eighteenth-century colonial Jewish settlements like Lancaster and Reading revolved around these privately owned Torahs. Whenever a prayer quorum or *minyan* could be gathered, usually in the owner's private home, the presence of the Torah scroll defined the worship service as authentic, for the scroll contains the sacred teachings of Jewish religious life.[2]

While the ritualized public reading of the Torah from an ornamented scroll naturally focused attention on the first five books of the Bible, which Jews continue to privilege and know best, some early American Jews also possessed printed copies of all twenty-four books of the Hebrew Bible, imported from Europe. Others relied upon less expensive Christian editions of the Bible in English, even though these contained the Jewish Bible and New Testament bound together in one volume, according to the Christian canon, with headings that highlighted how the "Old Testament" prefigured the New.[3]

Millions of Christian Americans likewise possessed such Bibles, which they read, pondered, preached from, and debated. In the early decades of the nineteenth century, historian Mark Noll shows, belief in the "Bible alone" (*sola scriptura*) "constituted an anchor of religious authority in a churning sea of demographic, social and political turmoil."[4]

Even if they owned the same Bibles, however, American Jews never viewed them in precisely the same way as their neighbors did. They accorded sanctity only to the books that formed part of the Jewish Bible, resisted Christological interpretations, and recalled that their own tradition ordered the books of scripture in a different way than did Christians.[5]

Jewish biblical exegesis, by its very existence, complicated American Christian ideas of following the "Bible alone." If, after all, there were multiple texts and interpretations of the Bible, how could all of them be true? The *sola scriptura* concept, moreover, ran counter to Jewish teachings concerning the "Oral Torah." Judaism holds that there is a wealth of tradition preserved by the ancient rabbis of the Talmud that had been handed down at Sinai but not found in the written biblical text itself.

The "hidden meaning" of biblical texts even underlay many a synagogue name in early America. For example, Shearith Israel, Mikveh Israel, and Jeshuat Israel (the official names of synagogues in New York, Philadelphia, Savannah, and Newport) all reflected mystical understandings of the biblical text. Drawing upon the language of Jeremiah (14:8), Micah (2:12), and Psalms (14:7), they all hinted that the dispersion of Israel's remnant to the four corners of the world (including the New World) heralded the long-awaited ingathering of far-scattered Jews to the Land of Israel.[6]

For their part, Christians viewed Jews as "keepers of the Old Testament" who obstinately misunderstood the Jewish Bible's central message. William McGuffey's *Eclectic Third Reader* (1836-37), for example, taught a generation of American schoolchildren that the "Old Testament" was the Jews' "own sacred volume, which contained the most extraordinary predictions concerning the infidelity of their nation, and the rise, progress, and extensive prevalence of Christianity."[7] To Jews, of course, such Christological readings of the Jewish Bible were anathema.

Simultaneously, then, the Bible served both as a bridge and as a boundary marker between Jews and Christians in America. It linked the two great faiths around commonly cherished biblical teachings. And it demarcated differences over what the term "Bible" comprehends, and how the Bible's sacred words should be understood.

The vast majority of American Jews, until comparatively recent times, privileged the Jewish Bible over the Talmud, which few could read and which would not even be printed in the United States until 1919.[8] This distinguished American Jews from the mass of Eastern European Jews, whose educational priorities were precisely the reverse. In nineteenth-century America, it was the Bible and not the Talmud that bound Jews together and linked them to their neighbors. Leading Jews, like the editor, politician, and dramatist Mordecai Noah (1785-1851), believed that God's word, as found in the Jewish Bible, was "our safest guide." He once advised the American Jewish religious leader Isaac Leeser (1806-1868) to "shut the Talmud and open the Bible."[9]

Indeed, it was a Jew, Jonathan (Jonas) Horwitz (d. 1852), who, in 1812, "proposed the publication of an edition of the Hebrew Bible," the first of its kind in the United States. Many Christian clergy subscribed to the project, and it was brought to fruition two years later by the Scottish printer, Thomas Dobson.[10] In 1826, another Jew, printer Solomon Jackson (d. ca. 1847), proposed the publication of a Hebrew-English linear edition of the Pentateuch. Six leading Jews and three Christian clergy recommended the project, one of the latter highlighting the fact that the "author and editor belong to the *literal* family of Abraham."[11]

While Jackson's volume never appeared, Isaac Leeser of Philadelphia, the foremost traditionalist Jewish leader in America for over three decades, published numerous editions of the Bible, both in English and in Hebrew, during his lifetime. They formed part of his larger project aimed at educating American Jews so that they might understand and preserve their religion while luxuriating in the freedom that characterized the American setting. Having witnessed how effectively Christian evangelicals harnessed the printing press to spread the Gospel, and having experienced the joy as a young immigrant of seeing an article of his own in defense of the Jews widely distributed and reprinted, Leeser embraced the printed word with a vengeance.

Nobody in American Jewish life grasped the religious and educational potential of the printing press sooner or more effectively than Leeser. He wrote, translated, and edited more than one hundred volumes, including textbooks, prayer books, polemics, sermons, a wide-ranging journal (*The Occident*), a handsome five-volume Hebrew-English edition of the Pentateuch (1845), the first vocalized Hebrew Bible (*Biblia Hebraica*) ever printed in America (1848), and most significantly of all, the world's first full-scale English translation of the Hebrew Bible by a member of the Jewish community: *The Twenty-four Books of the Holy Scriptures; Carefully Translated According to the Massoretic Text, on the Basis of the English Version, After the Best Jewish Authorities; and Supplied with Short Explanatory Notes* (1853).[12]

The "Leeser Bible," as it came to be known, signified the arrival of Jews on the American scene. By the time it appeared, the number of Jews in the United States—most of them recent immigrants from Central Europe—was approaching 150,000, and Jewish communities had sprung up from coast to coast. Just as the construction of new synagogues announced the presence of Jews in places where none had previously reached, so too did the new Leeser Bible. No longer, Leeser exclaimed in 1856, would Jews have to defer to a translation authorized by "a deceased king of England [King James] who certainly was no prophet." His translation, made for Jews "by one of themselves," became in many ways, a Declaration of Religious Independence.[13]

Leeser's translation not only freed Jews from their reliance upon Christian translations of the Bible, it also taught the Christians who consulted it much about the Jewish view of scripture. Indeed, Leeser's biographer, Lance Sussman, characterized the translation and accompanying notes as nothing less than "an *Apologia Judaica*." It highlighted the views of traditional and modern Jewish Bible exegetes, rebutted Christian renderings that Jews found offensive, particularly in the case of controversial passages such as "until Shiloh come" (Gen. 49:10), and, as Sussman documented, "frequently explained biblical passages that might have appeared objectionable to a modern person in a way that made them more acceptable."[14] Modern critics have understandably complained that "Leeser's English was rather wooden and at many points essentially devoid of literary distinction."[15] Nevertheless, once Leeser's text appeared in a more affordable quarto edition with abbreviated notes, it stood as the standard Anglo-Jewish translation on both sides of the Atlantic for more than six decades.

Thanks in part to Leeser, many in America came to look upon Jews as experts on everything connected to the Hebrew Bible. When controversies arose over such topics as temperance and slavery, the Jewish view of scripture was often solicited, especially since leading rabbis could read its text in the original Hebrew and cite a chain of traditional Jewish authorities concerning what that text meant.[16]

In the case of slavery, Rabbi Morris Raphall (1798-1868) of New York, an ordained Orthodox rabbi with impressive university credentials, delivered a celebrated address in early 1861 that tried to prove, based on learned quotations from the Hebrew Bible, (1) that slavery had existed since antiquity; (2) that it was "no sin" as slave property was expressly placed under the protection of the Ten Commandments; and (3) that the slave should be considered a person with rights "not conflicting with the lawful exercise of the rights of his owner." He argued that this "Bible view" of slavery offered a sound basis for sectional reconciliation.[17] Raphall's address echoed familiar Protestant arguments, but nevertheless received wide circulation, coming as it did from a learned rabbi. One enthusiastic Protestant minister was so persuaded by the rabbi's close textual reading, based on the Hebrew original, that he declared the rabbi's lecture to be "as true almost as the word of God itself."[18]

Not surprisingly, opponents of slavery, significant Jewish leaders among them, condemned Raphall's literal reading of the biblical text and insisted on a more contextualized reading or one that focused on the spirit rather than on the letter of Divine law. Rabbi David Einhorn (1808-1879), a Reform rabbi and fierce opponent of slavery, argued vehemently, for example, that "the spirit of the law of God" enshrined in the creation story, where "God created man in his image" (Gen. 1:27), "can never approve of slavery."[19] What is significant is that both sides in this debate appealed to the Jewish Bible, as interpreted by rabbis who could read it in Hebrew and were familiar with its traditional commentaries.

Americans continued to look to Jews as experts on the Hebrew Bible long after the Civil War. Popular nineteenth-century Bible magazines, such as *The Old Testament Student*, welcomed Jewish participation and brought Jewish teachings concerning the Bible to non-Jewish readers. Chautauqua and other lecture forums regularly featured Jewish speakers on biblical subjects. Thanks to the Jewish philanthropist Jacob Schiff (1847-1920), Harvard University created its Semitics Museum and funded the first American archeological excavation in Palestine, which Schiff saw as the fountainhead of Semitic civilization.[20] Elsewhere, in many parts of the country, Christians consulted with knowledgeable Jews concerning what the Hebrew of the Jewish Bible originally meant and how Jews understood difficult biblical passages.[21]

These developments went hand-in-hand with the first flickers of Jewish Bible scholarship on American shores. These pioneering Jewish Bible scholars, trained in Europe, immigrated with the great wave of Central European Jews that swelled America's Jewish population from less than 15,000 in 1840 to about 250,000 just forty years later, and with the exception of Michael Heilprin (1823-1888) were active rabbis. Some, like Isidor Kalisch (1816-1886) and Isaac M. Wise (1819-1900), sought to strengthen the hands of the faithful against missionaries and higher biblical critics. Others, like Benjamin Szold (1829-1902), whose commentary on Job was the first commentary on a book of the Bible by an American Jew, wrote primarily for his peers abroad; he has been described as a "conservative critic." Michael Heilprin, meanwhile, enthusiastically promoted biblical criticism and did much to familiarize Americans of all faiths with the fruits of German scholarship. Perhaps the most creative of all the early Jewish Bible scholars in America was the eccentric Arnold Bogumil Ehrlich (1848-1919). His scholarly writings in German and Hebrew, replete with suggested emendations of the biblical text, continue to be widely consulted.[22]

The lonely efforts of these scholarly pioneers contrast with the pediatric knowledge of the Bible that characterized the mass of American Jews at that time. Like so many of their Protestant and Catholic peers, they revered the Bible more than they actually knew it. They formally studied the Bible for only a few years as youngsters in supplementary schools that met mostly on Sundays.

The textbooks Jews employed to teach the Bible were also similar to Christian volumes. Instead of word-for-word translations from the original Hebrew, common in traditional

Jewish pedagogy, American Jewish textbooks mostly relied upon catechisms with posed questions and memorized answers, as well as moralistic Bible stories (including folk legends such as the story of Abraham smashing his father's idols), and, for older children, abridged translations known as "junior Bibles." For all that these resembled Christian textbooks in form, the Jewish texts defiantly stood their ground against Christian interpretive traditions. They emphasized Jewish interpretations in place of Christian ones and sought to ensure that Jewish children identified the Bible as a Jewish book and the source of Jewish law. For example, the popular Protestant *Child's Scripture Question Book* (1853) depicted the prophet Malachi as foretelling the coming of John the Baptist, "to prepare the way before Christ." Its closely related Jewish counterpart, *Elementary Introduction to the Scriptures for the Use of Hebrew Children* (1854) depicted Malachi instead as one who came to "reform the people" and who foretold the coming of "Elijah the prophet."[23]

The mass migration of over two million Eastern European Jews to America's shores in the late nineteenth and early twentieth centuries brought to America a community of Jews who knew and respected the Jewish Bible; many of them could read it in the original. Their numbers elevated the American Jewish community into one of the world's largest, with a new responsibility to advance Jewish learning at all levels. Publication in New York of the *Jewish Encyclopedia* (1901-6), a grand summary of Jewish scholarship, reflected this responsibility and heralded American Jewry's cultural arrival. The encyclopedia devoted substantial attention to biblical subjects, making available to lay English readers traditional Jewish approaches to the Bible as well as the fruits of modern critical scholarship.[24]

The Jewish Publication Society (JPS), established in 1888, likewise committed itself to advancing knowledge of the Bible among Jews.[25] It was born amid signs of a Jewish religious revival, including newly popular adult education classes focused on the Bible sponsored by synagogues and Jewish organizations. The Leeser Bible failed to satisfy these eager students. In part, it was too expensive, many times more costly than the Bibles sold by the Protestant-sponsored American Bible Society. Even more important, in comparison with the sparklingly up-to-date scholarship of the 1885 "Revised Version" of the King James Bible, published in England, it seemed musty and obsolete. So, in 1893, the JPS began a long effort to produce a new Jewish translation of the Bible into English. After several false starts, the project came to successful fruition under the editorship of the Russian-born Max Margolis (1866-1932), one of America's foremost biblical scholars.[26]

Rather than basing his translation on the Leeser Bible or the original Hebrew text, Margolis began with the state-of-the-art Revised Version. He greatly admired its sound scholarship and majestic English. He then introduced changes—upward of 40,000 of them, by his count—to scrub away Christological readings, bow to traditional Jewish interpretations of scripture, and correct what he saw as scholarly or literary errors made by the Protestant translators. A committee of six scholars and rabbis—some traditional, some liberal—reviewed Margolis's draft and introduced further changes. Finally, in 1917, the translation was published to great fanfare. Along with other developments in the years immediately before and after World War I, the new Bible translation reflected American Jewry's changing self-image, its growing cultural independence, and its quest for preeminence. America's Jewish population had surpassed three million thanks to rapid immigration, and the community's scholarly reputation was growing.

A majority of the members of the translation committee for the new Bible, including Margolis, had received at least an important part of their formal Jewish education in the

United States, a signal of how quickly serious study of the Jewish Bible in the country had developed.[27] "We have applied ourselves to the sacred task of preparing a new translation of the Bible into the English language, which, unless all signs fail, is to become the current speech of the majority of the children of Israel," the translators boasted in their preface.[28] Looking back, in 1940, historian Abraham Neuman grasped the magnitude of their achievement: "It was a Bible translation to which American Jews could point with pride as the creation of the Jewish consciousness on a par with similar products of the Catholic and Protestant churches.... To the Jews it presented a Bible which combined the spirit of Jewish tradition with the results of biblical scholarship, ancient, mediaeval and modern. To the non-Jews it opened the gateway of Jewish tradition in the interpretation of the Word of God."[29]

The new Jewish Bible translation spawned renewed interest in the Bible at the popular level. The *American Jewish Year Book*, in 1923, provided a list of some sixty volumes on Bible and Biblical Literature, which it described as "standard books in English" on the subject, numbers of them written by American Jews. The Jewish Chautauqua Society produced educational materials on the Bible for teachers. Educator Joseph Magil (1871-1945) created a series of linear Bibles to facilitate word-by-word translations from biblical Hebrew into Yiddish or English. For Yiddish-speaking Jews, the poet Yehoash Solomon Bloomgarden (d. 1927) also produced a lyrical Yiddish translation of the Bible ("the greatest single achievement of American Yiddish poetry" according to David Roskies) that began to appear serially in the New York daily *Der Tog* from 1922. [30]

Popular interest in the Bible soon spilled over into American Jewish literature and popular culture. The poet Delmore Schwartz (1913-1966), for example, wrote a series of dramatic monologues expounding on the biblical stories of Abraham, Sarah, and Jacob. The prolific novelist Sholem Asch (1880-1957) produced, late in life, novels on Moses and Isaiah. Charles Reznikoff (1894-1976) penned *By the Waters of Manhattan*, as if reimagining Psalm 137 for a new diaspora land. Later, under the influence of the Holocaust, novelists like Bernard Malamud (1914-1986) drew upon themes from the book of Job.[31]

Filmmakers likewise turned to biblical themes. The world's first Yiddish talkie film, produced in the United States by Joseph Green (1900-1996), was entitled *Joseph in the Land of Egypt* (1932). Other Yiddish-language films featured titles like *The Sacrifice of Isaac* and *The Destruction of Jerusalem*, recycled from biblical epics originally produced for the silent screen. These stories from the Jewish Bible proved popular with Jewish audiences. They reinforced Judaism's central narratives and helped to legitimate film as an acceptable form of mass entertainment.[32]

The religious revival that followed World War II led to a series of film epics from the Jewish Bible for broader English-speaking audiences, notably such titles as *Samson and Delilah* (1949), *The Ten Commandments* (1956), and *Esther and the King* (1960). All three, according to film scholar Patricia Erens, employed biblical themes to "provide a commentary on the recent suffering of the Jewish people, their miraculous survival and their hope for reconstitution in the new State of Israel." To date, more than fifty films based on themes from the Jewish Bible have been produced in the United States. Their subjects, selected both for their dramatic power and for their familiarity to viewers, include widely known stories from Genesis and Exodus, the tale of Samson and Delilah from the Book of Judges, episodes from the lives of King David and King Solomon, and the thrilling story of Esther.[33]

The postwar revival also witnessed new interest on the part of Jews in the study of the Jewish Bible, paralleling renewed Christian interest in the "Book of Books." Rabbis in the 1950s spoke of the need "to reclaim the Bible for the Jews." Sales of the 1917 Jewish Bible translation boomed. A new Hebrew-English Bible was produced. An introduction to the Jewish Bible by Rabbi Mortimer Cohen (1894-1972), entitled *Pathways through the Bible* (1946), illustrated with Jewish themed "biblical pictures" by artist Arthur Szyk (1894-1951), became a Jewish bestseller. Synagogue Bible classes and home study programs (some of them linked to Cohen's book) proliferated. Bible-themed art books and illustrated Jewish editions of individual books of the Bible, such as Jonah and Ruth, sold thousands of copies.[34]

Against this background, the JPS decided, in 1953, to undertake a new Jewish translation of the Bible, on different principles than the 1917 translation.[35] Protestants had produced the highly successful Revised Standard Version (1952) and Catholics had likewise begun to translate the Bible anew (their New American Bible appeared in 1970). The Jewish translation promised to take full advantage of all modern scholarship, to render the Bible into modern (as opposed to King James) English, and to print the Bible according to the highest standards of contemporary typographical design. Harry Orlinsky (1908-1992), Professor of Bible at the Hebrew Union College-Jewish Institute of Religion in New York, spearheaded the new effort. He had been the lone Jew on the committee that produced the Protestant Revised Standard Version, and he insisted that the Jewish People now needed an up-to-date English translation of the Bible as well.[36]

The scholars and rabbis (Orthodox, Conservative, and Reform) who worked alongside him on the new translation were, for the most part, American-born and trained. Several taught at major universities, reflecting both the growing acceptance of Jewish studies as a legitimate academic discipline and the increased willingness on the part of universities to permit biblical studies to be taught by Jews. The goal of these rabbis and scholars was to produce a Jewish Bible translation, based on the canonical Hebrew text and sensitive to Jewish interpretive tradition, that would be respected by Jews and non-Jews alike.

That, in the end, proved easier said than done. The committee members' problems, perennial ones for Bible translators, concerned matters of principle. Should they strive above all to explain each word faithfully, or should they favor, instead, an idiomatic translation? Should they be guided by what they thought the Bible meant, or only by what the text actually said? Should their highest priority be accuracy, readability, or majesty of expression? And what about when ancient versions, like the Greek Septuagint, preserved variant readings? Might those be substituted for the traditional Hebrew text if they seemed to make more sense?

On the final point, the committee was unequivocal. Unlike its Catholic and Protestant counterparts, it undertook faithfully to follow the traditional (Masoretic) text. Every word was translated from the Hebrew original. Where committee members deviated from their Jewish predecessors was in their enthusiastic embrace of the idiomatic over the mechanical word-for-word translations that once had been normative. Instead of "Laban departed and returned unto his place," for example, the new translation crisply substituted, "Laban left on his journey homeward" (Gen. 32:1). Still, achieving agreement and compromise took years. The translation of Genesis alone went through thirteen different revisions before it won final committee approval.

When published in 1963, the translation of the Torah (Pentateuch) was warmly welcomed by Catholic and Protestant as well as Jewish scholars. Its appearance was judged an important historical event and it sold briskly. Harry Orlinsky went so far as to boast that it marked "a revolutionary breakthrough in Bible translation."[37]

The translation's opening words marked it as distinctive: "When God began to create," rather than "In the beginning." The translation avoided obsolete words and phrases and sought to render Hebrew idioms by means of their normal and most accurate English equivalents, regardless of how familiar the "standard" English of earlier translations was. In the Ten Commandments, for example, it rendered the third commandment as "You shall not *swear falsely* by the name of the LORD your God" (Exod. 20:7). The more familiar "take in vain," like other familiar but now discarded renderings, appeared only in a footnote. It also banished mechanical renderings of Hebrew particles, and archaic words like "thou" and "thy." In keeping with the linguistic spirit of the original Hebrew as well as contemporary usage, even God became a "You."[38]

Twenty more years would pass before the JPS celebrated the translation of the whole Bible in 1982, and that only came about because a second committee of translators, consisting of younger scholars, was recruited to translate the third section of the Hebrew Bible, known as the Writings. Three years later, in 1985, all three parts of the Bible translation, with revisions, were brought together in one volume entitled Tanakh—from the Hebrew acronym for Torah (Pentateuch), Nevi'im (Prophets), and Kethuvim (Writings). That title, carefully chosen, underscored the Jewishness of the new translation. A "Judeo-Christian" title like "The Holy Scriptures" was consciously rejected. Tanakh thus encapsulated an important message about the JPS Bible translation as a whole: that even though Jews had the Hebrew Bible in common with their Christian neighbors, they understood much of it differently, and even called it by a different name. A Hebrew-English edition of Tanakh followed in 1999.

Tanakh, unlike its Protestant and Catholic counterparts, was never an "authorized" Jewish translation. Although widely accepted by English-speaking Jews, no Jewish ecclesiastical body ever formally authorized it. Nor has it escaped competition and criticism.

Fervently Orthodox Jews, for example, criticized the translation for privileging modern scholarship over sacred tradition, and for deviating from classical Jewish interpretations of difficult words and passages. In 1996, Mesorah ("tradition") publications issued a rival translation, often called the Stone Tanach after the Cleveland family that funded it, that advertised itself as "faithful to the interpretation of the Sages and to the classic commentators." Part of the "ArtScroll" series, characterized by fidelity to Orthodox tradition and innovative formatting and design, it consciously eschewed critical scholarship. It also introduced Hebrew transliterations into its text, notably the word HA-SHEM, "the name," as the translation of the tetragrammaton, rendered by many English translations, including JPS, as LORD and by others as YHWH.[39]

Other critics faulted the JPS translation for its lack of attention to the aural aspects of the Hebrew text: the wordplay, the repetitions, the alliterations, the puns, and so forth. Influenced by Franz Rosenzweig and Martin Buber's translation of the Bible into German, Professor Everett Fox of Clark University created a new translation for Schocken Books—covering, so far, Genesis through Kings—that privileged the sound of the English. Although characterized in places by German-style compound adjectives and controversial neologisms, it is, more than many recent translations, one that is meant to be read aloud.[40]

Still others, most notably Professor Robert Alter (b. 1935), professor emeritus of Hebrew and Comparative Literature at the University of California-Berkeley, criticized the JPS translation on literary grounds. "Again and again," he charged, it "exhibits a tin ear for English." The Jewish translation, like its Protestant and Catholic counterparts, erred in his view in repackaging biblical syntax "to make it look as though it were composed in the twentieth century." By making the Bible's English thoroughly modern, he believes that translators sacrificed the rhythms and purposeful ambiguities of the original Hebrew. His own translation, now covering the bulk of the Bible, seeks to remedy that. Its goal, which he understands "can be only distantly realized," is "to fashion an English Bible that feels like the Hebrew, recovering the earthiness and the previous concreteness of the biblical language," with all its complexities and subtleties.[41]

More recently, the JPS Bible translation has also been criticized on feminist grounds, by those who consider the translation patriarchal, particularly since it genders God as masculine. David E. S. Stein and Carol L. Meyers, in response, published a "gender-sensitive" translation of the Pentateuch (2006), based on the JPS original, that changed words and phrases, particularly references to God, into gender-neutral terms. "Every man as he pleases," for example, became "each of us as we please" (Deut. 12:8). "Man and beast" became "human and beast" (Exod. 8:14). LORD was replaced with the word "God" along with the unvocalized tetragrammaton in Hebrew letters.[42]

Such contemporary debates over how the Bible should properly be translated and interpreted underscore the continuing relevance of the Bible to twenty-first-century American Jews. Regardless of how much they know of the Bible, and whether or not they can read it in the original, they appreciate, much as the first American Jews did back in the seventeenth century, that the Bible forms the foundation for Judaism and that Jewish communal life is impossible without it.

NOTES

1. Isaac S. Emmanuel, "New Light on American Jewry," *American Jewish Archives* 7 (January 1955): 17–23, 56; Jonathan D. Sarna, *American Judaism: A History* (New Haven, Conn.: Yale University Press, 2004), 10.
2. Jonathan D. Sarna, "Torah," in *Encyclopedia of Religion in America*, ed. Charles H. Lippy and Peter W. Williams (Washington, D.C.: CQ Press, 2010), 4:2194–97.
3. Jonathan D. Sarna and Nahum M. Sarna, "Jewish Bible Scholarship and Translations in the United States," in *The Bible and Bibles in America*, ed. Ernest S. Frerichs (Atlanta, Ga.: Scholars Press, 1988), 86–87.
4. Mark A. Noll, *America's God: From Jonathan Edwards to Abraham Lincoln* (New York: Oxford University Press, 2002), 373.
5. For a convenient guide to Jewish approaches to the Bible, see *The Jewish Study Bible*, 2nd ed., ed. Adele Berlin and Marc Zvi Brettler (New York: Oxford University Press, 2014).
6. Jonathan D. Sarna, "The Mystical World of Colonial American Jews," in *Mediating Modernity: Essays in Honor of Michael A. Meyer*, ed. Lauren B. Strauss and Michael Brenner (Detroit, Mich.: Wayne State University Press, 2008), 187–88.
7. William H. McGuffey, *The Eclectic Third Reader* (Cincinnati, Ohio: Truman and Smith, 1837; repr., Milford, Mich.: Mott Media, 1982), 69, 75; John H. Westerhoff, *McGuffey and His Readers: Piety, Morality, and Education in Nineteenth-Century America* (Nashville, Tenn.: Abingdon Press, 1978), 139. Lindley Murray's *The English Reader* (York: Longman and Rees, 1799; Stockbridge, Mass.: Charles Webster, 1822), another well-known textbook,

provided a much more positive biblically based view of the Jews; see Jonathan D. Sarna and Benjamin Shapell, *Lincoln and the Jews: A History* (New York: St. Martin's Press, 2015), 4.

8. Sharon Liberman Mintz and Gabriel M. Goldstein, *Printing the Talmud: From Bomberg to Schottenstein* (New York: Yeshiva University Museum, 2005).

9. *The Occident* 3 (April 1845): 34; Jonathan D. Sarna, *Jacksonian Jew: The Two Worlds of Mordecai Noah* (New York: Holmes & Meier, 1981), 139, 206n54.

10. M. Vaxer, "The First Hebrew Bible Printed in America," *Journal of Jewish Bibliography* 2, no. 1 (1940): 20–26; Jacob R. Marcus, *United States Jewry 1776-1985* (Detroit, Mich.: Wayne State University Press, 1989), 360–61; Sarna and Sarna, "Jewish Bible Scholarship," 90.

11. Solomon H. Jackson, *Proposals for Printing, by Subscription. . . the Hebrew Pentateuch, with the Literal Translation of Each Word in English, Above the Hebrew Word*, broadside (New York: 1826); on Jackson, see Marcus, *United States Jewry*, 193–94, emphasis in original.

12. Lance J. Sussman, *Isaac Leeser and the Making of American Judaism* (Detroit, Mich.: Wayne State University Press, 1995) is the standard biography. For a complete bibliography of Leeser's works, see the index to Robert Singerman, *Judaica Americana: A Bibliography of Publications to 1900*, 2 vols. (New York: Greenwood, 1990).

13. Sarna, *American Judaism*, 64–111, esp. 81.

14. Sussman, *Isaac Leeser*, 186–93; Lance J. Sussman, "Another Look at Isaac Leeser and the First Jewish Translation of the Bible in the United States," *Modern Judaism* 5 (May 1985): 176.

15. Leonard Greenspoon, "Jewish Translations of the Bible," in *The Jewish Study Bible*, 2nd ed., ed. Adele Berlin and Marc Zvi Brettler (New York: Oxford University Press, 2014), 2098.

16. Jonathan D. Sarna, "Passover Raisin Wine, the American Temperance Movement, and Mordecai Noah: The Origins, Meaning and Wider Significance of a Nineteenth-Century American Jewish Religious Practice," *Hebrew Union College Annual* 59 (1988): 269–88.

17. Morris J. Raphall, "Bible view of slavery: A discourse, delivered at the Jewish synagogue, 'Bnai Jeshurum,' New York, on the day of the national fast, Jan. 4, 1861" (New York: Rudd & Carleton, 1861), http://hdl.handle.net/2027/loc.ark:/13960/t6k076d64.

18. Rev. Hugh Brown, as quoted in Sarna and Shapell, *Lincoln and the Jews*, 71.

19. "David Einhorn's response to 'A Biblical View of Slavery,'" trans. from the German in *Sinai* 6 (1861): 2–22, http://www.jewish-history.com/civilwar/einhorn.html.

20. Rachel Hallote, "Jacob H. Schiff and the Beginning of Biblical Archeology in the United States," *American Jewish History* 95 (September 2009): 225–47.

21. Sarna and Sarna, "Jewish Bible Scholarship," 89–95.

22. Sarna and Sarna, "Jewish Bible Scholarship," 89–95; S. David Sperling, *Students of the Covenant: A History of Jewish Biblical Scholarship in North America* (Atlanta, Ga.: Scholar's Press, 1992), 33–67.

23. Jonathan D. Sarna, "'God Loves an Infant's Praise': Cultural Borrowing and Cultural Resistance in Two Nineteenth-Century American Jewish Sunday-School Texts." *Jewish History* 27, no. 1 (2013): 73–89, doi 10.1007/s10835-012-9168-0; Penny Schine Gold, *Making the Bible Modern: Children's Bibles and Jewish Education in Twentieth-Century America* (Ithaca, N.Y.: Cornell University Press, 2003).

24. Shuly Rubin Schwartz, *The Emergence of Jewish Scholarship in America: The Publication of the Jewish Encyclopedia* (Cincinnati, Ohio: Hebrew Union College Press, 1991), 134–45.

25. Jonathan D. Sarna, *JPS: The Americanization of Jewish Culture* (Philadelphia: Jewish Publication Society, 1989).

26. Leonard Greenspoon, *Max Leopold Margolis: A Scholar's Scholar* (New York: Society of Biblical Literature, 1987).

27. For the full story of the 1917 translation, see Sarna, *JPS*, 95–116.

28. *The Holy Scriptures* (Philadelphia: Jewish Publication Society, 1917), vi, viii.

29. Abraham A. Neuman, "Cyrus Adler—A Biographical Sketch," *American Jewish Year Book* 42 (1941): 107, http://www.bjpa.org/Publications/details.cfm?PublicationID=19828.

30. David Roskies, "Coney Island, USA: America in the Yiddish Literary Imagination," in *The Cambridge Companion to Jewish American Literature*, ed. Hana Wirth-Nesher and Michael P. Kramer (New York: Cambridge University Press, 2003), 84.

31. Schwartz's poems and many others are conveniently collected in Robert Atwan and Laurance Wieder, *Chapters into Verse: Poetry in English Inspired by the Bible*, 2 vols. (New York: Oxford University Press, 1993); Sholem Asch, *Moses* (New York: G. P. Putnam's Sons, 1951) and *The Prophet* (New York: G. P. Putnam's Sons, 1955); Charles Reznikoff, *By the Waters of Manhattan* (New York: Boni, 1930); Bernard Malamud, *Novels & Stories*, 2 vols. (New York: Library of America, 2014); Ita Sheres, "The Alienated Sufferer: Malamud's Novels from the Perspective of Old Testament and Jewish Mystical Thought," *Studies in American Jewish Literature* 4, no. 1 (1978): 68–76; see also Victoria Aarons, *What Happened to Abraham: Reinventing the Covenant in American Jewish Fiction* (Dover: University of Delaware Press, 2005).

32. J. Hoberman, *Bridge of Light: Yiddish Film between Two Worlds* (New York: Schocken, 1991), 71, 183, 236–37.

33. Patricia Erens, *The Jew in American Cinema* (Bloomington: Indiana University Press, 1984), 225–28, 355–56; see also Adele Reinhartz, *Bible and Cinema: Fifty Key Films* (New York: Routledge, 2013).

34. Sarna, *JPS*, 205–7, 233–34.

35. For what follows, see Sarna, *JPS*, 233–47.

36. Harry M. Orlinsky, "Wanted: A New English Translation of the Bible for the Jewish People," in *Essays in Biblical Culture and Bible Translation*, ed. Harry M. Orlinsky (New York: Ktav Publishing House, 1974), 349–62.

37. Quoted in Sarna, *JPS*, 242. See Orlinsky's *Notes on the New Translation of the Torah* (Philadelphia: Jewish Publication Society, 1969) for his perspective on the translation.

38. Greenspoon analyzes various passages from the translation in his "Jewish Translations of the Bible," 2100–103.

39. Nosson Scherman, *The Stone Edition of the Tanach* (Brooklyn, N.Y.: ArtScroll/Mesorah, 1996), quote is from p. xii. On ArtScroll, see Jeremy Stolow, *Orthodox by Design: Judaism, Print Politics and the ArtScroll Revolution* (Berkeley: University of California Press, 2010).

40. Everett Fox, *The Five Books of Moses: The Schocken Bible*, vol. 1 (New York: Schocken, 1995) and *The Early Prophets: The Schocken Bible*, vol. 2 (New York: Schocken, 2014).

41. Robert Alter, "Translating the Bible Again," *AJS Perspectives* (Fall 2015): 6–7. Alter's translations from the Bible include *The Five Books of Moses* (New York: Norton, 2004); *The Book of Psalms* (New York: Norton, 2007); *Ancient Israel: The Former Prophets* (New York: Norton, 2013); *The Wisdom Books* (New York: Norton, 2010); and *Strong as Death Is Love: The Song of Songs, Ruth, Esther, Jonah and Daniel* (New York: Norton, 2015).

42. E. S. Stein, ed., *The Contemporary Torah: A Gender-Sensitive Adaptation of the JPS Translation* (Philadelphia: Jewish Publication Society, 2006).

Bibliography

Aarons, Victoria. *What Happened to Abraham: Reinventing the Covenant in American Jewish Fiction*. Dover: University of Delaware Press, 2005.

Fox, Everett. *The Five Books of Moses*. Vol. 1 of *The Schocken Bible*. New York: Schocken, 1995.

———. *The Early Prophets*. Vol. 2 of *The Schocken Bible*. New York: Schocken, 2014.

Gold, Penny Schine. *Making the Bible Modern: Children's Bibles and Jewish Education in Twentieth-Century America*. Ithaca, N.Y.: Cornell University Press, 2003.

Greenspoon, Leonard. "Jewish Translations of the Bible." In *The Jewish Study Bible*, 2nd ed., edited by Adele Berlin and Marc Zvi Brettler, 2005–20. New York: Oxford University Press, 2014.

Orlinsky, Harry M. "Wanted: A New English Translation of the Bible for the Jewish People." In *Essays in Biblical Culture and Bible Translation*, edited by Harry M. Orlinsky, 349–62. New York: Ktav Publishing House, 1974.

Sarna, Jonathan D. *American Judaism: A History*. New Haven, Conn.: Yale University Press, 2004.

———. "'God Loves an Infant's Praise': Cultural Borrowing and Cultural Resistance in Two Nineteenth-Century American Jewish Sunday-School Texts." *Jewish History* 27, no. 1 (2013): 73–89, doi 10.1007/s10835-012-9168-0.

———. *Jacksonian Jew: The Two Worlds of Mordecai Noah*. New York: Holmes & Meier, 1981.

———. *JPS: The Americanization of Jewish Culture*. Philadelphia: Jewish Publication Society, 1989.

———. "The Mystical World of Colonial American Jews." In *Mediating Modernity: Challenges and Trends in the Jewish Encounter with the Modern World*, edited by Lauren B. Strauss and Michael Brenner, 185–94. Detroit, Mich.: Wayne State University Press, 2008.

Sarna, Jonathan D., and Benjamin Shapell. *Lincoln and the Jews: A History*. New York: St. Martin's Press, 2015.

Sarna, Jonathan D., and Nahum M. Sarna. "Jewish Bible Scholarship and Translations in the United States." In *The Bible and Bibles in America*, edited by Ernest S. Frerichs, 83–116. Atlanta, Ga.: Scholars Press, 1988.

Scherman, Nosson. *The Stone Edition of the Tanach*. Brooklyn, N.Y.: ArtScroll/Mesorah, 1996.

Schwartz, Shuly Rubin. *The Emergence of Jewish Scholarship in America: The Publication of the Jewish Encyclopedia*. Cincinnati, Ohio: Hebrew Union College Press, 1991.

Sperling, S. David. *Students of the Covenant: A History of Jewish Biblical Scholarship in North America*. Atlanta, Ga.: Scholar's Press, 1992.

Stein, E. S., ed. *The Contemporary Torah: A Gender-Sensitive Adaptation of the JPS Translation*. Philadelphia: Jewish Publication Society, 2006.

Sussman, Lance J. "Another Look at Isaac Leeser and the First Jewish Translation of the Bible in the United States." *Modern Judaism* 5 (May 1985): 159–90.

———. *Isaac Leeser and the Making of American Judaism*. Detroit, Mich.: Wayne State University Press, 1995.

CHAPTER 33

....

THE BIBLE
AND CATHOLICISM

....

DONALD SENIOR C.P.

THE role of the Bible in Roman Catholicism in the United States has been shaped both by the history and teaching of the universal Catholic Church and by the particular social and religious context of North America. The Bible has always had a substantial and definitive role in Catholic faith experience. Preaching and reflection on the scriptures were the heart and soul of theology from the patristic era up into the early medieval period. Prior to the advent of the printing press, the skilled scribes of monastic communities were the primary means through which the material writings of the Bible were preserved and transmitted over the centuries. Major theologians from Origen to Augustine to Aquinas produced commentaries on scripture and incorporated sermons and homilies into the body of their theological reflection.[1] Because most Christians up to the early modern period were illiterate, devotional reading of the Bible was not an option, but the content of the Bible was communicated through a number of oral and visual mediums. The Eucharistic liturgy included selections from scripture, and preaching in that context normally addressed biblical stories and teachings. Hymnody, too, drew from biblical texts and motifs; this was particularly true of the Gregorian chant that had widespread use in Catholic worship from the early medieval period until modern times.[2] As Christian art developed it, too, drew primarily on biblical subjects, with a particular emphasis on scenes from the life of Christ, Mary, and the saints.[3] The stained glass windows, mosaics, frescoes, paintings, and statuary of Christian churches traditionally portrayed biblical themes and served as a virtual catechism for congregants.[4]

CATHOLIC REACTION TO THE REFORMATION

....

The Reformation of the sixteenth century and its aftermath had a profound impact on Catholic attitudes toward and use of the Bible—a reaction that would also eventually influence the role of the Bible among Catholics in the United States. Two developments that would occur in the wake of the Protestant Reformation were especially significant.

First of all, the Protestant principle of "*sola scriptura*," that is, viewing the scriptures alone as the norm for Christian teaching and life, was a major point of contention. Martin Luther, in reaction to the perceived excesses of late medieval Catholicism (e.g., entrenched hierarchical authority, distorted popular devotions, and the exaggerated use of indulgences, etc.), appealed to the Bible as the sole normative source of Christian faith and as the touchpoint for ecclesiastical reform. In that same spirit, he considered only the books of the Old Testament included within the Hebrew canon to be inspired, moving away from the prevailing use of additional sacred books included in the Septuagint, which had also been incorporated in the Vulgate.[5] Luther compared the Catholicism of his day to his conception of Pharisaic Judaism, which he believed was legalistic and arrogant in its conviction that it could achieve salvation through works of the law. Luther, by contrast, emphasized what he considered the central message of Paul and the New Testament that salvation came through faith alone.

On its part, Catholicism reacted to the critiques of the Reformers through its "Counter-Reformation" spearheaded by the Council of Trent (1545–63). The Council disputed the notion of *sola scriptura*, insisting on the complementary role of tradition and the guiding teaching authority of the church's Magisterium, that is, official church teaching under the guidance of the pope and the bishops. The Council of Trent itself did not define the exact relationship between scripture and tradition, an issue that would continue to be a bone of contention both within Catholicism as well as between Catholic and Protestant theologians and would be one of the central issues in the discussions at the Second Vatican Council in the twentieth century. Trent also officially determined the books belonging to the inspired canon of scripture, confirming for the Old Testament the canonical list of the Septuagintal tradition that in fact had held sway in the church from the earliest centuries. One of the lasting, if not foreseen, impacts of Trent's actions was to create suspicion among Catholic religious authorities about "private interpretation" of scripture, by which was meant the kind of interpretations originating with individuals apart from the guidance of the Magisterium, which they saw as one of the ills of the Protestant approach.

A second important factor that followed upon the Reformation was the advent of the Enlightenment in Europe, with its emphasis on the rational and empirical. From this would eventually spring the development of the positive sciences, including critical historical inquiry, methods ultimately applied to the Bible itself with growing intensity in the eighteenth, nineteenth, and early twentieth centuries. The application of historical and literary critical methods to the scriptures themselves would be by most Catholic religious leaders of the time as a threat to faith and religious sensitivity. Study of the Bible from a critical historical viewpoint was judged to be excessively rationalistic in spirit and reductionist in intent. In fact, some of the practitioners of these empirical methods expressly did rule out the existence of the transcendent and thus confirmed the suspicions of Catholic authorities.[6]

Nevertheless, there were some Catholic scholars who employed historical-critical and literary methodologies in their exposition of the Bible and did so without finding these methods to be incompatible with faith in the sacred and inspired nature of the biblical texts. A notable example was Père Marie-Joseph Lagrange, OP, the French Dominican scholar and founder of what would become the prestigious École biblique in Jerusalem, a leading Catholic graduate school of biblical studies.[7] Lagrange did his professional work at the end of the nineteenth and the beginning of the twentieth centuries—a time when Catholic Church leaders were increasingly alarmed by historical-critical inquiry.

Lagrange, who believed that the Bible was best studied in the Middle Eastern context in which it was created, studied the creation narratives and legal texts of the Pentateuch in relationship to other ancient Middle Eastern creation mythologies and law codes. He also applied form, historical, and literary critical methods in the exposition of the Gospels, notably in his commentary on the Gospel of Mark. These initiatives of Lagrange and his growing influence in the world of Catholic biblical scholarship made him and the institution he founded the target of a number of repressive measures by church authorities. His commentaries were suppressed and he himself at one point was reassigned from his work in Jerusalem to teach mathematics in a high school in Toulouse! As his own journals attest, Lagrange suffered greatly from these censures by church leaders, but he was also a devout and faithful Catholic. Eventually his example of fidelity and his academic integrity, as well as that of other similar Catholic scholars of the time, would help turn the tide and persuade church leadership to be less suspicious of historical methods. But this would take time.

Suspicion of modern methods of biblical interpretation on the part of Catholic leadership reached its greatest intensity in the early decades of the twentieth century and would have strong reverberations in the United States as well as in Europe. In 1901 Pope Leo XIII established the "Pontifical Biblical Commission," a commission composed of various cardinals and bishops, along with some scholars as "consultants" to the Commission, whose purpose was to monitor Catholic biblical scholarship for any corrosive influence of a rationalistic or reductionist approach.[8] A particularly contested issue, and what would become a litmus test for orthodoxy on these matters, was the question of the Mosaic authorship of the Pentateuch. Catholic scholars who questioned this traditional view, suggesting, for example, the presence of various theological and literary traditions within the Pentateuchal corpus, fell under suspicion and were accused of questioning the historical truth of the Bible. Pope Pius X was particularly driven to combat such "errors" and in 1907 published an encyclical, *Pascendi Dominici Gregis*, that condemned a host of "modernist" errors including the questioning of the Mosaic authorship of the Pentateuch and the use of the methods of historical inquiry to analyze the Gospels.

This concern worked its way into the Catholic Church in the United States as well. Until the advent of the twentieth century, the Catholic Church in the United States was relatively small and was still considered "missionary territory" by the Vatican. Its pastoral concerns were mainly in building up a community that by the latter part of the nineteenth and early twentieth centuries was mushrooming in number under the tide of immigration; there was relatively little concern with issues of biblical scholarship, apart from the prevailing Catholic attitudes to the Bible since the time of the Council of Trent. But as the Catholic community matured, it too began to build institutions and professional associations of higher learning. The Catholic University of America was founded by the US bishops in 1887. Later, in 1936, the Catholic Biblical Association of America—a professional association of Catholic biblical scholars and teachers—was founded. In these settings, the storm created in the Catholic Church by historical-critical methods in Europe made its way to the American shores. In 1910, for example, a noted Dutch priest and biblical scholar, Henry Poels, who held the position of Professor of Old Testament at the Catholic University of America, was dismissed from his appointment after a long and arduous process because he was suspected of holding a too liberal and too "Protestant" view of biblical interpretation, including his position on the authorship of the Pentateuch.[9] The Catholic Biblical Association and its official publication, the *Catholic Biblical Quarterly*, was a battleground for these disputes, particularly as it began to be more and more populated by well-trained biblical scholars.

THE BIBLICAL REVOLUTION OF VATICAN II AND ITS IMPACT ON THE CHURCH IN THE UNITED STATES

It would be difficult to exaggerate the transforming effect of the Second Vatican Council on Catholic life and thought, especially in the area of the role of the Bible. In a certain sense, the fundamental purpose of the Council, convoked by Pope John XIII in 1959 and taking place in Rome from 1962 to 1965, was to bring Catholicism into the modern world. As in many other aspects, the deliberations of the Council had been prepared for by events and movements taking place much earlier in various parts of the Catholic world. A significant turning point regarding the Catholic view of the Bible came with the publication of an encyclical by Pope Pius XII, *Divino Afflante Spiritu*, in 1943 that effectively rejected the defensive posture the church had previously taken regarding the use of historical-critical methods in biblical interpretation. The pope called for a renewal of biblical study and devotion in the church, encouraged a new generation of biblical scholars, and called for translations based not solely on the Vulgate but on the original biblical languages. Although suspicion of modern biblical methodology and some continuing repression of Catholic biblical scholars on the part of some church officials remained, the tide had turned and the way was paved for a genuine biblical renewal within the Catholic Church.

The work of Pius XII came to full fruition with the Second Vatican Council's statement on Divine Revelation, entitled *Dei Verbum* (the "Word of God"). The original working schema for this key text was introduced at the very beginning of the Council but was ultimately rejected because it was deemed too defensive and rigid in its formulations.[10] The final and much richer version was approved by a near unanimous vote in the final session of the Council (November 1965). Several key affirmations of *Dei Verbum* continue to have a profound impact on Catholic views of the Bible and were a stimulus to a strong biblical renewal in the United States. First of all, *Dei Verbum* emphasized that "revelation" was not primarily a series of doctrinal propositions but a loving relationship between God and humanity, a relationship that issued in creation, reaching its summit in the creation of man and woman, formed in the "image and likeness" of God (Gen. 1:26). God's Word or creative impulse was also present within history, particularly within the chosen people Israel, and would come to its full embodiment in the person and mission of Jesus Christ, the Word Incarnate. The church itself would continue to proclaim the Word within unfolding history until the end of time.

Derived from this perspective, was the Council's new formulation of the relationship between scripture and tradition. Departing from a view that would see two independent sources of revelation, the Council affirmed that there was one "Word of God" expressed both in scripture and in tradition. Under the guidance of the Spirit present within the church, the Magisterium continued to play the role of guidance and discernment concerning the authentic interpretation of God's Word. The Council also emphasized that the Old Testament had revelatory value on its own and was not simply as an anticipation of the

New Testament—a point that would also be emphasized in subsequent church documents concerning the church's relationship with Judaism.[11]

During the course of the Council's deliberations and before the final formulation of *Dei Verbum*, the Pontifical Biblical Commission issued an important statement entitled "An Instruction on the Historical Truth of the Gospels" (1964), the contents of which would also influence *Dei Verbum* itself.[12] Here was a clear endorsement of the methodologies of form and redaction criticism and an assertion that the content of the Gospels themselves was formulated in an evolutionary pattern, beginning with the period of the historical Jesus and his disciples, extending into the preaching, religious instruction, and worship of the early church, and finally issuing in the literary compositions of the four evangelists—compositions that incorporated the historical traditions transmitted by the church but also shaped by the proclamation and faith experience of the apostolic church.

As important for Catholicism were the theological formulations of *Dei Verbum* and its endorsement of modern methods of biblical interpretation, equally significant were the pastoral initiatives urged by the Council in the final chapter of the decree, initiatives that would have a substantial influence on the role of the Bible in the post-conciliar church in the United States. The document called for a renewal of preaching that took its inspiration and content from the scriptures; it urged that "access to sacred Scripture ought to be open wide to the Christian faithful"—a recommendation that ran against the cautions about "private interpretation" that had prevailed in Catholic thinking; it called for updated translations into the vernacular based on the original biblical languages and encouraged that this be done with ecumenical collaboration; it urged theologians to enrich their reflections with attention to the Bible and reiterated that "the very soul of sacred theology" should be rooted in the study of the scriptures (evoking a style of theology that had characterized patristic theology); it encouraged priests, deacons, and catechists to "immerse themselves in the Scriptures by constant sacred reading and diligent study"; laity were encouraged to read the scriptures and to "become steeped in their spirit" through prayer and study; and it called for "editions of sacred Scripture, provided with suitable notes" for the use of even non-Christians and adopted to their circumstances.[13]

THE CATHOLIC BIBLICAL RENEWAL IN THE UNITED STATES

This remarkable list of pastoral recommendations was implemented in a robust way, particularly in the United States. Here, where many Protestants, particularly evangelical Christians, had a strong devotion to Bible reading and study, the recommendations of the Council were especially welcome. Already before the Council, the impact of Pius XII's encyclical in 1943 had inspired a whole new generation of Catholic scholars—at that time, mainly priests—to take up graduate study of the Bible. Most of these were trained in Catholic universities in Europe and at places like the Catholic University of America, but increasingly Catholics were trained in non-Catholics settings such as Johns Hopkins University and the divinity schools of Harvard, Princeton, Yale, and the University of Chicago. This wave of new scholars—trained in the modern methods of biblical interpretation—would also turn their energy to informing Catholic laity about the Bible. Popular workshops and study days and parochial Bible study groups began to appear throughout the country in the years immediately preceding the Vatican Council and would multiply thereafter.[14]

On the level of the church's official teaching, the impetus for a biblical renewal continued both during and after the Council. Most of the decrees of the Council itself drew deeply on biblical sources for their teaching on such issues as the nature of the church, the role of bishops and priests, the renewal of the church's liturgy, and the mission of the church in the modern world. After the Council, Pope Paul VI reorganized the function of the Pontifical Biblical Commission; what was previously meant to monitor the orthodoxy of biblical scholars was now composed of scholars themselves and was to serve as a kind of "think tank" or resource on biblical matters for the pope and his advisors. A series of important and substantial decrees would be published by the Biblical Commission: on methods of interpretation (1993—to commemorate the 50th anniversary of Pius XII's groundbreaking encyclical of 1943); on "the Jewish People and Their Sacred Scriptures in the Christian Bible" (2002), on the use of the Bible in addressing moral issues (2008), and on the question of biblical inspiration and inerrancy (2014).[15] Each of these documents was published for the sake of the wider church with the express approval of the pope and each of them reflected the strong influence of historical-critical methodology. The Commission's 1993 influential text on biblical interpretation emphatically stated that the historical-critical method and its focus on the literal meaning of the biblical text, although not the only valid approach to interpretation, was, nevertheless, foundational. At the same time, the Commission severely criticized a fundamentalist approach to biblical interpretation as incompatible with Catholic tradition because it was ahistorical and intellectually "suicidal"![16] It described "fundamentalist" as an approach that placed "undue stress" on the accuracy of certain details in the Bible, ignored textual problems found in the Hebrew or Greek, and refused to see the development of traditions found in both the Old and the New Testaments.

Another development in the wake of the Council, with great importance for the role of the Bible in Catholicism, was the institution of a three-year lectionary of readings for use in the Eucharist. Over a three-year cycle, selections from Matthew, Mark, and Luke were read each Sunday, as well as on a parallel track on weekdays. Selections from the Gospel of John appeared every year. These Gospel readings were paired with selections from the Old Testament, the Pauline writings, and other New Testament texts. Prior to the Council, the scripture readings at the Eucharist were on a single yearly cycle and in the years before the reforms of the Council the official readings were in Latin, with the faithful following along in vernacular translations available in so-called missals. Through the means of the lectionary, the vast number of Catholics in the United States who attended Sunday Eucharist on a regular basis was now exposed to a substantial portion of the Bible over the course of the three-year lectionary.[17]

No doubt influenced by Protestant devotion to Bible study, most Catholic parishes in the United States inaugurated Bible study groups. For many Catholics this would be their first experience of reading the biblical text on their own and, together with other adult Catholics, drawing their own reflections about the meaning of the biblical text for their everyday lives. In many instances, Catholics would join Bible study groups sponsored by neighboring Protestant congregations, a symptom of the mushrooming ecumenical spirit that for American Catholics was also a fruit of the Second Vatican Council. Also becoming popular was a method drawn from Catholic monastic tradition of *Lectio Divina* (literally, "Divine reading") that consisted of meditative reading and contemplation of the biblical text.[18]

For Catholic publishing houses in the United States, the biblical renewal also meant the development of a whole new set of catechetical and educational resources that incorporated biblical study within their content. Where prior to the Council, Catholic publications on scripture were sparse, an avalanche of biblical commentaries, dictionaries, study Bibles, video and audio tapes, and a host of other resources began to be available from Catholic sources. This was a phenomenon, while not absent on the European and other international arenas, that was strongly characteristic of the Catholic Church in the United States. The vast network of Catholic schools in the United States provided a ready audience for these materials. Likewise, some publishers developed correspondence courses on the Bible that could assist Bible study groups at the parish level, such as the Little Rock Scripture Study Program founded in 1974 and the Paulist Press Bible Study program. In the mid-1960s, directly influenced by the Council, the Benedictine Liturgical Press began the publication of a popular journal on the Bible, entitled *The Bible Today*—a project originally intended to be hosted by the Catholic Biblical Association of America.[19]

The biblical renewal in American Catholicism also has had a strong impact on the style and quality of preaching. The liturgical reforms of the Council had put an emphasis on the "homily" as distinct from the formal "sermon"—a feature of Catholic preaching that is different from that of usual Protestant practice. The role of the homily is to form something of an "interpretive bridge" between the biblical readings of the first part of the Eucharist (called, the "liturgy of the Word") and the Eucharistic prayer that followed. Thus, ideally, the homily was not to be topical or catechetical or provide moral instruction as such, but was to amplify the message of the lectionary readings for the day, show their connection to the Eucharist and to the lives of the worshippers. Two major documents on the renewal of preaching have been produced by the US bishops. The first, published in 1982, was entitled, "Fulfilled in Your Hearing: The Homily in the Sunday Assembly"; the second, more expansive text was published in 2013 and entitled, "Preaching the Mystery of Faith: The Sunday Homily."[20] Both emphasized the biblical roots of preaching and the particular qualities and liturgical context of the homily. "Preaching the Mystery of Faith" also provided an extensive biblical background for the preaching ministry and discussed the role of the scriptures in the formation and spirituality of priests and deacons authorized to preach at the Eucharist. In his first major exhortation entitled "The Joy of the Gospel" (2013) Pope Francis himself gave detailed attention to the ministry of preaching the homily and offered extended practical advice on the preparation and even the delivery of an effective homily.[21] The results of all this emphasis on the homily seem to be mixed. There is no doubt that Catholic preaching in the United States has become more biblically focused than ever before, but some priests find it difficult to adjust to the style and purpose of the homily and multiple surveys indicate that American Catholics continue to have complaints about the quality of the preaching they encounter at Sunday Mass.

Also as part of the biblical renewal, American Catholicism set about to provide a new translation of the Bible, that would first appear as the "New American Bible" in 1970. Prior to that American Catholics used an English translation whose roots went back to the early part of the seventeenth century with the translation of the Latin Vulgate New Testament into English at Reims, France; the Old Testament translation was produced at the English College in Douay, France—leading to the "Douay-Reims" translation. In the middle of the eighteenth century this translation would be revised by the respected English bishop Richard Challoner. The Douay-Reims translation, with its revision, would be the standard Catholic English version for nearly 300 years. Early in the twentieth century, some American Catholic scholars and church leaders decided to embark on a new translation, also from the Vulgate. It appeared in 1941 as the "Confraternity" version of the Bible. However, the mandate of Pius XII to base translations on the original biblical languages, a mandate renewed by Vatican II's *Dei Verbum*, led to the publication of the *New American Bible* that appeared in segments from 1952 until 1970 and would enjoy widespread use among Catholics in the United States. The New Testament portion was revised in 1986 and a revision of the Old Testament appeared in 2010. The quality of the NAB translation was comparable to that of such major Protestant translations such as the Revised Standard Version (RSV) and the more recent New Revised Standard Version (NRSV). The latter used more pronounced inclusive language, creating some controversy among more traditional readers. Two features of the NAB reflect its sponsorship by the Catholic bishops: it includes official explanatory footnotes that are intended to provide both essential background information but also support Catholic doctrinal perspectives, and it uses a modified form of inclusive language, reflecting official Catholic sensitivities on this point.[22]

Other trends in the use of the Bible within American Catholicism also reflect the particular social and religious context of the United States. Although feminism is not an exclusively American phenomenon, it remains particularly strong in the United States and probably found its original impetus there.[23] The feminist movement has certainly had an impact on the Catholic Church in the United States on a number of levels. The church's official stance on an all-male priesthood and the preponderance of male ecclesiastical leadership at both the international and local level have been a source of contention for many Catholic women. At the same time, Catholic women—particularly religious sisters—have exercised exceptional leadership in other areas of the church's institutional life such as healthcare and education. The number of Catholic women, both lay and religious, professionally trained in biblical studies over the past several decades has resulted in a strong presence of feminist biblical interpretation. The Pontifical Biblical Commission's 1993 statement on "The Interpretation of the Bible in the Church" had cited feminist methodology as a legitimate approach to biblical exegesis (although a footnote in the text stated that this was not the view of the entire commission!).[24] The ranks of the Catholic Biblical Association were also decidedly male (and clerical) for many decades; Sr. Kathryn Sullivan, RSCJ, one of the pioneer American Catholic women to have a prominent role in biblical interpretation after the Council, was elected vice president of the organization in 1958, but was not moved up to president—a move found to be too bold at the time. Subsequently, several women have served as presidents of the Catholic Biblical Association and its membership includes a substantial portion of women scholars. The continuing drive in the Catholic Church to include more women in the church's leadership and decision-making, particularly in the United States, has been sustained in part by the research of Catholic feminist scholars who have emphasized the significant role of women in the early church and thrown light on the often male bias of biblical interpretation.

Ecumenism as well as interreligious influence, as already noted, has also been an integral part of the more recent Catholic experience in the United States. Here again, the pluralistic social and religious context of the United States has had a significant influence. Particularly since the Vatican Council and its encouragement of ecumenical dialogue and collaboration, Protestant and Catholic scholars have worked closely together on biblical study and interpretation. The Catholic Biblical Association, for instance, has a significant number of Protestant scholars as full members. Presbyterian scholar Paul Achtemeier was elected the first non-Catholic president of the Association. Similarly, the Society of Biblical Literature (SBL) that was mainly Protestant in membership also counts numerous Catholic scholars as its members; in 1966 John McKenzie, SJ would become the SBL's first Catholic president. Virtually unheard of prior to the Council, now the collaboration of Protestant and Catholic scholars on various publishing projects and contributions in denominational biblical journals is routine.

The influence of interreligious perspectives in Catholic interpretation of the Bible has moved at a slower pace but has become increasingly significant; this is particularly true of the inclusion of Jewish scholarship. The catastrophic experience of the Holocaust (referred to in official Catholic documents as the *Shoah*—i.e., the "horror") has had a profound impact on biblical studies in general, resulting in a more accurate portrayal of first-century Judaism and a more nuanced understanding of the complex relationship between Judaism and emergent Christianity. This has been particularly true in the United States, not only because of the vitality and number of the Jewish community in this country but, in the case of Catholicism, also because of close ties between Catholics and Jews that has developed through involvement in common social causes such as the labor movement, and a mutual commitment to respectful dialogue. As a result, several Jewish scholars also participate as members and speakers in the meetings of the Catholic Biblical Association and pursue collaborative publication projects with Catholic and Protestant colleagues. Care about the portrayal of Jews and Judaism in Catholic catechetical and other educational materials has become normative. Without drawing too rosy a picture of such progress, nevertheless, in the areas of biblical study and devotion and in ecumenism and interreligious dialogue, Catholicism—and to a special degree, Catholicism in the United States—has undergone an exceptional and historic transformation in the period since the Second Vatican Council.

VERBUM DOMINI AND THE FUTURE OF CATHOLIC BIBLICAL INTERPRETATION IN THE UNITED STATES

In 2008 the Vatican hosted a general synod of bishops from around the world, an official meeting that occurs every few years. The topic of this particular synod was "The Role of the Bible in the Life and Mission of the Church." The impetus for this topic was the ongoing desire to deepen the role of the Bible in the life of the church and, particularly for Latin American bishops, the concern that Pentecostal Christian movements, with their strong and often fundamentalist biblical viewpoints, were eroding Catholic membership. The normal process is for the pope to consider the recommendations that arise from such synods and to offer a formal response. That is the case with Pope Benedict's 2010 "post-synodal exhortation" entitled, *Verbum Domini* ("the Word of the Lord").[25] Benedict, himself an accomplished theologian in his own right and one who made substantial use of the scriptures as a hallmark of his theology, produced a document that touches on several issues of particular significance for the role of the Bible in the church of the United States.

The pope reaffirmed the church's endorsement of the historical-critical methodology in interpretation of the Bible, noting that Christianity was a religion rooted in history and thus historical consciousness was essential in understanding the origin and development of Christian faith.[26] At the same time, the historical-critical method was not the only valid approach to the text, as the early patristic tradition in its approach to the Bible had already affirmed. The early church fathers made a distinction between the "literal" and "symbolic" dimensions of scripture. The latter dimension had a fourfold level of meaning (i.e., the spiritual, the moral, the allegorical, and the anagogical senses).[27] The pope cautioned that viewing the Bible only as a historical and cultural artifact was insufficient for the Catholic interpreter; rather, biblical interpretation had to be for the service of the faith community and move beyond simply historical inquiry into the question of meaning and the theological significance of the Bible for the life of faith. The interplay of faith and reason was a recurring motif of Pope Benedict's theological reflections prior to his becoming pope. Faith without reason, he noted, could lead to ideology and fanaticism; just as reason without faith and without acknowledgment of the transcendent led to an incomplete and misleading view of reality.

Here the pope addressed a concern that has significance for American Catholicism. In the United States, many biblical scholars and their students are enrolled in religious studies programs in public or secular schools and universities. In a context where the separation of church and state holds sway and where the normal classroom usually has students from diverse religious traditions or no tradition at all, engaging in biblical interpretation from a particular theological or ecclesial point of view is difficult, if not impossible. Many American Catholic students, unless they are enrolled in Catholic schools and universities, will have little or no thoughtful exposure to the Bible from a theological or faith perspective. At the same time, Catholic biblical scholars looking for professional advancement increasingly turn to more historical or literary research projects or to refined methodological reflections, rather than the theological significance of the Bible.

The welcome arrival of lay Catholics into the field of professional biblical studies also has had some collateral impacts. Prior to the Second Vatican Council (1960–65), most biblical scholars were Catholic priests or religious and had the benefit of theological studies at the masters or even doctoral level as preparation for specialized biblical study—a path that is not practical for most lay professionals entering the field. Thus, a new generation of Catholic scholars and teachers may have less theological background and may be more oriented to a "religious studies" approach to biblical interpretation.

Pope Benedict's exhortation also pointed to another challenge for the future of biblical interpretation in a Catholic context. The lure of biblical fundamentalism characteristic of some Pentecostal and evangelical approaches, with its robust confidence in the absolute inerrancy and objective historical value of the biblical text, has had an influence on many Catholics in the United States, notably among Hispanic Catholics who now form a substantial portion of the US Catholic population.[28] As noted earlier, the Catholic approach to the Bible makes room both for a nuanced view of the historical character of the Bible and for the role of tradition and church teaching in the interpretation of the biblical text. In some cases, the use of attractive non-Catholic educational materials on the Bible both in print and in other media, and even the popularity of some former evangelical scholars who have been converts to Catholicism but still retain their previous views of biblical interpretation, pose a challenge for the continuing authentic role of the Bible within Catholic tradition.

Conclusion

As noted at the outset, the role of the Bible in Catholicism in the United States is influenced both by the remarkable biblical renewal that has gripped the universal Catholic Church over the past half-century since the Second Vatican Council and by the particular social and religious context of the pluralistic and dynamic American society as a whole. In a global church such as Roman Catholicism, both streams of influence will continue to enrich, define, and challenge the essential place of the Bible in American Catholic faith.

Notes

1. Christopher A. Hall, *Reading Scripture with the Church Fathers* (Downers Grove, Ill.: InterVarsity Press, 1998), esp. 19–42; see also the multivolume series, *Ancient Christian Commentary on Scripture*, ed. Thomas C. Oden (Downers Grove, Ill.: InterVarsity Press), which provides multiple examples of patristic and early Christian theologians' commentaries on specific biblical books.
2. Katherine W. Le Mée, *Chant: The Origins, Form, Practice and Healing Power of Gregorian Chant* (London: Rider Books, Random House, 1994). On the overall development of Christian worship and its deep biblical roots, see Andrew B. McGowan, *Ancient Christian Worship: Early Church Practices in Social, Historical, and Theological Perspective* (Grand Rapids, MI: Baker Academic, 2014).
3. See Robin Margaret Jensen, *Understanding Early Christian Art* (New York: Routledge, 2000).
4. The fundamental message of salvation was transmitted through such media; see, for example, Christopher Irvine, *The Cross and Creation in Christian Liturgy and Art* (London: SPCK, 2013).
5. On formation of the canon, see Bruce M. Metzger, *The Canon of the New Testament: Its Origin, Development, and Significance* (New York: Oxford University Press, 1987); see also Lee Martin McDonald, *Formation of the Bible: The Story of the Church's Canon* (Peabody, Mass.: Hendrickson, 2012), 45–166.
6. A sensational example was the publication of the Tübingen scholar David Friederich Strauss's *Das Leben Jesu, kritisch bearbeitet* (*The Life of Jesus, Critically Examined*) published in 1836, which affirmed that the miraculous elements of the Gospel accounts were simply mythical interpretations of normal events. His work was translated into English in 1846 and had wide influence as a rational explanation of the Gospel miracles and other supernatural phenomena.
7. See Bernard Montagnes, OP, *The Story of Father Marie-Joseph Lagrange: Founder of Modern Catholic Bible Study* (New York: Paulist Press, 2006); Lagrange's own reflections on his ordeals can be found in *Père Lagrange: Personal Reflections and Memoirs* (New York: Paulist Press, 1985).
8. The format and purpose of the Pontifical Biblical Commission have radically changed since its founding. Today its membership consists of an international group of biblical scholars and its purpose is to advise the Vatican and the Pope on issues of biblical interpretation.
9. See Gerald P. Fogarty, SJ, *American Catholic Biblical Scholarship: A History from the Early Republic to Vatican II* (San Francisco, Calif.: Harper & Row, 1989), esp. 78–119.

10. An intervention of Pope John XXIII was decisive in withdrawing the schema and appointing a commission to formulate a new draft, which would be approved by a near unanimous vote at the very end of the Council in November 1965. On the history and content of this key Council document, see Ronald D. Witherup, *Scripture: Dei Verbum* (New York: Paulist Press, 2006), 1–132, and *The Word of God at Vatican II: Exploring Dei Verbum* (Collegeville, Minn.: Liturgical Press, 2014), 1–60.

11. See, particularly, the Pontifical Biblical Commission's, *The Jewish People and Their Sacred Scriptures in the Christian Bible* (Rome: Libreria Editrice Vaticana, 2002), esp. 15–41.

12. The Pontifical Biblical Commission's document *De Historica Evangeliorum Veritate* ("On the Historical Truth of the Gospels") was approved by Pope Paul VI, who ordered its publication on April 21, 1964. On the significance of this text for subsequent Catholic biblical interpretation, see Joseph Fitzmyer, SJ, "The Biblical Commission's Instruction on the Historical Truth of the Gospels," in *Theological Studies* 25 (1964): 386–408. Fitzmyer himself was a noted Catholic biblical scholar, a member of the Pontifical Biblical Commission, and a stout defender of the historical-critical method.

13. See "The Dogmatic Constitution on Divine Revelation" (*Dei Verbum*), ch. 6, ns 21–26, *Vatican Council II*, ed. Austin Flannery, OP (Collegeville, Minn.: Liturgical Press, 1975), 762–65.

14. Biblical institutes open to the laity as well as clergy and religious were founded throughout the country during this time, such as those at Mundelein Seminary in Chicago, Georgetown University in Washington, D.C., Misericordia College in Dallas, Pa., at Mercy College in Burlington, Vt., the Catholic Biblical Studies program in Buffalo, N.Y., The Denver Biblical School, and a host of others.

15. See the following official English titles of the Pontifical Biblical Commission's documents: *The Interpretation of the Bible in the Church* (1993); *The Jewish People and their Sacred Scriptures in the Christian Bible* (2002); *The Bible and Morality: Biblical Roots of Christian Conduct* (2008); and *The Inspiration and Truth of Sacred Scripture* (2014).

16. "Without saying as much in so many words, fundamentalism actually invites people to a kind of intellectual suicide. It injects into life a false certitude, for it unwittingly confuses the divine substance of the biblical message with what are in fact its human limitations." *The Interpretation of the Bible in the Church*, ed. J. L. Houlden (London: SCM Press, 1995), 46.

17. It should be noted that the institution of the lectionary also prompted a number of mainline Protestant denominations to do likewise, leading to a "common lectionary."

18. See, for example, M. Basil Pennington, *Lectio Divina: Renewing the Ancient Practice of Praying the Scriptures* (New York: Crossroad, 1998).

19. Fogarty, *American Catholic Biblical Scholarship*, 272–74.

20. USCCB, *Fulfilled in Your Hearing: The Homily in the Sunday Assembly* (Washington, D.C.: USCCB, 1982), and *Preaching the Mystery of Faith: The Sunday Homily* (Washington, D.C.: USCCB, 2013).

21. Pope Francis, *The Joy of the Gospel: Apostolic Exhortation* (Washington, D.C.: USCCB, 2013), 68–80.

22. The preface to the recent (2008) revision of the Old Testament states: "The present translation has generally made all references to human beings inclusive in the recognition that "man" and "he" are increasingly heard as gender-specific in North American English. Unfortunately, in literary/proverbial registers old usage of such works persists. It has not been possible in every instance to adopt inclusive language, for some circumlocutions

are awkward." See the *New American Bible*, Revised Edition, "Preface to the Revised New American Bible Old Testament."
23. Mary J. Henold, *Catholic and Feminist: The Surprising History of the American Catholic Feminist Movement* (Chapel Hill: University of North Carolina Press, 2012).
24. The PBC itself had an all-male and clerical membership until recently. The first woman member (and a lay person), Dr. Mary Healy, an American biblical scholar, was appointed in 2014.
25. Pope Benedict XVI, *The Word of the Lord* (*Verbum Domini*): *Post-Synodal Apostolic Exhortation* (Washington, D.C.: USCCB, 2010).
26. "For the Catholic understanding of sacred Scripture, attention to such methods [i.e., the historical-critical exegesis] is indispensable, linked as it is to the realism of the Incarnation: 'This necessity is a consequence of the Christian principle formulated in the Gospel of John 1:14: *Verbum caro factum est*. The historical fact is a constitutive dimension of the Christian faith. The history of salvation is not mythology, but a true history, and it should thus be studied with the methods of serious historical research.'" Pope Benedict XVI, 33–34, citing his own address to the Representatives of World Culture meeting in Paris in September 2008.
27. Pope Benedict XVI, *The Word*, 38–39.
28. Pope Benedict XVI, *The Word*, 45–46.

BIBLIOGRAPHY

Fogarty, Gerald P., SJ. *American Catholic Biblical Scholarship: A History from the Early Republic to Vatican II.* San Francisco, Calif.: Harper & Row, 1989.
Fitzmyer, Joseph, SJ. "The Biblical Commission's Instruction on the Historical Truth of the Gospels." *Theological Studies* 25 (1964): 386–408.
Hall, Christopher A. *Reading Scripture with the Church Fathers.* Downers Grove, Ill.: InterVarsity Press, 1998.
Harrington, Daniel J. "The Bible in Catholic Life," in *The Catholic Study Bible*, 2nd ed., edited by Donald Senior and John J. Collins, 16–29. New York: Oxford University Press, 2006.
Henold, Mary J. *Catholic and Feminist: The Surprising History of the American Catholic Feminist Movement.* Chapel Hill: University of North Carolina Press, 2012.
Irvine, Christopher. *The Cross and Creation in Christian Liturgy and Art.* London: SPCK, 2013.
Jensen, Robin Margaret. *Understanding Early Christian Art.* New York: Routledge, 2000.
Lagrange, Marie-Joseph, OP. *Père Lagrange: Personal Reflections and Memoirs.* New York: Paulist Press, 1985.
Le Mée, Katherine W. *Chant: The Origins, Form, Practice and Healing Power of Gregorian Chant.* London: Rider Books, Random House, 1994.
Levering, Matthew. *Engaging the Doctrine of Revelation: The Mediation of the Gospel through Church and Scripture.* Grand Rapids, Mich.: Baker Academic, 2014.
McDonald, Lee Martin. *Formation of the Bible: The Story of the Church's Canon.* Peabody, Mass.: Hendrickson, 2012.
McGowan, Andrew B. *Ancient Christian Worship: Early Church Practices in Social, Historical, and Theological Perspective.* Grand Rapids, Mich.: Baker Academic, 2014.
Metzger, Bruce M. *The Canon of the New Testament: Its Origin, Development, and Significance.* New York: Oxford University Press, 1987.

Moloney, Francis J., SDB. *Reading the New Testament in the Church. A Primer for Pastors, Religious Educators, and Believers*. Grand Rapids, Mich.: Baker Academic, 2015.

Montagnes, Bernard, OP. *The Story of Father Marie-Joseph Lagrange: Founder of Modern Catholic Biblical Study*. New York: Paulist, 2006.

Pennington, M. Basil. *Lectio Divina: Renewing the Ancient Practice of Praying the Scriptures*. New York: Crossroad, 1998.

Pontifical Biblical Commission. *The Interpretation of the Bible in the Church*. Edited by J. L. Houlden. London: SCM Press, 1995.

———. *The Jewish People and Their Sacred Scriptures in the Christian Bible*. Rome: Libreria Editrice Vaticana, 2002.

Pope Benedict XVI. *The Word of the Lord (Verbum Domini): Post-Synodal Apostolic Exhortation*. Washington, D.C.: US Conference of Catholic Bishops, 2010.

Pope Francis. *The Joy of the Gospel: Apostolic Exhortation*. Washington, D.C.: US Conference of Catholic Bishops, 2013.

Senior, Donald, and John J. Collins, eds. *The Catholic Study Bible*. 2nd ed. New York: Oxford University Press, 2006.

US Conference of Catholic Bishops. *Fulfilled in Your Hearing: The Homily in the Sunday Assembly*. Washington, D.C.: US Conference of Catholic Bishops, 1982.

———. *Preaching the Mystery of Faith: The Sunday Homily*. Washington, D.C.: US Conference of Catholic Bishops, 2013.

Witherup, Ronald D. *Scripture: Dei Verbum*. New York: Paulist Press, 2006.

———. *The Word of God at Vatican II: Exploring Dei Verbum*. Collegeville, Minn.: Liturgical Press, 2014.

CHAPTER 34

THE ORTHODOX CHRISTIANS AND THE BIBLE

A. G. ROEBER

WHOSE BIBLE?

To speak of Eastern Orthodox Christianity and "the Bible" has the potential to mislead the unwary reader. Orthodox Christianity—whether of the "Eastern" (Chalcedonian) or "Oriental" (non-Chalcedonian) variety—has historically emphasized the public proclamation of what its tradition incorporates as "Sacred Scripture" into its liturgical life.[1] As a result, various parts of Sacred Scripture have been, from ancient times, arranged in collections (eventually books) that the Orthodox would recognize because of having heard them proclaimed and expounded upon during worship. Thus, a book of New Testament epistles is known as the Apostolos; the book of the Gospels, the Evangelion; a "book of Hours" (Horologion) that provides the fixed texts for the daily cycle of services observed in monasteries (and in part, in parishes); the Prophetologion, selected readings from the Hebrew Bible now commonly used at vespers and other services; and the Psalter. If we were to try to follow the history of the Orthodox Bible in North America, therefore, we should be forced to reconstruct the history of what was available for the Divine Liturgy and other services in various forms of print starting in the late eighteenth century. By at least some estimates, the most commonly used Liturgy of the Eastern or Chalcedonian Orthodox, named in honor of St. John Chrysostom (ca. 349-407) but in actuality a redaction of the West Syrian School of Antioch's liturgical tradition, incorporates 98 quotations from the Old Testament and another 114 from the New Testament, with the morning and evening prayer services (matins, vespers) even more extensively dependent upon biblical texts.[2]

Even more unsettling for those unaware of the Orthodox is their conviction, as the late theologian John Meyendorff insisted, that "the written form of the apostolic message was always understood . . . in the framework of 'apostolic tradition'—the wider, living, and uninterrupted continuity of the apostolic Church." Pointing to the Cappadocian bishop Basil of Caesarea's (329?-379) *Treatise on the Holy Spirit*, Meyendorff emphasized that even prior to the act of reading, a community exists whose reception of what was spoken and then written determines the final status as scripture that in addition is supported by what Basil, in his defense of Nicaean doctrinal teaching was not bashful about calling "other doctrines," "the liturgical and sacramental traditions which, together with the more conceptual consensus found in the continuity of Greek patristic theology. . . [serve] as a living framework for the understanding of Scripture."[3]

In order to understand the history of the Bible among the Orthodox in North America, this essay advances a fourfold argument: first, the liturgical focus has influenced the subsequent history of the Orthodox production and usage of the Bible; second, that ethnic and linguistic issues predominated in shaping that history during the first century and a half of Orthodoxy's presence in North America; third, that the deference paid to patristic commentary impeded for some time engagement with non-Orthodox approaches to biblical scholarship, a hesitancy reinforced by the "neo-patristic" movement in mid-twentieth-century Orthodox theological circles; and finally, that New Testament scholarship, while moving toward a synthesis of reverence for patristic witness and contemporary standards of biblical scholarship, continues to overshadow a much-needed but largely absent Orthodox recovery and appropriation of the Hebrew Bible and Septuagint.

When speaking of what "Bible," the Orthodox regard as most influential (and it must be emphasized that there is no "official" or "authoritative" text for the Orthodox), the Septuagint, (the *koine* Greek translation of the Hebrew Bible by the fourth century along with the Greek New Testament). It is the Septuagint then, and the translations from its text, that most often is counted among the Orthodox as "Sacred Scripture."[4] Syriac, Armenian, Coptic, Georgian, Slavonic, and Ethiopian translations of both the Septuagint and the New Testament cannot, however, be allowed to disguise the indebtedness of the Orthodox to the Qumran and Proto-Masoretic textual streams as well.[5] Thus, although the Greek of both the Hebrew Bible and the New Testament remains a center of Orthodox reference, neither Eastern nor Oriental Orthodox views of the Septuagint or the New Testament matched, for example, the influence of Jerome's Latin translation of the *Vetus Latina* upon Western Christianity.

It may also surprise non-Orthodox readers that concern for the "canon" of Scripture did not manifest itself among the Orthodox until considerably later in the history of Christianity. Moreover, to this day there is no "official" canon in the sense of a specific list of numbered books. The Orthodox recognized Philo of Alexandria's notion of a "canon" as including "laws, prophets, hymns and others," paid attention to Athanasius's urging that there were books "worthy to be read," but followed neither the "ended" canon of Judaism nor that of the Roman Catholic or Protestant Christians.[6]

The Orthodox use of the Hebrew Bible's contents in liturgical worship also reveals a "canon within a canon" since the Psalms, Deuteronomy, Isaiah, and other messianic prophetic books played a far more central role than did the historic or the Wisdom literary works.[7] Whether the East Roman Church in its "cathedral" tradition actually dropped from the Divine Liturgy a selection from the Hebrew Bible after the seventh century in favor of a more compact, monastic tradition of readings as some have asserted, or whether the selections of the Prophetologion had always been read at other services, opens a question beyond the competence of this essay. Of considerably more significance for the later history of the Bible among the Orthodox, however, is the undisputed fact that with the advent of printing, the old manuscript tradition of the Prophetologion vanished and "the readings and rubrical material that once made up the text of the *Prophetologion* were transferred from the discrete Old Testament lectionary volume they had once constituted into other liturgical books used in Byzantine worship. . . the demise of the *Prophetologion* text tradition was therefore actually a transmigration."[8]

What we know about the transmigration of worship practices among Orthodox Christians in eighteenth-century North America, however, amounts to so little that the related question of the Orthodox Bible's story remains equally opaque. Furthermore, not until 1977 did an English translation of the Septuagint receive Orthodox approval, and that version did not come from Orthodox, but from the predominantly Protestant efforts in the form of the *New Oxford Annotated Bible*.[9] For that reason, the history of the Orthodox and the Bible in North America can only be appreciated by noting particular periods and episodes that have shaped that story following the four points of the argument outlined in this section.

The Long Eighteenth-Century Developments

While English-speaking residents of North America—including the formidable eighteenth-century Puritan theologian Cotton Mather—continued to debate the relationship between ancient Hebrew and pagan rituals in the shaping of the Mosaic Law, that very focus revealed the low level of interest among Protestant Christians in the Septuagint as a testimony of the Jewish diaspora's massive impact upon the Hellenistic culture of Second Temple Judaism in which Christianity itself was born.[10] In the case of the Orthodox and their relationship to scripture, a convention among historians who speak of a "long eighteenth century" normally thought to have ended by the 1830s proved in the North American context to have lasted even longer.[11] The London conversion to Orthodox Christianity in 1738 of the colonial Briton Philip Ludwell III of Virginia (1716 -1767) resulted in Ludwell's 1760 handwritten translation of the Presanctified Liturgy, the Liturgy of St. John Chrysostom and the Liturgy of St. Basil. Since these translations never saw publication, their biblical texts exercised no further influence on the history of scripture within Orthodox liturgical or biblical literacy.

The same applied to Ludwell's published catechism volume that appeared in 1762. Ludwell used a Greek text to make his translation of Peter Mohila's (1596-1646) 1640 Catechism that appeared as *The Orthodox Confession of the Catholic and Apostolic Eastern Church*. If one studies the verses of scripture Mohila chose to illustrate his catechetical points, the results reveal a "canon within the canon" principle. When drawing upon the Old Testament, Mohila included a total of 39 citations to the Psalms; another 12 to Isaiah; 11 to Genesis, 3 each to Deuteronomy and Proverbs, and 4 to Exodus. A scattering of one to two citations ranged from the major and minor prophets, Kings, Wisdom, Tobit, 2 Samuel, Job, Sirach, and Ecclesiastes. Mohila's references to the New Testament texts give pride of place to the Gospel of Matthew with 67 quotations, followed by the Gospel of John, 1 Corinthians, Romans, the Gospel of Luke, and Acts (35, 30, 29, 26, and 21, respectively.) The overwhelming emphasis upon the Matthean texts and the didactic tone of Mohila's Catechism reflected Mohila's concerns for an ordered family, state, and society. This emphasis on familial and civil order would find its way into the biblical missionary messages first announced to the First Peoples of North America as well.[12]

A London publication had appeared in 1723 of an Orthodox catechism in English (that included large excerpts from a German, then a French commentary on Russian Orthodoxy) authored by the Archbishop of Novgorod Feofan Prokopovich (1681-1736). Controversial because of his endorsement of the pro-Western reforms of Czar Peter the Great, Prokopovich's Catechism and the commentary were intended by the English translator to acquaint British Protestants with the Russian Church as another ally against Roman Catholicism. The Catechism itself emphasized obedience to the law and the Czar in its exposition of the Decalogue, the Lord's Prayer, and the Nicaean Creed. Prokopovich himself recognized that such instruction had to be in Russian, not Slavonic, if the church now had any chance of reaching its youth. The additional exposition on church government bemoaned the lack of preaching and the lamentable state of clergy who "being utterly unlearned both in the Scriptures and all other sorts of Knowledge; by consequence, the People being so indifferently instructed, live in gross Ignorance."

The French commentary cited by Prokopovich in his catechism explained further that "the Russians never expound any Parts of Scripture in their Churches, neither do they preach, because they hold, that by this Means Heresies and erroneous opinions in regard to the Faith, are published to the World." Inept preaching meant that "the House of God is prophaned thereby, the Preacher, as his Passions move him, being apt to vent whatever comes uppermost, to raise Questions and Disputes." Instead, "the Reading the New-Testament, as used in their Churches, is sufficient to teach them good Manners, and instruct them in all Christian Virtues . . . if the Scripture must needs be interpreted, it is much better (according to their Custom) to read in their Churches the Homilies of the Holy Fathers, than to permit very ignorant Priest, who loves Wrangling" to mislead people. Nonetheless, Peter the Great, seeing the "usefulness" of preaching had now ordered young priests to Kiev to learn the art of preaching under Popovich's tutoring.[13] These early publications in English translation illustrate succinctly the priority given to doctrine and catechesis handed down as patristic witness, as opposed to concern about producing an authoritative biblical text among the Orthodox in Europe or early North America.

The only known version of an early North American Septuagint Bible was Charles Thomson's translation into English that appeared in Philadelphia. Thomson, the Secretary to the Continental Congress, began this effort in 1789. His four-volume work appeared nearly twenty years later in 1808, without a preface or explanation regarding the importance of the Septuagint. Since no community of Orthodox believers existed in the then-United States, however, Thomson's translation also played no part in shaping the later history of the Orthodox Bible. Thomson's labor was highly regarded in Great Britain, but ironically, not in North America.[14]

By the time missionaries from the Russian monastery at Valaam arrived in present-day Alaska in 1794, they brought with them the Slavonic version of liturgical books including scripture readings. That early effort, however, ended in disaster when the leading monastics perished in 1799 in a shipwreck while attempting to return to Russia to protest the abuse of Alaska's First Peoples by unscrupulous Russian traders. By the 1820s both Father Jacob Netsevetov's ability to preach the Gospel of Matthew in the Atka/Aleut and the creation of an Aleut alphabet by the priest and later Bishop John (Innocent) Veniaminov (1797-1879) who had arrived in Alaska in 1824 allowed the latter to begin by 1828 the translation of the Bible into the Unagan dialect of the Aleut language. It was on this basis that over the next twenty years he could translate a catechism, some of the Gospel of Luke, Acts, and a Bible history as well.[15] Innocent's treatise, the "Indication of the Pathway into the Kingdom of

Heaven," revealed a similar pattern with the Gospel of Matthew earning 14 citations; Luke, 9; John, 7; and Genesis, 6.[16]

Another important Orthodox translation of the Bible which would be used in the United States came from the Russian Bible Society at St. Petersburg, an organization that had been authorized from its founding in 1812 to translate the Slavonic Bible into Russian. After starting with the New Testament, however, translators had to abandon the effort in order to avoid prosecution under harsher censorship laws imposed by the Russian monarchy in the 1820s. A version of the Septuagint was approved by the Holy Synod and appeared in Moscow in 1821 and this version also received endorsement by the new Church of Greece in 1843. Although by 1904 an approved "Patriarchal" text for the Greek New Testament appeared, however, no equivalent for the Septuagint has ever been approved by the Ecumenical Patriarchate in Istanbul (Constantinople). Not until 1876 did a full Russian version of the Bible appear under the authority of the Holy Synod of the Russian Orthodox Church.

By 1831, the Gospel was heard in Slavonic, Russian, and fox-Aleut in the Russian mission; by 1833 the Gospel of Matthew was translated into Aleut, and by 1840, Veniamin translated the service books into several of the indigenous languages of North America, including parts of the Bible, relying on the Greek or Slavonic Septuagint text. That same year the Gospel of Matthew was finally published in the western Aleut dialect at St. Petersburg. By 1857 Bishop Innocent had translated the Bible into Yakut (the Sakha language).[17] To what extent service books in Slavonic made their way south into the Russian territory along the Pacific Coast of the Continent also remains unknown. That services were held at Fort Ross, and that by 1857 Russians in San Francisco heard services led by Russian priests on board Russian ships at anchor, is a matter of historical record. But no surviving evidence exists of an actual published liturgy or version of the Bible in either Slavonic or Russian.

At the same time, roughly between 1860 and 1866, Greek Orthodox residents of New Orleans began gathering for lay-led services and some version of the Greek Septuagint scriptures must have been used in those meetings. Similarly, a mixed language group of Orthodox gathered at Galveston, Texas, to hold lay-led reader services, but in what language no one knows. The first priest sent to serve these Texans was Greek-speaking, but a petition to the Russian Tsar Nicholas I for support suggests that whatever version of the scriptures was being read could have been in either Slavonic or Greek. In any event, no version of an Orthodox Bible emerged from any publisher in any language in North America prior to the American Civil War. No complete version of the Bible translated into modern Greek and sanctioned by the Orthodox hierarchs exists even in the twenty-first century.

THE ORTHODOX BIBLE IN THE ERA OF ETHNIC FRAGMENTATION (1880–1945)

The upsurge in immigration to the United States from both Eastern and Southern Europe during the last third of the nineteenth century forced the relocation of the original Russian Orthodox Mission that had become the "Russian Orthodox Diocese of the Aleutian Islands and Alaska," from Alaska to San Francisco, and subsequently to New York City. This unexpected turn of events shifted attention away from liturgical and Bible translation into the languages of the First Peoples of North America to those of the various European and Middle Eastern arrivals.

By 1895 the Arabic priest Raphael Hawaweeny arrived in New York bringing with him Arabic liturgical books, one of which after its translation into English in the 1930s would have a profound impact upon English-language biblical knowledge two generations later. Among Arabic Orthodox, the famous Eli Smith-Cornelius Van Dyck translation of 1865 became the standard Arabic Bible in North America; the version remains the most commonly used among both Coptic and Antiochian Greek Orthodox Christians into the twenty-first century.[18] Three years later, Tikhon Bellavin arrived in America from Russia to begin his service as bishop over the Russian Diocese. Ordaining Hawaweeny to the episcopate, Bellavin initiated a visionary project to bring the various linguistic Orthodox communities under the umbrella of the Russian Diocese while encouraging each to continue worship either in their original language, or in English. Rather than producing an English version of the Septuagint, however, in keeping with the Orthodox priority upon liturgical worship and catechetical instruction, the translation of the major liturgical services by the Episcopalian admirer of Orthodoxy, Isabel Florence Hapgood (1851-1928), began to spread an English-language version of scripture among the Orthodox. Hapgood's 1906 effort enjoyed the personal financial support of Tsar Nicholas II. Its appearance signaled the beginning of Orthodox translation of various parts of scripture into English, but Greek, Slavonic, Arabic, Romanian, Armenian, and other languages from traditionally Orthodox regions of the world continued to dominate the liturgical life of North American Orthodoxy.[19]

The catastrophic impact of the Bolshevik Revolution of 1917 upon the history of the Orthodox in North America can hardly be exaggerated. With the collapse of the Russian Diocese, fragmentation and retreat into ethnic enclaves halted scholarly work in biblical studies or translations, as well as their extension into parish life over the next generation. With the closure of St. Platon's Orthodox Theological Seminary, the only Orthodox seminary in the United States (Minneapolis, 1905, to Tenafly, New Jersey, 1912-24), biblical instruction and study effectively ceased. Not until the late 1930s when the Greek Orthodox Archdiocese that had been formed in 1921 established its theological school at Pomfret, Connecticut, and finally Holy Cross School of Theology in 1947 at Brookline, Massachusetts, did the Orthodox begin to reclaim the systematic study of scripture. By 1938 the remnants of the Russian Missionary Diocese (referred to as the Metropolia) founded St. Vladimir's Seminary in New York City and a pastoral Seminary at St. Tikhon's monastery in South Canaan, Pennsylvania. By 1948 the Russian Church Outside Russia also established Holy Trinity Seminary on the grounds of its monastery at Jordanville, New York. None of these institutions, however, emerged as centers of biblical scholarship or translation until after World War II.[20]

In keeping with the priority of scripture translations appearing first in liturgical form, the Arab-American priest Constantine Nassar undertook in the 1920s the translation into English of the 1898 Arabic work of Raphael Hawaweeny. That translation, which included the scripture readings assigned for the Sundays and Great Feasts of the liturgical year, was laboriously typed into an English manuscript by three sisters in Spring Valley, Illinois. What appeared in 1938 as *Divine Prayers and Services* confirmed a pattern that had begun during the Russian Diocese's happier days. English had been used in services alongside Slavonic at its seminary in Minneapolis. But the impact of the Russian Revolution had driven the competing factions within the exiled Russian community deeper into a defense of Old Church Slavonic and Russian. As a result, the Arabic-American communities emerged by the late 1930s as the parishes most likely to use English translations of the Bible or Bible commentaries.[21]

No discussion of the Orthodox and its use of the Bible during these decades can be conducted apart from recognizing the gradual influence exercised by renewed international attention given to the Septuagint scriptures. The American Bible Society continued to issue reprints of Alfred Rahlfs's nineteenth-century two-volume edition of the Septuagint, and the sixth edition of that work appeared in 1959. Before his own death in 1935, Rahlfs had begun the project that would become internationally known as the "Göttingen" edition whose first volume appeared in 1931. Only those Orthodox fluent in German would have profited from Eberhard Nestle's first edition of the *Novum Testamentum Graece* (1898). But by the 1950s, the 21st edition of that text undertaken by Kurt Aland provided a basis for cooperative work with the Greek New Testament committee that included American scholars and—eventually—the Greek Orthodox participant Johannes Karavidopoulos.[22] Since few of the Orthodox hierarchs or clergy who served in North America prior to World War II were fluent in English, the Cambridge edition that began publication in 1906 (that eventually collapsed in 1940) also exercised no influence on the Orthodox Bible in North America. But the impact of these developments in North America and abroad would be felt in a profound, if delayed manner in the quarter century following the end of World War II.

THE FOUNDATIONAL GENERATION OF ORTHODOX BIBLICAL STUDY 1945-1970

Only in retrospect can one appreciate the significant influence upon biblical study among the Orthodox of the Russian Orthodox émigré Georges Florovsky. Florovsky aimed at nothing less than to elevate Orthodox standards of post-graduate education in the United States to international levels. That vision profoundly affected the standing of scripture study from the level of seminary training to parish educational efforts, although the impact only became manifest a generation after the end of World War II.

Florovsky's underlying assumptions, however, did not envision an unqualifiedly cooperative effort in integrating biblical scholarship with the patristic heritage of Orthodoxy. Florovsky figured as only the most "prominent patristic theoretician" among many who bemoaned what they believed had been a corruption of Orthodox theology due to the adoption by the Orthodox of "logical categories developed in the European West during the period of institutional and cultural estrangement between the two major branches of Christianity." This "neopatristic synthesis" undoubtedly helped to focus attention on "the resources expended on biblical scholarship," but for some time "this theological resurgence ultimately proved to be of ambiguous value in advancing the field."[23] Moreover, it was New Testament studies, and not a rediscovery of the Hebrew Bible that emerged from this synthesis. Nonetheless, in the opinion of at least one contemporary, Florovsky did help "to anchor the use of historical and critical standards in both patristic and biblical fields."[24]

Florovsky's efforts as the dean of St. Vladimir's Seminary were cut short—ironically in a clash with his most distinguished student Alexander Schmemann, who had been called to St. Vladimiar's by Florovsky to teach liturgical theology. Whatever their differences regarding the shape of theological training—"Florovsky was more inclined to emphasize the academic rigor, Schmemann the pastoral formation"—they agreed on the importance of recovering the patristic witness in the study of scripture.[25]

Florovsky's determination to advance biblical studies was bolstered by the arrival of the New Testament scholars Veselin Kesich and Nicholas Arseniev and the former Protestant William Schneirla at St. Vladimir's, the latter asked to be responsible for Old Testament courses, signaling the beginning of heightened academic standards in the study of scripture. That development in turn touched off a long struggle to reconcile approaches committed to the historical-critical methods of biblical scholarship with the long-standing Orthodox determination to read scripture from the patristic perspective, one that regarded the Hebrew Bible as significant only to the extent that it pointed to, and confirmed, the salvific person and role of Jesus. In the hands of the less skillful, the latter approach had often resulted in reducing scripture to useful proof texts that undergirded dogmatic theology and catechetics. Between 1953 and the late 1970, the first tentative steps were taken that would stimulate an explosion of both scholarly and popular writing in English on both Old and New Testament books and themes among the Orthodox.[26]

Attention to Orthodox biblical literacy did not remain solely within the bounds of the seminaries that became fully accredited institutions of higher learning between 1950 and up through the 1970s. Parish-level materials, however, were few and far between during the foundational years. The Department of Christian Education of the Antiochian Orthodox Archdiocese eventually emerged in the 1970s and called as its first chair W. S. Paul Schneirla (1907-2014). Schneirla also served during his Department of Christian Education tenure as professor of Old Testament at St. Vladimir's Seminary. The focus of education in that department, however, remained catechetics, and no texts promoting biblical literacy emerged despite the pioneering work done by Arabic Orthodox in translating the liturgical pericopes into English in the 1930s. In the Greek Orthodox Archdiocese, the Greek Theological Institute Press—the precursor to the eventual Holy Cross Press—did publish a handful of biblical stories, but the actual publication of full-length books on either Old or New Testament themes did not begin until the 1980s.[27] Similarly, the Orthodox Church in America (the former Metropolia) also began expanding its contributions to biblical studies beginning in the 1990s.

THE ORTHODOX AND THE BIBLE
IN NORTH AMERICA, 1970-PRESENT

In some respects, the history of the Orthodox and the Bible in North America depended upon the ability of a younger generation of both scholars and regular parishioners to set aside the specific ethnic-linguistic issues that had significantly hampered Orthodox life for half a century. The First International Conference of Orthodox Theologians in America that met in 1970 included papers by Savas Agourides, Veselin Kesich, and Theodore Stylianopoulos, where both of the latter challenged the notion that Orthodox biblical interpreters should be primarily concerned about making sure their "research would be conducive to the church's life." Instead, biblical texts as well as patristic commentaries "were both candidates for exegesis."[28] Two years later, in 1972 the first International Orthodox Biblical Conference met in Athens, Greece.

In quick succession, the former Metropolia of the Russian Diocese became in 1970 the Orthodox Church in America and by 1975 the two Arabic dioceses that had been split in allegiance to Damascus or Moscow, successfully merged into the Antiochian Christian Archdiocese of North America. Although the Greek Archdiocese (the largest "jurisdiction" among the North American Orthodox) still remained committed to the use of *koine* Greek in liturgical services, it too, with the two other jurisdictions, now made a significant move toward English-language biblical scholarship. This scholarship concerned itself mainly with the New Testament.

Significantly, although the Society of Biblical Literature initiated both its "Septuagint & Cognate Studies" and its "Masoretic Studies" series in 1972, a retrospective of the Society published in 1982 noted the gradual inclusion of Jewish and Catholic scholars; the Orthodox are conspicuously absent.[29] Only more recently have members of both the Oriental and Chalcedonian churches participated in the Society of Biblical Literature meetings that have developed a "Bible in the Eastern and Oriental Orthodox Traditions" unit as part of its annual sessions. Nevertheless, an internationally recognized and professionally trained group of Orthodox biblical scholars emerged in the 1970s that included John Breck, Theodore Stylianopoulos, George Barrois, and Paul Tarazi who began their teaching careers at St. Vladimir's Seminary or Holy Cross, the latter institution having hosted as visiting professor Savas Agourides in 1962–63. Agourides, Greek by birth and initial education, obtained his doctorate at Duke, but returned to Greece where he taught at Thessaloniki until his retirement in 1985, recognized as one of the foremost Orthodox biblical scholars of his generation. It was this small group of scholars who transformed the standing and the approach to biblical studies and literacy among the Orthodox in North America.[30]

Among the Oriental or non-Chalcedonian Orthodox, the 1970s witnessed a similar transformation. Established in 1961, St. Nersess Armenian Orthodox Seminary established a relationship with St. Vladimir's in 1967, one that was refined in 1982 and again in 2007 that allowed Armenian Orthodox students to study at St. Vladimir's. Vahan Hovhanessian, who earned his doctorate in Biblical Studies at Fordham, served as a founding biblical scholar among the Armenians, initiating the "Bible in the Christian Orthodox Tradition" series before being elected Primate of Great Britain.[31] Since his departure, adjunct faculty in New Testament and access to courses at St. Vladimir's have helped to grow biblical literacy among the Armenian communities.

Despite real advances in integrating neo-patristic recovery with the approaches and perspectives of contemporary biblical scholarship, New Testament studies has remained the dominant emphasis among the Orthodox. With the exception of Tarazi, who began his teaching career only in 1977, none of the above-named scholars identified himself primarily as an expert in the Hebrew Bible. To this group, however, one should add Harry Pappas who received his doctorate in Hebrew Bible from Yale University, taught Old Testament courses at Holy Cross during the 1980s, and has written on Old Testament topics. But the Romanian-born Eugen Pentiuc emerged during that decade as the most distinguished Orthodox scholar of the Septuagint and Hebrew Bible. He would be joined by his fellow Romanian Nicolae Roddy, and the former Lutheran pastor and professor of Old Testament Studies, Gabriel Rochelle, who became a faculty member at the St. Sophia Ukrainian Orthodox seminary in South Bound Brook, New Jersey. Timothy Clark, after receiving his doctorate in Old Testament from Emory University, guest-lectured at St. Vladimir's Seminary.

Some effort to redress this imbalance in favor of New Testament Studies emerged with the founding of the Orthodox Center for the Advancement of Biblical Studies (where Clark serves as book review editor), but the emphasis on New Testament Studies continues. To date, doctoral-level faculty posts in Old Testament have been created neither at St. Tikhon's Seminary in South Canaan, Pennsylvania, nor Holy Trinity Orthodox Seminary in Jordanville, New York. Holy Cross Press published some fourteen titles on Sacred Scripture between 1980 and 2011, ten of them on New Testament topics.

With the conversion of the large group of former evangelical Protestants in 1986, Conciliar Press (founded in 1982) devoted itself to publishing accessible books and instructional materials on Sacred Scripture. This emphasis led to the publication by Thomas Nelson (with whom many of the former evangelicals enjoyed a close relationship) of the *Orthodox Study Bible* that appeared first as the *New Testament and the Psalms* (1993) and eventually, the entire Bible (2008).[32] Conciliar Press (since incorporated into Ancient Faith Ministries) injected a vigorous former-Protestant interest in, and dedication to, scriptural literacy at the level of parish study as well as scholarship, a focus that continues to inform especially the Orthodox Church in America and the Antiochian Christian Orthodox Archdiocese. Here too, however, the companion series to the *Orthodox Study Bible* provides thirteen titles on New Testament books, but only five for the entire Hebrew Bible. Other works on scripture reflect a preference for publishing commentaries by medieval Orthodox fathers as opposed to the work of contemporary Orthodox scholars. The Orthodox Christian Archdiocese's St. Vladimir Seminary Press has long led the English-language publication of books in the United States. But even in this instance, its catalogues reflect the emphasis on New Testament books (some twenty-three titles) versus a mere ten volumes on the books of the Hebrew Bible.

On balance, however, the deepening awareness of and dedication to biblical literacy among the Orthodox in North America; the willingness to engage both patristic witness as well as confront the hermeneutical and methodological implications of contemporary biblical scholarship that is not explicitly Orthodox; and the decline of specifically ethnic and linguistic concerns have together contributed to an Orthodox engagement with the Bible in America that is incomparably greater today than at any time in the history of that faith since its late eighteenth-century arrival in the New World.

NOTES

1. John Breck, *Scripture in Tradition: The Bible and Its Interpretation in the Orthodox Church* (Crestwood, N.Y.: St. Vladimir's Seminary Press, 2001), 33–44.
2. The estimates are taken from the citations provided in Constantine Nasr, *The Bible in the Liturgy* (Oklahoma City, Okla.: Theosis, 1988).
3. John Meyendorff, *Byzantine Theology: Historical Trends and Doctrinal Themes*, 2nd ed. (New York: Fordham University Press, 1979), 8.
4. See, for example, the summary provided in Timothy Michael Law, *When God Spoke Greek: The Septuagint and the Making of the Christian Bible* (New York: Oxford University Press, 2013).

5. Eugen J. Pentiuc, *The Old Testament in Eastern Orthodox Tradition* (New York: Oxford University Press, 2014), 62–70.

6. The standard works on the development of the Canon in Western Christianity remain Geoffrey Mark Hahneman, *The Muratorian Fragment and the Development of the Canon* (Oxford: Clarendon Press, 1992) and Bruce Metzger, *The Canon of the New Testament: Its Origin, Significance, and Development* (Oxford: Clarendon Press, 1997). For the Orthodox position, see Pentiuc, *The Old Testament*, especially Philo of Alexandria's definition (111) and Athanasius's "worthy to be read" (115–16).

7. Martin Hengel, *The Septuagint as Christian Scripture: Its Prehistory and the Problem of Its Canon*, trans. Mark E. Biddle, intro. Robert Hanhart (Edinburgh: T. & T. Clark, 2002), 107.

8. Paul Magdalino and Robert Nelson, "Introduction," and James Miller, "The Prophetologion: The Old Testament of Byzantine Christianity?," in *The Old Testament in Byzantium*, ed. Paul Magdalino and Robert Nelson (Washington, D.C.: Dumbarton Oaks Research Library and Collection, 2010), 30, 65.

9. Harold P. Scanlin, "The Old Testament Canon in the Orthodox Churches," in *New Perspectives on Historical Theology: Essays in Memory of John Meyendorff*, ed. Bradley Nassif (Grand Rapids, Mich.: William B. Eerdmans, 1996), 300.

10. Reiner Smolinski, "'Eager Imitators of the Egyptian Inventions': Cotton Mather's Engagement with John Spencer and the Debate about the Pagan Origin of the Mosaic Laws, Rites, and Customs," in *Cotton Mather and Biblia Americana: America's First Bible Commentary*, ed. Reiner Smolinski and Jan Stievermann (Grand Rapids, Mich.: Baker Academic, 2010), 295–335.

11. I use the term in the sense employed by Frank O'Gorman, *The Long Eighteenth Century: British Political and Social History, 1688-1832* (London: Bloomsbury Academic, 1997).

12. When Ludwell died in London, the 1767 inventory of his estate revealed nothing about a version of scripture in Greek or Slavonic, nor did his neighbor Charles Carroll of Carrollton specify which books of a religious nature he chose to take from Ludwell's library, as the deceased had invited him to do in his will. Philip Ludwell, *The Orthodox Confession of the Catholic and Apostolic Eastern Church* (London, 1762); Ronald Hoffman, ed., *Dear Papa, Dear Charlie: The Papers of Charles Carroll* (Chapel Hill: University of North Carolina Press, 2001), 3:1564–69. For more details, see Nicholas Chapman, "Early Orthodox in British America," *Road to Emmaus* 46 (2011): 3–25, http://www.roadtoemmaus.net/back_issue_articles/RTE_46/EARLY_ORTHODOXY_IN_BRITISH_AMERICA.pdf; and Mark A. Lamport, "Philip Ludwell III," in *Encyclopedia of Christianity in the United States*, ed. George Thomas Kurian and Mark A. Lamport (New York: Routledge, 2016).

13. Feofan Prokopovich, *The Russian Catechism, Composed and Published by order of the Czar, To Which is annex'd a short Account of the Church government, and ceremonies of the Moscovites*, trans. Jenkin Thomas Philipps (London: W. Meadows, 1723), xi, 49, 50, 51, 52, 53.

14. Kendrick Grobel, "Charles Thomson, First American N.T. Translator—An Appraisal," *Journal of Bible & Religion* 11, no. 3 (1943): 151. The English translation of the Septuagint by Sir Lancelot Brenton in 1844 probably had the most long-term impact, since it forms the basis for the 2008 edition of the *Orthodox Study Bible*. See also E. B. O'Callaghan, *A List of Editions of the Holy Scriptures and parts Thereof, Printed in American Previous to 1860: with introduction and bibliographical notes* (Albany: Munsell & Rowland, 1861), 91–92.

15. Gregory Afonsky, *A History of the Orthodox Church in Alaska (1794–1917)* (Kodiak, Alaska: St. Herman's Theological Seminary, 1977), 44, 48.

16. John Veniaminov, "Indication of the Pathway into the Kingdom of Heaven," in *Alaskan Missionary Spirituality*, ed. Michael J. Oleksa (New York: Paulist Press, 1987), 80–119.

17. John H. Erickson, "Eastern Orthodox Christianity in America," in *The Cambridge History of Religions in America*, ed. Stephen J. Stein (New York: Cambridge University Press, 2012), 2:324–43. Paul Garrett, *St. Innocent Apostle to America* (Crestwood, N.Y.: St. Vladimir's Seminary Press, 1979), 73–74, 97–98, 118–21, 257–61.

18. Azar Ajaj, "The Van Dyck Bible Translation: The American Mission Board and the Translation of the Bible into Arabic," *St. Francis Magazine* 11, no. 1 (2015): 7–11, http://spotidoc.com/doc/749188/the-pdf---st.francis-magazine.

19. Isabel Florence Hapgood, *Service Book of the Holy Orthodox-Catholic Apostolic Church: Compiled, Translated, and Arranged from the Old Church-Slavonic Service Books of the Russian Church, and Collated with the Service Books of the Greek Church* (Boston: Houghton, Mifflin and Company, 1906).

20. For two summaries of this history, see Mark Stokoe and Leonid Kishkovsky, *Orthodox Christians in North America, 1794–1994* (Brooklyn, Ohio: Orthodox Christian Publications Center, 1995); and Thomas E. Fitzgerald, *The Orthodox Church* (Westport, Conn.: Greenwood Press, 1995).

21. Orthodox Eastern Church and Seraphim Nassar, *Divine Prayers and Services of the Catholic Orthodox Church of Christ: Comprising the Most Important of the Private and Public Prayers; Services of the Dominical Feasts of the Distinguished Saints; and of All Sundays of the Year; in the Order Ordained by the Holy Orthodox Church of Christ; to Which Are Appended an Index and a Table for Finding Easter, Covering a Period of Twenty Years, 1938 to 1958* (New York: Blackshaw Press, 1938).

22. Kurt Aland et al., *Novum Testamentum Graece post Eberhard et Erwin Nestle editione vicesima septima revisa* (Stuttgart: Deutsche Bibelgesellschaft, 1979), 1–3.

23. Timothy Clark, "Recent Eastern Orthodox Interpretation of the New Testament," *Currents in Biblical Research* 5, no. 3 (2007): 324, 325. doi:10.1177/1476993X7077964.

24. Theodore G. Stylianopoulos, "Orthodox Biblical Interpretation," in *Dictionary of Biblical Interpretation*, 2 vols., ed. John H. Hayes (Nashville, Tenn.: Abingdon Press, 1999), 2:229. For reflection on the issue of patristic views of scripture, see Oliver Herbel, "A 'Doctrine of Scripture' from the Eastern Orthodox Tradition: A Reflection on the Desert Father Saint Serapion of Thmuis," in *What Is the Bible? The Patristic Doctrine of Scripture*, ed. Matthew Baker and Mark Mourachian (Minneapolis, Minn.: Fortress Press, 2016), 21–34.

25. Paul L. Gavrilyuk, *Georges Florovsky and the Russian Religious Renaissance* (Oxford: Oxford University Press, 2014), 243.

26. These are the conclusions offered by the late Dr. Veselin Kesich, "St. Vladimir's in the 'Fifties,'" in *A Legacy of Excellence: St. Vladimir's Orthodox Theological Seminary, 1938–1988*, ed. John Meyendorff (Crestwood, N.Y.: St. Vladimir Seminary Press, 1988), 24–31.

27. I am indebted to Dr. Anton Vrame, Director of Holy Cross Press for this information gleaned from the Press archives at Holy Cross Orthodox School of Theology, Brookline, Mass.

28. Clark, "Recent Eastern Orthodox Interpretation," 326, 327.

29. Ernest W. Saunders, *Searching the Scriptures: A History of the Society of Biblical Literature, 1880–1980* (Chico, Calif.: Scholars Press, 1982), 83, 84, 91.

30. See the essays in Theodore G. Stylianopoulos, ed., *Sacred Text and Interpretation: Perspectives in Orthodox Biblical Studies: Papers in Honor of Professor Savas Agourides* (Brookline, Mass.: Holy Cross Orthodox Press, 2006).

31. Vahan S. Hovhanessian, ed., *The Old Testament as Authoritative Scripture in the Early Churches of the East* (New York: Peter Lang, 2010).

32. *The Orthodox Study Bible* (Nashville, Tenn.: Thomas Nelson, 2008); see the introduction for the Editors' acknowledgment of reliance upon Sir Lancelot Brenton's English translation (1844), xi.

BIBLIOGRAPHY

Afonsky, Gregory. *A History of the Orthodox Church in Alaska (1794–1917)*. Kodiak, Alaska: St. Herman's Theological Seminary, 1977.

Ajaj, Azar. "The Van Dyck Bible Translation: The American Mission Board and the Translation of the Bible into Arabic." *St. Francis Magazine* 11, no. 1 (2015): 7–11. http://spotidoc.com/doc/749188/the-pdf---st.francis-magazine.

Aland, Kurt, et al. *Novum Testamentum Graece post Eberhard et Erwin Nestle editione vicesima septima revisa*. Stuttgart: Deutsche Bibelgesellschaft, 1979.

Barrois, Georges Augustin. *The Face of Christ in the Old Testament*. Crestwood, N.Y.: St. Vladimir Seminary Press, 1974.

Breck, John. *Scripture in Tradition: The Bible and Its Interpretation in the Orthodox Church*. Crestwood, N.Y.: St. Vladimir's Seminary Press, 2001.

Chapman, Nicholas. "Early Orthodox in British America." *Road to Emmaus* 46 (2011): 3–25. http://www.roadtoemmaus.net/back_issue_articles/RTE_46/EARLY_ORTHODOXY_IN_BRITISH_AMERICA.pdf.

Clark, Timothy. "Recent Eastern Orthodox Interpretation of the New Testament." *Currents in Biblical Research* 5, no. 3 (2007): 322–40. doi:10.1177/1476993X7077964.

Coniaris, Anthony M. *Introducing the Orthodox Church: Its Faith and Life*. Minneapolis, Minn.: Light and Life, 1982.

Erickson, John H. "Eastern Orthodox Christianity in America." In *The Cambridge History of Religions in America*, edited by Stephen J. Stein, 2:324–43. New York: Cambridge University Press, 2012.

Fitzgerald, Thomas E. *The Orthodox Church*. Westport, Conn.: Greenwood Press, 1995.

Florovsky, Georges. *Bible, Church, Tradition: An Eastern Orthodox View*. Belmont, Mass.: Nordland, 1972.

Garrett, Paul. *St. Innocent Apostle to America*. Crestwood, N.Y.: St. Vladimir's Seminary Press, 1979.

Gavrilyuk, Paul L. *Georges Florovsky and Russian Religious Renaissance*. Oxford: Oxford University Press, 2014.

Grobel, Kendrick. "Charles Thomson, First American N.T. Translator—An Appraisal." *Journal of Bible & Religion* 11, no. 3 (1943): 145–51.

Hahneman, Geoffrey Mark. *The Muratorian Fragment and the Development of the Canon*. Oxford: Clarendon Press, 1992.

Hapgood, Isabel Florence. *Service Book of the Holy Orthodox-Catholic Apostolic Church: Compiled, Translated, and Arranged from the Old Church-Slavonic Service Books of the Russian Church, and Collated with the Service Books of the Greek Church*. Boston: Houghton, Mifflin, 1906.

Hengel, Martin. *The Septuagint as Christian Scripture: Its Prehistory and the Problem of Its Canon*. Trans. Mark E. Biddle. Edinburgh: T. & T. Clark, 2002.

Herbel, Oliver. "A 'Doctrine of Scripture' from the Eastern Orthodox Tradition." In *What Is the Bible? The Patristic Doctrine of Scripture*, edited by Matthew Baker and Mark Mourachian, 21–34. Minneapolis, Minn.: Fortress Press, 2016.

Hoffman, Ronald. *Dear Papa, Dear Charlie: The Papers of Charles Carroll*. 3 vols. Chapel Hill: University of North Carolina Press, 2001.

Hovhanessian, Vahan S., ed. *The Old Testament as Authoritative Scripture in the Early Churches of the East*. New York: Peter Lang, 2010.

Kesich, Veselin. "St. Vladimir's in the 'Fifties.'" In *A Legacy of Excellence: St. Vladimir's Orthodox Theological Seminary, 1938-1988*, edited by John Meyendorff, 28–31. Crestwood, N.Y.: St. Vladimir Seminary Press, 1988.

Lamport, Mark A. "Philip Ludwell III." In *Encyclopedia of Christianity in the United States*, edited by George Thomas Kurian and Mark A. Lamport. New York: Routledge, 2016.

Law, Timothy Michael. *When God Spoke Greek: The Septuagint and the Making of the Christian Bible*. New York: Oxford University Press, 2013.

Ludwell, Philip. *The Orthodox Confession of the Catholic and Apostolic Eastern Church*. London, 1762.

Manley, Johanna, comp. and ed. *The Bible and the Holy Fathers for Orthodox: Daily Scripture Readings and Commentary for Orthodox Christians*. Crestwood, N.Y.: Monastery Books, 1984.

Miller, James. "The Prophetologion: The Old Testament of Byzantine Christianity?" In *The Old Testament in Byzantium*, edited by Paul Magdalino and Robert Nelson, 55–76. Washington, D.C.: Dumbarton Oaks Research Library and Collection, 2010.

Metzger, Bruce. *The Canon of the New Testament: Its Origin, Significance, and Development*. Oxford: Clarendon Press, 1997.

Meyendorff, John. *Byzantine Theology: Historical Trends and Doctrinal Themes*. 2nd ed. New York: Fordham University Press, 1979.

Nasr, Constantine. *The Bible in the Liturgy*. Oklahoma City, Okla.: Theosis, 1988.

O'Callaghan, E. B. *A List of Editions of the Holy Scriptures and Parts Thereof, Printed in America Previous to 1860*. Albany: Munsell & Rowland, 1861.

O'Gorman, Frank. *The Long Eighteenth Century: British Political and Social History, 1688-1832*. London: Bloomsbury Academic, 1997.

Orthodox Eastern Church, and Seraphim Nassar. *Divine Prayers and Services of the Catholic Orthodox Church of Christ: Comprising the Most Important of the Private and Public Prayers; Services of the Dominical Feasts of the Distinguished Saints; and of All Sundays of the Year; in the Order Ordained by the Holy Orthodox Church of Christ; to Which Are Appended an Index and a Table for Finding Easter, Covering a Period of Twenty Years, 1938 to 1958*. New York: Blackshaw Press, 1938.

Pentiuc, Eugen J. *The Old Testament in Eastern Orthodox Tradition*. New York: Oxford University Press, 2014.

Pietersma, Albert, and Benjamin G. Wright, eds. *A New English Translation of the Septuagint and the Other Greek Translations Traditionally Included under That Title*. New York: Oxford University Press, 2007.

Prokopovich, Feofan. *The Russian Catechism, Composed and Published by order of the Czar, To Which is annex'd a short Account of the Church government, and ceremonies of the Moscovites*. Translated by Jenkin Thomas Philipps. London: W. Meadows, 1723.

Rahlfs, Alfred, ed. *Septuaginta: Id Est Vetus Testamentum Grace justa LXX Interpretes*. 2 vols. Stuttgart: Privilegierte Wurttembergische Bibelanstalt, for the American Bible Society, 1959.

———, ed. *Septuaginta: Vetus Testamentum Graecum Auctoritate Academiae Scientiarum Gottingensis editum*. 20 vols. Göttingen: Vandenhoeck & Ruprecht, 1931.

Saunders, Ernest W. *Searching the Scriptures: A History of the Society of Biblical Literature, 1880–1980*. Chico, Calif.: Scholars Press, 1982.

Scanlin, Harold P. "The Old Testament Canon in the Orthodox Churches." In *New Perspectives on Historical Theology: Essays in Memory of John Meyendorff*, edited by Bradley Nassif, 300–312. Grand Rapids, Mich.: William B. Eerdmans, 1996.

Smolinski, Reiner. "'Eager Imitators of the Egyptian Inventions': Cotton Mather's Engagement with John Spencer and the Debate about the Pagan Origin of the Mosaic Laws, Rites, and Customs." In *Cotton Mather and Biblia Americana: America's First Bible Commentary*, edited by Reiner Smolinski and Jan Stievermann, 295–335. Grand Rapids, Mich.: Baker Academic, 2010.

Stokoe, Mark, and Leonid Kishkovsky. *Orthodox Christians in North America, 1794–1994*. Brooklyn, Ohio: Orthodox Christian Publications Center, 1995.

Stylianopoulos, Theodore G. "Orthodox Biblical Interpretation." In *Dictionary of Biblical Interpretation*, 2 vols., edited by John H. Hayes. Nashville, Tenn.: Abingdon Press, 1999.

———, ed. *Sacred Text and Interpretation: Perspectives in Orthodox Biblical Studies: Papers in Honor of Professor Savas Agourides*. Brookline, Mass.: Holy Cross Orthodox Press, 2006.

Veniaminov, John. "Indication of the Pathway into the Kingdom of Heaven." In *Alaskan Missionary Spirituality*, edited by Michael J. Oleksa, 80–119. New York: Paulist Press, 1987.

CHAPTER 35

....

THE BIBLE AND THE
MAINLINE DENOMINATIONS

....

ELESHA COFFMAN

THE National Council of Churches (NCC) holds the copyright to the Revised Standard and New Revised Standard versions of the Bible. This fact speaks volumes about the mainline Protestant approach to the Bible, which emphasizes scholarly expertise, institutional authorization, and ecumenical cooperation. This essay explains how these three emphases shaped the mainline in the late nineteenth and early twentieth centuries, and how the mainline continued to rely on them amid dramatic cultural changes in the later twentieth century. The essay closes by exploring ways the Bible has been both a unifying and divisive force among mainline Protestants in more recent history.

Before proceeding, it is worth noting some complexities of the category "mainline denominations." The word "mainline" was not applied to a subset of American Protestant churches until 1960. When the term came into use, though, its meaning stabilized quickly, thanks to affinities that had been building for decades within the denominations to which the label was most commonly applied: the Episcopal Church, the Congregational Church/ United Church of Christ, the United Methodist Church, the Presbyterian Church (USA), northern Baptists, Disciples of Christ, and the Evangelical Lutheran Church in America. Other denominations are sometimes labeled "mainline" as well, typically on the basis of membership in the NCC. The institutional and ideological affinities among these churches will be addressed in this essay.[1]

There is another way in which "mainline" is a complicated category. Unlike other major categories within American Protestantism, such as evangelical or Pentecostal, "mainline" almost always applies to whole denominations rather than to individuals. (One does not use "mainliner" as a singular noun.) This use of the term is significant. Mainline churches tend to have hierarchical structures into which they have invested substantial authority, not to mention substantial money. What happens at the top of these organizations, at the level of the bishop or general assembly or denominational seminary, matters. This commitment to structure does not mean, however, that what is true of mainline leaders is reliably true of mainline laity. In fact, mainline laity (and the clergy of smaller churches) have frequently been unaware of, or even hostile to, the ideas advanced by their leaders. Because the story of this disjuncture entwines with the story of mainline engagement with the Bible, it, too, appears in this essay.

REVISING THE BIBLE, CREATING DIVISIONS

The history of the Revised Version of the Bible gives a good sense of where and how main-line affinities began to develop. In 1870, American "divines"—learned churchmen—were invited to join a project of Bible revision that had been launched by the Church of England and funded by Oxford and Cambridge University presses. While on a trip to New York for a meeting of the Evangelical Alliance, English Baptist biblical scholar Joseph Angus issued this invitation personally to Philip Schaff, a Swiss-born, German Reformed historian and theologian who had just taken a teaching position at Union Theological Seminary. Schaff became president of the American revision committee, whose members represented prominent theological schools, including Andover, Harvard, Princeton, Rochester, Union, and Yale; colleges, including Columbia, Haverford, the University of Pennsylvania, and Yale College; and church positions (a member of the Old Testament committee led Collegiate Reformed Dutch Church in New York; a member of the New Testament committee served as the Episcopal Bishop of Delaware).

The revision project bore all three hallmarks of the mainline Protestant approach to the Bible, scholarly expertise, institutional authorization, and ecumenical cooperation.

Revision organizers privileged academic expertise over confessional loyalty, seeking the input "of any eminent for scholarship, to whatever nation or religious body they might belong." Naturally, then, most American committee members were attached to educational institutions, and all held at least one graduate degree. Other major institutions—the Church of England, university presses—backed the endeavor, while an ecumenical group, the Evangelical Alliance, facilitated interpersonal connections among the revisers. In all of these ways, the project was the antithesis of the populist, democratized religion that had swept the United States in the earlier nineteenth century. Revivalists cared about personal testimony and piety; the revision committee cared about scholarship, credentials, and institutional connections.[2]

The revised New Testament made a big splash, selling an estimated quarter of a million copies on the day it appeared in May 1881. The revised Old Testament was welcomed almost as enthusiastically in July 1885. The revisions were moderate, incorporating insights from textual ("lower") criticism but not historical ("higher") criticism and retaining archaic *thee* and *thou*. The revisions also proved deeply divisive. Granted, new translations of the Bible had provoked heated reactions since the fifth century, when Jerome's choice to call the plant in Jonah 4:6 *hedera* (ivy) instead of *cucurbita* (gourd) prompted riots and several angry letters from Augustine. Complaints in the 1880s concerned different issues, but were no less sharp. The Revised Version sounded strange and inelegant, critics charged. The Protestant clergy of New Haven, Connecticut, rejected the new Bible two months after their hometown university, Yale, adopted it for use in chapel, preferring the beauty of the King James Version to the purported accuracy of the new text.[3]

Revisers had anticipated this kind of resistance from, in the impolitic words of one member of the New Testament committee, "old grannies and croakers," but felt confident that the new translation would prevail in a decade or so. (Faith in the eventual triumph of sound scholarship has been a constant refrain among the leaders of mainline Protestant denominations.) A more intractable form of resistance also emerged, however, attacking not just the word choices but the elitism of the revision project. Reverend T. DeWitt

Talmage, a social reformer and noted orator who presided over the massive Brooklyn Tabernacle, joined this battle with a sermon titled "The New Revision: A Mutilation and Profanation." "All Christendom was satisfied with the [King James Version] translation except a few doctors of divinity," Talmage charged. Those experts then labored in secret for ten years, building readers' curiosity and anxiety, before unleashing their revision on the public. Talmage likened the experts' tactics to the operation of corrupt political machines, warning that "there is as much *bossism* in the church of God as in the world, and monopoly would rule the kingdom of Christ, if it could, as it rules the money market and legislatures of the world." Talmage allied himself with the 999 out of 1,000 Christians who, he predicted, would defy this outrage by holding fast to the King James Version.[4]

Within churches that would later be called mainline, reactions to the new Bible varied. Theological schools and many church periodicals embraced it, but only one denomination, the American Baptist Church, officially endorsed it. The views of laypeople are more difficult to determine, but the Revised Version captured only 5 to 10 percent of the Bible market by the late 1890s, so it is clear that the majority of American Protestants remained skeptical. (The fact that publishers could print the King James Version without worrying about copyright influenced market share as well.) Meanwhile, Protestants who agreed with Talmage's critique began to wear their allegiance to the King James Version as a badge of orthodoxy. This emerging division should not be overstated; several contributors to *The Fundamentals*, published 1910-15, quoted the Revised Version in their essays, while many pro-scholarship ministers continued to quote the King James Version from the pulpit for poetic effect. Nevertheless, acceptance or rejection of the Revised Version sifted American Protestants into different camps, sketching in the fault lines that would come to separate modernists from fundamentalists. These lines emerged within, rather than between, denominations.[5]

BATTLES FOR THE BIBLE

Differing views of the Bible contributed to a number of high-profile conflicts in Protestant churches and seminaries in the late nineteenth and early twentieth centuries. Other issues, not to mention egos, were involved as well, but often the crux of the argument came down to the reading of specific biblical passages or to the articulation of biblical authority. Protestants had wrestled with the latter question since the sixteenth century, when Martin Luther rejected the authority of popes and church councils in favor of *sola scriptura*, the Bible alone. This stance made it vitally important to determine what, exactly, the biblical text said, what those words meant, and, if Christians disagreed on either the words or the meaning, how their argument might be adjudicated. In the United States, the Supreme Court settled such questions regarding the Constitution. How would mainline denominations settle them regarding the Bible?

The first big conflict of this sort erupted at Union Seminary in 1891. Presbyterian scholar Charles A. Briggs, appointed to the school's newly created endowed professorship in Biblical Theology, titled his inaugural address "The Authority of Holy Scripture." Briggs used the address to argue that the Bible was not verbally inspired, inerrant, or self-authenticating. Higher Criticism had proven that biblical books were not written by their putative authors, he stated, and science had exposed miracles as human inventions. Briggs claimed to be rescuing the Bible from traditionalist obstructions, as a farmer cleared dead wood from his fields, and opening the scriptures up to modern minds. He closed on an incendiary note: "Let us burn up every form of false doctrine, false religion, and false practice. Let us remove every incumbrance [sic] out of the way for a new life; the life of God is moving throughout Christendom, and the spring-time of a new age is about to come upon us."[6]

Briggs's ideas, as well as his optimistic belief that their adoption would grow and unify churches, can be labeled theological modernism, the acceptance of which is a hallmark of mainline Protestantism. But not everyone in his church, or even at Union Seminary, accepted these ideas. Briggs's students cheered during his address, but many guests and other faculty members squirmed. Journalists covered the brewing controversy extensively in a slow news year, and opposition to Briggs mounted, resulting in a multi-year investigation of Briggs by the Presbyterian General Assembly. Finding Briggs's statements incompatible with the Westminster Confession (the authoritative Presbyterian statement of faith), delegates at the 1891 assembly voted overwhelmingly to remove Briggs from his professorship and to scrutinize Union, which, though interdenominational, had come under partial Presbyterian control in 1870. Union defended its professor and its independence, as theologians on both sides of the modernism question articulated their views of biblical authority and pressed for the official position of the Presbyterian Church to align with their own. After much wrangling, Briggs was suspended from Presbyterian ministry in 1893 on grounds of heresy.

The Briggs controversy, which hinged on the academic study of the Bible, fractured the Presbyterian Church while also spurring ecumenical cooperation. Opposition to Briggs emanated largely from the Midwest, while his support centered in New York. When conservative Midwestern presbyteries declared a boycott of Union Seminary, Union broke its ties with the Presbyterian Church and began to attract liberal students from a wider variety of denominations. Briggs himself switched his ordination to the Protestant Episcopal Church. This pattern was repeated in several other cases in the early twentieth century, as modernists Arthur Cushman McGiffert (Presbyterian, Union Seminary), Hinckley Gilbert Thomas Mitchell (Methodist, Boston University), Algernon Sidney Crapsey (Episcopal priest), George Burman Foster (Baptist, University of Chicago), and John H. Dietrich (Reformed Church minister) either faced heresy trials or withdrew from their churches to avoid them. McGiffert remained at Union but became a Congregationalist; Dietrich left his church and became a Unitarian. These trials, which occurred in other countries as well, eventually exhausted their participants. Then, after a lull of a few years, heresy investigations swung the other way. In 1932, J. Gresham Machen (Presbyterian, founder of Westminster Seminary) was forced out of the Presbyterian Church for rejecting modernism. In 1939, charges against four modernist professors at Mercer University (Baptist) produced only a mild warning from trustees—and, implicitly, a rebuke to the conservative students whose complaints initiated the investigation.[7]

Given this complicated history, it is difficult to generalize about the Bible and the mainline denominations in the early twentieth century. Modernism made significant inroads and also met fierce opposition. There were regional differences, as well as differences between metropolitan areas and smaller towns. Seminaries were among the most liberal of church institutions and also among the most conservative. It is fair to say that seminaries often became a locus of conflict because of mainline emphasis on scholarly expertise and institutional authorization, and it is also worth noting that modernists facing hostility within their churches frequently made common cause with other modernists across denominational lines. The modernist editors of the Disciples of Christ magazine, *The Christian Century*, recognized the value of this realignment after contributor and University of Chicago biblical scholar Herbert Willett was nearly cut from the program of the 1909 Disciples Centennial because he embraced higher criticism and doubted biblical miracles. After additional fights with its denomination, *The Christian Century* rebranded itself in 1917 as the "undenominational" organ of Protestant liberalism.[8]

While the finer points of modernist biblical scholarship (much of which was written in German) were mostly only debated in seminaries, academic commitment to progress as the lens through which the Bible—and all of human history—should be viewed was diffused much more widely through the mainline denominations. Faith in progress was hardly unique to mainline Protestantism in this era of social reform, as seen in a widespread cultural optimism captured by the French psychologist Émile Coué's famous mantra, "Every day, in every way, I'm getting better and better."

There were, however, competing perspectives on the Bible and history within American Protestantism. A strain of primitivism running from the Puritans through the restorationist churches of the nineteenth century (among them the Disciples of Christ, Mormons, and Adventists) elevated the early church as the ideal from which later history degenerated. In other words, older was better, and reinvigorated ancient traditions were to be pursued. Another competing perspective, dispensationalism, held that God had divided history into periods with different modes of divine governance, and, while human awareness of God grew through progressive revelation, sinfulness persisted. The present was not necessarily better than the past, and the future was apt to get worse before God set everything to rights.

Rejecting these other views, the mainline denominations in the early twentieth century adopted the progressive approach to the Bible popularized by the foremost liberal Protestant of the day, Harry Emerson Fosdick. Fosdick, a 1904 Union Seminary graduate, was ordained a Baptist and then called, in 1918, to First Presbyterian Church in Manhattan. From that pulpit he delivered his widely circulated sermon "Shall the Fundamentalists Win?"—a modernist plea that earned him an investigation by his presbytery. He avoided censure by leaving First Presbyterian for Park Avenue Baptist Church and then, in 1930, for the new, ecumenical Riverside Church. Fosdick explained his perspective on the Bible in a set of Lyman Beecher lectures at Yale, published in 1924 as *The Modern Use of the Bible*. Thanks to advanced critical methods, Fosdick explained, scholars were finally able to put all of the biblical texts in chronological order, which enabled readers to see the progression from the coarse Old Testament to the hopeful and forward-looking New Testament. All of the parts that seemed backward were obsolete and could safely be set aside: "We know now that every idea in the Bible started from primitive and childlike origins and, with however many setbacks and delays, grew in scope and height toward the culmination in Christ's Gospel. We know now that the Bible is the record of an amazing spiritual development." Scholarship liberated Christians from the intellectually untenable portions of their holy book, enabling them to proclaim a faith suited to their modern age.[9]

MORE REVISION, MORE DIVISIONS

The decade after World War II was, numerically and financially, the high point for the institutional, ecumenical Protestantism favored by the mainline denominations, and these years yielded yet another revision of the Bible: the Revised Standard Version (RSV). Discussion of a new, American translation, reflecting post-1885 critical and archaeological discoveries, had begun back in the early 1930s, but the project was delayed by the economic depression. When a revision committee formed, in 1937, it resembled the group from the 1870s: all members were white, male professors at research-oriented seminaries or universities, and they hailed from a variety of mainline churches. Union Seminary once again served as the translation effort's headquarters. The funding structure for this project, however, differed from the previous effort. American publisher Thomas Nelson and Sons supported the committee in exchange for the exclusive rights to publish its product. The entity behind the revision was the Chicago-based International Council of Religious Education (ICRE), which wanted a fresh, up-to-date Bible for use in Sunday schools.[10]

Reaction to the RSV New Testament, which appeared (several years behind schedule) in 1946, was more muted than reaction to the Revised Version New Testament in 1881, but similarly mixed. Officials at the sorts of religious institutions involved in the new translation loved it, some traditionalists pined for the mellifluous King James Version, and conservatives were generally wary of what they saw as the machinations of a few liberal eggheads. A new phase in both acceptance and opposition began in 1950 with the formation of the NCC, a large and complex organization encompassing representatives from more than thirty denominations ("communions," in NCC parlance) and multiple ecumenical agencies, including the ICRE, which became the NCC's Division of Education. In the merger, the NCC assumed sponsorship of the ICRE-led translation project, which is why it holds the copyright to the RSV.

In 1952 the NCC authorized publication of the new Bible, including a revised Old Testament, and promoted its use through its many agencies, giving members of the affiliated communions a strong reason to adopt it. Thomas Nelson even marketed its Bible as a "new authorized version," appropriating the title previously held by the King James Version. This was a bolder endorsement than the Revised Version ever received, but this endorsement generated massive backlash. Institutional imprimatur gave opponents of the NCC—which was deemed by conservatives to be a hyper-liberal, probably Communist, "superchurch"—overwhelming reason to reject the RSV. Reverend Martin Luther Hux, a North Carolina Baptist, reprised and enlarged the role previously played by T. DeWitt Talmage, going so far as to publicly burn the RSV page bearing Isaiah 7:14, which, in the new rendering, prophesied that Jesus Christ would be born not of a "virgin" but merely a "young woman." A deluge of anti-RSV polemics, by Hux and many other writers, ensued. By 1953, members of the RSV translation committee found themselves under investigation by the House Un-American Activities Committee.[11]

As this external drama raged, the mainline denominations faced internal difficulties related to the Bible, too. In the realm of mainline biblical interpretation, Fosdick's fervent attachment to progress had given way to more nuanced, and more varied, approaches. Interpretive variation within and among mainline denominations had never been absent, of course, and, to an extent, the multiplicity that surfaced in the 1950s could be attributed to the denominational mixing enabled by ecumenical institutions. As the preface to a 1951 World Council of Churches (WCC) volume of essays on biblical authority put it, "Every confession looks at the Bible from the point of view of its own tradition or customary ways of interpretation. Were it not so, there would be no need for ecumenical Bible study at all." But mainline Protestantism had also seen the rise of neo-orthodoxy, the theology principally associated with Karl Barth and Reinhold Niebuhr. Whereas the liberalism of a figure like Fosdick pared the Bible into a shape that made sense to modern readers, neo-orthodoxy emphasized the sometimes inscrutable otherness of both God and his word. When liberal/neo-orthodox divisions were added to churches whose humbler members had never even embraced modernism, it became less clear to anyone what the Bible said or meant.[12]

Theologically, this mid-century uncertainty was defensible, even commendable. The world had just suffered greatly at the hands of men who were unswervingly sure of their own beliefs. Additionally, the socially prominent, white Americans who made up the bulk of mainline membership were becoming increasingly aware of the continued suffering of the minorities in their own midst, thanks to the early civil rights movement. The American Methodist contributor to the 1951 WCC volume, Clarence T. Craig of Drew University, warned readers to recall "the long history of the use of the Bible to defend ethical standards advantageous to powerful, dominant groups," singling out the biblical case for slavery once argued in the American South. In Craig's view, advancing academic knowledge could not prevent more errors of this sort because the Bible contained too many contradictory statements for fallible humans to parse perfectly. In short, the Bible was complicated, and so were all of the people trying to interpret it. Clarion calls were in short supply. Recognizing that this conclusion might be dispiriting, Craig cited 1 Corinthians 14:8: "If the bugle gives an indistinct sound, who will get ready for battle?" Yet he would not give an easy answer, insisting that "it is far better to admit the obscurities in our sources of guidance than to claim the possession of a clear-cut direction."[13]

Principled ambiguity was not a popular stance amid aggressive Cold War piety and the frequent televised appearances of evangelist Billy Graham, poking his finger at the camera and repeating his catchphrase, "The Bible Says." Nor did mid-century academic efforts to scrutinize the derivations and redactions of biblical texts, or to capture the "historical Jesus," inspire much lay enthusiasm. Consequently, ambitious mainline campaigns to encourage Bible reading in churches and homes fell far short of their organizers' hopes. For example, beginning in 1948, the Presbyterian Church USA rolled out "Christian Faith and Life: A Program for Home and Church," a package of Sunday school lessons and take-home books aimed at improving biblical understanding among children and their parents. By 1951, more than 6,000 Presbyterian churches were using the curriculum, and it was both adopted and imitated in other mainline denominations. Supporters lavished praise on the program's comprehensiveness, sophistication, and verve. But it did not work. Parents did not use the materials at home. The Bible did not become more central in mainline Protestant family life, and church members reported alarming rates of theological confusion. As described by historian Margaret Lamberts Bendroth, in her book *Growing Up Protestant* (2002), drawing on church-sponsored research from the later 1950s:

> Instead of training their children in Christian theology, Protestant parents waffled around matters of religious truth; their children spent many more hours at Little League games or in

front of the ubiquitous television set than they did at the family altar. Even worse, the suburban parents interviewed in surveys had little sense of participation in an ongoing tradition. As one mildly distressed Presbyterian father admitted, "I don't have any sense of carrying on anything."[14]

Presbyterians abandoned the Christian Faith and Life program by the end of the decade. Meanwhile, conservative Protestants launched highly successful programs like Awana, an organization that worked with churches to create clubs where children memorized significant chunks of the Bible, and Bible Quiz (or Bible Bowl), where young people competed to display their mastery of Bible verses and Bible trivia. Mainline Protestants likely shuddered at the literalist view to the Bible embodied by these conservative programs, but they could only have envied the result: millions of children, and their supportive parents, reading the Bible regularly.

In subsequent decades, perspectives on the Bible within the mainline denominations continued to multiply, further eroding certainty among clergy or laypeople. A 1978 study of Chicago-area mainline clergy, replicating a 1928 study, found significant decreases in affirmation of such statements as "the New Testament is, and always will remain, the final revelation of the will of God to humanity" (-25 percent), "the Bible was written by men chosen and supernaturally endowed by God for that purpose, and by him given the exact message they were to write" (-26 percent), and "the selection and collection of the sacred books known as the Bible was by the direct will and authority of God, and is infallibly correct as determining what should be the content of the Bible" (-20 percent), along with an increase in affirmation of the statement, "the principles of criticism and evaluation applied to other literature and history should be applied to the Bible" (+12 percent). The same study summarized, "The 1960s saw malaise in the institutional churches and radicalism in theology. And the 1970s saw a decline and loss of nerve in the Protestant mainline."

A 1985 book by Donald McKim, a Presbyterian theologian, offered an overview of *What Christians Believe about the Bible*, giving two chapters to fundamentalist and evangelical perspectives and eight to perspectives present within mainline denominations: liberal theology, scholastic theology (the "Old Princeton" tradition), neo-orthodox theology, existential theology, process theology, story theology, liberation theology, and feminist theology. Early twenty-first century data on mainline Protestant laypeople revealed high reverence for the Bible ("The Bible is the inspired word of God," 92 percent) but low confidence in its literal accuracy ("Everything in the Bible should be taken literally, word for word," 28 percent) and an odd equivocation about the centrality of Christian doctrine ("Christianity is the best way to understand God," 79 percent; "All religions are equally good ways of knowing about God," 70 percent). The strongest point of agreement among these mainline Protestants, in a faint echo of Harry Emerson Fosdick, was the absolute importance of spiritual growth. Truth claims faltered, but faith in progress remained.[15]

A New Resource: The Lectionary

A notable counter-trend to this disengagement of mainline Protestants from the Bible, as well as the disjuncture between scholars, denominational executives, and the rank-and-file, was the gradual adoption of the Revised Common Lectionary. A lectionary lists selected scripture texts for every day or week. It might include all scriptures or only portions, and it might schedule the texts to repeat annually or less frequently—often, on a three-year cycle. Jews and Christians representing various traditions developed numerous lectionaries from the medieval period onward. Occasionally, important though not sacred texts were also organized in a lectionary format, such as the 52-week Heidelberg Catechism used in Reformed churches.

One of the liturgical innovations of the Second Vatican Council was a new, three-year lectionary for use in Roman Catholic Mass, and some ecumenical Protestants quickly grew interested in adapting a version for use in their own worship services. A group of Catholic and Protestant liturgical scholars, called the Consultation on Common Texts (CCT), formed in 1969. The group worked first on harmonizing disparate versions of liturgical texts (such as the Lord's Prayer, also known as the "Our Father") before turning its attention to a version of the Catholic lectionary that could be used in participating Protestant churches—initially, Episcopal, Lutheran, Presbyterian, and United Methodist. The Common Lectionary appeared in 1983, a three-year cycle of Old Testament and New Testament texts, plus a weekly psalm, arranged to follow the basic liturgical year (Advent, Christmas, Lent, Easter, Pentecost, and few other special observances). After several years of feedback from churches using the lectionary, and after the 1989 publication of the New Revised Standard Version of the Bible, the CCT issued a Revised Common Lectionary, using the NRSV, in 1992. This lectionary is used widely, though not universally, in all mainline denominations. (A separate effort, undertaken in the early 1980s by a division of the NCC, to publish a lectionary using gender-inclusive language generated more controversy than traction. The Revised Common Lectionary is more gender-inclusive than the earlier version, because the NRSV is more gender-inclusive than the RSV.)

The Revised Common Lectionary is not theologically directive, in that pastors who favor any of the approaches listed by Donald McKim (or any others) can apply those approaches to the weekly texts. Sermons can focus on the Old or New Testament selections, emphasizing narrative, doctrine, contemporary application, or whatever the preacher chooses to highlight. Copious liturgical aids, in print and available online, allow further variation in worship services, and mainline hymnals correlate songs to the scheduled texts. Perhaps the only perspective not accommodated by the lectionary is the dismissiveness toward the Old Testament expressed by some of the more strident supersessionists of the early twentieth century.

Instead, the lectionary reflects a mid-century ecumenical consensus, set down in 1949 as "Guiding Principles for the Interpretation of the Bible," that sound analysis requires moving back and forth between the Old and New Testaments, seeing every passage in its fullest context. Still, acute discomfort persists among mainline Christians regarding texts, particularly though not exclusively in the Old Testament, that seem to advocate violence, belittle women, or condemn homosexuality. Many of these texts are simply omitted from the scheduled Sunday readings.[16]

All three key aspects of the mainline approach to the Bible—scholarly expertise, institutional authorization, and ecumenical cooperation—come together in the lectionary. Scholars compiled the lists of texts and produce many of the resources that supplement it. (*The Christian Century* has carried a regular column of lectionary reflections, usually written by professors or pastors with advanced degrees, since 2008.) The lectionary has institutional authorization from dozens of churches in the United States and throughout the English-speaking world. Finally, the lectionary is a concrete example of ecumenism in action. Few church members have any meaningful connection to the NCC, WCC, or other acronymic organizations, but every Sunday they can get the sense that they are participating in common worship with Christians across confessional and national boundaries.

Conclusion

Mainline Protestants' trifold commitments to scholarly expertise, institutional authorization, and ecumenical cooperation predisposed them to certain accomplishments and challenges over the past 150 years. These Protestants were consistently at the forefront of biblical studies, producing insights from which even Christians hostile to mainline theology benefited. For example, evangelical study Bibles routinely include information on the historical background of each book, and members of the Evangelical Theological Society (cautiously) embraced higher criticism toward the end of the twentieth century. Mainline institutional backing facilitated complex, multi-year projects of translation and resource development while also supporting the seminaries and divinity schools where scholarship flourished. Ecumenical cooperation tempered the atomistic interpretive tendencies present within Protestantism ever since Martin Luther proclaimed the "priesthood of all believers." At the same time, an expert-heavy, top-down approach to the Bible (and to church life more generally) frequently alienated laypeople, discouraging them from engaging scriptures on their own. The "logic of mainline churchliness," as one scholar dubbed it, created a tradition in which members are most likely to encounter the Bible not on their nightstand, but in a public worship service, where the words are read aloud by someone else.[17]

Notes

1. Elesha J. Coffman, *"The Christian Century" and the Rise of the Protestant Mainline* (New York: Oxford University Press, 2013), 213–16. For variant definitions of "mainline," see, e.g., Glenn Utter, *Mainline Christians and U.S. Public Policy* (Santa Barbara, Calif.: ABC-CLIO, 2007); Peter W. Williams, *America's Religions: From Their Origins to the Twenty-First Century*, 3rd ed. (Urbana: University of Illinois Press, 2008); and Jason S. Lantzer, *Mainline Christianity: The Past and Future of America's Majority Faith* (New York: New York University Press, 2012).

2. Philip Schaff, *Historical Account of the American Committee of Revision of the Authorized English Version of the Bible* (New York: Scribner's, 1885), esp. 32; Nathan O. Hatch, *The Democratization of American Christianity* (New Haven, Conn.: Yale University Press, 1989).

3. Peter J. Thuesen, *In Discordance with the Scriptures: American Protestant Battles over Translating the Bible* (New York: Oxford University Press, 1999), 54.

4. Thuesen, *Discordance with the Scriptures*, 49; DeWitt Talmage, "Refuge of Superstition," *Free Religious Index*, June 16, 1881, 610–11.

5. Thuesen, *Discordance with the Scriptures*, 55n50, 59.

6. Charles A. Briggs, *Inaugural Address and Defense*, 1891/1893 (New York: Arno Press, 1972), 67. See also Carl E. Hatch, *The Charles A. Briggs Heresy Trial: Prologue to Twentieth-Century Liberal Protestantism* (New York: Exposition Press, 1969).

7. George H. Shriver, *A Dictionary of Heresy Trials in American Christianity* (Westport, Conn.: Greenwood Press, 1997).

8. Coffman, *Christian Century*, 57.

9. Harry Emerson Fosdick, *The Modern Use of the Bible* (1924; repr., New York: Macmillan, 1940), 11–12. Incidentally, when Fosdick quoted from the Bible in this book, he used the words of the King James Version. For a folksier, though still mainline (Congregationalist) appropriation of the lens of progress and the insights of higher criticism in the same era, see Bruce Barton, *The Book Nobody Knows* (Indianapolis, Ind.: Bobbs-Merrill, 1926).

10. Thuesen, *Discordance with the Scriptures*, 69–73.

11. Thuesen, *Discordance with the Scriptures*, 91, 97, 101. See also Ralph Lord Roy, *Apostles of Discord: A Study of Organized Bigotry and Disruption on the Fringes of Protestantism* (Boston, Mass.: Beacon Press, 1953).

12. Alan Richardson and Wolfgang Schweitzer, eds. *Biblical Authority for Today: A World Council of Churches Symposium on "The Biblical Authority for the Churches' Social and Political Message for Today"* (London: SCM Press, 1951), 11.

13. Clarence Tucker Craig, "A Methodist Contribution," in Richardson and Schweitzer, *Biblical Authority for Today*, 30–44.

14. Margaret Lamberts Bendroth, *Growing Up Protestant: Parents, Children, and Mainline Churches* (New Brunswick, N.J.: Rutgers University Press, 2002), 115.

15. Dean R. Hoge and John E. Dyble, "The Influence of Assimilation on American Protestant Ministers' Beliefs, 1928-1978," *Journal for the Scientific Study of Religion* 20, no. 1 (March 1981): 64–77; Donald K. McKim, *What Protestants Believe about the Bible* (Nashville, Tenn.: Thomas Nelson, 1985); Robert Wuthnow and John H. Evans, eds., *The Quiet Hand of God: Faith-Based Activism and the Public Role of Mainline Protestantism* (Berkeley: University of California Press, 2002), 8–10.

16. Richardson and Schweitzer, *Biblical Authority for Today*, 240–44. On omitted texts, see Roger Beckwith, "The Revised Common Lectionary," *Churchman* 112, no. 2 (1998): 117–23.

17. Grant R. Osborne, "Historical Criticism and the Evangelical," *Journal of the Evangelical Theological Society* 42, no. 2 (March 1999): 193–210; Christopher M. Hays and Christopher B. Ansberry, eds., *Evangelical Faith and the Challenge of Historical Criticism* (Grand Rapids, Mich.: Baker, 2013); Peter J. Thuesen, "The Logic of Mainline Churchliness: Historical Background since the Reformation," in Wuthnow and Evans, *The Quiet Hand of God*, 27–53.

BIBLIOGRAPHY

Bendroth, Margaret Lamberts. *Growing Up Protestant: Parents, Children, and Mainline Churches*. New Brunswick, N.J.: Rutgers University Press, 2002.

Bowman, Matthew. *The Urban Pulpit: New York City and the Fate of Liberal Evangelicalism*. New York: Oxford University Press, 2014.

Coffman, Elesha J., *"The Christian Century" and the Rise of the Protestant Mainline*. New York: Oxford University Press, 2013.

Dorrien, Gary. *The Making of American Liberal Theology: Idealism, Realism and Modernity*. Louisville, Ky.: Westminster John Knox, 2003.

Hollinger, David. *After Cloven Tongues of Fire: Protestant Liberalism in Modern American History*. Princeton, N.J.: Princeton University Press, 2013.

Hutchison, William R., ed. *Between the Times: The Travail of the Protestant Establishment, 1900–1960*. Cambridge: Cambridge University Press, 1989.

———. *The Modernist Impulse in American Protestantism*. Cambridge, Mass.: Harvard University Press, 1976.

Lantzer, Jason S. *Mainline Christianity: The Past and Future of America's Majority Faith*. New York: New York University Press, 2012.

Longfield, Bradley J. *The Presbyterian Controversy: Fundamentalists, Modernists, and Moderates*. New York: Oxford University Press, 1991.

Pietsch, B. M. *Dispensational Modernism*. New York: Oxford University Press, 2015.

Schmidt, Leigh Eric, and Sally Promey, eds. *American Religious Liberalism*. Bloomington: Indiana University Press, 2012.

Thuesen, Peter J. *In Discordance with the Scriptures: American Protestant Battles over Translating the Bible*. New York: Oxford University Press, 1999.

White, Heather Rachelle. *Reforming Sodom: Protestants and the Rise of Gay Rights*. Chapel Hill: University of North Carolina Press, 2015.

Wuthnow, Robert, and John H. Evans, eds., *The Quiet Hand of God: Faith-Based Activism and the Public Role of Mainline Protestantism*. Berkeley: University of California Press, 2002.

Zeller, Benjamin E. "American Postwar 'Big Religion': Reconceptualizing Twentieth-Century American Religion Using Big Science as a Model." *Church History* 80, no. 2 (June 2011): 321–51.

CHAPTER 36

....

THE BIBLE
AND EVANGELICALISM

....

JOHN G. STACKHOUSE JR.

The B-I-B-L-E
Yes, that's the book for me!
I stand alone on the Word of God
The B-I-B-L-E!

ALL Christians love and venerate the Bible. But no tradition of Christianity loves and venerates it more than evangelical Protestantism. The renowned English pastor and writer John R. W. Stott, one of the previous generation's leading evangelical statesmen, pronounces evangelicals to be, above all, "Bible people."[1] Lutheran sociologist Peter Berger famously writes of Protestants purging Roman Catholicism of most of its myth and mystery, leaving the Bible at the core of humanity's revelational connection with God.[2] Evangelicals "stand alone on the Word of God" as faithfully as any Protestant—even to what many Protestants would deem an extreme.

Precisely because of this setting aside of other religious resources such as liturgies, creedal statements, and sacramental rituals in favor of the Bible, the identity, activity, and vitality of evangelicals has depended crucially upon the Bible in their midst. This chapter surveys how the Bible has figured in evangelical life and suggests how the role of the Bible is under stress amid sweeping changes in contemporary evangelicalism.

WHO ARE THE EVANGELICALS?

....

An academic cottage industry has sprung up in this last generation of historians, sociologists, and theologians to answer the question: Who are the evangelicals? Since it is only preliminary to our purposes, however, let us agree on a widely accepted general definition.[3]

Historically, evangelicalism emerged in the eighteenth-century revivals associated with the work of John and Charles Wesley, George Whitefield, and Jonathan Edwards. Individuals and movements who descend from these origins and who have not departed from the concerns that marked them can be called "evangelicals," along with those groups that latterly identified with these concerns and the network of groups that espouse them. Evangelicals thus would be found among Methodists, Presbyterians, and Baptists in the former set, and among Mennonite Brethren and the Christian Reformed in the latter.

Evangelical concerns are perhaps best seen as a cluster of five. First, "evangelical" comes from *evangel*, or "gospel." Evangelicals prize the classic good news of God being "in Christ, reconciling the world to himself" (2 Cor. 5:19). Doctrinally, then, evangelicals are creedally orthodox (whether or not they happen to recognize the authority of the Apostles', Nicene, and Chalcedonian symbols, which many do not) and concentrate particularly on the career of Jesus Christ—his incarnation, life, death, resurrection, and ascension. Evangelicals believe that only in the work of Christ is salvation secured, and only through faith in Christ is salvation received.

Second, evangelicals hold to these beliefs, as well as all of their other religious tenets, because they believe that the Bible teaches them, and the Bible is the Word of God in written form. The Bible is fully inspired by God such that it is God's own book. Most evangelicals specify that the Holy Spirit inspired the very words of Hebrew, Aramaic, and Greek in the Bible's canonical form, while others believe that God allowed the limitations of the human authors to show up in relatively minor matters. All agree, however, that the Bible is the fundamental and supremely authoritative reference for the key issues of life, given by God in inspiration and subsequently illuminating through the Holy Spirit all who read it in faith.

Third, evangelicals believe in conversion, and they believe in it in two respects. Because of each person's inherited sinfulness and many individual acts of willful sin, he or she must be converted away from sin and toward God, raised from spiritual death to eternal life—in a phrase, they must be "born again." Furthermore, evangelicals believe in "full conversion"— a life of increasing holiness, of disciplined and fervent piety that conforms increasingly to Christ's example of obedience and goodness. This aspect of conversion involves an ongoing journey toward complete maturity in Christ, a process known as "sanctification."

Fourth, evangelicals believe in mission. They particularly support the work of evangelism, the act of proclaiming the Gospel and calling for decision regarding it. But they also have been busy cooperating on other fronts to accomplish what they see to be the divine mission in the world, especially in ameliorating evils. Thus, they have sponsored hospitals, schools, farms, and other institutions that care for the body and mind, as well as the spirit.

So far, of course, these four emphases are generically Protestant and, with the exception of the emphasis placed on the supremacy of scriptural authority, basically Christian. What makes evangelicalism distinctive is its fifth emphasis, namely, a cooperative transdenominationalism that holds the other four concerns as so primary that evangelicals recognize anyone else who holds them also as spiritual kin and are willing to work together with them in a wide range of modes on that basis. Thus, evangelical Pentecostals, Methodists, Anglicans, and Mennonites, for example, all share the first four concerns and go on to cooperate in the World Evangelical Fellowship, in World Vision, in parachurch missionary endeavors such as InterVarsity Christian Fellowship, and in a multitude of other institutions and movements. Those Christians who happen to hold the first four concerns with evangelicals but who do not privilege them and who do not see them as a sufficient basis for fellowship and service together (for example, some Mennonite, Baptist, and Lutheran groups) would thus properly not be called "evangelicals" in this context, however truly "Gospel-oriented" and thus "evangelical" they are in a more basic sense. Having offered this generic definition, because of the arrangement of topics in this volume I will be focusing upon white, Anglophone evangelicals in America.

EVANGELICALS AND THE BIBLE: THE HERITAGE

Christ and Salvation

The "original evangelicals" were, of course, the sixteenth-century Protestant Reformers who saw themselves as champions of the true Gospel against Roman Catholic distortions and accretions. The famous Reformation slogans—*sola fide, sola gratia*, and *sola scriptura* (faith alone, grace alone, and the Bible alone)—epitomized the Protestant agenda of stripping away the husk of medieval superstition that had obscured the Gospel kernel for centuries.

Modern evangelicals have continued to understand Christ and salvation in terms that self-consciously reject Roman Catholicism's putative excesses: all those intermediary saints and clergy; all those rituals, pilgrimages, and relics; all those extra duties entailed by confession and penance; all those elaborations of the cosmos such as limbo, purgatory, and various angelic realms; and all those dubious additional doctrines, whether the Immaculate Conception of Mary or the infallibility of the pope. Indeed, it is this last doctrine that highlights the role that the Bible has played in the evangelical articulation of the Gospel. Evangelicals have understood themselves to teach what the Bible teaches—nothing more and nothing less. Roman Catholics, however, have taught much more, drawing as they have on what they understand to be divinely inspired tradition mediated by the church through the centuries and clarified particularly in the *magisterium*, or "teaching office," of the Catholic Church personified by the pope. Evangelicals have been radically Protestant in this respect: the Bible is a sword that evangelicals have used to cut off all of Roman Catholic teaching and practice that was not conformed—to evangelical satisfaction, at least—to the teaching of the Bible alone.

Evangelicals have seen a symmetry here. Roman Catholics teach "too much," adding unhelpfully to the Gospel message, because they draw on "too many" extra-biblical revelational resources. Disqualifying tradition as inspired revelation and ignoring Catholic claims of papal authority has reduced evangelicals to sorting out what the Bible says and thus reduce the version of the Gospel they have preached to a simpler, starker message.

The other group, however, over against whom evangelicals have defined themselves since the origin of "evangelicalism" in the eighteenth century, is the tradition of liberal theology. To be sure, most textbooks trace the origins of liberal theology to the career of F. D. E. Schleiermacher, whose first book was not published until 1799. Yet some of the polemics of Jonathan Edwards—perhaps most famously his treatise *On the Freedom of the Will* (1754)—are addressed to theological positions that clearly anticipate nineteenth-century liberalism. And whereas evangelicals have seen Roman Catholics as adding improperly to the "store" of God-given revelation and thus end up with a theology and piety that is too elaborate, evangelicals have seen liberals as subtracting from the Bible's authority and thus commending a theology that is attenuated and anemic when it comes to the Bible's most important teachings.

In the evangelical view of liberal theology, the Incarnate Son of God is diminished into a "very, very, very good man," in the droll phrase of Reinhold Niebuhr.[4] Salvation becomes merely our imitation of Jesus's example of godliness—without need of the Atonement (Christ's death on the cross to turn away God's judgment of sin). In many versions of liberalism, the Christian religion itself becomes just one of many salvific paths to God. Given the acids of what evangelicals have called "irreverent" and "destructive" historical criticism of the Bible and the preference for the deliverances of contemporary reason and experience over the orthodox doctrine harvested faithfully from the pages of scripture over the centuries, liberalism is left with a thin theology and a merely moralistic (and perhaps mystical) piety wrought out of a thoroughly degraded view of the Bible's salvific message.

Positively, then, evangelical summaries of doctrine typically provide "proof-texts" for each proposition, not only as glosses but as authorities: We believe *X* because the Bible teaches it right here. Orthodoxy is not merely the position of the strongest party in church disputes. Evangelicals have maintained instead that orthodoxy is simply a digest of the Bible in correct delineation and emphasis.

The Bible

The evangelical commitment to *sola scriptura* has played out in a number of respects, some of them paradoxical, some of them even contradictory. Evangelical theology was formed in the crucible of the Enlightenment, and much of it continues to show traits of that movement. Evangelical sermons and Bible study materials, for example, typically have emphasized "word studies," the tracing of etymologies and semantics through the Bible. Such word studies often depend on Enlightenment-style univocity in which "one word means one thing." Thus, many evangelicals confidently have discussed a term such as "glory" or "righteousness," flipping lightly over vast tracts of scriptural material with the aid of their concordances. Here, ironically, is a built-in disregard for hermeneutical context, a disregard that punishes the blithe exegete all the more when multivalent symbols are in play: thus, "fire" *always* connotes "judgment," and "leaven" *always* connotes "sin."

The most obvious sign of evangelical deference to the text of scripture is the habit of proof-texting. Evangelicals have assumed that truth is found in the very words of scripture, and every truth (at least, every truth of faith and religious practice) therefore can be demonstrated as emerging from particular texts of the Bible, cited by chapter and verse. Such an inclination has not been confined to the more radical "biblicistic" evangelical traditions, whether Plymouth Brethren, Mennonites, or Baptists. Evangelical theologians, scholarly or popular, whether Luther and Wesley, or Whitefield and Moody, habitually cite actual verses of scripture as the authority for whatever point they wish to make.

Many evangelicals, however, have been slow to take stock of just what role should be played, and in fact is played, by reason, experience, and tradition in their theologies. Wesley formulated his famous "quadrilateral" to coordinate these four resources, but few evangelicals outside the academy have explicated just what goes on in their theology besides mere Bible study. Thus, the dispensationalist has believed that his theological scheme is merely the end result of careful exegesis, not a paradigm that, once adopted, bends recalcitrant texts to its pattern. The Calvinist has done the same, ingenuously claiming that his system is merely the distillation of Biblical truth.

The most obvious giveaway of such a lack of theological self-consciousness has been the widely recommended evangelical practice of so-called inductive Bible study. Taught in dispensational Bible schools, denominational seminaries, and transdenominational Bible study guides alike, the practice seeks to expose the Bible reader to the text without the "interference" of "theology" or "tradition." Readers instead are given a select passage to read and a few "guiding questions" meant to help the reader come to his or her own conclusions (albeit within the terms of the questions thus interposed between the reader and the text). The Reformation doctrine of the "perspicuity of Scripture"—the idea that the scripture is sufficiently plain in its meaning that no official interpreter (= Roman Catholic clergy) must be interposed between the faithful reader and God—therefore has played out in ways that are sometimes perplexing and even self-defeating.

The authority of the Bible as evangelicalism's primary theological resource has been reinforced in evangelical use of the scriptural text symbolically. Scripture texts have been calligraphed or cross-stitched for decorating rooms both domestic and ecclesiastical. And Bible texts in some evangelical churches have replaced even the cross as the symbol emblazoned upon the front wall of the sanctuary—in an aesthetic that oddly resembles Islam's resistance to pictorial representation and embrace of the Qur'anic text for both ornamentation and devotional focus.

What has been true of the biblical text has been true also of the Bible itself as a holy object. A massive Bible typically has resided upon a prominent lectern at the front of the church—occupying the place of honor reserved in other churches for the elements of the Eucharist. In traditional evangelical homes, one could count on each family member owning a leather-bound, gilt-edged Bible. One also could count on these Bibles being shelved in places of honor, with many evangelicals practicing the folkway that no other book would be placed on top of it. Each family member often also possessed more than one personal copy of the Bible because evangelicals typically have marked important rites of passage with the presentation of new Bibles: birth and (perhaps) infant baptism, beginning a new phase of education, believer's baptism or confirmation, graduation from school, and marriage. Such personal Bibles frequently include pages for recording the milestones in one's life such as the births and deaths of loved ones, just as the family Bible has served as the register to record a family's genealogical history. In these and other ways, then, evangelicals have affirmed the preeminence of the Bible both practically and symbolically.[5]

Conversion

Conversion in the sense of evangelism will be discussed in the "Mission" section. Conversion in the sense of the progressive transformation of the sinner into the image of Christ is an equally important theme in evangelicalism.

When evangelicals have assembled to worship, the Bible always has figured prominently. Evangelicals have long championed preaching as the focus of the worship service. Good preachers are valued everywhere, but in no tradition more than evangelicalism—so much so that the pastor has sometimes been called "the preacher." The sermon normally has been positioned at the climax of liturgies and worship services, and evangelical sermons have almost always lasted longer than they have in non-evangelical churches.

Evangelical sermons have tended also to feature the actual words of scripture. Many preachers simply have exposited the Bible book by book, chapter by chapter, and verse by verse. Others have followed a lectionary or set of themes, but the evangelical impulse has always been to refer frequently to the text of the day. "Let's look now at verse *x*" has been a familiar phrase in evangelical churches, with the expectation that congregants will have their Bibles open throughout the sermon to follow along with the preacher to see that the Bible does, in fact, say what the preacher has said it does. Evangelical churches typically offer pew Bibles accessible in every seat, but regular attendees are expected to bring their own Bibles and take notes on the sermon either in the margins of those Bibles or in pads brought along expressly for that purpose. People in evangelical churches typically expect to learn more about the Bible each time they hear a sermon.

Scriptural knowledge was to be gained in other ways as well. Children in evangelical Sunday schools have heard Bible stories, not just cute fictions meant to illustrate generic spiritual or ethical truths. They have learned the order of the books of the Bible, engaged in contests (known colloquially as "sword drills") to find a particular passage first, and been encouraged to memorize scripture, whether key verses or whole passages such as the Ten Commandments or the Beatitudes. Adults also typically have engaged in Bible study in a small group, whether in a Sunday morning class or in a midweek home fellowship. Laypeople commonly have owned at least one single-volume commentary on the Bible and often have invested considerable sums in a reference library of Bible commentaries, concordances, and other study aids. Such aids have assisted them in their personal study and devotional reading that, again, normally focus upon scripture—as opposed to, for example, devotional readings from the Church Fathers or contemporary spiritual writers.

Scripture has also been embedded into music. Adults have sung scripture in church—from sixteenth-century Psalters to contemporary songs based on Bible verses by such popular institutions as Hillsong Church and Vineyard Christian Fellowship USA. Sunday schools and vacation Bible clubs for children have also featured specially composed, simple songs based on scripture. Indeed, many evangelical children have learned most of the "memory verses" they know by singing them rather than merely reading them.

The role of scripture in forming the beliefs and behaviors of evangelical Christians, whether individually or in community, can also be seen in how scripture passages are frequently used in any number of church-related settings. For example, ethical issues discussed in church boardrooms, at annual meetings, or in Christian homes often reference snatches of scripture, whether that be a proverb here or a beatitude there. Allusions and catchphrases have shown up as a matter of course in informal speech at church dinners and in correspondence with other believers. And jokes have been made, whether from the pulpit or over Sunday lunch, that presume a general knowledge of the Bible that is sometimes quite specific and might even include a particular knowledge of a specific Bible translation like the King James Version (e.g., "What man had no parents in the Bible? Joshua, the son of Nun [none]").

Mission

The Bible has been woven throughout the evangelical subculture. It naturally has played a large role, then, in the witness of this tradition to the larger world. Evangelicals have a long record of providing for the needs of others at home and around the globe. But when evangelicals have offered help—such as medicine, education, or food—they typically have tied it to evangelism. Furthermore, evangelicals have not merely commended the Gospel to others. They have argued for its validity and virtue, and they have done so typically with open

Bibles. So the apologetic as well as the evangelistic modes of evangelical mission deserve a look, and both show once again just how important the Bible is to evangelicalism.

In apologetics, evangelicals typically have concentrated attention on the Bible because it is the supreme guide to their faith. Thus, evangelicals have argued for the historical reliability of the Bible's accounts, the prophetic accuracy of its predictions, the beauty of its poetry and prose, the glory of its moral teachings, and the fundamental reality of its divine inspiration and authority. On the basis of this peerless volume, others have been invited to look at the Bible's central subject, Jesus Christ, and come to faith in him.

Evangelicals have used the Bible in Gospel preaching quite directly, as the very instrument of God's voice. Heeding promises such as "my word shall not return unto me void" (Isa. 55:11), evangelicals have freely salted their sermons with phrases, verses, and even whole chapters of scripture. Billy Graham has epitomized the evangelical who confidently proclaims, "The Bible says. . ." even to audiences who are not yet convinced of the Bible's authority. Graham is convinced, and so he speaks and reads from it with assurance that the very words of the Bible are charged with divine blessing and will be used for the divine mission by the Holy Spirit in the evangelistic encounter. Evangelicals at Bible schools and evangelism training workshops offered by groups such as the Billy Graham Evangelistic Association have been taught to memorize key scripture texts at the heart of the Gospel and urged to deploy them in evangelistic conversations. The Bible is not seen as magical here, as a book of charms merely to be recited to affect the desired outcome, but as a trusted vehicle through which God has promised to work.

Thus, evangelicals have both learned the Bible themselves to aid them in witnessing to the Gospel and encouraged their neighbors to read it in the course of their investigation of the Christian faith. Such reading means that evangelicals have worked hard to make scripture available to their neighbors, a fact that brings us to our next heading.

Transdenominationalism

In order to venerate and use the Bible, and in order to learn, memorize, teach, and evangelize from its pages, the Bible has to be intelligible and available. Thus, evangelicals have enthusiastically supported means of translating and disseminating the Bible. Whether as individuals struggling to produce translations for missionary frontiers—with missionary pioneer William Carey's Bengali translation as one of the great early translation efforts—or as major international organizations (with the Wycliffe Bible Translators/Summer Institute of Linguistics perhaps the best known), evangelicals have worked hard and often sacrificially to render the Bible into hundreds of languages around the world.

Evangelicals have worked no less diligently at the tasks of producing and transporting Bibles. Colporteurs in the nineteenth century brought Bibles to the borderlands of rural and urban America alike, to both remote farmers and forgotten slum-dwellers.[6] In the next century, Brother Andrew, "God's Smuggler," inspired a generation of evangelicals with his swashbuckling escapades on behalf of scripture distribution behind the Iron Curtain.[7] In these tasks, then, evangelicals typically have worked cooperatively with other evangelicals. For nothing is more basic, more uniting, and less contentious among evangelicals than the value of the Bible. So the great Bible societies arose as mainstays of evangelical ecumenism. Translation projects became one of the few enterprises in which evangelical scholars of various traditions worked together, partnering to produce the New American Standard Bible (1960), the New International Version (1973), and the Living Bible (notably its revised edition, 1997), among numerous other versions issued by Anglophone North Americans.

The culture of North American evangelicalism, then, features the Bible in every important respect. But in those same respects, the place of the Bible is under challenge in North American evangelicalism today.

Evangelicals and the Bible: Today and Tomorrow

While the traditions of evangelical regard for, and use of, the Bible continue to the present, in each area of concern new challenges have arisen.

Christ and Salvation

The first question deals with world religions and the fate of the unevangelized. All evangelicals reject the option of "pluralism," the position associated with scholars such as Wilfred Cantwell Smith and John Hick, and with varieties of Hindu and New Age religion. Pluralism affirms all spiritual paths as salvific—or, at least, affirms all good spiritual paths as salvific. (No one wants to endorse, say, infant sacrifice to Moloch in the ancient world or the religious aspects of Hitler's National Socialism in our own era.) But evangelicals divide into two broad camps of "exclusivists" and "inclusivists" on the question of the salvation of those who do not hear and understand the propositions of the Christian Gospel.[8]

These two camps have radically divergent views when it comes to who might be saved. Exclusivists maintain that hearing and responding to the Gospel is normally required for salvation (hardliners would remove the qualifier "normally"), and that the best one can hope for others is that God might do some mysteriously gracious thing about which we have no clue. Exclusivists, of course, have their proof texts, such as Romans 10:14 ("How shall they hear without a preacher?") and Acts 4:12 ("for there is no other name under heaven given among mortals by which we may be saved"). Inclusivists respond that the Bible is full of examples of people who have saving faith without knowledge of Jesus Christ: most obviously, every believer in the Old Testament qualifies as such. Furthermore, what about infants, or the mentally incompetent, or the schizophrenic, or others who are incapacitated and cannot understand the propositions of the Gospel? Surely God will not abandon them all? Both sides, to be sure, deploy both proof texts and examples. Exclusivists point to Cornelius as an example of a God-fearer who nonetheless had Peter sent to him by God to bring him the Gospel (Acts 10); inclusivists wield verses such as John 10:16—"I have sheep not of this fold."

This debate has yet to mature into a full-blown theology of religions, although there are some new ventures in that direction.[9] Neither side, however, is challenging fundamental orthodoxies regarding Christ or salvation. And both clearly see the Bible as the fundamental resource for exploring and resolving this conflict. Thus evangelicals are poised finally to answer the questions being raised throughout the world: Why this Book instead of that (sacred) book? Why this faith instead of that?

A controversy much more far-reaching than the inclusivism–exclusivism debate has been led by theologians Clark Pinnock and Gregory Boyd, reacting strongly against what they see to be a view of God distorted by Platonism via the Augustinian tradition.[10] This view of God, they believe, portrays him as static in his timelessness, loveless in his impassibility, and utterly domineering in his sovereignty. Instead, Pinnock, Boyd, and their followers recommend that evangelicals stress the "openness" of God. They aver that God goes through time as we do. In some way, he feels as we do (whether love or hate, dismay or celebration) as events come and go and as his purposes are frustrated or fulfilled, and most important, he cooperates with his creation toward an ultimately beneficent end.

The majority of evangelical theologians currently look askance at this "openness" movement. Some share its displeasure toward the classical categories of timelessness, impassibility, and so on, but believe that many streams of evangelical orthodoxy provide the resources to differ with those categories without adopting what seems dangerously close to the categories of process thought, albeit without all of the vocabulary and detail typical of its heritage in the complex philosophy of A. N. Whitehead. Others denounce the whole enterprise as simply heretical, compromising the glory of God both metaphysically and morally. They see the "openness" movement as characterizing God as no longer omniscient and omnipotent, himself subject to doubt, confusion, and fits of rage from which he needs sometimes to be helped by men and women who are able to communicate with him (Exod. 32.7–14).

These stories of God's creatures negotiating with him provide grist for the "openness" mill. And those aligned with the "openness" movement assert that they are simply reading the Bible better than their opponents and that they are more faithful to the biblical text and less dominated by non-Christian philosophical presuppositions.

No one in this debate doubts the creedal affirmations regarding Christ and salvation as far as they go. Clearly, however, the nature of God's work in Christ, the nature of God's program of salvation, the nature of the church's relationship with God, and the eschatological hope of the church all are affected by the change in viewpoint advocated in the "openness" model. The controversy has sometimes been bitter, but one pastor involved in this discussion reported to me that this was the first time in his twenty-year career that his congregants were fascinated by a theological subject and were reading and discussing the Bible as never before on matters that, he concluded with satisfaction, really matter.

The Bible

The third leading edge of evangelical theological development is one entirely of methodology. Whether in the championing of Karl Barth's theology by an earlier generation of evangelical theologians, most notably Bernard Ramm and Donald Bloesch, or in the exploration of post-liberal views in the current one, evangelical theologians have been wondering aloud about just what biblical inspiration and authority mean.[11] Some have come to the conclusion that the Barthian/post-liberal acceptance of higher criticism followed by a kind of "second naïveté" that affirms the Bible's truth and authority within the discourse of the Christian community points the way out of two hundred years of controversy between evangelicals and liberals. Many evangelicals, however, wonder if this is merely a sidestep around the question both traditional evangelicals and liberals want to keep asking: However "true" the Bible seems to be for those within the Christian fold, what claims can be made, if any, for the truth of the Bible in the world at large?[12]

Such methodological debates have yet to seep deeply into evangelical popular culture. What is striking in some cutting-edge evangelical churches is a sort of embarrassment toward, or at least a downplaying of, the Bible as symbol. "Seeker-sensitive" churches typically avoid any traditional religious symbolism, including the Bible. No great Bible sits splendidly at the front of these auditoriums. Rarely are there Bibles available for those in the pew to read. Instead, if viewing any biblical text is deemed necessary, it is projected onto a screen for a few moments and then, surely with unintentional irony, extinguished. Or perhaps a few verses are printed in the program for that service, only to be discarded as trash once the service is finished. In such "seeker-sensitive" churches it remains a matter of fact that the Bible is purposely much less evident than in traditional evangelical services and sanctuaries.

As for the Bible in the private lives of evangelicals, the practice of posting scripture texts on the walls of one's home seems to be fading fast. As for other kinds of adornment, evangelicals do not typically go to the Hasidic extreme of binding actual texts to their bodies, of course—except that some now do: in T-shirts or phone cases emblazoned with snatches of scripture; pens and pencils imprinted with Bible passages; and even candy that "bears witness" via Bible verses on their wrappers. The "Jesus junk" of contemporary evangelical paraphernalia thus contrasts sharply with former evangelical traditions of the Bible as holy object. More radical, hipster evangelicals, both male and female, have symbols, words, and even whole phrases tattooed on their bodies, often in the original Hebrew or Greek.

Critics of various displays and physical manifestations of scripture must be careful, however, to ensure that their criticism is not just a matter of aesthetic taste dressed up in theological robes. What to one person may be a sacrilegiously tacky bathroom mirror scripture text or T-shirt slogan might be another person's daily reminder to piety or a heartfelt testimony to salvation. Some uses of the Bible might well be the result of misplaced zeal or crass commercialism, but these phenomena challenge everyone to recall just what the Bible is given us to do and to beware of an excessive reverence that might keep the Bible from functioning as it ought.

Among evangelicals who do want to consider the great teachings of theology in some detail, doctrine is often reduced merely to the adducing, arranging, and commenting on biblical texts—as in the very popular "systematic theology" of New Testament scholar Wayne Grudem, or even less conservative authorities such as N. T. Wright and John Stott himself.[13] Very little attention is paid to the two thousand years of church experience and reflection that intervene between the Bible and humankind, much less the deliverances of contemporary philosophy, literature, or the natural and social sciences. Nor is there much consciousness of the hermeneutical effects of ethnicity, class, and gender, categories so familiar in the secular academy as to verge on cliché. Since evangelical belief is rooted in and governed by the Bible, evangelicals seem to think we need expertise only in biblical studies to articulate doctrine.

Other evangelicals, however, are deeply interested in tradition and particularly in those traditions of Christianity and of biblical interpretation that are traditionally viewed by evangelicals as polar opposites of evangelicalism: Roman Catholicism, Orthodoxy, and the patristic and medieval authorities. Largely as a reaction against the desiccated historicism of academic historical criticism, "spiritual" or "theological" interpretation of scripture now enjoys a new vogue among academic theologians and increasingly among pastors as well.[14] Even the once-derided category of allegory has returned, somewhat ironically, in an age dominated by ultramodern visual electronic media and by hyper- and inter-textual richness. Evangelical theologians debate how far allegory properly can take us in explicating particularly the Christological content in Old Testament texts while avoiding the hermeneutical nightmare of "anything can be said. . . about anything" (George Steiner).[15] But allegorical interpretation's traditional concern for doctrinal import and ethical impact resonates nicely with an age of storytelling homiletics, big-screen churches, and, among the more intellectually minded, a growing stress on narrative theology.[16]

Curiously, increasing numbers of evangelicals are apparently not interested in biblical study even on the things that matter most to them. Particularly in debates over sexual ethics and identities, but on other fronts as well including politics, parenting, and bioethics, many American evangelicals no longer feel obliged to mount careful and detailed biblical arguments for their views. In terms more familiar to scholars of Romanticism than of the Enlightenment, this or that conviction is right because it is obviously, intuitively right. Jesus was kind, and good, and loving, and affirming, and inclusive, and so our particular position on this or that contested ethical topic clearly follows this view of Jesus's benevolent character. It seems not to occur to these evangelicals that Jesus, as a member of the Trinity, troubled himself to compose, collect, edit, transmit, and preserve a large and complicated set of books called the Bible, and by doing so offered a range of teachings that might challenge our easy generalizations, particularly when those generalizations (a) conform to the aspects of culture we find most attractive, and (b) justify our personal preferences. It is this recourse to intuition and "broad themes" rather than the authority of particular biblical texts that is one of the most striking changes in American evangelicalism in the last generation.

Conversion

Evangelical preaching in many places is as traditionally expositional as ever. But two other traditions of preaching vie increasingly with it. One such tradition includes evangelicals influenced by the "narrative" school of homiletics (American Fred Craddock is perhaps the best known of these) who are encouraged to reach the postmodern mind by jettisoning the old, linear, argumentative form of preaching and adopting an impressionistic, quick-cutting style that emphasizes story-telling over declamation.[17] The other tradition is on display in the Pentecostal and charismatic wings of evangelicalism in which preachers still unabashedly wave open Bibles about as they speak and still quote scripture aplenty. The Bible, that is, continues to occupy the sermon both symbolically and materially. But many of these preachers perpetuate a "ranting" tradition of homiletics that ironically also fits into some people's understanding of the postmodern mind: its preference for the episodic, allusive, and affective. In this style of preaching, the speaker selects a theme and then proceeds to make his points in turn while studding each one with select phrases of scripture. The effect is not unlike the more refined homiletics of the "narrative" school in the combination of story-telling (or "testimonies"), scriptural allusions, and punchy exhortations.

What is difficult to judge in either form of such quickly changing, kaleidoscopic presentations is whether what the preacher is saying really emerges from the authoritative Word of God or whether the preacher might just be grabbing convenient bits from here and there to justify a point he was going to make anyway. In sermons that increasingly resemble music videos as nonsequential, rapid-fire "experiences," it is also unclear here whether anyone is learning much about the Bible.

Evangelicals apparently are still learning about the Bible in small group studies. Yet many of these groups read other sorts of books together, whether guides to healthier marriage or family life, handbooks on evangelism or apologetics, or even popular Christian novels. To be sure, any and all of these pursuits can be part of a good program of adult Christian education. But an observer might still wonder where, if not in these groups, evangelicals are engaged in an ongoing study of the Bible.

Preachers and pollsters alike report that both churchgoers and non-churchgoers show a declining grasp of even basic Bible content. The experiential-cum-therapeutic cultural wave of the late twentieth century has tended to turn even genuine Bible studies into encounter groups in which people offer their impressions of "what this Bible passage means to me" or perhaps, in good evangelical pragmatist fashion, "what this Scripture encourages me to do," without lingering upon the prior question of "what the Bible actually says." "Sword drills" are quaint relics of a rapidly disappearing subculture, along with the discipline of scripture memorization. Indeed (to take humor seriously as an anthropological marker), one could not tell a joke to a typical church audience today that assumed any particular item of scriptural knowledge with confidence that most people would get it. Evangelicals can no longer be accused of "biblicism" and even "bibliolatry," and it is not because evangelicals generally have become more theologically sophisticated.

Mission

In apologetics and evangelism, traditional methods and resources still prevail. Evidentialist and rationalist apologetics dominate, and most evangelistic programs still emphasize proof texts as part of an appropriate Gospel presentation. Amid these apologetic strains has been a rise in what has become known as "friendship evangelism," a school of outreach that concentrates on personal relationships over the brute force means of disseminating the Gospel through tracts, door-to-door visitations, and revival preaching. The rise of "friendship evangelism," however, is not without its ambiguities. At its best, such an emphasis encourages evangelicals to eschew the bad old days of seeing neighbors as souls to be saved, as targets for proselytization by relentless messaging. The Gospel is lived out, and in time is articulated within the context of genuine love for one's neighbor. At its worst, however, such an approach allows for the benign and inoffensive vagueness of mere goodwill to substitute for a scripturally informed conversation.

Another popular means of evangelistic endeavor is the wildly popular "Alpha" program originating from Holy Trinity–Brompton (HTB) Anglican Church in London, England, and imported to North America. Drawing on previous evangelistic programs, most notably the supper meetings of the Oxford Group Movement of the mid-twentieth century, the Alpha program has been employed enthusiastically by groups that share neither HTB's

Anglicanism nor its charismatic emphasis. It features smaller groups dining together before a short theological lecture is given and then discussed.

And therein lies the rub when it comes to the Bible's role in evangelism. The Alpha program's Gospel presentation of "basic Christianity" is largely devoted to a charismatic presentation of the work of the Holy Spirit in the individual and the church, from teaching about the "Baptism of the Holy Spirit" in classical Pentecostal terms to extended discussions of spiritual gifts. Such teachings, however true they might be to the charismatic tradition in its distinctive cultivation of believers, seem oddly prominent in a program designed to evangelize those who do not attend church and are not confessing Christians of any sort. Indeed, they seem oddly out of keeping with the evangelistic emphases of the New Testament itself, which concentrates instead on the saving work of Jesus Christ, particularly in its accounts of apostolic proclamation. One wonders in both cases, then, how deeply informed by the Bible evangelical thinking has become in contemporary society even regarding the fundamental enterprise of Christian mission.

Transdenominationalism

When it comes to the projects of translating and disseminating the Bible as key zones of evangelical transdenominational cooperation, one might conclude that the evangelical story is an entirely happy one. Domestic translations have proliferated with huge sales across denominational lines. Publishers have devised more and more ingenious Bible "products," including a variety of smartphone and laptop applications. And global translation continues apace, with Wycliffe Bible Translators weathering various storms, from accusations of complicity with the CIA overseas to the kidnapping and even murder of some of their staff.[18]

Yet all has not been well even here. Controversy rocked American evangelicalism over the proposals to use inclusive language for human beings in the revision of the New International Version (NIV). (The New Revised Standard Version [1989] had anticipated this change by a decade.) In regard to revising the NIV, some prominent evangelicals took umbrage at what they saw to be the not-so-thin edge of a feminist wedge that would perhaps lead to outright goddess worship. Many evangelicals saw these fears as hysterical, but the American publisher backed off and refused to print the new edition. (The British publisher had already begun distribution.) Actual matters of Bible translation are indeed at stake in good faith: there might well be something important lost, for example, in rendering Psalm 1 as "Blessed are those" (that is, a group) rather than the more literal "Blessed is the man..." (that is, a faithful individual). But more than a few observers have seen the conservative reaction as beholden at least as much to anti-feminist ideology as to scriptural fidelity. In that respect, this was the first translation controversy not clearly about orthodox doctrine of God, Christ, and salvation, but perhaps about secondary or even tertiary matters of differing evangelical opinion.[19]

Other critics have found the very proliferation of translations to have affected evangelical piety and community. No longer are the cadences of a single translation (the King James Version or KJV) familiar to everyone, and therefore useful for reference and allusion. Evangelical congregations now are filled with people having to do their own quick translating between the version they had brought to church and the version from which the preacher is reading. Furthermore, the new translations have aimed so obviously, and generally successfully, at contemporary idiomatic and accessible English that many observers bemoan the loss of nuance and poetic singularity of expression that had made the KJV a classic of English literature. "Who wants to memorize this banality?" some ask.

Still, as revisers of the KJV itself have agreed through the centuries, there is little to be spiritually gained by memorizing words that in fact have changed their meanings over time, let alone become simply opaque. Furthermore, the Bible itself is not uniformly written in fine style. So there is a fundamental translation question here not to be overlooked: if Peter or John wrote like fishermen, should not their epistles sound that way? Perhaps "committee" translations of the Bible ought to emerge from individual translators emulating the particular styles of the Biblical books so as to relay something of the rhetorical differences between, say, Peter and Paul—rather than everything sounding like it emerged from a single committee.

Finally, the wide range of study Bibles prompts some to wonder whether evangelicals are now unwittingly reintroducing a whole new set of intermediaries between the reader and the text. Moreover, these intermediaries are not nearly as distinguished as, say, Augustine, Aquinas, Luther, or Wesley, but are merely contemporary Bible scholars, popular pastors, or even hack writers hired to produce material somehow germane to the target group. Furthermore, the very attempt to package these Bibles in various covers and designs in order to appeal to a particular taste has had the unfortunate symbolic effect of conforming the Bible to an individual's own chosen "lifestyle," rather than marking it out as a holy object to which one ought to conform oneself.[20]

CONCLUSION

To remark that evangelicalism has changed is to spout a truism. Every movement changes over time, and evangelicalism has taken on the contours of a succession of cultural impulses from its eighteenth-century origins to its current position at the beginning of a new century and millennium. So, too, has evangelicalism's relationship to the Bible varied over time. The mere fact, then, that the present does not look like the past should not necessarily provoke either dismay or joy. Historical awareness, however, should bring into relief aspects of current thought and practice that can too easily be assumed as "obviously right" when, in fact, they are artifacts of our particular cultural moment. With that awareness evangelicals are at least better equipped to read, understand, champion, share, and live in the light of their Bibles.

NOTES

1. John Stott, *Evangelical Truth: A Personal Plea for Unity, Integrity and Faithfulness* (Downers Grove, Ill.: InterVarsity, 1999), 65.
2. Peter L. Berger, *The Sacred Canopy: Elements of a Sociological Theory of Religion* (Garden City, N.Y.: Doubleday, 1967), 110–13.

3. David W. Bebbington, *Evangelicalism in Modern Britain: A History from the 1730s to the 1980s* (London: Unwin Hyman, 1989), 1–19; George M. Marsden, ed., introduction to *Evangelicalism and Modern America* (Grand Rapids, Mich.: Eerdmans, 1984), viii–xvi; and John G. Stackhouse, Jr., "Generic Evangelicalism," in *Four Views on the Spectrum of Evangelicalism*, ed. Andrew David Naselli and Collin Hansen (Grand Rapids, Mich.: Zondervan, 2011), 56–61.

4. Reinhold Niebuhr, *The Nature and Destiny of Man: A Christian Interpretation*, vol. 1: *Human Nature*, 2 vols. (1941; repr., New York: Scribner's, 1964), 146.

5. Colleen McDannell, *Material Christianity: Religion and Popular Culture in America* (New Haven, Conn.: Yale University Press, 1995), 67–102.

6. David Paul Nord, "The Evangelical Origins of Mass Media in America, 1815-1835," *Journalism Monographs* 88 (May 1984), 1-30.

7. Brother Andrew et al., *God's Smuggler* (New York: New American Library, 1987).

8. John Sanders, *No Other Name: An Investigation into the Destiny of the Unevangelized* (Grand Rapids, Mich.: Eerdmans, 1992); John Sanders, ed., *What about Those Who Have Never Heard? Three Views on the Destiny of the Unevangelized* (Downers Grove, Ill.: InterVarsity, 1995).

9. Gerald D. McDermott and Harold A. Netland, *A Trinitarian Theology of Religions: An Evangelical Proposal* (Oxford: Oxford University Press, 2014); John G. Stackhouse, Jr., ed., *No Other Gods before Me?: Evangelicals and the Challenge of World Religions* (Grand Rapids, Mich.: Baker Academic, 2001).

10. Clark H. Pinnock, ed., *The Openness of God: A Biblical Challenge to the Traditional Understanding of God* (Downers Grove, Ill.: InterVarsity, 1994); Gregory A. Boyd, *God of the Possible: A Biblical Introduction to the Open View of God* (Grand Rapids, Mich.: Baker, 2000).

11. Gary Dorrien, *The Remaking of Evangelical Theology* (Louisville, Ky.: Westminster John Knox, 1998).

12. Timothy R. Phillips and Dennis L. Okholm, eds., *The Nature of Confession: Evangelicals and Postliberals in Conversation* (Downers Grove, Ill.: InterVarsity, 1996).

13. Wayne Grudem, *Systematic Theology: An Introduction to Biblical Doctrine* (Grand Rapids, Mich.: Zondervan, 1995).

14. Daniel J. Treier, *Introducing Theological Interpretation of Scripture: Recovering a Christian Practice* (Grand Rapids, Mich.: Baker Academic, 2008); Kevin J. Vanhoozer, ed., *Dictionary for Theological Interpretation of the Bible* (Grand Rapids, Mich.: Baker Academic, 2005); see also the multivolume series *Brazos Theological Commentary on the Bible* (Grand Rapids, Mich.: Baker Publishing/Brazos Press, 2005–14).

15. George Steiner, *Real Presences* (Chicago: University of Chicago Press, 1989), 53.

16. Gerard Loughlin, *Telling God's Story: Bible, Church and Narrative Theology* (New York: Cambridge University Press, 1999).

17. Fred Craddock, *Preaching* (Nashville, Tenn.: Abingdon Press, 2010).

18. William Lawrence Svelmoe, *A New Vision for Missions: William Cameron Townsend, the Wycliffe Bible Translators, and the Culture of Early Evangelical Faith Missions, 1917-1945* (Tuscaloosa: University of Alabama Press, 2008).

19. John G. Stackhouse, Jr., *Partners in Christ: A Conservative Case for Egalitarianism* (Downers Grove, Ill.: InterVarsity, 2015), ch. 17.

20. Paul C. Gutjahr, "From Monarch to Democracy: The Dethroning of the King James Bible in the United States," in *The King James Bible after 400 Years*, ed. Hannibal Hamlin and Norman W. Jones (New York: Cambridge University Press, 2010), 173.

Bibliography

Bebbington, David W. *Evangelicalism in Modern Britain: A History from the 1730s to the 1980s.* London: Unwin Hyman, 1989.

Berger, Peter L. *The Sacred Canopy: Elements of a Sociological Theory of Religion.* Garden City, N.Y.: Doubleday, 1967.

Bielo, James. *Words upon the Word: An Ethnography of Evangelical Group Bible Study.* New York: New York University Press, 2009.

Boyd, Gregory A. *God of the Possible: A Biblical Introduction to the Open View of God.* Grand Rapids, Mich.: Baker, 2000.

Brother Andrew et al. *God's Smuggler.* New York: New American Library, 1987.

Craddock, Fred. *Preaching.* Nashville, Tenn.: Abingdon Press, 2010.

Dayton, Donald W., and Robert K. Johnston, eds. *The Variety of American Evangelicalism.* Downers Grove, Ill.: InterVarsity, 1991.

Dorrien, Gary. *The Remaking of Evangelical Theology.* Louisville, Ky.: Westminster John Knox, 1998.

Grudem, Wayne. *Systematic Theology: An Introduction to Biblical Doctrine.* Grand Rapids, Mich.: Zondervan, 1995.

Gutjahr, Paul C. "From Monarch to Democracy: The Dethroning of the King James Bible in the United States." In *The King James Bible after 400 Years,* edited by Hannibal Hamlin and Norman W. Jones. New York: Cambridge University Press, 2010.

Harris, Harriet. *Fundamentalism and Evangelicals.* Oxford : Oxford University Press, 2008.

Hatch, Nathan O., and Mark A. Noll, eds. *The Bible in America: Essays in Cultural History.* New York: Oxford University Press, 1982.

Loughlin, Gerard. *Telling God's Story: Bible, Church and Narrative Theology.* New York: Cambridge University Press, 1999.

Marsden, George M., ed. Introduction to *Evangelicalism and Modern America.* Grand Rapids, Mich.: Eerdmans, 1984.

McDannell, Colleen. *Material Christianity: Religion and Popular Culture in America.* New Haven, Conn.: Yale University Press, 1995.

McDermott, Gerald D., and Harold A. Netland. *A Trinitarian Theology of Religions: An Evangelical Proposal.* Oxford: Oxford University Press, 2014.

Niebuhr, Reinhold. *The Nature and Destiny of Man: A Christian Interpretation,* vol. 1: *Human Nature* (1941). 2 vols. Repr. New York: Scribner's, 1964.

Noll, Mark A., *Between Faith and Criticism: Evangelicals, Scholarship, and the Bible in America.* San Francisco, Calif.: Harper & Row, 1986.

Nord, David Paul. "The Evangelical Origins of Mass Media in America, 1815–1835." *Journalism Monographs* 88 (May 1984), 1–30.

Phillips, Timothy R., and Dennis L. Okholm, eds. *The Nature of Confession: Evangelicals and Postliberals in Conversation.* Downers Grove, Ill.: InterVarsity, 1996.

Pinnock, Clark H., ed. *The Openness of God: A Biblical Challenge to the Traditional Understanding of God.* Downers Grove, Ill.: InterVarsity, 1994.

Sanders, John Sanders. *No Other Name: An Investigation into the Destiny of the Unevangelized.* Grand Rapids, Mich.: Eerdmans, 1992.

———, ed. *What about Those Who Have Never Heard? Three Views on the Destiny of the Unevangelized.* Downers Grove, Ill.: InterVarsity, 1995.

Sparks, Kenton L. *God's Word in Human Words: An Evangelical Appropriation of Critical Biblical Scholarship.* Grand Rapids, Mich.: Baker Academic, 2008.

Stackhouse, John G., Jr. "Generic Evangelicalism." In *Four Views on the Spectrum of Evangelicalism*, edited by Andrew David Naselli and Collin Hansen. Grand Rapids, Mich.: Zondervan, 2011.

——, ed. *No Other Gods before Me?: Evangelicals and the Challenge of World Religions*. Grand Rapids, Mich.: Baker Academic, 2001.

——. *Partners in Christ: A Conservative Case for Egalitarianism*. Downers Grove, Ill.: InterVarsity, 2015.

Steiner, George. *Real Presences*. Chicago: University of Chicago Press, 1989.

Stott, John. *Evangelical Truth: A Personal Plea for Unity, Integrity and Faithfulness*. Downers Grove, Ill.: InterVarsity, 1999.

Svelmoe, William Lawrence. *A New Vision for Missions: William Cameron Townsend, the Wycliffe Bible Translators, and the Culture of Early Evangelical Faith Missions, 1917–1945*. Tuscaloosa: University of Alabama Press, 2008.

Treier, Daniel J. *Introducing Theological Interpretation of Scripture: Recovering a Christian Practice*. Grand Rapids, Mich.: Baker Academic, 2008.

Vanhoozer, Kevin J., ed. *Dictionary for Theological Interpretation of the Bible*. Grand Rapids, Mich.: Baker Academic, 2005.

CHAPTER 37

....

THE BIBLE
AND FUNDAMENTALISM

....

RANDALL J. STEPHENS

INTRODUCTION

....

AMERICAN Protestant fundamentalists ground their beliefs, behavior, and denominational identity on a strict interpretation of the Bible. Fiercely biblicist, and reading their sacred text with a literalist eye, fundamentalist Christians often see scripture as a kind of puzzle to be solved but also certainly a book to be obeyed. Fundamentalists declare that they read the Bible straight, unmediated by priests, professors, or liberal intellectuals, and that they live their lives in accordance to their straightforward reading of the Bible.

Central to understanding the emergence of American Protestant fundamentalism is an appreciation of the importance of the Scofield Reference Bible. First published in 1909, the Scofield Reference Bible sold 10 million copies by 2011 and became Oxford University Press's most popular title in its 500-year history.[1] C. I. Scofield (1843–1921) hoped his study Bible would clearly lay out the prophetic truths of the good book. The enormously influential volume came to embody some basic characteristics of fundamentalism as the movement relates to scripture: emphasizing premillennialism (or the bodily return of Jesus before the start of the millennium), stressing the coherence of the entirety of scripture, holding the truth found in its interpretation over and against other versions of truth, and following a literalist way of reading and understanding scripture. "The remarkable results of the modern study of the Prophets," the introduction to the reference Bible laid out, "in recovering to the church not only a clear and coherent harmony of the predictive portions, but also great treasures of ethical truth, are indicated in expository notes." For too long "fanciful and allegorical schemes of interpretation" had clouded a more accurate view of passages.[2] The notes themselves—concise, clear, and appearing in the same typeface as the scriptural text—assumed a significant authority and power. For one early critic this approach audaciously claimed to be "nothing more than a transcript of what the Bible itself says."[3]

DEFINITIONS

Although a view of the Bible as free of any error, or inerrant, is rudimentary to American fundamentalism, there are additional ways to define the movement. For instance, they have been united around certain common themes, reacting to and against mass culture as well as standing firmly against liberal and moderate Protestants. Common prohibitions against alcohol, Sabbath desecration, theater attendance, dancing, extravagant dress, and much more have been common. The faithful have pointed to the stern logic of New Testament verses like 1 Corinthians 3:16-17: "Know ye not that ye are the temple of God, and that the Spirit of God dwelleth in you? If any man defile the temple of God, him shall God destroy; for the temple of God is holy, which temple ye are."

Beyond doctrinal purity and biblicism, it is useful to think of fundamentalism as a style of engagement, a set of behaviors, and in some cases a sense of embattlement. Fundamentalists hold to a kind of canon within the canon. Certain books of the Bible and certain passages have received more attention than others. Leaders and laypeople, for instance, taking the great commission of Matthew 28:19-20 to heart, have been staunchly committed to evangelism and church growth since the beginning of the movement. They have also offered strict interpretations of Old Testament and New Testament passages concerning gender and sexuality. In practical terms this has limited the roles of women in the church and subordinated them in society. Two of the most common passages used include Paul's first letter to the Corinthians 14:34: "Let your women keep silence in the churches: for it is not permitted unto them to speak; but they are commanded to be under obedience, as also saith the law"; and Genesis 3:16, in which God chastises Adam and Eve following their temptation and sin in the Garden of Eden: "Unto the woman he said, I will greatly multiply thy sorrow and thy conception; in sorrow thou shalt bring forth children; and thy desire shall be to thy husband, and he shall rule over thee." Fundamentalism's biblical gender conservatism has remained one of the defining features of the movement. So has the separatism of fundamentalists who often shun working with other non-fundamentalist churches or ministers and have held out some of their fiercest criticism for Catholicism. Opposition to major modern intellectual developments—including Darwinian evolutionary theory, higher criticism of the Bible, and more—also mark off believers from other Christians.[4]

Such defining characteristics, according to fundamentalists themselves, are drawn from a clear, basic view of scripture. W. Paul Williamson and Ralph W. Hood suggest that fundamentalists see scripture as basically "self-interpretive." That would be the case, of course, even when and where believers do interpret. In the words of Hood and Williamson:

> The sacred text is sufficient in and of itself for understanding the divine intent and meaning of the author. For the fundamentalist, no outside sources, such as scholarly criticism, science, or history, are necessary for deriving the true interpretation of the text. Outside sources may be consulted, although their offerings are accepted only in so far as they support and illuminate what is perceived as the abiding truth in the text.[5]

The historian George Marsden observed that fundamentalists "were more prone to interpret Scripture according to the principle of 'literal when possible' so that any seeming historical or prophetic narrative (as opposed to unmistakable metaphor) should be interpreted as literally and exactly true." Says Marsden, "Moderate evangelicals, in the meantime, allowed more leeway in interpreting what the Bible meant to say or teach."[6] In certain cases, then, their view of scripture is a qualified literalism, even if unacknowledged.

Fundamentalism, by these lights, is a subspecies of evangelicalism. Sociologist Christian Smith describes the umbrella term "biblicism," by which he means:

> a theory about the Bible that emphasizes together its exclusive authority, infallibility, perspicuity, self-sufficiency, internal consistency, self-evident meaning, and universal applicability. Different communities within American evangelicalism emphasize various combinations of these points differently. But all together they form a constellation of assumptions and beliefs that define a particular theory and practice.[7]

The literal truth of the Bible is a constant, recurring theme within fundamentalist circles. It ranges from those belonging to the formal, doctrinally driven Reformed end of the spectrum to those occupying the more experiential, Pentecostal end. Pentecostalism was a new mass religious movement that developed in the United States in the early twentieth century. Believers pursued greater works of the spirit beyond salvation and sanctification. A focus on the Holy Spirit and the miraculous workings of God featured strongly for followers. Inspired by the biblical books of Acts and Revelation in particular, Pentecostals thought that they were living in the last days of world history, before the return of Jesus. Adherents spoke in tongues, believed in and practiced healing, and looked for miraculous signs of the "latter days." Some of the movement's largest denominations included the mostly white Assemblies of God and the predominately African American Church of God in Christ. By the end of the century the Pentecostalism, which grew rapidly in the global South, claimed approximately 500 million followers, making it the second largest subgrouping of global Christianity.[8] Many stalwarts were staunch biblicists. Pentecostal television preacher and Christian Zionist John Hagee, for instance, summed up that view well when criticizing President Obama for his policies on Israel. "The truth is not what you think that it is," remarked the Texas minister, "it's what the Bible says."[9] And it is not just end-times warriors like Hagee who make that point. Such biblicism shades from fundamentalism into evangelicalism. For instance, when comedian and filmmaker Woody Allen interviewed Billy Graham on television in the late 1960s, America's Pastor, the chief voice of evangelicalism, offered his take on biblical truth. In jest Allen asked Graham what his favorite commandment was. Graham said the first may be the most important: "Thou shalt have no other gods before me." To which Allen shot back: "Really, that one bothers you the most?" Graham responded, not missing a beat, "No, that doesn't bother me it bothers the scriptures. It bothers God."[10]

Fundamentalists engage the past and the world of the Bible in myriad ways, though quite often at odds with scholarly, mainline Protestant or even evangelical views. In basic ways a fundamentalist understanding of Christianity and the past is both historical and ahistorical. Whether believers are dealing with ancient history, premillennialism, contemporary events, the age of the earth or human origins, they do so through a biblical lens.

578   RANDALL J. STEPHENS

HISTORICAL ANTECEDENTS

Historian Richard Hofstadter's (1916–1970) classic work *Anti-Intellectualism in American Life*, winner of the 1964 Pulitzer Prize, examined America's "national disrespect for the mind." Early twentieth-century celebrity preacher and staunch biblical literalist Billy Sunday (1862–1935) emerged as one of Hofstadter's chief culprits. "The feeling that rationalism and modernism could no longer be answered in debate," Hofstadter ventured, "led to frantic efforts to overwhelm [the enemies of fundamentalism] by sheer violence of rhetoric and finally by efforts of suppression and intimidation."[11] In Hofstadter's telling, fundamentalists were allergic to intellectual engagement with the Bible and hostile to the life of the mind in general. Yet as historians like Ernest Sandeen, George Marsden, Matthew Sutton, and B. M. Pietsch have pointed out, fundamentalism rested on a long-standing and vibrant intellectual tradition, though one that Hofstadter would not have recognized as such. It is true that the movement itself is of relative recent vintage. It was only in 1920 that the Baptist pastor and newspaper editor Curtis Lee Laws wrote in the *Watchmen-Examiner*: "We suggest that those who still cling to the great fundamentals and who mean to do battle royal for the fundamentals be called 'Fundamentalists.'"[12] In the hands of Jazz Age gadfly H. L. Mencken (1880–1956) or novelist Sinclair Lewis (1885–1951) or Hofstadter, the term would take on the character of a bleak epithet. Regardless of the relative newness of the movement and its contested legacy, fundamentalism and its view of scripture have a deep history. A brief survey of the movement and fundamentalist interpretation and understanding of the Bible helps situate fundamentalism in the broader history of the West and the United States.

SCOTTISH COMMON SENSE PHILOSOPHY

Even up to the present, fundamentalists tend to argue that the Bible must be read in a plain sense, minus the flourish of allegory, mythology, or modern glosses. Such views demonstrate the influence of the Scottish Enlightenment, an influence that fostered the belief that the real world and the clear meaning of scripture were directly accessible to believers. In 1970 the fundamentalist Bible scholar David L. Cooper even developed a standard "Golden Rule of Biblical Interpretation" that guides many: "When the plain sense of Scripture makes common sense, seek no other sense; therefore, take every word at its primary, ordinary, usual, literal meaning unless the facts of the immediate context, studied in the light of related passages and axiomatic and fundamental truths, indicate clearly otherwise."[13]

Such a style of reading and interpreting owes something to the Scottish Common Sense philosophy of Thomas Reid (1710–1796), Adam Ferguson (1723–1816), and Dugald Stewart (1753–1828), which held sway over much of American thought and belief from the late eighteenth through the nineteenth century. For what might be called proto-fundamentalists, writes Marsden, "Two premises were absolutely fundamental—that God's truth was a single unified order and that all persons of common sense were capable of knowing that truth."[14] Armed with this philosophy, whether acknowledged or not, conservative evangelicals in the late nineteenth century resisted new historical critical studies of scripture. The Bible, according to the latest scholarship of the age, was now being viewed as one among many other ancient texts.

What would come to be called Princeton Theology, associated as it was with Princeton Theological Seminary in the nineteenth and early twentieth centuries, translated Scottish Common Sense philosophy into the conservative American Protestant context. Key figures associated with the school—such as Archibald Alexander (1772–1851), Charles Hodge (1797–1878), Benjamin Warfield (1851–1921), and J. Gresham Machen (1881–1937)—defended Presbyterian orthodoxy and the inerrancy of the Bible and fought against the encroachments of new school revivalism, and later, liberalism and modernism. Hodge summed up the biblicist approach in the decade after the Civil War: "It is plain that complete havoc must be made of the whole system of revealed truth, unless we consent to derive our philosophy from the Bible, instead of explaining the Bible by our philosophy."[15]

Other influences from overseas would dramatically shape the later movement and strongly influence fundamentalist views of scripture. John Nelson Darby (1800–1882), an influential member of the Plymouth Brethren sect in England, introduced the theological novelty of dispensationalism to a subset of evangelicals in his home country and in America. World history, in this context, could be broken up into distinct eras, or dispensations. God dealt with humankind differently in each era. Darby and his enthusiastic readers imagined that they were in the last days before Christ's return and the judgment of humankind. "From the time of the exaltation of Jesus to the right hand of God, and the association of the Church with Him, Christ has been ready to judge," wrote Darby in his *Notes on the Book of Revelations* (1839). "And now in the manifested failure of the Church on earth . . . though the bridegroom might tarry, the Church, knowing His mind, had but one cry, 'Come quickly!' "[16] Darby also popularized the belief in the Rapture, or God's spiriting of the saints into heaven before calamity on earth, drawing upon passages found in 1st Thessalonians, Matthew, Daniel, and Revelation.[17] In the coming decades key conservative evangelicals like Dwight L. Moody (1837–1899) and James H. Brookes (1830–1897) came under the influence of Darby and incorporated his apocalyptic ideas to help foster a larger conservative Protestant movement.

In other quarters, fundamentalism's roots rested deep in American soil. A contemporary of Darby's, William Miller (1782–1849), was an autodidact who delved into Bible study after his conversion. Miller, and his so-called Millerite followers, understood passages from the Old Testament book of Daniel as critical for unlocking the date of Christ's return. Two subsequent dates in 1843 and 1844 proved as false as they were demoralizing for Miller and his band. Adventist church factions rose from the ashes of Miller's movement. Yet his general ideas and biblical calculations, if not his exact predictions, had some influence on evangelicals and later fundamentalists. The travails of a bloody Civil War, social unrest, and the dislocations of the late nineteenth century would bring Miller's ideas, once relatively obscure, a new energy and relevance. In the coming years, Presbyterians, Baptists, holiness believers like the Wesleyan Methodists, and others came to believe that the world was largely irredeemable. For these, the promises of antebellum reform and the hope of Christendom, intended to make society more holy and more just, evaporated like so much steam. One holiness minister from the American South summed up this new pessimism. Thinking back on the tumultuous late nineteenth century he intoned: "Looking into this writhing, hopeless human vortex and seeing that boasted Christendom was ecclesiastical, formal, worldly, proud, and fallen, my heart would have sunk in despair had I not caught sight of this 'Blessed Hope' of His glorious appearing."[18] It was the hope of Jesus's return to rescue the faithful remnant from a corrupt, dying world.

BIBLE CONFERENCES AND BIBLE SCHOOLS

Spanning across the Atlantic in the late nineteenth century, a series of conferences devoted to scripture, spreading the doctrine of premillennialism, and promoting holiness and what was called the higher Christian life captured the imagination of conservative American evangelicals.[19] The influence of such conferences spread from the United Kingdom to first the northern parts of the United States and then throughout the entire nation. Popular books, pamphlets, and periodicals—the *Christian Herald* among them—further inspired Americans to embrace a new kind apocalypticism.

The Niagara Bible Conference, one of the most influential and popular Bible-centered gatherings, first formed in the late 1860s and subsequently met from 1883 to 1900 in Niagara-on-the-Lake, Ontario. Meetings here and at Northfield Bible Conference (Northfield, Massachusetts) and Winona Lake Bible Conference (Winona Lake, Indiana) featured preaching, Bible study, and a focus on prophecy and the last dispensation of human history. Such readings had a strong Reformed, Calvinistic imprint. Some of the foremost Americans attached to the Bible conference movement included the Presbyterian author and preacher A. T. Pierson (1837–1911), Baptist minister A. J. Gordon (1836–1895), the Methodist premillennialist theologian and bestselling author W. E. Blackstone (1841–1935), and most critically, Dwight L. Moody. These participants and others like them unanimously held that the era in which they lived—riled by immigration, filled with apostasy much like what they saw described in scripture, labor strife, and political radicalism—marked the final hour of humankind before the return of Jesus. Hence, they likened salvation to being "rescued" from a dying and irredeemable world. "I look on this world as a wrecked vessel," Moody announced. "God has given me a life-boat, and said to me, 'Moody, save all you can.'"[20]

Moody called for the training of what he referred to as "gap men," who would bridge the gap between lay people and seminary-trained scholars. The latter, in his view, had lost touch with regular believers. "Never mind the Greek and Hebrew," Moody advised with a sense of end-times urgency. In newly established Bible schools, Moody proclaimed: "give them plain English and good Scripture. It is the Sword of the Lord that cuts deep. If you have men trained for that kind of work, there is no trouble about reaching the men who do not go into churches."[21] One early academic observer of this educational trend noted that "in Bible schools scholastic requirements for matriculation, promotion and graduation, were not exacted as in theological seminaries. Revivalistic and missionary zeal was stressed." Fitting that pattern, "Students were called upon to 'attempt great things for God.'"[22] By the late nineteenth and early twentieth centuries, a number of Bible institutes and schools were established around the country, which would help foster a new generation of conservative Protestant leaders. These schools included A. B. Simpson's Missionary and Training Institute (New York City), A. J. Gordon's Boston Missionary

Training School, the Moody Bible Institute (Chicago), and the Bible Institute of Los Angeles.

THE TWENTIETH CENTURY

Following the preaching and literary successes of key figures like Dwight Moody, William Blackstone, R. A. Torrey (1856–1928), and others, conservative evangelical Protestantism grew in both numeric strength and in force of conviction in the opening years of the twentieth century. Yet stalwarts were uneasy. Between 1910 and 1915, a group of leading evangelicals in England and the United States published a collection of twelve booklets titled *The Fundamentals: Testimony to Truth*. With the backing of oil barons Lyman Stewart (1840–1923) and Milton Stewart (1838–1923), the collection was meant to stem the tide of liberalism and theological modernism that conservative critics thought was swamping Protestant churches. Although Protestant fundamentalism did not properly exist in these years, *The Fundamentals* helped define and set a defensive tone for the subsequent movement. Among other things, the authors championed several aspects of true Christian faith: the Bible as the inerrant word of God, the doctrine of hell and judgment, the virgin birth of Jesus, the divinity of Jesus, the veracity of Jesus's miracles, and the bodily second coming of Christ.[23] One contributor summed up the views of many others who took a defensive posture when it came to biblical inspiration:

> In this paper the authenticity and credibility of the Bible are assumed, by which is meant (1), that its books were written by the authors to whom they are ascribed, and that their contents are in all material points as when they came from their hands; and (2), that those contents are worthy of entire acceptance as to their statements of fact. Were there need to prove these assumptions, the evidence is abundant, and abler pens have dealt with it.[24]

Leaders of this nascent fundamentalist movement distrusted the new higher critics and the expertise of university-based Bible scholars. The reading and interpretation of the word of God, they argued, was now less accessible to common readers. Yet the historian Timothy Weber notes an irony here. "As dispensationalism became more dominant in militant fundamentalist circles in the 1920s," says Weber, "people actually had less control of their Bibles than before." The tangled subtleties of the inductive system of fundamentalist logic meant that churchgoers "were only slightly less reliant on their Bible teachers than liberal lay people were on the higher critics."[25]

During the 1920s, fundamentalists and their many foes battled over the teaching of evolutionary biology in public schools. Former populist politician and presidential candidate, congressman, and secretary of state William Jennings Bryan (1860–1925), known as the Great Commoner, took up the cause on the side of newly dubbed fundamentalists. In the now-famous 1925 Scopes Trial in Dayton, Tennessee, Bryan faced off against the defense led by noted liberal and self-professed agnostic Clarence Darrow (1857-1938) to determine the lawfulness of teaching Darwinian evolution in schools. In the public eye, the trial soon became a contest between science on one side and biblical, literalist Christianity on the other. Darrow, after being forbidden to have scientific expert witnesses placed on the witness stand, was able to put Bryan on the witness stand and question him. In a clumsy defense of inerrancy, Bryan was forced by Darrow to stretch the meaning of literalism:

> Q—Would you say that the earth was only 4,000 years old?
> A—Oh, no; I think it is much older than that.
> Q—How much?
> A—I couldn't say.
> Q—Do you say whether the Bible itself says it is older than that?
> A—I don't think it is older or not.
> Q—Do you think the earth was made in six days?
> A—Not six days of twenty-four hours.
> Q—Doesn't it say so?
> A—No, sir.[26]

Despite such scenes, Bryan and the prosecution won the case. Yet there is considerable evidence that public opinion and the press turned against the doctrinaire fundamentalists. The faithful were savaged in these years for their attachment to biblical certitudes and for their moralizing. Sinclair Lewis's novel *Elmer Gantry* (1927), a merciless satire of fundamentalism and one of the bestsellers of the decade, followed the antics of a jackleg preacher in Kansas. In one typical passage a scoffer lobs questions about the Bible at the protagonist: "You believe a thing like that? And do you believe that Samson lost all his strength just because his gal cut off his hair? Do you, eh? Think hair had anything to do with his strength?"[27]

It would be a mistake to say, as historians once did with far too much certainty, that fundamentalists retreated into the defensive comforts of their churches and Bible schools after the stinging defeat of the Scopes Trial and the eventual failure of prohibition. Certainly, Billy Sunday and others staked much of their reputation on teetotalism and had scripture ready at-hand in their defense. "Jesus Christ was God's revenue officer," Sunday told crowds. "Now the Jews were forbidden to eat pork, but Jesus Christ came and found that crowd buying and selling and dealing in pork, and confiscated the whole business, and he kept within the limits of the law when he did it . . . . And they told Jesus to leave the country. They said: 'You are hurting our business.'"[28] It is true that the rosy, near-millennial predictions concerning prohibition failed to materialize. Yet that did not deter fundamentalists for long. The twenty-first Amendment of 1933 that repealed Prohibition was a setback, but stalwarts still were occupied with the cultures around them. They were ready to do battle with new foes and they still remained steadfast in their opposition to demon rum.

Believers remained politically and socially engaged in the intervening years. Over the last 100 years, liberal critics and what might be called—in the words of fundamentalists— evangelical accommodationists, have driven fundamentalists to a further sense of embattlement. Fundamentalists have felt besieged and have taken to finding comfort in various Bible passages and stories such as the Jewish people's captivity in Egypt and Babylon, as well as the persecution of the early church. The embattled feeling of fundamentalists found some of their most vivid manifestations in their battles with school boards, moderate to liberal denominations, and secular groups over the meaning of the past and the historical claims of the Bible, whether those pertain to the creation story, Noah and the flood, miracles, or the resurrection of Jesus.

CONTEMPORARY IMPACT

Clearly in the latter half of the twentieth century, fundamentalism made national news as well as broadened its appeal to the American public. At the same time, fundamentalist views of the Bible and ideas about how scripture should direct belief and behavior entered the public realm in new and powerful ways.

Charting the influence and scope of biblical fundamentalism through the twentieth century might be done in numerous ways. The extent of parents who homeschool their children with fundamentalist curriculums from publishers such as A Beka Book or Bob Jones University Press reveals the appeal of the movement. So does the variety of Christian bookstores and outlets that have cropped up around the country since the 1970s. Even before the 1970s, national figures like Charles Fuller (1887–1968) and his Old Fashioned Revival Hour or the success of literalist preachers like Billy Sunday, Billy Graham, or Oral Roberts was evidence of a large constituency. Fundamentalists reached out to new generations as well, with the founding in 1942 of Youth for Christ, a massive and staunchly conservative national teen and young adult ministry.

New denominations, like the Independent Fundamental Churches of America and the General Association of Regular Baptist Churches, thrived. Even the landscape of American higher education bore the influence of fundamentalist biblical doctrine, with key seminaries and colleges becoming battlegrounds over theology and interpretation. A sampling of schools that have been historically the most closely linked with fundamentalist views of scripture include: Bob Jones University (Greenville, S.C.), Bryan College (Dayton, Tenn.), Liberty University (Lynchburg, Va.), Dallas Theological Seminary (Dallas, Tex.), and Pensacola Christian College (Pensacola, Fla.).

Beyond the establishment of colleges, Bible schools, and universities, fundamentalists targeted baby boomers in new ways in the 1960s and 1970s, even making some concessions to the counterculture. The bestselling nonfiction title of the 1970s was Hal Lindsey's *The Late Great Planet Earth*, which borrowed from youth slang and the ideas of the Jesus People movement to refashion premillennialism for a new crowd. Lindsey read prophetic passages from the Old and New Testaments into the geopolitics of the modern age. But even the success of that popular book was overshadowed by the series of *Left Behind* apocalyptic thrillers authored by fundamentalist minster Tim LaHaye and writing partner/journalist Jerry Jenkins. As of 2009, the sixteen novels had sold 70 million copies.[29]

The 1979 formation of the Moral Majority, a political and religious lobbying group, led and organized by the fundamentalist Baptist preacher Jerry Falwell (1933–2007), marked a new stage in public visibility and the politicization of conservative Protestantism. Falwell and like-minded conservatives called for a greater role for the Bible in national life, support for the state of Israel, a fusion of hyper-patriotism and conservative Christianity, and the reinstitution of prayer in public schools along with the teaching of creation science. Falwell—who founded Lynchburg Baptist College in 1971, later rechristened Liberty University—spelled out his fundamentalist educational ideals in 1981. "Our unique philosophy of education," he wrote, "rests upon our belief that the Bible is the authentic and reliable guide and authority for all areas of life."[30]

From the 1970s forward, with the advent of the culture wars, fundamentalists became far more vocal in opposing secular humanism, legalized abortion, and feminism. The support of the Moral Majority for Ronald Reagan and his subsequent landslide presidential victory in 1980 made conservative Christians a new political force to be reckoned with. Reagan himself, not an active church member, as was his predecessor Carter, sought out the assistance of fundamentalists and spoke their language of moral and biblical certainty. There is also evidence that he was influenced by the popular millennialism that followed the publication of *The Late Great Planet Earth*. Reagan ruminated with foreign officials on how the battle of Armageddon, described in the New Testament book of Revelation, would take place. He also spoke with his staff about other details of the apocalypse. At the same time the president publicly sided with the cause of creationism.[31]

MILITANCY

Over the many decades since the fundamentalist movement first made national headlines in the 1920s, one theme has remained consistent. Fundamentalists, especially in their defense of an unmediated, common sense approach to the Bible, have militantly defended their cause. As the historian and religion scholar Grant Wacker has pointed out, the fundamentalist-turned-evangelical Billy Graham certainly mellowed with age.[32] His anti-communist crusading in the late 1940s and 1950s was replaced with a more pacific evangelicalism in later years. In many ways Graham lost his fighting, contentious spirit, putting him at odds with the fundamentalists who first nourished his faith.

"A fundamentalist is an evangelical who is angry," wrote Marsden, with tongue perhaps in cheek.[33] This righteous rage, or holy indignation is, at least in part, linked to what religious studies scholar Jason Bivins calls a religion of fear. "In the politically coded drama of Hell Houses, in the pages of apocalyptic novels or Jack Chick's cartoon tracts, and in the public denunciations of popular music," Bivins notes "there is far more at work than simply Christian kitsch or crude anti-modernism. Creators provide for audiences and readers an interpretive template that posits demonological causes for political decline, and they situate readers in a historical framework and define for audiences a coherent, unchanging place therein."[34]

Military metaphors and talk of battles suffuse fundamentalist rhetoric. Pastors and youth leaders return again and again to the New Testament passage Ephesians 6:12-13: "For we wrestle not against flesh and blood, but against principalities, against powers, against the rulers of the darkness of this world, against spiritual wickedness in high places. Wherefore take unto you the whole armour of God, that ye may be able to withstand in the evil day, and having done all, to stand." Articles from key publications like the *King's Business, Moody Monthly*, and *Sword of the Lord* typically employed spiritual warfare and military metaphors. The combat theme inspired Frank E. Peretti's multimillion-dollar-selling novel, *This Present Darkness* (1986). The book's praying heroes and heroines battle a number of villains, including new age gurus, public school educators, psychologists, and academics, all under the influence of Satan.

Ken Ham is America's foremost young-earth creationist, believing that the earth is only 6,000 to 10,000 years old, not the billions of years old, as modern geology would have it. He has been vocal about threats that he sees to his multimillion-dollar Answers in Genesis ministry and creationist museum. In November 2011, Ham confided to his website's readers: "Some days in this ministry, I frankly feel exhausted. There seems to be constant daily battles! But I remind myself that Answers in Genesis, a Bible-upholding ministry, is engaged in an ongoing spiritual war; when one battle is over, another front opens."[35]

New Interpretations
and Contemporary Influence

Critics have long claimed that true believers were at war with modernity.[36] Media and religious studies scholar Heidi Campbell remarks that "there's been a tendency throughout history to see science, technology, and modernity as essentially in conflict with religion and religious communities. . . . This continues to be a popular and often overarching characterization in contemporary times."[37] Such assumptions, as Campbell and others contend, are largely wrong.

For much of the twentieth century, historians had classed fundamentalists as anti-modernists. The pronouncements of believers, stridently opposed as they were to theological modernism and liberalism, seemed to make them anything but modern. A new wave of scholarship, though, is showing that fundamentalists can quite accurately be described as modernists.[38] The late Harvard University religious studies scholar William R. Hutchison defined modernism in relation to religion as involving "the conscious, intended adaptation of religious ideas to modern culture . . . the idea that God is immanent in human cultural development and revealed through it . . . [and] a belief that human society is moving toward realization (even though it may never attain the reality) of the Kingdom of God."[39] The way that fundamentalists and evangelicals have used media technology, theological and historical categories, and conceived of an imminent God, place them squarely within Hutchinson's modernist framework.

A raft of recent studies makes strong links between modernism, innovation, and the purported old-time religion.[40] Conservative believers' relationship to modern consumer capitalism, their media savvy, and theological orientation formed a kind of "alternate modernity." B. M. Pietsch, for instance, points out the "modernist assumptions" of dispensationalists. Their systems of "classification, enumeration, cross-referencing, and taxonomic comparisons of literary units" reveal modernist ideas of interpretation.[41] Similarly, Timothy Gloege notes that "corporate evangelicals" were well placed to remold an old-time faith and an ancient text to fit a modern age. Writes Gloege about the founding documents of the movement: "*The Fundamentals* thus pointed the way forward for modern conservative evangelicalism by modeling the methodology for creating, and constantly recreating whatever 'orthodoxy' the present moment required."[42]

Perhaps this flexibility and innovativeness, along with a commitment to evangelism and church growth, helps explain the movement's successes throughout the twentieth and into the twenty-first centuries. The conservative takeover of the largest Protestant denomination in the country, the Southern Baptist Convention (SBC), and the consistent election of conservatives to this denomination's presidency since 1979, tells part of that story. Yet since fundamentalism is a somewhat amorphous movement, it is difficult to estimate an exact number of American Christians who would identify with it and its strict interpretation of the Bible. In 2000, the historian Martin Marty figured that when including the SBC and numerous other religious bodies that identify in some way with the fundamentalist tradition, there were likely 20 to 30 million fundamentalists in the United States.[43]

Another way to estimate the movement's influence, especially with regard to views of scripture, is through polling data. According to a Gallup Poll in 2014, 28 percent of Americans surveyed believed that "the Bible is the actual word of God, to be taken literally." It is not possible to tell how many of those belonged to a fundamentalist or evangelical church. Yet the figure reveals the continued influence of literalistic, fundamentalist views of the Bible, perhaps well beyond the walls of fundamentalist churches. At the same time this percentage was markedly lower than the 38-40 percent that answered the question the same way in the 1970s. Indeed, as of 2014 a larger group (47 percent) felt most comfortable saying, "The Bible is the inspired word of God but not everything in it should be taken literally."[44] The appeal of a fundamentalist reading of the Bible—combining religious certainty, urgent millennial expectation, and a strong sense of embattlement—is still compelling for large portions of the American population.

NOTES

1. B. M. Pietsch, *Dispensational Modernism* (New York: Oxford University Press, 2015), 249–50.
2. Pietsch, *Dispensational Modernism*, 194–95; C. I. Scofield, introduction to *The Scofield Reference Bible* (1909; repr., New York: Oxford University Press, 1945), iv; Harris Franklin Rall, "Premillennialism: II. Premillennialism and the Bible," *Biblical World* 53, no. 5 (September 1919): 459.
3. Rall, "Premillennialism and the Bible," 459.
4. Brenda Brasher, ed., introduction to *Encyclopedia of Fundamentalism* (New York: Routledge, 2001), xv–xviii.
5. W. Paul Williamson et al., "The Intratextual Fundamentalism Scale: Cross-Cultural Application, Validity Evidence, and Relationship with Religious Orientation and the Big 5 Factor Markers," *Mental Health, Religion & Culture* 13, no. 7–8 (2010): 723.
6. George M. Marsden, *Fundamentalism and American Culture: The Shaping of Twentieth Century Evangelicalism, 1870–1925* (New York: Oxford University Press, 1980), 323.
7. Christian Smith, *The Bible Made Impossible: Why Biblicism Is Not a Truly Evangelical Reading of Scripture* (Grand Rapids, Mich.: Brazos Press, 2011), viii.
8. Grant Wacker, *Heaven Below: Early Pentecostals and American Culture* (Cambridge, Mass.: Harvard University Press, 2001), 271; Todd M. Johnson, "Global Pentecostal Demographics," in *Spirit and Power: The Growth and Global Impact of Pentecostalism*, ed. Donald E. Miller, Kimon H. Sargeant, and Richard Flory (New York: Oxford University Press, 2013), 319–20.
9. Quoted by Natasha Mozgovaya, "Christian Zionists Unite in D.C. to Express Support for Israel," *Haaretz*, July 20, 2011, http://www.haaretz.com/news/diplomacy-defense/christian-zionists-unite-in-d-c-to-express-support-for-israel-1.374161.

10. Billy Graham, interview by Woody Allen, YouTube video, 5:56, from *The Woody Allen Special* televised by CBS on September 21, 1969, posted by "komman3008," http://www.youtube.com/watch?v=K_poGsbBgpE.

11. Richard Hofstadter, *Anti-Intellectualism in American Life* (New York: Alfred A. Knopf, 1969), 3, 123, 145–49, 30–31. See also, Stephen J. Whitfield, "The Eggheads and the Fatheads," *Change* 10, no. 4 (April 1978): 64–66.

12. Quoted in C. Douglas Weaver, *In Search of the New Testament Church: The Baptist Story* (Macon, Ga.: Mercer University Press, 2008), 132.

13. David L. Cooper, *The World's Greatest Library Graphically Illustrated* (Los Angeles: Biblical Research Society, 1970), 11; Mark A. Noll, "Common Sense Traditions and American Evangelical Thought," *American Quarterly* 37, no. 2 (1985): 220, 224, 230.

14. George M. Marsden, *Fundamentalism and American Culture: The Shaping of Twentieth Century Evangelicalism, 1870–1925* (New York: Oxford University Press, 1980), 14.

15. Charles Hodge, *Systematic Theology*, vol. 1 (New York: Scribner, Armstrong, 1873), 14.

16. John Nelson Darby, *Notes on the Book of Revelations: To Assist Inquirers in Searching into that Book* (London: Central Tract Depôt, 1839), 169–71.

17. Matthew Avery Sutton, *American Apocalypse: A History of Modern Evangelicalism* (Cambridge, Mass.: Belknap Press of Harvard University Press, 2014), 17–20.

18. B. F. Haynes, *Tempest Tossed on Methodist Seas; or, A Sketch of My Life* (Louisville, Ky.: Pentecostal Publishing Company, 1921), 232–33, 71–74.

19. Melvin E. Dieter, *The Holiness Revival of the Nineteenth Century* (Lanham, Md.: Scarecrow Press, 1996), 248–50; Randall J. Stephens, *The Fire Spreads: Holiness and Pentecostalism in the American South* (Cambridge, Mass.: Harvard University Press, 2010), 146, 162.

20. Ernest R. Sandeen, *The Roots of Fundamentalism: British and American Millenarianism, 1800–1930* (Chicago: University of Chicago Press, 1970), 132–61; Timothy P. Weber, *Living in the Shadow of the Second Coming: American Premillennialism, 1875–1925* (Chicago: University of Chicago Press, 1987), 10; Dwight L. Moody, *New Sermons* (New York: Henry S. Goodspeed, 1880), 535.

21. "Dwight Moody's Vision of a Bible School," in Brasher, *Fundamentalism*, 60.

22. Stewart G. Cole, *The History of Fundamentalism* (1931; repr., Westport, Conn.: Greenwood Press, 1971), 43.

23. Dixon, Amzi C., Louis Meyer, and Reuben A. Torrey, eds., *The Fundamentals: A Testimony to the Truth*, 12 vols. (Chicago: Testimony, 1910-15).

24. James M. Gray, "The Inspiration of the Bible—Definition, Extent, and Proof," in *Evangelicalism and Fundamentalism: A Documentary Reader*, ed. Barry Hankins (New York: New York University Press, 2008), 10.

25. Timothy P. Weber, "The Two-Edged Sword: The Fundamentalist Use of the Bible," in *The Bible in America: Essays in Cultural History*, ed. Nathan O. Hatch and Mark A. Noll (New York: Oxford University Press, 1982), 116.

26. "The State of Tennessee vs. John Scopes," in *The South in Perspective: An Anthology of Southern Literature*, ed. Edward Francisco, Robert Vaughan, and Linda Francisco (Upper Saddle River, N.J.: Prentice Hall, 2001), 577.

27. Sinclair Lewis, *Elmer Gantry* (1927; repr., New York: Penguin Books, 1967), 36–37.

28. Billy Sunday and William Thomas Ellis, *Billy Sunday, the Man and His Message: With His Own Words which Have Won Thousands for Christ* (Chicago: John C. Winston, 1917), 86.

29. Melani McAlister, "Prophecy, Politics, and the Popular: The *Left Behind* Series and Christian Fundamentalism's New World Order," *South Atlantic Quarterly* 102, no. 4 (Fall 2003): 773.

30. Jerry Falwell, "Future-World: An Agenda for the Eighties," in *The Fundamentalist Phenomenon: The Resurgence of Conservative Christianity*, ed. Jerry Falwell, Edward E. Hindson, and Ed Dobson (Garden City, N.Y.: Doubleday Books, 1981), 219.

31. Ronald Reagan, *The Reagan Diaries*, ed. Douglas Brinkley (New York: HarperCollins, 2007), 19, 24; Constance Holden, "Republican Candidate Picks Fight with Darwin," *Science* 209, no. 4462 (1980): 1214, doi:10.1126/science.209.4462.1214.

32. Grant Wacker, *America's Pastor: Billy Graham and the Shaping of a Nation* (Cambridge, Mass.: Belknap Press of Harvard University Press, 2014), 244–45, 287–89.

33. George M. Marsden, *Understanding Fundamentalism and Evangelicalism* (Grand Rapids, Mich.: William B. Eerdmans, 1991), 1.

34. Jason Bivins, *Religion of Fear: The Politics of Horror in Conservative Evangelicalism* (New York: Oxford University Press, 2008), 9.

35. Ken Ham, "Are You Aware of the Battles against AiG and the Truth of God's Word?" "Letter from Ken," November 14, 2011, http://www.answersingenesis.org/articles/2011/11/14/are-you-aware-of-battles-letter.

36. Edward J. Larson, *Summer for the Gods: The Scopes Trial and America's Continuing Debate over Science and Religion* (New York: Basic Books, 2006), 33–36.

37. Heidi Campbell, *When Religion Meets New Media* (New York: Routledge, 2010), 5.

38. Mark Elvin, "Viewpoint: A Working Definition of 'Modernity'?" *Past and Present* 113 (1986): 209; Richard Madsen et al., introduction to *Meaning and Modernity: Religion, Polity, and Self*, ed. Richard Madsen, William M. Sullivan, Ann Swidler, and Steven M. Tipton (Berkeley: University of California Press, 2002), ix; Jeffrey C. Alexander and Steven J. Sherwood, "'Mythic Gestures': Robert N. Bellah and Cultural Sociology," in Masden, *Meaning and Modernity*, 6.

39. William R. Hutchison, *The Modernist Impulse in American Protestantism* (Durham, N.C.: Duke University Press, 1992), 2; see also 11, 182, 298.

40. Bethany Moreton, *To Serve God and Wal-Mart: The Making of Christian Free Enterprise* (Cambridge, Mass.: Harvard University Press, 2009); Timothy Gloege, *Guaranteed Pure: The Moody Bible Institute, Business, and the Making of Modern Evangelicalism* (Chapel Hill, NC: University of North Carolina Press, 2015); B. M. Pietsch, *Dispensational Modernism* (New York: Oxford University Press, 2015); Matthew Avery Sutton, *American Apocalypse: A History of Modern Evangelicalism* (Cambridge, Mass.: Belknap Press of Harvard University Press, 2014); Darren Dochuk, *From Bible Belt to Sunbelt: Plain-Folk Religion, Grassroots Politics, and the Rise of Evangelical Conservatism* (New York: W. W. Norton, 2010); Kate Bowler, *Blessed: A History of the American Prosperity Gospel* (New York: Oxford University Press, 2013); William K. Kay, "Pentecostalism and Religious Broadcasting," *Journal of Beliefs & Values: Studies in Religion & Education* 30, no. 3 (2009): 245–54; Josh McMullen, *Under the Big Top: Big Tent Revivalism and American Culture, 1885-1925* (New York: Oxford University Press, 2015); Kathryn Lofton, "Commonly Modern: Rethinking the Modernist-Fundamentalist Controversies," *Church History* 83, no. 1 (2014): 137–44.

41. Pietsch, *Dispensational Modernism*, 4, 14–16.

42. Gloege, *Guaranteed Pure*, 10.

43. Martin Marty, "Fundamentalist Christianity," in *Contemporary American Religion*, ed. Wade Clark Roof (New York: Macmillan Reference, 2000), 1:272.

44. Lydia Saad, "Three in Four in U.S. Still See the Bible as Word of God," Gallup, June 4, 2014, http://www.gallup.com/poll/170834/three-four-bible-word-god.aspx. See a related

Pew poll from 2013 in which 33 percent of respondents agreed that "humans existed in present form since the beginning of time." Pew Research Center, "Public's Views on Human Evolution," December 30, 2015, http://pewrsr.ch/KflcPb.

BIBLIOGRAPHY

Ammerman, Nancy. *Bible Believers: Fundamentalists in the Modern World.* New Brunswick, N.J.: Rutgers University Press, 1987.

Balmer, Randall. *Encyclopedia of Evangelicalism.* 2nd ed. Waco, Tex.: Baylor University Press, 2004.

Bendroth, Margaret Lamberts. *Fundamentalism and Gender, 1875 to the Present.* New Haven, Conn.: Yale University Press, 1993.

Blackstone, W. E. *Jesus is Coming.* New York: Fleming H. Revell, 1908.

Brekke, Torkel. *Fundamentalism: Prophecy and Protest in the Age of Globalization.* New York: Cambridge University Press, 2012.

Dalhouse, Mark Taylor. *An Island in the Lake of Fire: Bob Jones University, Fundamentalism and the Separatist Movement.* Athens, GA: University of Georgia Press, 1996.

DeBerg, Betty. *Ungodly Women: Gender and the First Wave of American Fundamentalism.* Minneapolis, Minn.: Fortress Press, 1990.

Dixon, Amzi C., Louis Meyer, and Reuben A. Torrey, eds. *The Fundamentals: A Testimony to the Truth.* 12 vols. Chicago: Testimony, 1910-15.

Evensen, Bruce. *God's Man for the Gilded Age: D. L. Moody and the Rise of Modern Mass Evangelism.* New York: Oxford University Press, 2003.

Falwell, Jerry. *Listen, America!* Garden City, N.Y.: Doubleday, 1980.

—— Edward E. Hindson, and Ed Dobson, eds. *The Fundamentalist Phenomenon: The Resurgence of Conservative Christianity.* Garden City, N.Y.: Doubleday Books, 1981.

Hankins, Barry, ed. *Evangelicalism and Fundamentalism: A Documentary Reader.* New York: New York University Press, 2008.

——. *God's Rascal: J. Frank Norris and the Beginnings of Southern Fundamentalism.* Lexington: University Press of Kentucky, 1996.

Harding, Susan Friend. *The Book of Jerry Falwell: Fundamentalist Language and Politics.* Princeton, N.J.: Princeton University Press, 2000.

Henry, Carl F. H. *The Uneasy Conscience of Modern Fundamentalism* (1947). Repr. Grand Rapids, Mich.: Eerdmans, 2003.

Katz, David S. *God's Last Words: Reading the English Bible from the Reformation to Fundamentalism.* New Haven, Conn.: Yale University Press, 2004.

Larson, Edward J.. *Summer for the Gods: The Scopes Trial and America's Continuing Debate over Science and Religion.* New York: Basic Books, 2006.

Longfield, Bradley J. "For Church and Country: The Fundamentalist–Modernist Conflict in the Presbyterian Church." *Journal of Presbyterian History* 78, no. 1 (Spring 2000): 35–50.

Machen, J. Gresham. *Christianity and Liberalism* (1923). Repr. Grand Rapids, Mich.: William B. Eerdmans, 1946.

Marsden, George. *Fundamentalism and American Culture: The Shaping of Twentieth-Century American Evangelicalism, 1870–1925.* New York: Oxford University Press, 1980.

——. *Understanding Fundamentalism and Evangelicalism.* Grand Rapids, Mich.: William B. Eerdmans, 1991.

Marty, Martin, and R. Scott Appleby, eds. *Fundamentalisms Comprehended.* Chicago: University of Chicago Press, 1995.

Noll, Mark A. *Between Faith and Criticism: Evangelicals, Scholarship, and the Bible in America.* New York: Harper Collins, 1986.

Pietsch, B. M. *Dispensational Modernism.* New York: Oxford University Press, 2015.

Sandeen, Ernest. *The Roots of Fundamentalism: British and American Millenarianism, 1800–1930.* Chicago: University of Chicago Press, 1970.

Smith, Christian. *American Evangelicalism: Embattled and Thriving.* Chicago: University of Chicago Press, 1998.

Stephens, Randall J. *The Fire Spreads: Holiness and Pentecostalism in the American South.* Cambridge, Mass.: Harvard University Press, 2010.

———, and Karl Giberson. *The Anointed: Evangelical Truth in a Secular Age.* Cambridge, Mass.: Belknap Press of Harvard University Press, 2011.

Sutton, Matthew Avery. *American Apocalypse: A History of Modern Evangelicalism.* Cambridge, Mass.: Belknap Press of Harvard University Press, 2014.

Weber, Timothy. *Standing in the Shadow of the Second Coming: American Premillennialism, 1875–1982.* Chicago: University of Chicago Press, 1987.

———. "The Two-Edged Sword: The Fundamentalist Use of the Bible." In *The Bible in America: Essays in Cultural History*, edited by Nathan O. Hatch and Mark A. Noll, 101–20. New York: Oxford University Press, 1982.

CHAPTER 38

....

THE BIBLE AND
PENTECOSTALISM

....

MICHAEL J. MCCLYMOND

FROM its early twentieth-century origins, the North American Pentecostal movement began with an experience—Spirit baptism as evidenced by speaking in tongues. This experience supported a premise—that God was again pouring out the Holy Spirit, as at the church's beginnings, on the Day of Pentecost (Acts 2). The premise of an end-times outpouring of the Spirit involved an interpretation—"this is that which was spoken" (Acts 2:16).[1] Pentecostals interpreted their experience—occurring through their own lungs, larynx, and lips—as fulfilling the biblical prophecies of a "latter rain" outpouring of the Spirit, just prior to Christ's Second Coming.[2] This prophetic fulfillment was supernatural. Their utterances were "the language of the Holy Ghost." When asked about the Spirit, Pentecostals did not have to open a book. They had only to open their mouths and to declare God's ineffable praise. They did not have to rehearse ancient accounts, but they could recount their own stories of what God had done right in their midst, in the here and now. Pentecostals presumed that, in the words of Mark McLean, "God is as much an active causative agent today as He is pictured in the biblical writings."[3]

In seeking a deeper encounter with God, Pentecostals did not set aside their Bibles—a common criticism and caricature that has persisted. Walter Hollenweger wrote:

> The critics of the Pentecostal movement who accuse it of neglecting the written word in favour of individual illuminations by the Spirit are ignorant of the role which the Bible plays in the Pentecostal movement. Pentecostals live with the Bible. They read it every day and know many passages by heart. . . . Many of them hardly read any books apart from the Bible.[4]

The mutual interplay between biblical texts and present-day experiences was what made possible the "this is that" interpretation—simply that this experience is that very thing to which the Bible bears witness. While Pentecostal experiences occurred in modern times, their assigned meanings depended on what stands written in the Bible, and so the biblical texts were read, scrutinized, and applied. All the same, there was a here-and-now-ness to

Pentecostal biblical interpretation that derived from the view that present-day experiences were prefigured in the scriptures.

A Hermeneutics of Fulfillment, Enactment, and Affection

To summarize, one might say that Pentecostal biblical interpretation rests on a "hermeneutics of fulfillment." The fundamental assumption is that an outpouring of the Holy Spirit is already in process, just as the kingdom of God on earth is already being realized. Alongside this stress on "fulfillment"—and partially overlapping with it—is what we might call a "hermeneutics of enactment." Pentecostals are better described as "people of the word" than as "people of the book."[5] It is not merely the letters on the page that matter, but the word of God as spoken, heard, sung, analogized, typologized, enacted, or practiced. In a text often cited by Pentecostals, the Apostle Paul wrote, "The word is nigh thee, even in thy mouth, and in thy heart: that is, the word of faith, which we preach" (Rom. 10:8). One notices that the apostle did not say that the word is "on the page" or "in the book," but in the three non-textual locations of "in thy mouth," "in thy heart," and "the word . . . we preach."[6]

Pentecostals construe the Bible not as a set of ideas or abstract, detached, cognitive content, but as a living, active, and efficacious power. The Old Testament prophets had declared: "My word . . . shall accomplish that which I please, and it shall prosper in the thing whereto I sent it" (Isa. 55:11), and "I will hasten my word to perform it" (Jer. 1:12). The Isaiah text presented "the word of God" in quasi-personal terms, as able to "prosper," even as a human being does. These texts presume that God's word accomplishes something, even if we cannot always see what that is. The assumption is that God is at work in our own age, bringing his purposes and his word to pass. Believers play a subordinate role, by discerning God's ways, following God's initiative, and enacting God's kingdom. Yet God's word always retains priority over any merely human word. It is not that we read the Bible but rather that the Bible "reads" us—revealing and exposing us for who we truly are (Heb. 4:12).

A third principle in Pentecostal biblical interpretation is its "hermeneutics of affect or affection." In a well-known study of Pentecostal spirituality, Steven J. Land characterized Pentecostalism by distinguishing orthodoxy (right beliefs) from orthopraxy (right actions) and orthopathy (right affections).[7] The last member of the trio—orthopathy—tends to be emphasized in Pentecostalism. Neither intellectual and doctrinal understanding nor ethical principles of behavior are as important as the congruity of Pentecostal experience with biblical experience. To be Pentecostal has meant, in Andrew Davies's words, to have "music in your heart and poetry in your soul."[8] A witness to the Azusa Street Revival wrote: "We have no need of organs and pianos, for the Holy Ghost plays the piano in all our hearts . . . it is so sweet. It is heaven below."[9] This affective stress is why Pentecostals generally were interested neither in historical-critical analysis of the Bible (as in Protestant modernism) nor in evidentialist apologetics to demonstrate the Bible's historical accuracy (as in fundamentalism). Neither side in these twentieth-century debates paid much attention to orthopathy, and so Pentecostals generally remained on the sidelines of the controversy.

Untraditional, Christocentric, and Narratival Hermeneutics

Pentecostal approaches to the Bible tend to be untraditional, Christocentric, and narratival. Because Pentecostals presumed that the restored gifts of the Holy Spirit included new and deeper insights into the Bible, all previous—pre-Pentecostal—readings of the Bible were either false or incomplete. Assemblies of God historian and pastor B. F. Lawrence captured the Pentecostal ethos when he wrote in 1916:

> The older denominations have a past which is their own... [and] have become possessed of a two-fold inheritance, a two-fold guide of action, a two-fold criterion of doctrine—the New Testament and the church position. [In contrast], the Pentecostal Movement has no such history; it leaps the intervening years crying, "Back to Pentecost." In the minds of these honest-hearted thinking men and women, this [present-day] work of God is immediately connected with the work of God in New Testament days.[10]

Pentecostals set aside the apparatus of creeds, confessions, and formally defined dogmas in their quest for a new encounter with God.

In approaching the Bible, therefore, Pentecostals felt unconstrained by past definitions and interpretations, and this often resulted in fresh and creative re-readings of the biblical texts. The non-Pentecostal theologian, Clark Pinnock, commended Pentecostal biblical interpretation by saying that "Pentecostalism... has not only restored joy and power to the church but a clearer reading to the Bible as well."[11] On the other hand, Pentecostal non-traditionalism or anti-traditionalism has had the potential to reignite old controversies. In the "New Issue" debate, beginning in 1915, one branch of Pentecostalism jettisoned belief in doctrine of the Trinity and shifted toward a non-Trinitarian "Oneness" position—a new theological formulation that closely resembled the ancient heresy of modalism.[12]

Pentecostal attitudes toward church history and church tradition showed divergent tendencies, and one may discern a difference between what we might term restorationist and successionist approaches.[13] Restorationists wanted to leapfrog across the centuries and to return to first-century church experience. As I have indicated, B. F. Lawrence sounded the note of restorationism, and yet this was not the only Pentecostal view. Successionists perceived a stepwise progression in church history (or at least in Protestant history), as an early *Apostolic Faith* author explained:

> All along the ages men have been preaching a partial Gospel... God has from time to time raised up men to bring back the truth to the church. He raised up Luther to bring back to the world the doctrine of justification by faith. He raised up another reformer in John Wesley to establish Bible holiness in the church. Then he raised up Dr. [Charles] Cullis who brought back to the world the wonderful doctrine of divine healing. Now he is bringing back the Pentecostal Baptism to the church.[14]

Restorationists and successionists both wanted to re-experience the pristine purity and spiritual authority of the early church. The former thought that this re-experiencing would come through a radical rejection of church history and church traditions, while the latter anticipated it as the outcome of a centuries-long process that could be discerned within history. The former approach tended to become exclusive and sectarian, while the latter was more inclusive and ecumenical.[15]

It may be surprising to hear the Pentecostal approach to the Bible described as Christ-centered, because the movement is so often described as Spirit-centered. Yet the nearest thing to an early Pentecostal confession of faith was the so-called Five-Fold (sometimes Four-Fold) Gospel—Christ the Savior, Christ the Sanctifier, Christ the Baptizer (in the Spirit), Christ the Healer, and Christ the Coming King.[16] Pentecostal preaching was like classic evangelical teaching—and like early Christian exegesis—in seeking to discern the presence and activity of Christ in all portions of the Bible. The Pentecostal movement, in most of its expressions, was deeply Christ-centered and Christ-focused.

Pentecostal biblical interpretations have usually highlighted the Bible's narrative arc or aspect. Christian ministries professor Scott Ellington wrote that "understanding the Bible as story rather than 'pure' history frees the reader from the need to defend a model of historical truth that seems alien to the biblical writers." To be sure, Pentecostals were not uninterested in what really happened. Yet the concern for what really happened among Pentecostals did not engender efforts at verification through historical-critical analysis.[17] The theme of narrative carried over from the Bible into Pentecostal community life, where personal testimony concerning God's work in one's own life was foundational. To be a Pentecostal is to have a story to tell, which is as much a story of one's own life and experiences as it is a story of what God did in the days of Israel, Jesus, and the early church.

The Word Constrained—Ambivalence between Pentecostals and Evangelicals

Early Pentecostalism emerged from the radical, Holiness wing of North American evangelicalism, and yet soon it was an outcast from most church congregations. In the United States and Canada, the Pentecostals were generally not "come-outers" but "thrown-outers," who left because they were longer welcome in the churches. There was little tolerance for "tongue-speakers," who were regarded as religious fanatics, or even as mentally ill or demonically possessed.[18] Barred from existing Protestant denominations, schools, and colleges, and lacking in financial resources, the early Pentecostals were not equipped to establish their own theological seminaries and to devote time and energy to intellectual activities. As a result, they maintained their distinctive belief in Spirit baptism and the contemporary experience and expression of the charismatic gifts, and yet largely carried over into their own pulpits and Sunday schools the biblical interpretation and hermeneutical system of Protestant fundamentalism.

The union of Pentecostal experience with fundamentalist Bible interpretation was a marriage of convenience and not a satisfactory arrangement. Systematic theology professor Veli-Matti Kärkkäinen observed that "no other movement has ever been so hostile to Pentecostal distinctives. . . [as] reactionary Fundamentalism."[19] The supernaturalism of early Pentecostalism scandalized conservative Christians. The fundamentalists were "cessationists," holding that the miracles reported in the first-century church had ceased shortly after the New Testament was completed.[20] Moreover, their premillennialist view of the church's history was pessimistic. Fundamentalists believed that things would get worse before they got better. Only Christ's glorious Second Coming would bring radical improvement. The core Pentecostal conviction—that the Holy Spirit today was newly manifested in tongues-speaking and other signs and wonders—involved an optimistic perspective on history that contradicted premillennialist pessimism, just as the idea of modern-day miracles contradicted cessationism.

Fundamentalists had insisted—counter to liberal Protestant views—that the miracles and unusual events recorded in the Bible had truly and literally occurred. Methuselah lived to be 969 years old (Gen. 5:27). Noah's flood covered the entire earth and destroyed all but eight people (Gen. 6-9). God divided the Red Sea into two parts, and the children of Israel were supernaturally saved (Exod. 14:21-31). Jesus's Virgin birth, his healings, resurrection from the dead, and ascension into heaven all occurred as historical events. The apostles healed the sick in Jesus's name. Taking a cessationist view, the fundamentalists—and their evangelical successors—held that the biblical miracles were God's way of attesting to the revelation contained in the Bible. Yet once the Bible was completed, there was no further need of miracles. The book was a clearer revelation than the miracles could ever be. Fundamentalists and evangelicals argued that the basic hermeneutical error of the Pentecostals was to focus on narrative portions of the Bible, and especially the Acts of the Apostles, and to treat the experiences recorded there as normative. A 1970s evangelical saying held that we should not "teach the *experience* of the apostles" but rather "experience the *teaching* of the apostles."[21] The New Testament's didactic sections, and especially the epistles, had interpretive priority over the narrative or historical portions.

Scholars debated as to whether Pentecostals had erred by mandating that people today should have the same experiences as those recorded in biblical times. Theologian and seminary professor Gordon Fee—though Pentecostal—agreed substantially with the evangelical critique, writing that Pentecostals are "noted for bad hermeneutics" and that "experience has preceded their hermeneutics. In a sense, the Pentecostal tends to exegete his experience." The Book of Acts, he claimed, is "not an epistle, nor a theological treatise" and "drawing universal norms from particular events produces a *non sequitur*."[22]

In response to Fee, Canadian Pentecostal theologian Roger Stronstad argued that Pentecostalism did not rest on the unwarranted assumption that believers today need to replicate the first-century experiences of the apostles by speaking in tongues and healing the sick. What the Acts of the Apostles gave to Pentecostals was not a simple summons to imitate the early church but an interpretive template linking biblical texts to later experiences. In Acts 2:16, Peter had interpreted the church's first Pentecost with a "this is that" statement interpreting the tongues-speaking of the first disciples in light of Joel's ancient prophecy. Later in Acts, when the Gentile household of Cornelius unexpectedly received the Holy Spirit, Peter inferred that their Spirit baptism happened according to the earlier pattern of Pentecost (Acts 11:15-17). Stronstad noted that it was "Peter, and not the Pentecostals, who established the principle of a pattern for the various episodes of the pouring forth of the Spirit."[23] Pentecostals were thus not imitating Peter's experience of the Spirit but following Peter's instruction on the Spirit. Stronstad's interpretation blurred Fee's clear line between apostolic narrative in Acts and apostolic instruction in the New Testament epistles. Moreover, Fee offered a counterargument to his own stated position in acknowledging that "the Pentecostal may justify his speaking in tongues not only from precedent (in Acts) but also from the teaching about spiritual gifts in 1 Corinthians 12-14."[24]

Given the New Testament interweaving of charismatic experiences, Hebrew Bible citations, and apostolic instructions, Pentecostal interpretations of the Bible had arguably a firmer exegetical basis than competing, cessationist interpretations. Pentecostal theologian and seminary professor John Christopher Thomas extrapolated Stronstad's line of argument with an appeal to the Jerusalem Council in Acts 15.[25] In this biblical chapter, the Gentiles' positive response to Gospel preaching led James to quote from the Book of Amos, and—in another "this is that" moment—to reinterpret the present circumstance not as a church problem needing to be fixed but as a providential event requiring acknowledgment. For John Christopher Thomas, this Lucan interpretive template—linking scripture (the Books of Joel and Amos), to later experiences and to doctrinal teaching—found support in Acts 15 as well as in Acts 2.

Formal relations between American Pentecostals and other conservative Protestants went through ups and downs. The low ebb came in 1918, when the World Christian Fundamentals Association voted to disfellowship all Pentecostals, referring to as them "fanatics."[26] By the 1940s, the Pentecostals were tired of being rejected and their leaders sought a strategic alliance with the increasingly respected and respectable "evangelicals"—the new name for the former fundamentalists. The 1942 admission of the Assemblies of God into the National Association of Evangelicals (NAE) was a watershed moment. From the 1940s onward, an "evangelicalization of Pentecostalism" made denominational Pentecostals in North America seem much more like their evangelical cousins. Charismatic gifts were deemphasized.[27] Yet from the 1970s onward, a reverse process also became visible: the "Pentecostalization of evangelicalism." Many evangelical churches embraced "contemporary worship," whose style (people standing, hands aloft, loud instrumentation, followed by quiet meditative music) was a clear reflection of Pentecostal and charismatic influences.

During the 1970s, two major, largely white Pentecostal denominations in the United States—the Assemblies of God and the Church of God (Cleveland, Tennessee)—founded their own accredited theological seminaries.[28] As American Pentecostalism has gained greater cultural and theological self-confidence, it began searching for its own theological method and a way of reading the scriptures that was more congruent with its own presuppositions.[29] Some even spoke of the Pentecostal approach to the Bible not as "modernist" but "postmodernist."[30] The Pentecostal-evangelical hermeneutical "marriage of convenience" arrived at either a "separation" or an "annulment," depending on one's view of the union that had preceded.

THE WORD ENACTED AND CONTEMPORIZED— EXPERIENCING AND PRACTICING THE BIBLE

In Pentecostal life and experience, scripture becomes script. The Bible is not only to be believed; it must also be lived. Religious studies scholar and anthropologist Simon Coleman's field research during the 1990s in a charismatic (or neo-Pentecostal) congregation highlights the theme of enactment, as already noted.[31] Coleman uses the term "dramatization" to refer to "the ways in which biblical exegesis is achieved through an acting out of the text, whether in sermons or in other areas of life." In this way, "believers come to see themselves as representing—perhaps even embodying—characters in a biblical drama whose episodes can be replayed again and again throughout history." This "use of scripture as script" relies on an identification of "the self with the biblical characters who are regarded as undergoing analogous experiences to one's own." Thus "the Bible [serves] as the textual catalyst for the telling of stories that can be applied directly . . . to the self, encouraging the believer to take a particular course of action, remain firm in the faith, discover the reason for a particular event, and so on."[32]

Preaching in this context requires the speaker "to extemporize on familiar biblical themes," and to engage in "the direct application of scriptural narrative to the present." Listeners are informed that by acting "as" Jesus—or Moses, or Abraham, or some other biblical figure—they can achieve the same results that the biblical characters achieved, inasmuch as God's power is still at work in the world today. Any portion of scripture—however small—can be applied to contemporary life. Coleman speaks of "the insertion of the self into 'living' biblical drama." People think of themselves as living vehicles or representatives of God's word—or perhaps of a specific biblical text. This "insertion" into the biblical drama takes on a yet more radical form when Pentecostals seek guidance through dreams or visions. Some persons—and especially certain leading pastors—claim that they have encountered Jesus or other biblical figures in dreams or visions.[33]

Pentecostals do not regard themselves as "interpreting" biblical texts. Using oral-aural language, they say rather that the text is "speaking" to them. One interesting image is that of "ingestion," referring to "the ways in which people come to regard themselves as physically assimilating and . . . becoming constituted by [biblical] . . . words." Scripture in this sense has "a performative force . . . appropriated by the person." Pentecostals see the Bible as nurturant—feeding and sustaining the human self, soul, or spirit. Occasionally one encounters reproductive metaphors—the Bible as seminal. God's word is said to be a seed that enters the self to make it pregnant with truth. Pentecostals do not only read the Bible, but memorize it, transcribe it, sing it, and speak it aloud, in order to release its power into their lives. As in British philosopher of language J. L. Austin's speech act theory, Pentecostal proclamation of God's word is thought to effect or produce that which it names. Adherents of the so-called prosperity Gospel practice "positive confession," whereby the words they pronounce are said to create the very realities that they describe. Coleman sees here a collapse between symbols and realities, the metaphorical and the material. People sometimes speak of "walking on the Word"—as it were some kind of material support for their feet and for the rest of their physical bodies.[34]

For Pentecostals, the repetition of God's word does not render it trivial or banal, but allows it to exercise and pool its holy influence and power—as though one were accumulating quantities of some resource. Verses of scripture spoken in faith help to create the health and well-being desired by the speaker. These can be passed on to other hearers too. Romans 5:17, for example, speaks of "reigning in life," and by declaring aloud this text one can acquire the spiritual authority denoted in the verses.[35] Ulf Ekman—founder of the Word of Life organization in Sweden—stressed the interiority and spirituality of God's word: "Somewhere God's Word comes and it goes in and . . . reaches into your spirit. And when it reaches into your spirit it explodes on the inside and God's Word which is eternal has become an eternal truth in your spirit."[36]

Black Pentecostal churches in the United States and Canada have distinctive ways of preaching through, living out, and applying the Bible to contemporary experience. One finds an immediacy, vividness, and urgency in black preaching generally, and this applies especially to black Pentecostal preaching. Using technical language, the phenomenon can be called a "fusion of horizons" (in German: *Horizontverschmelzung*) in which the distinction vanishes between biblical history and the contemporary setting.[37] In preaching on the Israelites' deliverance at the Red Sea (Exod. 14), a black preacher might communicate that we (the preacher and hearers) are the children of Israel, our adversaries are the Egyptians chariots pursuing us, and our situation is that of Israelites at the Red Sea, hemmed in and doomed to defeat. Yet God assuredly will part the waters for us, so that our escape from adversaries is just as certain as that of the Israelites. A black church sermon is not an invitation to enter the past or to inhabit the biblical world. It is rather a creative reimagining and redeployment of the biblical text for the present-day situation. The "fusion of horizons" occurs in a forward direction—not toward the there-and-then but toward the here-and-now. The ancient author speaks, and the twentieth- or twenty-first-century believer hears and believes.

When performed by a skillful practitioner, and when spoken out of a life experience and social context that is congruent with the message, a black church sermon is often spellbinding. The hearer feels personally empowered and affectively equipped to endure hardship, difficulty, and setbacks in the days ahead, convinced that God—the God-of-Exodus, the-God-Who-Parted-the-Waters—is present and is superintending all of life's circumstances for his or her benefit and blessing. Black church biblical interpretation, preaching, and worship includes many aspects that cannot be explored here, including the "chanted" or "performed sermon" (a kind of sung, semi-musical, and/or rhythmic presentation), the call-and-response in worship (interplay of preacher with congregation), the respective roles of lamentation and celebration in preaching the Bible, and sociopolitical or liberationist messages or subtexts in preaching and interpreting scripture.[38]

One of the more complex questions regarding Pentecostals and the Bible pertains to the question of contemporary "prophecy." Self-described Pentecostals do not agree among themselves on this issue. Some accept that God today speaks in a more-or-less direct way to certain people, while others—standing closer to the evangelicals—are skeptical regarding such claims. On the other hand, most Pentecostals display a flexibility in thinking about divine revelation that one does not find among evangelicals.

"God speaking" is an elastic category. God may "speak" to someone not only through the text of the Bible but also through life circumstances, events in the news, a random saying in a book or magazine, a dream, a stranger's comment (even if not spoken with the meaning later assigned to the comment), or extraordinary experiences of seeing a vision or hearing God in a seemingly auditory way. One is tempted to say that almost anything that a Pentecostal Christian encounters in everyday life might be construed as God's act of "speaking." This does not mean that the Bible has no normative value or significance, but rather that the discernment process—"what is God saying to me right now?"—is enlarged and complicated by the explicit incorporation of contextual factors in interpreting the Bible.

In various ways, the word of God is contemporized so that it is not only an ancient text but a "right-now-word" that applies immediately to the believer's life situation. A Pentecostal in reading the Bible will sometimes say that God has underscored a particular verse or passage—as though God had applied a colored marker or highlighter to the printed page. Some call this a *rhema*-word, because *rhema* is a Greek New Testament term for "saying," and in this usage it suggests a divine message that is situational and specific.

The *rhema*-word represents, on the Pentecostal view, a happy conjunction and harmonization of the Holy Spirit with the Holy Bible. A Pentecostal might say—"while I was praying this morning, God gave me a word"—referring in this instance not to words that are wholly new, but to a passage of scripture that seems to address some situation in the believer's own life. The *rhema*-word does not always occur when someone is reading the Bible, but can be a matter of later remembrance—a recalling of a particular text, with Spirit-given emphasis, as applying to the present set of circumstances.[39]

Evangelical Christians—in contrast to Pentecostals—draw a clear distinction between "inspiration" and "illumination." That is, the work of the Holy Spirit in guiding the original authors of the Bible in their writing ("inspiration") is a work of the Holy Spirit wholly different from the conferring of insight and understanding in reading the texts of the Bible today ("illumination"). The Pentecostal *rhema*-word blurs this sharp boundary. Even more disconcerting—from the evangelical point of view—is the notion prevalent among some Pentecostals that God might somehow be communicating wholly new facts or ideas to people alive today.[40] To evangelical ears, this makes it sound as though the biblical canon is not closed and new scriptural and authoritative revelation is still being given through God-ordained prophets, as in the biblical epoch.

With only rare exceptions, however, Pentecostals reject the idea that contemporary "prophecy" stands on the same level of authority as the Bible. Instead, they hold that the Spirit works in various people in various manners and degrees, and that Spirit-guided ideas, impressions, and images are not to be shunned, but can serve a subordinate role in guiding believers through the complexities of daily life and Christian service. No one today, that is, has a universal teaching office—like that of the biblical David, Isaiah, Matthew, or Paul. What is today called "prophecy" is occasional and situational in scope, even though Spirit-conferred.[41]

THE WORD TYPOLOGIZED, LYRICIZED, AND WEAPONIZED—THE "DAVIDIC" MOTIF

Pentecostals love King David. The biblical David not only authored scripture but also fought the Lord's battles and was a "man after God's heart" (1 Sam. 13:14). From the overflow of his worshipful heart, he composed the music used in Israel's public worship. While the musical tones and rhythms of the ancient songs are lost to us, the Book of Psalms preserves the lyrics attributed to David. Many independent charismatic congregations—including especially the "house of prayer" and 24/7 prayer and worship movements—are deeply Davidic.[42] Clustering around David are a set of themes near and dear to Pentecostals—affective spirituality, the heart aflame, music and singing, day and night worship, the composition of new songs, spiritual battle, power through praising God, and victory over adversaries. Pentecostal biblical interpretation includes not only Lucan themes (such as the Day of Pentecost, Spirit baptism, tongues-speaking, and evangelism) but also the Davidic themes just mentioned.[43]

In independent charismatic churches one finds a surprising focus on the little-known biblical book of First Chronicles, inasmuch as this book describes how David appointed the singers and instrumentalists for worship in the tabernacle. The spiritual goal is to become, like David, a "worshipping warrior," a person so full of praise for God that he or she overcomes every spiritual obstacle that comes along. Women as well as men can be "warriors" in this way, and indeed—in many churches and especially in the prayer groups—the women warriors far outnumber the men. Through prayer, singing, instrumental music, and spoken biblical texts (seen as having power to effect change), Davidic-style worshippers engage in spiritual battle against their perceived adversaries. Affirmatively, they may pray for the salvation of a loved one, world evangelization, for the healing of illnesses, or the end of drug addiction. Negatively, they pray against Satan and his demonic hordes, and against social ills (including abortion, crime, human trafficking, pornography, racial division, and social strife), while citing biblical texts that promise victory over enemies. "No weapon that is formed against thee shall prosper" (Isa. 54:17). "Behold, I give unto you power to tread on serpents and scorpions... and nothing shall... hurt you" (Luke 10:19). "And they overcame him [i.e., Satan] by the blood of the Lamb" (Rev. 12:11). Language and imagery from the Book of Joshua and the Israelite conquest of the Canaanites is also sometimes invoked.[44] The contemporary Davidic-style worshipper reenacts the life of the biblical David, sings songs in praise of God, and thereby defeats the devil. In this way, the Bible is typologized, lyricized, and weaponized in the believer's own experience and practice.

The roots of Davidic teaching go back several decades, at least to the 1970s and perhaps earlier to the "Latter Rain" revival in Canada during the late 1940s.[45] Two authors—both associated with the Portland Bible College (Portland, Ore.)—published books expounding this teaching, Dick Iverson's *Present Day Truths* (1976), and Kevin J. Connor's *Tabernacle of David* (1976) and *Tabernacle of Moses* (1976). Iverson did not believe that God was presently giving new biblical revelation, and yet he held that there are elements in the Bible that need to be reemphasized in any given age: "In every generation, God specifically moves with a fresh 'rhema' [Gk., 'word'] from Heaven. The emphasis of the Spirit is very important to the Church in each generation.... What is 'present truth'? It is that portion of God's Word that the Holy Spirit is emphasizing at this time." Right worship among God's people was "the heart desire of God from Genesis to Revelation."[46] All of biblical revelation somehow addressed the one question—How does one worship God? Iverson proposed that "the restoration of the tabernacle of David," or a recovery of genuine, heartfelt, and uninhibited worship, was "present truth" or God's particular purpose at the present time.

Iverson developed an elaborate account of the biblical Tabernacle of David in a twofold typological relation to Christ and to the Christian life. The brazen altar represented Christ as our sacrifice and Christian repentance. The brazen laver was Christ our sanctifier and Christian baptism. The golden candlestick depicted Christ our light and the apostles' teaching. The table of showbread prefigured Christ the bread of life and the Eucharist. The altar of incense anticipated Christ our intercessor and Christian prayer.[47] The ark of the covenant was a type of Christ our life and of Christian fellowship. For Iverson, the "Tabernacle of Moses" was an early and inadequate form of Israelite worship. David's music, instrumentation, and psalmody were innovations that brought greater depth to the worship experience. Iverson's biblical exegesis suggested that today's Christians need to move from the "Tabernacle of Moses" (dutiful, perfunctory, church attendance) to the "Tabernacle of David" (heartfelt and exuberant worship). As David danced before God "with all his might" (2 Sam. 6:14), so ought God's worshippers to do today. These Davidic teachings from the 1970s encouraged the development of contemporary Christian music and helped to shape the worship ethos of recent Pentecostal revivals, such as the Toronto Blessing of the mid-1990s and subsequently.[48]

TENTATIVE CONCLUSIONS

Modern biblical scholarship tells us that the Bible is not a book of timeless truths, detached from social and historical contexts. The "good book" did not fall to us from heaven. Pentecostals agree. Yet their preoccupation is with present-day situations rather than ancient history—the contemporary "horizon" of meaning rather than the text's ancient "horizon." They seek to discern where and how the Bible's living God is at work in the world, fulfilling the ancient prophecies, transforming human lives, and judging, hindering, enabling, or blessing peoples and nations. The Pentecostals' Bible is a book filled with movement—not like a fixed outline of a static object, but more like an athlete's instructional video, showing how to execute a back flip, spike a volleyball, or dance a pirouette. Since on the Pentecostal view the Holy Spirit allows for continually new interpretations of the Bible, the instructional video—to adapt the analogy—will have to be updated and uploaded in new format every day. It is no wonder that Pentecostals have adapted so well to the Internet age. Their worldview, idea of God, and approach to the Bible underscore change and alteration. Images of rivers and flowing water often recur in Pentecostal hymns and devotional writing, highlighting the themes of flux and fluidity. Similarly, the common Pentecostal image of fire also reveals a dynamic picture of God and spiritual life

During the early twentieth century, fundamentalist Christians held fast to the literal text of the Bible, while modernist or liberal Christians based their opinions and theology on contemporary religious experience. In the midst of the fundamentalist-modernist controversy, these emphases appeared irreconcilable. Pentecostalism accomplished what seemed impossible by *combining biblical literalism with open-ended experientialism*. Pentecostalism, L. William Oliverio commented, points "toward a way beyond the divide between the biblical propositionalism of conservative Protestantism and the placing of the locus of divine revelation on religious experience as in liberal Protestantism." The hermeneutic movement of Pentecostalism, adds Oliverio, was "not. . . consciously theoretical," in contrast to twentieth-century so-called neo-Orthodoxy or Barthianism, and yet in the long run it was a vastly more successful movement, if we judge in terms of the numbers of people affected.[49]

By taking the supernaturalism of the New Testament texts with absolute seriousness, and insisting that the first-century experiences were normative and had to be replicated in contemporary life, the early Pentecostals succeeded in being just as biblically literalistic as the fundamentalists and yet just as experientialist and as contemporaneous as the liberals or modernists. The Pentecostal leap across the centuries—though bypassing historical investigation—shaped a religious ethos that was highly attuned to the present. Throughout the last century, the adaptability of Pentecostals in various missionary and cultural settings around the world corroborated the point. While fundamentalist and evangelical Protestants from British, European, or North American cultures struggled to establish new inculturated congregations in African, Asian, and Latin American contexts, Pentecostal evangelists with only a modicum of cultural or linguistic training generally achieved this goal more fully and swiftly. The surviving and thriving global Pentecostal movement thus shows an irony. The biblical supernaturalism that—to many scholars—seemed wholly irrelevant to modern humanity proved instead to be highly relevant to great masses of people in the twentieth- and twenty-first centuries.[50]

Notes

1. This and all other biblical citations are to the King James Bible or Authorized Version.
2. Space limitations will not allow me to delve into the complex uses of such terms as "Pentecostal," "charismatic," "neo-Pentecostal," and "Spirit-filled." In this essay I will use the word "Pentecostal" to cover all Christians designated under these terms. Allan Anderson speaks of those "concerned primarily with the *experience* of the working of the Holy Spirit and the *practice* of spiritual gifts." Allan Anderson, "Varieties, Taxonomies, Definitions," in *Studying Global Pentecostalism: Theories and Methods*, ed. Allan Anderson et al. (Berkeley: University of California Press, 2010), 16–17. Douglas Jacobsen admits that "Pentecostal" as a term is "essentially contested," yet describes it as applying to someone who is "committed to a Spirit-centered, miracle-affirming, praise-oriented version of Christian faith." Douglas Jacobsen, *Thinking in the Spirit: Theologies of the Early Pentecostal Movement* (Bloomington: Indiana University Press, 2001), 12. For further discussion of terminology, see Michael J. McClymond, "Charismatic Renewal and Neo-Pentecostalism: From American Origins to Global Permutations," in *The Cambridge Companion to Pentecostalism*, ed. Cecil M. Robeck and Amos Yong (Cambridge, UK: Cambridge University Press, 2014), 31–51, and esp., "The Challenge of Taxonomy and Terminology," 32–34. For definition and discussion of "spiritual gifts" or "charismatic gifts," see Michael J. McClymond, "Charismatic Gifts: Healing, Tongues-Speaking, Prophecy, and Exorcism," in *The Wiley-Blackwell Companion to World Christianity*, ed. Lamin Sanneh and Michael J. McClymond (Oxford, UK: Wiley-Blackwell, 2016), 399–418.
3. Mark McLean, "Toward a Pentecostal Hermeneutic," *Pneuma* 6, no. 2 (1984): 38; cited in David Kling, *The Bible in History: How the Texts Have Shaped the Times* (New York: Oxford University Press, 2004), 238. The presumption that God is active today, in supernatural ways, is foundational to Pentecostalism. Andrew Davies writes, "Pentecostalism requires a God on the loose, involving himself with the fine details of our earthly existence and actively transformed lives." Davies, "What Does It Mean to Read the Bible as a Pentecostal?" *Journal of Pentecostal Theology* 18, no. 2 (2009): 220. Scott A. Ellington comments, "The common thread that allows the bringing together of the worldview(s) of the biblical writers and the worldview(s) of Pentecostals is a commonly held belief that God remains an active agent (indeed the primary active agent) in the biblical stories." Ellington, "History, Story, and Testimony: Locating Truth in a Pentecostal Hermeneutic," *Pneuma* 23, no. 1 (2001): 262.
4. Walter Hollenweger, *The Pentecostals: The Charismatic Movement in the Churches* (Minneapolis, Minn.: Augsburg, 1972), 321–22; Hollenweger wrote in the dedication, "To my friends and teachers in the Pentecostal Movement who taught me to love the Bible and to my teachers and friends in the Presbyterian Church who taught me to understand it" (xvi).
5. James K. A. Smith, "The Closing of the Book: Pentecostals, Evangelicals, and the Sacred Writings," *Journal of Pentecostal Theology* 5, no. 11 (1997): 49–51.

6. Limited space in this essay will not allow me to address the possible parallels between the Pentecostal and Barthian approaches to the Bible. Beginning with his *Epistle to the Romans* (1918) and continuing into his multivolume *Church Dogmatics* (1934-1968), Swiss theologian Karl Barth presented God's Word as dynamic rather than static—not as a thing but rather as an event (Ger. *Ereignis*). Like Pentecostals, Barth stressed the word of God in its *spoken or preached* rather than written form. To oversimplify: while conservative Protestantism had said that "the Bible *is* the word of God," Barth affirmed that "the Bible *becomes* the word of God." This contrast is too glib and yet the saying raises a question: What analogy might there be between the dynamic understanding of God's word in Pentecostalism and in Barthianism? On Barth as biblical interpreter, see Gary J. Dorrien, "Dialectics of the Word: Crisis Theology," in *The Barthian Revolt in Modern Theology: Theology without Weapons* (Louisville, Ky.: Westminster John Knox, 2000), 47–80; and Richard Burnett, *Karl Barth's Theological Exegesis: The Hermeneutical Principles of the Römerbrief Period* (Tübingen: Mohr Siebeck, 2001). In general Barth held to a dialectic of crisis or judgment, while Pentecostalism manifested a dialectic of grace. God's grace—by the Holy Spirit—was already being poured out, and there was more grace to come. If Barth in his biblical interpretation sought to afflict the comfortable, then the Pentecostals sought to comfort the afflicted. Western cultural elites—with their preening pride and presumption—were the focus of Barth's devastating attack in his *Epistle to the Romans*. Early Pentecostals would not have understood Barth's writings, but even if they had, his message was really not for them, as outsiders to the cultural and educational hierarchy of their day. One cannot repent of cultural pretensions or theological errors that one has never had.

7. Steven J. Land writes, "This theological task demands the ongoing integration of beliefs, affections and actions lest the spirituality and theology fragment into intellectualism, sentimentalism and activism respectively. . . . Experience of the Spirit, who is the agent of mutuality and relatedness in the Trinity and the church, drives toward and requires this integration of. . . orthodoxy (right praise-confession), orthopathy (right affections) and orthopraxy (right praxis)." Land, *Pentecostal Spirituality: A Passion for the Kingdom* (Sheffield, UK: Sheffield Academic Press, 1993), 41. Pentecostal communities often focus on orthopathy, yet Land highlights not only orthopathy but the integration of orthodoxy, orthopraxy, and orthopathy.

8. Davies, "What Does it Mean," 216.

9. *Apostolic Faith* [newsletter], December 1906, 2. This quotation was excerpted in the title of Grant Wacker's monograph, *Heaven Below: Early Pentecostals and American Culture* (Cambridge, Mass.: Harvard University Press, 2001).

10. Bennett F. Lawrence, *The Apostolic Faith Restored* (St. Louis, Mo.: Gospel Publishing House, 1916), n.p.; cited in L. William Oliverio, *Theological Hermeneutics in the Classical Pentecostal Tradition: A Typological Account* (Leiden: Brill, 2012), 19.

11. Clark Pinnock, foreword to Roger Stronstad, *The Charismatic Theology of St. Luke* (Peabody, Mass.: Hendrickson Publishers, 1984), viii.

12. The outstanding account of Oneness Pentecostalism is David A. Reed, *"In Jesus' Name": The History and Beliefs of Oneness Pentecostals* (Blandford Forum, UK: Deo Publishing, 2008). Reed does not see Pentecostal "Oneness" teaching as a modern form of modalism, but as a third alternative to modalist heresies and traditional Trinitarian formulations. David A. Reed, in conversation with the author, at the Society for Pentecostal Studies meeting, at Southeastern University, Lakeland, Fla., USA, March 12–14, 2015.

13. The term "restorationist" is well established and widely used, and I am here proposing the term "successionist" to name what I view as a countervailing tendency in Pentecostalism.

14. *Apostolic Faith* [newsletter], October 1906, 1.

15. The Latter Rain Revival (1948-1950) in Canada followed a successionist rather than restorationist interpretation of church history, and this may be one reason that Pentecostal denominations in Canada and the United States—Pentecostal Assemblies of Canada (PAOC) and Assemblies of God (AG)—rejected the Latter Rain and disfellowshipped its leaders. See Richard M. Riss, "The Latter Rain Movement of 1948," *Pneuma* 4 (1982): 32–45; and Riss, *Latter Rain: The Latter Rain Movement of 1948 and the Mid-Twentieth Century's Evangelical Awakening* (Mississauga, Ont.: Honeycomb Visual Production, 1987). In Latter Rain successionism, Spirit baptism and speaking in tongues in the early twentieth century were only a start, and further gifts and graces from God were to be expected. Latter Rain Charismatics aided the early stages of the mainline Charismatic Renewal, and their ecumenical interpretation of church history allowed them to affirm the Spirit's work in traditional churches.

16. The fourfold or four-square Gospel typified the non-Wesleyan Pentecostals, who did not believe in "sanctification" as a distinct experience subsequent to conversion, but viewed it as a gradual, lifelong process. In the fourfold Gospel, Christ the Sanctifier drops out, and only four attributions remain.

17. Ellington, "History, Story, and Testimony," 262.

18. Reactions against early Pentecostalism are documented through primary sources, with commentary, in "Disorder, Dementia, and Demons: Early Critics of Pentecostalism," in *Encyclopedia of Religious Revivals in America*, 2 vols., ed. Michael J. McClymond (Westport, Conn.: Greenwood Press, 2007), 2:255–59.

19. Veli-Matti Kärkkäinen, "Pentecostal Hermeneutics in the Making: On the Way from Fundamentalism to Postmodernism," *Journal of the European Pentecostal Theological Association* 18, no. 1 (1998): 96.

20. On cessationism and its origins, see Jon Ruthven, *On the Cessation of Charismata: The Protestant Polemic on Postbiblical Miracles* (Sheffield, UK: Sheffield Academic Press, 1993).

21. The 1970s saying is quoted from memory. Donald A. Carson summarized evangelical arguments by saying that Pentecostals "have succumbed to the modern love of 'experience,' even at the expense of truth." D. A. Carson, *Showing the Spirit: A Theological Exposition of 1 Corinthians 12–14* (Grand Rapids, Mich.: Baker Book House, 1987), 12.

22. Gordon D. Fee, "Hermeneutics and Historical Precedent—A Major Problem in Pentecostal Hermeneutics," in *Perspectives on the New Pentecostalism*, ed. Russell D. Spittler (Grand Rapids, Mich.: Baker Book House, 1976), 119, 122, 124–25, 128.

23. Roger Stronstad, "Pentecostal Hermeneutics: A Review Essay of Gordon D. Fee, *Gospel and Spirit*," *Pneuma* 15, no. 2 (1993): 221; see also Roger Stronstad, "Pentecostal Experience and Hermeneutics," *Paraclete* 26, no. 1 (Winter 1992): 14–30.

24. Fee, "Hermeneutics," 119–20.

25. John Christopher Thomas, "Women, Pentecostals and the Bible: An Experiment in Pentecostal Hermeneutics," *Journal of Pentecostal Theology* 5 (1994): 41–56.

26. William Atkinson, "Worth a Second Look? Pentecostal Hermeneutics," *Evangel* 21 (Summer 2003): 51.

27. On the "evangelicalization" of Pentecostalism, see William M. Menzies, *Anointed to Serve: The Story of the Assemblies of God* (Springfield, Mo.: Gospel Publishing House, 1971), 177–227; and Edith L. Blumhofer, *The Assemblies of God: A Chapter in the Story*

of *American Pentecostalism*, 2 vols. (Springfield, Mo.: Gospel Publishing House, 1989), 2:13–49.

28. The Assemblies of God (USA) formally founded their seminary in 1973, while the Church of God (Cleveland, Tenn.) did so in 1975. The latter seminary was later renamed as Pentecostal Theological Seminary. Timothy B. Cargal, "Beyond the Fundamentalist-Modernist Controversy: Pentecostals and Hermeneutics in a Postmodern Age," *Pneuma* 15 (1993): 169n18.

29. Works reflecting the recent Pentecostal quest for hermeneutical and methodological self-definition include: Kenneth J. Archer, *A Pentecostal Hermeneutic: Spirit, Scripture, and Community* (Cleveland, Tenn.: CPT Press, 2009); Oliverio, *Theological Hermeneutics*; Lee Roy Martin, ed., *Pentecostal Hermeneutics: A Reader* (Leiden: Brill, 2013); and Kenneth J. Archer and L. William Oliverio Jr., eds., *Constructive Pneumatological Hermeneutics in Pentecostal Christianity* (New York: Palgrave Macmillan, 2016). The elite, scholarly conversation occurring in these books and the related journal articles has not yet had much impact on Pentecostal preaching and teaching on the grass-roots level. Kärkkäinen aptly speaks of a "growing divergence in the practice of biblical interpretation between Pentecostals in the parish and in the academy." Kärkkäinen, "Pentecostal Hermeneutics," 82.

30. Kärkkäinen noted that "the alleged similarities between Pentecostalism and Postmodernism are not that obvious when the issues are pressed." Kärkkäinen, "Pentecostal Hermeneutics," 97. For in postmodernism, there is no macro-narrative or "big story," as in Pentecostalism, nor any concept of objective truth.

31. Simon Coleman, "Textuality and Embodiment among Charismatic Christians," in *Reading Religion in Text and Context: Reflections on Faith and Practice in Religious Materials*, ed. Elisabeth Arweck and Peter Collins (Aldershot, UK: Ashgate, 2006), 157–68. This essay draws from Coleman's research, published previously as *The Globalisation of Charismatic Christianity: Spreading the Gospel of Prosperity* (Cambridge: Cambridge University Press, 2000). The Word of Life (*Livets Ord*) congregation is located in Uppsala, Sweden, and yet its founding pastor was educated at the Rhema Bible Institute in Tulsa, Oklahoma, and Coleman's generalizations about the role of Bible/Word/word apply to US as well as Swedish Pentecostalism.

32. Coleman, "Textuality and Embodiment," 162.

33. Coleman, "Textuality and Embodiment," 161–62.

34. Coleman, "Textuality and Embodiment," 163, 165. On "performative" language—so important in Pentecostalism—see the classic work by J. L. Austin, *How To Do Things with Words* (Cambridge, Mass.: Harvard University Press, 1962). On the prosperity Gospel, see Kate Bowler, *Blessed: A History of the American Prosperity Gospel* (New York: Oxford University Press, 2013).

35. Coleman, "Textuality and Embodiment," 165.

36. Ulf Ekman, as cited (from a message delivered in Swedish) in Coleman, "Textuality and Embodiment," 163; the word "spirit" is capitalized in the original and is here de-capitalized, since it refers to the human "spirit."

37. The classic account of the "fusion of horizons" appears in Hans-Georg Gadamer, *Truth and Method*, 2nd rev. ed., trans. Joel Weinsheimer and Donald G. Marshall (New York: Crossroad, 1989).

38. On black church preaching and black church use of scripture, a rich literature exists: Warren H. Stewart, *Interpreting God's Word in Black Preaching* (Valley Forge, Pa.: Judson Press,

1984); Gerald L. Davis, *I Got the Word in Me and I Can Sing It, You Know: A Study of the Performed African-American Sermon* (Philadelphia: University of Pennsylvania Press, 1985); Jon Michael Spencer, *Sacred Symphony: The Chanted Sermon of the Black Preacher* (New York: Greenwood Press, 1988); William H. Pipes, *Say Amen, Brother!: Old-Time Negro Preaching, A Study in American Frustration* (Detroit, Mich.: Wayne State University Press, 1992); Crawford E. Evans, *The Hum: Call and Response in African American Preaching* (Nashville, Tenn.: Abingdon Press, 1995); James H. Harris, *Preaching Liberation* (Minneapolis, Minn.: Fortress Press, 1995); Glenn Hinson, *Fire in My Bones: Transcendence and the Holy Spirit in African American Gospel* (Philadelphia: University of Pennsylvania Press, 2000), 43–52; Susan L. Bond, *Contemporary African American Preaching: Diversity in Theory and Style* (St. Louis, Mo.: Chalice Press, 2003); Cleophus James LaRue, *I Believe I'll Testify: The Art of African American Preaching* (Louisville, Ky.: Westminster John Knox Press, 2011); Kenyatta R. Gilbert, *The Journey and Promise of African American Preaching* (Minneapolis, Minn.: Fortress Press, 2011); Luke A. Powery, *Dem Dry Bones: Preaching, Death, and Hope* (Minneapolis, Minn.: Fortress Press, 2012); Frank A. Thomas, *They Like to Never Quit Praisin' God: The Role of Celebration in Preaching* (Cleveland, Ohio: Pilgrim Press, 2013).

39. Pentecostals invoke a passage from the Gospel of John in support of their idea that the Holy Spirit reminds them of things written in the Bible: "But the Comforter, which is the Holy Ghost, whom the Father will send in my name, he shall teach you all things, and bring all things to your remembrance, whatsoever I have said unto you" (John 14:26, AV). The *rhema*-word is an important concept in Pentecostal use of the Bible, yet I have been unable to find any academic literature devoted to this theme. Reflecting on the 1740s New England revivals, Jonathan Edwards noted that some participants claimed that God brought certain texts of scripture to their minds, applying them directly to their own situation. Jonathan Edwards, *The Works of Jonathan Edwards*, vol. 2: *Religious Affections*, ed. John E. Smith (New Haven, Conn.: Yale University Press, 1959), 218–39. John Smith, in the "Editor's Introduction" to this volume, noted that Edwards "attacked affections [i.e., religious experiences] based on texts of Scripture coming suddenly and miraculously to mind and giving people the idea that God was communicating his special favor to them individually." These 1740s experiences sounded much like later Pentecostal *rhema*-word experiences. Yet for Edwards, unlike Pentecostals, the "extraordinary manner in which something comes to mind is of no account" (Smith, "Editor's Introduction," 31). Here Edwards reflected a characteristic evangelical caution in seeing sudden, dramatic experiences as God's way of speaking to individual or giving them guidance.

40. As to any "revelation of secret facts by immediate suggestion," Edwards stated that there was nothing in this "spiritual and divine, in that sense wherein gracious affections and operations are." Edwards, *Religious Affections*, 226. For Edwards, neither the experience of recalling biblical words (the Pentecostal *rhema*), nor the more overt claims in his own day to revelation of wholly new truths, could be reliably identified as the work of the Holy Spirit.

41. For a general account of contemporary Pentecostal prophecy, by a former-evangelical-turned-Pentecostal, see Jack Deere, *Surprised by the Voice of God: How God Speaks Today through Prophecies, Dreams, and Visions* (Grand Rapids, Mich.: Zondervan, 1996). See also Wayne A. Grudem, *The Gift of Prophecy in the New Testament and Today* (Wheaton, Ill.: Crossway Books, 2000), and the cautious affirmation by the classical Pentecostal scholar, Cecil M. Robeck Jr., in "Written Prophecies: A Question of Authority," *Pneuma* 2 (1980): 26–45.

42. A key center of 24/7 prayer is the International House of Prayer (or IHOP), in Kansas City, Missouri, which claims to have had non-stop, uninterrupted prayer and worship at its facility since 1999 (http://www.ihopkc.org). As of 2016, about a thousand people live near the facility and serve as scheduled worshippers each week. Lou Engel, one of the leaders, has led large stadium prayer rallies around the world. Mike Bickle, another key leader, teaches on the need for the church to recover a deeper love for God. Relatively little has been written on this group, but the Davidic teaching described here is central to IHOP's ethos.

43. Many Pentecostal-Charismatic Christians are pro-Jewish and/or pro-Israel or Zionist in their politics. These sociopolitical views are not essential to the "Davidic" stand-point described here, and yet the elements easily blend. In Charismatic worship, one sometimes sees dancers carrying a Star of David or an Israeli flag. Gentile Christians in the "Hebrew roots" movement go a step further by observing at least some elements of Jewish and halakhic practice, e.g., the Saturday Sabbath, dietary laws, annual festivals, prayers in Hebrew, and interpretations of the Bible through the lens of Jewish tradition.

44. Pentecostal culture warriors often invoke the Book of Joshua, as Lloyd K. Pietersen notes, in one of the few essays on the phenomenon: "The violent language contained in the biblical texts is reinterpreted as spiritual warfare against demonic forces. However, the way in which such demonic forces are perceived as affecting society renders this interpretation as a narrative politics which calls for political action and informs the worldview of the Religious Right." Lloyd K. Pietersen, "Joel's/Elijah's Army or the Joshua Generation: The Military Rhetoric of Third Wave Neo-Pentecostalism," *Relegere: Studies in Religion and Reception* 3 (2013): 99–120. In the nineteenth-century Holiness movement, there were symbolic or typological appeals to the Book of Joshua, and yet these generally had to do with the Christian's internal struggle to overcome besetting sins, and to defeat the "Canaanite" within, e.g., Chester Briggs, *The Canaanite Exterminated; or, A Practical Treatise on Present and Entire Sanctification* (Dayton, Ohio: Conference Printing Establishment of the United Brethren in Christ, 1854). This interiorized interpretation followed precedents from Origen and other early Christian writers. See John R. Franke, ed., *Ancient Christian Commentary on Scripture, Old Testament*, vol. 4: *Joshua, Judges, Ruth, 1–2 Samuel* (Downers Grove, Ill.: InterVarsity Press, 2005).

45. See note 15 on the "Latter Rain" revival.

46. Dick Iverson, with Bill Scheidler, *Present Day Truths* (Portland, Ore.: City Bible Publishing, 1976), v–vi. On the Tabernacle teaching, see also Kevin J. Connor, *The Tabernacle of David* (Portland, Ore.: Bible Temple, 1976); and *The Tabernacle of Moses: The Riches of Redemption's Story as Revealed in the Tabernacle* (Portland, Ore.: City Bible Publishing, 1976).

47. Iverson, *Present Day Truths*, 188.

48. On the wide-ranging contemporary Christian music (CCM) phenomenon, see Mark Allen Powell, ed., *Encyclopedia of Contemporary Christian Music* (Peabody, Mass.: Hendrickson Publishers, 2002). On Davidic-style worship and "intimacy with God" as the foundation for Christian ministry and mission, see Michael J. McClymond, "After Toronto: Randy Clark's Global Awakening, Heidi and Rolland Baker's Iris Ministries, and the Post-1990s Global Charismatic Networks," *Pneuma* 38 (2016): 1–27.

49. Oliverio, *Theological Hermeneutics*, 34. On Barthianism in comparison with Pentecostalism, see 34–35.

50. The German New Testament scholar Rudolf Bultmann (1884-1976) was well known for his argument that the Bible could be relevant to twentieth-century people only if its supernaturalistic elements were eliminated in a process that Bultmann called "de-mythologization." See Rudolf Bultmann, "The New Testament and Mythology," in *Kerygma and Myth: A Theological Debate*, ed. Rudolf Bultmann et al. (New York: Harper and Row, 1961), 1–44. While claims regarding the supernatural continue to be disputed in twenty-first-century academic contexts, the rapid and widespread growth of twentieth-century Pentecostalism suggests that Bultmann's reticence over miracles was less widely shared by "modern man" than his arguments had suggested. For an extensive analysis, see Craig S. Keener, *Miracles: The Credibility of the New Testament Accounts*, 2 vols. (Grand Rapids, Mich.: Baker Academic, 2011).

BIBLIOGRAPHY

Anderson, Allan. "Varieties, Taxonomies, Definitions." In *Studying Global Pentecostalism: Theories and Methods*, edited by Allan Anderson et al., 13–39. Berkeley: University of California Press, 2010.

Archer, Kenneth J. *A Pentecostal Hermeneutic: Spirit, Scripture, and Community*. Cleveland, Tenn.: CPT Press, 2009.

Archer, Kenneth J., and L. William Oliverio Jr., eds., *Constructive Pneumatological Hermeneutics in Pentecostal Christianity*. New York: Palgrave Macmillan, 2016.

Arweck, Elisabeth, and Peter Collins, eds. *Reading Religion in Text and Context: Reflections on Faith and Practice in Religious Materials*. Aldershot, UK: Ashgate, 2006.

Austin, J. L. *How To Do Things with Words*. Cambridge, Mass.: Harvard University Press, 1962.

Bond, Susan L. *Contemporary African American Preaching: Diversity in Theory and Style*. St. Louis, Mo.: Chalice Press, 2003.

Bowler, Kate. *Blessed: A History of the American Prosperity Gospel*. New York: Oxford University Press, 2013.

Bultmann, Rudolf. "The New Testament and Mythology." In *Kerygma and Myth: A Theological Debate*, edited by Rudolf Bultmann et al., 1–44. New York: Harper and Row, 1961.

Burnett, Richard. *Karl Barth's Theological Exegesis: The Hermeneutical Principles of the Römerbrief Period*. Tübingen: Mohr Siebeck, 2001.

Coleman, Simon. *The Globalisation of Charismatic Christianity: Spreading the Gospel of Prosperity*. Cambridge, UK: Cambridge University Press, 2000.

———. "Textuality and Embodiment among Charismatic Christians." In *Reading Religion in Text and Context: Reflections on Faith and Practice in Religious Materials*, edited by Elisabeth Arweck and Peter Collins, 157–68. Aldershot, UK: Ashgate, 2006.

Connor, Kevin J. *The Tabernacle of David*. Portland, Ore.: Bible Temple, 1976.

———. *The Tabernacle of Moses: The Riches of Redemption's Story as Revealed in the Tabernacle*. Portland, Ore.: City Bible Publishing, 1976.

Davies, Andrew. "What Does It Mean to Read the Bible as a Pentecostal?." *Journal of Pentecostal Theology* 18, no. 2 (2009): 216–29.

Deere, Jack. *Surprised by the Voice of God: How God Speaks Today through Prophecies, Dreams, and Visions*. Grand Rapids, Mich.: Zondervan, 1996.

Dorrien, Gary J. "Dialectics of the Word: Crisis Theology." In *The Barthian Revolt in Modern Theology: Theology without Weapons*, 47–80. Louisville, Ky.: Westminster John Knox, 2000.

Edwards, Jonathan. *The Works of Jonathan Edwards*, vol. 2: *Religious Affections*. Edited by John E. Smith. New Haven, Conn.: Yale University Press, 1959.

Ellington, Scott A. "History, Story, and Testimony: Locating Truth in a Pentecostal Hermeneutic." *Pneuma* 23, no. 1 (2001): 245–63.

Gadamer, Hans-Georg. *Truth and Method*. 2nd rev. ed. Translated by Joel Weinsheimer and Donald G. Marshall. New York: Crossroad, 1989.

Gilbert, Kenyatta R. *The Journey and Promise of African American Preaching*. Minneapolis, Minn.: Fortress Press, 2011.

Grudem, Wayne A. *The Gift of Prophecy in the New Testament and Today*. Wheaton, Ill.: Crossway Books, 2000.

Harris, James H. *Preaching Liberation*. Minneapolis, Minn.: Fortress Press, 1995.

Hinson, Glenn. *Fire in My Bones: Transcendence and the Holy Spirit in African American Gospel*. Philadelphia. University of Pennsylvania Press, 2000.

Hollenweger, Walter. *The Pentecostals: The Charismatic Movement in the Churches*. Minneapolis, Minn.: Augsburg, 1972.

Iverson, Dick, with Bill Scheidler. *Present Day Truths*. Portland, Ore.: City Bible Publishing, 1976.

Jacobsen, Douglas. *Thinking in the Spirit: Theologies of the Early Pentecostal Movement*. Bloomington: Indiana University Press, 2001.

Kärkkäinen, Veli-Matti. "Pentecostal Hermeneutics in the Making: On the Way from Fundamentalism to Postmodernism." *Journal of the European Pentecostal Theological Association* 18, no. 1 (1998): 76–115.

Keener, Craig S. *Miracles: The Credibility of the New Testament Accounts*. 2 vols. Grand Rapids, Mich.: Baker Academic, 2011.

Kling, David. *The Bible in History: How the Texts Have Shaped the Times*. New York: Oxford University Press, 2004.

Land, Stephen J. *Pentecostal Spirituality: A Passion for the Kingdom*. Sheffield, UK: Sheffield Academic Press, 1993.

LaRue, Cleophus James. *I Believe I'll Testify: The Art of African American Preaching* Louisville, Ky.: Westminster John Knox Press, 2011.

McClymond, Michael J. "After Toronto: Randy Clark's Global Awakening, Heidi and Rolland Baker's Iris Ministries, and the Post-1990s Global Charismatic Networks." *Pneuma* 38 (2016): 1–27.

———. "Charismatic Gifts: Healing, Tongues-Speaking, Prophecy, and Exorcism." In *The Wiley-Blackwell Companion to World Christianity*, edited by Lamin Sanneh and Michael J. McClymond, 399–418. Oxford, UK: Wiley-Blackwell, 2016.

———. "Charismatic Renewal and Neo-Pentecostalism: From American Origins to Global Permutations." In *The Cambridge Companion to Pentecostalism*, edited by Cecil M. Robeck and Amos Yong, 31–51. Cambridge, UK: Cambridge University Press, 2014.

McLean, Mark. "Toward a Pentecostal Hermeneutic." *Pneuma* 6, no. 2 (1984): 35–56.

Oliverio, L. William. *Theological Hermeneutics in the Classical Pentecostal Tradition: A Typological Account*. Leiden: Brill, 2012.

Pietersen, Lloyd K. "Joel's/Elijah's Army or the Joshua Generation: The Military Rhetoric of Third Wave Neo-Pentecostalism." *Relegere: Studies in Religion and Reception* 3 (2013): 99–120.

Powery, Luke A. *Dem Dry Bones: Preaching, Death, and Hope*. Minneapolis, Minn.: Fortress Press, 2012.

Reed, David A. *"In Jesus' Name": The History and Beliefs of Oneness Pentecostals*. Blandford Forum, UK: Deo Publishing, 2008.

Riss, Richard M. "The Latter Rain Movement of 1948." *Pneuma* 4 (1982): 32–45.

——. *Latter Rain: The Latter Rain Movement of 1948 and the Mid-Twentieth Century's Evangelical Awakening.* Mississauga, Ont.: Honeycomb Visual Production, 1987.

Robeck, Cecil M., Jr. "Written Prophecies: A Question of Authority." *Pneuma* 2 (1980): 26–45.

Ruthven, Jon. *On the Cessation of Charismata: The Protestant Polemic on Postbiblical Miracles* Sheffield, UK: Sheffield Academic Press, 1993.

Smith, James K. A. "The Closing of the Book: Pentecostals, Evangelicals, and the Sacred Writings." *Journal of Pentecostal Theology* 5, no. 11 (1997): 49–71.

Thomas, Frank A. *They Like to Never Quit Praisin' God: The Role of Celebration in Preaching.* Cleveland, Ohio: Pilgrim Press, 2013.

Thomas, John Christopher. "Women, Pentecostals and the Bible: An Experiment in Pentecostal Hermeneutics." *Journal of Pentecostal Theology* 5 (1994): 41–56.

Wacker, Grant. *Heaven Below: Early Pentecostals and American Culture.* Cambridge, Mass.: Harvard University Press, 2001.

CHAPTER 39

···

THE BIBLE AND MORMONISM

···

DAVID HOLLAND

LIKE so much else in the annals of American religion, the story of the Church of Jesus Christ of Latter-day Saints begins with the Bible. But the Bible that emerges from the early narratives of Mormonism is of a distinctive character. Divinely authoritative and fundamentally vulnerable, it both exudes great strength and evinces certain deficiencies. It has retained this contrapuntal character over the course of its usage among the Latter-day Saints. And this Bible of counterpoints has shaped a religion given to paradox. The most fundamental of these paradoxes lies within a lasting Mormon struggle to retain rather than disentangle the Good Book's intertwined commitments to particularity and universality. The persistence of these competing elements should not suggest, however, that the Saints' biblical approaches remained static or unitary over time. The Mormons and the Bible have a history.

FIRST VISIONS

···

Joseph Smith recorded in his personal history that, as a young man coming of age in rural New York, he had observed the intense religious conflict of the Second Great Awakening and quickly perceived the Bible's place at the heart of it. "The teachers of religion of the different sects understood the same passages of scripture so differently as to destroy all confidence in settling the question by an appeal to the Bible," he recalled. The unspoken backstory to this "destruction" of Smith's biblical confidence includes a long-standing Protestant promise that the Christian's Holy Bible could interpret itself. Scripture, various Reformers declared, must surely be clear enough for every sincere believer to comprehend. Many Christians of the early United States clung to that democratizing promise, and its hermeneutical implications, with extraordinary resolve. At the same time, the intense denominational competition of antebellum American religion put that assurance to a severe test.

While competing denominations and their interpretations raised serious questions about the Bible's self-interpreting sufficiency for Smith, this constant disputation did little to challenge his faith in its essential truthfulness. Smith still reflexively appealed to biblical passages for answers to his most pressing questions. "While I was laboring under the extreme difficulties caused by the contests of these parties of religionists," he reported, "I was one day reading the Epistle of James, first chapter and fifth verse, which reads: *If any of you lack wisdom, let him ask of God, that giveth to all men liberally, and upbraideth not; and it shall be given him.*" Smith determined to follow the Bible's instructions. He prayed. In return he received a grand theophany, the beginning of a new faith. These aspects of the Bible's complex character, its textual liabilities and its divine authority, serve as the essential pistons driving Smith's narrative.[1] Over the course of his life, Smith came to understand the Bible as pointing to revelations that lay beyond its own pages.

The prophetic trajectory that began in these early encounters with the Bible ultimately led to the founding of a new church and the writing of new scripture. Smith's account records that, a few years after his initial vision, a resurrected prophet from ancient America named Moroni appeared to him. This angelic visitor told of a forgotten civilization whose sacred history ran on a parallel track to the one contained in the biblical record. He directed Smith to a set of gold plates chronicling this history and thus declared, well before Smith had even begun to contemplate the creation of a church, that the canon of scripture could be augmented. Smith would translate the record to which Moroni referred, ultimately publishing it as *The Book of Mormon*, named after Moroni's father, the chief compiler of his people's history.

This early encounter with *The Book of Mormon* reinforced the Bible's divine centrality as a testament of God's work of salvation while also casting it as one imperfect witness among others. For instance, when Moroni first visited Smith, he repeatedly quoted a passage from the biblical prophet Malachi, among other portions of the Bible. While Moroni's rendition of Malachi's words adhered quite closely to the phrasing of the King James Version, it did contain some significant distinctions. In recalling his experience, and noting these variations, Smith conveyed his and his culture's familiarity with the passages' form and location in the common translation.[2] This broad knowledge of the Bible served as an essential part of the backdrop against which he made sense of the canon-altering implications embedded in Moroni's visit. An American steeped in the Bible, a sense of sacred history that embraced but could not be contained in Old World sources, a biblical text that served as both the model and the stimulus for ongoing revelations: Of such material was Mormonism made.

Over the course of his prophetic ministry, lasting until his murder at age 38, Smith produced four lasting pieces of sacred text: *The Book of Mormon*, the antique record of an American Israel; the *Doctrine and Covenants*, mostly a volume of contemporary revelations received directly by Smith; the *Book of Abraham*, a rendering of Egyptian manuscripts attributed to the ancient patriarch; and an inspired translation of the Bible.[3] Each of these texts relates to the Bible somewhat differently. Each of them speaks most directly to a key aspect of the Latter-day Saints' biblical understanding. And they all inform a distinctive Mormon engagement with the Bible's enduring questions about historical particulars and universal claims.

The Universal and the Particular: A Biblical Dilemma

Understanding the key features of the Latter-day Saints' approach to the Bible requires some consideration of the Bible itself, a book that contains endemic points of contrast between the particular and the universal. Its very nature raised a series of questions that achieved prominence among a diverse array of nineteenth-century Christians. One of these involved the matter of God's special relationship with Israel as contrasted to his paternal concern for all humanity. At mid-century the English theologian Frederick Denison Maurice sought to reconcile what many saw as the contrasting messages of the Old and the New Testaments with a rhetorical question: "Is there no universal family which is implied in the existence of all particular families?"⁴ A related question wondered why a God of universal love and unchanging character would speak so freely in one particular time and place and then cease to do so in other times and places. The venerable nineteenth-century American poet James Russell Lowell raised this concern in first-person verse: "God of all the olden prophets, wilt thou speak with men no more? Have I not as truly served thee as thy chosen ones of yore?"⁵

Another concern questioned whether the particular ethical demands of one era could be universalized to all eras. Antebellum Americans confronted this query with special urgency and eventually great violence as they argued about whether the Bible's primitive validations of human bondage justified the United States' modern institutions of chattel slavery. Could these scriptural stories and commands apply across time and space, or had history so distanced modern America from ancient Israel that some of the Bible's content no longer directly applied?

A concern for how to connect the Bible's text to contemporary life was hardly unique to Americans of that era. Bible readers possessed long-cherished interpretive strategies, ranging from literalistic primitivism to allegorical typology, to which they could appeal in the face of these intensified questions. Many nineteenth-century Americans simply grasped these extant methods of reading more tightly. Others, including some liberal Christians and evangelical innovators, began to emphasize the New Testament to almost the complete disregard of the Old. The justification for such a move was a heightened sense of "progressive revelation," in which God's truth became clearer, purer, and more universal as the Bible moved from what they saw as the inwardly oriented tribalism of ancient Israel to the universal mission of the early Christian church.⁶ Even more radical readers, however, argued that even the early Christian texts reflected their own provincialisms and took a further step of insisting that all of the Bible's historical particularities in both testaments should be disregarded in pursuit of only those universally recognizable truths that a careful reader could find embedded in the cultural chaff of the text. From the deistical Thomas Jefferson to the transcendentalist Theodore Parker, this response had a variety of American expressions.⁷

Such struggles between the universal and particular elements of scripture were reaching new levels of intensity in the times and places from which Mormonism emerged. While they have remained at the heart of much biblical inquiry, a broad trend in the critical scholarship has been to break down the stark binaries of the question. The influential scholar of the Hebrew Bible Jon Levenson, for instance, has recurrently invited us to consider the ways the robust particularism of Israel's national chosenness coexists in a complex biblical matrix with a universalizing sense of God's relationship to all humanity.

New Testament studies have produced similar efforts to disrupt simplistic dichotomies. Against those who see the New Testament as following a rigid sequence in which the particularism of Jesus gives way to the universalism of Paul, some have insisted that Jesus's apparent particularism was more universally oriented than such a schema would suggest, while critical developments from the opposite angle have increasingly questioned the very nature of Paul's universality, seeing in his teachings a persistent Abrahamic particularism. ⁸ Much of the more careful biblical scholarship is thus inclined to see the particularistic and universalizing elements of the Bible not in clearly delineated chronological segments or testamental categories but in complex relationships that bend, blend, and intertwine throughout scripture. Mormon engagements with the Bible suggest their own distinguishing approaches to its entangled particulars and universals. These may be illustrated most clearly through the Latter-day Saints' additional works of scripture.

THE BOOK OF MORMON: A MATTER OF BIBLICAL SPACE

"And what thank they the Jews for the Bible which they receive from them?" The God of *The Book of Mormon* thus reproves the failure of the Gentile nations to appreciate the work of the Jewish people in preparing and preserving the scriptures. Christendom, the Almighty continues, has neglected "the travails, and the labors, and the pains of the Jews, and their diligence unto me, in bringing forth salvation unto the Gentiles."[9] According to *The Book of Mormon*, the Bible carried salvation and the Jews carried the Bible: Historical Israel therefore deserves the deep gratitude of all biblical believers. Yet even as these words appear to build toward a statement that is very much in keeping with a stereotypical antebellum American culture of single-minded biblical devotion, the context of *The Book of Mormon* dramatically shifts its significance. This divine call to recognize the contributions of the Jews occurs in a chapter devoted to the importance of extra-biblical sources of revelation.

If Christians could overcome their prejudice and give Jews proper credit for the Bible, the chapter continues, they would more fully realize that their Book of Books is the product of one particular nation in one particular place. Anti-Semitism had prevented Gentile believers from acknowledging the obvious implications of the Bible's history, *The Book of Mormon* argues. Full recognition of the Hebraic particularity of the Bible, in light of the universality of God, could only lead to one logical conclusion: There must be other books out there, other records of the Deity's interaction with His scattered chosen people, containing additional witnesses of Jesus Christ's atoning mission and the divine plan of redemption. Because of the diaspora, Israel was global, the particular was universal. The Saints were far from the first to argue that the diaspora had universalized Jehovah—Jonathan Edwards, for one, made a similar argument—but *The Book of Mormon* was unique in making the diasporic claim that every nation thus had its own scripture. The emphasis on Israel perpetuates the particular, but the rhetoric becomes universal: "I . . . speak unto all nations of the earth," God explains, "and they shall write it."[10] In *The Book of Mormon*, the millennium would be brought to pass not by the spreading influence of one universal scripture, but by the cumulative effect of various holy books from around the globe. The Bible, as the first of many such works destined to come to light, thus becomes the pattern by which other books of scripture might be recognized. It emerges as a particular book of timeless truths, a universal example with a specific history.

Part of that specific history includes its textual vulnerability. *The Book of Mormon* explains that after the Bible moved from the care of the Jews to the keeping of medieval Christians the text became corrupted. "Thou seest that after the book hath gone forth through the hands of the great and abominable church, that there are many plain and precious things taken away from the book, which is the book of the Lamb of God."[11] Elsewhere, Joseph Smith made clear that he shared *The Book of Mormon*'s understanding of the Bible's textual history. "I believe the Bible as it read when it came from the pen of the original writers," he reportedly said toward the end of his life. "Ignorant translators, careless transcribers, or designing and corrupt priests have committed many errors."[12]

The Book of Mormon demonstrated that even the most inspired books, when left in the hands of uninspired guardians, require a certain degree of caution from readers. It also insists that the additional books of scripture, destined to come forth from Israel's diasporic presence in every nation, would both declare the Bible's truth and help repair its vitiated texts. One of its prophets foresaw "other books, which came forth by the power of the Lamb," which "shall establish the truth of the first [biblical records], . . . and shall make known the plain and precious things which have been taken away from them."[13] The solution to the Bible's textual damage was not more handling by uninspired translators or self-important scholars; its full meaning would be restored by the revelatory production of more books like it. The Bible here appears as the noble but wounded ancestor of all true scripture, rescued by a world of reinforcing texts that will emerge in the last days to follow its lead and hail its truths.

The Book of Mormon thus speaks to one of the chief complaints that Enlightenment-era critics lodged against biblical faith. God's universal love and justice struck them as at odds with the Bible's particular geography of revelation. Conversely, the God of *The Book of Mormon* promised to live up to his universal obligations by bringing numerous books of scripture "unto the children of men, yea, even upon all the nations of the earth."[14] Remarkably, given the early modern intellectual context of its publication and its own repeatedly disparaging tone toward Jews, it does so with an overtly philo-Semitic twist. While *The Book of Mormon* also argues that God will speak in all times, its most striking statement of divine universality is that God will speak in all nations, albeit through the blood of Israel. Thus, its God has words for the whole world, not to come through one biblical voice, but through a global chorus of many textual expressions.

THE DOCTRINE AND COVENANTS: A MATTER OF BIBLICAL TIME

The early modern critics of the Bible pointed to more than just the matter of limited geography. They also challenged the Bible's temporal particularity, its limitation to a specific season in the history of the world. If *The Book of Mormon* spoke most pointedly to the problem of the Bible's geographical limitations, the *Doctrine and Covenants* spoke most explicitly to the question of its dating. Indeed, even in its discussion of *The Book of Mormon*, the *Doctrine and Covenants* shifts its focus from space to time, bearing witness that "God does inspire men and call them to his holy work in this age and generation, as well as in generations of old; thereby showing that he is the same God yesterday, today, and forever."[15] In the Latter-day Saints' collection of modern-day revelations, this contemporary proof of a revelatory God served not as a slight to the Bible but as a defense of it. To those who were dismissing the Good Book because its tales of revelations seemed the vestige of a primitive people in a faraway time, the *Doctrine and Covenants* offered a rebuttal.

Beyond its basic witness to a timelessly revelatory God, the *Doctrine and Covenants* reinforced the Bible in a host of other ways: by answering some of its chief exegetical questions, or by replicating its calls to build temples and ordain high priests, or—most notoriously—by offering a divine justification for its polygamous patriarchs. In the process, this modern-day book of revelations also established a distinctive conception of time in which all of the eras depicted in the Bible became key elements in the millennial fulfillment of God's plan for humanity. The Latter-day Saints were not alone in thinking of biblical time in terms of such dispensations, but they were unusual in the extent to which they saw this dispensational schema as one of convergence rather than sequence. "It is necessary in the ushering in of the dispensation of the fullness of times," reads one section of the *Doctrine and Covenants*, "which dispensation is now beginning to usher in, that a whole and complete and perfect union, and welding together of dispensations, and keys, and powers, and glories should take place, and be revealed from the days of Adam even to the present time."[16] This Latter-day Saint idea that the millennial moment did not entail the supersession of previous dispensations, but rather the unification of every scriptural epoch, brought all of biblical history into contemporary importance.

Mormons conferred blessings like the patriarchs, they wore priestly robes like Aaron's, they washed feet like Jesus, they preached to the nations like Paul. They even spoke of restoring animal sacrifice in some form.[17] In this sense, their new revelations were not designed to supplant the Bible, but to provide the authoritative framework in which all of the lasting biblical truths might be fit together. Just as *The Book of Mormon* promised that a diverse world of local scriptures would ultimately contribute in their own voices to a millennial and universal culmination, so the *Doctrine and Covenants* proclaimed that the revealed truths of every era would coalesce into the dispensation of the fullness of times. The Mormon millennium would include not just a geographically comprehensive chorus, but it would also include voices from across time. In both cases, the Bible sang the lead melody, imperfectly, but indispensably.

The revelatory economy of Mormonism thus began to address both the geographical and the temporal challenge of biblical particularity not by jettisoning the local and the historical in favor of one universal text, or a transcendent sense of dehistoricized truth, but by proliferating particular scriptures and restoring particular dispensations into an inductive millennium. The Bible thus could no longer be criticized for its particularity even as it also could no longer be celebrated for its complete sufficiency or its utter exceptionality.

JOSEPH SMITH TRANSLATION: A MATTER OF BIBLICAL LANGUAGE

Along with the Enlightenment's criticism of biblical particularity in time and place came a related complaint about the particularity of language. As Thomas Paine wrote in *The Age of Reason*, his late eighteenth-century critique of biblical religion, "The continually progressive change to which the meaning of words is subject, the want of a universal language which renders translation necessary, the errors to which translations are again subject, the mistakes of copyists and printers, together with the possibility of willful alteration, are of themselves evidences that the human language, whether in speech or in print, cannot be the vehicle of the word of God."[18] In the nineteenth century, Paine's words were followed by a growing number of biblical renditions available to Americans, illustrating the very linguistic mutability to which Paine spoke. In contrast, Joseph Smith's translations of the Bible and other ancient texts suggested a conception of translation that rested more on perceptions of universal truth than on particular ancient languages, even as it retained an emphasis on the historical artifacts from which those truths derived.

As Smith undertook his most ambitious scriptural project, a retranslation of the Bible, it quickly became apparent that this was not a traditional rendering of the text. The project bore a certain resemblance to targumic translation, a tradition of expansive interpretation that often meant the pursuit not just of what the Bible had originally said, but of what the Bible should have said. The very nature of Smith's process and the resulting lines of text suggested that particular sacred books could be the pretext for an encounter with the divine that provided truths well beyond the words on the page.

Smith's translation of the Bible not only altered certain phrases and reworked particular passages; it created entire new chapters. Engagement with the text became the setting for both exegesis and ongoing revelation. Most of the textual changes that emerged from his translation drew more heavily from Smith's sense of inspiration than his philology. Most famously, his version radically expanded the biblical references to Enoch's prophetic call and mission, producing some of the most memorable scenes in all of the Mormon canon, including an encounter with a God who weeps over the suffering and enmity of his children. In Enoch's story, as elsewhere in the translation, Christian themes conspicuously appear in Hebrew scripture settings. Kathleen Flake has noted of Smith's translation that the process demonstrated "Smith's prophetic authority to divine the truth about God's past acts within the narrative limits of ancient, prophetic history." In relation to the Bible, Smith's translation was "both governed by the text and productive of it."[19]

As the biblical scholar Krister Stendahl observed in the context of his encounter with Mormon scripture, such targumic efforts are usually intended to make an ancient record more relevant to the community needs or theological interests of the peoples of later times.[20] Certainly Smith's translation brought the Bible into greater harmony with itself and with new Mormon concepts of the Gospel. But Smith's translation effort in nineteenth-century America stands in illuminating contrast to the work of other prophetic figures of his period who likewise undertook to use their revelatory powers to amplify the Bible's resonances for modern Americans. Ellen White, a founder of Seventh-day Adventism, and Mary Baker Eddy, the founder of Christian Science, were born two decades after Smith but their generation was confronted with many of the same questions about the Bible's particularity and the universality of God's care. Like Smith, they both spoke to those questions through their very identities: they each insisted that God had spoken again and thus broken out of the ancient context that lay at the heart of the critics' complaints. And like Smith, they both published material meant to make the Bible more meaningful and accessible to their contemporaries.

The contrasting ways in which they did so tells us much about their moment and sets Mormon approaches in sharper relief. Ellen White, for example, had a series of visions that filled in some of the historical detail missing from the biblical record. Through her visionary experiences we learn more about the lives of the ancient kings and prophets; rendered in modern language, her summaries and elaborations of biblical figures and stories sought to draw universal lessons from particular histories. Of Solomon she wrote, "In the midst of prosperity lurks danger. Throughout the ages, riches and honor have ever been attended with peril to humility and spirituality."[21] More accessible, rendered in modern English, illustrative of readily applicable lessons, White's biblical figures conspicuously take on universal meaning.

Mary Baker Eddy had a different approach. She produced a scriptural glossary in her magnum opus, *Science and Health with Key to the Scriptures*, that universalized the Bible's figures by thoroughly downplaying their personal, historical details. Scriptural characters became less important as real people and more important as transcendent symbols. Her biblical glossary contained such entries as, "Adam: Error; a falsity; the belief of 'original sin,' sickness, and death.... Canaan (the son of Ham). A sensuous belief; the testimony of what is termed material sense.... Eve. A beginning; mortality; that which does not last forever."[22] These names connoted general lessons more than particular personalities.

Smith's translations came from yet another angle. Generally retaining archaic scriptural language, depicting scriptural characters who still seem distant and ancient, but giving us more of their words, words that tended to harmonize their teachings with those of other prophets of other times and places, Smith's translations implied that the problem of the universal and the particular would not be solved by eliminating the particular (as Eddy did) or by explicitly drawing universalizing conclusions (as White did) but by giving us more and more of the uncommented upon particulars. The largest published portion of his translation—and the only one to achieve canonical status—eventually appeared in a volume the Utah Saints called the *Pearl of Great Price*, where it was paired with an entirely other work of scripture, the *Book of Abraham*, which Smith produced in what appears again to be a radically targumic translation of antique sources. Indeed, in the case of the *Book of Abraham*, there seems to be very little linguistic relationship between the ancient artifacts and the narrative Smith produced. For Smith, translation was unbound from the particularities of text though dependent on the presence of the material object; truth was necessarily tied to but not strictly representative of the historical document.[23] The Mormons' *Book of Abraham* addresses the tensions between the Bible's particularism and universalism not by downplaying one or another, but by amplifying both.

The Mormon restoration approached the universal by a proliferation of the particulars, generating or promising so much new data that God's universal plan would appear by induction rather than deduction. This reflected Smith's sense of his own prophetic project in which, to borrow Philip Barlow's helpful phrase, all the gaps of a "fractured reality" began to fill: *The Book of Mormon* promises to close the gaps of space, the *Doctrine and Covenants* promises to close the gaps of time, the *Pearl of Great Price* promises to close the gaps of language. [24] And they all keep the biblical narratives near the center of this project. Tellingly, they all also remain open ended: *The Book of Mormon* promises books that have yet to appear; the *Doctrine and Covenants* promises revelations yet to be received; the Joseph Smith translation left passages yet to consider. By implication, the Mormon pursuit of more particulars remains ever in effect.

A Universe of Particulars

This triple combination of new scriptures—*The Book of Mormon*, the *Doctrine and Covenants*, and the Inspired Translation—speaks directly to the Bible's essential questions of particularity and universality. And different Mormon denominations have emphasized different parts of that conversation. The Community of Christ (formerly known as the Reorganized Church of Jesus Christ of Latter Day Saints) has relatively downplayed Smith's ancient extra-biblical texts—such as *The Book of Mormon* and the *Book of Abraham*—while placing comparatively more emphasis on his inspired translation of the Bible. Conversely, the Latter-day Saint Church (typically styled the LDS Church of "Utah Church") has emphasized *The Book of Mormon*, defended the *Book of Abraham*, and proved relatively ambivalent about the biblical translation.

These decisions on questions of canon shaped and reflected church cultures in the two denominations, forming a crucial part of their differing theological responses to Smith's scriptural legacy. Their respective treatments of the *Book of Abraham*, the patriarch of particular covenants, symbolize much of the contrast between the two churches. As its choice of scriptural emphases might suggest, the Community of Christ developed a greater quest for biblical universality that over its history has drawn the faith closer to normative Protestantism.[25] The LDS Church, by contrast, retained a greater affinity for particularities that left them further beyond the pale of mainstream American Christianity. For the LDS Church—which has some seventy times more members than the Community of Christ—the Bible's place has undergone a series of historical shifts, but it has never escaped its role as the justifier of the universal God's particular interests. The Utah church has seen this as an indispensable part of Joseph Smith's legacy.

Following Smith's murder in 1844, Latter-day Saints had a choice to make about the leader who should succeed their prophet. Those who followed Brigham Young into the valleys of Utah were led by a man of distinctive candor or even coarseness in his consideration of the Bible's mixed character. Although he cited biblical texts at length, he also dismissed parts of the Bible as folkloric clutter that scattered throughout an otherwise true account of God's dealings in history. In the same discourse, Young could on the one hand pose,

> What do the infidel world say about the Bible? They say that the Bible is nothing better than last year's almanac; it is nothing but a fable and priestcraft, and it is good for nothing. The Book of Mormon, however, declares that the Bible is true, and it proves it; and the two prove each other true.

and on the other hand also declare,

> I believe that the Bible contains the word of God, and the words of good men and the words of bad men; the words of good angels and the words of bad angels and words of the devil; and also the words uttered by the ass when he rebuked the prophet in his madness. I believe the words of the Bible are just what they are; but aside from that I believe the doctrines concerning salvation contained in that book are true, and that their observance will elevate any people, nation or family that dwells on the face of the earth.[26]

While Young's rhetoric was rather more vivid than most Mormons' would later be, he effectively captured a Latter-day Saint view of scripture that perceived a combination of cultural refuse and transcendent principle.

Because of this combination, embedded so deeply in the marrow of their movement, the LDS Church had mixed and rather muted reactions to the higher criticism that began to emerge in American biblical discourse during Young's presidency and subsequent decades. Mormons' relative equanimity in the face of the new scholarship reflected their sense that their faith was not wholly dependent on one text. Many of the questions posed by early biblical critics of the higher criticism school of thought—about textual corruptions and historical change—seemed familiar to inquisitive Latter-day Saints like the Mormon authority B. H. Roberts, who endorsed the methods of biblical criticism but criticized what he saw as its extreme conclusions.[27]

In the era when American Christianity began splitting along lines of fundamentalism and liberalism, largely hinging on how one read the Bible, Latter-day Saints faced their own crisis about fundamentals, but theirs largely focused on whether to retain the practice of polygamy rather than on what to make of historical criticism. Once again, the distinctive theological culture of the LDS Church kept it at an arm's remove from the pressing biblical conversations of its Protestant neighbors; ironically, this distance derived from the fact that Mormonism had so scandalously brought the Bible about which others debated into an immediate, plurally married embodiment. That sense of radical recovery of patriarchal dispensations, however, would not last forever.

More explicit Latter-day Saint engagement with questions of higher biblical criticism emerged just as the passing of polygamy at the turn of the twentieth century allowed Mormons new opportunities to reconnect with the rest of America. But even then the Latter-day Saint response proved rather ambivalent. Some, like William H. Chamberlin—a professor at the church-owned Brigham Young University and a prominent advocate of the new biblical learning—staked out an early position on the liberal side of the Latter-day Saint spectrum. Thinkers of this sort, who found a sympathetic hearing even within the highest leadership councils of the church, could make the case that biblical criticism only reinforced Mormons' extant views of the Bible as a mix of divine truth embedded in a historicized past and an imperfect text.

For others, like the instinctively conservative scion of the Smith family and eventual LDS Church president, Joseph Fielding Smith, biblical scholarship in the twentieth century had pushed too far beyond the point where Latter-day Saints could see it as an ally in the battle for truth. Like Christian conservatives all around the country, Smith believed the most fundamental doctrines to be at stake in the question of biblical historicity. As Barlow has documented in his defining treatment of *Mormons and the Bible*, many leading Latter-day Saints' voices in the early twentieth century took up their places somewhere between the poles represented by Chamberlin and Smith, with most seeing critical scholarship as a significant threat.[28]

An especially illustrative artifact from the first half of the twentieth century, a letter from the church's First Presidency (a trio of leaders who compose the highest authority in the LDS Church) in 1921, reflected a dialectical Mormon stance. "The Bible," they wrote, "contains the word of God so far as it is translated correctly. That does not positively make the book as a whole an inspired presentation of the word of God. There are matters in it that are historical, and some of them may be of the character set forth by the 'higher criticism.'" Yet the letter then went on to condemn those aspects of the new scholarship that they found detrimental to faith. This strategy of a strictly constrained openness to biblical criticism, acknowledging it only insofar as it did not threaten the authenticity of other latter-day revelations or central Mormon doctrines, captured much of the church's response and its sense of the scholarly future. "'Higher criticism,'" the letter asserted, "has lost ground as time goes on."[29]

As the Latter-day Saints in the twentieth century shifted an increasing amount of their polemical energy away from sectarian Christianity and toward secular humanism, they had stronger motives to make common cause with biblical conservatives in other denominations. A choice to join the brewing cultural war against the corrosions of modernity led some Saints to rein in the latitudes of their earlier positions. For example, in response to the publication of the Revised Standard Version of the Bible at mid-century—a translation widely denounced by traditional Christians of various denominational stripes—LDS leaders began more heavily emphasizing the King James Version as a bulwark against skepticism.[30] They thus positioned themselves more firmly as the conservers of a certain Christian tradition. In the process, Latter-day Saints' culture softened the spotlight it had traditionally focused on the particular limitations of all translations and instead raised the King James Version to something approaching universal textual authority.

If such moves seemed to augur a rapprochement between Latter-day Saints and evangelical Christians, as both camps resisted the inroads of a common foe, they each still understood that a shared concern for the preservation of biblical faith would not overcome the profound theological differences that separated them. Indeed, a common defense of the Bible could illustrate rather than resolve their most basic points of contention. Latter-day Saints always knew, and their evangelical counterparts remained well aware, that in defending the Bible in general and the King James Version (KJV) in particular, Mormons were also defending the additional books of scripture that traditional Christians found so objectionable. To insist on the historical literalness of the Tower of Babel story was to protect a *Book of Mormon* narrative that seemed to depend on it. To preserve the language of the KJV was to defend the divinity of those *Doctrine and Covenants* revelations that echoed its wording. Mormon defenses of the Bible, even those that sounded like others in the evangelical camps around them, were never independent of the uniquely crowded scriptural terrain in which the Latter-day Saints lived. As the First Presidency affirmed in an official statement in 1992, "In doctrinal matters, Latter-day revelation supports the KJV in preference to other English translations."[31] Among traditional Christians, even for those who share the Saints' passion for the continuity of the KJV, such a line is more likely to be alienating than allying.

Too conservative in their biblical approaches to attract the sympathy of cutting-edge scholars, too heretical in their extra-biblical devotions to win true friendship among conservative Christians, the Latter-day Saints' understanding of the Bible leaves them in a category of their own. Among their idiosyncratic cultural elements is the remarkable absence of internal debates about hermeneutics. Largely this reflects the authority of the LDS Church's prophets and apostles, whom the Saints trust to provide any necessary salvific gloss on scriptural meaning. The theologically inflected headnotes placed at the top of every chapter in the Mormon canon—largely written by the influential and doctrinally conservative apostle Bruce R. McConkie—symbolize the exegetical influence of the church hierarchy and the scriptural apparatus that helps restrain hermeneutical argument in the church.[32]

Furthermore, a Latter-day Saint canon that includes everything from Solomon's "uninspired" erotic poetry to extended allegories on olive trees to personal histories to policy statements to apparently targumic renderings of Egyptian funerary texts have placed the prospect of rigid exegetical consistency so far beyond the realm of reasonability as to render hermeneutical debates moot. Mormons typically care whether a person has arrived at orthodox practice. The interpretive strategy that leads to that practice is of relatively little concern. This may be pragmatically advantageous in a church of lay local ministry wherein radically untrained amateurs—often of strikingly limited experience—explicate an extremely complex set of scriptures for one another on a regular basis. If you asked most Mormons, even the bishops and stake presidents that wield great authority over local organization, what the best principles of biblical interpretation are, they would—after a quizzical look—likely offer some form of the same simple answer: read the scriptures and pray to God and listen to the living prophet.

A BIBLICAL ONTOLOGY

In a 2010 survey conducted by the Pew Research Center, designed to test American levels of familiarity with the Bible, Latter-day Saints scored higher than all other groups. The survey was so brief, and of such a rudimentary nature, as to raise serious questions about the conclusions one might draw from it. But it is suggestive in some respects. For instance, evangelical Protestants nearly matched Mormons on New Testament questions, but the evangelical respondents fell much further behind when it came to the Hebrew scriptures. Conversely, the edge Mormons had over Jews on the Hebrew scriptures grew significantly larger when the questions shift to the New Testament. To some degree, the data bear out a Mormon theology that sees the biblical dispensations as constituent pieces of one culminating millennial whole rather than as sequential chapters of increasing or decreasing value. Mormons also position all such biblical chapters, however, as equally subject to the interpretive and cohering force of a living revelation. It is precisely this last point that will leave Latter-day Saints as suspect students of the Bible in the eyes of many Christians regardless of survey data or Mormon protestations to the contrary.[33]

Those perceptions matter to Latter-day Saints, but they seem to locate their biblical bona fides more in the very nature of their church rather than in any specific act of exegesis. They insist that the belief in a living prophet makes them more biblical rather than less. They see a theological imperative to embody many dispensations' worth of biblical forms, an effort that has generated both some of their most distinctive doctrines and some of their most profound internal challenges. By explicitly embracing the identities of both ancient Israel and the early Christian church, the Latter-day Saints in the fullness of times have simultaneously cultivated both a sense of distinctive peoplehood and an indefatigable quest for universal conversion.

It is in its often unsettling mix of universalism and particularity that Mormonism most resembles the Bible. Inwardly oriented and outwardly reaching, tribalistic and transcendent, actively isolated and insistently involved, it exemplifies the Bible's conflicting messages. Just as scholars long did for the Bible, so observers of Mormonism have seen emphases on universality and particularity rising and falling in chronological sequence, especially on the painful Mormon matter of racial hierarchicalism, the place where ethnic particularity has run most devastatingly and disturbingly into the Latter-day Saints' emphasis on universal divine parenthood. Again, as with the Bible, many evidences sustain this view that the church's early "Old Testament" focus on patriarchal blessings and ancestral curses and exclusive covenants has unevenly given way to a later twentieth-century focus on human equality and global unity. Paralleling the work of biblical scholars, however, a closer look at Mormonism suggests that both forces have always been present and both remain locked in unrelenting struggle.[34] Just as Moses and Micah and Jesus and Paul approached the question of the relationship between the God of Israel and the Lord of all nations differently, so Mormon thinkers have long wrestled with the challenges of simultaneously believing that their Lord has particular relationships with them—because of their ties to a specific tribe of Israel, or their unique access to priesthood authority, or their defining experiences in a carefully bounded temple—and that each of God's children is the object of His perfect love. Mormonism, at its root, is both about a people and about all people. And here lies its most formative debt to the Bible.

NOTES

1. *Joseph Smith—History*, 1:11, 12, 17. Originally published in serialized form in *The Times and Seasons* (ca. 1842), the history was eventually added by the Utah Saints to the canonized *Pearl of Great Price* (1851), https://www.lds.org/scriptures/pgp/js-h/1?lang=eng. On the democratized hermeneutic that prevailed in the early national period, see Mark A. Noll, *America's God: From Jonathan Edwards to Abraham Lincoln* (New York: Oxford University Press, 2002), 367–85; and Elisabeth Schüssler Fiorenza, *Democratizing Biblical Studies: Toward an Emancipatory Educational Space* (Louisville, Ky.: Westminster John Knox Press, 2009), 64–65.
2. *Joseph Smith—History*, 1:36–39.
3. The largest body of Latter-day Saints, the Utah-based LDS Church, has bound passages of the biblical translation together with the Abrahamic text to comprise a canonized volume they today call *The Pearl of Great Price*. The second largest denomination within Mormonism, the Community of Christ, rejects the canonicity of the *Book of Abraham* but has canonized the entirety of Smith's biblical translation. The exact compositions of the two groups' editions of the *Doctrine and Covenants* also differ. Despite such variations of canon, these texts comprise the shared inheritance of those who trace their scriptural lineage back to Joseph Smith. William D. Russell, "The LDS Church and Community of Christ: Clearer Differences, Closer Friends," *Dialogue: A Journal of Mormon Thought* 36, no. 4 (2003): 177–190; Royal Skousen, "The Earliest Textual Sources for Joseph Smith's 'New Translation' of the King James Bible," *Farms Review* 17, no. 2 (2005): 451–70.
4. Frederick Denison Maurice, *The Church a Family* (Cambridge: Macmillan, 1850), 3–4.
5. James Russell Lowell, "A Parable," in *The Poetical Works of James Russell Lowell* (Boston: Houghton Mifflin, 1882), 18.
6. Richard A. Grusin, *Transcendentalist Hermeneutics: Institutional Authority and the Higher Criticism of the Bible* (Durham, N.C.: Duke University Press, 1991), 64–65.
7. Consider Theodore Parker from his *A Discourse of Matters Pertaining to Religion* (Boston: American Unitarian Assoc., 1907), 340: "Men justify slavery out of the New Testament, because Paul had not his eye open to the evil, but sent back a fugitive!"

8. For a sense of this debate, as well as a recent contribution to it, see Jon Levenson, "The Universal Horizon of Biblical Particularism," in *Ethnicity and the Bible*, ed. Mark G. Brett (Boston: Brill, 2002), 143–69; Michael F. Bird, *Jesus and the Origins of the Gentile Mission* (London: T & T Clark, 2006), 13–14; and Anders Runesson, "Particularistic Judaism and Universalistic Christianity?: Some Critical Remarks on Terminology and Theology," *Studia Theologica-Nordic Journal of Theology* 54, no. 1 (2000): 55–75.
9. 2 Nephi 29:4–5.
10. 2 Nephi 29:12.
11. 1 Nephi 12:28.
12. Joseph Smith, *Teachings of the Prophet Joseph Smith* (Salt Lake City, Utah: Deseret Book, 1976), 327.
13. 1 Nephi 13:39.
14. 2 Nephi 29:7.
15. *Doctrine and Covenants*, https://www.lds.org/scriptures/dc-testament/dc, 20:11.
16. *Doctrine and Covenants*, 128:18.
17. Smith, *Teachings of the Prophet Joseph Smith*, 172–73.
18. Thomas Paine, *The Age of Reason* (1794); repr., in *The Complete Religious and Theological Works of Thomas Paine* (New York: P. Eckler, 1892), 22.
19. Kathleen Flake, "Translating Time: The Nature and Function of Joseph Smith's Narrative Canon," *Journal of Religion* 87, no. 4 (2007): 508.
20. Krister Stendahl, "The Sermon on the Mount and Third Nephi," in *Reflections on Judaeo-Christian Parallels*, ed. Truman G. Madsen (Provo, Utah: Religious Studies Center, 1978), 139–54.
21. Ellen G. White, *Prophets and Kings* (Nampa, Idaho: Pacific Press Publishing, 2005), 59–60
22. Mary Baker Eddy, *Science and Health with Key to the Scriptures* (Boston: Christian Science Board of Directors, 2013), 575–89.
23. Smith's interest in Abraham—marked by his ability to find him in even those sources where he appears textually absent—speaks again to this distinctive approach to the Bible's universal particulars. Abraham's individual covenant had long been seen as the ultimate expression of tribalistic Hebrew particularity; Mormons used this biblical legacy to talk at great length about specific blood lines and the particular blessings of particular lineages, and this Abrahamic emphasis even fueled the Utah church's notorious discourse on race, but they also emphasized a part of the covenant in which Abraham was told his posterity would "in their hands. . . bear this ministry and Priesthood unto all nations." Abraham 2:9; the Latter-day Saints Church has recently published a new synopsis of the official range of positions on the *Book of Abraham* on its website, https://www.lds.org/topics/translation-and-historicity-of-the-book-of-abraham.
24. Philip L. Barlow, "To Mend a Fractured Reality: Joseph Smith's Project," *Journal of Mormon History* 38, no. 3 (Summer 2012): 28–50.
25. See, for instance, Roger D. Launius, *Joseph Smith III: Pragmatic Prophet* (Urbana: University of Illinois Press, 1988), 152–55; Russell, "LDS Church and Community of Christ," 451–70.
26. Brigham Young, *Journal of Discourses*, 26 vols. (Liverpool, UK: 1871), 13:175.
27. Philip L. Barlow, *Mormons and the Bible: The Place of the Latter-day Saints in American Religion* (New York: Oxford University Press, 2013), 122–33.
28. Barlow, *Mormons and the Bible*, 133–61.
29. Charles W. Penrose [For the First Presidency] to Joseph W. McMurrin, October 31, 1921, Church Historian's Office. Facsimile in author's possession.
30. Barlow, *Mormons and the Bible*, 162–97.

31. Ezra Taft Benson, Gordon B. Hinckley and Thomas S. Monson, "First Presidency Statement on the King James Version of the Bible," August 1992.
32. That is not to say, of course, that individual Latter-day Saints have not thought carefully about the unspoken hermeneutical categories of the faith. See, for instance, Anthony A. Hutchinson, "LDS Approaches to the Holy Bible," *Dialogue: A Journal of Mormon Thought* 15, no. 1 (1982): 101–26.
33. "Who Knows What about Religion," Pew Research Center, September 28, 2010, http://www.pewforum.org/2010/09/28/u-s-religious-knowledge-survey-who-knows-what-about-religion.
34. See Armand L. Mauss, *All Abraham's Children: Changing Mormon Conceptions of Race and Lineage* (Urbana: University of Illinois Press, 2003), 23–24.

BIBLIOGRAPHY

Barlow, Philip L. *Mormons and the Bible: The Place of the Latter-day Saints in American Religion*. New York: Oxford University Press, 2013.
———. "To Mend a Fractured Reality: Joseph Smith's Project." *Journal of Mormon History* 38, no. 3 (Summer 2012): 28–50.
Bird, Michael F. *Jesus and the Origins of the Gentile Mission*. London: T & T Clark, 2006.
Eddy, Mary Baker. *Science and Health with Key to the Scriptures*. Boston: Christian Science Board of Directors, 2013.
Flake, Kathleen. "Translating Time: The Nature and Function of Joseph Smith's Narrative Canon." *Journal of Religion* 87, no. 4 (2007): 497–527.
Grusin, Richard A. *Transcendentalist Hermeneutics: Institutional Authority and the Higher Criticism of the Bible*. Durham, N.C.: Duke University Press, 1991.
Holland, David F. *Sacred Borders: Continuing Revelation and Canonical Restraint*. New York: Oxford University Press, 2011.
Hutchinson, Anthony A. "LDS Approaches to the Holy Bible." *Dialogue: A Journal of Mormon Thought* 15, no. 1 (1982): 101–26.
Launius, Roger D. *Joseph Smith III: Pragmatic Prophet*. Urbana: University of Illinois Press, 1988.
Levenson, Jon. "The Universal Horizon of Biblical Particularism." In *Ethnicity and the Bible*, edited by Mark G. Brett, 143–69. Boston: Brill, 2002.
Lowell, James Russell. "A Parable." In *The Poetical Works of James Russell Lowell*, 18. Boston: Houghton Mifflin, 1882.
Maurice, Frederick Denison. *The Church a Family*. Cambridge: Macmillan, 1850.
Mauss, Armand L. *All Abraham's Children: Changing Mormon Conceptions of Race and Lineage*. Urbana: University of Illinois Press, 2003.
Noll, Mark A. *America's God: From Jonathan Edwards to Abraham Lincoln*. New York: Oxford University Press, 2002.
Paine, Thomas. *The Age of Reason* (1794). Repr. in *The Complete Religious and Theological Works of Thomas Paine*. New York: P. Eckler, 1892.
Runesson, Anders. "Particularistic Judaism and Universalistic Christianity?: Some Critical Remarks on Terminology and Theology." *Studia Theologica-Nordic Journal of Theology* 54, no. 1 (2000): 55–75.
Russell, William D. "The LDS Church and Community of Christ: Clearer Differences, Closer Friends." *Dialogue: A Journal of Mormon Thought* 36, no. 4 (2003): 177–90.

Shüssler Fiorenza, Elizabeth. *Democratizing Biblical Studies: Toward an Emancipatory Educational Space*. Louisville, Ky.: Westminster John Knox Press, 2009.

Skousen, Royal. "The Earliest Textual Sources for Joseph Smith's 'New Translation' of the King James Bible." *Farms Review* 17, no. 2 (2005): 451–79.

Smith, Joseph. *Teachings of the Prophet Joseph Smith*. Salt Lake City, Utah: Deseret Book, 1976.

Stendahl, Krister. "The Sermon on the Mount and Third Nephi." In *Reflections on Judaeo-Christian Parallels*, edited by Truman G. Madsen, 139–54. Provo, Utah: Religious Studies Center, 1978.

White, Ellen G. *Prophets and Kings*. Nampa, Idaho: Pacific Press Publishing Association, 2005.

"Who Knows What about Religion." Pew Research Center. September 28, 2010. http://www.pew-forum.org/2010/09/28/u-s-religious-knowledge-survey-who-knows-what-about-religion.

Young, Brigham. *Journal of Discourses*. 26 vols. Liverpool, UK: 1871.

CHAPTER 40

···

THE BIBLE AND
SEVENTH-DAY ADVENTISTS

···

NICHOLAS MILLER

THE Seventh-day Adventist Church—currently with nearly 20 million members world-wide, and operating the most widespread Protestant systems of education and health care in the world—was a somewhat exotic, but not entirely unique plant in the nineteenth-century hothouse of American evangelicalism.[1] That nurturing spiritual soil was particularly fruitful in the first third or so of that century—a period of such religious blooming and buzzing that historians have dubbed it the Second Great Awakening.[2]

Adventism has been described as a biblically conservative, evangelical, Arminian, American-based denomination with its roots in the religious ferment and social reform of the latter end of that Awakening.[3] There is enough truth to this picture that the study of Adventism and its relation to the Bible can illuminate the experience of other conservative evangelical denominations from the same period. Adventism is different enough, however, that a study of Adventism and the Bible provides unique insights into the social forces that shaped modern American Christianity.[4]

Along with its observance of the Saturday Sabbath, probably the main difference noted by an outsider to Adventism would be the church's claim to have had a live, functioning, albeit non-canonical, prophet, in the person of Ellen G. White. American evangelicals have argued over the years whether this feature of Adventism should keep it from full evangelical membership. Adventists note that the mere existence of a claim to prophecy should not disqualify a group from being an authentic expression of New Testament Christianity. After all, the early church had such a gift, as have many Christian traditions and Christian revival movements since the time of Christ. Thus, most evangelicals have generally come to accept Adventists as at least "friendly fellow traveler[s]" on the evangelical Christian pilgrimage.[5]

The question of prophecy, however, gives Adventism a somewhat unique experience in relating to questions of inspiration and authority. Unlike most evangelicals in the nineteenth century who were theorizing about revelation and inspiration, Adventists believed they were directly experiencing it as a phenomenon. This gave their engagement with the topic of divine inspiration—including that of the Bible—a particular urgency and immediacy.

It is Adventism's similarities with certain strands of American evangelicalism that makes its story relevant for many other Christians. We will therefore begin with Adventism's continuities with nineteenth-century conservative evangelicalism's view of the Bible. Of course, there is not, and was not, a single conservative evangelical view of the Bible in the nineteenth century. Certainly by the late 1800s, when the challenges of higher criticism to biblical authority were being felt with ever greater force in North America, conservative Protestant Christians found different ways to respond to it. Almost all these groups claimed to support the Protestant standard of *sola scriptura* (the Bible alone), but what exactly *sola scriptura* meant would differ from church to church.[6]

Often as important as a particular name or category of belief about divine inspiration were the unspoken philosophical assumptions of the interpretive community in which Bible readers operate. Scholars have recognized that Adventism was heir of at least three very distinct religious and theological communities: Methodism (the heirs of the movement started by John and Charles Wesley), the American Restorationist movement (Christian primitivists who desired to return to the purity and order of the New Testament Church), and the Millerite Movement (pre-millennialists led by Baptist preacher William Miller who believed that Christ would return in the 1840s).[7] These three movements were made up largely of believers in the Arminian tradition—the belief that Christ died for all, not just an elect few, and that every person, through God's prevenient grace, had free will and could choose to partake of the redemptive work of Christ. These Arminian groups also implicitly operated within a Scottish Common Sense philosophical framework, in both its epistemological and ethical dimensions. Such a Scottish Common Sense orientation held that basic moral truths were often self-evident, discoverable by reason, or apprehended through intuition, and that everyone who chose to make the effort could learn and understand these truths.[8]

It is beyond the scope of this chapter to examine in detail the approach to Scripture of even this subset of evangelicalism. But it is possible to sketch the main outline or pillars of the general, philosophical approach that they shared in their approach to revelation and biblical interpretation. In brief, three main points characterized their approach. First, despite living in an era which is often described as being characterized by a philosophical foundationalism—a demand for an objective certainty in matters of knowledge—most of these groups were willing to live with something less than objective certainty. They embraced an evidentiary approach that did not offer absolute, mathematical proof, but made room for faith and internal judgment.[9] This stood in contrast to other, often Calvinistic strands of Protestantism that tended to make a certain science of knowledge, both natural and revealed.[10] As the Enlightenment began to make ever more aggressive claims to knowledge and certainty, this other strand culminated in the development of modern conceptions of verbal inerrancy in the halls of Princeton Seminary, which served as the foundations of twentieth-century Christian fundamentalism.[11]

The second feature shared in common by Methodists, Restorationists, and Millerites was a willingness to accept the validity of knowledge attainable from God's other book, that of nature. These traditions held a belief in the validity of truths discoverable by human reason, moral sense, and intuition. This view was an expression of the ethical common sense strand of the Scottish Common Sense philosophy, and it supported eighteenth- and nineteenth-century Protestant beliefs in the importance of both natural law and moral philosophy in the construction of laws and for ethical reflection.[12]

The third point was theological and flowed from the first two and became a guiding hermeneutical principle. If God could and did communicate reliable truths, and did so through multiple sources, then one could use these sources to understand and assess claims about God, whether from nature or the Bible itself (or some combination of the two). If the Bible said that God was just, moral, and good, then he could be understood, at least in part, to be just and moral, even by fallen human reason. In the end, Scottish Common Sense argued that the teachings of the Bible were consistent with moral reason, once moral reason and the Bible were properly understood.

This biblical and moral reasoning supported the adoption of a theological and interpretive system known as the moral government of God. If God was moral, loving, and good, then his written revelation should be interpreted to make those truths about him clearer. It also provided a framework to think about issues of society and the state. If God himself was willing to be assessed by the moral framework that he had imbedded into the universe, and made accessible to the mind of man, then how could human governments escape this standard?[13]

It was no coincidence, then, that there was a strong correlation between those Christians that accepted this moral government of God hermeneutic and those Christians that participated in antislavery and social welfare activism. In such a moral worldview, it was manifestly clear to such Christians that slavery was a practice that had no place in how God had established his morally based universe.

This correlation can be found at many different times and places. Puritan preacher and theologian Jonathan Edwards, was a slaveholder. His son, Jonathan Edwards Jr., however, adopted the moral government of God view of the Atonement and wrote a treatise opposing slavery.[14] William Wilberforce, the famed British antislavery activist, was raised a Methodist and was urged by John Wesley to end the evil institution.[15] Further, "virtually all antislavery Presbyterians and Congregationalists came from the New School," including biblical scholar Albert Barnes and the famous evangelist Charles Finney, who helped found Oberlin College of Ohio, a hotbed of antislavery activity.[16]

Early Adventist thought came down squarely amidst the Arminian/New School Presbyterian approach to the Bible and social issues. Sea Captain Joseph Bates, health reformer, abolitionist, and bringer of the Sabbath into Adventism, was from the Christian Connection, part of the Restorationist movement; Hiram Edson, who first gave expression to the Adventist doctrine regarding the heavenly sanctuary, had a Methodist background; James White was an ordained minister with the Christian Connection before becoming an Adventist; and Ellen White had been raised in the Methodist Church and was known to read New School theologians.[17]

All four of these Adventist founders had grown up in an area of New England so impacted by the fires of revival that it came to be known as the "burned-over" district. It was home to the renewal efforts of Charles Finney and others who created an ecumenical spirit of revival, consisting of new birth conversion, God as a moral governor, and his children as agents of godly spiritual and social reform.[18] So, despite, or perhaps because of, being "biblical conservative," the Adventists held to quite progressive social positions at the time. They not only opposed slavery and supported abolition, but they called for civil disobedience to fugitive slave laws. They did not ordain women ministers, but their position toward women in teaching, preaching, and evangelizing was progressive by the standards of the day. They wrote strongly against the restrictive teachings, promoted by Christian social conservatives, which defended slavery and that limited women to the teaching of women and children.[19]

Over time, however, Adventists did not consistently keep to their socially progressive positions. Adventist history reveals that a shift in approaches to the biblical text correlates with a shift in the church's approach to social questions. Adventism's vision of the Bible at any given time impacted the vision the church fostered of the role of their members in American life. To understand the impact of Adventism's shifting view of the Bible, it is helpful to see their changing view of the church's social role.

For these purposes, the Adventist approach to the Bible during the century and a half since its founding in the middle of the nineteenth century can be divided into five chronological periods:[20]

A. Confident Beginnings: Firm Foundations, 1849–1883
B. Growing Pains: Liberalism and Fundamentalism, 1883–1919
C. Arrested Development: Against Modernity, 1919–1966
D. Delayed Adolescence: The Center Holds? 1967–1988
E. Tentative Maturity: The World and America, 1988–2015

Confident Beginnings: Firm Foundations, 1849–1883

In antebellum America, a quite simple approach to the Bible prevailed among serious Christians. The Bible was treated largely as a pure and uncorrupted text, with the real work of Bible study being to seek to understand what the text actually taught. This stood in contrast to an emergent new German or "higher criticism," which stressed the historicizing Scripture by examining its transmission throughout the centuries and studying the impact of human thought and culture on its construction and teachings. Higher criticism was slow to come to Britain and America. Its rise in Germany began in the late eighteenth and early nineteenth centuries, but it did not get serious and widespread attention in Britain until the *Essays and Reviews* of 1859, the same year that Darwin's *Origin of the Species* was published. The distractions of the Civil War slowed a serious engagement with higher biblical criticism for several more years in America.[21]

William Miller, the prophetic expositor and key forerunner to the Adventist tradition whose studies led to a series of religious revivals surrounding 1844, was a typical example of this approach to Scripture. In his twenties, Miller had become a deist and had given up his faith in Scripture as divine revelation. After a conversion experience in his mid-thirties, Miller came back to the study of Scripture, and he became convinced that "if the Bible was the word of God, every thing contained therein might be understood, and all its parts be made to harmonize."[22] Early Adventists inherited this high view of Scripture from Miller and his followers, the Millerites. They held the foundational belief that, as expressed by cofounder James White, "the Bible is a perfect, and complete revelation . . . our only rule of faith and practice."[23] Any Adventist elaboration of scripture during this period came almost always in defense against attacks by infidels and deists.[24]

Yet, despite this high view of Scripture, the most formal Adventist statement onScripture during this time stayed away from strong claims about verbally inerrant inspiration that was becoming common in some evangelical circles. The third article of an 1872 statement of

Adventist beliefs said simply that the Scriptures are "given by inspiration of God, contain a full revelation of his will to man, and are the only infallible rule of faith and practice."[25] The social attitudes of Adventists also differed quite markedly from those Christians in America who were advancing a more absolutist, mechanical version of inspiration. Adventist favorable attitudes toward the role of woman in preaching and teaching, their staunch opposition to slavery, and their desire for government to protect children and families from the use of alcohol contrasted with those holding to a verbal inerrancy outlook, such as those in the Old School Presbyterian tradition.[26]

GROWING PAINS: LIBERALISM AND FUNDAMENTALISM, 1883–1919

It was the role of Adventism's prophet within the church that precipitated its first significant internal encounter with a more liberal view of scriptural authority. Such views had begun to make their way into mainstream evangelical thought after the Civil War had ended.[27] But these new views were not entertained seriously inside the Adventist Church until the early 1880s.

At that time, certain church leaders had grown impatient regarding criticisms leveled at them by Ellen White. It was hard to argue with a prophetic voice that the church at large considered inspired. To strengthen their positions, certain leaders, including the church's president, proposed a theory that while Ellen White's visions were inspired, her "testimony letters to leaders and others" were not inspired to the same degree.[28] This theory of "levels of inspiration" gained some traction in Adventist circles into the late 1880s and was applied to the Bible as well. But in 1889, Ellen White herself spoke to the question directly. She wrote, with a certain sense of irony, that "the Lord did not inspire the articles on inspiration published in the *Review*." No person, she continued, should "pronounce judgment" on the Bible, "selecting some things as inspired and discrediting others as uninspired."[29] The church generally embraced her cautionary guidance.

But Ellen White also played a part in pushing back against the other extreme—that of literal, mechanical, verbal inspiration. It was at the 1883 General Conference Session where it was proposed that there be revision of certain of Ellen White's books to correct grammatical errors.[30] The wording of the motion for revision spoke directly to the process of inspiration. "We believe the light given by God to his servants is by the enlightenment of the mind, thus imparting the thoughts, and not (except in rare cases) the very words in which the ideas should be expressed."[31] Again, this understanding of inspiration as functioning at the level of thought, and not word choice, was also applied to Scripture. For instance, Adventist scholar Uriah Smith wrote that except where a writer quoted God or an angel, that the "mere language" of neither White nor the Scriptures were directly God's words. Rather, he said, though the exact "words may not be inspired,... at the same time, the facts, the truths, which those words convey, may be divinely communicated."[32]

It was at this time, where both more liberal and fundamentalists views of inspiration where pressing in, that Ellen White made her first extended remarks about the nature of inspiration.[33] Her comments reveal a connection with an existing strand of moderate

Protestant thought on the topic. Scholars have since recognized White's use of New School Presbyterian Calvin Stowe's book *Origin and History of the Books of the Bible* in setting out her own views of inspiration.[34]

Stowe represented a middle ground between the liberalism of the higher critics, and the verbal inerrancy being developed and promoted by more conservative American Protestants such as the Old School Presbyterians of Princeton Seminary. He drew an analogy between Christ being fully divine and fully human, with the limitations and shortcomings implied by human flesh, and the divine message, but human words and frame, of the written Word.[35] Ellen White used very similar language and imagery to Stowe. "Jesus, in order to reach man where he is," she wrote, "took humanity." Similarly, "the Bible must be given in the language of men. Everything that is human is imperfect. Different meanings are expressed by the same word; there is not one word for each distinct idea." White also revealed her non-foundationalist view of truth—that it was given not for absolute, perfect precision, but for use in ordinary life—concluding that in what was almost a direct quote from Stowe, "The Bible was given for practical purposes."[36]

Ellen White did not, however, merely parrot or crib from Stowe. She differed with him on important points. She refused to follow his claim that "thoughts" were not inspired, but only the men.[37] She distinctly said that God did inspire thoughts. She also allowed a greater role for the Holy Spirit in influencing, though not dictating, the choice of words.[38]

Stowe and White agreed on a non-foundationalist, non-absolutist epistemology (Scripture is for "practical" purposes), as well as a recognition of the human aspects of Scripture. Both interpreted Scripture with a moral government of God hermeneutic that resulted in opposition to slavery. Calvin Stowe is most well-known, of course, as being the husband of Harriet Beecher-Stowe, the woman who wrote *Uncle Tom's Cabin*—the book that widely influenced abolitionist sentiment leading up to the Civil War. Stowe and his New School colleagues were supportive of these abolitionist views.[39]

Stowe's and White's views on biblical language reveals why those holding a moderate, non-inerrant view of inspiration were more open to a Bible reading that criticized establishment institutions like slavery than their inerrantist brethren. There is a simple explanation. Those committed to absolute, inerrant, verbal precision will be more likely to believe they are eschewing interpretation, and reading the "plain meaning" of the text. The problem is, of course, that the "obvious" meaning of a word or passage will often turn out to be the meaning proposed and understood by the social and cultural majority of those in a given interpretative community at a given historical moment.

For instance, the words "slave" or "slavery," read against an early nineteenth-century American backdrop, especially in the South, would make it appear that the Bible supported the racialized, chattel, man-stealing slavery, rather than the economic serfdom of ancient Israel. But an approach to inspiration that recognizes the flexibility, imprecision, and semantic range of language and words will be open to interpreting those words according to larger principles, even if that meant looking for a secondary or less well-known meaning to a word or passage. For those adopting the moral government of God hermeneutic, this view of Scripture meant that difficult texts about human freedom and slavery were interpreted in a manner that, while faithful to the text and context, would also maximize the fairness, justice, and love of God in dealing with humanity, and of humans with each other.

Based on this approach, Ellen White herself had counseled that Adventists had a duty to disobey fugitive slave laws, as they were an affront to God's laws.[40] Later, after slavery was abolished in the United States, she continued to be a strong advocate for the education and uplifting of the former slaves. Her son, Edson White, risked his life in taking a boat to the South to serve as a floating school in which to educate and empower former slaves.[41]

ARRESTED DEVELOPMENT: AGAINST MODERNITY, 1919–1966

There were those within early Adventism that promoted a verbal, mechanical view of inspiration, but they had been kept largely on the margins by the moderating influence of Ellen White and those close to her. But after her death in 1915, that began to change. Her inner circle, including her son, Willie White, and General Conference President A. G. Daniells, worked to keep alive her moderate views on the topic. They found themselves under increasing pressure, however, by a more extreme conservative view, newly energized by an escalation in the fundamentalist-modernist conflict in Christianity and society at large.[42]

It was also in 1915 that the final volume of the series *The Fundamentals* was published. This was the widely circulated (three million volumes distributed) defense of Christian orthodoxy by a consortium of conservative evangelical pastors, scholars, and laymen.[43] There was much that Adventists could accept in *The Fundamentals*. It defended the virgin birth and deity of Christ, Christ's atoning death and resurrection, the Trinity, and the historicity of the Bible.

Three articles criticized even "Christianized" versions Darwinian thought concerning evolution.[44] This stout defense of special creation, a doctrine of particular importance to Adventism—because of its connection with the Seventh-day Sabbath and the character of God—that likely caused the books in *The Fundamentals* series to be of influence in Adventist circles. Whatever the cause, Adventists began to espouse more frequently the views of verbal inspiration defended in *The Fundamentals*.

Matters came to a head in 1919, when Adventists held a Bible Conference for its editors, religion teachers, and church administrators. It was here that the old guard of moderates who had worked closely with Ellen White attempted to head off a growing move in the church to embrace a fundamentalist outlook on inerrant verbal inspiration as to both the Bible and Ellen White.[45] Ultimately, the Conference discussions were inconclusive. Records from this Conference, where the facts of Ellen White's use of sources and editors was freely acknowledged, were not made public until 1974.[46] The overall effect of this conservative turn was that the growing forces of inerrancy and fundamentalism continued to spread throughout Adventism.[47] Official publications for the next two decades often espoused the verbal inerrancy position.[48]

This shift profoundly influenced not just Adventist biblical exegesis and interpretation but also larger theological and social outlooks throughout the denomination. Previously, Ellen White and those close to her had been open to the use of new translations of the Bible as they came out. Within Protestant fundamentalism more generally, however, there arose a strong "King James only" movement that soon found its way into the Adventist Church.[49]

The church also moved from a pragmatically progressive outlook on issues of social justice, especially in relation to race and gender, to one that was distinctly socially conservative and even regressive. At the time of Ellen White's death, while the Adventist Church had not ordained women to the Gospel ministry, many women functioned as licensed ministers and evangelists, rising through the ranks to become administrators. At one point, they held as many as one-quarter to one-third of church administrative offices as treasurers, department secretaries, and educational department leaders.[50] But after the 1920s, women began to disappear from these positions. Very few remained by the 1930s, and all were gone a decade later. They vanished not only from administrative leadership but also no longer functioned as licensed ministers, being limited to the roles of deaconess or Bible worker.[51]

A similar thing happened on the racial front. Early Adventism had moved forward with pragmatic, yet hopeful, progress in dealing with race questions. While recognizing the dangers of a frontal assault on the southern color line, Ellen White and other leaders sought to elevate the freed slaves through education and evangelism. Their pragmatic and progressive ministry in these regards, however, was turned in a conservative direction as the church entered the 1920s and 1930s. Adventist institutions that had not practiced segregation in the early twentieth century began to do so in the 1930s. This continued into the 1960s, even as society itself became more open to greater equality.[52]

What happened? Certainly the nationwide economic depression of the 1930s created a culture-wide pull toward more conservative social values. But given Adventism's socially progressive past, a full explanation must take into account Adventism's growing experimentation with Protestant fundamentalism and the theological rigid and socially conservative outlook that came with it. This fundamentalist status quo was to be challenged, however, by the events of the next period.

DELAYED ADOLESCENCE: THE CENTER HOLDS?
1967–1988

The re-marginalization of verbal inerrancy in mainstream Adventism came at a turbulent time in American. In 1966, *Time* magazine ran its famous cover, asking "Is God Dead?" The assassinations of Robert Kennedy and Martin Luther King Jr. were to shortly take place, opposition to Vietnam would coalesce into a popular protest movement, and flower power, Woodstock, and the summer of love would challenge basic Christian moral outlooks.[53]

It was not a time when Americans were attracted to affirmations of moderation, and currents within Adventism reflected this. The denomination's strongly conservative bent shielded it from truly liberal theology, but it began to move away from some fundamentalist positions. This move was begun in the mid-1950s, when Adventist scholars published the SDA Bible Commentary. In wrestling with the choice of various textual readings, word translations, and interpretations, verbal inerrancy was hard to maintain. But the re-marginalization of verbal inerrancy in popular, mainstream Adventism was signaled by two events in 1966. The first was the publication of the *Seventh-day*

Adventist Encyclopedia, which stated that the church did "not believe in verbal inspiration, according to the usual meaning of the term, but in what may be properly called thought inspiration."[54]

The second was a lecture by Arthur L. White, grandson of Ellen White at Andrews University, the church's flagship theological institution. Arthur White stated that "Ellen G. White's statements concerning the Bible and her work indicate that the concept of verbal inspiration is without support in either the Bible writers' or her own word."[55] After this time, it became increasingly difficult to find claims or affirmations of verbal inerrancy in official, institutional Adventist circles.

But some Adventist scholars went further. They were attracted by neo-orthodox theology and encounter views of inspiration—emphasizing revelation as experiential encounter rather than propositional exchange—which were considered liberal in Adventist circles. These new theologies were given a platform by the creation in 1967 by some Adventist academics of the Association of Adventism Forums. Two years later, the association began publishing its journal, *Spectrum*, which assumed a "revisionist-critical stand," and began critiquing traditional Adventist beliefs from the neo-orthodox and encounter theology perspectives.[56] What followed was a series of volleys between left-leaning Adventist academics and more conservative scholars at the Adventist Seminary and church headquarters. The former wanted to emphasize revelation as encounter, the latter tended to defend a both/and position, arguing that revelation could be both encounter with God and productive of propositional, doctrinal information.[57]

Those leaning toward neo-orthodoxy also began making greater use of higher-critical biblical analysis than Adventism had previously done. Views of inspiration became bound up with methods of Bible study and how Scripture should be analyzed. The first target of such inspiration deconstruction was Ellen White and her writings. Triggered by a 1970 *Spectrum* article entitled "Ellen White: A Subject for Adventist Scholarship," a veritable avalanche of articles appeared in the journal critiquing Ellen White's use of the Bible, history, health science, her own visions, and other authors. These were responded to in turn by articles and materials from the church and its denominational scholars.[58]

Thus again it was disputes over Adventism's experience with inspiration that impacted its discussion about the approach to all revelation, including Scripture. Three distinct groups began to take shape. The first group was made up of those who had embraced an overly rigid view of inspiration, found it untrue, and reacted by viewing all revelation as either operating at the level of encounter, or as almost entirely historically conditioned, or both. This was a relatively small, but influential group clustered in Adventist academic centers and large urban churches in North American and Western Europe. A positive aspect of this group was that it tended to be socially and racially progressive, supportive of the equal treatment of blacks, women, and other minorities. Many mainstream church members wondered, however, if this was the progressivism of evangelical, biblical thought, or that of socially liberal politics, especially as this group began to espouse elements of the sexual revolution, including the LGBT movement.[59]

The second group included those who reacted against the observations of *Spectrum* and the left-wing revisionists by doubling down on an inerrant view of inspiration, in regard to both the Bible and Ellen White. Given Adventism's extended liaison with Protestant fundamentalism, especially at the popular levels of the church, this group was somewhat larger than the first, but did not represent the moderate, institutional core. Instead, this second group fed into an existing strand within Adventism of independent institutions, medical and educational, that largely supported the work and beliefs of the church, but operated outside its organizational structure.[60]

In the 1970s, a number of these independent organizations became havens for those Adventists who felt that the growing moderate view of inspiration in the institutional church was a capitulation to the forces of liberalism. This group tended to stay out of social and racial matters, viewing the church's shortcomings as primarily spiritual and theological. They viewed calls for racial or social justice with some suspicion and as being part of the biblically liberal "social gospel."[61]

The third group included those who held to the moderate view of plenary thought inspiration. It was by far the largest group although not necessarily the loudest. It included most of Adventism's official publications and institutional voices, as well as some of the more moderate independent institutions and ministries. Elements of the more extreme first and second groups could be found in this third group, causing the third group to sometimes feel significant internal tension over how the official publications and institutions within the church should address various conflicts and viewpoints.

For example, the consortium of Adventist religion and theology professors, the Adventist Society for Religious Studies, founded in 1979 in conjunction with the Society of Biblical Literature, did harbor some left-wing voices.[62] So much so, that in 1988, more conservative members of the group split off and formed a competing, more conservative group called the Adventist Theological Society.[63] Certainly both groups had elements from groups one or two within them, but most of the membership of both groups would be more accurately described as moderate in their views of revelation and inspiration.[64] Both these groups and their institutions became more progressive in matters of race and gender equity as they became increasingly aware of the unfortunate impact of fundamentalism on the church over the previous half-century.

With the formation of these two separate theological societies within the church, it might appear that 1988 represented the beginning of a new and higher level of conflict between left-leaning and right-leaning groups within the church. The subsequent years did witness some conflict, but an event two years earlier in Rio de Janeiro—where the world church voted on a document entitled "Methods of Bible Study"—actually presaged a more united future than the theological society split appeared to indicate.

The very location of the Rio event revealed the reality of the growing international nature of the Adventist Church. The new international balance of influence represented a boost for the moderate to conservative side of the church. It turned out, however, that fundamentalist views of inerrant inspiration were primarily a North American phenomenon. Adventist scholars outside North American were not generally supporters of the verbal inerrantists. The Rio document clearly denied verbal inspiration, acknowledged minor discrepancies in the Bible, and acknowledged multiple sources of revelation.[65]

The Rio document showed the church moving toward an era of moderate conservatism. The growing clamor of the extremes on both sides of the inspiration issue heralded an increasing loss of influence of either of these extremes on the Adventist mainstream, as a theologically conservative, but socially and culturally diverse, overseas contingent played an increasingly important role in church affairs.

Tentative Maturity: The World Comes to America, 1988–2015

In the fifty years since the mid-twentieth century, the average Adventist Church member went from being a white male of European descent to an African or Hispanic woman. During this period, the internationalization of Adventist Church membership was its most striking feature. In 1960, total membership stood at about 1.2 million, with 43 percent of that found in North America and Europe. Forty years later in 2001, the church had grown dramatically by over 1,000 percent, with membership totaling about 12.3 million.[66] In a shift almost as dramatic as this phenomenal growth rate, the population center moved decisively from the Europe and North American to South America and Africa. In 2001, North America and Europe's share of the membership had declined to about 11 percent. Africa and South America, conversely, came to account for 67 percent of the Adventist membership, while Asia composed an additional 19 percent.[67]

At gatherings of the Adventist Church, theological leaders and Bible scholars from Africa, South America, and Asia began to have a larger influence. The demographic and geographical shift did no favors for the left, progressive wing of the Western Adventist Church. Somewhat more surprisingly, the fundamentalist wing of the church did not find totally sympathetic allies among the church's new international membership, as many had thought they would.

The more moderate international stance on inspiration can, in part, be attributed to the mission history of the Adventist Church. The vast majority of the overseas growth in the church occurred in the 1950s and after; but the vast majority of Adventist missions were founded in the early twentieth century, at a time when the theologically moderate view of inspiration had been in its ascendancy. Thus, Adventist missions had proceeded largely on this earlier, more moderate platform. The overseas church had been less influenced than the American by fundamentalist influences of the 1930s, 1940s, and 1950s. The result was that by the end of the twentieth century, the left-right biblical conflict so prevalent in the North American and European churches began to be overshadowed and tempered by a moderately conservative influence from overseas.

This pattern was vividly illustrated by the discussion and conflict over the question of whether the church should ordain women ministers. Western leaders and scholars had raised this issue since the 1970s in reaction against the fundamentalist culture that had marginalized women in Adventism from the 1920s to the 1960s. Conferences were convened, scholars were commissioned, and church councils were held. But whenever a vote was taken, a substantial margin, especially those from overseas, initially resisted the movement to ordain female ministers.[68]

The issue persisted, however, and in 2010 the church voted to engage in a formal, church-wide discussion on the matter of female ordination. A truly international study body was convened to study and work over a two-year period, and make recommendations to the church at large. What resulted provided a fascinating insight into the engagement of a truly worldwide, multicultural church with issues of biblical interpretation and application.[69] Many of the North American and European delegates assumed a pro-ordination position, but there were a significant number of North American conservatives who held a fundamentalist-inspired outlook and mounted strong opposition to female ordination. This group made a series of presentations that reflected not the moderate, early historic position of the church, but rather a more conservative, fundamentalist view of gender roles. For instance, they not only argued that women should not be ordained to the gospel ministry, but some also insisted, contrary to the Adventist pioneers, that women could and should teach only other women or children.

What was most interesting was the reaction of the international delegates to this split. Most of them did not side with the pro-ordination progressives, but many of them did not find the extreme anti-position acceptable either. Over the course of the two years of meetings and discussions, a third group spontaneously emerged that received formal recognition from the church committee leadership. This third group took a somewhat conservative reading of the Bible and gender roles, but did so in a less dogmatic and inflexible way than the North American conservatives.[70] For example, they were willing to allow the ordination of women in those regions where local leadership deemed it essential to the mission of the church. Ultimately, this third group received the second largest number of votes in the committee, somewhat behind the pro-ordination group, but significantly ahead of the anti-ordination crowd.[71]

In the General Conference session that followed in the summer of 2015 in San Antonio, Texas, where the recommendations were passed on to the full church, the no-ordination vote prevailed. But the margin was significantly smaller than in the past. Earlier General Conference votes had denied ordination by 75 and 70 percent. But this time, the "no" vote came in at about 59 percent (and this vote included an Adventist Church that had grown significantly overseas in the more than two decades since the earlier votes).[72] It appeared that once the overseas members came into contact with a fundamentalist approach to Scripture and social issues, they shied away from it, and sought out a more moderate alternative.

CONCLUSION: A MISSION TO THE WORLD COMES HOME

In the 1880s and 1890s, Adventist pioneers started on a mission to the world, which at the time seemed ambitious, audacious, and quixotic. The church persisted in this global effort when other, larger Protestant churches decided to split up mission territories among themselves. The Adventist pioneers endured two World Wars, numerous other regional conflicts and civil wars, and many other trials and hardships, establishing beachheads in most countries of six continents. When the old colonial worlds collapsed after World War II, local leaders stepped forward, and the next fifty years turned into a half-century of dramatic missions' growth.[73]

This growth is coming back to the American Adventist Church in two distinct ways. First, the immigration of Adventists from overseas is causing American Adventism to continue to be the fastest-growing American Protestant denomination.[74] Second, and more important to Adventism and the Bible, the international influence is reminding American

Adventists of their heritage of a moderately conservative approach to biblical inspiration and interpretation and the pragmatically progressive social values that went with it.

Those who the Adventist Church touched with its missionary endeavors have themselves become the missionaries and the teachers. The experience of Adventism illustrates in miniature the larger story of the impact of the Great Awakenings on the Bible in America. The biblically based social renewal movements of the Second Great Awakening and the missionary impulses found throughout the late nineteenth and early twentieth centuries in what some have called a Third Great Awakening have combined and coalesced in what could be termed the Fourth Great Awakening—the Christianization of the southern hemisphere in the second half of the twentieth century.

The story of the Christianized global South confronting an increasingly secularized West is not just the story of the future of the Bible in Adventism—but of the Bible and Christianity in America itself. We will do well to pay it close attention.

Notes

1. The Adventist Church currently has a worldwide membership of nearly 20 million members. It is the most widespread Protestant denomination in the world, having a presence in 216 countries. It currently has the largest and most widespread system of primary and secondary schools and colleges, clinics and hospitals, and publishing houses of any Protestant denomination. *Seventh-day Adventist Yearbook* (Nampa, Idaho: Pacific Press Publishing Association, 2016), 4, http://documents.adventistarchives.org/Statistics/ASR/ ASR2016.pdf; "Protestant School Systems," *Educational Encyclopedia*, http://education. stateuniversity.com/pages/2339/Protestant-School-Systems.html; "13 Largest Non-Profit Hospital Systems by Number of Hospitals," *Beckers Hospital Review*, September 4, 2009, http://www.beckershospitalreview.com/lists-and-statistics/13-largest-non-profit-hospital-systems-by-number-of-hospitals.html.
2. David Kling, "The Second Great Awakening," in *Encyclopedia of Religious Revivals in America*, ed. Michael McClymond (Westport, Conn.: Greenwood Press, 2007), 384–89.
3. Jerry Moon, "Seventh-day Adventists," in McClymond, *Religious Revivals in America*, 391–92.
4. A helpful overview of the Adventist roots in the Second Great Awakening can be found in Everett Dick, "The Millerite Movement, 1830-1845," and Godfrey Anderson, "Sectarianism and Organization, 1846-1864," the first two chapters in *Adventism in America: A History*, ed. Gary Land, rev. ed. (Berrien Springs, Mich.: Andrews University Press, 1998), 1–52; also see George R. Knight, *Millennial Fever and the End of the World: A Study of Millerite Adventism* (Nampa, Idaho: Pacific Press Publishing Association, 1993).
5. Thomas Kidd quoted in Alan Rappeport, "Ben Carson Puts Spotlight on Seventh-day Adventists," *New York Times*, October 27, 2015, http://nyti.ms/1kNfTZt; also see Walter Martin and Donald Barnhouse, *The Truth about Seventh-day Adventism* (White Fish, Mont.: Literary Licensing, LLC, 2013).
6. Mark A. Noll, *In the Beginning Was the Word* (New York: Oxford University Press, 2015), 331–33; also see Ronald F. Satta, *The Sacred Text: Biblical Authority in Nineteenth-Century America* (Eugene, Ore.: Pickwick, 2007), xiv, 43–73.
7. Also see Rolf J. Pöhler, *Continuity and Change in Adventist Teaching: A Case Study in Doctrinal Development* (Frankfurt am Main: Lang, 2000), 21–31; George R. Knight,

A Search for Identity: The Development of Seventh-day Adventist Beliefs (Hagerstown, Md.: Review and Herald, 2000), 28–37.

8. Mark Noll, "Common Sense Traditions and American Evangelical Thought," *American Quarterly* 37, no. 2 (Summer 1985): 220–22. An additional movement which impacted Adventism, but that has received less attention, is the Calvinist-based New School Presbyterian movement that became active and influential in the revivals surrounding the Second Great Awakening in the 1820s and 1830s. Nicholas Miller, "Alongside Foundationalism: Adventism's Alternate Protestant Philosophical Path," *Andrews University Seminary Studies* 53, no. 1 (2015): 37–54.

9. Douglas Casson, *Liberating Judgment: Fanatics, Skeptics, and John Locke's Politics of Probability* (Princeton, N.J.: Princeton University Press, 2011), 21–22; Elmer H. Duncan, ed., *Thomas Reid's Lectures on Natural Theology* (1780; repr. Washington, D.C.: University Press of America, 1981), xxxxv; see discussion by Miller, "Alongside Foundationalism," 41–44.

10. Reformed theologian Francis Turretin (1623-1687) is said to be one of the first formulators of the verbal inspiration of the Scriptures, and his *Institutio Thelogiae Elencticae* was used as a standard text in "Reformed Christian circles until it was replaced by Charles Hodge's *Systematic Theology* in the late 19ᵗʰ century." "Francis Turretin," *Theopedia*, http://www.theopedia.com/francis-turretin.)

11. George Marsden, *Fundamentalism and American Culture*, 2nd ed. (New York: Oxford University Press, 2006).

12. While nearly all biblically conservative nineteenth-century Protestants drew from Scottish Common Sense epistemology, traditional reformed thinkers, including those at early to mid-nineteenth-century Princeton, became increasingly resistant to the ethical arguments of Common Sense theory. They viewed this method of moral reasoning as an intrusion on the teaching role reserved, in their minds, primarily, if not exclusively for Scripture. Mark Noll, ed., *The Princeton Theology: 1812-1921* (Grand Rapids, Mich.: Baker Academic, 1983, 2001), 30–33, 165–66, 218–20.

13. The moral government of God theory was articulated initially by Hugo Grotius, building on Jacob Arminius's free-will theology, and developed by John Wesley, Thomas Reid, John Locke, and other Arminian-leaning thinkers, including New England's Nathaniel Taylor. Miller "Alongside Foundationalism," 47–50.

14. Jonathan Edwards Jr., "The Injustice and Impolicy of the Slave Trade, and of Slavery," in *The Works of Jonathan Edwards*, 2 vols., ed. Tryon Edwards (Andover, Mass.: Allen, Morrill & Wardwell, 1842; repr. New York: Garland, 1987), 2:75–90.

15. John Wesley to William Wilberforce, February 24, 1791, quoted in Eric Metaxas, *Amazing Grace: William Wilberforce and the Heroic Campaign to End Slavery* (New York: Harper Collins, 2007), 144.

16. Leo Hirrel, *Children of Wrath* (Lexington, Ky.: University Press of Kentucky, 1998), 136; T. H. Olbricht, "Barnes, Albert (1798-1870)," in *Historical Handbook of Major Biblical Interpreters*, ed. Donald K. McKim (Downers Grove, Ill.: InterVarsity Press, 1998), 281–84; E. Brooks Holifield, *Theology in America: Christian Thought from the Age of the Puritans to the Civil War* (New Haven, Conn.: Yale University Press, 2003), 501; Keith J. Hardman, *Charles Grandison Finney: 1792-1875: Revivalist and Reformer* (Syracuse, N.Y.: Syracuse University Press, 1987), 271–74; J. Brent Morris, *Oberlin, Hotbed of Abolitionism: College, Community, and the Fight for Freedom and Equality in Antebellum America* (Chapel Hill: University of North Carolina Press, 2014), 81–89.

17. Sketches of these pioneer Adventists can be found in Gary Land, *Historical Dictionary of the Seventh-day Adventists* (Lanham, Md.: Scarecrow Press, 2005).

18. Hardman, *Charles Grandison Finney*, 61–76, 150–58.

19. On slavery and fugitive slave laws, see Ellen White, *Testimonies for the Church*, vol. 1 (1859; repr. Mountain View, Calif.: Pacific Press Publishing, 1948), 201–2; Samuel G. London Jr., *Seventh-day Adventists and the Civil Rights Movement* (Jackson: University of Mississippi Press, 2009), 44–56; on women, see the entry in Land, *Historical Dictionary*, 329–30.

20. The rest of this chapter draws on Alberto R. Timm, "A History of Seventh-day Adventist Views on Biblical and Prophetic Inspiration (1844-2000)," *Journal of the Adventist Theological Society* 10, nos. 1-2 (1999): 486–542.

21. On the slow reception of higher biblical criticism in America, see Holifield, *Theology in America*, 192–95; Noll, *In the Beginning*, 333–39.

22. William Miller, *Apology and Defence* (Boston: Joshua V. Himes, 1845), 5–6.

23. James White, *A Word to the "Little Flock"* (Brunswick, Maine: printed by author, 1847), 13.

24. Moses Hull, *The Bible from Heaven; or, a Dissertation on the Evidences of Christianity* (Battle Creek, Mich.: Seventh-day Adventist Publishing Association, 1863), 79.

25. Uriah Smith, *A Declaration of the Fundamental Principles Taught and Practiced by the Seventh-day Adventists* (Battle Creek, Mich.: Steam Press of the Seventh-Day Adventist Publishing Association, 1872), 5.

26. Holifield, *Theology in America*, 370–80, 500–502; see note 19.

27. Timm, "History of Seventh-day Adventist Views," 492n38, citing Daniel Wilson, *The Evidences of Christianity*, 5th ed. (Boston: Crocker and Brewster, 1845), 1:278–89.

28. Timm, "A History of Adventist Views," 491–92.

29. E. G. White to R. A. Underwood, January 18, 1889, Ellen G. White Research Center, Andrews University (EGWRC-AU).

30. Timm, "A History of Adventist Views," 493.

31. "General Conference Proceedings," *Review and Herald*, November 27, 1883, 741–42.

32. Uriah Smith, "Which Are Revealed, Words or Ideas?" *RH*, March 13, 1888, 168–69.

33. Ellen G. White [1886] MS 24, reprinted in *Selected Messages, Book 1* (Washington, D.C.: Review and Herald, 1958), 19–21, http://media4.egwwritings.org/pdf/en_1SM.pdf.

34. Robert M. Johnston, "The Case for a Balanced Hermeneutic," *Ministry: International Journal for Pastors* 72, no. 3 (March 1999): 11–12; David Neff, "Ellen G. White's Theological and Literary Indebtedness to Calvin Stowe," unpublished paper, The Ellen G. White Estate [DF 65], 1979, http://ellenwhite.org/library/Calvin%20Stowe?sqid=1799797490.

35. C. E. Stowe, *Origin and History of the Books of the Bible* (Hartford, Conn.: Hartford Pub. Co., 1867), 19.

36. Ellen White, *Selected Messages, Book 1*, 20, compare with Stowe, *Origin and History of the Books of the Bible*, 15–16, 18.

37. Compare Stowe, *Origin and History of the Books of the Bible*, 20, with White, *Selected Messages, Book 1*, 21; Neff, "Literary Indebtedness to Calvin Stowe," 16–19.

38. Ellen White, *Selected Messages, Book 1*, 21; Neff, "Literary Indebtedness to Calvin Stowe," 16–18.

39. See Daniel R. Vollaro, "Lincoln, Stowe, and the 'Little Woman/Great War' Story: The Making, and Breaking, of a Great American Anecdote," *Journal of the Abraham Lincoln Association* 30, no. 1 (Winter 2009): 18–34, http://hdl.handle.net/2027/spo.2629860.0030.104.

40. White, *Testimonies for the Church*, 1:201–2.

41. London, *Seventh-day Adventists and the Civil Rights Movement*, 44–56.
42. George Marsden, *Fundamentalism and American Culture* (New York: Oxford University Press, 2006).
43. Marsden, *Fundamentalism and American Culture*, 119.
44. Henry H. Beach, "The Decadence of Darwinism," in *The Fundamentals*, 4 vols., ed. R. A. Torrey and A. C. Dixon (1910–1915; repr. Grand Rapids, Mich.: Baker Books, 2008), 4:59–71; George Frederick Wright, "The Passing of Evolution," in *The Fundamentals*, 4:72–87; and By an Occupant of the Pew, "Evolutionism in the Pulpit," in *The Fundamentals*, 4:88–96.
45. Allan Lindsay, "Bible Conference of 1919," in *The Ellen White Encyclopedia*, ed. Denis Fortin and Jerry Moon (Hagerstown, Md.: Review and Herald, 2014), 657–58.
46. Lindsay, "Bible Conference of 1919," 657–58.
47. Timm, "A History of Seventh-day Adventist Views," 500–503.
48. Timm, "A History of Seventh-day Adventist Views," 502–3.
49. Timm, "A History of Seventh-day Adventist Views," 505.
50. Land, *Historical Dictionary*, 329.
51. Land, *Historical Dictionary*, 329–30.
52. London, *Adventists and the Civil Rights Movement*, 69, 76–77, 83–88, 100–106, 109.
53. "Is God Dead?" *Time*, April 8, 1966, http://content.time.com/time/covers/0,16641,19660408,00.html.
54. Don F. Neufeld, ed., *Seventh-day Adventist Encyclopedia* (Washington, D.C.: Review & Herald, 1966), 585.
55. Arthur L. White, *The Ellen G. White Writings* (Washington, D.C.: Review and Herald, 1973), 13.
56. Land, *Historical Dictionary*, 27, 283–84; Timm, "A History of Seventh-day Adventist Views," 513–14.
57. Timm, "A History of Seventh-day Adventist Views," 515–16.
58. Malcolm Bull and Keith Lockhart, *Seeking a Sanctuary: Seventh-day Adventism and the American Dream*, 2nd ed. (Bloomington: Indiana University Press, 2007), 33.
59. Jared Wright, "Why Adventists Should Consider Supporting Gay Marriage," *Spectrum*, June 16, 2008, http://spectrummagazine.org/article/jared-wright/2008/06/16/why-adventists-should-consider-supporting-gay-marriage; Jonathan Cook, "Voting for Same-Sex Marriage: An Adventist Perspective," *Spectrum*, November 4, 2012, http://spectrummagazine.org/article/jonathan-cook/2012/11/04/voting-same-sex-marriage-adventist-perspective.
60. Bull and Lockhart, *Seeking a Sanctuary*, 333–35.
61. Bull and Lockhart, *Seeking a Sanctuary*, 341.
62. "Adventist Society for Religious Studies," in Land, *Historical Dictionary*, 14.
63. "Adventist Society for Religious Studies," in Land, *Historical Dictionary*, 326; "Adventist Theological Society," in Land, *Historical Dictionary*, 15.
64. Membership of the two groups overlaps considerably and they have begun fellowshipping together on a yearly basis.
65. "Methods of Bible Study Committee (GCC-A)—Report" [2(a)(2)], *Adventist Review*, January 22, 1987, 18, http://adventistdigitallibrary.org/adl-355695/adventist-review-january-22-1987.
66. Lowell Cooper, "Profile of a Changing Church," *Dialogue* 15, no. 1 (2003): 5–8, http://dialogue.adventist.org/en/articles/15-1/cooper/profile-of-a-changing-church.

67. Cooper, "Profile of a Changing Church."

68. General Conference Committee, Tenth Business Session, 55th General Conference Session, Indianapolis, Ind., July, 11, 1990, 1039–040, http://docs.adventistarchives.org/docs/GCC/GCC1990-07.pdf; 56th General Conference, *General Conference Bulletin*, July 11, 1995, 30, http://docs.adventistarchives.org/docs/GCB/GCB1995-08.pdf.

69. Documents regarding the Theology of Ordination Study Committee can be found here: "2013-14 GC Theology of Ordination Study Committee," Office of Archives, Statistics, and Research (Seventh-day Adventist Church, 2015), https://www.adventistarchives.org/gc-tosc.

70. David Read, "Surprise 'Third Way' Option Emerges at Final TOSC Meeting," *ADvindicate*, June 7, 2014, http://advindicate.com/articles/2014/6/6/surprise-third-way-option-emerges-at-final-tosc-meeting.

71. The author of this chapter was a member of the TOSC, and one of the leaders and organizers of the third, moderate group. The anti-ordination group received a total of 34 votes, the pro-ordination group received 52 votes, and the moderate group received 41 votes. "Importance of TOSC Report," *EqualOrdination*, June 1, 2015, http://equalordination.com/importance-of-tosc.

72. Andrew McChesney and Marcos Paseggi, "Delegates Vote 'No' on Issue of Women's Ordination," *Adventist Review*, July 8, 2015, http://www.adventistreview.org/church-news/story2988-%E2%80%8Bgc-delegates-vote-'no'-on-issue-of-women's-ordination.

73. D. J. B. Trim, "Adventist Church Growth and Mission since 1863: An Historical-Statistical Analysis," *Journal of Adventist Mission Studies* 8, no. 2, Art. 5 (2012), http://digitalcommons.andrews.edu/cgi/viewcontent.cgi?article=1209&context=jams.

74. G. Jeffrey MacDonald, "Adventists' Back-to-Basics Faith Is Fastest Growing U.S. Church," *USA Today*, March 17, 2011, http://usatoday30.usatoday.com/news/religion/2011-03-18-Adventists_17_ST_N.htm.

BIBLIOGRAPHY

Bull, Malcolm, and Keith Lockhart. *Seeking a Sanctuary: Seventh-day Adventism and the American Dream*. 2nd ed. Bloomington: Indiana University Press, 2007.

Casson, Douglas. *Liberating Judgment: Fanatics, Skeptics, and John Locke's Politics of Probability*. Princeton, N.J.: Princeton University Press, 2011.

Fortin, Denis, and Jerry Moon, eds. *The Ellen White Encyclopedia*. Hagerstown, Md.: Review and Herald, 2014.

Holifield, E. Brooks. *Theology in America: Christian Thought from the Age of the Puritans to the Civil War*. New Haven, Conn.: Yale University Press, 2003.

Johnston, Robert M. "The Case for a Balanced Hermeneutic." *Ministry: International Journal for Pastors* 72, no. 3 (March 1999): 11–12.

Kling, David. "The Second Great Awakening." In McClymond, *Religious Revivals in America*, 384–89.

Knight, George R. *Millennial Fever and the End of the World: A Study of Millerite Adventism*. Nampa, Idaho: Pacific Press Publishing Association, 1993.

——. *A Search for Identity: The Development of Seventh-day Adventist Beliefs*. Hagerstown, Md.: Review and Herald, 2000.

Land, Gary, ed. *Adventism in America: A History.* Rev. ed. Berrien Springs, Mich.: Andrews University Press, 1998.

———. *Historical Dictionary of the Seventh-day Adventists.* Lanham, Md.: Scarecrow Press, 2005.

London, Samuel G., Jr. *Seventh-day Adventists and the Civil Rights Movement.* Jackson: University of Mississippi Press, 2009.

Marsden, George. *Fundamentalism and American Culture.* 2nd ed. New York: Oxford University Press, 2006.

Martin, Walter, and Donald Barnhouse. *The Truth about Seventh-day Adventism.* White Fish, Mont.: Literary Licensing, LLC, 2013.

McClymond, Michael, ed. *Encyclopedia of Religious Revivals in America.* Westport, Conn.: Greenwood Press, 2007.

McKim, Donald K., ed. *Historical Handbook of Major Biblical Interpreters.* Downers Grove, Ill.: InterVarsity Press, 1998.

Miller, Nicholas. "Alongside Foundationalism: Adventism's Alternate Protestant Philosophical Path." *Andrews Univ. Seminary Studies* 53, no. 1 (2015): 37–54.

Miller, William. *Apology and Defence.* Boston, Mass.: Joshua V. Himes, 1845.

Moon, Jerry. "Seventh-day Adventists." In McClymond, *Religious Revivals in America,* 391–92.

Neufeld, Don F., ed. *Seventh-day Adventist Encyclopedia.* Washington, D.C.: Review & Herald, 1966.

Noll, Mark. "Common Sense Traditions and American Evangelical Thought." *American Quarterly* 37, no. 2 (Summer 1985): 220–22.

———. *In the Beginning Was the Word.* New York: Oxford University Press, 2015.

Numbers, Ronald. *Prophetess of Health: A Study of Ellen G. White.* New York: Harper and Row, 1976.

Pöhler, Rolf J. *Continuity and Change in Adventist Teaching: A Case Study in Doctrinal Development.* Frankfurt am Main: Lang, 2000.

Satta, Ronald F. *The Sacred Text: Biblical Authority in Nineteenth-Century America.* Eugene, Ore.: Pickwick, 2007.

Stowe, C. E. *Origin and History of the Books of the Bible.* Hartford, Conn.: Hartford Pub. Co., 1867.

Timm, Alberto R. "A History of Seventh-day Adventist Views on Biblical and Prophetic Inspiration (1844-2000)." *Journal of the Adventist Theological Society* 10, nos. 1-2 (1999): 486–542.

Torrey, R. A., and A. C. Dixon, eds. *The Fundamentals.* 4 vols. (1910-1915). Repr. Grand Rapids, Mich.: Baker Books, 2008.

Vollaro, Daniel R. "Lincoln, Stowe, and the 'Little Woman/Great War' Story: The Making, and Breaking, of a Great American Anecdote." *Journal of the Abraham Lincoln Association* 30, no. 1 (Winter 2009): 18–34.

White, Ellen. *Testimonies for the Church.* Vol. 1 (1859). Repr. Mountain View, Calif.: Pacific Press Publishing, 1948.

CHAPTER 41

....

THE BIBLE AND JEHOVAH'S WITNESSES

....

MICHAEL J. GILMOUR

THE Watch Tower Bible and Tract Society, or the Jehovah's Witnesses, is a millenarian religion within the Christian tradition tracing its origins back to late nineteenth-century America and the teachings of Charles Taze Russell (1852–1916). By millenarian in this context, I mean a religious movement that fixates on end-times themes including the judgment of the wicked and the vindication of the righteous, and I locate the group within the Christian tradition only in the loosest sense. In their own teachings, they are unambiguous about their independence from all other faiths: "We are an international organization unaffiliated with other religious groups."[1] Jehovah's Witnesses stand apart from other Christian movements in many ways but three in particular deserve notice.

First, Russell and a number of writers informing his thought believed most churches throughout history to be erroneous on matters of doctrine.[2] For this reason, and because they reject the historical creeds and refuse to entertain any ecumenical dialogue, Watch Tower interpretation of the Bible is idiosyncratic in many respects. They are a reform movement, but they do not seek to work inside the Christian tradition to obtain their reformation. Theirs is a complete break with other religionists reading the Old and New Testaments.

Second, a strong fixation on eschatological cataclysm characterizes the movement. There is a sustained energy and fervency to Jehovah's Witnesses' proselytizing efforts and a tendency to underscore "last days" themes, including a penchant for assigning dates to looming apocalyptic events. This sets Watch Tower biblical interpretation apart from most Bible-reading communities, with only rare equivalents in other contemporary Christian movements.

Third, the Watch Tower Bible and Tract Society is "top down" and hierarchical with respect to organizational and doctrinal matters. Bible reading and exegesis for Jehovah's Witnesses is not a matter of independent study by individuals or local communities gathered in neighborhood Kingdom Halls (their local places of worship). It involves, rather, engagement with scripture guided by the Society's Brooklyn-based Governing Body through their prolific publishing efforts, which includes numerous books, pamphlets, web-based articles (see http://www.jw.org), and widely distributed magazines such as *Awake!* and *The Watchtower*.

For these and other reasons, and given that the organization frequently defines itself over and against traditional Christianity, comparisons of Jehovah's Witnesses with other Bible-based belief systems potentially mislead. There are overlaps with the beliefs of mainstream, traditional Christianity to be sure—God as creator, humanity's sinfulness, the writings of the prophets and apostles as inspired scripture, the resurrection of Jesus, a coming judgment—but in many other respects their beliefs and praxis are quite distinct from Christianity as defined by the historic creeds and practiced by contemporary churches.

The focus of this chapter is the place of the Bible in the belief system and worldview of the Watch Tower Bible and Tract Society. A few pages is hardly space enough to do justice to more than a century of doctrinal developments, so I gravitate toward a few examples of where and how Jehovah's Witnesses differ from historic, traditional Christianity in their understandings of the Bible. Before proceeding further, however, a brief caveat is in order.

JEHOVAH'S WITNESSES AND SCHOLARSHIP

There is a lot of excellent scholarly work discussing the Jehovah's Witnesses from a range of disciplinary perspectives. For instance, historians naturally discuss the origins of the movement in the context of nineteenth-century American millenarianism, and legal specialists examine the implications of their disengagement from politics and refusal to serve in the military in terms of constitutional concerns centered on freedom of religious expression.[3] Scholars interested in medical practice and ethics have focused on the Witnesses' refusal to accept blood transfusions (especially when parents make decisions about the care of children), and sociologists study the makeup of the community and its behaviors within the societies where they congregate and proselytize.[4] But when it comes to religious studies, and more specifically, biblical and theological studies, there is a conspicuous dearth of scholarly treatment.

Studies in comparative religion necessarily include some treatment of the movement.[5] It is not large compared to the major world religions (according to their own numbers, there are 8,220,105 Jehovah's Witnesses worldwide[6]). That said, they are well established in many countries and language groups, have an enormous publishing operation, a robust Internet presence, and an aggressive proselytizing culture that means their distinctive teachings circulate widely and persistently. Standard textbooks and encyclopedias usually include at least a cursory overview.[7]

Most publications that do analyze their beliefs tend to be polemical and produced by ex-members or those wanting to convert Witnesses to other faith traditions (often Christian fundamentalism). There seems to be no end of such books, challenging the organization's interpretations and often ridiculing parts of the movement's story, particularly their date-specific eschatological speculations. The term "cult" often appears in such literature with all the negative baggage that term carries.[8]

With respect to scholarly research into the Jehovah's Witnesses' reading of the Bible, there is relatively little dispassionate enquiry. I suspect there are at least three reasons for this. First, Jehovah's Witnesses rarely engage non-member biblical scholarship. There is no formal representation of the group within the Society of Biblical Literature (SBL) or the

American Academy of Religion (AAR), or within its affiliates. These are the largest professional societies of biblical and religious studies in the world, and the great majority of biblically based religious traditions participate in SBL or AAR, so the non-participation of Jehovah's Witnesses is conspicuous. For the most part, the only time Jehovah's Witnesses discuss the Bible with non-members is in the context of their proselytizing efforts.

Second, publications produced by the Watch Tower reveal a deep suspicion of, and often open hostility toward, biblical scholarship outside the organization. They occasionally cite non-*Watchtower* scholarly works in support of arguments, though such choices for outside support show a clear preference for older publications. In general, Jehovah's Witnesses are dismissive and condemning of outside scholarship, often calling it the work of "worldly commentators."[9]

Finally, there is the challenge of examining the ideas of a group that is somewhat closed and secretive. Their publications, including their *New World Translation of the Holy Scriptures*, do not identify the authors and translators involved, a practice started in 1942.[10] A consequence of this anonymity is that any evaluative remarks by reviewers potentially come across as a criticism of the entire religion. This presents a dilemma for modern academic study because conventionally responding to, and dialoguing with, a signed paper or book amounts to a conversation with the author or authors. When the entire organization or at least its leadership is the *de facto* "author" of the magazine, pamphlet, book, or Bible translation in question, the perception of religious intolerance is inevitably a risk.

A quick note about nomenclature is also in order. Although most know the religious tradition discussed here by the name Jehovah's Witnesses, the legal names of the organization are confusing. Early on, as the movement grew, there was a need to formalize the association of like-minded congregations. The Watch Tower Bible and Tract Society of Pennsylvania (incorporated 1884) "long remained the primary publishing and administrative organization of the men who oversaw the affairs of the Bible Student–Jehovah's Witnesses." In 1939, The Watchtower Bible and Tract Society of New York, Incorporated (note the spelling variation) "became the primary owner of Witness properties in the United States and was used to direct the activities of Jehovah's Witnesses throughout the world."[11] For convenience, as this is not an attempt to tell the full story of the movement but rather a consideration of their use of the Bible, I usually use various terms interchangeably, without attempts to distinguish different periods of the group's evolution over the last century and a half. These include Jehovah's Witnesses, the Watch Tower Bible and Tract Society, the Watch Tower, the Bible Student movement, the movement, or the organization. Furthermore, my approach is largely synchronic, focusing on teachings reflected in recent publications, as opposed to a more diachronic approach that would trace the development of their ideas over the decades.[12]

THE BIBLE AND THE JEHOVAH'S WITNESSES

As noted, a comprehensive introduction to this topic is not possible in such a brief chapter, so what follows are a few specific illustrations of the Watch Tower Bible and Tract Society's interpretation of the Bible along with general observations about tendencies within their exegesis. As much as possible I draw on material published by the organization and available at https://www.jw.org. Any publications listed without page numbers come from that website.

Finding Its Story within Biblical Literature: The Appeal to Analogy and Prophecy

Perhaps the best place to begin is with a deeply entrenched assumption that gives a distinctive shape to most biblical interpretation by the Watch Tower Bible and Tract Society. Jehovah's Witnesses are adamant that they alone possess the truth. They believe that God speaks directly to them through scripture as interpreted by the organization's theocratic hierarchy. All other religions, including Jewish and Christian traditions relying on the Old and New Testaments, misunderstand or reject Jehovah's message for the world. Although its history is relatively short, with 1879—the year Russell first published *Zion's Watch Tower and Herald of Christ's Presence*, later renamed *The Watchtower*—usually identified as its beginning, the Bible Student movement of the late nineteenth century (as it was then called) and its subsequent growth represents the fruition, a latter-day response, to revelation signaling the approaching end of Jehovah's work in the world.

The prophets themselves anticipate the events culminating in the Bible Student movement and the teachings of its founding members, and here we find a key hermeneutical lens employed often by Jehovah's Witnesses. We see it in two ways. First, if Jehovah's faithful prophets and apostles embody appropriate responses to divine revelation and obedience within a sinful world, it follows that their true heirs ought to resemble them in various respects. For this reason, we find numerous appeals to analogy within the Society's publications. Jeremiah was a faithful prophet called by Jehovah (Jer. 1:7) who suffered because of obedience to the divine mandate, so naturally the call and experiences of Jehovah's faithful representatives in the modern world resemble Jeremiah's life experience. As one study of this prophet succinctly puts it: "There are many parallels between Jeremiah's assignment and the public ministry of Jehovah's Witnesses today. Like him, you serve the true God during a time of judgment."[13]

Presumably, the analogy reinforces a sense of identity among Witnesses, fostering a self-understanding that has them part of a faithful remnant reaching back to antiquity. Comments about Jeremiah's faithful scribe Baruch provide another such occasion connecting past and present:

> If we were to cultivate a strong attachment to material things, it could be hard for us to apply Jesus' words. But do not forget—Baruch took to heart God's warning and stayed alive as a result. Consider the situation of the brothers in Romania during the Communist regime. While raiding the homes of Witnesses, government agents sometimes seized personal belongings . . . still, they kept their integrity to Jehovah.[14]

Such easy linkages between Bible stories and present-day experience, the constant paralleling of Witnesses with the ancients, serve a pedagogical end. Most if not all Watch Tower publications include leading questions that invite readers to draw out life lessons from biblical stories: "How did Jehovah kindly correct Baruch's inclination to seek 'great things'? Why do you feel that accepting divine correction is wise?"[15]

Along with constant appeal to analogy, the second way the Bible anticipates and links directly to Jehovah's Witnesses is through passages referring specifically to events in the movement's history. This phenomenon started early with some Bible Students concluding Charles Taze Russell was the "discreet slave whom his master appointed over his domestics, to give them their food at the proper time," mentioned by Jesus in Matthew 24:45. This reading changed in later years. They now understand Jesus's words to indicate the 144,000, a group sometimes referred to as the slave class (Rev. 7:4–8, 14:1–3). As one publication puts it, the discreet slave is "a small group of anointed brothers who are directly involved in preparing and dispensing spiritual food during Christ's presence," which began, according to Watch Tower chronology, in 1914. Soon after that, in 1919, "Jesus selected capable anointed brothers to be his faithful and discreet slave," individuals that are part of the 144,000 faithful servants. "In keeping with Jesus' pattern of feeding many through the hands of a few," the explanation continues, "that slave is made up of a small group of anointed brothers who are directly involved in preparing and dispensing spiritual food during Christ's presence. Throughout the last days, the anointed brothers who make up the faithful slave have served together at [the Brooklyn] headquarters."[16]

Another interesting example of reading the movement's activities and history into the pages of scripture is their interpretation of the trumpet blasts described in Revelation 8:1–9 and 11:15–19. Their official commentary of John's apocalypse aligns these passages with a series of Bible Student conventions held between 1922 and 1928: "When the sounding of the seven trumpets got under way in 1922, the Bible Students' convention at Cedar Point, Ohio, featured a talk by the president of the Watch Tower Society, J. F. Rutherford.... The trumpet blast of the seventh angel was reflected in highlights of the Bible Students' convention in Detroit, Michigan, July 30–August 6, 1928."[17]

Visual Aids and Biblical Interpretation

Most publications from the Watch Tower Bible and Tract Society are readily recognizable by their use of pictures, something more important for understanding their engagement with the Bible than may first appear. On occasion, there are photographs of members from bygone days, but more often than not, publications include simple, cartoon-like (and rather unattractive) drawings that represent biblical characters and scenes, or illustrate various lessons taken from them.[18] These visuals inevitably mediate the "experience" of the Bible for Jehovah's Witnesses and reinforce certain values and interpretations. For instance, Jehovah's Witnesses believe the world to be evil and under the rule of Satan, so many of these pictures serve to underline this assumption. Representations of nonbelievers tend to involve markers of worldliness, such as alcohol, cigarettes, violence, and promiscuous behavior. If Witnesses appear in such scenes, they are objects of ridicule because they choose not to participate in sinful activities.

These published drawings also reinforce the urgency to respond to the Gospel and remain faithful to it, so they are important for the organization's proselytizing efforts and self-regulation. Pictures of cemeteries, war, poverty, environmental disasters, and the like remind readers that humanity is in desperate straits, unable to deliver itself from cataclysm, and in need of divine rescue.

The drawings demarcate Jehovah's Witnesses from other belief systems as well. Religious leaders in ecclesial regalia or other markings of the world's diverse religions serve as indicators of demonic activity. They also highlight particular interpretive emphases that distinguish Jehovah's Witnesses from other parts of Christendom. Pictures of Jesus's crucifixion, for instance, always show him on a single post or stake, reinforcing their claim that the Greek word *stauros* in the New Testament does not indicate two pieces of crossed wood but rather an upright post. This curious detail arises from concern that the cross is an idolatrous symbol of pagan origin, and that use of it by Christians is a late development, originating in the days of Constantine. In support, they observe that the Greek word *xylon* (stick, timber, tree) also appears in some passages with reference to Jesus's execution (e.g., Acts 5:30, 10:39, 13:29; Gal. 3:13; 1 Pet. 2:24), a word indicating a single piece of wood.[19]

This seemingly minor detail about the appearance of the device used by Jesus's Roman executors deserves further comment because their rejection and condemnation of Christianity's ubiquitous cross, combined with pictorial depictions of the single post in their literature, clearly demarcates Jehovah's Witnesses from others in rather striking fashion. Disdain for the cross symbol emerged in the 1930s. Before that, Bible Students wore a badge with a cross in a crown, and the same symbol appeared on the front cover of some Watch Tower publications. This practice changed in 1936, however, when "it was pointed out that the evidence indicates that Christ died on a stake, not a two-beamed cross."[20] Furthermore, any executed man "hung... upon a stake" is "accursed of God" (Deut. 21:22–23), a passage Paul cites with reference to Christ (Gal. 3:13). Since this is the case, "it would not be proper for Christians to decorate their homes with images of Christ on a cross."[21]

The Jehovah's Witnesses' unique *New World Translation* version of the Bible reflects this position by avoiding the term "cross":

> Then Jesus said to his disciples: "If anyone wants to come after me, let him disown himself and pick up his torture stake and keep following me." (Matt. 16:24)

And again:

> So they took charge of Jesus. Bearing the torture stake for himself, he went out to the so-called Skull Place.... There they nailed him to the stake. (John 19:17–18)

Regardless of the Jehovah's Witnesses' assertion in these passages that there is "no evidence that the Greek word meant a cross,"[22] the word "torture" in these and other passages of their *New World Translation* has no basis in the Greek text. This avoidance of the word "cross" and disdain for iconography using that symbol, serve to differentiate Jehovah's Witnesses from Christian groups that do, particularly Roman Catholics.

An Illustration of Watch Tower Society Interpretation: The 144,000 of Revelation

Watch Tower Society exegesis is at times literal, at times allegorical, but it always appeals to a complex cross-referencing system. The Society makes this hermeneutical practice clear when it states: "If the surrounding verses do not make the meaning of a particular statement clear, compare that statement with others in the Bible that discuss the same subject. In this way, we let the Bible, not personal opinion, guide our thinking."[23] The Jehovah's Witnesses' interpretation, thus, has a certain leveling quality. It pays little attention to the distinctive message of, say, Matthew in contrast to Mark. All scripture speaks with one voice and the particular nuances of individual authors or texts are a nonissue. To read one writer is to read them all. Interpretation of the Bible means fitting the individual puzzle pieces together so the larger picture emerges. The stress is always on the larger picture, not the smaller pieces.

The Jehovah's Witnesses' interpretation of Revelation 7 and 14 illustrates some of these tendencies. Here one finds some of the most fascinating teachings of the movement and a window into the Witnesses' understanding of the true community of faith. Their conclusions are so unlike other interpretations of these chapters that a closer look is rewarding.

(a) As is often the way with Watch Tower Bible teaching, interpretation of one passage begins with another. Two important remarks by Jesus are critical to an understanding of the 144,000 mentioned in the Book of Revelation. The first is Luke 12:32 and specifically, the identity of those he addresses: "Have no fear, *little flock*, for your Father has approved of giving you the Kingdom" (italics added). The second is John 14:2 concerning Jesus's promise concerning his Father's house: "I am going my way to prepare a place for you." There is, argues the Watch Tower, a small group, a little flock distinct from the larger community of those following Jesus. The disciples are among them. It is this "little flock," a select few, that comprises the 144,000 mentioned in the Book of Revelation.

The 144,000 who have the seal of God on their foreheads mentioned in Revelation 7 and 14 are "faithful followers of Jesus Christ specially chosen to rule in heaven with him."[24] The number is literal, not symbolic, and refers to an "actual heavenly government with a King—Jesus Christ—and 144,000 corulers."[25] Elsewhere the literature refers to them as "underpriests" and "the Israel of God."[26] Paul and Timothy are among this select group: "if we go on enduring, we will also rule together as kings; if we deny, he will also deny us" (2 Tim. 2:12; Rev. 5:10).

(b) The selection of the 144,000, a number that includes Jesus's faithful apostles, began at Pentecost and continues through to the present. Speculation about when the gathering of the full number is to be completed is an ongoing question among Witnesses, with views changing over the decades. Russell taught the gathering ended in 1881 and later President Joseph. F. Rutherford identified 1935 as the critical date.[27] Subsequent publications indicate the number of chosen ones remains incomplete: "Those few remaining ones of the 144,000 who die in our day are instantly resurrected to life in heaven."[28] However, 1935 remains significant in relation to the 144,000 because since that year, "a growing great crowd of other sheep has heard their triumphant song and been moved to join with them in publicizing God's Kingdom." More specifically, "at a historic convention of Jehovah's Witnesses . . . emphasis was shifted to the ingathering of a great crowd with earthly life prospects."[29] Here we see a distinction among different classes of Jehovah's faithful witnesses; while the vast majority awaits resurrection to an earthly paradise, only a comparative few await a heavenly one.

652   MICHAEL J. GILMOUR

(c) The calculation of important dates based on biblical numbers is a long-standing tradition among Jehovah's Witnesses. A number of claims regarding Jehovah's work in
the world attached to specific years illustrate the presupposition that the Bible is a
book of hidden, but ultimately, decipherable meanings. These calculations are also
pertinent to an understanding of the 144,000 because they are to be co-rulers with
Christ in the anticipated new world. If scripture reveals the timing of the latter, it
does also for the gathering of the former.

The year 1914 is particularly important in Jehovah's Witnesses' eschatology. Their arguments
about its significance stem from the meaning of Jesus's words in Luke 21:24: "Jerusalem
will be trampled on by the nations until the appointed times of the nations are fulfilled." In
short, this verse indicates the time between the overthrow of the house of David and the
coming of Jesus as King in 1914, a period of 2,520 years.[30]

Although Charles Taze Russell maintained 1914 would be the end of the present world,
later Society publications necessarily backed away from that interpretation to one a little
more defensible, namely that the year marked the beginning of the last days.[31] The logic
behind setting dates based on biblical writings is problematic for many reasons, but the
calculations leading to 1914 as either the date for the end of the present world or the beginning of the last days rests on the (highly contentious) claim that the Babylonians under
Nebuchadnezzar destroyed Jerusalem in 607 B.C.E. This date appears constantly in Watch
Tower literature,[32] including the 2013 revision of *The New World Translation*.[33] Much rests on
assigning the fall of the city to this date:

> From the mid-1870's, Jehovah's people had been anticipating that catastrophic events would
> start in 1914 and would mark the end of the Gentile Times. This is the period of 'seven times'
> (2,520 years) running from the overthrow of the Davidic kingdom in Jerusalem in 607 B.C.E.
> to Jesus' enthronement in heavenly Jerusalem in 1914 C.E.[34]

In 1914, God's heavenly kingdom commenced, with Christ established as King with his
co-rulers at his side (Rev. 14:1, 4). John's vision of the birth of a male child in Revelation
12 indicates "the birth of God's Kingdom in 1914." The removal of Satan from heaven (Rev.
12:9) accounts for the horrendous violence of that time (i.e., the outbreak of World War I)
because Satan's "ouster" from heaven means "woe for the literal earth."[35]

(d) Somewhat unexpectedly for those not familiar with the Jehovah's Witnesses' worship life, the interpretation of Revelation 7 and 14 and the image of the 144,000 have
implications for the practice of the Lord's Supper. Jesus refers to the bread as his body
and the wine as "my blood of the covenant, which is to be poured out in behalf of
many for forgiveness of sins" (Matt. 26:26–28). This ritual of wine makes it possible
to be clean in the eyes of God and enter the new covenant with Jehovah (Heb. 9:14;
10:16–17). But it is not for everyone: "This covenant, or contract, makes it possible for
144,000 faithful Christians to go to heaven." Only those in the new covenant, "that
is, those who have the hope of going to heaven—should partake of the bread and
the wine." This is an interesting, almost mystical way of thinking about the sacred
meal because the Jehovah's Witnesses maintain, "God's holy spirit convinces such
ones that they have been selected to be heavenly kings."[36] When the faithful gather

at Kingdom Halls once a year to celebrate the Lord's Evening Meal (as they call it), most if not all are there only as "respectful observers," not partakers, as "only a few thousand worldwide profess to have the heavenly hope."[37]

The Bible and the Jehovah's Witnesses in Contemporary Society

The Bible is the word of God for Jehovah's Witnesses, so naturally it serves as the basis for questions of ethics and expressions of piety. While the previous section identifies a few ways their distinctive theological and doctrinal conclusions employ scripture, this section considers ways the interpretation of certain passages shapes the community's interactions with the outside world. In a number of ways, these interpretations differ sharply from those of other Christian groups that read the same texts. The Jehovah's Witnesses thus use their scriptural interpretations to separate themselves from those they consider to be of Babylon and the harlot of Revelation.

Certain beliefs result in uneasy relationships between individual adherents and the wider, non-Watch Tower community. The historian of religion Joseph Zygmunt reflects on their determination to maintain a polarity between themselves and the world, and the organization's practice of cultivating various "marks of distinctiveness, to put greater symbolic distance between itself and the world."[38] The interpretation of the Bible is simply one way they maintain their separation from society. There are numerous examples of Watch Tower biblical interpretations that have repercussions for the movement's interactions with non-Witnesses.

Witnesses do not recognize the Christian Calendar. They do not mark Christmas because the early church did not do so, the exact date of Jesus's birth is unknown, and there was a pagan Roman festival associated with December 25. Similar reasoning applies to Easter ("It is rooted in pagan worship"), New Year's celebrations, and Halloween.[39] They do not celebrate birthdays either.[40]

The organization's views on the sacredness of blood and their extension of prohibitions about consuming it (Gen. 9:3–4; Lev. 17:13–14; Acts 15:28–29, 21:25) to blood transfusions is highly contentious. This position often pushes the limits of religious freedom in certain jurisdictions, especially when children are involved. That said, despite repeated insistence on the importance of this issue, and frequent claims that "faithful servants of God firmly resolve to follow his direction regarding blood [and] will not eat it in any form,"[41] there is no expectation that Witnesses be vegan. Consequently, the prohibition against the consumption of blood sometimes involves ambiguities in practice.[42]

Jehovah's Witnesses view the state and patriotism with great disdain. Their theology identifies governments as instruments of the Devil. They refuse to salute the flag, sing national anthems, or participate in the military. Watch Tower exegesis reinforces this anti-state bias. This is particularly explicit in the oft-repeated claim that the beast with ten horns in the Book of Revelation (13:1, 17:3, 5, 11) is the United Nations.[43] The reading of Revelation 17:8 ("The wild beast that you saw was, but is not, and yet is about to ascend out of the abyss, and it is to go off into destruction") illustrates how Watch Tower interpretation allows for literal, specific, and identifiable fulfillments of the language of the apostles and prophets. Here, the beast that "was" refers to the League of Nations (established 1920), a union that dissolved during World War II. The beast ascending out of the abyss indicates a new satanic organization: "On June 26, 1945, with noisy fanfare in San Francisco, U.S.A., 50 nations voted to accept the Charter of the United Nations organization.... The UN, then, is actually a revival of the scarlet-colored wild beast."[44]

THE NEW WORLD TRANSLATION

As the organization's very name suggests, scripture is central to the activities of the Watch Tower Bible and Tract Society. Jehovah's Witnesses also recognize proclamation of the Gospel and proselytizing as their raison d'être: "Perhaps nothing distinguishes us as much as our extensive preaching work—from house to house, in public places, and wherever people are found."[45] Following from these two emphases, Jehovah's Witnesses place high value on publishing Bibles and printing literature explaining God's message to the world. The official website and numerous publications frequently highlight the numbers of magazines and other items produced and distributed, as an evidence of the organization's faithfulness in fulfilling the Great Commission.

Early on, the emphasis was on publishing and distributing Bibles as opposed to printing and binding them. They used many translations, "working out specifications, providing valuable supplementary features," and then arranging with commercial firms to produce the books.[46] In 1926, they began printing and binding their own materials in Brooklyn, New York.

Whereas the earliest decades of the movement's history focused on distributing the Bible, there was a growing awareness of the need to circulate a correct Bible. Suspicions of corruption in the text and the influence of paganism on Christianity (like the use of the terms "Trinity" and "cross") are frequent themes in their literature, and this is no less true for the history of Bible translation as they see it. By the mid-twentieth century, the need for a Bible free of theological distortion was a priority:

> Was there really a need for another translation? Already at that time [the 1940s], the complete Bible had been published in 190 languages, and at least part of it had been translated into 928 additional languages and dialects. Jehovah's Witnesses have at various times used most of these translations. But the fact is that most of these were made by clergymen and missionaries of Christendom's religious sects, and to varying degrees their translations were *influenced by the pagan philosophies and unscriptural traditions* that their religious systems had inherited from the past.... Jehovah's Witnesses wanted a translation... not colored by the creeds and traditions of Christendom.[47]

Although they continue to use other versions—the full text of the King James or Authorized Version (1611), the American Standard Version (1901), and the Bible in Living English (1972) are all available on the official website—their concerns resulted in a new, highly distinctive publication.

Jehovah's Witnesses now have their own Bible translation.[48] The full *New World Translation of the Holy Scriptures* first appeared in English in 1961 and the latest edition in 2013.[49] The Appendix A1 in the *New World Translation* outlines some of its general characteristics, although it does not mention a few emendations introduced to the most recent edition. For instance, the *New World Translation* omits the shorter and longer endings of the Gospel of Mark (16:9–20), whereas these verses appeared in previous *New World Translation* editions with notes explaining variants in the manuscript tradition as is typical of modern English Bibles. Earlier *New World Translation* editions also included the story of the woman caught in adultery (John 7:53–8:11), though relegating the passage to a footnote with an explanation of manuscript discrepancies. The 2013 edition cuts the episode entirely. Such decisions indicate a high degree of confidence on the part of Watch Tower leaders in their ability to reconstruct an authoritative biblical text.

There are frequent criticisms of other Bible translations in Watch Tower publications, as in the oft-repeated concern that modern Bibles "sacrifice faithfulness to God's message in favor of following human traditions . . . by replacing God's personal name, Jehovah, with titles such as Lord or God"[50] This use of the term "Jehovah" in both testaments is perhaps the most striking feature of the *New World Translation*. The convention of using LORD for YHWH in modern English Bibles has its origin with the Masoretes of the sixth through tenth centuries who introduced vowel marks to help preserve pronunciations of the consonantal Hebrew text. To avoid speaking the divine name, they applied the vowels for *adonai* (lord) to the Tetragrammaton. Although the actual pronunciation is uncertain, it is conventional to read and spell the Tetragrammaton with the vowels of *adonai* as Yahweh, or, as Witnesses prefer, Jehovah. The use of this spelling and pronunciation in the New Testament (often rendering the Greek word *kurios*, lord, as Jehovah) is unusual and reflects foundational beliefs.

Jehovah's Witnesses are not Trinitarian and there are occasions when this theological presupposition determines their translation decisions. Acts 7:59–60 is a case in point:

> As they were stoning Stephen, he made this appeal: "Lord [*Kurie*] Jesus, receive my spirit." Then, kneeling down, he cried out with a strong voice: "Jehovah [*Kurie*], do not charge this sin against them."

The translators assume these two uses of *kurios* (lord) in close proximity represent two different entities, the first Jesus and the second Jehovah. The first vocative unambiguously refers to Jesus because that name appears alongside it, but why translate the second *Kurie* as "Jehovah" instead of Lord?

A note at this second *Kurie* in the 2013 edition of *The New World Translation* (but not the 1984 edition) directs readers to the Appendix titled, "The Divine Name in the Christian Greek Scriptures."[51] Here readers find the suggestion that "Bible scholars" and the "translators" of other versions of the Bible misunderstand "the original Greek manuscripts" of the New Testament. The misunderstanding in question concerns the history behind extant manuscripts of the New Testament. Earlier manuscripts, the Appendix claims, used the name Jehovah, not *kurios* (lord). Said differently, the appearance of the second *Kurie* in the passage above is a corruption of the (now lost) original form of the text. The *New World Translation* is thus a corrective restoration reflecting the biblical text's original wording.

> Bible scholars acknowledge that God's personal name, as represented by the Tetragrammaton . . . appears almost 7,000 times in the original text of the Hebrew Scriptures [i.e., the Old Testament]. However, many feel that it did not appear in the original text of the Christian Greek Scriptures. For this reason, most modern English Bibles do not use the name Jehovah when translating the so-called New Testament.

The translators of the *New World Translation*, by contrast, introduce the term "Jehovah" 237 times to the New Testament on the assumption the Tetragrammaton "did appear in the original Greek manuscripts," and that later copyists—those responsible for the extant manuscripts on which all translations depend—substituted "Lord" for Yahweh/Jehovah.[52] Luke's language in Acts 7:60 is one such example.

Appealing to an "original" manuscript that no longer exists, of course, is not likely to convince many. It seems likely that changing *kurios* to Jehovah in Acts 7:60 helps safeguard against deifying Jesus by making it clear that Stephen is not praying to Jesus alone. In Watch Tower theology, Jesus is not divine, nor is the Holy Spirit. The non-Trinitarian theology of Jehovah's Witnesses informs the language of the *New World Translation* in various other passages as well.

Watch Tower publications frequently point out that the word "Trinity" does not appear in the Bible and that it is, in fact, a term that only appears later in the Christian Church's (by then corrupted) history. Jehovah's Witnesses maintain Jesus is a created being and so the translation reflects this in the much-discussed rendering of the anarthrous *theos* of John 1:1 ("the Word was with God, and the Word was *a god*," italics added) and the presentation of Colossians 1:16–20:

> by means of him all [other] things were created in the heavens and upon the earth. . . . All [other] things have been created through him and for him. Also, he is before all [other] things and by means of him all [other] things were made to exist . . . through him to reconcile again to himself all [other] things by making peace through the blood.[53]

I cite the latter from the 1984 edition of the *New World Translation*, which includes the brackets because there is no equivalent to "other" in the Greek text. It is interesting to find the 2013 revision omits these brackets entirely in these verses. Readers simply see "all other things," the effect of which is to reinforce the view that Jesus is simply one of many things God created.

Or consider the translation of Psalm 2:12, another instance of this preference for language that resists Trinitarian interpretation:

> Kiss the son, that He may not become incensed (Ps. 2:12a; *New World Translation*, 1984)
> Honor the son, or God will become indignant (Ps. 2:12a; *New World Translation*, 2013)

Translators of the newer version incorporate here a small change in order to prevent readers from making a theological misstep by confusing the created son with the divine God.[54] This care to avoid possible Trinitarian confusions shows up in various places. Another example is 1 Peter 1:11 where the phrase "spirit of Christ" in the 1984 edition becomes simply "spirit" in the 2013 edition.

CONCLUSION

Historian M. James Penton observes that "dealing with the doctrinal concepts of Jehovah's Witnesses is a most difficult matter, even for one thoroughly familiar with them. The Witnesses have no systematic theologians and systematic theology." Furthermore, "since their doctrines are constantly in flux, it is really impossible to discuss Witness theology in the same way that one can discuss the more stable doctrinal systems of the great churches."[55] This presents considerable challenges for outsiders wanting to explore Jehovah's Witnesses' interpretations of the Bible. Yet, because the Watchtower remains a growing part of the religious fabric of many societies across the world, their continuous engagement with biblical literature merits careful attention.

NOTES

1. Watchtower Bible and Tract Society of New York, "What Sort of People Are Jehovah's Witnesses?," *The Watchtower: Announcing Jehovah's Kingdom*, September 1, 2015, 4. Similar assertions are commonplace in the organization's writings.
2. Self-definition in the literature often stresses this break with the history of Christianity and the recovery of truth by Jehovah's Witnesses. As one pamphlet puts it, "in the 1870's a small group of Bible students began rediscovering long-lost Bible truths." Watch Tower Bible and Tract Society of Pennsylvania, "Good News from God!" (Brooklyn, N.Y.: Watchtower Bible and Tract Society of New York, 2012), 29.
3. Of course, the nature of the debates vary depending on the jurisdiction. On this issue, with reference to the United States, see, e.g., David R. Manwaring, *Render unto Caesar: The Flag Salute Controversy* (Chicago: University of Chicago Press, 1962); and Merlin Owen Newton, *Armed with the Constitution: Jehovah's Witnesses in Alabama and the U.S. Supreme Court, 1939-1946* (Tuscaloosa: University of Alabama Press, 1995). For discussion of legal challenges in the Canadian context, see, e.g., William Kaplan, *State and Salvation: The Jehovah's Witnesses and Their Fight for Civil Rights* (Toronto: University of Toronto Press, 1989); M. James Penton, *Jehovah's Witnesses in Canada: Champions of Freedom of Speech and Worship* (Toronto: Macmillan, 1976); and Gary Botting, *Fundamental Freedoms and Jehovah's Witnesses* (Calgary: University of Calgary Press, 1993).
4. See, for instance, Alan Aldridge, *Religion in the Contemporary World: A Sociological Introduction* (Cambridge: Polity, 2013); and Andrew Holden, *Jehovah's Witnesses: Portrait of a Contemporary Religious Movement* (London: Routledge, 2002).
5. E.g., Catherine L. Albanese, *America: Religions and Religion*, 5th ed. (Boston: Wadsworth, 2013). See esp. ch. 7, "Visions of Paradise Planted: Nineteenth-Century New Religions."
6. This figure comes from the Watch Tower Bible and Tract Society's official website, https://www.jw.org. See "Fast Facts—Worldwide," under the tab "About," https://www.jw.org/en/jehovahs-witnesses.
7. E.g., M. James Penton, with Michael J. Gilmour, "Christianity: Jehovah's Witnesses," in *Worldmark Encyclopedia of Religious Practices*, vol. 1: *Religions and Denominations*, 2nd ed., edited by Thomas Riggs (Detroit, Mich.: Gale, 2014), 248-55.
8. A well-known example is Walter R. Martin's *The Kingdom of the Cults*, which first appeared in 1965. See the revised, updated, and expanded edition, edited by Ravi Zacharias (Bloomington, Ind.: Bethany House, 2003).
9. For use of this term, see, e.g., Watch Tower Bible and Tract Society of Pennsylvania, *Revelation: Its Grand Climax at Hand!* (Brooklyn, N.Y.: Watchtower Bible and Tract Society of New York, 1988), 120.
10. On this, see M. James Penton, *Apocalypse Delayed: The Story of Jehovah's Witnesses*, 3rd ed. (Toronto: University of Toronto Press, 2015), 106.

11. Penton, *Apocalypse Delayed*, xix. See also page 8. The term "Bible Students" described adherents of the movement prior to July 26, 1931. On that date, a resolution passed at a convention in Columbus, Ohio, to adopt the name Jehovah's Witnesses, a term derived from Isaiah 43:12: "'you are my witnesses,' declares Jehovah, 'and I am God'" (*New World Translation*, 2013 edition—unless otherwise stated, I use this version of the Bible throughout). For the story of the name change, see "This Is Our Spiritual Heritage," in *The Watchtower* (February 15, 2013), 4.

12. With respect to changes in the Jehovah's Witnesses' biblical interpretation and doctrine over time, see Penton, *Apocalypse Delayed*, esp. 233–88.

13. Watch Tower Bible and Tract Society of Pennsylvania, *God's Word for Us through Jeremiah* (Brooklyn, N.Y.: Watchtower Bible and Tract Society of New York, 2010), 191.

14. Watch Tower, *Jeremiah*, 111.

15. Watch Tower, *Jeremiah*, 106.

16. "Who Really Is the Faithful and Discreet Slave?," in *The Watchtower: Announcing Jehovah's Kingdom*, July 15, 2013, 22.

17. Watch Tower, *Revelation*, 172.

18. Watch Tower, *Jeremiah*, 111.

19. For the rationale, see the section "Why True Christians Do Not Use the Cross in Worship," in Watch Tower Bible and Tract Society of Pennsylvania, *What Does the Bible Really Teach?* (Brooklyn, N.Y.: Watchtower Bible and Tract Society of New York, 2014), 204–6.

20. Watch Tower Bible and Tract Society of Pennsylvania, *Jehovah's Witnesses: Proclaimers of God's Kingdom* (Brooklyn, N.Y.: Watchtower Bible and Tract Society of New York, 1993), 200. Photographs of the badge and cover logo appear here as well.

21. Watch Tower, *What Does the Bible Really Teach?*, 205.

22. A claim made in the glossary entry for "Torture stake" in the 2013 edition of *The New World Translation*. Watch Tower Bible and Tract Society of Pennsylvania, *New World Translation of the Holy Scriptures*, revised (Brooklyn, N.Y.: Watchtower Bible and Tract Society of New York, 2013), 1714.

23. "A Key to Understanding the Bible," *Awake!*, November 2012, 28, http://wol.jw.org/en/wol/d/r1/lp-e/102012416.

24. Watch Tower, *What Does the Bible Really Teach?*, 78.

25. "What Do Jehovah's Witnesses Believe?" *Awake!*, August 2010, 8–9, http://wol.jw.org/en/wol/d/r1/lp-e/102010283.

26. E.g., Watch Tower, *Jeremiah*, 181, and "You Will Become 'a Kingdom of Priests,'" in *The Watchtower*, October 15, 2014, 13–17, respectively.

27. See Penton, *Apocalypse Delayed*, 36–37, 141.

28. Watch Tower, *What Does the Bible Really Teach?*, 74.

29. Watch Tower, *Revelation*, 201, 117.

30. For some of the reasoning and strategies involved in their calculations, see, e.g., Watch Tower, *What Does the Bible Really Teach?*, 217.

31. Penton, *Apocalypse Delayed*, 138.

32. The more likely date of the destruction of Jerusalem, according to scholarly consensus, is 587 or 586 B.C.E.

33. See "Chart: Prophets and Kings of Judah and Israel," Appendix 6 in Watch Tower Bible and Tract Society of Pennsylvania, *New World Translation*, 2013.

34. Watch Tower, *Revelation*, 105; cf. 179.

35. Watch Tower, *Revelation*, 180, 183.

36. Watch Tower, *What Does the Bible Really Teach?*, 207.

37. Watch Tower, *What Does the Bible Really Teach?*, 208.

38. Joseph F. Zygmunt, "Jehovah's Witnesses in the U.S.A. 1942–1976," *Social Compass* 24 (1977): 54. As cited in Penton, *Apocalypse Delayed*, 229. For various observations on the function of boundaries for this religion, see too Holden, *Jehovah's Witnesses*, 41, 77–81, 106–12, and throughout.

39. Watch Tower, *What Does the Bible Really Teach?*, 157–58, 223.

40. Four principal concerns result in this position, according to the short entry "Why Don't Jehovah's Witnesses Celebrate Birthdays?," https://www.jw.org/en/jehovahs-witnesses/faq/birthdays. While acknowledging the Bible does not explicitly condemn the practice, the article notes (a) that birthdays have pagan roots with ties to magical practice, and the Bible condemns magic (citing Deut. 18:14 and Gal. 5:19–21 in support); (b) early Christians did not celebrate birthdays; (c) the only commemoration required of Christians is remembrance of Jesus's death; and (d) the Bible never mentions a servant of God celebrating a birthday, though there are two stories of wicked men who do so, and "those events are presented in a bad light" (i.e., Pharaoh's birthday in Gen. 4:20–22, and Herod Antipas's in Mark 6:21–29). See too Watch Tower Bible and Tract Society of Pennsylvania, *Jehovah's Witnesses: Proclaimers*, 199, and Holden, *Jehovah's Witnesses*, 25.

41. Watch Tower, *What Does the Bible Really Teach?*, 131.

42. Penton, "Christianity: Jehovah's Witnesses," 254.

43. E.g., Watch Tower Bible and Tract Society of Pennsylvania, *God's Kingdom Rules!* (Brooklyn, N.Y.: Watchtower Bible and Tract Society of New York, 2014), 223. Despite this association of the United Nations with satanic activities, this same book cites statistics taken from that organization (83).

44. Watch Tower, *Revelation*, 248.

45. Watchtower Bible and Tract Society of New York, "Why Do We Preach?," *The Watchtower: Announcing Jehovah's Kingdom*, September 1, 2015, 7.

46. Watch Tower, *Jehovah's Witnesses: Proclaimers*, 603, 605.

47. Watch Tower, *Jehovah's Witnesses: Proclaimers*, 608–609, italics added.

48. For a helpful introduction to the *New World Translation*, see Penton, *Apocalypse Delayed*, 249–53.

49. Available as a PDF at https://www.jw.org.

50. "Is the *New World Translation* Accurate?" This article appears under Frequently Asked Questions at https://www.jw.org. Cf. various remarks in the appendices of the most recent edition, such as: "Quite a number of Bible translators have taken the unjustifiable liberty of omitting God's name, Jehovah, from modern translations" (Watch Tower Bible and Tract Society of Pennsylvania, *New World Translation*, 1721).

51. "The Divine Name in the Christian Greek Scriptures," Appendix 5 in Watch Tower Bible and Tract Society of Pennsylvania, *New World Translation*, 1736–1743.

52. Watch Tower Bible and Tract Society of Pennsylvania, *New World Translation*, 1736.

53. Watch Tower Bible and Tract Society of Pennsylvania, *New World Translation*, 1984 edition.

54. This remark rests on the following observations. (a) The translators clearly read this passage through a Christological lens, because one of the cross-references provided is Philippians 2:10 ("in the name of Jesus every knee should bend"). Whatever else the verse means, the translators believe "son" indicates or foreshadows Jesus in some sense. (b) The close proximity of the capitalized "He" after "son" in 2:12 (1984 edition) is potentially

confusing. "He" presumably refers back to "Jehovah" in the previous verse, where the poet says, "Serve Jehovah with fear." The 1984 translators understood it this way, which explains their decision to capitalize "He" (i.e., it refers to God). However, might some readers miss this, since the nearest antecedent to "He" is "son"? If so, they put "Jehovah" and "the son"/"He" in parallel, possibly blurring the distinction between them and thus attributing divinity to "the son." (c) Certainly this was not the intent of the 1984 edition and the 2013 revision removes the ambiguity entirely by changing "He" to "God," thus distinguishing clearly the two persons mentioned in Psalm 2:11–12.

55. Penton, *Apocalypse Delayed*, 233; cf. 256.

BIBLIOGRAPHY

Gilmour, Michael J. "An Outsider's Notes on the Jehovah's Witnesses' *Revelation: Its Grand Climax at Hand!*" *Journal of Religion and Society* 8 (2006), http://hdl.handle.net/10504/64551.

Holden, Andrew. *Jehovah's Witnesses: Portrait of a Contemporary Religious Movement.* London: Routledge, 2002.

Penton, M. James. *Apocalypse Delayed: The Story of Jehovah's Witnesses.* 3rd ed. Toronto: University of Toronto Press, 2015.

——, updated and revised by Michael J. Gilmour. "Christianity: Jehovah's Witnesses." In *Worldmark Encyclopedia of Religious Practices*, vol. 1: *Religions and Denominations*, edited by Thomas Riggs, 248–55. Detroit, Mich.: Gale Research, 2014.

Watch Tower Bible and Tract Society of Pennsylvania. *God's Word for Us Through Jeremiah.* Brooklyn, N.Y.: Watchtower Bible and Tract Society of New York, 2010.

——. *Jehovah's Witnesses: Proclaimers of God's Kingdom.* Brooklyn, N.Y.: Watchtower Bible and Tract Society of New York, 1993.

——. *Revelation: Its Grand Climax at Hand!* Brooklyn, N.Y.: Watchtower Bible and Tract Society of New York, 1988.

——. *What Does the Bible Really Teach?* Brooklyn, N.Y.: Watchtower Bible and Tract Society of New York, 2014.

Zygmunt, Joseph F. "Jehovah's Witnesses in the U.S.A. 1942–1976." *Social Compass* 24 (1977): 44–57.

CHAPTER 42

....

THE BIBLE AND CHRISTIAN SCIENTISTS

....

MICHAEL W. HAMILTON

CHRISTIAN Scientists read and study the Bible in conjunction with *Science and Health with Key to the Scriptures* by Mary Baker Eddy, a book first published in 1875. The weekly Bible lesson in the *Christian Science Quarterly* includes selections from both books and constitutes the basis of individual study and of the sermon read at Sunday services. Mary Baker Eddy claimed unique authority for her primary work, and this has brought attention to *Science and Health* and its place in Christian Science.[1]

Scholars interested in Christian Science have paid less attention to the influence of the Bible on Eddy and on *Science and Health*. In part, this is because analyses that make Eddy's primary influences such figures as Emanuel Swedenborg, Phineas P. Quimby, and various American Transcendentalists tend to ignore her debt to the Hebrew and Christian scriptures.[2] Such treatments make the Bible appear almost incidental to her book. On the other hand, some critics see Eddy's ideas as occult distortions of biblical teachings.[3] Others tend to classify Christian Scientists as faith healers whose practices spring from Eddy's misuse of the Bible.[4] Still others have portrayed *Science and Health* as a new American scripture.[5] All this tends to disregard the experience of Eddy and of her followers with the Bible, especially the words and works of Jesus. The Christian Science historian Stephen Gottschalk, however, highlights this dependence:

> Eddy did not believe she was so much adding to scriptural truth as throwing new light upon it, making explicit what was already in substance there. It would never have occurred to her to view her teachings as a personal religious philosophy of her own devising, independent of biblical truth and precedent.[6]

Christian Scientists generally resist categorizations that separate Christian Science from biblical religion, as well as associations with occultism or faith healing, and they do not usually refer to *Science and Health* as scripture. Eddy's published writings and her voluminous correspondence point to the Hebrew and Christian Bible as the most significant source for her ideas.[7]

At the same time, it is vital to understand the factors that mediated her approach to these texts. Two influences stand out: (1) Eddy's Puritan heritage, including her rebellion against the doctrine of predestination; (2) the convergence of Eddy's religious commitments with her desire to regain her own health and to more generally relieve human suffering. This led her to homeopathy and to Phineas Quimby, a mental healer; but, as Eddy later explained, "here I found not Christianity."[8] These influences both problematized and catalyzed her research in the Bible that consumed three years in the 1860s; that research supplied the dominant motifs for her later study, teaching, writing, preaching, and organizing.

When the Christian Science Church was founded in 1879 with few resources and fewer talented preachers, it was not clear how the new sect could compensate for this pastoral deficit. Eddy preached regularly on Bible texts in rented halls during the 1880s, but even at the center of the new movement, it was hard to supply the pulpit with those who could preach sermons that Eddy believed accurately represented her discovery.[9] So, in 1895, as pastor of her church, she ordained the scriptures and her book, a change that publicly yoked the Bible to *Science and Health*.[10] This deeply influenced the development of Christian Science as a religious movement, as a healing system, and as a way of understanding the Bible. It also promoted spiritual entrepreneurship as followers initiated healing practices and started churches. An 1891 testimony is typical:

> I had always been sick, but found no relief in drugs; still, I thought that if the Bible was true, God could heal me. So, when my attention was called to Christian Science, I at once bought "Science and Health with Key to the Scriptures," studied it, and began to improve in health. I seemed to see God so near and so dear, —so different from the God I had been taught to fear. I studied alone night and day, until I found I was healed, both physically and mentally.
>
> Then came a desire to tell everyone of this wonderful truth. I expected all to feel just as pleased as I did; but to my sorrow none would believe. Some, it is true, took treatment and were helped, but went on in the old way, without a word of thanks. But still I could not give up. I seemed to know that this was the way, and I had rather live it alone than to follow the crowd the other way. But as time passed, I had some good demonstrations of this Love that is our Life.
>
> I am the only Scientist in Le Roy, [Michigan] as yet, but the good seed has been sown, and where the people once scoffed at this "silly new idea," they are becoming interested, and many have been healed, and some are asking about it. One dear old lady and I study the Bible Lessons every Tuesday afternoon. She came to call, and as we talked, she told me of her sickness of years' standing; and was healed during our talk, so that she has never felt a touch of the old trouble since.[11]

Of course, the role of the Bible in Christian Science is not just about the past. When reporting physical cure, moral regeneration, or poverty overcome, a significant percentage of writers in Christian Science magazines continue to emphasize their renewed interest in the Bible. For example, one wrote in 2016, "Since that day I was healed, I have had a voracious appetite for learning as much as I can about God's divine harmony and love. Although I had read the Bible since childhood, I started reading it with new insight. I now understand more deeply the lessons that Christ Jesus was teaching and the true nature of the Gospels' 'good news.' "[12] While understanding the Bible in the light of Christian Science is reputed to bring healing, for many the experience of healing leads to a new appreciation for the Bible. The ability of Christian Science to connect seekers with the Bible is a consistent thread in testimonies for over a century.

In the Christian Science Church archives at The Mary Baker Eddy Library in Boston, one is able to find a King James Bible printed at Edinburgh in 1795. It belonged to Mary Baker Eddy's paternal grandparents, Joseph Baker and Maryann Moore Baker of New Hampshire.

The book, bound in worn brown leather, is surprisingly lightweight. The signatures of Eddy's grandparents inside the front cover indicate their ownership. Eddy signed her own name decades later and wrote: "A holy book and a family treasure."

Eddy's father, Mark Baker, read a chapter of the Bible to his wife and six children every morning, followed by a lengthy extemporaneous prayer.[13] The absolute sovereignty of God, the total depravity of man, and the authority of Bible formed the foundation of the Bakers' religious life. If predestinarian theology was fading in much of nineteenth-century New England, it still held sway in the Baker household, and it provoked lively discussion and debate with friends, relatives, and visiting ministers.[14] This theology was also a primary source of conflict between young Mary and her father. She later wrote, "My father's relentless theology emphasized belief in a final judgment-day, in the danger of endless punishment, and in a Jehovah merciless towards unbelievers." [15] Her mother, Abigail Baker, held a more nuanced view of God's sovereignty. On one occasion, after a debate between father and daughter, the adolescent Mary became ill. In later years, she concluded that the chronic sickness that she endured was related to the theology of her childhood.[16] But she also remembered the relief that came in response to her mother's prompting:

> My mother, as she bathed my burning temples, bade me lean on God's love, which would give me rest, if I went to Him in prayer, as I was wont to do, seeking His guidance. I prayed; and a soft glow of ineffable joy came over me. The fever was gone, and I rose and dressed myself, in a normal condition of health. Mother saw this, and was glad. The physician marvelled; and the "horrible decree" of predestination—as John Calvin rightly called his own tenet—forever lost its power over me.[17]

Eddy, however, did retain some of her theological inheritance. She believed, along with many other Puritan descendants, that the Bible "was to be taken with desperate seriousness."[18] In 1846, when she was twenty-five, Eddy wrote this poem:

The Bible

> Word of God! What condescension,
> Infinite with finite mind,
> To commune, sublime conception.
> Canst thou fathom love divine?
> Oracle of God-like wonder,
> Frame-work of His mighty plan,
> Chart and compass for the wanderer,
> Safe obeying thy command.
>
> By Omniscience veiled in glory,
> 'Neath the Omnipresent eye—
> Kingdoms, empires, bow before thee,
> Sceptic, truth immortal see!
> Spare O then the querist's cavil,
> Search in faith—obey, adore!
> Ponder, pause, believe and "marvel
> Not, I say," forevermore.[19]

At the time of writing, Eddy was already immersed in the difficulties that characterized her life for the next twenty years: deaths of loved ones, poverty, and chronic illness. The Bible was a constant, especially when things fell apart. She was groping toward a faith that would liberate both body and mind. Later, she referred to 1846 as the start of her practical quest to "trace all physical effects to a mental cause."[20]

During these difficult years, she used homeopathy to help herself and others.[21] Her successful treatment of a woman for edema, combining placebos with homeopathic remedies, made Eddy question the efficacy of drugs and the physical basis of disease.[22] She called that experience "a falling apple to me—it made plain to me that mind governed the whole question of her recovery. I was always praying to be kept from sin, and I waited and prayed for God to direct me."[23] It was around this time that Eddy said that she vowed to herself that "if [God] restored her to health, she would devote her remaining years to helping sick and suffering humanity."[24] She also reputedly cured by prayer alone, including the 1860 case of a baby with an eye infection.[25] Eddy remembered, "I gave the infant no drugs,—held her in my arms a few moments while lifting my thoughts to God," and the child was quickly healed.

While she was at times able to help others, Eddy was at first less effective in her own case, perhaps a result of the unresolved questions endemic to this period of her life. This led to her most important therapeutic contact up to that time, with Phineas P. Quimby, a self-taught mental healer in Maine. After seeing him for treatment in 1862, she temporarily regained her strength and climbed a towering 182 steps to the top of the Portland City Hall dome. She wrote that she felt like a bird uncaged and compared Quimby's method to Christ's: "As he speaks as never man before spake, and heals as never man healed since Christ, is he not identified with truth? And is not this the Christ which is in him?"[26] What followed became one of the most contested periods of Eddy's life. Later critics claimed that she had stolen Quimby's ideas and passed them off as her own.[27] Debate continued for decades. One of the severest early critics of Eddy and of Christian Scientists, H. A. L. Fisher, nonetheless observed, "When we ask what was the inner source of her power, the answer can only be that it was religion. . . . What exactly her book owes to Quimby remains, and will probably continue to remain, a matter of doubt: nor does it much signify. . . Quimby would certainly never have written Science and Health."[28] More recently, Gill writes,

> the New Testament dimension of Quimby's work, his distinction between Jesus and the Christ, and his readiness to interpret the Bible and accept or reject Protestant religious orthodoxy had a special resonance with the deeply religious [Eddy]. Already in November 1862 she was focusing on the triangular relationship among patient, healer, and God as the key to cure, and this idea was not something she learned from Quimby but, if anything, something which she brought to him.[29]

Carefully sorting through documentary evidence, Gill concludes that the idea that Eddy replicates Quimby's ideas and writings in her own was "largely rigged."[30]

Eddy's skyrocketing freedom plummeted back to earth when she returned home, and she was again sick much of the time. While this seesaw did not immediately dampen her faith in Quimby, it must have sown seeds of doubt that she had arrived at a real solution to her own problems, and to the larger problem of human suffering. But she was spiritually energized, if perplexed. She later wrote of herself, "As early as 1862 she began to write down and give to friends the results of her Scriptural study, for the Bible was her sole teacher; but these compositions were crude,—the first steps of a child in the newly discovered world of Spirit."[31]

It was a crisis that pushed Eddy's own thinking about God's healing touch forward. When she fell on the ice on a cold winter evening in 1866 at Lynn, Massachusetts, she was knocked unconscious and carried to a nearby house. The next two days were tenuous. Quimby had died only weeks earlier and could not help her. The *Lynn Reporter* described her grave condition.[32] Hovering friends and her minister prepared her for the worst. Instead, Eddy rallied enough to ask for her Bible and a little privacy. When she read the account of one of Jesus's healings, she later claimed, things suddenly came into focus. She said that her thought was filled with the "allness" of God—not for the first time, but in a way that spoke uniquely to her need. She got up, dressed, and walked out of her sickroom.[33] She later said that she was not even sure how her recovery had happened except that God had done it.[34]

Eddy's papers show that there was only one source to which she believed she could go for answers: the Bible. In an undated document she summarized her experience:

> I was never luke-warm but always fervid. I had not found all that I desired in the orthodox church and I examined Spiritualism with utter disappointment. Homeopathy was my last step in medicine and Quimbyism was my next in healing but here I found not Christianity. Yet I lauded his courage in believing that mind made disease and that mind healed disease. . . . Yet lacked I yet some thing, the one thing needed, and again my health declined. Then came the accident and injury called fatal and the Bible healed me, and from Quimbyism to the Bible was like turning from Leviticus to St. John in the Scripture.[35]

She plunged into a period of intensive research. She wrote in her autobiography, *Retrospection and Introspection*: "The Bible was my textbook. It answered my questions as to how I was healed; but the Scriptures had to me a new meaning, a new tongue. Their spiritual signification appeared; and I apprehended for the first time, in their spiritual meaning, Jesus' teaching and demonstration, and the Principle and rule of spiritual Science and metaphysical healing—in a word, Christian Science."[36]

Eddy made copious notes on Genesis for a planned book called "The Bible in its Spiritual Meaning."[37] It was never completed, but the title captures Eddy's focus.[38] She healed people. An infected finger, clubfeet, a dislocated hip, yielded to her prayers.[39] She became convinced that while the nature of disease was mental, the unaided human mind could not cure the suffering it engendered. Instead, the limited human mind and all its debris had to yield to the cleansing action of the divine Mind, God.[40]

She moved frequently over the next decade and found interest, opposition, and indifference in the homes and boarding houses that sheltered her. Even sympathetic auditors often found Eddy's ideas inexplicable. She would write all day in her room and then share the product with those around her, inviting—"almost demanding," one remembered—their feedback.[41] Eddy was seeking not only to understand but also to communicate what came to her. She wrote of her healing, "That short experience included a glimpse of the great fact that I have since tried to make plain to others, namely, Life in and of Spirit; this Life being the sole reality of existence."[42] Charles Alan Taber remembered her at that time:

> Mrs. Winslow, a broad minded and well educated member of the Society of Friends, and my wife a zealous church member, had both made a careful study of the Bible, but Mrs. Glover led us toward an understanding of the Bible which neither of us had ever reached. The central principle of her conversation seemed to be the power over, the control of our physical and mental faculties, through the study of, the belief in and the daily practice of the teachings of

Christ as she understood them. We said she was reading more into the Bible than we could find in the text, but we had to admit that her ideas had a good foundation on the Bible and in the writings of some of the greatest religious teachers in the world. She made a protest against the belief, then somewhat prevalent, that we should take but little thought as to our bodies and our earthly lives, and consider only the life to come.... Her intellect and spiritual nature had evidently absorbed certain Christian principles, which were not set forth in the Bible or in the theology of any church known to her as fully as she desired, and which she was trying to put into language more acceptable to her.[43]

Eddy reached a milestone in her interpretation of the Bible when she published her primary work, *Science and Health*, in 1875.[44] She would revise it constantly over the next thirty-five years, until her death in 1910.[45] The first edition began with this credo: "Leaning on the sustaining infinite with loving trust, the trials of to-day are brief, and tomorrow is big with blessings." For confirmation she turned to the Nativity, and compared the shepherds' night vigil near Bethlehem to the contemporary seeker waiting and watching for the Truth her book delivered—the Truth that would explain the mission of Jesus anew. "The time for thinkers has come; and the time for revolutions, ecclesiastic and social, must come. Truth, independent of doctrines or time-honored systems, stands at the threshold of history." Following the preface were eight chapters: "Natural Science," "Imposition and Demonstration," "Spirit and Matter," "Creation," "Prayer and Atonement," "Marriage," "Physiology," and "Healing the Sick." Eddy described the development of her hermeneutic in an undated fragment: "The Scriptures were the arm to my system of metaphysics, Christian Science," she wrote, "as step by step I walked toward God. And proportionally as all my thoughts revolved around this common centre of their spiritual signification it threw the light of penetration on the page."[46]

She added a *Key to the Scriptures* to the sixth edition in 1883, including the chapter "Genesis," which drew on her intensive study of the Bible in the 1860s. Although apparently unaware of the Graf-Wellhausen Genesis hypothesis that the book contained markedly different creation stories, she wrote that Genesis included two distinct—and to her, irreconcilable—accounts of creation.[47] The first account, including the decree that all that God had made was "very good," was the spiritual and true record, and the basis of Christian Science. The second narrative, featuring Adam and Eve, was an "inverted" view of creation.[48] If Spirit was real and All-in-all, then matter and its conglomeration of sin, sickness, and death must be fundamentally unreal, the dust to dust of nothingness, and Genesis supplied the typology for this truth.[49] Her interpretation of selected verses of Genesis, chapters 1-4, included the following:

Genesis 1.1. In the beginning, God created the heaven and the earth.
The infinite has no beginning. This word *beginning* is employed to signify the only—that is, the eternal verity and unity of God and man, including the universe. The creative Principle—Life, Truth, and Love—is God. The universe reflects God. There is but one creator and one creation. This creation consists of the unfolding of spiritual ideas and their identities, which are embraced in the infinite Mind and forever reflected. These ideas range from the infinitesimal to infinity, and the highest ideas are the sons and daughters of God.[50]

Genesis 2.6. But there went up a mist from the earth, and watered the whole face of the ground.
The Science and truth of the divine creation have been presented in the verses already considered, and now the opposite error, a material view of creation, is to be set forth. The second

chapter of Genesis contains a statement of this material view of God and the universe, a statement which is the exact opposite of scientific truth as before recorded. The history of error or matter, if veritable, would set aside the omnipotence of Spirit; but it is the false history in contradistinction to the true.

The Science of the first record proves the falsity of the second. If one is true, the other is false, for they are antagonistic. The first record assigns all might and government to God, and endows man out of God's perfection and power. The second record chronicles man as mutable and mortal, — as having broken away from Deity and as revolving in an orbit of his own. Existence, separate from divinity, Science explains as impossible.[51]

Eddy had a basic knowledge of Greek and Hebrew and of the higher criticism sweeping biblical scholarship.[52] She was not a literalist, but neither was her exegesis entirely figurative. She argued for the basic authenticity of the scriptures, especially the New Testament. An unpublished manuscript explained:

the strongest proof to my mind of the genuineness in the main of the scriptures is that the views of their writers exposed them to suffering and violent deaths, yet they held steadfastly to the facts which they recorded.

. . .

Jesus the great teacher and demonstrator of Truth recognized the Old Testament as inspired in some of its parts where the good old patriarchs and prophets spake as they were moved by the Holy Ghost, the science of being showing conclusively that amid diversity of form, style, and mode of thought, one Mind, even the Intelligence that made man and the universe, through more than fifteen hundred years was inspiring some author to utter the Truth that has since been rent and divided even as the garment of Jesus, and falsely rendered through isms and ologies.[53]

Eddy hoped that her book would cut through "isms and ologies" and encourage people to read the Bible, and later she included testimonies at the end of *Science and Health* that confirmed this result.[54] "A.F." of Sioux City, Iowa, wrote, "The Bible, which I regarded with suspicion, has become my guide, and Christianity has become a sweet reality, because the Christian Science textbook has indeed been a 'Key to the Scriptures' and has breathed through the Gospel pages a sweet sense of harmony."[55] "S.H.L." of North Pittston, Maine, told of a first encounter with the book:

When I reached the place where Mrs. Eddy says she found this truth in the Bible, I began comparing the two books. I read passages which looked very reasonable to me, and said to myself, This is nearer to the truth than anything I have ever seen. I continued to read all day, stopping only long enough to eat my dinner. As I read on, everything became clearer to me, and I felt that I was healed. During the evening a neighbor came in, and I said, "I am healed, and that book has healed me."[56]

Various religious leaders and metaphysical thinkers had different responses to Eddy. Her interpretation of the Bible appalled many among Boston's Protestant clergy.[57] Rev. A. J. Gordon was particularly acerbic: "One has only to open the published volumes of its lady apostle in this city to find such a creed of pantheism and blasphemy as has been rarely compounded."[58] Rev. Alvin E. Bell asked, "How could anyone who knows what God's Word teaches. . . believe the word of any woman?"[59] Some liberal Protestant leaders, however, were guardedly sympathetic.[60] On Eddy's other flank were the mind curers, forerunners of New Thought, who found her insistence on a biblical basis for metaphysics too confining.[61]

Their emerging eclecticism might acknowledge the Bible as a sacred text, but they placed it on a continuum of multiple revelations with many texts, especially those from the East. Eddy's book was not like that. While New Thought extolled the "god within," *Science and Health* insisted on Mosaic monotheism.[62] Eddy wrote: "The First Commandment is my favorite text. It demonstrates Christian Science."[63]

Eddy and her students founded the Church of Christ, Scientist in 1879, in Massachusetts. Christian Science gradually grew in the United States and Canada, and by 1900, in other parts of the world, as well. Although early church services were often patterned after evangelical Protestant worship, there were few trained ministers among the converts. Preaching was important to Eddy, but more vital were the "signs following" of healing, what Christian Science terms "demonstration." She wrote to two students:

> *Demonstration* is the whole of Christian Science, nothing else proves it, nothing else will save it and continue it with us. God has said this—and Christ Jesus has proved it. Preaching and teaching are of no use without proof of what is taught and said. . . . One case *healed* is more than other denominations can do, whereas all sects can preach and teach more scholarly than the majority of Christian Scientists.[64]

The danger that preaching might overtake healing, that talking might supersede doing, and that words might swamp the provable Word of Scripture was not a concern unique to Christian Science. But Eddy developed a novel solution. When her followers built The Mother Church in Boston in 1895, Eddy moved to institute a new kind of service: "The Bible and 'Science and Health with Key to the Scriptures' shall henceforth be the Pastor of the Mother Church. This will tend to spiritualize thought. Personal preaching has more or less of human views grafted into it. Whereas the pure Word contains only the living, health-giving Truth."[65]

Eddy's unconventional solution was to place books, not preachers or rituals, at the center of worship.[66] Churches appointed lay readers from among their members, usually a man and a woman. They read selections from the Bible and *Science and Health*. These lessons had been in use among Christian Scientists for several years, adapted from the Protestant New International Series of Sunday School lessons, augmented with excerpts from *Science and Health*. Eddy soon developed her own Bible lesson subjects and appointed a committee to select and arrange relevant passages. Some predicted that these liturgical changes would bring disaster. The churches, however, adjusted and a new kind of church service developed.[67] The emergence of a Protestant clerical class in Christian Science was quashed and greater uniformity introduced through Eddy's move to place books at the center of the church's worship services.

While some saw this action as further evidence of emerging authoritarianism, others saw it as an innovative and divinely ordained way to elevate the Bible to a place of unrivalled prominence and power within the church. The effect of instituting the Bible lesson was far-reaching, emphasizing both the autonomy and the unity of Christian Scientists around the world who studied them. A modern church website explains a system unchanged since Eddy's time:

> There are 26 subjects which repeat twice a year and explore the primary themes of Christian Science, including the nature of God, the healing and redeeming power of the Christ, and our spiritual identity as the children of God. Each week, a new Lesson with passages from

the Bible and *Science and Health* offers practical, healing ideas that apply to issues people face every day—from sickness and injury to financial problems, unhappy relationships, and many more. Beyond meeting individual needs, these spiritual truths apply equally and just as effectively to widespread issues such as crime, environmental concerns, war, and poverty.[68]

Bible texts used in the lessons extend from Genesis to Revelation (but exclude the Apocrypha) and include a substantial amount of material from the Hebrew scriptures. All lessons use material from both Testaments.

Each Bible lesson opens with a "Golden Text," a brief Bible passage that sets the theme. For example, a lesson might open with part of this verse from Galatians: "he that soweth to the Spirit shall of the Spirit reap life everlasting," followed by a responsive reading that amplifies it. The lesson is developed in a series of sections treating the theme. A Bible account of healing is usually included, and Christ Jesus is always featured as a central exponent of the lesson's main ideas. It requires about 30 minutes to thoughtfully read the lesson; in-depth study of its citations can occupy more time. These Bible lessons put *Science and Health* in continuous conversation with the scriptures in the practice and teaching of Christian Science. Eddy packed her book with scriptural quotes, allusions, metaphors, and references. For Eddy, her book was the "Key to the Scriptures," and it was a text born out of spiritual necessity. She wrote that "if the Bible were understood [*Science and Health*] would never have been written. Every inspired sentence in the Bible has a spiritual meaning and it means nothing that the [five] material so-called senses can grasp or interpret."[69]

By the time of Eddy's death in 1910, *Science and Health* was in some ways a very different book than when it was first published in 1875. Through dozens of revisions and with editorial help, its rough swaddling clothes had been smoothed into a more polished garment. But the book's debt to the Bible remained evident, and her other published writings showed the same lineage. In about 1,900 pages of published works, she quotes the Hebrew and Christian scriptures over 2,100 times, favoring the New Testament, especially Matthew and John, over the Old, where she most often quotes Genesis and Psalms. Paul's writings were important in her output; she quotes from his seven undisputed letters over 200 times, favoring Romans and 1 Corinthians, and frequently mentions Paul.[70]

Science and Health expanded from eight to eighteen chapters. New material had been gradually added, but much had also been outgrown and removed.[71] Every chapter title was followed by passages from the Bible. The opening words of the 1875 Preface remained in revised form: "To those leaning on the sustaining infinite, today is big with blessings." The book was more hospitable to inquirers and to basic Christian concerns, opening with the chapters "Prayer," "Atonement and Eucharist," and "Marriage."[72] Eddy identified systems in opposition to her Science in "Christian Science versus Spiritualism" and "Animal Magnetism Unmasked." What followed was an in-depth statement of Christian Science: "Science, Theology, Medicine," "Physiology," "Footsteps of Truth," "Creation," "Science of Being," "Some Objections Answered," "Christian Science Practice," "Teaching Christian Science," and the summative "Recapitulation." The three-chapter "Key to the Scriptures" section included "Genesis," "The Apocalypse," and "Glossary." She began that section by writing that

> Scientific interpretation of the Scriptures properly starts with the beginning of the Old Testament, chiefly because the spiritual import of the Word, in its earliest articulations, often seems so smothered by the immediate context as to require explication; whereas the

New Testament narratives are clearer and come nearer the heart. Jesus illumines them, showing the poverty of mortal existence, but richly recompensing human want and woe with spiritual gain.[73]

The acts, even more than the words, of Jesus were the touchstone for the practice of healing outlined in the book. While an understanding of the Principle and rules of the Science was requisite, Eddy resisted creating formulas for success and started her chapter, "Christian Science Practice," by retelling the encounter recorded in Luke, chapter seven, between Jesus, Simon the Pharisee, and the woman who washed his feet with tears and wiped them "with the hairs of her head." Interestingly, it was the repentant woman—and Jesus's response to her—who she put forward as the model for aspiring Christian Science practitioners.

The book ended with "Fruitage," an appendix of over eighty letters from people who had benefited by *Science and Health*. Three Bible verses opened the chapter; the first was, "By their fruits ye shall know them." This was the promise and challenge of Christian Science. Eddy offered, "You can prove for yourself, dear reader, the Science of healing, and so ascertain if the author has given you the correct interpretation of Scripture."[74]

Christian Science invites people, however modestly, to approach the teachings of the Bible pragmatically. *Science and Health* was designed to show them how to do it. Testimonies and reminiscences from any period could illustrate how Christian Scientists believe that they are following Jesus.[75] Times of war are especially evocative because of the extremities often involved, and so a sampling of testimonies from World War I concludes this chapter.[76]

Christian Scientists' self-consciousness as religious outsiders in the United States was lessened by the Mother Church's philanthropy during World War I. In 1914, the church asked members to contribute to relief efforts overseas. Six months after the first call to help, they had raised over $100,000 ($2.3 million in 2016 dollars). Volunteers distributed clothes, money, and other goods through an international network of centers during and after the conflict. Several Christian Scientists served as military chaplains. Testimonies given at Wednesday evening meetings and in print dramatized the role of the Bible and *Science and Health* in healing. Christian Scientist soldiers used small editions that fit in rucksacks and sometimes introduced others to their religion simply by reading from their books.[77]

The war also helped American Christian Scientists to see themselves as part of a global religious movement. A French soldier recounted in 1918, "Since the beginning of the war I have been protected in many painful circumstances, from dysentery and other ills. Whenever I can do so I study the Lesson-Sermons, as I brought my books with me to the front, although at first this seemed impossible."[78] An American ambulance driver at the Front gave an account of how he drew on the Bible:

> When under shellfire for the first time, I huddled at the base of a wall, wanting nothing but to go to sleep and be oblivious to the threat of danger. Here I was, face to face with what I had really enlisted for—to prove the actuality of divine Love in spite of every seeming condition to the contrary. That sense of my purpose woke me out of my dormancy.... On the Somme front we had fourteen days and nights of incessant activity and of unforgettable proofs of God's care. Never was a patient wounded en route.... The fellows often remarked about our good fortune. They knew I thought it was divine protection.... On a later front...a shell exploded nearby, and imbedded a fragment of rock in my shoulder. I was able to man a stretcher and carry more seriously wounded French soldiers to the dressing room and drive them in my ambulance to the hospital, where the fragment was removed from my shoulder. Then I had time to face the error which, undetected, had crept into my thinking. It was a

complacent sense of personal immunity, a deceptive counterfeit of that spiritual understanding of God's presence which had been my genuine protection. Jesus' meek words, 'I can of mine own self do nothing,' restored a sense of true humility; and his amplifying statement, 'What things soever [the Father] doeth, these also doeth the Son likewise,' renewed the assurance of unity with Principle.[79]

Wartime volunteers wrote of their healing experiences with soldiers, including this account of a person who delivered *The Christian Science Monitor* to hospital wards:[80]

> The *Monitor* distributor left a message of love one day for a soldier who was unconscious and appeared to be passing on. On the next visit the lad was quite well. He had heard that one word "love," he said, and he was sure he must be home again, so he decided it was best to wake up and see what was going on. On another day the supervising nurse asked the *Monitor* distributor to say a few words to another lad who was expected to live but a few hours. This wounded soldier had lost his Bible at Château-Thierry and then, he explained, "he knew he would not live." He was reminded that he had not lost the Lord's Prayer and that he [could] avail himself of these living words. He promised to say the Lord's Prayer all day—to substitute its words for what appeared to be a shortness of breath. This obedient soldier did exactly as he promised and his healing came that day. Two weeks later a small consignment of Bibles came from Boston.... When the Bible was given to the lad, he quickly removed the outer box and threw it under his cot. The Book itself he held for some time caressingly against his face, and then slipped it securely under his pillow.[81]

Each of these vignettes offers the voice of individuals who believed that they were empowered to interpret the Bible and experience its meaning in a way that intervened in crisis and brought them through it. In their own ways, each agreed that *Science and Health* enabled them to move from a passive to an active faith. The intent of Eddy was to promote the kind of individual agency in everyday life that would allow readers of her book to make the Bible their own. In that sense she sought to replicate her own experience in the lives of her followers—to make the scriptures more authoritative through claiming that it was the spiritual, not the literal meaning that really counted.

Notes

1. For example, see Mary Baker Eddy, *The First Church of Christ, Scientist and Miscellany* (Boston, Mass.: First Church of Christ, Scientist, 1913), 115. H. A. L. Fisher is representative: "in the development of Christian Science that book, and that book only, has been of decisive importance." *Our New Religion* (London: E. Benn Limited, 1929), 40. Mark Twain observed, "There are plenty of people who imagine they understand [*Science and Health*]; I know this, for I have talked with them;... they seem to know the volume by heart, and to revere it as they would a Bible—another Bible, perhaps I ought to say." *Christian Science* (New York: Harper and Brothers, 1907), 23. Here was a charge that was to shadow Eddy and Christian Scientists: that they regarded *Science and Health* as a new scripture and its author as a second Christ. The apotheosis heaped on Eddy by her most intemperate followers solidified this impression. But her correspondence shows that she was nearly driven to distraction at times by those who parroted her words, talked too much, and did too little to demonstrate what *Science and Health* actually taught. These enthusiasts often lurched from adoration to acrimony, reviling the woman they had once

exalted. Eddy had a decidedly different view of herself, and, by extension, of her book. Replying to Twain in the *New York Herald* she wrote, "What I am remains to be proved by the good I do" (Eddy, *Miscellany*, 303).

2. This line of argument began with Julius Dresser, *The True History of Mental Science* (Boston, Mass.: A Mudge and Son, 1887) and was crystallized in Georgine Milmine, *The Life of Mary Baker Eddy and the History of Christian Science* (New York: Doubleday, 1909) and Frederick Peabody, *The Religio-Medical Masquerade: A Complete Exposure of Christian Science* (Boston, Mass.: Hancock Press, 1915). These polemical works have informed much subsequent literature on Eddy and Christian Science; their influence is traceable in Edward Franden Dakin, *Mary Baker Eddy: The Biography of a Virginal Mind* (New York: Blue Ribbon Books, 1929); Ernest S. Bates and John V. Dittemore, *Mary Baker Eddy: The Truth and the Tradition* (New York: Alfred A. Knopf, 1932); Julius Silsberger Jr., *Mary Baker Eddy: An Interpretive Biography of the Founder of Christian Science* (New York: Little Brown, 1980). Robert Peel, *Christian Science: Its Encounter with American Culture* (New York: Henry Holt, 1958) and Stephen Gottschalk, *The Emergence of Christian Science in American Religious Life* (Berkeley: University of California Press, 1973) treat Eddy and her religion with scholarly, if sympathetic, care that challenges the Dresser-Milmine-Peabody hypotheses.

3. See Walter Martin and Ravi Zacharias, *Kingdom of the Cults* (Minneapolis, Minn.: Bethany House, 2003). Catherine Albanese reaches a similar, though secular, conclusion in *Republic of Mind and Spirit: A Cultural History of American Metaphysical Religion* (New Haven, Conn.: Yale University Press, 2008).

4. This has been part of the approach of several memoirists, such as Caroline Fraser, *God's Perfect Child: Living and Dying in the Christian Science Church* (New York: Henry Holt, 1999). DeWitt John, *The Christian Science Way of Life* (Boston, Mass.: Christian Science Publishing Society, 1962) offers a more positive assessment.

5. See, e.g., Laurie F. Maffly-Kipp, *American Scriptures: An Anthology of Sacred Writings* (New York: Penguin Classics, 2010), 194.

6. Stephen Gottschalk, *Rolling Away the Stone: Mary Baker Eddy's Challenge to Materialism* (Bloomington: Indiana University Press, 2005), 125.

7. Martin E. Marty writes, "If reasons exist for defensiveness, for seizing occasions to explain oneself, reasons also exist for seeing these habits as intrinsic to the character of Christian Science. If not proselytizing or missionary, if never aggressive or belligerent. . . it is always quietly setting out to revise or correct the settled world views others take so for granted. . . . Although this faith, with its radical spirituality, contains real challenges to 'orthodox' Christianity, there are also more points of contact than one might previously have guessed." Introduction to Robert Peel, *Health and Medicine in the Christian Science Tradition: Principle, Practice, and Challenge* (New York: Crossroad, 1988), viii–ix. The Mary Baker Eddy Papers (https://mbepapers.org) is gradually making available annotated versions of Eddy's incoming and outgoing correspondence, sermons, and other documents.

8. A10409, The Mary Baker Eddy Collection.

9. Daisette D. S. McKenzie, "The Writings of Mary Baker Eddy," in *We Knew Mary Baker Eddy*, vol. 1 (Boston, Mass.: Christian Science Publishing Society, 2011), 252.

10. See Richard A. Nenneman, *The New Birth of Christianity: Why Religion Persists in a Scientific Age* (San Francisco, Calif.: HarperSanFrancisco, 1992), 236–37.

11. Florence Williams, in Mary Baker Eddy, *Miscellaneous Writings, 1883-1896* (Boston, Mass.: First Church of Christ, Scientist, 1896), 431–32; originally in *The Christian Science Journal*, November 1891.

12. Cynthia Kains, "Testimony," *Christian Science Journal*, April 2016, 34–35.

13. Robert Peel, *Mary Baker Eddy: The Years of Discovery* (Boston, Mass.: Holt, Rinehart, and Winston, 1966), 23; Robert David Thomas, *With Bleeding Footsteps: Mary Baker Eddy's Path to Religious Leadership* (New York: Alfred A. Knopf, 1994), 4–5.

14. Peel, *Years of Discovery*, 19; Gillian Gill, *Mary Baker Eddy* (Reading, Mass.: Perseus Books, 1998), 11; Jewel Spangler Smaus, *Mary Baker Eddy: The Golden Days* (Boston: Christian Science Publishing Society, 1966), 29.

15. Mary Baker Eddy, *Retrospection and Introspection* (Boston: First Church of Christ, Scientist, 1891), 13.

16. "Extracts from Sermon," in Eddy, *Miscellaneous Writings*, 169, explained that, "Within Bible pages she [Eddy] had found all the divine Science she preaches. . . Early training, through misinterpretation of the Word, had been the underlying cause of the long years of invalidism she endured before Truth dawned upon her understanding, through right interpretation. With the understanding of Scripture-meanings, had come physical rejuvenation."

17. Eddy, *Miscellaneous Writings*, 13–14.

18. Peel, *Years of Discovery*, 22.

19. See John 3:7.

20. Peel, *Years of Discovery*, 24.

21. See Yvonne Caché von Fettweis and Robert Townsend Warneck, *Mary Baker Eddy: Christian Healer*, amplified ed. (Boston, Mass.: Christian Science Publishing Society, 2009), 41; Eddy was introduced to homeopathy by her cousin by marriage, Dr. Alpheus Morrill. For histories of this system in the United States, see John S. Haller Jr., *The History of American Homeopathy* (New Brunswick, N.J.: Rutgers University Press, 2009); and Natalie Robbins, *Copeland's Cure: Homeopathy and the War between Conventional and Alternative Medicine* (New York: Alfred A. Knopf, 1994).

22. Mary Baker Eddy, *Science and Health with Key to the Scriptures* (Boston, Mass.: First Church of Christ, Scientist, 1875), 156; Gill, *Mary Baker Eddy*, 109.

23. Sibyl Wilbur, *The Life of Mary Baker Eddy* (Boston: Christian Science Publishing Company), 347. Note the juxtaposition of Eddy's medical and religious observations. Thomas believes that homeopathy was not as important to Eddy at that period as she later portrayed it to be (Thomas, *Bleeding Footsteps*, 79).

24. L10106, The Mary Baker Eddy Collection.

25. Von Fettweis and Warneck, *Christian Healer*, esp. 45.

26. Peel, *Years of Discovery*, 167.

27. This was the position of Julius and Annetta Dresser and later of their son, Horatio Dresser, ed., *The Quimby Manuscripts* (New York: Thomas Y. Crowell, 1921), as well as of most of the leaders of New Thought. Keith McNeill rebuts Dresser in his exhaustive analysis of Quimby documents, *A Story Untold: The History of the Quimby-Eddy Debate*, https://ppquimby-mbeddydebate.com.

28. Fisher, *Our New Religion*, 40.

29. Gill, *Mary Baker Eddy*, 132.

30. Gill, *Mary Baker Eddy*, 146. Fraser and Gill engaged in a spirited exchange over their opposing assessments of Eddy in "Mrs. Eddy's Voices," *New York Times Review of Books*, June 29, 2000.

31. Eddy, *Science and Health*, viii.
32. Peel, *Years of Discovery*, 195.
33. Eddy, *Miscellaneous Writings*, 24.
34. Eddy, *Miscellaneous Writings*, 109.
35. A10409, The Mary Baker Eddy Collection.
36. Eddy, *Retrospection and Introspection*, 25; Thomas explains: "Her only source for the Science of man was the Bible, but Science was not to be found in the usual interpretations, the common beliefs, and the accepted opinions regarding the Scriptures" (*Bleeding Footsteps*, 134).
37. Gottschalk, *Rolling Away the Stone*, 125; *In My True Light and Life* includes this description: "She apparently first envisioned giving a metaphysical exegesis of the entire Bible, but only completed a portion of the book of Genesis. Still, the manuscript as she left it runs to over 600 pages. It represents her earliest effort to conceptualize in writing the truths she had seen during her healing in 1866, and some of the ideas in it are contrary to her final formulation of her metaphysics in the various editions of Science and Health." Mary Baker Eddy, *In My True Light and Life: Mary Baker Eddy Collections* (Boston, Mass.: The Writings of Mary Baker Eddy and The Mary Baker Eddy Library, 2002), 177.
38. As Thomas points out, "reinterpreting the Bible, especially the book of Genesis, was not out of the ordinary in the decades after the Civil War" (*Bleeding Footsteps*, 124). Responding to Darwinism's challenge to religion motivated many of those efforts. However, Eddy's approach to Genesis differed from that of allegorists and literalists in that she saw it as a foundational text for her therapeutics. Peel writes that Eddy "readily granted that Darwin. . . might have given a reasonable explanation of the evolution of mortal man, but this, in her view, was not the man God had made in His own image and likeness. Although the words 'evolve' and 'evolution' occurred in her book again and again. . . they were used metaphorically to describe the gradual appearing in human experience of the image, the true idea, of God" (*Years of Discovery*, 280).
39. Von Fettweiss and Warneck, *Mary Baker Eddy*, 65–68. On the other hand, Milmine and later biographers who accepted her damning portrait of Eddy dismissed this early healing work, and, in fact, all Christian Science healing accounts, as anecdotal and unreliable. Twain took the ambivalent position that, while Christian Science healing was real, Eddy was an imposter. William James made little distinction between Christian Science and New Thought, but acknowledged the "patent and startling" fact of its healing and urged further examination of the phenomenon. See Robert Peel, *Mary Baker Eddy: The Years of Authority* (Boston, Mass.: Holt, Rinehart, and Winston, 1977), 98–99. Peel argues for the continuing relevance of Christian Science healing in *Spiritual Healing in a Scientific Age* (New York: Harper and Row, 1988), as does Nenneman in *The New Birth of Christianity*, 149–75.
40. Eddy's notes on Genesis, as well as her early teaching manuscript, *The Science of Man*, contain ideas from her contact with Quimby as well as an emerging theology at odds with his "errors." See Peel, *Years of Discovery*, 231–36, on the development of *The Science of Man*. She may have been describing this tension when she wrote, "When the Science of Mind was a fresh revelation to the author, she had to impart, while teaching its grand facts, the hue of spiritual ideas from her own spiritual condition, and she had to do this orally through the meagre channel afforded by language and by her manuscript circulated among the students. As former beliefs were expelled from her thought, the teaching

became clearer, until finally the shadow of old errors was no longer cast upon divine Science" (Eddy, *Science and Health*, 460).

41. Peel, *Years of Discovery*, esp. 204.

42. Eddy, *Miscellaneous Writings*, 24.

43. Peel, *Years of Discovery*, esp. 209. A very different account of Eddy's ideas during this period was given by disaffected student Wallace Wright in letters to the Lynn Transcript; he maintained that Eddy was a mesmerist. Her spirited response is the first published statement of her early teachings and includes reference to *Science and Health*: "I am preparing a work on Moral and Physical Science, that I shall submit to the public as soon as it is completed. This work is laborious." "To The Public: Moral Science and Mesmerism," February 3, 1872 (V05003, The Mary Baker Eddy Collection).

44. The book sold only 200 copies out of a printing of 1,000 in the first year, in spite of a favorable review in the *Boston Investigator* (Thomas, *Bleeding Footsteps*, 149) and the *Christian Advocate*. However, the reformer and philosopher Bronson Alcott encouraged Eddy, writing her:

The sacred truths which you announce, sustained by facts of the Immortal Life, give to your work the seal of inspiration—reaffirm in modern phrase the Christian revelations. In times like ours, so sunk in sensualism, I hail with joy any voice speaking an assured word for God and Immortality. And my joy is heightened the more when I find the blessed words are of woman's divinings. (Peel, *Years of Discovery*, 292)

For more on Alcott and the relationship between Transcendentalism and Christian Science, see Peel, *Christian Science*, 47–67, 87–103. Georgine Milmine calls the first edition of *Science and Health*, "hardly more than a tangle of words and theories, faulty in grammar and construction, and singularly contradictory in its statements." *The Life of Mary Baker Eddy and the History of Christian Science* (New York: Doubleday, 1909), 178. Gill claims that "the real issue is the author's audacity, her daring to think that a woman like her, with her resources, could write, not the expected textbook on mental healing techniques, not the comfortable compendium of healing anecdotes, but a book that takes on the great questions of God and man, good and evil, and that rejects orthodox verities" (*Mary Baker Eddy*, 217).

45. Amy Black Voorhees offers a comprehensive treatment of early editions of *Science and Health*. "Writing Revelation: Mary Baker Eddy and Her Early Editions of Science and Health, 1875-1891" (PhD diss., UC, Santa Barbara, 2013). Peel, *Years of Authority*, 183–90. Gill points out that Eddy's process also did not fit conventional definitions of revelatory experience: "Revealed truth, according to the implied criteria of Mrs. Eddy's critics, must come swiftly and definitively, under exceptional, even mystic, circumstances, not over forty years of unremitting labor, copious drafts, and constant erasures" (*Mary Baker Eddy*, 219).

46. A10934, The Mary Baker Eddy Collection.

47. Robert Peel, *Mary Baker Eddy: Years of Trial* (Boston, Mass.: Holt, Rinehart, and Winston, 1977), 188.

48. Eddy, *Science and Health*, 502. Gill, *Mary Baker Eddy*, 227–30.

49. Stephen Gottschalk discusses Eddy's typology as an outgrowth of "the Edwardian tradition in which she was raised." He maintains that Edwards's definition of typology as applying primarily to the Elect is broadened by Eddy: "She believed that biblical events could be taken as foreshadowing what all practicing Christians could and would experience

in whatever era they lived." *Rolling Away the Stone: Mary Baker Eddy's Challenge to Materialism* (Bloomington: Indiana University Press, 2006), 126–27.

50. Eddy, *Science and Health*, 502–3.

51. Eddy, *Science and Health*, 521.

52. In an undated document probably dating from the 1890s, Eddy writes of herself: "The higher criticism was not extant prior to Mary Baker G. Eddy's discovery of Christian Science. Nothing can breathe more bravely the higher criticism than her spiritual version of the Lord's Prayer, Exegesis of the Scriptures, etc." (A10253, The Mary Baker Eddy Collection). Here she appears to compare the advent of Christian Science with the challenge posed to traditional religion by modern biblical scholarship. Her spiritual sense of the Lord's Prayer concludes the first chapter of *Science and Health*, "Prayer"; the text from Matthew 5 is interlined with her interpretation, and begins,

> Our Father which art in heaven,
> Our Father-Mother God, all-harmonious. (16)

Eddy's occasional use of the term "higher criticism" shows her appropriating it for her own purposes while acknowledging its more general meaning. See, e.g., *Christian Science versus Pantheism* (Boston, Mass.: First Church of Christ, Scientist, 1898), 6; *Message to the Mother Church* (Boston, Mass.: First Church of Christ, Scientist, 1900), 11; *The First Church of Christ, Scientist, and Miscellany*, 3, 118, 136, 237, 240.

53. A10070, The Mary Baker Eddy Collection.

54. "The question, 'What is Truth,' convulses the world. . . . The efforts of error to answer this question by some ology are vain. Spiritual rationality and free thought accompany approaching Science, and cannot be put down" (Eddy, *Science and Health*, 223).

55. Eddy, *Science and Health*, 657.

56. Eddy, *Science and Health*, 642, lines 1–10, http://concordexpress.christianscience.com/?query=SH%20642. See also 615–16, 620–21, 627, 640, 643, 645, 654, 657, 663, 665, 672, 675–76, 689, 691–92, 694, 698.

57. See Thomas, *Bleeding Footsteps*, 304.

58. Peel, *Years of Trial*, 155. The charge of pantheism was rejected by Eddy. She responded to another salvo referring to her as "the pantheistic and prayerless Mrs. Eddy, of Boston," by writing that "it would be difficult to build a sentence of so few words conveying ideas more opposite to the fact" (Eddy, *Miscellaneous Writings*, 133).

59. Barry Huff, "Mary Baker Eddy: Liberating Interpreter of the Pauline Corpus," in *Strangely Familiar: Protofeminist Interpretations of Patriarchal Biblical Texts*, ed. Nancy Calvert-Koyzis and Heather Weir (Atlanta, Ga.: Society of Biblical Literature, 2009), 250. McDonald argues that the misogyny articulated by Rev. Bell also infected twentieth-century feminist scholars' appraisal of Eddy.

60. Gottschalk notes that "even in the hostile Protestant literature on Christian Science, there is one frequently sounded note of guarded approval. Ministers of varying orientations who found themselves in almost complete disagreement with Mrs. Eddy's teaching sometimes saw limited value in it as a protest against materialism" (*Emergence of Christian Science*, 207). See also Gottschalk, *Rolling Away the Stone*, 337–38; Peel, *Christian Science*, 105–6.

61. Charles S. Braden distinguishes New Thought from Christian Science partly based on the "authoritarianism" of the latter, *Spirits in Rebellion: The Rise and Development of New Thought* (Dallas, Tex.: Southern Methodist University Press, 1963). Organizational differences between New Thought and Christian Science and Eddy's role as leader of her

church are relevant, but the exclusively biblical claims Eddy made for her metaphysics are the important source of distinctions between Christian Science and New Thought theology and praxis.

62. Braden, *Spirits in Rebellion*, 138ff.

63. Eddy, *Science and Health*, 340. In addition to Protestants and the unchurched, Christian Science has also attracted many Jews to its ranks. John J. Appel cites cure for nervous debilities and desire for assimilation as driving the phenomena in the early twentieth century, "Christian Science and the Jews," *Jewish Social Studies* (1969): 100–21. My own sense is that Jewish attraction to Christian Science has had more to do with shared emphases on continuous study of the scriptures as key to spiritual development, on affirmations of scientific sensibility and applicability, and on textualism in worship. Eddy offered her own explanation in *Science and Health*, 360–61.

64. L08352, The Mary Baker Eddy Collection.

65. Peel, *Years of Authority*, 72.

66. Gill omits the role of the Bible in the new arrangement but points out a paradox: "More and more convinced that the book was the product of revelation, that, in the final sense, it was God's work and not her own, she saw no contradiction in her increasing denunciation of 'personality' and her institutionalized ban in Christian Science worship of any words but those she had penned" (*Mary Baker Eddy*, 369). On Eddy's concept of spiritual authority, see Peel, *Years of Authority*, 4–5.

67. Irving C. Tomlinson, *Twelve Years with Mary Baker Eddy*, amplified ed. (Boston, Mass.: Christian Science Publishing Society, 1994), 183–86.

68. "Christianscience.com," First Church of Christ, Scientist, http://www.christianscience.com.

69. A10245, The Mary Baker Eddy Collection.

70. See Christopher Langton, "Mary Baker Eddy and the Bible: Some General Statistics," unpublished manuscript (Elsah, Ill.: no date). Eddy's use of Paul's letters offers insight into her hermeneutics. Huff calls her "a liberating interpreter" of Paul because of her use of his writings to promote equal religious, marital, and legal rights for women ("Liberating Interpreter," 245–58).

71. See Gill, *Mary Baker Eddy*, 218.

72. However, it is hard to see how Dresser, Milmine, Peabody, et al., could plausibly claim that Eddy simply backfilled later editions of her book with Christian concepts and vocabulary to hide the supposedly mesmeric nature of her early teachings. Eddy grapples with religious themes in *Science and Health* in the first and all subsequent editions.

73. Eddy, *Science and Health*, 501.

74. Eddy, *Science and Health*, 547.

75. Testimonies of healing appear in every edition of the weekly *Christian Science Sentinel*, the monthly *Christian Science Journal*, and the various international language editions of the *Herald of Christian Science*. Spontaneous oral testimonies are also a regular part of the Wednesday evening meetings held in Christian Science churches.

76. For a detailed account of Christian Science activities during World War I and World War II, see *Christian Science Wartime Activities* (Boston, Mass.: Christian Science Publishing Society, 1922). Kim M. Schuette offers a comprehensive treatment in *Christian Science Military Ministry, 1917–2004* (Indianapolis, Ind.: Brockton Publishing, 2008).

77. *The Christian Science Quarterly* was also printed in a reduced size.

78. *A Century of Christian Science Healing* (Boston, Mass.: Christian Science Publishing Society, 1966), 74. An American soldier gave a similar account: "During the second battle of the Marne I lost everything I had except my equipment, rifle, *Science and Health*, and Bible, and if I had been forced to discard anything else, I am sure that my rifle would have gone before my *Science and Health* and Bible. For four days we were without a meal, but what little reading I could do seemed to take the place of food and sleep and it kept me contented under all conditions" (Chalmers, "War Relief Work in France," *Christian Science Sentinel*, December 1, 1918).

79. Chalmers, "War Relief Work," 76.

80. Founded by Mary Baker Eddy in 1908, with the object "to injure no man, but to bless all mankind," the newspaper early gained and continues to draw its readership from the general public as well as from Christian Scientists.

81. Chalmers, "War Relief Work."

BIBLIOGRAPHY

Albanese, Catherine. *Republic of Mind and Spirit: A Cultural History of American Metaphysical Religion*. New Haven, Conn.: Yale University Press, 2008.

Appel, John J. "Christian Science and the Jews." *Jewish Social Studies* 31, no. 2 (1969): 100-121.

Bates, Ernest S., and John V. Dittemore. *Mary Baker Eddy: The Truth and the Tradition*. New York: Alfred A. Knopf, 1932.

Bloom, Harold. *The American Religion*. 2nd ed. New York: Chu Hartley, 2006.

Braden, Charles S. *Spirits in Rebellion: The Rise and Development of New Thought*. Dallas, Tex.: Southern Methodist University Press, 1963.

A Century of Christian Science Healing. Boston, Mass.: Christian Science Publishing Society, 1966.

Christian Science Wartime Activities. Boston, Mass.: Christian Science Publishing Society, 1922.

Dakin, Edwin Franden. *Mrs. Eddy: The Biography of a Virginal Mind*. New York: Blue Ribbon Books, 1930.

Dresser, Horatio W., ed. *The Quimby Manuscripts*. New York: Thomas Y. Crowell, 1921.

Dresser, Julius A. *The True History of Mental Science*. Boston, Mass.: George H. Ellis, 1899.

Eddy, Mary Baker. *Christian Science versus Pantheism*. Boston, Mass.: First Church of Christ, Scientist, 1898.

———. *The First Church of Christ, Scientist and Miscellany*. Boston, Mass.: First Church of Christ Scientist, 1913.

———. *In My True Light and Life: Mary Baker Eddy Collections*. Boston, Mass.: The Writings of Mary Baker Eddy and The Mary Baker Eddy Library, 2002.

———. *Message to the Mother Church*. Boston, Mass.: First Church of Christ, Scientist, 1900.

———. *Miscellaneous Writings, 1883–1896*. Boston, Mass.: First Church of Christ, Scientist, 1896.

———. *Retrospection and Introspection*. Boston, Mass.: First Church of Christ, Scientist, 1891.

———. *Science and Health with Key to the Scriptures*. Boston, Mass.: First Church of Christ, Scientist, 1875.

Fisher, H. A. L. *Our New Religion*. London: E. Benn Limited, 1929.

Fraser, Caroline. *God's Perfect Child: Living and Dying in the Christian Science Church*. New York: Henry Holt, 1999.

Gill, Gillian. *Mary Baker Eddy*. Reading, Mass.: Perseus Books, 1998.

Gottschalk, Stephen. *The Emergence of Christian Science in American Religious Life.* Berkeley: University of California Press, 1973.

———. *Rolling Away the Stone: Mary Baker Eddy's Challenge to Materialism.* Bloomington: Indiana University Press, 2005.

Haller, John S., Jr. *The History of American Homeopathy.* New Brunswick, N.J.: Rutgers University Press, 2009.

Huff, Barry. "Mary Baker Eddy: Liberating Interpreter of the Pauline Corpus." In *Strangely Familiar: Protofeminist Interpretations of Patriarchal Biblical Texts,* edited by Nancy Calvert-Koyzis and Heather Weir, 245-58. Atlanta, Ga.: Society of Biblical Literature, 2009.

John, DeWitt. *The Christian Science Way of Life.* Boston, Mass.: Christian Science Publishing Society, 1962.

Langton, Christopher. "Mary Baker Eddy and the Bible: Some General Statistics." Unpublished manuscript. Elsah, Ill.: n.d.

Maffly-Kipp, Laurie F., ed. *American Scriptures: An Anthology of Sacred Writings.* New York: Penguin Classics, 2010.

Martin, Walter, and Ravi Zacharias. *The Kingdom of the Cults.* Minneapolis, Minn.: Bethany House, 2003.

McDonald, Jean A. "Mary Baker Eddy and the Nineteenth-Century 'Public' Woman: A Feminist Reappraisal." *Journal of Feminist Studies in Religion* 2, no. 1 (1986): 89-111.

McKenzie, Daisette D. S. "The Writings of Mary Baker Eddy." In *We Knew Mary Baker Eddy,* expanded ed., 1:246-55. Boston, Mass.: Christian Science Publishing Society, 2011.

McNeill, Keith. *A Story Untold: The History of the Quimby-Eddy Debate.* 2015. https://ppquimby-mbeddydebate.com.

Milmine, Georgine. *The Life of Mary Baker Eddy and the History of Christian Science.* New York: Doubleday, 1909.

Nenneman, Richard A. *The New Birth of Christianity: Why Religion Persists in a Scientific Age.* San Francisco, Calif.: HarperSanFrancisco, 1992.

———. *Persistent Pilgrim: The Life of Mary Baker Eddy.* Etna, N.H.: Nebadoon Press, 1997.

Peabody, Frederick W. *The Religio-Medical Masquerade: A Complete Exposure of Christian Science.* Boston, Mass.: Hancock Press, 1915.

Peel, Robert. *Christian Science: Its Encounter with American Culture.* New York: Henry Holt, 1958.

———. *Health and Medicine in the Christian Science Tradition.* New York: Crossroad, 1988.

———. *Mary Baker Eddy: The Years of Discovery.* Boston, Mass.: Holt, Rinehart, and Winston, 1966.

———. *Mary Baker Eddy: The Years of Trial.* Boston, Mass.: Holt, Rinehart, and Winston, 1971.

———. *Mary Baker Eddy: The Years of Authority.* Boston, Mass.: Holt, Rinehart, and Winston, 1977.

———. *Spiritual Healing in a Scientific Age.* New York: Harper and Row, 1988.

Robbins, Natalie. *Copeland's Cure: Homeopathy and the War between Conventional and Alternative Medicine.* New York: Alfred A. Knopf, 2005.

Schuette, Kim M. *Christian Science Military Ministry, 1917-2004.* Indianapolis, Ind.: Brockton, 2008.

Silsberger, Julius, Jr. *Mary Baker Eddy: An Interpretive Biography of the Founder of Christian Science.* New York: Little Brown, 1980.

Smaus, Jewel Spangler. *Mary Baker Eddy: The Golden Days.* Boston, Mass.: Christian Science Publishing Society, 1966.

Thomas, Robert David. *With Bleeding Footsteps: Mary Baker Eddy's Path to Religious Leadership*. New York: Alfred A. Knopf, 1994.

Tomlinson, Irving C. *Twelve Years with Mary Baker Eddy*. Amplified ed. Boston, Mass.: Christian Science Publishing Society, 1994.

Twain, Mark. *Christian Science*. New York: Harper and Brothers, 1907.

Von Fettweis, Yvonne Caché, and Robert Townsend Warneck. *Mary Baker Eddy: Christian Healer*. Amplified ed. Boston, Mass.: Christian Science Publishing Society, 2009.

Voorhees, Amy Black. "Writing Revelation: Mary Baker Eddy and Her Early Editions of Science and Health, 1875–1891." PhD diss., University of California, Santa Barbara, 2013.

Wilbur, Sibyl. *The Life of Mary Baker Eddy*. Boston, Mass.: Christian Science Publishing Society, 1907.

Index

primer, 85, 96, 265
primitivism, 79, 105, 550
Princeton Theological Seminary, 123, 131,
    136, 216
  Bible translation, 547
  Princeton Theology, 119, 553,
    579, 628, 632
  students, 521
progressive creationism, 219–220
progressive revelation, 613
Prokopovich, Norgorod Feofan, 534
prophecy, 437–438, 575, 580
  African Americans, 200, 202, 362
  Anne Hutchinson, 87
  art, 409, 416, 456, 459–461
  Bible conferences, 125, 131
  Edwards, Jonathan, 440
  Pentecostalism, 595, 598–599
  Scofield, C.I., 131, 218
  second coming, 591
  Seventh-day Adventism, 627
  skepticism concerning, 101
  women, 163, 247
providentialism, 335–336, 362–363
Psalter, 97, 123, 531, 563
  Lutheran, 98
  music, 470–471
  Native American, 47
  puritan, 81–83
  Scottish, 388
Puritans, xx, 82–89, 470, 533, 550, 661
  African Americans, 292, 443, 629
  biblical literacy, 80–81, 99, 102
  covenantalism, 106
  education, 25, 264
  eschatology, 439
  laws, 263, 278–279
  literature, 440, 442, 446
  missions, 3, 62
  piety, 97, 265
  politics, 89, 106, 250, 278–279,
    290–291, 346
  preaching, 242–247, 250–251
  primitivism, 79, 99, 550
  sports, 323–324, 326
  typology, 101, 199
Putnam, Robert, 251

Quakerism, 88–89, 104, 243, 265
  art, 411–413
  inner light, 248
  Pacificism, 107
queer theory, 175, 187–191
Quimby, Phineas P., 661, 664–665
Qur'an, 33, 562

Ramm, Bernard, 219, 222, 566
Rand, Archie, 408
rap music, 175, 198, 473, 475
Rattner, Abraham, 416–417
Rauschenbusch, Walter, 293–294, 296, 325
Reagan, Ronald, 375, 584
Red-letter Bible, 12
Reformed tradition, 86, 97, 101, 549, 577
  education, 265
  environmentalism, 389, 391
  evangelicalism, 238
  politics, 346
Reims-Douay Bible, 5, 63, 97, 523–524.
    See also Catholic Bible
  translation, 125, 205
religious education, 19, 266–267, 452
Religious Right, 338, 370–379
Republican party, 373–374
republicanism, 130, 277, 279, 353–354
  artistic expression, 410, 441
  classical, 349–350
  Christian, 106–107
  Hebrew, 106
  opposed to monarchy, 107
  Whig, 96, 105
restorationism, 117–118, 593, 628–629
Revised Version, 9, 125, 130
Revised Standard Version, 10, 229, 511,
    524, 554
  Isaiah controversy, 132, 235–236, 551
  language of, 24
  mormonism, 621
  National Council of Churches, 546
Rhode Island, 48, 88–89, 99
Riley, William Bell, 219, 221
Rimmer, Harry, 219, 222
Riplinger, Gail, 233
Roberts, Oral, 149, 583
Robertson, Pat, 297